1st Joint Conference on Lexical and Computational Semantics 2012

(SEM 2012)

Montreal, Canada
7-8 June 2012

ISBN: 978-1-62276-502-7

Printed from e-media with permission by:

Curran Associates, Inc.
57 Morehouse Lane
Red Hook, NY 12571

Some format issues inherent in the e-media version may also appear in this print version.

Printed by Curran Associates, Inc. (2013)

Association for Computational Linguistics
209 N. Eighth Street
Stroudsburg, Pennsylvania 18360

Phone: 1-570-476-8006
Fax: 1-570-476-0860

acl@aclweb.org

Additional copies of this publication are available from:

Curran Associates, Inc.
57 Morehouse Lane
Red Hook, NY 12571 USA
Phone: 845-758-0400
Fax: 845-758-2634
Email: curran@proceedings.com
Web: www.proceedings.com

Introduction to *SEM 2012

In the summer of 2011, the idea of having a joint conference covering two ACL Special Interest Groups, namely SIGLEX and SIGSEM, was born. Traditionally, the SIGLEX has been concerned with issues of the lexicon and computational lexical semantics, while SIGSEM has been engaged with issues of computational modeling of semantics. The need for an umbrella conference on semantics was growing not only because of the many recent exciting developments in the field of computational linguistics, but also because of the growing number of shared tasks and workshops, of which many show points of contact with semantics in its various forms.

We name just three of these exciting and promising developments. First, Recognizing Textual Entailment, which started as a shared task, has established itself as an active area of research in semantics. Second, following syntactic parsing, robust, broad-coverage systems for shallow (and reasonably deep) semantics have been developed over the last years and are still being improved as observed in the SemEval competitions. And third, statistical semantics has emerged as a hot topic, in particular distributional approaches. All of these research directions touch upon both lexical and modeling aspects. Progress in either of these fields needs input from both.

At the same time, we clearly recognized that the current venues for publishing research and meeting fellow semanticists wasn't satisfactory. SIGSEM organizes a successful biennial workshop (recently rechristened as a conference) on computational semantics, IWCS, which however sees a small number of lexically-oriented researchers attending, and moreover has been geographically restricted since it started in 1994. SIGLEX, on the other hand, has organized the widely attended SemEval evaluation exercises organized by active communities of researchers, but has not been very successful in attracting computational modeling semanticists from the SIGSEM community. Hence, we came to the conclusion that the time is ripe for a more synergistic effort where we combine our events.

An explosion of emails followed between SIGLEX & SIGSEM board members and not long after *SEM came to the world. The organizational tasks were carefully split between members of SIGLEX and SIGSEM to ensure optimal collaboration and exchange of ideas. The conference is coordinated by one person — the general chair — with the idea to let this position alternate by a SIGLEX and SIGSEM representative in future editions of *SEM. For the first edition of *SEM, NAACL in Montreal seemed a natural choice. As a satellite event of a larger event *SEM could benefit from the organizational know-how of ACL experts and we could leverage the NAACL community presence as a way of popularizing our ideas.

*SEM received 79 long and 29 short papers. Three long papers were withdrawn leaving 76 long papers. We accepted 21 long and 13 short papers. These numbers translate in acceptance rates of 27.6% (long) and 44.8% (short papers).

*SEM is also hosting a shared task on Resolving the Scope and Focus of Negation, organized by Roser Morante and Eduardo Blanco. 10 teams participated, together submitting 14 runs. The task and system descriptions papers for this event are included in these proceedings.

In addition, *SEM is hosting the last edition of SemEval, whose proceedings are published in an accompanying volume. The proceedings include 8 task description papers and 56 system description papers.

∗SEM took a tremendous effort to conceive. It would not have been possible without the vision of the CL community at large but the NAACL executive board chaired by Rebecca Hwa (through December 2011), the ACL business manager Priscilla Rasmussen, and the NAACL 2012 General Chair Jennifer Chu-Carrol as well as the ACL executive board as chaired by Kevin Knight, all allowed for it to come to reality so quickly. We are deeply grateful for the vote of confidence and support from the various semantics workshop organizers from previous years like RTE, MWE, DISCO and GEMS for rallying their subcommunities to support our initiative.

There are many individuals to thank for their contributions to the conference program. First and foremost, we would like to thank the authors who submitted their work to ∗SEM. We are deeply indebted to the area chairs and the reviewers for their hard work. The area chairs (Timothy Baldwin, Marco Baroni, Johan Bos, Philipp Cimiano, Ido Dagan, Christiane Fellbaum, Carlos Ramisch) and reviewers did a fantastic job. They enabled us to select an exciting program and to provide valuable feedback to the authors.

We are very grateful to Sara Barcena, who designed the ∗SEM logo. We would like to thank Roberto Basili in his role as sponsorship chair. We also would like to thank Priscilla Rasmussen who provided a reliable and fast human interface with the local organization. Suresh Manandhar and Deniz Yuret (chairs of the task committee) ensured a smooth integration with the shared task and SemEval activities. Roser Morante and Eduardo Blanco organized the shared task. Finally, Yuval Marton, the publication chair, did an amazing job in putting the proceedings together. No hanging word or dangling footnote escaped his attention.

Finally, last but not least, we would like to acknowledge sponsors from both the academic and industrial worlds. The logo design for ∗SEM is sponsored by the Groningen Meaning Bank Project of the University of Groningen. ∗SEM is supported by the European project INSEARCH (FP7 262491) and, in particular, by its contributing partners of the Department of Enterprise Engineering of the University of Rome, Tor Vergata (Italy) and CiaoTech s.r.l.

We hope this will be the first of an exciting series of conferences.

Eneko Agirre (General Chair)
Johan Bos (PC chair)
Mona Diab (PC chair)

Introduction to SemEval

The Semantic Evaluation (SemEval) series of workshops focus on the evaluation of semantic analysis systems with the aim of comparing systems that can analyse diverse semantic phenomena in text. SemEval provides an exciting forum for researchers to propose challenging research problems in semantics and to build systems/techniques to address such research problems. This volume contains papers accepted for presentation at the SemEval-2012 International Workshop on Semantic Evaluation Exercises. SemEval-2012 is co-organized with the *Sem The First Joint Conference on Lexical and Computational Semantics. SemEval-2012 immediately follows the North American Chapter of the Association for Computational Linguistics - Human Language Technologies (NAACL HLT) 2012 conference.

SemEval-2012 included the following 8 tasks for evaluation:

- English Lexical Simplification
- Measuring Degrees of Relational Similarity
- Spatial Role Labeling
- Evaluating Chinese Word Similarity
- Chinese Semantic Dependency Parsing
- Semantic Textual Similarity
- COPA: Choice Of Plausible Alternatives An evaluation of commonsense causal reasoning
- Cross-lingual Textual Entailment for Content Synchronization

This volume contains both Task Description papers that describe each of the above tasks and System Description papers that describe the systems that participated in the above tasks. A total of 8 task description papers and 56 system description papers are included in this volume. Task 6 on "Semantic Textual Similarity" was the most successful task attracting over half of the total submissions.

We are indebted to all program committee members for their high quality, elaborate and thoughtful reviews. The papers in this proceedings have surely benefited from this feedback.

We are grateful to *SEM 2012 and NAACL-HLT 2012 conference organizers for local organization and the forum. We most gratefully acknowledge the support of our sponsors, the ACL Special Interest Group on the Lexicon (SIGLEX) and the ACL Special Interest Group on Computational Semantics (SIGSEM).

Welcome to SemEval-2012!

Suresh Manandhar and Deniz Yuret

Organizers:

General Chair:

Eneko Agirre (University of the Basque Country)

Program Committee Chairs:

Johan Bos (University of Groningen)

Mona Diab (Columbia University)

Shared Task Committee Chairs:

Suresh Manandhar (University of York)

Deniz Yuret (Koç University)

Publications Chair:

Yuval Marton (IBM Watson Research Center)

Sponsorship Chair:

Roberto Basili (University of Rome "Tor Vergata")

Area Chairs:

Timothy Baldwin (University of Melbourne)

Marco Baroni (University of Trento)

Johan Bos (University of Groningen)

Philip Cimiano (University of Bielefield)

Ido Dagan (Bar Ilan University)

Christiane Fellbaum (Princeton University)

Carlos Ramisch (University of Rio Grande do Sul)

Program Committee:

Samir AbdelRahman, Amjad Abu-Jbara, Nitish Aggarwal, Eneko Agirre, Iñaki Alegria, Enrique Amigo, Marilisa AMOIA, Dimitra Anastasiou, Mark Andrews, Daniel Baer, Collin Baker, Tim Baldwin, Miguel Ballesteros, Carmen Banea, Srinivas Bangalore, Pierpaolo Basile, Valerio Basile, Luciana Benotti, Luisa Bentivogli, Jonathan Berant, Raffaella Bernardi, Steven Bethard, Arindam Bhattacharya, Pushpak Bhattacharyya, Chris Biemann, Eduardo Blanco, Gemma Boleda, Francis Bond, Johan Bos, Jordan Boyd-Graber, Antonio Branco, Paul Buitelaar, Aljoscha Burchardt, Davide Buscaldi, Alastair Butler, Miriam Butt, Elena Cabrio, Aoife Cahill, Chris Callison-Burch, Nicoletta Calzolari, Jose' Guilherme Camargo de Souza, Annalina Caputo, Julio Castillo, Daniel Cer, Rui Chaves, Wanxiang Che, David Chen, Md. Faisal Mahbub Chowdhury, Grzegorz Chrupala, Peter Clark, Stephen Clark, Paul Cook, Crit Cremers, Danilo Croce, Noa P. Cruz Díaz, Walter Daelemans, Béatrice Daille, Marie-Catherine de Marneffe, Rodolfo Delmonte, Gerard deMelo, Leon Derczynski, Gaël Dias, Georgiana Dinu, Bill Dolan, Markus Egg, Katrin Erk, Miquel Espla, Kilian Evang, Stefan Evert, James Fan, Christiane Fellbaum, Ana Fernandez, Raquel Fernandez, Antonio C. Fernández, Tim Fernando, Darja Fiser, Anette Frank,

Diego Frassinelli, Claire Gardent, Danilo Giampiccolo, Eugenie Giesbrecht, Claudio Giuliano, Demetrios Glinos, Alfio Gliozzo, Aitor Gonzalez Agirre, Travis Goodwin, Edward Grefenstette, Karl Grieser, Yoan Gutiérrez Vázquez, Binod Gyawali, Sanda Harabagiu, Chikara Hashimoto, Michael Heilman, Aurelie Herbelot, Erhard Hinrichs, Graeme Hirst, Nancy Ide, Hitoshi Isahara, Suhel Jaber, Sujay Kumar Jauhar, Sergio Jimenez, Peng Jin, Anders Johannsen, David Jurgens, Kyo Kageura, Kyoko Kanzaki, Mladen Karan, Adam Kilgarriff, Su Nam Kim, Parisa Kordjamshidi, Valia Kordoni, Ioannis Korkontzelos, Milen Kouylekov, Zornitsa Kozareva, Gerhard Kremer, Brigitte Krenn, Alberto Lavelli, Alessandro Lenci, Mike Lewis, Bin Li, Anne-Laure Ligozat, Krister Lindén, Ting Liu, Bernardo Magnini, Nikos Malandrakis, Manuel J. Maña López, Suresh Manandhar, Alessandro Marchetti, David Martinez, Yannick Mathieu, Takuya Matsuzaki, Diana McCarthy, Yashar Mehdad, Rada Mihalcea, Yusuke Miyao, Marie-Francine Moens, Saif Mohammad, Shaabi Mohammed, Michael Mohler, Dan Moldovan, Roser Morante, Alessandro Moschitti, Brian Murphy, Preslav Nakov, Roberto Navigli, Matteo Negri, Guenter Neumann, David Newman, Sanni Nimb, Diarmuid Ó Séaghdha, Sam Oakley, Jan Odjik, Stephan Oepen, Ekaterina Ovchinnikova, Lilja Øvrelid, Partha Pakray, Martha Palmer, Pavel Pecina, Bolette Pedersen, Ted Pedersen, Yves Peirsman, Anselmo Peñas, Alpar Perini, Emanuele Pianta, Scott Piao, Maciej Piasecki, Manfred Pinkal, Paul Piwek, Simone Paolo Ponzetto, Octavian Popescu, Stephen Pulman, Zhou Qiaoli, Ari Rappoport, Jonathon Read, Siva Reddy, Joe Reisinger, Bryan Rink, Miguel Rios, Kirk Roberts, Melissa Roemmele, Sabine Rosenberg, Magnus Sahlgren, Manfred Sailer, Mark Sammons, Frane Šarić, Shrutiranjan Satapathy, Agata Savary, Lenhart Schubert, Sabine Schulte im Walde, Hinrich Schütze, H. Andrew Schwartz, Satoshi Sekine, Violeta Seretan, Chung-chieh Shan, Vera Sheinman, Eyal Shnarch, Ekaterina Shutova, Janardhan Singh, Ravi Sinha, Richard Socher, Artem Sokolov, Daniel Sonntag, Anders Soogard, Virach Sornlertlamvanich, Marc Spaniol, Lucia Specia, Mark Steedman, Asher Stern, Matthew Stone, Carlo Strapparava, Luke Stringer, Michael Strube, Sara Stymne, Stan Szpakowicz, Idan Szpektor, Alex Tantos, Stefan Thater, Zhu Tiantian, Sara Tonelli, Mireya Tovar, Beata Trawinski, Vivian Tsang, Peter Turney, Kyioko Uchiyama, Lyle Ungar, Christina Unger, Ruben Urizar, Tim Van de Cruys, Benjamin Van Durme, Gloria Vazquez, Sonia Vázquez, Tony Veale, Erik Velldal, Noortje Venhuizen, Yannick Versley, Darnes Vilarino Ayala, Begoña Villada Moirón, Aline Villavicencio, Martin Volk, Piek Vossen, Katharina Waeschle, Rui Wang, james White, Michael White, Yunfang Wu, Zhijun Wu, Hao Xiong, Willy Yap, Eric Yeh, Deniz Yuret, Fabio Zanzotto, Konstantin Zuyev.

Additional Reviewers:

Mehmet Ali Yatbaz, Paolo Annesi, Kartik Asooja, Pierpaolo Basile, Sumit Bhagwani, Chris Biemann, Sam Biggins, Olivia Buzek, Marina Elizabeth Cardenas, Jinho Choi, Maximilian Dylla, Paula Estrella, Sascha Fendrich, Fanpeng Guo, Elias Iosif, Sigrid Klerke, Héctor Martínez, Rada Mihalcea, Azucena Montes Rendon, Snehasis Neogi, Magdalena Plamada, Barbara Plank, Michael Roth, João Silva, Guangchao Tang, Sara Tonelli, Olga Uryopina, Svitlana Volkova, Torsten Zesch.

Invited Speaker:

Jerry Hobbs

Table of Contents

Conference Program Summary

	*SEM Main Conference (Drummond Center/East)		Shared Task and SemEval (Drummond West)	
Day 1: Thursday June 7th 2012				
08:00--09:15	Registration			
09:15--10:30	Opening Remarks and Keynote Address (Plenary PLN1)			
10:30--11:00	Coffee Break			
11:00--12:40	Long Papers 1: Linking and Anaphora	*SEM2	SemEval Session 1	SE1
12:40--2:00	Lunch			
2:00--3:30	Short Papers Boasters and Posters	*SEM3	SemEval Session 2	SE2
3:30--4:00	Coffee Break			
4:00--6:05	Long Papers 2: Semantic Models	*SEM4	SemEval Session 3	SE3

	*SEM Main Conference (Drummond Center/East)		Shared Task and SemEval (Drummond West)	
Day 2: Friday June 8th 2012				
08:15--09:15	Best Papers and Shared Task (Plenary PLN2)			
09:15--10:30	Long Papers 3: Lexical Semantics	*SEM6	Shared Task	TSK1
10:30--11:00	Coffee Break			
11:00--12:15 / 12:30	Long Papers 4: Lexical Semantics	*SEM7	Shared Task	TSK2
12:15--2:00	Lunch			
2:00--3:15 / 3:30	Long Papers 5: Semantic Parsing	*SEM8	SemEval Poster Session 1 (Salons 6/7)	SE4
3:15--4:00	Coffee Break			
4:00--5:15	Long Papers 6: Semantic Inference	*SEM9	SemEval Poster Session 2 (Salons 6/7)	SE5
5:15--6:00	Plenary Panel and Closing: *SEM and the Future (PLN3)			

Conference Program

***SEM Main Conference View**

Day 1: Thursday June 7th 2012 (*SEM Main Conference View)

(08:00–09:15) Registration

Session PLN1: (09:15–10:30) Opening Remarks and Keynote Address (Plenary)

09:15–09:30 *SEM Opening

09:30–10:30 Keynote Address by Jerry Hobbs

(10:30–11:00) Coffee Break

Session *SEM2: (11:00–12:40) Long Papers 1: Linking and Anaphora

11:00–11:25 *Casting Implicit Role Linking as an Anaphora Resolution Task*
Carina Silberer and Anette Frank

11:25–11:50 *Adaptive Clustering for Coreference Resolution with Deterministic Rules and Web-Based Language Models*
Razvan Bunescu

11:50–12:15 *Measuring Semantic Relatedness using Multilingual Representations*
Samer Hassan, Carmen Banea and Rada Mihalcea

12:15–12:40 *Towards Building a Multilingual Semantic Network: Identifying Interlingual Links in Wikipedia*
Bharath Dandala, Rada Mihalcea and Razvan Bunescu

Session SE1: (11:00–12:40) SemEval Session 1

(See SemEval View for details)

(12:40–2:00) Lunch

Session *SEM3: (2:00–3:30) Short Papers Boasters and Posters

Day 1: Thursday June 7th 2012 (*SEM Main Conference View) (continued)

Session SE2: (2:00–3:30) SemEval Session 2

(See SemEval View for details)

(3:30–4:00) Coffee Break

Session *SEM4: (4:00–6:05) Long Papers 2: Semantic Models

4:00–4:25 *Annotating Preferences in Negotiation Dialogues*
Anais Cadilhac, Nicholas Asher and Farah Benamara

4:25–4:50 *Selecting Corpus-Semantic Models for Neurolinguistic Decoding*
Brian Murphy, Partha Talukdar and Tom Mitchell

4:50–5:15 *Simple and Phrasal Implicatives*
Lauri Karttunen

5:15–5:40 *An Unsupervised Ranking Model for Noun-Noun Compositionality*
Karl Moritz Hermann, Phil Blunsom and Stephen Pulman

5:40–6:05 *Expanding the Range of Tractable Scope-Underspecified Semantic Representations*
Mehdi Manshadi and James Allen

Session SE3: (4:00–6:00) SemEval Session 3

(See SemEval View for details)

Day 2: Friday June 8th 2012 (*SEM Main Conference View)

Session PLN2: (08:15–09:15) Best Paper Awards and Shared Task (Plenary)

08:15–08:20 Announcement of Best Papers

08:20–08:30 Best Short Paper Speech

08:30–08:45 Best Long Paper Speech

08:45–09:10 Shared Task: Resolving the Scope and Focus of Negation

Session *SEM6: (09:15–10:30) Long Papers 3: Lexical Semantics

09:15–09:40 *Regular polysemy: A distributional model*
Gemma Boleda, Sebastian Padó and Jason Utt

09:40–10:05 *Extracting a Semantic Lexicon of French Adjectives from a Large Lexicographic Dictionary*
Selja Seppälä, Lucie Barque and Alexis Nasr

10:05–10:30 *Modelling selectional preferences in a lexical hierarchy*
Diarmuid Ó Séaghdha and Anna Korhonen

Session TSK1: (09:15–10:30) Shared Task

(See *SEM Shared Task View for details)

(10:30–11:00) Coffee Break

Session *SEM7: (11:00–12:15) Long Papers 4: Lexical Semantics

11:00–11:25 *Unsupervised Induction of a Syntax-Semantics Lexicon Using Iterative Refinement*
Hagen Fürstenau and Owen Rambow

11:25–11:50 *An Evaluation of Graded Sense Disambiguation using Word Sense Induction*
David Jurgens

11:50–12:15 *Ensemble-based Semantic Lexicon Induction for Semantic Tagging*
Ashequl Qadir and Ellen Riloff

Session TSK2: (11:00–12:30) Shared Task

(See *SEM Shared Task View for details)

Day 2: Friday June 8th 2012 (*SEM Main Conference View) (continued)

(12:15–2:00) Lunch

Session *SEM8: (2:00–3:15) Long Papers: Semantic Parsing

2:00–2:25 *An Exact Dual Decomposition Algorithm for Shallow Semantic Parsing with Constraints*
Dipanjan Das, André F. T. Martins and Noah A. Smith

2:25–2:50 *Aligning Predicate Argument Structures in Monolingual Comparable Texts: A New Corpus for a New Task*
Michael Roth and Anette Frank

2:50–3:15 *The Effects of Semantic Annotations on Precision Parse Ranking*
Andrew MacKinlay, Rebecca Dridan, Diana McCarthy and Timothy Baldwin

Session SE4: (2:00–3:30) SemEval Poster Session 1

(See SemEval View for details)

(3:15–4:00) Coffee Break

Session *SEM9: (4:00–5:15) Long Papers 6: Semantic Inference

4:00–4:25 *A Probabilistic Lexical Model for Ranking Textual Inferences*
Eyal Shnarch, Ido Dagan and Jacob Goldberger

4:25–4:50 *#Emotional Tweets*
Saif Mohammad

4:50–5:15 *Monolingual Distributional Similarity for Text-to-Text Generation*
Juri Ganitkevitch, Benjamin Van Durme and Chris Callison-Burch

Session SE5: (4:00–5:15) SemEval Poster Session 2

(See SemEval View for details)

Session PLN3: (5:15–6:00) Plenary Panel and Closing: *SEM and the Future

—- End of *SEM Main Conference View —-

***SEM Shared Task View**

Day 1: Thursday June 7th 2012 (*SEM Shared Task View)

(Same as *SEM Main Conference View)

Day 2: Friday June 8th 2012 (*SEM Shared Task View)

Session PLN2: (08:15–09:15) Best Paper Awards and Shared Task (Plenary)

08:15–08:20 Announcement of Best Papers

08:20–08:30 Best Short Paper Speech

08:30–08:45 Best Long Paper Speech

08:45–09:10 Shared Task: Resolving the Scope and Focus of Negation

Session TSK1: (09:15–10:30) Shared Task Session 1

09:15–09:30 **SEM 2012 Shared Task: Resolving the Scope and Focus of Negation*
Roser Morante and Eduardo Blanco

09:30–09:45 *UABCoRAL: A Preliminary study for Resolving the Scope of Negation*
Binod Gyawali and Thamar Solorio

09:45–10:00 *UCM-I: A Rule-based Syntactic Approach for Resolving the Scope of Negation*
Jorge Carrillo de Albornoz, Laura Plaza, Alberto Díaz and Miguel Ballesteros

10:00–10:15 *UCM-2: a Rule-Based Approach to Infer the Scope of Negation via Dependency Parsing*
Miguel Ballesteros, Alberto Díaz, Virginia Francisco, Pablo Gervás, Jorge Carrillo de Albornoz and Laura Plaza

10:15–10:30 *UConcordia: CLaC Negation Focus Detection at *Sem 2012*
Sabine Rosenberg and Sabine Bergler

(10:30–11:00) Coffee Break

Day 2: Friday June 8th 2012 (*SEM Shared Task View) (continued)

Session TSK2: (11:00–12:30) Shared Task Session 2

11:00–11:15 *UGroningen: Negation detection with Discourse Representation Structures*
Valerio Basile, Johan Bos, Kilian Evang and Noortje Venhuizen

11:15–11:30 *UiO1: Constituent-Based Discriminative Ranking for Negation Resolution*
Jonathon Read, Erik Velldal, Lilja Øvrelid and Stephan Oepen

11:30–11:45 *UiO 2: Sequence-labeling Negation Using Dependency Features*
Emanuele Lapponi, Erik Velldal, Lilja Øvrelid and Jonathon Read

11:45–12:00 *UMichigan: A Conditional Random Field Model for Resolving the Scope of Negation*
Amjad Abu Jbara and Dragomir Radev

12:00–12:15 *UWashington: Negation Resolution using Machine Learning Methods*
James Paul White

FBK: Exploiting Phrasal and Contextual Clues for Negation Scope Detection
Md. Faisal Mahbub Chowdhury

12:15–12:30 Discussion

(12:30–2:00) Lunch

– no Shared Task-specific afternoon sessions –

(See *SEM Main Conference and SemEval Views for details)

Session PLN3: (5:15–6:00) Plenary Panel and Closing: *SEM and the Future

—- End of *SEM Shared Task View —-

SemEval View

Day 1: Thursday June 7th 2012 (SemEval View)

(08:00–09:15) Registration

Session PLN1: (09:15–10:30) Opening Remarks and Keynote Address (Plenary)

09:15–09:30 *SEM Opening

09:30–10:30 Keynote Address by Jerry Hobbs

(10:30–11:00) Coffee Break

Session SE1: (11:00–12:40) SemEval Session 1

11:00–11:10 Welcome to SemEval-2012

11:10 *SemEval-2012 Task 1: English Lexical Simplification*
Lucia Specia, Sujay Kumar Jauhar and Rada Mihalcea

11:25 *SemEval-2012 Task 2: Measuring Degrees of Relational Similarity*
David Jurgens, Saif Mohammad, Peter Turney and Keith Holyoak

11:40 *SemEval-2012 Task 3: Spatial Role Labeling*
parisa kordjamshidi, steven bethard and Marie-Francine Moens

11:55 *SemEval-2012 Task 4: Evaluating Chinese Word Similarity*
Peng Jin and Yunfang Wu

12:10 *SemEval-2012 Task 5: Chinese Semantic Dependency Parsing*
Wanxiang Che, Meishan Zhang, Yanqiu Shao and Ting Liu

12:25 *SemEval-2012 Task 6: A Pilot on Semantic Textual Similarity*
Eneko Agirre, Daniel Cer, Mona Diab and Aitor Gonzalez-Agirre

(12:40–2:00) Lunch

Day 1: Thursday June 7th 2012 (SemEval View) (continued)

5:00	*UNED: Improving Text Similarity Measures without Human Assessments* Enrique Amigó, Jesus Gimenez, Julio Gonzalo and Felisa Verdejo
5:15	*UTDHLT: COPACETIC System for Choosing Plausible Alternatives* Travis Goodwin, Bryan Rink, Kirk Roberts and Sanda Harabagiu
5:30	*HDU: Cross-lingual Textual Entailment with SMT Features* Katharina Wäschle and Sascha Fendrich
5:45	*UAlacant: Using Online Machine Translation for Cross-Lingual Textual Entailment* Miquel Esplà-Gomis, Felipe Sánchez-Martínez and Mikel L. Forcada

Day 2: Friday June 8th 2012 (SemEval View)

Session PLN2: (08:15–09:15) Best Paper Awards and Shared Task (Plenary)

08:15–08:20	Announcement of Best Papers
08:20–08:30	Best Short Paper Speech
08:30–08:45	Best Long Paper Speech
08:45–09:10	Shared Task: Resolving the Scope and Focus of Negation

– No SemEval-specific morning sessions –

(See *SEM Main Conference and Shared Task Views for details)

(12:15–2:00) Lunch

Day 2: Friday June 8th 2012 (SemEval View) (continued)

Session SE4: (2:00–3:30) SemEval Poster Session 1

Day 2: Friday June 8th 2012 (SemEval View) (continued)

LIMSI: Learning Semantic Similarity by Selecting Random Word Subsets
Artem Sokolov

ATA-Sem: Chunk-based Determination of Semantic Text Similarity
Demetrios Glinos

IRIT: Textual Similarity Combining Conceptual Similarity with an N-Gram Comparison Method
Davide Buscaldi, Ronan Tournier, Nathalie Aussenac-Gilles and Josiane Mothe

DSS: Text Similarity Using Lexical Alignments of Form, Distributional Semantics and Grammatical Relations
Diana McCarthy, Spandana Gella and Siva Reddy

DeepPurple: Estimating Sentence Semantic Similarity using N-gram Regression Models and Web Snippets
NIkos Malandrakis, Elias Iosif and Alexandros Potamianos

JU_CSE_NLP: Multi-grade Classification of Semantic Similarity between Text Pairs
Snehasis Neogi, Partha Pakray, Sivaji Bandyopadhyay and Alexander Gelbukh

Tiantianzhu7:System Description of Semantic Textual Similarity (STS) in the SemEval-2012 (Task 6)
Zhu Tiantian and Lan Man

sranjans : Semantic Textual Similarity using Maximal Weighted Bipartite Graph Matching
Sumit Bhagwani, Shrutiranjan Satapathy and Harish Karnick

Weiwei: A Simple Unsupervised Latent Semantics based Approach for Sentence Similarity
Weiwei Guo and Mona Diab

UNIBA: Distributional Semantics for Textual Similarity
Annalina Caputo, Pierpaolo Basile and Giovanni Semeraro

UNITOR: Combining Semantic Text Similarity functions through SV Regression
Danilo Croce, Paolo Annesi, Valerio Storch and Roberto Basili

Saarland: Vector-based models of semantic textual similarity
Georgiana Dinu and Stefan Thater

(3:30–4:00) Coffee Break

Day 2: Friday June 8th 2012 (SemEval View) (continued)

Session SE5: (4:00–5:15) SemEval Poster Session 2

UMCC_DLSI: Multidimensional Lexical-Semantic Textual Similarity
Antonio Fernández, Yoan Gutiérrez, Héctor Dávila, Alexander Chávez, Andy González, Rainel Estrada, Yenier Castañeda, Sonia Vázquez, Andrés Montoyo and Rafael Muñoz

SRIUBC: Simple Similarity Features for Semantic Textual Similarity
Eric Yeh and Eneko Agirre

FBK: Machine Translation Evaluation and Word Similarity metrics for Semantic Textual Similarity
José Guilherme Camargo de Souza, Matteo Negri and Yashar Mehdad

FCC: Three Approaches for Semantic Textual Similarity
Maya Carrillo, Darnes Vilariño, David Pinto, Mireya Tovar, Saul León and Esteban Castillo

UNT: A Supervised Synergistic Approach to Semantic Text Similarity
Carmen Banea, Samer Hassan, Michael Mohler and Rada Mihalcea

DERI&UPM: Pushing Corpus Based Relatedness to Similarity: Shared Task System Description
Nitish Aggarwal, Kartik Asooja and Paul Buitelaar

Stanford: Probabilistic Edit Distance Metrics for STS
Mengqiu Wang and Daniel Cer

University_Of_Sheffield: Two Approaches to Semantic Text Similarity
Sam Biggins, Shaabi Mohammed, Sam Oakley, Luke Stringer, Mark Stevenson and Judita Preiss

janardhan: Semantic Textual Similarity using Universal Networking Language graph matching
Janardhan Singh, Arindam Bhattacharya and Pushpak Bhattacharyya

SAGAN: An approach to Semantic Textual Similarity based on Textual Entailment
Julio Castillo and Paula Estrella

UOW: Semantically Informed Text Similarity
Miguel Rios, Wilker Aziz and Lucia Specia

Penn: Using Word Similarities to better Estimate Sentence Similarity
Sneha Jha, Hansen A. Schwartz and Lyle Ungar

Day 2: Friday June 8th 2012 (SemEval View) (continued)

Session PLN3: (5:15–6:00) Plenary Panel and Closing: *SEM and the Future

—- End of SemEval View —-

Casting Implicit Role Linking as an Anaphora Resolution Task

Carina Silberer*
School of Informatics
University of Edinburgh
Edinburgh, UK
c.silberer@ed.ac.uk

Anette Frank
Department of Computational Linguistics
Heidelberg University
Heidelberg, Germany
frank@cl.uni-heidelberg.de

Abstract

Linking implicit semantic roles is a challenging problem in discourse processing. Unlike prior work inspired by SRL, we cast this problem as an anaphora resolution task and embed it in an entity-based coreference resolution (CR) architecture. Our experiments clearly show that CR-oriented features yield strongest performance exceeding a strong baseline. We address the problem of data sparsity by applying heuristic labeling techniques, guided by the anaphoric nature of the phenomenon. We achieve performance beyond state-of-the art.

1 Introduction

A widespread phenomenon that is still poorly studied in NLP is the meaning contribution of unfilled semantic roles of predicates in discourse interpretation. Such roles, while linguistically unexpressed, can often be anaphorically bound to antecedent referents in the discourse context. Capturing such implicit semantic roles and linking them to their antecedents is a challenging problem. But it bears immense potential for establishing discourse coherence and for getting closer to the aim of true NLU.

Linking of implicit semantic roles in discourse has recently been introduced as a shared task in the SemEval 2010 competition *Linking Events and Their Participants in Discourse* (Ruppenhofer et al., 2009, 2010). The task consists in detecting unfilled semantic roles of events and determining antecedents in the discourse context that these roles can be understood to refer to. In (1), e.g., the predicate *jealousy* introduces two implicit roles, one for the experiencer, the other for the object of jealousy involved. These roles can be bound to *Watson* and the speaker (*I*) in the non-local preceding context.

(1) Watson won't allow that I know anything of art but that is mere *jealousy* because our views upon the subject differ.

(2) I_{Reader} was sitting *reading* in the chair_{Place}.

In contrast to implicit roles that can be *discourse-bound* to an antecedent as in (1), roles can be interpreted *existentially*, as in (2), with an unfilled TEXT role of the READING frame that cannot be anchored in prior discourse. The FrameNet paradigm (Fillmore et al., 2003) that was used for annotation in the SemEval task classifies these interpretation differences as definite (DNI) vs. indefinite (INI) null instantiations (NI) of roles, respectively.

2 Implicit Role Reference: A Short History

Early studies. The phenomenon of implicit role reference is not new. It has been studied in a number of early approaches. Palmer et al. (1986) treated unfilled semantic roles as special cases of anaphora and coreference resolution (CR). Resolution was guided by domain knowledge encoded in a knowledge-based system. Similarly, Whittemore et al. (1991) analyzed the resolution of unexpressed event roles as a special case of CR. A formalization in DRT was fully worked out, but automation was not addressed.

Later studies emphasize the role of implicit role reference in a frame-semantic discourse analysis. Fillmore and Baker (2001) provide an analysis of

* The work reported in this paper is based on a Master's Thesis conducted at Heidelberg University (Silberer, 2011).

a newspaper text that indicates the importance of frames and roles in establishing discourse coherence. Burchardt et al. (2005) offer a formalization of the involved factors: the interplay of frames and frame relations with factors of contextual contiguity. The work includes no automation, but suggests a corpus-based approach using antecedent-role coreference patterns collected from corpora.

Tetreault (2002), finally, offers an automated analysis for resolving implicit role reference. The small-scale study is embedded in a rule-based CR setup.

SemEval 2010 Task 10: Linking Roles. Triggered by the SemEval 2010 competition (Ruppenhofer et al., 2010), research on resolving implicit role reference has gained momentum again, in a field where both semantic role labeling (SRL) and coreference resolution have seen tremendous progress. However, the systems that participated in the *NI-only* task on implicit role resolution achieved moderate success in the initial subtasks: (i) recognition of implicit roles and (ii) classification as discourse-bound vs. existential interpretation (DNI vs. INI). Yet, (iii) identification of role antecedents was bluntly unsuccessful, with around 1% F-score.

Ruppenhofer et al. clearly relate the task to coreference resolution. The participating systems, though, framed the task as a special case of SRL.

Chen et al. (2010) participated with their SRL system SEMAFOR (Das et al., 2010). They cast the task as one of extended SRL, by admitting constituents from a larger context. To overcome the lack and sparsity of syntactic path features, they include lexical association and similarity scores for semantic roles and role fillers; classical SRL order and distance features are adapted to larger distances.

VENSES++ by Tonelli and Delmonte (2010) is a semantic processing system that includes lexico-semantic processing, anaphora resolution and deep semantic resolution components. Anaphora resolution is performed in a rule-based manner; pronominals are replaced with their antecedents' lexical information. For role linking, the system applies diverse heuristics including search for predicate-argument structures with compatible arguments, as well as semantic relatedness scores between potential fillers of (overt and implicit) semantic roles.

More recently Tonelli and Delmonte (2011) recur to a leaner approach for role binding, estimating a relevance score for potential antecedents from role fillers observed in training. They report an F-score of 8 points for role binding on SemEval data. However, being strongly lexicalized, their trained model seems heavily dependent on the training data.

Ruppenhofer et al. (2011) use semantic types for identifying DNI role antecedents, reporting an error reduction of 14% on Chen et al. (2010)'s results.

The poor performance results in the SemEval task clearly indicate the difficulty of resolving implicit role reference. A major factor seems to relate to data sparsity: the training set covers only 245 DNI annotations linked to an antecedent.

Linking implicit arguments of nominals. Gerber and Chai (2010) (G&C henceforth) investigate a closely related task of argument binding, tied to the linking of implicit arguments for *nominal predicates* using the PropBank role labeling scheme. In contrast to the SemEval task, which focuses on a verbs and nouns, their system is only applied to nouns and is restricted to 10 predicates with substantial training set sizes (avg: 125, median: 103).

G&C propose a discriminative model that selects an antecedent for an implicit role from an extended context window. The approach incorporates some aspects relating to CR that go beyond the SRL-oriented SemEval systems: A candidate representation includes information about all the candidates' coreferent mentions (determined by automatic CR), in particular their semantic roles (provided by gold annotations) and WordNet synsets. Patterns of semantic associations between filler candidates and implicit roles are learned for *all* mentions contained in the candidate's entity chain. They achieve an F-score of 42.3, against a baseline of 26.5.

Gerber (2011) presents an extended model that incorporates strategies suggested in Burchardt et al. (2005): using frame relations as well as coreference patterns acquired from large corpora. This model achieves an F-score of 50.3 (baseline: 28.9).

3 Casting Implicit Role Linking as an Anaphora Resolution Task

3.1 Implicit role = anaphora resolution

Recent models for role binding mainly draw on techniques from SRL, enriched with concepts from CR.

In this paper, we explicitly formulate implicit role linking as an anaphora resolution task. This is in line with the predominant conception in early work, and also highlights the close relationship with zero anaphora (Kameyama, 1985). Computational treatments of zero anaphora (e.g., Imamura et al. (2009)) are in fact employing techniques well-known from SRL. Recent work by Iida and Poesio (2011), by contrast, offers an analysis of zero anaphora in a CR architecture. Further support comes from psycholinguistic studies in Garrod and Terras (2000), who establish commonalities between implicit role reference and other types of anaphora resolution.

The contributions of our work are as follows:

i. We cast implicit role binding as a CR task, using an *entity-mention* model and discriminative classification for antecedent selection.

ii. We examine the effectiveness of model features for classical SRL vs. CR features to clarify the nature of this special phenomenon.

iii. We automatically acquire heuristically labeled data to address the sparse data problem.

i. An entity-mention model for anaphoric role resolution. In our model implicit roles that are discourse-bound (i.e. classified as DNI) are treated as anaphoric, similar to zero anaphora: the implicit role will be bound to a discourse antecedent.

In line with recent research in CR, we adopt an *entity-mention* model, where an *entity* is represented by all mentions pertaining to a coreference chain (see i.a. Rahman and Ng (2011), Cai and Strube (2010)). Our model is based on binary classifier decisions that take as input the anaphoric role and an entity candidate from the preceding discourse. The final classification of a role linking to an entity is obtained by discriminative ranking of the binary classifiers' probability estimates. Details on the system architecture are given in Section 3.2.

ii. SRL vs. CR: Analysis of feature sets. The linking of implicit semantic roles represents an interesting mixture of SRL and CR that displays exceptional characteristics of both types of phenomena.

In contrast to classical SRL, the relation between a predicate's semantic role and a candidate role filler – being realized outside the local syntactic context – cannot be characterized by syntactic path features. But similar to SRL we can compute a semantic class type expected by the role and determine which candidate is most appropriate to fill the semantic role.

Anaphoric binding of unfilled roles also diverges from classical CR in that the anaphoric element is not overtly expressed. This excludes typical CR features that refer to overt realization, such as agreement or string overlap. Again, we can make use of a semantic characterization of role fillers to determine the role's most appropriate antecedent entity in the discourse. This closely relates to semantic class features employed in CR (e.g., Rahman and Ng (2011)).

Thus, semantic association features are important modeling aspects, but they do not contribute to clarifying the nature of the phenomenon. We will include additional properties that are considered characteristic for CR, such as the semantics of an *entity* (as opposed to individual mentions), or salience properties of antecedents (cf. Section 4.3). Thus, the model we propose substantially differs from prior work.

We classify the features of our models as SRL vs. CR features, plus a mixture class that relates to both phenomena. We examine which type of features is most effective for resolving implicit role reference.

iii. Heuristic data acquisition. In response to the sparse data problem encountered with the SemEval data set and the general lack of annotated resources for implicit role binding, we experiment with techniques for heuristic data acquisition. The strategy we apply builds on our working hypothesis that implicit role reference is best understood as a special case of (zero) anaphora resolution.

We process manually annotated coreference data sets that are jointly labeled with semantic roles. From these we extract entity chains that contain anaphoric pronouns that fill a predicate's semantic role. We artificially delete the pronoun's role label and transfer it to its closest antecedent in its chain. In this way, we convert the example to an instance that is structurally similar to one involving a locally unfilled semantic role that is bound to an overt antecedent. An example is given below: in (3.a) we identify a pronoun that fills the SPEAKER role of the frame STATEMENT. We transfer this role label to its closest antecedent (3.b).

(3) a. Riady$_k$ spoke in his$_k$ 21-story office building on the outskirts of Jakarta. [...] The timing of his$_{k,Speaker}$ statement$_{Statement}$ is important.

b. Riady$_k$ spoke in his$_{k,Speaker}$ 21-story office building on the outskirts of Jakarta. [...] The timing of $\emptyset$ statement$_{Statement}$ is important.

Clearly such artificially created annotation instances are only approximations of naturally occurring cases of implicit role binding. But we expect to acquire numerous data points for relevant features: semantic class information for the antecedent entity, the predicate's frame and roles and coherence properties.

3.2 System Architecture

Our approach is embedded in an architecture for supervised CR using an entity-mention model. The main processing steps of the system include: (1) entity detection, (2) instance creation with feature extraction and (3) classification. As we are focusing on the resolution of implicit DNI roles, we assume that the text is already augmented with standard CR information (we make use of gold data and automatically assigned coreference chains). Accordingly, the description of modules focuses exclusively on the resolution of DNIs.

(1) Entity Detection. We first collect the entire entity set $\mathcal{E}$ mentioned in the discourse. This set forms the overall set of candidates to consider for DNI linking. For each DNI d_k to be linked, a subset of candidates $\mathcal{E}_k \subset \mathcal{E}$ is chosen as candidate search space for resolving d_k. We experiment with different strategies for constructing $\mathcal{E}_k$ (cf. Section 4).

(2) Instance Creation. The next step consists in the creation of (training) instances for classification including the extraction of features for all instances.

An instance $inst_{e_j,d_k}$ consists of the active DNI d_k, its frame and a candidate entity $e_j \in \mathcal{E}_k$. Instance creation follows an entity-based adaption of the standard procedure of Soon et al. (2001), which has been applied by Yang et al. (2004, 2008). Processing the discourse from left to right, for each DNI d_k, instances $\mathcal{I}_k$ are created by processing $\mathcal{E}_k$ from right to left according to each entity's most recent mention, starting with the entity closest to d_k. Note that, as entities instead of mentions are considered, only one instance is created for an entity which is mentioned several times in the search space.

In training, the instance creation stops when the correct antecedent, i.e. a positive instance, as well as at least one negative instance have been found.[1]

(3) Classification. From the acquired training instances we learn a binary classifier that predicts for an instance $inst_{e_j,d_k}$ whether it is positive, i.e. entity e_j is a correct antecedent for DNI d_k. Further, the classifier provides a probability estimate for $inst_{e_j,d_k}$ being positive. We obtain classifications for all instances in $\mathcal{I}_k$. Among the positive classified instances, we select the antecedent e with the highest estimate. That is, we apply the *best-first* strategy (Ng and Cardie, 2002). In case of a tie, we choose the antecedent which is closer to the target. If no instance is classified as positive, d_k is left unfilled.

4 Data and Experiments

4.1 SEMEVAL 2010 task and data set

We adhere to the SemEval 2010 task by Ruppenhofer et al. (2009) as test bed for our experiments. The main focus of our work is on part (iii), the identification of antecedents for DNIs. Subtasks (i) and (ii), the recognition and interpretation of NIs will be only tackled to enable comparison to the participating systems of the SemEval *NI-only* task.

The SemEval task is based on fiction stories by A. C. Doyle, one story as training data and another two chapters as test set, enriched with coreference and FrameNet-style frame annotations. Information about the training section is found in Table 1. The test data comprise 710 NIs (349 DNIs, 361 INIs), of which 259 DNIs are linked.

4.2 Heuristic data acquisition

Since the training data has a critically small amount of linked DNIs, we heuristically labeled training data on the basis of data sets with manually annotated coreference information: OntoNotes 3.0 (Hovy et al., 2006), as well as ACE-2 (Mitchell et al., 2003) and MUC-6 (Chinchor and Sundheim, 2003).

OntoNotes 3.0 was merged with gold SRL annotations from the CoNLL-2005 shared task. By means of SemLink-1.1 (Loper et al., 2007) and a mapping included in the SemEval data, these PropBank (PB, Palmer et al. (2005)) annotations were

[1] We additionally impose several restrictions, e.g., a valid candidate must not already fill another role of the active frame.

	#ent	avg #ent/doc	avg size	#frames	#frame types	#DNI	#DNI types
SemEval	141	141	9	1,370	317	245	155
ONotes	7899	23	3	12,770	258	2,220	270
ACE-2	3564	11	4	58,204	757	4,265	578
MUC-6	1841	15	3	20,140	654	997	310

corpus	coref	semantic roles
ONotes	manual	manual PB CoNLL05, ported to FN
ACE-2	manual	automatic FN (Semafor)
MUC-6	manual	automatic FN (Semafor)

Table 1: SemEval vs. heuristically acquired data

mapped to their FrameNet (FN) counterparts, if existent. For the ACE-2 and MUC-6 corpora, we used Semafor (Das and Smith, 2011) for automatic annotation with FN semantic roles. From these data sets we acquired heuristically annotated instances of role linking using the strategy explained in 3.1.

Table 1 summarizes the resulting training data. The heuristically labeled data extends the manually labeled DNI instances by an order of magnitude.

4.3 Model parameters

Entity sets $\mathcal{E}_{dni}$. For definition of the set of candidate entities to consider for DNI linking, $\mathcal{E}_{dni}$, we determined different parameter settings with restrictions on the types, distances and prominence of candidate antecedents. For instance, unlike in noun phrase CR, antecedents for a DNI can be realized by a wide range of constituents other than NPs, such as prepositional (`PP`), adverbial (`ADVP`), verb phrases (`VP`) and even sentences (`S`) referring to propositions.

These settings, stated in Table 2, were inferred by experiments on the training data and by examining its statistics: *AllChains* is motivated by the fact that 72% of the DNIs are linked to referents with non-singleton chains. On the other hand, the majority of DNI antecedents – not only non-singletons, but also phrases of a certain type or terminals that overtly fill other roles – are located in the current and the two preceding sentences (69.6%), which motivates *SentWin*. However, antecedents are also located far beyond this window span which is probably due to the nature of the SemEval texts, with prominent entities being accessible over longer stretches of discourse. *Chains+Win* is designed by taking into account all previous observations.

AllChains This set contains all the entities represented by non-singleton coreference chains that were introduced in the discourse up to the current DNI position, assuming that this way only more salient entities are considered.

SentWin Comprises constituents with a certain phrase type[2] or terminals that overtly fill a role, occurring within the current or the preceding two sentences.

Chain+Win This set comprises **SentWin** plus all entities mentioned at least five times up to the current DNI position (i.e. salient entities).

Table 2: Entity set settings $\mathcal{E}_{dni}$

Training data sets. We made use of different mixtures of training data: SemEval plus different extensions using the heuristically acquired data summarized in Table 1.

4.4 Feature sets: SRL, mixed and CR-oriented

Table 3 lists the most important features used for training our models. Features 1-13 were used in the best model and are ordered by their strength based on feature ablation experiments (cf. Section 5). All features are marked for their general type; the last column marks features employed by G&C.[3]

Below we give some details for selected features.

Feat. 1: Prominence. We first compute average prominence of an entity e (Eq. 2) by summing over the size (= nb. of mentions) of all entities e in a window w[4] of preceding sentences and dividing by the nb. of entities E in w. Prominence of e (Eq. 1) is set to the difference between its size in w and the average prominence score.[5] The final feature value records the relative rank of e's prominence score compared to the scores of the other candidates.

$$prom(e,w) = \#mentions(e,w) - avg\ prom(w) \quad (1)$$

$$avg\ prom(w) = \frac{\sum_{e \in E} \#mentions(e,w)}{|E|} \quad (2)$$

[2]The phrase type must be `NPB`, `S`, `VP`, `SBAR`, or `SG`.

[3]$\sim$ marks features that are similar to G&C features. Note that their only CR features are distance features.

[4]We set $w = 2$ based on experiments on the training data.

[5]This prominence score was proposed by Dolata (2010) within an entity grid approach to role linking.

nr	feature		type	G&C
1	prominence	prominence score of the entity in the current discourse position	CR	-
2	pos.dist_mention	PoS or phrase type of the most recent explicit mention concatenated with sentence distance to the target	(CR)	-
3	dist_mentions	minimum distance between DNI and entity in mentions	CR	-
4	dist_sentences	minimum distance between DNI and entity in sentences	CR	+
5	vnroles_dni.entity	the counterparts of the DNI in VerbNet (VN, Kipper et al. (2000)) concatenated with the VN roles the entity already instantiates	mixed	+
6	roles_dni.entity	concatenation of the DNI with the FN roles the entity already instantiates	mixed	~
7	semType_dni.entity	semantic type of the DNI concatenated with the semantic types of the roles the entity already instantiates	mixed	-
8	avgDist_sentences	average sentence distance between the entity and the DNI	CR	+
9	sp_supersense	agreement of the selectional preferences for the DNI and the most frequent supersense of the entity	mixed	-
10	function (target)	grammatical function of the target	SRL	-
11	wnss_ent.st_dni	pointwise mutual information between the entity's WN supersense ss and the DNI's FN semantic type st: $pmi(ss, st) = log_2 P(ss\|st)/P(ss)$	mixed	-
12	nbRoles_dni.entity	like feature 5, but with NomBank arguments 0 and 1	mixed	~
13	frame.dni	frame name concatenated with the DNI	SRL	-

Table 3: Best features used for training. Feat. 11 was computed on the FN dataset and the SemEval training data.

Feat. 9: SelPrefs. We compute selectional preferences following the information-theoretic approach of Resnik (1993, 1996). Similar to Erk (2007), we used an adapted version which we computed for semantic roles by means of the FN database rather than for verb argument positions. The WordNet classes over which the preferences are defined are WordNet lexicographer's files (supersenses).

The selectional association values $\Lambda(dni, ss)$ of the DNI's selectional preferences are retrieved for the supersense ss of each candidate antecedent's head. As for Feat. 1, we define a candidate's feature value by its rank in the ordered list of these Λs.

4.5 Experiments

Evaluation measures. We adopt the precision (P), recall (R) and F_1 measures in Ruppenhofer et al. (2010). A true positive is a DNI which has been linked to the correct entity as given by the gold data.

Classifiers and feature selection. For DNI linking, we use BayesNet (Cooper and Herskovits, 1992) as classifier, implemented in Weka (Witten and Frank, 2000).[6] For each parameter combination, we perform feature selection by means of leave-one-out 10-fold cross-validation on the SemEval training data with successively removing/determining the best features. The resulting models M_i are then evaluated on the SemEval test data in different setups:

Exp1: Linking DNIs. Exp1 evaluates our models on the DNI linking task proper (NI-only step (iii)). This setting uses the gold coreference, SRL and DNI information in the test data.

Exp2: Full NI-only. For benchmarking on the SemEval task, we perform the complete NI-only task. Here, the test data is only enriched w/ SRL labeling. Each frame *f* in the test corpus is processed, involving the following steps:

(i) *Recognition of NIs* is performed by consulting the FN database[7] and determining the FN core roles that are unfilled. From this NI set, roles that are conceptually redundant or competing with *f*'s overt roles are rejected as they don't need to or must not be linked, respectively.

(ii) For predicting the *interpretation of an NI*, we use LibSVM (Chang and Lin, 2001) as classifier which further assigns each NI a probability estimate of the NI being definite. We use a small set of features: the FN semantic type of the NI and a boolean feature indicating whether the target is in passive voice and the agent (object) not realized. Further, we use a statistical feature which gives the relative

[6]We experimented with different learners and selected the algorithm that performed best for the different subtasks.

[7]We used the FrameNetAPI by Reiter (2010).

model	add. data	entity set	frame anno.	DNI Linking (%) P	R	F_1
M_0	-	AllChains	gold	25.6	25.1	25.3
M_1	ON2-10	Chains+Win	proj	30.8	**25.1**	**27.7**
$M_{1'}$	ON2-24	AllChains	proj	**35.6**	20.1	25.7
$M_{1''}$	ON2-24	SentWin	proj	23.3	22.4	22.8
M_2	MUC	Chains+Win	auto	26.1	24.3	25.3
M_3	ACE	AllChains	auto	24.0	21.2	22.5
Prom	–	Chains+Win	–	20.5	20.5	20.5

Table 4: Exp1: Best performing models for different entity and data settings. Test data contain gold CR chains.

frequency of the role's realization as DNI and INI, respectively, in the training data.

(iii) *DNI linking* is performed for each of *f*'s predicted DNIs $\mathcal{D}_f$ in descending order of their probability estimates. If an antecedent e_m can be determined for a predicted DNI, the role is labeled as such and linked to e_m. As the DNI's role has been filled now, competing or redundant DNIs are removed from $\mathcal{D}_f$ before moving to the next predicted DNI. Only DNIs for which an antecedent is found are labeled as such.

Exp2 is evaluated on both gold coreference annotation and automatically assigned coreference chains, using the CR system of Cai et al. (2011).

5 Evaluation and Results

5.1 Exp1: DNI linking evaluation

Table 4 shows the best performing models for DNI linking for each parameter setting[8]. We compare them to a strong baseline *Prom* (last row) that links each DNI to the antecedent candidate with highest prominence score. Its F_1-score is beaten by the other models, with a gain of 7.2 points for model M_1. The high performance of the baseline can be taken as evidence that salience factors are crucial for this task.

The best performing model M_1 (27.7 F_1) uses about a fifth of the ON data with *Chains+Win*. When using *SentWin* as entity set, F_1 drops to 18.5 (not shown). The best performing model using *SentWin* ($M_{1''}$) performs 4.9 points below M_1. Hence, reliance on the *Chains+Win* set seems beneficial. Performance of the *AllChains* setting varies over the different data sets: the strongest model is M_0 without additional data. An explanation could be the different data domains (story vs. news), leading to a different nature (length and number) of the entities.

In general, the models seem to profit from heuristically labeled training data. We note strong gains (up to 10 pts) in precision for 3 of these 5 best models, compared to M_0. Finally, we observe higher performance when using additional data with gold/ projected semantic frame annotations (M_1, $M_{1'}$).

Features	P (%)	R (%)	F_1 (%)
all	30.8	25.1	27.7
- 1-4,8 (CR)	21.6	8.1	11.8
- 10,13 (SRL)	31.0	25.9	28.2
- 5-7,9,11-12 (mixed)	20.6	20.5	20.5

Table 5: Results of ablation study.

Analysis of the best model. Table 5 states the results for M_1 when leaving out one of the feature types at a time. The serious drop of F_1 from 27.7% to 11.8% when omitting CR features clearly demonstrates that this feature type has by far the greatest impact on the task performance. Rejection of the mixed features decreases F_1 to a score equal to the prominence baseline, whereas leaving out the SRL-features even slightly increases F_1. The weakness of Feature 13 could still be attributed to data sparsity.

5.2 Exp2: Full NI-only evaluation

Table 6 lists the results for the full NI-only task obtained with the presented models with different additional training data sets (lines 2-5). When performing all three steps, the F_1-score of the best model M_1 drops to 10.1% (-17.6 pts, col. 10) under usage of automatic coreference annotations in the test data (i.e. under the real task conditions). When using gold coreference annotations, the F_1-score is at 18.1% (col. 11), which can be seen as an upper bound for our current models on this task. The difference of 9.6 points between only performing DNI linking (Table 4) and the full NI-only task reflects the fact that recognizing (step i) and interpreting (step ii) NIs bear difficulties on their own.[9]

Comparison of our models with the two SemEval

[8]We consider the 3 types of entity sets and different training setups ± additional data (Section 4.3); additional data with gold, projected or automatic frame annotations. The ON data was also evaluated with roughly a fifth of ON to evaluate the effect of different amounts of data of the same type of data.

[9]When not performing step (iii), NI recognition achieves 77.6% recall and 67% relative precision.

model	add. data	entity set	frame anno.	Null Instantiations (%) recogn. recall	interpret. (precision) relative	absolute	DNI Linking (%) P	R	F_1	F_1(crf)
M_0	-	AllChains	gold	58	68	40	6.0	8.9	7.1	12.5
M_1	ON2-10	Chains+Win	proj	56	69	38	9.2	11.2	10.1	18.1
M_2	MUC	Chains+Win	auto	52	70	36	7.0	8.5	7.6	11.0
M_3	ACE	AllChains	auto	56	68	38	5.9	8.1	6.8	11.3
$M_{3'}$	ACE	Chains+Win	auto	56	68	38	6.9	9.7	8.0	9.5
SEMAFOR		–		63	55	35			1.40	
VENSES++		–		8	64	5			1.21	
T&D		–		54	75	40	13.0	6.0	8	

Table 6: Exp2 results obtained for our models (lines 1-5) and comparable systems (lines 6-8). Column 5 gives the score for correctly recognized NIs. Cols. 6 and 7 report precision for correctly interpreted NIs on the basis of the correctly recognized (relative) vs. all gold NIs to be recognized (absolute). The scores in the last column (F_1(crf)) were obtained with gold CR annotations.

task participants[10] (lines 7-8) shows that our models clearly outperform these systems – with a gain of +5.7 and +8.89 points in F_1-score in DNI linking.[11]

Compared to Tonelli and Delmonte (2011) (T&D), M_1 has a higher F_1-score in linking of +2.1 points. In contrast to our method, their linking approach is (admittedly) heavily lexicalized and strongly tailored to the domain of the used data.

6 Conclusion

We cast the problem of linking implicit semantic roles as a special case of (zero) anaphora resolution, drawing on insights from earlier work and parallels observed with zero anaphora. Our results strongly support this analysis: (i) Feature selection clearly determines CR-related features as strongest support for DNI linking. (ii) Our models beat a strong baseline using a prominence score to determine DNI reference. (iii) We devise a method for heuristically labeling training data that simulates implicit role reference. Using this data we obtain system performance beyond state-of-the-art, with high gains in precision.

While these findings clearly corroborate our conceptual approach, overall performance is still meager. Comparison to G&C's setting suggests that training data is a serious issue. We addressed the problem of training set size using heuristic data acquisition. The nature of semantic role annotations may be another problem, as FrameNet-style roles do not generalize well. Finally, implicit roles pertaining to nominalizations tend to be more local than those pertaining to verbs[12] and might be less diverse.

Our model is closer in spirit to G&C than the SemEval systems, but differs by being embedded in an entity-based CR architecture using discriminative antecedent selection. Also, we address a more principled issue, by exploring the nature of the task using a qualitative feature analysis. Our system compares favorably to related work. Benchmarking against the SemEval participants and T&D shows clear improvements. Also, T&D's model is closely tied to domain data, while ours is enhanced with out-of-domain data. Exact comparison to G&C needs to be conducted on the same data set and labeling scheme.

In sum, within the chosen setting we can show that implicit role reference is best modeled as a special case of anaphora resolution. We observe that models trained on cleaner data perform better than on larger, but more noisy data sets. Thus, it is essential to further enhance the quality of heuristically labeled data. Applying the classifiers for steps (i) and (ii) as a filter could help to better constrain the data to the target phenomenon.

Acknowledgements. We would like to thank Mateusz Dolata for his help with salience and coherence features, and Michael Roth for his server support.

[10]The F_1-scores are from `http://semeval2.fbk.eu/semeval2.php?location=Rankings/ranking10.html`

[11]Moreover, note that Ruppenhofer et al. describe a weaker evaluation, that judges DNI linkings as correct if the span of the linked referent contains the gold referent. Further, they consider 14 linked INIs in the test data, although linking INIs conflicts with the definition of INIs.

[12]This is confirmed by analysis of the SemEval vs. NomBank corpus of G&C.

References

Aljoscha Burchardt, Anette Frank, and Manfred Pinkal. 2005. Building Text Meaning Representations from Contextually Related Frames – A Case Study. In *Proceedings of the 6th International Workshop on Computational Semantics*, IWCS-6, pages 66–77, Tilburg, The Netherlands.

Jie Cai and Michael Strube. 2010. End-to-end coreference resolution via hypergraph partitioning. In *Proceedings of the 23rd International Conference on Computational Linguistics*, pages 143–151, Beijing, China.

Jie Cai, Eva Mújdricza-Maydt, and Michael Strube. 2011. Unrestricted coreference resolution via global hypergraph partitioning. In *Proceedings of the Shared Task of 15th Conference on Computational Natural Language Learning*, pages 56–60, Portland, Oregon.

Chih-Chung Chang and Chih-Jen Lin, 2001. *LIBSVM: a Library for Support Vector Machines*. Software available at `http://www.csie.ntu.edu.tw/~cjlin/libsvm`.

Desai Chen, Nathan Schneider, Dipanjan Das, and Noah A. Smith. 2010. SEMAFOR: Frame Argument Resolution with Log-Linear Models. In *Proceedings of the 5th International Workshop on Semantic Evaluation*, pages 264–267, Uppsala, Sweden, July.

Nancy Chinchor and Beth Sundheim, 2003. *Message Understanding Conference (MUC) 6*. Linguistic Data Consortium, Philadelphia.

Gregory F. Cooper and Edward Herskovits. 1992. A Bayesian Method for the Induction of Probabilistic Networks from Data. *Machine Learning*, 9(4):309–347.

Dipanjan Das and Noah A. Smith. 2011. Semi-supervised frame-semantic parsing for unknown predicates. In Dekang Lin, Yuji Matsumoto, and Rada Mihalcea, editors, *ACL*, pages 1435–1444. The Association for Computer Linguistics.

Dipanjan Das, Nathan Schneider, Desai Chen, and Noah A. Smith. 2010. Probabilistic Frame-Semantic Parsing. In *Human Language Technologies: The 2010 Annual Conference of the North American Chapter of the Association for Computational Linguistics*, pages 948–956, Los Angeles, California, June.

Mateusz Dolata. 2010. *Extending the Entity-Grid Model for the Processing of Implicit Roles in Discourse*. Bachelor's thesis, Department of Computational Linguistics, Heidelberg University, Germany.

Katrin Erk. 2007. A Simple, Similarity-based Model for Selectional Preferences. In *Proceedings of the 45th Annual Meeting of the Association for Computational Linguistics*, ACL '07, pages 216–223, Prague, Czech Republic, June.

Charles J. Fillmore and Collin F. Baker. 2001. Frame Semantics for Text Understanding. In *Proceedings of the NAACL 2001 Workshop on WordNet and Other Lexical Resources*, Pittsburgh, June.

Charles J. Fillmore, Christopher R. Johnson, and Miriam R. L. Petruck. 2003. Background to Framenet. *International Journal of Lexicography*, 16(3):235–250.

Simon Garrod and Melody Terras. 2000. The Contribution of Lexical and Situational Knowledge to Resolving Discourse Roles: Bonding and Resolution. *Journal of Memory and Language*, 42(4):526–544.

Matthew Gerber and Joyce Chai. 2010. Beyond NomBank: A Study of Implicit Arguments for Nominal Predicates. In *Proceedings of the 48th Annual Meeting of the Association for Computational Linguistics*, pages 1583–1592, Uppsala, Sweden, July.

Matthew Steven Gerber. 2011. *Semantic Role Labeling of Implicit Arguments for Nominal Predicates*. Ph.D. thesis, Michigan State University.

Eduard Hovy, Mitchell Marcus, Martha Palmer, Lance Ramshaw, and Ralph Weischedel. 2006. OntoNotes: The 90% Solution. In *Proceedings of the Human Language Technology Conference of the North American Chapter of the Association for Computational Linguistics*, HLT-NAACL '06, pages 57–60, New York, New York, June.

Ryu Iida and Massimo Poesio. 2011. A Cross-Lingual ILP Solution to Zero Anaphora Resolution. In *Proceedings of the 49th Annual Meeting of the Association for Computational Linguistics*, pages 804–813, Portland, Oregon.

Kenji Imamura, Kuniko Saito, and Tomoko Izumi. 2009. Discriminative Approach to Predicate-Argument Structure Analysis with Zero-Anaphora Resolution. In *Proceedings of the Joint Conference of the 47th Annual Meeting of the Association for Computational Linguistics and the 4th International Joint Conference on Natural Language Processing of the Asian Federation of Natural Language Processing*, ACL-IJCNLP '09, pages 85–88, Suntec, Singapore, August.

Megumi Kameyama. 1985. *Zero Anaphora: The case of Japanese*. Ph.D. thesis, Stanford University.

Karin Kipper, Hoa Trang Dang, and Martha Palmer. 2000. Class-Based Construction of a Verb Lexicon. In *Proceedings of the 17th National Conference on Artificial Intelligence and 12th Conference on Innovative Applications of Artificial Intelligence*, pages 691–696, Austin, Texas. AAAI Press. `http://verbs.colorado.edu/~mpalmer/projects/verbnet.html`.

Edward Loper, Szu ting Yi, and Martha Palmer. 2007. Combining Lexical Resources: Mapping between

PropBank and VerbNet. In *Proceedings of the 7th International Workshop on Computational Linguistics*.

Alexis Mitchell, Stephanie Strassel, Mark Przybocki, JK Davis, George Doddington, Ralph Grishman, Adam Meyers, Ada Brunstein, Lisa Ferro, and Beth Sundheim, 2003. *ACE-2 Version 1.0*. Linguistic Data Consortium, Philadelphia.

Vincent Ng and Claire Cardie. 2002. Improving Machine Learning Approaches to Coreference Resolution. In *Proceedings of the 40th Annual Meeting of the Association for Computational Linguistics*, ACL '02, pages 104–111, Philadelphia, Pennsylvania.

Martha S. Palmer, Deborah A. Dahl, Rebecca J. Schiffman, Lynette Hirschman, Marcia Linebarger, and John Dowding. 1986. Recovering Implicit Information. In *Proceedings of the 24th Annual Meeting of the Association for Computational Linguistics*, pages 10–19, New York, New York, USA.

Martha Palmer, Daniel Gildea, and Paul Kingsbury. 2005. The Proposition Bank: An Annotated Corpus of Semantic Roles. *Computational Linguistics*, 31(1):71–106, March.

Altaf Rahman and Vincent Ng. 2011. Narrowing the modeling gap: A cluster-ranking approach to coreference resolution. *Journal of Artificial Intelligence Research*, 40:469–521.

Nils Reiter. 2010. FrameNet API. `http://www.cl.uni-heidelberg.de/trac/FrameNetAPI`.

Philip Resnik. 1996. Selectional Constraints: an Information-theoretic Model and its Computational Realization. *Cognition*, 61(1-2):127–159, November.

Josef Ruppenhofer, Caroline Sporleder, Roser Morante, Collin Baker, and Martha Palmer. 2009. SemEval-2010 Task 10: Linking Events and Their Participants in Discourse. In *Proceedings of the NAACL-HLT 2009 Workshop on Semantic Evaluations: Recent Achievements and Future Directions (SEW-09)*, pages 106–111, Boulder, Colorado, June.

Josef Ruppenhofer, Caroline Sporleder, Roser Morante, Collin Baker, and Martha Palmer. 2010. SemEval-2010 Task 10: Linking Events and Their Participants in Discourse. In *Proceedings of the 5th International Workshop on Semantic Evaluations*, pages 45–50, Uppsala, Sweden, July.

Josef Ruppenhofer, Philip Gorinski, and Caroline Sporleder. 2011. In Search of Missing Arguments: A Linguistic Approach. In *Proceedings of the International Conference Recent Advances in Natural Language Processing*, pages 331–338, Hissar, Bulgaria, September.

Carina Silberer. 2011. *Linking Implicit Semantic Roles in Discourese Using Coreference Resolution Methods*. Master's thesis, Department of Computational Linguistics, Heidelberg University, Germany.

Wee Meng Soon, Hwee Tou Ng, and Daniel Chung Yong Lim. 2001. A Machine Learning Approach to Coreference Resolution of Noun Phrases. *Computational Linguistics*, 27:521–544, December.

Joel R. Tetreault. 2002. Implicit Role Reference. In *International Symposium on Reference Resolution for Natural Language Processing*, pages 109–115, Alicante, Spain.

Sara Tonelli and Rodolfo Delmonte. 2010. VENSES++: Adapting a Deep Semantic Processing System to the Identification of Null Instantiations. In *Proceedings of the 5th International Workshop on Semantic Evaluations*, pages 296–299, Uppsala, Sweden, July.

Sara Tonelli and Rodolfo Delmonte. 2011. Desperately Seeking Implicit Arguments in Text. In *Proceedings of the ACL 2011 Workshop on Relational Models of Semantics*, pages 54–62, Portland, Oregon, USA, June.

G. Whittemore, M. Macpherson, and G. Carlson. 1991. Event-building through role filling and anaphora resolution. In *Proceedings of the 29th Annual Meeting on Association for Computational Linguistics*, pages 17–24, Morristown, NJ, USA.

Ian H. Witten and Eibe Frank. 2000. *Data Mining: Practical Machine Learning Tools and Techniques with Java Implementations*. Morgan Kaufmann, San Francisco, CA, USA.

Xiaofeng Yang, Jian Su, Guodong Zhou, and Chew Lim Tan. 2004. An NP-cluster Based Approach to Coreference Resolution. In *Proceedings of the 20th International Conference on Computational Linguistics*, COLING '04, pages 226–232, Geneva, Switzerland.

Xiaofeng Yang, Jian Su, Jun Lang, Chew Lim Tan, Ting Liu, and Sheng Li. 2008. An Entity-Mention Model for Coreference Resolution with Inductive Logic Programming. In *Proceedings of the 46th Annual Meeting of the Association for Computational Linguistics: Human Language Technologies*, ACL '08:HLT, pages 843–851, Columbus, Ohio, June.

Adaptive Clustering for Coreference Resolution with Deterministic Rules and Web-Based Language Models

Razvan C. Bunescu
School of EECS
Ohio University
Athens, OH 45701, USA
bunescu@ohio.edu

Abstract

We present a novel adaptive clustering model for coreference resolution in which the expert rules of a state of the art deterministic system are used as features over pairs of clusters. A significant advantage of the new approach is that the expert rules can be easily augmented with new semantic features. We demonstrate this advantage by incorporating semantic compatibility features for neutral pronouns computed from web n-gram statistics. Experimental results show that the combination of the new features with the expert rules in the adaptive clustering approach results in an overall performance improvement, and over 5% improvement in F_1 measure for the target pronouns when evaluated on the ACE 2004 newswire corpus.

1 Introduction

Coreference resolution is the task of clustering a sequence of textual entity mentions into a set of maximal non-overlapping clusters, such that mentions in a cluster refer to the same discourse entity. Coreference resolution is an important subtask in a wide array of natural language processing problems, among them information extraction, question answering, and machine translation. The availability of corpora annotated with coreference relations has led to the development of a diverse set of supervised learning approaches for coreference. While learning models enjoy a largely undisputed role in many NLP applications, deterministic models based on rich sets of expert rules for coreference have been shown recently to achieve performance rivaling, if not exceeding, the performance of state of the art machine learning approaches (Haghighi and Klein, 2009; Raghunathan et al., 2010). In particular, the top performing system in the CoNLL 2011 shared task (Pradhan et al., 2011) is a multi-pass system that applies tiers of deterministic coreference sieves from highest to lowest precision (Lee et al., 2011). The PRECISECONSTRUCTS sieve, for example, creates coreference links between mentions that are found to match patterns of apposition, predicate nominatives, acronyms, demonyms, or relative pronouns. This is a high precision sieve, correspondingly it is among the first sieves to be applied. The PRONOUNMATCH sieve links an anaphoric pronoun with the first antecedent mention that agrees in number and gender with the pronoun, based on an ordering of the antecedents that uses syntactic rules to model discourse salience. This is the last sieve to be applied, due to its lower overall precision, as estimated on development data. While very successful, this deterministic multi-pass sieve approach to coreference can nevertheless be quite unwieldy when one seeks to integrate new sources of knowledge in order to improve the resolution performance. Pronoun resolution, for example, was shown by Yang et al. (2005) to benefit from semantic compatibility information extracted from search engine statistics. The semantic compatibility between candidate antecedents and the pronoun context induces a new ordering between the antecedents. One possibility for using compatibility scores in the deterministic system is to ignore the salience-based ordering and replace it with the new compatibility-based ordering. The drawback of this simple approach is that now discourse salience, an important signal in pronoun resolution, is completely ignored. Ideally, we would want to use both discourse salience and semantic compatibility when ranking the candidate antecedents of the pronoun, something that can be achieved naturally in a discriminative learning approach that uses the two rankings as different, but overlapping, features. Consequently, we propose an adaptive clustering model for coreference in which the expert rules are successfully supplemented by semantic compatibility features obtained from limited history web n-gram statistics.

2 A Coreference Resolution Algorithm

From a machine learning perspective, the deterministic system of Lee et al. (2011) represents a trove of coreference resolution features. Since the deterministic sieves use not only information about a pair of mentions, but also the clusters to which they have been assigned so far, a learning model that utilized the sieves as features would need to be able to work with features defined on pairs of clusters. We therefore chose to model coreference resolution as the greedy clustering process shown in Algorithm 1. The algorithm starts by initializing the clustering C with a set of singleton clusters. Then, as long as the clustering contains more than one cluster, it repeatedly finds the highest scoring pair of clusters $\langle C_i, C_j \rangle$. If the score passes the threshold $\tau = f(\emptyset, \emptyset)$, the clusters C_i, C_j are joined into one cluster and the process continues with another highest scoring pair of clusters.

Algorithm 1 CLUSTER(X,f)

Input: A set of mentions $X = \{x_1, x_2, ..., x_n\}$;
A measure $f(C_i, C_j) = \mathbf{w}^T \Phi(C_i, C_j)$.
Output: A greedy agglomerative clustering of X.

for $i = 1$ **to** n **do**
  $C_i \leftarrow \{x_i\}$
$C \leftarrow \{C_i\}_{1 \le i \le n}$
$\langle C_i, C_j \rangle \leftarrow \operatorname{argmax}_{p \in \mathcal{P}(C)} f(p)$
while $|C| > 1$ **and** $f(C_i, C_j) > \tau$ **do**
  replace C_i, C_j in C with $C_i \cup C_j$
  $\langle C_i, C_j \rangle \leftarrow \operatorname{argmax}_{p \in \mathcal{P}(C)} f(p)$
return C

The scoring function $f(C_i, C_j)$ is a linearly weighted combination of features $\Phi(C_i, C_j)$ extracted from the cluster pair, parametrized by a weight vector $\mathbf{w}$. The function $\mathcal{P}$ takes a clustering C as argument and returns a set of cluster pairs $\langle C_i, C_j \rangle$ as follows:

$$\mathcal{P}(C) = \{\langle C_i, C_j \rangle \mid C_i, C_j \in C,\ C_i \neq C_j\} \cup \{\langle \emptyset, \emptyset \rangle\}$$

$\mathcal{P}(C)$ contains a special cluster pair $\langle \emptyset, \emptyset \rangle$, where $\Phi(\emptyset, \emptyset)$ is defined to contain a binary feature uniquely associated with this empty pair. Its corresponding weight is learned together with all other weights and will effectively function as a clustering threshold $\tau = f(\emptyset, \emptyset)$.

Algorithm 2 TRAIN($\mathcal{C}$,T)

Input: A dataset of training clusterings $\mathcal{C}$;
The number of training epochs T.
Output: The averaged parameters $\overline{\mathbf{w}}$.

$\mathbf{w} \leftarrow \mathbf{0}$
for $t = 1$ **to** T **do**
  for all $C \in \mathcal{C}$ **do**
    $\mathbf{w} \leftarrow$ UPDATE(C,$\mathbf{w}$)
return $\overline{\mathbf{w}}$

Algorithm 3 UPDATE(C,$\mathbf{w}$)

Input: A gold clustering $C = \{C_1, C_2, ..., C_m\}$;
The current parameters $\mathbf{w}$.
Output: The updated parameters $\mathbf{w}$.

$X \leftarrow C_1 \cup C_2 \cup ... \cup C_m = \{x_1, x_2, ..., x_n\}$
for $i = 1$ **to** n **do**
  $\hat{C}_i \leftarrow \{x_i\}$
$\hat{C} \leftarrow \{\hat{C}_i\}_{1 \le i \le n}$
while $|\hat{C}| > 1$ **do**
  $\langle \hat{C}_i, \hat{C}_j \rangle = \operatorname{argmax}_{p \in P(\hat{C})} \mathbf{w}^T \Phi(p)$
  $\mathcal{B} \leftarrow \{\langle \hat{C}_k, \hat{C}_l \rangle \in \mathcal{P}(\hat{C}) \mid g(\hat{C}_k, \hat{C}_l | C) > g(\hat{C}_i, \hat{C}_j | C)\}$
  if $\mathcal{B} \neq \emptyset$ **then**
    $\langle \hat{C}_k, \hat{C}_l \rangle = \operatorname{argmax}_{p \in \mathcal{B}} \mathbf{w}^T \Phi(p)$
    $\mathbf{w} \leftarrow \mathbf{w} + \Phi(\hat{C}_k, \hat{C}_l) - \Phi(C_i, C_j)$
  if $\langle \hat{C}_i, \hat{C}_j \rangle = \langle \emptyset, \emptyset \rangle$ **then**
    return $\mathbf{w}$
  replace $\hat{C}_i, \hat{C}_j$ in $\hat{C}$ with $\hat{C}_i \cup \hat{C}_j$
return $\mathbf{w}$

Algorithms 2 and 3 show an incremental learning model for the weight vector w that is parametrized with the number of training epochs T and a set of training clusterings C in which each clustering contains the true coreference clusters from one document. Algorithm 2 repeatedly uses all true clusterings to update the current weight vector and instead of the last computed weights it returns an averaged weight vector to control for overfitting, as originally proposed by Freund and Schapire (1999). The core of the learning model is in the update procedure shown in Algorithm 3. Like the greedy clustering of Algorithm 1, it starts with an initial system clustering $\hat{C}$ that contains all singleton clusters. At every step in the iteration (lines 5–13), it joins the highest scoring pair of clusters $\langle \hat{C}_i, \hat{C}_j \rangle$, computed according to the current parameters. The iteration ends when either the empty pair obtains the highest score or everything has been joined into only one cluster. The weight update logic is implemented in lines 7–10: if a more accurate pair $\langle \hat{C}_k, \hat{C}_l \rangle$ can be found, the highest scoring such pair is used in the perceptron update in line 10. If multiple cluster pairs obtain the maximum score in lines 6 and 9, the algorithm selects one of them at random. This is useful especially in the beginning, when the weight vector is zero and consequently all cluster pairs have the same score of 0. We define the goodness $g(\hat{C}_k, \hat{C}_l | C)$ of a proposed pair $\langle \hat{C}_k, \hat{C}_l \rangle$ with respect to the true clustering C as the accuracy of the coreference pairs that would be created if $\hat{C}_k$ and $\hat{C}_l$ were joined:

$$g(\cdot) = \frac{\left| \{(x,y) \in \hat{C}_k \times \hat{C}_l \mid \exists C_i \in C : x, y \in C_i\} \right|}{|\hat{C}_k| \cdot |\hat{C}_l|} \tag{1}$$

It can be shown that this definition of the goodness function selects a cluster pair (lines 7–9) that, when joined, results in a clustering with a better pairwise accuracy. Therefore, the algorithm can be seen as trying to fit the training data by searching for parameters that greedily maximize the clustering accuracy, while overfitting is kept under control by computing an averaged version of the parameters. We have chosen to use a perceptron update for simplicity, but the algorithm can be easily instantiated to accommodate other types of incremental updates, e.g. MIRA (Crammer and Singer, 2003).

3 Expert Rules as Features

With the exception of mention detection which is run separately, all the remaining 12 sieves mentioned in (Lee et al., 2011) are used as Boolean features defined on cluster pairs, i.e. if any of the mention pairs in the cluster pair $\langle \hat{C}_i, \hat{C}_j \rangle$ were linked by sieve k, then the corresponding sieve feature $\Phi_k(\hat{C}_i, \hat{C}_j) = 1$. We used the implementation from the Stanford CoreNLP package[1] for all sieves, with a modification for the PRONOUNMATCH sieve which was split into 3 different sieves as follows:

- ITPRONOUNMATCH: this sieve finds antecedents only for neutral pronouns *it*.
- ITSPRONOUNMATCH: this sieve finds antecedents only for neutral possessive pronouns *its*.
- OTHERPRONOUNMATCH: this is a catch-all sieve for the remaining pronouns.

This 3-way split was performed in order to enable the combination of the discourse salience features captured by the pronoun sieves with the semantic compatibility features for neutral pronouns that will be introduced in the next section. The OTHERPRONOUNMATCH sieve works exactly as the original PRONOUNMATCH: for a given non-neutral pronoun, it searches in the current sentence and the previous 3 sentences for the first mention that agrees in gender and number with the pronoun. The candidate antecedents for the pronoun are ordered based on a notion of discourse salience that favors syntactic salience and document proximity (Raghunathan et al., 2010).

4 Discourse Salience Features

The IT/SPRONOUNMATCH sieves use the same implementation for finding the first matching candidate antecedent as the original PRONOUNMATCH. However, unlike OTHERPRONOUNMATCH and the other sieves that generate Boolean features, the neutral pronoun sieves are used to generate real valued features. If the neutral pronoun is the leftmost mention in the cluster $\hat{C}_j$ from a cluster pair $\langle \hat{C}_i, \hat{C}_j \rangle$, the corresponding normalized feature is computed as follows:

[1] http://nlp.stanford.edu/software/corenlp.shtml

1. Let $S_j = \langle S_j^1, S_j^2, ..., S_j^n \rangle$ be the sequence of candidate mentions that precede the neutral pronoun and agree in gender and number with it, ordered from most salient to least salient.

2. Let $A_i \subseteq \hat{C}_i$ be the set of mentions in the cluster $\hat{C}_i$ that appear before the pronoun and agree with it.

3. For each mention $m \in A_i$, find its rank in the sequence S_j:

$$rank(m, S_j) = k \Leftrightarrow m = S_j^k \quad (2)$$

4. Find the minimum rank across all the mentions in A_i and compute the feature as follows:

$$\Phi_{it/s}(\hat{C}_i, \hat{C}_j) = \left(\min_{m \in A_i} rank(m, S_j) \right)^{-1} \quad (3)$$

If A_i is empty, set $\Phi_{it/s}(\hat{C}_i, \hat{C}_j) = 0$.

The discourse salience feature described above is by definition normalized in the interval $[0, 1]$. It takes the maximum value of 1 when the most salient mention in the discourse at the current position agrees with the pronoun and also belongs to the candidate cluster. The feature is 0 when the candidate cluster does not contain any mention that agrees in gender and number with the pronoun.

5 Semantic Compatibility Features

Each of the two types of neutral pronouns is associated with a new feature that computes the semantic compatibility between the syntactic head of a candidate antecedent and the context of the neutral pronoun. If the neutral pronoun is the leftmost mention in the cluster $\hat{C}_j$ from a cluster pair $\langle \hat{C}_i, \hat{C}_j \rangle$ and c_j is the pronoun context, then the new normalized features $\Psi_{it/s}(\hat{C}_i, \hat{C}_j)$ are computed as follows:

1. Compute the maximum semantic similarity between the pronoun context and any mention in $\hat{C}_i$ that precedes the pronoun and is in agreement with it:

$$M_j = \max_{m \in A_i} comp(m, c_j)$$

2. Compute the maximum and minimum semantic similarity between the pronoun context and any mention that precedes the pronoun and is in agreement with it:

$$M_{all} = \max_{m \in S_j} comp(m, c_j)$$
$$m_{all} = \min_{m \in S_j} comp(m, c_j)$$

3. Compute the semantic compatibility feature as follows:

$$\Psi_{it/s}(\hat{C}_i, \hat{C}_j) = \frac{M_j - m_{all}}{M_{all} - m_{all}} \quad (4)$$

To avoid numerical instability, if the overall maximum and minimum similarities are very close ($M_{all} - m_{all} < 1e{-4}$) we set $\Psi_{it/s}(\hat{C}_i, \hat{C}_j) = 1$.

Like the salience feature $\Phi_{it/s}$, the semantic compatibility feature $\Psi_{it/s}$ is normalized in the interval $[0, 1]$. Its definition assumes that we can compute $comp(m, c_j)$, the semantic compatibility between a candidate antecedent mention m and the pronoun context c_j. For the possessive pronoun its, we extract the syntactic head h of the mention m and replace the pronoun with the mention head h in the possessive context. We use the resulting possessive pronoun context $pc_j(h)$ to define the semantic compatibility as the following conditional probability:

$$\begin{aligned} comp(m, c_j) &= \log P(pc_j(h)|h) \quad (5) \\ &= \log P(pc_j(h)) - \log P(h) \end{aligned}$$

To compute the n-gram probabilities $P(pc_j(h))$ and $P(h)$ in Equation 6, we use the language models provided by the Microsoft Web N-Gram Corpus (Wang et al., 2010), as described in the next section.

Figure 1 shows an example of a possessive neutral pronoun context, together with the set of candidate antecedents that agree in number and gender with the pronoun, from the current and previous 3 sentences. Each candidate antecedent is given an index that reflects its ranking in the discourse salience based ordering. We see that discourse salience does not help here, as the most salient mention is not the correct antecedent. The figure also shows the

In 1946, the nine justices dismissed a $case_{[7]}$ involving the $apportionment_{[8]}$ of congressional districts. That $view_{[6]}$ would slowly change. In 1962, the $court_{[3]}$ abandoned $its_{[5]}$ $caution_{[4]}$. Finding remedies to the unequal $distribution_{[1]}$ of political $power_{[2]}$ was indeed within ***its*** constitutional authority.

[3] P(*court's constitutional authority* | *court*) $\approx exp(-5.91)$
[5] P(*court's constitutional authority* | *court*) (*) $\approx exp(-5.91)$
[7] P(*case's constitutional authority* | *case*) $\approx exp(-8.32)$
[2] P(*power's constitutional authority* | *power*) $\approx exp(-9.30)$
[8] P(*app-nt's constitutional authority* | *app-nt*) $\approx exp(-9.32)$
[4] P(*caution's constitutional authority* | *caution*) $\approx exp(-9.39)$
[1] P(*dist-ion's constitutional authority* | *dist-ion*) $\approx exp(-9.40)$
[6] P(*view's constitutional authority* | *view*) $\approx exp(-9.69)$

Figure 1: Possessive neutral pronoun example.

The $letter_{[5]}$ appears to be an $attempt_{[6]}$ to calm the concerns of the current American $administration_{[7]}$. "I confirm my $commitment_{[1]}$ to the points made therein," Aristide said in the $letter_{[2]}$, "confident that they will help strengthen the ties between our two nations where $democracy_{[3]}$ and $peace_{[4]}$ will flourish." Since 1994, when ***it*** sent 20,000 troops to restore Aristide to power, the administration ...

[7] P(*administration sent troops* | *administration*) $\approx exp(-6.00)$
[2] P(*letter sent troops* | *letter*) $\approx exp(-6.57)$
[5] P(*letter sent troops* | *letter*) $\approx exp(-6.57)$
[4] P(*peace sent troops* | *peace*) $\approx exp(-7.92)$
[6] P(*attempt sent troops* | *attempt*) $\approx exp(-8.26)$
[3] P(*democracy sent troops* | *democracy*) $\approx exp(-8.30)$
[1] P(*commitment sent troops* | *commitment*) $\approx exp(-8.62)$

Figure 2: Neutral pronoun example.

compatibility score computed for each candidate antecedent, using the formula described above. In this example, when ranking the candidate antecedents based on their compatibility scores, the top ranked mention is the correct antecedent, whereas the most salient mention is down in the list.

When the set of candidate mentions contains pronouns, we require that they are resolved to a nominal or named mention, and use the head of this mention to instantiate the possessive context. This is the case of the pronominal mention [5] in Figure 1, which we assumed was already resolved to the noun *court* (even if the pronoun [5] were resolved to an incorrect mention, the noun *court* would still be ranked first due to mention [3]). This partial ordering between coreference decisions is satisfied automatically by setting the semantic compatibility feature $\Psi_{it/s}(\hat{C}_i, \hat{C}_j) = 0$ whenever the antecedent cluster $\hat{C}_i$ contains only pronouns.

A similar feature is introduced for all neutral pronouns *it* appearing in subject-verb-object triples. The new pronoun context $pc_j(h)$ is obtained by replacing the pronoun *it* in the subject-verb-object context c_j with the head h of the candidate antecedent mention. Figure 2 shows a neutral pronoun context, together with the set of candidate antecedents that agree in number and gender with the pronoun, from an abridged version of the original current and previous 3 sentences. Each candidate antecedent is given an index that reflects its ranking in the discourse salience based ordering. Discourse salience does not help here, as the most salient mention is not the correct antecedent. The figure shows the compatibility score computed for each candidate antecedent, using Equation 6. In this example, the top ranked mention in the compatibility based ordering is the correct antecedent, whereas the most most salient mention is at the bottom of the list.

To summarize, in the last two sections we described two special features for neutral pronouns: the discourse salience feature $\Phi_{it/s}$ and the semantic compatibility feature $\Psi_{it/s}$. The two real-valued

Candidate mentions	Original context	N-gram context
capital, store, GE, side, offer	with ***its*** corporate tentacles reaching	GE's corporate tentacles
AOL, Microsoft, Yahoo, product	***its*** substantial customer base	AOL's customer base
regime, Serbia, state, EU, embargo	meets ***its*** international obligations	Serbia's international obligations
company, secret, internet, FBI	***it*** was investigating the incident	FBI was investigating the incident
goal, team, realm, NHL, victory	something ***it*** has not experienced since	NHL has experienced
Onvia, line, Nasdaq, rating	said Tuesday ***it*** will cut jobs	Onvia will cut jobs
coalition, government, Italy	but ***it*** has had more direct exposure	Italy has had direct exposure
Pinochet, arrest, Chile, court	while ***it*** studied a judge 's explanation	court studied the explanation

Table 1: N-gram generation examples.

features are computed at the level of cluster pairs as described in Equations 3 and 4. Their computation relies on the mention level rank (Equation 2) and semantic compatibility (Equation 6) respectively.

6 Web-based Language Models

We used the Microsoft Web N-Gram Corpus[2] to compute the pronoun context probability $P(pc_j(h))$ and the candidate head probability $P(h)$. This corpus provides smoothed back-off language models that are computed dynamically from N-gram statistics using the CALM algorithm (Wang and Li, 2009). The N-grams are collected from the tokenized versions of the billions of web pages indexed by the Bing search engine. Separate models have been created for the document body, the document title and the anchor text. In our experiments, we used the April 2010 version of the document body language models. The number of words in the pronoun context and the antecedent head determine the order of the language models used for estimating the conditional probabilities. For example, to estimate $P(\textit{administration sent troops} \mid \textit{administration})$, we used a trigram model for the context probability $P(\textit{administration sent troops})$ and a unigram model for the head probability $P(\textit{administration})$. Since the maximum order of the N-grams available in the Microsoft corpus is 5, we designed the context and head extraction rules to return N-grams with size at most 5. Table 1 shows a number of examples of N-grams generated from the original contexts, in which the pronoun was replaced with the correct antecedent. To get a sense of the utility of each context in matching the right antecedent, the table also shows a sample of candidate antecedents.

[2]http://web-ngram.research.microsoft.com

For possessive contexts, the N-gram extraction rules use the head of the NP context and its closest premodifier whenever available. Using the premodifier was meant to increase the discriminative power of the context. For the subject-verb-object N-grams, we used the verb at the same tense as in the original context, which made it necessary to also include the auxiliary verbs, as shown in lines 4–7 in the table. Furthermore, in order to keep the generated N-grams within the maximum size of 5, we did not include modifiers for the subject or object nouns, as illustrated in the last line of the table. Some of the examples in the table also illustrate the limits of the context-based semantic compatibility feature. In the second example, all three company names are equally good matches for the possessive context. In these situations, we expect the discourse salience feature to provide the additional information necessary for extracting the correct antecedent. This combination of discourse salience with semantic compatibility features is done in the adaptive clustering algorithm introduced in Section 2.

7 Experimental Results

We compare our adaptive clustering (AC) approach with the state of the art deterministic sieves (DT) system of Lee et al. (2011) on the newswire portion of the ACE-2004 dataset. The newswire section of the corpus contains 128 documents annotated with gold mentions and coreference information, where coreference is marked only between mentions that belong to one of seven semantic classes: person, organization, location, geo-political entity, facility, vehicle, and weapon. This set of documents has been used before to evaluate coreference resolution sys-

System	Mentions	P	R	F_1
DT	Gold, all	88.1	73.3	80.0
AC	Gold, all	**88.7**	**73.5**	**80.4**
DT	Gold, neutral	82.5	51.5	63.4
AC	Gold, neutral	**83.0**	**52.1**	**64.0**
DT	Auto, neutral	84.4	34.9	49.3
AC	Auto, neutral	**86.1**	**40.0**	**54.6**

Table 2: B^3 comparative results on ACE 2004.

tems in (Poon and Domingos, 2008; Haghighi and Klein, 2009; Raghunathan et al., 2010), with the best results so far obtained by the deterministic sieve system of Lee at al. (2011). There are 11,398 annotated gold mentions, out of which 135 are possessive neutral pronouns *its* and 88 are neutral pronouns *it* in a subject-verb-object triple. Given the very small number of neutral pronouns, in order to obtain reliable estimates for the model parameters we tested the adaptive clustering algorithm in a 16 fold cross-validation scenario. Thus, the set of 128 documents was split into 16 folds, where each fold contains 120 documents for training and 8 documents for testing. The final results were pooled together from the 16 disjoint test sets. During training, the AC's update procedure was run for 10 epochs. Since the AC algorithm does not need to tune any hyper parameters, there was no need for development data.

Table 2 shows the results obtained by the two systems on the newswire corpus under three evaluation scenarios. We use the B^3 version of the precision (P), recall (R), and F_1 measure, computed either on all mention pairs (all) or only on links that contain at least one neutral pronoun (neutral) marked as a mention in ACE. Furthermore, we report results on gold mentions (Gold) as well as on mentions extracted automatically (Auto). Since the number of neutral pronouns marked as gold mentions is small compared to the total number of mentions, the impact on the overall performance shown in the first two rows is small. However, when looking at coreference links that contain at least one neutral pronoun, the improvement becomes substantial. AC increases F_1 with 5.3% when the mentions are extracted automatically during testing, a setting that reflects a more realistic use of the system. We have also evaluated the AC approach in the Gold setting using only the original DT sieves as features, obtaining an F_1 of 80.3% for all mentions and 63.4% – same as DT – for neutral pronouns.

By matching the performance of the DT system in the first two rows of the table, the AC system proves that it can successfully learn the relative importance of the deterministic sieves, which in (Raghunathan et al., 2010) and (Lee et al., 2011) have been manually ordered using a separate development dataset. Furthermore, in the DT system the sieves are applied on mentions in their textual order, whereas the adaptive clustering algorithm AC does not assume a predefined ordering among coreference resolution decisions. Thus, the algorithm has the capability to make the first clustering decisions in any section of the document in which the coreference decisions are potentially easier to make. We have run experiments in which the AC system was augmented with a feature that computed the normalized distance between a cluster and the beginning of the document, but this did not lead to an improvement in the results, lending further credence to the hypothesis that a strictly left to right ordering of the coreference decisions is not necessary, at least with the current features.

The same behavior, albeit with smaller increases in performance, was observed when the DT and AC approaches were compared on the newswire section of the development dataset used in the CoNLL 2011 shared task (Pradhan et al., 2011). For these experiments, the AC system was trained on all 128 documents from the newswire portion of ACE 2004. On gold mentions, the DT and AC systems obtained a very similar performance. When evaluated only on links that contain at least one neutral pronoun, in a setting where the mentions were automatically detected, the AC approach improved the F_1 measure over the DT system from 58.6% to 59.1%. One reason for the smaller increase in performance in the CoNLL experiments could be given by the different annotation schemes used in the two datasets. Compared to ACE, the CoNLL dataset does not include coreference links for appositives, predicate nominals or relative pronouns. The different annotation schemes may have led to mismatches in the training and test data for the AC system, which was trained on ACE and tested on CoNLL. While we tried to control for these conditions during the evaluation of the AC system, it is conceivable that the differ-

System	Mentions	P	R	F_1
DT	Auto, *its*	86.0	46.9	60.7
AC	Auto, *its*	**91.7**	**47.5**	**62.6**

Table 3: B^3 comparative results on CoNLL 2011.

ences in annotation still had some effect on the performance of the AC approach. Another cause for the smaller increase in performance was that the pronominal contexts were less discriminative in the CoNLL data, especially for the neutral pronoun *it*. When evaluated only on links that contained at least one possessive neutral pronoun *its*, the improvement in F_1 increased at 1.9%, as shown in Table 3.

8 Related Work

Closest to our clustering approach from Section 2 is the error-driven first-order probabilistic model of Culotta et al. (2007). Among significant differences we mention that our model is non-probabilistic, simpler and easier to understand and implement. Furthermore, the update step does not stop after the first clustering error, instead the algorithm learns and uses a clustering threshold τ to determine when to stop during training and testing. This required the design of a method to order cluster pairs in which the clusters may not be consistent with the true coreference chains, which led to the introduction of the goodness function in Equation 1 as a new scoring measure for cluster pairs. The strategy of continuing the clustering during training as long as a an adaptive threshold is met better matches the training with the testing, and was observed to lead to better performance. The cluster ranking model of Rahman and Ng (2009) proceeds in a left-to-right fashion and adds the current discourse old mention to the highest scoring preceding cluster. Compared to it, our adaptive clustering approach is less constrained: it uses only a weak, partial ordering between coreference decisions, and does not require a singleton cluster at every clustering step. This allows clustering to start in any section of the document where coreference decisions are easier to make, and thus create accurate clusters earlier in the process.

The use of semantic knowledge for coreference resolution has been studied before in a number of works, among them (Ponzetto and Strube, 2006), (Bengtson and Roth, 2008), (Lee et al., 2011), and (Rahman and Ng, 2011). The focus in these studies has been on the semantic similarity between a mention and a candidate antecedent, or the parallelism between the semantic role structures in which the two appear. One of the earliest methods for using predicate-argument frequencies in pronoun resolution is that of Dagan and Itai (1990). Closer to our use of semantic compatibility features for pronouns are the approaches of Kehler et al. (2004) and Yang et al. (2005). The last work showed that pronoun resolution can be improved by incorporating semantic compatibility features derived from search engine statistics in the twin-candidate model. In our approach, we use web-based language models to compute semantic compatibility features for neutral pronouns and show that they can improve performance over a state-of-the-art coreference resolution system. The use of language models instead of search engine statistics is more practical, as they eliminate the latency involved in using search engine queries. Web-based language models can be built on readily available web N-gram corpora, such as Google's Web 1T 5-gram Corpus (Brants and Franz, 2006).

9 Conclusion

We described a novel adaptive clustering method for coreference resolution and showed that it can not only learn the relative importance of the original expert rules of Lee et al. (2011), but also extend them effectively with new semantic compatibility features. Experimental results show that the new method improves the performance of the state of the art deterministic system and obtains a substantial improvement for neutral pronouns when the mentions are extracted automatically.

Acknowledgments

We would like to thank the anonymous reviewers for their helpful suggestions. This work was supported by grant IIS-1018590 from the NSF. Any opinions, findings, and conclusions or recommendations expressed in this material are those of the author and do not necessarily reflect the views of the NSF.

References

Eric Bengtson and Dan Roth. 2008. Understanding the value of features for coreference resolution. In *Proceedings of the Conference on Empirical Methods in Natural Language Processing*, pages 294–303, Honolulu, Hawaii, October. Association for Computational Linguistics.

Thorsten Brants and Alex Franz. 2006. Web 1t 5-gram version 1.

Koby Crammer and Yoram Singer. 2003. Ultraconservative online algorithms for multiclass problems. *J. Mach. Learn. Res.*, 3:951–991.

Aron Culotta, Michael Wick, and Andrew McCallum. 2007. First-order probabilistic models for coreference resolution. In *Human Language Technologies 2007: The Conference of the North American Chapter of the Association for Computational Linguistics; Proceedings of the Main Conference*, pages 81–88, Rochester, New York, April. Association for Computational Linguistics.

Ido Dagan and Alon Itai. 1990. Automatic processing of large corpora for the resolution of anaphora references. In *Proceedings of the 13th conference on Computational linguistics - Volume 3*, COLING'90, pages 330–332.

Yoav Freund and Robert E. Schapire. 1999. Large margin classification using the perceptron algorithm. *Machine Learning*, 37:277–296.

Aria Haghighi and Dan Klein. 2009. Simple coreference resolution with rich syntactic and semantic features. In *Proceedings of the 2009 Conference on Empirical Methods in Natural Language Processing*, pages 1152–1161, Singapore, August.

Andrew Kehler, Douglas Appelt, Lara Taylor, and Aleksandr Simma. 2004. The (non)utility of predicate-argument frequencies for pronoun interpretation. In *HLT-NAACL 2004: Main Proceedings*, pages 289–296, Boston, Massachusetts, USA. Association for Computational Linguistics.

Heeyoung Lee, Yves Peirsman, Angel Chang, Nathanael Chambers, Mihai Surdeanu, and Dan Jurafsky. 2011. Stanford's multi-pass sieve coreference resolution system at the conll-2011 shared task. In *Proceedings of the Fifteenth Conference on Computational Natural Language Learning: Shared Task*, pages 28–34.

Simone Paolo Ponzetto and Michael Strube. 2006. Exploiting semantic role labeling, wordnet and wikipedia for coreference resolution. In *Proceedings of the Human Language Technology Conference of the North American Chapter of the Association of Computational Linguistics*, pages 192–199.

Hoifung Poon and Pedro Domingos. 2008. Joint unsupervised coreference resolution with markov logic. In *Proceedings of the 2008 Conference on Empirical Methods in Natural Language Processing*, Honolulu, Hawaii, October.

Sameer Pradhan, Lance Ramshaw, Mitchell Marcus, Martha Palmer, Ralph Weischedel, and Nianwen Xue. 2011. Conll-2011 shared task: modeling unrestricted coreference in ontonotes. In *Proceedings of the Fifteenth Conference on Computational Natural Language Learning: Shared Task*, pages 1–27.

Karthik Raghunathan, Heeyoung Lee, Sudarshan Rangarajan, Nate Chambers, Mihai Surdeanu, Dan Jurafsky, and Christopher D. Manning. 2010. A multi-pass sieve for coreference resolution. In *Proceedings of the 2010 Conference on Empirical Methods in Natural Language Processing (EMNLP'10)*, pages 492–501.

Altaf Rahman and Vincent Ng. 2009. Supervised models for coreference resolution. In *Proceedings of the 2009 Conference on Empirical Methods in Natural Language Processing*, pages 968–977, Singapore, August. Association for Computational Linguistics.

Altaf Rahman and Vincent Ng. 2011. Coreference resolution with world knowledge. In *Proceedings of the 49th Annual Meeting of the Association for Computational Linguistics: Human Language Technologies*, pages 814–824, Stroudsburg, PA, USA. Association for Computational Linguistics.

Kuansan Wang and Xiaolong Li. 2009. Efficacy of a constantly adaptive language modeling technique for web-scale applications. In *Proceedings of the 2009 IEEE International Conference on Acoustics, Speech and Signal Processing*, ICASSP '09, pages 4733–4736, Washington, DC, USA. IEEE Computer Society.

Kuansan Wang, Christopher Thrasher, Evelyne Viegas, Xiaolong Li, and Bo-june (Paul) Hsu. 2010. An overview of microsoft web n-gram corpus and applications. In *Proceedings of the NAACL HLT 2010 Demonstration Session*, HLT-DEMO '10, pages 45–48, Stroudsburg, PA, USA. Association for Computational Linguistics.

Xiaofeng Yang, Jian Su, and Chew Lim Tan. 2005. Improving pronoun resolution using statistics-based semantic compatibility information. In *Proceedings of the 43rd Annual Meeting on Association for Computational Linguistics*, pages 165–172.

Measuring Semantic Relatedness using Multilingual Representations

Samer Hassan
University of North Texas
Denton, TX
samer@unt.edu

Carmen Banea
University of North Texas
Denton, TX
carmenbanea@my.unt.edu

Rada Mihalcea
University of North Texas
Denton, TX
rada@cs.unt.edu

Abstract

This paper explores the hypothesis that semantic relatedness may be more reliably inferred by using a multilingual space, as compared to the typical monolingual representation. Through evaluations using several state-of-the-art semantic relatedness systems, applied on standard datasets, we show that a multilingual approach is better suited for this task, and leads to improvements of up to 47% with respect to the monolingual baseline.

1 Introduction

Semantic relatedness is the task of quantifying the strength of the semantic connection between textual units, be they words, sentences, or documents. For instance, one may want to determine how semantically related are two words such as *car* and *automobile*, or two pieces of text such as *I love animals* and *I own a pet.* It is one of the main tasks explored in the field of natural language processing, as it lies at the core of a large number of applications such as information retrieval (Ponte and Croft, 1998), query reformulation (Metzler et al., 2007; Yih and Meek, 2007; Sahami and Heilman, 2006; Broder et al., 2008), image retrieval (Leong and Mihalcea, 2009; Goodrum, 2000), plagiarism detection (Hoad and Zobel, 2003; Shivakumar and Garcia-Molina, 1995; Broder et al., 1997; Heintze, 1996; Brin et al., 1995; Manber, 1994), information flow (Metzler et al., 2005), sponsored search (Broder et al., 2008), short answer grading (Mohler and Mihalcea, 2009a; Pulman and Sukkarieh, 2005; Mitchell et al., 2002), and textual entailment (Dagan et al., 2005).

The typical approach to semantic relatedness is to either measure the distance between the constituent words by using a knowledge base such as WordNet or Roget (e.g., (Leacock and Chodorow, 1998; Lesk, 1986; Jarmasz and Szpakowicz, 2003; Pedersen et al., 2004)), or to calculate the similarity between the word distributions in very large corpora (e.g., (Landauer et al., 1991; Lin, 1998; Gabrilovich and Markovitch, 2007)). With almost no exception, these methods have been applied on one language at a time – English, most of the time, although measures of relatedness have also been explored on languages such as German (Zesch et al., 2007), Chinese (Li et al., 2005), Japanese (Kazama et al., 2010), and others.

In this paper, we take a step further and explore a joint multilingual semantic relatedness metric, which aggregates semantic relatedness scores measured on several different languages. Specifically, in our method, in order to measure the relatedness of two textual units, we first determine their relatedness in multiple languages, and consequently infer a final relatedness score by averaging the scores calculated in the individual languages.

Our hypothesis is that a multilingual representation can enrich the relatedness space and address relevant issues such as *polysemy* (i.e., find that two occurrences of the same word in language L1 represent two different meanings because of different translations in language L2) and *synonymy* (i.e., find that two words in language L1 are related because they have the same translation in language L2). We show that by measuring relatedness in a multilingual space, we are able to improve over a traditional relatedness measure that relies exclusively on a monolingual representation.

Through experiments using several state-of-the-art measures of relatedness, applied on a multilingual space including English, Arabic, Spanish, and Romanian, we aim to answer the following research questions: (1) Does the task of semantic relatedness benefit from a multilingual representation, as compared to a monolingual one? (2) Does the translation quality affect the results? and (3) Do the findings hold for different relatedness datasets?

The paper is organized as follows. First, we overview related work on word and text relatedness, and on multilingual natural language processing. We then briefly describe three corpus-based measures of relatedness, and present several word and text datasets that have been used in the past to evaluate relatedness. We then present evaluations and experiments addressing each of the three research questions, and discuss our findings.

2 Related Work

Semantic relatedness. The approaches for semantic relatedness that have been considered to date can be grouped into knowledge-based and corpus-based. Knowledge-based methods derive a measure of relatedness by utilizing lexical resources and ontologies such as WordNet (Miller, 1995) to measure definitional overlap (Lesk, 1986), term distance within a graphical taxonomy (Leacock and Chodorow, 1998), term depth in the taxonomy as a measure of specificity (Wu and Palmer, 1994), and others. The application of such measures to a language other than English requires the availability of the lexical resource in that language; furthermore, even though taxonomies such as WordNet (Miller, 1995) are available in a number of languages[1], their coverage is still limited, and often times they are not publicly available. For these reasons, in multilingual settings, these measures often become untractable.

On the other side, corpus-based measures such as Latent Semantic Analysis (LSA) (Landauer et al., 1991), Explicit Semantic Analysis (ESA) (Gabrilovich and Markovitch, 2007), Salient Semantic Analysis (SSA) (Hassan and Mihalcea, 2011), Pointwise Mutual Information (PMI) (Church and Hanks, 1990), PMI-IR (Turney, 2001), Second Order PMI (Islam and Inkpen, 2006), Hyperspace Analogues to Language (HAL) (Burgess et al., 1998) and distributional similarity (Lin, 1998) employ probabilistic approaches to decode the semantics of words. They consist of unsupervised methods that utilize the contextual information and patterns observed in raw text to build semantic profiles of words, and thus they can be easily transferred to a new language provided that a large corpus in that language is available.

Multilingual natural language processing. Also relevant is the work done on multilingual text processing, which attempts to improve the performance of different natural language processing tasks by integrating information drawn from multiple languages. For instance, (Cohn and Lapata, 2007) explore the use of triangulation for machine translation, where multiple translation models are learned using multilingual parallel corpora. The model was found especially beneficial for languages where the training dataset was small, thus suggesting that this method may be particularly useful for languages with scarce resources. (Davidov and Rappoport, 2009) experiment with the use of multiple languages to enhance an existing lexicon. In their experiments, using three source languages and 45 intermediate languages, they find that the multilingual resources can lead to significant improvements in concept expansion. (Banea et al., 2010) explore the use of parallel multilingual corpora to improve subjectivity classification in a target language, finding that the use of multilingual representations for subjectivity analysis improves over the monolingual classifiers. Similarly, (Banea and Mihalcea, 2011) investigate the use of multilingual contexts for word sense disambiguation. By leveraging on the translations of the annotated contexts in multiple languages, a multilingual thematic space emerges that better disambiguates target words.

Finally, there are two lines of work that explore semantic distances in a multilingual space. First, (Besançon and Rajman, 2002) examine the notion that the distances between document vectors within a language correlate with the distances between their corresponding vectors in a parallel corpus. These findings provide clues about the possibility of reliable semantic knowledge transfer across language boundaries. Second, (Hassan and Mihalcea, 2009) propose a framework to compute semantic relatedness between two words in different languages, by considering Wikipedia articles in multiple languages. The method differs from the one proposed here, as we aggregate relatedness over monolingual spaces rather than measuring cross-lingual relatedness, and we do not specifically use the inter-wiki links between Wikipedia pages.

[1] http://www.illc.uva.nl/EuroWordNet/

3 Measures of Text Relatedness

In this work, we focus on corpus-based metrics because of their unsupervised nature, their flexibility, scalability, and portability to different languages. Specifically, we utilize three popular models, LSA (Landauer et al., 1991), ESA (Gabrilovich and Markovitch, 2007), and SSA (Hassan and Mihalcea, 2011). In these models, the semantic profile of a word is expressed in terms of the explicit (ESA), implicit (LSA), or salient (SSA) concepts. All three models are trained on the Wikipedia 2010 corpora corresponding to the four languages of interest (English, Arabic, Spanish, Romanian).

Explicit Semantic Analysis. ESA (Gabrilovich and Markovitch, 2007) uses encyclopedic knowledge in an information retrieval framework to generate a semantic interpretation of words. Since encyclopedic knowledge is typically organized into concepts (or topics), each concept is described using definitions and examples. ESA relies on the distribution of words inside the encyclopedic descriptions. It builds semantic representations for a given word using a word-document association, where each document represents a Wikipedia article. In this vector representation, the semantic interpretation of a text can be modeled as an aggregation of the semantic vectors of its individual words.

Latent Semantic Analysis. In LSA (Landauer et al., 1991), term-context associations are captured by means of a dimensionality reduction operated by a singular value decomposition (SVD) on the term-by-context matrix $\mathbf{T}$, where the matrix is induced from a large corpus. This reduction entails the abstraction of meaning by collapsing similar contexts and discounting noisy and irrelevant ones, hence transforming the real world term-context space into a word-latent-concept space which achieves a much deeper and concrete semantic representation of words.

Salient Semantic Analysis. SSA (Hassan and Mihalcea, 2011) incorporates a similar semantic abstraction and interpretation of words, by using salient concepts gathered from encyclopedic knowledge, where a concept is defined as an unambiguous word or phrase with a concrete meaning, which can afford an encyclopedic definition. The links available between Wikipedia articles, obtained either through manual annotation by the Wikipedia users or using an automatic annotation process, are regarded as clues or salient features within the text that help define and disambiguate its context. This method seeks to determine the semantic relatedness of words by measuring the distance between their concept-based profiles, where a profile consists of co-occurring salient concepts found within a given window size in a very large corpus.

4 Datasets

To evaluate the representation strength of a multilingual semantic relatedness model we employ several standard word-to-word and text-to-text datasets. For each of these datasets, we make use of their representation in the four languages of interest.

4.1 Word Relatedness

We construct our multilingual word-to-word datasets building upon three word relatedness datasets that have been widely used in the past.

Rubenstein and Goodenough (Rubenstein and Goodenough, 1965) **(RG65)** consists of 65 word pairs ranging from synonymy pairs (e.g., *car - automobile*) to completely unrelated words (e.g., *noon - string*). The participating terms in all the pairs are non-technical nouns annotated by 51 human judges on a scale from 0 (unrelated) to 4 (synonyms).

Miller-Charles (Miller and Charles, 1991) **(MC30)** is a subset of $RG65$, consisting of 30 word pairs annotated for relatedness by 38 human subjects, using the same 0 to 4 scale.

WordSimilarity-353 (Finkelstein et al., 2001) **(WS353)**, also known as Finkelstein-353, consists of 353 word pairs annotated by 13 human experts, on a scale from 0 (unrelated) to 10 (synonyms). While containing the $MC30$ set, it poses an additional degree of difficulty by also including phrases (e.g., *"Wednesday news"*), proper names and technical terms.

To enable a multilingual representation, we use the multilingual datasets introduced by (Hassan and Mihalcea, 2009), which are based upon $MC30$ and $WS353$. These multilingual datasets are built using manual translations, following the same guidelines adopted for the generation and the annotation of their original English counterparts. These manually translated collections, available in Arabic, Spanish, and Romanian, allow us to infer an upper bound for the multilingual semantic relatedness model.

Moreover, in order to provide a more realistic scenario, where manual translations are not available, we also create multilingual datasets by automatically translating the three English datasets into

Arabic, Spanish and Romanian.[2] Similar to how the manually translated datasets were created by providing the bilingual speakers with one word pair at a time, for the automatic translation each word pair is processed as a single query to the translation engine. Thus, the co-occurrence metrics derived from large corpora are able to play a role in providing a disambiguated translation instead of defaulting to the most frequently used sense if the words were to be processed individually. This allows for the embedded word pair relatedness to be transferred to other languages as well.

4.2 Text Relatedness

We use three standard text-to-text datasets.

Lee50 (Lee and Welsh, 2005) is a compilation of 50 documents collected from the Australian Broadcasting Corporation's news mail service. Each document is scored by ten annotators on a scale from 1 (unrelated) to 5 (alike) based on its semantic relatedness to all the other documents. The users' annotation is then averaged per document pair, resulting in 2,500 document pairs annotated with their similarity scores. Since it was found that there was no significant difference between annotations given a different order of the documents in a pair (Lee and Welsh, 2005), the evaluations are carried out on only 1225 document pairs after ignoring duplicates.

Li30 (Li et al., 2006) is a sentence pair similarity dataset obtained by replacing each of the $RG65$ word-pairs with their respective definitions extracted from the Collins Cobuild dictionary (Sinclair, 2001). Each sentence pair was scored between 0 (unrelated) to 4 (alike) by 32 native English speakers, and their annotations were averaged. Due to the skew in the scores toward low similarity sentence-pairs, they selected a subset of 30 sentences from the 65 sentence pairs to maintain an even relatedness distribution.

AG400 (Mohler and Mihalcea, 2009b) is a domain specific dataset from the field of computer science, used to evaluate the application of semantic relatedness measures to real world applications such as short answer grading. We employ the version proposed by (Hassan and Mihalcea, 2011) which consists of 400 student answers along with the corresponding questions and correct instructor answers. Each student answer was graded by two judges on a scale from 0 (completely wrong) to 5 (perfect answer). The correlation between human judges was measured at 0.64.

First, we construct a multilingual, manually translated text-to-text relatedness dataset based on the standard $Li30$ corpus.[3] Native speakers of Spanish, Romanian and Arabic, who were also highly proficient in English, were asked to translate the entries drawn from the English collection. They were presented with one sentence at a time, and asked to provide the appropriate translation into their native language. Since we had five Spanish, two Arabic, and two Romanian translators, an arbitrator (native to the language) was charged with merging the candidate translations by proposing one sentence per language.

Furthermore, to test the abstraction of semantics from the choice of underlying language, we asked three different Spanish human experts to re-score the Spanish text-pair translations on the same scale used in the construction of the English collection. The correlation between the relatedness scores assigned during this experiment and the scores assigned to the original English experiment was $0.77 - 0.86$, indicating that the translations provided by the bilingual judges were correct and preserved the semantics of the original English text-pairs. As was the case for the manually constructed word-to-word datasets previously described, the metrics obtained on the manually translated $Li30$ dataset will also act as an upper bound for the text-to-text evaluations.

Finally, for a more sensible scenario where the text fragments do not require manual translations in order to compute their semantic relatedness, we create a multilingual version of the three English datasets by employing statistical machine translation to translate the texts into the other three languages. Each text pair was processed through two separate queries to the translation engine, since the two text fragments contain sufficient information to prompt an in-context translation on their own.

5 Framework

We generate SSA, LSA and ESA vectorial models for English, Romanian, Arabic, and Spanish, using the same Wikipedia 2010 versions for all the systems (e.g., the SSA, LSA and ESA relatedness measures for Spanish are all trained on the same Spanish Wikipedia version).

We construct a multilingual model by considering a word- or text-pair from a source language along

[2]For all the automatic translations we used the Google Translate service.

[3]Dataset is available for download at `lit.csci.unt.edu/index.php?P=research/downloads`

with its translations in the other languages. To evaluate this multilingual model in a way that reduces the bias that may arise from choosing one language over the other, we do the following: we start from a source language and generate all the possible combinations of this language with the available language set $\{ar, en, es, ro\}$. Within each combination, we average the monolingual model scores for the languages in this combination with respect to the target word- or text-pair into a final relatedness score.

For example, let us consider Spanish as the source language, then the possible combinations of the languages that include the source language will be $\{\{es\}, \{es, ar\}, \{es, ro\}, \{es, en\}, \{es, ar, en\}, \{es, ar, ro\}, \{es, en, ro\}$, and $\{es, ar, en, ro\}\}$. For each possible combination, we aggregate the scores of the languages in that combination. In this setting, a combination of size (cardinality) one will always be the source language and will serve as the baseline. For every combination (e.g. $\{es, ar\}$), we average the individual monolingual relatedness scores for a given word- or text-pair in this set.

Finally, to calculate the overall correlation of these generated multilingual models (one system per combination size) with the human scores, we average the correlation scores achieved over all the datasets in a given combination (e.g., $\{es, ar\}$) with all correlation scores achieved under other combinations of the same size (e.g., $\{es, ro\}, \{es, en\}$). This in effect allows us to observe the cumulative performance irrespective of language choice, as we extend the multilingual model to include more languages.

Formally, let N be the number of languages, C_n be the set of all language combinations of size n, and c_i be one of the possible combinations of size n,

$$C_n = \{c_i \mid |c_i| = n, 0 < i < \binom{N}{n}\} \quad (1)$$

then the relatedness of a word- or text-pair p from the dataset P under this combination can be represented as:

$$Sim_{c_i}(p) = \frac{1}{|c_i|} \sum_{l \in c_i} Sim_l(p) \quad (2)$$

where $Sim_l(p)$ is the relatedness score of the word- or text-pair p in the monolingual model of language l. To evaluate the performance of the multilingual model, let D_i be the generated relatedness distribution for the dataset P using the combination c_i:

$$D_i = \{\langle p, Sim_{c_i}(p)\rangle \mid p \in P\}. \quad (3)$$

Then, the correlation between the gold standard distribution G and the generated scores can be calculated as follows:

$$Correl_{C_n}(D, G) = \frac{1}{|C_n|} \sum_{c_i \in C_n} Correl_{c_i}(D_i, G), \quad (4)$$

where $Correl$ can stand for Pearson (r), Spearman (ρ), or their harmonic mean (μ), as also reported in (Hassan and Mihalcea, 2011).

6 Evaluations

In this section we revisit the questions formulated in the introduction, and based on different experiment setups following the framework introduced in Section 5, we provide an answer to each one of them.

Does the task of semantic relatedness benefit from a multilingual representation? We evaluate the three semantic relatedness models, namely LSA, ESA and SSA on our manually constructed multilingual word relatedness ($MC30$, $WS353$) and text relatedness datasets ($LI30$), as described in Section 4.

Figure 1 plots the correlation scores achieved across all the languages against the gold standard and then averaged across all the multilingual datasets. The figure shows a clear and steady improvement (25% - 28% with respect to the monolingual baseline) achieved when more languages are incorporated into the relatedness model. It is worth noting that both the Pearson and Spearman correlations exhibit the same improvement pattern, which confirms our hypothesis that adding more languages has a positive impact on the relatedness scores. The fact that this trend is visible across all the systems supports the idea that a multilingual representation constitutes a better model for determining semantic relatedness. Furthermore, we notice that SSA is the best performing system under these settings, with a correlation improvement of approximately 15%.

To further analyze the role of the multilingual model and to explore whether some languages benefit from using this abstraction more than others, we plot the correlation scores achieved by the individual languages averaged over all the systems and the datasets in Figure 2. We notice a sharp rise in performance associated with the addition of more languages to the Arabic (42%) and the Romanian (47%) models, and a slower rise for Spanish (23%). The performance of English is also affected, but on a smaller scale (4%) when compared to the other

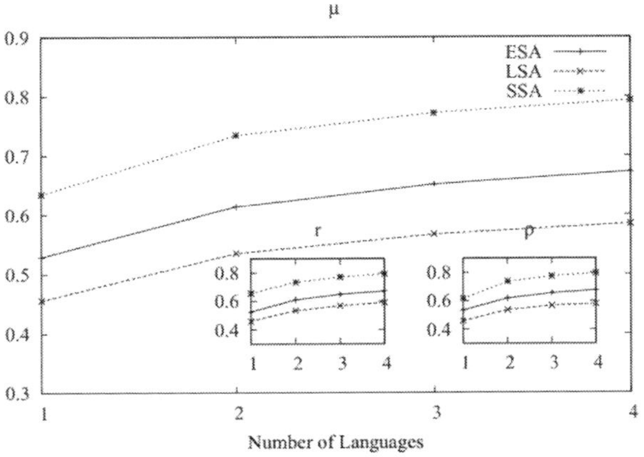

Figure 1: Manual translation - average correlation (μ, r, ρ) obtained from incorporating scores from models in other languages

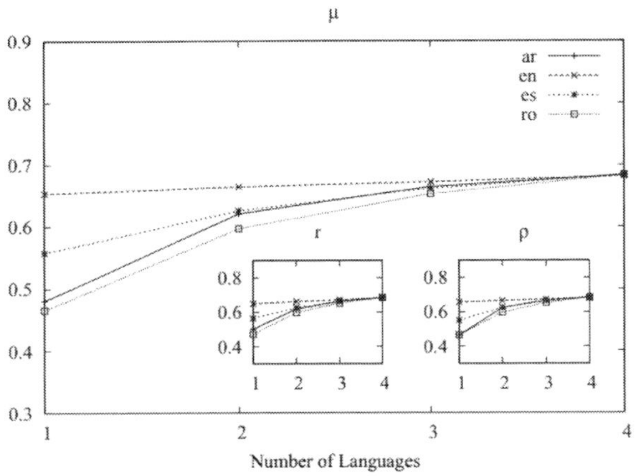

Figure 2: Manual translation - average correlation (μ, r, ρ) obtained by supplementing a source language with scores from other languages

languages. Not surprisingly, this correlates with the size of each corpus, where Arabic and Romanian are the smallest, while English is the largest.

The results support the notion that resource poor languages can benefit from languages with richer and larger resources, such as English or Spanish. Furthermore, incorporating additional languages to English also leads to small improvements, which indicates that the benefit, while disproportionate, is mutual.

Does the quality of translations affect the results? As a natural next step, we investigate the role played by the manual translations in the performance of the multilingual model. Since the previous evaluations require the availability of the word- or text-pairs in multiple languages, we attempt to see if we can eliminate this restriction by automating the translation process using statistical machine translation (MT). Therefore, for a multilingual model employing automated settings, the manual models proposed previously constitute an upper bound.

We use the Google MT engine[4] to translate our multilingual datasets into the target languages (en, es, ar, and ro). We then repeat all the evaluations using the newly constructed datasets.

Figure 3 shows the correlation scores achieved across all the languages and averaged across all the multilingual datasets constructed using automatic translation. We again see a clear and steady improvement (12% - 35% with respect to the monolingual baseline) similar to the observed pattern in the corresponding manual evaluations (Figure 1). While the overall achieved performance for SSA has dropped (from $\mu = 0.793$ to $\mu = 0.71$) when compared to the manual settings, we are still able to improve over the baseline ($\mu = 0.635$). LSA seems to experience the highest relative improvement (35%), which might be due to its ability to handle noise in these automatic settings. Overall Pearson and Spearman correlations exhibit the same improvement pattern, which supports the notion that even with the possibility of introducing noise through miss-translations, the models overall benefit from the additional clues provided by the multilingual representation.

To explore the effect of automatic translation on the individual languages, we plot the correlation scores achieved vis-à-vis a reference language, and average over all the systems and the automatically translated datasets in Figure 4, in a similar fashion to Figure 2.

We notice the similar rise in performance associated with the addition of more languages to the Arabic (20%) and the Romanian (37%) models, and a slower rise for Spanish (16%) and English (8%). The effect of the automatic translation quality is evident for the Arabic language where the automatic translation seems to slow down the improvement when compared to the manual translations (Figure 2). A similar behavior is also observed in Spanish and Romanian but on a lower scale.

[4]This API is now offered as a paid service; Microsoft or Babelfish automatic translation services are publicly available.

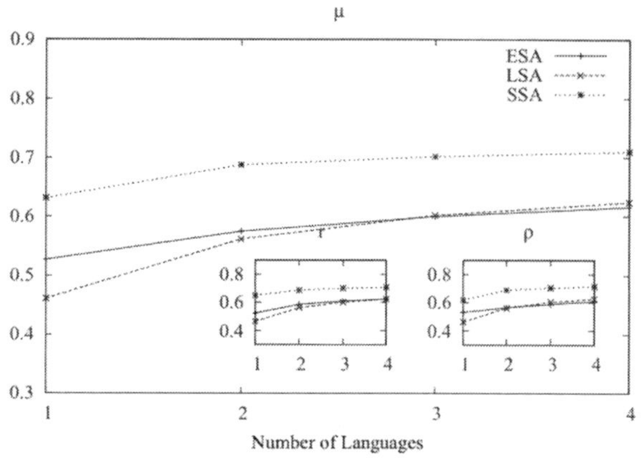

Figure 3: Automatic translation - average correlation (μ, r, ρ) obtained from incorporating scores from models in other languages

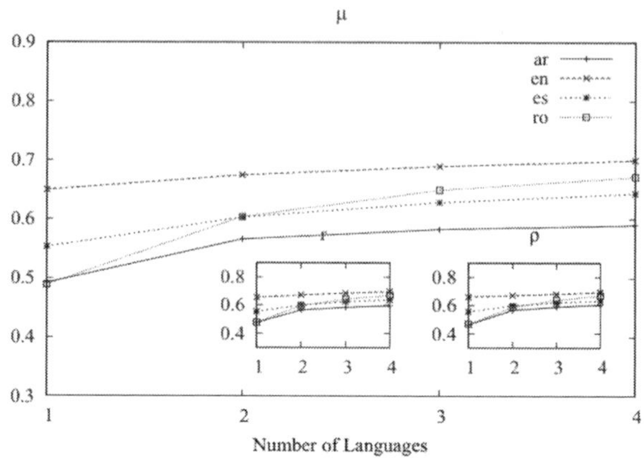

Figure 4: Automatic translation - average correlation (μ, r, ρ) obtained by supplementing a source language with scores from other languages

A very interesting consideration is that English experiences a stronger improvement when using automatic translations (8%) compared to manual translations (4%). This can be attributed to the translation engine quality in transferring English text to other languages and to the fact that the statistical translation (when accurate) can lead to a translation that makes use of more frequently used words, which contribute to more robust relatedness measures. When presented with a word pair, human judges may provide a translation influenced by the form/root of the word in the source language, which may not be as commonly used as the output of a MT system. For example, when presented with the pair "coast - shore," a Romanian translator may be tempted to provide "coastă" as a translation candidate for the first word in the pair, as it resembles the English word in form. However, the Romanian word is highly ambiguous, and in an authoritative Romanian dictionary[5] its primary sense is that of rib, followed by side, slope, and ultimately coast. Thus, a MT system using a statistical inference may provide a stronger translation such as "ţărm" that is far less ambiguous, and whose primary meaning is the one intended by the original pair.

Overall, the trend is positive and follows the pattern previously observed on the manually constructed datasets. This suggests that an automatic translation, even if more noisy, is beneficial and provides a way to reinforce semantic relatedness in a given language with information coming from multiple languages with no manual effort.

Do our findings hold for different relatedness datasets? At last, encouraged by the small performance difference between the use of manual versus automatic translations, we seek to explore how this multilingual model behaves under the different paradigms dictated by word relatedness versus text relatedness scenarios. Since our previous experiments were constrained to collections for which we also had a manual translation, we perform a larger scale evaluation by including automatically translated word relatedness ($RG65$) and text relatedness ($LEE50$ and $AG400$) datasets into all the languages in our language set, and repeat all the word-to-word and text-to-text evaluations.

Table 1 shows the correlation scores achieved using automatic translations on the word relatedness datasets. Most models on most datasets benefit from the multilingual representation (as shown by the figures in bold). Specifically, the SSA model has an improvement in μ of 26% for WS353 and 15% for $MC30$. This improvement is most evident in the case of the largest dataset $WS353$, where all the multilingual models exhibit a consistent and strong performance.

Table 2 reports the results obtained for the text relatedness datasets using automatic translation. While the ESA performance suffers in the multilingual model, it is overshadowed by the improvement experienced by LSA and SSA. The multilin-

[5] http://dexonline.ro/definitie/coasta

	r			ρ			μ		
Models	**MC30**	**RG65**	**WS353**	**MC30**	**RG65**	**WS353**	**MC30**	**RG65**	**WS353**
ESA_{en}	0.645	0.644	0.487	0.742	**0.768**	**0.525**	0.690	0.701	0.506
ESA_{ml}	**0.723**	**0.741**	**0.515**	**0.766**	0.759	0.519	**0.744**	**0.75**	**0.517**
LSA_{en}	0.509	0.450	0.435	**0.525**	0.499	0.436	**0.517**	0.473	0.436
LSA_{ml}	**0.538**	**0.566**	**0.487**	0.484	**0.569**	**0.517**	0.510	**0.567**	**0.502**
SSA_{en}	0.771	**0.824**	0.543	0.688	0.772	0.553	0.727	0.797	0.548
SSA_{ml}	**0.873**	0.807	**0.674**	**0.803**	**0.795**	**0.713**	**0.836**	**0.801**	**0.693**

Table 1: Automatic translation - r, ρ, μ correlations on the word relatedness datasets using multilingual models.

	r			ρ			μ		
Models	**LI30**	**LEE50**	**AG400**	**LI30**	**LEE50**	**AG400**	**LI30**	**LEE50**	**AG400**
ESA_{en}	**0.792**	**0.756**	**0.434**	**0.797**	**0.48**	**0.392**	**0.795**	**0.587**	**0.412**
ESA_{ml}	0.776	0.648	0.382	0.742	0.339	0.358	0.759	0.445	0.369
LSA_{en}	0.829	**0.776**	0.400	0.824	**0.523**	0.359	0.826	**0.625**	0.379
LSA_{ml}	**0.856**	0.765	**0.46**	**0.855**	0.502	**0.404**	**0.856**	0.606	**0.43**
SSA_{en}	**0.840**	**0.744**	0.520	0.843	0.371	0.501	0.841	0.495	0.510
SSA_{ml}	0.829	0.743	**0.539**	**0.87**	**0.41**	**0.521**	**0.849**	**0.528**	**0.53**

Table 2: Automatic translation - r, ρ, μ correlations on the text relatedness datasets using multilingual models.

gual model reports some of the best scores in the literature, such as a correlations of $r = 0.856$ and $\rho = 0.87$ for $LI30$ achieved by LSA and SSA, respectively. Not surprisingly, SSA is still a top contender, achieving the highest scores for $AG400$ and $LI30$. In $AG400$, SSA reports a μ of 0.53 which represents a 4% improvement over the English SSA model ($\mu = 0.51$) and a 16% improvement over the best knowledge-based system $J\&C$ ($\mu = 0.457$).

It is important to note that the evaluation in Tables 1 and 2 are restricted to data translated from English into a target language. English, as a resource-rich language, has an extensive and robust monolingual model, yet it can still be enhanced with additional clues originating from other languages. Accordingly, we only expected small improvements in these two experiments, unlike the cases where we start from resource-poor languages such as Romanian or Arabic (see Figures 2 and 4).

7 Conclusion

In this paper, we showed how a semantic relatedness measure computed in a multilingual space is able to acquire and leverage additional information from the multilingual representation, and thus be strengthened as more languages are taken into consideration. Our experiments seem to suggest that combinations of multiple languages supply additional information to derive a semantic relatedness between texts in an automatic framework. Since establishing semantic relatedness requires us to employ cognitive processes that are in large part independent of the language that we speak, it comes at no surprise that using relatedness clues originating from more than one language allows for a better identification of relationships between texts. While efficiency may be a concern, it is worth noting that the method is highly parallelizable, as the individual relatedness measures obtained before the aggregation step can be calculated in parallel.

Notably, all the relatedness measures that we experimented with exhibited the same improvement trend. While this framework allows languages with scarce electronic resources, such as Romanian and Arabic, to obtain very large improvements in semantic relatedness as compared to the monolingual measures, improvements are also noticed for languages with richer resources such as English.

Acknowledgments

This material is based in part upon work supported by the National Science Foundation CAREER award #0747340 and IIS award #1018613. Any opinions, findings, and conclusions or recommendations expressed in this material are those of the authors and do not necessarily reflect the views of the National Science Foundation.

References

C. Banea and R. Mihalcea. 2011. Word sense disambiguation with multilingual features. In *International Conference on Semantic Computing*, Oxford, UK.

C. Banea, R. Mihalcea, and J. Wiebe. 2010. Multilingual subjectivity: Are more languages better? In *Proceedings of the 23rd International Conference on Computational Linguistics (Coling 2010)*, pages 28–36, Beijing, China, August.

R. Besançon and M. Rajman. 2002. Evaluation of a vector space similarity measure in a multilingual framework. In *Proceedings of the Third International Conference on Language Resource and Evaluation (LREC 2002)*, Las Palmas, Spain.

S. Brin, J. Davis, and H. Garcia-Molina. 1995. Copy detection mechanisms for digital documents. In *ACM International Conference on Management of Data (SIGMOD 1995)*.

A. Z. Broder, S. C. Glassman, M. S. Manasse, and G. Zweig. 1997. Syntactic clustering of the web. *Comput. Netw. ISDN Syst.*, 29(8-13):1157–1166.

A Z. Broder, P. Ciccolo, M. Fontoura, E. Gabrilovich, V. Josifovski, and L. Riedel. 2008. Search advertising using web relevance feedback. In *CIKM '08: Proceeding of the 17th ACM conference on Information and knowledge management*, pages 1013–1022, New York, NY, USA. ACM.

C. Burgess, K. Livesay, and K. Lund. 1998. Explorations in context space: words, sentences, discourse. *Discourse Processes*, 25(2):211–257.

K. Church and P. Hanks. 1990. Word association norms, mutual information, and lexicography. *Computational Linguistics*, 16(1):22–29.

T. Cohn and M. Lapata. 2007. Machine translation by triangulation: making effective use of multi-parallel corpora. In *Proceedings of the 45th Annual Meeting of the Association of Computational Linguistics*, pages 728–735, Prague, Czech Republic.

I. Dagan, O. Glickman, and B. Magnini. 2005. The PASCAL recognising textual entailment challenge. In *Proceedings of the PASCAL Workshop*.

D. Davidov and A. Rappoport. 2009. Enhancement of lexical concepts using cross-lingual web mining. In *Proceedings of the 2009 Conference on Empirical Methods in Natural Language Processing*, pages 852–861, Singapore.

L. Finkelstein, E. Gabrilovich, Y. Matias, E. Rivlin, Z. Solan, G. Wolfman, and E. Ruppin. 2001. Placing search in context: the concept revisited. In ACM Press, editor, *The Tenth International World Wide Web Conference*, pages 406–414, Hong Kong.

E. Gabrilovich and S. Markovitch. 2007. Computing semantic relatedness using Wikipedia-based explicit semantic analysis. In *Proceedings of the 20th International Joint Conference on Artificial Intelligence*, pages 1606–1611, Hyderabad, India.

A. Goodrum. 2000. Image information retrieval: An overview of current research. *Informing Science*, 3(2):63–66.

S. Hassan and R. Mihalcea. 2009. Cross-lingual semantic relatedness using encyclopedic knowledge. In *Proceedings of the 2009 Conference on Empirical Methods in Natural Language Processing*, pages 1192–1201, Singapore. Association for Computational Linguistics.

S. Hassan and R. Mihalcea. 2011. Measuring semantic relatedness using salient encyclopedic concepts. *Artificial Intelligence, Special Issue*, xx(xx).

N. Heintze. 1996. Scalable document fingerprinting. In *In Proc. USENIX Workshop on Electronic Commerce*.

T. C. Hoad and J. Zobel. 2003. Methods for identifying versioned and plagiarized documents. *J. Am. Soc. Inf. Sci. Technol.*, 54(3):203–215.

A. Islam and D. Inkpen. 2006. Second order co-occurrence PMI for determining the semantic similarity of words. In *Proceedings of the Fifth Conference on Language Resources and Evaluation*, volume 2, Genoa, Italy, July.

M. Jarmasz and S. Szpakowicz. 2003. Roget's thesaurus and semantic similarity. In *Proceedings of the conference on Recent Advances in Natural Language Processing RANLP-2003*, Borovetz, Bulgaria, September.

J. Kazama, S. De Saeger, K. Kuroda, M. Murata, and K. Torisawa. 2010. A bayesian method for robust estimation of distributional similarities. In *Proceedings of the 48th Annual Meeting of the Association for Computational Linguistics*, Uppsala, Sweden.

T. K. Landauer, D. Laham, B. Rehder, and M. E. Schreiner. 1991. How well can passage meaning be derived without using word order? A comparison of latent semantic analysis and humans. In *Proceedings of the 19th annual meeting of the Cognitive Science Society*, pages 412–417, Mawhwah, N. Erlbaum.

C. Leacock and M. Chodorow, 1998. *Combining local context and WordNet similarity for word sense identification*, pages 305–332.

M. D. Lee and M. Welsh. 2005. An empirical evaluation of models of text document similarity. In *Proceedings of the 27th annual meeting of the Cognitive Science Society*, pages 1254–1259, Stresa, Italy.

C. W. Leong and R. Mihalcea. 2009. Explorations in automatic image annotation using textual features. In *Proceedings of the Third Linguistic Annotation Workshop*, pages 56–59, Suntec, Singapore, August. Association for Computational Linguistics.

M. Lesk. 1986. Automatic sense disambiguation using machine readable dictionaries. In *Proceedings of the 5th annual international conference on Systems documentation - SIGDOC '86*, pages 24–26, Toronto, Ontario. ACM Press.

W. Li, Q. Lu, and R. Xu. 2005. Similarity based chinese synonym collocation extraction. *International Journal of Computational Linguistics and Chinese Language Processing*, 10(1).

Y. Li, D. McLean, Z. A. Bandar, J. D. O'Shea, and K. Crockett. 2006. Sentence similarity based on semantic nets and corpus statistics. *IEEE Transactions on Knowledge and Data Engineering*, 18(8):1138–1150, August.

D. Lin. 1998. An information-theoretic definition of similarity. In *Proceedings of the Fifteenth International Conference on Machine Learning*, pages 296–304, Madison, Wisconsin.

U. Manber. 1994. Finding similar files in a large file system. In *USENIX WINTER 1994 TECHNICAL CONFERENCE*, pages 1–10.

D. Metzler, Y. Bernstein, W. Bruce Croft, A. Moffat, and J. Zobel. 2005. Similarity measures for tracking information flow. In *CIKM '05: Proceedings of the 14th ACM international conference on Information and knowledge management*, pages 517–524, New York, NY, USA. ACM.

D. Metzler, S. T. Dumais, and C. Meek. 2007. Similarity measures for short segments of text. In Giambattista Amati, Claudio Carpineto, and Giovanni Romano, editors, *ECIR*, volume 4425 of *Lecture Notes in Computer Science*, pages 16–27. Springer.

G. A. Miller and W. G. Charles. 1991. Contextual correlates of semantic similarity. *Language and Cognitive Processes*, 6(1):1–28.

G. A. Miller. 1995. WordNet: a Lexical database for english. *Communications of the Association for Computing Machinery*, 38(11):39–41.

T. Mitchell, T. Russell, P. Broomhead, and N. Aldridge. 2002. Towards robust computerised marking of free-text responses. In *roceedings of the 6th International Computer Assisted Assessment (CAA) Conference*, Loughborough, UK. Loughborough University.

M. Mohler and R. Mihalcea. 2009a. Text-to-text semantic similarity for automatic short answer grading. In *EACL*, pages 567–575. The Association for Computer Linguistics.

M. Mohler and R. Mihalcea. 2009b. Text-to-text semantic similarity for automatic short answer grading. In *Proceedings of the 12th Conference of the European Chapter of the Association for Computational Linguistics*, pages 567–575, Stroudsburg, PA, USA.

T. Pedersen, S. Patwardhan, and J. Michelizzi. 2004. WordNet::Similarity - measuring the relatedness of concepts. In *Proceedings of the Nineteenth National Conference on Artificial Intelligence (AAAI-04), demonstrations*, San Jose, CA.

J. Ponte and W. Croft. 1998. A language modeling approach to information retrieval. In *Proceedings of the Annual International SIGIR Conference on Research and Development in Information Retrieval*, pages 275–281, Melbourne, Australia.

S. G. Pulman and J. Z. Sukkarieh. 2005. Automatic short answer marking. In *EdAppsNLP 05: Proceedings of the second workshop on Building Educational Applications Using NLP*, pages 9–16, Morristown, NJ, USA. Association for Computational Linguistics.

H. Rubenstein and J. B. Goodenough. 1965. Contextual correlates of synonymy. *Communications of the ACM*, 8(10):627–633, October.

M. Sahami and T. D. Heilman. 2006. A web-based kernel function for measuring the similarity of short text snippets. In *WWW '06: Proceedings of the 15th international conference on World Wide Web*, pages 377–386, New York, NY, USA. ACM.

N. Shivakumar and H. Garcia-Molina. 1995. Scam: A copy detection mechanism for digital documents. In *2nd International Conference in Theory and Practice of Digital Libraries (DL 1995)*.

J. Sinclair. 2001. *Collins cobuild English dictionary for advanced learners*. Harper Collins, 3rd edition.

P. D. Turney. 2001. Mining the Web for Synonyms: PMI-IR versus LSA on TOEFL. In *Proceedings of the 12th European Conference on Machine Learning*, pages 491–502, Freiburg, Germany.

Z. Wu and M. Palmer. 1994. Verbs semantics and lexical selection. In *Proceedings of the 32nd annual meeting on Association for Computational Linguistics*, pages 133—-138, Las Cruces, New Mexico.

W. T. Yih and C. Meek. 2007. Improving similarity measures for short segments of text. In *AAAI'07: Proceedings of the 22nd national conference on Artificial intelligence*, pages 1489–1494. AAAI Press.

T. Zesch, I. Gurevych, and M. Mühlhäuser. 2007. Comparing Wikipedia and German Wordnet by Evaluating Semantic Relatedness on Multiple Datasets. In *Proceedings of Human Language Technologies: The Annual Conference of the North American Chapter of the Association for Computational Linguistics*.

Towards Building a Multilingual Semantic Network: Identifying Interlingual Links in Wikipedia

Bharath Dandala
Dept. of Computer Science
University of North Texas
Denton, TX
BharathDandala@my.unt.edu

Rada Mihalcea
Dept. of Computer Science
University of North Texas
Denton, TX
rada@cs.unt.edu

Razvan Bunescu
School of EECS
Ohio University
Athens, Ohio
bunescu@ohio.edu

Abstract

Wikipedia is a Web based, freely available multilingual encyclopedia, constructed in a collaborative effort by thousands of contributors. Wikipedia articles on the same topic in different languages are connected via interlingual (or translational) links. These links serve as an excellent resource for obtaining lexical translations, or building multilingual dictionaries and semantic networks. As these links are manually built, many links are missing or simply wrong. This paper describes a supervised learning method for generating new links and detecting existing incorrect links. Since there is no dataset available to evaluate the resulting interlingual links, we create our own gold standard by sampling translational links from four language pairs using distance heuristics. We manually annotate the sampled translation links and used them to evaluate the output of our method for automatic link detection and correction.

1 Introduction

In recent years, Wikipedia has been used as a resource of world knowledge in many natural language processing applications. A diverse set of tasks such as text categorization, information extraction, information retrieval, question answering, word sense disambiguation, semantic relatedness, and named entity recognition have been shown to benefit from the semi-structured text of Wikipedia. Most approaches that use the world knowledge encoded in Wikipedia are statistical in nature and therefore their performance depends significantly on the size of Wikipedia. Currently, the English Wikipedia alone has four million articles. However, the combined Wikipedias for all other languages greatly exceed the English Wikipedia in size, yielding a combined total of more than 10 million articles in more than 280 languages.[1] The rich hyperlink structure of these Wikipedia corpora in different languages can be very useful in identifying various relationships between concepts.

Wikipedia articles on the same topic in different languages are often connected through interlingual links. These links are the small navigation links that show up in the "Languages" sidebar in most Wikipedia articles, and they connect an article with related articles in other languages. For instance, the interlingual links for the Wikipedia article about "Football" connect it to 20 articles in 20 different languages. In the ideal case, a set of articles connected directly or indirectly via such links would all describe the same entity or concept. However, these links are produced either by polyglot editors or by automatic bots. Editors commonly make mistakes by linking articles that have conceptual drift, or by linking to a concept at a different level of granularity. For instance, if a corresponding article in one of the languages does not exist, a similar article or a more general article about the concept is sometimes linked instead. Various bots also add new interlingual links or attempt to correct existing ones. The downside of a bot is that an error in a translational link created by editors in Wikipedia for one language propagates to Wikipedias in other languages. Thus, if a bot introduces a wrong link, one may have to search for

[1] http://en.wikipedia.org/wiki/Wikipedia:Size_of_Wikipedia

Language	Code	Articles	Redirects	Users
English	en	4,674,066	4,805,557	16,503,562
French	fr	3,298,615	789,408	1,250,266
German	de	3,034,238	678,288	1,398,424
Italian	it	2,874,747	319,179	731,750
Polish	pl	2,598,797	158,956	481,079
Spanish	es	2,587,613	504,062	2,162,925
Dutch	nl	2,530,250	226,201	446,458
Russian	ru	2,300,769	682,402	819,812
Japanese	jp	1,737,565	372,909	607,152
Chinese	cn	1,199,912	333,436	1,171,148

Table 1: Number of articles, redirects, and users for the top nine Wikipedia editions plus Chinese. The total number of articles also includes the disambiguation pages.

the underlying error in a different language version of Wikipedia.

The contributions of the research described in this paper are two-fold. First, we describe the construction of a dataset of interlingual links that are automatically sampled from Wikipedia based on a set of distance heuristics. This dataset is manually annotated in order to enable the evaluation of methods for translational link detection. Second, we describe an automatic model for correcting existing links and creating new links, with the aim of obtaining a more stable set of interlingual links. The model's parameters are estimated on the manually labeled dataset using a supervised machine learning approach.

The remaining of this paper is organized as follows: Section 2 briefly describes Wikipedia and the relevant terminology. Section 3 introduces our method of identifying a candidate set of translational links based on distance heuristics, while Section 4 introduces the methodology for building a manually annotated dataset. Section 5 describes the machine learning experiments for detecting or correcting interlingual links. Finally, we present related work in Section 6, and concluding remarks in Section 7.

2 Wikipedia

Wikipedia is a free online encyclopedia, representing the outcome of a continuous collaborative effort of a large number of volunteer contributors. Virtually any Internet user can create or edit a Wikipedia webpage, and this "freedom of contribution" has a positive impact on both the quantity (fast-growing number of articles) and the quality (potential errors are quickly corrected within the collaborative environment) of this online resource.

The basic entry in Wikipedia is an *article* (or *page*), which defines and describes an entity or an event, and consists of a hypertext document with hyperlinks to other pages within or outside Wikipedia. The role of the hyperlinks is to guide the reader to pages that provide additional information about the entities or events mentioned in an article. Articles are organized into *categories*, which in turn are organized into category hierarchies. For instance, the article *automobile* is included in the category *vehicle*, which in turn has a parent category named *machine*, and so forth.

Each article in Wikipedia is uniquely referenced by an identifier, consisting of one or more words separated by spaces or underscores and occasionally a parenthetical explanation. For example, the article for *bar* with the meaning of *"counter for drinks"* has the unique identifier *bar (counter)*.

Wikipedia editions are available for more than 280 languages, with a number of entries varying from a few pages to three millions articles or more per language. Table 1 shows the nine largest Wikipedias (as of March 2012) and the Chinese Wikipedia, along with the number of articles and approximate number of contributors.[2]

The ten languages mentioned above are also the languages used in our experiments. Note that Chi-

[2]http://meta.wikimedia.org/wiki/List_of_Wikipedias#Grand_Total

Relation	Exists	Via
SYMMETRY		
en=Ball de=Ball	Yes	-
en=Hentriacontane it=Entriacontano	No	-
TRANSITIVITY		
en=Deletion (phonology) fr=Amuïssement	Yes	nl=Deletie (taalkunde)
en=Electroplating fr=Galvanoplastie	No	-
REDIRECTIONS		
en=Gun Dog de=Schiesshund	Yes	de=Jagdhund
en=Ball de=Ball	No	-

Table 2: Symmetry, transitivity, and redirections in Wikipedia

nese is the twelfth largest Wikipedia, but we decided to include it at the cost of not covering the tenth largest Wikipedia (Portuguese), which has close similarities with other languages already covered (e.g., French, Italian, Spanish).

Relevant for the work described in this paper are the *interlingual links*, which explicitly connect articles in different languages. For instance, the English article for *bar (unit)* is connected, among others, to the Italian article *bar (unitá di misura)* and the Polish article *bar (jednostka)*. On average, about half of the articles in a Wikipedia version include interlingual links to articles in other languages. The number of interlingual links per article varies from an average of five in the English Wikipedia, to ten in the Spanish Wikipedia, and as many as 23 in the Arabic Wikipedia.

3 Identifying Interlingual Links in Wikipedia

The interlingual links connecting Wikipedias in different languages should ideally be symmetric and transitive. The symmetry property indicates that if there is an interlingual link $A_\alpha \rightarrow A_\beta$ between two articles, one in language α and one in language β, then the reverse link $A_\alpha \leftarrow A_\beta$ should also exist in Wikipedia. According to the transitivity property, the presence of two links $A_\alpha \rightarrow A_\beta$ and $A_\beta \rightarrow A_\gamma$ indicates that the link $A_\alpha \rightarrow A_\gamma$ should also exist in Wikipedia, where α, β and γ are three different languages. While these properties are intuitive, they are not always satisfied due to Wikipedia's editorial policy that accredits editors with the responsibility of maintaining the articles. Table 2 shows actual cases in Wikipedia where these properties fail due to missing interlingual links. The table also shows examples where the editors link an article from one language to a redirect page in another language.

Link type	Total number of links	Newly added links
DL	26,836,572	-
RL	26,836,572	1,277,760
DP_2/RP_2	25,763,689	853,658
DP_3/RP_3	23,383,535	693,262
DP_4/RP_4	21,560,711	548,354

Table 3: Number of links identified in Wikipedia, as direct, symmetric, or transitional links. The number of newly added links, not known in the previous set of links, is also indicated (e.g., DP_3/RP_3 adds 693,262 new links not found by direct or symmetric links, or by direct or reverse paths of length two).

In order to generate a normalized set of interlingual links between Wikipedias, we replace all the redirect pages with the corresponding original articles, so that each concept in a language is represented by one unique article. We then identify the following four types of simple interlingual paths between articles in different languages:

DL: Direct links $A_\alpha \rightarrow A_\beta$ between two articles.

RL: Reverse links $A_\alpha \leftarrow A_\beta$ between two articles.

DP_k: Direct, simple paths of length k between two articles.

RP_k: Reverse, simple paths of length k between two articles.

Relation	Number of paths
DL	
en=Ball de=Ball	1
en=Ball it=Palla (sport)	1
en=Ball fr=Boule (solide)	0
de=Ball fr=Ballon (sport)	0
RL	
en=Ball de=Ball	1
en=Ball it=Palla(sport)	1
en=Ball fr=Boule (solide)	0
de=Ball fr=Ballon (sport)	0
DP_2	
en=Ball de=Ball	1
en=Ball it=Palla (sport)	2
en=Ball fr=Boule (solide)	1
de=Ball fr=Ballon (sport)	2
DP_3	
en=Ball de=Ball	1
en=Ball it=Palla (sport)	0
en=Ball fr=Boule (solide)	1
de=Ball fr=Ballon (sport)	1
DP_4	
en=Ball de=Ball	0
en=Ball it=Palla (sport)	0
en=Ball fr=Boule (solide)	1
de=Ball fr=Ballon (sport)	0
RP_2	
en=Ball de=Ball	1
en=Ball it=Palla (sport)	2
en=Ball fr=Boule (solide)	0
de=Ball fr=Ballon (sport)	2
RP_3	
en=Ball de=Ball	1
en=Ball it=Palla (sport)	0
en=Ball fr=Boule (solide)	0
de=Ball fr=Ballon (sport)	1
RP_4	
en=Ball de=Ball	0
en=Ball it=Palla (sport)	0
en=Ball fr=Boule (solide)	0
de=Ball fr=Ballon (sport)	0

Table 4: A subset of the direct links, reverse links, and inferred direct and reverse paths for the graph in Figure 1

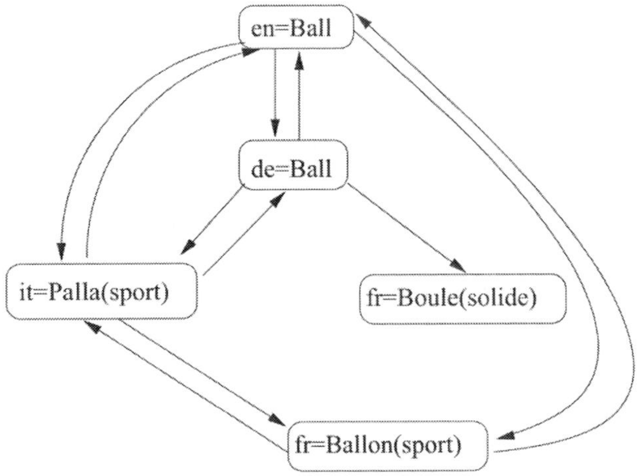

Figure 1: A small portion of the multilingual Wikipedia graph.

Figure 1 shows a small portion of the Wikipedia graph, connecting Wikipedias in four languages: English, German, Italian, and French. Correspondingly, Table 4 shows a subset of the direct links DL, reverse links RL, direct translation paths DP_k and reverse translation paths RP_k of lengths $k = 2, 3, 4$ for the graph in the figure.

Using these distance heuristics, we are able to extract or infer a very large number of interlingual links. Table 3 shows the number of direct links extracted from the ten Wikipedias we currently work with, as well as the number of paths that we add by enforcing the symmetry and transitivity properties.

4 Manual Evaluation of the Interlingual Links

The translation links in Wikipedia, whether added by the Wikipedia editors (direct links), or inferred by the heuristics described in the previous section, are not guaranteed for quality. In fact, previous work (de Melo and Weikum, 2010b) has shown that a large number of the links created by the Wikipedia users are incorrect, connecting articles that are not translations of each other, subsections of articles, or disambiguation pages. We have therefore decided to run a manual annotation study in order to determine the quality of the interlingual links. The resulting annotation can serve both as a gold standard for evaluating the quality of predicted links, and as supervision for a machine learning model that would automatically detect translation links.

Language pair	0	1	2	3	4
(English, German)	46	8	29	2	110
(English, Spanish)	22	19	19	13	123
(Italian, French)	30	7	19	7	132
(Spanish, Italian)	21	8	17	13	136

Table 6: Number of annotations on a scale of 0-4 for each pair of languages

From the large pool of links directly available in Wikipedia or inferred automatically through symmetry and transitivity, we sampled and then manually annotated 195 pairs of articles for each of four language pairs: (English, German), (English, Spanish), (Italian, French), and (Spanish, Italian). The four language pairs were determined based on the native or near-native knowledge available in the group of annotators in our research group. The sampling of the article pairs was done such that it covers all the potentially interesting cases obtained by combining the heuristics used to identify interlingual links. The left side of Table 5 shows the combination of heuristics used to select the article pairs. For each such combination, and for each language pair, we randomly selected 15 articles. Furthermore, we added 15 randomly selected pairs for the highest quality combination (Case 1).

For each language pair, the sampled links were annotated by one human judge, with the exception of the (English, Spanish) dataset, which was annotated by two judges so that we could measure the inter-annotator agreement. The annotators were asked to check the articles in each link and annotate the link on a scale from 0 to 4, as follows:

4: Identical concepts that are perfect translations of each other.

3: Concepts very close in meaning, which are good translations of each other, but a better translation for one of the concepts in the pair also exists. The annotators are not required to identify a better translation in Wikipedia, they only have to use their own knowledge of the language, e.g. "building" (English) may be a good translation for "tore" (Spanish), yet a better translation is known to exist.

2: Concepts that are closely related but that are not translations of each other.

1: Concepts that are remotely related and are not translations of each other.

0: Completely unrelated concepts or links between an article and a portion of another article.

To determine the quality of the annotations, we ran an inter-annotator study for the (English-Spanish) language pair. The two annotators had a Pearson correlation of 70%, which indicates good agreement. We also calculated their agreement when grouping the ratings from 0 to 4 in only two categories: 0, 1, and 2 were mapped to *no translation*, whereas 3 and 4 were mapped to *translation*. On this coarse scale, the annotators agreed 84% of the time, with a kappa value of 0.61, which once again indicate good agreement.

The annotations are summarized in the right side of Table 5. For each quality rating, the table shows the number of links annotated with that rating. Note that this is a summary over the annotations of five annotators, corresponding to the four language pairs, as well as an additional annotation for (English, Spanish).

Not surprisingly, the links that are "supported" by all the heuristics considered (Case 1) are the links with the highest quality. These are interlingual links that are present in Wikipedia and that can also be inferred through transitive path heuristics. Interestingly, links that are only guaranteed to have a direct link (DL) and no reverse link (RL) (Case 2) have a rather low quality, with only 68% of the links being considered to represent a perfect or a good translation (score of 3 or 4).

Table 6 summarizes the annotations per language pair. There appear to be some differences in the quality of interlingual links extracted or inferred for different languages, with (Spanish, Italian) being the pair with the highest quality of links (76% of the links are either perfect or good translations), while English to German seems to have the lowest quality (only 57% of the links are perfect or good). For the (English, Spanish) pair, we used the average of the two annotators' ratings, rounded up to the nearest integer.

Cases	Combinations of heuristics to extract or infer interlingual links									Link quality on a 0-4 scale				
	DL	RL	DP_2	RP_2	DP_3	RP_3	DP_4	RP_4	Samples	0	1	2	3	4
Case 1	y	y	y	y	y	y	y	y	30	6	3	6	6	129
Case 2	y	n	-	-	-	-	-	-	15	15	3	6	3	48
Case 3	n	y	-	-	-	-	-	-	15	13	3	8	4	47
Case 4	n	n	y	y	-	-	-	-	15	6	3	16	4	46
Case 5	n	n	-	-	y	y	-	-	15	13	9	12	4	28
Case 6	n	n	-	-	-	-	y	y	15	15	8	3	8	37
Case 7	n	n	n	n	-	-	-	-	15	19	8	11	5	31
Case 8	n	n	-	-	n	n	-	-	15	13	8	11	5	32
Case 9	n	n	-	-	-	-	n	n	15	25	4	11	2	33
Case 10	y	y	n	n	-	-	-	-	15	6	3	4	3	59
Case 11	y	y	-	-	n	n	-	-	15	6	2	3	0	64
Case 12	y	y	-	-	-	-	n	n	15	3	6	2	4	60

Table 5: Left side of the table: distance heuristics and number of samples based on each distance heuristic. 'y' indicates that the corresponding path should exist, 'n' indicates that the corresponding path should not exist, '-' indicates that we don't care whether the corresponding path exists or not. Right side of the table: manual annotations of the quality of links, on a scale of 0 to 4, with 4 meaning perfect translations.

5 Machine Learning Experiments

The manual annotations described above are good indicators of the quality of the interlingual links that can be extracted and inferred in Wikipedia. But such manual annotations, because of the human effort involved, do not scale up, and therefore we cannot apply them on the entire interlingual Wikipedia graph to determine the links that should be preserved or the ones that should be removed.

Instead, we experiment with training machine learning models that would automatically determine the quality of an interlingual link. As features, we use the presence or absence of direct or symmetric links, along with the number of inferred paths of length $k = 2, 3, 4$, as defined in Section 3. Table 7 shows the feature vectors for the same four pairs of articles that were used in Table 4. The feature values are computed based on the sample network of interlingual links from Figure 1. Each feature vector is assigned a numerical class, corresponding to the manual annotation provided by the human judges.

We conduct two experiments, at a fine-grained and a coarse-grained level. In both experiments, we use all the annotations for all four language pairs together (i.e., a total of 780 examples), and perform evaluations in a ten-fold cross validation scenario.

For the fine-grained experiments, we use all five numerical classes in a linear regression model.[3] We determine the correctness of the predictions on the test data by calculating the Pearson correlation with respect to the gold standard. The resulting correlation was measured at 0.461. For comparison, we also run an experiment where we only keep the presence or absence of the direct links as a feature (DL). In this case, the correlation was measured at 0.418, which is substantially below the correlation obtained when using all the features. This indicates that the interlingual links inferred through our heuristics are indeed useful.

In the coarse-grained experiments, the quality ratings 0, 1, and 2 are mapped to the *no translation* label, while ratings 3 and 4 are mapped to the *translation* label. We used the Ada Boost classifier with decision stumps as the binary classification algorithm. When using the entire feature vectors, the accuracy is measured at 73.97%, whereas the use of only the direct links results in an accuracy of 69.35%. Similar to the fine-grained linear regression experiments, these coarse-grained experiments further validate the utility of the interlingual links inferred through the transitive path heuristics.

[3]We use the Weka machine learning toolkit.

Concept pair	DL	RL	DP_2	DP_3	DP_4	RP_2	RP_3	RP_4	Class
en=Ball de=Ball	1	1	1	1	0	1	1	0	4
en=Ball it=Palla (sport)	1	1	2	0	0	2	0	0	4
en=Ball fr=Boule (solide)	0	0	1	1	1	0	0	0	1
de=Ball fr=Ballon (sport)	0	0	2	1	0	2	1	0	4

Table 7: Examples of feature vectors generated for four interlingual links, corresponding to the concept pairs listed in Table 4

6 Related Work

The multilingual nature of Wikipedia has been already exploited to solve several number of language processing tasks. A number of projects have used Wikipedia to build a multilingual semantic knowledge base by using the existing multilingual nature of Wikipedia. For instance, (Ponzetto and Strube, 2007) derived a large scale taxonomy from the existing Wikipedia. In related work, (de Melo and Weikum, 2010a) worked on a similar problem in which they combined all the existing multilingual Wikipedias to build a stable, large multilingual taxonomy.

The interlingual links have also been used for cross-lingual information retrieval (Nguyen et al., 2009) or to generate bilingual parallel corpora (Mohammadi and QasemAghaee, 2010). (Ni et al., 2011) used multilingual editions of Wikipedia to mine topics for the task of cross lingual text classification, while (Hassan and Mihalcea, 2009) used Wikipedias in different languages to measure cross-lingual semantic relatedness between concepts and texts in different languages. (Bharadwaj et al., 2010) explored the use of the multilingual links to mine dictionaries for under-resourced languages. They developed an iterative approach to construct a parallel corpus, using the interlingual links, info boxes, category pages, and abstracts, which they then be used to extract a bilingual dictionary. (Navigli and Ponzetto, 2010) explored the connections that can be drawn between Wikipedia and WordNet. While no attempts were made to complete the existing link structure of Wikipedia, the authors made use of machine translation to enrich the resource.

The two previous works most closely related to ours are the systems introduced in (Sorg and Cimiano, 2008) and (de Melo and Weikum, 2010a; de Melo and Weikum, 2010b). (Sorg and Cimiano, 2008) designed a system that predicts new interlingual links by using a classification based approach. They extract certain types of links from bilingual Wikipedias, which are then used to create a set of features for the machine learning system. In follow-up work, (Erdmann et al., 2008; Erdmann et al., 2009) used an expanded set of features, which also accounted for direct links, redirects, and links between articles in Wikipedia, to identify entries for a bilingual dictionary. In this line of work, the focus is mainly on article content analysis, as a way to detect new potential translations, rather than link analysis as done in our work.

Finally, (de Melo and Weikum, 2010b) designed a system that detects errors in the existing interlingual links in Wikipedia. They show that there are a large number of links that are imprecise or wrong, and propose the use of a weighted graph to produce a more consistent set of consistent interlingual links. Their work is focusing primarily on correcting existing links in Wikipedia, rather than inferring new links as we do.

7 Conclusions

In this paper, we explored the identification of translational links in Wikipedia. By using a set of heuristics that extract and infer links between Wikipedias in different languages, along with a machine learning algorithm that builds upon these heuristics to determine the quality of the interlingual links, we showed that we can both correct existing translational links in Wikipedia as well as discover new interlingual links. Additionally, we have also constructed a manually annotated dataset of interlingual links, covering different types of links in four pairs of languages, which can serve as a gold standard for evaluating the quality of predicted links, and as supervision for the machine learning model.

In future work, we plan to experiment with additional features to enhance the performance of the classifier. In particular, we would like to also include content-based features, such as content overlap and interlinking.

The collection of interlingual links for the ten Wikipedias considered in this work, as well as the manually annotated dataset are publicly available at http://lit.csci.unt.edu.

Acknowledgments

This material is based in part upon work supported by the National Science Foundation IIS awards #1018613 and #1018590 and CAREER award #0747340. Any opinions, findings, and conclusions or recommendations expressed in this material are those of the authors and do not necessarily reflect the views of the National Science Foundation.

References

G.R. Bharadwaj, N. Tandon, and V. Varma. 2010. An iterative approach to extract dictionaries from Wikipedia for under-resourced languages. Kharagpur, India.

G. de Melo and G. Weikum. 2010a. MENTA: inducing multilingual taxonomies from Wikipedia. In *Proceedings of the 19th ACM international conference on Information and knowledge management*, pages 1099–1108, New York, NY, USA. ACM.

G. de Melo and G. Weikum. 2010b. Untangling the cross-lingual link structure of Wikipedia. In *Proceedings of the 48th Annual Meeting of the Association for Computational Linguistics*, pages 844–853, Stroudsburg, PA, USA. Association for Computational Linguistics.

M. Erdmann, K. Nakayama, T. Hara, and S. Nishio. 2008. An approach for extracting bilingual terminology from Wikipedia. In *Proceedings of the 13th International Conference on Database Systems for Advanced Applications*.

M. Erdmann, K. Nakayama, T. Hara, and S. Nishio. 2009. Improving the extraction of bilingual terminology from Wikipedia. *ACM Transactions on Multimedia Computing, Communications and Applications*, 5(4):31:1–31:17.

S. Hassan and R. Mihalcea. 2009. Cross-lingual semantic relatedness using encyclopedic knowledge. In *Proceedings of the Conference on Empirical Methods in Natural Language Processing (EMNLP)*, Suntec, Singapore.

M. Mohammadi and N. QasemAghaee. 2010. Building bilingual parallel corpora based on Wikipedia. *International Conference on Computer Engineering and Applications*, 2:264–268.

R. Navigli and S. Ponzetto. 2010. Babelnet: Building a very large multilingual semantic network. In *Proceedings of the 48th Annual Meeting of the Association for Computational Linguistics*, Uppsala, Sweden.

D. Nguyen, A. Overwijk, C. Hauff, D. Trieschnigg, D. Hiemstra, and F. De Jong. 2009. WikiTranslate: query translation for cross-lingual information retrieval using only Wikipedia. In *Proceedings of the 9th Cross-language evaluation forum conference on Evaluating systems for multilingual and multimodal information access*, pages 58–65, Berlin, Heidelberg. Springer-Verlag.

X. Ni, J. Sun, J. Hu, and Z. Chen. 2011. Cross lingual text classification by mining multilingual topics from Wikipedia. In *Proceedings of the fourth ACM international conference on Web search and data mining*, pages 375–384, New York, NY, USA. ACM.

S. Ponzetto and M. Strube. 2007. Deriving a large scale taxonomy from Wikipedia. In *Proceedings of the 22nd national conference on Artificial intelligence - Volume 2*, pages 1440–1445. AAAI Press.

P. Sorg and P. Cimiano. 2008. Enriching the crosslingual link structure of Wikipedia - a classification-based approach. In *Proceedings of the AAAI 2008 Workshop on Wikipedia and Artificial Intelligence*.

Sentence Clustering via Projection over Term Clusters

Lili Kotlerman, Ido Dagan
Bar-Ilan University
Israel
Lili.Kotlerman@biu.ac.il
dagan@cs.biu.ac.il

Maya Gorodetsky, Ezra Daya
NICE Systems Ltd.
Israel
Maya.Gorodetsky@nice.com
Ezra.Daya@nice.com

Abstract

This paper presents a novel sentence clustering scheme based on projecting sentences over term clusters. The scheme incorporates external knowledge to overcome lexical variability and small corpus size, and outperforms common sentence clustering methods on two real-life industrial datasets.

1 Introduction

Clustering is a popular technique for unsupervised text analysis, often used in industrial settings to explore the content of large amounts of sentences. Yet, as may be seen from the results of our research, widespread clustering techniques, which cluster sentences directly, result in rather moderate performance when applied to short sentences, which are common in informal media.

In this paper we present and evaluate a novel sentence clustering scheme based on projecting sentences over term clusters. Section 2 briefly overviews common sentence clustering approaches. Our suggested clustering scheme is presented in Section 3. Section 4 describes an implementation of the scheme for a particular industrial task, followed by evaluation results in Section 5. Section 6 lists directions for future research.

2 Background

Sentence clustering aims at grouping sentences with similar meanings into clusters. Commonly, vector similarity measures, such as cosine, are used to define the level of similarity over bag-of-words encoding of the sentences. Then, standard clustering algorithms can be applied to group sentences into clusters (see Steinbach et al. (2000) for an overview).

The most common practice is representing the sentences as vectors in term space and applying the K-means clustering algorithm (Shen et al. (2011); Pasquier (2010); Wang et al. (2009); Nomoto and Matsumoto (2001); Boros et al. (2001)). An alternative approach involves partitioning a sentence connectivity graph by means of a graph clustering algorithm (Erkan and Radev (2004); Zha (2002)).

The main challenge for any sentence clustering approach is language variability, where the same meaning can be phrased in various ways. The shorter the sentences are, the less effective becomes exact matching of their terms. Compare the following newspaper sentence "*The bank is phasing out the EZ Checking package, with no monthly fee charged for balances over $1,500, and is instead offering customers its Basic Banking account, which carries a fee*" with two tweets regarding the same event: "*Whats wrong.. charging $$ for checking a/c*" and "*Now they want a monthly fee!*". Though each of the tweets can be found similar to the long sentence by exact term matching, they do not share any single term. Yet, knowing that the words *fee* and *charge* are semantically related would allow discovering the similarity between the two tweets.

External resources can be utilized to provide such kind of knowledge, by which sentence representation can be enriched. Traditionally, WordNet (Fellbaum, 1998) has been used for this purpose (Shehata (2009); Chen et al. (2003); Hotho et al. (2003); Hatzivassiloglou et al. (2001)). Yet, other resources of semantically-related terms can be beneficial, such as WordNet::Similarity (Pedersen et al., 2004), statistical resources like that of Lin (1998) or DIRECT (Kotlerman et al., 2010), thesauri, Wikipedia (Hu et al., 2009), ontologies (Suchanek et al., 2007) etc.

3 Sentence Clustering via Term Clusters

This section presents a generic sentence clustering scheme, which involves two consecutive steps: (1) generating relevant term clusters based on lexical semantic relatedness and (2) projecting the sentence set over these term clusters. Below we describe each of the two steps.

3.1 Step 1: Obtaining Term Clusters

In order to obtain term clusters, a term connectivity graph is constructed for the given sentence set and is clustered as follows:

1. Create initially an undirected graph with sentence-set terms as nodes and use lexical resources to extract semantically-related terms for each node.
2. Augment the graph nodes with the extracted terms and connect semantically-related nodes with edges. Then, partition the graph into term clusters through a graph clustering algorithm.

Extracting and filtering related terms. In Section 2 we listed a number of lexical resources providing pairs of semantically-related terms. Within the suggested scheme, any combination of resources may be utilized.

Often resources contain terms, which are semantically-related only in certain contexts. E.g., the words *visa* and *passport* are semantically-related when talking about tourism, but cannot be considered related in the banking domain, where *visa* usually occurs in its *credit card* sense. In order to discard irrelevant terms, filtering procedures can be employed. E.g., a simple filtering applicable in most cases of sentence clustering in a specific domain would discard candidate related terms, which do not occur sufficiently frequently in a target-domain corpus. In the example above, this procedure would allow avoiding the insertion of *passport* as related to *visa*, when considering the banking domain.

Clustering the graph nodes. Once the term graph is constructed, a graph clustering algorithm is applied resulting in a partition of the graph nodes (terms) into clusters. The choice of a particular algorithm is a parameter of the scheme. Many clustering algorithms consider the graph's edge weights. To address this trait, different edge weights can be assigned, reflecting the level of confidence that the two terms are indeed validly related and the reliability of the resource, which suggested the corresponding edge (e.g. WordNet synonyms are commonly considered more reliable than statistical thesauri).

3.2 Step 2: Projecting Sentences to Term Clusters

To obtain sentence clusters, the given sentence set has to be projected in some manner over the term clusters obtained in Step 1. Our projection procedure resembles unsupervised text categorization (Gliozzo et al., 2005), with categories represented by term clusters that are not predefined but rather emerge from the analyzed data:

1. Represent term clusters and sentences as vectors in term space and calculate the similarity of each sentence with each of the term clusters.
2. Assign each sentence to the best-scoring term cluster. (We focus on hard clustering, but the procedure can be adapted for soft clustering).

Various metrics for feature weighting and vector comparison may be chosen. The top terms of term-cluster vectors can be regarded as labels for the corresponding sentence clusters.

Thus each sentence cluster corresponds to a single coherent cluster of related terms. This is contrasted with common clustering methods, where if sentence *A* shares a term with *B*, and *B* shares another term with *C*, then *A* and *C* might appear in the same cluster even if they have no related terms in common. This behavior turns out harmful for short sentences, where each incidental term is influential. Our scheme ensures that each cluster contains only sentences related to the underlying term cluster, resulting in more coherent clusters.

4 Application: Clustering Customer Interactions

In industry there's a prominent need to obtain business insights from customer interactions in a contact center or social media. Though the number of key sentences to analyze is often relatively small, such as a couple hundred, manually analyzing just a handful of clusters is much preferable. This section describes our implementation of the scheme described in Section 3 for the task of clustering customer interactions, as well as the data used for evaluation. Results and analysis are presented in Section 5.

4.1 Data

We apply our clustering approach over two real-life datasets. The first one consists of 155 sentences containing reasons of account cancelation, retrieved from automatic transcripts of contact center interactions of an Internet Service Provider (ISP). The second one contains 194 sentences crawled from Twitter, expressing reasons for customer dissatisfaction with a certain banking company. The sentences in both datasets were gathered automatically by a rule-based extraction algorithm. Each dataset is accompanied by a small corpus of call transcripts or tweets from the corresponding domain.[1]

The goal of clustering these sentences is to identify the prominent reasons of cancelation and dissatisfaction. To obtain the gold-standard (GS) annotation, sentences were manually grouped to clusters according to the reasons stated in them.

Table 1 presents examples of sentences from the ISP dataset. The sentences are short, with only one or two words expressing the actual reason stated in them. We see that exact term matching is not sufficient to group the related sentences. Moreover, traditional clustering algorithms are likely to mix related and unrelated sentences, due to matching non-essential terms (e.g. *husband* or *summer*). We note that such short and noisy sentences are common in informal media, which became a most important channel of information in industry.

4.2 Implementation of the Clustering Scheme

Our proposed sentence clustering scheme presented in Section 3 includes a number of choices. Below we describe the choices we made in our current implementation.

Input sentences were tokenized, lemmatized and cleaned from stopwords in order to extract content-word terms. Candidate semantically-related terms

he hasn't been using it all summer long *it's been sitting idle for about it almost a year*
I'm getting married my husband has a computer *yeah I bought a new laptop this summer so*
when I said faces my husband got laid off from work *well I'm them going through financial difficulties*

Table 1: Example sentences expressing 3 reasons for cancelation: the customer (1) does not use the service, (2) acquired a computer, (3) cannot afford the service.

were extracted for each of the terms, using WordNet synonyms and derivations, as well as DIRECT[2], a directional statistical resource learnt from a news corpus. Candidate terms that did not appear in the accompanying domain corpus were filtered out as described in Section 3.1.

Edges in the term graph were weighted with the number of resources supporting the corresponding edge. To cluster the graph we used the Chinese Whispers clustering tool[3] (Biemann, 2006), whose algorithm does not require to pre-set the desired number of clusters and is reported to outperform other algorithms for several NLP tasks.

To generate the projection, sentences were represented as vectors of terms weighted by their frequency in each sentence. Terms of the term-cluster vectors were weighted by the number of sentences in which they occur. Similarity scores were calculated using the cosine measure. Clusters were labeled with the top terms appearing both in the underlying term cluster and in the cluster's sentences.

5 Results and Analysis

In this section we present the results of evaluating our projection approach, compared to the common K-means clustering method[4] applied to:

(A) Standard bag-of-words representation of sentences;

[1]The bank dataset with the output of the tested methods will be made publicly available.

[2]Available for download at www.cs.biu.ac.il/~nlp/downloads/DIRECT.html. For each term we extract from the resource the top-5 related terms.

[3]Available at http://wortschatz.informatik.uni-leipzig.de/~cbiemann/software/CW.html

[4]We use the Weka (Hall et al., 2009) implementation. Due to space limitations and for more meaningful comparison we report here one value of K, which is equal to the number of clusters returned by projection (60 for the ISP and 65 for the bank dataset). For K = 20, 40 and 70 the performance was similar.

(B) Bag-of-words representation, where sentence's words are augmented with semantically-related terms (following the common scheme of prior work, see Section 2). We use the same set of related terms as is used by our method.

(C) Representation of sentences in term-cluster space, using the term clusters generated by our method as vector features. A feature is activated in a sentence vector if it contains a term from the corresponding term cluster.

Table 2 shows the results in terms of Purity, Recall (R), Precision (P) and F1 (see "Evaluation of clustering", Manning et al. (2008)). Projection significantly[5] outperforms all baselines for both datasets.

Dataset	Algorithm	Purity	R	P	F1
ISP	**Projection**	**.74**	**.40**	**.68**	**.50**
	K-means A	.65	.18	.22	.20
	K-means B	.65	.13	.24	.17
	K-means C	.65	.18	.26	.22
Bank	**Projection**	**.79**	**.26**	**.53**	**.35**
	K-means A	.61	.14	.14	.14
	K-means B	.64	.13	.19	.16
	K-means C	.67	.17	.21	.19

Table 2: Evaluation results.

For completeness we experimented with applying Chinese Whispers clustering to sentence connectivity graphs, but the results were inferior to K-means.

Table 3 presents sample sentences from clusters produced by projection and K-means for illustration. Our initial analysis showed that our approach indeed produces more homogenous clusters than the baseline methods, as conjectured in Section 3.2. We consider it advantageous, since it's easier for a human to merge clusters than to reveal sub-clusters. E.g., a GS cluster of 20 sentences referring to fees and charges is covered by three projection clusters labeled *fee*, *charge* and *interest rate*, with 9, 8 and 2 sentences correspondingly. On the other hand, K-means C method places 11 out of the 20 sentences in a messy cluster of 57 sentences (see Table 3), scattering the remaining 9 sentences over 7 other clusters.

In our current implementation *fee*, *charge* and *interest rate* were not detected by the lexical resources we used as semantically similar and thus were not grouped in one term cluster. However, adding more resources may introduce additional noise. Such dependency on coverage and accuracy of resources is apparently a limitation of our approach. Yet, as our experiments indicate, using only two generic resources already yielded valuable results.

[5]p=0.001 according to McNemar test (Dietterich, 1998).

a. Projection

credit card, card, mastercard, visa (38 sentences)
XXX has the worst credit cards ever
XXX MasterCard is the worst credit card I've ever had
ntuc do not accept XXX visa now I have to redraw $150...
XXX card declined again , $40 dinner in SF...

b. K-means C

fee, charge (57 sentences)
XXX playing games wit my interest
arguing w incompetent pol at XXX damansara perdana
XXX's upper management are a bunch of rude pricks
XXX are ninjas at catching fraudulent charges.

Table 3: Excerpt from resulting clusterings for the bank dataset. Bank name is substituted with XXX. Cluster labels are given in italics. Two most frequent terms are assigned as cluster labels for K-means C.

6 Conclusions and Future Work

We presented a novel sentence clustering scheme and evaluated its implementation, showing significantly superior performance over common sentence clustering techniques. We plan to further explore the suggested scheme by utilizing additional lexical resources and clustering algorithms. We also plan to compare our approach with co-clustering methods used in document clustering (Xu et al. (2003), Dhillon (2001), Slonim and Tishby (2000)).

Acknowledgments

This work was partially supported by the MAGNETON grant no. 43834 of the Israel Ministry of Industry, Trade and Labor, the Israel Ministry of Science and Technology, the Israel Science Foundation grant 1112/08, the PASCAL-2 Network of Excellence of the European Community FP7-ICT-2007-1-216886 and the European Community's Seventh Framework Programme (FP7/2007-2013) under grant agreement no. 287923 (EXCITEMENT).

References

Chris Biemann. 2006. Chinese whispers - an efficient graph clustering algorithm and its application to natural language processing problems. In *Proceedings of TextGraphs: the Second Workshop on Graph Based Methods for Natural Language Processing*, pages 73–80, New York City, USA.

Endre Boros, Paul B. Kantor, and David J. Neu. 2001. A clustering based approach to creating multi-document summaries.

Hsin-Hsi Chen, June-Jei Kuo, and Tsei-Chun Su. 2003. Clustering and visualization in a multi-lingual multi-document summarization system. In *Proceedings of the 25th European conference on IR research*, ECIR'03, pages 266–280, Berlin, Heidelberg. Springer-Verlag.

Inderjit S. Dhillon. 2001. Co-clustering documents and words using bipartite spectral graph partitioning. In *Proceedings of the seventh ACM SIGKDD international conference on Knowledge discovery and data mining*, KDD '01, pages 269–274, New York, NY, USA. ACM.

Thomas G. Dietterich. 1998. Approximate statistical tests for comparing supervised classification learning algorithms.

Günes Erkan and Dragomir R. Radev. 2004. Lexrank: graph-based lexical centrality as salience in text summarization. *J. Artif. Int. Res.*, 22(1):457–479, December.

C. Fellbaum. 1998. *WordNet – An Electronic Lexical Database*. MIT Press.

Alfio Massimiliano Gliozzo, Carlo Strapparava, and Ido Dagan. 2005. Investigating unsupervised learning for text categorization bootstrapping. In *HLT/EMNLP*.

Mark Hall, Eibe Frank, Geoffrey Holmes, Bernhard Pfahringer, Peter Reutemann, and Ian H. Witten. 2009. The weka data mining software: an update. *SIGKDD Explor. Newsl.*, 11(1):10–18.

Vasileios Hatzivassiloglou, Judith L. Klavans, Melissa L. Holcombe, Regina Barzilay, Min yen Kan, and Kathleen R. McKeown. 2001. Simfinder: A flexible clustering tool for summarization. In *In Proceedings of the NAACL Workshop on Automatic Summarization*, pages 41–49.

A. Hotho, S. Staab, and G. Stumme. 2003. Wordnet improves text document clustering. In Ying Ding, Keith van Rijsbergen, Iadh Ounis, and Joemon Jose, editors, *Proceedings of the Semantic Web Workshop of the 26th Annual International ACM SIGIR Conference on Research and Development in Informaion Retrieval (SIGIR 2003), August 1, 2003, Toronto Canada*. Published Online at `http://de.scientificcommons.org/608322`.

Xiaohua Hu, Xiaodan Zhang, Caimei Lu, E. K. Park, and Xiaohua Zhou. 2009. Exploiting wikipedia as external knowledge for document clustering. In *Proceedings of the 15th ACM SIGKDD international conference on Knowledge discovery and data mining*, KDD '09, pages 389–396, New York, NY, USA. ACM.

Lili Kotlerman, Ido Dagan, Idan Szpektor, and Maayan Zhitomirsky-Geffet. 2010. Directional distributional similarity for lexical inference. *JNLE*, 16:359–389.

Dekang Lin. 1998. Automatic retrieval and clustering of similar words. In *Proceedings of the 17th international conference on Computational linguistics - Volume 2*, COLING '98, pages 768–774, Stroudsburg, PA, USA. Association for Computational Linguistics.

Christopher D. Manning, Prabhakar Raghavan, and Hinrich Schütze. 2008. *Introduction to Information Retrieval*. Cambridge University Press, Cambridge, Juli.

Tadashi Nomoto and Yuji Matsumoto. 2001. A new approach to unsupervised text summarization. In *Proceedings of the 24th annual international ACM SIGIR conference on Research and development in information retrieval*, SIGIR '01, pages 26–34, New York, NY, USA. ACM.

Claude Pasquier. 2010. Task 5: Single document keyphrase extraction using sentence clustering and latent dirichlet allocation. In *Proceedings of the 5th International Workshop on Semantic Evaluation*, SemEval '10, pages 154–157, Stroudsburg, PA, USA. Association for Computational Linguistics.

Ted Pedersen, Siddharth Patwardhan, and Jason Michelizzi. 2004. Wordnet::similarity: measuring the relatedness of concepts. In *Demonstration Papers at HLT-NAACL 2004*, HLT-NAACL–Demonstrations '04, pages 38–41, Stroudsburg, PA, USA. Association for Computational Linguistics.

Shady Shehata. 2009. A wordnet-based semantic model for enhancing text clustering. *Data Mining Workshops, International Conference on*, 0:477–482.

Chao Shen, Tao Li, and Chris H. Q. Ding. 2011. Integrating clustering and multi-document summarization by bi-mixture probabilistic latent semantic analysis (plsa) with sentence bases. In *AAAI*.

Noam Slonim and Naftali Tishby. 2000. Document clustering using word clusters via the information bottleneck method. In *Proceedings of the 23rd annual international ACM SIGIR conference on Research and development in information retrieval*, SIGIR '00, pages 208–215, New York, NY, USA. ACM.

M. Steinbach, G. Karypis, and V. Kumar. 2000. A comparison of document clustering techniques. *KDD Workshop on Text Mining*.

Fabian M. Suchanek, Gjergji Kasneci, and Gerhard Weikum. 2007. Yago: A large ontology from wikipedia and wordnet.

Dingding Wang, Shenghuo Zhu, Tao Li, and Yihong Gong. 2009. Multi-document summarization using sentence-based topic models. In *Proceedings of the ACL-IJCNLP 2009 Conference Short Papers*, ACLShort '09, pages 297–300, Stroudsburg, PA, USA. Association for Computational Linguistics.

Wei Xu, Xin Liu, and Yihong Gong. 2003. Document clustering based on non-negative matrix factorization. In *Proceedings of the 26th annual international ACM SIGIR conference on Research and development in informaion retrieval*, SIGIR '03, pages 267–273, New York, NY, USA. ACM.

Hongyuan Zha. 2002. Generic summarization and keyphrase extraction using mutual reinforcement principle and sentence clustering. In *SIGIR*, pages 113–120.

The Use of Granularity in Rhetorical Relation Prediction

Blake Stephen Howald and Martha Abramson
Ultralingua, Inc.
1313 SE Fifth Street, Suite 108
Minneapolis, MN 55414
{howald, abramson}@ultralingua.com

Abstract

We present the results of several machine learning tasks designed to predict rhetorical relations that hold between clauses in discourse. We demonstrate that organizing rhetorical relations into different granularity categories (based on relative degree of detail) increases average prediction accuracy from 58% to 70%. Accuracy further increases to 80% with the inclusion of clause types. These results, which are competitive with existing systems, hold across several modes of written discourse and suggest that features of information structure are an important consideration in the machine learnability of discourse.

1 Introduction

The rhetorical relations that hold between clauses in discourse index temporal and event information and contribute to a discourse's pragmatic coherence (Hobbs, 1985). For example, in (1) the NARRATION relation holds between (1a) and (1b) as (1b) temporally follows (1a) at event time.

(1) a. Pascale closed the toy chest.
 b. She walked to the gate.
 c. The gate was locked securely.
 d. So she couldn't get into the kitchen.

The ELABORATION relation, describing the surrounding state of affairs, holds between (1b) and (1c). (1c) is temporally inclusive (subordinated) with (1b) and there is no temporal progression at event time. The RESULT relation holds between (1b-c) and (1d). (1d) follows (1b) and its subordinated ELABORATION relation (1c) at event time.

Additional pragmatic information is encoded in these relations in terms of granularity. Granularity refers to the relative increases or decreases in the level of described detail. For example, moving from (1b) to (1c), we learn more information about *the gate* via the ELABORATION relation. Also, moving from (1b-c) to (1d) there is a consolidation of information associated with the RESULT relation.

Through several supervised machine learning tasks, we investigate the degree to which granularity (as well as additional elements of discourse structure (e.g. tense, aspect, event)) serves as a viable organization and predictor of rhetorical relations in a range of written discourses. This paper is organized as follows. Section 2 reviews prior research on rhetorical relations, discourse structure, granularity and prediction. Section 3 discusses the analyzed data, the selection and annotation of features, and the construction of several machine learning tasks. Section 4 provides the results which are then discussed in Section 5.

2 Background

Rhetorical relation prediction has received considerable attention and has been shown to be useful for text summarization (Marcu, 1998). Prediction tasks rely on a number of features (discourse connectives, part of speech, etc.) (Marcu and Echihabi, 2002; Lapata and Lascarides, 2004). A wide range of accuracies are also reported - 33.96% (Marcu and Echihabi, 2002) to 70.70% (Lapata and Lascarides, 2004) for all rhetorical relations and, for individual relations, CONTRAST (43.64%) and CONTINUATION (83.35%) (Sporleder and Lascarides, 2005).

We seek to predict the inventory of rhetorical relations defined in Segmented Discourse Representation Theory ("SDRT") (Asher and Lascarides, 2003). In addition to the relations illustrated in (1), we consider: BACKGROUND: *It was Christmas. Pascale got a new toy.*; EXPLANATION: *The aardvark was dirty. It fell into a puddle.*; CONSEQUENCE: *If the aardvark fell in the puddle, then it got dirty.*; ALTERNATION: *Pascale got an aardvark or a stuffed bunny.*; and CONTINUATION: *Pascale got an aardvark. Grimsby got a rawhide.*

Discourses were selected based on Smith (2003) who defines five primary discourse modes by: (1) the *situations* (events and states) they describe; (2) the overarching *temporality* (tense, aspect); and (3) the type of text *progression* (temporal - text and event time progression are similar; atemporal - text and event time progression are not similar). These contrastive elements inform the features selected for the machine learning tasks discussed in Section 3.2. The five modes, *narratives, reports* (news articles), *description* (recipes), *information* (scientific essays), and *argument* (editorials) were selected to ensure a balanced range of theoretically supported discourse types.

2.1 Granularity of Information

Granularity in discourse refers to the relative degree of detail. The higher the level of detail, the more informative the discourse is. We assume that there will be some pragmatic constraints on the informativeness of a discourse (e.g., consistent with Grice's (1975) Maxim of Quantity). For our purposes, we rely specifically on granularity as defined in Mulkar-Mehta et al. (2011) ("MM") who characterize granularity in terms of entities and events.

To illustrate, consider (2) where the rhetorical structure indicates that (2b) is an ELABORATION of (2a), the NARRATION relation holds between (2b) and (2c) and (2c) and (2d), and the RESULT relation between (2d) and (2e).

(2) a. The Pittsburgh Steelers needed to win.
b. Batch took the first snap.
c. Then he threw the ball into the endzone.
d. Ward caught the ball.
e. A touchdown was scored.

Entities and events can stand in *part-whole* and *causality* relationships with entities and events in subsequent clauses. A *positive* granularity shift indicates movement from whole to part (more detail) - e.g., Batch (2b) is a *part* of the *whole* Pittsburgh Steelers (2a). A *negative* granularity shift indicates movement from part to whole (less detail), or if one event *causes* a subsequent event (if an event is caused by a subsequent event, this is a *positive* shift) - e.g., Ward's catching of the ball (2d) *caused* the scoring of the touchdown (2e). *Maintained* granularities (not considered by MM) are illustrated in (2b-c) and (2c-d). Clauses (2b) through (2d) are temporally linked events, but there is no *part-whole* shift in, nor a *causal* relationship between, the entities or events; the granularity remains the same.

We maintain that there is a close relationship between rhetorical relations and granularity. Consequently, rhetorical relations can be organized as follows: *positive*: BACKGROUND, ELABORATION, EXPLANATION; *negative*: CONSEQUENCE, RESULT; and *maintained*: ALTERNATION, CONTINUATION, NARRATION. The machine learning tasks discussed in the remainder of the paper consider this information in the prediction of rhetorical relations.

3 Data and Methods

Five written discourses of similar sentence length were selected from each mode for 25 total discourses. The discourses were segmented by independent or dependent (subordinate) clauses, if the clauses contained discourse markers (*but, however*), and if the clauses were embedded in the sentence provided in the orginal written discourse (e.g., John, *who is the director of NASA*, gave a speech on Friday). The total number of clauses is 1090, averaging 43.6 clauses per discourse (σ=7.2).

3.1 Feature Annotation

For prediction, we use a feature set distilled from Smith's classification of discourses: TENSE and ASPECT; EVENT (from the TimeML annotation scheme (Pustejovksy, et al., 2005), *Aspectual, Occurence, States*, etc.); SEQUENCE information as the clause position normalized to the unit interval; and discourse MODE. We also include CLAUSE type - independent (*IC*) or dependent clauses (*DC*) with the inclusion of a discourse marker (*M*) or not,

Table 1: Distribution of Relations by Granularity Type.

Relation	Number (Avg.)
Positive	**515 (47%)**
BACKGROUND	315 (61%)
ELABORATION	161 (31%)
EXPLANATION	39 (7%)
Negative	**59 (5%)**
CONSEQUENCE	16 (26%)
RESULT	43 (71%)
Maintenance	**490 (44%)**
ALTERNATION	76 (14%)
CONTINUATION	30 (6%)
NARRATION	384 (78%)

embedded (*EM*) or not - and GRANULARITY shift categories which are an organization of the SDRT rhetorical relations (Asher and Lascarides, 2003), summarized in Table 1.

All 25 discourses were annotated by one of the authors using only a reference sheet. The other author independently coded 80% of the data (20 discourses, four from each mode). Average agreement and Cohen's Kappa (Cohen, 1960) statistics were computed and are within acceptable ranges: TENSE (99.65 / .9945), ASPECT (99.30 / .9937), SDRT (77.42 / .6850), and EVENT (75.88 / .6362).

These results are consistent with previously reported annotations for rhetorical relations (Sporleder and Lascarides, 2005; Howald and Katz, 2011), event verbs and durations, tense and aspect (Puscasu and Mititelu, 2008; Wiebe et al., 1997). *Positive, negative* and *maintained* granularities were not annotated, but MM report a Kappa between .8500 and 1. The distribution of these granularities, based on the organization of the annotated rhetorical relations is presented in Table 1.

3.2 Machine Learning

Three supervised machine learning tasks were constructed to predict SDRT relations. The first task (**Uncollapsed**) created a 8-way classifier to predict the SDRT relations based on the feature set, omitting the GRANULARITY feature. The second task (**Collapsed**) created a 3-way classifier to predict the GRANULARITY categories (the SDRT feature was omitted). The third task (**Combined**) included

Table 2: Relation Prediction - Combined Modes.

Feature	J48	K*	NB	MCB
Uncollapsed	**58.99**	55.41	56.69	35
Collapsed	69.90	**70.18**	69.81	41
Combined	78.62	71.92	**80.00**	35 (70)

the GRANULARITY feature back into the **Uncollapsed** 8-way classifier. We utilized the WEKA toolkit (Witten and Frank, 2005) and treated each clause as a vector of information (SDRT, EVENT, TENSE, ASPECT, SEQUENCE, CLAUSE, MODE, GRANULARITY), illustrated in (3)[1]:

(3) a. The Pittsburgh Steelers needed to win.
START, *State, Pa., N, .200, IC, NA, start*
b. Batch took the first snap.
ELAB., *Occ., Pa., N, .400, IC, NA, pos.*
c. Then he threw the ball into the endzone.
NAR., *Asp., Pa., N, .600, IC-M, NA, main.*
d. Ward caught the ball.
NAR., *Occ., Pa., N, .800, IC, NA, main.*
e. A touchdown was scored.
RESULT, *Occ., Pa., Perf., 1.00, IC, NA, neg.*

We report results from the Naïve Bayes (NB), J48 (C4.5 decision tree (Quinlan, 1993)) and K* (Cleary and Trigg, 1995) classifiers, run at 10-fold cross-validation.

4 Results

Table 2 indicates that the best average accuracy for the **Uncollapsed** task is 58.99 (J48). The accuracy increases to 70.18 (K*) for the **Collapsed** task. The accuracy increases further to 80.00 (NB) for the **Combined** task. All accuracies are statistically significant over majority class baselines ("MCB"): **Uncollapsed** (MCB = 35) - χ^2 = 15.11, d.f. = 0, $p \leq$ .001; **Collapsed** (MCB = 41) - χ^2 = 20.51, d.f. = 0, $p \leq$ .001; and **Combined** (treating the best **Collapsed** accuracy as the new baseline (MCB = 70)) - χ^2 = 1.43, d.f. = 0, $p \leq$ .001.

As shown in Table 3, based on the NB 8-way **Combined** classifier, the prediction accuracies of

[1]Note that what is being predicted is the rhetorical relation, or associated granularity, with the second clause in a clause pair. Tasks were performed where clause information was paired, but this did not translate into improved accuracies.

Table 3: Individual Relation Prediction Accuracies (%).

Relation	A	I	D	N	R	T
NAR.	73	55	100	100	94	**96**
RES.	75	88	85	100	100	**93**
BACK.	93	92	96	87	94	**92**
ELAB.	57	41	69	21	48	**69**
CONSEQ.	20	0	0	0	0	**37**
ALTER.	50	42	0	0	43	**27**
CONTIN.	8	0	0	0	0	**23**
EXPLAN.	0	20	0	9	0	**2**
Total	**68**	**72**	**92**	**74**	**74**	**80**

the individual modes are no more than 12 percentage points off of the average (80.00). Accuracies range from 68% **A(rgument)** (σ=-12) to 92% **D(escription)** (σ=+12) with **N(arrative), R(eport)**, and **I(nformation)** being closest to average (σ=-6-8). For individual relation predictions, NARRATION, RESULT and BACKGROUND have the highest total accuracies followed by ELABORATION and CONTRAST. Performing less well is CONSEQUENCE, ALTERNATION and CONTINUATION with EXPLANATION performing the worst. All accuracies are statistically significant above baseline ($\chi^2 = 341.89$, d.f. = 7, $p \leq .001$).

5 Discussion and Conclusion

Using the **Collapsed** performance as a baseline for the **Combined** classifier, we discuss the features contributing to the 10 percentage point increase as well as the optimal (minimal) set of features for prediction. The best accuracies for the **Combined** experiment only require CLAUSE and GRANULARITY information; achieving 79.08% (NB - 44 above MCB, *f*-score=.750). Both CLAUSE and GRANULARITY are necessary. Relying only on CLAUSE achieves a 48.25% accuracy (J48) and relying only on GRANULARITY achieves 70.36% for all classifiers, but this higher accuracy is an artifact of the organization as evidenced by the *f*-score (.585).

The relationship between CLAUSE and the rhetorical relations is straightforward. For example, the CONSEQUENCE relation is often an "intersentential" relation (*if the aardvark fell in the puddle, then it got dirty*), each of the 16 CONSEQUENCE relations are embedded. Similarly, 93% of all ELABORATION relations, which are temporally subordinating, are embedded. Clause types appear to be a viable source of co-varying information in rhetorical relation prediction in the tasks under discussion.

The aspects of syntactic-semantic form and pragmatic function in the relationship between granularity and rhetorical relations is of central interest in this investigation. Asher and Lascarides represent discourses hierarchically through coordination and subordination of information which corresponds to changes in granularity. However, while the notion of granularity enters into the motivation and formulation of the SDRT inventory, it is not developed further. These results potentailly allow us to say something deeper about the structural organization of discourse as it relates to granularity.

In particualr, while there is some probabilistic leverage in collapsing categories, it is not the case that arbitrary categorizations will perform similarly. This observation holds true even for theoretically informed categorizations. For example, organizing the SDRT inventory into *coordinated* and *subordinated* relations yields lower performance on relation prediction. *Coordinated* and *subordinated* can be predicted with 80% accuracy, but the prediction of the individual relations given the category performs only at 70%. Since the granularity-based organization presented here performs better, we suggest that the pragmatic *function* of the relation is more systematic than the syntactic-semantic *form* of the relation.

Future research will focus on more data, different machine learning techniques (e.g. unsupervised learning) and automatization. Where clause, tense, aspect and event are readily automatable, rhetorical relations and granularity are less so. Automatically extracting such information from an annotated corpus such as the Penn Discourse Tree Bank is certainly feasible. However, the distribution of genres in this corpus is somewhat limited (i.e., predominately news text (Webber, 2009)) and calls into question the generalizeability of results to other modes of discourse. Overall, we have demonstrated that the inclusion of a granularity-based organization in the machine learning prediction of rhetorical relations increases performance by 37%, which is roughly 14% above previous reported results for a broader range of discourses and relations.

Acknowledgments

Thank you to Jeff Ondich and Ultralingua for facilitating this research and to four anonymous *SEM reviewers for insightful and constructive comments.

References

Nicholas Asher and Alex Lascarides. 2003. *Logics of Conversation.* Cambridge University Press, Cambridge, UK.

John G. Cleary and Leonard E. Trigg 1995. K*: An Instance-based Learner Using an Entropic Distance Measure. In *Proceedings of the 12 International Conference on Machine Learning*, 108–113.

Jacob Cohen. 1960. A Coefficient of Agreement for Nominal Scales. *Educational and Psychological Measurement*, 20(1):37–46.

H. Paul Grice. 1975. *Logic and Conversation.* In *Syntax and Semantics, Vol. 3, Speech Acts*, 43–85. Academic Press, New York.

Jerry R. Hobbs. 1985. On The Coherence and Structure of Discourse. *CSLI Technical Report*, CSLI-85-37.

Blake Stephen Howald and Graham Katz. 2011. The Exploitation of Spatial Information in Narrative Discourse. In *Proceedings of the Ninth International Workshop on Computational Semantics*, 175–184.

Mirella Lapata and Alex Lascarides. 2004. Inferring Sentence Internal Temporal Relations. In *Proceedings of the North American Association of Computational Linguistics (NAACL-04) 2004*, 153–160.

Daniel Marcu. 1998. Improving Summarization Through Rhetorical Parsing Tuning. In *Proceedings of The 6th Workshop on Very Large Corpora*, 206–215.

Daniel Marcu and Abdessamad Echihabi. 2002. An Unsupervised Approach to Recognizing Discourse Relations. In *Proceedings of the Association of Computational Linguistics (ACL-02) 2002*, 368–375.

Rutu Mulkar-Mehta, Jerry R. Hobbs and Eduard Hovy. 2011. Granulairty in Natural Language Discourse. In *Proceedings of the Ninth International Conference on Computational Semantics (IWCS 2011) 2011*, 195–204.

Georgiana Puscasu and Verginica Mititelu. 2008. Annotation of WordNet Verbs with TimeML Event Classes. *Proceedings of the Sixth International Language Resources and Evaluation (LREC08)*

James Pustejovsky, José Castaño, Robert Ingria, Roser Saur, Robert Gaizauskas, Andrea Setzer, and Graham Katz. 2005. TimeML: Robust Specification of Event and Temporal Expressions in Text. In *Proceedings of the Fith International Conference on Computational Semantics (IWCS 2005)*

Ross Quinlan. 1993 *C4.5: Programs for Machine Learning.* Morgan Kaufmann, San Francisco, CA.

Carlota Smith. 2003. *Modes of Discourse: The Local Structure of Texts.* Cambridge University Press, Cambridge, UK.

Caroline Sporleder and Alex Lascarides. 2005. Exploiting Linguistic Cues to Classify Rhetorical Relations. In *Proceedings of Recent Advances in Natural Language Processing (RANLP-05)*, 532–539.

Caroline Sporleder and Alex Lascarides. 2008. Using Automatically Labelled Examples to Classify Rhetorical Relations: An Assessment. *Natural Language Engineering*, 14:369–416.

Janyce Wiebe, Thomas O'Hara, Thorsten Öhrström-Sandgren and Kenneth McKeever. 1997. An Empirical Approach to Temporal Reference Resolution. In *Proceedings of the 2nd Conference on Empirical Methods in Natural Language Processing (EMNLP-97)*, 174–186.

Ian Witten and Eibe Frank. 2005. *Data Mining: Practical Machine Learning Techniques with Java Implementation (2nd Ed.)* Morgan Kaufmann, San Francisco, CA.

Bonnie Webber 2009. Genre Distictions for Discourse in the Penn TreeBank. In *Proceedings of the 47th ACL Conference*, 674–682.

"Could you *make* me a favour and *do* coffee, please?": Implications for Automatic Error Correction in English and Dutch

Sophia Katrenko
UiL-OTS
Utrecht University
s.katrenko@uu.nl

Abstract

The correct choice of words has proven challenging for learners of a second language and errors of this kind form a separate category in error typology. This paper focuses on one known example of two verbs that are often confused by non-native speakers of Germanic languages, *to make* and *to do*. We conduct experiments using syntactic information and immediate context for Dutch and English. Our results show that the methods exploiting syntactic information and distributional similarity yield the best results.

1 Introduction

When learning a second language, non-native speakers make errors at all levels of linguistic analysis, from pronunciation and intonation to language use. Word choice errors form a substantial part of all errors made by learners and may also be observed in writing or speech of native speakers. This category of errors includes homophones. Some commonly known confusions in English are *accept-except*, *advice-advise*, *buy-by-bye*, *ate-eight*, to name but a few. Other errors can be explained by a non-native speaker's inability to distinguish between words because there exists only one corresponding word in their native language. For example, Portuguese and Spanish speakers have difficulties to differentiate between *te doen (to do)* and *te maken (to make)*, and Turkish between *kunnen (can)*, *weten (to know)* and *kennen (to know)* in Dutch (Coenen et al., 1979). Adopting terminology from Golding and Roth (1999) and Rozovskaya and Roth (2010), *do/make* and *kunnen/kennen/weten* form two confusion sets. However, unlike the case of *kunnen/kennen/weten*, where the correct choice is often determined by syntactic context [1], the choice between *to make* and *to do* can be motivated by semantic factors. It has been argued in the literature that the correct use of these verbs depends on what is being expressed: *to do* is used to refer to daily routines and activities, while *to make* is used to describe constructing or creating something. Since word choice errors have different nature, we hypothesize that there may exist no uniform approach to correct them.

State-of-the-art spell-checkers are able to detect spelling and agreement errors but fail to find words used incorrectly, e.g. to distinguish *to make* from *to do*. Motivated by the implications that the correct prediction of two verbs of interest may have for automatic error correction, we model the problem of choosing the correct verb in a similar vein to selectional preferences. The latter has been considered for a variety of applications, e. g. semantic role labeling (Zapirain et al., 2009). Words such as *be* or *do* have been often excluded from consideration because they are highly polysemous and "do not select strongly for their arguments" (McCarthy and Carroll, 2003). In this paper, we study whether semantic classes of arguments may be used to determine the correct predicate (e.g., *to make* or *to do*) and consider the following research questions:

1. Can information on semantic classes of direct

[1] *Kunnen* is a modal verb followed by the main verb, *kennen* takes a direct object as in, e.g., *to know somebody*, and *weten* is often followed by a clause (as in *I know that*).

objects potentially help to correct verb choice errors?

2. How do approaches using contextual and syntactic information compare when predicting *to make* vs. *to do*?

The paper is organised as follows. Section 2.1 discusses the methods, followed by Section 2.2 on data. The experimental findings are presented in Section 2.3. We conclude in Section 3.

2 Experiments

We re-examine several approaches to selectional preferences in the context of error correction. Existing methods fall into one of two categories, either those relying on information from WordNet (McCarthy and Carroll, 2003), or data-driven (Erk, 2007; Schulte im Walde, 2010; Pado et al., 2007). For the purpose of our study, we focus on the latter.

2.1 Methods

For each verb in question, we have a frequency-based ranking list of nouns co-occurring with it (verb-object pairs) which we use for the first two methods.

Latent semantic clustering (LSC) Rooth et al. (1999) have proposed a soft-clustering method to determine selectional preferences, which models the joint distribution of nouns n and verbs v by conditioning them on a hidden class c. The probability of a pair (v, n) then equals

$$P(v,n) = \sum_{c \in C} P(c)P(v|c)P(n|c) \qquad (1)$$

Similarity-based method The next classifier we use combines similarity between nouns with ranking information and is a modification of the method described in (Pado et al., 2007). First, for all words n_i on the ranking list their frequency scores are normalised between 0 and 1, f_i. Then, they are weighed by the similarity score between a new noun n_j and a corresponding word on the ranking list, n_i, and the noun with the highest score (1-nearest neighbour) is selected:

$$\arg\max_{n_i} f_i \times sim(n_j, n_i) \qquad (2)$$

Finally, two highest scores for each verb's ranking list are compared and the verb with higher score is selected as a preferred one.

In addition, if we sum over all seen words instead of choosing the nearest neighbour, this will lead to the original approach by Pado et al. (2007). In the experimental part we consider both approaches (the original method is referred to as **SMP** while the nearest neighbour approach is marked by **SMknn**) and study whether there is any difference between the two when a verb that allows many different arguments is considered (e.g., it may be better to use the nearest neighbour approach for *to do* rather than aggregating over all similarity scores).

Bag-of-words (BoW) approach This widely used approach to document classification considers contextual words and their frequencies to represent documents (Zellig, 1954). We restrict the length of the context around two verbs (within a window of ± 2 and ± 3 around the focus word, *make* or *do*) and build a Naive Bayes classifier.

2.2 Data

Both verbs, *to make* and *to do*, license complements of various kinds, e. g. they can be mono-transitive, ditransitive, and complex transitive (sentences 1, 2, and 3, respectively). Furthermore, *make* can be part of idiomatic ditransitives (e.g., *make use of*, *make fun of*, *make room for*) and phrasal mono-transitives (e.g., *make up*) .

1. Andrew made [a cake]$_{dobj}$.
2. Andrew made [his mum]$_{iobj}$ [a cake]$_{dobj}$.
3. Andrew made [his mum]$_{dobj}$ happy.

For English, we use one of the largest corpora available, the PukWAC (over 2 billion words, 30GB) (Baroni et al., 2009), which has been parsed by MaltParser (Nivre and Scholz, 2004). We extract all sentences with *to do* or *to make* (based on lemmata). The verb *to make* occurs in 2,13% of sentences, and the verb *to do* in 3,27% of sentences in the PukWAC corpus. Next, we exclude from consideration phrasal mono-transitives and select sentences where verb complements are nouns (Table 1).

For experiments in Dutch, we use the "Wikipedia Dump Of 2010" corpus, which is a part of Lassy Large corpus (159 million tokens), and is parsed by

LANG	# sent	# dobj (*to make*)	# dobj (*to do*)
EN	181,813,571	1,897,747	881,314
NL	8,639,837	15,510	6,197

Table 1: The number of sentences in English (EN) and Dutch (NL) corpora (the last two columns correspond to the number of sentences where direct objects are nouns).

the Alpino parser (Bouma et al., 2001). Unlike in English data, *to make* occurs here more often than *to do* (3,3% vs. 1%). This difference can be explained by the fact that *to do* is also an auxiliary verb in English which leads to more occurrences in total. Similarly to the English data set, phrasal monotransitives are filtered out. Finally, the sentences that contain either *to make* or *to do* from wiki01 up to wiki07 (19,847 sentences in total) have been selected for training and wiki08 (1,769 sentences in total) for testing. To be able to compare our results against the performance on English data, we sample a subset from PukWAC which is of the same size as Dutch data set and is referred to as *EN (sm)*.

To measure distributional similarity for the nearest neighbour method, we use first-order and second-order similarity based on Lin's information theoretic measure (Lin, 1998). For both languages, similarity scores have been derived given a subset of Wikipedia (276 million tokens for English and 114 million tokens for Dutch) using the DISCO API (Kolb, 2009).

2.3 Results

Table 2 and Table 3 summarize our results. When referring to similarity-based methods, the symbols **(f)** and **(s)** indicate first-order and second-order similarity. For the BoW models, ± 2 and ± 3 corresponds to the context length. The performance is measured by true positive rate (*TP*) per class, overall accuracy (*Acc*) and coverage (*Cov*). The former indicates in how many cases the correct class label (*make* or *do*) has been predicted, while the latter shows how many examples a system was able to classify. Coverage is especially indicative for LCS and semantic similarity approaches because they may fail to yield predictions. For these methods, we provide two evaluations. First, in order to be able to compare results against the BoW approach, we measure accuracy and coverage on all test examples. In such a case, if some direct objects occur very often in the test set and are classified correctly, accuracy scores will be boosted. Therefore, we also provide the second evaluation where we measure accuracy and coverage on (unique) test examples regardless of how frequent they are. This evaluation will give us a better insight into how well LCS and similarity-based methods work. Finally, we tested several settings for the LSC method and the results presented here are obtained for 20 clusters and 50 iterations. We remove stop words [2] but do not take any other preprocessing steps.

For both languages, it is more difficult to predict *to do* than *to make*, although the differences in performance on Dutch data (NL) are much smaller than on English data (EN (sm)). An interesting observation is that using second-order similarity slightly boosts performance for *to make* but is highly undesirable for predicting *to do* (decrease in accuracy for around 15%) in Dutch. This may be explained by the fact that the objects of *to do* are already very generic. Our findings on English data are that the similarity-based approach is more sensitive to the choice of aggregating over all words in the training set or selecting the nearest neighbour. In particular, we obtained better performance when choosing the nearest neighbour for *to do* but aggregating over all scores for *to make*. The results on Dutch and English data are in general not always comparable. In addition to the differences in performance of similarity-based methods, the BoW models work better for predicting *to do* in English but *to make* in Dutch.

As expected, similarity-based approaches yield higher coverage than LSC, although the latter is superior in terms of accuracy (in all cases but *to do* in English). Since LSC turned out to be the most computationally efficient method, we have also run it on larger subsets of the PukWAC data set, up to the entire corpus. We have not noticed any signifi-

[2] We use stop word lists for English and Dutch from `http://snowball.tartarus.org/algorithms/`.

LANG	Method	TP (*to make*)	Cov (*to make*)	TP (*to do*)	Cov (*to do*)	Acc (all)	Cov (all)
EN (all)	LSC	91.70	98.75	73.40	97.16	85.90	98.24
EN (sm)	LSC	89.81	90.00	75.81	86.70	86.91	89.30
	SMP (f)	84.89	98.82	69.89	95.14	81.78	98.03
	SMP (s)	82.92	98.82	55.65	95.14	77.27	98.03
	SMknn (f)	62.61	98.82	91.13	95.14	68.52	98.03
	SMknn (s)	4.36	98.82	99.46	95.14	24.07	98.03
	BoW ± 2	36.41	100	82.21	100	46.01	100
	BoW ± 3	32.26	100	84.10	100	43.13	100
NL	LSC	98.75	91.79	95.74	93.37	98.09	92.13
	SMP (f)	95.64	95.82	92.97	98.14	95.06	96.32
	SMP (s)	97.52	95.82	76.75	98.14	93.00	96.32
	SMknn (f)	94.14	95.82	92.97	98.14	93.89	96.32
	SMknn (s)	96.09	95.82	78.64	98.14	92.30	96.32
	BoW ± 2	89.34	100	61.19	100	83.44	100
	BoW ± 3	91.06	100	54.18	100	83.32	100

Table 2: True positive rate (*TP*, %), accuracy (*Acc*, %) and coverage (*Cov*, %) for the experiments on English (*EN*) and Dutch (*NL*) data.

LANG	Method	TP (*to make*)	Cov (*to make*)	TP (*to do*)	Cov (*to do*)	Acc (all)	Cov (all)
EN (sm)	LSC	80.88	77.12	52.60	74.76	73.73	76.51
	SMP (f)	73.17	97.29	45.99	90.78	66.49	95.60
	SMP (s)	77.00	97.29	33.69	90.78	66.36	95.60
	SMknn (f)	31.18	97.29	82.35	90.78	43.76	95.60
	SMknn (s)	4.36	98.82	98.93	90.78	25.76	95.60
NL	LSC	94.85	63.40	86.59	76.64	92.39	66.83
	SMP (f)	87.55	81.37	77.00	93.45	84.24	84.50
	SMP (s)	91.16	81.37	54.00	93.45	80.52	84.50
	SMknn (f)	80.72	81.37	76.00	93.45	79.66	84.50
	SMknn (s)	85.54	81.37	55.00	93.45	76.79	84.50

Table 3: True positive rate (*TP*, %), accuracy (*Acc*, %) and coverage (*Cov*, %) for the experiments on English (*EN*) and Dutch (*NL*) unique direct objects.

cant changes in performance; the results for the entire data set, EN (all), are given in the first row of Table 2. Table 3 shows the results for the methods using direct object information on unique objects, which gives a more realistic assessment of their performance. At closer inspection, we noticed that many non-classified cases in Dutch refer to compounds. For instance, *bluegrassmuziek (bluegrass music)* cannot be compared against known words in the training set. In order to cover such cases, existing methods may benefit from morphological analysis.

3 Conclusions

In order to predict the use of two often confused verbs, *to make* and *to do*, we have compared two methods to modeling selectional preferences against the bag-of-words approach. The BoW method is always outperformed by LCS and similarity-based approaches, although the differences in performance are much larger for *to do* in Dutch and for *to make* in English. In this study, we do not use any corpus of non-native speakers' errors and explore how well it is possible to predict one of two verbs provided that the context words have been chosen correctly. In the future work, we plan to label all incorrect uses of *to make* and *to do* and to correct them.

Acknowledgments

The author thanks anonymous reviewers for their valuable comments. This work is supported by a VICI grant number 277-80-002 by the Netherlands Organisation for Scientific Research (NWO).

References

Marco Baroni and Silvia Bernardini and Adriano Ferraresi and Eros Zanchetta. 2009. *The WaCky Wide Web: A Collection of Very Large Linguistically Processed Web-Crawled Corpora.* Language Resources and Evaluation 43(3), pp. 209-226.

Gosse Bouma, Gertjan van Noord, and Robert Malouf. 2001. *Alpino: Wide-coverage Computational Analysis of Dutch.* In Computational Linguistics in the Netherlands 2000. Enschede.

Josée A. Coenen, W. van Wiggen, and R. Bok-Bennema. 1979. *Leren van fouten: een analyse van de meest voorkomende Nederlandse taalfouten, die gemaakt worden door Marokkaanse, Turkse, Spaanse en Portugese kinderen.* Amsterdam: Stichting ABC, Contactorgaan voor de Innovatie van het Onderwijs.

Katrin Erk. 2007. *A simple, similarity-based model for selectional preferences.* In Proceedings of ACL 2007. Prague, Czech Republic, 2007.

Andrew R. Golding and Dan Roth. 1999. *A Winnow-Based Approach to Context-Sensitive Spelling Correction.* Machine Learning 34(1-3), pp. 107-130.

Peter Kolb. 2009. *Experiments on the difference between semantic similarity and relatedness.* In Proceedings of the 17th Nordic Conference on Computational Linguistics - NODALIDA '09, Odense, Denmark, May 2009.

Dekang Lin. 1998. *Automatic Retrieval and Clustering of Similar Words.* In Proceedings of COLING-ACL 1998, Montreal.

Diana McCarthy and John Carroll. 2003. *Disambiguating nouns, verbs and adjectives using automatically acquired selectional preferences.* Computational Linguistics, 29(4), pp. 639-654.

Joakim Nivre and Mario Scholz. 2004. *Deterministic dependency parsing of English text.* In Proceedings of COLING 04.

Sebastian Padó, Ulrike Padó and Katrin Erk. 2007. *Flexible, Corpus-Based Modelling of Human Plausibility Judgements.* In Proceedings of EMNLP/CoNLL 2007. Prague, Czech Republic, pp. 400-409.

Mats Rooth, Stefan Riezler and Detlef Prescher. 1999. *Inducing a Semantically Annotated Lexicon via EM-Based Clustering.* In Proceedings of ACL 99.

Anna Rozovskaya and Dan Roth. 2010. *Generating Confusion Sets for Context-Sensitive Error Correction.* In Proceedings of EMNLP, pp. 961-970.

Sabine Schulte im Walde. 2010. *Comparing Computational Approaches to Selectional Preferences – Second-Order Co-Occurrence vs. Latent Semantic Clusters.* In Proceedings of the 7th International Conference on Language Resources and Evaluation, Valletta, Malta, pp. 1381–1388.

Beñat Zapirain, Eneko Agirre and Lluís Màrquez. 2009. *Generalizing over Lexical Features: Selectional Preferences for Semantic Role Classification.* In Proceedings of the ACL-IJCNLP 2009 Conference Short Papers. Suntec, Singapore, pp. 73-76.

Harris Zellig. 1954. *Distributional Structure.* Word 10 (2/3), p. 146-62.

Detecting Text Reuse with Modified and Weighted N-grams

Rao Muhammad Adeel Nawab*, **Mark Stevenson*** and **Paul Clough**†
*Department of Computer Science and †iSchool
University of Sheffield, UK.
{r.nawab@dcs, m.stevenson@dcs, p.d.clough@}.shef.ac.uk

Abstract

Text reuse is common in many scenarios and documents are often based, at least in part, on existing documents. This paper reports an approach to detecting text reuse which identifies not only documents which have been reused verbatim but is also designed to identify cases of reuse when the original has been rewritten. The approach identifies reuse by comparing word n-grams in documents and modifies these (by substituting words with synonyms and deleting words) to identify when text has been altered. The approach is applied to a corpus of newspaper stories and found to outperform a previously reported method.

1 Introduction

Text reuse is the process of creating new document(s) using text from existing document(s). Text reuse is standard practice in some situations, such as journalism. Applications of automatic detection of text reuse include the removal of (near-)duplicates from search results (Hoad and Zobel, 2003; Seo and Croft, 2008), identification of text reuse in journalism (Clough et al., 2002) and identification of plagiarism (Potthast et al., 2011).

Text reuse is more difficult to detect when the original text has been altered. We propose an approach to the identification of text reuse which is intended to identify reuse in such cases. The approach is based on comparison of word n-grams, a popular approach to detecting text reuse. However, we also account for synonym replacement and word deletion, two common text editing operations (Bell, 1991). The relative importance of n-grams is accounted for using probabilities obtained from a language model. We show that making use of modified n-grams and their probabilities improves identification of text reuse in an existing journalism corpus and outperforms a previously reported approach.

2 Related Work

Approaches for identifying text reuse based on word-level comparison (such as the SCAM copy detection system (Shivakumar and Molina, 1995)) tend to identify topical similarity between a pair of documents, whereas methods based on sentence-level comparison (e.g. the COPS copy detection system (Brin et al., 1995)) are unable to identify when text has been reused if only a single word has been changed in a sentence.

Comparison of word and character n-grams has proven to be an effective method for detecting text reuse (Clough et al., 2002; Cedeño et al., 2009; Chiu et al., 2010). For example, Cedeño et al. (2009) showed that comparison of word bigrams and trigrams are an effective method for detecting reuse in journalistic text. Clough et al. (2002) also applied n-gram overlap to identify reuse of journalistic text, combining it with other approaches such as sentence alignment and string matching algorithms. Chiu et al. (2010) compared n-grams to identify duplicate and reused documents on the web. Analysis of word n-grams has also proved to be an effective method for detecting plagiarism, another form of text reuse (Lane et al., 2006).

However, a limitation of n-gram overlap approach is that it fails to identify reuse when the original text has been altered. To overcome this problem we propose using modified n-grams, which have been altered by deleting or substituting words in the n-gram. The modified n-grams are intended to improve matching with the original document.

3 Determining Text Reuse with N-gram Overlap

3.1 N-grams Overlap (NG)

Following Clough et al. (2002), the asymmetric containment measure (eqn 1) was used to quantify the degree of text within a document (A) that is likely to have been reused in another document (B).

$$score_n(A, B) = \frac{\sum_{ngram \in B} count(ngram, A)}{\sum_{ngram \in B} count(ngram, B)} \quad (1)$$

where $count(ngram, A)$ is the number of times $ngram$ appears in document A. A score of 1 means that document B is contained in document A and a score of 0 that none of the n-grams in B occur in A.

3.2 Modified N-grams

N-gram overlap has been shown to be useful for measuring text reuse as derived texts typically share longer n-grams ($\geq$ 3 words). However, the approach breaks down when an original document has been altered. To counter this problem we applied various techniques for modifying n-grams that allow for word deletions (Deletions) and word substitutions (WordNet and Paraphrases), two common text editing operations.

Deletions (Del) Assume that $w_1, w_2, ...w_n$ is an n-gram. Then a set of modified n-grams can be created by removing one of the w_2 ... w_{n-1}. The first and last words in the n-gram are not removed since they will also be generated as shorter n-grams. An n-gram will generate $n - 2$ deleted n-grams and no deleted n-grams will be generated for unigrams and bigrams.

Substitutions Further n-grams can be created by substituting one of the words in an n-gram with one of its synonyms from **WordNet (WN)**. For words with multiple senses we use synonyms from *all senses*. Modified n-grams are created by substituting one of the words in the n-gram with one of its synonyms from WordNet.

Similarly to the WordNet approach, n-grams can be created by substituting one of the words with an equivalent term from a paraphrase lexicon, which we refer to as **Paraphrases (Para)**. A paraphrase lexicon was generated automatically (Burch, 2008) and ten lexical equivalents (the default setting) produced for each word. Modified n-grams were created by substituting one of the words in the n-gram with one of the lexical equivalents.

3.3 Comparing Modified N-grams

The modified n-grams are applied in the text reuse score by generating modified n-grams for the document that is suspected to contain reused text. These n-grams are then compared with the original document to determine the overlap. However, the techniques in Section 3.2 generate a large number of modified n-grams which means that the number of n-grams that overlap with document A can be greater than the total number of n-grams in B, leading to similarity scores greater than 1. To avoid this the n-gram overlap counts are constrained in a similar way that they are clipped in BLEU and ROUGE (Papineni et al., 2002; Lin, 2004).

For each n-gram in B, a set of modified n-grams, $mod(ngram)$, is created.[1] The count for an individual n-gram in B, $exp\_count(ngram, B)$, can be computed as the number of times any n-gram in $mod(ngram)$ occurs in A, see equation 2.

$$\sum_{ngram' \in mod(ngram)} count(ngram', A) \quad (2)$$

However, the contribution of this count to the text reuse score has to be bounded to ensure that the combined count of the modified n-grams appearing in A does not exceed the number of times the original n-gram occurs in B. Consequently the text reuse score, $score_n(A, B)$, is computed using equation 3.

$$\frac{\sum_{ngram \in B} min(exp\_count(ngram, A), count(ngram, B))}{\sum_{ngram \in B} count(ngram, B)} \quad (3)$$

3.4 Weighting N-grams

Probabilities of each n-gram, obtained using a language model, are used to increase the importance of

[1] This is the set of n-grams that could have been created by modifing an n-gram in B and includes the original n-gram itself.

rare n-grams and decrease the contribution of common ones. N-gram probabilities are computed using the SRILM language modelling toolkit (Stolcke, 2002). The score for each n-gram is computed as its Information Content (Cover and Thomas, 1991), ie. $-log(P)$. When the **language model (LM)** is applied the scores associated with each n-gram are used instead of counts in equations 2 and 3.

4 Experiments

4.1 METER Corpus

The METER corpus (Gaizauskas et al., 2001) contains 771 *Press Association (PA)* articles, some of which were used as source(s) for 945 news stories published by nine British newspapers.

These 945 documents are classified as *Wholly Derived (WD)*, *Partially Derived (PD)* and *Non Derived (ND)*. WD means that the newspaper article is likely derived entirely from the PA source text; PD reflects the situation where some of the newspaper article is derived from the PA source text; news stories likely to be written independently of the PA source fall into the category of ND. In our experiments, the 768 stories from court and law reporting were used (WD=285, PD=300, ND=183) to allow comparison with Clough et al. (2002). To provide a collection to investigate binary classification we aggregated the WD and PD cases to form a Derived set. Each document was pre-processed by converting to lower case and removing all punctuation marks.

4.2 Determining Reuse

The text reuse task aims to distinguish between levels of text reuse, i.e. WD, PD and ND. Two versions of a classification task were used: binary classification distinguishes between Derived (i.e. WD $\cup$ PD) and ND documents, and ternary classification distinguishes all three levels of reuse.

A Naive Bayes classifier (Weka version 3.6.1) and 10-fold cross validation were used for the experiments. Containment similarity scores between all PA source texts and news articles on the same story were computed for word uni-grams, bi-grams, tri-grams, four-grams and five-grams. These five similarity scores were used as features. Performance was measured using precision, recall and F_1 measures with the macro-average reported across all classes.

The language model (Section 3.4) was trained using 806,791 news articles from the Reuters Corpus (Rose et al., 2002). A high proportion of the news stories selected were related to the topics of entertainment and legal reports to reflect the subjects of the new articles in the METER corpus.

5 Results and Analysis

Tables 1 and 2 show the results of the binary and ternary classification experiments respectively. "NG" refers to the comparison of n-grams in each document (Section 3.1), while "Del", "WN" and "Para" refer to the modified n-grams created using deletions, WordNet and paraphrases respectively (Section 3.2). The prefix "LM" (e.g. "LM-NG") indicates that the n-grams are weighted using the language model probability scores (Section 3.4).

For the binary classification task (Table 1) it can be observed that including modified n-grams improves performance. This improvement is observed when each of the three types of modified n-grams is applied individually, with a greater increase being observed for the n-grams created using the WordNet and paraphrase approaches. Further improvement is observed when different types of modified n-grams are combined with the best performance obtained when all three types are used. All improvements over the baseline approach (NG) are statistically significant (Wilcoxon signed-rank test, $p < 0.05$). These results demonstrate that the various types of modified n-grams all contribute to identifying when text is being reused since they capture different types of rewrite operations.

In addition, performance consistently improves when n-grams are weighted using language model scores. The improvement is significant for all types of n-grams. This demonstrates that the information provided by the language model is useful in determining the relative importance of n-grams.

Several of the results are higher than those reported by Clough et al. (2002) (F_1=0.763), despite the fact their approach supplements n-gram overlap with additional techniques such as sentence alignment and string search algorithms.

Results of the ternary classification task are shown in Table 2. Results show a similar pattern to those observed for the binary classification task

Approach	P	R	F_1
NG	0.836	0.706	0.732
LM-NG	0.846	0.722	0.746
Del	0.851	0.745	0.767
LM-Del	0.858	0.765	0.785
WN	0.876	0.801	0.817
LM-WN	0.879	0.810	0.825
Para	0.884	0.821	0.834
LM-Para	0.888	0.831	0.843
Del+WN	0.889	0.835	0.847
LM-Del+WN	0.884	0.848	0.855
Del+Para	0.892	0.841	0.853
LM-Del+Para	0.896	0.849	0.860
WN+Para	0.894	0.848	0.858
LM-WN+Para	0.896	0.865	0.871
Del+WN+Para	0.897	0.856	0.865
LM-Del+WN+Para	**0.903**	**0.876**	**0.882**
(Clough et al., 2002)	—	—	0.763

Table 1: Results for binary classification

Approach	P	R	F_1
NG	0.596	0.557	0.551
LM-NG	0.615	0.579	0.574
Del	0.612	0.584	0.579
LM-Del	0.633	0.611	0.606
WN	0.644	0.636	0.631
LM-WN	0.649	0.640	0.635
Para	0.662	0.653	0.647
LM-Para	0.669	0.659	0.654
Del+WN	0.655	0.649	0.643
LM-Del+WN	0.668	0.656	0.650
Del+Para	0.665	0.658	0.652
LM-Del+Para	0.661	0.662	0.655
WN+Para	0.668	0.661	0.655
LM-WN+Para	0.680	0.675	0.668
Del+WN+Para	0.669	0.666	0.660
LM-Del+WN+Para	**0.688**	**0.689**	**0.683**
(Clough et al., 2002)	—	—	0.664

Table 2: Results for ternary classification

Classified as	WD	PD	ND
WD	139	94	14
PD	57	206	54
ND	1	13	191

Table 3: Confusion matrix when "LM-Del+WN+Para" approach used for ternary classification

and the best result is also obtained when all three types of modified n-grams are included and n-grams are weighted with probability scores. Once again weighting n-grams with language model scores improves results for all types of n-gram and this improvement is significant. Results for several types of n-gram are also better than those reported by Clough et al. (2002) (F_1=0.664).

Results for all approaches are lower for the ternary classification. This is because the binary classification task involves distinguishing between two classes of documents which are relatively distinct (derived and non-derived) while the ternary task divides the derived class into two (WD and PD) which are more difficult to separate (see Table 3 showing confusion matrix for the approach which gave best results for ternary classification).

6 Conclusion

This paper describes an approach to the analysis of text reuse which is based on comparison of n-grams. This approach is augmented by modifying the n-grams in various ways and weighting them with probabilities derived from a language model. Evaluation is carried out on a standard data set containing examples of reused journalistic texts. Making use of modified n-grams with appropriate weights is found to improve performance when detecting text reuse and the approach described here outperforms an existing approach. In future we plan to experiment with other methods for modifying n-grams and also to apply this approach to other types of text reuse.

Acknowledgments

This work was funded by the COMSATS Institute of Information Technology, Islamabad, Pakistan under the Faculty Development Program (FDP) and a Google Research Award.

References

Alberto B. Cedeño, Paolo Rosso, and Jose M. Bened 2009. *Reducing the Plagiarism Detection Search Space on the basis of the Kullback-Leibler Distance* Proceedings of CICLing-09, 523–534.

Allan Bell 1991. *The Language of News Media*. Blackwell.

Andreas Stolcke. 2002. *SRILM - An Extensible Language Modeling Toolkit*. In Proceedings of the International Conference on Spoken Language Processing, 901–904.

Chin-Yew Lin. 2004. *Rouge: A Package for Automatic Evaluation of Summaries*. In Proceedings of the ACL-04 Workshop, 74–81.

Chris Callison-Burch. 2008. *Syntactic Constraints on Paraphrases Extracted from Parallel Corpora*. In Proceedings of EMNLP'08, 196–205.

Jangwon Seo and W. Bruce Croft. 2008. *Local Text Reuse Detection*. In Proceedings of SIGIR'08, 571–578. In Proceedings of the 31st Annual International ACM SIGIR Conference on Research and Development in Information Retrieval, 571–578.

Kishore Papineni, Salim Roukos, Todd Ward, and Wei J. Zhu. 2002. *Bleu: A Method for Automatic Evaluation of Machine Translation*. In Proceedings of ACL'02, 311–318.

Martin Potthast, Andreas Eiselt, Alberto Barrón-Cedeño, Benno Stein and Paolo Rosso. 2011. *Overview of the 3rd International Competition on Plagiarism Detection*. Notebook Papers of CLEF 11 Labs and Workshops.

Narayanan Shivakumar and Hector G. Molina. 1995. *SCAM: A Copy Detection Mechanism for Digital Documents*. Proceedings of the 2nd Annual Conference on the Theory and Practice of Digital Libraries, Texas, USA.

Paul Clough, Robert Gaizauskas, Scott S.L. Piao, and Yorick Wilks. 2002. *Measuring Text Reuse*. In Proceedings of ACL'02, Philadelphia, USA, 152–159.

Peter C. R. Lane, Caroline M. Lyon, and James A. Malcolm. 2006. *Demonstration of the Ferret plagiarism detector*. Proceedings of the 2nd International Plagiarism Conference, Newcastle, UK.

Robert Gaizauskas, Jonathan Foster, Yorick Wilks, John Arundel, Paul Clough, and Scott S.L. Piao. 2001. *The METER Corpus: A Corpus for Analysing Journalistic Text Reuse*. In Proceedings of the Corpus Linguistics Conference, 214–223.

Sergey Brin, James Davis and Hector G. Molina. 1995. *Copy Detection Mechanisms for Digital Documents*. Proceedings ACM SIGMOD'95, 398–409.

Stanford Chiu, Ibrahim Uysal, Bruce W. Croft. 2010. *Evaluating text reuse discovery on the web*. In Proceedings of the third symposium on Information interaction in context, 299–304.

Thomas M. Cover, Joy A. Thomas. 1991. *Elements of Information Theory*. Wiley, New York, USA.

Timothy C. Hoad and Justin Zobel. 2003. *Methods for Identifying Versioned and Plagiarized Documents*. Journal of the American Society for Information Science and Technology, 54(3):203–215.

Tony Rose, Mark Stevenson, Miles Whitehead. 2002. *The Reuters Corpus Volume 1 - from Yesterday's news to tomorr ow's language resources*. In Proceedings of the Third International Conference on Language Resources and Evaluation (LREC-02), 827–832.

Statistical Thesaurus Construction for a Morphologically Rich Language

Chaya Liebeskind, Ido Dagan and Jonathan Schler
Computer Science Department
Bar-Ilan University
Ramat-Gan, Israel
liebchaya@gmail.com, dagan@cs.biu.ac.il, schler@gmail.com

Abstract

Corpus-based thesaurus construction for Morphologically Rich Languages (MRL) is a complex task, due to the morphological variability of MRL. In this paper we explore alternative term representations, complemented by clustering of morphological variants. We introduce a generic algorithmic scheme for thesaurus construction in MRL, and demonstrate the empirical benefit of our methodology for a Hebrew thesaurus.

1 Introduction

Corpus-based thesaurus construction has been an active research area (Grefenstette, 1994; Curran and Moens, 2002; Kilgarriff, 2003; Rychly and Kilgarriff, 2007). Typically, two statistical approaches for identifying semantic relationships between words were investigated: first-order, co-occurrence-based methods which assume that words that occur frequently together are topically related (Schutze and Pederson, 1997) and second-order, distributional similarity methods (Hindle, 1990; Lin, 1998; Gasperin et al, 2001; Weeds and Weir, 2003; Kotlerman et al., 2010), which suggest that words occurring within similar contexts are semantically similar (Harris, 1968).

While most prior work focused on English, we are interested in applying these methods to MRL. Such languages, Hebrew in our case, are characterized by highly productive morphology which may produce as many as thousands of word forms for a given root form.

Thesauri usually provide *related terms* for each entry term (denoted *target term*). Since both target and related terms correspond to word lemmas, statistics collection from the corpus would be most directly applied at the lemma level as well, using a morphological analyzer and tagger (Linden and Piitulainen, 2004; Peirsman et al., 2008; Rapp, 2009). However, due to the rich and challenging morphology of MRL, such tools often have limited performance. In our research, the accuracy of a state-of-the-art modern Hebrew tagger on a cross genre corpus was only about 60%.

Considering such limited performance of morphological processing, we propose a schematic methodology for generating a co-occurrence based thesaurus in MRL. In particular, we propose and investigate three options for term representation, namely surface form, lemma and multiple lemmas, supplemented with clustering of term variants. While the default lemma representation is dependent on tagger performance, the two other representations avoid choosing the right lemma for each word occurrence. Instead, the multiple-lemma representation assumes that the right analysis will accumulate enough statistical prominence throughout the corpus, while the surface representation solves morphological disambiguation "in retrospect", by clustering term variants at the end of the extraction process. As the methodology provides a generic scheme for exploring the alternative representation levels, each corpus and language-specific tool set might yield a different optimal configuration.

2 Methodology

Thesauri usually contain thousands of entries, termed here *target terms*. Each entry holds a list of *related terms*, covering various semantic relations. In this paper we assume that the list of target terms is given as input, and focus on the process of extracting a ranked list of candidate related terms (termed *candidate terms*) for each target term. The top ranked candidates may be further examined (manually) by a lexicographer, who will select the eventual related terms for the thesaurus entry.

Our methodology was applied for statistical measures of first order similarity (word co-occurrence). These statistics consider the number of times each candidate term co-occurs with the target term in the same document, relative to their total frequencies in the corpus. Common co-occurrence metrics are *Dice coefficient* (Smadja et al, 1996), *Pointwise Mutual Information* (PMI) (Church and Hanks, 1990) and *log-likelihood test* (Dunning, 1993).

2.1 Term Representation

Statistical extraction is affected by term representation in the corpus. Usually, related terms in a thesaurus are lemmas, which can be identified by morphological disambiguation tools. However, we present two other approaches for term representation (either a target term or a candidate related term), which are less dependent on morphological processing.

Typically, a morphological analyzer produces all possible analyses for a given token in the corpus. Then, a *Part Of Speech* (POS) tagger selects the most probable analysis and solves morphology disambiguation. However, considering the poor performance of the POS tagger on our corpus, we distinguish between these two analysis levels. Consequently, we examined three levels of term representation: (i) Surface form (*surface*) (ii) Best lemma, as indentified by a POS tagger (*best*), and (iii) All possible lemmas, produced by a morphological analyzer (*all*).

2.2 Algorithmic Scheme

We used the following algorithmic scheme for thesaurus construction. Our input is a target term in one of the possible term representations (*surface*, *best* or *all*). For each target term we retrieve all the documents in the corpus where the target term appears. Then, we define a set of candidate terms that consists of all the terms that appear in all these documents (this again for each of the three possible term representations). Next, a co-occurrence score between the target term and each of the candidates is calculated. Then, candidates are sorted, and the highest rated candidate terms are clustered into lemma-oriented clusters. Finally, we rank the clusters according to their members' co-occurrence scores and the highest rated clusters become related terms in the thesaurus.

Figure 1 presents the algorithm's pseudo code. The notion *rep*(term) is used to describe the possible term representations and may be either *surface*, *best* or *all*. In our experiments, when *rep*(target_term)=*best*, the correct lemma was manually assigned (assuming a lexicographer involvement with each thesaurus entry in our setting). While, when *rep*(word)=*best*, the most probable lemma is assigned by the tagger (since there are numerous candidates for each target term we cannot resort the manual involvement for each of them). The two choices for *rep*(term) are independent, resulting in nine possible configurations of the algorithm for representing both the target term and the candidate terms. Thus, these 9 configurations cover the space of possibilities for term representation. Exploring all of them in a systematic manner would reveal the best configuration in a particular setting.

```
Input: target term, corpus, a pair of values for
rep(target_term) and rep(word)
Output: clusters of related terms

target_term ← rep(target_term)
docs_list ← search(target_term)
FOR doc IN docs_list
  FOR word IN doc
    add rep(word) to candidates
  ENDFOR
ENDFOR
compute co-occurrence scores for all candidates
sort(candidates) by score
clusters ←cluster(top(candidates))
rank(clusters)
related terms ← top(clusters)
```

Figure 1: Methodology implementation algorithm

2.3 Clustering

The algorithm of Figure 1 suggests clustering the extracted candidates before considering them for the thesaurus. Clustering aims at grouping together related terms with the same lemma into clusters, using some measure of morphological equivalence. Accordingly, an equivalence measure between related terms needs to be defined, and a clustering algorithm needs to be selected. Each obtained cluster is intended to correspond to the lemma of a single candidate term. Obviously, clustering is mostly needed for surface-level representation, in order to group all different inflections of the same lemma. Yet, we note that it was also found necessary for the lemma-level representations, because the tagger often identifies slightly different lemmas for the same term.

The equivalence measure is used for building a graph representation of the related terms. We represented each term by a vertex and added an edge between each pair of terms that were deemed equivalent. We investigated alternative equivalence measures for measuring the morphological distance between two vertices in our graph. We considered the string edit distance measure and suggested two morphological-based equivalence measures. The first measure, given two vertices' terms, extracts all possible lemmas for each term and searches for an overlap of at least one lemma. The second measure considers the most probable lemma of the vertices' terms and checks whether these lemmas are equal. The probability of a lemma was defined as the sum of probabilities for all morphological analyses containing the lemma, using a morpho-lexical context-independent probabilities approximation (Goldberg et al., 2008). The clustering was done by finding the connected components in our graph of terms using the JUNG[1] implementation (WeakComponentVertexClusterer algorithm with default parameters). The connected components are expected to correspond to different lemmas of terms. Hierarchical clustering methods (Jain et al., 1999) were examined as well (Single-link and Complete-link clustering), but they were inferior.

After applying the clustering algorithm, we re-ranked the clusters aiming to get the best clusters at the top of clusters list. We investigated two scoring approaches for cluster ranking; maximization and averaging. The maximization approach assigns the maximal score of the cluster members as the cluster score. While the averaging approach assigns the average of the cluster members' scores as the cluster score. The score obtained by either of the approaches may be scaled by the cluster length, to account for the accumulative impact of all class members (corresponding to morphological variants of the candidate term).

3 Case Study: Cross-genre Hebrew Thesaurus

Our research targets the construction of a cross genre thesaurus for the Responsa project[2]. The corpus includes questions posed to rabbis along with their detailed rabbinic answers, consisting of various genres and styles. It contains 76,710 articles and about 100 million word tokens, and was used for previous IR and NLP research (Choueka, 1972; Fraenkel, 1976; Choueka et al., 1987; Kernel et al, 2008).

Unfortunately, due to the different genres in the Responsa corpus, available tools for Hebrew processing perform poorly on this corpus. In a preliminary experiment, the POS tagger (Adler and Elhadad, 2006) accuracy on the Responsa Corpus was less than 60%, while the accuracy of the same tagger on modern Hebrew corpora is ~90% (Bar-Haim et al., 2007).

For this project, we utilized the MILA Hebrew Morphological Analyzer[3] (Itai and Wintner, 2008; Yona and Wintner, 2008) and the (Adler and Elhadad 2006) POS tagger for lemma representation. The latter had two important characteristics: The first is flexibility- This tagger allows adapting the estimates of the prior (context-independent) probability of each morphological analysis in an unsupervised manner, from an unlabeled corpus of the target domain (Goldberg et al., 2008). The second advantage is its mechanism for analyzing unknown tokens (Adler et al., 2008). Since about 50% of the words in our corpora are unknown (with respect to MILA's lexicon), such mechanism is essential.

For statistics extraction, we used Lucene[4]. We took the top 1000 documents retrieved for the target term and extracted candidate terms from them. Dice coefficient was used as our co-occurrence measure, most probable lemma was considered for clustering equivalence, and clusters were ranked based on maximization, where the maximal score was multiplied by cluster size.

[1] http://jung.sourceforge.net/

[2] Corpus kindly provided - http://www.biu.ac.il/jh/Responsa/

[3] http://mila.cs.technion.ac.il/mila/eng/tools_analysis.html

[4] http://lucene.apache.org/

4 Evaluation

4.1 Dataset and Evaluation Measures

The results reported in this paper were obtained from a sample of 108 randomly selected terms from a list of 5000 terms, extracted from two publicly available term lists: the University of Haifa's entry list[5] and Hebrew Wikipedia entries[6].

In our experiments, we compared the performance of the alternative 9 configurations by four commonly used IR measures: precision (P), relative recall (R), F1, and Average Precision (AP). The scores were macro-averaged. We assumed that our automatically-generated candidate terms will be manually filtered, thus, recall becomes more important than precision. Since we do not have any pre-defined thesaurus, we evaluated the relative-recall. Our relative-recall considered the number of suitable related terms from the output of all methods as the full set of related terms. As our system yielded a ranked sequence of related terms clusters, we also considered their ranking order. Therefore, we adopted the recall-oriented AP for ranking (Voorhees and Harman, 1999).

4.2 Annotation Scheme

The output of the statistical extraction is a ranked list of clusters of candidate related terms. Since manual annotation is expensive and time consuming, we annotated for the gold standard the top 15 clusters constructed from the top 50 candidate terms, for each target term. Then, an annotator judged each of the clusters' terms. A cluster was considered as relevant if at least one of its terms was judged relevant[7].

4.3 Results

Table 1 compares the performance of all nine term representation configurations. Due to data sparseness, the lemma-based representations of the target term outperform its surface representation. However, the best results were obtained from candidate representation at the surface level, which was complemented by grouping term variants to lemmas in the clustering phase.

Target \ Candidate		surface	best	All
Surface	R	36.59	29.37	26.68
	P	24.29	21.09	18.71
	F1	29.20	24.55	21.99
	AP	20.87	15.83	14.13
Best lemma	R	46.70	39.88	36.97
	P	**25.03**	23.08	20.94
	F1	**32.59**	29.24	26.74
	AP	26.84	20.86	19.32
All lemmas	R	**47.13**	42.52	42.13
	P	23.72	22.47	21.23
	F1	31.56	29.40	28.24
	AP	**27.86**	22.99	21.14

Table 1: Performances of the nine configuratrions

Furthermore, we note that the target representation by all possible lemmas (all) yielded the best R and AP scores, which we consider as most important for the thesaurus construction setting. The improvement over the common default best lemma representation, for both target and candidate, is notable (7 points) and is statistically significant according to the two-sided Wilcoxon signed-rank test (Wilcoxon, 1945) at the 0.01 level for AP and 0.05 for R.

5 Conclusions and Future Work

We presented a methodological scheme for exploring alternative term representations in statistical thesaurus construction for MRL, complemented by lemma-oriented clustering at the end of the process. The scheme was investigated for a Hebrew cross-genre corpus, but can be generically applied in other settings to find the optimal configuration in each case.

We plan to adopt our methodology to second order distributional similarity methods as well. In this case there is an additional dimension, namely feature representation, whose representation level should be explored as well. In addition, we plan to extend our methods to deal with Multi Word Expressions (MWE).

Acknowledgments

This work was partially supported by the PASCAL-2 Network of Excellence of the European Community FP7-ICT-2007-1-216886.

[5] http://lib.haifa.ac.il/systems/ihp.html
[6] http://he.wikipedia.org
[7] This was justified by empirical results that found only a few clusters with some terms judged positive and others negative

References

Adler Meni and Michael Elhadad. 2006. An Unsupervised Morpheme-Based HMM for Hebrew Morphological Disambiguation, in *Proceedings of COLING-ACL*, Sydney, Australia.

Adler Meni, Yoav Goldberg, David Gabay and Michael Elhadad. 2008. Unsupervised Lexicon-Based Resolution of Unknown Words for Full Morphological Analysis, in *Proceedings of ACL*.

Bar-Haim Roy, Khalil Sima'an, and Yoad Winter. 2007. Part-of-speech tagging of Modern Hebrew text. *Natural Language Engineering*, 14(02):223.251.

Choueka, Yaacov. 1972. Fast searching and retrieval techniques for large dictionaries and concordances. *Hebrew Computational Linguistics*, 6:12–32, July.

Choueka, Y., A.S. Fraenkel, S.T. Klein and E. Segal. 1987. Improved techniques for processing queries in full-text systems. *Proceedings of the 10th annual international ACM SIGIR conference on Research and development in information retrieval.*

Church, K. W., and Hanks, P. 1990. Word association norms, mutual information and lexicography. *Computational Linguistics* 16(1): 22–29.

Curran, James R. and Marc Moens. 2002. Improvements in automatic thesaurus extraction. In *Proceedings of the ACL-SIGLEX Workshop on Unsupervised Lexical Acquisition*, pages 59–67, Philadelphia, PA.

Dunning, T.E. 1993. Accurate methods for the statistics of surprise and coincidence. *Computational Linguistics* 19, 61–74 (1993).

Fraenkel, Aviezri S. 1976. All about the Responsa retrieval project – what you always wanted to know but were afraid to ask. *Jurimetrics Journal*, 16(3):149–156, Spring.

Gasperin, C., Gamallo, P., Agustini, A., Lopes, G., and de Lima, V. 2001. Using syntactic contexts for measuring word similarity. In *the Workshop on Semantic Knowledge Acquisition and Categorisation (ESSLI 2001)*, Helsinki, Finland.

Goldberg Yoav, Meni Adler and Michael Elhadad, 2008. EM Can Find Pretty Good HMM POS-Taggers (When Given a Good Start), in *Proceedings of ACL*.

Grefenstette, G. 1994. Explorations in Automatic Thesaurus Construction. *Kluwer Academic Publishers*, Boston, USA

Harris, Zelig S. 1968. *Mathematical Structures of Language*. John Wiley, New York.

Hindle, D. 1990. Noun classification from predicate argument structures. In *Proceedings of ACL*.

Itai Alon and Shuly Wintner. 2008. Language Resources for Hebrew. *Language Resources and Evaluation* 42(1):75-98, March 2008.

Jain, A. K., M. N. Murty, P. J. Flynn. 1999. Data Clustering: A Review. *ACM Computing Surveys* 31(3):264-323.

Kerner Yaakov HaCohen, Ariel Kass, Ariel Peretz. 2008. Combined One Sense Disambiguation of Abbreviations. In *Proceedings of ACL (Short Papers)*, pp. 61-64.

Kilgarriff, Adam. 2003. Thesauruses for natural language processing. In *Proceedings of the Joint Conference on Natural Language Processing and Knowledge Engineering*, pages 5–13, Beijing, China.

Kotlerman Lili, Dagan Ido, Szpektor Idan, and Zhitomirsky-Geffet Maayan. 2010. Directional Distributional Similarity for Lexical Inference. *Natural Language Engineering*, 16(4):359–389.

Linden Krister, and Jussi Olavi Piitulainen. 2004. Discovering Synonyms and Other Related Words. In Proceedings of COLING 2004 : CompuTerm 2004: 3rd International Workshop on Computational Terminology, Pages 63-70, Geneva, Switzerland

Lin, D. 1998. Automatic retrieval and clustering of similar words. In *Proceedings of COLING-ACL.*

Peirsman Yves, Kris Heylen, and Dirk Speelman. 2008. Putting things in order. first and second order contexts models for the calculation of semantic similarity. In Actes des 9i`emes Journ´ees internationales d'Analyse statistique des Donn´ees Textuelles (JADT 2008), pages 907–916.

Rapp, R. 2009. The Automatic Generation of Thesauri of Related Words for English, French, German, and Russian, *International Journal of Speech Technology*, 11, 3-4, 147-156.

Rychly, P. and Kilgarriff, A. 2007. An efficient algorithm for building a distributional thesaurus (and other Sketch Engine developments). In *Proceedings of ACL-07*, demo session. Prague, Czech Republic.

Schutze Hinrich and Jan 0. Pederson. 1997. A cooccurrence-based thesaurus and two applications to information retrieval. *Information Processing and Management*, 33(3):307-318.

Smadja, F., McKeown, K.R., Hatzivassiloglou, V. 1996. Translating collocations for bilingual lexicons: A statistical approach. *Computational Linguistics* 22, 1–38

Voorhees E.M. and D. Harman. 1999. Overview of the seventh text retrieval conference . In *Proceedings of the Seventh Text Retrieval 73 Conference*, 1999. NIST Special Publication. 58.

Weeds, J., and Weir, D. 2003. A general framework for distributional similarity. In *Proceedings of EMNLP*, Sapporo, Japan.

Wilcoxon F. 1945. Individual comparisons by ranking methods. *Biometrics Bulletin*, 1:80–83.

Yona Shlomo and Shuly Wintner. 2008. A Finite-State Morphological Grammar of Hebrew. *Natural Language Engineering* 14(2):173-190, April 2008. *Language Resources and Evaluation* 42(1):75-98, March 2008.

Sorting out the Most Confusing English Phrasal Verbs

Yuancheng Tu
Department of Linguistics
University of Illinois
ytu@illinois.edu

Dan Roth
Department of Computer Science
University of Illinois
danr@illinois.edu

Abstract

In this paper, we investigate a full-fledged supervised machine learning framework for identifying English phrasal verbs in a given context. We concentrate on those that we define as *the most confusing* phrasal verbs, in the sense that they are the most commonly used ones whose occurrence may correspond either to a true phrasal verb or an alignment of a simple verb with a preposition.

We construct a benchmark dataset[1] with 1,348 sentences from BNC, annotated via an Internet crowdsourcing platform. This dataset is further split into two groups, more *idiomatic* group which consists of those that tend to be used as a true phrasal verb and more *compositional* group which tends to be used either way. We build a discriminative classifier with easily available lexical and syntactic features and test it over the datasets. The classifier overall achieves 79.4% accuracy, 41.1% error deduction compared to the corpus majority baseline 65%. However, it is even more interesting to discover that the classifier learns more from the more *compositional* examples than those *idiomatic* ones.

1 Introduction

Phrasal verbs in English, are syntactically defined as combinations of verbs and prepositions or particles, but semantically their meanings are generally not the direct sum of their parts. For example, *give in* means *submit, yield* in the sentence, *Adam's saying it's important to stand firm , not give in to terrorists.* Adam was not *giving* anything and he was not *in* anywhere either. (Kolln and Funk, 1998) uses *the test of meaning* to detect English phrasal verbs, i.e., each phrasal verb could be replaced by a single verb with the same general meaning, for example, using *yield* to replace *give in* in the aforementioned sentence. To confuse the issue even further, some phrasal verbs, for example, *give in* in the following two sentences, are used either as a true phrasal verb (the first sentence) or not (the second sentence) though their surface forms look cosmetically similar.

1. How many Englishmen **gave in** to their emotions like that ?
2. It is just this denial of anything beyond what is directly **given in** experience that marks Berkeley out as an empiricist .

This paper is targeting to build an automatic learner which can recognize a true phrasal verb from its orthographically identical construction with a verb and a prepositional phrase. Similar to other types of MultiWord Expressions (MWEs) (Sag et al., 2002), the syntactic complexity and semantic idiosyncrasies of phrasal verbs pose many particular challenges in empirical Natural Language Processing (NLP). Even though a few of previous works have explored this identification problem empirically (Li et al., 2003; Kim and Baldwin, 2009) and theoretically (Jackendoff, 2002), we argue in this paper that this context sensitive identification problem is not so easy as conceivably shown before, especially when it is used to handle those more *compositional* phrasal verbs which are empirically used either way in the corpus as a true phrasal verb or a simplex verb with a preposition combination. In addition, there is still a lack of adequate resources or benchmark datasets to identify and treat phrasal

[1] http://cogcomp.cs.illinois.edu/page/resources/PVC_Data

verbs within a given context. This research is also an attempt to bridge this gap by constructing a publicly available dataset which focuses on some of the most commonly used phrasal verbs within their most confusing contexts.

Our study in this paper focuses on six of the most frequently used verbs, *take*, *make*, *have*, *get*, *do* and *give* and their combination with nineteen common prepositions or particles, such as *on, in, up* etc. We categorize these phrasal verbs according to their continuum of compositionality, splitting them into two groups based on the biggest gap within this scale, and build a discriminative learner which uses easily available syntactic and lexical features to analyze them comparatively. This learner achieves 79.4% overall accuracy for the whole dataset and learns the most from the more *compositional* data with 51.2% error reduction over its 46.6% baseline.

2 Related Work

Phrasal verbs in English were observed as one kind of composition that is used frequently and constitutes the greatest difficulty for language learners more than two hundred and fifty years ago in Samuel Johnson's *Dictionary of English Language*[2]. They have also been well-studied in modern linguistics since early days (Bolinger, 1971; Kolln and Funk, 1998; Jackendoff, 2002). Careful linguistic descriptions and investigations reveal a wide range of English phrasal verbs that are syntactically uniform, but diverge largely in semantics, argument structure and lexical status. The complexity and idiosyncrasies of English phrasal verbs also pose a special challenge to computational linguistics and attract considerable amount of interest and investigation for their extraction, disambiguation as well as identification. Recent computational research on English phrasal verbs have been focused on increasing the coverage and scalability of phrasal verbs by either extracting unlisted phrasal verbs from large corpora (Villavicencio, 2003; Villavicencio, 2006), or constructing productive lexical rules to generate new cases (Villanvicencio and Copestake, 2003). Some other researchers follow the semantic regularities of the particles associated with these phrasal verbs and concentrate on disambiguation of phrasal verb semantics, such as the investigation of the most common particle *up* by (Cook and Stevenson, 2006).

Research on token identification of phrasal verbs is much less compared to the extraction. (Li et al., 2003) describes a regular expression based simple system. Regular expression based method requires human constructed regular patterns and cannot make predictions for *Out-Of-Vocabulary* phrasal verbs. Thus, it is hard to be adapted to other NLP applications directly. (Kim and Baldwin, 2009) proposes a memory-based system with post-processed linguistic features such as selectional preferences. Their system assumes the perfect outputs of a parser and requires laborious human corrections to them.

The research presented in this paper differs from these previous identification works mainly in two aspects. First of all, our learning system is fully automatic in the sense that no human intervention is needed, no need to construct regular patterns or to correct parser mistakes. Secondly, we focus our attention on the comparison of the two groups of phrasal verbs, the more *idiomatic* group and the more *compositional* group. We argue that while more *idiomatic* phrasal verbs may be easier to identify and can have above 90% accuracy, there is still much room to learn for those more *compostional* phrasal verbs which tend to be used either positively or negatively depending on the given context.

3 Identification of English Phrasal Verbs

We formulate the context sensitive English phrasal verb identification task as a supervised binary classification problem. For each target candidate within a sentence, the classifier decides if it is a true phrasal verb or a simplex verb with a preposition. Formally, given a set of n labeled examples $\{x_i, y_i\}_{i=1}^n$, we learn a function $f : \mathcal{X} \rightarrow \mathcal{Y}$ where $\mathcal{Y} \in \{-1, 1\}$. The learning algorithm we use is the soft-margin SVM with L2-loss. The learning package we use is LIBLINEAR (Chang and Lin, 2001)[3].

Three types of features are used in this discriminative model. (1)*Words*: given the window size from the one before to the one after the target phrase, *Words* feature consists of every surface string of all shallow chunks within that window. It can be an n-word chunk or a single word depending on

[2]It is written in the Preface of that dictionary.

[3]http://www.csie.ntu.edu.tw/~cjlin/liblinear/

the the chunk's bracketing. (2)*ChunkLabel*: the chunk name with the given window size, such as *VP*, *PP*, etc. (3)*ParserBigram*: the bi-gram of the non-terminal label of the parents of both the verb and the particle. For example, from this partial tree *(VP (VB get)(PP (IN through)(NP (DT the)(NN day)))*, the parent label for the verb *get* is *VP* and the parent node label for the particle *through* is *PP*. Thus, this feature value is *VP-PP*. Our feature extractor is implemented in Java through a publicly available NLP library[4] via the tool called Curator (Clarke et al., 2012). The shallow parser is publicly available (Punyakanok and Roth, 2001)[5] and the parser we use is from (Charniak and Johnson, 2005).

3.1 Data Preparation and Annotation

All sentences in our dataset are extracted from BNC (XML Edition), a balanced synchronic corpus containing 100 million words collected from various sources of British English. We first construct a list of phrasal verbs for the six verbs that we are interested in from two resources, WN3.0 (Fellbaum, 1998) and DIRECT[6]. Since these targeted verbs are also commonly used in English Light Verb Constructions (LVCs), we filter out LVCs in our list using a publicly available LVC corpus (Tu and Roth, 2011). The result list consists of a total of 245 phrasal verbs. We then search over BNC and find sentences for all of them. We choose the frequency threshold to be 25 and generate a list of 122 phrasal verbs. Finally we manually pick out 23 of these phrasal verbs and sample randomly 10% extracted sentences for each of them for annotation.

The annotation is done through a crowdsourcing platform[7]. The annotators are asked to identify true phrasal verbs within a sentence. The reported inner-annotator agreement is 84.5% and the gold average accuracy is 88%. These numbers indicate the good quality of the annotation. The final corpus consists of 1,348 sentences among which, 65% with a true phrasal verb and 35% with a simplex verb-preposition combination.

[4]http://cogcomp.cs.illinois.edu/software/edison/

[5]http://cogcomp.cs.illinois.edu/page/software_view/Chunker

[6]http://u.cs.biu.ac.il/~nlp/downloads/DIRECT.html

[7]crowdflower.com

3.2 Dataset Splitting

Table 1 lists all verbs in the dataset. *Total* is the total number of sentences annotated for that phrasal verb and *Positive* indicated the number of examples which are annotated as containing the true phrasal verb usage. In this table, the decreasing percentage of the true phrasal verb usage within the dataset indicates the increasing compositionality of these phrasal verbs. The natural division line with this scale is the biggest percentage gap (about 10%) between *make_out* and *get_at*. Hence, two groups are split over that gap. The more *idiomatic* group consists of the first 11 verbs with 554 sentences and 91% of these sentences include true phrasal verb usage. This data group is more biased toward the positive examples. The more *compositional* data group has 12 verbs with 794 examples and only 46.6% of them contain true phrasal verb usage. Therefore, this data group is more balanced with respective to positive and negative usage of the phrase verbs.

Verb	Total	Positive	Percent(%)
get_onto	6	6	1.00
get_through	61	60	0.98
get_together	28	27	0.96
get_on_with	70	67	0.96
get_down_to	17	16	0.94
get_by	11	10	0.91
get_off	51	45	0.88
get_behind	7	6	0.86
take_on	212	181	0.85
get_over	34	29	0.85
make_out	57	48	0.84
get_at	35	26	0.74
get_on	142	103	0.73
take_after	10	7	0.70
do_up	13	8	0.62
get_out	206	118	0.57
do_good	8	4	0.50
make_for	140	65	0.46
get_it_on	9	3	0.33
get_about	20	6	0.30
make_over	12	3	0.25
give_in	118	27	0.23
have_on	81	13	0.16
Total: 23	1348	878	0.65

Table 1: The top group consists of the more *idiomatic* phrasal verbs with 91% of their occurrence within the dataset to be a true phrasal verb. The second group consists of those more *compositional* ones with only 46.6% of their usage in the dataset to be a true phrasal verb.

3.3 Experimental Results and Discussion

Our results are computed via 5-cross validation. We plot the classifier performance with respect to the overall dataset, the more *compositional* group and the more *idiomatic* group in Figure 1. The classifier only improves 0.6% when evaluated on the *idiomatic* group. Phrasal verbs in this dataset are more biased toward behaving like an idiom regardless of their contexts, thus are more likely to be captured by rules or patterns. We assume this may explain some high numbers reported in some previous works. However, our classifier is more effective over the more *compositional* group and reaches 73.9% accuracy, a 51.1% error deduction comparing to its majority baseline. Phrasal verbs in this set tend to be used equally likely as a true phrasal verb and as a simplex verb-preposition combination, depending on their context. We argue phrasal verbs such as these pose a real challenge for building an automatic context sensitive phrasal verb classifier. The overall accuracy of our preliminary classifier is about 79.4% when it is evaluated over all examples from these two groups.

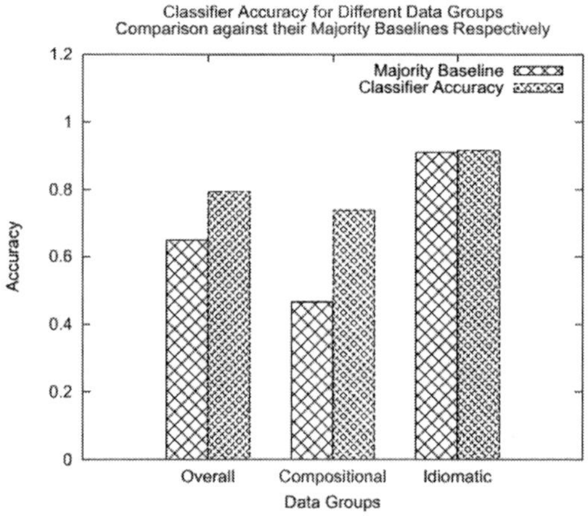

Figure 1: Classifier Accuracy of each data group, comparing with their baseline respectively. Classifier learns the most from the more *compositional* group, indicated by its biggest histogram gap.

Finally, we conduct an ablation analysis to explore the contributions of the three types of features in our model and their accuracies with respect to each data group are listed in Table 2 with the boldfaced best performance. Each type of features is used individually in the classifier. The feature type *Words* is the most effective feature with respect to the *idiomatic* group and the overall dataset. And the *chunk* feature is more effective towards the *compositional* group, which may explain the linguistic intuition that negative phrasal verbs usually do not belong to the same syntactic chunk.

	Datasets		
	Overall	Compositional	Idiom.
Baseline	65.0%	46.6%	91%
Words	**78.6%**	70.2%	**91.4%**
Chunk	65.6%	**70.7%**	89.4%
ParserBi	64.4%	67.2%	89.4%

Table 2: Accuracies achieved by the classifier when tested on different data groups. Features are used individually to evaluate the effectiveness of each type.

4 Conclusion

In this paper, we build a discriminative learner to identify English phrasal verbs in a given context. Our contributions in this paper are threefold. We construct a publicly available context sensitive English phrasal verb dataset with 1,348 sentences from BNC. We split the dataset into two groups according to their tendency toward idiosyncrasy and compositionality, and build a discriminative learner which uses easily available syntactic and lexical features to analyze them comparatively. We demonstrate empirically that high accuracy achieved by models may be due to the stronger idiomatic tendency of these phrasal verbs. For many of the more *ambiguous* cases, a classifier learns more from the *compositional* examples and these phrasal verbs are shown to be more challenging.

Acknowledgments

The authors would like to thank four annonymous reviewers for their valuable comments. The research in this paper was supported by the Multimodal Information Access & Synthesis Center at UIUC, part of CCICADA, a DHS Science and Technology Center of Excellence and the Defense Advanced Research Projects Agency (DARPA) Machine Reading Program under Air Force Research Laboratory (AFRL) prime contract no. FA8750-09-C-0181. Any opinions and findings expressed in this material are those of the authors and do not necessarily reflect the view of DHS, DARPA, AFRL, or the US government.

References

D. Bolinger. 1971. *The Phrasal Verb in English.* Harvard University Press.

C. Chang and C. Lin, 2001. *LIBSVM: a library for support vector machines.* Software available at http://www.csie.ntu.edu.tw/~cjlin/libsvm.

E. Charniak and M. Johnson. 2005. Coarse-to-fine n-best parsing and maxent discriminative reranking. In *Proceedings of ACL-2005.*

J. Clarke, V. Srikumar, M. Sammons, and D. Roth. 2012. An NLP curator: How I learned to stop worrying and love NLP pipelines. In *Proceedings of LREC-2012.*

P. Cook and S. Stevenson. 2006. Classifying particle semantics in English verb-particle constructions. In *Proceedings of the Workshop on Multiword Expressions: Identifying and Exploiting Underlying Properties*, pages 45–53, Sydney, Australia.

C. Fellbaum, editor. 1998. *WordNet: An Electronic Lexical Database.* MIT Press.

R. Jackendoff. 2002. English particle constructions, the lexicon, and the autonomy of syntax. In N. Dehé, R. Jackendoff, A. McIntyre, and S. Urban, editors, *Verb-Particle Explorations*, pages 67–94. Mouton de Gruyter.

S Kim and T. Baldwin. 2009. How to pick out token instances of English verb-particle constructions. *Journal of Language Resources and Evaluation.*

M. Kolln and R. Funk. 1998. *Understanding English Grammar.* Allyn and Bacon.

W. Li, X. Zhang, C. Niu, Y. Jiang, and R. Srihari. 2003. An expert lexicon approach to identifying English phrasal verbs. In *Proceedings of the 41st Annual Meeting of ACL*, pages 513–520.

V. Punyakanok and D. Roth. 2001. The use of classifiers in sequential inference. In *NIPS*, pages 995–1001.

I. Sag, T. Baldwin, F. Bond, and A. Copestake. 2002. Multiword expressions: A pain in the neck for NLP. In *Proc. of the 3rd International Conference on Intelligent Text Processing and Computational Linguistics (CICLing-2002)*, pages 1–15.

Y. Tu and D. Roth. 2011. Learning english light verb constructions: Contextual or statistica. In *Proceedings of the ACL Workshop on Multiword Expressions: from Parsing and Generation to the Real World.*

A. Villanvicencio and A. Copestake. 2003. Verb-particle constructions in a computational grammar of English. In *Proceedings of the 9th International Conference on HPSG*, pages 357–371.

A. Villavicencio. 2003. Verb-particle constructions and lexical resources. In *Proceedings of the ACL 2003 Workshop on Multiword Expressions: Analysis, Acquisition and Treatment*, pages 57–64.

A. Villavicencio, 2006. *Computational Linguistics Dimensions of the Syntax and Semantics of Prepositions*, chapter Verb-Particel Constructions in the World Wide Web. Springer.

Learning Semantics and Selectional Preference of Adjective-Noun Pairs

Karl Moritz Hermann
Department of Computer Science
University of Oxford
Oxford OX1 3QD, UK
karl.moritz.hermann@cs.ox.ac.uk

Chris Dyer
Language Technologies Institute
Carnegie Mellon University
Pittsburgh, PA, 15213, USA
cdyer@cs.cmu.edu

Phil Blunsom
Department of Computer Science
University of Oxford
Oxford OX1 3QD, UK
phil.blunsom@cs.ox.ac.uk

Stephen Pulman
Department of Computer Science
University of Oxford
Oxford OX1 3QD, UK
stephen.pulman@cs.ox.ac.uk

Abstract

We investigate the semantic relationship between a noun and its adjectival modifiers. We introduce a class of probabilistic models that enable us to to simultaneously capture both the semantic similarity of nouns and modifiers, and adjective-noun selectional preference. Through a combination of novel and existing evaluations we test the degree to which adjective-noun relationships can be categorised. We analyse the effect of lexical context on these relationships, and the efficacy of the latent semantic representation for disambiguating word meaning.

1 Introduction

Developing models of the meanings of words and phrases is a key challenge for computational linguistics. Distributed representations are useful in capturing such meaning for individual words (Sato et al., 2008; Maas and Ng, 2010; Curran, 2005). However, finding a compelling account of semantic *compositionality* that utilises such representations has proven more difficult and is an active research topic (Mitchell and Lapata, 2008; Baroni and Zamparelli, 2010; Grefenstette and Sadrzadeh, 2011). It is in this area that our paper makes its contribution.

The dominant approaches to distributional semantics have relied on relatively simple frequency counting techniques. However, such approaches fail to generalise to the much sparser distributions encountered when modeling compositional processes and provide no account of selectional preference. We propose a probabilistic model of the semantic representations for nouns and modifiers. The foundation of this model is a latent variable representation of noun and adjective semantics together with their compositional probabilities. We employ this formulation to give a dual view of noun-modifier semantics: the induced latent variables provide an explicit account of selectional preference while the marginal distributions of the latent variables for each word implicitly produce a distributed representation.

Most related work on selectional preference uses class-based probabilities to approximate (sparse) individual probabilities. Relevant papers include Ó Séaghdha (2010), who evaluates several topic models adapted to learning selectional preference using co-occurence and Baroni and Zamparelli (2010), who represent nouns as vectors and adjectives as matrices, thus treating them as functions over noun meaning. Again, inference is achieved using co-occurrence and dimensionality reduction.

2 Adjective-Noun Model

We hypothesize that *semantic classes* determine the semantic characteristics of nouns and adjectives, and that the distribution of either with respect to other components of the sentences they occur in is also mediated by these classes (i.e., not by the words themselves). We assume that in general nouns select for adjectives,[1] and that this selection is dependent on both their latent semantic classes. In the next section, we describe a model encoding our hypotheses.

2.1 Generative Process

We model a corpus $\mathcal{D}$ of tuples of the form $(n, m, c_1 \dots c_k)$ consisting of a noun *n*, an adjective *m* (modifier), and k words of context. The context variables $(c_1 \dots c_k)$ are treated as a bag of words and

[1] We evaluate this hypothesis as well as its inverse.

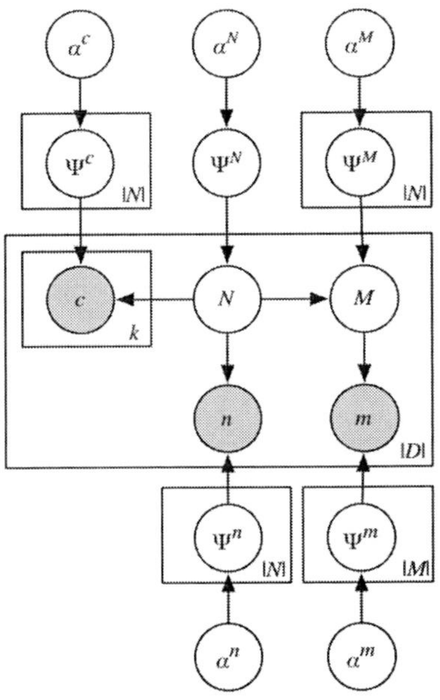

Figure 1: Plate diagram illustrating our model of noun and modifier semantic classes (designated N and M, respectively), a modifier-noun pair (m,n), and its context.

include the words to the left and right of the noun, its siblings and governing verbs. We designate the vocabulary V_n for nouns, V_m for modifiers and V_c for context. We use z_i to refer to the ith tuple in $\mathcal{D}$ and refer to variables within that tuple by subscripting them with i, e.g., n_i and $c_{3,i}$ are the noun and the third context variable of z_i. The latent noun and adjective class variables are designated N_i and M_i.

The corpus $\mathcal{D}$ is generated according to the plate diagram in figure 1. First, a set of parameters is drawn. A multinomial Ψ^{N} representing the distribution of noun semantic classes in the corpus is drawn from a Dirichlet distribution with parameter α^{N}. For each noun class i we have distributions Ψ_i^{M} over adjective classes, Ψ_i^{n} over V_n and Ψ_i^{c} over V_c, also drawn from Dirichlet distributions. Finally, for each adjective class j, we have distributions Ψ_j^{m} over V_m.

Next, the contents of the corpus are generated by first drawing the length of the corpus (we do not parametrise this since we never generate from this model). Then, for each i, we generate noun class N_i, adjective class M_i, and the tuple z_i as follows:

$$\begin{aligned} N_i \mid \Psi^{\text{N}} &\sim \text{Multi}(\Psi^{\text{N}}) \\ M_i \mid \Psi^{\text{M}}_{N_i} &\sim \text{Multi}(\Psi^{\text{M}}_{N_i}) \\ n_i \mid \Psi^{\text{n}}_{N_i} &\sim \text{Multi}(\Psi^{\text{n}}_{N_i}) \\ m_i \mid \Psi^{\text{m}}_{M_i} &\sim \text{Multi}(\Psi^{\text{m}}_{M_i}) \\ \forall k\colon c_{k,i} \mid \Psi^{\text{c}}_{N_i} &\sim \text{Multi}(\Psi^{\text{c}}_{N_i}) \end{aligned}$$

2.2 Parameterization and Inference

We use Gibbs sampling to estimate the distributions of N and M, integrating out the multinomial parameters Ψ^x (Griffiths and Steyvers, 2004). The Dirichlet parameters $\boldsymbol{\alpha}$ are drawn independently from a $\Gamma(1,1)$ distribution, and are resampled using slice sampling at frequent intervals throughout the sampling process (Johnson and Goldwater, 2009). This "vague" prior encourages sparse draws from the Dirichlet distribution. The number of noun and adjective classes $\mathcal{N}$ and $\mathcal{M}$ was set to 50 each; other sizes (100,150) did not significantly alter results.

3 Experiments

As our model was developed on the basis of several hypotheses, we design the experiments and evaluation so that these hypotheses can be examined on their individual merit. We test the first hypothesis, that nouns and adjectives can be represented by semantic classes, recoverable using co-occurence, using a sense clustering evaluation by Ciaramita and Johnson (2003). The second hypothesis, that the distribution with respect to context and to each other is governed by these semantic classes is evaluated using pseudo-disambiguation (Clark and Weir, 2002; Pereira et al., 1993; Rooth et al., 1999) and bigram plausibility (Keller and Lapata, 2003) tests.

To test whether noun classes indeed select for adjective classes, we also evaluate an inverse model (Mod_i), where the adjective class is drawn first, in turn generating both context and the noun class. In addition, we evaluate copies of both models ignoring context (Mod_{nc} and Mod_{inc}).

We use the British National Corpus (BNC), training on 90 percent and testing on 10 percent of the corpus. Results are reported after 2,000 iterations including a burn-in period of 200 iterations. Classes are marginalised over every 10th iteration.

4 Evaluation

4.1 Supersense Tagging

Supersense tagging (Ciaramita and Johnson, 2003; Curran, 2005) evaluates a model's ability to cluster words by their semantics. The task of this evaluation is to determine the WORDNET supersenses of a given list of nouns. We report results on the WN1.6 test set as defined by Ciaramita and Johnson (2003), who used 755 randomly selected nouns with a unique supersense from the WORDNET 1.6

corpus. As their test set was random, results weren't exactly replicable. For a fair comparison, we select all suitable nouns from the corpus that also appeared in the training corpus. We report results on type and token level (52314 tokens with 1119 types). The baseline[2] chooses the most common supersense.

	k	Token	Type
Baseline		.241	.210
Ciaramita & Johnson		.523	.534
Curran		-	**.680**
Mod	10	**.592**	.517
Mod_{nc}	10	.473	.410

Table 1: Supersense evaluation results. Values are the percentage of correctly assigned supersenses. k indicates the number of nearest neighbours considered.

We use cosine-similarity on the marginal noun class vectors to measure distance between nouns. Each noun in the test set is then assigned a supersense by performing a distance-weighted voting among its k nearest neighbours. Results of this evaluation are shown in Table 1, with Figure 2 showing scores for model Mod across different values for k.

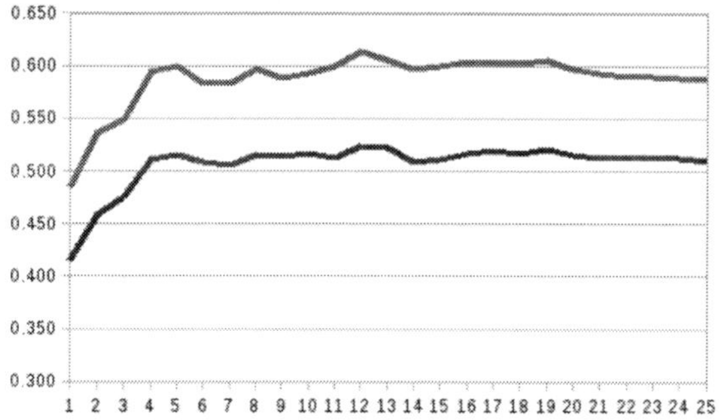

Figure 2: Scores of Mod on the supersense task. The upper line denotes token-, the lower type-level scores. The y-axis is the percentage of correct assignments, the x-axis denotes the number of neighbours included in the vote.

The results demonstrate that nouns can semantically be represented as members of latent classes, while the superiority of Mod over Mod_{nc} supports our hypothesis that context co-occurence is a key feature for learning these classes.

4.2 Pseudo-Disambiguation

Pseudo-disambiguation was introduced by Clark and Weir (2002) to evaluate models of selectional preference. The task is to select the more probable of two candidate arguments to associate with a given predicate. For us, this is to decide which adjective, a_1 or a_2, is more likely to modify a noun n.

We follow the approach by Clark and Weir (2002) to create the test data. To improve the quality of the data, we filtered using bigram counts from the Web1T corpus, setting a lower bound on the probable bigram (a_1, n) and chosing a_2 from five candidates, picking the lowest count for bigram (a_2, n).

We report results for all variants of our model in Table 2. As baseline we use unigram counts in our training data, chosing the more frequent adjective.

L-bound	0	100	500	1000
Size	5714	5253	3741	2789
Baseline	.543	.543	.539	.550
Mod	**.783**	**.792**	**.810**	**.816**
Mod_i	.781	.787	.800	.810
Mod_{nc}	.720	.728	.746	.750
Mod_{inc}	.722	.730	.747	.752

Table 2: Pseudo-disambiguation: Percentage of correct choices made. L-bound denotes the Web1T lower bound on the (a_1, n) bigram, size the number of decisions made.

While all models decisively beat the baseline, the models using context strongly outperform those that do not. This supports our hypothesis regarding the importance of context in semantic clustering.

The similarity between the normal and inverse models implies that the direction of the noun-adjective relationship has negligible impact for this evaluation.

4.3 Bigram Plausibility

Bigram *plausibility* (Keller and Lapata, 2003) is a second evaluation for selectional preference. Unlike the frequency-based pseudo-disambiguation task, it evaluates how well a model matches human judgement of the plausibility of adjective-noun pairs. Keller and Lapata (2003) demonstrated a correlation between frequencies and plausibility, but this does not sufficiently explain human judgement. An example taken from their *unseen* data set illustrates the dissociation between frequency and plausibility:

- Frequent, implausible: "educational water"
- Infrequent, plausible: "difficult foreigner"[3]

The plausibility evaluation has two data sets of 90 adjective-noun pairs each. The first set (*seen*) contains random bigrams from the BNC. The second set (*unseen*) are bigrams not contained in the BNC.

[2]The baseline results are from Ciaramita and Johnson (2003). Using the majority baseline on the full test set, we only get .176 and .160 for token and type respectively.

[3]At the time of writing, Google estimates 56,900 hits for "educational water" and 575 hits for "difficult foreigner". "Educational water" ranks bottom in the gold standard of the *unseen* set, "difficult foreigner" ranks in the top ten.

Recent work (Ó Séaghdha, 2010; Erk et al., 2010) approximated plausibility with joint probability (JP). We believe that for semantic *plausibility* (not *probability*!) mutual information (MI), which factors out acutal frequencies, is a better metric.[4] We report results using JP, MI and MI^2.

	Seen		Unseen	
	r	ρ	r	ρ
AltaVista	.650	—	.480	—
BNC (Rasp)	.543	.622	.135	.102
Padó et al.	.479	.570	.120	.138
LDA	.594	.558	.468	.459
ROOTH-LDA	.575	.599	**.501**	**.469**
DUAL-LDA	.460	.400	.334	.278
Mod (JP)	.495	.413	.286	.276
Mod (MI)	.394	.425	<u>.471</u>	<u>.457</u>
Mod (MI^2)	.575	.501	.430	.408
Mod_{nc} (JP)	.626	.505	.357	.369
Mod_{nc} (MI)	.628	.574	.427	.385
Mod_{nc} (MI^2)	<u>**.701**</u>	<u>**.623**</u>	.423	.394

Table 3: Results (Pearson r and Spearman ρ correlations) on the Keller and Lapata (2003) plausibility data. Bold indicates best scores, underlining our best scores. High values indicate high correlation with the gold standard.

Table 3 shows the performance of our models compared to results reported in Ó Séaghdha (2010). As before, results between the normal and the inverse model (omitted due to space) are very similar. Surprisingly, the no-context models consistently outperform the models using context on the *seen* data set. This suggests that the *seen* data set can quite precisely be ranked using frequency estimates, which the no-context models might be better at capturing without the 'noise' introduced by context.

	Standard		Inverse (i)	
	r	ρ	r	ρ
Mod (JP)	.286	.276	.243	.245
Mod (MI)	.471	.457	.409	.383
Mod (MI^2)	.430	.408	.362	.347
Mod_{nc} (JP)	.357	.369	.181	.161
Mod_{nc} (MI)	.427	.385	.220	.209
Mod_{nc} (MI^2)	.423	.394	.218	.185

Table 4: Results on the *unseen* plausibility dataset.

The results on the *unseen* data set (Table 4) prove interesting as well. The inverse no-context model is performing significantly poorer than any of the other models. To understand this result we must investigate the differences between the *unseen* data set and the *seen* data set and to the pseudo-disambiguation evaluation. The key difference to pseudo-disambiguation is that we measure a human plausibility judgement, which — as we have demonstrated — only partially correlates with bigram frequencies. Our models were trained on the BNC, hence they could only learn frequency estimates for the *seen* data set, but not for the *unseen* data.

Based on our hypothesis about the role of context, we expect Mod and Mod_i to learn semantic classes based on the distribution of context. Without the access to that context, we argued that Mod_{nc} and Mod_{inc} would instead learn frequency estimates.[5] The hypothesis that nouns generally select for adjectives rather than vice versa further suggests that Mod and Mod_{nc} would learn semantic properties that Mod_i and Mod_{inc} could not learn so well.

In summary, we hence expected Mod to perform best on the *unseen* data, learning semantics from both context and noun-adjective selection. Also, as supported by the results, we expected Mod_{inc} to performs poorly, as it is the model least capable of learning semantics according to our hypotheses.

5 Conclusion

We have presented a class of probabilistic models which successfully learn semantic clusterings of nouns and a representation of adjective-noun selectional preference. These models encoded our beliefs about how adjective-noun pairs relate to each other and to the other words in the sentence. The performance of our models on estimating selectional preference strongly supported these initial hypotheses.

We discussed plausibility judgements from a theoretical perspective and argued that frequency estimates and JP are imperfect approximations for plausibility. While models can perform well on some evaluations by using either frequency estimates or semantic knowledge, we explained why this does not apply to the *unseen* plausibility test. The performance on that task demonstrates both the success of our model and the shortcomings of frequency-based approaches to human plausibility judgements.

Finally, this paper demonstrated that it is feasible to learn semantic representations of words while concurrently learning how they relate to one another.

Future work will explore learning words from broader classes of semantic relations and the role of context in greater detail. Also, we will evaluate the system applied to higher level tasks.

[4]See (Evert, 2005) for a discussion of these metrics.

[5]This could also explain their weaker performance on pseudo-disambiguation in the previous section, where the negative examples had zero frequency in the training corpus.

References

Marco Baroni and Roberto Zamparelli. 2010. Nouns are vectors, adjectives are matrices: representing adjective-noun constructions in semantic space. In *Proceedings of the 2010 Conference on Empirical Methods in Natural Language Processing*, EMNLP '10, pages 1183–1193, Stroudsburg, PA, USA. Association for Computational Linguistics.

Massimiliano Ciaramita and Mark Johnson. 2003. Supersense tagging of unknown nouns in wordnet. In *Proceedings of the 2003 conference on Empirical methods in natural language processing*, EMNLP '03, pages 168–175, Stroudsburg, PA, USA. Association for Computational Linguistics.

Stephen Clark and David Weir. 2002. Class-based probability estimation using a semantic hierarchy. *Comput. Linguist.*, 28:187–206, June.

James R. Curran. 2005. Supersense tagging of unknown nouns using semantic similarity. In *Proceedings of the 43rd Annual Meeting on Association for Computational Linguistics*, ACL '05, pages 26–33, Stroudsburg, PA, USA. Association for Computational Linguistics.

Katrin Erk, Sebastian Padó, and Ulrike Padó. 2010. A flexible, corpus-driven model of regular and inverse selectional preferences. *Computational Linguistics*, 36:723–763.

Stefan Evert. 2005. *The statistics of word cooccurrences: word pairs and collocations*. Ph.D. thesis, Universität Stuttgart, Holzgartenstr. 16, 70174 Stuttgart.

Edward Grefenstette and Mehrnoosh Sadrzadeh. 2011. Experimental support for a categorical compositional distributional model of meaning. In *Proceedings of the Conference on Empirical Methods in Natural Language Processing*, EMNLP '11, pages 1394–1404, Stroudsburg, PA, USA. Association for Computational Linguistics.

Thomas L. Griffiths and Mark Steyvers. 2004. Finding scientific topics. *Proceedings of the National Academy of Sciences*, 101:5228–5235.

Mark Johnson and Sharon Goldwater. 2009. Improving nonparameteric bayesian inference: experiments on unsupervised word segmentation with adaptor grammars. In *Proceedings of Human Language Technologies: The 2009 Annual Conference of the North American Chapter of the Association for Computational Linguistics*, NAACL '09, pages 317–325, Stroudsburg, PA, USA. Association for Computational Linguistics.

Frank Keller and Mirella Lapata. 2003. Using the web to obtain frequencies for unseen bigrams. *Computational Linguistics*, pages 459–484.

Andrew L. Maas and Andrew Y. Ng. 2010. A probabilistic model for semantic word vectors. In *Workshop on Deep Learning and Unsupervised Feature Learning*, NIPS '10.

Jeff Mitchell and Mirella Lapata. 2008. Vector-based models of semantic composition. In *ACL-HLT'08*, pages 236 – 244.

Diarmuid Ó Séaghdha. 2010. Latent variable models of selectional preference. In *Proceedings of the 48th Annual Meeting of the Association for Computational Linguistics*, ACL '10, pages 435–444, Stroudsburg, PA, USA. Association for Computational Linguistics.

Fernando Pereira, Naftali Tishby, and Lillian Lee. 1993. Distributional clustering of English words. In *Proceedings of the 31st annual meeting on Association for Computational Linguistics*, ACL '93, pages 183–190, Stroudsburg, PA, USA. Association for Computational Linguistics.

Mats Rooth, Stefan Riezler, Detlef Prescher, Glenn Carroll, and Franz Beil. 1999. Inducing a semantically annotated lexicon via EM-based clustering. In *Proceedings of the 37th annual meeting of the Association for Computational Linguistics on Computational Linguistics*, ACL '99, pages 104–111, Stroudsburg, PA, USA. Association for Computational Linguistics.

Issei Sato, Minoru Yoshida, and Hiroshi Nakagawa. 2008. Knowledge discovery of semantic relationships between words using nonparametric bayesian graph model. In *Proceeding of the 14th ACM SIGKDD international conference on Knowledge discovery and data mining*, KDD '08, pages 587–595, New York, NY, USA. ACM.

Identifying hypernyms in distributional semantic spaces

Alessandro Lenci
University of Pisa, Dept. of Linguistics
via S. Maria 36
I-56126, Pisa, Italy
alessandro.lenci@ling.unipi.it

Giulia Benotto
University of Pisa, Dept. of Linguistics
via S. Maria 36
I-56126, Pisa, Italy
mezzanine.g@gmail.com

Abstract

In this paper we apply existing directional similarity measures to identify hypernyms with a state-of-the-art distributional semantic model. We also propose a new directional measure that achieves the best performance in hypernym identification.

1 Introduction and related works

Distributional Semantic Models (DSMs) measure the semantic similarity between words with proximity in distributional space. However, semantically similar words in turn differ for the type of relation holding between them: e.g., *dog* is strongly similar to both *animal* and *cat*, but with different types of relations. Current DSMs accounts for these facts only partially. While they may correctly place both *animal* and *cat* among the nearest distributional neighbors of *dog*, they are not able to characterize the different semantic properties of these relations, for instance the fact that hypernymy is an asymmetric semantic relation, since being a dog entails being an animal, but not the other way round.

The purpose of this paper is to explore the possibility of identifying hypernyms in DSMs with *directional (or asymmetric) similarity measures* (Kotlerman et al., 2010). These measures all rely on some variation of the **Distributional Inclusion Hypothesis**, according to which if u is a semantically narrower term than v, then a significant number of salient distributional features of u is included in the feature vector of v as well. Since hypernymy is an asymmetric relation and hypernyms are semantically broader terms than their hyponyms, then we can predict that directional similarity measures are better suited to identify terms related by the hypernymy relation.

Automatic identification of hypernyms in corpora is a long-standing research line, but most methods have adopted semi-supervised, pattern-based approaches (Hearst, 1992; Pantel and Pennacchiotti, 2006). Fully unsupervised hypernym identification with DSMs is still a largely open field. Various models to represent hypernyms in vector spaces have recently been proposed (Weeds and Weir, 2003; Weeds et al., 2004; Clarke, 2009), usually grounded on the Distributional Inclusion Hypothesis (for a different approach based on representing word meaning as "regions" in vector space, see Erk (2009a; 2009b)). The same hypothesis has been adopted by Kotlerman *et al.* (2010) to identify (substitutable) lexical entailments" . Within the context of the Textual Entailment (TE) paradigm, Zhitomirsky-Geffet and Dagan (2005; 2009) define *(substitutable) lexical entailment* as a relation holding between two words, if there are some contexts in which one of the words can be substituted by the other and the meaning of the original word can be inferred from the new one. Its relevance for TE notwithstanding, this notion of lexical entailment is more general and looser than hypernymy. In fact, it encompasses several standard semantic relations such as synonymy, hypernymy, metonymy, some cases of meronymy, etc.

Differently from Kotlerman *et al.* (2010), here we focus on applying directional, asymmetric similarity measures to identify hypernyms. We assume the classical definition of a hypernymy, such that Y is an hypernym of X if and only if X is a kind of Y, or equivalently every X is a Y.

2 Directional similarity measures

In the experiments reported in section 3 we have applied the following directional similarity measures (F_x is the set of distributional features of a term x, $w_x(f)$ is the weight of the feature f for x):

WeedsPrec (M1) - this is a measure that quantifies the weighted inclusion of the features of a term u within the features of a term v (Weeds and Weir, 2003; Weeds et al., 2004; Kotlerman et al., 2010):

$$WeedsPrec(u, v) = \frac{\sum_{f \in F_u \cap F_v} w_u(f)}{\sum_{f \in F_u} w_u(f)} \quad (1)$$

cosWeeds (M2) - this measure corresponds to the geometrical average of *WeedsPrec* and the symmetric similarity between u and v, measured by their vectors' cosine:

$$cosWeeds(u, v) = \sqrt{M1(u, v) * cos(u, v)} \quad (2)$$

This is actually a variation of the *balPrec* measure in Kotlerman *et al.* (2010), the difference being that cosine is used as a symmetric similarity measure instead of the *LIN* measure (Lin, 1998).

ClarkeDE (M3) - a close variation of M1, proposed by Clarke (2009):

$$ClarkeDE(u, v) = \frac{\sum_{f \in F_u \cap F_v} min(w_u(f), w_v(f))}{\sum_{f \in F_u} w_u(f)} \quad (3)$$

invCL (M4) - this a new measure that we introduce and test here for the first time. It takes into account not only the inclusion of u in v, but also the *non-inclusion* of v in u, both measured with *ClarkeDE*:

$$invCL(u, v) = \sqrt{M3(u, v) * (1 - M3(v, u))} \quad (4)$$

The intuition behind *invCL* is that, if v is a semantically broader term of u, then the features of u are included in the features of v, but crucially the features of v are also *not* included in the features of u. For instance, if *animal* is a hypernym of *lion*, we can expect i.) that a significant number of the *lion*-contexts are also *animal*-contexts, and ii.) that a significant number of *animal*-contexts are not *lion*-contexts. In fact, being a semantically broader term of *lion*, *animal* should also be found in contexts in which animals other than lions occur.

3 Experiments

The main purpose of the experiments reported below is to investigate the ability of the directional similarity measures presented in section 2 to identify the hypernyms of a given target noun, and to discriminate hypernyms from terms related by symmetric semantic relations, such as coordinate terms.

We have represented lexical items with distributional feature vectors extracted from the *TypeDM* tensor (Baroni and Lenci, 2010). TypeDM is a particular instantiation of the *Distributional Memory* (DM) framework. In DM, distributional facts are represented as a *weighted tuple structure* T, a set of weighted word-link-word tuples $\langle\langle w_1, l, w_2\rangle, \sigma\rangle$, such that w_1 and w_2 are content words (e.g. nouns, verbs, etc.), l is a syntagmatic co-occurrence links between words in a text (e.g. syntactic dependencies, etc.), and σ is a weight estimating the statistical salience of that tuple. The TypeDM word set contains 30,693 lemmas (20,410 nouns, 5,026 verbs and 5,257 adjectives). The TypeDM link set contains 25,336 direct and inverse links formed by (partially lexicalized) syntactic dependencies and patterns. The weight σ is the *Local Mutual Information* (LMI) (Evert, 2005) computed on link type frequency (negative LMI values are raised to 0).

3.1 Test set

We have evaluated the directional similarity measures on a subset of the BLESS data set (Baroni and Lenci, 2011), consisting of tuples expressing a **relation** between a target concept (henceforth referred to as **concept**) and a relatum concept (henceforth referred to as **relatum**). BLESS includes 200 distinct English concrete nouns as target concepts, equally divided between living and non-living entities, and grouped into 17 broader classes (e.g., BIRD, FRUIT, FURNITURE, VEHICLE, etc.).

For each concept noun, BLESS includes several

relatum words, linked to the concept by one of 5 semantic relations. Here, we have used the BLESS subset formed by 14,547 tuples with the relatum attested in the TypeDM word set, and containing one of these relations: COORD: the relatum is a noun that is a co-hyponym (coordinate) of the concept: $\langle alligator, coord, lizard \rangle$; HYPER: the relatum is a noun that is a hypernym of the concept: $\langle alligator, hyper, animal \rangle$; MERO: the relatum is a noun referring to a part/component/organ/member of the concept, or something that the concept contains or is made of: $\langle alligator, mero, mouth \rangle$; RANDOM-N: the relatum is a random noun holding no semantic relation with the target concept: $\langle alligator, random - n, message \rangle$.

Kotlerman *et al.* (2010) evaluate a set of directional similarity measure on a data set of valid and invalid (substitutable) lexical entailments (Zhitomirsky-Geffet and Dagan, 2009). However, as we said above, lexical entailment is defined as an asymmetric relation that covers various types of classic semantic relations, besides hypernymy . The choice of BLESS is instead motivated by the fact that here we focus on the ability of directional similarity measure to identify hypernyms.

3.2 Evaluation and results

For each word x in the test set, we represented x in terms of a set F_x of distributional features $\langle l, w_2 \rangle$, such that in the TypeDM tensor there is a tuple $\langle \langle w_1, l, w_2 \rangle, \sigma \rangle$, $w_1 = x$. The feature weight $w_x(f)$ is equal to the weight σ of the original DM tuple. Then, we applied the 4 directional similarity measures in section 2 to BLESS, with the goal of evaluating their ability to discriminate hypernyms from other semantic relations, in particular co-hyponymy. In fact, differently from hypernyms, coordinate terms are not related by inclusion. Therefore, we want to test whether directional similarity measures are able to assign higher scores to hypernyms, as predicted by the Distributional Inclusion Hypothesis. We used the *Cosine* as our baseline, since it is a symmetric similarity measure and it is commonly used in DSMs.

We adopt two different evaluation methods. The first is based on the methodology described in Baroni and Lenci (2011). Given the similarity scores for a concept with all its relata across all relations in our test set, we pick the relatum with the highest score (nearest neighbour) for each relation. In this way, for each of the 200 BLESS concepts, we obtain 4 similarity scores, one per relation. In order to factor out concept-specific effects that might add to the overall score variance, we transform the 8 similarity scores of each concept onto standardized z scores (mean: 0; s.d: 1) by subtracting from each their mean, and dividing by their standard deviation. After this transformation, we produce a **boxplot** summarizing the distribution of scores per relation across the 200 concepts.

Boxplots for each similarity measure are reported in Figure 1. They display the median of a distribution as a thick horizontal line within a box extending from the first to the third quartile, with whiskers covering 1.5 of the interquartile range in each direction from the box, and values outside this extended range – extreme outliers – plotted as circles (these are the default boxplotting option of the R statistical package). To identify significant differences between relation types, we also performed pairwise comparisons with the Tukey Honestly Significant Difference test, using the standard $\alpha = 0.05$ significance threshold.

In the boxplots we can observe that all measures (either symmetric or not) are able to discriminate truly semantically related pairs from unrelated (i.e. random) ones. Crucially, *Cosine* shows a strong tendency to identify coordinates among the nearest neighbors of target items. This is actually consistent with its being a symmetric similarity measure. Instead, directional similarity measures significantly promote hypernyms over coordinates. The only exception is represented by *cosWeeds*, which again places coordinates at the top, though now the difference with hypernyms is not significant. This might be due to the cosine component of this measure, which reduces the effectiveness of the asymmetric *WeedsPrec*. The difference between coordinates and hypernyms is slightly bigger in *invCL*, and the former appear to be further downgraded than with the other directional measures. From the boxplot analysis, we can therefore conclude that similarity measures based on the Distributional Inclusion Hypothesis do indeed improve hypernym identification in context-feature semantic spaces, with respect to other types of semantic relations, such as COORD.

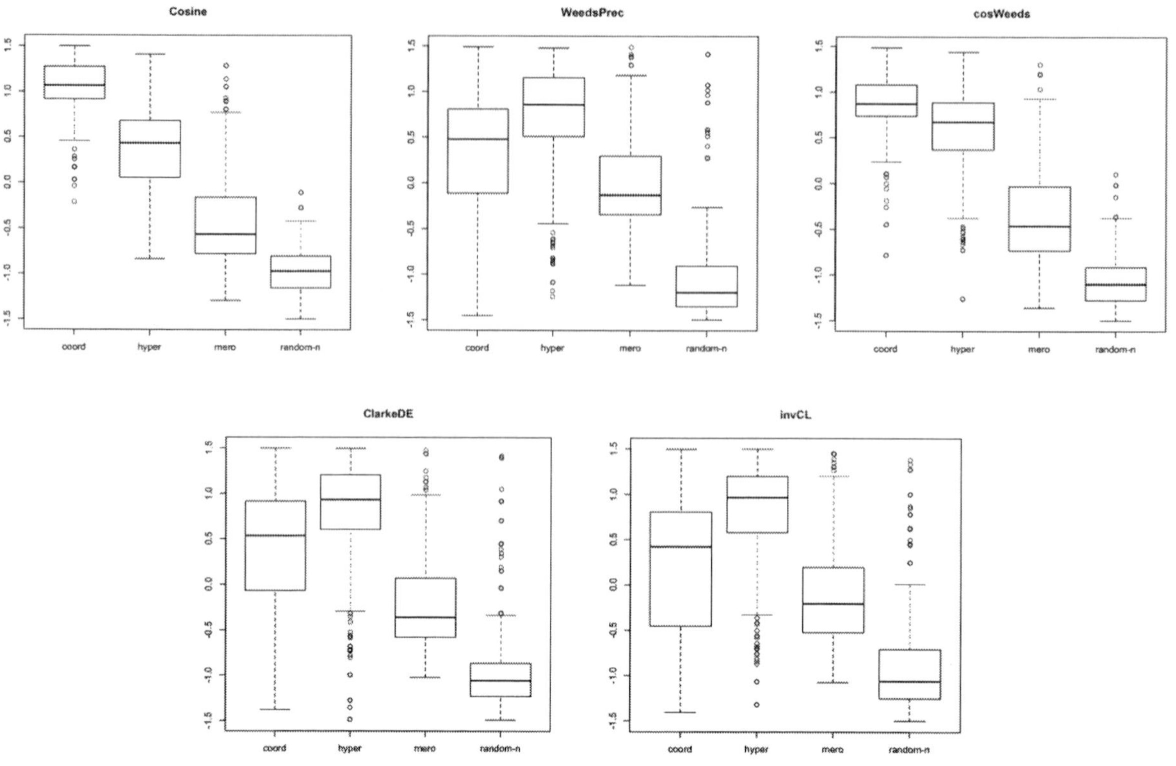

Figure 1: Distribution of relata similarity scores across concepts (values on ordinate are similarity scores after concept-by-concept z-normalization).

The second type of evaluation we have performed is based on Kotlerman *et al.* (2010). The similarity measures have been evaluated with **Average Precision** (AP), a method derived from Information Retrieval and combining precision, relevance ranking and overall recall. For each similarity measure, we computed AP with respect to the 4 BLESS relations. The best possible score (AP = 1) for a given relation (e.g., HYPER) corresponds to the ideal case in which all the relata belonging to that relation have higher similarity scores than the relata belonging to the other relations. For every relation, we calculated the AP for each of the 200 BLESS target concepts.

In Table 1, we report the AP values averaged over the 200 concepts. On the one hand, these results confirm the trend illustrated by the boxplots, in particular the fact that directional similarity measures clearly outperform *Cosine* (or cosine-based measures such as *cosWeeds*) in identifying hypernyms, with no significant differences among them. However, a different picture emerges by comparing the AP values for HYPER with those for COORD. since in this case important distinctions among the directional measures emerge. In fact, even if *WeedsPrec* and *ClarkeDE* increase the AP for HYPER, still they assign even higher AP values to COORD. Conversely, *invCL* is the only measure that assigns to HYPER the top AP score, higher than COORD too.

measure	COORD	HYPER	MERO	RANDOM-N
Cosine	0.79	0.23	0.21	0.30
WeedsPrec	0.45	0.40	0.31	0.32
cosWeeds	0.69	0.29	0.23	0.30
ClarkeDE	0.45	0.39	0.28	0.33
invCL	**0.38**	**0.40**	0.31	0.34

Table 1: Mean AP values for each semantic relation reported by the different similarity scores.

The new directional similarity measure we have proposed in this paper, *invCL*, thus reveals a higher ability to set apart hypernyms from other relations, coordinates terms included. The latter are expected to share a large number of contexts and this is the reason why they are strongly favored by symmetric similarity measures, such as *Cosine*. Asymmetric measures like *cosWeeds* and *ClarkeDE* also fall short of distinguishing hypernyms from coordinates because the condition of feature inclusion they test is satisfied by coordinate terms as well. If two sets share a high number of elements, then many elements of the former are also included in the latter, and vice versa. Therefore, coordinate terms too are expected to have high values of feature inclusions. Conversely, *invCL* takes into account not only the inclusion of u into v, but also the amount of v that is not included in u. Thus, *invCL* provides a better distributional correlate to the central property of hypernyms of having a broader semantic content than their hyponyms.

4 Conclusions and ongoing research

The experiments reported in this paper support the Distributional Inclusion Hypothesis as a viable approach to model hypernymy in semantic vector spaces. We have also proposed a new directional measure that actually outperforms the state-of-the-art ones. Focusing on the contexts that broader terms do not share with their narrower terms thus appear to be an interesting direction to explore to improve hypernym identification. Our ongoing research includes testing *invCL* to recognize lexical entailments and comparing it with the *balAPinc* measured proposed by Kotlerman *et al.* (2010) for this task, as well as designing new distributional methods to discriminate between various other types of semantic relations.

Acknowledgments

We thank the reviewers for their useful and insightful comments on the paper.

References

Marco Baroni and Alessandro Lenci. 2010. Distributional Memory: A general framework for corpus-based semantics. *Computational Linguistics*, 36(4): 673–721.

Marco Baroni and Alessandro Lenci. 2011. How we BLESSed distributional semantic evaluation. In *Proceedings of the GEMS 2011 Workshop on Geometrical Models of Natural Language Semantics, EMNLP 2011*, Edinburgh, Scotland, UK: 1–10.

Daoud Clarke. 2009. Context-theoretic semantics for natural language: an overview. In *Proceedings of the EACL 2009 Workshop on GEMS: GEometrical Models of Natural Language Semantics*, Athens, Greece: 112–119.

Katrin Erk. 2009a. Supporting inferences in semantic space: representing words as regions. In *Proceedings of the 8th International Conference on Computational Semantics*, Tilburg, January: 104–115.

Katrin Erk. 2009b. Representing words as regions in vector space. In *Proceedings of the Thirteenth Conference on Computational Natural Language Learning (CoNLL)*, Boulder, Colorado: 57–65.

Stefan Evert. 2005. *The Statistics of Word Cooccurrences*. Ph.D. dissertation, Stuttgart University.

Marti Hearst. 1992. Automatic acquisition of hyponyms from large text corpora. In *Proceedings of COLING 1992*, Nantes, France: 539–545.

Lili Kotlerman, Ido Dagan, Idan Szpektor, and Maayan Zhitomirsky-Geffet. 2010. Directional distributional similarity for lexical inference. *Natural Language Engineering*, 16(04): 359–389.

Dekang Lin. 1998. Automatic Retrieval and Clustering of Similar Words. In *Proceedings of the COLING-ACL 1998*, Montreal, Canada: 768–774.

Patrick Pantel and Marco Pennacchiotti. 2006. Espresso: Leveraging generic patterns for automatically harvesting semantic relations. In *Proceedings of the COLING-ACL 2006*, Sydney, Australia: 113–120.

Idan Szpektor and Ido Dagan. 2008. Learning Entailment Rules for Unary Templates. In *Proceedings of COLING 2008*, Manchester, UK: 849–856.

Julie Weeds and David Weir. 2003. A general framework for distributional similarity. In *Proceedings of the EMNLP 2003*, Sapporo, Japan: 81–88.

Julie Weeds, David Weir, and Diana McCarthy. 2004. Characterising measures of lexical distributional similarity. In *Proceedings of COLING 2004*, Geneva, Switzerland: 1015–1021.

Maayan Zhitomirsky-Geffet and Ido Dagan. 2005. The distributional inclusion hypotheses and lexical entailment. In *Proceedings of ACL 2005*, Ann Arbor, MI: 107–114.

Maayan Zhitomirsky-Geffet and Ido Dagan. 2009. Bootstrapping distributional feature vector quality. *Computational Linguistics*, 35(3): 435-461.

Towards a Flexible Semantics: Colour Terms in Collaborative Reference Tasks

Bert Baumgaertner
University of California, Davis
bbaum@ucdavis.edu

Raquel Fernández
University of Amsterdam
raquel.fernandez@uva.nl

Matthew Stone
Rutgers University
matthew.stone@rutgers.edu

Abstract

We report ongoing work on the development of agents that can implicitly coordinate with their partners in referential tasks, taking as a case study colour terms. We describe algorithms for generation and resolution of colour descriptions and report results of experiments on how humans use colour terms for reference in production and comprehension.

1 Introduction

Speakers do not always share identical semantic representations nor identical lexicons. For instance, a subject may refer to a shape as a diamond while another subject may call that same shape a square (which just happens to be tilted sidewise); or someone may refer to a particular colour with *'light pink'* while a different speaker may refer to it as *'salmon'*. Regardless of these differences, which seem common place, speakers in dialogue are able to communicate successfully most of the time. Successful communication exploits interlocutors' abilities to negotiate referring expressions interactively through grounding (Clark and Wilkes-Gibbs, 1986; Clark and Schaefer, 1989), but in many cases interlocutors can already make a good guess at their partners' intentions by relaxing the interpretation of their utterances and looking for the referent that best matches this looser interpretation. We are interested in modelling this second kind of behaviour computationally, to get a better understanding of it and to contribute to the development of dialogue systems that are able to better coordinate with their human partners.

In this paper we focus on collaborative referential tasks (akin to the classic matching tasks introduced by Krauss and Weinheimer (1966) and Clark and Wilkes-Gibbs (1986)) and take as a case study colour terms. Our focus here is not on the explicit joint negotiation of effective terms, but rather on the deployment of flexible semantic representations that can adapt to the constraints imposed by the context and to the dialogue partner's language use.

We start by describing our algorithms for generation and resolution of colour descriptions in the next section. In sections 3 and 4, we present results of experiments that investigate how humans use colour terms for reference in production and comprehension. Section 5 compares our model against the experimental data we have collected so far and discusses some directions for future work. We end with a short conclusion in section 6.

2 Reference to Colours: Our Model

Our view of how colour terms are used in referential tasks follows the basic tenets of Gricean pragmatics (Grice, 1975) and collaborative reference theories (Clark and Wilkes-Gibbs, 1986), according to which speakers and addressees tend to maximize the success of their joint task while minimizing costs.

In the domain of colour terms, we take this to mean that speakers tend use a basic colour term (e.g., *'red'* or *'blue'*) whenever this is enough to identify the target object and resort to an alternative, more specific or complex term (e.g., *'bordeaux'* or *'navy blue'*) in other contexts where the basic term is deemed insufficient. Non-basic terms can be considered more costly because they are less frequent and thus more difficult to retrieve.

Similar ideas are at the core of models for the generation of referring expressions that build on the seminal work of Dale and Reiter (1995). These approaches, however, rely on a lexicon or database where the properties of potential target objects are associated with specific, predefined terms.[1] Our aim is to develop dialogue agents that employ more flexible semantic representations, allowing them to (a) refer to target colours with different terms in different contexts, and (b) resolve the reference of colour terms produced by the dialogue partner by picking up targets that are not rigidly linked to the term in the agent's lexicon.

2.1 Algorithms

Data. To develop the generation and resolution algorithms of our agent, we used a publicly available database of RGB codes and colour terms generated from a colour naming survey created by Randall Monroe (author of the webcomic `xkcd.com`) and taken by around two hundred thousand participants.[2] This database contains a total of 954 colour terms (corresponding to the colour terms most frequently used by the participants) paired with a unique RGB code corresponding to the location in the RGB colour space which was most frequently named with the colour term in question.

We use this database as the default lexicon of our agent. Amongst the colour terms in the lexicon, we distinguish between basic and non-basic colours. We selected the following as our basic colours: red, purple, pink, magenta, brown, orange, yellow, green, teal, blue, and grey. This selection takes into account the high frequency of these terms in English and is in line with the literature on basic colour terms (Berlin and Kay, 1967; Berlin and Kay, 1991).

Resolution Algorithm. ALIN (ALgorithm for INterpretation) is given as input a scene of coloured squares and a colour term. Its output is the square it takes to be the intended target, generated as follows. Assuming the input term is in the lexicon, ALIN compares every colour in the scene to the RGB value of the input (the *anchor*). ALIN considers a colour c the intended target if, (a) c is nearest the anchor within a certain distance threshold, and (b) for any other colour c' in the scene within the given distance threshold of the anchor, c' is far enough away from both the anchor and c. We say more about distance thresholds below.

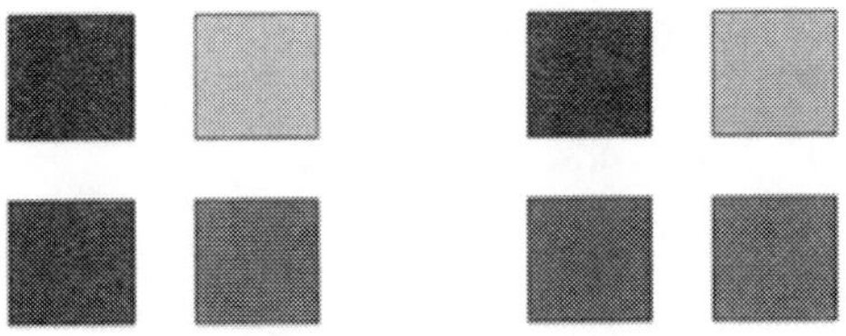

Figure 1: Two scenes with the brown square (top left in both scenes) as the target; no competitors (left scene) and one potential competitor (right scene).

Generation Algorithm. Unless there are competitors (colours relatively close to the target), GENA (GENeration Algorithm) is disposed to output a basic colour term if the target is acceptably close to a basic colour (if not, it selects the default term associated with the RGB code in the lexicon). In case there are competitor colours in the scene, if the target is a basic colour, GENA will attempt to select a non-basic colour term closest to the target but still further away from the competitor(s). If the target is not a basic colour, GENA simply selects the default term in the lexicon.

Measuring Colour Distance. We treat colours in our model as points in a conceptual space (Gärdenfors, 2000; Jäger, 2009). As a first approximation, we measure colour proximity in terms of Euclidean distances between RGB values.[3] Three variables were used to set the thresholds required by ALIN and GENA: i) *bc* is the maximum range to search for basic colours; ii) *min* is the minimum distance required between two colours to be considered minimally different; and iii) *max* is the maximum range of allowable search for alternative colours. We conducted two pilot studies to establish reasonable values for these variables, which we then set as: *bc* = 100; *min* = 25; *max* = 75.[4]

3 Experimental Methodology

We conducted two small experiments to collect data about how speakers and addressees use colour terms in referential tasks.

[1]See, however, van Deemter (2006) for an attempt to deal with vague properties such as *size* within this framework.

[2]For further details visit `http://blog.xkcd.com/2010/05/03/color-survey-results/`.

[3]We recognize Euclidean distances between RGB values assumes colour space is uniform, which is not the case in human vision (Wyszecki and Stiles, 2000). See section 5.

[4]RGB codes scaled at 0–255.

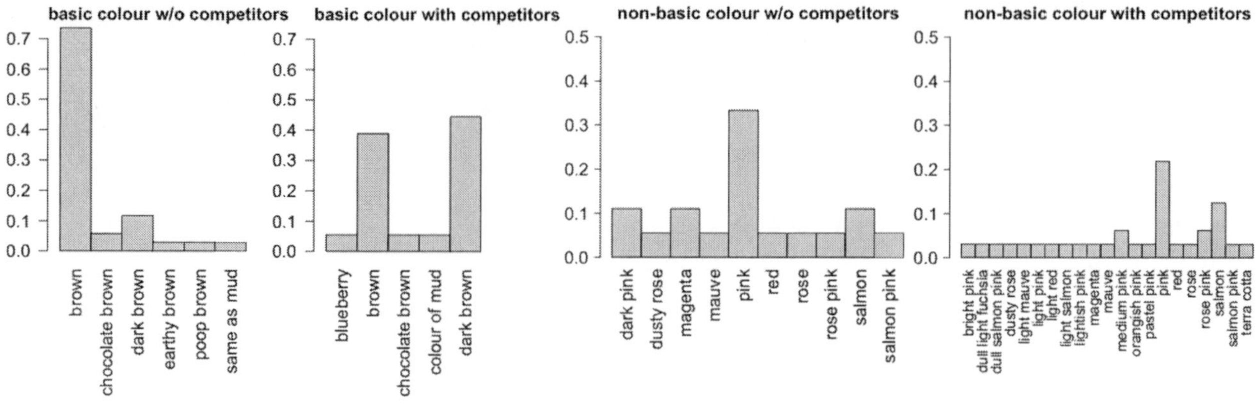

Figure 2: Sample of results from ExpA, for a basic and a non-basic colour.

Materials & Setup. We created 12 different scenes, each consisting of four solid coloured squares, one of them the target (see Figure 1 for sample scenes). Scenes were designed to take into account two parameters: basic and non-basic target colours, and without or with a competitor – a colour at a distance threshold from the target.[5] The target basic colours used were *'brown'* and *'magenta'* and the non-basic ones, *'rose'* and *'sea blue'*.[6] Each target colour appeared at least in one scene where there were no competitors.

We run a generation experiment (ExpA) and a resolution experiment (ExpB). In ExpA, participants were shown our 12 scenes and were asked to refer to the target with a colour term that would allow a potential addressee to identify it in the current context, but without reference to the other colours in the scene (to avoid comparatives such as *'the bluer square'*). In ExpB, participants were shown a scene and a colour term and were asked to pick up the intended referent. The colour terms used in this second experiment were selected from those produced in ExpA – 29 scene-term pairs in total. Each scene appeared at least twice, once with a term with high occurrence frequency in ExpA, and once or twice with one or two terms that had been produced with low frequency. To minimize chances that subjects recognize the same scene more than once, we rotated and dispersed them evenly throughout.

[5]Any colour within a Euclidean distance of 125 from the target was considered a competitor.

[6]Compositional phrases may introduce more sophisticated effects. However, the data on which our lexicon is based abstracted away from such details, treating them as simples.

Participants. A total of 36 native-English participants took part in the experiments: 19 in ExpA and 17 in ExpB. Subjects for both experiments included undergraduate students, graduates students, and university faculty. Both experiments were run online.

4 Experimental Results

ExpA Generation. ExpA revealed there is high variability in the terms produced to refer to a single colour. As expected, variability of terms generated for non-basic colours was higher than for basic colours. For non-basic colours, variability of terms in scenes with competitors was higher. Figure 2 shows the different terms produced for a basic colour (*'brown'*) and a non-basic colour (*'rose'*) in scenes without and with competitors, together with the proportional frequency of each term.

For the brown square target in a scene without competitors, the basic-colour term *'brown'* was used with high frequency (72% of the time) while any other terms were used 1 or 2 times only. In scenes with competitors, *'dark brown'* had highest frequency with *'brown'* almost as much (43% vs. 40%). For the rose square target in a scene without competitors, there was also one term that stood out as the most frequent, *'pink'*, although its frequency (30%) is substantially lower to that of the basic-colour *'brown'*. In scenes with competitors there is an explosion in variation, with *'pink'* still standing out but only with a proportional frequency of 21%.

Overall, ExpA showed that speakers attempt to adapt their colour descriptions to the context and that there is high variability in the terms they choose to do this.

ExpB: Resolution. ExpB showed that reference resolution is almost always successful despite the variation in colour terms observed in ExpA. For the basic colours in scenes with no competitors, participants successfully identified the targets in all cases, while in scenes with competitors they did so 98% of the time. This was the case for both terms with proportionally high and low frequency.

For the non-basic colours in scenes with no competitors, the success rate in identifying the target was again 100% for both high and low frequency terms. For scenes with competitors, there were differences depending on the frequency of the terms used: for high frequency terms there were once more no resolution errors, while the resolution success rate dropped to 78% where we used terms with low proportional frequency scores. A summary of these results is shown in Table 1, together with the success rate of our resolution algorithm ALIN.

	Basic Colours				Non-basic Colours			
	high freq.		low freq.		high freq.		low freq.	
	nc	c	nc	c	nc	c	nc	c
ExpB	1	0.98	1	0.98	1	1	1	0.78
ALIN	1	0.71	1	0.71	0.5	1	0.75	0.71

Table 1: Resolution success rate by human participants and ALIN in scenes without and with competitors (nc/c).

5 Discussion

The data we collected allows us to make informative comparisons between humans and our model in collaborative reference tasks. Although we do not believe the data is sufficient for an evaluation, the comparison illuminates how the model can be refined and the setup required for a proper evaluation.

Regarding resolution, we note that an algorithm that rigidly associates colours and terms would have successfully resolved only 4 of the 29 cases, 3 of which were basic colours with no distractors – a 7.25% success rate. In our scenarios with four potential targets, a random algorithm would have an average success rate of 25%. ALIN is closer to our human data (see Table 1), though anomalies exist. One problem is the lack of compositional semantics in our current model. ALIN failed to resolve complex phrases like *'dull salmon pink'* and *'deep gray blue'*, which were terms produced by humans for non-basic colours with competitors, simply because the terms were not in the agent's lexicon. Other anomalies seem to be consequences of taking Euclidean distances over RGB values, which may be too crude. In the future, our intent is to convert RGB values to Lab values and then use Delta-E values to measure distances. First, however, we need a more sophisticated analysis of the thresholds that we used for ALIN and GENA.

As for generation, given the amount of variation observed in the terms produced by our subjects, it is not clear how human performance ought to be compared to GENA's. For instance, in scenes with competitors, GENA produced *'reddish brown'* for the basic colour *'brown'* and *'coral'* for the non-basic colour *'rose'*. These did not appear in our human-generated data but still seem to our lights reasonable descriptions. GENA also produced *'gray'* to refer to *'rose'* in a different scene, which seems less appropriate and may be due to our current way of calculating colour distances and setting up the thresholds.

We believe that instead of comparing GENA's output to human output, it makes more sense to evaluate GENA by testing how well humans can resolve terms produced by it. We intend to carry out this evaluation in the future.

6 Conclusions

We have focused on the specific case of colours where speakers differ in the referring expressions they generate, but addressees are nevertheless able to relax the interpretations of the expressions in order to coordinate. We believe this implicit adaptability is part of our semantic representation more broadly. The case of colour provides us with a starting point for studying and modelling computationally this flexibility we possess.

Acknowledgements

This work has been partially supported by grant 632.002.001 from the Netherlands Organisation for Scientific Research (NWO) and by grant IIS-1017811 from the National Science Foundation (NSF).

References

Brent Berlin and Paul Kay. 1967. *Universality and evolution of basic color terms*. Laboratory for Language-Behavior Research.

Brent Berlin and Paul Kay. 1991. *Basic color terms: Their universality and evolution*. Univ of California Pr.

Herbert H. Clark and Edward F. Schaefer. 1989. Contributing to discourse. *Cognitive Science*, 13(2):259–294.

Herbert H. Clark and Donna Wilkes-Gibbs. 1986. Referring as a collaborative process. *Cognition*, 22:1–39.

Robert Dale and Ehud Reiter. 1995. Computational interpretations of the Gricean Maxims in the Generation of Referring Expressions. *Cognitive Science*, 18:233–266.

Peter Gärdenfors. 2000. *Conceptual Spaces*. MIT Press, Cambridge.

Paul Grice. 1975. Logic and conversation. In D. Davidson and G. Harman, editors, *The Logic of Grammar*, pages 64–75. Dickenson, Encino, California.

Gerhard Jäger. 2009. Natural color categories are convex sets. In *Logic, Language and Meaning: 17th Amsterdam Colloquium, Amsterdam, The Netherlands, December 16-18, 2009, Revised Selected Papers*, pages 11–20. Springer.

Robert Krauss and Sidney Weinheimer. 1966. Concurrent feedback, confirmation, and the encoding of referents in verbal communication. *Journal of Personality and Social Psychology*, 4(3):343–346.

Kees van Deemter. 2006. Generating referring expressions that involve gradable properties. *Computational Lingustics*, 32(2):195–222.

Günter Wyszecki and Walter S. Stiles. 2000. *Color science: concepts and methods, quantitative data and formulae*. Wiley Classics Library.

Unsupervised Disambiguation of Image Captions

Wesley May, Sanja Fidler, Afsaneh Fazly, Sven Dickinson, and Suzanne Stevenson
Department of Computer Science
University of Toronto
Toronto, Ontario, Canada, M5S 3G4
{wesley, fidler, afsaneh, sven, suzanne}@cs.toronto.edu

Abstract

Given a set of images with related captions, our goal is to show how visual features can improve the accuracy of unsupervised word sense disambiguation when the textual context is very small, as this sort of data is common in news and social media. We extend previous work in unsupervised text-only disambiguation with methods that integrate text and images. We construct a corpus by using Amazon Mechanical Turk to caption sense-tagged images gathered from ImageNet. Using a Yarowsky-inspired algorithm, we show that gains can be made over text-only disambiguation, as well as multimodal approaches such as Latent Dirichlet Allocation.

1 Introduction

We examine the problem of performing unsupervised word sense disambiguation (WSD) in situations with little text, but where additional information is available in the form of an image. Such situations include captioned newswire photos, and pictures in social media where the textual context is often no larger than a tweet.

Unsupervised WSD has been shown to work very well when the target word is embedded in a large quantity of text (Yarowsky, 1995). However, if the only available text is "The crane was so massive it blocked the sun" (see Fig. 1), then text-only disambiguation becomes much more difficult; a human could do little more than guess. But if an image is available, the intended sense is much clearer. We develop an unsupervised WSD algorithm based on Yarowsky's that uses words in a short caption along with "visual words" from the captioned image to choose the best of two possible senses of an ambiguous keyword describing the content of the image.

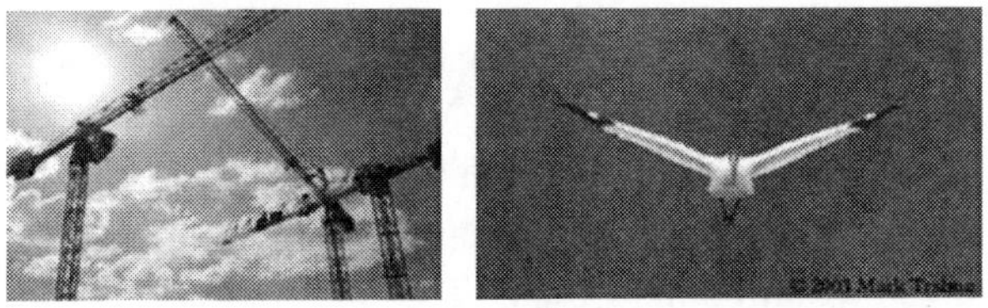

Figure 1: "The crane was so massive it blocked the sun." Which sense of crane? With images the answer is clear.

Language-vision integration is a quickly developing field, and a number of researchers have explored the possibility of combining text and visual features in various multimodal tasks. Leong and Mihalcea (2011) explored semantic relatedness between words and images to better exploit multimodal content. Jamieson et al. (2009) and Feng and Lapata (2010) combined text and vision to perform effective image annotation. Barnard and colleagues (2003; 2005) showed that supervised WSD by could be improved with visual features. Here we show that unsupervised WSD can similarly be improved. Loeff, Alm and Forsyth (2006) and Saenko and Darrell (2008) combined visual and textual information to solve a related task, image sense disambiguation, in

We thank NSERC and U. Toronto for financial support. Fidler and Dickinson were sponsored by the Army Research Laboratory and this research was accomplished in part under Cooperative Agreement Number W911NF-10-2-0060. The views and conclusions contained in this document are those of the authors and should not be interpreted as representing the official policies, either express or implied, of the Army Research Laboratory or the U.S. Government.

an unsupervised fashion. In Loeff et al.'s work, little gain was realized when visual features were added to a great deal of text. We show that these features have more utility with small textual contexts, and that, when little text is available, our method is more suitable than Saenko and Darrell's.

2 Our Algorithm

We model our algorithm after Yarowsky's (1995) algorithm for unsupervised WSD: Given a set of documents that contain a certain ambiguous word, the goal is to label each instance of that word as some particular sense. A seed set of collocations that strongly indicate one of the senses is initially used to label a subset of the data. Yarowsky then finds new collocations in the labelled data that are strongly associated with one of the current labels and applies these to unlabelled data. This process repeats iteratively, building a decision list of collocations that indicate a particular sense with a certain confidence.

In our algorithm (Algorithm 1), we have a document collection D of images relevant to an ambiguous keyword k with senses s_1 and s_2 (though the algorithm is extensible to more than two senses). Such a collection might result from an internet image search using an ambiguous word such as "mouse".

Each D_i is an image–caption pair repsented as a bag-of-words that includes both lexical words from the caption, and "visual words" from the image. A visual word is simply an abstract representation that describes a small portion of an image, such that similar portions in other images are represented by the same visual word (see Section 3.2 for details). Our seed sets consist of the words in the definitions of s_1 and s_2 from WordNet (Fellbaum, 1998). Any document whose caption contains more words from one sense definition than the other is initially labelled with that sense. We then iterate between two steps that (i) find additional words associated with s_1 or s_2 in currently labelled data, and (ii) relabel all data using the word sense associations discovered so far.

We let V be the entire vocabulary of words across all documents. We run experiements both with and without visual words, but when we use visual words, they are included in V. In the first step, we compute a confidence C_i for each word V_i. This confidence is a log-ratio of the probability of seeing V_i in documents labelled as s_1 as opposed to documents labelled as s_2. That is, a positive C_i indicates greater association with s_1, and vice versa. In the second step we find, for each document D_j, the word $V_i \in D_j$ with the highest magnitude of C_i. If the magnitude of C_i is above a labelling threshold τ_c, then we label this document as s_1 or s_2 depending on the sign of C_i. Note that all old labels are discarded before this step, so labelled documents may become unlabelled, or even differently labelled, as the algorithm progresses.

Algorithm 1 Proposed Algorithm

D: set of documents D_1 ... D_d
V: set of lexical and visual words V_1 ... V_v in D
C_i: log-confidence V_i is sense 1 vs. sense 2
S_1 and S_2: bag of dictionary words for each sense
L_1 and L_2: documents labelled as sense 1 or 2

for all D_i **do** ▷ Initial labelling using seed set
  if $|D_i \cap S_1| > |D_i \cap S_2|$ **then**
    $L_1 \leftarrow L_1 \cup \{D_i\}$
  else if $|D_i \cap S_1| < |D_i \cap S_2|$ **then**
    $L_2 \leftarrow L_2 \cup \{D_i\}$
  end if
end for

repeat
  for all $i \in 1..v$ **do** ▷ Update word conf.
    $C_i \leftarrow log\left(\frac{P(V_i|L_1)}{P(V_i|L_2)}\right)$
  end for

  $L_1 \leftarrow \emptyset$, $L_2 \leftarrow \emptyset$ ▷ Update document conf.
  for all D_i **do**
    ▷ Find word with highest confidence
    $m \leftarrow \underset{j \in 1..v, V_j \in D_i}{\arg\max} |C_j|$
    if $C_m > \tau_c$ **then**
      $L_1 \leftarrow L_1 \cup \{D_i\}$
    else if $C_m < -\tau_c$ **then**
      $L_2 \leftarrow L_2 \cup \{D_i\}$
    end if
  end for
until no change to L_1 or L_2

3 Creation of the Dataset

We require a collection of images with associated captions. We also require sense annotations for the keyword for each image to use for evaluation. Barnard and Johnson (2005) developed the

"Music is an important means of expression for many teens."

"Keeping your office supplies organized is easy, with the right tools."

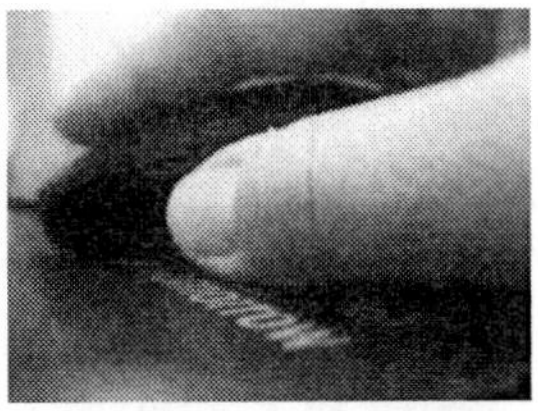

"The internet has opened up the world to people of all nationalities."

"When there is no cheese I will take over the world."

Figure 2: Example image-caption pairs from our dataset, for "band" (top) and "mouse" (bottom).

ImCor dataset by associating images from the Corel database with text from the SemCor corpus (Miller et al., 1993). Loeff et al. (2006) and Saenko and Darrell (2008) used Yahoo!'s image search to gather images with their associated web pages. While these datasets contain images paired with text, the textual contexts are much larger than typical captions.

3.1 Captioning Images

To develop a large set of sense-annotated image–caption pairs with a focus on caption-sized text, we turned to ImageNet (Deng et al., 2009). ImageNet is a database of images that are each associated with a synset from WordNet. Hundreds of images are available for each of a number of senses of a wide variety of common nouns. To gather captions, we used Amazon Mechanical Turk to collect five sentences for each image. We chose two word senses for each of 20 polysemous nouns and for each sense we collected captions for 50 representative images. For each image we gathered five captions, for a total of 10,000 captions. As we have five captions for each image, we split our data into five sets. Each set has the same images, but each image is paired with a different caption in each set.

We specified to the Turkers that the sentences should be relevant to, but should not talk directly about, the image, as in "In this picture there is a blue fish", as such captions are very unnatural. True captions generally offer orthogonal information that is not readily apparent from the image. The keyword for each image (as specified by ImageNet) was not presented to the Turkers, so the captions do not necessarily contain it. Knowledge of the keyword is presumed to be available to the algorithm in the form of an image tag, or filename, or the like. We found that forcing a certain word to be included in the caption also led to sentences that described the picture very directly. Sentences were required to be a least ten words long, and have acceptable grammar and spelling. We remove stop words from the captions and lemmatize the remaining words. See Figure 2 for some examples.

3.2 Computing the Visual Words

We compute visual words for each image with ImageNet's feature extractor. This extractor lays down a grid of overlapping squares onto the image and computes a SIFT descriptor (Lowe, 2004) for each square. Each descriptor is a vector that encodes the edge orientation information in a given square. The descriptors are computed at three scales: 1x, 0.5x and 0.25x the original side lengths. These vectors are clustered with k-means into 1000 clusters, and the labels of these clusters (arbitrary integers from 1 to 1000) serve as our visual words.

It is common for each image to have a "vocabulary" of over 300 distinct visual words, many of which only occur once. To denoise the visual data, we use only those visual words which account for at least 1% of the total visual words for that image.

4 Experiments and Results

To show that the addition of visual features improves the accuracy of sense disambiguation for image–caption pairs, we run our algorithm both with and without the visual features. We also compare our results to three different baseline methods: K-means (K-M), Latent Dirichlet Allocation (LDA) (Blei et al., 2003), and an unsupervised WSD algorithm (PBP) explained below. We use accuracy to measure performance as it is commonly used by the WSD community (See Table 1).

For K-means, we set $k = 2$ as we have two senses, and represent each document with a V-dimensional

Table 1: Results (Average accuracy across all five sets of data). Bold indicates best performance for that word.

	Ours text	Ours w/vis	K-M text	K-M w/vis	LDA text	LDA w/vis	PBP text
band	.80	**.82**	.66	.65	.64	.56	.73
bank	.77	**.78**	.71	.59	.52	.67	.62
bass	**.94**	**.94**	.90	.88	.61	.62	.49
chip	**.90**	**.90**	.73	.58	.57	.66	.75
clip	.70	**.79**	.65	.58	.48	.53	.65
club	.80	**.84**	.80	.81	.61	.73	.63
court	.79	.79	.61	.53	.62	**.82**	.57
crane	.62	.67	**.76**	**.76**	.52	.54	.66
game	**.78**	**.78**	.60	.66	.60	.66	.70
hood	**.74**	.73	.73	.70	.51	.45	.55
jack	**.76**	.74	.62	.53	.58	.66	.47
key	.81	**.92**	.79	.54	.57	.70	.50
mold	.67	**.68**	.59	.67	.57	.66	.54
mouse	**.84**	**.84**	.71	.62	.62	.69	.68
plant	.54	.54	.56	.53	.52	.50	**.72**
press	.60	.59	.60	.54	.58	**.62**	.48
seal	.70	**.80**	.61	.67	.55	.53	.62
speaker	**.70**	.69	.57	.53	.55	.62	.63
squash	.89	**.95**	.84	.92	.55	.67	.79
track	.78	**.85**	.71	.66	.51	.54	.69
avg.	.76	**.78**	.69	.65	.56	.63	.62

vector, where the ith element is the proportion of word V_i in the document. We run K-means both with and without visual features.

For LDA, we use the dictionary sense model from Saenko and Darrell (2008). A topic model is learned where the relatedness of a topic to a sense is based on the probabilities of that topic generating the seed words from its dictionary definitions. Analogously to k-means, we learn a model for text alone, and a model for text augmented with visual information.

For unsupervised WSD (applied to text only), we use WordNet::SenseRelate::TargetWord, hereafter PBP (Patwardhan et al., 2007), the highest scoring unsupervised lexical sample word sense disambiguation algorithm at SemEval07 (Pradhan et al., 2007). PBP treats the nearby words around the target word as a bag, and uses the WordNet hierarchy to assign a similarity score between the possible senses of words in the context, and possible senses of the target word. As our captions are fairly short, we use the entire caption as context.

The most important result is the gain in accuracy after adding visual features. While the average gain across all words is slight, it is significant at $p < 0.02$ (using a paired t-test). For 12 of the 20 words, the visual features improve performance, and in 6 of those, the improvement is 5–11%.

For some words there is no significant improvement in accuracy, or even a slight decrease. With words like "bass" or "chip" there is little room to improve upon the text-only result. For words like "plant" or "press" it seems the text-only result is not strong enough to help bootstrap the visual features in any useful way. In other cases where little improvement is seen, the problem may lie with high intra-class variation, as our visual words are not very robust features, or with a lack of orthogonality between the lexical and visual information.

Our algorithm also performs significantly better than the baseline measurements. K-means performs surprisingly well compared to the other baselines, but seems unable to make much sense of the visual information present. Saenko and Darrell's (2008) LDA model makes substansial gains by using visual features, but does not perform as well on this task. We suspect that a strict adherence to the seed words may be to blame: while both this LDA model and our algorithm use the same seed definitions initially, our algorithm is free to change its mind about the usefulness of the words in the definitions as it progresses, whereas the LDA model has no such capacity. Indeed, words that are intuitively non-discriminative, such as "carry", "lack", or "late", are not uncommon in the definitions we use.

5 Conclusion and Future Work

We present an approach to unsupervised WSD that works jointly with the visual and textual domains. We showed that this multimodal approach makes gains over text-only disambiguation, and outperforms previous approaches for WSD (both text-only, and multimodal), when textual contexts are limited.

This project is still in progress, and there are many avenues for further study. We do not currently exploit collocations between lexical and visual information. Also, the bag-of-SIFT visual features that we use, while effective, have little semantic content. More structured representations over segmented image regions offer greater potential for encoding semantic content (Duygulu et al., 2002).

References

Kobus Barnard and Matthew Johnson. 2005. Word sense disambiguation with pictures. In *Artificial Intelligence*, volume 167, pages 13–130.

Kobus Barnard, Matthew Johnson, and David Forsyth. 2003. Word sense disambiguation with pictures. In *Workshop on Learning Word Meaning from Non-Linguistic Data*, Edmonton, Canada.

David M. Blei, Andrew Ng, and Michael I. Jordan. 2003. Latent dirichlet allocation. In *JMLR*, volume 3, pages 993–1022.

Jia Deng, Wei Dong, Richard Socher, Li-Jia Li, Kai Li, and Li Fei-Fei. 2009. Imagenet: A large-scale hierarchical image database. In *IEEE Conference on Computer Vision and Pattern Recognition.*

Pinar Duygulu, Kobus Barnard, Nando de Freitas, and David Forsyth. 2002. Object recognition as machine translation: Learning a lexicon for a fixed image vocabulary. In *European Conference on Computer Vision*, Copenhagen, Denmark.

Christiane Fellbaum. 1998. Wordnet: An electronic lexical database. In *Bradford Books.*

Yansong Feng and Mirella Lapata. 2010. Topic models for image annotation and text illustration. In *Annual Conference of the North American Chapter of the ACL*, pages 831–839, Los Angeles, California.

Michael Jamieson, Afsaneh Fazly, Suzanne Stevenson, Sven Dickinson, and Sven Wachsmuth. 2009. Using language to learn structured appearance models for image annotation. *IEEE Transactions on Pattern Analysis and Machine Intelligence*, 32(1):148–164.

Chee Wee Leong and Rada Mihalcea. 2011. Measuring the semantic relatedness between words and images. In *International Conference on Semantic Computing*, Oxford, UK.

Nicolas Loeff, Cecilia Ovesdotter Alm, and David Forsyth. 2006. Discriminating image senses by clustering with multimodal features. In *Proceedings of the COLING/ACL 2006 Main Conference Poster Sessions*, pages 547–554, Sydney, Australia.

David Lowe. 2004. Distinctive image features from scale-invariant keypoints. *International Journal of Computer Vision*, 60(2):91–110.

George Miller, Claudia Leacock, Randee Tengi, and Ross Bunker. 1993. A semantic concordance. In *Proceedings of the 3rd DARPA Workshop on Human Language Technology*, pages 303–308.

Siddharth Patwardhan, Satanjeev Banerjee, and Ted Pedersen. 2007. UMND1: Unsupervised word sense disambiguation using contextual semantic relatedness. In *Proceedings of SemEval-2007*, pages 390–393, Prague, Czech Republic.

Sameer Pradhan, Edward Loper, Dmitriy Dligach, and Martha Palmer. 2007. Task 17: English lexical sample, SRL and all words. In *Proceedings of SemEval-2007*, pages 87–92, Prague, Czech Republic.

Kate Saenko and Trevor Darrell. 2008. Unsupervised learning of visual sense models for polysemous words. In *Proceedings of Neural Information Processing Systems*, Vancouver, Canada.

David Yarowsky. 1995. Unsupervised word sense disambiguation rivaling supervised methods. In *Proceedings of the 33rd Annual Meeting of the ACL*, pages 189–196, Cambridge, Massachusetts.

Lexical semantic typologies from bilingual corpora — A framework

Steffen Eger
Department of Computer Science / Carnegie Mellon University
5404 Gates Hillman Complex / Pittsburgh, PA 15213, USA
seger@cs.cmu.edu

Abstract

We present a framework, based on Sejane and Eger (2012), for inducing lexical semantic typologies for groups of languages. Our framework rests on lexical semantic association networks derived from encoding, via bilingual corpora, each language in a common reference language, the *tertium comparationis*, so that distances between languages can easily be determined.

1 Introduction

Typologocial classifications have a long tradition in linguistics. For example, typologies based on syntactic categories have been proposed e.g. by Greenberg (1961), leading a.o. to 'word order' categorizations of natural languages as belonging to SVO, VSO, etc. types. Relatedly, genealogical classification systems based on phonological and morphological similarities date back at least to the comparatists of the nineteenth centuries, among them Jacob Grimm (1785-1863), Rasmus Rask (1787-1832), and Karl Verner (1846-1896). Typological investigations into (lexical) semantic relations across languages have, in contrast, attracted little attention. Still, some results have been established such as classifications based upon treatment of animal concepts and corresponding meat concepts (see the excellent introduction to lexical typologies by Koch, 2001). As further exceptions, based on computational principles, may be considered Mehler et al. (2011), who analyze conceptual networks derived from the Wikipedia topic classification systems for different languages; Gaume et al. (2008), who propose (but do not realize, to the best of our knowledge) to compare distances between selected word pairs such as *meat/animal*, *child/fruit*, *door/mouth* across language-specific monolingual dictionaries in order to categorize the associated languages and, partly, Cooper (2008), who computes semantic distances between languages based on the curvature of translation histograms in bilingual dictionaries.

Recently, Sejane and Eger (2012) have outlined a novel approach to establishing semantic typologies based upon the language-specific polysemy relation of lexical units which entails language-dependent 'lexical semantic association networks'. To illustrate, French *bœuf* has two meanings, which we may gloss as 'cow' and 'beef' in English. Similarly, French *langue* and Spanish *lingua* mean both 'language' and 'tongue', whereas Chinese *huà* means both 'language' and 'picture'. Sejane and Eger's (2012) key idea is then that this language-specific polysemy can be made observable via the translation relation implied e.g. by a bilingual dictionary. For instance, using a Chinese-English dictionary, one might be able to uncover the polysemy of *huà* by assessing its two English translations, as given above. More formally, one might create a link (in a network) between two English words if they have a common translation in Chinese (cf. Eger and Sejane, 2010); doing the same with a Spanish-English and French-English dictionary, one would obtain three different lexical semantic association networks, all encoded in the English language, the *tertium comparationis* or *reference language* in this case. In the English networks based upon Spanish and French — Sejane and Eger (2012) call these networks the Spanish and French *versions* of English, respectively — 'language' and 'tongue' would have a link, whereas in the Chinese version of English, 'language' and 'picture' would have a link (see also Figure 1 where we illustrate this idea for English and Latin versions of German). Then, comparing these networks across languages may allow establishing a typology of lexical semantic associations.

In the current paper, we deliberate on Sejane and Eger's (2012) idea, suggesting ways to adequately formalize their approach (Section 2) and propose data sources suitable for their framework (Section 3). Moreover, in Section 4 we shortly discuss how network versions of a given reference language can be formally contrasted and suggest solutions for the *tertium comparationis* problem. In Section 5, we conclude.

2 Formal approach to lexical semantic association networks

We propose the following mathematical framework for representing lexical semantic association networks. Given n languages $L_1, \ldots, L_n$, $n \geq 2$, plus a selected reference language R distinct from $L_1, \ldots, L_n$, and bilingual translation operators $T_1, \ldots, T_n$, where T_i, $i = 1, \ldots, n$, maps (or, translates) from language L_i to the reference language R, create network graphs

$$G_i = (V_i, E_i)$$

with

$$V_i = W[R],$$

and

$$E_i = \{(u, v) \mid u, v \in V_i, uT_ix, xT_iv \text{ for some } x \in W[L_i]\},$$

where by $W[L]$ we denote the words of language L and by aT_ib we denote that a translates into b under T_i; moreover, we assume T_i to be symmetric such that the G_i's may be considered undirected graphs.

To generalize this a bit, we may consider *weighted graphs* where for network i, $i = 1, \ldots, n$, V_i is as above, $E_i = \{(u, v) \mid u, v \in V_i\}$, and each edge $(u, v) \in E_i$ has weight (being a function of)

$$d_i(u, v) = |\{x \mid uT_ix,\ xT_iv\}|. \qquad (1)$$

Then, if u and v have no common translation x, $d_i(u, v) = 0$ and generally $d_i(u, v)$ counts the number of common translations x between u and v, entailing a generalization of the setting above, which may allow for a more fine-grained analysis and may be of importance for example for outlining semantic many-to-one relationships between a language L_i and the reference language R.

3 Possible data sources

Sejane and Eger (2012) conduct a preliminary study of their approach on the open-source bilingual dictionaries *dicts.info* (http://www.dicts.info/uddl.php). The disadvantage with using bilingual dictionaries is of course that they are scarcely available (and much less *freely* available); moreover, for the above described semantic association networks, it may be of crucial importance to have *comparable* data sources; e.g. using a general-purpose dictionary in one case and a technical dictionary in the other, or using dictionaries of vastly different sizes may severely affect the quality of results.[1]

We more generally propose to use bilingual corpora for the problem of inducing semantic association networks, where we particularly have e.g. sentence-aligned corpora like the Europarl corpus (Koehn, 2005) in mind (see also the study of Rama and Borin (2011) on cognates, with Europarl as the data basis). Then, translation relations T_i may be induced from these corpora by applying a statistical machine translation approach such as the Moses toolkit (Koehn et al., 2007). The translation relations may thus be probabilistic instead of binary, which may either be resolved via thresholding or by modifying Equation (1) as in

$$d_i(u, v) = \sum_{x \in W[L_i]} \frac{\Pr[uT_ix] + \Pr[xT_iv]}{2}$$

or

$$d_i(u, v) = \sum_{x \in W[L_i]} \Pr[uT_ix] \cdot \Pr[xT_iv],$$

both of which have (1) as special cases.

[1] As another aspect, Sejane and Eger (2012) concluded that the sizes and partly the qualities of their bilingual dictionaries were, throughout, not fully adequate for their intentions.

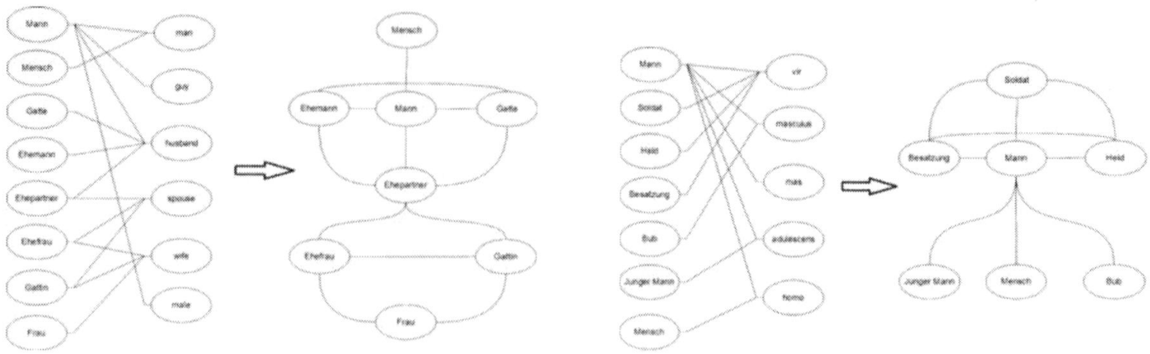

Figure 1: Bilingual dictionaries German-English and German-Latin and induced lexical semantic association networks, English and Latin versions of German. Note the similarities and differences; *Mann* 'man' and *Mensch* 'human' have a link in both versions but there is a path between *Mann* and *Frau* 'woman' only in the English version of German, whereas there exists e.g. a path between *Mann* and *Held* 'hero' only in the Latin version. Reprinted from Sejane and Eger (2012).

Using the Europarl corpus would both address the problem of size and comparability raised above; moreover, corpora may better reflect actual language use than dictionaries, which oftentimes document idiosyncractic, normative or assumed language conditions. A problem with the Europarl corpus is that it covers just a very small (and selected) subset of the world's languages, whereas it might be of particular interest for (semantic) typology to contrast large, heterogeneous classes of languages.

4 Network distance measures and the problem of *tertium comparationis*

In order to be able to induce a semantic typology from the above described lexical semantic association networks, a distance metric δ on network graphs is required,[2] that is, a function δ that maps network graphs G_i, G_j, $1 \leq i, j \leq n$, to numbers

$$\delta_{ij} = \delta(G_i, G_j) \in \mathbb{R}.$$

Such distance measures may be derived from general network statistics such as the *number of edges*, the *diameters* of the networks, network *density*, *graph entropy* via information functionals (cf. Dehmer, 2008) or *clustering coefficients* (cf. Watts and Strogatz, 1998). We believe, however, that such abstract measures can be useful only for a preliminary examination of the data. A more in-depth analysis should be based on comparing individual network vertices in two versions of the reference language. For example, we could ask about the lexical semantic difference between French and Chinese with respect to the lexical unit 'language'. One way of realizing such an analysis would be by making use of *shortest distances* between network vertices. To be more precise, let G_i and G_j be two lexical semantic network versions of a reference language R. Assume that G_i and G_j have the same number, N, of vertices, with the same labels (i.e. names of vertices such as 'language'). Let u_k, $1 \leq k \leq N$, be the k-th vertex in both graphs, with identical label across the two graphs. Moreover, let $s_i(u_k)$ and $s_j(u_k)$ be vectors whose l-th component, $1 \leq l \leq N$, is given as the shortest distance between vertex u_k and vertex u_l in graphs G_i and G_j, respectively,

$$(s_i(u_k))_l = \text{shortest distance between } u_k \text{ and } u_l \text{ in } G_i,$$

and analogously for $s_j(u_k)$. We could then define the difference between network version G_i and G_j with respect to vertex u_k as e.g. the Euclidean distance between these two vectors,

$$\|s_i(u_k) - s_j(u_k)\|.$$

However, as useful as shortest distances may be, they do not seem to fully capture the topological structure of a network. For example, they do not indicate whether there are many or few (short) paths between two vertices, etc. (see also the discussion

[2]In this context, we identify languages with their lexical semantic association networks.

in Gaume et al., 2008). Therefore, we propose a Page-rank like (see Brin and Page, 1998; Gaume and Mathieu, 2012) procedure to compare network vertices of networks G_i and G_j. To this end, let $p_i(u_k)$, a vector of dimension N, denote the probability distribution that if, starting from vertex u_k, one may reach any of the other vertices of network G_i (and analogously for network G_j), under the following rules. In each step, starting at vertex u_k, with probability α, a 'random surfer' on the network G_i may pass from its current vertex v to any of v's neighbors with equal probability (if there are no neighbors, the surfer passes to a random vertex), and with probability $(1-\alpha)$ the surfer 'teleports' to an arbitrary vertex. The probability distribution $p_i(u_k)$, for α close to 1, may then neatly represent topological properties of network G_i, from the 'perspective' of vertex u_k. On this basis, we can, as above, determine the difference between network versions G_i and G_j with respect to vertex u_k as

$$\delta_{u_k}(G_i, G_j) = \|p_i(u_k) - p_j(u_k)\| \,. \qquad (2)$$

Finally, we define the (global) distance between G_i and G_j as the average over all such (local) distances,

$$\delta_{ij} = \frac{1}{N}\sum_{k=1}^{N} \delta_{u_k}(G_i, G_j). \qquad (3)$$

If, as mentioned above, we have weighted graphs, we slightly modify the random surfer's behavior. Instead of passing with uniform probability from vertex v to a neighbor vertex w of v, the surfer passes to w with probability proportional to the weight between v and w; the larger the weight the higher is the probability that the surfer ends up at w.

Then, once distance metric values δ_{ij} are given, an $n \times n$ distance matrix D may be defined whose entry (i, j) is precisely δ_{ij},

$$D_{ij} = \delta_{ij}.$$

On D, standard e.g. hierarchical clustering algorithms may be applied in order to deduce a lexical semantic typology.

Finally, we address the *tertium comparationis* problem: Given a set of languages, which one should be chosen as reference language? It might be tempting to believe that the choice of the reference language should not matter much for the resulting lexical semantic association networks, but the reference language may certainly have *some* impact. For example, if English is the reference language, the Chinese version of English might not only have a link between 'language' and 'picture' but also between 'language' and 'tongue', because of the polysemy of 'tongue' in English. If, in contrast, German was the reference language, the Chinese version of German should not have a link between *Zunge* 'tongue' and *Sprache* 'language' because *Zunge*, in German, does not mean 'language' (any more).

Thus, to avoid misspecifications based on a particular choice of reference language, we propose the following. Let $L_1, \ldots, L_n, L_{n+1}, n \geq 2$, be $(n+1)$ languages for which bilingual translation operators $T_{A,B}$ exist for any two languages A, B from the $(n+1)$ languages. Then let the distance between languages i and j, $1 \leq i, j \leq n+1$, be defined as

$$\Delta_{ij} = \frac{1}{n-1} \sum_{R \in L \setminus \{L_i, L_j\}} \delta(G_i^R, G_j^R),$$

where by G_i^R we denote the L_i version of R, and by L we denote the set of languages $\{L_1, \ldots, L_n, L_{n+1}\}$; in other words, we specify the distance between languages i and j as the average distance over all possible reference languages, which excludes languages i and j themselves. As above, Δ_{ij} induces a distance matrix, with which clustering can be performed.

5 Conclusion

We have presented a framework for inducing lexical semantic typologies based on the idea of Sejane and Eger (2012) to represent lexical semantic spaces of different languages in a common reference language in order to be able to contrast them. We have extended Sejane and Eger's (2012) approach by giving it a solid mathematical foundation, by suggesting more suitable data bases on which to implement their study, and by outlining adequate network distance metrics on this data. Moreover, we have addressed the *tertium comparationis* problem of the choice of the reference language. In follow-up work, we intend to bring the idea to the data, from which we expect very interesting cross-lingual lexical semantic insights.

References

S. Brin, and L. Page. 1998. The Anatomy of a Large-Scale Hypertextual Web Search Engine. In *Seventh International World-Wide Web Conference (WWW 1998)*.

M.C. Cooper. 2008. Measuring the Semantic Distance between Languages from a Statistical Analysis of Bilingual Dictionaries. *Journal of Quantitative Linguistics*, 15 (1): 1–33.

M. Dehmer. 2008. Information processing in complex networks: Graph entropy and information functionals. *Applied Mathematics and Computation* 201: 82–94.

S. Eger, and I. Sejane. 2010. Computing semantic similarity from bilingual dictionaries. In *Proceedings of the 10th International Conference on statistical analysis of textual data (JADT 2010)*: 1217–1225.

B. Gaume, K. Duvignau, and M. Vanhove. 2008. Semantic associations and confluences in paradigmatic networks. In *From Polysemy to Semantic Change: Towards a typology of lexical semantic associations*, Amsterdam: John Benjamins: 233–267.

B. Gaume, and F. Mathieu. 2012. PageRank Induced Topology for Real-World Networks. To appear.

J. H. Greenberg. 1961. Some universals of grammar with particular reference to the order of meaningful elements. In *Universals of language*, Joseph H. Greenberg (ed.), Cambridge, MA: MIT Press: 73–113.

P. Koch. 2001. Lexical typology from a cognitive and linguistic point of view. In *Language Typology and Language Universals*, Martin Haspelmath, Ekkehard Knig, Wulf Oesterreicher, and Wolfgang Raible (eds.), Berlin: Mouton de Gruyter: 1142–1178.

P. Koehn. 2005. Europarl: A Parallel Corpus for Statistical Machine Translation. In *MT Summit 2005*.

P. Koehn, H. Hoang, A. Birch, C. Callison-Burch, M. Federico, N. Bertoldi, B. Cowan, W. Shen, C. Moran, R. Zens, C. Dyer, O. Bojar, A. Constantin, and E. Herbst. 2007. Moses: Open Source Toolkit for Statistical Machine Translation. In *Annual Meeting of the Association for Computational Linguistics (ACL), demonstration session*, Prague, Czech Republic, June 2007.

A. Mehler, O. Pustylnikov, and N. Diewald. 2011. Geography of Social Ontologies: Testing a Variant of the Sapir-Whorf Hypothesis in the Context of Wikipedia. *Computer Speech and Language*, 25: 716–740.

T. Rama, and L. Borin. 2011. Estimating language relationships from a parallel corpus. A study of the Europarl corpus. In *NEALT Proceedings Series (NODALIDA 2011 Conference Proceedings)*: 161–167.

I. Sejane, and S. Eger. 2012. Semantic typologies from bilingual dictionaries. To appear.

D.J. Watts, S. Strogatz. 1998. Collective dynamics of 'small-world' networks. *Nature* 393 (6684): 440–442.

Non-atomic Classification to Improve a Semantic Role Labeler for a Low-resource Language

Richard Johansson
Språkbanken, Department of Swedish, University of Gothenburg
Box 100, SE-40530 Gothenburg, Sweden
richard.johansson@gu.se

Abstract

Semantic role classification accuracy for most languages other than English is constrained by the small amount of annotated data. In this paper, we demonstrate how the frame-to-frame relations described in the FrameNet ontology can be used to improve the performance of a FrameNet-based semantic role classifier for Swedish, a low-resource language. In order to make use of the FrameNet relations, we cast the semantic role classification task as a *non-atomic label prediction task*. The experiments show that the cross-frame generalization methods lead to a 27% reduction in the number of errors made by the classifier. For previously unseen frames, the reduction is even more significant: 50%.

1 Introduction

The FrameNet lexical database and annotated corpora, based on the theory of semantic frames (Fillmore et al., 2003), have allowed the implementation of automatic systems to extract *semantic roles* (Gildea and Jurafsky, 2002; Johansson and Nugues, 2007; Màrquez et al., 2008; Das et al., 2010).

Since the original FrameNet is developed for the English language, most research on semantic role extraction has focused exclusively on English. However, the English FrameNet has inspired similar efforts for other languages. For instance, the ongoing development of a Swedish FrameNet (Borin et al., 2010) allows us to investigate the feasibility of using this resource in constructing an automatic role-semantic analyzer for Swedish. However, due to the fact that the Swedish FrameNet annotation process is in a fairly early stage, not much annotated material is available, and this limits the performance attainable by automatic classifiers trained on these data. In particular, the scarce amount of data makes it very hard for the machine learning methods to discern general linguistic facts concerning the syntactic–semantic linking patterns, such as the relation between the voice of a verb, the syntactic functions of its arguments, and the semantic roles of the arguments (Dowty, 1991).

In this paper, we show that the inter-frame relations described in the FrameNet ontology allow us to generalize across frames. This allows the classifier to learn general linguistic facts, and it also leads to more efficient use of the annotated data. To allow this kind of generalization, we formulate the semantic role selection problem as a classification task with non-atomic labels. This cross-frame generalization method reduces the number of errors made by the classifier by 27%, improving the accuracy from 54.4 to 66.5. When evaluating on frames for which the classifier has not been trained, the accuracy improves from 7.2 (random performance) to 53.4, a 50% error reduction.

2 The Swedish FrameNet

The Swedish FrameNet, SweFN, is a lexical resource under development (Friberg Heppin and Toporowska Gronostaj, 2012), based on the English version of FrameNet constructed by the Berkeley research group (Baker et al., 1998). It is found on the SweFN website[1], and is available as a free resource.

The SweFN frames and frame names correspond to the English ones, with some exceptions, as do the selection of frame elements including definitions and internal relations. The meta-information about the frames, such as semantic relations between frames, is also transferred from the Berkley FrameNet. Compared to the Berkeley FrameNet, SweFN is expanded with information about the domain of the frames, at present: general language, the medical and the art domain.

[1] http://spraakbanken.gu.se/eng/swefn

At the time of writing this paper, SweFN covered 519 frames with around 18,000 lexical units. The lexical units are gathered from SALDO, a free Swedish electronic association lexicon (Borin and Forsberg, 2009). A lexical unit from SALDO cannot populate more than one frame. At present there are 31 frames in SweFN which do not match a frame in the Berkeley FrameNet. Of these, there are eight completely new frames while the others have been modified in some way.

Crucially for the work presented in this paper, each frame is exemplified with at least one sentence. The number of sentences is currently 2,974. The most well-annotated frames are EXPERIENCER_OBJ with 38 sentences, CAUSE_MOTION with 21, and CAUSE_HARM with 19. These sentences form the training material used in the following sections.

3 System Implementation

In this section, we describe the implementation of our semantic role labeling system. In order to be useful on its own, such a system needs to solve several tasks: (1) identification of predicate words; (2) assignment of frames to predicate words; (3) identification of role fillers; (4) assignment of semantic role labels to role fillers. In this paper, we focus exclusively on the semantic role classification task.

3.1 Baseline: A Classifier for Swedish Semantic Roles

Following most previous implementations, we used a syntactic parse tree as the basis of the semantic role extraction; we assumed that every semantic role span coincides with the projection of a subtree in the syntactic tree. The tasks of segmentation and labeling then reduce to a classification problem on syntactic tree nodes. Each sentence was parsed by the LTH dependency parser (Johansson and Nugues, 2008a), which we trained on a Swedish treebank (Nilsson et al., 2005). Figure 1 shows a sentence annotated with a dependency tree and semantic roles.

The semantic role labeling classifier was implemented as a linear multiclass classifier with a flexible output space depending on the frame of the given predicate; we trained this classifier using an online learning algorithm (Crammer et al., 2006). In addition, we imposed a uniqueness constraint on the labels output by the classifier, so that every role may appear only once for a given predicate.

We considered a large number of features for the classifier (Table 1). Most of these are commonly used features taken from the standard literature on semantic role labeling. We then applied a standard greedy forward feature selection procedure to determine which of them to use. The features containing SALDO ID refer to the entry identifiers in the SALDO lexicon. Note that the POS tags have coarse and fine variants, such as VERB and VERB-FINITE-PRESENT-ACTIVE respectively, and we used both of them.

Semantic role classifiers rely heavily on lexical features (Johansson and Nugues, 2008b), and this may lead to brittleness; in order to increase robustness, we added features based on hierarchical clusters constructed using the Brown algorithm (Brown et al., 1992). The Brown algorithm clusters word into hierarchies represented as bit strings. Based on tuning on a development set, we found that it was best not to use the full bit string, but only a prefix if the string was longer than 12 bits.

FRAME
DEPENDENCY RELATION PATH
FRAME ELEMENTS
POSITION
VOICE
ARGUMENT HEAD SALDO ID
ARGUMENT HEAD LEMMA
ARGUMENT HEAD POS (FINE)
PREDICATE POS (FINE)
ARGUMENT POS (COARSE)
ARGUMENT RIGHT CHILD POS (COARSE)
ARGUMENT WORD
PREDICATE WORD CLUSTER
ARGUMENT WORD CLUSTER

Table 1: List of classifier features.

3.2 A Classifier Using Non-atomic Semantic Role Labels

The classifier described above is a quite typical example of how semantic role classifiers are normally implemented: each frame is independent of all other frames. However, in our case, when the amount of training data is quite small, the limitations of this standard approach become apparent:

- Since there are many frames, the amount of training data for each frame is very limited.

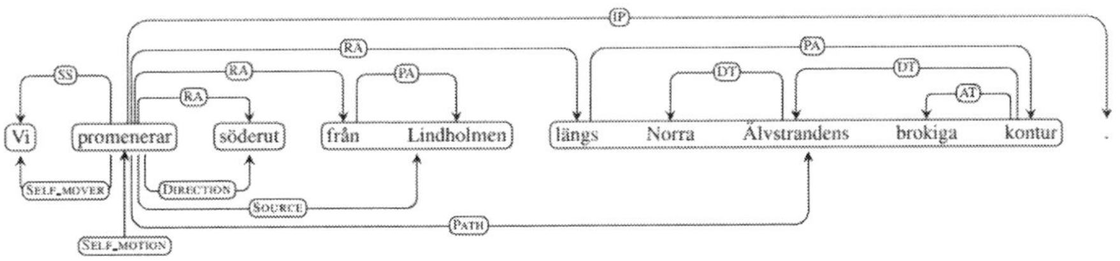

Figure 1: A sentence with dependency syntax (above) and semantic role structure (below).

- Basic linguistic facts, such as which roles are likely to appear in subject position, have to be relearned for each frame.

To remedy these problems, we developed a classifier using *non-atomic labels*: instead of just a simple label INGESTION:INGESTOR, the classifier can predict several labels, using some sort of decomposition into meaningful parts. In §3.3, we will describe several such decompositions.

As described above, our baseline classifier is a standard linear classifier. Assume that the frame F defines a set of semantic roles $r_1, \ldots, r_n$, then the classifier predicts a semantic role r^* for a given argument a using this model:

$$r^* = \arg\max_{r \in F} w \cdot \Phi(a, r)$$

Here Φ is a feature function describing features of the argument a taking the semantic role r, and w is a weight vector produced by some training algorithm.

This classifier model can easily be generalized to the non-atomic case. We then assume that each role r can be decomposed using a decomposition function D, which returns a set of labels. We now apply the feature function to each sub-label l instead of the main label r.

$$r^* = \arg\max_{r \in F} \sum_{l \in D(r)} w \cdot \Phi(a, l)$$

Non-atomic classification has been described in a number of publications. It is fairly common in text categorization, where *hierarchical* classification is probably the most common type. One of the most similar to ours is the action classifier by Roth and Tu (2009), which handled a large label set by decomposing the labels into meaningful parts.

3.3 Generalization Methods

We investigated several ways of analyzing the labels, and most of them were based on the properties of the frames, defined in the FrameNet ontology. The Swedish FrameNet currently does not define such properties, but since the frames and frame elements are for the most part based on their English counterparts, we used the English ontology. In case of mismatch, we just left the label in its original state.

The first method we tried was based on frame-to-frame relations. We used the following relations:

INHERITANCE: specific to general, e.g. COMMUNICATION_NOISE to COMMUNICATION.

SUBFRAME: from component to complex, e.g. SETTING_OUT to TRAVEL.

CAUSATIVE-OF: causative to inchoative, e.g. CAUSE_TEMPERATURE_CHANGE to INCH._CHANGE_OF_TEMP..

INCHOATIVE-OF: inchoative to stative, e.g. INCH._CHANGE_OF_TEMP. to TEMPERATURE.

USING: child to parent, e.g. COMMUNICATION_NOISE to MAKE_NOISE.

PERSPECTIVE-ON: perspectivized to neutral, e.g. RIDE_VEHICLE to USE_VEHICLE.

To analyze a label in terms of frame-to-frame relations, we applied the transitive closure of each relation and returned the resulting set. For instance, when applying the Inheritance relation to the INGESTION:INGESTOR label, we get the following set: { INGESTION:INGESTOR, INGEST_SUBSTANCE:INGESTOR, MANIPULATION:AGENT, INTENT._AFFECT:AGENT, INTENT._ACT:AGENT, TRANS._ACTION:AGENT }.

The second method was based on the *semantic type* of the semantic role. For instance, the INGESTION:INGESTOR role needs to be filled by an entity of the semantic type SENTIENT. The decomposition of this role then simply becomes { INGESTION:INGESTOR, SENTIENT }.

The third method was based on the simple notion *label generalization*: if two semantic roles in two different frames have the same name, then we use the same label. For instance, we change the INGESTION:INGESTOR and INGEST_SUBSTANCE:INGESTOR to INGESTOR. We normalized the spelling, punctuation, and capitalization of the labels before generalizing.

4 Experiments

We evaluated the classifier on the example sentences in the Swedish FrameNet. The frame and the argument were given to the classifier, which then had to predict the semantic role. We evaluated in two different ways: *In-frame* evaluation, where a 5-fold cross-validation was carried out over the set of sentences, and *Out-frame* evaluation, where the cross-validation was done over the set of frames. The out-frame setting simulates the situation where a new frame has been defined, but no training data have been annotated. Without any sort of cross-frame generalization, the classification in the out-frame setting becomes a random baseline.

Table 2 shows the results of using the frame-to-frame relations for analyzing the semantic role labels. We see that decomposition based on Inheritance is by far the most effective of these, although the highest performance is obtained when combining all types of relation-based decompositions.

Classifier	In-frame	Out-frame
Baseline	54.4	7.2
Inheritance	58.7	28.1
Using	55.8	20.5
Subframe	54.8	11.5
Causative-of	54.5	9.7
Perspective-on	54.5	8.1
Inchoative-of	54.4	8.0
All except Inheritance	56.0	24.0
All relations	59.6	36.9

Table 2: Classification results with generalization based on frame-to-frame relations.

The effect of analyzing labels in terms of semantic type is similar. The in-frame performance is higher than that of relation-based decomposition, while the out-frame performance is a bit lower. The two generalization methods seem to complement each other, since we get a higher performance by combining them. Table 3 shows the results.

Classifier	In-frame	Out-frame
Semantic type	61.7	31.7
Semantic type + relations	63.5	42.6

Table 3: Adding semantic type generalization.

Finally, Table 4 shows the effect of using label generalization. This is by far the most effective method. However, we get even higher performance by combining it with the other two methods.

Classifier	In-frame	Out-frame
Label generalization	65.9	51.5
LG + ST + relations	66.5	53.4

Table 4: Results with label generalization.

5 Discussion

When developing NLP systems for a low-resource language, it is crucial to make effective use of the available data. In the case of FrameNet semantic role classification, one way to improve the use of the data is to generalize the roles across the frames. This also makes sense from a theoretical point of view, since predicting multiple labels allows the machine learner to learn general facts as well as specifics.

This work builds on previous work in multi-label classification. For the task of FrameNet semantic role classification, the work most closely related to ours is that by Matsubayashi et al. (2009), which defined a classifier making use of *role groups*; the effect of the role groups turns out to be similar to our non-atomic classification approach.

Our experiments showed very significant error reductions. This was especially notable in the case of out-frame evaluation, which is to be expected since the baseline in this case was a random selection. The best classifier used all three types of label decomposition, and achieved a 26% in-frame and a 50% out-frame error reduction.

Acknowledgements

The research presented here was supported by the Swedish Research Council (the project *Swedish Framenet++*, VR dnr 2010-6013) and by the University of Gothenburg through its support of the Centre for Language Technology and Språkbanken (the Swedish Language Bank).

References

Collin F. Baker, Charles J. Fillmore, and John B. Lowe. 1998. The Berkeley FrameNet project. In *Proceedings of the 36th Annual Meeting of the Association for Computational Linguistics and 17th International Conference on Computational Linguistics*, pages 86–90, Montréal, Canada.

Lars Borin and Markus Forsberg. 2009. All in the family: A comparison of SALDO and WordNet. In *Proceedings of the Nodalida 2009 Workshop on WordNets and other Lexical Semantic Resources – between Lexical Semantics, Lexicography, Terminology and Formal Ontologies*, Odense, Denmark.

Lars Borin, Dana Dannélls, Markus Forsberg, Maria Toporowska Gronostaj, and Dimitrios Kokkinakis. 2010. The past meets the present in the Swedish FrameNet++. In *Proceedings of EURALEX*.

Peter F. Brown, Peter V. deSouza, Robert L. Mercer, Vincent J. Della Pietra, and Jenifer C. Lai. 1992. Class-based n-gram models of natural language. *Computational Linguistics*, 18(4):467–479.

Koby Crammer, Ofer Dekel, Joseph Keshet, Shai Shalev-Schwartz, and Yoram Singer. 2006. Online passive-aggressive algorithms. *Journal of Machine Learning Research*, 2006(7):551–585.

Dipanjan Das, Nathan Schneider, Desai Chen, and Noah A. Smith. 2010. Probabilistic frame-semantic parsing. In *Human Language Technologies: The 2010 Annual Conference of the North American Chapter of the Association for Computational Linguistics*, pages 948–956, Los Angeles, United States.

David R. Dowty. 1991. Thematic proto-roles and argument selections. *Language*, 67(3):574–619.

Charles Fillmore, Christopher Johnson, and Miriam Petruck. 2003. Background to FrameNet. *International Journal of Lexicography*, 16(3):235–250.

Karin Friberg Heppin and Maria Toporowska Gronostaj. 2012. The rocky road towards a Swedish FrameNet. In *Proceedings of LREC-2012 (to appear)*.

Daniel Gildea and Daniel Jurafsky. 2002. Automatic labeling of semantic roles. *Computational Linguistics*, 28(3):245–288.

Richard Johansson and Pierre Nugues. 2007. Semantic structure extraction using nonprojective dependency trees. In *Proceedings of SemEval-2007*, pages 227–230, Prague, Czech Republic, June 23-24.

Richard Johansson and Pierre Nugues. 2008a. Dependency-based syntactic–semantic analysis with PropBank and NomBank. In *Proceedings of the CoNLL Shared Task*, pages 183–187, Manchester, United Kingdom.

Richard Johansson and Pierre Nugues. 2008b. The effect of syntactic representation on semantic role labeling. In *Proceedings of the 22nd International Conference on Computational Linguistics (Coling 2008)*, pages 393–400, Manchester, United Kingdom.

Lluís Màrquez, Xavier Carreras, Ken Litkowski, and Suzanne Stevenson. 2008. Semantic role labeling: An introduction to the special issue. *Computational Linguistics*, 34(2):145–159.

Yuichiroh Matsubayashi, Naoaki Okazaki, and Jun'ichi Tsujii. 2009. A comparative study on generalization of semantic roles in FrameNet. In *Proceedings of the Joint Conference of the 47th Annual Meeting of the ACL and the 4th International Joint Conference on Natural Language Processing of the AFNLP*, pages 19–27, Suntec, Singapore.

Jens Nilsson, Johan Hall, and Joakim Nivre. 2005. MAMBA meets TIGER: Reconstructing a Swedish treebank from antiquity. In *Proceedings of NODALIDA Special Session on Treebanks*.

Dan Roth and Yuancheng Tu. 2009. Aspect guided text categorization with unobserved labels. In *Proceedings of the IEEE Conference on Data Mining*, Miami, United States.

Combining resources for MWE-token classification

Richard Fothergill and Timothy Baldwin
Department of Computing and Information Systems
The University of Melbourne
VIC 3010 Australia
r.fothergill@student.unimelb.edu.au, tb@ldwin.net

Abstract

We study the task of automatically disambiguating word combinations such as *jump the gun* which are ambiguous between a literal and MWE interpretation, focusing on the utility of type-level features from an MWE lexicon for the disambiguation task. To this end we combine gold-standard idiomaticity of tokens in the *OpenMWE* corpus with MWE-type-level information drawn from the recently-published *JDMWE* lexicon. We find that constituent modifiability in an MWE-type is more predictive of the idiomaticity of its tokens than other constituent characteristics such as semantic class or part of speech.

1 Introduction

A **multiword expression (MWE)** is a phrase or sequence of words which exhibits idiosyncratic behaviour (Sag et al., 2002; Baldwin and Kim, 2009). The nature of this idiosyncracy may be purely distributional — such as *hot and cold* being more common than *cold and hot* — but in this paper we study MWEs with idiosyncratic semantics. Specifically we are concerned with expressions such as *jump the gun* which are ambiguous between a literal interpretation of "to leap over a firearm", and an idiomatic interpretation of "to act prematurely".

While MWEs are increasingly entering the mainstream of NLP, the accurate identification of MWEs remains elusive for current methods, particularly in the absence of MWE type-specialised training data. This paper builds on the work of Hashimoto et al. (2006) and Fothergill and Baldwin (2011) in exploring whether type-level MWE properties sourced from an idiom dictionary can boost the accuracy of crosstype MWE-token classification. That is, we attempt to determine whether token occurrences of ambiguous expressions such as *Kim jumped the gun on this issue* are idiomatic or literal, based on: (a) annotated instances for MWEs other than *jump the gun* (e.g. we may only have token-level annotations for *kick the bucket* and *throw in the towel*), and (b) dictionary-based information on the syntactic properties of the idiom in question.

We find that constituent modifiability judgments extracted from the idiom dictionary are more predictive of the idiomaticity of tokens than other features of the idiom's constituents such as part of speech or lexeme. However, violations of the dictionary's modifiability rules have variable utility for machine learning classification, being suggestive of the literal class but not definitive. Finally, we present novel results illuminating the effectiveness of contextual semantic vectors at MWE-token classification.

2 Related Work

The *OpenMWE* corpus (Hashimoto and Kawahara, 2009) is a gold-standard corpus of over $100,000$ Japanese MWE-tokens covering 146 types. It is the largest resource we are aware of which has hand-annotated instances of MWEs which are ambiguous between a literal and idiomatic interpretation, and has been used by Hashimoto and Kawahara (2009) and Fothergill and Baldwin (2011) for supervised classification of MWE-tokens using features capturing lexico-syntactic variation and traditional semantic features borrowed from **word sense disambiguation (WSD)**. Similar work in other languages has been performed by Li and Sporleder (2010) and Diab and Bhutada (2009). We build on this work in exploring the use of MWE-type-level features drawn from an idiom dictionary for MWE identification.

Hashimoto and Kawahara (2009) developed a variety of features capturing lexico-syntactic variation but only one — a Boolean feature for "internal modification", which fired only when a non-constituent word appeared between constituent words in an MWE-token — had an appreciable impact on classification. However, they found that this effect was far overshadowed by semantic context features inspired by WSD. That is, treating each MWE-type as a word with two senses and performing sense disambiguation was far more successful than any features based on lexico-syntactic characteristics of idioms. Intuitively, we would expect that if we had access to a rich inventory of expression-specific type-level features encoding the ability of the expression to participate in different syntactic alternations, we should be better equipped to disambiguate token occurrences of that expression. Indeed, the work of Fazly et al. (2009) would appear to support this hypothesis, in that the authors used unsupervised methods to learn type-level preferences for a range of MWE types, and demonstrated that these could be successfully applied to a token-level disambiguation task.

Hashimoto and Kawahara (2009) trained individual classifiers for each MWE-type in their corpus and tested them only on instances of the type they were trained on. In contrast to this **type-specialised classification**, Fothergill and Baldwin (2011) trained classifiers on a subset of MWE-types and tested on instances of the remaining held-out MWE-types. The motivation for this **crosstype classification** was to test the use of data from the *OpenMWE* corpus for MWE-token classification of MWE-types with no gold-standard data available (which are by far the majority). Fothergill and Baldwin (2011) introduced features for crosstype classification which captured features of the MWE-type, reasoning that similar expressions would have similar propensity for idiomaticity. We introduce new MWE-type features expressing the modifiability of constituents based on information extracted from an MWE dictionary with wide coverage.

Fothergill and Baldwin (2011) expected that WSD features — however successful at type specialised classification — would lose their advantage in crosstype classification because of the lack of a common semantics between MWE-types. However, this turned out not to be the case, with by far the most successful results arising again from use of WSD features. This surprising result raises the possibility of distributional similarity between the contexts of idiomatic MWE-tokens of different MWE-types, however the result was not explained or explored further. In this paper we offer new insights into the distributional similarity hypothesis.

The recently-published *JDMWE* (*Japanese Dictionary of Multiword Expressions*) encodes type-level information on thousands of Japanese MWEs (Shudo et al., 2011). A subset of the dictionary has been released, and overlaps to some extent with the MWE-types in the *OpenMWE* corpus. *JDMWE* encodes information about lexico-syntactic variations allowed by each MWE-type it contains. For example, the expression *hana wo motaseru* — literally "to have [someone] hold flowers" but figuratively "to let [someone] take the credit" — has the syntactic form entry *[N wo] *V30*. The asterix indicates modifiability, telling us that the head [V]erb *motaseru* "cause to hold" allows modification by non-constituent dependents – such as adverbs – but the dependent [N]oun *hana* "flowers" does not.

3 Features for classification

We introduce features based on the lexico-syntactic flexibility constraints encoded in *JDMWE* and compare them with similar features from related work.

3.1 Type-level features

We extracted the modifiability flags from the syntactic field of entries in *JDMWE* and generated a feature for each modifiable constituent, identified by its position in the type's parse tree. The motivation for this is to allow machine learning algorithms to capture any similarities in idiomaticity between MWE-types with similar modifiability.

Fothergill and Baldwin (2011) also aimed to exploit crosstype similarity with their *type* features. They extracted lexical features (part-of-speech, lemma and semantic category) of the type headword and other constituents. We use these features as point of contrast.

3.2 Token features

An **internal modifier** is a dependent of a constituent which is not a constituent itself but divides an MWE-token into two parts, such as the word *seven* in *kick* *seven buckets*. Features in related work have flagged the presence of any internal modifier unconditionally (Hashimoto and Kawahara, 2009; Fothergill and Baldwin, 2011). We introduce a refined feature which fires only when a MWE-token has an internal modifier which violates the constituent modification constraints encoded in *JDMWE*.

JDMWE modifiability constraints could also be construed to proscribe *external* modifiers. Sentential subjects and other external arguments of the head verb are too common to be sensibly proscribed but we did include a feature flagging proscribed external modification of leaf constituents such as *water* in *kick the bucket of water*. This feature effectively refines the **adnominal modification** feature of Hashimoto and Kawahara (2009) which indiscriminately flags external modifications on a leaf noun.

We include in our analysis a contrast of these features to token-based features in related work. The closest related features are those focussed on the MWE characteristic of lexico-syntactic fixedness termed **idiom** features by Hashimoto and Kawahara (2009) and Fothergill and Baldwin (2011):

- the flag for internal modification;
- the flag for adnominal modification;
- lexical features such as part-of-speech, lemma and semantic category extracted from an internal or adnominal modifier;
- inflections of the head constituent.

Additionally, we include WSD-inspired features used by Hashimoto and Kawahara (2009) and Fothergill and Baldwin (2011). These are all lexical features extracted from context, including part-of-speech, lemma and semantic category of words in the paragraph, local and syntactic contexts of the MWE-token. These features set the high water mark for classification accuracy in both type-specialised and crosstype classification scenarios.

3.3 Example JDMWE feature extraction

The following is a short literal token of the example type from Section 2, with numbered constituents: *kireina hanawo(2) motaseta(1)* ("[He] had [me] hold the pretty flowers"). The *JDMWE* features emitted for this token are the type feature *modifiable(1)* and the token feature *proscribed_premodifier(2)*.

4 Results

We worked with a subset of the *OpenMWE* corpus comprising those types having: (a) an entry in the released subset of the *JDMWE*, and (b) both literal and idiomatic classes represented by at least 50 MWE-tokens each in the corpus. This leaves only 27 MWE-types and 23,392 MWE-tokens and means that our results are not directly comparable to those of Hashimoto and Kawahara (2009) and Fothergill and Baldwin (2011). The release of the full *JDMWE* should enable more comparable results.

We constructed a crosstype classification task by ten-fold cross validation of the MWE-types in the *OpenMWE* subset, with micro-averaged results. Training sets were the union of all MWE-tokens of MWE-types in a partition. The majority class was the idiomatic sense and provided a baseline accuracy of 0.594. *Support Vector Machine* models with linear kernels were trained on various feature combinations using the *libSVM* package.

Our *JDMWE* type-level features performed comparatively well at the crosstype task, with an accuracy of 0.647, at 5.3 percentage points above the baseline. This is a marked improvement on the lexical type-level features from related work, which achieved an accuracy of 4.0 points above baseline. As has been observed in related work, the accuracy gained by using type-level features is much smaller than the token-level WSD features. However, the relative performance of the *JDMWE* type features to the lexical type features is sustained in combination with other feature types, as shown in Figure 1a.

Our *JDMWE* token-level features on the other hand perform quite badly at crosstype classification. When measured against the baseline or used to augment other token features, they degraded or only marginally improved performance. The fact that using these features resulted in worse-than-baseline performance suggests that the constituent modifiability features extracted from *JDMWE* may not be strict constraints as they are construed.

To better examine the quality of the *JDMWE* constituent modifiability constraint features, we constructed a heuristic classifier. The classifier applies the idiomatic class by default, but the literal class to any MWE-token which violates the *JDMWE* constituent modifiability constraints. This classifier's

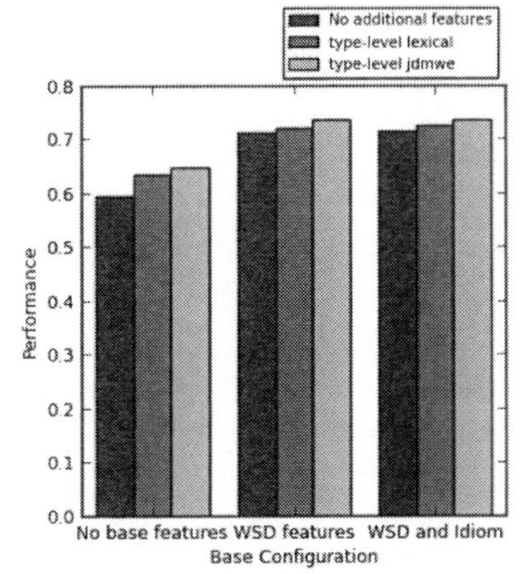

(a) Accuracy using *JDMWE* type-level features and lexical type-level features in combination with various token-level features

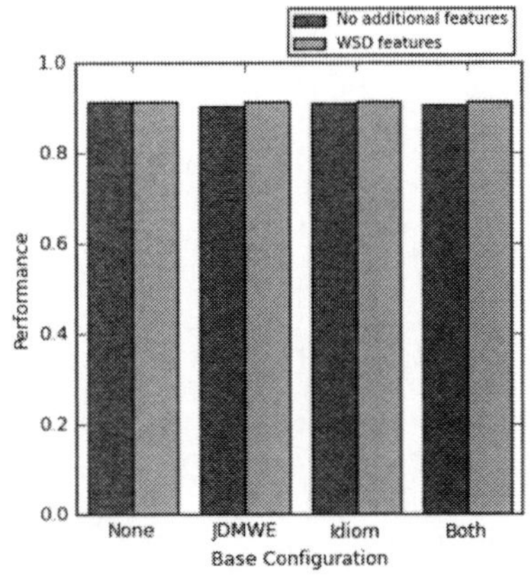

(b) Recall for idiomatic instances for various feature combinations with and without WSD context features, in a type-specialised classification setting

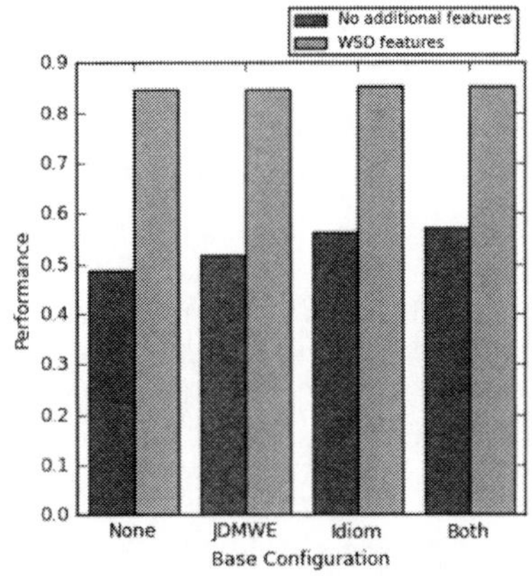

(c) Recall for literal instances for various feature combinations with and without WSD context features, in a type-specialised classification setting.

Figure 1: Results

precision on the literal class was 0.624, meaning that fully 0.376 of modifiability constraint violations in the corpus occured for idiomatic tokens.

However, the classifier was correct in its literal class labels more than half the time so it achieved a better accuracy than the majority class classifer, at 0.612. As such, the heuristic classifier comfortably outperformed the *Support Vector Machine* classifier based on the same features. This shows that our poor results with regards to the *JDMWE* constraint violation features are due mainly to failures of the machine learning model to take advantage of them.

As to the strength of the constraints encoded in *JDMWE*, we found that 4.4% of all idiomatic tokens in the corpus violated constituent modification constraints, and 10.8% of literal tokens. Thus the constraints seem sound but not as rigid as presented by the *JDMWE* developers.

Figure 1a shows that even with our improvements to type-level features, the finding of Fothergill and Baldwin (2011) that WSD context features perform best at crosstype classification still holds. We cannot fully account for this, but one observation regarding the results of our type-specialised evaluation may have bearing on the crosstype scenario.

For our type-specialised classification task we performed cross-validation for each MWE-type in isolation, aggregating final results. Some types had a literal majority class, so the baseline accuracy was 0.741. Figure 1b shows that type-specialised classification performance is basically constant when restricting analysis to only the idiomatic test instances. The huge performance boost produced through the use of WSD features occurs only on literal instances (see Figure 1c). That is, our type-specialised classifiers are capturing distributional similarity of context for the literal instances of a MWE-type but not for the idiomatic instances. Since the contexts of idiomatic instances of the same MWE-type do not exhibit a usable distributional similarity, it is unlikely that crosstype similarities between *idiomatic* MWE-token contexts can explain the efficacy of WSD features for crosstype classification.

5 Conclusion

Using a MWE dictionary as input to a supervised crosstype MWE-token classification task we have shown that the constituents' modifiability characteristics tell more about idiomaticity than their lexical characteristics. We found that the constituent modification constraints in *JDMWE* are not hard-and-fast rules but do show up statistically in the *OpenMWE* corpus. Finally, we found that distributional similarity of the contexts of idiomatic MWE-tokens is unlikely to be the source of the success of WSD features on MWE-token classification accuracy.

References

Timothy Baldwin and Su Nam Kim. 2009. Multiword expressions. In Nitin Indurkhya and Fred J. Damerau, editors, *Handbook of Natural Language Processing*, pages 267–292. CRC Press, Boca Raton, USA, 2nd edition.

Mona T. Diab and Pravin Bhutada. 2009. Verb noun construction MWE token supervised classification. In *MWE '09: Proceedings of the Workshop on Multiword Expressions*, pages 17–22, Singapore.

Afsaneh Fazly, Paul Cook, and Suzanne Stevenson. 2009. Unsupervised type and token identification of idiomatic expressions. *Computational Linguistics*, 35(1):61–103.

Richard Fothergill and Timothy Baldwin. 2011. Fleshing it out: A supervised approach to MWE-token and MWE-type classification. In *Proceedings of 5th International Joint Conference on Natural Language Processing*, Chiang Mai, Thailand.

Chikara Hashimoto and Daisuke Kawahara. 2009. Compilation of an idiom example database for supervised idiom identification. *Language Resources and Evaluation*, 43:355–384.

Chikara Hashimoto, Satoshi Sato, and Takehito Utsuro. 2006. Detecting Japanese idioms with a linguistically rich dictionary. *Language Resources and Evaluation*, 40:243–252.

Linlin Li and Caroline Sporleder. 2010. Linguistic cues for distinguishing literal and non-literal usages. In *Coling 2010: Posters*, pages 683–691, Beijing, China.

Ivan Sag, Timothy Baldwin, Francis Bond, Ann Copestake, and Dan Flickinger. 2002. Multiword expressions: A pain in the neck for NLP. In *Computational Linguistics and Intelligent Text Processing*, pages 189–206, Mexico City, Mexico.

Kosho Shudo, Akira Kurahone, and Toshifumi Tanabe. 2011. A comprehensive dictionary of multiword expressions. In *Proceedings of the 49th Annual Meeting of the Association for Computational Linguistics: Human Language Technologies*, Portland, USA.

Annotating Preferences in Negotiation Dialogues

Anaïs Cadilhac, Nicholas Asher and Farah Benamara
IRIT, CNRS and University of Toulouse
118, route de Narbonne
31062 Toulouse, France
{cadilhac, asher, benamara}@irit.fr

Abstract

Modeling user preferences is crucial in many real-life problems, ranging from individual and collective decision-making to strategic interactions between agents and game theory. Since agents do not come with their preferences transparently given in advance, we have only two means to determine what they are if we wish to exploit them in reasoning: we can infer them from what an agent says or from his nonlinguistic actions. In this paper, we analyze how to infer preferences from dialogue moves in actual conversations that involve bargaining or negotiation. To this end, we propose a new annotation scheme to study how preferences are linguistically expressed in two different corpus genres. This paper describes the annotation methodology and details the inter-annotator agreement study on each corpus genre. Our results show that preferences can be easily annotated by humans.

1 Introduction

Modeling user preferences is crucial in many real-life problems, ranging from individual and collective decision-making (Arora and Allenby, 1999) to strategic interactions between agents (Brainov, 2000) and game theory (Hausman, 2000). A web-based recommender system can, for example, help a user to identify (among an optimal ranking) the product item that best fits his preferences (Burke, 2000). Modeling preferences can also help to find some compromise or consensus between two or more agents having different goals during a negotiation (Meyer and Foo, 2004).

Working with preferences involves three subtasks (Brafman and Domshlak, 2009): *preference acquisition*, which extracts preferences from users, *preference modeling* where a model of users' preferences is built using a preference representation language and *preference reasoning* which aims at computing the set of optimal outcomes. We focus in this paper on the first task.

Handling preferences is not easy. First, specifying an ordering over acceptable outcomes is not trivial especially when multiple aspects of an outcome matter. For instance, choosing a new camera to buy may depend on several criteria (e.g. battery life, weight, etc.), hence, ordering even two outcomes (cameras) can be cognitively difficult because of the need to consider trade-offs and dependencies between the criteria. Second, users often lack complete information about preferences initially. They build a partial description of agents' preferences that typically changes over time. Indeed, users often learn about the domain, each others' preferences and even their own preferences during a decision-making process. Since agents don't come with their preferences transparently given in advance, we have only two means to determine what they are if we wish to exploit them in reasoning: we can infer them from what an agent says or from his nonlinguistic actions. In this paper, we analyze how to infer preferences from dialogue moves in actual conversations that involve bargaining or negotiation.

Within the Artificial Intelligence community, preference acquisition from nonlinguistic actions has been performed using a variety of specific tasks, including preference learning (Fürnkranz and

Hüllermeier, 2011) and preference elicitation methods (Chen and Pu, 2004) (such as query learning (Blum et al., 2004), collaborative filtering (Su and Khoshgoftaar, 2009) and qualitative graphical representation of preferences (Boutilier et al., 1997)). However, these tasks don't occur in actual conversations about negotiation. We are interested in how agents learn about preferences from actual conversational turns in real dialogue (Edwards and Barron, 1994), using NLP techniques.

To this end, we propose a new annotation scheme to study how preferences are linguistically expressed in dialogues. The annotation study is performed on two different corpus genres: the Verbmobil corpus (Wahlster, 2000) and a booking corpus, built by ourselves. This paper describes the annotation methodology and details the inter-annotator agreement study on each corpus genre. Our results show that preferences can be easily annotated by humans.

2 Background

2.1 What are preferences?

A preference is commonly understood as an ordering by an agent over outcomes, which are understood as actions that the agent can perform or goal states that are the direct result of an action of the agent. For instance, an agent's preferences may be defined over actions like *buy a new car* or by its end result like *have a new car*. The outcomes over which a preference is defined will depend on the domain or task.

Among these outcomes, some are acceptable for the agent, i.e. the agent is ready to act in such a way as to realize them, and some outcomes are not. Among the acceptable outcomes, the agent will typically prefer some to others. Our aim is not to determine the most preferred outcome of an agent but follows rather the evolution of their commitments to certain preferences as the dialogue proceeds. To give an example, if an agent proposes to meet on a certain day X and at a certain time Y, we learn that among the agent's acceptable outcomes is a meeting on X at Y, even if this is not his most preferred outcome. We are interested in an ordinal definition of preferences, which consists in imposing a ranking over all (relevant) possible outcomes and not a cardinal definition which is based on numerical values that allow comparisons.

More formally, let Ω be a set of possible outcomes. A *preference relation*, written $\succeq$, is a reflexive and transitive binary relation over elements of Ω. The preference orderings are not necessarily complete, since some candidates may not be comparable by a given agent. Given the two outcomes o_1 and o_2, $o_1 \succeq o_2$ means that outcome o_1 is equally or more preferred to the decision maker than o_2. *Strict preference* $o_1 \succ o_2$ holds iff $o_1 \succeq o_2$ and not $o_2 \succeq o_1$. The associated *indifference relation* is $o_1 \sim o_2$ if $o_1 \succeq o_2$ and $o_2 \succeq o_1$.

2.2 Preferences vs. opinions

It is important to distinguish preferences from opinions. While opinions are defined as a point of view, a belief, a sentiment or a judgment that *an agent may have about an object or a person*, preferences, as we have defined them, involve an ordering on behalf of an agent and thus are *relational and comparative*. Hence, opinions concern absolute judgments towards objects or persons (positive, negative or neutral), while preferences concern relative judgments towards actions (preferring them or not over others). The following examples illustrate this:

(a) The movie is not bad.

(b) The scenario of the first season is better than the second one.

(c) I would like to go to the cinema. Let's go and see *Madagascar 2*.

(a) expresses a direct positive opinion towards the movie but we do not know if this movie is the most preferred. (b) expresses a comparative opinion between two movies with respect to their shared features (scenarios) (Ganapathibhotla and Liu, 2008). If actions involving these movies (e.g. seeing them) are clear in the context, such a comparative opinion will imply a preference, ordering the first season scenario over the second. Finally, (c) expresses two preferences, one depending on the other. The first is that the speaker prefers to go to the cinema over other alternative actions; the second is, given that preference, that he wants to see Madagascar 2 over other possible movies.

Reasoning about preferences is also distinct from reasoning about opinions. An agent's preferences determine an order over outcomes that predicts how the agent, if he is rational, will act. This is not true for opinions. Opinions have at best an indirect link to action: I may hate what I'm doing, but do it anyway because I prefer that outcome to any of the alternatives.

3 Data

Our data come from two corpora: one already-existing, `Verbmobil` (C_V), and one that we created, `Booking` (C_B).

The first corpus is composed of 35 dialogues randomly chosen from the existing corpus Verbmobil (Wahlster, 2000), where two agents discuss on when and where to set up a meeting. Here is a typical fragment:

π_1 A: Shall we meet sometime in the next week?
π_2 A: What days are good for you?
π_3 B: I have some free time on almost every day except Fridays.
π_4 B: Fridays are bad.
π_5 B: In fact, I'm busy on Thursday too.
π_6 A: Next week I am out of town Tuesday, Wednesday and Thursday.
π_7 A: So perhaps Monday?

The second corpus was built from various English language learning resources, available on the Web (e.g., `www.bbc.co.uk/worldservice/learningenglish`). It contains 21 randomly selected dialogues, in which one agent (the customer) calls a service to book a room, a flight, a taxi, etc. Here is a typical fragment:

π_1 A: Northwind Airways, good morning. May I help you?
π_2 B: Yes, do you have any flights to Sydney next Tuesday?
π_3 A: Yes, there's a flight at 16:45 and one at 18:00.
π_4 A: Economy, business class or first class ticket?
π_5 B: Economy, please.

Our approach to preference acquisition exploits discourse structure and aims to study the impact of discourse for extracting and reasoning on preferences. Cadilhac et al. (2011) show how to compute automatically preference representations for a whole stretch of dialogue from the preference representations for elementary discourse units. Our annotation here concentrates on the commitments to preferences expressed in elementary discourse units or EDUs. We analyze how the outcomes and the dependencies between them are linguistically expressed by performing, on each corpus, a two-level annotation. First, we perform a segmentation of the dialogue into EDUs. Second, we annotate preferences expressed by the EDUs.

The examples above show the effects of segmentation. Each EDU is associated with a label π_i. For `Verbmobil`, we rely on the already available discourse annotation of Baldridge and Lascarides (2005). For `Booking`, the segmentation was made by consensus.

We detail, in the next section, our preference annotation scheme.

4 Preference annotation scheme

To analyze how preferences are linguistically expressed in each EDU, we must: (1) identify the set Ω of outcomes, on which the agent's preferences are expressed, and (2) identify the dependencies between the elements of Ω by using a set of specific operators, i.e. identifying the agent's preferences on the stated outcomes. Consider the segment "Let's meet Thursday or Friday". We have $\Omega = \{$*meet Thursday*, *meet Friday*$\}$ where outcomes are linked by a disjunction that means the agent is ready to act for one of these outcomes, preferring them equally.

Within an EDU, preferences can be expressed in different ways. They can be atomic preference statements or complex preference statements.

4.1 Atomic preferences

Atomic preference statements are of the form "I prefer X", "Let's X", or "We need X", where X describes an outcome. X may be a definite noun phrase ("Monday", "next week", "almost every day"), a prepositional phrase ("at my office") or a verb phrase ("to meet"). They can be expressed within comparatives and/or superlatives ("a cheaper room" or "the cheapest flight").

Preferences can also be expressed in an indirect way using questions. Although not all questions entail that their author commits to a preference, in many cases they do. That is, if A asks "can we meet next week?" he implicates a preference for meeting. For negative and wh-interrogatives, the implication is even stronger. Expressions of sentiment or politeness can also be used to indirectly introduce preferences. In `Booking`, the segment "economy please" indicates the agent's preference to be in an economy class.

EDUs can also express preferences via free-choice modalities; "I am free on Thursday" or "I can meet on Thursday" tells us that Thursday is a possible day to meet, it is an acceptable outcome.

A negative preference expresses an unacceptable outcome, i.e. what the agent does not prefer. Negative preference can be expressed explicitly with negation words ("I don't want to meet on Friday") or inferred from the context ("I am busy on Monday").

While the logical form of an atomic preference statement is something of the form $Pref(X)$, we abbreviate this in the annotation language, using just the outcome expression X to denote that the agent prefers X to the alternatives, i.e. $X \succ \overline{X}$. If X is an unacceptable outcome, we use the non-boolean operator *not* to denote that the agent prefers *not X* to other alternatives, i.e. $\overline{X} \succ X$. In our `Verbmobil` annotation, X is typically an NP denoting a time or place; X as an outcome is thus shorthand for *meet on* X or *meet at* X. For `Booking`, X is short for *reserve* or *book* X.

4.2 Complex preferences

Preference statements can also be complex, expressing dependencies between outcomes. Borrowing from the language of *conditional preference networks* or CP-nets (Boutilier et al., 2004), we recognize that some preferences may depend on another action. For instance, given that I have chosen to eat fish, I will prefer to have white wine over red wine—something which we express as *eat fish* : *drink white wine* $\succ$ *drink red wine*.

Among the possible combinations, we find conjunctions, disjunctions and conditionals. We examine these conjunctive, disjunctive and conditional operations over outcomes and suppose a language with non-boolean operators &, $\bigtriangledown$ and $\mapsto$ taking outcome expressions as arguments.

With conjunctions of preferences, as in "Could I have a breakfast and a vegetarian meal?" or in "Mondays and Fridays are not good?", the agent expresses two preferences (respectively over the acceptable outcomes breakfast and vegetarian meal and the non acceptable outcomes not Mondays and not Fridays) that he wants to satisfy and he prefers to have one of them if he can not have both. Hence o_1 & o_2 means $o_1 \succ \overline{o_1}$ and $o_2 \succ \overline{o_2}$.

The semantics of a disjunctive preference is a free choice one. For example in "either Monday or Tuesday is fine for me" or in "I am free Monday and Tuesday", the agent states that either Monday or Tuesday is an acceptable outcome and he is indifferent between the choice of the outcomes. Hence $o_1 \bigtriangledown o_2$ means $o_2 : o_1 \sim \overline{o_1}, \overline{o_2} : o_1 \succ \overline{o_1}$ and $o_1 : o_2 \sim \overline{o_2}, \overline{o_1} : o_2 \succ \overline{o_2}$.

Finally, some EDUs express conditional among preferences. For example, in the sentence "What about Monday, in the afternoon?", there are two preferences: one for the day Monday, and, given the Monday preference, one for the time afternoon (of Monday), at least for one syntactic reading of the utterance. Hence $o_1 \mapsto o_2$ means $o_1 \succ \overline{o_1}$ and $o_1 : o_2 \succ \overline{o_2}$.

For each EDU, annotators identify how outcomes are expressed and then indicate if the outcomes are acceptable, or not, using the operator *not* and how the preferences on these outcomes are linked using the operators &, $\bigtriangledown$ and $\mapsto$.

4.3 Example

We give below an example of how some EDUs are annotated. <*o*>_*i* indicates that o is the outcome number i in the EDU, the symbol // is used to separate the two annotation levels and brackets indicate how outcomes are attached.

π_1 : <Tuesday the sixteenth>_1 I got class <from nine to twelve>_2? // 1 $\mapsto$ not 2

π_2 : What about <Friday afternoon>_1, <at two thirty>_2 or <three>_3, // 1 $\mapsto$ (2 $\bigtriangledown$ 3)

π_3 : <The room with balcony>_1 should be equipped <with a queen size bed>_2, <the other one>_3 <with twin beds>_4, please. // (1 $\mapsto$ 2) & (3 $\mapsto$ 4)

In π_1, the annotation tells us that we have two outcomes and that the agent prefers outcome 1 over any other alternatives and given that, he does not prefer outcome 2. In π_2, the annotation tells us that the agent prefers to have one of outcome 2 and outcome 3 satisfied given that he prefers outcome 1. In this example, the free choice between outcome 2 and outcome 3 is lexicalized by the coordinating conjunction "or". On the contrary, π_3 is a more complex example where there is no discursive marker to find that the preference operator between the couples of outcomes 1 and 2 on one hand, and 3 and 4 on the other hand, is the conjunctive operator &.

5 Inter-annotator agreements

Our two corpora (`Verbmobil` and `Booking`) were annotated by two annotators using the previously described annotation scheme. We performed an intermediate analysis of agreement and disagreement between the two annotators on two `Verbmobil` dialogues. Annotators were thus trained only for `Verbmobil`. The aim is to study to what extent our annotation scheme is genre dependent. The training allowed each annotator to understand the reason of some annotation choices. After this step, the dialogues of our corpora have been annotated separately, discarding those two dialogues. Table 1 presents some statistics about the annotated data in the gold standard.

	C_V	C_B
No. of dialogues	35	21
No. of outcomes	1081	275
No. of EDUs with outcomes	776	182
% with 1 outcome	71%	70%
% with 2 outcomes	22%	19%
% with 3 or more outcomes	8%	11%
No. of unacceptable outcomes (not)	266	9
No. of conjunctions (&)	56	31
No. of disjunctions ($\bigtriangledown$)	75	29
No. of conditionals ($\mapsto$)	184	37

Table 1: Statistics for the two corpora.

We compute four inter-annotator agreements: on outcome identification, on outcome acceptance, on outcome attachment and finally on operator identification. Table 2 summarizes our results.

5.1 Agreements on outcome identification

Two inter-annotator agreements were computed using Cohen's Kappa. One based on an *exact* matching between two outcome annotations (i.e. their corresponding text spans), and the other based on a *lenient* match between annotations (i.e. there is an overlap between their text spans as in "2p.m" and "around 2p.m"). This approach is similar to the one used by Wiebe, Wilson and Cardie (2005) to compute agreement when annotating opinions in news corpora. We obtained an exact agreement of 0.66 and a lenient agreement of 0.85 for both corpus genres.

	C_V	C_B
Outcome identification (Kappa)	exact : 0.66 lenient : 0.85	
Outcome acceptance (Kappa)	0.90	0.95
Outcome attachment (F-measure)	93%	82%
Operator identification (Kappa)	0.93	0.75

Table 2: Inter-annotator agreements for the two corpora.

We made the gold standard after discussing cases of disagreement. We observed four cases. The first one concerns redundant preferences which we decided not to keep in the gold standard. In such cases, the second EDU π_2 does not introduce a new preference, neither does it correct the preferences stated in π_1; rather, the agent just wants to insist by repeating already stated preferences, as in the following example:

π_1 A: Thursday, Friday, and Saturday I am out.

π_2 A: So those days are all out for me,

The second case of disagreement comes from anaphora which are often used to introduce new, to make more precise or to accept preferences. Hence, we decided to annotate them in the gold standard. Here is an example:

π_1 A: One p.m. on the seventeenth?

π_2 B: That sounds fantastic.

The third case of disagreement concerns preference explanation. We chose not to annotate these expressions in the gold standard because they are used to explain already stated preferences. In the following example, one judge annotated "from nine to twelve" to be expressions of preferences while the other did not :

π_1 A: Monday is really not good,

π_2 A: I have got class from nine to twelve.

Finally, the last case of disagreement comes from preferences that are not directly related to the action of fixing a date to meet but to other actions, such as having lunch, choosing a place to meet, etc. Even though those preferences were often missed by annotators, we decided to keep them, when relevant.

5.2 Agreements on outcome acceptance

The aim here is to compute the agreement on the *not* operator, that is if an outcome is acceptable, as in "<Mondays>_1 are good // 1", or unacceptable, as in "<Mondays>_1 are not good // not 1". We get a Cohen's Kappa of 0.9 for `Verbmobil` and 0.95 for `Booking`. The main case of disagreement concerns anaphoric negations that are inferred from the context, as in π_2 below where annotators sometimes fail to consider "in the morning" as unacceptable outcomes:

π_1 A: Tuesday is kind of out,

π_2 A: Same reason in the morning

Same case of disagreement in this example where "Monday" is an unacceptable outcome:

π_1 well, I am, busy <in the afternoon of the twenty sixth>_1, // not 1

π_2 that is <Monday>_1 // not 1

5.3 Agreements on outcome attachment

Since this task involves structure building, we compute the agreement using the F-score measure. The agreement was computed on the previously built gold standard once annotators discussed cases of outcome identification disagreements. We compare how each outcome is attached to the others within the same EDU. This agreement concerns EDUs that contain at least three outcomes, that is 8% of EDUs from `Verbmobil` and 11% of EDUs from `Booking`. When comparing annotations for the example π_1 below, there is three errors, one for outcome 2, one for 3 and one for 4.

π_1 <for the next week>_1 the only days I have open are <Monday>_2 or <Tuesday>_3 <in the morning>_4.

- Annotation 1 : $1 \mapsto (2 \bigtriangledown (3 \mapsto 4))$
- Annotation 2 : $1 \mapsto ((2 \bigtriangledown 3) \mapsto 4)$

We obtain an agreement of 93% for `Verbmobil` and 82% for `Booking`.

5.4 Agreements on outcome dependencies

Finally, we compute the agreements for each couple of outcomes on which annotators agreed about how they are attached.

In `Verbmobil`, the most frequently used binary operator is $\mapsto$. Because the main purpose of the agents in this corpus is to schedule an appointment, the preferences expressed by the agents are mainly focused on concepts of time and there are many conditional preferences since it is common that preferences on specific concepts depend on more broad temporal concepts. For example, preferences on hours are generally conditional on preferences on days. In `Booking`, there are almost as many & as $\mapsto$ because independent and dependent preferences are more balanced in this corpus. The agents discuss preferences about various criteria that are independent. For example, to book a hotel, the agent express his preferences towards the size of the bed (single or double), the quality of the room (smoker or nonsmoker), the presence of certain conveniences (TV, bathtub), the possibility to have breakfast in his room, etc. Within an EDU, such preferences are often expressed in different sentences (compared to `Verbmobil` where segments' lengths are smaller) which lead annotators to link those preferences with the operator &. Conditionals between preferences hold when decision criteria are dependent. For example, the preference for having a vegetarian meal is conditional on the preference for having lunch. There also are conditionals between temporal concepts, for example, to choose the time of a flight.

Table 3 shows the Kappa for each operator on each corpus genre. The Cohen's Kappa, averaged over all the operators, is 0.93 for `Verbmobil` and 0.75 for `Booking`. We observe two main cases of disagreement: between $\bigtriangledown$ and &, and between & and $\mapsto$. These cases are more frequent for `Booking` mainly because annotators were not trained on this corpus. This is why the Kappa was lower than for `Verbmobil`. We discuss below the main two cases of disagreement.

Confusion between $\bigtriangledown$ and &. The same linguistic realizations do not always lead to the same operator. For instance, in "<Monday>_1 and <Wednesday>_2 are good" we have $1 \bigtriangledown 2$ whereas in "<Monday>_1 and <Wednesday>_2 are not

	C_V	C_B
&	0.90	0.66
$\triangledown$	0.97	0.89
$\mapsto$	0.92	0.71

Table 3: Agreements on binary operators.

good" or in "I would like a <single room>_1 and a <taxi>_2" we have respectively *not* 1 & *not* 2 and 1 & 2.

The coordinating conjunction "**or**" is a strong predictor for recognizing a disjunction of preferences, at least when the "or" is clearly outside of the scope of a negation[1], as in the examples below (in π_1, the negation is part of the wh-question, and not boolean over the preference):

π_1 Why don't we <meet, either Thursday the first>_1, or <Thursday the eighth>_2 // 1 $\triangledown$ 2

π_2 Would you like <a single>_1 or <a double>_2? // 1 $\triangledown$ 2

The coordinating conjunction "**and**" is also a strong indication, especially when it is used to link two acceptable outcomes that are both of a single type (e.g., day of the week, time of day, place, type of room, etc.) between which an agent wants to choose a single realization. For example, in Verbmobil, agents want to fix a single appointment so if there is a conjunction "and" between two temporal concepts of the same level, it is a disjunction of preference (see π_3 below). It is also the case in Booking when an agent wants to book a single plane flight (see π_4).

π_3 <Monday>_1 and <Tuesday>_2 are good for me // 1 $\triangledown$ 2

π_4 You could <travel at 10am.>_1, <noon>_2 and <2pm>_3 // 1 $\triangledown$ (2 $\triangledown$ 3)

The acceptability modality distributes across the conjoined NPs to deliver something like $\Diamond(\textit{meet Monday}) \wedge \Diamond(\textit{meet Tuesday})$ in modal logic (clearly acceptability is an existential rather than universal modality), and as is known from studies of free choice modality (Schulz, 2007), such a conjunction translates to $\Diamond(\textit{meet Monday} \vee \textit{meet Tuesday})$, which expresses our free choice disjunction of preferences, $o_1 \triangledown o_2$.

On the other hand, when the conjunction "and" links two outcomes referring to a single concept that are not acceptable, it gives a conjunction of preferences, as in π_5. Once again thinking in terms of modality is helpful. The "not acceptable" modality distributes across the conjunction, this gives something like $\Box\neg o_1 \wedge \Box\neg o_2$ (where $\neg$ is truth conditional negation) which is equivalent to $\Box(\neg o_1 \wedge \neg o_2)$, i.e. *not* o_1 & *not* o_2 and not equivalent to $\Box(\neg o_1 \vee \neg o_2)$, i.e. *not* $o_1 \triangledown$ *not* o_2.

The connector "and" also involves a conjunction of preferences when it links two independent outcomes that the agent wants to satisfy simultaneously. For example, in π_6, the agent wants to book two hotel rooms, and so the outcomes are independent. In π_7, the agent expresses his preferences on two different features he wants for the hotel room he is booking.

π_5 <Thursday the thirtieth>_1, and <Wednesday the twenty ninth>_2 are, booked up // not 1 & not 2

π_6 Can I have one room< with balcony>_1 and <one without balcony>_2? // 1 & 2

π_7 <Queen>_1 and <nonsmoking>_2 // 1 & 2

Confusion between & and $\mapsto$. In this case, disagreements are mainly due to the difficulty for annotators to decide if preferences are dependent, or not. For example, in "I have a meeting <starting at three>_1, but I could meet <at one o'clock>_2", one annotator put *not* 1 $\mapsto$ 2 meaning that the agent is ready to meet at one o'clock because he can not meet at three, while the other annotated *not* 1 & 2 meaning that the agent is ready to meet at one o'clock independently of what it will do at three.

Some connectors introduce contrast between the preferences expressed in a segment as "**but**", "**although**" and "**unless**". In the annotation, we can model it thanks to the operator $\mapsto$. When it is used between two conflicting values, it represents a correction. Thus, the annotation $o_1 \mapsto$ *not* o_1 means we need to replace in our model of preferences $o_1 \succ \overline{o_1}$ by $\overline{o_1} \succ o_1$. And vice versa for *not* $o_1 \mapsto o_1$.

π_8 I have class <on Monday>_1, but, <any time, after one or two>_2 I am free. // not 1 $\mapsto$ (1 $\mapsto$ 2)

[1]When there is a propositional negation over the disjunction as in "I don't want sheep or wheat", which occurs frequently in a corpus in preparation, we no longer have a disjunction of preferences.

π_9 <Friday>_1 is a little full, although there is some possibility, <before lunch>_2 // not 1 $\mapsto$ (1 $\mapsto$ 2)

π_{10} we're full <on the 22nd>_1, unless you want <a smoking room>_2 // not 1 $\mapsto$ (1 $\mapsto$ 2)

However, it is important to note that the coordinating conjunction "but" does not always introduce contrast, as in the example below, where it introduces a conjunction of preferences.

π_{11} I am busy <on Monday>_1, but <Tuesday afternoon>_2, sounds good // not 1 & 2

The subordinating conjunctions "**if**", "**because**" and "**so**" are indications for detecting conditional preferences. The preferences in the main clause depend on the preferences in the subordinate clause (if-clause, because-clause, so-clause), as in the examples below.

π_{12} so if we are going to be able to meet <that, last week in January>_1, it is going have to be <the, twenty fifth>_2 // 1 $\mapsto$ 2

π_{13} <the twenty eighth>_1 I am free, <all day>_2, if you want to go for <a Sunday meeting>_3 // 3 $\mapsto$ (2 $\mapsto$ 1)

π_{14} it is going to have to be <Wednesday the third>_1 because, I am busy <Tuesday>_2 // not 2 $\mapsto$ 1

π_{15} I have a meeting <from eleven to one>_1, so we could, meet <in the morning from nine to eleven>_2, or, <in the afternoon after one>_3 // not 1 $\mapsto$ (2 $\bigtriangledown$ 3)

Whether or not there are some discursive markers between two outcomes, to find the appropriate operator, we need to answer some questions : does the agent want to satisfy the two outcomes at the same time ? Are the preferences on the outcomes dependent or independent ?

We have shown in this section that it is difficult to answer the second question and there is quite some ambiguity between the operators & et $\mapsto$. This ambiguity can be explained by the fact that both operators model the same optimal preference. Indeed, we saw in section 4.2 that for two outcomes o_1 and o_2 linked by a conjunction of preferences (o_1 & o_2), we have $o_1 \succ \overline{o_1}$ and $o_2 \succ \overline{o_2}$. For two outcomes o_1 and o_2 where o_2 is linked to o_1 by a conditional preference ($o_1 \mapsto o_2$), we have $o_1 \succ \overline{o_1}$ and $o_1 : o_2 \succ \overline{o_2}$. In both cases, the best possible world for the agent is the one where o_1 and o_2 are both satisfied at the same time.

6 Conclusion and Future Work

In this paper, we proposed a linguistic approach to preference aquisition that aims to infer preferences from dialogue moves in actual conversations that involve bargaining or negotiation. We studied how preferences are linguistically expressed in elementary discourse units on two different corpus genres: one already available, the `Verbmobil` corpus and the `Booking` corpus purposely built for this project. Annotators were trained only for `Verbmobil`. The aim is to study to what extent our annotation scheme is genre dependent.

Our preference annotation scheme requires two steps: identify the set of acceptable and non acceptable outcomes on which the agents preferences are expressed, and then identify the dependencies between these outcomes by using a set of specific non-boolean operators expressing conjunctions, disjunctions and conditionals. The inter-annotator agreement study shows good results on each corpus genre for outcome identification, outcome acceptance and outcome attachment. The results for outcome dependencies are also good but they are better for `Verbmobil`. The difficulties concern the confusion between disjunctions and conjunctions mainly because the same linguistic realizations do not always lead to the same operator. In addition, annotators often fail to decide if the preferences on the outcomes are dependent or independent.

This work shows that preference acquisition from linguistic actions is feasible for humans. The next step is to automate the process of preference extraction using NLP methods. We plan to do it using an hybrid approach combining both machine learning techniques (for outcome extraction and outcome acceptance) and rule-based approaches (for outcome attachment and outcome dependencies).

References

Neeraj Arora and Greg M. Allenby. 1999. Measuring the influence of individual preference structures in group decision making. *Journal of Marketing Research*, 36:476–487.

Jason Baldridge and Alex Lascarides. 2005. Annotating discourse structures for robust semantic interpretation. In *Proceedings of the 6th IWCS*.

Avrim Blum, Jeffrey Jackson, Tuomas Sandholm, and

Martin Zinkevich. 2004. Preference elicitation and query learning. *Journal of Machine Learning Research*, 5:649–667.

Craig Boutilier, Ronen Brafman, Chris Geib, and David Poole. 1997. A constraint-based approach to preference elicitation and decision making. In *AAAI Spring Symposium on Qualitative Decision Theory*, pages 19–28.

Craig Boutilier, Craig Brafman, Carmel Domshlak, Holger H. Hoos, and David Poole. 2004. Cp-nets: A tool for representing and reasoning with conditional *ceteris paribus* preference statements. *Journal of Artificial Intelligence Research*, 21:135–191.

Ronen I. Brafman and Carmel Domshlak. 2009. Preference handling - an introductory tutorial. *AI Magazine*, 30(1):58–86.

Sviatoslav Brainov. 2000. The role and the impact of preferences on multiagent interaction. In *Proceedings of ATAL*, pages 349–363. Springer-Verlag.

Robin Burke. 2000. Knowledge-based recommender systems. In *Encyclopedia of Library and Information Science*, volume 69, pages 180–200. Marcel Dekker.

Anaïs Cadilhac, Nicholas Asher, Farah Benamara, and Alex Lascarides. 2011. Commitments to preferences in dialogue. In *Proceedings of SIGDIAL*, pages 204–215. ACL.

Li Chen and Pearl Pu. 2004. Survey of preference elicitation methods. Technical report.

Ward Edwards and F. Hutton Barron. 1994. Smarts and smarter: Improved simple methods for multiattribute utility measurement. *Organizational Behavior and Human Decision Processes*, 60(3):306–325.

Johannes Fürnkranz and Eyke Hüllermeier, editors. 2011. *Preference Learning*. Springer.

Murthy Ganapathibhotla and Bing Liu. 2008. Mining opinions in comparative sentences. In *Proceedings of the 22nd International Conference on Computational Linguistics - Volume 1*, COLING '08, pages 241–248, Stroudsburg, PA, USA. Association for Computational Linguistics.

Daniel M. Hausman. 2000. Revealed preference, belief, and game theory. *Economics and Philosophy*, 16(01):99–115.

Thomas Meyer and Norman Foo. 2004. Logical foundations of negotiation: Strategies and preferences. In *In Proceedings of the Ninth International Conference on Principles of Knowledge Representation and Reasoning (KR04*, pages 311–318.

Katrin Schulz. 2007. *Minimal Models in Semantics and Pragmatics: Free Choice, Exhaustivity, and Conditionals*. PhD thesis, ILLC.

Xiaoyuan Su and Taghi M. Khoshgoftaar. 2009. A survey of collaborative filtering techniques. *Advances in Artificial Intelligence*, 2009:1–20.

Wolfgang Wahlster, editor. 2000. *Verbmobil: Foundations of Speech-to-Speech Translation*. Springer.

Janyce Wiebe, Theresa Wilson, and Claire Cardie. 2005. Annotating expressions of opinions and emotions in language. *Language Resources and Evaluation*, 39(2-3):165–210.

Selecting Corpus-Semantic Models for Neurolinguistic Decoding

Brian Murphy
Machine Learning Dept.
Carnegie Mellon University
Pittsburgh, USA
brianmurphy@cmu.edu

Partha Talukdar
Machine Learning Dept.
Carnegie Mellon University
Pittsburgh, USA
ppt@cs.cmu.edu

Tom Mitchell
Machine Learning Dept.
Carnegie Mellon University
Pittsburgh, USA
tom.mitchell@cs.cmu.edu

Abstract

Neurosemantics aims to learn the mapping between concepts and the neural activity which they elicit during neuroimaging experiments. Different approaches have been used to represent individual concepts, but current state-of-the-art techniques require extensive manual intervention to scale to arbitrary words and domains. To overcome this challenge, we initiate a systematic comparison of automatically-derived corpus representations, based on various types of textual co-occurrence. We find that dependency parse-based features are the most effective, achieving accuracies similar to the leading semi-manual approaches and higher than any published for a corpus-based model. We also find that simple word features enriched with directional information provide a close-to-optimal solution at much lower computational cost.

1 Introduction

The cognitive plausibility of computational models of word meaning has typically been tested using behavioural benchmarks, such as identification of synonyms among close associates (the TOEFL task for language learners, see e.g. Landauer and Dumais, 1997); emulating elicited judgments of pairwise similarity (such as Rubenstein and Goodenough, 1965); judgments of category membership (e.g. Battig and Montague, 1969); and word priming effects (Lund and Burgess, 1996). Mitchell et al. (2008) introduced a new task in *neurosemantic decoding* – using models of semantics to learn the mapping between concepts and the neural activity which they elicit during neuroimaging experiments. This was achieved with a linear model which used training data to find neural basis images that correspond to the assumed semantic dimensions (for instance, one such basis image might be the activity of the brain for words representing animate concepts), and subsequently used these general patterns and known semantic dimensions to infer the fMRI activity that should be elicited by an unseen stimulus concept. Follow-on work has experimented with other neuroimaging modalities (Murphy et al., 2009), and with a range of semantic models including elicited property norms (Chang et al., 2011), corpus derived models (Devereux and Kelly, 2010; Pereira et al., 2011) and structured ontologies (Jelodar et al., 2010).

The current state-of-the-art performance on this task is achieved using models that are hand-tailored in some respect, whether using manual annotation tasks (Palatucci et al., 2009), use of a domain-appropriate curated corpus (Pereira et al., 2011), or selection of particular collocates to suit the concepts to be described (Mitchell et al., 2008). While these approaches are clearly very successful, it is questionable whether they are a general solution to describe the various parts-of-speech and semantic domains that make up a speaker's vocabulary. The Mitchell et al. (2008) 25-verb model would probably have to be extended to describe the lexicon at large, and it is unclear whether such a compact model could be maintained. While Wikipedia (Pereira et al., 2011) has very broad and increasing coverage, it is possible that it will remain inadequate for specialist vocabularies, or for less-studied languages. And while the method used by Palatucci et al. (2009) distributes the annotation task efficiently by crowd-sourcing, it still requires that appropriate questions are compiled by researchers, a task that is both difficult to perform in a systematic way, and which may not generalize to more abstract concepts.

In this paper we examine a representative set of corpus-derived models of meaning, that require no manual intervention, and are applicable to any syntactic and semantic domain. We concentrate on which types of basic corpus pattern perform well on the neurosemantic decoding task: LSA-style **word-region** co-occurrences, and various HAL-style **word-collocate** features including raw tokens, POS tags, and a full dependency parse. Otherwise a common feature extraction and preprocessing pipeline is used: a co-occurrence frequency cutoff, application of a frequency normalization weighting, and dimensionality reduction with SVD.

The following section describes how the brain activity data was gathered and processed; the construction of several corpus-derived models of meaning; and the regression-based methods used to predict one from the other, evaluated with a brain-image matching task (Mitchell et al., 2008). In section 3 we report the results, and in the Conclusion we discuss both the practical implications, and what this works suggests for the cognitive plausibility of distributional models of meaning.

2 Methods

2.1 Brain activity features

The dataset used here is that described in detail in (Mitchell et al., 2008) and released publicly[1] in conjunction with the NAACL 2010 Workshop on Computational Neurolinguistics (Murphy et al., 2010). Functional MRI (fMRI) data was collected from 9 participants while they performed a property generation task. The stimuli were line-drawings, accompanied by their text label, of everyday concrete concepts, with 5 exemplars of each of 12 semantic classes (mammals, body parts, buildings, building parts, clothes, furniture, insects, kitchen utensils, miscellaneous functional artifacts, work tools, vegetables, and vehicles). Stimuli remained on screen for three seconds, and each was each presented six times, in random order, to give a total of 360 image presentations in the session.

The fMRI images were recorded with 3.0T scanner at 1 second intervals, with a spatial resolution of 3x3x6mm. The resulting data was preprocessed with the SPM package (Friston et al., 2007); the blood-oxygen-level response was approximated by taking a boxcar average over a sequence of brain images in each trial; percent signal change was calculated relative to rest periods, and the data from each of the six repetitions of each stimulus were averaged to yield a single brain image for each concept. Finally, a grey-matter anatomical mask was used to select only those voxels (three-dimensional pixels) that overlap with cortex, yielding approximately 20 thousand features per participant.

2.2 Models of semantics

Our objective is to compare current semantic representations that get state-of-the-art performance on the neuro-semantics task with representative distributional models of semantics that can be derived from arbitrary corpora, using varying degrees of linguistic preprocessing. A series of candidate models were selected to represent the variety of ways in which basic textual features can be extracted and represented, including token co-occurrence in a small local window, dependency parses of whole sentences, and document co-occurrence, among others. Other parameters were kept fixed in a way that the literature suggests would be neutral to the various models, and so allow a fair comparison among them (Sahlgren, 2006; Bullinaria and Levy, 2007; Turney and Pantel, 2010).

All textual statistics were gathered from a set of 50m English-language web-page documents consisting of 16 billion words. Where a fixed text window was used, we chose an extent of ± 4 lower-case tokens either side of the target

[1] http://www.cs.cmu.edu/afs/cs/project/theo-73/www/science2008/data.html

word of interest, which is in the mid-range of optimal values found by various authors (Lund and Burgess, 1996; Rapp, 2003; Sahlgren, 2006). Positive pointwise-mutual-information (1,2) was used as an association measure to normalize the observed co-occurrence frequency $p(w, f)$ for the varying frequency of the target word $p(w)$ and its features $p(f)$. PPMI up-weights co-occurrences between rare words, yielding positive values for collocations that are more common than would be expected by chance (i.e. if word distributions were independent), and discards negative values that represent patterns of co-occurrences that are *rarer* than one would expect by chance. It has been shown to perform well generally, with both word- and document-level statistics, in raw and dimensionality reduced forms (Bullinaria and Levy, 2007; Turney and Pantel, 2010).[2]

$$\text{PPMI}_{wf} = \begin{cases} \text{PMI}_{wf} & \text{if PMI}_{wf} > 0 \\ 0 & \text{otherwise} \end{cases} \quad (1)$$

$$\text{PMI}_{wf} = log\left(\frac{p(w,f)}{p(w)p(f)}\right) \quad (2)$$

A frequency threshold is commonly applied for three reasons: low-frequency co-occurrence counts are more noisy; PMI is positively biased towards hapax co-occurrences; and due to Zipfian distributions a cut-off dramatically reduces the amount of data to be processed. Many authors use a threshold of approximately 50-100 occurrences for word-collocate models (Lund and Burgess, 1996; Lin, 1998; Rapp, 2003). Since Bullinaria and Levy (2007) find improving performance with models using progressively lower cutoffs we explored two cut-offs of 20 and 50 which equate to low co-occurrences thresholds of 0.00125 or 0.003125 per million respectively; for the word-region model we chose a threshold of 2 occurrences of a target term in a document, to keep the input features to a reasonable dimensionality (Bradford, 2008).

After applying these operations to the input data from each model, the resulting dimensionality ranged widely, from about 500 thousand, to tens of millions. A singular value decomposition (SVD) was applied to identify the 1000 dimensions within each model with the greatest explanatory power, which also has the effect of combining similar dimensions (such as synonyms, inflectional variants, topically similar documents) into common components, and discarding more noisy dimensions in the data. Again there is variation in the number of dimension that authors use: here we experiment with 300 and 1000. For decomposition we used a sparse SVD method, the Implicitly Restarted Arnoldi Method (Lehoucq et al., 1998; Jones et al., 2001), which was coherent with the PPMI normalization used, since a zero value represented both negative target-feature associations, and those that were not observed or fell below the frequency cut-off. We also streamlined the task by reducing the input data C (of n target words by m co-occurrence features) to a square matrix CC^T of size $n \times n$, taking advantage of the equality of their left singular vectors U. For SVD to generalize well over the many input features, it is also important to have more training cases that the small set of 60 concrete nouns used in our evaluation task. Consequently we gathered all statistics over a set of the 40,000 most frequent word-forms found in the American National Corpus (Nancy Ide and Keith Suderman, 2006), which should approximate the scale and composition of the vocabulary of a university-educated speaker of English (Nation and Waring, 1997), and over 95% of tokens typically encountered in English.

2.2.1 Hand-tailored benchmarks

The state-of-the-art models on this brain activity prediction task are both hand-tailored. Mitchell et al. (2008) used a model of semantics based on co-occurrence in the Google 1T 5-gram corpus of English (Brants and Franz, 2006) with a small set of **25 Verbs** chosen to represent everyday sensory-motor interaction with concrete objects, such as *see, move, listen.* We recreated this using our current parameters (web document corpus, co-occurrence frequency cut-off, PPMI normalization). The second hand-

[2]Preliminary analyses confirmed that PPMI performed as well or better than alternatives including log-likelihood, TF-IDF, and log-entropy.

tailored dataset we used was a set of **Elicited Properties** inspired by the *20 Questions* game, and gathered using Mechanical Turk (Palatucci et al., 2009; Palatucci, 2011). Multiple informants were asked to answer one or more of 218 questions "related to size, shape, surface properties, and typical usage" such as *Do you see it daily?, Is it wild?, Is it man-made?* with a scalar response ranging from 1 to 5. The resulting responses were then averaged over informants, and then the values of each question were grouped into 5 bins, giving all dimensions similar mean and variance.

2.2.2 Word-Region Model

Latent Semantic Analysis (Deerwester et al., 1990; Landauer and Dumais, 1997), and its probabilistic cousins (Blei et al., 2003; Griffiths et al., 2007), express the meaning of a word as a distribution of co-occurrence across a set of documents, or other text-regions such as paragraphs. This word-region matrix instantiates the assumption that words that share a topical domain (such as medicine, entertainment, philosophy) would be expected to appear in similar sub-sets of text-regions. In such a model, the nearest neighbors of a target word are syntagmatically related (i.e. appear alongside each other), and for *judge* might include *lawyer, court, crime,* or *prison.*

The **Document** model used here is loosely based on LSA, taking the frequency of occurrence of each of our 40,000 vocabulary words in each of 50 million documents as its input data, and it follows Bullinaria and Levy (2007); Turney and Pantel (2010) in using PPMI as a normalization function. We have not investigated variations on the decomposition algorithm in any detail, such as those using non-negative matrix factorization, probabilistic LSA or LDA topic models, as the objective in this paper is to provide a direct comparison between the different types of basic collocation information encoded in corpora, rather than evaluate the best algorithmic means for discovering latent dimensions in those co-occurrences. Nor have we evaluated performance on a more structured corpus input (Pereira et al., 2011). However preliminary tests with the Wikipedia corpus, and with LDA, using the Gensim package (Rehurek and Sojka, 2010) yielded similar performances.

2.2.3 Word-Collocate Models

Word-collocate models make a complementary assumption to that of the document model: that words with closely-related categorical or taxonomic properties should appear in the same position of similar sentences. In a basic word-collocate model, based on a word-word co-occurrence matrix, the nearest neighbors of *judge* might be *athlete, singer,* or *fire-fighter,* reflecting paradigmatic relatedness (i.e. substitutability). Word-collocate models are further differentiated by the amount of linguistic annotation attached to word features, ranging from simple word-form features in a fixed-width window around the concept word, to more elaborate word sequence patterns and parses including parts of speech and dependency relation tags. Among these alternatives, we might expect a dependency model to be the most powerful. Intuitively, the information that *John* is sentient is similarly encoded in the text *John likes cake* and *John seems to really really like cake,* and a suitably effective parser should be able to generalize over this variation, to extract the same dependency relationship of *John-subject-like.* In contrast a narrow window-based model might exclude informative features (such as *like* in the second example), while including presumably uninformative ones (such as *really*). However parsers have the disadvantage of being computationally expensive (meaning that they typically are applied to smaller corpora) and usually introduce some noise through their errors. Consequently, simpler window-based models have often been found to be as effective.

The most basic model considered is the **Word-Form** model, in which all lower-case tokens (word forms and punctuation) found within four positions left and right of the target word are recorded, yielding simple features such as {*john, likes*}. It may also be termed a 'flat' model in contrast to those which assign a variable weight to collocates, progressively lower as one moves further than the target position (e.g.

Lund et al., 1995). We did not use a stop-list, as Bullinaria and Levy (2007) found co-occurrence with very high frequency words also to be informative for semantic tasks. We also expect that the subsequent steps of normalizing with PPMI, reduction with SVD, and use of regularised regression should be able to recognize when such high-frequency words are not informative and then discount these, without the need for such assumptions upfront.

The **Stemmed** model is a slight variation on the Word-Form model, where the same statistics are aggregated after applying Lancaster stemming (Paice, 1990; Loper and Bird, 2002).

The **Directional** model, inspired by Schütze and Pedersen (1993), is also derived from the word-form model, but differentiates between co-occurrence to the left or to the right of the target word, with features such as {*john_L, cake_R*}.

The **Part-of-Speech** model (Kanejiya et al., 2003; Widdows, 2003) replaces each lower-case word-token with its part-of-speech disambiguated form (e.g. *likes_VBZ, cake_NN*). These annotations were extracted from the full dependency parse described below.

The **Sequence** model draws on a range of work that uses word sequence patterns (Lin and Pantel, 2001; Almuhareb and Poesio, 2004; Baroni et al., 2010), and may also be considered an approximation of models that use shallow syntactic analysis (Grefenstette, 1994; Curran and Moens, 2002). All distinct token sequences up to length 4 either side of the target word were counted.

Finally the **Dependency** model uses a full dependency parse, which might be considered the most informed representation of the word-collocate relationships instantiated in corpus sentences, and this approach has been used by several authors (Lin, 1998; Padó and Lapata, 2007; Baroni and Lenci, 2010). The features used are pairs of dependency relation and lexeme corresponding to each edge linked to a target word of interest (e.g. *likes_subj*). The parser used here was Malt, which achieves accuracies of 85% when deriving labelled dependencies on English text (Hall et al., 2007). The features produced by this module are much more limited, to those words that have a direct dependency relation with the word of interest.

2.3 Linear Learning Model

A linear regression model will allow us to evaluate how well a given model of word semantics can be used to predict brain activity. We follow the analysis in Mitchell et al. (2008) and subsequently adopted by several other research groups (see Murphy et al., 2010). For each participant and selected fMRI feature (i.e. each voxel, which records the time-course of neural activity at a fixed location in the brain), we train a model where the level of activation of the latter (the blood oxygenation level) in response to different concepts is approximated by a regularised linear combination of their semantic features:

$$f = \mathbf{C}\beta + \lambda||\beta||^2 \qquad (3)$$

where f is the vector of activations of a specific fMRI feature for different concepts, the matrix $\mathbf{C}$ contains the values of the semantic features for the same concepts, β is the vector of weights we must learn for each of those (corpus-derived) features, and λ tunes the degree of regularisation. We can illustrate this with a toy example, containing several stimulus concepts and their attributes on three semantic dimensions: *cat* (*+animate, -big, +moving*); *phone* (*-animate, -big, -moving*); elephant (*+animate, +big, +moving*); skate-board (*-animate, -big, +moving*). After training over all the voxels in our fMRI data with this simple semantic model, we can derive whole brain images that are typical of each of the semantic dimensions. The power of the model is its ability to predict activity for concepts that were not in the training set – for instance the brain activation elicited by the word *car* might be approximated by combining the images see for *-animate, +big, +moving*, even though this combination of properties was not observed during training.

The linear model was estimated with a least squared errors method and $L2$ regularisation, selecting the lambda parameter from the range 0.0001 to 5000 using Generalized Cross-Validation (see Hastie et al., 2011, p.244). The activation of each fMRI voxel in response to a new concept that was not in the training data was predicted by a β-weighted sum of the values on each semantic dimension, building a picture of expected the global neural activity response for an arbitrary concept. Again following Mitchell et al. (2008) we use a leave-2-out paradigm in which a linear model for each neural feature is trained in turn on all concepts minus 2, having selected the 500 most stable voxels in the training set using the same correlational measure across stimulus presentations. For each of the 2 left-out concepts, we predict the global neural activation pattern, as just described. We then try to correctly match the predicted and observed activations, by measuring the cosine distance between the model-generated estimate of fMRI activity and the that observed in the experiment. If the sum of the matched cosine distances is lower than the sum of the mismatched distances, we consider the prediction successful – otherwise as failed. At chance levels, expected matching accuracy is 50%, and significant performance above chance can be estimated using the binomial test, once variance had been verified over independent trials (i.e. where no single stimulus concept is shared between pairs).

3 Results

Table 1 shows the main results of the leave-two-out brain-image matching task. They show the mean classification performance over 1770 word pairs (60 select 2) by 9 participants. All of these classification accuracies are highly significant at $p \ll 0.001$ over test trials (binomial, chance 50%, n=1770*9) and $p < 0.001$ over words (binomial, chance 50%, n=60). There were some significant differences between models when making inferences over trials, but for the small set of words used here it is not possible to make firm conclusions about the superiority of one model over the other, that could be confidently expected to generalize to other stimuli or experiments. However, we do achieve classification accuracies that are as high, or higher than any previously published (Palatucci et al., 2009; Pereira et al., 2011), while models based on very different basic features (directional word-forms; dependency relations; document co-occurrence) yield very similar performance.

Semantic Models	Features	Accuracy
25 Verbs	25	78.5
Elicited Properties	218	83.5
Document (f2)	1000	76.2
Word Form	1000	80.0
Stemmed	1000	76.2
Direction	1000	80.2
Part-of-Speech	1000	80.0
Sequence	1000	78.5
Dependency	1000	**83.1**

Table 1: Brain activity prediction accuracy on leave-2-out pair-matching task. A frequency cutoff of 20 was used for all 1000 dimensional models.

Semantic Models	300 Feats.	1000 Feats.
Document (f2)	79.9	76.2
Word Form	78.1	80.0
Stemmed	77.9	76.2
Direction	80.0	80.2
Part-of-Speech	77.9	80.0
Sequence	72.9	78.5
Dependency	81.6	83.1

Table 2: Effect of SVD dimensionality in the leave-2-out pair-matching setting; frequency cutoff of 20.

3.1 Effect of Number of Dimensions

Here we evaluate what effect the number of SVD dimensions used has on the final performance of various semantic models. Experimental results comparing 300 and 1000 dimensions are presented in Table 2, all based on a frequency cutoff of 20. We observe that performance improves in 5 out of 7 semantic models compared, with the highest performance achieved by the Dependency model when 1000 SVD dimensions were used.

3.2 Effect of Frequency Cutoff

In this section, we evaluate what effect frequency cutoff has on the brain prediction accuracy of various semantic models. From the results in Table 3, we observe only marginal changes as the frequency cutoff varied from 20 to 50. This suggests that the semantic models of this set of

Semantic Models	Cutoff = 50	Cutoff = 20
Document (f2)	79.9	79.9
Word Form	78.5	78.1
Stemmed	78.2	77.9
Direction	80.8	80.0
Part-of-Speech	77.5	77.9
Sequence	74.4	72.9
Dependency	81.3	81.6

Table 3: Effect of frequency cutoff in the leave-2-out pair-matching setting; 300 SVD dimensions.

words are not very sensitive to variations in the frequency cutoff under current experimental settings, and do not benefit clearly from the decrease in sparsity and increase in noise that a lower threshold produces.

3.3 Information Overlap Analysis

To verify that the models are in fact substantially different, we performed a follow-on analysis that measured the informational overlap between the corpus-derived models. Given two models A and B, both with dimensionality 40 thousand words by 300 SVD dimensions, we can evaluate the extent to which A (used as the predictor semantic representation) contains the information encoded in B (the explained representation). As shown in (4), for each SVD component c, we take the left singular vector b_c as a dependent variable and fit it with a linear model, using the matrix A (all left singular vectors) as independent variables. The explained variance for this column is weighted by its squared singular value s_c^2 in B, and the sum of these component-wise variances gives the total variance explained $R^2_{A \to B}$.

$$R^2_{A \to B} = \sum_{c=1}^{300} \frac{s_c^2}{\sum s_c^2} R_{A \to b_c} \quad (4)$$

Figure 1 indicates that the first three models, which are all derived from token occurrences in a ± 4 window, are close to identical. The sequence and document models are relatively dissimilar, and the dependency model occupies a middle ground, with some similarity to all the models. It is also interesting to note that the among the first cluster of word-form derived models, the

Figure 1: Informational Overlap between Corpus-Derived Datasets, in R^2

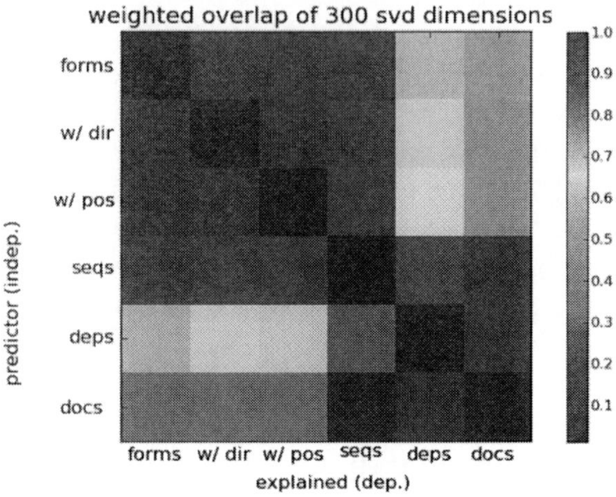

directional one has the highest similarity to the dependency model.

4 Conclusion

The main result of this study was that we achieved classification accuracies as high as any published, and within a fraction of a percentage point of the human benchmark *20 Questions* data, using completely unsupervised, data-driven models of semantics based on a large random sample of web-text. The most linguistically informed among the models (and so, perhaps the most psychologically plausible), based on dependency parses, is the most successful. Still the performance of sometimes radically different models, from Document-based (syntagmatic) and Word-Form-based (paradigmatic), is surprisingly similar. One reason for this may be that we have reached a ceiling in performance on the fMRI data, due to its inherent noise – in this regard it is interesting to note that an attempt to classify individual concepts using this data directly, without an intervening model of semantics, also achieves about 80% (though on a different task, Shinkareva et al., 2008). Another possible explanation is that both methods reveal equivalent sets of underlying semantic dimensions, but figure 1 suggests not. Alternatively, it may be that the small set of 60 words examined here may be as well-distinguished by means of their taxonomic differences, as by their topical differences, a suggestion supported by the results in Pereira et al. (2011, see Figure 2A).

From the perspective of computational efficiency however, some of the models have clearer advantages. The Dependency and Part-of-Speech models are processing-intensive, since the broad vocabulary considered requires that the very large quantities of text pass through a parsing or tagging pipeline (though these tasks can be parallelized). The Sequence and Document models conversely require very large amounts of memory to store all their features during SVD. In comparison, the Direction model is impressive, as it achieves close to optimal performance, despite being very cheap to produce in terms of processor time and memory footprint. Its relatively superior performance may be due to the relatively fixed word-order of English, making it a good approximation of a Dependency model. For instance, given the narrow ±4 token windows used here, the Direction features *shaky_Left* and *donate_Right* (relative to a target noun) are probably nearly identical to the Dependency features *shaky_Adj* and *donate_Subj*. The Sequence model might also be seen as an approximate Dependency model, but one with the addition of more superficial collocations such as "fish and chips" or "Judge Judy", which are less relevant to our semantic task.

The evidence for the influence of the scaling parameters (number of SVD dimensions, frequency cutoff) is mixed: cut-off appears to have little effect either way, and increasing the number of dimensions can help or hinder (compare the Sequence and Document models). We can speculate that the Document model is already "saturated" with 300 dimensions/topics, but that the other models based on properties have a higher inherent dimensionality. It may also be a lower cut-off and higher dimensionality would show clearer benefits over a larger set of semantic/syntactic domains, including lower-frequency words (the lowest frequency work in the set of 60 used here was *igloo*, which has an incidence of 0.3 per million words in the ANC).

PPMI appears to be both effective, and parsimonious with assumptions one might make about conceptual representations, where it would be cognitively onerous and unnecessary to encode all *negative* features (such as the facts that *dogs* do not have wheels, are not communication events, and do not belong in the aviation domain). But while SVD is certainly effective in dealing with the pervasive synonymy and polysemy seen in corpus-feature sets, it is less clear that it reveals psychologically plausible dimensions of meaning. Alternatives such as non-negative matrix factorization (Lee and Seung, 1999) or Latent Dirichlet Allocation (Blei et al., 2003) might extract more readily interpretable dimensions; or alternative regularisation methods such as Elastic Nets, Lasso (Hastie et al., 2011), or Network Regularisation (Sandler et al., 2009) might even be capable of identifying meaningful clusters of features when learning directly on co-occurrence data. Finally, we should consider whether more derived datasets could be used as input data in place of the basic corpus features used here, such as the full facts learned by the NELL system (Carlson et al., 2010), or crowd-sourced data which can be easily gathered for any word (e.g. association norms, Kiss et al., 1973), though different algorithmic means would be needed to deal with their extreme degree of sparsity.

The results also suggest a series of follow-on analyses. A priority should be to test these models against a wider range of neuroimaging data modalities (e.g. MEG, EEG) and stimulus sets, including abstract kinds (see Murphy et al. 2012, for a preliminary study), and parts-of-speech beyond nouns. It may be that a putative complementarity between word-region and word-collocate models is only revealed when we look at a broader sample of the human lexicon. And beyond establishing what informational content is required to make semantic distinctions, other factorisation methods (e.g. sparse or non-negative decompositions) could be applied to yield more interpretable dimensions. Other classification tasks might also be more sensitive for detecting differences between models, such as the test of word identification among a set by rank accuracy, as used in (Shinkareva et al., 2008).

References

Almuhareb, A. and Poesio, M. (2004). Attribute-based and value-based clustering: An evaluation. In *Proceedings of EMNLP*, pages 158–165.

Baroni, M. and Lenci, A. (2010). Distributional Memory : A General Framework for Corpus-Based Semantics. *Computational Linguistics*, 36(4):673–721.

Baroni, M., Murphy, B., Barbu, E., and Poesio, M. (2010). Strudel: A corpus-based semantic model based on properties and types. *Cognitive Science*, 34(2):222–254.

Battig, W. F. and Montague, W. E. (1969). Category Norms for Verbal Items in 56 Categories: A Replication and Extension of the Connecticut Category Norms. *Journal of Experimental Psychology Monographs*, 80(3):1–46.

Blei, D. M., Ng, A. Y., and Jordan, M. I. (2003). Latent Dirichlet Allocation. *Journal of Machine Learning Research*, 3(4-5):993–1022.

Bradford, R. B. (2008). An empirical study of required dimensionality for large-scale latent semantic indexing applications. *Proceeding of the 17th ACM conference on Information and knowledge mining CIKM 08*, pages 153–162.

Brants, T. and Franz, A. (2006). Web 1T 5-gram Version 1.

Bullinaria, J. A. and Levy, J. P. (2007). Extracting semantic representations from word co-occurrence statistics: A computational study. *Behavior Research Methods*, 39(3):510–526.

Carlson, A., Betteridge, J., Kisiel, B., Settles, B., Jr., E. R. H., and Mitchell, T. M. (2010). Toward an Architecture for Never-Ending Language Learning. *Artificial Intelligence*, 2(4):3–3.

Chang, K.-m. K., Mitchell, T., and Just, M. A. (2011). Quantitative modeling of the neural representation of objects: how semantic feature norms can account for fMRI activation. *NeuroImage*, 56(2):716–727.

Curran, J. R. and Moens, M. (2002). Improvements in automatic thesaurus extraction. In *SIGLEX*, pages 59–66.

Deerwester, S., Dumais, S., Landauer, T., Furnas, G., and Harshman, R. (1990). Indexing by Latent Semantic Analysis. *Journal of the American Society of Information Science*, 41(6):391 – 407.

Devereux, B. and Kelly, C. (2010). Using fMRI activation to conceptual stimuli to evaluate methods for extracting conceptual representations from corpora. In Murphy, B., Korhonen, A., and Chang, K. K.-M., editors, *1st Workshop on Computational Neurolinguistics*.

Friston, K. J., Ashburner, J. T., Kiebel, S. J., Nichols, T. E., and Penny, W. D. (2007). *Statistical Parametric Mapping: The Analysis of Functional Brain Images*, volume 8. Academic Press.

Grefenstette, G. (1994). *Explorations in Automatic Thesaurus Discovery*. Kluwer, Dordrecht.

Griffiths, T. L., Steyvers, M., and Tenenbaum, J. B. (2007). Topics in semantic representation. *Psychological Review*, 114(2):211–244.

Hall, J., Nilsson, J., Nivre, J., Eryigit, G., Megyesi, B., Nilsson, M., and Saers, M. (2007). Single Malt or Blended? A Study in Multilingual Parser Optimization. *CoNLL Shared Task Session*, pages 933–939.

Hastie, T., Tibshirani, R., and Friedman, J. (2011). *The Elements of Statistical Learning*, volume 18 of *Springer Series in Statistics*. Springer, 5th edition.

Jelodar, A. B., Alizadeh, M., and Khadivi, S. (2010). WordNet Based Features for Predicting Brain Activity associated with meanings of nouns. In Murphy, B., Korhonen, A., and Chang, K. K.-M., editors, *1st Workshop on Computational Neurolinguistics*, pages 18–26.

Jones, E., Oliphant, T., Peterson, P., and Et Al. (2001). SciPy: Open source scientific tools for Python.

Kanejiya, D., Kumar, A., and Prasad, S. (2003). Automatic evaluation of students' answers using syntactically enhanced LSA. *Building educational applications, NAACL*, 2:53–60.

Kiss, G. R., Armstrong, C., Milroy, R., and Piper, J. (1973). An associative thesaurus of English and its computer analysis. In Aitken, A. J., Bailey, R. W., and Hamilton-Smith, N., editors, *The Computer and Literary Studies*. Edinburgh University Press.

Landauer, T. and Dumais, S. (1997). A solution to Plato's problem: the latent semantic analysis theory of acquisition, induction, and representation of knowledge. *Psychological Review*, 104(2):211–240.

Lee, D. D. and Seung, H. S. (1999). Learning the parts of objects by non-negative matrix factorization. *Nature*, 401(6755):788–91.

Lehoucq, R. B., Sorensen, D. C., and Yang, C. (1998). *Arpack users' guide: Solution of large scale eigenvalue problems with implicitly restarted Arnoldi methods*. SIAM.

Lin, D. (1998). Automatic Retrieval and Clustering of Similar Words. In *COLING-ACL*, pages 768–774.

Lin, D. and Pantel, P. (2001). DIRT – discovery of inference rules from text. *Proceedings of the seventh ACM SIGKDD international conference on Knowledge discovery and data mining KDD 01*, datamining:323–328.

Loper, E. and Bird, S. (2002). {NLTK}: The natural language toolkit. In *ACL Workshop*, volume 1, pages 63–70. Association for Computational Linguistics.

Lund, K. and Burgess, C. (1996). Producing high-dimensional semantic spaces from lexical co-occurrence. *Behavior Research Methods, Instruments, and Computers*, 28:203–208.

Lund, K., Burgess, C., and Atchley, R. (1995). Semantic and associative priming in high dimensional semantic space. In *Proceedings of the 17th Cognitive Science Society Meeting*, pages 660–665.

Mitchell, T. M., Shinkareva, S. V., Carlson, A., Chang, K.-M., Malave, V. L., Mason, R. A., and Just, M. A. (2008). Predicting Human Brain Activity Associated with the Meanings of Nouns. *Science*, 320:1191–1195.

Murphy, B., Baroni, M., and Poesio, M. (2009). EEG responds to conceptual stimuli and corpus semantics. In *Proceedings of EMNLP*, pages 619–627. ACL.

Murphy, B., Korhonen, A., and Chang, K. K.-M., editors (2010). *Proceedings of the 1st Workshop on Computational Neurolinguistics, NAACL-HLT*, Los Angeles. ACL.

Murphy, B., Talukdar, P., and Mitchell, T. (2012). Comparing Abstract and Concrete Conceptual Representations using Neurosemantic Decoding. In *NAACL Workshop on Cognitive Modelling and Computational Linguistics.*

Nancy Ide and Keith Suderman (2006). The American National Corpus First Release. *Proceedings of the Fifth Language Resources and Evaluation Conference (LREC).*

Nation, P. and Waring, R. (1997). Vocabulary size, text coverage and word lists. In Schmitt, N. and McCarthy, M., editors, *Vocabulary Description acquisition and pedagogy*, pages 6–19. Cambridge University Press.

Padó, S. and Lapata, M. (2007). Dependency-based construction of semantic space models. *Computational Linguistics*, 33(2):161–199.

Paice, C. D. (1990). Another stemmer. *SIGIR Forum*, 24(3):56–61.

Palatucci, M., Hinton, G., Pomerleau, D., and Mitchell, T. M. (2009). Zero-Shot Learning with Semantic Output Codes. *Advances in Neural Information Processing Systems*, 22:1–9.

Palatucci, M. M. (2011). *Thought Recognition: Predicting and Decoding Brain Activity Using the Zero-Shot Learning Model.* PhD thesis, Carnegie Mellon University.

Pereira, F., Detre, G., and Botvinick, M. (2011). Generating Text from Functional Brain Images. *Frontiers in Human Neuroscience*, 5:1–11.

Rapp, R. (2003). Word Sense Discovery Based on Sense Descriptor Dissimilarity. *Proceedings of the Ninth Machine Translation Summit*, pp:315–322.

Rehurek, R. and Sojka, P. (2010). Software Framework for Topic Modelling with Large Corpora. In *New Challenges, LREC 2010*, pages 45–50. ELRA.

Rubenstein, H. and Goodenough, J. B. (1965). Contextual correlates of synonymy. *Communications of the ACM*, 8(10):627–633.

Sahlgren, M. (2006). *The Word-Space Model: Using distributional analysis to represent syntagmatic and paradigmatic relations between words in high-dimensional vector spaces.* Dissertation, Stockholm University.

Sandler, T., Talukdar, P. P., Ungar, L. H., and Blitzer, J. (2009). Regularized Learning with Networks of Features. *Advances in Neural Information Processing Systems 21*, 4:1401–1408.

Schütze, H. and Pedersen, J. (1993). A Vector Model for syntagmatic and paradigmatic relatedness. In *Making Sense of Words Proceedings of the 9th Annual Conference of the University of Waterloo Centre for the New OED and Text Research*, pages 104–113.

Shinkareva, S. V., Mason, R. A., Malave, V. L., Wang, W., Mitchell, T. M., and Just, M. A. (2008). Using fMRI Brain Activation to Identify Cognitive States Associated with Perception of Tools and Dwellings. *PloS ONE*, 3(1).

Turney, P. D. and Pantel, P. (2010). From Frequency to Meaning: Vector Space Models of Semantics. *Artificial Intelligence*, 37(1):141–188.

Widdows, D. (2003). Unsupervised methods for developing taxonomies by combining syntactic and statistical information. In *NAACL*, pages 197–204. Association for Computational Linguistics.

Simple and Phrasal Implicatives

Lauri Karttunen
Stanford University
CSLI, 210 Panama St.
Stanford, CA 94305, USA
laurik@stanford.edu

Abstract

This paper complements a series of works on implicative verbs such as *manage to* and *fail to*. It extends the description of simple implicative verbs to phrasal implicatives as *take the time to* and *waste the chance to*. It shows that the implicative signatures of over 300 verb-noun collocations depend both on the semantic type of the verb and the semantic type of the noun in a systematic way.

1 Introduction

There is a substantial body of literature on the semantics of English complement constructions starting with (Kiparsky and Kiparsky, 1970) and (Karttunen, 1971; Karttunen, 1973), including (Rudanko, 1989; Rudanko, 2002; Nairn et al., 2006; Egan, 2008). These studies have developed a semantic classification of verbs and verb-noun collocations that take sentential complements. They focus on constructions that give rise to implied commitments that the author cannot disavow without being incoherent or without contradicting herself. For example, (1a) presupposes that Kim had not rescheduled the meeting, (1b) entails that she didn't and presupposes that she intended to reschedule it.

(1) a. Kim forgot that she had not rescheduled the meeting.

b. Kim forgot to reschedule the meeting.

FACTIVE constructions like *forget that X* involve presuppositions, IMPLICATIVE constructions like *forget to X* give rise to entailments and may carry presuppositions.

Presuppositions persist under negation, in questions and if-clauses, entailments do not. For example, the negation of (1b), *Kim did not forget to reschedule the meeting*, entails that Kim did reschedule the meeting and presupposes, as (1b) does, that it was her intention to do so.

Implicative constructions involve entailments. The entailment may be positive or negative depending on the polarity of the containing clauses. Replacing *forget* by *didn't forget* in (1b) gives an entailment of the opposite polarity. Questions and if-clauses do not yield any entailments.

2 Simple implicatives

The constructions *forget to X* and *remember to X* are two-way implicative constructions. They yield an entailment about the truth or falsity of X both in affirmative and in negative sentences. We use the notation $+- \mid -+$ for the verb *forget to* to indicate that *forget to X* yields a negative entailment for X in a positive context, $+-$, and a positive entailment in a negative context, $-+$. The first sign stands for the polarity of the embedding context, the second sign for the polarity of the entailment. We code the verb *remember to* as $++ \mid --$ because in a positive context *remember to X* yields a positive entailment about X, $++$, and the opposite, $--$, in a negative context.

There are two major types of implicative constructions. TWO-WAY IMPLICATIVES like *forget to* and *remember to* yield an entailment both in positive and negative contexts, ONE-WAY IMPLICATIVES yield an entailment only under one polarity. Karttunen (1971; 1973) and Nairn *et al.* (2006) list verbs of both types. Table 1 gives a few examples of two-way implicatives.

++ | −− implicatives	+− | −+ implicatives
turn out that	
manage to	fail to
succeed in	neglect to
remember to	forget to
deign to	refrain from ... ing
happen to	avoid ... ing

Table 1: Types of two-way implicative verbs

2.1 Two-way implicatives

The type of the complementizer that a verb takes may change the semantic type of the construction. *forget that X* is factive but *forget to X* is a + − | − + implicative construction. (1a) presupposes that Kim had not rescheduled the meeting, (1b) entails that she didn't.[1] If we replace *forgot* in (1) by *didn't forget*, the presupposition of (1a) remains intact but the entailment of (1b) reverses polarity: Kim did reschedule the meeting.[2] In contrast to *forget*, *pretend that X* and *pretend to X* are both counterfactive. The sentences in (2) and their affirmative counterparts presuppose that Kim did not have everything figured out.

(2) a. Kim didn't pretend that she had everything figured out.

b. Kim didn't pretend to have everything figured out.

The polarity of a clause is determined from top down. (3) entails that Kim ate breakfast because the two negative polarities of *almost* and *fail* cancel out and *fail to X* and *remember to X* are both two-way implicative constructions.

(3) Kim almost failed to remember to eat breakfast.

The chain of inferences is sketched in (4) where [+] marks the top-level expression as true. The subsequent [+] and [−] signs indicate the entailed polarity of each subordinate clause.

(4) [+] almost(fail-to(remember-to(X)))
[−] fail-to(remember-to(X))
[+] remember-to(X)
[+] X

In short, *almost(X)* and *fail-to(X)* switch the polarity of the entailment, *remember-to(X)* preserves it. Omitting *almost* (or *fail to*) from (3) reverses the entailed polarity of the eat-clause.

(5) Kim failed to remember to eat breakfast.

(6) [+] fail-to(remember-to(X))
[−] remember-to(X)
[−] X

2.2 One-way implicatives

Constructions such as *manage to X* and *fail to X* are perfectly symmetrical in that they yield an entailment both in affirmative and negative contexts. As noted early on, (Karttunen, 1971; Karttunen, 1973), there are four types of verbs that yield an entailment about their complement clause only under one or the other polarity.

++ implicatives	+− implicatives
cause NP to	refuse to
force NP to	prevent NP from
make NP to	keep NP from
−− implicatives	−+ implicatives
can (= be able to)	hesitate to

Table 2: Types of one-way implicative verbs

The ++ and some of the +− implicatives in Table 2 are causatives.[3] (7a) entails that Mary left, (7b) entails that she didn't. (7c) and (7d) are consistent with Mary leaving or not leaving.

(7) a. Kim forced Mary to leave. (*but she didn't)

b. Kim prevented Mary from leaving.

c. Kim did not force Mary to leave.

d. Kim did not prevent Mary from leaving.

The +− implicatives switch the polarity of the entailment from positive to negative. (8) does not tell us whether Dave left or not because *force to* does not yield any entailment under negative polarity about its complement.

[1]All the two-way implicatives in Table 1 also give rise to a presupposition. (1b) and its negative counterpart presuppose that Kim had intended to reschedule the meeting.

[2]It is possible to interpret the example differently by focusing the negation on the word *forget*: *Kim did not* FORGET *to reschedule the meeting. She never intended to do that.* See (Karttunen and Peters, 1979), (Horn, 1985) for further discussion of this type of "metalinguistic negation" that objects to the use of a particular word or locution but not necessarily to what the sentence entails.

[3]Rudanko (2002) points out that there is a causative construction that is not associated with any particular verb: *She bullied him into marrying her* entails that he married her. It appears that all constructions of the type TV NP *into X* are ++ implicatives.

(8) Kim prevented Mary from forcing Dave to leave.

(9) [+] prevent-to(X, force-to(Y, Z))
[−] force-to(Y, Z)
[ ] Z

The −− implicatives express a necessary condition for the truth of the complement clause. If the host clause is under negative polarity, the complement clause is false. (10) entails that Kim did not finish her sentence.

(10) Kim could not finish her sentence.

It appears that *hesitate to* is the only −+ implicative verb in English. (11) entails that Kim spoke her mind.

(11) Kim did not hesitate to speak her mind.

Omitting the negation in (11) makes it non-committal as to whether Kim spoke her mind or not.[4] There are other verbs such as *shy away from* and *shrink from* that yield a positive entailment under negation but they are two-way implicatives like *avoid to*. The verb *wait to* has one interpretation that has the same implicative signature as *not hesitate to* but the construction *not wait to* is ambiguous.

2.3 Ambiguity of *not wait to X*

The construction *not wait to X* can be understood in two ways. The example in (12a) could be continued either with (12b) or (12c).

(12) a. Ed did not wait to call for help.

b. ...Instead he left the scene in a hurry.

c. ...But it was too late.

The continuation (12b) implies that Ed did not call for help, (12c) implies that Ed called for help right away. The word *instead* in (12b) and the anaphoric *it* in (12c) are clues that indicate whether Ed made a call or not.

A Google search finds numerous examples of both types. The sentences in (13) contain *wait to X* in the −− sense, in the the examples in (14) it has the −+ interpretation.

(13) a. Deena did not wait to talk to anyone. Instead, she ran home.

b. He did not wait to hear Ms. Coulter's response, but immediately walked up the balcony stairs and left.

c. He was so excited to get his Thomas set that he didn't wait to take off his coat.

(14) a. It hurt like hell, but I'm glad she didn't wait to tell me.

b. Kalamazoo didn't wait to strike back. The K-Wings scored two goals in less than 90 seconds.

c. I didn't wait to open the gift. Heck, I didn't even wait to wear them. They're the softest most comfy overalls I've ever owned.

The construction *not wait to X* is not vague about the truth or falsity of the complement. Either it means that X was not done at all or it means that X was done right away without delay. In most contexts it is immediately clear which interpretation the author has in mind. The ambiguity mostly goes unnoticed.

The source of the ambiguity can be seen in examples where *wait to* has two infinitival complements.

(15) a. "My biggest regret is that I didn't wait [to get married] [to have kids]" says Gerald, a father of three. "If I had it to do over again, I'd wait until I was married to become a father."

b. Chances are, you probably didn't wait [to get permission from the scientific establishment] [to start believing in the creative power of thought and the underlying spirituality of the universe].

c. I raised my hand above my head, as if I were in school or something, but didn't wait [for anyone to give me the "okay"] [to start talking].

The examples in (15) have the form *not wait [to X] [to Y]*. They entail that X did not happen but Y is true. In other words *wait to* is −− with respect to its first complement and −+ with respect to the second. In (15a) Gerald did not get married but had kids. In (15b) the addressee probably started believing without the permission of the scientific establishment.

The implicit assumption in these cases is that one might see X as a precondition for Y but the protagonist skipped X and proceeded directly to Y. The ambiguity arises from the fact that syntactically the two complements of *wait to* are both optional.

In the case of (15a), Gerald might have said *My greatest regret is that I didn't wait to get married* leaving out the second complement, or he might have said *My greatest regret is that I didn't wait to have kids* leaving out the first.

(13c) came with a picture of a boy with his blue coat still on playing with his new Thomas train set. (14c) came with a picture of a girl wearing her comfy birthday gift overalls in advance of her birthday.

[4] Although *not hesitate to X* seems to deny that there was any hesitation to X, many examples from the web suggest otherwise: *When I got the paper back I almost hesitated to see the grade, but when I saw the A on the title page, that hesitation quickly turned into relief. Not hesitate to X* is an idiom, it is not compositional.

In the case of (12a) that is ambiguous without a context, the reader has to guess whether it should be read as *Ed did not wait [to call for help][. . .]* or *Ed did not wait [. . .] [to call for help]*. The continuation (12b) is consistent with the first option, (12c) with the second.

The fact that the ambiguity of (12a) is syntactic rather than semantic explains why it is not possible to translate this sentence to languages such as Finnish, German and French in a way that preserves the ambiguity. The translator has to decide which of the two interpretations is the right one because they translate differently. In this respect (12a) is similar to well known examples such as *time flies like an arrow* and *I saw her duck* that have no ambiguity-preserving translations in other languages because the ambiguity comes from accidental lexical and syntactic overlaps that are language-specific.

2.4 Invited inferences

Although one-way implicatives yield a definite entailment only under one polarity, in many contexts they are interpreted as if they were two-way implicatives. For example, the complement of *prevent from* in negative sentences such as (16) is likely to be understood to be true and the author probably intended the sentence to be interpreted in that way.

(16) The language barrier did not prevent us from having a few laughs together.

If something was not prevented or if someone could do it, it may have happened. If someone was not forced to do something or hesitated doing it, maybe she did not do it. However, an explicit denial is possible as in (17) showing that the inference about the veridicality of the complement is pragmatically based, not truth-conditional.

(17) a. Her mother did not prevent her from visiting her father, but she never did.

b. He showed he could jab, but didn't. He showed he could work the body, but didn't.

c. The school had not forced the students to leave, but they left on their own.

d. She hesitated to ask, but had to: "Stateside?"

The promotion of *can* and *be able to* from a one-way implicative to a two-way implicative is similar to the phenomenon that (Geis and Zwicky, 1971) discuss under the label of INVITED INFERENCE. What they observe is the tendency to read conditionals as biconditionals. For example, *If you mow my lawn I will give you $5* is usually interpreted as *I will give you $5 if and only if you mow my lawn*. Invited inferences may be explicitly cancelled. as in (17), and they do not even arise in contexts where they would conflict with what is known: *Firms were allowed to earn more than they did earn*. Obviously, firms did not earn more than they earned. No invited inference in this case.

The phenomenon of invited inferences is much more prevalent than has been recognized and it has not been systematically studied except for SCALAR IMPLICATURES for which there is a vast literature.[5]

3 Phrasal implicatives

There is a large class of multiword constructions that are semantically similar to the single verbs in Tables 1 and 2. We call them PHRASAL IMPLICATIVES. They are composed of a transitive verb such as *have*, *make*, *take* and *use*, and a noun phrase headed by a noun such as *attempt*, *effort* and *opportunity* that can take sentential complements. The "implicative signature" of such a phrase depends both on the type of verb and the type of the noun. We organize the presentation by the nouns.

3.1 attempt, effort, trouble, initiative

In the case of *attempt* the relation between a single verb implicative and a phrasal one is obvious. For example, *attempt to X* and *make an attempt to X* are virtually synonymous.[6]

(18) a. Kim didn't attempt to hide her feelings.

b. Kim didn't make any attempt to hide her feelings.

c. Kim made no effort to hide her feelings.

All the examples in (18) entail that Kim did not hide her feelings. The affirmative versions of these sentences are non-committal with respect to the complement clause. Attempts and efforts can fail. Consequently, *attempt to X*, *make an attempt to X* and *make an effort to X* are all −− implicatives like *allow* NP *to X* in Table 2. The phrasal version provides more ways to express negation than the simple verb. It can be expressed by the determiner as in (18c).

Another way to bring about a negative entailment in this construction is to indicate by an adjective such as *futile* that an attempt was made but it failed.

(19) Convair made a futile attempt to save their bomber program.

---

[5] http://en.wikipedia.org/wiki/Scalar_implicature

[6] We assume here that the infinitival clause is syntactically a complement to the noun. In (18b), (18c) and in all the later examples in this section there is an alternative syntactic analysis under which the to-complement expresses a purpose. In that sense it does not modify the noun but the verb. The purpose clause could be fronted separately, as in *To hide her feelings, Kim turned away*. Purpose clauses are non-committal as to whether the intended purpose was achieved.

Conversely, *make a successful attempt to X* entails that X came about. Attempts can be described as bungled, defeated, foiled, etc. that all yield a negative entailment for the complement.

Complement taking nouns tend to occur with specific verbs. *Attempt* can appear with *have*, *make* and *take* but *make* is by far the most common collocate verb for this noun. Semantically *have/make/take an attempt to X* are all $--$ implicatives.

The choice of the collocate verb makes a difference for many other nouns. In particular, *make an effort to X* is a $--$ implicative but *take an effort to X* is a two-way implicative. It has the signature $++ \mid --$ as illustrated in (20).

(20) a. He took an effort to bring me to the butterfly garden.

b. She took no effort to dress in style.

In these examples *take an effort to X* is an equi-construction. They are in contrast with the *take an effort* sentences in (21).

(21) a. Before people had computers, it took an effort to infringe copyright.

b. It took no effort to unscrew the bolt.

c. Did it take an effort to be so clever?

The examples in (21) do not contain phrasal implicatives, they have an extraposed complement clause. Extraposition is a factive construction. The extraposed infinitival clauses in (21) are presupposed.

The nouns *trouble* and *initiative* are like *effort* in that they form a $++ \mid --$ implicative phrase with *take*.

(22) a. She took the trouble to iron all the clothes.

b. Napoleon didn't take the trouble to study the country he was going to invade.

3.2 opportunity, chance, occasion

The phrase *take the/an opportunity to X* is a two-way $++ \mid --$ implicative whereas *have the/an opportunity to X* is only a $--$ implicative. (23a) entails that Kim expressed her feelings, (23b) entails the opposite.

(23) a. Kim took the opportunity to express her feelings.

b. Kim didn't take the opportunity to express her feelings.

Replacing *took* by *have* as in (24) takes away the positive entailment. (24a) is non-commital with respect to the veridicality of the complement, (24b) has the same negative entailment as (23b).

(24) a. Kim had the opportunity to express her feelings.

b. Kim didn't have the opportunity to express her feelings.

In (24) one could substitute *get* for *have* as getting something entails having it and not getting something entails not having it. The substitution of *lack* or *miss* or *lose* for *have* in (24) turns the $--$ implicative into a $+-$ implicative. In (25) we get a negative entailment in the affirmative and no entailment under negation.

(25) a. The Belarusians lacked the opportunity to create a distinctive national identity.

b. I didn't lack the opportunity to engage in a relationship, I just felt no desire to.

There are several verbs that can substitute for *take* in (23) without changing the entailments. They include more descriptive synonyms for *take* such as *seize*, *grab* and *snap*. There is also another family of verbs, *use*, *utilize*, *exploit* and *expend*, that yield a two-way $++ \mid --$ implicative phrase with *the/an opportunity to X*.

(26) a. Randy used the opportunity to toot his own horn.

b. Randy didn't use the opportunity to toot his own horn.

Here *use* could be replaced by *make use of*, itself a $++ \mid --$ implicative phrase.

Another class of verbs that yield implicative constructions with *the/a opportunity to X* consists of *lose*, *miss*, *squander* and *waste* that entail either not having or not using an opportunity.

(27) a. Mr. Spitzer wasted the opportunity to drive a harder bargain.

b. Galileo did not waste the opportunity to aim a funny mock-syllogism at Grassi's flying eggs.

Although *WordNet* classifies the verb *waste* as a hyponym of the verb *use*, the two constructions, *use the opportunity to X* and *waste the opportunity to X*, have opposite entailment signatures. (27a) entails that Spitzer did not drive a harder bargain. Replacing *waste* by *did not use* in (27a) yields the same entailment as the original: he didn't. Similarly, (27b) entails that Galileo aimed a mock syllogism at this opponent but replacing *waste* by *use* in (27b) entails that he did not do that. In other words, *use the/an opportunity to X* is a $++ \mid --$ implicative, but *waste the/an opportunity to X* is a $+- \mid -+$ implicative construction.

Table 3 below summarizes the observations in this section. HAVE stands for *have* and *get*; LACK for *lack, miss, give up, throw away* and *discard*; TAKE for *take, seize, grab* and *snap*; USE for *use, utilize, exploit* and *expend*;

WASTE for *waste*, *squander* and *drop*; OPPORTUNITY for *opportunity*, *chance* and *occasion*. Altogether Table 3 lists the signatures of 54 implicative constructions.

Construction	Implicative signature
HAVE OPPORTUNITY to X	−−
LACK OPPORTUNITY to X	+−
TAKE/USE OPPORTUNITY to X	++ | −−
WASTE OPPORTUNITY to X	+− | −+

Table 3: Phrasal implicatives with OPPORTUNITY nouns

3.3 asset, money, time

As the the contrast between examples in (27) and (28) show, wasting money is different from wasting a chance.

(28) a. I wasted the money to buy a game that I cannot play.

b. I wasted $10 to buy it.

c. I am thrilled I didn't waste $10 to see it in the theater.

d. I'm so glad I didn't waste money to have someone else do it.

(28a) and (28b) entail that I bought the game, (28c) and (28d) yield a negative entailment.

Constructions *waste* NP *to X* where NP is headed by a noun that describes something of value like *asset*, *money*, *time*. *perks* seem all to be + + | − − implicatives.

(29) a. I wasted the time to read through the whole thing.

b. He didn't waste time to stop and look for signs of her trail.

c. I read that it did not work, so didn't waste perks to get it.

d. I'm glad I didn't waste 90 minutes to see this film.

e. I wasted an hour to play this game.

But *waste time to X* is a special case. It has an alternative idiomatic reading in negative sentences as illustrated in (30).

(30) a. Dunning didn't waste any time to begin writing his second film.

b. Madonna didn't waste time to move on to her next single.

c. Secularists wasted no time to jump in flawed study's bandwagon.

Wasting no time to X in the sense of 'quickly do X' is an idiomatic use of *waste*. The examples in (30) do not mean the opposite if the negation is removed. To express the idea opposite to (30b), for example, you have to resort to another idiom, *Madonna took her time to move on to her next single*, it is not correct to say that she wasted time. Without the possessive, *take the time to X* is a straightforward ++ | −− implicative construction, *have the time to X* is −−.

3.4 ability, power, means, oomph

Having the ability to do something is a precondition for doing it. Lacking or losing the ability to X precludes doing X. Both examples in (31) yield a negative entailment for the complement clause.

(31) a. The defendant had no ability to pay a fine.

b. The crickets were there, but they had lost the ability to sing.

The affirmative cases are less clear. (32a) does not entail that Google has been tracking you, but an affirmative answer to the on-line survey in (32b) would interpreted by the author of the survey to mean that the Helpdesk actually solved your issues.

(32) a. Google has had the ability to track your online behavior.

b. The Helpdesk had the ability to solve your issues. Yes or No?

We classify *have the ability to X* as a −− implicative and *lose the ability to X* as a +− implicative. But perhaps *ability* and *power* should also be included in the next class of nouns to accommodate the interpretation of (32b) and similar cases.

3.5 courage, audacity, guts, gall, impudence, chutzpah, gumption, good sense, foresight, wisdom, nerve, stamina, endurance

This set of nouns describes character traits that "manifest themselves" in acts that presuppose them. That is, if someone had the courage to testify, she must have testified. If she didn't testify, then she didn't have the courage to do so, or she lacked whatever other quality the act would have required in her.

(33) a. Julie had the chutzpah to ask the meter maid for a quarter.

b. I didn't have the courage to tell her I love her.

have COURAGE *to X* is a + + | − − implicative construction. It also carries the presupposition that the act in question requires the character trait described by the noun. *Did you have the foresight to invest in Apple?* asks whether the addressee invested in Apple and presupposes that it would have been a good idea. *I managed to get the courage to brave the hot tub* has two presuppositions, one coming from *manage to*, the other from *get the courage to*.

3.6 hesitation, reluctance, qualms, scruples

Like the simple implicative *hesitate to X*, under negative polarity *have/show/display hesitation/reluctance/qualms/scruples to X* entail the complement clause. They are −+ implicative constructions.

(34) a. She did not have any hesitation to don the role of a seductress.

b. Fonseka displayed no reluctance to carry out his orders.

c. Lauren showed no qualms to confess that she fell for it.

3.7 obligation, responsibility, duty

Responsibilities and obligations to do something can be accepted and taken on, or refused and declined. The examples in (35) are future-oriented statements. They do not entail the truth or falsity of the complement clause at the time referred to by the sentence even if there is an invited inference about what might or might not be the case.

(35) a. The Government accepted the obligation to see that fair and reasonable wages were paid to railwaymen.

b. The bank who owns the foreclosed property has refused the responsibility to maintain and clean it up.

But statements about meeting or doing an obligation, responsibility or duty are $++ \mid --$ implicative constructions.

(36) a. We clearly met the obligation to pass a balanced, on-time budget.

b. Strausser hasn't met his responsibility to make improvements.

c. The cyclist met his duty to be seen, and the motorist did not meet his corresponding duties to keep a proper lookout and to exercise due care.

d. Gosling certainly did his duty to pitch the movie to the masses.

4 Conclusion and future work

Table 4 summarizes the findings of the previous section for some of the most common verbs that appear in phrasal implicative constructions and the semantic types of nouns they collocate with.

Verb family	Noun family	Implicative signature
HAVE	ABILITY	−−
HAVE	COURAGE	$++ \mid --$
HAVE	OPPORTUNITY	−−
LACK	ABILITY	+−
LACK	COURAGE	+−
LACK	OPPORTUNITY	+−
MAKE	EFFORT	−−
MEET	OBLIGATION	$++ \mid --$
SHOW	HESITATION	−+
TAKE	EFFORT	$++ \mid --$
TAKE	ASSET	$++ \mid --$
TAKE	OPPORTUNITY	$++ \mid --$
USE	ASSET	$++ \mid --$
USE	OPPORTUNITY	$++ \mid --$
WASTE	ASSET	$++ \mid --$
WASTE	OPPORTUNITY	$+- \mid -+$

Table 4: Implicative signatures for verb-noun collocations

This table lists the implicative signatures of over three hundred phrasal implicative verb-noun collocations. On the level of surface strings the number of constructions is of course much larger because of different tenses for the verb and the many ways of fleshing a noun into a noun phrase. For example, the verb *waste* expands to *wasted, has wasted, did not waste*, etc. The noun *chance* expands to *a chanche, the chance, his chance, her last chance*, etc.

The verb-noun collocations are publicly available.[7] It is a much larger class than the simple implicatives discussed in Section 2 but it is not complete. From a linguistic point of view finding all the specimens is not important if the conceptual classification is done correctly. For computational applications completeness does matter. We plan to continue to expand the list in the near future.

The noun and verb classes discussed in Section 3 contain items that are not together in any *WordNet* (Fellbaum, 1998) SYNSET class. For example, *acquit, fulfill, meet*, and *perform* are interchangeable in sentences such as

[7] http://www.stanford.edu/group/csli_lnr/Lexical_Resources/phrasal-implicatives/

(37) a. He conscientiously acquitted his duty to inform and educate the Court.

b. He fulfilled his duty to cremate his dead brother's body.

c. The officer met his duty to investigate and had probable cause to arrest Kim.

As far as *WordNet* is concerned, the verbs *acquit, fulfill, meet*, and *perform* are totally unrelated. Nevertheless they constitute an equivalence class for this particular phrasal implicative collocation, the MEET OBLIGATION *to X* construction.

The same holds for the noun classes in Section 3. The class in 3.5 includes *chutzpah* and *foresight*. Substituting *foresight* for *chutzpah* in (33a) would retain the entailment, that Julie asked the meter maid for a quarter, but it would bring in a different presupposition.

Some computational systems already take advantage of the semantic classification of simple and phrasal implicatives. PARC's *Bridge* system (Nairn et al., 2006) implements the simple implicatives discussed in Section 2. A few of the phrasal implicatives discussed in Section 3 have also been implemented in *Bridge* (Pichotta, 2008). The *NatLog* system (MacCartney, 2009) implements the same simple implicatives as *Bridge* but in a different way.

But neither *Bridge* nor *NatLog* does anything with presuppositions. *NatLog* takes (1b), *Kim forgot to reschedule the meeting*, as a paraphrase of what it entails, *Kim did not reschedule the meeting*, *Bridge* doesn't. But neither system recognizes the presupposition of intent that comes with the construction *forget to X*.

One area that remains to be systematically explored is the complements of adjectives. It is known that there are factive adjectives such as *strange*, as in *It is strange that Federer has never suffered a major injury*, and two-way implicative adjectives such as *lucky*, as in *He was lucky to break even*, and phrasal adjective $++ \mid --$ constructions such as *see (it) fit to X*, as in *He saw fit to laugh and sneer at us*.

Another unexplored topic is phrasal factives such as *make pretense to X* that is counterfactive, a paraphrase of *pretend to X*.

We will address these issues in future work with the Language and Natural Reasoning group at CSLI.[8]

Acknowledgments

Thanks to my fellow participants in the Linguistics and Natural Reasoning group at CSLI (Cleo Condoravdi, Stanley Peters, Tania Rojas-Esponda and Annie Zaenen) for their help on the content and style of this article. Thanks also to the four anonymous reviewers of this paper for their comments and suggestions.

[8] http://www.stanford.edu/group/csli_lnr/

The author gratefully acknowledges the support of Defense Advanced Research Projects Agency (DARPA) Machine Reading Program under Air Force Research Laboratory (AFRL) prime contract no. FA8750-09-C-0181. Any opinions, findings, and conclusions or recommendations expressed in this material are those of the author and do not necessarily reflect the view of DARPA, AFRL, or the US government.

References

Thomas Egan. 2008. *Non-finite complementation: A usage-based study of infinitive and -ing clauses in English*. Rodopi, Amserdam.

Christiane Fellbaum. 1998. *WordNet: An Electronic Lexical Database*. Bradford Books.

Michael L. Geis and Arnold M. Zwicky. 1971. On invited inferences. *Linguistic Inquiry*, 2(4):561–566. http://www.jstor.org/stable/4177664.

Laurence Horn. 1985. Metalinguistic negation and pragmatic ambiguity. *Language*, 61(1):121–174.

Lauri Karttunen and Stanley Peters. 1979. Conventional implicature. In Choon-Kyu Oh and David A. Dinneen, editors, *Syntax and Semantics, Volume 11: Presupposition*, pages 1–56. Academic Press, New York.

Lauri Karttunen. 1971. Implicative verbs. *Language*, 47:340–358.

Lauri Karttunen. 1973. La logique des constructions anglaises à complément prédicatif. *Langages*, 8:56–80. Published originally as "The Logic of English Predicate Complement Constructions" by the Indiana University Linguistics Club in 1971.

Paul Kiparsky and Carol Kiparsky. 1970. Fact. In M. Bierwisch and K. E. Heidolph, editors, *Progress in Linguistics*, pages 143–173. Mouton, Hague.

Bill MacCartney. 2009. *Natural language inference*. Ph.D. thesis, Stanford University.

Rowan Nairn, Cleo Condoravdi, and Lauri Karttunen. 2006. Computing relative polarity for textual inference. In *Proceedings of the Fifth International workshop on Inference in Computational Semantics (ICoS-5)*, pages 67–76.

Karl Pichotta. 2008. Processing paraphrases and phrasal implicatives in the Bridge question-answering system. Undergraduate Honors Thesis, Symbolic Systems Program, Stanford University.

Juhani Rudanko. 1989. *Complementation and Case Grammar*. State University of New York Press, Albany, New York.

Juhani Rudanko. 2002. *Complements and Constructions. Corpus-Based Studies on Sentential Complements in English in Recent Centuries*. University of Press of America, Lanham, Maryland.

An Unsupervised Ranking Model for Noun-Noun Compositionality

Karl Moritz Hermann, Phil Blunsom, and Stephen Pulman
Department of Computer Science
University of Oxford
Wolfson Building, Parks Road
Oxford OX1 3QD, UK
{karl.moritz.hermann,phil.blunsom,stephen.pulman}@cs.ox.ac.uk

Abstract

We propose an unsupervised system that learns continuous degrees of lexicality for noun-noun compounds, beating a strong baseline on several tasks. We demonstrate that the distributional representations of compounds and their parts can be used to learn a fine-grained representation of semantic contribution. Finally, we argue such a representation captures compositionality better than the current status-quo which treats compositionality as a binary classification problem.

1 Introduction

A Multiword Expressions (MWE) can be defined as a sequence of words whose meaning cannot necessarily be derived from the meaning of the words making up that sequence, for example:

Rat Race — self-defeating or pointless pursuit[1]

MWEs are considered a "key problem for the development of large-scale, linguistically sound natural language processing technology" (Sag et al., 2002). The challenge posed by MWEs is threefold, consisting of MWE identification, classification and interpretation. Following the identification of a MWE, it needs to be established whether the expression should be treated as lexical (idiomatic) or as compositional. The final step, learning the semantics of the MWE, strongly depends on this decision.

The problem posed by MWEs is considered hard, but at the same time it is highly relevant and interesting. MWEs occur frequently in language and interpreting them correctly would directly improve results in a number of tasks in NLP such as translation and parsing (Korkontzelos and Manandhar, 2010). By extension this makes deciding the lexicality of MWEs an important challenge for various fields including machine translation, question answering and information retrieval. In this paper we discuss compositionality with respect to noun-noun compounds.

Most Computational Linguistics literature treats compositionality as a binary problem, classifying compounds as either lexical or compositional. We show that this approach is too simplistic and argue for the real-valued treatment of compositionality.

We propose two unsupervised models that learn compositionality rankings for compounds, placing them on a scale between lexical and compositional extremes. We develop a fine-grained representation of compositionality using a novel generative approach that models context as generated by compound constituents. This representation differentiates between the semantic contribution of both compound constituents as well as the compound itself.

Comparing it with existing work in the field, we demonstrate the competitiveness of our approach. We evaluate on an existing corpus of noun compounds with ranked compositionality data, as well as on a large corpus with a binary annotation for lexical and compositional compounds. We analyse the impact of data sparsity and propose an interpolation approximation which significantly reduces the effect of sparsity on model performance.

[1] Definition taken from Wikipedia, and clearly not recoverable if one only knows the meaning of the words 'rat' and 'race'.

2 Related Work

Interpreting MWEs is a difficult task as "compound nouns can be freely constructed" (Spärck Jones, 1985), and are thus able to proliferate infinitely. At the same time, semantic composition can take many different forms, making uniform interpretation of compounds impossible (Zanzotto et al., 2010).

Most current work on MWEs focuses on interpreting compounds and sidesteps the task of determining whether a compound is compositional in the first place (Butnariu et al., 2010; Kim and Baldwin, 2008). Such methods, aimed at learning the semantics of compounds, can roughly be divided into two major strands of research.

One group relies on data intensive methods to extract semantics vectors from large corpora (Baroni and Zamparelli, 2010; Zanzotto et al., 2010; Giesbrecht, 2009). The focus of these approaches is to develop methods for composing the vectors of unigrams into a semantic vector representing a compound. Some of the work in this area touches on the issue of lexicality, as models learning distributional representations of MWEs ideally would first establish whether a given MWE is compositional or not (Mitchell and Lapata, 2010).

The other group are knowledge intensive approaches collecting linguistic features (Kim and Baldwin, 2005; Korkontzelos and Manandhar, 2009). Tratz and Hovy (2010), for instance, train a classifier for noun compound interpretation on a large set of WordNet and Thesaurus features.

Combined approaches include Kim and Baldwin (2008), who interpret noun compounds by extrapolating their semantics from observations where the two nouns forming a compound are in an intransitive relationship. For example extracting the phrase 'the family owns a car' from the training data would help learn that the compound 'family car' describes a Possessor-Owned/Possessed relationship.

Some of these supervised classifiers include lexicality as a classification option, considering it jointly with the actual compound interpretation.

Next to the work on MWE interpretation there has been some work focused on determining lexicality in its own right (Reddy et al., 2011; Bu et al., 2010; Kim and Baldwin, 2007).

One possibility is to exploit special properties of lexical MWEs such as high statistical association of their constituents (Pedersen, 2011) or syntactic rigidity (Fazly et al., 2009; McCarthy et al., 2007). However, these approaches are limited in their applicability to compound nouns (Reddy et al., 2011).

Another method is to compare the semantics of a compound and its constituents to decide compositionality. The approaches used to determine those semantics can again be divided into knowledge intensive and data-driven methods. Depending on the chosen representation of semantics these approaches can either be used for supervised classifiers or together with a distance metric comparing vector space representations of semantics. In a binary setting, a threshold would then be applied to the result of that distance function (Korkontzelos and Manandhar, 2009). In a real-valued setting the distance metric itself can be used as a measure for compositionality (Reddy et al., 2011). Related to the vector space based models, some research focuses on improving the distance metrics used to compare induced semantics (Bu et al., 2010).

3 Methodology

English noun-noun compounds are majority left-branching (Lauer, 1995), with a head (the second element), modified by an attributive noun (first element). For example:

Ground Floor — The floor of a building at or nearest ground level.[2]

In this paper, we will use the terms attributive noun (AN) and head noun (HN) to refer to the first and second noun in a noun compound.

3.1 Real-Valued Representation

Lexicality of MWEs is frequently treated as a binary property (Tratz and Hovy, 2010; Ó Séaghdha, 2007). We argue that lexicality should instead be treated as a graded property, as most compound semantics exhibit a mixture of compositional and lexical influences. For example, '*cocktail dress*' derives a large part of its semantics from '*dress*', but the compound also contributes an idiosyncratic element to its meaning.

[2] Definition from http://www.thefreedictionary.com

We define lexicality as the degree to which idiosyncrasy contributes to a compound's semantics. Inversely phrased, the compositionality of a compound can be defined as the degree to which its sense is related to the senses of its constituents.[3]

This graded representation follows Spärck Jones (1985), who argued that "it is not possible to maintain a principled distinction between lexicalised and non-lexicalised compounds". Some recent work also supports this view (Reddy et al., 2011; Bu et al., 2010; Baldwin, 2006). From a practical perspective, a real-valued representation of compositionality should help improve interpretation of compounds. This is especially true when factoring in the respective semantic contributions of its parts.

3.2 Context Generation

According to the distributional hypothesis, the semantics of a lexical item can be expressed by its context. We apply this hypothesis to the problem of noun compound compositionality by using a generative model on compound context. Our model allows context to be generated by the compound itself or by either one of its constituents. By learning which element of the compound generates which part of its context we effectively determine the semantic contribution of each element. This in turn gives us a fine-grained, graded representation of a compound's lexicality.

4 Corpora for Evaluation

4.1 Ranked Corpus — REDDY

As we want to evaluate our models' ability to learn lexicality as a real-valued property, we require an annotated data set of noun compounds ranked by lexicality. To the best of our knowledge the only such data set was developed by Reddy et al. (2011). This data set contains 90 distinct noun compounds with real-valued gold standard scores ranking from 0 (lexical) to 5 (compositional). The compounds are nearly linearly distributed across the [0;5] range, with inter annotator agreement (Spearman's ρ) of 0.522. We refer to this data set and evaluation as REDDY throughout this paper.

4.2 Binary Corpora — TRATZ

We also apply our models to a second, binary classification task. Tratz and Hovy (2010) compiled a data set for noun compound interpretation, which classifies noun compounds based on their internal structure. We use this corpus to extract lexical and compositional noun compounds.

After some pre-processing[4] the data set contains 18,858 compositional and 118 lexical noun compounds. We believe this to more accurately represent the real world distribution of lexical and compositional noun compounds: Tratz and Hovy (2010) extracted noun compounds from several large corpora including the Wall Street Journal section of the Penn Treebank, thus obtaining a reasonable approximation of real world occurrence. Other collections of noun compounds (Ó Séaghdha, 2007) feature similar proportions of lexical and compositional noun compounds.

The large bias towards compositional noun compounds does not support the status-quo of treating compositionality as a binary property. As discussed earlier, we assume that most compounds have a compositional as well as a lexical element. While the compositional aspect may be larger for most compounds this alone does not suffice as a reason to disregard the lexical element contained in these compounds.

In order to evaluate our system on the TRATZ data, we use receiving operator characteristic (ROC) curves. ROC analysis enables us to evaluate a ranking model without setting an artificial threshold for the compositionality/lexicality decision.

5 Baseline Approach

We develop a set of advanced baselines related to the semi-supervised models presented by Reddy et al. (2011). We define the context K of a noun compound as all words in all sentences the compound appears in. From this we calculate distributional representations of a compound ($c = \langle a, h \rangle$) and its constituent elements a, h. We refer to these representations as $\vec{c}$ for the compound and $\vec{a}$, $\vec{h}$ for the

[3]For example, the meaning of '*gravy train*' has hardly any relation to either '*gravy*' or '*train*'. Its semantics are thus highly dependent on the compound in its own right. On the other end of the spectrum, '*climate change*' is significantly related to both '*climate*' and '*change*', contributing little inherent semantics to its overall meaning.

[4]We removed trigrams from the data set.

Name	$\oplus$	r	ρ
ADD	$w.S_{ac} + (1 - w).S_{hc}$	.323	**.567**
MULT	$S_{ac}.S_{hc}$	**.379**	.551
MIN	$min(S_{ac}, S_{hc})$	.343	.550
MAX	$max(S_{ac}, S_{hc})$	.299	.505
COMB	$w_1.S_{ac}+w_2.S_{hc}+w_3.S_{ac}.S_{hc}$	.366	.556

Table 1: Results of CosLex with different operators on the REDDY data set, reporting Pearson's r and Spearman's ρ correlations. Weights for operators ADD ($w = 0.3$) and COMB ($\mathbf{w} = \langle 0.3, 0.1, 0.6 \rangle$) are manually optimised. Values range from -1 (negative correlation) to +1 (perfect correlation) with 0 describing random data.

attributive and head noun, respectively. We can calculate the cosine similarity based lexicality score (CosLex) by combining the cosine similarity of the compound's distribution with each of its two constituents (Reddy et al., 2011).

$$S_{ac} = \text{sim}(\vec{a}, \vec{c})$$
$$S_{hc} = \text{sim}(\vec{h}, \vec{c})$$
$$\text{CosLex}(c) = S_{ac} \oplus S_{hc}$$

We evaluate a number of alternative operators $\oplus$ for combining S_{ac} and S_{hc}. Results for this baseline on the REDDY corpus are in Table 1,[5] with weights w_i on the combination operators manually optimised for Spearman's ρ on that data set. In effect this renders this baseline into a supervised approach, so we would expect it to perform very well. We use the best performing operators (ADD with $w = 0.3$, MULT) as baselines for this paper.

6 Generative Models

We exploit the distributional hypothesis to model the semantic contribution of the different elements of a noun compound. For this, we require a system that treats a noun compound as a vector of three semantics-bearing units: the compound itself, its head and its attributive noun. This system should then model the relationship between the context of the compound and these three units, deciding which of them is responsible for each context element.

[5]Reddy et al. (2011) report higher figures on our baseline models. The differences are attributed to differences in training data and parametrization.

6.1 3-way Compound Mixture

We model a corpus $\mathcal{D}$ of tuples $d = \{c, k_1, ..., k_n\}$. Each tuple d contains a noun compound $c = \langle a, h \rangle$ and its context words $\mathbf{K} = (k_1, ..., k_n)$. We use vocabularies V_c for noun compounds, V_a for attributive nouns, V_h for head nouns and V_k for context.

We condition our generative model on the noun compounds. Given an observation d of a compound c, we generate each context word in two steps. First, we choose one of the compounds three elements[6] to generate the next context word. Second, we generate a new context word conditioned on that element. Formally, the context is generated as follows.

We draw three multinomial parameters Ψ^c, Ψ^a and Ψ^h from Dirichlet distributions with parameters α^c, α^a and α^h. Ψ^c represents the distribution over context words V_k given compound c. Ψ^a and Ψ^h are distributions over V_k given attributive noun a and head noun h, respectively. These three distributions form the mixture components of our model.

A fourth multinomial parameter Ψ^z, drawn from a Dirichlet distribution with parameter α^z, controls the distribution over the mixture components. Ψ^z is specific to each compound c, so multiple observations of the same compound share this parameter.

For each context word we draw a mixture component $z_{c,i} \in \{\check{c}, \check{a}, \check{h}\}$ from the multinomial distribution with parameter Ψ^z. $z_{c,i}$ determines which distribution the context word itself will be drawn from. Finally, we draw the context word:

$$\forall i \colon k_i \mid \Psi^{\{z_{c,i}\}} \sim \text{Multi}(\Psi^{\{z_{c,i}\}})$$

Thus, for each observation of a compound noun we have a vector $\mathbf{z_c} = \langle \mathbf{z_1}, ..., \mathbf{z_n} \rangle$ detailing how its context words were created either by the compound itself or by one of its constituents. To determine lexicality, we are interested in learning the multinomial parameter Ψ^z, which describes to what extent the compound and its constituents contribute to the generation of the context (i.e. semantics). We can approximate Ψ^z from the vector $\mathbf{z_c}$.

We define the lexicality score $Lex(c)$ for a compound as the percentage of context words created by

[6]The compound itself, its attributive noun and its head noun

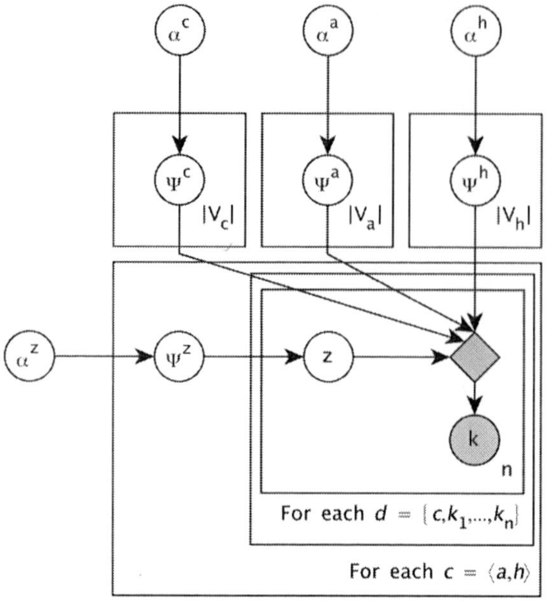

Figure 1: Plate diagram illustrating the MULT-CMPD model with context words k_i drawn from a mixture model with three components controlled by z_i.

the compound and not one of its constituents:

$$Lex(c) = p(z{=}\check{c}|\langle a, h\rangle), \quad \text{where } c = \langle a, h\rangle \tag{1}$$

Figure 1 shows a plate diagram of this model, which we will refer to as MULT-CMPD.

One hypothesis encoded in model MULT-CMPD is that deciding which part of a compound (the compound itself, the head or the attributive noun) generates context is a single decision. An alternative representation could treat this as a two-step process, which we encode in a second model BIN-CMPD. The intuition behind the BIN-CMPD model is that there are two distinct decisions. First, whether a compound is compositional or not. Second, whether (in the compositional case) its semantics stem from its head or attributive noun

Where MULT-CMPD uses a three component mixture to determine which multinomial distribution to use, BIN-CMPD uses two cascaded binary mixtures (see Figure 2). The BIN-CMPD model first chooses whether to treat a compound as compositional or lexical. If the compound is determined as compositional, a second binary mixture determines whether to generate a context word using the attributive (Ψ^a) or head multinomial (Ψ^h). For the lexical case, the model remains unchanged.

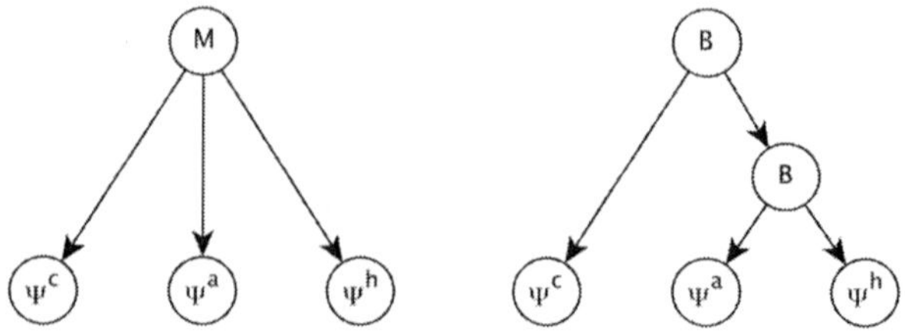

Figure 2: Schematic description of compositionality/lexicality decision for models MULT-CMPD and BIN-CMPD.

Model	r	ρ
COSLEX (ADD)	.323	**.567**
COSLEX (MULT)	**.379**	.551
MULT-CMPD	.141	.435
BIN-CMPD	.168	.410

Table 2: Results on the REDDY data set, reporting Pearson's r and Spearman's ρ correlations. Values range from -1 (negative correlation) to +1 (perfect correlation).

6.1.1 Inference and Sampling

We use Gibbs sampling to learn the vectors **z** for each instance d, integrating out the parameters Ψ^x. We train our models on the British National Corpus (BNC), extracting all noun-noun compounds from a parsed version of the corpus.

In order to speed up convergence of the sampler, we use simulated annealing over the first 20 iterations (Kirkpatrick et al., 1983), helping the randomly initialised model reach a mode faster. We report results using marginal distributions after a further 130 iterations, excluding the counts of the annealing stage.

6.1.2 Evaluation

We evaluate our two models on the REDDY data set by comparing its scores for lexicality ($Lex(c)$) with the annotated gold standard. The aim of this evaluation is to determine how accurately the models can capture gradual distinctions in lexicality. The ROC analysis on the TRATZ data set furthermore informs us how precise the models are at distinguishing lexical from compositional compounds.

Results of the REDDY evaluation are in Table 2. We use Spearman's ρ to measure the monotonic correlation of our data to the gold standard. Pearson's r additionally captures the linear relationship between the data, taking into account the relative differences in $Lex(c)$ scores among noun compounds.

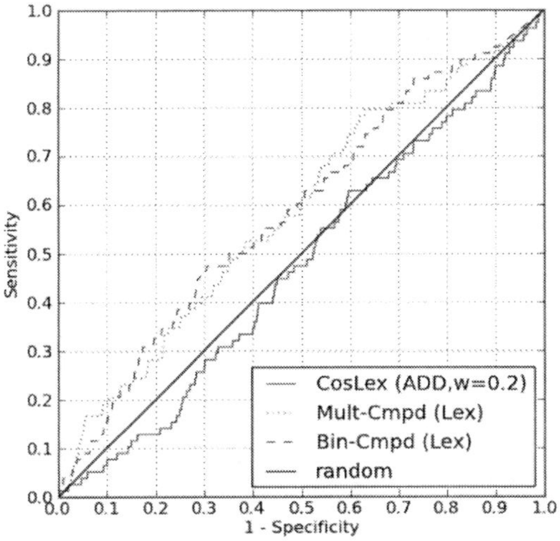

Figure 3: ROC analysis of models MULT-CMPD and BIN-CMPD versus the best COSLEX baseline (ADD) on the TRATZ data set

While both models, BIN-CMPD and MULT-CMPD, clearly learn a correlation with lexicality rankings, they underperform the strong, semi-supervised COSLEX baselines described earlier in this paper. The second evaluation, on the binary TRATZ data set shows a different picture (see Figure 3). The best COSLEX baseline (ADD with $w = 0.2$) fails to outperform random choice on this task. Both generative models clearly beat COSLEX on this task, with MULT-CMPD in particular performing very well for low sensitivity.

There is no clear distinction in performance between the two generative approaches. Further analysis might help us to separate the two more clearly, and we will continue using both models throughout this paper.

It is important to note the different performance of the generative models vs. the cosine similarity approach on two tasks. The REDDY data set has a nearly linear distribution of compositionality scores, while the TRATZ data set is overwhelmingly compositional, which more closely represents the real world distribution of compounds. The poor performance of the cosine similarity approach (COSLEX) on the TRATZ evaluation suggests the limitations of this approach when applied to more realistic data such as this data set. An additional explanation for the semi-supervised baseline's poorer result is that the effect of parameter tuning decreases on larger data.

Investigating the errors made by the models MULT-CMPD and BIN-CMPD gives rise to a number of possible explanations for their performance. The most promising lead is related to data sparsity, with many of the evaluated noun-noun compounds only appearing once or twice in the corpus. This makes it harder for our generative approach to learn sensible context distributions for these instances.

We will next investigate how to reduce the effects encountered by sparsity.

6.2 Interpolation

Working on problems related to non-unigram data, sparsity is a frequently encountered problem. As already explored in the previous section, this is also the case for our generative models of lexicality.

It would be possible to use an even larger training corpus, but there are limitations as to what extent this is possible. The BNC, containing 100 million words, is already one of the largest corpora regularly used in Computational Linguistics. However, adding more data in an unsupervised sense is unlikely to significantly improve results (Brants et al., 2007).

Alternatively, it would be possible to add specific training data that included the noun compounds from the evaluation data sets. This would, however, compromise the unsupervised nature of our approach, and it thus not an option either.

In this paper, we will instead focus on extenuating the effects of data sparsity through other unsupervised means. For this purpose we investigate interpolating on a larger set of noun compounds.

Kim and Baldwin (2007) observed that semantic similarity of verb-particle compounds correlates with their lexicality. We extend this observation for noun compounds, hypothesising that the lexicality of similar words will be similar. We combine this with the assumption that noun compounds sharing a constituent are likely to be semantically similar (Korkontzelos and Manandhar, 2009).

Using this idea, we can approximate the lexicality of a given compound with the lexicality scores of all compounds sharing either of its constituents. So far we have calculated the lexicality of a given compound using the formula $Lex(c)$ in Equation 1. The formula $Clex(c)$ in Equation 2 averages the lexicality scores of a compound with those of its related

Function and Model		r	ρ
	CosLex (ADD)	.323	.567
	CosLex (MULT)	.379	.551
$Lex(c)$	Mult-Cmpd	.141	.435
	Bin-Cmpd	.168	.410
$Clex(c)$	Mult-Cmpd	.357	.596
	Bin-Cmpd	.400	.592
$Ilex(c)$	Mult-Cmpd	.422	.621
	Bin-Cmpd	**.538**	**.623**

Table 3: Results on the REDDY data set, reporting Pearson's r and Spearman's ρ correlations, comparing $Ilex(c)$ and $Clec(c)$ interpolations with $Lex(c)$.

compounds. As $p(z=1|\langle a,h\rangle)$ directly influences both $p(z=1|\langle a,\cdot\rangle)$ and $p(z=1|\langle \cdot,h\rangle)$, we can also consider dropping it from the approximation such as in Equation 3. This approach trades some specificity in favour of reducing sparsity, as we observe more instances of such related compounds than of a particular noun compound itself only.

$$Lex(c) \approx Clex(c) \quad (2)$$

$$Clex(c) = \frac{p(z=1|\langle a,\cdot\rangle) + p(z=1|\langle \cdot,h\rangle) + p(z=1|\langle a,h\rangle)}{3}, \text{ where } c = \langle a,h\rangle$$

$$Lex(c) \approx Ilex(c) \quad (3)$$

$$Ilex(c) = \frac{p(z=1|\langle a,\cdot\rangle) + p(z=1|\langle \cdot,h\rangle)}{2}, \text{ where } c = \langle a,h\rangle$$

Both formulations enable us to better deal with sparse data as decisions are made based on a wider range of observations. At the same time, we avoid a loss of specificity as the models and scores are still highly dependent on the individual noun compound.

We avoid introducing additional degrees of freedom by using uniform weights only. However, it would be simple to turn this approach into a semi-supervised model by tuning the weights for the different probabilities involved in calculating $Clex(c)$ and $Lex(c)$. That approach would be comparable to the operators used on our CosLex baselines.

Results on the REDDY data set using $Clex(c)$ and $Ilex(c)$ are in Table 3. Figure 4 shows the impact of these approximations on the Tratz data for the Bin-Cmpd model. These interpolations suggest strong improvements in performance. It should especially be noted that $Ilex(c)$ consistently outperforms $Clex(c)$, which indicates the strength of the related-compound probabilities over the individual compound probabilities.

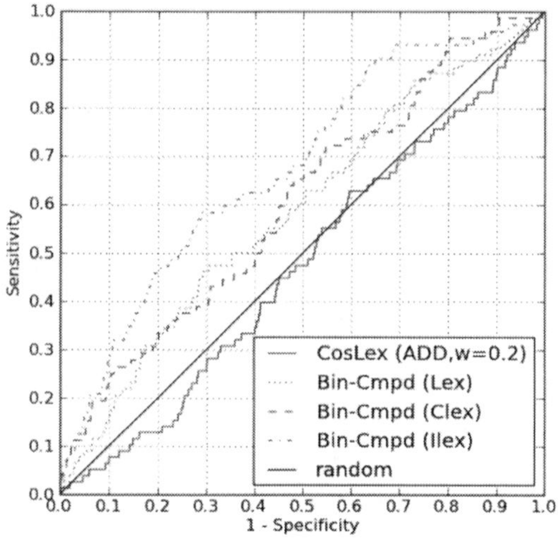

Figure 4: ROC analysis of model Bin-Cmpd on the TRATZ data set, comparing $Ilex(c)$ and $Clec(c)$ interpolations with $Lex(c)$.

These results confirm our suspicion that sparsity was a major factor affecting our models' performance. Furthermore, they strengthen our hypothesis about the relatedness of semantic similarity and lexicality and demonstrate a sensible approach for exploiting this relationship.

7 Analysis

We use this section for qualitative evaluation, complementing the quantitative evaluation in the previous sections. The purpose of the qualitative evaluation is to better understand exactly what it is our models are learning.

Table 5 lists the compounds that model Bin-Cmpd considers the most lexical and the most compositional. The list of compounds with the high lexicality scores is dominated by proper nouns such as countries, companies and persons. This is in line with expectation as compounds of proper nouns are fully lexical. Removing proper nouns (also in Table 5), we get a slightly more ambiguous list. For example, 'study design' is not considered a lexical compound, but rather a highly institutionalized, compositional MWE (Sag et al., 2002). Using $Lex(c)$ 'study design' is ranked as such, so this appears to be a case where interpolation has a negative impact.

In this paper we argued for a finer grained analysis of compositionality, taking into account the differ-

Context of 'flea market' generated by

flea	market	flea market
canal, wall, incline, campsite	stall, Paris, sale, Saturday, week, Sunday, quarter, damage, change	barter, souvenir, launderette, Lamine, Canet, Kouyate, Plage

Context of 'memory lane' generated by

memory	lane	memory lane
take, story, about, tell, real, glimpse, Britain, reminiscence	village, protection, drive, catwalk, plant	war, justify, bill, Campbell, rude-boys

Context of 'night owl' generated by

night	owl	night owl
court, fee, guest, early, day, Baden, membership, life, game	waive, player, Halikarnas, bar, bird, unbooked, Vienna	adventurous

Context of 'melting pot' generated by

melting	pot	melting pot
forest, racial, caribbean, plan, programme, reality, arrangement	in, into, put, political, community, prepare	ethnic, greatest, drawing, liaise, pan-european, myth

Table 4: Overview over context words generated by model BIN-CMPD. We list a selection of words predominately generated by each of the mixture components of the given noun-noun compound.

Most Compositional
labour union, tax authority, health council, market counterparty, employment policy

Most Lexical
study design, family motto, wood shaving, avoidance behaviour, smash hit

Most Lexical (including Proper Nouns)
Vo Quy, Bonito Oliva, Mamur Zapt, Evander Holyfield, Saudi Arabia

Table 5: Top lexical and compositional nouns for the BIN-CMPD model using $Ilex(c)$

ent impact of both constituents. We tried to achieve this by modelling a compound's context as generated from its various semantic constituents. Table 4 highlights the impact of this method for a number of noun compounds, showing which context words were predominately generated by each constituent.

Due to the nature of the context used, some of the links are semantically not obvious (e.g. the relationship between owls and Vienna). In some cases the semantic contribution of the parts is more clearly separated, such as the contributions of '*memory*' and '*lane*' to the semantics of '*memory lane*'. In summary, these examples clearly suggest that our models learn to associate context with compound elements and that this association is an informed one.

8 Conclusion

We proposed a novel approach for learning lexicality scores for noun compounds and empirically demonstrated the feasiblity of this approach. Using a generative model we were able to beat a strong, semi-supervised baseline with an unsupervised model.

We discussed the issue of data sparsity in depth and proposed several approaches for overcoming this problem. Focusing on unsupervised approaches, we demonstrated how interpolation can be used to tackle sparsity. The two interpolation methods that we implemented helped us to strongly improve overall model performance. Our empirical evaluation of interpolation metrics $Clex(c)$ and $Ilex(c)$ also gives credence to the hypothesis that lexicality is related to semantic similarity.

On the theoretical side, we offered further support to the real-valued treatment of lexicality.

Further work will include using larger training corpora. While the BNC is a popular corpus in Computational Linguistics, it proved to be too small to learn sensible representations for a number of compounds encountered in the test data. Using larger corpora will also allow us to further study and reduce the sparsity issues encountered.

To study the relationship between constituent and compound compositionality in greater depth, we will also investigate alternative approaches for interpolation. Similarity measures that consider the semantic relevance of individual context elements should also be considered as a next step.

Another obvious source of future work is to apply our approach to general collocations beyond the special case of noun compounds only.

Acknowledgments

The authors would like to acknowledge the use of the Oxford Supercomputing Centre (OSC) in carrying out this work.

References

Timothy Baldwin. 2006. Compositionality and multiword expressions: Six of one, half a dozen of the other? In *Proceedings of the Workshop on Multiword Expressions: Identifying and Exploiting Underlying Properties*, page 1, Sydney, Australia. Association for Computational Linguistics.

Marco Baroni and Roberto Zamparelli. 2010. Nouns are vectors, adjectives are matrices: representing adjective-noun constructions in semantic space. In *Proceedings of the 2010 Conference on Empirical Methods in Natural Language Processing*, EMNLP '10, pages 1183–1193, Stroudsburg, PA, USA. Association for Computational Linguistics.

Thorsten Brants, Ashok C. Popat, Peng Xu, Franz J. Och, and Jeffrey Dean. 2007. Large Language Models in Machine Translation. In *Proceedings of the 2007 Joint Conference on Empirical Methods in Natural Language Processing and Computational Natural Language Learning (EMNLP-CoNLL)*, pages 858–867.

Fan Bu, Xiaoyan Zhu, and Ming Li. 2010. Measuring the non-compositionality of multiword expressions. In *Proceedings of the 23rd International Conference on Computational Linguistics*, COLING '10, pages 116–124, Stroudsburg, PA, USA. Association for Computational Linguistics.

Cristina Butnariu, Su Nam Kim, Preslav Nakov, Diarmuid Ó. Séaghdha, Stan Szpakowicz, and Tony Veale. 2010. Semeval-2010 task 9: The interpretation of noun compounds using paraphrasing verbs and prepositions. In *Proceedings of the 5th International Workshop on Semantic Evaluation*, SemEval '10, pages 39–44, Stroudsburg, PA, USA. Association for Computational Linguistics.

Afsaneh Fazly, Paul Cook, and Suzanne Stevenson. 2009. Unsupervised type and token identification of idiomatic expressions. *Computational Linguistics*, 35(1):61–103.

Eugenie Giesbrecht. 2009. In search of semantic compositionality in vector spaces. In *Proceedings of the 17th International Conference on Conceptual Structures: Conceptual Structures: Leveraging Semantic Technologies*, ICCS '09, pages 173–184, Berlin, Heidelberg. Springer-Verlag.

Su Nam Kim and Timothy Baldwin. 2005. Automatic interpretation of noun compounds using wordnet similarity. In *In Proceedings of the 2nd International Joint Conference on Natural Language Processing, Jeju Island, South Korea, 1113*, pages 945–956.

Su Nam Kim and Timothy Baldwin. 2007. Detecting compositionality of English verb-particle constructions using semantic similarity. In *Proceedings of the 7th Meeting of the Pacific Association for Computational Linguistics*, PACLING '07, pages 40–48.

Su Nam Kim and Timothy Baldwin. 2008. An unsupervised approach to interpreting noun compounds. In *Natural Language Processing and Knowledge Engineering, 2008. NLP-KE '08. International Conference on*, pages 1–7.

S. Kirkpatrick, C. D. Gelatt, and M. P. Vecchi. 1983. Optimization by simulated annealing. *Science*, 220(4598):671–680.

Ioannis Korkontzelos and Suresh Manandhar. 2009. Detecting compositionality in multi-word expressions. In *Proceedings of the ACL-IJCNLP 2009 Conference Short Papers*, ACLShort '09, pages 65–68, Stroudsburg, PA, USA. Association for Computational Linguistics.

Ioannis Korkontzelos and Suresh Manandhar. 2010. Can recognising multiword expressions improve shallow parsing? In *Human Language Technologies: The 2010 Annual Conference of the North American Chapter of the Association for Computational Linguistics*, HLT '10, pages 636–644, Stroudsburg, PA, USA. Association for Computational Linguistics.

Mark Lauer. 1995. Corpus statistics meet the noun compound: some empirical results. In *Proceedings of the 33rd annual meeting on Association for Computational Linguistics*, ACL '95, pages 47–54, Stroudsburg, PA, USA. Association for Computational Linguistics.

Diana McCarthy, Sriram Venkatapathy, and Aravind Joshi. 2007. Detecting compositionality of verb-object combinations using selectional preferences. In *Proceedings of the 2007 Joint Conference on Empirical Methods in Natural Language Processing and Computational Natural Language Learning (EMNLP-CoNLL)*, pages 369–379, Prague, Czech Republic. Association for Computational Linguistics.

Jeff Mitchell and Mirella Lapata. 2010. Composition in distributional models of semantics. *Cognitive Science*, 34(8):1388–1429.

Diarmuid Ó Séaghdha. 2007. Annotating and learning compound noun semantics. In *Proceedings of the 45th Annual Meeting of the ACL: Student Research Workshop*, ACL '07, pages 73–78, Stroudsburg, PA, USA. Association for Computational Linguistics.

Ted Pedersen. 2011. Identifying collocations to measure compositionality: shared task system description. In *Proceedings of the Workshop on Distributional Semantics and Compositionality*, DiSCo '11, pages 33–37, Stroudsburg, PA, USA. Association for Computational Linguistics.

Siva Reddy, Diana McCarthy, and Suresh Manandhar. 2011. An empirical study on compositionality in compound nouns. In *Proceedings of The 5th International Joint Conference on Natural Language Processing 2011 (IJCNLP 2011)*, Chiang Mai, Thailand.

Ivan A. Sag, Timothy Baldwin, Francis Bond, Ann Copestake, and Dan Flickinger. 2002. Multiword expressions: A pain in the neck for NLP. In *In Proc. of the 3rd International Conference on Intelligent Text Processing and Computational Linguistics (CICLing-2002*, pages 1–15.

Karen Spärck Jones. 1985. Compound noun interpretation problems. In Frank Fallside and William A. Woods, editors, *Computer speech processing*, pages 363–381. Prentice Hall International (UK) Ltd., Hertfordshire, UK, UK.

Stephen Tratz and Eduard Hovy. 2010. A taxonomy, dataset, and classifier for automatic noun compound interpretation. In *Proceedings of the 48th Annual Meeting of the Association for Computational Linguistics*, ACL '10, pages 678–687, Stroudsburg, PA, USA. Association for Computational Linguistics.

Fabio Massimo Zanzotto, Ioannis Korkontzelos, Francesca Fallucchi, and Suresh Manandhar. 2010. Estimating linear models for compositional distributional semantics. In *Proceedings of the 23rd International Conference on Computational Linguistics*, COLING '10, pages 1263–1271, Stroudsburg, PA, USA. Association for Computational Linguistics.

Expanding the Range of Tractable Scope-Underspecified Semantic Representations

Mehdi Manshadi and James Allen
Department of Computer Science
University of Rochester
Rochester, NY 14627
{mehdih, james}@cs.rochester.edu

Abstract

Over the past decade, several underspecification frameworks have been proposed that efficiently solve a big subset of scope-underspecified semantic representations within the realm of the most popular constraint-based formalisms. However, there exists a family of coherent natural language sentences whose underspecified representation does not belong to this subset. It has remained an open question whether there exists a tractable superset of these frameworks, covering this family. In this paper, we show that the answer to this question is yes. We define a superset of the previous frameworks, which is solvable by similar algorithms with the same time and space complexity.

1 Introduction

Scope ambiguity is a major source of ambiguity in semantic representation. For example, the sentence

1. *Every politician has a website.*

has at least two possible interpretations, one in which each *politician* may have a different *website* (i.e., *Every* has **wide scope**) and one in which there is a unique *website* for all the *politicians* (i.e., *Every* has **narrow scope**). Since finding the most preferred reading automatically is very hard, the most widely adopted solution is to use an **Underspecified Representation (UR)**, that is to encode the ambiguity in the semantic representation and leave scoping **underspecified**.

In an early effort, Woods (1986) developed an unscoped logical form where the above sentence is represented (roughly) as the formula:

2. $Has(\langle Every\ x\ Politician\rangle, \langle A\ y\ Website\rangle)$

To obtain a fully scoped formula, the quantifiers are pulled out one by one and wrapped around the formula. If we pull out *Every* first, we produce the fully-scoped formula:

3. $A(y, Website(y),$
$Every(x, Politician(x), Has(x, y))$

If we had pulled out A first, we would have had the other reading, with *Every* having wide scope.

Hobbs and Shieber (1987) extend this formalism to support operators (such as *not*) and present an enumeration algorithm that is more efficient than the naive wrapping approach.

Since the introduction of Quasi Logical Form (Alshawi and Crouch, 1992), there has been a lot of work on designing constraint-based underspecification formalisms where the readings of a UR are not defined in a constructive fashion as shown above, but rather by a set of constraints. A fully-scoped structure is a reading iff it satisfies all the constraints. The advantage of these frameworks is that as the processing goes deeper, new (say pragmatically-driven) constraints can be added to the representation in order to filter out unwanted readings. **Hole Semantics** (Bos, 1996; Bos, 2002), Constraint Language for Lambda Structures (**CLLS**) (Egg et al., 2001), and Minimal Recursion Semantics (**MRS**) (Copestake et al., 2001) are among these frameworks.

In an effort to bridge the gap between the above formalisms, a graph theoretic model of scope underspecification was defined by Bodirsky et al. (2004), called **Weakly Normal Dominance Graphs**. This

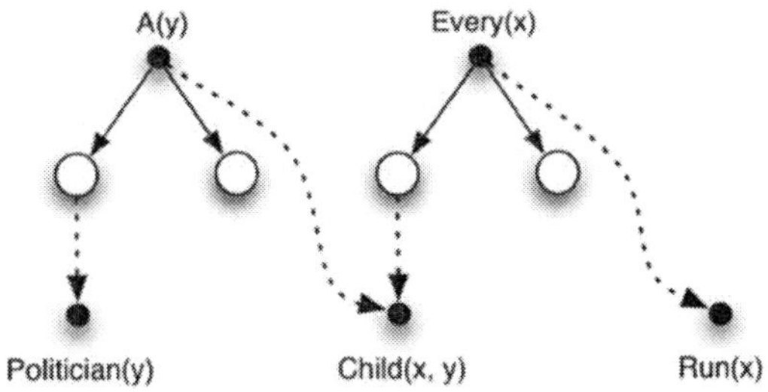

Figure 1: UG for *Every child of a politician runs.*

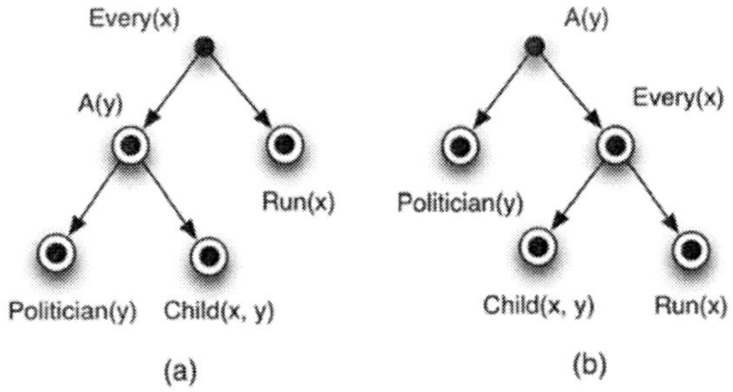

Figure 2: Solutions of the UG in Figure 1.

framework and its ancestor, **Dominance Constraints** (Althaus et al., 2003), are broad frameworks for solving constrained tree structures in general. When it comes to scope underspecification, some of the terminology becomes counter-intuitive. Therefore, here we first define (scope) **Underspecification Graphs (UG)**, a notational variant of weakly normal dominance graphs, solely defined to model scope underspecification.[1] Figure 1 shows a UG for the following sentence.

4. *Every child of a politician runs.*

The big circles and the dot nodes are usually referred to as the **hole** nodes (or simply holes) and the **label** nodes (or simply labels) respectively. The left and the right holes of each quantifier are placeholders for the **restriction** and the **body** of the quantifier. A fully scoped structure is built by **plugging** labels into holes, as shown in Figure 2(a). The dotted edges represent the **constraints**. For example, the constraint from the restriction hole of *Every(x)* to the node *Politician(x)* states that this label node must be within the scope of the restriction of *Every(x)* in every reading of the sentence. The constraint edge from *Every(x)* to *Run(x)* forces the binding constraint for variable x; that is variable x in *Run(x)* must be within the scope of its quantifier. Figure 2(b) represents the other possible reading of the sentence. Now consider the sentence:

5. *Every politician, whom I know a child of, probably runs.*

with its UG shown in Figure 3. This sentence contains a scopal adverbial (a.k.a. **fixed-scopal**; cf. Copestake et al. (2005)), the word *Probably*. Since in general, quantifiers can move inside or outside a scopal operator, the scope of *Probably* is left underspecified, and hence represented by a hole. It is easy to verify that the corresponding UG has five possible readings, two of which are shown in Figure 4.

There are at least two major algorithmic problems that need to be solved for any given UG U: the **satisfiability** problem; that is whether there exists any reading satisfying all the constraints in U, and the **enumeration** problem; that is enumerating all the possible readings of a satisfiable U. Unfortunately, both problems are NP-complete for UG in its general form (Althaus et al., 2003). This proves that Hole Semantics and Minimal Recursion Semantics are also intractable in their general form (Thater, 2007). In the last decade, there has been a series of interesting work on finding a tractable subset of those frameworks, broad enough to cover most structures occurring in practice. Those efforts resulted in two closely related **tractable** frameworks: (dominance) **net** and **weak** (dominance) **net**. Intuitively, the net condition requires the following property. Given a UG U, for every label node in U with n holes, if the node together with all its holes is removed from U, the remaining part is composed of at most n (weakly) connected components. A difference between net and weak net is that in nets, label-

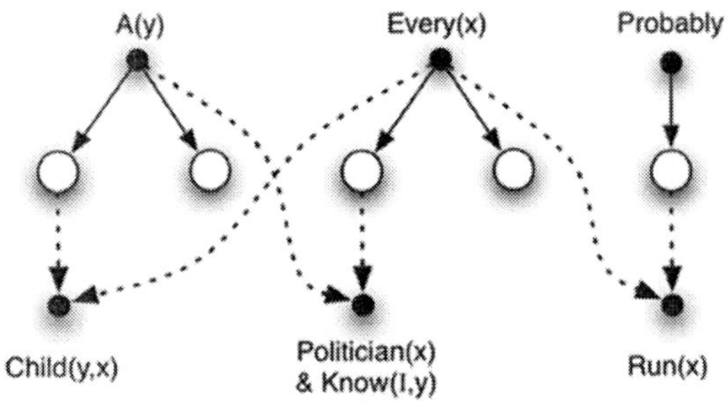

Figure 3: UG for the sentence in (5).

[1]The main difference is in the concept of solution in the two frameworks. See Section 4.3 for details.

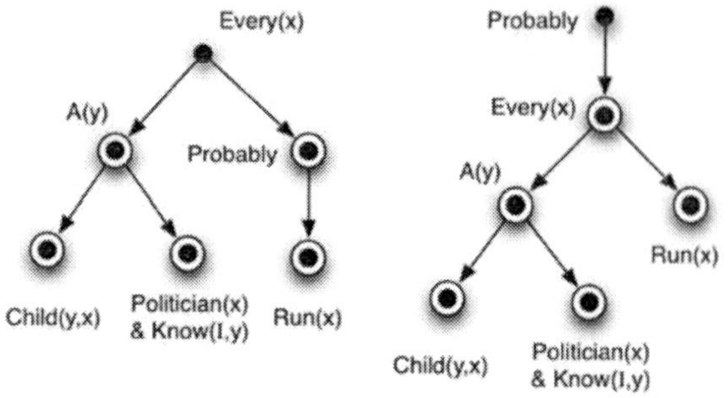

Figure 4: Two of the solutions to the UG in Figure 3.

to-label constraints (e.g. the constraint between *Every(x)* and *Run(x)* in Figure 1) are not allowed.

Using a sample grammar for CLLS, Koller et al. (2003) conjecture that the syntax/semantics interface of CLLS only generates underspecified representations that follow the definition of net and hence can be solved in polynomial time. They also prove that the same efficient algorithms can be used to solve the underspecification structures of Hole Semantics which satisfy the net condition.

Unlike Hole Semantics and CLLS, MRS implicitly carries label-to-label constraints; hence the concept of net could not be applied to MRS. In order to address this, Niehren and Thater (2003) define the notion of weak net and conjecture that it covers all semantically complete MRS structures occurring in practice. Fuchss et al. (2004) supported the claim by investigating MRS structures in the Redwoods corpus (Oepen et al., 2002). Later coherent sentences were found in other corpora or suggested by other researchers (see Section 6.2.2 in Thater (2007)), whose UR violates the net condition, invalidating the conjecture. However, violating the net condition occurs in a similar way in those examples, suggesting a family of non-net structures, characterized in Section 4.2. Since then, it has been an open question whether there exists a tractable superset of weak nets, covering this family of non-net UGs.

In the rest of this paper, we answer this question. We modify the definition of weak net to define a superset of it, which we call **super net**. Super net covers the above mentioned family of non-net structures, yet is solvable by (almost) the same algorithms as those solving weak nets with the same time and space complexity.

The structure of the paper is as follows. We define our framework in Section 2 and present the polynomial-time algorithms for its satisfiability and enumeration problems in Section 3. In Section 4, we compare our framework with nets and weak nets. Section 5 discusses the related work, and Section 6 summarizes this work and discusses future work.

2 Super net

We first give a formal definition of underspecification graph (UG). We then define super net as a subset of UG. In the following definitions, we openly borrow the terminology from Hole Semantics, Dominance Constraints, and MRS, in order to avoid inventing new terms to name old concepts.

Definition 1 (Fragments). *Consider L a set of labels, H a set of holes, and S a set of directed* solid *edges from labels to holes, such that $\mathcal{F} = (L \uplus H, S)$ is a forest of* ordered *trees of depth at most 1, whose root and only the root is a label node. Each of these trees is called a **fragment**.*

Following this definition, the number of trees in $\mathcal{F}$ (including single-node trees) equals the number of labels. For example, if we remove all the dotted edges in Figure 1, we obtain a forest of 5 fragments.

Definition 2 (Underspecification Graph). *Let $\mathcal{F} = (L \uplus H, S)$ be a forest of fragments and C be a set of directed* dotted *edges from $L \uplus H$ to L, called the set of **constraints**.*[2] *$U = (L \uplus H, S \uplus C)$ is called an **underspecification graph** or **UG**.*

Figures 1 and 3 each represent a UG.

Definition 3 (Plugging). (Bos, 1996)
*Given a UG $U = (L \uplus H, S \uplus C)$, a **plugging** P is a total one-to-one function from H to L.*

In Figure 1, if l_A, l_E, l_P, l_C, and l_R represent the nodes labeled by *A(y)*, *Every(x)*, *Politician(y)*, *Child(x,y)*, and *Run(x)* respectively and h^r_A (h^b_A) and h^r_E (h^b_E) represent the restriction (body) hole of *A* and *Every* respectively, then P in (6) is a plugging.

6. $P = \{(h^r_A, l_P), (h^b_A, l_C), (h^r_E, l_A), (h^b_E, l_R)\}$

We use $\boldsymbol{T_{U,P}}$ to refer to the graph, formed from U by removing all the constraints and plugging $P(h)$ into h for every hole h. For example if U is the UG in Figure 1 and P is the plugging in (6), then $T_{U,P}$ is the graph shown in Figure 2(a).

[2]We assume that there is no constraint edge between two nodes of the same fragment.

Definition 4 (Permissibility/Solution). *$T_{U,P}$ **satisfies** the constraint (u,v) in U, iff u* dominates[3] *v in $T_{U,P}$*.[4] *A plugging P is **permissible**, iff $T_{U,P}$ is a* forest *satisfying all the constraints in U. $T_{U,P}$ is called a **solution** of U iff P is a permissible plugging. In informal contexts, solutions are sometimes referred to as **readings**.*

It is easy to see that the plugging in (6) is a permissible plugging for the UG in Figure 1, and hence Figure 2(a) is a solution of this UG. Similarly, Figures 4(a,b) represent two solutions of the UG in Figure 3. The solutions in Figures 2 and 4 are all *tree* structures. This is because UGs in Figures 1 and 3 are *weakly connected*.[5] Lemma 2 proves that this holds in general, that is:

Proposition 1. *Every solution of a weakly connected UG is a tree.*

Throughout the rest of this paper, unless otherwise specified, UGs are assumed to be weakly connected, hence solutions are tree structures.[6]

Lemma 2. (Bodirsky et al., 2004)
Given a UG U and a solution T of U, if the nodes u and v in U are connected using an undirected path p, there exists a node w on p such that w dominates both u and v in T.

This Lemma is proved using induction on the length of p. As mentioned before, *satisfiability* and *enumeration* are two fundamental problems to be solved for a UG. A straightforward approach is depicted in Figure 5. We pick a label l; remove it from U; recursively solve each of the resulting *weakly connected components* (*WCC*s; cf. footnote 2) and plug the root of the returned trees into the corresponding holes of l. A problem to be addressed though is whether there exists any solution rooted at l. This leads us to the following definition.

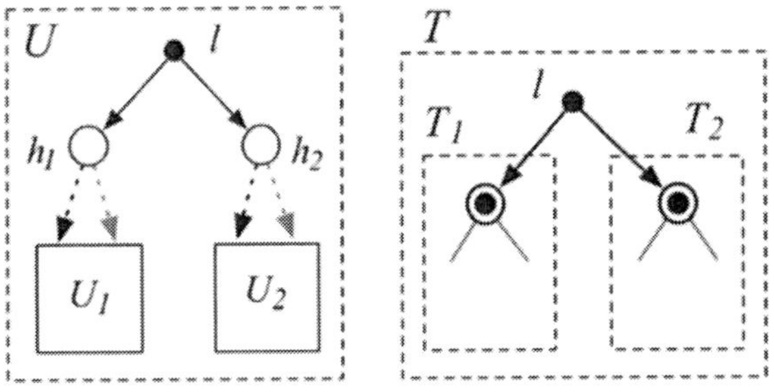

Figure 5: Recursively solving UGs.

Definition 5 (Freeness). (Bodirsky et al., 2004)
*A label l in U is called a **free node**, iff there exists some solution of U rooted at l. The fragment rooted at l is called a **free fragment**.*

The following proposition states the necessary conditions for a label (or fragment) to be free.[7]

Proposition 3. *Let l in U be the root of a fragment F with m holes. l is a free node of U, only if*

P3a. l has no incoming (constraint) edge;

P3b. Every distinct hole of F lies in a distinct WCC in $U-l$;

P3c. $U-F$ consists of at least m WCCs.

Proof. The first condition is trivial. To see why the second condition must hold, let T be a solution rooted at l, and assume to the contrary that h_1 and h_2 lie in the same WCC in $U-l$. From Lemma 2, all the nodes in this WCC must be in the scope of both h_1 and h_2. But this is not possible, because T is a tree. The third condition is proved similarly. Assume to the contrary that $U-F$ has $m-1$ WCCs. From Lemma 2, all the nodes in a WCC must be in the scope of a single hole of F. But there are m holes and only $m-1$ WCCs. It means that one of the holes in T is left unplugged. Contradiction! □

The motivation behind defining super nets is to find a subset of UG for which these conditions are also sufficient. The following concept from Althaus et al. (2003) plays an important role.

[3] u dominates v in the directed graph G, iff u reaches v in G by a *directed* path.

[4] Here, we are referring to the nodes in $T_{U,P}$ by calling the nodes u and v in U. This is a sound strategy, as every node in U is mapped into a unique node in $T_{U,P}$. The inverse is not true though, as every node (except the root) in $T_{U,P}$ corresponds to one hole and one label in U. Addressing $T_{U,P}$'s nodes in this way is convenient, so we practice that throughout the paper.

[5] Given a directed graph G and the nodes u and v in G, u is said to be *weakly connected* to v (and vice versa), iff u and v are connected in the underlying undirected graph of G. A *weakly connected graph* is a graph in which every two nodes are weakly connected. Since weak connectedness is an equivalence relation, it partitions a directed graph into equivalent classes each of which is called a *weakly connected component* or *WCC*.

[6] Since fragments are ordered trees, solutions are ordered trees as well.

[7] Necessary conditions of freeness in a UG are not exactly the same as the ones in a weakly normal dominance graph, as depicted in Bodirsky et al. (2004), because the definition of solution is different for the two frameworks (c.f. Section 4.3).

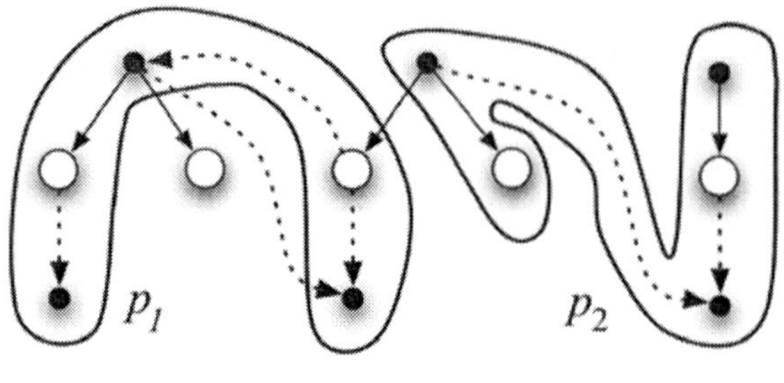

Figure 6: UG for *Illustration of hypernormal path.*

Definition 6 (Hypernormal Connectedness). *Given a UG U, a* ***hypernormal path*** *is an undirected path*[8] *with no two consecutive constraint edges emanating from the same node. Node u is* ***hypernormally connected*** *to node v iff there is at least one hypernormal path between the two. U is called* ***hypernormally connected*** *iff every pair of nodes in U are hypernormally connected.*

For example, in Figure 2, p_2 is a hypernormal path, but p_1 is not. In spite of that, the whole graph is hypernormally connected.[9] The following simple notion will also come handy.

Definition 7 (Openness). (Thater, 2007) *A node u of a fragment F is called an* ***open node*** *iff it has no outgoing constraint edge.*

For example, l in Figure 5(a) is an open label node. In Figure 2(b), h_2 is an open hole. We are finally ready to define super net.

Definition 8 (Super net). *A UG U is called a* ***super net*** *if for every fragment F rooted at l:*

D8a. F has at most one open node.

D8b. If l_1 and l_2 are two dominance children of a hole h of F, then l_1 and l_2 are hypernormally connected in $U-h$.

D8c.
- *Case 1: F has no open hole.* *Every* dominance child[10] *of l is hypernormally connected to some hole of F in U–l.*
- *Case 2: F has an open hole.* *All dominance children of l, not hypernormally connected to a hole of F in U–l, are hypernormally connected together.*

[8]Throughout this paper, by path we always mean a simple path, that is no node may be visited more than once on a path.

[9]Note that even though p_1 is not a hypernormal path, there is another hypernormal path connecting the same two nodes

[10]v is a dominance child of u in a UG U, if (u, v) is a constraint edge in U.

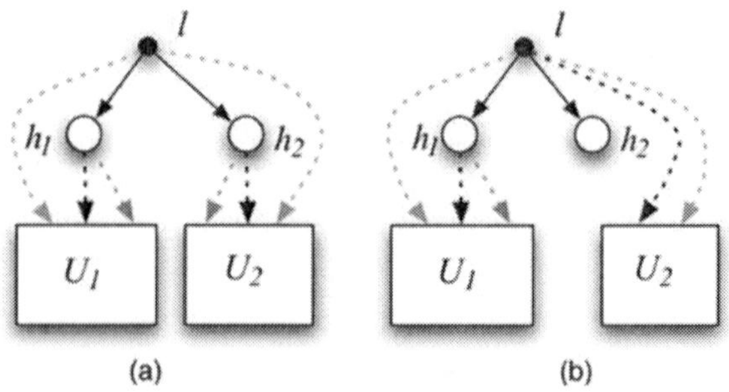

Figure 7: Illustration of super net conditions.

Definition 9 (Types of fragment). *Following Definition 8, super net allows for three possible types of fragment:*

D9a. ***Open-root****: Only the root is open (Figure 5a)*

D9b. ***Open-hole****: Only a hole is open (Figure 2b)*

D9c. ***Closed****: F There is no open node. (Figure 2a)*

Definition 8 guarantees the following property.

Lemma 4. *For a super net U and a fragment F of U with m holes, which satisfies the conditions in Proposition 3, $U-F$ consists of exactly m WCCs, each of which is a super net.*

Proof sketch. The detailed proof of this Lemma is long. Therefore, we sketch the proof here and leave the details for a longer paper. First, we show that $U-F$ consists of exactly m WCCs. Following conditions (D8b) and (D8c), no matter what structure F has, U–F consists of at most m WCCs. On the other hand, based on condition (P3c), U–F has at least m WCCs. Therefore, $U-F$ has exactly m WCCs. To prove that each WCC in $U-F$ is a super net, all we need to prove is that if two nodes u and v, which do not belong to F, are hypernormally connected in U, they are also hypernormally connected in U–F. This is proved by showing that there is no hypernormal path between u and v in U that visits some node of F. Suppose that F is an open-hole fragment rooted at l, as in Figure 2(b) (the two other cases are proved similarly) and assume to the contrary that there is a hypernormal path p between u and v that visits some node of F. One of the following three cases holds.

i. p visits exactly one node of F.
ii. p visits (at least) two holes of F.
iii. p visits l and exactly one hole of F.

All the three cases results in a contradiction: (i) proves that p is not hypernormal; (ii) proves that F

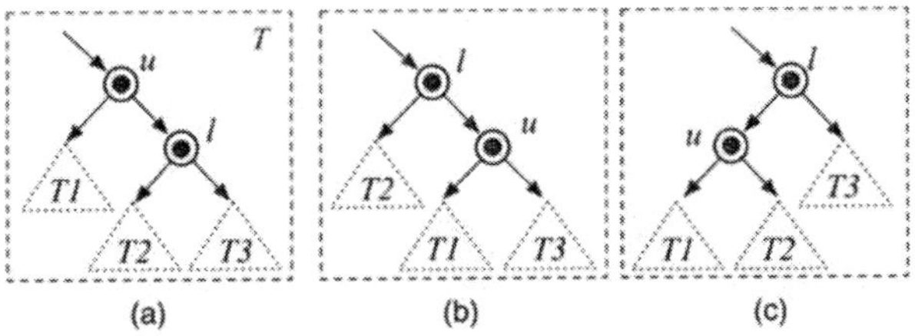

Figure 8: Proof of Proposition 5

is not a free fragment because it violates condition (P3b); and (iii) proves that U is not a super net because F violates condition (D8c).

Proposition 5. *If U is a satisfiable super net, the necessary freeness conditions in Proposition 3 are also sufficient.*

Proof sketch. Let F rooted at l be a fragment satisfying the three conditions in Proposition 3. Among all the solutions of U, we pick a solution T in which the depth d of l is minimal. Using proof by contradiction, we show that $d = 0$, which proves l is the root of T. If $d > 0$, there is some node u that outscopes l (Figure 8(a)). Lemma 2 and 4 guarantee that at least one of the trees in Figures 8(b,c) is a solution of U. So U has a solution in which, the depth of l is smaller than d. Contradiction!

3 SAT and ENUM algorithms

Following Lemma 4 and Proposition 5, Table 1 gives the algorithms for the satisfiability (**SAT**), and the enumeration (**ENUM**) of super nets.

Theorem 6. *ENUM and SAT are correct.*

Proof sketch. Using Lemma 4 and induction on the depth of the recursion, it is easy to see that if ENUM or SAT returns a tree T, T is a solution of U. This proves that ENUM and SAT are sound. An inductive proof is used to prove the completeness as well. Consider a solution T of depth n of U (Figure 5). It can be shown that T_1 and T_2 must be the solutions to U_1 and U_2. Therefore based on the induction assumption they are generated by $Solve(G)$, hence T is also generated by $Solve(G)$.

Let $U = (L \uplus H, S \uplus C)$. The running time of the algorithms depends on the depth of the recursion which is equal to the number of fragments/labels, $|L|$. At each depth it takes $O(|U|)$ to find the set of free fragments (Bodirsky et al., 2004) and also to compute $U - F$ for some free fragment F.

Solve(U)
1. If U contains a single (label) node, return U.
2. Pick a free fragment F with m holes rooted at l, otherwise fail.
// For SAT: pick arbitrarily.
// For ENUM: pick non-deterministically.
3. Let $U_1, U_2, \cdots, U_m$ be WCCs of $U - F$.
4. Let $T_i = Solve(U_i)$ for $i = 1 \cdots m$.
5. Let h_i be the hole of F connected to U_i in $U - l$, for $i = 1 \cdots m$.
(If for some k, U_k is not connected to any hole of F in $U - l$, let h_k be the open hole of F.)
6. Build T by plugging the root of T_i into h_i, for $i = 1 \cdots m$.
7. Return T.

Table 1: ENUM and SAT algorithms

($|U| =_{def} |V| + |E|$, where $|V| =_{def} |L| + |H|$, and $|E| =_{def} |S| + |C|$). Therefore SAT (and each branch of ENUM) run(s) in $O(|L|.|U|)$ step. Therefore the worst-case time complexity of SAT and each branch of ENUM is quadratic in the size of U.

4 Super net versus weak net

Although net is a subset of weak net, to better understand the three frameworks, we first define net.

4.1 Net

Net was first defined by Koller et al. (2003), in order to find a subset of Hole Semantics that can be solved in polynomial-time. Nets do not contain any label-to-label constraints. In fact, out of the three possible structures that super net allows for a fragment F (Definition 9), net only allows for the first one, that is open-root.

Definition 10 (Net). (Thater, 2007)
*Let U be a UG with no label-to-label constraints. U is called a **net** iff for every fragment F:*

D10a. *F has no open hole.*

D10b. *If l_1, l_2 are two dominance children of a hole h of F, then l_1 and l_2 are hypernormally connected in $U - h$.*

The root of F is open, therefore (D8a) subsumes (D10a). Condition (D10b) is exactly the same as (D8b). Therefore, super net is a superset of net. Strictness of the superset relationship is trivial.

4.2 Weak net

Weak net was first introduced by Niehren and Thater (2003), in order to find a tractable subset of MRS. In order to model MRS, weak net allows for label-to-label constraints, but to stay a tractable framework it forces the following restrictions.

Definition 11 (Weak net). (Thater, 2007)
A UG U is a weak net iff for every fragment F:

D11a. *F has exactly one open node.*

D11b. *If l_1, l_2 are two dominance children of a node u of F, then l_1 and l_2 are hypernormally connected in $U - u$.*

Weak nets suffer from two limitations with respect to super nets.

First, out of the three possible types of fragment allowed by super net (Definition 9), weak net only allows for the first two; open-root and open-hole. In practice this becomes an issue only if new constraints are to be added to a UG after syntax/semantic interface. Since weak net requires one node of every fragment to be open, a constraint cannot be added if it violates this condition.[11]

Second, open-hole fragments in weak nets are more restricted than open-hole fragments in super nets. This is the Achilles' heel of weak nets (D11b). To see why, consider the UG in Figure 3 for the sentence *Every politician, whom I know a child of, runs* which we presented in Section 1. If F is the fragment for the quantifier *Every* and l is the root of F, the two dominance children of l are not (hypernormally) connected in $U - l$. Therefore, U is not a weak net. All the non-net examples we have found so far behave similarly. That is, there is a quantifier with more than one outgoing dominance edge. Once you remove the quantifier node, the dominance children are no longer weakly (and hence hypernormally) connected, violating condition (D11b). In super net, however, we define case 2 of condition (D8c) such that it does not force dominance children of l to be (hypernormally) connected, allowing for non-net structures such as the one in Figure 3.[12]

[11] As discussed in Section 5, by defining the notion of *downward connectedness*, Koller and Thater (2007) address this issue of weak nets, at the expense of cubic time complexity.

[12] For simplicity, throughout this paper we have used the term non-net to refer to non-(weak net) UGs.

Proposition 7. *Weak net is a strict subset of super net.*

Proof. Consider an arbitrary weak net U, and let F be an arbitrary fragment of U rooted at l.

(i). F has exactly one open node, so it satisfies condition (D8a).

(ii). For every two holes of F, condition (D11b) guarantees that condition (D8b) holds.

(iii).
- Case 1) F has no open hole:
  Based on condition (D11a) the root of F is open, hence it has no dominance children. (D8c) trivially holds in this case.
- Case 2) F has an open hole:
  Based on condition (D11b) every two dominance children of l are hypernormally connected, so (D8c) holds in this case too.

Therefore, every fragment F satisfies all the conditions in Definition 8, hence U is a super net. This and the fact that Figure 3 is a super net but not a weak net complete the proof. □

4.3 Underspecification graph vs. weakly normal dominance graph

Dominance graphs and their ancestor, dominance constraints, are designed for solving constrained tree structures in general. Therefore, some of the terminology of dominance graph may seem counter-intuitive when dealing with scope underspecification. For example the notion of **solution** in that formalism is broader than what is known as solution in scope underspecification formalisms. As defined there (but translated into our terminology), a solution may contain unplugged holes, or holes plugged with more than one label. This broad notion of solution is computationally less expensive such that an algorithm very similar to the one in Table 1 can be used to solve every weakly normal dominance graph (Bodirsky et al., 2004). Solution, as defined in this paper (Definition 4), corresponds to the notion of **simple leaf-labeled solved forms** (a.k.a. **configuration**) in dominance graphs. Although solutions of a weakly normal dominance graph can be found in polynomial time, finding configurations is NP-complete. Solvability of underspecification graphs is equivalent to configurability of weakly normal dominance graphs, and hence NP-complete.

5 Related work

We already compared our model with nets and weak nets. Koller and Thater (2007) present another extension of weak nets, downward connected nets. They show that if a *dominance graph* has a subgraph which is a weak net, it can be solved in polynomial time. This addresses the first limitation of weak nets, discussed in Section 4.2, but it does not solve the second one, because the graph in Figure 3 neither is a weak net, nor has a weak-net subgraph.

Downward connected dominance graph, in its general form, goes beyond weakly normal dominance graph (and hence UG), incorporating label-to-hole constraints. It remains for future work to investigate whether allowing for label-to-hole constraints adds any value to the framework within the context of scope underspecified semantics, or whether it is possible to model the same effect using hole-to-label and label-to-label constraints. In any case, the same extension can be applied to super nets as well, defining downward connected super nets, a strict super set of downward connected nets, solvable using similar algorithms with the same time/space complexity.

Another tractable framework presented in the past is our own framework, Canonical Form Underspecified Representation (**CF-UR**) (Manshadi et al., 2009), motivated by Minimal Recursion Semantics. CF-UR is defined to characterize the set of all MRS structures generated by the MRS semantic composition process (Manshadi et al., 2008). CF-UR in its general form is not tractable. Therefore, we define a notion of coherence called **heart-connectedness** and show that all heart-connected CF-UR structures can be solved efficiently. We also show that heart-connected CF-UR covers the family of non-net structures, so CF-UR is in fact the first framework to address the non-net structures. In spite of that, CF-UR is quite restricted and does not allow for adding new constraints after semantic composition.

In recent work, Koller et al. (2008) suggest using Regular Tree Grammars for scope underspecification, a probabilistic version of which could be used to find the best reading. The framework goes beyond the formalisms discussed in this paper and is expressively complete in Ebert (2005)'s sense of completeness, i.e. it is able to describe any subset of the readings of a UR. However, this power comes at the cost of exponential complexity. In practice, RTG is built on top of weak nets, benefiting from the compactness of this framework to remain tractable. Being a super set of weak net, super net provides a more powerful core for RTG.

Koller and Thater (2010) address the problem of finding the weakest readings of a UR, which are those entailed by some reading(s), but not entailing any other reading of the UR. By only considering the weakest readings, the space of solutions will be dramatically reduced. Note that entailment using the weakest readings is sound but not complete.

6 Summary and Future work

Weakly normal dominance graph brings many current constraint-based formalisms under a uniform framework, but its configurability is intractable in its general form. In this paper, we present a tractable subset of this framework. We prove that this subset, called super net, is a strict superset of weak net, a previously known tractable subset of the framework, and that it covers a family of coherent natural language sentences whose underspecified representation are known not to belong to weak nets.

As mentioned in Section 5, another extension of weak nets, downward connected nets, has been proposed by Koller and Thater (2007), which addresses some of the limitations of weak nets, yet is unable to solve the known family of non-net structures. A thorough comparison between super nets and downward connected nets remains for future work.

Another interesting property of super nets to be explored is how they compare to heart-connected graphs. Heart-connectedness has been introduced as a mathematical criterion for verifying the coherence of an underspecified representation within the framework of underspecification graph (Manshadi et al., 2009). Our early investigation shows that super nets may contain all heart-connected UGs. If this conjecture is true, super net would be broad enough to cover every coherent natural language sentence (under this notion of coherence). We leave a detailed investigation of this conjecture for the future.

Acknowledgments

This work was support in part by NSF grant 1012205, and ONR grant N000141110417.

References

Hiyan Alshawi and Richard Crouch. 1992. Monotonic semantic interpretation. In *Proceedings of ACL '92*, pages 32–39.

Ernst Althaus, Denys Duchier, Alexander Koller, Kurt Mehlhorn, Joachim Niehren, and Sven Thiel. 2003. An efficient graph algorithm for dominance constraints. *J. Algorithms*, 48(1):194–219, August.

Manuel Bodirsky, Denys Duchier, Joachim Niehren, and Sebastian Miele. 2004. An efficient algorithm for weakly normal dominance constraints. In *In ACM-SIAM Symposium on Discrete Algorithms*. The ACM Press.

J. Bos. 1996. Predicate logic unplugged. In *In Proceedings of the 10th Amsterdam Colloquium*, pages 133–143.

J. Bos. 2002. *Underspecification and Resolution in Discourse Semantics*. Saarbrücken dissertations in computational linguistics and language technology. DFKI.

Ann Copestake, Alex Lascarides, and Dan Flickinger. 2001. An algebra for semantic construction in constraint-based grammars. In *Proceedings of ACL '01*, pages 140–147.

Christian Ebert. 2005. Formal investigations of underspecified representations. Technical report, King's College, London, UK.

M. Egg, A. Koller, and J. Niehren. 2001. The constraint language for lambda structures. *J. of Logic, Lang. and Inf.*, 10(4):457–485, September.

Ruth Fuchss, Alexander Koller, Joachim Niehren, and Stefan Thater. 2004. Minimal recursion semantics as dominance constraints: Translation, evaluation, and analysis. In *Proceedings of the 42nd Meeting of the Association for Computational Linguistics (ACL'04), Main Volume*, pages 247–254, Barcelona, Spain, July.

Jerry R. Hobbs and Stuart M. Shieber. 1987. An algorithm for generating quantifier scopings. *Comput. Linguist.*, 13(1-2):47–63, January.

Alexander Koller and Stefan Thater. 2007. Solving unrestricted dominance graphs. In *Proceedings of the 12th Conference on Formal Grammar*, Dublin.

Alexander Koller and Stefan Thater. 2010. Computing weakest readings. In *Proceedings of the 48th ACL*, Uppsala.

Alexander Koller, Joachim Niehren, and Stefan Thater. 2003. Bridging the gap between underspecification formalisms: Hole semantics as dominance constraints. In *Proceedings of the 11th EACL*, Budapest.

Alexander Koller, Michaela Regneri, and Stefan Thater. 2008. Regular tree grammars as a formalism for scope underspecification. In *Proceedings of ACL-08: HLT*, Columbus, Ohio.

Mehdi H. Manshadi, James F. Allen, and Mary Swift. 2008. Toward a universal underspecified semantic representation. In *Proceedings of the 13th Conference on Formal Grammar*, Hamburg, Germany, August.

Mehdi H. Manshadi, James F. Allen, and Mary Swift. 2009. An efficient enumeration algorithm for canonical form underspecified semantic representations. In *Proceedings of the 14th Conference on Formal Grammar*, Bordeaux, France, July.

Joachim Niehren and Stefan Thater. 2003. Bridging the gap between underspecification formalisms: minimal recursion semantics as dominance constraints. In *Proceedings of the 41st Annual Meeting on Association for Computational Linguistics - Volume 1*, ACL '03, pages 367–374, Stroudsburg, PA, USA. Association for Computational Linguistics.

S. Oepen, K. Toutanova, S. Shieber, C. Manning, D. Flickinger, and T. Brants. 2002. The lingo redwoods treebank motivation and preliminary applications. In *Proceedings of COLING '02*, pages 1–5.

S. Thater. 2007. *Minimal Recursion Semantics as Dominance Constraints: Graph-theoretic Foundation and Application to Grammar Engineering*. Saarbrücken dissertations in computational linguistics and language technology. Universität des Saarlandes.

W A Woods. 1986. Semantics and quantification in natural language question answering. In Barbara J. Grosz, Karen Sparck-Jones, and Bonnie Lynn Webber, editors, *Readings in natural language processing*, pages 205–248. Morgan Kaufmann Publishers Inc., San Francisco, CA, USA.

Regular polysemy: A distributional model

Gemma Boleda
Dept. of Linguistics
University of Texas at Austin
gemma.boleda@upf.edu

Sebastian Padó
ICL
University of Heidelberg
pado@cl.uni-heidelberg.de

Jason Utt
IMS
University of Stuttgart
uttjn@ims.uni-stuttgart.de

Abstract

Many types of polysemy are not word specific, but are instances of general sense alternations such as ANIMAL-FOOD. Despite their pervasiveness, regular alternations have been mostly ignored in empirical computational semantics. This paper presents (a) a general framework which grounds sense alternations in corpus data, generalizes them above individual words, and allows the prediction of alternations for new words; and (b) a concrete unsupervised implementation of the framework, the Centroid Attribute Model. We evaluate this model against a set of 2,400 ambiguous words and demonstrate that it outperforms two baselines.

1 Introduction

One of the biggest challenges in computational semantics is the fact that many words are *polysemous*. For instance, *lamb* can refer to an animal (as in *The lamb squeezed through the gap*) or to a food item (as in *Sue had lamb for lunch*). Polysemy is pervasive in human language and is a problem in almost all applications of NLP, ranging from Machine Translation (as word senses can translate differently) to Textual Entailment (as most lexical entailments are sense-specific).

The field has thus devoted a large amount of effort to the representation and modeling of word senses. The arguably most prominent effort is Word Sense Disambiguation, WSD (Navigli, 2009), an *in-vitro* task whose goal is to identify which, of a set of predefined senses, is the one used in a given context.

In work on WSD and other tasks related to polysemy, such as word sense induction, sense alternations are treated as *word-specific*. As a result, a model for the meaning of *lamb* that accounts for the relation between the animal and food senses cannot predict that the same relation holds between instances of *chicken* or *salmon* in the same type of contexts.

A large number of studies in linguistics and cognitive science show evidence that there are regularities in the way words vary in their meaning (Apresjan, 1974; Lakoff and Johnson, 1980; Copestake and Briscoe, 1995; Pustejovsky, 1995; Gentner et al., 2001; Murphy, 2002), due to general analogical processes such as regular polysemy, metonymy and metaphor. Most work in theoretical linguistics has focused on *regular*, *systematic*, or *logical* polysemy, which accounts for alternations like ANIMAL-FOOD. Sense alternations also arise from metaphorical use of words, as *dark* in *dark glass-dark mood*, and also from metonymy when, for instance, using the name of a place for a representative (as in *Germany signed the treatise*). Disregarding this evidence is empirically inadequate and leads to the well-known *lexical bottleneck* of current word sense models, which have serious problems in achieving high coverage (Navigli, 2009).

We believe that empirical computational semantics could profit from a model of polysemy[1] which (a) is applicable across individual words, and thus capable of capturing general patterns and generalizing to new

[1] Our work is mostly inspired in research on regular polysemy. However, given the fuzzy nature of "regularity" in meaning variation, we extend the focus of our attention to include other types of analogical sense construction processes.

words, and (b) is induced in an unsupervised fashion from corpus data. This is a long-term goal with many unsolved subproblems.

The current paper presents two contributions towards this goal. First, since we are working on a relatively unexplored area, we introduce a formal framework that can encompass different approaches (Section 2). Second, we implement a concrete instantiation of this framework, the unsupervised Centroid Attribute Model (Section 3), and evaluate it on a new task, namely, to detect which of a set of words instantiate a given type of polysemy (Sections 4 and 5). We finish with some conclusions and future work (Section 7).

L	set of lemmas
I_L	set of (lemma-wise) instances
S_L	set of (lemma-wise) senses
$\mathrm{inst}: L \rightarrow \wp(I_L)$	mapping lemma → instances
$\mathrm{sns}: L \rightarrow \wp(S_L)$	mapping lemma → senses
M	set of meta senses
$\mathrm{meta}: S_L \rightarrow M$	mapping senses → meta senses
$A \subseteq M \times M$	set of meta alternations (MAs)
$\mathfrak{A}$	set of MA representations
$\mathrm{score}: A \times S_L^2 \rightarrow \mathbb{R}$	scoring function for MAs
$\mathrm{rep_A}: A \rightarrow \mathfrak{A}$	MA representation function
$\mathrm{comp}: \mathfrak{A} \times S_L^2 \rightarrow \mathbb{R}$	compatibility function

Table 1: Notation and signatures for our framework.

2 Formal framework

In addition to introducing formal definitions for terms commonly found in the literature, our framework provides novel terminology to deal with regular polysemy in a general fashion (cf. Table 1; capital letters designate sets and small letters elements of sets).[2]

For a lemma l like *lamb*, we want to know how well a **meta alternation** (such as ANIMAL-FOOD) explains a pair of its senses (such as the animal and food senses of *lamb*).[3] This is formalized through the function score, which maps a meta alternation and two senses onto a score. As an example, let $lamb_{\mathrm{anm}}$ denote the ANIMAL sense of *lamb*, $lamb_{\mathtt{fod}}$ the FOOD sense, and $lamb_{\mathrm{hum}}$ the PERSON sense. Then, an appropriate model of meta alternations should predict that $\mathrm{score}(\mathtt{animal}, \mathtt{food}, lamb_{\mathrm{anm}}, lamb_{\mathtt{fod}})$ is greater than $\mathrm{score}(\mathtt{animal}, \mathtt{food}, lamb_{\mathrm{anm}}, lamb_{\mathrm{hum}})$.

Meta alternations are defined as unordered pairs of **meta senses**, or cross-word senses like ANIMAL. The meta senses M can be defined a priori or induced from data. They are equivalence classes of senses to which they are linked through the function meta. A sense s *instantiates* a meta sense m iff $\mathrm{meta}(s) = m$. Functions inst and sns allow us to define meta senses and lemma-specific senses in terms of actual instances, or occurrences of words in context.

[2]We re-use inst as a function that returns the set of instances for a sense: $S_L \rightarrow \wp(I_L)$ and assume that senses partition lemmas' instances: $\forall l : \mathrm{inst}(l) = \bigcup_{s \in \mathrm{sns}(l)} \mathrm{inst}(s)$.

[3]Consistent with the theoretical literature, this paper focuses on two-way polysemy. See Section 7 for further discussion.

We decompose the score function into two parts: a *representation* function $\mathrm{rep_A}$ that maps a meta alternation into some suitable representation for meta alternations, $\mathfrak{A}$, and a *compatibility* function comp that compares the relation between the senses of a word to the meta alternation's representation. Thus, $\mathrm{comp} \circ \mathrm{rep_A} = \mathrm{score}$.

3 The Centroid Attribute Model

The *Centroid Attribute Model (CAM)* is a simple instantiation of the framework defined in Section 2, designed with two primary goals in mind. First, it is a data-driven model. Second, it does not require any manual sense disambiguation, a notorious bottleneck.

To achieve the first goal, CAM uses a distributional approach. It represents the relevant entities as *co-occurrence vectors* that can be acquired from a large corpus (Turney and Pantel, 2010). To achieve the second goal, CAM represents meta senses using *monosemous* words only, that is, words whose senses all correspond to one meta sense. [4] Examples are *cattle* and *robin* for the meta sense ANIMAL. We define the vector for a meta sense as the *centroid* (average vector) of the monosemous words instantiating it. In turn, meta alternations are represented by the centroids of their meta senses' vectors.

This strategy is not applicable to test lemmas, which instantiate some meta alternation and are by definition ambiguous. To deal with these without

[4]10.8% of noun types in the corpus we use are monosemous and 2.3% are disemous, while, on a token level, 23.3% are monosemous and 20.2% disemous.

$\mathrm{vec}_I : I_L \rightarrow \mathbb{R}^k$	instance vector computation
$\mathfrak{C} : \mathbb{R}^{k \times m} \rightarrow \mathbb{R}^k$	centroid computation
$\mathrm{vec}_L : L \rightarrow \mathbb{R}^k$	lemma (type) vector computation
$\mathrm{rep}_\mathrm{M} : M \rightarrow \mathbb{R}^k$	meta sense representation

Table 3: Additional notation and signatures for CAM

explicit sense disambiguation, CAM represents lemmas by their type vectors, i.e., the *centroid* of their instances, and compares their vectors (*attributes*) to those of the meta alternation – hence the name.

CoreLex: A Semantic Inventory. CAM uses CoreLex (Buitelaar, 1998) as its meta sense inventory. CoreLex is a lexical resource that was designed specifically for the study of polysemy. It builds on WordNet (Fellbaum, 1998), whose sense distinctions are too fine-grained to describe general sense alternations. CoreLex defines a layer of abstraction above WordNet consisting of 39 *basic types*, coarse-grained ontological classes (Table 2). These classes are linked to one or more Wordnet *anchor nodes*, which define a mapping from WordNet synsets onto basic types: A synset s maps onto a basic type b if b has an anchor node that dominates s and there is no other anchor node on the path from b and s.[5]

We adopt the WordNet synsets as S, the set of senses, and the CoreLex basic types as our set of meta senses M. The meta function (mapping word senses onto meta senses) is given directly by the anchor mapping defined in the previous paragraph. This means that the set of meta alternations is given by the set of pairs of basic types. Although basic types do not perfectly model meta senses, they constitute an approximation that allows us to model many prominent alternations such as ANIMAL-FOOD.

Vectors for Meta Senses and Alternations. All representations used by CAM are co-occurrence vectors in R^k (i.e., $\mathfrak{A} := R^k$). Table 3 lists new concepts that CAM introduces to manipulate vector representations. vec_I returns a vector for a lemma instance, vec_L a (type) vector for a lemma, and $\mathfrak{C}$ the centroid of a set of vectors.

We leave vec_I and $\mathfrak{C}$ unspecified: we will experiment with these functions in Section 4. CAM does fix the definitions for vec_L and rep_A. First, vec_L defines a lemma's vector as the centroid of its instances:

$$\mathrm{vec}_L(l) = \mathfrak{C}\{\mathrm{vec}_I(i) \mid i \in \mathrm{inst}(l)\} \quad (1)$$

Before defining rep_A, we specify a function rep_M that computes vector representations for meta senses m. In CAM, this vector is defined as the centroid of the vectors for all monosemous lemmas whose WordNet sense maps onto m:

$$\mathrm{rep}_\mathrm{M}(m) = \mathfrak{C}\{\mathrm{vec}_L(l) \mid \mathrm{meta}(\mathrm{sns}(l)) = \{m\}\} \quad (2)$$

Now, rep_A can be defined simply as the centroid of the meta senses instantiating a:

$$\mathrm{rep}_\mathrm{A}(m_1, m_2) = \mathfrak{C}\{\mathrm{rep}_\mathrm{M}(m_1), \mathrm{rep}_\mathrm{M}(m_2)\} \quad (3)$$

Predicting Meta Alternations. The final component of CAM is an instantiation of comp (cf. Table 1), i.e., the degree to which a sense pair (s_1, s_2) matches a meta alternation a. Since CAM does not represent these senses separately, we define comp as

$$\mathrm{comp}(a, s_1, s_2) = \mathrm{sim}(a, \mathrm{vec}_L(l)) \text{ so that } \{s_1, s_2\} = \mathrm{sns}(l) \quad (4)$$

The complete model, score, can now be stated as:

$$\mathrm{score}(m, m', s, s') = \mathrm{sim}(\mathrm{rep}_\mathrm{A}(m, m'), \mathrm{vec}_L(l)) \text{ so that } \{s, s'\} = \mathrm{sns}(l) \quad (5)$$

CAM thus assesses how well a meta alternation $a = (m, m')$ explains a lemma l by comparing the centroid of the meta senses m, m' to l's centroid.

Discussion. The central feature of CAM is that it avoids word sense disambiguation, although it still relies on a predefined sense inventory (WordNet, through CoreLex). Our use of monosemous words to represent meta senses and meta alternations goes beyond previous work which uses monosemous words to disambiguate polysemous words in context (Izquierdo et al., 2009; Navigli and Velardi, 2005).

Because of its focus on avoiding disambiguation, CAM simplifies the representation of meta alternations and polysemous words to single centroid vectors. In the future, we plan to induce word senses (Schütze, 1998; Pantel and Lin, 2002; Reisinger and Mooney, 2010), which will allow for more flexible and realistic models.

[5] This is necessary because some classes have non-disjoint anchor nodes: e.g., ANIMALs are a subset of LIVING BEINGs.

abs	ABSTRACTION	ent	ENTITY	loc	LOCATION	prt	PART
act	ACT	evt	EVENT	log	GEO. LOCATION	psy	PSYCHOL. FEATURE
agt	AGENT	fod	FOOD	mea	MEASURE	qud	DEFINITE QUANTITY
anm	ANIMAL	frm	FORM	mic	MICROORGANISM	qui	INDEFINITE QUANTITY
art	ARTIFACT	grb	BIOLOG. GROUP	nat	NATURAL BODY	rel	RELATION
atr	ATTRIBUTE	grp	GROUPING	phm	PHENOMENON	spc	SPACE
cel	CELL	grs	SOCIAL GROUP	pho	PHYSICAL OBJECT	sta	STATE
chm	CHEMICAL	hum	HUMAN	plt	PLANT	sub	SUBSTANCE
com	COMMUNICATION	lfr	LIVING BEING	pos	POSSESSION	tme	TIME
con	CONSEQUENCE	lme	LINEAR MEASURE	pro	PROCESS	pro	PROCESS

Table 2: CoreLex's basic types with their corresponding WordNet anchors. CAM adopts these as meta senses.

4 Evaluation

We test CAM on the task of identifying which lemmas of a given set instantiate a specific meta alternation. We let the model rank the lemmas through the score function (cf. Table (1) and Eq. (5)) and evaluate the ranked list using Average Precision. While an alternative would be to rank meta alternations for a given polysemous lemma, the method chosen here has the benefit of providing data on the performance of individual meta senses and meta alternations.

4.1 Data

All modeling and data extraction was carried out on the written part of the British National Corpus (BNC; Burnage and Dunlop (1992)) parsed with the C&C tools (Clark and Curran, 2007). [6]

For the evaluation, we focus on *disemous words*, words which instantiate exactly two meta senses according to WordNet. For each meta alternation (m, m'), we evaluate CAM on a set of disemous *targets* (lemmas that instantiate (m, m')) and disemous *distractors* (lemmas that do not). We define three types of distractors: (1) distractors sharing m with the targets (but not m'), (2) distractors sharing m' with the targets (but not m), and (3) distractors sharing neither. In this way, we ensure that CAM cannot obtain good results by merely modeling the similarity of targets to either m or m', which would rather be a coarse-grained word sense modeling task.

To ensure that we have enough data, we evaluate CAM on all meta alternations with at least ten targets that occur at least 50 times in the corpus, discarding nouns that have fewer than 3 characters or contain non-alphabetical characters. The distractors are chosen so that they match targets in frequency. This leaves us with 60 meta alternations, shown in Table 5. For each meta alternation, we randomly select 40 lemmas as experimental items (10 targets and 10 distractors of each type) so that a total of 2,400 lemmas is used in the evaluation.[7] Table 4 shows four targets and their distractors for the meta alternation ANIMAL-FOOD.[8]

4.2 Evaluation Measure and Baselines

To measure success on this task, we use Average Precision (AP), an evaluation measure from IR that reaches its maximum value of 1 when all correct items are ranked at the top (Manning et al., 2008). It interpolates the precision values of the top-n prediction lists for all positions n in the list that contain a target. Let $T = \langle q_1, \dots, q_m \rangle$ be the list of targets, and let $P = \langle p_1, \dots, p_n \rangle$ be the list of predictions as ranked by the model. Let $I(x_i) = 1$ if $p_i \in T$, and zero otherwise. Then $AP(P,T) = \frac{1}{m} \sum_{i=1}^{m} I(x_i) \frac{\sum_{j=1}^{i} I(x_i)}{i}$. AP measures the quality of the ranked list for a single meta alternation. The overall quality of a model is given by Mean Average Precision (MAP), the mean of the AP values for all meta alternations.

We consider two baselines: (1) A *random baseline* that ranks all lemmas in random order. This baseline is the same for all meta alternations, since the distribution is identical. We estimate it by sampling. (2) A meta alternation-specific *frequency baseline* which orders the lemmas by their corpus frequencies. This

[6]The C&C tools were able to reliably parse about 40M words.

[7]Dataset available at `http://www.nlpado.de/~sebastian/data.shtml`.

[8]Note that this experimental design avoids any overlap between the words used to construct sense vectors (one meta sense) and the words used in the evaluation (two meta senses).

Targets	Distractors with meta sense anm	Distractors with meta sense fod	Random distractors
carp	*amphibian* (anm-art)	*mousse* (art-fod)	*appropriation* (act-mea)
duckling	*ape* (anm-hum)	*parsley* (fod-plt)	*scissors* (act-art)
eel	*leopard* (anm-sub)	*pickle* (fod-sta)	*showman* (agt-hum)
hare	*lizard* (anm-hum)	*pork* (fod-mea)	*upholstery* (act-art)

Table 4: Sample of experimental items for the meta alternation anm-fod. (Abbreviations are listed in Table 2.)

baseline uses the intuition that frequent words will tend to exhibit more typical alternations.

4.3 Model Parameters

There are four more parameters to set.

Definition of vector space. We instantiate the vec_I function in three ways. All three are based on dependency-parsed spaces, following our intuition that topical similarity as provided by window-based spaces is insufficient for this task. The functions differ in the definition of the space's dimensions, incorporating different assumptions about distributional differences among meta alternations.

The first option, gram, uses grammatical paths of lengths 1 to 3 as dimensions and thus characterizes lemmas and meta senses in terms of their grammatical context (Schulte im Walde, 2006), with a total of 2,528 paths. The second option, lex, uses words as dimensions, treating the dependency parse as a co-occurrence filter (Padó and Lapata, 2007), and captures topical distinctions. The third option, gramlex, uses lexicalized dependency paths like *obj–see* to mirror more fine-grained semantic properties (Grefenstette, 1994). Both lex and gramlex use the 10,000 most frequent items in the corpus.

Vector elements. We use "raw" corpus co-occurrence frequencies as well as log-likelihood-transformed counts (Lowe, 2001) as elements of the co-occurrence vectors.

Definition of centroid computation. There are three centroid computations in CAM: to combine instances into lemma (type) vectors (function vec_L in Eq. (1)); to combine lemma vectors into meta sense vectors (function rep_M in Eq. (2)); and to combine meta sense vectors into meta alternation vectors (function rep_A in Eq. (3)).

For vec_L, the obvious definition of the centroid function is as a *micro-average*, that is, a simple average over all instances. For rep_M and rep_A, there is a design choice: The centroid can be computed by micro-averaging as well, which assigns a larger weight to more frequent lemmas (rep_M) or meta senses (rep_A). Alternatively, it can be computed by *macro-averaging*, that is, by normalizing the individual vectors before averaging. This gives equal weight to the each lemma or meta sense, respectively. Macro-averaging in rep_A thus assumes that senses are equally distributed, which is an oversimplification, as word senses are known to present skewed distributions (McCarthy et al., 2004) and vectors for words with a predominant sense will be similar to the dominant meta sense vector. Micro-averaging partially models sense skewedness under the assumption that word frequency correlates with sense frequency.

Similarity measure. As the vector similarity measure in Eq. (5), we use the standard cosine similarity (Lee, 1999). It ranges between -1 and 1, with 1 denoting maximum similarity. In the current model where the vectors do not contain negative counts, the range is $[0; 1]$.

5 Results

Effect of Parameters The four parameters of Section 4.3 (three space types, macro-/micro-averaging for rep_M and rep_A, and log-likelihood transformation) correspond to 24 instantiations of CAM.

Figure 1 shows the influence of the four parameters. The only significant difference is tied to the use of lexicalized vector spaces (gramlex / lex are better than gram). The statistical significance of this difference was verified by a t-test ($p < 0.01$). This indicates that meta alternations can be characterized better through fine-grained semantic distinctions than by syntactic ones.

The choice of micro- vs. macro-average does not have a clear effect, and the large variation observed in Figure 1 suggests that the best setup is dependent on the specific meta sense or meta alternation being

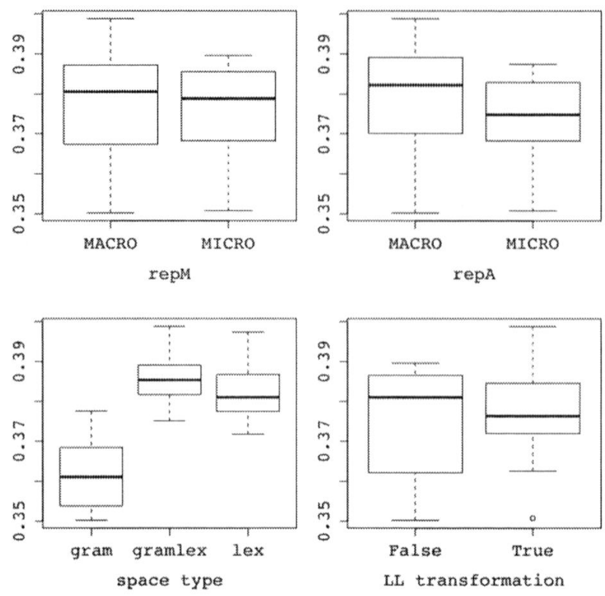

Figure 1: Effect of model parameters on performance. A data point is the mean AP (MAP) across all meta alternations for a specific setting.

modeled. Focusing on meta alternations, whether the two intervening meta senses should be balanced or not can be expected to depend on the frequencies of the concepts denoted by each meta sense, which vary for each case. Indeed, for AGENT-HUMAN, the alternation which most benefits from the micro-averaging setting, the targets are much more similar to the HUMAN meta sense (which is approximately 8 times as frequent as AGENT) than to the AGENT meta sense. The latter contains anything that can have an effect on something, e.g. *emulsifier, force, valium*. The targets for AGENT-HUMAN, in contrast, contain words such as *engineer, manipulator, operative*, which alternate between an agentive role played by a person and the person herself.

While lacking in clear improvement, log-likelihood transformation tends to reduce variance, consistent with the effect previously found in selectional preference modeling (Erk et al., 2010).

Overall Performance Although the performance of the CAM models is still far from perfect, all 24 models obtain MAP scores of 0.35 or above, while the random baseline is at 0.313, and the overall frequency baseline at 0.291. Thus, all models consistently outperform both baselines. A bootstrap resampling test (Efron and Tibshirani, 1994) confirmed that the difference to the frequency baseline is significant at $p < 0.01$ for all 24 models. The difference to the random baseline is significant at $p < 0.01$ for 23 models and at $p < 0.05$ for the remaining model. This shows that the models capture the meta alternations to some extent. The best model uses macro-averaging for rep_{M} and rep_{A} in a log-likelihood transformed `gramlex` space and achieves a MAP of 0.399.

Table 5 breaks down the performance of the best CAM model by meta alternation. It shows an encouraging picture: CAM outperforms the frequency baseline for 49 of the 60 meta alternations and both baselines for 44 (73.3%) of all alternations. The performance shows a high degree of variance, however, ranging from 0.22 to 0.71.

Analysis by Meta Alternation Coherence Meta alternations vary greatly in their difficulty. Since CAM is an attribute similarity-based approach, we expect it to perform better on the alternations whose meta senses are ontologically more similar. We next test this hypothesis.

Let $D_{m_i} = \{d_{ij}\}$ be the set of distractors for the targets $T = \{t_j\}$ that share the meta sense m_i, and $D_R = \{d_{3j}\}$ the set of random distractors. We define the coherence κ of an alternation a of meta senses m_1, m_2 as the mean (ø) difference between the similarity of each target vector to a and the similarity of the corresponding distractors to a, or formally $\kappa(a) = ø\ \text{sim}(\text{rep}_{\text{A}}(m_1, m_2), \text{vec}_L(t_j)) - \text{sim}(\text{rep}_{\text{A}}(m_1, m_2), \text{vec}_L(d_{ij}))$, for $1 \leq i \leq 3$ and $1 \leq j \leq 10$. That is, κ measures how much more similar, on average, the meta alternation vector is to the target vectors than to the distractor vectors. For a meta alternation with a higher κ, the targets should be easier to distinguish from the distractors.

Figure 2 plots AP by κ for all meta alternations. As we expect from the definition of κ, AP is strongly correlated with κ. However, there is a marked Y shape, i.e., a divergence in behavior between high-κ and mid-AP alternations (upper right corner) and mid-κ and high-AP alternations (upper left corner).

In the first case, meta alternations perform worse than expected, and we find that this typically points to missing senses, that is, problems in the underlying lexical resource (WordNet, via CoreLex). For instance, the FOOD-PLANT distractor *almond* is given

grs-psy	0.709	**com-evt**	0.501	**art-com**	0.400	**atr-com**	0.361	art-frm	0.286
pro-sta	0.678	**art-grs**	0.498	**act-pos**	0.396	**atr-sta**	0.361	**act-hum**	0.281
fod-plt	0.645	**hum-psy**	0.486	**phm-sta**	0.388	**act-phm**	0.339	art-fod	0.280
psy-sta	0.630	**hum-nat**	0.456	**atr-psy**	0.384	**anm-art**	0.335	**grs-hum**	0.272
hum-prt	0.602	**anm-hum**	0.448	**fod-hum**	0.383	**art-atr**	0.333	act-art	0.267
grp-psy	0.574	**com-psy**	0.443	**plt-sub**	0.383	**act-psy**	0.333	art-grp	0.258
grs-log	0.573	**act-grs**	0.441	**act-com**	0.382	**agt-hum**	0.319	art-nat	0.248
act-evt	0.539	**atr-rel**	0.440	**grp-grs**	0.379	**art-evt**	0.314	act-atr	0.246
evt-psy	0.526	**art-qui**	0.433	**art-psy**	0.373	**atr-evt**	0.312	art-hum	0.240
act-tme	0.523	**act-sta**	0.413	**art-prt**	0.364	**art-sta**	0.302	art-loc	0.238
art-pho	0.520	**art-sub**	0.412	**evt-sta**	0.364	act-grp	0.296	art-pos	0.228
act-pro	0.513	**art-log**	0.407	**anm-fod**	0.361	**com-hum**	0.292	com-sta	0.219

Table 5: Meta alternations and their average precision values for the task. The random baseline performs at 0.313 while the frequency baseline ranges from 0.255 to 0.369 with a mean of 0.291. Alternations for which the model outperforms the frequency baseline are in boldface (mean AP: 0.399, standard deviation: 0.119).

grs-psy	*democracy, faculty, humanism, regime,*
pro-sta	*bondage, dehydration, erosion,urbanization*
psy-sta	*anaemia,delight, pathology, sensibility*
hum-prt	*bum, contractor, peter, subordinate*
grp-psy	*category, collectivism, socialism, underworld*

Table 6: Sample targets for meta alternations with high AP and mid-coherence values.

a PLANT sense by WordNet, but no FOOD sense. In the case of SOCIAL GROUP-GEOGRAPHICAL LOCATION, distractors *laboratory* and *province* are missing SOCIAL GROUP senses, which they clearly possess (cf. *The whole laboratory celebrated Christmas*). This suggests that our approach can help in Word Sense Induction and thesaurus construction.

In the second case, meta alternations perform better than expected: They have a low κ, but a high AP. These include grs-psy, pro-sta, psy-sta, hum-prt and grp-psy. These meta alternations involve fairly abstract meta senses such as PSYCHOLOGICAL FEATURE and STATE.[9] Table 6 lists a sample of targets for the five meta alternations involved. The targets are clearly similar to each other on the level of their meta senses. However, they can occur in very different semantic contexts. Thus, here it is the underlying model (the gramlex space) that can explain the lower than average coherence. It is striking that CAM can account for abstract words and meta alternations between these, given that it uses first-order co-occurrence information only.

[9]An exception is hum-prt. It has a low coherence because many WordNet lemmas with a PART sense are body parts.

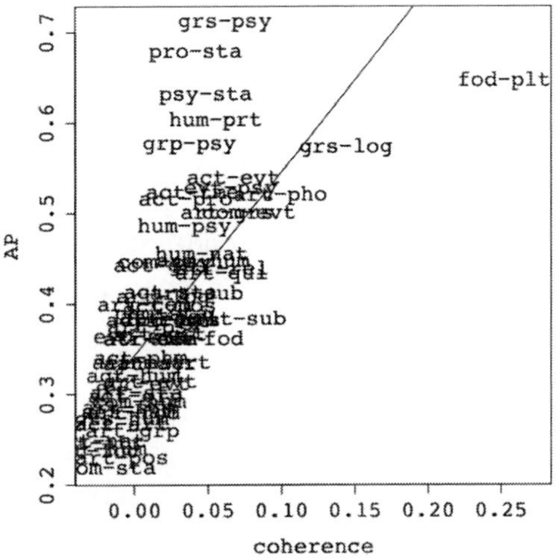

Figure 2: Average Precision and Coherence (κ) for each meta alternation. Correlation: $r = 0.743$ ($p < 0.001$)

6 Related work

As noted in Section 1, there is little work in empirical computational semantics on explicitly modeling sense alternations, although the notions that we have formalized here affect several tasks across NLP subfields.

Most work on regular sense alternations has focused on regular polysemy. A pioneering study is Buitelaar (1998), who accounts for regular polysemy through the CoreLex resource (cf. Section 3). A similar effort is carried out by Tomuro (2001), but he represents regular polysemy at the level of senses. Recently, Utt and Padó (2011) explore the differences between between idiosyncratic and regular polysemy patterns building on CoreLex. Lapata (2000) focuses on the default meaning arising from word combinations, as opposed to the polysemy of single words as in this study.

Meta alternations other than regular polysemy, such as metonymy, play a crucial role in Information Extraction. For instance, the meta alternation SOCIAL GROUP-GEOGRAPHICAL LOCATION corresponds to an ambiguity between the LOCATION-ORGANIZATION Named Entity classes which is known to be a hard problem in Named Entity Recognition and Classification (Markert and Nissim, 2009). Metaphorical meta alternations have also received attention recently (Turney et al., 2011)

On a structural level, the prediction of meta alternations shows a clear correspondence to analogy prediction as approached in Turney (2006) (*carpenter:wood* is analogous to *mason:stone*, but not to *photograph:camera*). The framework defined in Section 2 conceptualizes our task in a way parallel to that of analogical reasoning, modeling not "first-order" semantic similarity, but "second-order" semantic relations. However, the two tasks cannot be approached with the same methods, as Turney's model relies on contexts linking two nouns in corpus sentences (*what does A do to B*?). In contrast, we are interested in relations *within* words, namely between word senses. We cannot expect two different senses of the same noun to co-occur in the same sentence, as this is discouraged for pragmatic reasons (Gale et al., 1992).

A concept analogous to our notion of meta sense (i.e., senses beyond single words) has been used in previous work on class-based WSD (Yarowsky, 1992; Curran, 2005; Izquierdo et al., 2009), and indeed, the CAM might be used for class-based WSD as well. However, our emphasis lies rather on modeling polysemy across words (meta alternations), something that is absent in WSD, class-based or not. The only exception, to our knowledge, is Ando (2006), who pools the labeled examples for all words from a dataset for learning, implicitly exploiting regularities in sense alternations.

Meta senses also bear a close resemblance to the notion of semantic class as used in lexical acquisition (Hindle, 1990; Merlo and Stevenson, 2001; Schulte im Walde, 2006; Joanis et al., 2008). However, in most of this research polysemy is ignored. A few exceptions use soft clustering for multiple assignment of verbs to semantic classes (Pereira et al., 1993; Rooth et al., 1999; Korhonen et al., 2003), and Boleda et al. (to appear) explicitly model regular polysemy for adjectives.

7 Conclusions and Future Work

We have argued that modeling regular polysemy and other analogical processes will help improve current models of word meaning in empirical computational semantics. We have presented a formal framework to represent and operate with regular sense alternations, as well as a first simple instantiation of the framework. We have conducted an evaluation of different implementations of this model in the new task of determining whether words match a given sense alternation. All models significantly outperform the baselines when considered as a whole, and the best implementation outperforms the baselines for 73.3% of the tested alternations.

We have two next steps in mind. The first is to become independent of WordNet by unsupervised induction of (meta) senses and alternations from the data. This will allow for models that, unlike CAM, can go beyond "disemous" words. Other improvements on the model and evaluation will be to develop more informed baselines that capture semantic shifts, as well as to test alternate weighting schemes for the co-occurrence vectors (e.g. PMI) and to use larger corpora than the BNC.

The second step is to go beyond the limited in-vitro evaluation we have presented here by integrating alternation prediction into larger NLP tasks. Knowledge about alternations can play an important role in counteracting sparseness in many tasks that involve semantic compatibility, e.g., testing the applicability of lexical inference rules (Szpektor et al., 2008).

Acknowledgements

This research is partially funded by the Spanish Ministry of Science and Innovation (FFI2010-15006, TIN2009-14715-C04-04), the AGAUR (2010 BP-A00070), the German Research Foundation (SFB 732), and the EU (PASCAL2; FP7-ICT-216886). It is largely inspired on a course by Ann Copestake at U. Pompeu Fabra (2008). We thank Marco Baroni, Katrin Erk, and the reviewers of this and four other conferences for valuable feedback.

References

Rie Kubota Ando. 2006. Applying alternating structure optimization to word sense disambiguation. In *Proceedings of the 10th Conference on Computational Natural Language Learning*, pages 77–84, New York City, NY.

Iurii Derenikovich Apresjan. 1974. Regular polysemy. *Linguistics*, 142:5–32.

Gemma Boleda, Sabine Schulte im Walde, and Toni Badia. to appear. Modeling regular polysemy: A study of the semantic classification of Catalan adjectives. *Computational Linguistics*.

Paul Buitelaar. 1998. CoreLex: An ontology of systematic polysemous classes. In *Proceedings of Formal Ontologies in Information Systems*, pages 221–235, Amsterdam, The Netherlands.

Gavin Burnage and Dominic Dunlop. 1992. Encoding the British National Corpus. In Jan Aarts, Pieter de Haan, and Nelleke Oostdijk, editors, *English Language Corpora: Design, Analysis and Exploitation, Papers from the Thirteenth International Conference on English Language Research on Computerized Corpora*. Rodopi, Amsterdam.

Stephen Clark and James R. Curran. 2007. Wide-coverage efficient statistical parsing with ccg and log-l inear models. *Computational Linguistics*, 33(4).

Ann Copestake and Ted Briscoe. 1995. Semi-productive Polysemy and Sense Extension. *Journal of Semantics*, 12(1):15–67.

James Curran. 2005. Supersense tagging of unknown nouns using semantic similarity. In *Proceedings of the 43rd Annual Meeting of the Association for Computational Linguistics (ACL'05)*, pages 26–33, Ann Arbor, Michigan.

Bradley Efron and Robert Tibshirani. 1994. *An Introduction to the Bootstrap*. Monographs on Statistics and Applied Probability 57. Chapman & Hall.

Katrin Erk, Sebastian Padó, and Ulrike Padó. 2010. A flexible, corpus-driven model of regular and inverse selectional preferences. *Computational Linguistics*, 36(4):723–763.

Christiane Fellbaum, editor. 1998. *WordNet: an electronic lexical database*. MIT, London.

William A. Gale, Kenneth W. Church, and David Yarowsky. 1992. One sense per discourse. In *Proceedings of the 1992 ARPA Human Language Technologies Workshop*, pages 233–237, Harriman, NY.

Dedre Gentner, Brian F. Bowdle, Phillip Wolff, and Consuelo Boronat. 2001. Metaphor is like analogy. In D. Gentner, K. J. Holyoak, and B. N. Kokinov, editors, *The analogical mind: Perspectives from Cognitive Science*, pages 199–253. MIT Press, Cambridge, MA.

Gregory Grefenstette. 1994. *Explorations in Automatic Thesaurus Discovery*. Kluwer Academic Publishers.

Donald Hindle. 1990. Noun classification from predicate-argument structures. In *Proceedings of the 28th Meeting of the Association for Computational Linguistics*, pages 268–275.

Rubén Izquierdo, Armando Suárez, and German Rigau. 2009. An empirical study on class-based word sense disambiguation. In *Proceedings of the 12th Conference of the European Chapter of the ACL (EACL 2009)*, pages 389–397, Athens, Greece.

Eric Joanis, Suzanne Stevenson, and David James. 2008. A general feature space for automatic verb classification. *Natural Language Engineering*, 14(03):337–367.

Anna Korhonen, Yuval Krymolowski, and Zvika Marx. 2003. Clustering polysemic subcategorization frame distributions semantically. In *Proceedings of the 41st Annual Meeting of the Association for Computational Linguistics*, pages 64–71.

George Lakoff and Mark Johnson. 1980. *Metaphors We Live By*. University of Chicago Press.

Mirella Lapata. 2000. *The Acquisition and Modeling of Lexical Knowledge: A Corpus-based Investigation of Systematic Polysemy*. Ph.D. thesis, University of Edinburgh.

Lillian Lee. 1999. Measures of distributional similarity. In *Proceedings of the 37th Annual Meeting on Association for Computational Linguistics*, pages 25–32, College Park, MA.

Will Lowe. 2001. Towards a theory of semantic space. In *Proceedings of the 23rd Annual Meeting of the Cognitive Science Society*, pages 576–581, Edinburgh, UK.

Christopher D. Manning, Prabhakar Raghavan, and Hinrich Schütze. 2008. *Introduction to Information Retrieval*. Cambridge University Press, Cambridge, UK, 1st edition.

Katja Markert and Malvina Nissim. 2009. Data and models for metonymy resolution. *Language Resources and Evaluation*, 43(2):123–138.

Diana McCarthy, Rob Koeling, Julie Weeds, and John Carroll. 2004. Using automatically acquired predominant senses for word sense disambiguation. In *Proceedings of the ACL SENSEVAL-3 workshop*, pages 151–154.

Paola Merlo and Suzanne Stevenson. 2001. Automatic verb classification based on statistical distributions of argument structure. *Computational Linguistics*, 27(3):373–408.

Gregory L. Murphy. 2002. *The Big Book of Concepts*. MIT Press, Cambridge, MA.

Roberto Navigli and Paola Velardi. 2005. Structural semantic interconnections: a knowledge-based approach to word sense disambiguation. *IEEE Transactions on Pattern Analysis and Machine Intelligence*, 27(7):1075–1086, July.

Roberto Navigli. 2009. Word sense disambiguation: A survey. *ACM Computing Surveys*, 41:10:1–10:69, February.

Sebastian Padó and Mirella Lapata. 2007. Dependency-based construction of semantic space models. *Computational Linguistics*, 33(2):161–199.

Patrick Pantel and Dekang Lin. 2002. Discovering word senses from text. In *Proceedings of ACM SIGKDD Conference on Knowledge Discovery and Data Mining 2002*, pages 613–619, Edmonton.

Fernando C. N. Pereira, Naftali Tishby, and Lillian Lee. 1993. Distributional clustering of English words. In *Proceedings of the 31st Meeting of the Association for Computational Linguistics*, pages 183–190, Columbus, OH.

James Pustejovsky. 1995. *The Generative Lexicon*. MIT Press, Cambridge, MA.

Joseph Reisinger and Raymond J. Mooney. 2010. Multi-prototype vector-space models of word meaning. In *Proceedings of the 11th Annual Conference of the North American Chapter of the Association for Computational Linguistics (NAACL-2010)*, pages 109–117.

Mats Rooth, Stefan Riezler, Detlef Prescher, Glenn Carroll, and Franz Beil. 1999. Inducing a semantically annotated lexicon via EM-based clustering. In *Proceedings of the 37th Annual Meeting of the Association for Computational Linguistics*, College Park, MD.

Sabine Schulte im Walde. 2006. Experiments on the automatic induction of German semantic verb classes. *Computational Linguistics*, 32(2):159–194.

Hinrich Schütze. 1998. Automatic word sense discrimination. *Computational Linguistics*, 24(1):97–123.

Idan Szpektor, Ido Dagan, Roy Bar-Haim, and Jacob Goldberger. 2008. Contextual preferences. In *Proceedings of the 46th Annual Meeting of the Association for Computational Linguistics*, pages 683–691, Columbus, Ohio.

Noriko Tomuro. 2001. Tree-cut and a lexicon based on systematic polysemy. In *Proceedings of the second meeting of the North American Chapter of the Association for Computational Linguistics on Language technologies*, NAACL '01, pages 1–8, Stroudsburg, PA, USA. Association for Computational Linguistics.

Peter D. Turney and Patrick Pantel. 2010. From frequency to meaning: Vector space models of semantics. *Journal of Artificial Intelligence Research*, 37:141–188.

Peter Turney, Yair Neuman, Dan Assaf, and Yohai Cohen. 2011. Literal and metaphorical sense identification through concrete and abstract context. In *Proceedings of the Conference on Empirical Methods in Natural Language Processing*, pages 680–690, Edinburgh, Scotland, UK.

Peter D. Turney. 2006. Similarity of semantic relations. *Computational Linguistics*, 32:379–416.

Jason Utt and Sebastian Padó. 2011. Ontology-based distinction between polysemy and homonymy. In *Proceedings of the 9th International Conference on Computational Semantics*, Oxford, UK.

David Yarowsky. 1992. Word-sense disambiguation using statistical models of Roget's categories trained on large corpora. In *Proceedings of the 14th conference on Computational linguistics - Volume 2*, COLING '92, pages 454–460, Stroudsburg, PA, USA. Association for Computational Linguistics.

Extracting a Semantic Lexicon of French Adjectives from a Large Lexicographic Dictionary

Selja Seppälä and Alexis Nasr
Laboratoire d'Informatique Fondamentale
Aix Marseille Université
163, avenue de Luminy
F-13288 Marseille Cedex 9
alexis.nasr@lif.univ-mrs.fr
selja.seppala@lif.univ-mrs.fr

Lucie Barque
Lexiques Dictionnaires Informatique
Université Paris 13
99, avenue Jean-Baptiste Clément
F-93430 Villetaneuse
lucie.barque@univ-paris13.fr

Abstract

We present a rule-based method to automatically create a large-coverage semantic lexicon of French adjectives by extracting paradigmatic relations from lexicographic definitions. Formalized adjectival resources are, indeed, scarce for French and they mostly focus on morphological and syntactic information. Our objective is, therefore, to contribute enriching the available set of resources by taking advantage of reliable lexicographic data and formalizing it with the well-established *lexical functions* formalism. The resulting semantic lexicon of French adjectives can be used in NLP tasks such as word sense disambiguation or machine translation. After presenting related work, we describe the extraction method and the formalization procedure of the data. Our method is then quantitatively and qualitatively evaluated. We discuss the results of the evaluation and conclude on some perspectives.

1 Introduction

Formalized semantic resources are highly valuable in areas such as NLP, linguistic analysis or language acquisition. However, creating such resources from scratch is time-consuming and generally yields limited-size lexicons. Existing lexicographic dictionaries do have a large coverage and present a reliable content. They lack nevertheless the sufficient formalization. In this paper, we present a rule-based method to automatically create a large-coverage semantic lexicon of French adjectives by extracting paradigmatic relations from lexicographic definitions using lexico-syntactic patterns. Formalized adjectival resources are, indeed, scarce for French and they mostly focus on morphological and syntactic information. Our goal is, therefore, to contribute enriching the available set of resources by taking advantage of reliable lexicographic data and formalizing it with the well-established *lexical functions* formalism of the Meaning-Text theory (Mel'čuk, 1996). The resulting semantic lexicon of French adjectives can be used in NLP tasks such as word sense disambiguation or machine translation[1]. In section 2, we present related work. In section 3, we expose the method used to build the lexicon, i.e. the extraction method and the formalization procedure of the data, and outline the main results. Finally, in section 4, we present a quantitative evaluation of our method and a qualitative evaluation of our data, and discuss their results. We conclude on some perspectives for future work.

2 Related Work

It is well established that there are different types of adjectives distinguished by properties, such as *gradation* and *markedness*, and by their semantic and syntactic behaviors (*antonymy*, *selectional preferences*) (Fellbaum et al., 1993; Raskin and Nirenburg, 1996). WordNet, for example, distinguishes different types of adjectives according to their semantic and syntactic behaviors: *descriptive*, *reference-modifying*, *color* and *relational adjectives* (Fellbaum et al., 1993). However, it mainly accounts for the first and the last types of adjectives. Descrip-

[1] For other possible NLP applications of lexicons encoded with the lexical function formalism, see Schwab and Lafourcade (2007).

tive adjectives are organized in adjectival synsets that are mostly related through antonymy (*heavy–light*); synsets of relational adjectives are linked to a related noun by a pointer (*fraternal–brother*). Fellbaum et al. (1993:36) acknowledge the existence of more diverse relations to nominal synsets, but, to our knowledge, these are not accounted for in WordNet. This limitation is also present in the open access French version of the Princeton WordNet, WOLF (Sagot and Fišer, 2012). This limitation has led projects extending WordNet to other languages, like *EuroWordNet*, *ItalWordNet* or *WordNet.PT*, to add a few more relations to account for this diversity (Alonge et al., 2000; Marrafa and Mendes, 2006; Vossen, 2002). The number of new relations is however limited. As can be seen, WordNet-type approaches focus on relating adjectival synsets using a few semantic relations, mostly *antonymy* and plain *related_to* relations.

Our goal is to achieve a finer, and thus richer, semantic characterization of the relations holding between French adjectives and other words from all syntactic categories using the formalism of lexical functions. We assume that the type of the adjective is reflected in the structure of its lexicographic definition. Thus, to extract semantically relevant information from adjectival definitions, we propose to create different types of rules accounting for this diversity of defining structures.

Formalized French lexicons contain rather limited adjectival data. One can cite the morphological lexicon that links French denominal adjectives to the nouns they are derived from (Strnadovà and Sagot, 2011) or the syntactic characterization of French adjectives based on an automatic extraction of subcategorization frames proposed in Kupść (2008). Our method is meant to complete this set of resources with an adjectival lexicon that is not limited to certain types of adjectives (like *descriptive* or *denominal*) nor to morphologically related adjectives, and which provides semantic information.

3 Method and Results

The method we use to extract formalized semantic information from unformalized lexicographic definitions follows two steps : extracting relations between defined adjectives and elements of their definitions using lexico-syntactic rules (section 3.1) and mapping these relations to regular relations that can be expressed in terms of lexical functions (section 3.2).

3.1 Extracting Paradigmatic Relations from Lexicographic Definitions

The dictionary used in this project is the *Trésor de la langue française informatisé*[2] (TLFi). It is the electronic version of a 100,000 word lexicographic dictionary of 19th and 20th century French, the *Trésor de la langue française* (Dendien and Pierrel, 2003).

The TLFi contains a total of 13,513 adjectival entries, among which 6,425 entries correspond to mere adjectives and 7,088 to adjectives and other parts of speech (generally nouns)[3]. Each of these entries includes one or more definitions, which add up to 44,410 definitions, among which 32,475 are estimated to be adjectival. This approximation is obtained after filtering out 11,935 non-adjectival definitions from the mixed entries using a lexico-syntactic definition parsing program aimed at detecting nominal definitions. The remaining definitions are mostly adjectival, with exceptions due to more complex definition structures that are not accounted for by the filtering method. Table 1 sums up the main figures.

Adjectival entries	6,425
Not only adjectival entries	7,088
Estimated adjectival definitions	32,475

Table 1: Adjectives in the TLFi

To extract semantically relevant information from adjectival definitions, we use a lexico-syntactic adjectival definition parsing program which uses lexico-syntactic rules that are linearly matched to syntactically annotated adjectival definitions[4]. The extraction method consists of the following steps:

1. First, tagging and lemmatizing the definition so

[2]TLFi, http://atilf.atilf.fr/tlf.htm.

[3]It is difficult to determine exactly how many adjectives are defined in the TLFi since the dictionary often joins together words that can be both used as a noun or an adjective (for example JEUNE-*young*).

[4]The definitions are syntactically annotated with the Macaon tool suite (Nasr et al., 2010) that was adapted to the special sublanguage of lexicographic definitions.

that each word is related to a part of speech tag (POS).

(1) RETENU = Qui fait preuve de modération. (*restrained = Who shows moderation.*)
Qui/prorel fait/v preuve/nc de/prep modération/nc ./poncts

2. Second, running the adjectival definition parsing program to obtain a triplet composed of the defined adjective (`<adj>`), a relation (`<rel>`) and an argument (`<arg>`), i.e. a word or group of words that is linked by the extracted relation to the defined adjective.

(2)
```
<adj>retenu</adj>
<rel>fait preuve de</rel>
<arg>modération</arg>
```

A lexico-syntactic rule extracts from a definition the `<rel>` and `<arg>` elements. As can be seen in figure 1, each lexico-syntactic rule is composed of a left-hand side (LHS) containing either a lexical unit (`lex`), such as *qui*, or a POS tag (`cat`) like *v* (*verb*), both of which can be optional (`op="y"`), and a right-hand side (RHS) specifying which elements of the LHS are to be extracted as semantically relevant: a relation (REL) and/or an argument (ARG)[5].

In figure 1, the denominal rule 2.2 identifies adjectival definitions corresponding to the lexico-syntactic pattern stated by the LHS of the rule, such as that of the adjective RETENU in example 2 above[6]. The LHS contains nine elements, where the first two correspond to lexical items and the remaining ones to POS tags. Five elements are marked as optional, since a definition may for example start by the formula *Qui est* (*Which/Who is*) followed by some verb, or it may directly begin with a verb. This verb has to be followed by a noun (*nc*) and a preposition (*prep*), which may be followed by a determinant and/or an adjective, but which has to be followed by a noun, etc. The RHS of the rule states that the relation to be extracted corresponds to elements 3, 4 and 5 of the LHS, and that the argument is composed of elements 7, 8 and 9[7].

```
<regle num="2.2" rel="denominal">
  <lhs>
    <elt lex="qui" op="y" />
    <elt lex="est" op="y" />
    <elt cat="v" />
    <elt cat="nc" />
    <elt cat="prep" />
    <elt cat="det" op="y" />
    <elt cat="adj" op="y" />
    <elt cat="nc" />
    <elt cat="adj" op="y" />
  </lhs>
  <rhs>
    <rel>
      <elt num="3" />
      <elt num="4" />
      <elt num="5" />
    </rel>
    <arg>
      <elt num="7" />
      <elt num="8" />
      <elt num="9" />
    </arg>
  </rhs>
</regle>
```

Figure 1: Example of Lexico-Syntactic Rule

The relation extraction program reads the dictionary definition from the beginning of the sentence checking whether it contains the elements specified in the LHS of the rule. In case the rule matches the lexico-syntactic elements composing the definition, it outputs the lexical elements of the definition corresponding to the lexical or syntactic information specified in the RHS of the rule in the form REL(ARG)=ADJ, where ADJ stands for the adjective of the dictionary entry. For instance, applying the rule from figure 1 to the definition of the adjective RETENU returns the relation *fait_preuve_de* and the argument *modération* (example 2).

A total of 109 lexico-syntactic rules have been designed. These rules cover 76.1 % of the adjectival definitions (24,716/32,475 definitions). The rules can broadly be grouped into four categories corresponding to different adjectival definition structures. This categorization is done according to the type of defining information matched by the rules:

[5]For definitions by synonymy, only the argument is specified, the default semantic relation being *synonymy*.

[6]Note that the adjective RETENU (*retained*) is, morphologically speaking, not a denominal. However, the rule extracts a noun to which this adjective is related in its definition, i.e. MODÉRATION (*moderation*). It is, therefore, the rule that is considered denominal.

[7]In the RHS, the number assigned as a value to the `num` attribute corresponds to the line number of the `elt` in the LHS.

1. The adjective is defined by one or more synonyms.
→ REL = *synonymy*; ARG = adjective

(3) DIAGONAL = Transversal, oblique. (*diagonal = Transversal, oblique.*)
⇒ syn(transversal) = DIAGONAL; syn(oblique) = DIAGONAL (*syn(transversal) = diagonal; syn(oblique) = diagonal*)

2. The adjective is defined by another adjective modified by an adverb.
→ REL = adverb; ARG = adjective

(4) KILOMÉTRIQUE = Qui est très long, qui n'en finit pas. (*kilometric = Which is very long, never-ending.*)
⇒ très(long) = KILOMÉTRIQUE (*very(long) = kilometric*)

3. The adjective is defined by a relation to a property of the thing denoted by the modified noun. The argument of this complex REL consists of a noun phrase (NP), a verbal phrase (VP) or an adjective (ADJ).
→ REL = relation + property; ARG = NP/VP/ADJ

(5) AGRÉGATIF = Qui a la faculté d'agréger. (*aggregative = Which has the power to aggregate.*)
⇒ a_la_faculté_de(agréger) = AGRÉGATIF (*has_power_to(aggregate) = aggregative*)
VERSICOLORE = Dont la couleur est changeante. (*versicolor = Which color is changing.*)
⇒ dont_la_couleur_est(changeante) = VERSICOLORE (*which_color_is(changing) = versicolor*)

4. The adjective is defined by a relation having as argument a noun phrase, a verbal phrase or an adjective.
→ REL = relation; ARG = NP/VP/ADJ

(6) ACADÉMIQUE = Qui manque d'originalité, de force; conventionnel. (*academic = Which lacks originality, strength; conventional.*)
⇒ manque_de(originalité) = ACADÉMIQUE (*lacks(originality) = academic*)
INANALYSABLE = Qui ne peut être analysé, qui ne peut être décomposé en ses éléments distinctifs. (*unanalyzable = Which cannot be analyzed, which cannot be decompozed in its distinctive elements.*)
⇒ ne_peut_être(analysé) = INANALYSABLE (*cannot_be(analyzed) = unanalyzable*)

The rules extract a total of 5,284 different relation types in the form (REL, ARG), where REL is a lexicalized expression and ARG a phrasal type, as illustrated in example (7).

(7)

(capable de, VPinf)	(*capable of, VPinf*)
(constitué de, NP)	(*constituted by, NP*)
(couvert de, NP)	(*covered with, NP*)
(fondé sur, NP)	(*founded on, NP*)
(peu, ADJ)	(*not very, ADJ*)
(propre à, NP)	(*particular to, NP*)
(propre à, VPinf)	(*capable of, VPinf*)
(relatif à, NP)	(*relating to, NP*)

One can note that the lexicalized relation is sometimes followed by different phrasal types, as can be seen for *propre à* in example (7). In those cases, each (REL, ARG) pair is considered as a distinct relation type.

3.2 Formalizing Paradigmatic Relations with Lexical Functions

Lexical functions (LF) are a formal tool designed to describe all types of genuine lexical relations (paradigmatic and syntactic ones) between lexical units of any language (Mel'čuk, 1996). Some of the standard lexical functions that often return adjectival values are briefly presented below:

- **A0** – This paradigmatic lexical function returns the adjective that semantically corresponds to the argument. E.g. A0(CHAT) = FÉLIN (*A0(cat) = feline*); A0(CRIME) = CRIMINEL (*A0(crime) = criminal*)
- **A1/A2** – These paradigmatic lexical functions return the adjectives that typically characterize, respectively, the first and second argument of the predicate given as argument to the functions. This predicate can be nominal, adjectival or verbal. For example, given that the nominal predicate DÉCEPTION (*disappointment*) has two arguments, the person that is disappointed and the reason of the disappointment, function A1 applied to DÉCEPTION returns the adjective DÉÇU (*disappointed*), while function A2 returns DÉCEVANT (*disappointing*). E.g. A1(DÉCEPTION) = DÉÇU (*A2(disappointment) = disappointed*); A2(DÉCEPTION) = DÉCEVANT (*A2(disappointment) = disappointing*)

- **Able1/Able2** – Closely related to A1 and A2, these functions return the adjective that means that the first (Able1) or the second (Able2) argument of the predicate P "might P or is likely to P" (whereas A1 just means "arg1 that P" and A2 "arg2 that is P-ed"). E.g. Able1(CRAINDRE) = PEUREUX *(Able1(to fear) = coward)*; Able2(CRAINDRE) = EFFRAYANT *(Able2(to fear) = frightening)*
- **Magn** – This function returns an intensificator of the predicate. This intensificator can modify the argument, as in *heavy rain* (Magn expresses then a syntagmatic relation), or can be another adjective that intensifies the meaning of the argument (Magn expresses then a paradigmatic relation). E.g. Magn(MAUVAIS) = AFFREUX *(Magn(bad) = awful)*
- **Anti** – This function returns the argument's antonym(s). E.g. Anti(ABSENT) = PRÉSENT *(Anti(absent) = present)*
- **AntiA1** – This complex lexical function returns the adjective that means that the first argument of the predicate P "is not P (anymore)". E.g. AntiA1(FAIM) = REPU *(AntiA1(hunger) = full)*

We use this formalism to describe the paradigmatic relations between adjectives and the arguments extracted in the previous step. These relations are formulated in a non-systematic way in the TLFi's definitions. Definitions in traditional dictionaries are written in natural language and, thus, are not formal enough to be used as such, for example, in NLP tasks. In order to formalize the lexicon, a mapping is done between lexical functions describing paradigmatic relations and the different ways of expressing these relations in the TLFi's definitions (see *relation types* in example 7), as illustrated in table 2.

This REL-LF mapping covers 67.3 % of the extracted relations (16,646/24,716 extracted relations). Table 3 shows the complete list of lexical functions used in our lexicon and their distribution: the three lexical functions A0, A1 and QSyn represent around 90 % of the relations.

4 Evaluation

The method and the data have been evaluated in two ways. The method has first been evaluated by comparing our data to an external resource, the *Dictionnaire de combinatoire*[8] (DiCo), a French lexicographic dictionary describing words with their paradigmatic and syntagmatic relations expressed in the LF formalism. In this first evaluation, we determine the performance of the method by quantifying the number of reference elements from the DiCo that can be extracted from the TLFi with our rules (section 4.1). Since relations involving adjectives are scarce in the DiCo, our data has then been qualitatively evaluated by an expert familiar with the formalism of lexical functions[9] (section 4.2). The expert evaluates the relevance of the argument and the adequacy of the proposed lexical function to describe the relation between the defined adjective and the argument.

A0	(qui) est relatif à, est propre à + N, se rapporte à, . . . *(who/that is related to, particular to . . .)*
A1	(qui) a la forme de, est atteint de, . . . *(who/that has the shape of, suffers from . . .)*
A2	(qui) produit, provoque, a reçu, . . . *(who/that causes, has obtained . . .)*
Able1	qui peut, est propre à + V, susceptible de, . . . *(who/that can, is likely to . . .)*
Able2	que l'on peut, . . . *(who/that can be . . .)*
Anti	qui n'est pas, qui s'oppose à, . . . *(that is not, that is opposed to . . .)*
AntiA1	(qui) n'a pas de, est dépourvu de, manque de, . . . *(who/that has no, is un-sthg, lacks sthg . . .)*

Table 2: LFs and Their Glosses in the TLFi Definitions

A0	**A1**	**A2**	**Able1**	**Able2**
28.8 %	27.71 %	4.38 %	6.65 %	0.37 %
Anti	**AntiA1**	**AntiA2**	**AntiAble1**	**AntiAble2**
1.64 %	3.49 %	0.21 %	1.24 %	1.04 %
QSyn	**Magn**	**Ver**	**AntiMagn**	**AntiVer**
21.73 %	1.60 %	0.62 %	0.35 %	0.20 %

Table 3: LF's Distribution in the French Adjectival Lexicon

4.1 Comparison With the DiCo Data

The first evaluation procedure is meant to measure the performance of the extraction program against an existing resource. The reference is constituted by selecting 240 triplets in the form LF(ARG)=ADJ from the DiCo. An automatic evaluation script compares these reference triplets with the hypothesized triplets extracted from the TLFi. The system catego-

[8]The electronic version of the DiCo can be accessed here: http://olst.ling.umontreal.ca/dicouebe/index.php.

[9]The expert is not an author of this paper.

rizes the reference triplets in one of three large categories explained below: "Impossible", "Yes" and "No", the latter ones indicating whether the method allows to extract the reference triplets from the TLFi or not. In the "No" cases, the evaluation system subcategorizes the reference triplet according to a possible explanation of the failure of the extraction method.

1. **IMPOSSIBLE** (42.9 %, 103/240 triplets)

   Cases where the reference triplets cannot be used as an evaluation reference because either the adjective of the reference is absent from the TLFi dictionary (5 %, 12/240 triplets, example 8) or the reference argument is absent from the definition(s) of the corresponding adjective in the TLFi (37.9 %, 91/240 triplets, example 9).

   (8) **DiCo-reference**
   QSyn(humain) = philanthrope
   (QSyn(human) = philanthropic)
   TLFi-hypothesis
   ø(ø) = ø
   The adjective *philanthrope* (*philanthropic*) does not have an entry in the TLFi.

   (9) **DiCo-reference**
   A1(richesse) = riche
   (A1(wealth) = rich)
   TLFi-hypothesis
   A1Perf(fortune) = riche
   (A1Perf(fortune) = rich)
   In this example, the argument *richesse* (*wealth*) does not exist in any of the 15 definitions of *riche* (*rich*) in the TLFi.

2. **YES** (20.4 %, 49/240 triplets)

   (a) Total matches: these cases correspond to the intersection of the two resources, i.e. cases where the triplets are identical on both sides (16.3 %, 39/240 triplets).

   (10) **DiCo-reference**
   A1(faute) = fautif
   TLFi-hypothesis
   A1(faute) = fautif
   (A1(fault) = guilty)

   (b) Partial matches: cases where the adjectives and LFs are identical on both sides and where the reference argument is included in the hypothesis argument (4.2 %, 10/240 triplets).

   (11) **DiCo-reference**
   A1(défaite) = vaincu
   (A1(defeat) = vanquished)
   TLFi-hypothesis
   A1(défaite militaire) = vaincu
   (A1(military defeat) = vanquished)

3. **NO** (36.7 %, 88/240 triplets) Four types of cases can be distinguished:

   (a) Cases where the reference adjective is in the TLFi but absent from the set of hypothesis adjectives. These cases can be explained by the fact that the extraction rules did not match a definition in the TLFi or by the fact that no LF has been mapped to the lexical relation that was extracted from the TLFi definitions (13.8 %, 33/240 triplets).

   (12) **DiCo-reference**
   A0(lait) = lactique
   (A0(milk) = lactic)
   TLFi-hypothesis
   ø(ø) = ø

   (b) Cases where the adjective and the argument of the reference and of the hypothesis are identical or where the arguments match partially, but the LFs are different (11.3 %, 27/240 triplets, example 13). This divergence might indicate an erroneous mapping between the extracted lexicalized relation and the LF. It could also be explained by the possibility of describing the same pair of ADJ-ARG with two different LFs.

   (13) **DiCo-reference**
   Able1(haine) = haineux
   TLFi-hypothesis
   A1(haine) = haineux
   (A1(hate) = hateful)

   (c) Cases where the extraction rule outputs an ill-formed hypothesis argument resulting from some problem in the extraction rule (example 14), or where the hypothesis triplet is not erroneous as such but corresponds to a new triplet-variant for a particular adjective (example 15) (11.7 %, 28/240 triplets).

   (14) **DiCo-reference** A0(sucre) = sucrier
   (A0(sugar) = sugar (nominal adjective))

TLFi-hypothesis
A0(production) = sucrier
(A0(production) = sugar)
TLFi-definition
SUCRIER = Qui est relatif à la production, à la fabrication du sucre.
(sugar (adj.) = Related to the production, the manufacture of sugar.)

In example 14, the TLFi definition for *sucrier* contains the reference argument *sucre*, but the extraction rule did not match the right string, resulting in an ill-formed hypothesis argument.

(15) **DiCo-reference** A1(enthousiasme) = enthousiaste
(A1(enthusiasm) = enthusiastic)
TLFi-hypothesis
A1(admiration passionnée) = enthousiaste
(A1(passionate admiration) = enthusiastic)

In example 15, the hypothesis argument extracted by the rule is well-formed but does not correspond to the reference argument. The hypothesis triplet can thus be considered as a new variant for the adjective *enthousiaste* (*enthusiastic*).

The most significant results of the first evaluation are synthesized in table 4. Note that the reference does not cover every relation type that has been taken into account in our lexicon: among the 15 relation types listed in table 3 above, only ten are present in the DiCo resource and six illustrated in table 4.

Eval.	%	A1	A0	QSyn	Able2	A2	Able1
Imp.	42.9	33	10	31	7	12	6
Yes	20.4	18	24	0	1	2	2
No	36.7	29	16	10	14	6	8
Total	100	80	50	41	22	20	16

Table 4: Results of the First Evaluation Against the DiCo

If the reference triplets marked "Impossible" (Imp.) are excluded, this evaluation shows that the simple rule-based system proposed to extract semantically relevant information from lexicographic definitions of adjectives covers 35.8 % of the 137 reference triplets that can be used for the evaluation. The analysis of the 88 "No" cases shows that most of the problems are due to insufficient rule-coverage and/or REL-LF mapping (37.5 %, 33/88). This figure could be reduced by further analyzing the definitions that are not accounted for by the rules in order to add more rules, and by mapping more lexicalized relations to LFs. The latter solution might, however, prove difficult due to the high frequency of reduced- or single-occurrence relations extracted. 30.7 % (27/88) of the "No" cases correspond to a difference in LFs and 31.8 % (28/88) to either ill-formed arguments or to new variant-triplets. A manual check of the 53 hypothesis triplets extracted for the 28 adjectives of the latter types of cases shows that in only 12 cases the hypothesis arguments are ill-formed (corresponding to 6/28 reference triplets); the rest corresponds to, *a priori*, acceptable arguments, i.e. to new triplet variants (41/53 cases), although a few of them are technically speaking ill-formed. Therefore, most of the remaining 55.7 % (49/88) "No" cases should be qualitatively evaluated.

These mitigated quantitative results have to be put in perspective. The first evaluation was meant to test the performance of the extraction rules against data from an existing resource, but, as the figures show, the vast majority of the reference triplets cannot be tested. This quantitative evaluation thus highlights the difficulty of using existing resources for this kind of task (particularly when such resources are scarce). Moreover, it proves insufficient to measure the actual performance of the rules. Two types of cases are indeed unaccounted for: first, there might be many *correct* hypothesis triplets that are not in the reference, since there is a huge discrepancy in the number of triplets between the reference and the hypotheses; second, the hypothesis triplets that don't match to the reference might still be correct. Therefore, other qualitative evaluation methods have to be used.

4.2 Evaluation by an LF Expert

An expert of the LF formalism has evaluated the quality of 150 triplets taken from the 16,646 LF(ARG)=ADJ triplets of the lexicon. First, he evaluated the argument (0 for a *wrong argument*, 1 for a *valid argument*) and, when he judged that the argument was correct, he evaluated the LF: 2 for a *good*

LF, 1 for a *partially satisfying LF* and 0 for an *invalid LF*. To sum up, four configurations are possible:

- **Case 1 – ARG:0**

  E.g. A2(*converti*-converted) = AGATISÉ-agatized

  The expert considers that the argument is invalid. Indeed, AGATISÉ means *converted into an agate* but the program extracted *converted* as an argument instead of *agate*.

- **Case 2 – ARG:1 LF:0**

  E.g. Able1(*admiration*) = ADMIRABLE

  The expert considers that the argument is valid but the LF is not the right one: the adjective ADMIRABLE characterizes the second argument of *admiration* and not the first one. The correct LF should therefore be Able2.

- **Case 3 – ARG:1 LF:1**

  A1(*trouble*-confusion) = AHURI-dazed

  The expert considers that the argument is valid but the LF is incomplete: it is true that the adjective AHURI qualifies the first argument of *confusion* but, more precisely, it conveys information on the manifestation of the emotion. So a more precise LF should be A1-Manif.

- **Case 4 – ARG:1 LF:2**

  Magn(*agité*-upset) = AFFOLÉ-distraught

  The expert considers that the argument and the LF are valid since AFFOLÉ indeed means *very upset*.

Table 5 shows the results of the qualitative evaluation of lexical functions. Cases 3 and 4 are considered to be accurate.

Case 1	Case 2	Case 3	Case 4	Total	Accuracy
11	34	32	73	150	70.5 %

Table 5: Evaluation by the Expert

When confronted to cases 2 and 3, the expert was invited to give the correct LF. This information will be processed in order to improve the matching between relations extracted from the TLFi and appropriate lexical functions.

5 Conclusion

In this article, we presented a rule-based method to automatically extract paradigmatic relations from lexicographic definitions of adjectives using lexico-syntactic patterns. This method was completed with a manual mapping of the most frequently extracted lexicalized relations (which are quite heterogenous) to formal lexical functions. Our goal is to automatically create a formalized semantic lexicon of French adjectives that would be complementary to the few existing adjectival resources that can be used, for instance, in NLP tasks. The adjectival lexicon, in which each adjective is related by a lexical function to an NP/VP/adjectival/adverbial argument, was quantitatively and qualitatively evaluated.

The first evaluation, entirely automatic, was aimed at testing the performance of the method. It yielded rather inconclusive results mainly due to the scarcity of the external data available for the task. A thorough analysis of the different types of "errors" showed that the number of "technical problems" can be reduced by refining the extraction rules, by adding more of them, and by completing the mapping of extracted relations to LFs. It also highlighted the necessity to evaluate the method qualitatively. The second evaluation was, thus, aimed at rating the acceptability of the extracted relations. It was realized by an expert of the lexical functions formalism and gave good results, with a precision of around 70 %.

The automatically created adjectival lexicon presented in this paper can be easily extended by a straightforward inversion of the LF(ARG)=ADJ triplets. The resulting triplets would either complete existing lexical entries if integrated into a similarly encoded nominal and verbal lexicon, or constitute new entries in the adjectival lexicon, thus extending the syntactic categories represented in the lexicon. The LF formalism could also be used to further enrich adjectival entries by making automatic inferences between adjective-argument pairs and their respective synonyms. E.g. infer *A0(kitty)=feline* from *A0(cat)=feline* and *syn(cat)=kitty*. Finally, mapping LFs with the existing relations in WordNet could allow to integrate this adjectival lexicon to the French WOLF.

Acknowledgements

This work has been funded by the French Agence Nationale pour la Recherche, through the project EDYLEX (ANR-08-CORD-009).

References

Alonge A., Bertagna F., Calzolari N., Roventini A., and Zampolli A. 2000. Encoding information on adjectives in a lexical-semantic net for computational applications. In *Proceedings of the 1st North American chapter of the Association for Computational Linguistics conference*, NAACL 2000, pages 42–49, Stroudsburg, PA, USA. Association for Computational Linguistics.

Dendien J. and Pierrel J.-M. 2003. Le Trésor de la Langue Française informatisé : un exemple d'informatisation d'un dictionnaire de langue de référence. *Traitement Automatique des Langues.* 44(2):11-37.

Fellbaum C., Gross D. and Miller K. J. 1993. *Adjectives in WordNet.* Technical report, Cognitive Science Laboratory, Princeton University, 26–39.

Kupść A. 2008. *Adjectives in TreeLex.* In M. Klopotek, A. Przepiórkowski, S. Wierzchoń et K. Trojanowski (eds.), 16th International Conference Intelligent Information Systems. Zakopane, Poland, 16-18 juin, Academic Publishing House EXIT, 287–296.

Marrafa, P. and Mendes, S. 2006. Modeling adjectives in computational relational lexica. In *Proceedings of the COLING/ACL on Main conference poster sessions*, COLING-ACL '06, pages 555–562, Stroudsburg, PA, USA. Association for Computational Linguistics.

Mel'čuk I. 1996. Lexical Functions: A Tool for the Description of Lexical Relations in the Lexicon. In: L. Wanner (ed.). *Lexical Functions in Lexicography and Natural Language Processing.* Amsterdam/Philadelphia: Benjamins, 37-102.

Nasr A., Béchet F., Rey J.-F., Favre B. and Le Roux J. 2011. MACAON: An NLP tool suite for processing word lattices. *The 49th Annual Meeting of the Association for Computational Linguistics.*

Raskin V. and Nirenburg S. 1996. Adjectival Modification in Text Meaning Represention. *Proceedings of COLING '96.*

Sagot B. and Fišer D. 2012. Automatic extension of WOLF. *6th International Global Wordnet Conference (GWC2012).* Matsue, Japan.

Schwab D. and Lafourcade M. 2011. Modelling, Detection and Exploitation of Lexical Functions for Analysis. *ECTI Journal.* Vol.2. 97-108.

Strnadová J. and Sagot B. 2011. Construction d'un lexique des adjectifs dénominaux. *Actes de TALN 2011.* Vol.2. 69-74. Montpellier, France.

Vossen, P. 2002. WordNet, EuroWordNet and Global WordNet. *Revue française de linguistique appliquée,* 7(1):27–38.

Modelling selectional preferences in a lexical hierarchy

Diarmuid Ó Séaghdha
Computer Laboratory
University of Cambridge
Cambridge, UK
do242@cam.ac.uk

Anna Korhonen
Computer Laboratory
University of Cambridge
Cambridge, UK
Anna.Korhonen@cl.cam.ac.uk

Abstract

This paper describes Bayesian selectional preference models that incorporate knowledge from a lexical hierarchy such as WordNet. Inspired by previous work on modelling with WordNet, these approaches are based either on "cutting" the hierarchy at an appropriate level of generalisation or on a "walking" model that selects a path from the root to a leaf. In an evaluation comparing against human plausibility judgements, we show that the models presented here outperform previously proposed comparable WordNet-based models, are competitive with state-of-the-art selectional preference models and are particularly well-suited to estimating plausibility for items that were not seen in training.

1 Introduction

The concept of *selectional preference* captures the intuitive fact that predicates in language have a better semantic "fit" for certain arguments than others. For example, the direct object argument slot of the verb *eat* is more plausibly filled by a type of food (*I ate a pizza*) than by a type of vehicle (*I ate a car*), while the subject slot of the verb *laugh* is more plausibly filled by a person than by a vegetable. Human language users' knowledge about selectional preferences has been implicated in analyses of metaphor processing (Wilks, 1978) and in psycholinguistic studies of comprehension (Rayner et al., 2004). In Natural Language Processing, automatically acquired preference models have been shown to aid a number of tasks, including semantic role labelling (Zapirain et al., 2009), parsing (Zhou et al., 2011) and lexical disambiguation (Thater et al., 2010; Ó Séaghdha and Korhonen, 2011).

It is tempting to assume that with a large enough corpus, preference learning reduces to a simple language modelling task that can be solved by counting predicate-argument co-occurrences. Indeed, Keller and Lapata (2003) show that relatively good performance at plausibility estimation can be attained by submitting queries to a Web search engine. However, there are many scenarios where this approach is insufficient: for languages and language domains where Web-scale data is unavailable, for predicate types (e.g., inference rules or semantic roles) that cannot be retrieved by keyword search and for applications where accurate models of rarer words are required. Ó Séaghdha (2010) shows that the Web-based approach is reliably outperformed by more complex models trained on smaller corpora for less frequent predicate-argument combinations. Models that induce a level of semantic representation, such as probabilistic latent variable models, have a further advantage in that they can provide rich structured information for downstream tasks such as lexical disambiguation (Ó Séaghdha and Korhonen, 2011) and semantic relation mining (Yao et al., 2011).

Recent research has investigated the potential of Bayesian probabilistic models such as Latent Dirichlet Allocation (LDA) for modelling selectional preferences (Ó Séaghdha, 2010; Ritter et al., 2010; Reisinger and Mooney, 2011). These models are flexible and robust, yielding superior performance compared to previous approaches. In this paper we present a preliminary study of analogous models that make use of a lexical hierarchy (in our case the WordNet hierarchy). We describe two broad classes of probabilistic models over WordNet and how they can be implemented in a Bayesian framework. The two main potential advantages of incorporating WordNet information are: (a) improved predictions about rare and out-of-vocabulary arguments; (b) the ability to perform syntactic word sense disambiguation with a principled probabilistic model and without the need for an additional step that heuristically maps latent variables onto WordNet senses. Focussing here on (a), we demonstrate that our models attain better performance than previously-proposed WordNet-based methods on a plausibility estimation task and are particularly well-suited to estimating plausibility for arguments that were not seen in training and for which LDA cannot make useful predictions.

2 Background and Related Work

The WordNet lexical hierarchy (Fellbaum, 1998) is one of the most-used resources in NLP, finding many applications in both the definition of tasks (e.g. the SENSEVAL/SemEval word sense disambiguation tasks) and in the construction of systems. The idea of using WordNet to define selectional preferences was first implemented by Resnik (1993), who proposed a measure of *associational strength* between a semantic class s and a predicate p corresponding to a relation type r:

$$A(s,p,r) = \frac{1}{\eta} P(s|p,r) \log_2 \frac{P(s|p,r)}{P(s|r)} \quad (1)$$

where η is a normalisation term. This measure captures the degree to which the probability of seeing s given the predicate p differs from the prior probability of s. Given that we are often interested in the preference of p for a word w rather than a class and words generally map onto multiple classes, Resnik suggests calculating $A(s,p,r)$ for all classes that could potentially be expressed by w and predicting the maximal value.

Cut-based models assume that modelling the selectional preference of a predicate involves finding the right "level of generalisation" in the WordNet hierarchy. For example, the direct object slot of the verb *eat* can be associated with the subhierarchy rooted at the synset **food#n#1**, as all hyponyms of that synset are assumed to be edible and the immediate hypernym of the synset, **substance#n#1**, is too general given that many substances are rarely eaten.[1] This leads to the notion of "cutting" the hierarchy at one or more positions (Li and Abe, 1998). The modelling task then becomes that of finding the cuts that are maximally general without overgeneralising. Li and Abe (1998) propose a model in which the appropriate cut c is selected according to the Minimum Description Length principle; this principle explicitly accounts for the trade-off between generalisation and accuracy by minimising a sum of *model description length* and *data description length*. The probability of a predicate p taking as its argument an synset s is modelled as:

$$P_{la}(s|p,r) = P(s|c_{s,p,r})P(c|p) \quad (2)$$

where $c_{s,p,r}$ is the portion of the cut learned for p that dominates s. The distribution $P(s|c_{s,p,r})$ is held to be uniform over all synsets dominated by $c_{s,p,r}$, while $P(c|p)$ is given by a maximum likelihood estimate.

Clark and Weir (2002) present a model that, while not explicitly described as cut-based, likewise seeks to find the right level of generalisation for an observation. In this case, the hypernym at which to "cut" is chosen by a chi-squared test: if the aggregate preference of p for classes in the subhierarchy rooted at c differs significantly from the individual preferences of p for the immediate children of c, the hierarchy is cut below c. The probability of p taking a synset s as its argument is given by:

$$P_{cw}(s|p,r) = \frac{P(p|c_{s,p,r},r)\frac{P(s|r)}{P(p|r)}}{\sum_{s' \in S} P(p|c_{s',p,r},r)\frac{P(s'|r)}{P(p|r)}} \quad (3)$$

where $c_{s,p,r}$ is the root node of the subhierarchy containing s that was selected for p.

An alternative approach to modelling with WordNet uses its hierarchical structure to define a Markov model with transitions from senses to senses and from senses to words. The intuition here is that each observation is generated by a "walk" from the root of the hierarchy to a leaf node and emitting the word

[1] In this paper we use WordNet version 3.0, except where stated otherwise.

corresponding to the leaf. Abney and Light (1999) proposed such a model for selectional preferences, trained via EM, but failed to achieve competitive performance on a pseudodisambiguation task.

The models described above have subsequently been used in many different studies. For example: McCarthy and Carroll (2003) use Li and Abe's method in a word sense disambiguation setting; Schulte im Walde et al. (2008) use their MDL approach as part of a system for syntactic and semantic subcategorisation frame learning; Shutova (2010) deploys Resnik's method for metaphor interpretation. Brockmann and Lapata (2003) report a comparative evaluation in which the methods of Resnik and Clark and Weir outpeform Li and Abe's method on a plausibility estimation task.

Much recent work on preference learning has focused on purely distributional methods that do not use a predefined hierarchy but learn to make generalisations about predicates and arguments from corpus observations alone. These methods can be vector-based (Erk et al., 2010; Thater et al., 2010), discriminative (Bergsma et al., 2008) or probabilistic (Ó Séaghdha, 2010; Ritter et al., 2010; Reisinger and Mooney, 2011). In the probabilistic category, Bayesian models based on the "topic modelling" framework (Blei et al., 2003b) have been shown to achieve state-of-the-art performance in a number of evaluation settings; the models considered in this paper are also related to this framework.

In machine learning, researchers have proposed a variety of topic modelling methods where the latent variables are arranged in a hierarchical structure (Blei et al., 2003a; Mimno et al., 2007). In contrast to the present work, these models use a relatively shallow hierarchy (e.g., 3 levels) and any hierarchy node can in principle emit any vocabulary item; they thus provide a poor match for our goal of modelling over WordNet. Boyd-Graber et al. (2007) describe a topic model that is directly influenced by Abney and Light's Markov model approach; this model (LDAWN) is described further in Section 3.3 below. Reisinger and Paşca (2009) investigate Bayesian methods for attaching attributes harvested from the Web at an appropriate level in the WordNet hierarchy; this task is related in spirit to the preference learning task.

3 Probabilistic modelling over WordNet

3.1 Notation

We assume that we have a lexical hierarchy in the form of a directed acyclic graph $G = (S, E)$ where each node (or *synset*) $s \in S$ is associated with a set of words W_n belonging to a large vocabulary V. Each edge $e \in E$ leads from a node n to its children (or *hyponyms*) Ch_n. As G is a DAG, a node may have more than one parent but there are no cycles. The ultimate goal is to learn a distribution over the argument vocabulary V for each predicate p in a set P, through observing predicate-argument pairs. A predicate is understood to correspond to a pairing of a lexical item v and a relation type r, for example $p = (eat, direct\_object)$. The list of observations for a predicate p is denoted by $Observations(p)$.

3.2 Cut-based models

Model 1 Generative story for WN-CUT

```
for cut c ∈ {1...|C|} do
    Φ_c ~ Multinomial(β_c)
end for
for predicate p ∈ {1...|P|} do
    θ_p ~ Dirichlet(α)
    for argument instance i ∈ Observations(p) do
        c_i ~ Multinomial(θ_p)
        w_i ~ Multinomial(Φ_{c_i})
    end for
end for
```

The first model we consider, WN-CUT, is directly inspired by Li and Abe's model (2). Each predicate p is associated with a distribution over "cuts", i.e., complete subgraphs of G rooted at a single node and containing all nodes dominated by the root. It follows that the number of possible cuts is the same as the number of synsets. Each cut c is associated with a non-uniform distribution over the set of words W_c that can be generated by the synsets contained in c. As well as the use of a non-uniform emission distribution and the placing of Dirichlet priors on the multinomial over cuts, a significant difference from Li and Abe's model is that overlapping cuts are permitted (indeed, every cut has non-zero probability given a predicate). For example, the model may learn that the direct object slot of *eat* gives high probability to the cut rooted at **food#n#1** but also that the cut rooted at **substance#n#1** has non-negligible probability, higher than that assigned to **phenomenon#n#1**. It follows that the estimated probability of p taking argument w takes into account all possible cuts, weighted by their probability given p.

The generative story for WN-CUT is given in Algorithm 1; this describes the assumptions made by the model about how a corpus of observations is generated. The probability of predicate p taking argument w is defined as (4); an empirical posterior estimate of this quantity can be computed from a Gibbs sampling state via (5):

$$P(w|p) = \sum_c P(c|p)P(w|c) \quad (4)$$

$$\propto \sum_c \frac{f_{cp} + \alpha}{f_{\cdot p} + |C|\alpha} \frac{f_{wc} + \beta}{f_{\cdot c} + |W_c|\beta} \quad (5)$$

where f_{cw} is the number of observations containing argument w that have been assigned cut c, f_{cp} is the number of observations containing predicate p that have been assigned cut c and $f_{c\cdot}$, $f_{\cdot p}$ are the marginal counts for cut c and predicate p, respectively. The two terms that are multiplied in (4) play complementary roles analogous to those of the two description lengths in Li and Abe's MDL formulation; $P(c|p)$ will prefer to reuse more general cuts, while $P(w|c)$ will prefer more specific cuts with a smaller associated argument vocabulary.

As the number of words $|W_c|$ that can be emitted by a cut $|c|$ varies according to the size of the subhierarchy under the cut, the proportion of probability mass accorded to the likelihood and the prior in (5) is not constant. An alternative formulation is to keep the distribution of mass between likelihood and prior constant but vary the value of the individual β_c parameters according to cut size. Experiments suggest that this alternative does not differ in performance.

The second cut-based model, WN-CUT-TOPICS, extends WN-CUT by adding two extra layers of latent variables. Firstly, the choice of cut is conditional on a "topic" variable z rather than directly conditioned on the predicate; when the topic vocabulary Z is much smaller than the cut vocabulary C, this has the effect of clustering the cuts. Secondly, instead of immediately drawing a word once a cut has been chosen, the model first draws a synset s and then draws a word from the vocabulary W_s associated with that synset. This has two advantages; it directly disambiguates each observation to a specific synset rather than to a region of the hierarchy and it should also improve plausibility predictions for rare synonyms of common arguments. The generative story for WN-CUT-TOPICS is given in Algorithm 2; the distribution over arguments for p is given in (6) and the corresponding posterior estimate in (7):

Model 2 Generative story for WN-CUT-TOPICS

```
for topic z ∈ {1...|Z|} do
  Ψ_z ~ Dirichlet(α)
end for
for cut c ∈ {1...|C|} do
  Φ_c ~ Dirichlet(γ_c)
end for
for synset s ∈ {1...|S|} do
  Ξ_s ~ Dirichlet(β_s)
end for
for predicate p ∈ {1...|P|} do
  θ_p ~ Dirichlet(κ)
  for argument instance i ∈ Observations(p) do
    z_i ~ Multinomial(θ_p)
    c_i ~ Multinomial(Ψ_z)
    s_i ~ Multinomial(Φ_c)
    w_i ~ Multinomial(Ξ_s)
  end for
end for
```

$$P(w|p) = \sum_z P(z|p) \sum_c P(c|z) \sum_s P(s|c)P(w|s) \quad (6)$$

$$\propto \sum_z \frac{f_{zp} + \kappa_z}{f_{\cdot p} + \sum_{z'} \kappa_{z'}} \sum_c \frac{f_{cz} + \alpha}{f_{\cdot z} + |C|\alpha} \times \sum_s \frac{f_{sc} + \gamma}{f_{\cdot c} + |S_c|\gamma} \frac{f_{ws} + \beta}{f_{\cdot s} + |W_s|\beta} \quad (7)$$

As before, f_{zp}, f_{cz}, f_{sc} and f_{ws} are the respective co-occurrence counts of topics/predicates, cuts/topics, synsets/cuts and words/synsets in the sampling state and $f_{\cdot p}$, $f_{\cdot z}$, $f_{\cdot c}$ and $f_{\cdot s}$ are the corresponding marginal counts.

Since WN-CUT and WN-CUT-TOPICS are constructed from multinomials with Dirichlet priors, it is relatively straightforward to train them by collapsed Gibbs sampling (Griffiths and Steyvers, 2004), an iterative method whereby each latent variable in the model is stochastically updated according to the distribution given by conditioning on the current latent variable assignments of all other tokens. In the case of WN-CUT, this amounts to updating the cut assignment c_i for each token in turn. For WN-CUT-TOPICS there are three variables to update; c_i and s_i must be updated simultaneously, but z_i can be updated independently for the benefit of efficiency. Although WordNet contains 82,115 noun synsets, updates for c_i and s_i can be computed very efficiently, as there are typically few possible synsets for a given word type and few possible cuts for a given synset (the maximum synset depth is 19).

The hyperparameters for the various Dirichlet priors are also reestimated in the course of learning; the values of these hyperparameters control the degree of sparsity preferred by the model. The "top-level" hyperparameters α in WN-CUT and κ in WN-CUT-TOPICS are estimated using a fixed-point iteration proposed by Wallach (2008); the other hyperparameters are learned by slice sampling (Neal, 2003).

3.3 Walk-based models

Abney and Light (1999) proposed an approach to selectional preference learning in which arguments are generated for predicates by following a path $\lambda = (l_1, \ldots, l_{|\lambda|})$ from the root of the hierarchy to a leaf node and emitting the corresponding word. The path is chosen according to a Markov model with transition probabilities specific to each predicate. In this model, each leaf node is associated with a single word; the synsets associated with that word are the immediate parent nodes of the leaf. Abney and Light found that their model did not match the performance of Resnik's (1993) simpler method. We have had a similar lack of success with a Bayesian version of this model, which we do not describe further here.

Boyd-Graber et al. (2007) describe a related topic model, LDAWN, for word sense disambiguation that adds an intermediate layer of latent variables Z on which the Markov model parameters are conditioned. In their application, each document in a corpus is associated with a distribution over topics and each topic is associated with a distribution over paths. The clustering effect of the topic layer allows the documents to "share" information and hence alleviate problems due to sparsity. By analogy to Abney and Light, it is a short and intuitive step to apply LDAWN to selectional preference learning. The generative story for LDAWN is given in Algorithm 3; the probability model for $P(w|p)$ is defined by (8) and the posterior estimate is (9):

Model 3 Generative story for LDAWN

for topic $z \in \{1 \ldots |Z|\}$ **do**
  for synset $s \in \{1 \ldots |S|\}$ **do**
    Draw transition probabilities $\Psi_{z,s} \sim Dirichlet(\sigma\alpha_s)$
  end for
end for
for predicate $p \in \{1 \ldots |P|\}$ **do**
  $\theta_p \sim Dirichlet(\kappa)$
  for argument instance $i \in Observations(p)$ **do**
    $z_i \sim Multinomial(\theta_p)$
    Create a path starting at the root synset λ_0:
    while not at a leaf node **do**
      $\lambda_{t+1} \sim Multinomial(\Psi_{z_i,\lambda_t})$
    end while
    Emit the word at the leaf as w_i
  end for
end for

$$P(w|p) = \sum_z P(z|p) \sum_\lambda \mathbb{1}[\lambda \rightarrow w] P(\lambda|z) \quad (8)$$

$$\propto \sum_z \frac{f_{zp} + \kappa_z}{f_{\cdot p} + \sum_{z'} \kappa_{z'}} \sum_\lambda \mathbb{1}[\lambda \rightarrow w] \times \prod_{i=1}^{|\lambda|-1} \frac{f_{z,l_i \rightarrow l_{i+1}} + \sigma\alpha_{l_i \rightarrow l_{i+1}}}{f_{z,l_i \rightarrow \cdot} + \sigma} \quad (9)$$

where $\mathbb{1}[\lambda \rightarrow w] = 1$ when the path λ leads to leaf node w and has value 0 otherwise. Following Boyd-Graber et al. the Dirichlet priors on the transition probabilities are parameterised by the product of a strength parameter σ and a distribution α_s, the latter being fixed according to relative corpus frequencies to "guide" the model towards more fruitful paths.

Gibbs sampling updates for LDAWN are given in Boyd-Graber et al. (2007). As before, we reestimate

SEEN:	
staff morale	0.4889
team morale	0.5945
issue morale	0.0595
UNSEEN:	
pupil morale	0.4318
minute morale	-0.0352
snow morale	-0.2748

Table 1: Extract from the noun-noun section of Keller and Lapata's (2003) dataset, with human plausibility scores

the hyperparameters during learning; κ is estimated by Wallach's fixed-point iteration and σ is estimated by slice sampling.

4 Experiments

4.1 Experimental procedure

We evaluate our methods by comparing their predictions to human judgements of predicate-argument plausibility. This is a standard approach to selectional preference evaluation (Keller and Lapata, 2003; Brockmann and Lapata, 2003; Ó Séaghdha, 2010) and arguably yields a better appraisal of a model's intrinsic semantic quality than other evaluations such as pseudo-disambiguation or held-out likelihood prediction.[2] We use a set of plausibility judgements collected by Keller and Lapata (2003). This dataset comprises 180 predicate-argument combinations for each of three syntactic relations: verb-object, noun-noun modification and adjective-noun modification. The data for each relation is divided into a "seen" portion containing 90 combinations that were observed in the British National Corpus and an "unseen" portion containing 90 combinations that do not appear (though the predicates and arguments do appear separately). Plausibility judgements were elicited from a large group of human subjects, then normalised and log-transformed. Table 1 gives a representative illustration of the data. Following the evaluation in Ó Séaghdha (2010), with which we wish to compare, we use Pearson r and Spearman ρ correlation coefficients as performance measures.

All models were trained on the 90-million word written component of the British National Corpus,[3] lemmatised, POS-tagged and parsed with the RASP toolkit (Briscoe et al., 2006). We removed predicates occurring with just one argument type and all tokens containing non-alphabetic characters. The resulting datasets consist of 3,587,172 verb-object observations (7,954 predicate types, 80,107 argument types), 3,732,470 noun-noun observations (68,303 predicate types, 105,425 argument types) and 3,843,346 adjective-noun observations (29,975 predicate types, 62,595 argument types).

All the Bayesian models were trained by Gibbs sampling, as outlined above. For each model we run three sampling chains for 1,000 iterations and average the plausibility predictions for each to produce a final prediction $P(w|p)$ for each predicate-argument item. As the evaluation demands an estimate of the joint probability $P(w,p)$ we multiply the predicted $P(w|p)$ by a predicate probability $P(p|r)$ estimated from relative corpus frequencies. In training we use a burn-in period of 200 iterations, after which hyperparameters are reestimated and $P(p|r)$ predictions are sampled every 50 iterations. All probability estimates are log-transformed to match the gold standard judgements.

In order to compare against previously proposed selectional preference approaches based on WordNet we also reimplemented the methods that performed best in the evaluation of Brockmann and Lapata (2003): Resnik (1993) and Clark and Weir (2002). For Resnik's model we used WordNet 2.1 rather than WordNet 3.0 as the former has multiple roots, a property that turns out to be necessary for good performance. Clark and Weir's method requires that the user specify a significance threshold α to be used in deciding where to cut; to give it the best possible chance we tested with a range of values $(0.05, 0.3, 0.6, 0.9)$ and report results for the best-performing setting, which consistently was $\alpha = 0.9$. One can also use different statistical hypothesis tests; again we choose the test giving the best results, which was Pearson's chi-squared test. As this method produces a probability estimate conditioned on the predicate p we multiply by a MLE estimate of $P(p|r)$ and log-transform the result.

[2] For a related argument in the context of topic model evaluation, see Chang et al. (2009).

[3] http://www.natcorp.ox.ac.uk/

eat	**food#n#1, aliment#n#1, entity#n#1, solid#n#1, food#n#2**
drink	**fluid#n#1, liquid#n#1, entity#n#1, alcohol#n#1, beverage#n#1**
appoint	**individual#n#1, entity#n#1, chief#n#1, being#n#2, expert#n#1**
publish	**abstract_entity#n#1, piece_of_writing#n#1, communication#n#2, publication#n#1**

Table 2: Most probable cuts learned by WN-CUT for the object argument of selected verbs

	Verb-object				Noun-noun				Adjective-noun			
	Seen		Unseen		Seen		Unseen		Seen		Unseen	
	r	ρ	r	ρ	r	ρ	r	ρ	r	ρ	r	ρ
WN-CUT	.593	.582	.514	.571	.550	.584	.564	.590	.561	.618	.453	.439
WN-CUT-100	.500	.529	**.575**	**.630**	**.619**	.639	**.662**	**.706**	.537	.510	.464	.431
WN-CUT-200	.538	.546	.557	.608	.595	.632	.639	.669	.585	.587	.435	.431
LDAWN-100	.497	.538	.558	.594	.605	.619	.635	.633	.549	.545	.459	.462
LDAWN-200	.546	.562	.508	.548	.610	**.654**	.526	.568	.578	.583	.453	.450
Resnik	.384	.473	.469	.470	.242	.187	.152	.037	.309	.388	.311	.280
Clark/Weir	.489	.546	.312	.365	.441	.521	.543	.576	.440	.476	.271	.242
BNC (MLE)	**.620**	**.614**	.196	.222	.544	.604	.114	.125	.543	**.622**	.135	.102
LDA	.504	.541	.558	.603	.615	.641	.636	.666	**.594**	.558	**.468**	**.459**

Table 3: Results (Pearson r and Spearman ρ correlations) on Keller and Lapata's (2003) plausibility data; underlining denotes the best-performing WordNet-based model, boldface denotes the overall best performance

4.2 Results

Table 2 demonstrates the top cuts learned by the WN-CUT model from the verb-object training data for a selection of verbs. Table 3 gives quantitative results for the WordNet-based models under consideration, as well as results reported by Ó Séaghdha (2010) for a purely distributional LDA model with 100 topics and a Maximum Likelihood Estimate model learned from the BNC. In general, the Bayesian WordNet-based models outperform the models of Resnik and Clark and Weir, and are competitive with the state-of-the-art LDA results. To test the statistical significance of performance differences we use the test proposed by Meng et al. (1992) for comparing correlated correlations, i.e., correlation scores with a shared gold standard. The differences between Bayesian WordNet models are not significant ($p > 0.05$, two-tailed) for any dataset or evaluation measure. However, all Bayesian models improve significantly over Resnik's and Clark and Weir's models for multiple conditions. Perhaps surprisingly, the relatively simple WN-CUT model scores the greatest number of significant improvements over both Resnik (7 out of 12 conditions) and Clark and Weir (8 out of 12), though the other Bayesian models do follow close behind. This may suggest that the incorporation of WordNet structure into the model in itself provides much of the clustering benefit provided by an additional layer of "topic" latent variables.[4]

In order to test the ability of the WordNet-based models to make predictions about arguments that are absent from the training vocabulary, we created an artificial out-of-vocabulary dataset by removing each of the Keller and Lapata argument words from the input corpus and retraining. An LDA selectional preference model will completely fail here, but we hope that the WordNet models can still make relatively accurate predictions by leveraging the additional lexical knowledge provided by the hierarchy. For example, if one knows that a tomatillo is classed as a vegetable in WordNet, one can predict a relatively high probability that it can be eaten, even though the word *tomatillo* does not appear in the BNC.

As a baseline we use a BNC-trained model that

[4] An alternative hypothesis is that samplers for the more complex models take longer to "mix". We have run some experiments with 5,000 iterations but did not observe an improvement in performance.

	Verb-object				Noun-noun				Adjective-noun			
	Seen		Unseen		Seen		Unseen		Seen		Unseen	
	r	ρ	r	ρ	r	ρ	r	ρ	r	ρ	r	ρ
WN-CUT	**.334**	.326	**.518**	**.569**	.252	.212	.254	.274	**.451**	**.397**	**.471**	**.458**
WN-CUT-100	.308	**.357**	.459	.489	.223	.207	.126	.074	.285	.264	.234	.226
WN-CUT-200	.273	.321	.452	.482	.192	.174	.115	.053	.266	.212	.220	.214
LDAWN-100	.223	.235	.410	.391	**.259**	**.220**	.132	.138	.016	.037	.264	.254
LDAWN-200	.291	.285	.392	.379	.240	.163	.118	.131	.041	.078	.209	.212
Resnik	.203	.341	.472	.497	.054	-.054	.184	.089	.353	.393	.333	.365
Clark/Weir	.222	.287	.201	.235	.225	.162	**.279**	**.304**	.313	.202	.190	.148
BNC	.206	.224	.276	.240	.256	.240	.223	.225	.088	.103	.220	.231

Table 4: Forced-OOV results (Pearson r and Spearman ρ correlations) on Keller and Lapata's (2003) plausibility data

predicts $P(w, p)$ proportional to the MLE predicate probability $P(p)$; a distributional LDA model will make essentially the same prediction. Clark and Weir's method does not have full coverage; if no sense s of an argument appears in the data then $P(s|p)$ is zero for all senses and the resulting prediction is zero, which cannot be log-transformed. To sidestep this issue, unseen senses are assigned a pseudofrequency of 0.1. Results for this "forced-OOV" task are presented in Table 4. WN-CUT proves the most adept at generalising to unseen arguments, attaining the best performance on 7 of 12 dataset/evaluation conditions and a statistically significant improvement over the baseline on 6. We observe that estimating the plausibility of unseen arguments for noun-noun modifiers is particularly difficult. One obvious explanation is that the training data for this relation has fewer tokens per predicate, making it more difficult to learn their preferences. A second, more hypothetical, explanation is that the ontological structure of WordNet is a relatively poor fit for the preferences of nominal modifiers; it is well-known that almost any pair of nouns can combine to produce a minimally plausible noun-noun compound (Downing, 1977) and it may be that this behaviour is ill-suited by the assumption that preferences are sparse distributions over regions of WordNet.

5 Conclusion

In this paper we have presented a range of Bayesian selectional preference models that incorporate knowledge about the structure of a lexical hierarchy. One motivation for this work was to test the hypothesis that such knowledge can be helpful in constructing robust models that can handle rare and unseen arguments. To this end we have reported a plausibility-based evaluation in which our models outperform previously proposed WordNet-based preference models and make sensible predictions for out-of-vocabulary items. A second motivation, which we intend to explore in future work, is to apply our models in the context of a word sense disambiguation task. Previous studies have demonstrated the effectiveness of distributional Bayesian selectional preference models for predicting lexical substitutes (Ó Séaghdha and Korhonen, 2011) but these models lack a principled way to map a word onto its most likely WordNet sense. The methods presented in this paper offer a promising solution to this issue. Another potential research direction is integration of semantic relation extraction algorithms with WordNet or other lexical resources, along the lines of Pennacchiotti and Pantel (2006) and Van Durme et al. (2009).

Acknowledgements

The work in this paper was funded by the EPSRC (UK) grant EP/G051070/1, EU grant 7FP-ITC-248064 and the Royal Society, (UK).

References

Steven Abney and Marc Light. 1999. Hiding a semantic hierarchy in a Markov model. In *Proceedings of the ACL-99 Workshop on Unsupervised Learning in NLP*, College Park, MD.

Shane Bergsma, Dekang Lin, and Randy Goebel. 2008. Discriminative learning of selectional preferences from unlabeled text. In *Proceedings of EMNLP-08*, Honolulu, HI.

David M. Blei, Thomas L. Griffiths, Michael I. Jordan, and Joshua B. Tenenbaum. 2003a. Hierarchical topic models and the nested Chinese Restaurant Process. In *Proceedings of NIPS-03*, Vancouver, BC.

David M. Blei, Andrew Y. Ng, and Michael I. Jordan. 2003b. Latent Dirichlet allocation. *Journal of Machine Learning Research*, 3:993–1022.

Jordan Boyd-Graber, David Blei, and Xiaojin Zhu. 2007. A topic model for word sense disambiguation. In *Proceedings of EMNLP-CoNLL-07*, Prague, Czech Republic.

Ted Briscoe, John Carroll, and Rebecca Watson. 2006. The second release of the RASP system. In *Proceedings of the ACL-06 Interactive Presentation Sessions*, Sydney, Australia.

Carsten Brockmann and Mirella Lapata. 2003. Evaluating and combining approaches to selectional preference acquisition. In *Proceedings of EACL-03*, Budapest, Hungary.

Jonathan Chang, Jordan Boyd-Graber, Sean Gerrish, Chong Wang, and David M. Blei. 2009. Reading tea leaves: How humans interpret topic models. In *Proceedings of NIPS-09*, Vancouver, BC.

Stephen Clark and David Weir. 2002. Class-based probability estimation using a semantic hierarchy. *Computational Linguistics*, 28(2), 187–206.

Pamela Downing. 1977. On the creation and use of English compound nouns. *Language*, 53(4):810–842.

Katrin Erk, Sebastian Padó, and Ulrike Padó. 2010. A flexible, corpus-driven model of regular and inverse selectional preferences. *Computational Linguistics*, 36(4):723–763.

Christiane Fellbaum, editor. 1998. *WordNet: An Electronic Lexical Database*. MIT Press, Cambridge, MA.

Thomas L. Griffiths and Mark Steyvers. 2004. Finding scientific topics. *Proceedings of the National Academy of Sciences*, 101(suppl. 1):5228–5235.

Frank Keller and Mirella Lapata. 2003. Using the Web to obtain frequencies for unseen bigrams. *Computational Linguistics*, 29(3):459–484.

Hang Li and Naoki Abe. 1998. Generalizing case frames using a thesaurus and the MDL principle. *Computational Linguistics*, 24(2):217–244.

Diana McCarthy and John Carroll. 2003. Disambiguating nouns, verbs and adjectives using automatically acquired selectional preferences. *Computational Linguistics*, 29(4):639–654.

Xiao-Li Meng, Robert Rosenthal, and Donald B. Rubin. 1992. Comparing correlated correlation coefficients. *Psychological Bulletin*, 111(1):172–175.

David Mimno, Wei Li, and Andrew McCallum. 2007. Mixtures of hierarchical topics with Pachinko allocation. In *Proceedings of ICML-07*, Corvallis, OR.

Radford M. Neal. 2003. Slice sampling. *Annals of Statistics*, 31(3):705–767.

Diarmuid Ó Séaghdha and Anna Korhonen. 2011. Probabilistic models of similarity in syntactic context. In *Proceedings of EMNLP-11*, Edinburgh, UK.

Diarmuid Ó Séaghdha. 2010. Latent variable models of selectional preference. In *Proceedings of ACL-10*, Uppsala, Sweden.

Marco Pennacchiotti and Patrick Pantel. 2006. Ontologizing semantic relations. In *Proceedings of COLING-ACL-06*, Sydney, Australia.

Keith Rayner, Tessa Warren, Barbara J. Juhasz, and Simon P. Liversedge. 2004. The effect of plausibility on eye movements in reading. *Journal of Experimental Psychology: Learning Memory and Cognition*, 30(6):1290–1301.

Joseph Reisinger and Raymond Mooney. 2011. Cross-cutting models of lexical semantics. In *Proceedings of EMNLP-11*, Edinburgh, UK.

Joseph Reisinger and Marius Paşca. 2009. Latent variable models of concept-attribute attachment. In *Proceedings of ACL-IJCNLP-09*, Suntec, Singapore.

Philip Resnik. 1993. *Selection and Information: A Class-Based Approach to Lexical Relationships*. Ph.D. thesis, University of Pennsylvania.

Alan Ritter, Mausam, and Oren Etzioni. 2010. A latent Dirichlet allocation method for selectional preferences. In *Proceedings ACL-10*, Uppsala, Sweden.

Sabine Schulte im Walde, Christian Hying, Christian Scheible, and Helmut Schmid. 2008. Combining EM training and the MDL principle for an automatic verb classification incorporating selectional preferences. In *Proceedings of ACL-08:HLT*, Columbus, OH.

Ekaterina Shutova. 2010. Automatic metaphor interpretation as a paraphrasing task. In *Proceedings of NAACL-HLT-10*, Los Angeles, CA.

Stefan Thater, Hagen Fürstenau, and Manfred Pinkal. 2010. Contextualizing semantic representations using syntactically enriched vector models. In *Proceedings of ACL-10*, Uppsala, Sweden.

Benjamin Van Durme, Philip Michalak, and Lenhart K. Schubert. 2009. Deriving generalized knowledge from corpora using WordNet abstraction. In *Proceedings of EACL-09*, Athens, Greece.

Hanna Wallach. 2008. *Structured Topic Models for Language*. Ph.D. thesis, University of Cambridge.

Yorick Wilks. 1978. Making preferences more active. *Artificial Intelligence*, 11:197–225.

Limin Yao, Aria Haghighi, Sebastian Riedel, and Andrew McCallum. 2011. Structured relation discovery using generative models. In *Proceedings of EMNLP-11*, Edinburgh, UK.

Beñat Zapirain, Eneko Agirre, and Lluís Màrquez. 2009. Generalizing over lexical features: Selectional preferences for semantic role classification. In *Proceedings of ACL-IJCNLP-09*, Singapore.

Guangyou Zhou, Jun Zhao, Kang Liu, and Li Cai. 2011. Exploiting web-derived selectional preference to improve statistical dependency parsing. In *Proceedings of ACL-11*, Portland, OR.

Unsupervised Induction of a Syntax-Semantics Lexicon Using Iterative Refinement

Hagen Fürstenau
CCLS
Columbia University
New York, NY, USA
hagen@ccls.columbia.edu

Owen Rambow
CCLS
Columbia University
New York, NY, USA
rambow@ccls.columbia.edu

Abstract

We present a method for learning syntax-semantics mappings for verbs from unannotated corpora. We learn *linkings*, i.e., mappings from the syntactic arguments and adjuncts of a verb to its semantic roles. By learning such linkings, we do not need to model individual semantic roles independently of one another, and we can exploit the relation between different mappings for the same verb, or between mappings for different verbs. We present an evaluation on a standard test set for semantic role labeling.

1 Introduction

A verb can have several ways of mapping its semantic arguments to syntax ("diathesis alternations"):

(1) a. We increased the response rate with SHK.
b. SHK increased the response rate.
c. The response rate increased.

The subject of *increase* can be the agent (1a), the instrument (1b), or the theme (what is being increased) (1c). Other verbs that show this pattern include *break* or *melt*.

Much theoretical and lexicographic (descriptive) work has been devoted to determining how verbs map their lexical predicate-argument structure to syntactic arguments (Burzio, 1986; Levin, 1993). The last decades have seen a surge in activity on the computational front, spurred in part by efforts to annotate large corpora for lexical semantics (Baker et al., 1998; Palmer et al., 2005). Initially, we have seen computational efforts devoted to finding classes of verbs that share similar syntax-semantics mappings from annotated and unannotated corpora (Lapata and Brew, 1999; Merlo and Stevenson, 2001). More recently, there has been an explosion of interest in semantic role labeling (with too many recent publications to cite).

In this paper, we explore learning syntax-semantics mappings for verbs from unannotated corpora. We are specifically interested in learning *linkings*. A linking is a mapping for one verb from its syntactic arguments and adjuncts to *all* of its semantic roles, so that individual semantic roles are not modeled independently of one another and so that we can exploit the relation between different mappings for the same verb (as in (1) above), or between mappings for different verbs. We therefore follow Grenager and Manning (2006) in treating linkings as first-class objects; however, we differ from their work in two important respects. First, we use semantic clustering of head words of arguments in an approach that resembles topic modeling, rather than directly modeling the subcategorization of verbs with a distribution over words. Second and most importantly, we do not make any assumptions about the linkings, as do Grenager and Manning (2006). They list a small set of rules from which they derive all linkings possible in their model; in contrast, we are able to learn any linking observed in the data. Therefore, our approach is language-independent. Grenager and Manning (2006) claim that their rules represent "a weak form of Universal Grammar", but their rules lack such common linking operations as the addition of an accusative reflexive for the unaccusative (Romance) or case marking (many languages), and they include a specific (English) preposition. We have no objection to using linguistic knowledge, but we do not feel that we have the empirical basis as of now to provide a set of Universal Grammar rules relevant for our task.

A complete syntax-semantics lexicon describes how lexemes syntactically realize their semantic arguments, and provides selectional preferences on these dependents. Though rich lexical resources exist (such as the PropBank rolesets, the FrameNet lexicon, or VerbNet, which relates and extends these sources), none of them is complete, not even for English, on which most of the efforts have focused. However, if a complete syntax-semantics lexicon did exist, it would be an extremely useful resource: the task of shallow semantic parsing (semantic argument detection and semantic role labeling) could be reduced to determining the best analysis according to this lexicon. In fact, the learning model we present in this paper is itself a semantic role labeling model, since we can simply apply it to the data we want to label semantically.

This paper is a step towards the unsupervised induction of a complete syntax-semantics lexicon. We present a unified procedure for associating verbs with linkings and for associating the discovered semantic roles with selectional preferences. As input, we assume a syntactic representation scheme and a parser which can produce syntactic representations of unseen sentences in the chosen scheme reasonably well, as well as unlabeled text. We do not assume a specific theory of lexical semantics, nor a specific set of semantic roles. We induce a set of linkings, which are mappings from semantic role symbols to syntactic functions. We also induce a lexicon, which associates a verb lemma with a distribution over the linkings, and which associates the sematic role symbols with verb-specific selectional preferences (which are distributions over distributions of words). We evaluate on the task of semantic role labeling using PropBank (Palmer et al., 2005) as a gold standard.

We focus on semantic arguments, as they are defined specifically for each verb and thus have verb-specific mappings to syntactic arguments, which may further be subject to diathesis alternations. In contrast, semantic adjuncts (modifiers) apply (in principle) to all verbs, and do not participate in diathesis alternations. For this reason, the PropBank lexicon includes arguments but not adjuncts in its framesets. The method we present in this paper is designed to find verb-specific arguments, and we therefore take the results on semantic arguments (Arg$n$) as our primary result. On these, we achieve a 20% F-measure error reduction over a high syntactic baseline (which maps each syntactic relation to a single semantic argument).

2 Related Work

As mentioned above, our approach is most similar to that of Grenager and Manning (2006). However, since their model uses hand-crafted rules, they are able to predict and evaluate against actual PropBank role labels, whereas our approach has to be evaluated in terms of clustering quality.

The problem of unsupervised semantic role labeling has recently attracted some attention (Lang and Lapata, 2011a; Lang and Lapata, 2011b; Titov and Klementiev, 2012). While the present paper shares the general aim of inducing semantic role clusters in an unsupervised way, it differs in treating syntax-semantics linkings explicitly and modeling predicate-specific distributions over them.

Abend et al. (2009) address the problem of unsupervised argument recognition, which we do not address in the present paper. For the purpose of building a complete unsupervised semantic parser, a method such as theirs would be complementary to our work.

3 Model

In this section, we decribe a model that generates arguments for a given predicate instance. Specifically, this generative model describes the probability of a given set of argument head words and associated syntactic functions in terms of underlying semantic roles, which are modelled as latent variables. The semantic role labeling task is therefore framed as the induction of these latent variables from the observed data, which we assume to be preprocessed by a syntactic parser.

The basic idea of our approach is to explicitly model *linkings* between the syntactic realizations and the underlying semantic roles of the arguments in a predicate-argument structure. Since our model of argument classification is completely unsupervised, we cannot assign familiar semantic role labels like *Agent* or *Instrument*, but rather aim at inducing *role clusters*, i.e., clusters of argument instances that share a semantic role. For example, each of the three instances of *response rate* in (1) should be assigned to the same cluster. We assume a fixed maximum number R of semantic roles per predicate and formulate argument classification as the task of assigning each argument in a predicate-argument structure to one of the numbered roles $1, \ldots, R$. Such an assignment can therefore be represented by an R-tuple, where each role position is either filled by one of the arguments or empty (denoted as ϵ). We represent each argument by its *head word* and its *syntactic function*, i.e., the path of syntactic dependency relations leading to it from the predicate. In our example (1a), a possible assignment of arguments to semantic roles could therefore be represented by a head word tuple $(\text{we}, \text{rate}, \epsilon, \text{SHK})$ and a corresponding tuple of syntactic functions $(\text{nsubj}, \text{dobj}, \epsilon, \text{prep\_with})$, where for the sake of the example we have chosen $R = 4$ and the third semantic role slot is empty. Note that this ordered R-tuple thus represents a semantic labeling of the unordered set of arguments, which our model takes as input. While in the case of a single predicate-argument structure the assignment of arguments to arbitrary semantic role numbers does not provide additional information, its value lies in the consistent assignment of arguments to specific roles *across instances of the same predicate*. For example, to be consistent with the assignment above, (1b) would have to be represented by $(\epsilon, \text{rate}, \epsilon, \text{SHK})$ and $(\epsilon, \text{dobj}, \epsilon, \text{nsubj})$.

To formulate a generative model of argument tuples, we separately consider the tuple of argument head words and the tuple of syntactic functions. The following two subsections will address each of these in turn.

3.1 Selectional Preferences

The probability of an argument in a certain semantic role depends strongly on the *selectional preferences* of the predicate with respect to this role. In the context of our model, we therefore need to describe the probability $P(w_r|p, r)$ of an argument head word w_r depending on the predicate p and the role r. Instead of directly modeling predicate- and role-specific distributions over head words, however, we model selectional preferences as distributions $\chi_{p,r}(c)$ over *semantic word classes* $c = 1, \ldots, C$ (with C being a fixed model parameter), each of which is in turn associated with a distribution $\psi_c(w_r)$ over the vocabulary. They are thus similar to topics in semantic topic models. An advantage of this approach is that semantic word classes can be shared among different predicates, which facilitates their inference. Technically, the introduction of semantic word classes can be seen as a factorization of the probability of the argument head $P(w_r|p, r) = \sum_{c=1}^{C} \chi_{p,r}(c)\psi_c(w_r)$.

3.2 Linkings

Another important factor for the assignment of arguments to semantic roles are their syntactic functions. While in the preceding subsection we considered selectional preferences for each semantic role separately (assuming their independence), the interdependence between syntactic functions is crucial and cannot be ignored: The assignment of an argument does not depend solely on its own syntactic function, but on the whole *subcategorization frame* of the predicate-argument structure. We therefore have to model the probability of the whole tuple $y = (y_1, \ldots, y_R)$ of syntactic functions.

We assume that for each predicate there is a relatively small number of ways in which it realizes its arguments syntactically, i.e., in which semantic roles are linked to syntactic functions. These may correspond to alternations like those shown in (1). Instead of directly modeling the predicate-specific probability $P(y|p)$, we consider predicate-specific distributions $\phi_p(l)$ over linkings $l = (x_1, \ldots, x_R)$. Such a linking then gives rise to the tuple $y = (y_1, \ldots, y_R)$ by way of probability distributions $P(y_r|x_r) = \eta_{x_r}(y_r)$. This allows us to keep the number of possible linkings l per predicate relatively small (by setting $\phi_p(l) = 0$ for most l), and generate a wide variety of syntactic function tuples y from them.

3.3 Structure of the Model

Figure 1 presents our linking model. For each predicate-argument structure in the corpus, it contains observable variables for the predicate p and the unordered set s of arguments, and further shows latent variables for the linking l and (for each role r) the semantic word class c, the head word w, and the syntactic function y.

The distributions $\chi_{p,r}(c)$ and $\psi_c(w)$ are drawn from Dirichlet priors with symmetric parameters α and β, respectively. In the case of the linking dis-

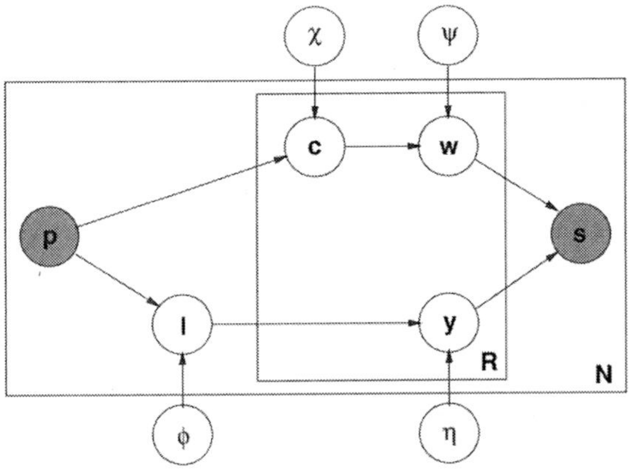

Figure 1: Representation of our linking model as a Bayesian network. The nodes p and s are observed for each of the N predicate-argument structures in the corpus. The latent variables c, w, l, and y are inferred from the data along with their distributions χ, ψ, ϕ, and η.

tribution $\phi_p(l)$, we are faced with an exponentially large space of possible linkings (considering a set G of syntactic functions, there are $(|G|+1)^R$ possible linkings). This is both computationally problematic and counter-intuitive. We therefore maintain a global list L of permissible linkings and enforce $\phi_p(l) = 0$ for all $l \notin L$. On the set L we then draw $\phi_p(l)$ from a Dirichlet prior with symmetric parameter γ. In Section 3.5, we will describe how the linking list L is iteratively induced from the data.

We introduced the distribution η_x to allow for incidental changes when generating the tuple of syntactic functions out of the linking. If this process were allowed to arbitrarily change any syntactic function in the linking, the linkings would be too unconstrained and not reflect the syntactic functions in the corpus. We therefore parameterize η_x in such a way that the only allowed modifications are the addition or removal of syntactic functions from the linking, but no change from one syntactic function to another. We attain this by parameterizing η_x as follows:

$$\eta_x(y) = \begin{cases} \eta^\epsilon & \text{if } x = y = \epsilon \\ \frac{1-\eta^\epsilon}{|G|} & \text{if } x = \epsilon \text{ and } y \in G \\ 1 - \eta^x & \text{if } x \in G \text{ and } y = \epsilon \\ \eta^x & \text{if } x = y \in G \\ 0 & \text{else} \end{cases}$$

Here, G again denotes the set of all syntactic functions. The parameter η^ϵ is drawn from a uniform prior on the interval $[0.0, 1.0]$ and the $|G|$ parameters η^x for $x \in G$ have uniform priors on $[0.5, 1.0]$. This has the effect that no syntactic function can change into another, that a syntactic function is never more probable to disappear than to stay, and that all syntactic functions are added with the same probability. This last property will be important for the iterative refinement process described in Section 3.5.

3.4 Training

In this subsection, we describe how we train the model described so far, assuming that we are given a fixed linking list L. The following subsection will address the problem of infering this list. In Section 3.6, we will then describe how we apply the trained model to infer semantic role assignments for given predicate-argument structures.

To train the linking model, we apply a Gibbs sampling procedure to the latent variables shown in Figure 1. In each sampling iteration, we first sample the values of the latent variables of each predicate-argument structure based on the current distributions, and then the latent distributions based on counts obtained over the corpus. For each predicate-argument structure, we begin with a blocked sampling step, simultaneously drawing values for w and y, while summing out c. This gives us

$$P(w, y|p, l, s) \propto \prod_{r=1}^{R} \eta_{x_r}(y_r) \sum_{c=1}^{C} \chi_{p,r}(c)\psi_c(w_r)$$

where we have omitted the factor $P(s|w, y)$, which is uniform as long as we assume that w and y indeed represent permutations of the argument set s. To sample efficiently from this distribution, we precompute the inner sum (as a tensor contraction or, equivalently, R matrix multiplications). We then enumerate all permutations of the argument set and compute their probabilities, defaulting to an approximative beam search procedure in cases where the space of permutations is too large.

Next, the linking l is sampled according to

$$P(l|p, y) \propto P(l|p)P(y|l) = \phi_p(l) \prod_{r=1}^{R} \eta_{x_r}(y_r)$$

Since the space L of possible linkings is small, completely enumerating the values of this distribution is not a problem.

After sampling the latent variables w, y, and l for each corpus instance, we go on to apply Gibbs sampling to the latent distributions. For example, for ϕ_p we obtain

$$P(\phi_p|p^1, l^1, \ldots, p^N, l^N) \propto P(\phi_p) \prod_{i=1}^{N} P(l^i|p^i)$$

$$\propto \mathrm{Dir}(\gamma)(\phi_p) \cdot \prod_{l \in L} [\phi_p(l)]^{n_p(l)} = \mathrm{Dir}(\vec{n}_p + \gamma)(\phi_p)$$

Here $n_p(l)$ is the number of corpus instances with predicate p and latent linking l, and $\vec{n}_p$ is the vector of these counts for a fixed p, indexed by l. Hence, ϕ_p is drawn from the Dirichlet distribution parameterized by this vector, smoothed in each component by γ.

In the same way, the sampling distributions for $\chi_{p,r}$ and ψ_c are determined as $\mathrm{Dir}(\vec{n}_{p,r} + \alpha)$ and $\mathrm{Dir}(\vec{n}_c + \beta)$, where each $\vec{n}_{p,r}$ is a vector of counts[1] indexed by word classes c and each $\vec{n}_c$ is a vector of counts indexed by head words w_r. Similarly, we draw the parameter η^ϵ in the parameterization of η_x from $\mathrm{Beta}\left(n(\epsilon, \epsilon) + 1, \sum_{x \in G} n(\epsilon, x) + 1\right)$ and approximate η^x by drawing η^x from $\mathrm{Beta}\left(n(x, x) + 1, n(x, \epsilon) + 1\right)$ and redrawing it uniformly from $[0.5, 1.0]$, if it is smaller than 0.5. In this context, $n(x, y)$ refers to the number of times the syntactic relation x is turned into y, counted over all corpus instances and semantic roles.

To test for convergence of the sampling process, we monitor the log-likelihood of the data. For each predicate-argument structure with predicate p^i and argument set s^i, we have

$$P(p^i, s^i) \propto \sum_l P(l|p^i) P(s^i|l) \approx P(s^i|l^i)$$

$$= \sum_{w,y} P(w, y, s^i|l^i) = \sum_{w,y \Rightarrow s^i} P(w, y|l^i) =: L_i$$

The approximation is rather crude (replacing an expected value by a single sample from $P(l|p^i)$), but we expect the errors to mostly cancel out over the instances of the corpus. The last sum ranges over all pairs (w, y) that represent permutations of the argument set s, and this can be computed as a by-product of the sampling process of w and y. We then compute $L := \log \prod_{i=1}^{N} L_i = \sum_{i=1}^{N} \log L_i$, and terminate the sampling process if L does not increase by more than 0.1% over 5 iterations.

3.5 Iterative Refinement of Possible Linkings

In Section 3.3, we have addressed the problem of the exponentially large space of possible linkings by introducing a subset $L \subset G^R$ from which linkings may be drawn. We now need to clarify how this subset is determined. In contrast to Grenager and Manning (2006), we do not want to use any linguistic intuitions or manual rules to specify this subset, but rather automatically infer it from the data, so that the model stays agnostic to the language and paradigm of semantic roles. We therefore adopt a strategy of *iterative refinement*.

We start with a very small set that only contains the trivial linking $(\epsilon, \ldots, \epsilon)$ and one linking for each of the R most frequent syntactic functions, placing the most frequent one in the first slot, the second one in the second slot etc. We then run Gibbs sampling. When it has converged in terms of log-likelihood, we add some new linkings to L. These new linkings are inferred by inspecting the action of the step from l to y in the generative model. Here, a syntactic function may be added to or deleted from a linking. If a particular syntactic function is frequently added to some linking, then a corresponding linking, i.e., one featuring this syntactic function and thus not requiring such a modification, seems to be missing from the set L. We therefore count for each linking l how often it is either reduced by the deletion of any syntactic function or expanded by the addition of a syntactic function. We then rank these modifications in descending order and for each of them determine the semantic role slot in which the modification (deletion or addition) occured most frequently. By applying the modification to this slot, each of the linkings gives rise to a new one. We add the first a of those, skipping new linkings if they are duplicates of those we already have in the linking set. We iterate this procedure, alternating between Gibbs sampling to convergence and the addition of a new linkings.

3.6 Inference

To predict semantic roles for a given predicate and argument set, we maximize $P(l, w, y|p, s)$. If the

[1] Since we do not sample c, we use pseudo-counts based on $P(c_r|p, r, w_r)$ for each instance.

space of permutations is too large for exhaustive enumeration, we apply a similar beam search procedure as the one employed in training to approximately maximize $P(w, y|p, s, l)$ for each value of l. For efficiency, we do not marginalize over l. This has the potential of reducing prediction quality, as we do not predict the most likely role assignment, but rather the most likely combination of role assignment and latent linking.

In all experiments we averaged over 10 consecutive samples of the latent distributions, at the end of the sampling process (i.e., when convergence has been reached).

4 Experimental Setup

We train and evaluate our linking model on the data set produced for the CoNLL-08 Shared Task on Joint Parsing of Syntactic and Semantic Dependencies (Surdeanu et al., 2008), which is based on the PropBank corpus (Palmer et al., 2005). This data set includes part-of-speech tags, lemmatized tokens, and syntactic dependencies, which have been converted from the manual syntactic annotation of the underlying Penn Treebank (Marcus et al., 1993).

4.1 Data Set

As input to our model, we decided not to use the syntactic representation in the CoNLL-08 data set, but instead to rely on Stanford Dependencies (de Marneffe et al., 2006), which seem to facilitate semantic analysis. We thus used the Stanford Parser[2] to convert the underlying phrase structure trees of the Penn Tree Bank into Stanford Dependencies. In the resulting dependency analyses, the syntactic head word of a semantic role may differ from the syntactic head according to the provided syntax. We therefore mapped the semantic role annotation onto the Stanford Dependency trees by identifying the tree node that covers the same set of tokens as the one marked in the CoNLL-08 data set.

The focus of the present work is on the linking behavior and classification of semantic arguments and not their identification. The latter is a substantially different task, and likely to be best addressed by other approaches, such as that of (Abend et al., 2009). We therefore use gold standard information of the CoNLL-08 data set for identifying argument sets as input to our model. The task of our model is then to *classify* these arguments into semantic roles.

We train our model on a corpus consisting of the training and the test part of the CoNLL-08 data set, which is permissible since as a unsupervised system our model does not make any use of the annotated argument labels for training. We test the model performance against the gold argument classification on the test part. For development purposes (both designing the model and tuning the parameters as described in Section 4.4), we train on the training and development part and test on the development part.

4.2 Evaluation Measures

As explained above, our model does not predict specific role labels, such as those annotated in PropBank, but rather aims at clustering like argument instances together. Since the (numbered) labels of these clusters are arbitrary, we cannot evaluate the predictions of our model against the PropBank gold annotation directly. We follow Lang and Lapata (2011b) in measuring the quality of our clustering in terms of cluster purity and collocation instead.

Cluster purity is a measure of the degree to which the predicted clusters meet the goal of containing only instances with the same gold standard class label. Given predicted clusters $C_1, \ldots, C_{n_C}$ and gold clusters $G_1, \ldots, G_{n_G}$ over a set of n argument instances, it is defined as

$$\text{Pu} = \frac{1}{n} \sum_{i=1}^{n_C} \max_{j=1,\ldots,n_G} |C_i \cap G_j|$$

Similarly, cluster collocation measures how well the clustering meets the goal of clustering all gold instances with the same label into a single predicted cluster, formally:

$$\text{Co} = \frac{1}{n} \sum_{j=1}^{n_G} \max_{i=1,\ldots,n_C} |C_i \cap G_j|$$

We determine purity and collocation separately for each predicate type and then compute their micro-average, i.e., weighting each score by the number of argument instances of this precidate. Just as precision and recall, purity and collocation stand in trade-off. In the next section, we therefore report their F_1 score, i.e., their harmonic mean $\frac{2 \cdot Pu \cdot Co}{Pu + Co}$.

[2]version 1.6.8, available at http://nlp.stanford.edu/software/lex-parser.shtml

4.3 Syntactic Baseline

We compare the performance of our model with a simple syntactic baseline that assumes that semantic roles are identical with syntactic functions. We follow Lang and Lapata (2011b) in clustering argument instances of each predicate by their syntactic functions. We do not restrict the number of clusters per predicate. In contrast, Lang and Lapata (2011b) restrict the number of clusters to 21, which is the number of clusters their system generates. We found that this reduces the baseline by 0.1% F_1-score (Arg$n$ on the development set, c.f. Table 1). If we reduce the number of clusters in the baseline to the number of clusters in our system (7), the baseline is reduced by another 0.8% F_1-score. These lower baselines are due to lower purity values. In general, we find that a smaller number of clusters results in lower F_1 measure for the baseline; the reported baseline therefore is the strictest possible.

4.4 Parameters and Tuning

For all experiments, we fixed the number of semantic roles at $R = 7$. This is the maximum size of the argument set over all instances of the data set and thus the lower limit for R. If R was set to a higher value, the model would be able to account for the possibility of a larger number of roles, out of which never more than 7 are expressed simultaneously. We leave such investigation to future work. We set the symmetric parameters for the Dirichlet distributions to $\alpha = 1.0$, $\beta = 0.1$, and $\gamma = 1.0$. This corresponds to uninformative uniform priors for $\chi_{p,r}$ and ϕ_p, and a prior encouraging a sparse lexical distribution ψ_c, similar as in topic models such as LDA (Blei et al., 2003).

The number C of word classes, the number a of additional linkings in each refinement of the linking set L, and the number k of refinement steps were tuned on the development set. We first fixed $a = 10$ and trained models for $C = 10, 20, \ldots, 100$, performing 50 refinement steps. The best F_1 score was obtained with $C = 10$ after $k = 20$ refinements (i.e., with 200 linkings). Next, we fixed these two parameters and trained models for $a = 5, 10, 15, 20, 25$. Here, we confirmed an optimal value of $a = 10$.

5 Results

In this section, we give quantitative results, comparing our system to the syntactic baseline in terms of cluster purity and collocation, and a qualitative discussion of some phenomena observed in the performance of the model.

5.1 Quantitative Results

Table 1 shows the results of applying our models to the CoNLL-08 test with the parameter values tuned in Section 4.4. For comparison, we also show results on the development set. The table is divided into three parts, one only considering semantic arguments (Arg$n$), one considering adjuncts (ArgM), and one aggregating results over both kinds of PropBank roles (Arg*). It can be seen that our model consistently outperforms the syntactic baseline in terms of collocation (by 10% on Arg$n$, 3% on ArgM, and 8.2% overall). In terms of purity, however, it falls short of the baseline. As mentioned above, there is a trade-off between purity and collocation. Compared to our model, which we run with a total of 7 semantic role slots, the baseline predicts a large number of small argument clusters for each predicate, whereas our model tends to group arguments together based on selectional preferences.

In terms of F_1 score, our model outperforms the baseline by 3.6% on Arg$n$, which translates into a relative error reduction by 20%. On adjuncts, on the other hand, our model falls short of the baseline by almost 10% F_1 score. This indicates that our approach based on explicit representations of linkings is most suited to the classification of arguments rather than adjuncts, which do not participate in diathesis alternations and do therefore not profit as much from our explicit induction of linkings.

5.2 Qualitative Observations

Among the verbs with at least 10 test instances, *include* shows the largest gain in F_1 score over the baseline. In the test corpus, we find an interesting pair of sentences for this predicate:

(2) a. *Mr. Herscu proceeded to launch an ambitious, but ill-fated, $1 billion acquisition binge that included Bonwit Teller and B. Altman & Co. [...]*

	Arg$n$			ArgM			Arg*		
Test Set	Pu	Co	F_1	Pu	Co	F_1	Pu	Co	F_1
Syntactic Baseline	**90.6**	75.4	82.3	**87.0**	73.3	**79.6**	**88.0**	74.9	**80.9**
Linking Model	86.4	**85.4**	**85.9**	64.4	**76.3**	69.8	74.5	**83.1**	78.6
Development Set	Pu	Co	F_1	Pu	Co	F_1	Pu	Co	F_1
Syntactic Baseline	**91.5**	73.9	81.8	**88.7**	78.6	**83.3**	**89.2**	75.1	**81.5**
Linking Model	85.6	**84.4**	**85.0**	67.7	**79.9**	73.3	75.2	**83.2**	79.0

Table 1: Purity (Pu), collocation (Co), and F_1 scores of our model and the syntactic baseline in percent. Performance on arguments (Arg$n$), adjuncts (ArgM), and overall results (Arg*) are shown separately.

b. *Not included in the bid are Bonwit Teller or B. Altman & Co. [...]*

The first of these two sentences is generated from the linking (nsubj, dobj, ϵ, ϵ, ϵ, ϵ, -rcmod), which does not need to be modified in any way to account for the subject *that* (coreferent with the head of the predicate in the modifying relative clause, *binge*) and the direct object *Teller* (head of the phrase *Bonwit Teller and B. Altman & Co.*). These are assigned to the first and second role slots, respectively. The second sentence, on the other hand, is generated out of the linking (prep_in, nsubjpass, ϵ, ϵ, ϵ, ϵ, ϵ). Here, the passive subject *Teller* is assigned to the second role slot (which we may interpret as the *Includee*), while the first semantic role (the *Includer*) is labeled on *bid*, which is realized in a prepositional phrase headed by the preposition *in*. Note that this alternation is not the general passive alternation though, which would have led to *Teller is not included* **by** *the bid*. Instead, the model learned a specific alternation pattern for the predicate *include*.

But even where a specific linking has not been learned, the model can often still infer a correct labeling by virtue of its selectional preference component. In our corpus, the predicate *give* occurs mostly with a direct and an indirect object as in *CNN recently gave most employees raises of as much as 15%*. The model therefore learns a linking (nsubj, dobj, ϵ, ϵ, ϵ, ϵ, iobj), but fails to learn that the *Beneficient* role can also be expressed with the preposition *to* as in

(3) *[...] only 25% give $2,500 or more to charity each year.*

However, when applying our model to this sentence, it nonetheless assigns *charity* to the last role slot (the same one previously occupied by the indirect object). This is due to the fact that *charity* is a good fit for the selectional preference of this role slot of the predicate *give*.

6 Conclusions

We have presented a novel generative model of predicate-argument structures that incorporates selectional preferences of argument heads and explicitly describes linkings between semantic roles and syntactic functions. The model iteratively induces a lexicon of possible linkings from unlabeled data. The trained model can be used to cluster given argument instances according to their semantic roles, outperforming a competitive syntactic baseline.

The approach is independent of any particular language or paradigm of semantic roles. However, in its present form the model assumes that each predicate has its own set of semantic roles. In formalisms such as Frame Semantics (Baker et al., 1998), semantic roles generalize across semantically similar predicates belonging to the same *frame*. A natural extension of our approach would therefore consist in modeling predicate groups that share semantic roles and selectional preferences.

Acknowledgments. This work was supported by the Intelligence Advanced Research Projects Activity (IARPA) via Department of Interior National Business Center (DoI/NBC) contract number D11PC20153. The U.S. Government is authorized to reproduce and distribute reprints for Governmental purposes notwithstanding any copyright annotation thereon. Disclaimer: The views and conclusions contained herein are those of the authors and should not be interpreted as necessarily representing the official policies or endorsements, either expressed or implied, of IARPA, DoI/NBC, or the U.S. Government.

References

Omri Abend, Roi Reichart, and Ari Rappoport. 2009. Unsupervised argument identification for semantic role labeling. In *Proceedings of the Joint Conference of the 47th Annual Meeting of the ACL and the 4th International Joint Conference on Natural Language Processing of the AFNLP*, pages 28–36, Singapore.

Collin F. Baker, J. Fillmore, and John B. Lowe. 1998. The Berkeley FrameNet project. In *36th Meeting of the Association for Computational Linguistics and 17th International Conference on Computational Linguistics (COLING-ACL'98)*, pages 86–90, Montréal.

David M. Blei, Andrew Y. Ng, and Michael I. Jordan. 2003. Latent dirichlet allocation. *Journal of Machine Learning Research*, 3:993–1022.

Luigi Burzio. 1986. *Italian Syntax: A Government-Binding Approach*. Reidel, Dordrecht.

Marie-Catherine de Marneffe, Bill MacCartney, and Christopher D. Manning. 2006. Generating typed dependency parses from phrase structure parses. In *Proceedings of LREC 2006*.

Trond Grenager and Christopher D. Manning. 2006. Unsupervised discovery of a statistical verb lexicon. In *Proceedings of the 2006 Conference on Empirical Methods in Natural Language Processing*, pages 1–8, Sydney, Australia.

Joel Lang and Mirella Lapata. 2011a. Unsupervised semantic role induction via split-merge clustering. In *Proceedings of the 49th Annual Meeting of the Association for Computational Linguistics: Human Language Technologies*, pages 1117–1126, Portland, Oregon, USA.

Joel Lang and Mirella Lapata. 2011b. Unsupervised semantic role induction with graph partitioning. In *Proceedings of the 2011 Conference on Empirical Methods in Natural Language Processing*, pages 1320–1331, Edinburgh, Scotland, UK.

Maria Lapata and Chris Brew. 1999. Using subcategorization to resolve verb class ambiguity. In *In Proceedings of Joint SIGDAT Conference on Empirical Methods in Natural Language Processing and Very Large Corpora*, pages 266—-274, College Park, MD.

Beth Levin. 1993. *English Verb Classes and Alternations: A Preliminary Investigation*. The University of Chicago Press.

Mitchell M. Marcus, Beatrice Santorini, and Mary Ann Marcinkiewicz. 1993. Building a Large Annotated Corpus of English: The Penn Treebank. *Computational Linguistics*, 19.2:313–330, June.

Paola Merlo and Suzanne Stevenson. 2001. Automatic verb classification based on statistical distributions of argument structure. *Computational Linguistics*, 27(3).

Martha Palmer, Daniel Gildea, and Paul Kingsbury. 2005. The Proposition Bank: An annotated corpus of semantic roles. *Computational Linguistics*, 31(1):71–106.

Mihai Surdeanu, Richard Johansson, Adam Meyers, Lluís Màrquez, and Joakim Nivre. 2008. The conll 2008 shared task on joint parsing of syntactic and semantic dependencies. In *CoNLL 2008: Proceedings of the Twelfth Conference on Computational Natural Language Learning*, pages 159–177, Manchester, England.

Ivan Titov and Alexandre Klementiev. 2012. A bayesian approach to unsupervised semantic role induction. In *Proceedings of the Conference of the European Chapter of the Association for Computational Linguistics*, Avignon, France, April.

An Evaluation of Graded Sense Disambiguation using Word Sense Induction

David Jurgens[1,2]
[1]HRL Laboratories, LLC
Malibu, California, USA
[2]Department of Computer Science
University of California, Los Angeles
jurgens@cs.ucla.edu

Abstract

Word Sense Disambiguation aims to label the sense of a word that best applies in a given context. Graded word sense disambiguation relaxes the single label assumption, allowing for multiple sense labels with varying degrees of applicability. Training multi-label classifiers for such a task requires substantial amounts of annotated data, which is currently not available. We consider an alternate method of annotating graded senses using Word Sense Induction, which automatically learns the senses and their features from corpus properties. Our work proposes three objective to evaluate performance on the graded sense annotation task, and two new methods for mapping between sense inventories using parallel graded sense annotations. We demonstrate that sense induction offers significant promise for accurate graded sense annotation.

1 Introduction

Word Sense Disambiguation (WSD) aims to identify the sense of a word in a given context, using a predefined sense inventory containing the word's different meanings (Navigli, 2009). Traditionally, WSD approaches have assumed that each occurrence of a word is best labeled with a single sense. However, human annotators often disagree about which sense is present (Passonneau et al., 2010), especially in cases where some of the possible senses are closely related (Chugur et al., 2002; McCarthy, 2006; Palmer et al., 2007).

Recently, Erk et al. (2009) have shown that in cases of sense ambiguity, a *graded* notion of sense labeling may be most appropriate and help reduce the ambiguity. Specifically, within a given context, multiple senses of a word may be salient to the reader, with different levels of applicability. For example, in the sentence

- The athlete **won** the gold metal due to her hard work and dedication.

multiple senses could be considered applicable for "won" according to the WordNet 3.0 sense inventory (Fellbaum, 1998):

1. win (be the winner in a contest or competition; be victorious)
2. acquire, win, gain (win something through one's efforts)
3. gain, advance, win, pull ahead, make headway, get ahead, gain ground (obtain advantages, such as points, etc.)
4. succeed, win, come through, bring home the bacon, deliver the goods (attain success or reach a desired goal)

In this context, many annotators would agree that the athlete has both won an object (the gold metal itself) and won a competition (signified by the gold medal). Although contexts can be constructed to elicit only one of these senses, in the example above, a graded annotation best matches human perception.

Graded word sense (GWS) annotation offers significant advantages for sense annotation with a fine-grained sense inventory. However, creating a sufficiently large annotated corpus for training supervised GWS disambiguation models presents a significant challenge, i.e., the laborious task of gathering annotations for all combinations of a word's senses, along with variation in those senses applicabilities. To our knowledge, Erk et al. (2009) have provided the only data set with GWS annotations for 11 terms.

Therefore, we consider the use of Word Sense Induction (WSI) for GWS annotation. WSI removes the need for substantial training data by automatically deriving a word's senses and associated sense features through examining its contextual uses. Furthermore, the data-driven sense discovery defines senses as they are present in the corpus, which may identify usages not present in traditional sense inventories (Lau et al., 2012). Last, many WSI models represent senses loosely as abstractions over usages, which potentially may transfer well to expressing GWS annotations as a blend of their sense usages.

In this paper, we consider the performance of WSI models on a GWS task. The contributions of this paper are as follows. First, in Sec. 2, we motivate three GWS annotation objectives and propose corresponding measures that provide fine-grained analysis of the capabilities of different WSI models. Second, in Sec. 4, we propose two new sense mapping procedures for converting an induced sense inventory to a reference sense inventory when GWS annotations are present, and demonstrate significant performance improvement using these procedures on GWS annotation. Last, in Sec. 5, we demonstrate a complete evaluation framework using three graph-based WSI models as examples, generating several insights for how to better evaluate GWS disambiguation systems.

2 Evaluating GWS Annotations

Graded word sense annotation conveys multiple levels of information, both in which senses are present and their relative levels of applicability; and so, no single evaluation measure alone is appropriate for assessing GWS annotation capability. Therefore, we propose three objectives for the evaluating the sense labeling: (1) Detection of which senses are present, (2) Ranking senses according to applicability, and (3) Perception of the graded presence of each sense. We separate the three objectives as a way to evaluate how well different techniques perform on each aspect individually, which may encourage future work in ensemble WSD methods that use combinations of the techniques. Figure 1 illustrates each evaluation on example annotations. We note that Erk and McCarthy (2009) have also proposed an alternate set of evaluation measures for GWS annotations. Where applicable, we describe and compare their measures to ours for the three objectives.

In the following definitions, let S^i_G refer to the set of senses $\{s_1, \ldots, s_n\}$ present in context i according to the gold standard, and similarly, let S^i_L refer to the set of senses for context i as labeled by a WSD system using the same sense inventory. Let $per_i(s_j)$ refer to the perceived numeric applicability rating of sense s_j in context i.

Detection measures the ability to accurately identify which senses are applicable in a given context, independent of their applicability. While the most basic of the evaluations, systems that are highly accurate at multi-sense detection could be used for recognizing ambiguous contexts where multiple senses are applicable or for evaluating the granularity of sense ontologies by testing for correlations between senses in a multi-sense labeling. Detection is measured using the Jaccard Index between S^i_G and S^i_L for a given context i: $\frac{S^i_G \cap S^i_L}{S^i_G \cup S^i_L}$

Ranking measures the ability to order the senses present in context i according to their applicability but independent of their quantitative applicability scores. Even though multiple senses are present, a context may have a clear primary senses. By providing a ranking in agreement with human judgements, systems create a primary sense label for each context. When the induced senses are mapped to a sense inventory, selecting the primary sense is analogous to non-graded WSD where a context is labeled with its most applicable sense.

To compare sense rankings, we use Goodman and Kruskal's γ, which is related to Kendall's τ rank correlation. When the data has many tied ranks, γ is preferable to both Kendall's τ as well as Spearman's ρ rank correlation (Siegel and Castellan Jr., 1988), the latter of which is used by Erk and McCarthy (2009) for evaluating sense rankings. The use of γ was motivated by our observation that in the GWS dataset (described later in Section 5.1), roughly 65% of the instances contained at least one tied ranking between senses.

To compute γ, we examine all pair-wise combinations of senses (s_i, s_j) of the target word. Let $r_G(s_i)$ and $r_L(s_i)$ denote the ranks of sense s_i in the gold standard and provided annotations. In the event that a ranking does not include senses, all of the inapplicable senses are assigned a tied rank

Instance	Gold Standard Annotation
The athlete **won** the gold metal due to her hard work and dedication.	win.v.1: 0.6, win.v.2: 0.4 (not applicable: win.v.3, win.v.4)

Test Annotation	Detection	Ranking	Perception
win.v.1: 0.7, win.v.2: 0.3	1.0	1.0	0.983
win.v.1: 1.0	0.5	1.0	0.832
win.v.2: 1.0	0.5	0.333	0.554
win.v.3: 0.5, win.v.1: 0.3, win.v.4: 0.2	0.25	-0.2	0.405

Figure 1: Example annotations of the same context compared with the gold standard according to Detection, Ranking, and Perception.

lower than the least applicable sense; i.e., for m applicable senses, all inapplicable senses have rank $m+1$. A pair of senses, (s_i, s_j) is said to be concordant if $r_G(s_i) < r_G(s_j)$ and $r_L(s_i) < r_L(s_j)$ or $r_G(s_i) > r_G(s_j)$ and $r_L(s_i) > r_L(s_j)$, and discordant otherwise. γ is defined as $\frac{c-d}{c+d}$ where c is the number of concordant pairs and d is the number of discordant.

Perception measures the ability to equal human judgements on the levels of applicability for each sense in a context. Unlike ranking, this evaluation quantifies the difference in sense applicability. As a potential application, these differences can be used to quantify the contextual ambiguity. For example, the relative applicability differences can be used to distinguish between ambiguous contexts where multiple highly-applicable senses exist and unambiguous contexts where a single main sense exists but other senses are still minimally applicable.

To quantify Perception, we compare sense labelings using the cosine similarity. Each labeling is represented as a vector with a separate component for each sense, whose value is the applicability of that sense. The Perception for two annotations of context j is then calculated as

$$\frac{\sum_i per_j(s_i^G) \times per_j(s_i^L)}{\sqrt{\sum_i per_j(s_i^G)^2} \times \sqrt{\sum_i per_j(s_i^L)^2}}.$$

Note that because all sense perceptibilities are non-negative, the cosine similarity is bounded to $[0, 1]$.

Erk and McCarthy (2009) propose an alternate measure for comparing the applicability values using the Jensen-Shannon divergence. The sense annotations are normalized to probability distributions, denoted G and L, and the divergence is computed as:

$$JSD(G||L) = \frac{1}{2}D_{KL}(G||M) + \frac{1}{2}D_{KL}(L||M)$$

where M is the average of the distributions G and L and D_{KL} denotes the Kullback-Leibler divergence. While both approaches are similar in intent, we find that the cosine similarity better matches the expected difference in Perception for cases where two annotations use different numbers of senses. For example, the fourth test annotation in Fig. 1 has a JSS[1] of 0.593, despite its significant differences in ordering and the omission of a sense. Indeed, in cases where the set of senses in a test annotation is completely disjoint from the set of gold standard senses, the JSS will be positive due to comparing the two distributions against their average; In contrast, the cosine similarity in such cases will be zero, which we argue better matches the expectation that such an annotation does not meet the Perception objective.

3 WSI Models

For evaluation we adapt three recent graph-based WSI methods for the task of graded-sense annotation: Navigli and Crisafulli (2010), referred to as *Squares*, Jurgens (2011), referred to as *Link*, and UoY (Korkontzelos and Manandhar, 2010). At an abstract level, these methods operate in two stages. First, a graph is built, using either words or word pairs as vertices, and edges are added denoting some form of association between the vertices. Second, senses are derived by clustering or partitioning the graph. We selected these methods based on their superior performance on recent benchmarks and also

[1]The JSD is a distance measure in $[0, 1]$, which we convert to a similarity $JSS = 1 - JSD$ for easier comparison.

for their significant differences in approach. Following, we briefly summarize each method to highlight its key parameters and then describe its adaptation to GWS annotation.

Squares Navigli and Crisafulli (2010) propose a method that builds a separate graph for each term for sense induction. First, a large corpus is used to identify associated terms using the Dice coefficient: For two terms w_1, w_2, $Dice(w_1, w_2) = \frac{2c(w_1,w_2)}{c(w_1)+c(w_2)}$ where $c(w)$ is the frequency of occurrence. Next, for a given term w the initial graph, G, is constructed by adding edges to every term w_2 where $Dice(w, w_2) \geq \delta$, and then the step is repeated for the neighbors of each term w_2 that was added.

Once the initial graph is constructed, edges are pruned to separate the graph into components. Navigli and Crisafulli (2010) found improved performance on their target application using a pruning method based on the number of squares (closed paths of length 4) in which an edge participates. Let s denote the number of squares that an edge e participates in and p denote the number of squares that would be possible from the set of neighbors of e. Edges with $\frac{s}{p} < \sigma$ are removed. The remaining connected components in G denote the senses of w.

Sense disambiguation on a context of w is performed by computing the intersection of the context's terms with the terms in each of the connected components. As originally specified, the component with the largest overlap is labeled as the sense of w. We adapt this to graded senses by returning all intersecting components with applicability proportional to their overlap. Furthermore, for efficiency, we use only noun, verb, and adjective lemmas in the graphs.

Link Jurgens (2011) use an all-words method where a single graph is built in order to derive the senses of all words in it. Here, the graph's clusters do not correspond to a specific word's senses but rather to contextual features that can be used to disambiguate any of the words in the cluster.

In its original specification, the graph is built with edges between co-occurring words and edge weights corresponding to co-occurrence frequency. Edges below a specified threshold τ are removed, and then link community detection (Ahn et al., 2010) is applied to discover sense-disambiguating word communities, which are overlapping cluster of vertices in the graph, rather than hard partitions. Once the set of communities is produced, communities with three or fewer vertices are removed, under the assumption that these communities contain too few features to reliably disambiguate.

Senses are disambiguated by finding the community with the largest overlap score, computed as the weighted Jaccard Index. For a context with the set of features F_i and a community with features F_j, the overlap is measured as $|F_j| \cdot \frac{|F_i \cap F_j|}{|F_i \cup F_j|}$.

We adapt this algorithm in three ways. First, rather than use co-occurrence frequency to weight edges between terms, we weight edges accord to their statistical association with the G-test (Dunning, 1993). The G-test weighting helps remove edges whose large edge weights are due to high corpus frequency but provide no disambiguating information, and the weighting also allows the τ parameter to be more consistently set across corpora of different sizes. Second, while Jurgens (2011) used only nouns as vertices in the graph, we include both verbs and adjectives due to needing to identify senses for both. Third, for graded senses, we disambiguate a context by reporting all overlapping communities, weighted by their overlap score.

UoY Korkontzelos and Manandhar (2010) propose a WSI model that builds a graph for each term for disambiguation. The graph is built in four stages, with four main tuning parameters, summarized next. First, using a reference corpus, all contexts of the target word w are selected to build a list of co-occurring noun lemmas, retaining all those with frequency above P_1. Second, the Log-Likelihood ratio (Dunning, 1993) is computed between all selected nouns and w, retaining only those with an association above P_2. Third, all remaining nouns are used to create all $\binom{n}{2}$ noun pairs. Next, each term and pair is mapped to the set of contexts in the reference corpus in which it is present. A pair (w_i, w_j) is retained only if its set of contexts is dissimilar to the sets of contexts of both its member terms, using the Dice coefficient to measure the similarity of the sets. Pairs with a Dice coefficient above P_4 with either of its constituent terms are removed. Last, edges are added between nouns and noun pairs according to their conditional probabilities of occurring with each other. Edges with a conditional probability less than

P_3 are not included.

Once the graph has been constructed, the Chinese Whispers graph partitioning algorithm (Biemann, 2006) is used to identify word senses. Each graph partition is assigned a separate sense of w. Next, each partition is mapped to the set of contexts in the reference corpus in which at least one of its vertices occurs. Partitions whose context sets are a strict subset of another are merged with the subsuming partition.

Word sense disambiguation occurs by counting the number of overlapping vertices for each partition and selecting the partition with the highest overlap as the sense of w. We extend this to graded annotation by selecting all partitions with at least one vertex present and set the applicability equal to the degree of overlap.

4 Evaluation Across Sense Inventories

Directly comparing GWS annotations from the induced and gold standard sense inventories requires first creating a mapping from the induced senses to the gold standard inventory. Agirre et al. (2006) propose a sense-mapping procedure, which was used in the previous two SemEval WSI Tasks (Agirre and Soroa, 2007; Manandhar et al., 2010). We consider this procedure and two extensions of it to support learning a mapping from graded sense annotations.

The procedure of Agirre et al. (2006) uses three corpora: (1) a base corpus from which the senses are derived, (2) a mapping corpus annotated with both gold standard senses, denoted gs, and induced senses, denoted is, and (3) a test corpus annotated with is senses that will be converted to gs senses.

Once the senses are induced from the base corpus, the mapping corpus is annotated with is senses and a matrix M is built where cell i, j initially contains the counts of each time gs_j and is_i were used to label the same instance. The rows of this matrix are then normalized such that each cell now represents $p(gs_j|is_i)$. The final mapping selects the most probable gs sense for each is sense.

To label the test corpus, each instance that is labeled with is_i is relabeled with the gs sense with the highest conditional probability given is_i. When a context c is annotated by a set of labels $L = \{is_i, \ldots, is_j\}$, the final sense labeling contains the set of all gs to which the is senses were mapped, weighted by their mapping frequencies: $per_c(gs_j) = \frac{1}{|L|}\sum_{is_i \in L} \delta(is_i, gs_j)$ where δ returns 1 if is_i is mapped to gs_j and 0 otherwise.

The original algorithm of Agirre et al. (2006) does not consider the role of applicability in evaluating whether an is sense should be mapped to a gs sense; is senses with different levels of applicability in the same context are treated equivalently in updating M. Therefore, as a first extension, referred to as *Graded*, we revise the update rule for constructing M where for the set of contexts C labeled by both is_i and gs_j, $M_{i,j} = \sum_{c \in C} per_c(is_i) \times per_c(gs_j)$. As in (Agirre et al., 2006), M is normalized and each is sense is mapped to its most probable gs sense.

To label the test corpus using the *Graded* method, the applicability of the is sense is also included. For a context c is annotated with senses $L = \{is_i, \ldots, is_j\}$, the final sense labeling contains the set of all gs senses to which the is senses were mapped, weighted by their mapping frequencies: $per_c(gs_j) = \sum_{is_i \in L} [\delta(is_i, gs_j) \times per_c(is_i)]$. The applicabilities are then normalized to sum to 1.

The prior two methods restrict an is sense to mapping to only a single gs sense. However, an is sense may potentially correspond to multiple gs senses, each with different levels of applicability. Therefore, we consider a second extension, referred to as *Distribution*, that uses the same matrix construction as the Graded procedure, but rather than mapping each is to a single sense, maps it to a distribution over all gs senses for which it was co-annotated, which is the normalized row vector in M for an is sense. Labeling in the test corpus is then done by summing the distributions of the is senses annotated in the context and normalizing to create a probability distribution over the union of their gs senses.

5 Experiments

We adapt the supervised WSD setting used in prior SemEval WSI Tasks (Agirre and Soroa, 2007; Manandhar et al., 2010) to evaluation the models according to the three proposed objectives. In the supervised setting, WSI systems provide GWS annotation of their induced senses for the test corpus, which is already labeled with the gold-standard GWS annotations. Then, a portion of the test corpus with gold standard annotations is used to build a mapping from induced senses to the reference sense inven-

Term	PoS	# senses	Avg. # Senses per Instance
add	verb	6	4.18
ask	verb	7	5.98
win	verb	4	3.98
argument	noun	7	5.18
interest	noun	7	5.12
paper	noun	7	5.54
different	adj.	5	4.98
important	adj.	5	4.82

Table 1: The terms from the GWS dataset (Erk et al., 2009) used in this evaluation

tory using one of the three algorithms described in Section 4. The remaining, held-out test corpus instances have their induced senses converted to the gold standard sense inventory and the sense labelings are evaluated for the three objectives from Section 2. In our experiments we divide the reference corpus into five evenly-sized segments and then use four segments (80% of the test corpus) for constructing the mapping and then evaluate the converted GWS annotations of the remaining segment.

5.1 Graded Annotation Data

The gold standard GWS annotations are derived from a subset of the GWS data provided by Erk et al. (2009). Here, three annotators rated the applicability of all WordNet 3.0 senses of a word in a single sentence context. Ratings were done using a 5-point ordinal ranking according to the judgements from 1 – this sense is not applicable to 5 – this usage exactly reflects this sense. Annotators used a wide-range of responses, leading to many applicable senses per instance. We selected the subset of the GWS dataset where each term has 50 annotated contexts, which were distributed evenly between SemCor (Miller et al., 1993) and the SENSEVAL-3 lexical substitution corpus (Mihalcea et al., 2004). Table 1 summarizes the target terms in this context.

To prepare the data for evaluation, we constructed the gold standard GWS annotations using the mean applicability ratings of all three annotators for each context. Senses that received a mean rating of 1 (not applicable) were not listed in gold standard labeling for that instance. All remaining responses were normalized to sum to 1.

5.2 Model Configuration

For consistency, all three WSI models were trained using the same reference corpus. We used a 2009 snapshot of Wikipedia,[2] which was PoS tagged and lemmatized using the TreeTagger (Schmid, 1994). All of target terms occurred over 12,000 times. The G-test between terms was computed using a three-sentence sliding window within each article in the corpus. The Dice coefficient was calculated using a single sentence as context.

For all three models, we performed a limited grid search to find the best performing system parameters, within reasonable computational limits. We summarize the parameters and models, selecting the configuration with the highest average Perception score. For all models, the applicability ratings for each instance are normalized to sum to 1.

Model	Parameter Range	Selected
Squares	$\delta=\{0.008, 0.009, \ldots, 0.092\}$	0.037
	$\sigma=\{0.25, 0.30, \ldots, 0.50, 0.55\}$	0.55
Link	$\tau=\{400, 500, \ldots, 900, 1000\}$	500
UoY	$P_1=\{10, 20\}$	20
	$P_2=\{10, 20, 30\}$	20
	$P_3=\{0.2, 0.3, 0.4\}$	0.3
	$P_4=\{0.4, 0.6, 0.8\}$	0.4

5.3 Baselines

Prior WSI evaluations have used the Most Frequent Sense (MFS) labeling a strong baseline in the supervised WSD task. For the GWS setting, we consider five other baselines that select one, some, or all of the sense of the target word, with different ordering strategies. In the six baselines, each instance is labeled as follows:

MFS: the most frequent sense of the word
RS: a single, randomly-selected sense
ASF: all senses, ranked in order of frequency starting with the most frequent
ASR: all senses, randomly ranked
ASE: all senses, ranked equally
RSM: a random number of senses, ranked arbitrarily

To establish applicability values from a ranking of n senses, we set applicability to the ith ranked sense of $\frac{(n-i)+1}{\sum_{k=1}^{n} k}$, where rank 1 is the highest ranked sense.

[2] http://wacky.sslmit.unibo.it/

Model	Agirre et al. (2006) Mapping D	R	P	Graded Mapping D	R	P	Distribution Mapping D	R	P	Recall
Squares	0.192	-0.024	0.382	0.198	0.555	0.504	**0.879**	**0.562**	**0.925**	0.560
Link	0.282	0.081	0.454	0.335	0.436	0.528	0.854	0.503	0.907	0.800
UoY	0.238	0.116	0.445	0.244	0.486	0.528	0.848	0.528	0.907	**0.940**

Table 2: Average performance of the three WSI models according to **D**etection, **R**anking, and **P**ercetion

Baseline	Detection	Ranking	Perception
MFS	0.204	**0.334**	0.469
RS	0.167	-0.036	0.363
ASF	**0.846**	0.218	0.830
ASR	**0.846**	0.006	0.776
ASE	**0.846**	0.000	**0.862**
RSM	0.546	0.005	0.632

Table 3: Average performance of the six baselines

5.4 Results and Discussion

Each WSI model was trained and then used to label the sense of each target term in the GWS corpus. The three sense-mapping procedures were then applied to the induced sense labels on the held-out instances to perform a comparison in the graded sense annotations. Table 2 reports the performance for the three evaluation measures for each model and mapping configuration on all instances where the sense mapping is defined. The sense mapping is undefined when (1) a WSI model cannot match an instance's features to any of its senses therefore leaves the instance unannotated or (2) when an instance is labeled with an is sense not seen in the training data. Therefore, we report the additional statistic, Recall, that indicates the percentage of instances that were both labeled by the WSI model and mapped to gs senses. Table 3 summarizes the baselines' performance.

The results show three main trends. First, introducing applicability into the sense mapping process noticeably improves performance. For almost all models and scores, using the Graded Mapping improves performance a small amount. However, the largest increase comes from using the Distribution mapping where induced senses are represented as distributions over the gold standard senses.

Second, performance was well ahead of the baselines across the three evaluations, when considering the models' best performances. The Squares and Link models were able to outperform the baselines that list all senses on the Detection objective, which the UoY model only improves slightly from this baseline. For the Ranking objective, all models substantially outperform the best baseline, MFS; and similarly, for the Perception objective, all models outperform the best performing baseline, ASE. Overall, these performance suggest that induce senses can be successfully used to produce quality GWS annotations.

Third, the WSI models themselves show significant differences in their recall and multi-labeling frequencies. The Squares model is only able to label approximately 56% of the GWS instances due to sparseness in its sense representation. Indeed, only 12 of its 237 annotated instances received more than one sense label, revealing that the model's performance is mostly based on correctly identifying the primary sense in a context and not on identifying the less applicable senses. The UoY model shows a similar trend, with most instances being assigned a median of 2 senses. However, its sense representation is sufficiently dense to have the highest recall of any of the models. In contrast to the other two models, the Link model varies significantly in the number of induced senses assigned: "argument," "ask," "different," and "win" were assigned over 60 senses on average to each of their instances, with "different" having an average of 238, while the remaining terms were assigned under two senses on average.

Furthermore, the results also revealed two unexpected findings. First, the ASE baseline performed unexpectedly high in Perception, despite its assignment of uniform applicability to all senses. We hypothesize this is due to the majority of instances in the GWS dataset being labeled with most of a word's senses, as indicated by Table 1, which results in their perceptibilities becoming normalized to small values. Because the ASE solution has applicability ratings for all senses, normalization brings the ratings close to those of the gold standard solution, and furthermore, the difference in score between applicable and inapplicable senses become too small to significantly affect the resulting cosine similarity. As an alternate model, we reevaluated the baselines against the gold standard using the Jensen-Shannon divergence as proposed by Erk and McCarthy (2009). Again, ASE is still the highest performing baseline on Perception. The high performance for both evaluation measures suggests that an alternate measure may be better suited for quantifying the difference in solutions' GWS applicabilities.

Second, performance was higher on the Perception task than on Ranking, the former of which was anticipated being more difficult. We attribute the lower Ranking performance to two factors. First, the GWS data contains main tied rank senses; however, ties in sense ranks after the mapping process are relatively rare, which reduces γ. Second, instances in the GWS often have senses within close applicability ranges. When scoring an induced annotation that swaps the applicability, the Perception is less affected by the small change in applicability magnitude, whereas Ranking is more affected due to the change in ordering.

6 Conclusion and Future Work

GWS annotations offer great potential for reliably annotating using fine-grained sense inventories, where word instance may elicit several concurrent meanings. Given the expense of creating annotated training corpora with sufficient examples of the graded senses, WSI offers significant promise for learning senses automatically while needing only a small amount GWS annotated data to learn the sense mapping for a WSD task.

In this paper, we have carried out an initial study on the performance of WSI systems on a GWS annotation task. Our primary contribution is an end-to-end framework for mapping and evaluating induced GWS data. We first proposed three objectives for graded sense annotation along with corresponding evaluation measures that reliably convey the effectiveness given the nature of GWS annotations. Second, we proposed two new mapping procedures that use graded sense applicability for converting induced senses into a reference sense inventory. Using three graph-based WSI models, we demonstrated that incorporating graded sense applicability into the sense mapping significantly improves GWS performance over the commonly used method of Agirre et al. (2006). Furthermore, our study demonstrated the potential of WSI systems, showing that all the models were able to outperform all six of the proposed baseline on the Ranking and Perception objectives.

Our findings raise several avenues for future work. First, our study only considered three graph-based WSI models; future work is needed to assess the capabilities other WSI approaches, such as vector-based or Bayesian. We are also interested in comparing the performance of the Link model with other recently developed all-words WSI approaches such as Van de Cruys and Apidianaki (2011).

Second, the proposed evaluation relies on a supervised mapping to the gold standard sense inventory, which has potential to lose information and incorrectly map new senses not in the gold standard. While unsupervised clustering evaluations such as the V-measure (Rosenberg and Hirschberg, 2007) and paired Fscore (Artiles et al., 2009) are capable of evaluating without such a mapping, future work is needed to test extrinsic soft clustering evaluations such as BCubed (Amigó et al., 2009) or develop analogous techniques that take into account graded class membership used in GWS annotations.

Last, we note that our setup normalized the GWS ratings into probability distribution, which is standard in the SemEval evaluation setup. However, this normalization incorrectly transforms GWS annotations where no predominant sense was rated at the highest value, e.g., an annotation of only two senses rated as 3 on a scale of 1 to 5. While these perceptibilities may be left unnormalized, it is not clear how to compare the induced GWS annotations with such mid-interval values, or when the rating scale of the WSI system is potentially unbounded. Future work is needed both in GWS evaluation and in quantifying applicability along a range in GWS-based WSI systems to address this issue.

All models and data will be released as a part of the S-Space Package (Jurgens and Stevens, 2010).[3]

[3]https://github.com/fozziethebeat/S-Space

References

Eneko Agirre and Aitor Soroa. 2007. Semeval-2007 task 02: Evaluating word sense induction and discrimination systems. In *Proceedings of the Fourth International Workshop on Semantic Evaluations*, pages 7–12. ACL, June.

Eneko Agirre, David Martínez, Oier ó de Lacalle, and Aitor Soroa. 2006. Evaluating and optimizing the parameters of an unsupervised graph-based WSD algorithm. In *Proceedings of TextGraphs: the First Workshop on Graph Based Methods for Natural Language Processing*, pages 89–96. Association for Computational Linguistics.

Yong-Yeol Ahn, James P. Bagrow, and Sune Lehmann. 2010. Link communities reveal multiscale complexity in networks. *Nature*, (466):761–764, August.

Enrique Amigó, Julio Gonzalo, Javier Artiles, and Felisa Verdejo. 2009. A comparison of extrinsic clustering evaluation metrics based on formal constraints. *Information Retrieval*, 12(4):461–486.

Javier Artiles, Enrique Amigó, and Julio Gonzalo. 2009. The role of named entities in web people search. In *Proceedings of EMNLP*, pages 534–542. Association for Computational Linguistics.

Chris Biemann. 2006. Chinese whispers: an efficient graph clustering algorithm and its application to natural language processing problems. In *Proceedings of the First Workshop on Graph Based Methods for Natural Language Processing*, pages 73–80. Association for Computational Linguistics.

Irina Chugur, Julio Gonzalo, and Felisa Verdejo. 2002. Polysemy and sense proximity in the senseval-2 test suite. In *Proceedings of the ACL-02 workshop on Word sense disambiguation: recent successes and future directions - Volume 8*, WSD '02, pages 32–39, Stroudsburg, PA, USA. Association for Computational Linguistics.

Ted Dunning. 1993. Accurate methods for the statistics of surprise and coincidence. *Computational linguistics*, 19(1):61–74.

Katrin Erk and Diana McCarthy. 2009. Graded word sense assignment. In *Proceedings of the 2009 Conference on Empirical Methods in Natural Language Processing: Volume 1*, pages 440–449. Association for Computational Linguistics.

Katrin Erk, Diana McCarthy, and Nicholas Gaylord. 2009. Investigations on word senses and word usages. In *Proceedings of the Joint Conference of the 47th Annual Meeting of the ACL and the 4th International Joint Conference on Natural Language Processing of the AFNLP: Volume 1*, pages 10–18. Association for Computational Linguistics.

Christine Fellbaum, editor. 1998. *WordNet: An Electronic Lexical Database*. The MIT Press.

David Jurgens and Keith Stevens. 2010. The S-Space Package: An Open Source Package for Word Space Models. In *Proceedings of the ACL 2010 System Demonstrations*. Association for Computational Linguistics.

David Jurgens. 2011. Word sense induction by community detection. In *Proceedings of Sixth ACL Workshop on Graph-based Methods for Natural Language Processing (TextGraphs-6)*. Association for Computational Linguistics.

Ioannis Korkontzelos and Suresh Manandhar. 2010. Uoy: Graphs of unambiguous vertices for word sense induction and disambiguation. In *Proceedings of the 5th International Workshop on Semantic Evaluation*, pages 355–358. Association for Computational Linguistics.

Jey Han Lau, Paul Cook, Diana McCarthy, David Newman, and Timothy Baldwin. 2012. Word sense induction for novel sense detection. In *Proceedings of the 13th Conference of the European Chapter of the Association for computational Linguistics (EACL 2012)*.

Suresh Manandhar, Ioannis P. Klapaftis, Dmitriy Dligach, and Sameer S. Pradhan. 2010. SemEval-2010 task 14: Word sense induction & disambiguation. In *Proceedings of the 5th International Workshop on Semantic Evaluation*, pages 63–68. Association for Computational Linguistics.

Diana McCarthy. 2006. Relating WordNet senses for word sense disambiguation. *Making Sense of Sense: Bringing Psycholinguistics and Computational Linguistics Together*, page 17.

Rada Mihalcea, Timothy Chklovski, and Adam Kilgarriff. 2004. The senseval-3 english lexical sample task. In *Senseval-3: Third International Workshop on the Evaluation of Systems for the Semantic Analysis of Text*, pages 25–28. Barcelona, Spain, Association for Computational Linguistics.

George A. Miller, Claudia Leacock, Randee Tengi, and Ross T. Bunker. 1993. A semantic concordance. In *Proceedings of the workshop on Human Language Technology*, pages 303–308. Association for Computational Linguistics.

Roberto Navigli and Giuseppe Crisafulli. 2010. Inducing word senses to improve web search result clustering. In *Proceedings of the 2010 Conference on Empirical Methods in Natural Language Processing*, pages 116–126. Association for Computational Linguistics.

Roberto Navigli. 2009. Word sense disambiguation: A survey. *ACM Computing Surveys (CSUR)*, 41(2):10.

Martha Palmer, Hoa Trang Dang, and Christiane Fellbaum. 2007. Making fine-grained and coarse-grained sense distinctions, both manually and automatically. *Natural Language Engineering*, 13(02):137–163.

Rebecca J. Passonneau, Ansaf Salleb-Aoussi, Vikas Bhardwaj, and Nancy Ide. 2010. Word sense annotation of polysemous words by multiple annotators. In *Proceedings of Seventh International Conference on Language Resources and Evaluation (LREC-7)*.

Andrew Rosenberg and Julia Hirschberg. 2007. V-measure: A conditional entropy-based external cluster evaluation measure. In *Proceedings of the 2007 Joint Conference on Empirical Methods in Natural Language Processing and Computational Natural Language Learning (EMNLP-CoNLL)*. ACL, June.

Helmut Schmid. 1994. Probabilistic part-of-speech tagging using decision trees. In *Proceedings of the International Conference on New Methods in Language Processing*.

Sidney Siegel and N. John Castellan Jr. 1988. *Nonparametric Statistics for the Behavioral Sciences*. McGraw-Hill, second edition.

Tim Van de Cruys and Marianna Apidianaki. 2011. Latent Semantic Word Sense Induction and Disambiguation. In *Proceedings of the 49th Annual Meeting of the Association for Computational Linguistics: Human Language Technologies (ACL/HLT)*, pages 1476–1485.

Ensemble-based Semantic Lexicon Induction for Semantic Tagging

Ashequl Qadir
University of Utah
School of Computing
Salt Lake City, UT 84112, USA
asheq@cs.utah.edu

Ellen Riloff
University of Utah
School of Computing
Salt Lake City, UT 84112, USA
riloff@cs.utah.edu

Abstract

We present an ensemble-based framework for semantic lexicon induction that incorporates three diverse approaches for semantic class identification. Our architecture brings together previous bootstrapping methods for pattern-based semantic lexicon induction and contextual semantic tagging, and incorporates a novel approach for inducing semantic classes from coreference chains. The three methods are embedded in a bootstrapping architecture where they produce independent hypotheses, consensus words are added to the lexicon, and the process repeats. Our results show that the ensemble outperforms individual methods in terms of both lexicon quality and instance-based semantic tagging.

1 Introduction

One of the most fundamental aspects of meaning is the association between words and semantic categories, which allows us to understand that a "cow" is an *animal* and a "house" is a *structure*. We will use the term *semantic lexicon* to refer to a dictionary that associates words with semantic classes. Semantic dictionaries are useful for many NLP tasks, as evidenced by the widespread use of WordNet (Miller, 1990). However, off-the-shelf resources are not always sufficient for specialized domains, such as medicine, chemistry, or microelectronics. Furthermore, in virtually every domain, texts contain lexical variations that are often missing from dictionaries, such as acronyms, abbreviations, spelling variants, informal shorthand terms (e.g., "abx" for "antibiotics"), and composite terms (e.g., "may-december" or "virus/worm"). To address this problem, techniques have been developed to automate the construction of semantic lexicons from text corpora using bootstrapping methods (Riloff and Shepherd, 1997; Roark and Charniak, 1998; Phillips and Riloff, 2002; Thelen and Riloff, 2002; Ng, 2007; McIntosh and Curran, 2009; McIntosh, 2010), but accuracy is still far from perfect.

Our research explores the use of *ensemble* methods to improve the accuracy of semantic lexicon induction. Our observation is that semantic class associations can be learned using several fundamentally different types of corpus analysis. Bootstrapping methods for semantic lexicon induction (e.g., (Riloff and Jones, 1999; Thelen and Riloff, 2002; McIntosh and Curran, 2009)) collect corpus-wide statistics for individual words based on shared contextual patterns. In contrast, classifiers for semantic tagging (e.g., (Collins and Singer, 1999; Niu et al., 2003; Huang and Riloff, 2010)) label *word instances* and focus on the local context surrounding each instance. The difference between these approaches is that semantic taggers make decisions based on a single context and can assign different labels to different instances, whereas lexicon induction algorithms compile corpus statistics from multiple instances of a word and typically assign each word to a single semantic category.[1] We also hypothesize that coreference resolution can be exploited to infer semantic

[1]This approach would be untenable for broad-coverage semantic knowledge acquisition, but within a specialized domain most words have a dominant word sense. Our experimental results support this assumption.

class labels. Intuitively, if we know that two noun phrases are coreferent, then they probably belong to the same high-level semantic category (e.g., "dog" and "terrier" are both *animals*).

In this paper, we present an ensemble-based framework for semantic lexicon induction. We incorporate a pattern-based bootstrapping method for lexicon induction, a contextual semantic tagger, and a new coreference-based method for lexicon induction. Our results show that coalescing the decisions produced by diverse methods produces a better dictionary than any individual method alone.

A second contribution of this paper is an analysis of the effectiveness of dictionaries for semantic tagging. In principle, an NLP system should be able to assign different semantic labels to different senses of a word. But within a specialized domain, most words have a dominant sense and we argue that using domain-specific dictionaries for tagging may be equally, if not more, effective. We analyze the tradeoffs between using an instance-based semantic tagger versus dictionary lookup on a collection of disease outbreak articles. Our results show that the induced dictionaries yield better performance than an instance-based semantic tagger, achieving higher accuracy with comparable levels of recall.

2 Related Work

Several techniques have been developed for *semantic class induction* (also called *set expansion*) using bootstrapping methods that consider co-occurrence statistics based on nouns (Riloff and Shepherd, 1997), syntactic structures (Roark and Charniak, 1998; Phillips and Riloff, 2002), and contextual patterns (Riloff and Jones, 1999; Thelen and Riloff, 2002; McIntosh and Curran, 2008; McIntosh and Curran, 2009). To improve the accuracy of induced lexicons, some research has incorporated negative information from human judgements (Vyas and Pantel, 2009), automatically discovered negative classes (McIntosh, 2010), and distributional similarity metrics to recognize concept drift (McIntosh and Curran, 2009). Phillips and Riloff (2002) used co-training (Blum and Mitchell, 1998) to exploit three simple classifiers that each recognized a different type of syntactic structure. The research most closely related to ours is an ensemble-based method for automatic thesaurus construction (Curran, 2002). However, that goal was to acquire fine-grained semantic information that is more akin to synonymy (e.g., words similar to "house"), whereas we associate words with high-level semantic classes (e.g., a "house" is a *transient structure*).

Semantic class tagging is closely related to *named entity recognition* (NER) (e.g., (Bikel et al., 1997; Collins and Singer, 1999; Cucerzan and Yarowsky, 1999; Fleischman and Hovy, 2002)). Some bootstrapping methods have been used for NER (e.g., (Collins and Singer, 1999; Niu et al., 2003) to learn from unannotated texts. However, most NER systems will not label nominal noun phrases (e.g., they will not identify "the dentist" as a *person*) or recognize semantic classes that are not associated with proper named entities (e.g., symptoms).[2] ACE mention detection systems (e.g., (ACE, 2007; ACE, 2008)) can label noun phrases that are associated with 5-7 semantic classes and are typically trained with supervised learning. Recently, (Huang and Riloff, 2010) developed a bootstrapping technique that induces a semantic tagger from unannotated texts. We use their system in our ensemble.

There has also been work on extracting semantic class members from the Web (e.g., (Paşca, 2004; Etzioni et al., 2005; Kozareva et al., 2008; Carlson et al., 2009)). This line of research is fundamentally different from ours because these techniques benefit from the vast repository of information available on the Web and are therefore designed to harvest a wide swath of general-purpose semantic information. Our research is aimed at acquiring domain-specific semantic dictionaries using a collection of documents representing a specialized domain.

3 Ensemble-based Semantic Lexicon Induction

3.1 Motivation

Our research combines three fundamentally different techniques into an ensemble-based bootstrapping framework for semantic lexicon induction: pattern-based dictionary induction, contextual semantic tagging, and coreference resolution. Our motivation for using an ensemble of different tech-

[2]Some NER systems will handle special constructions such as dates and monetary amounts.

niques is driven by the observation that these methods exploit different types of information to infer semantic class knowledge. The coreference resolver uses features associated with coreference, such as syntactic constructions (e.g., appositives, predicate nominals), word overlap, semantic similarity, proximity, etc. The pattern-based lexicon induction algorithm uses corpus-wide statistics gathered from the contexts of all instances of a word and compares them with the contexts of known category members. The contextual semantic tagger uses local context windows around words and classifies each word instance independently from the others.

Since each technique draws its conclusions from different types of information, they represent independent sources of evidence to confirm whether a word belongs to a semantic class. Our hypothesis is that, combining these different sources of evidence in an ensemble-based learning framework should produce better accuracy than using any one method alone. Based on this intuition, we create an ensemble-based bootstrapping framework that iteratively collects the hypotheses produced by each individual learner and selects the words that were hypothesized by at least 2 of the 3 learners. This approach produces a bootstrapping process with improved precision, both at the critical beginning stages of the bootstrapping process and during subsequent bootstrapping iterations.

3.2 Component Systems in the Ensemble

In the following sections, we describe each of the component systems used in our ensemble.

3.2.1 Pattern-based Lexicon Induction

The first component of our ensemble is Basilisk (Thelen and Riloff, 2002), which identifies nouns belonging to a semantic class based on collective information over lexico-syntactic pattern contexts. The patterns are automatically generated using AutoSlog-TS (Riloff, 1996). Basilisk begins with a small set of seed words for each semantic class and a collection of unannotated documents for the domain. In an iterative bootstrapping process, Basilisk identifies candidate nouns, ranks them based on its scoring criteria, selects the 5 most confident words for inclusion in the lexicon, and this process repeats using the new words as additional seeds in subsequent iterations.

3.2.2 Lexicon Induction with a Contextual Semantic Tagger

The second component in our ensemble is a contextual semantic tagger (Huang and Riloff, 2010). Like Basilisk, the semantic tagger also begins with seed nouns, trains itself on a large collection of unannotated documents using bootstrapping, and iteratively labels new instances. This tagger labels noun instances and does not produce a dictionary.

To adapt it for our purposes, we ran the bootstrapping process over the training texts to induce a semantic classifier. We then applied the classifier to the same set of training documents and compiled a lexicon by collecting the set of nouns that were assigned to each semantic class. We ignored words that were assigned different labels in different contexts to avoid conflicts in the lexicons. We used the identical configuration described by (Huang and Riloff, 2010) that applies a 1.0 confidence threshold for semantic class assignment.

3.2.3 Coreference-Based Lexicon Construction

The third component of our ensemble is a new method for semantic lexicon induction that exploits coreference resolution. Members of a coreference chain represent the same entity, so all references to the entity should belong to the same semantic class. For example, suppose *"Paris"* and *"the city"* are in the same coreference chain. If we know that *city* is a *Fixed Location*, then we can infer that *Paris* is also a *Fixed Location*.

We induced lexicons from coreference chains using a similar bootstrapping framework that begins with seed nouns and unannotated texts. Let S denote a set of semantic classes and W denote a set of unknown words. For any $s \in S$ and $w \in W$, let $N_{s,w}$ denote the number of instances of s in the current lexicon[3] that are coreferent with w in the text corpus. Then we estimate the probability that word w belongs to semantic class s as:

$$P(s|w) = \frac{N_{s,w}}{\sum_{s' \in S} N_{s',w}}$$

We hypothesize the semantic class of w, $SemClass(w)$ by:

$$SemClass(w) = \arg\max_s P(s|w)$$

[3]In the first iteration, the lexicon is initialized with the seeds.

To ensure high precision for the induced lexicons, we use a threshold of 0.5. All words with a probability above this thresold are added to the lexicon, and the bootstrapping process repeats. Although the coreference chains remain the same throughout the process, the lexicon grows so more words in the chains have semantic class labels as bootstrapping progresses. Bootstrapping ends when fewer than 5 words are learned for each of the semantic classes.

Many noun phrases are singletons (i.e., they are not coreferent with any other NPs), which limits the set of words that can be learned using coreference chains. Furthermore, coreference resolvers make mistakes, so the accuracy of the induced lexicons depends on the quality of the chains. For our experiments, we used Reconcile (Stoyanov et al., 2010), a freely available supervised coreference resolver.

3.3 Ensemble-based Bootstrapping Framework

Figure 1 shows the architecture of our ensemble-based bootstrapping framework. Initially, each lexicon only contains the seed nouns. Each component hypothesizes a set of candidate words for each semantic class, based on its own criteria. The word lists produced by the three systems are then compared, and we retain only the words that were hypothesized with the same class label by at least two of the three systems. The remaining words are discarded. The consenus words are added to the lexicon, and the bootstrapping process repeats. As soon as fewer than 5 words are learned for each of the semantic classes, bootstrapping stops.

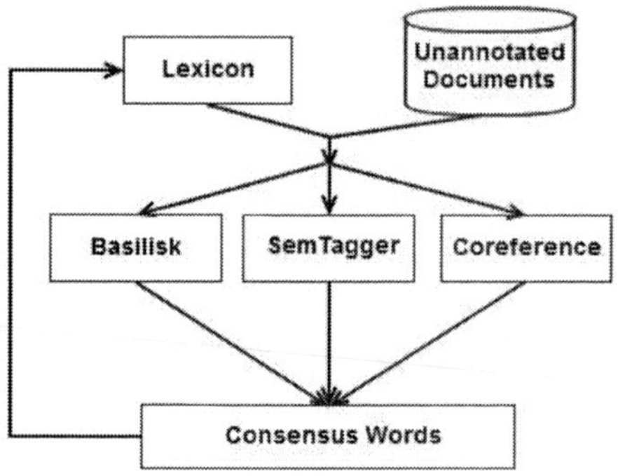

Figure 1: Ensemble-based bootstrapping framework

We ran each individual system with the same seed words. Since bootstrapping typically yields the best precision during the earliest stages, we used the semantic tagger's trained model immediately after its first bootstrapping iteration. Basilisk generates 5 words per cycle, so we report results for lexicons generated after 20 bootstrapping cycles (100 words) and after 80 bootstrapping cycles (400 words).

3.4 Co-Training Framework

The three components in our ensemble use different types of features (views) to identify semantic class members, so we also experimented with co-training. Our co-training model uses an identical framework, but the hypotheses produced by the different methods are all added to the lexicon, so each method can benefit from the hypotheses produced by the others. To be conservative, each time we added only the 10 most confident words hypothesized by each method.

In contrast, the ensemble approach only adds words to the lexicon if they are hypothesized by two different methods. As we will see in Section 4.4, the ensemble performs much better than co-training. The reason is that the individual methods do not consistently achieve high precision on their own. Consequently, many mistakes are added to the lexicon, which is used as training data for subsequent bootstrapping. The benefit of the ensemble is that consensus is required across two methods, which serves as a form of cross-checking to boost precision and maintain a high-quality lexicon.

4 Evaluation

4.1 Semantic Class Definitions

We evaluated our approach on nine semantic categories associated with disease outbreaks. The semantic classes are defined below.

Animal: Mammals, birds, fish, insects and other animal groups. (e.g., *cow, crow, mosquito, herd*)

[4] `http://www.nlm.nih.gov/research/umls/`

[5] `http://www.maxmind.com/app/worldcities`

[6] `http://www.listofcountriesoftheworld.com/`

[7] `http://names.mongabay.com/most_common_surnames.htm`

[8] `http://www.sec.gov/rules/other/4-460list.htm`

[9] `http://www.utexas.edu/world/univ/state/`

[10] `http://www.uta.fi/FAST/GC/usabacro.html/`

Semantic Class	External Word List Sources
Animal	**WordNet**: [animal], [mammal family], [animal group]
Body Part	**WordNet**: [body part], [body substance], [body covering], [body waste]
DisSym	**WordNet**: [symptom], [physical condition], [infectious agent]; **Wikipedia**: common and infectious diseases, symptoms, disease acronyms; **UMLS Thesaurus**[4]: diseases, abnormalities, microorganisms (Archaea, Bacteria, Fungus, Virus)
Fixed Loc.	**WordNet**: [geographic area], [land], [district, territory], [region]; **Wiki**:US-states; **Other**:cities[5], countries[6]
Human	**WordNet**: [person], [people], [personnel]; **Wikipedia**: people names, office holder titles, nationalities, occupations, medical personnels & acronyms, players; **Other**: common people names & surnames[7]
Org	**WordNet**: [organization], [assembly]; **Wikipedia**: acronyms in healthcare, medical organization acronyms, news agencies, pharmaceutical companies; **Other**: companies[8], US-universities[9], organizations[10]
Plant & Food	**WordNet**: [food], [plant, flora], [plant part]
Temp. Ref.	**WordNet**: [time], [time interval], [time unit],[time period] **TimeBank**: TimeBank1.2 (Pustejovsky et al., 2003) TIMEX3 expressions
Trans. Struct.	**WordNet**: [structure, construction], [road, route], [facility, installation], [work place]

Table 1: External Word List Sources

Body Part: A part of a human or animal body, including organs, bodily fluids, and microscopic parts. (e.g., *hand, heart, blood, DNA*)

Diseases and Symptoms (DisSym): Diseases and symptoms. We also include fungi and disease carriers because, in this domain, they almost always refer to the disease that they carry. (e.g. *FMD, Anthrax, fever, virus*)

Fixed Location (Fixed Loc.): Named locations, including countries, cities, states, etc. We also include directions and well-defined geographic areas or geo-political entities. (e.g., *Brazil, north, valley*)

Human: All references to people, including names, titles, professions, and groups. (e.g., *John, farmer, traders*)

Organization (Org.): An entity that represents a group of people acting as a single recognized body, including named organizations, departments, governments, and their acronyms. (e.g., *department, WHO, commission, council*)

Temporal Reference (Temp. Ref.): Any reference to a time or duration, including months, days, seasons, etc. (e.g., *night, May, summer, week*)

Plants & Food[11]**:** plants, plant parts, or any type of food. (e.g., *seed, mango, beef, milk*)

Transient Structures (Trans. Struct.): Transient physical structures. (e.g., *hospital, building, home*)

Additionally, we defined a **Miscellaneous** class for words that do not belong to any of the other categories. (e.g., *output, information, media, point*).

[11]We merged plants and food into a single category as it is difficult to separate them because many food items are plants.

4.2 Data Set

We ran our experiments on ProMED-mail[12] articles. ProMED-mail is an internet based reporting system for infectious disease outbreaks, which can involve people, animals, and plants grown for food. Our ProMED corpus contains 5004 documents. We used 4959 documents as (unannotated) training data for bootstrapping. For the remaining 45 documents, we used 22 documents to train the coreference resolver (Reconcile) and 23 documents as our test set. The coreference training set contains MUC-7 style (Hirschman, 1997) coreference annotations[13]. Once trained, Reconcile was applied to the 4959 unannotated documents to produce coreference chains.

4.3 Gold Standard Semantic Class Annotations

To obtain gold standard annotations for the test set, two annotators assigned one of the 9 semantic class labels, or Miscellaneous, to each head noun based on its surrounding context. A noun with multiple senses could get assigned different semantic class labels in different contexts. The annotators first annotated 13 of the 23 documents, and discussed the cases where they disagreed. Then they independelty annotated

[12]`http://www.promedmail.org/`

[13]We omit the details of the coreference annotations since it is not the focus of this research. However, the annotators measured their agreement on 10 documents and achieved MUC scores of Precision = .82, Recall = .86, F-measure = .84.

the remaining 10 documents and measured inter-annotator agreement with Cohen's Kappa (κ) (Carletta, 1996). The κ score for these 10 documents was 0.91, indicating a high level of agreement. The annotators then adjudicated their disagreements on all 23 documents to create the gold standard.

4.4 Dictionary Evaluation

To assess the quality of the lexicons, we estimated their accuracy by compiling external word lists from freely available sources such as Wikipedia[14] and WordNet (Miller, 1990). Table 1 shows the sources that we used, where the bracketed items refer to WordNet hypernym categories. We searched each WordNet hypernym tree (also, instance-relationship) for all senses of the word. Additionally, we collected the manually labeled words in our test set and included them in our gold standard lists.

Since the induced lexicons contain individual nouns, we extracted only the head nouns of multi-word phrases in the external resources. This can produce incorrect entries for non-compositional phrases, but we found this issue to be relatively rare and we manually removed obviously wrong entries. We adopted a conservative strategy and assumed that any lexicon entries not present in our gold standard lists are incorrect. But we observed many correct entries that were missing from the external resources, so our results should be interpreted as a lower bound on the true accuracy of the induced lexicons.

We generated lexicons for each method separately, and also for the ensemble and co-training models. We ran Basilisk for 100 iterations (500 words). We refer to a Basilisk lexicon of size N using the notation $B[N]$. For example, $B400$ refers to a lexicon containing 400 words, which was generated from 80 bootstrapping cycles. We refer to the lexicon obtained from the semantic tagger as *ST Lex*.

Figure 2 shows the dictionary evaluation results. We plotted *Basilisk's* accuracy after every 5 bootstrapping cycles (25 words). For *ST Lex*, we sorted the words by their confidence scores and plotted the accuracy of the top-ranked words in increments of 50. The plots for *Coref*, *Co-Training*, and *Ensemble B[N]* are based on the lexicons produced after each bootstrapping cycle.

[14] `www.wikipedia.org/`

The ensemble-based framework yields consistently better accuracy than the individual methods for *Animal*, *Body Part*, *Human* and *Temporal Reference*, and similar if not better for *Disease & Symptom*, *Fixed Location*, *Organization*, *Plant & Food*. However, relying on consensus from multiple models produce smaller dictionaries. Big dictionaries are not always better than small dictionaries in practice, though. We believe, it matters more whether a dictionary contains the most frequent words for a domain, because they account for a disproportionate number of instances. Basilisk, for example, often learns infrequent words, so its dictionaries may have high accuracy but often fail to recognize common words. We investigate this issue in the next section.

4.5 Instance-based Tagging Evaluation

We also evaluated the effectiveness of the induced lexicons with respect to instance-based semantic tagging. Our goal was to determine how useful the dictionaries are in two respects: (1) do the lexicons contain words that appear frequently in the domain, and (2) is dictionary look-up sufficient for instance-based labeling? Our bootstrapping processes enforce a constraint that a word can only belong to one semantic class, so if polysemy is common, then dictionary look-up will be problematic.[15]

The instance-based evaluation assigns a semantic label to each instance of a head noun. When using a lexicon, all instances of the same noun are assigned the same semantic class via dictionary look-up. The semantic tagger (SemTag), however, is applied directly since it was designed to label instances.

Table 2 presents the results. As a baseline, the *W.Net* row shows the performance of WordNet for instance tagging. For words with multiple senses, we only used the first sense listed in WordNet. The *Seeds* row shows the results when performing dictionary look-up using only the seed words. The remaining rows show the results for Basilisk (B100 and B400), coreference-based lexicon induction (Coref), lexicon induction using the semantic tagger (ST Lex), and the original instance-based tagger (SemTag). The following rows show the results for co-training (after 4 iterations and 20 iterations)

[15] Only coarse polysemy across semantic classes is an issue (e.g., "plant" as a living thing vs. a factory).

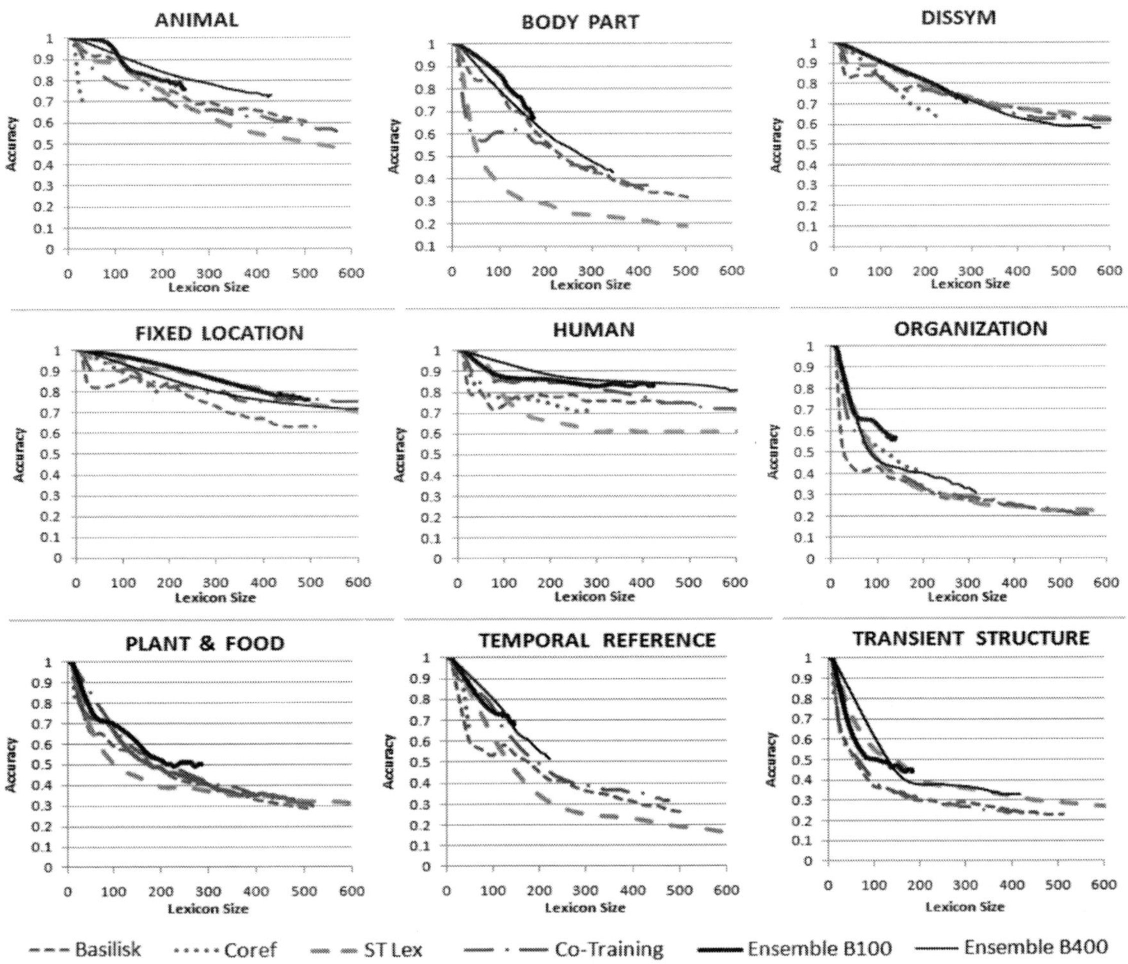

Figure 2: Dictionary Evaluation Results

and for the ensemble (using Basilisk size 100 and size 400). Table 3 shows the micro & macro average results across all semantic categories.

Table 3 shows that the dictionaries produced by the *Ensemble w/B100* achieved better results than the individual methods and co-training with an F score of 80%. Table 2 shows that the ensemble achieved better performance than the other methods for 4 of the 9 classes, and was usually competitive on the remaining 5 classes. WordNet *(W.Net)* consistently produced high precision, but with comparatively lower recall, indicating that WordNet does not have sufficient coverage for this domain.

4.6 Analysis

Table 4 shows the performance of our ensemble when using only 2 of the 3 component methods. Removing any one method decreases the average F-measure by at least 3-5%. Component pairs that include induced lexicons from coreference (*ST Lex+Coref* and *B100+Coref*) yield high precision but low recall. The component pair *ST Lex+B100* produces higher recall but with slightly lower accuracy. The ensemble framework boosted recall even more, while maintaining the same precision.

We observe that some of the smallest lexicons produced the best results for instance-based semantic tagging (e.g., *Organization*). Our hypothesis is that consensus decisions across different methods helps to promote the acquisition of high frequency domain words, which are crucial to have in the dictionary. The fact that dictionary look-up performed better than an instance-based semantic tagger also suggests that coarse polysemy (different senses that

Method	Animal	Body Part	DisSym	Fixed Loc.	Human	Org.	Plant & Food	Temp. Ref.	Trans. Struct.
	P R F	P R F	P R F	P R F	P R F	P R F	P R F	P R F	P R F
Individual Methods									
W.Net	92 88 90	93 59 72	99 77 87	86 58 69	83 55 66	86 44 59	65 79 71	93 85 **89**	85 64 73
Seeds	100 54 70	92 55 69	100 59 74	95 10 18	100 22 36	100 41 58	100 61 **76**	100 52 69	100 09 17
B100	99 77 86	94 73 **82**	100 66 80	96 23 37	96 31 47	91 58 71	82 64 72	68 83 75	67 22 33
B400	94 90 92	51 86 64	100 69 81	97 35 51	91 51 65	79 77 78	46 82 59	49 94 64	83 78 **80**
Coref	90 67 77	92 55 69	66 83 73	65 46 54	57 50 53	54 68 60	81 61 69	60 74 67	45 09 15
ST Lex	94 89 91	68 77 72	80 91 85	91 74 82	79 43 55	84 62 71	51 68 58	73 91 81	82 49 61
SemTag	91 90 90	52 68 59	77 90 83	91 78 **84**	81 48 60	80 63 70	43 82 56	77 93 84	83 53 64
Co-Training									
pass4	64 76 70	67 73 70	91 79 85	91 39 54	98 44 61	83 69 76	43 68 53	73 94 82	49 36 42
pass20	60 89 71	56 91 69	88 91 90	83 64 72	92 54 68	72 77 74	28 71 40	65 98 78	46 40 43
Ensembles									
w/B100	93 94 **94**	74 77 76	93 81 86	92 73 81	94 55 **70**	90 78 **84**	56 89 68	55 94 70	79 75 77
w/B400	94 93 93	65 91 75	96 87 **91**	89 75 81	92 56 **70**	79 79 79	47 86 61	53 94 68	63 55 58

Table 2: Instance-based Semantic Tagging Results (P = Precision, R = Recall, F = F-measure)

Method	Micro Average	Macro Average
	P R F	P R F
Individual Systems		
W.Net	88 66 75	87 68 76
Seeds	99 35 52	99 40 57
B100	89 50 64	88 55 68
B400	77 66 71	77 74 75
Coref	65 59 62	68 57 62
ST Lex	82 72 77	78 72 75
SemTag	80 74 77	75 74 74
Co-Training		
pass4	77 61 68	73 64 68
pass20	69 74 71	65 75 70
Ensembles		
w/B100	83 77 **80**	81 80 **80**
w/B400	79 78 78	75 79 77

Table 3: Micro & Macro Average for Semantic Tagging

cut across semantic classes) is a relatively minor issue within a specialized domain.

5 Conclusions

Our research combined three diverse methods for semantic lexicon induction in a bootstrapped ensemble-based framework, including a novel approach for lexicon induction based on coreference chains. Our ensemble-based approach performed better than the individual methods, in terms of both dictionary accuracy and instance-based semantic tagging. In future work, we believe this approach could be enhanced further by adding new types of techniques to the ensemble and by investigating better methods for estimating the confidence scores from the individual components.

Method	Micro Average	Macro Average
	P R F	P R F
Ensemble with component pairs		
ST Lex+Coref	92 59 72	92 57 70
B100+Coref	92 40 56	94 44 60
ST Lex+B100	82 69 75	81 75 77
Ensemble with all components		
ST Lex+B100+Coref	83 77 **80**	81 80 **80**

Table 4: Ablation Study of the Ensemble Framework for Semantic Tagging

Acknowledgments

We are grateful to Lalindra de Silva for manually annotating data, Nathan Gilbert for help with Reconcile, and Ruihong Huang for help with the semantic tagger. We gratefully acknowledge the support of the National Science Foundation under grant IIS-1018314 and the Defense Advanced Research Projects Agency (DARPA) Machine Reading Program under Air Force Research Laboratory (AFRL) prime contract no. FA8750-09-C-0172. Any opinions, findings, and conclusions or recommendations expressed in this material are those of the authors and do not necessarily reflect the view of the DARPA, AFRL, or the U.S. government.

References

ACE. 2007. NIST ACE evaluation website. In *http://www.nist.gov/speech/tests/ace/2007.*

ACE. 2008. NIST ACE evaluation website. In *http://www.nist.gov/speech/tests/ace/2008.*

Daniel M. Bikel, Scott Miller, Richard Schwartz, and Ralph Weischedel. 1997. Nymble: a high-performance learning name-finder. In *Proceedings of ANLP-97*, pages 194–201.

A. Blum and T. Mitchell. 1998. Combining Labeled and Unlabeled Data with Co-Training. In *Proceedings of the 11th Annual Conference on Computational Learning Theory (COLT-98).*

Jean Carletta. 1996. Assessing agreement on classification tasks: the kappa statistic. *Comput. Linguist.*, 22:249–254, June.

Andrew Carlson, Justin Betteridge, Estevam R. Hruschka Jr., and Tom M. Mitchell. 2009. Coupling semi-supervised learning of categories and relations. In *HLT-NAACL 2009 Workshop on Semi-Supervised Learning for NLP.*

M. Collins and Y. Singer. 1999. Unsupervised Models for Named Entity Classification. In *Proceedings of the Joint SIGDAT Conference on Empirical Methods in Natural Language Processing and Very Large Corpora (EMNLP/VLC-99).*

S. Cucerzan and D. Yarowsky. 1999. Language Independent Named Entity Recognition Combining Morphologi cal and Contextual Evidence. In *Proceedings of the Joint SIGDAT Conference on Empirical Methods in Natural Language Processing and Very Large Corpora (EMNLP/VLC-99).*

J. Curran. 2002. Ensemble Methods for Automatic Thesaurus Extraction. In *Proceedings of the 2002 Conference on Empirical Methods in Natural Language Processing.*

O. Etzioni, M. Cafarella, D. Downey, A. Popescu, T. Shaked, S. Soderland, D. Weld, and A. Yates. 2005. Unsupervised named-entity extraction from the web: an experimental study. *Artificial Intelligence*, 165(1):91–134, June.

M.B. Fleischman and E.H. Hovy. 2002. Fine grained classification of named entities. In *Proceedings of the COLING conference*, August.

L. Hirschman. 1997. MUC-7 Coreference Task Definition.

Ruihong Huang and Ellen Riloff. 2010. Inducing domain-specific semantic class taggers from (almost) nothing. In *Proceedings of the 48th Annual Meeting of the Association for Computational Linguistics.*

Z. Kozareva, E. Riloff, and E. Hovy. 2008. Semantic Class Learning from the Web with Hyponym Pattern Linkage Graphs. In *Proceedings of the 46th Annual Meeting of the Association for Computational Linguistics: Human Language Technologies (ACL-08).*

T. McIntosh and J. Curran. 2008. Weighted mutual exclusion bootstrapping for domain independent lexicon and template acquisition. In *Proceedings of the Australasian Language Technology Association Workshop.*

T. McIntosh and J. Curran. 2009. Reducing Semantic Drift with Bagging and Distributional Similarity. In *Proceedings of the 47th Annual Meeting of the Association for Computational Linguistics.*

T. McIntosh. 2010. Unsupervised Discovery of Negative Categories in Lexicon Bootstrapping. In *Proceedings of the 2010 Conference on Empirical Methods in Natural Language Processing.*

G. Miller. 1990. Wordnet: An On-line Lexical Database. *International Journal of Lexicography*, 3(4).

V. Ng. 2007. Semantic Class Induction and Coreference Resolution. In *Proceedings of the 45th Annual Meeting of the Association for Computational Linguistics.*

Cheng Niu, Wei Li, Jihong Ding, and Rohini K. Srihari. 2003. A bootstrapping approach to named entity classification using successive learners. In *Proceedings of the 41st Annual Meeting on Association for Computational Linguistics (ACL-03)*, pages 335–342.

M. Paşca. 2004. Acquisition of categorized named entities for web search. In *Proc. of the Thirteenth ACM International Conference on Information and Knowledge Management*, pages 137–145.

W. Phillips and E. Riloff. 2002. Exploiting Strong Syntactic Heuristics and Co-Training to Learn Semantic Lexicons. In *Proceedings of the 2002 Conference on Empirical Methods in Natural Language Processing*, pages 125–132.

J. Pustejovsky, P. Hanks, R. Saurí, A. See, R. Gaizauskas, A. Setzer, D. Radev, B. Sundheim, D. Day, L. Ferro, and M. Lazo. 2003. The TIMEBANK Corpus. In *Proceedings of Corpus Linguistics 2003*, pages 647–656.

E. Riloff and R. Jones. 1999. Learning Dictionaries for Information Extraction by Multi-Level Bootstrapping. In *Proceedings of the Sixteenth National Conference on Artificial Intelligence.*

E. Riloff and J. Shepherd. 1997. A Corpus-Based Approach for Building Semantic Lexicons. In *Proceedings of the Second Conference on Empirical Methods in Natural Language Processing*, pages 117–124.

E. Riloff. 1996. Automatically Generating Extraction Patterns from Untagged Text. In *Proceedings of the Thirteenth National Conference on Artificial Intelligence*, pages 1044–1049. The AAAI Press/MIT Press.

B. Roark and E. Charniak. 1998. Noun-phrase Co-occurrence Statistics for Semi-automatic Semantic

Lexicon Construction. In *Proceedings of the 36th Annual Meeting of the Association for Computational Linguistics*, pages 1110–1116.

Veselin Stoyanov, Claire Cardie, Nathan Gilbert, Ellen Riloff, David Buttler, and David Hysom. 2010. Coreference resolution with Reconcile. In *Proceedings of the ACL 2010 Conference Short Papers*, pages 156–161.

M. Thelen and E. Riloff. 2002. A Bootstrapping Method for Learning Semantic Lexicons Using Extraction Pa ttern Contexts. In *Proceedings of the 2002 Conference on Empirical Methods in Natural Language Processing*, pages 214–221.

V. Vyas and P. Pantel. 2009. Semi-automatic entity set refinement. In *Proceedings of North American Association for Computational Linguistics / Human Language Technology (NAACL/HLT-09)*.

An Exact Dual Decomposition Algorithm for Shallow Semantic Parsing with Constraints

Dipanjan Das* **André F. T. Martins*†** **Noah A. Smith***
*Language Technologies Institute, Carnegie Mellon University, Pittsburgh, PA 15213, USA
†Instituto de Telecomunicações, Instituto Superior Técnico, Lisboa, Portugal
{dipanjan,afm,nasmith}@cs.cmu.edu

Abstract

We present a novel technique for jointly predicting semantic arguments for lexical predicates. The task is to find the best matching between semantic roles and sentential spans, subject to structural constraints that come from expert linguistic knowledge (e.g., in the FrameNet lexicon). We formulate this task as an integer linear program (ILP); instead of using an off-the-shelf tool to solve the ILP, we employ a dual decomposition algorithm, which we adapt for exact decoding via a branch-and-bound technique. Compared to a baseline that makes local predictions, we achieve better argument identification scores and avoid all structural violations. Runtime is nine times faster than a proprietary ILP solver.

1 Introduction

Semantic knowledge is often represented declaratively in resources created by linguistic experts. In this work, we strive to exploit such knowledge in a principled, unified, and intuitive way. An example resource where a wide variety of knowledge has been encoded over a long period of time is the FrameNet lexicon (Fillmore et al., 2003),[1] which suggests an analysis based on frame semantics (Fillmore, 1982). This resource defines hundreds of semantic **frames**. Each frame represents a gestalt event or scenario, and is associated with several semantic **roles**, which serve as participants in the event that the frame signifies (see Figure 1 for an example). Along with storing the above data, FrameNet also provides a hierarchy of relationships between frames, and semantic relationships between pairs of roles. In prior NLP research using FrameNet, these interactions have been largely ignored, though they have the potential to improve the quality and consistency of semantic analysis.

In this paper, we present an algorithm that finds the full collection of arguments of a predicate given its semantic frame. Although we work within the conventions of FrameNet, our approach is generalizable to other semantic role labeling (SRL) frameworks. We model this **argument identification** task as constrained optimization, where the constraints come from expert knowledge encoded in a lexicon. Following prior work on PropBank-style SRL (Kingsbury and Palmer, 2002) that dealt with similar constrained problems (Punyakanok et al., 2004; Punyakanok et al., 2008, *inter alia*), we incorporate this declarative knowledge in an integer linear program (ILP).

Because general-purpose ILP solvers are proprietary and do not fully exploit the structure of the problem, we turn to a class of optimization techniques called **dual decomposition** (Komodakis et al., 2007; Rush et al., 2010; Martins et al., 2011a). We derive a modular, extensible, parallelizable approach in which semantic constraints map not just to declarative components of the algorithm, but also to procedural ones, in the form of "workers." While dual decomposition algorithms only solve a relaxation of the original problem, we make a novel contribution by wrapping the algorithm in a branch-and-bound search procedure, resulting in *exact* solutions.

We experimentally find that our algorithm achieves accuracy comparable to a state-of-the-art system, while respecting all imposed linguistic constraints. In comparison to inexact beam search that violates many of these constraints, our exact decoder has less than twice the runtime; furthermore, it decodes nine times faster than CPLEX, a state-of-the-art, proprietary, general-purpose exact ILP solver.

[1] http://framenet.icsi.berkeley.edu

Agent SELF_MOTION COLLABORATION

Austria , once expected to **waltz** smoothly into the European Union , is elbowing its **partners** ,

Self_mover Manner Goal Manner CONDUCT Partner_1 Partner_2

treading on toes and pogo-dancing in a most un-Viennese **manner** .

Figure 1: An example sentence from the annotations released as part of FrameNet 1.5 with three predicates marked in bold. Each predicate has its evoked semantic frame marked above it, in a distinct color. For each frame, its semantic roles are shown in the same color, and the spans fulfilling the roles are underlined. For example, **manner** evokes the CONDUCT frame, and has the Agent and Manner roles fulfilled by Austria and most un-Viennese respectively.

2 Collective Argument Identification

Here, we take a declarative approach to modeling argument identification using an ILP and relate our formulation to prior work in shallow semantic parsing. We show how knowledge specified in a linguistic resource can be used to derive the constraints used in our ILP. Finally, we draw connections of our specification to graphical models, a popular formalism in AI, and describe how the constraints can be treated as factors in a factor graph.

2.1 Declarative Specification

Let us denote a predicate by t and the semantic frame it evokes within a sentence $\mathbf{x}$ by f. In this work, we assume that the semantic frame f is given, which is traditionally the case in controlled experiments used to evaluate SRL systems (Màrquez et al., 2008). Given the semantic frame of a predicate, the semantic roles that might be filled are assumed to be given by the lexicon (as in PropBank and FrameNet). Let the set of roles associated with the frame f be $\mathcal{R}_f$. In sentence $\mathbf{x}$, the set of candidate spans of words that might fill each role is enumerated, usually following an overgenerating heuristic;[2] let this set of spans be $\mathcal{S}_t$. We include the null span $\emptyset$ in $\mathcal{S}_t$; connecting it to a role $r \in \mathcal{R}_f$ denotes that the role is not overt. Our approach assumes a scoring function that gives a strength of association between roles and candidate spans. For each role $r \in \mathcal{R}_f$ and span $s \in \mathcal{S}_t$, this score is parameterized as:

$$c(r, s) = \boldsymbol{\psi} \cdot \mathbf{h}(t, f, \mathbf{x}, r, s), \qquad (1)$$

where $\boldsymbol{\psi}$ are model weights and $\mathbf{h}$ is a feature function that looks at the predicate t, the evoked frame f, sentence $\mathbf{x}$, and its syntactic analysis, along with r and s. The SRL literature provides many feature functions of this form and many ways to use machine learning to acquire $\boldsymbol{\psi}$. Our presented method does not make any assumptions about the score except that it has the form in Eq. 1.

We define a vector $\mathbf{z}$ of binary variables $z_{r,s} \in \{0, 1\}$ for every role and span pair. We have that: $\mathbf{z} \in \{0,1\}^d$, where $d = |\mathcal{R}_f| \times |\mathcal{S}_t|$. $z_{r,s} = 1$ means that role r is filled by span s. Given the binary $\mathbf{z}$ vector, it is straightforward to recover the collection of arguments by checking which components $z_{r,s}$ have an assignment of 1; we use this strategy to find arguments, as described in §4.2 (strategies 4 and 6). The joint argument identification task can be represented as a constrained optimization problem:

$$\begin{array}{rc} \text{maximize} & \sum_{r \in \mathcal{R}_f} \sum_{s \in \mathcal{S}_t} c(r, s) \times z_{r,s} \\ \text{with respect to} & \mathbf{z} \in \{0, 1\}^d \\ \text{such that} & \mathbf{A}\mathbf{z} \leq \mathbf{b}. \end{array} \qquad (2)$$

The last line imposes constraints on the mapping between roles and spans; these are motivated on linguistic grounds and are described next.[3]

Uniqueness: Each role r is filled by at most one span in $\mathcal{S}_t$. This constraint can be expressed by:

$$\forall r \in \mathcal{R}_f, \sum_{s \in \mathcal{S}_t} z_{r,s} = 1. \qquad (3)$$

There are $O(|\mathcal{R}_f|)$ such constraints. Note that since $\mathcal{S}_t$ contains the null span $\emptyset$, non-overt roles are also captured using the above constraints. Such a constraint is used extensively in prior literature (Punyakanok et al., 2008, §3.4.1).

Overlap: SRL systems commonly constrain roles to be filled by non-overlapping spans. For example, Toutanova et al. (2005) used dynamic programming over a phrase structure tree to prevent overlaps between arguments, and Punyakanok et al. (2008) used

[2] Here, as in most SRL literature, role fillers are assumed to be expressed as *contiguous* spans, though such an assumption is easy to relax in our framework.

[3] Note that equality constraints $\mathbf{a} \cdot \mathbf{z} = b$ can be transformed into double-side inequalities $\mathbf{a} \cdot \mathbf{z} \leq b$ and $-\mathbf{a} \cdot \mathbf{z} \leq -b$.

constraints in an ILP to respect this requirement. Inspired by the latter, we require that each input sentence position of $\mathbf{x}$ be covered by at most one argument. For each role $r \in \mathcal{R}_f$, we define:

$$\mathcal{G}_r(i) = \{s \mid s \in \mathcal{S}_t, s \text{ covers position } i \text{ in } \mathbf{x}\}. \quad (4)$$

We can define our overlap constraints in terms of $\mathcal{G}_r$ as follows, for every sentence position i:

$$\forall i \in \{1, \ldots, |\mathbf{x}|\}, \quad \sum_{r \in \mathcal{R}_f} \sum_{s \in \mathcal{G}_r(i)} z_{r,s} \leq 1, \quad (5)$$

This gives us $O(|\mathbf{x}|)$ constraints.

Pairwise "Exclusions": For many predicate classes, there are pairs of roles forbidden to appear together in the analysis of a single predicate token. Consider the following two sentences:

A blackberry **resembles** a loganberry. (6)
Entity_1 Entity_2

Most berries **resemble** each other. (7)
Entities

Consider the uninflected predicate **resemble** in both sentences, evoking the same meaning. In example 6, two roles, which we call Entity_1 and Entity_2 describe two entities that are similar to each other. In the second sentence, a phrase fulfills a third role, called Entities, that collectively denotes some objects that are similar. It is clear that the roles Entity_1 and Entities cannot be overt for the same predicate at once, because the latter already captures the function of the former; a similar argument holds for the Entity_2 and Entities roles. We call this phenomenon the "excludes" relationship. Let us define a set of pairs from $\mathcal{R}_f$ that have this relationship:

$$\mathit{Excl}_f = \{(r_i, r_j) \mid r_i \text{ and } r_j \textit{ exclude} \text{ each other}\}$$

Using the above set, we define the constraint:

$$\forall (r_i, r_j) \in \mathit{Excl}_f, \; z_{r_i,\emptyset} + z_{r_j,\emptyset} \geq 1 \quad (8)$$

In English: if both roles are overt in a parse, this constraint will be violated, and we will not respect the "excludes" relationship between the pair. If neither or only one of the roles is overt, the constraint is satisfied. The total number of such constraints is $O(|\mathit{Excl}_f|)$, which is the number of pairwise "excludes" relationships of a given frame.

Pairwise "Requirements": The sentence in example 6 illustrates another kind of constraint. The predicate **resemble** cannot have only one of Entity_1 and Entity_2 as roles in text. For example,

* A blackberry **resembles**. (9)
Entity_1

Enforcing the overtness of two roles sharing this "requires" relationship is straightforward. We define the following set for a frame f:

$$\mathit{Req}_f = \{(r_i, r_j) \mid r_i \text{ and } r_j \textit{ require} \text{ each other}\}$$

This leads to constraints of the form

$$\forall (r_i, r_j) \in \mathit{Req}_f, z_{r_i,\emptyset} - z_{r_j,\emptyset} = 0 \quad (10)$$

If one role is overt (or absent), so must the other be. A related constraint has been used previously in the SRL literature, enforcing joint overtness relationships between core arguments and referential arguments (Punyakanok et al., 2008, §3.4.1), which are formally similar to the example above.[4]

Integer Linear Program and Relaxation: Plugging the constraints in Eqs. 3, 5, 8 and 10 into the last line of Eq. 2, we have the argument identification problem expressed as an ILP, since the indicator variables $\mathbf{z}$ are binary. In this paper, apart from the ILP formulation, we will consider the following *relaxation* of Eq. 2, which replaces the binary constraint $\mathbf{z} \in \{0, 1\}^d$ by a unit interval constraint $\mathbf{z} \in [0, 1]^d$, yielding a *linear* program:

$$\begin{aligned} \text{maximize} \quad & \textstyle\sum_{r \in \mathcal{R}_f} \sum_{s \in \mathcal{S}_t} c(r, s) \times z_{r,s} \\ \text{with respect to} \quad & \mathbf{z} \in [0, 1]^d \\ \text{such that} \quad & \mathbf{Az} \leq \mathbf{b}. \end{aligned} \quad (11)$$

There are several LP and ILP solvers available, and a great deal of effort has been spent by the optimization community to devise efficient generic solvers. An example is CPLEX, a state-of-the-art solver for mixed integer programming that we employ as a baseline to solve the ILP in Eq. 2 as well as its LP relaxation in Eq. 11. Like many of the best implementations, CPLEX is proprietary.

[4] We noticed in the annotated data, in some cases, the "requires" constraint is violated by the FrameNet annotators. This happens mostly when one of the required roles is absent in the sentence containing the predicate, but is rather instantiated in an earlier sentence; see Gerber and Chai (2010). We apply the hard constraint in Eq. 10, though extending our algorithm to seek arguments outside the sentence is straightforward (Chen et al., 2010).

2.2 Linguistic Constraints from FrameNet

Although enforcing the four different sets of constraints above is intuitive from a general linguistic perspective, we ground their use in definitive linguistic information present in the FrameNet lexicon (Fillmore et al., 2003). FrameNet, along with lists of semantic frames, associated semantic roles, and predicates that could evoke the frames, gives us a small number of annotated sentences with frame-semantic analysis. From the annotated data, we gathered that only 3.6% of the time is a role instantiated multiple times by different spans in a sentence. This justifies the uniqueness constraint enforced by Eq. 3. Use of such a constraint is also consistent with prior work in frame-semantic parsing (Johansson and Nugues, 2007; Das et al., 2010a). Similarly, we found that in the annotations, no arguments overlapped with each other for a given predicate. Hence, the overlap constraints in Eq. 5 are also justified.

Our third and fourth sets of constraints, presented in Eqs. 8 and 10, come from FrameNet, too; moreover, they are explicitly mentioned in the lexicon. Examples 6–7 are instances where the predicate **resemble** evokes the SIMILARITY frame, which is defined in FrameNet as: "Two or more distinct entities, which may be concrete or abstract objects or types, are characterized as being similar to each other. Depending on figure/ground relations, the entities may be expressed in two distinct frame elements and constituents, Entity_1 and Entity_2, or jointly as a single frame element and constituent, Entities."

For this frame, the lexicon lists several roles other than the three roles we have already observed, such as Dimension (the dimension along which the entities are similar), Differentiating_fact (a fact that reveals how the concerned entities are similar or different), and so forth. Along with the roles, FrameNet also declares the "excludes" and "requires" relationships noted in our discussion in Section 2.1. The case of the SIMILARITY frame is not unique; in Fig. 1, the frame COLLABORATION, evoked by the predicate **partners**, also has two roles Partner_1 and Partner_2 that share the "requires" relationship. In fact, out of 877 frames in FrameNet 1.5, the lexicon's latest edition, 204 frames have at least a pair of roles that share the "excludes" relationship, and 54 list at least a pair of roles that share the "requires" relationship.

2.3 Constraints as Factors in a Graphical Model

The LP in Eq. 11 can be represented as a maximum *a posteriori* (MAP) inference problem in an undirected graphical model. In the factor graph, each component of $\mathbf{z}$ corresponds to a binary variable, and each instantiation of a constraint in Eqs. 3, 5, 8 and 10 corresponds to a factor. Smith and Eisner (2008) and Martins et al. (2010) used such a representation to impose constraints in a dependency parsing problem; the latter discussed the equivalence of linear programs and factor graphs for representing discrete optimization problems. Each of our constraints take standard factor forms we can describe using the terminology of Smith and Eisner (2008) and Martins et al. (2010). The uniqueness constraint in Eq. 3 corresponds to an XOR factor, while the overlap constraint in Eq. 5 corresponds to an ATMOSTONE factor. The constraints in Eq. 8 enforcing the "excludes" relationship can be represented with an OR factor. Finally, each "requires" constraints in Eq. 10 is equivalent to an XORWITHOUTPUT factor.

In the following section, we describe how we arrive at solutions for the LP in Eq. 11 using dual decomposition, and how we adapt it to efficiently recover the *exact* solution of the ILP (Eq. 2), without the need of an off-the-shelf ILP solver.

3 "Augmented" Dual Decomposition

Dual decomposition methods address complex optimization problems in the dual, by dividing them into simple worker problems, which are repeatedly solved until a consensus is reached. The most simple technique relies on the subgradient algorithm (Komodakis et al., 2007; Rush et al., 2010); as an alternative, an augmented Lagrangian technique was proposed by Martins et al. (2011a, 2011b), which is more suitable when there are many small components—commonly the case in declarative constrained problems, such as the one at hand. Here, we present a brief overview of the latter, which is called *Dual Decomposition with the Alternating Direction Method of Multipliers* (AD^3).

Let us start by establishing some notation. Let $m \in \{1, \ldots, M\}$ index a factor, and denote by $\mathbf{i}(m)$

the vector of indices of variables linked to that factor. (Recall that each factor represents the instantiation of a constraint.) We introduce a new set of variables, $\mathbf{u} \in \mathbb{R}^d$, called the "witness" vector. We split the vector $\mathbf{z}$ into M overlapping pieces $\mathbf{z}_1, \ldots, \mathbf{z}_M$, where each $\mathbf{z}_m \in [0,1]^{|\mathbf{i}(m)|}$, and add M constraints $\mathbf{z}_m = \mathbf{u}_{\mathbf{i}(m)}$ to impose that all the pieces must agree with the witness (and therefore with each other). Each of the M constraints described in §2 can be encoded with its own matrix $\mathbf{A}_m$ and vector $\mathbf{b}_m$ (which jointly define $\mathbf{A}$ and $\mathbf{b}$ in Eq. 11). For convenience, we denote by $\mathbf{c} \in \mathbb{R}^d$ the score vector, whose components are $c(r,s)$, for each $r \in \mathcal{R}_f$ and $s \in \mathcal{S}_t$ (Eq. 1), and define the following scores for the mth subproblem:

$$c_m(r,s) = \delta(r,s)^{-1} c(r,s), \ \forall (r,s) \in \mathbf{i}(m), \quad (12)$$

where $\delta(r,s)$ is the number of constraints that involve role r and span s. Note that according to this definition, $\mathbf{c} \cdot \mathbf{z} = \sum_{m=1}^{M} \mathbf{c}_m \cdot \mathbf{z}_m$. We can rewrite the LP in Eq. 11 in the following equivalent form:

$$\begin{aligned} \text{maximize} \quad & \sum_{m=1}^{M} \mathbf{c}_m \cdot \mathbf{z}_m \\ \text{with respect to} \quad & \mathbf{u} \in \mathbb{R}^d, \ \mathbf{z}_m \in [0,1]^{\mathbf{i}(m)}, \quad \forall m \\ \text{such that} \quad & \mathbf{A}_m \mathbf{z}_m \leq \mathbf{b}_m, \quad \forall m \\ & \mathbf{z}_m = \mathbf{u}_{\mathbf{i}(m)}, \quad \forall m. \end{aligned} \quad (13)$$

We next augment the objective with a quadratic penalty term $\frac{\rho}{2} \sum_{m=1}^{M} \|\mathbf{z}_m - \mathbf{u}_{\mathbf{i}(m)}\|^2$ (for some $\rho > 0$). This does not affect the solution of the problem, since the equality constraints in the last line force this penalty to vanish. However, as we will see, this penalty will influence the workers and will lead to faster consensus. Next, we introduce Lagrange multipliers $\boldsymbol{\lambda}_m$ for those equality constraints, so that the augmented Lagrangian function becomes:

$$\begin{aligned} L_\rho(\mathbf{z}, \mathbf{u}, \boldsymbol{\lambda}) = & \sum_{m=1}^{M} (\mathbf{c}_m + \boldsymbol{\lambda}_m) \cdot \mathbf{z}_m - \boldsymbol{\lambda}_m \cdot \mathbf{u}_{\mathbf{i}(m)} \\ & - \frac{\rho}{2} \|\mathbf{z}_m - \mathbf{u}_{\mathbf{i}(m)}\|^2. \end{aligned} \quad (14)$$

The AD^3 algorithm seeks a saddle point of L_ρ by performing alternating maximization with respect to $\mathbf{z}$ and $\mathbf{u}$, followed by a gradient update of $\boldsymbol{\lambda}$. The result is shown as Algorithm 1. Like dual decomposition approaches, it repeatedly performs a *broadcast* operation (the $\mathbf{z}_m$-updates, which can be done in parallel, one constraint per "worker") and a *gather* operation (the $\mathbf{u}$- and $\boldsymbol{\lambda}$-updates). Each $\mathbf{u}$-operation can be seen as an averaged voting which takes into consideration each worker's results.

Like in the subgradient method, the $\boldsymbol{\lambda}$-updates can be regarded as price adjustments, which will affect the next round of $\mathbf{z}_m$-updates. The only difference with respect to the subgradient method (Rush et al., 2010) is that each subproblem involved in a $\mathbf{z}_m$-update also has a quadratic penalty that penalizes deviations from the previous average voting; it is this term that accelerates consensus and therefore convergence. Martins et al. (2011b) also provide stopping criteria for the iterative updates using primal and dual residuals that measure convergence; we refer the reader to that paper for details.

A key attraction of this algorithm is all the components of the declarative specification remain intact

Algorithm 1 AD^3 for Argument Identification

input:
- role-span matching scores $\mathbf{c} := \langle c(r,s) \rangle_{r,s}$,
- structural constraints $\langle \mathbf{A}_m, \mathbf{b}_m \rangle_{m=1}^{M}$,
- penalty $\rho > 0$

initialize $\mathbf{u}$ uniformly (*i.e.*, $u(r,s) = 0.5, \ \forall r, s$)
initialize each $\boldsymbol{\lambda}_m = \mathbf{0}, \ \forall m \in \{1, \ldots, M\}$
initialize $t \leftarrow 1$
repeat
  for each $m = 1, \ldots, M$ **do**
    make a $\mathbf{z}_m$-update by finding the best scoring analysis for the mth constraint, with penalties for deviating from the consensus $\mathbf{u}$:

$$\mathbf{z}_m^{t+1} \leftarrow \underset{\mathbf{A}_m \mathbf{z}_m \leq \mathbf{b}_m}{\arg\max} \ (\mathbf{c}_m + \boldsymbol{\lambda}_m) \cdot \mathbf{z}_m - \frac{\rho}{2} \|\mathbf{z}_m - \mathbf{u}_{\mathbf{i}(m)}\|^2$$

  end for
  make a $\mathbf{u}$-update by updating the consensus solution, averaging $\mathbf{z}_1, \ldots, \mathbf{z}_m$:

$$u^{t+1}(r,s) \leftarrow \frac{1}{\delta(r,s)} \sum_{m:(r,s) \in \mathbf{i}(m)} z_m^{t+1}(r,s)$$

  make a $\boldsymbol{\lambda}$-update:

$$\boldsymbol{\lambda}_m^{t+1} \leftarrow \boldsymbol{\lambda}_m^{t} - \rho(\mathbf{z}_m^{(t+1)} - \mathbf{u}_{\mathbf{i}(m)}^{(t+1)}), \quad \forall m$$

  $t \leftarrow t + 1$
until convergence.
output: relaxed primal solution $\mathbf{u}^*$ and dual solution $\boldsymbol{\lambda}^*$. If $\mathbf{u}^*$ is integer, it will encode an assignment of spans to roles. Otherwise, it will provide an upper bound of the true optimum.

in the procedural form. Each worker corresponds exactly to one constraint in the ILP, which corresponds to one linguistic constraint. There is no need to work out *when*, during the procedure, each constraint might have an effect, as in beam search.

Solving the subproblems. In a different application, Martins et al. (2011b, §4) showed how to solve each $\mathbf{z}_m$-subproblem associated with the XOR, XORWITHOUTPUT and OR factors in runtime $O(|\mathbf{i}(m)| \log |\mathbf{i}(m)|)$. The only subproblem that remains is that of the ATMOSTONE factor, to which we now turn. The problem can be transformed into that of projecting a point $(a_1, \ldots, a_k)$ onto the set

$$\mathcal{S}_m = \left\{ \mathbf{z}_m \in [0,1]^{|\mathbf{i}(m)|} \mid \sum_{j=1}^{|\mathbf{i}(m)|} z_{m,j} \leq 1 \right\}.$$

This projection can be computed as follows:

1. Clip each a_j into the interval $[0,1]$ (*i.e.*, set $a'_j = \min\{\max\{a_j, 0\}, 1\}$). If the result satisfies $\sum_{j=1}^{k} a'_j \leq 1$, then return $(a'_1, \ldots, a'_k)$.
2. Otherwise project $(a_1, \ldots, a_k)$ onto the probability simplex:

$$\left\{ \mathbf{z}_m \in [0,1]^{|\mathbf{i}(m)|} \mid \sum_{j=1}^{|\mathbf{i}(m)|} z_{m,j} = 1 \right\}.$$

   This is precisely the XOR subproblem and can be solved in time $O(|\mathbf{i}(m)| \log |\mathbf{i}(m)|)$.

Caching. As mentioned by Martins et al. (2011b), as the algorithm comes close to convergence, many subproblems become unchanged and their solutions can be cached. By caching the subproblems, we managed to reduce runtime by about 60%.

Exact decoding. Finally, it is worth recalling that AD^3, like other dual decomposition algorithms, solves a *relaxation* of the actual problem. Although we have observed that the relaxation is often tight—cf. §4—this is not always the case. Specifically, a fractional solution may be obtained, which is not interpretable as an argument, and therefore it is desirable to have a strategy to recover the exact solution. Two observations are noteworthy. First, the optimal value of the relaxed problem (Eq. 11) provides an upper bound to the original problem (Eq. 2). This is because Eq. 2 has the additional integer constraint on the variables. In particular, any feasible dual point provides an upper bound to the original problem's optimal value. Second, during execution of the AD^3 algorithm, we always keep track of a sequence of feasible dual points. Therefore, each iteration constructs tighter and tighter upper bounds. With this machinery, we have all that is necessary for implementing a branch-and-bound search that finds the exact solution of the ILP. The procedure works recursively as follows:

1. Initialize $L = -\infty$ (our best value so far).
2. Run Algorithm 1. If the solution $\mathbf{u}^*$ is integer, return $\mathbf{u}^*$ and set L to the objective value. If along the execution we obtain an upper bound less than L, then Algorithm 1 can be safely stopped and return "infeasible"—this is the *bound* part. Otherwise (if $\mathbf{u}^*$ is fractional) go to step 3.
3. Find the "most fractional" component of $\mathbf{u}^*$ (call it u_j^*) and *branch*: constrain $u_j = 0$ and go to step 2, eventually obtaining an integer solution $\mathbf{u}_0^*$ or infeasibility; and then constrain $u_j = 1$ and do the same, obtaining $\mathbf{u}_1^*$. Return the $\mathbf{u}^* \in \{\mathbf{u}_0^*, \mathbf{u}_1^*\}$ that yields the largest objective value.

Although this procedure may have worst-case exponential runtime, we found it empirically to rapidly obtain the exact solution in all test cases.

4 Experiments and Results

4.1 Dataset, Preprocessing, and Learning

In our experiments, we use FrameNet 1.5, which contains a lexicon of 877 frames and 1,068 role labels, and 78 documents with multiple predicate-argument annotations (a superset of the SemEval shared task dataset; Baker et al., 2007). We used the same split as Das and Smith (2011), with 55 documents for training (containing 19,582 frame annotations) and 23 for testing (with 4,458 annotations). We randomly selected 4,462 predicates in the training set as development data. The raw sentences in all the training and test documents were preprocessed using MXPOST (Ratnaparkhi, 1996) and the MST dependency parser (McDonald et al., 2005).

The state-of-the-art system for this task is SEMAFOR, an open source tool (Das et al., 2010a)[5] that provides a baseline benchmark for our new algorithm. We use the components of SEMAFOR as-is to define the features $\mathbf{h}$ and train the weights ψ used in the scoring function c. We also use its

[5] http://www.ark.cs.cmu.edu/SEMAFOR

heuristic mechanism to find potential spans $\mathcal{S}_t$ for a given predicate t. SEMAFOR learns weights using ℓ_2-penalized log-likelihood; we augmented its dev set-tuning procedure to tune both the regularization strength and the AD^3 penalty strength ρ. We initialize $\rho = 0.1$ and follow Martins et al. (2011b) in dynamically adjusting it. Note that we do not use SEMAFOR's automatic frame identification component in our presented experiments, as we assume that we have gold frames on each predicate. This lets us compare the different argument identification methods in a controlled fashion.

4.2 Decoding Strategies

We compare the following algorithms:

1. **Local**: this is a naïve argument identification strategy that selects the best span for each role r, according to the score function $c(r, s)$. It ignores all constraints except "uniqueness."
2. **SEMAFOR**: this strategy employs greedy beam search to eliminate overlaps between predicted arguments (Das et al., 2010b, Algorithm 1). Note that it does not try to respect the "excludes" and "requires" constraints between pairs of roles. The default size of the beam in SEMAFOR was a safe 10,000; this resulted in extremely slow decoding times. We also tried beam sizes of 100 and 2 (the latter being the smallest size that achieves the same F_1 score on the dev set as beam width 100.)
3. **CPLEX**, *LP*: this uses CPLEX to solve the relaxed LP in Eq. 11. To handle fractional $\mathbf{z}$, for each role r, we choose the best span s^*, such that $s^* = \arg\max_{s \in \mathcal{S}_r} z_{r,s}$, solving ties arbitrarily.
4. **CPLEX**, *exact*: this tackles the actual ILP (Eq. 2) with CPLEX.
5. **AD^3**, *LP*: this is the counterpart of the LP version of CPLEX, where the relaxed problem is solved using AD^3. We choose the spans for each role in the same way as in strategy 3.
6. **AD^3**, *exact*: this couples AD^3 with branch-and-bound search to get the exact integer solution.

4.3 Results

Table 1 shows performance of the different decoding strategies on the test set. We report precision, recall, and F_1 scores.[6] Since these scores do not penalize structural violations, we also report the number of overlap, "excludes," and "requires" constraints that were violated in the test set. Finally, we tabulate each setting's decoding time in seconds on the whole test set averaged over 5 runs.[7] The Local model is very fast but suffers degradation in precision and violates one constraint roughly per nine predicates. SEMAFOR used a default beam size of 10,000, which is extremely slow; a faster version of beam size 100 results in the same precision and recall values, but is 15 times faster. Beam size 2 results in slightly worse precision and recall values, but is even faster. All of these, however, result in many constraint violations. Strategies involving CPLEX and AD^3 perform similarly to each other and SEMAFOR on precision and recall, but eliminate most or all of the constraint violations. SEMAFOR with beam size 2 is 11-16 times faster than the CPLEX strategies, but is only twice as fast than AD^3, and results in significantly more structural violations. The exact algorithms are slower than the LP versions, but compared to CPLEX, AD^3 is significantly faster and has a narrower gap between its exact and LP versions. We found that relaxation was tight 99.8% of the time on the test examples.

The example in Fig. 1 is taken from our test set, and shows an instance where two roles, Partner_1 and Partner_2 share the "requires" relationship; for this example, the beam search decoder misses the Partner_2 role, which is a violation, while our AD^3 decoder identifies both arguments correctly. Note that beam search makes plenty of linguistic violations, but has precision and recall values that are marginally better than AD^3. We found that beam search, when violating many "requires" constraints, often finds one role in the pair, which increases its recall. AD^3 is sometimes more conservative in such cases, predicting neither role. A second issue, as noted in footnote 4, is that the annotations sometimes violate these constraints. Overall, we found it interesting that imposing the constraints did not have much effect on standard measures of accuracy.

[6] We use the evaluation script from SemEval 2007 shared task, modified to evaluate only the argument identification output.

[7] We used a 64-bit machine with 2 2.6GHz dual-core CPUs (*i.e.*, 4 processors in all) with a total of 8GB of RAM. The workers in AD^3 were not parallelized, while CPLEX automatically parallelized execution.

Method	P	R	F_1	Violations: Overlap	Violations: Requires	Violations: Excludes	Time in Secs.
Local	67.69	59.76	63.48	441	45	15	1.26 ± 0.01
SEMAFOR (beam = 2)	70.18	59.54	64.42	0	49	0	2.74 ± 0.10
SEMAFOR (beam = 100)	70.43	59.64	64.59	0	50	1	29.00 ± 0.25
SEMAFOR (beam = 10000)	70.43	59.64	64.59	0	50	1	440.67 ± 5.53
CPLEX, *LP*	70.34	59.43	64.43	0	1	0	32.67 ± 1.29
CPLEX, *exact*	70.31	59.45	64.43	0	0	0	43.12 ± 1.26
AD^3, *LP*	70.30	59.45	64.42	2	2	0	4.17 ± 0.01
AD^3, *exact*	70.31	59.45	64.43	0	0	0	4.78 ± 0.04

Table 1: Comparison of decoding strategies in §4.2. We evaluate in terms of precision, recall and F_1 score on a test set containing 4,458 predicates. We also compute the number of structural violations each model makes: number of overlapping arguments and violations of the "requires" and "excludes" constraints of §2. Finally decoding time (without feature computation steps) on the *whole* test set is shown in the last column averaged over 5 runs.

5 Related Work

Semantic role labeling: Most SRL systems use conventions from PropBank (Kingsbury and Palmer, 2002) and NomBank (Meyers et al., 2004), which store information about verbal and nominal predicates and corresponding symbolic and meaning-specific semantic roles. A separate line of work, including this paper, investigates SRL systems that use FrameNet conventions; while less popular, these systems, pioneered by Gildea and Jurafsky (2002), consider predicates of a wider variety of syntactic categories, use semantic frame abstractions, and employ explicit role labels. A common trait in prior work has been the use of a two-stage model that identifies arguments first, then labels them. They are treated jointly here, unlike what has typically been done in PropBank-style SRL (Màrquez et al., 2008).
Dual decomposition: Rush et al. (2010) proposed subgradient-based dual decomposition as a way of combining models which are tractable individually, but not jointly, by solving a relaxation of the original problem. This was followed by work adopting this method for syntax and translation (Koo et al., 2010; Auli and Lopez, 2011; DeNero and Macherey, 2011; Rush and Collins, 2011; Chang and Collins, 2011). Recently, Martins et al. (2011b) showed that the success of subgradient-based dual decomposition strongly relies on breaking down the original problem into a "good" decomposition, *i.e.*, one with few overlapping components. This leaves out many declarative constrained problems, for which such a good decomposition is not readily available. For those, Martins et al. (2011b) proposed the AD^3 algorithm, which retains the modularity of previous methods, but can handle thousands of small overlapping components.
Exact decoding: This paper contributes an exact branch-and-bound technique wrapped around AD^3. A related line of research is that of Rush and Collins (2011), who proposed a tightening procedure for dual decomposition, which can be seen as a cutting plane method (another popular approach in combinatorial optimization).

6 Conclusion

We presented a novel algorithm for incorporating declarative linguistic knowledge as constraints in shallow semantic parsing. It outperforms a naïve baseline that is oblivious to the constraints. Furthermore, it is significantly faster than a decoder employing a state-of-the-art proprietary solver, and less than twice as slow as beam search, which is inexact and does not respect all linguistic constraints. Our method is easily amenable to the inclusion of more constraints, which would require minimal programming effort. Our implementation of AD^3 within SEMAFOR will be publicly released at `http://www.ark.cs.cmu.edu/SEMAFOR`.

Acknowledgments

We thank the three anonymous reviewers for their valuable feedback. This material is based upon work supported by NSF grant IIS-1054319, Google's support of the Wordly Knowledge Project, a FCT/ICTI grant through the CMU-Portugal Program, and by Priberam, through the Discooperio project, contract 2011/18501 of the EU/FEDER program.

References

M. Auli and A. Lopez. 2011. A comparison of loopy belief propagation and dual decomposition for integrated ccg supertagging and parsing. In *Proc. of ACL*.

C. Baker, M. Ellsworth, and K. Erk. 2007. SemEval-2007 Task 19: Frame semantic structure extraction. In *Proc. of SemEval*.

Y.-W. Chang and Michael Collins. 2011. Exact decoding of Phrase-Based translation models through lagrangian relaxation. In *Proc. of EMNLP*. Association for Computational Linguistics.

D. Chen, N. Schneider, D. Das, and N. A. Smith. 2010. SEMAFOR: Frame argument resolution with log-linear models. In *Proc. of SemEval*.

D. Das and N. A. Smith. 2011. Semi-supervised frame-semantic parsing for unknown predicates. In *Proc. of ACL*.

D. Das, N. Schneider, D. Chen, and N. A. Smith. 2010a. Probabilistic frame-semantic parsing. In *Proc. of NAACL-HLT*.

D. Das, N. Schneider, D. Chen, and N. A. Smith. 2010b. SEMAFOR 1.0: a probabilistic frame-semantic parser. Technical report, CMU-LTI-10-001.

J. DeNero and K. Macherey. 2011. Model-based aligner combination using dual decomposition. In *Proc. of ACL*.

C. J. Fillmore, C. R. Johnson, and M. R.L. Petruck. 2003. Background to FrameNet. *International Journal of Lexicography*, 16(3).

C. J. Fillmore. 1982. Frame Semantics. In *Linguistics in the Morning Calm*. Hanshin.

M. Gerber and J. Y. Chai. 2010. Beyond nombank: A study of implicit arguments for nominal predicates. In *ACL*.

D. Gildea and D. Jurafsky. 2002. Automatic labeling of semantic roles. *Computational Linguistics*, 28(3).

R. Johansson and P. Nugues. 2007. LTH: semantic structure extraction using nonprojective dependency trees. In *Proc. of SemEval*.

P. Kingsbury and M. Palmer. 2002. From TreeBank to PropBank. In *Proc. of LREC*.

N. Komodakis, N. Paragios, and G. Tziritas. 2007. MRF optimization via dual decomposition: Message-passing revisited. In *ICCV*.

T. Koo, A. M. Rush, M. Collins, T. Jaakkola, and D. Sontag. 2010. Dual decomposition for parsing with non-projective head automata. In *Proc. of EMNLP*.

L. Màrquez, X. Carreras, K. C. Litkowski, and S. Stevenson. 2008. Semantic role labeling: an introduction to the special issue. *Computational Linguistics*, 34(2).

A. F. T. Martins, N. A. Smith, E. P. Xing, M. A. T. Figueiredo, and P. M. Q. Aguiar. 2010. Turbo parsers: Dependency parsing by approximate variational inference. In *EMNLP*.

A. F. T. Martins, M. A. T. Figueiredo, P. M. Q. Aguiar, N. A. Smith, and E. P. Xing. 2011a. An augmented Lagrangian approach to constrained MAP inference. In *Proc. of ICML*.

A F. T. Martins, N. A. Smith, P. M. Q. Aguiar, and M. A. T. Figueiredo. 2011b. Dual decomposition with many overlapping components. In *Proc. of EMNLP*.

R. McDonald, K. Crammer, and F. Pereira. 2005. Online large-margin training of dependency parsers. In *Proc. of ACL*.

A. Meyers, R. Reeves, C. Macleod, R. Szekely, V. Zielinska, B. Young, and R. Grishman. 2004. The NomBank project: An interim report. In *Proc. of NAACL/HLT Workshop on Frontiers in Corpus Annotation*.

V. Punyakanok, D. Roth, W.-T. Yih, and D. Zimak. 2004. Semantic role labeling via integer linear programming inference. In *Proc. of COLING*.

V. Punyakanok, D. Roth, and W Yih. 2008. The importance of syntactic parsing and inference in semantic role labeling. *Computational Linguistics*, 34:257–287.

A. Ratnaparkhi. 1996. A maximum entropy model for part-of-speech tagging. In *Proc. of EMNLP*.

A. M. Rush and M. Collins. 2011. Exact decoding of syntactic translation models through lagrangian relaxation. In *Proc. of ACL*.

A. M. Rush, D. Sontag, M. Collins, and T. Jaakkola. 2010. On dual decomposition and linear programming relaxations for natural language processing. In *Proceedings of EMNLP*.

D. Smith and J. Eisner. 2008. Dependency parsing by belief propagation. In *EMNLP*.

K. Toutanova, A. Haghighi, and C. Manning. 2005. Joint learning improves semantic role labeling. In *Proc. of ACL*.

Aligning Predicate Argument Structures in Monolingual Comparable Texts: A New Corpus for a New Task

Michael Roth and **Anette Frank**
Department of Computational Linguistics
Heidelberg University
Germany
{mroth,frank}@cl.uni-heidelberg.de

Abstract

Discourse coherence is an important aspect of natural language that is still understudied in computational linguistics. Our aim is to learn factors that constitute coherent discourse from data, with a focus on how to realize predicate-argument structures (PAS) in a model that exceeds the sentence level. In particular, we aim to study the case of non-realized arguments as a coherence inducing factor. This task can be broken down into two subtasks. The first aligns predicates across comparable texts, admitting partial argument structure correspondence. The resulting alignments and their contexts can then be used for developing a coherence model for argument realization.

This paper introduces a large corpus of comparable monolingual texts as a prerequisite for approaching this task, including an evaluation set with manual predicate alignments. We illustrate the potential of this new resource for the empirical investigation of discourse coherence phenomena. Initial experiments on the task of predicting predicate alignments across text pairs show promising results. Our findings establish that manual and automatic predicate alignments across texts are feasible and that our data set holds potential for empirical research into a variety of discourse-related tasks.

1 Introduction

Research in the fields of discourse and pragmatics has led to a number of theories that try to explain and formalize the effect of discourse coherence inducing elements either locally or globally. For example, *Centering Theory* (Grosz et al., 1995) provides a framework to model local coherence by relating the choice of referring expressions to the salience of an entity at certain stages of a discourse. An example for a global coherence model would be *Rhetorical Structure Theory* (Mann and Thompson, 1988), which addresses overall text structure by means of *coherence relations* between the parts of a text.

In addition to such theories, computational approaches have been proposed to capture corresponding phenomena empirically. A prominent example is the entity-based model by Barzilay and Lapata (2008). In their approach, local coherence is modeled by the observation of sentence-to-sentence realization patterns of individual entities. The learned model reflects a key idea from Centering Theory, namely that adjacent sentences in a coherent discourse are likely to involve the same entities.

One shortcoming of Barzilay and Lapata's model (and extensions of it) is that it only investigates overt realization patterns in terms of grammatical functions. These functions reflect explicit realizations of predicate argument structures (PAS), but they do not capture the full range of salience factors. In particular, the model does not reflect the importance of discourse entities that fill core roles of the predicate, but that remain implicit in the predicate's local argument structure. We develop a specific set-up that allows us to further investigate the factors that govern such a null-instantiations of argument positions (cf. Fillmore et al. (2003)), as a special form of coherence inducing element in discourse. We henceforth refer to such cases as *non-realized arguments*.

Our main hypothesis is that context specific realization patterns for PAS can be automatically learned from a semantically parsed corpus of comparable text pairs. This assumption builds on the success of previous research, where comparable and parallel texts have been exploited for a range of related learning tasks, e.g., unsupervised discourse segmentation (Barzilay and Lee, 2004) and bootstrapping semantic analyzers (Titov and Kozhevnikov, 2010).

For our purposes, we are interested in finding corresponding PAS across comparable texts that are known to talk about the same events, and hence involve the same set of underlying event participants. By aligning predicates in such texts, we can investigate the factors that determine discourse coherence in the realization patterns for the involved participants. As a first step towards this overall goal, we describe the construction of a resource that contains more than 160,000 document pairs that are known to talk about the same events and participants. Example (1), extracted from our corpus of aligned texts, illustrates this point: Both texts report on the same event, in particular the (aligned) event of locating victims in an avalanche. While (1.a) explicitly talks about the location of this event, the role remains implicit in the second sentence of (1.b), given that it can be recovered from the preceding sentence. In fact, realization of this argument would impede the fluency of discourse by being overly repetitive.

(1) a. ...The official said that [no bodies]$_{\text{Arg1}}$ had been recovered [from the avalanches]$_{\text{Arg2}}$ which occurred late Friday in the Central Asian country near the Afghan border some 300 kilometers (185 miles) southeast of the capital Dushanbe.

b. Three other victims were trapped *in an avalanche* in the village of Khichikh. [None of the victims bodies]$_{\text{Arg1}}$ have been found [ ]$_{\text{Argm-loc}}$.

Our aim is to identify comparable predications across pairs of texts, and to study the coherence factors that determine the realization patterns of argument structures (including roles that remain implicit) in discourse. This can be achieved by considering the full set of arguments that can be recovered from the aligned predications, including both core and non-core (i.e. adjunct) roles. However, in order to relate PAS across texts to one another, we first need to identify corresponding predicates.

In this paper, we construct a large data set to be used for the induction of a coherence model for argument structure realization and related tasks. We discuss the prospects of this data set for the study of coherence factors in PAS realization. Finally, we present first results on the initial task of *predicate alignment* across comparable monolingual texts.

The remainder of this paper is structured as follows: In Section 2, we discuss previous work in related tasks. Section 3 introduces the new task together with a description of how we prepared a suitable data set. Section 4 discusses the potential benefits of the created resource in more detail. Section 5 presents experiments on predicate alignment using this new data set and outlines first results. Finally, we conclude in Section 6 and discuss future work.

2 Related Work

Data sets comprising parallel texts have been released for various different tasks, including paraphrase extraction and statistical machine translation (SMT). While corpora for SMT are typically multilingual (e.g. Europarl, Koehn (2005)), there also exist monolingual parallel corpora that consist of multiple translations of one text into the same language (Barzilay and McKeown, 2001; Huang et al., 2002, inter alia). Each translation can provide alternative verbalizations of the same events but little variation can be observed in context, as the overall discourse remains the same. A higher degree of variation can be found in the Microsoft Research Paraphrase Corpus (e.g. MSRPC, Dolan and Brockett (2005)), which consists of paraphrases automatically extracted from different sources. In the MSRPC, however, original discourse contexts are not provided for each sentence. In contrast to truly parallel monolingual corpora, there also exist a range of comparable corpora that have been used for tasks such as (multi-document) summarization (McKeown and Radev, 1995, inter alia). Corpora for this task are collected manually and hence are rather small. Our work presents a method to automatically construct a large corpus of text pairs describing the same underlying events.

In this novel corpus, we identify common events across texts and investigate the argument structures that were realized in each context to establish a coherent discourse. Different aspects related to this setting have been studied in previous work. For example, Filippova and Strube (2007) and Cahill and Riester (2009) examine factors that determine constituent order and Belz et al. (2009) study the conditions for the use of different types of referring expressions. The specific set-up we examine allows us to further investigate the factors that govern the *non-realization* of an argument position, as a special form of coherence inducing element in discourse. As in the aforementioned work, we are specifically interested in the generation of coherent discourses (e.g. for summarization). Yet, our work also complements research in discourse analysis. A recent example for such work is the Semeval 2010 Task 10 (Ruppenhofer et al., 2010), which aims at linking events and their participants in discourse. The provided data sets for this task, however, are critically small (438 train and 525 test sentences). Eventually, the corpus we present in this paper could also be beneficial for data-driven approaches to role linking in discourse.

3 A Corpus for Aligning Predications across Comparable Texts

Our aim is to construct a corpus of comparable texts that can be assumed to be about the same events, but include variation in textual presentation. This requirement fits well with the news domain, for which we can trace varying textual sources for the same underlying events.

The English Gigaword Fifth Edition (Parker et al., 2011) corpus (henceforth just *Gigaword*) is one of the largest corpus collections for English. It comprises a total of 9.8 million newswire articles from seven distinct sources. For construction of our corpus we make use of all combinations of agency pairs in Gigaword.

3.1 Corpus Creation

In order to extract pairs of articles describing the same news event, we implemented the pairwise similarity method presented by Wubben et al. (2009). The method is based on measuring word overlap in news headlines, weighting each word by its TF*IDF score to give a higher impact to words occurring with lower frequency. As our focus is to provide a high-quality data set for predicate alignment and follow-up tasks, we impose an additional date constraint to favor precision over recall. We apply this constraint by requiring a pair of articles to be published within a two-day time frame in order to be considered as pairs of comparable news items.

Following this two-step procedure, we extracted a total of 167,728 document pairs, an overall collection of 50 million word tokens. We inspected about 100 randomly selected document pairs and found only two of them describing different events. This is in line with the results of Wubben et al. who reported a precision of 93% without explicitly imposing a date constraint. Overall, we found that most text pairs share a high degree of similarity and vary only in length (up to 7.564 words with a mean and median of 301 and 213 words, respectively) and detail. Closer examination of a development set of 10 document pairs (described below) revealed that we can indeed find multiple cases where roles are not locally filled in predicate argument structures. We show instances of this phenomenon, in which aligned PAS help to resolve implicit role references, in Section 4.

3.2 Gold Standard Annotation

We pre-processed all texts using MATE tools (Bohnet, 2010; Björkelund et al., 2010), a pipeline of natural language processing modules including a state-of-the-art semantic role labeler that computes Prop/NomBank annotations (Palmer et al., 2005; Meyers et al., 2008). The output was used to provide pre-labeled verbal and nominal predicates for annotation. We asked two students[1] to tag alignments of corresponding predicates in 70 text pairs derived from the created corpus. All document pairs were randomly chosen from the AFP and APW sections of Gigaword with the constraint that each text consists of 100 to 300 words[2]. We chose this constraint as longer text pairs contain a high number of unrelated predicates, making this task difficult to manage for the annotators.

Sure and possible links. Following standard practice in word alignment tasks (cf. Cohn et al. (2008))

[1]Both annotators are students in Computational Linguistics, one undergraduate (A) and one postgraduate (B) student.

[2]This constraint is satisfied by 75.3% of the documents.

the annotators were instructed to distinguish between *sure* (S) and *possible* (P) alignments, depending on how certainly, in their opinion, two predicates (including their arguments) describe the same event. The following examples show cases of predicate pairings marked as sure (S link) (2) and as possible (P link) alignments (3):

(2) a. The regulator ruled on September 27 that Nasdaq too was qualified to bid for OMX [...][3]

b. The authority [...] had already approved a similar application by Nasdaq.[4]

(3) a. Myanmar's military government said earlier this year it has released some 220 political prisoners [...][5]

b. The government has been regularly releasing members of Suu Kyi's National League for Democracy party [...][6]

Replaceability. As a guideline for deciding whether two predicates are to be aligned, the annotators were given the following two criteria: 1) whether the predicates are replaceable in a given context and 2) whether they share (potentially implicit) arguments.

Missing context. In case one text does not provide enough context to decide whether two predicates in the paired documents refer to the same event, an alignment should not be marked as sure.

Similar predicates. Annotators were told explicitly that sure links can be used even if two predicates are semantically different but have the same meaning in context. Example (4) illustrates such a case:

(4) a. The volcano roared back to life two weeks ago.

b. It began erupting last month.

1-to-1 vs. n-to-m. We asked the annotators to find as many 1-to-1 correspondences as possible and to prefer 1-to-1 matches over n-to-m alignments. In case of multiple mentions (cf. Example (5)) of the same event, we further asked the annotators to provide only one S link per predicate and mark remaining cases as P links. If possible, the S link should be used for the pairing of PAS with the highest information overlap (e.g. "perform$_{a3}$"–"perform$_{b2}$" in (5)). If there is no difference in information overlap, the predicate pair that occurs first in both texts should be marked as a sure alignment (e.g. "sing$_{a1}$"–"perform$_{b1}$" in (5)). The intuition behind this guideline is that the first mention introduces the actual event while later mentions just (co-)refer or add further information.

(5) a. Susan Boyle said she will sing$_{a1}$ in front of Britain's Prince Charles (...) "It's going to be a privilege to be performing$_{a2}$ before His Royal Highness," the singer said (...) British copyright laws will allow her to perform$_{a3}$ the hit in front of the prince and his wife.[7]

b. British singing sensation Susan Boyle is going to perform$_{b1}$ for Prince Charles (...) The show star will perform$_{b2}$ her version of Perfect Day for Charles and his wife Camilla.[8]

3.3 Development and Evaluation Data Sets

In total, the annotators (A/B) aligned 487/451 sure and 221/180 possible alignments with a Kappa score (Cohen, 1960) of 0.86. Following Brockett (2007), we computed agreement on labeled annotations, including unaligned predicate pairs as an additional *null* category. For the construction of a gold standard, we merged the alignments from both annotators by taking the union of all possible alignments and the intersection of all sure alignments. Cases which involved a sure alignment on which the annotators disagreed were resolved in a group discussion with the first author. We split the final corpus into a development set of 10 document pairs and a test set of 60 document pairs.

Table 1 summarizes information about the resulting annotations in the development and test sets, respectively. It gives information about the paired texts (PT): number of predicates marked in preprocessing (nouns and verbs), the set of manual predicate alignments (PA): sure and possible, as well as information about whether they were annotated for predicates of the same PoS (N,V) or lemma.

Finally, as a rough indicator for diverging argument structures captured in the annotated align-

[3]Source document ID: AFP_ENG_20071112.0235
[4]Source document ID: APW_ENG_20071112.0645
[5]Source document ID: AFP_ENG_20020301.0041
[6]Source document ID: APW_ENG_20020301.0132
[7]Source document ID: AFP_ENG_20101102.0028
[8]Source document ID: APW_ENG_20101102.0923

	Dev Set	Test Set
nb. of PT	10	60
nb. marked predicates	395	3,453
nb. marked nouns	168	1,531
nb. marked verbs	227	1,922
sure PA/PT: avg. (total)	3.9 (35)	7.4 (446)
poss. PA/PT: avg. (total)	4.8 (43)	6.0 (361)
same PoS in PA (N/V)	88.5% (24/42)	82.4% (242/423)
same lemma in PA	53.8% (42)	47.5% (383)
unequal nb. args in PA	30.8% (24)	39.7% (320)

Table 1: Information on Paired Texts (PT) and manual Predicate Alignments (PA) in development and test set

ments, we analyzed the number of PAs that involve a different number of arguments.

4 Potential of Aggregation

In this section, we analyze the predicate alignments in our manually annotated data set, to illustrate the potential of aggregating corresponding PAS across comparable texts.

We are particularly interested in cases of non-realization of arguments, and thus take a closer look at alignments involving roles that are not filled in their local PAS. We extract a subset of such cases by extracting pairs of aligned predicates that contain a different number of realized arguments. We deliberately focus on the more restricted core roles in this exposition, but will consider the full range of roles for developing a comprehensive coherence model for argument structure realization.[9] Our selection of alignment examples is drawn from the development set.

The following excerpts are from a pair of comparable texts describing a news report on Chadian refugees crossing into Nigeria:

(6) a. The Chadians said [they]$_{\text{Arg0}}$ had fled [ ]$_{\text{Arg1}}$ in fear of their lives.[10]

b. The United Nations says [some 20,000 refugees]$_{\text{Arg0}}$ have fled [into Cameroon]$_{\text{Arg1}}$.[11]

In both examples, the Arg0 role of the predicate fled is filled, but Arg1 has not been realized in (6.a). Note that the sentence is still part of a coherent discourse as fillers for the omitted role can be inferred from the preceding discourse context. Aggregating the aligned PAS presents an effective means to identify such appropriate fillers.

Example (7) presents another text pair, reporting on elections in Iraq, in which role realizations differ for the same hold event.

(7) a. He said (...) [elections]$_{\text{Arg1}}$ will be held [ ]$_{\text{Arg0}}$ to form a government.[12]

b. The president (...) said Wednesday [his country]$_{\text{Arg0}}$ will definitely hold [elections]$_{\text{Arg1}}$ in 2004.[13]

Here, the changes in argument realization go along with a diathesis alternation, while the pair in (6) exemplifies a case of lexical licensing for omission of a role.[14]

Example (8.b) illustrates a case in which the Arg1 of a decline event is involved in a preceding predication (*rise*) and thus has already been overtly realized. The constructional properties of the subsequent predicates *decline* as a participle and noun, respectively, are more adverse to overt realization of the Arg1 role. Suppression of Arg1 in such cases yields a much more coherent discourse as compared to their realization. This is brought out by the constructed examples in (a'/b'), which are both highly repetitive.

(8) a. The closely watched [index]$_{\text{Arg1}}$ rose to 93.7 ... after declining for ... months.[15]

a'. ? ... after the index declining for ... months.

b. Consumer confidence rose ... following three months of dramatic decline [ ]$_{\text{Arg1}}$.[16]

b'. ? ... following three months of dramatic decline [of consumer confidence]$_{\text{Arg1}}$.

As showcased by the previous examples, the decision on whether to realize a role filler in a local PAS can be rather complex. Obviously, the

[9] Accordingly, the number of PAs involving diverging role realizations in Table 1 is strongly underestimated.

[10] Source document ID: AFP_ENG_20080205.0230

[11] Source document ID: APW_ENG_20080206.0766

[12] Source document ID: AFP_ENG_20031015.0353

[13] Source document ID: APW_ENG_20031015.0236

[14] These different configurations are termed *constructional* vs. *lexical licensors* in the SemEval 2010 Task 10 (Ruppenhofer et al., 2010).

[15] Source document ID: AFP_ENG_20011228.0365

[16] Source document ID: APW_ENG_20011228.0572

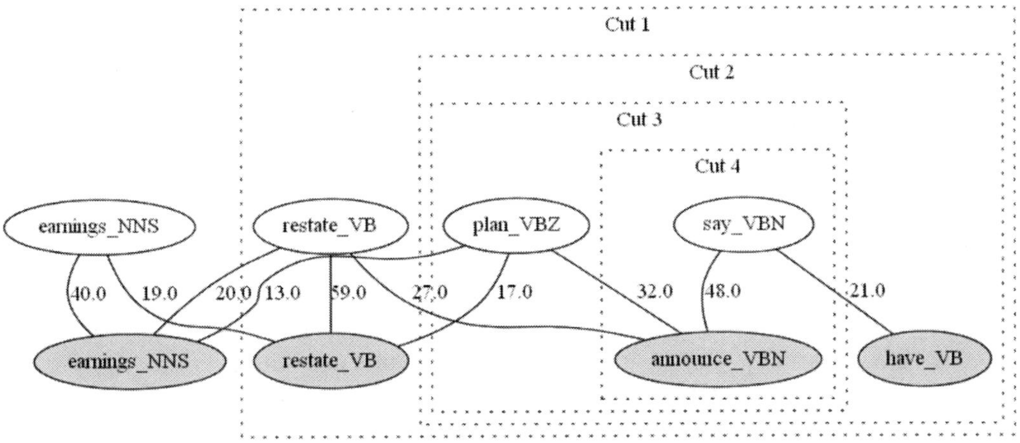

Figure 1: The predicates of two sentences (white: "The company has said it plans to restate its earnings for 2000 through 2002."; gray: "The company had announced in January that it would have to restate earnings (...)") from the Microsoft Research Paragraph Corpus are aligned by computing clusters with minimum cuts.

above instances do not provide exhaustive information for grounding all such decisions. A comprehensive model of discourse coherence will need to estimate the argument realization potential of different predicates and roles from larger corpora. But as can be seen from the discussed examples, training a semantic model with suitable discourse features on all predicate argument structures in a large corpus such as ours will provide indicative range of realization decisions.

5 Experiments

This section presents an initial experiment using an unsupervised graph-based clustering method for the task of aligning predicates across comparable texts. We describe the alignment model, two baselines as well as the experimental setting and results.[17]

5.1 Clustering Model

Similarity Measures. We define a number of similarity measures between predicates, which make use of complementary lexical information. One source of information are token-based frequency counts, which we compute over all documents from the AFP and APW sections of Gigaword[18]. Given two lemmatized predicates and their respective PAS, we employ the following four similarity measures: Similarity in WordNet ($\mathbf{sim_{WN}}$) and VerbNet ($\mathbf{sim_{VN}}$), distributional similarity ($\mathbf{sim_{Dist}}$) and bag-of-word similarity of arguments ($\mathbf{sim_{Args}}$). The first three measures are type-based, whereas the latter is token-based.

Graph Representation. The input for graph clustering is a bi-partite graph representation for pairs of texts to be predicate-aligned. In this graph, each node represents a PAS that was assigned during preprocessing (cf. Section 3). Edges are inserted between pairs of predicates that are from two distinct texts. A weight is assigned to each edge by a combination of the introduced similarity measures.

Clustering algorithm. The graph clustering method uses minimum cuts (or *Mincuts*) in order to partition the bipartite text graph into clusters of aligned predicates. Each Mincut operation divides a graph into two disjoint sub-graphs, such that the sum of weights of removed edges will be minimal. As the goal is to induce clusters consisting of pairs of similar predicates, a maximum number of two nodes per cluster is set as stopping criterion. We apply Mincut recursively to the input graph and resulting sub-graphs until we reach the stopping criterion. Figure 1 shows an example of a graph clustered by the Mincut approach.

5.2 Setting

We perform evaluations of the graph-based alignment model (henceforth called **Clustering**) on the

[17]The technicalities of this model, including detailed definitions of the similarity measures, are described elsewhere (manuscript, under submission).

[18]These sections make up 56.6% of documents in Gigaword.

task of inducing predicate alignments across comparable monolingual texts. We evaluate on the manually annotated gold alignments in the test data set described in Section 3.2.

Parameter Tuning. As the graph representation becomes rather inefficient to handle using edges between all predicate pairs, we use the development set of 10 text pairs to estimate a threshold for adding edges. We found the best similarity threshold to be an edge weight of 2.5. Note that the edge weights are calculated as a weighted linear combination of four different similarity measures. Subsequently, we also tune the weighting scheme for similarity measures on the development set. We found the best performing combination of weights to be 0.09, 0.19, 0.48 and 0.24 for $\mathbf{sim_{WN}}$, $\mathbf{sim_{VN}}$, $\mathbf{sim_{Dist}}$ and $\mathbf{sim_{Args}}$, respectively.

Baselines. A simple baseline for this task is to align all predicates whose lemmas are identical (**SameLemma**). As a more sophisticated baseline, we make use of alignment tools commonly used in statistical machine translation (SMT). We train our own word alignment model using the state-of-the-art tool Berkeley Aligner (Liang et al., 2006). As word alignment tools require pairs of sentences as input, we first extract paraphrases for this baseline using a re-implementation of the paraphrase detection system by Wan et al. (2006). In the following sections, we abbreviate this model as **WordAlign**.

5.3 Results

Following Cohn et al. (2008) we measure precision as the number of predicted alignments also annotated in the gold standard divided by the total number of predictions. Recall is measured as the number of correctly predicted *sure* alignments devided by the total number of sure alignments in the gold standard. We subsequently compute the F_1-score as the harmonic mean between precision and recall.

Table 2 presents the results for our model and the two baselines. From all four approaches, **WordAlign** performs worst. We identify two main reasons for this: On the one hand, the paraphrase detection does not perform perfectly. Hence, the extracted sentence pairs do not always contain gold alignments. On the other hand, even sentence pairs that contain gold alignments are generally less parallel compared to a typical SMT setting, which makes them harder to align.

	Precision	Recall	F1
WordAlign	19.7%	15.2%	17.2%
SameLemma	**40.3%**	**60.3%**	**48.3%**
Clustering	**59.7%**	50.7%	**54.8%**

Table 2: Results for all models on our test set; significant improvements (p<0.005) over the results given in each previous line are marked in bold face.

We observe that the majority of all sure alignments (60.3%) can be retrieved by applying the **SameLemma** model, yet at a low precision (40.3%). While the **Clustering** model only recalls 50.7% of all cases, it clearly outperforms **SameLemma** in terms of precision (+19.4% points), an important factor for us as we plan to use the alignments in subsequent tasks. With 54.8%, **Clustering** also achieves the best overall F_1-score. We computed statistical significance of result differences with a paired t-test (Cohen, 1995), yielding significance at the 99.5% level for precision and F_1-score.

5.4 Analysis of Results

We perform an analysis of the output of the **Clustering** model on the development set to categorize correct and incorrect alignment decisions.[19] In total, the model missed 13 out of 35 sure alignments (*Type I errors*) and predicted 23 alignments not annotated in the gold standard (*Type II errors*). Six Type I errors (46%) occurred when the lemma of an affected predicate occurred more than once in a text and the model missed the correct link. Vice versa, we find 18 Type II errors (78%) that were made because of a high predicate similarity despite low argument overlap. An example is given in (9).

(9) a. The US alert (...) followed intelligence <u>reports</u> that ...[20]

b. The Foreign Ministry <u>announcement</u> called on Japanese citizens to be cautious ...[21]

While argument overlap itself can be low even for correct alignments, the results clearly indicate that

[19] We decided to leave the test set untouched for further experiments. Due to parameter tuning, the results on the development set also provide us with an upper bound of the proposed model.

[20] Source document ID: AFP_ENG_20101004.0367

[21] Source document ID: APW_ENG_20101004.0207

a better integration of context is necessary: Example (10.a) illustrates a case in which the agent of a warning event is not realized. Here, contextual information is required to correctly align it to one of the warning events in (10.b). This involves inference beyond the local PAS.

(10) a. The US alert (...) is one step down from a full $[\text{travel}]_{\text{Arg1}}$ warning $[\ ]_{\text{Arg0}}$.[20]

b. Japan has issued a travel alert ...(which) follows similar warnings [from American and British $\text{authorities}]_{\text{Arg0}}$. (...) An official said it was highly unusual for $[\text{Tokyo}]_{\text{Arg0}}$ to issue such a warning ...[21]

On the positive side, **Clustering** achieves a precision of 61.4% and a recall of 65.7% on the development set. Example (11) shows a correctly aligned PAS pair that involves non-realized arguments:

(11) a. ...the Governing Council has established $[\text{a committee}]_{\text{Arg0}}$ to draft $[\text{a constitution}]_{\text{Arg1}}$.[22]

b. A .. resolution calls on the Governing Council for elections and the drafting $[\ ]_{\text{Arg0}}$ $[\text{of a new constitution}]_{\text{Arg1}}$.[23]

In (11.a), the follow-up sentences will refer back to the committee that will draft the new Iraqi constitution, hence the institution has to be introduced in the discourse at this point. In contrast, excerpt (11.b) is the last sentence of a news report. Since it presents a summary, introducing new (omissible) entities at this point would not concord with general coherence principles.

6 Conclusion

In this paper, we presented a novel corpus of comparable texts that provides full discourse contexts for alternative verbalizations. The motivation for the construction of this corpus is to acquire empirical data for studying discourse coherence factors related to argument structure realization. A special phenomenon we are interested in are discourse-related factors that license the omission of argument roles.

Our data set satisfies two conditions that are essential for the purported task: the texts are about the same events and constitute alternative verbalizations. Selected from the Gigaword corpus, the documents pertain to the news domain, and satisfy the further constraint that we have access to the full surrounding discourse context. The constructed corpus could thus be profitable for a range of other tasks that need to investigate factors for knowledge aggregation, such as summarization, or inference in discourse, such as textual entailment.

In total, we derived more than 160,000 document pairs from all pairwise combinations of newswire sources in the English Gigaword Fifth Edition. Using a subset of these pairs, we constructed a development and an evaluation data set with gold alignments that relate predications with (possibly partial) PAS correspondence. We established that the annotation task, while difficult, can be performed with good inter-annotator agreement (κ at 0.86).

We presented first experiments on the task of automatically predicting predicate alignments. This step is essential to gather empirical evidence of different PAS realizations for the same event, given varying discourse contexts. Analysis of the data shows that the aligned predications capture a wide variety of sources and variations of coherence effects, including constructional, lexical and discourse phenomena.

In future work, we will enhance our model by incorporating more refined semantic similarity measures including discourse-based criteria for establishing cross-document alignments. Given that our data set includes sets of aligned documents from several newswire sources, we will explore transitivity constraints across multiple document pairs in order to further enhance the precision of the alignment model. We will then proceed to the ultimate aim of our work: the development of a coherence model for argument structure realization, including the design of an appropriate task and evaluation setting.

Acknowledgements

We are grateful to the Landesgraduiertenförderung Baden-Württemberg for funding within the research initiative "Coherence in language processing" of Heidelberg University. We thank Danny Rehl and Lukas Funk for annotation and Kathrin Spreyer, Tae-Gil Noh and Carina Silberer for helpful discussion.

[22] Source document ID: AFP_ENG_20031015.0353

[23] Source document ID: APW_ENG_20031015.0236.

References

Regina Barzilay and Mirella Lapata. 2008. Modeling local coherence: An entity-based approach. *Computational Linguistics*, 34(1):1–34.

Regina Barzilay and Lillian Lee. 2004. Catching the drift: Probabilistic content models, with applications to generation and summarization. In *Proceedings of the Human Language Technology Conference of the North American Chapter of the Association for Computational Linguistics,* Boston, Mass., 2–7 May 2004, pages 113–120.

Regina Barzilay and Kathleen R. McKeown. 2001. Extracting paraphrases from a parallel corpus. In *Proceedings of the 39th Annual Meeting of the Association for Computational Linguistics,* Toulouse, pages 50–57.

Anja Belz, Eric Kow, Jette Viethen, and Albert Gatt. 2009. The grec main subject reference generation challenge 2009: overview and evaluation results. In *Proceedings of the 2009 Workshop on Language Generation and Summarisation*, pages 79–87.

Anders Björkelund, Bernd Bohnet, Love Hafdell, and Pierre Nugues. 2010. A high-performance syntactic and semantic dependency parser. In *Coling 2010: Demonstration Volume*, pages 33–36, Beijing, China, August. Coling 2010 Organizing Committee.

Bernd Bohnet. 2010. Top accuracy and fast dependency parsing is not a contradiction. In *Proceedings of the 23rd International Conference on Computational Linguistics (Coling 2010)*, pages 89–97, Beijing, China, August. Coling 2010 Organizing Committee.

Chris Brockett. 2007. *Aligning the RTE 2006 Corpus*. Microsoft Research.

Aoife Cahill and Arndt Riester. 2009. Incorporating information status into generation ranking. In *Proceedings of the Joint Conference of the 47th Annual Meeting of the ACL and the 4th International Joint Conference on Natural Language Processing of the AFNLP*, pages 817–825, Suntec, Singapore, August. Association for Computational Linguistics.

Jacob Cohen. 1960. A coefficient of agreement for nominal scales. *Educational and Psychological Measurement*, 20:37–46.

Paul R. Cohen. 1995. *Empirical methods for artificial intelligence*. MIT Press, Cambridge, MA, USA.

Trevor Cohn, Chris Callison-Burch, and Mirella Lapata. 2008. Constructing Corpora for Development and Evaluation of Paraphrase Systems. 34(4).

William B. Dolan and Chris Brockett. 2005. Automatically constructing a corpus of sentential paraphrases. In *Proceedings of the Third International Workshop on Paraphrasing*.

Katja Filippova and Michael Strube. 2007. Generating constituent order in German clauses. In *Proceedings of the 45th Annual Meeting of the Association for Computational Linguistics,* Prague, Czech Republic, 23–30 June 2007, pages 320–327.

Charles J. Fillmore, Christopher R. Johnson, and Miriam R.L. Petruck. 2003. Background to FrameNet. *International Journal of Lexicography*, 16.3:235–250.

Barbara J. Grosz, Aravind K. Joshi, and Scott Weinstein. 1995. Centering: A framework for modeling the local coherence of discourse. *Computational Linguistics*, 21(2):203–225.

Shudong Huang, David Graff, and George Doddington. 2002. *Multiple-Translation Chinese Corpus*. Linguistic Data Consortium, Philadelphia.

Philipp Koehn, 2005. *Europarl: A parallel corpus for statistical machine translation*, volume 5, pages 79–86.

Percy Liang, Benjamin Taskar, and Dan Klein. 2006. Alignment by agreement. In *North American Association for Computational Linguistics (NAACL)*, pages 104–111.

William C. Mann and Sandra A. Thompson. 1988. Rhetorical structure theory. Toward a functional theory of text organization. *Text*, 8(3):243–281.

Kathleen R. McKeown and Dragomir Radev. 1995. Generating summaries of multiple news articles. In *Proceedings of the 18th Annual International ACM-SIGIR Conference on Research and Development in Information Retrieval,* Seattle, Wash., 9–13 July 1995, pages 74–82. Reprinted in *Advances in Automatic Text Summarization*, Mani, I. and Maybury, M.T. (Eds.), Cambridge, Mass.: MIT Press, 1999, pp.381-389.

Adam Meyers, Ruth Reeves, and Catherine Macleod. 2008. *NomBank v1.0*. Linguistic Data Consortium, Philadelphia.

Martha Palmer, Daniel Gildea, and Paul Kingsbury. 2005. The proposition bank: An annotated corpus of semantic roles. *Computational Linguistics*, 31(1):71–105.

Robert Parker, David Graff, Jumbo Kong, Ke Chen, and Kazuaki Maeda. 2011. *English Gigaword Fifth Edition*. Linguistic Data Consortium, Philadelphia.

Josef Ruppenhofer, Caroline Sporleder, Roser Morante, Collin Baker, and Martha Palmer. 2010. SemEval-2010 Task 10: Linking Events and Their Participants in Discourse. In *Proceedings of the 5th International Workshop on Semantic Evaluations*, pages 45–50, Uppsala, Sweden, July.

Ivan Titov and Mikhail Kozhevnikov. 2010. Bootstrapping semantic analyzers from non-contradictory texts.

In *Proceedings of the 48th Annual Meeting of the Association for Computational Linguistics*, Uppsala, Sweden, 11–16 July 2010, pages 958–967.

Stephen Wan, Mark Dras, Robert Dale, and Cecile Paris. 2006. Using dependency-based features to take the "Para-farce" out of paraphrase. In *Proceedings of the Australasian Language Technology Workshop*, pages 131–138.

Sander Wubben, Antal van den Bosch, Emiel Krahmer, and Erwin Marsi. 2009. Clustering and matching headlines for automatic paraphrase acquisition. In *Proceedings of the 12th European Workshop on Natural Language Generation (ENLG 2009)*, pages 122–125, Athens, Greece, March. Association for Computational Linguistics.

The Effects of Semantic Annotations on Precision Parse Ranking

Andrew MacKinlay[◇♡], **Rebecca Dridan**[♠*], **Diana McCarthy**[♣†] **and Timothy Baldwin**[◇♡]
[◇] Dept. of Computing and Information Systems, University of Melbourne, Australia
[♡] NICTA Victoria Research Laboratories, University of Melbourne, Australia
[♠] Department of Informatics, University of Oslo, Norway
[♣] Computational Linguistics and Phonetics, Saarland University, Germany
amack@csse.unimelb.edu.au, rdridan@ifi.uio.no,
diana@dianamccarthy.co.uk, tb@ldwin.net

Abstract

We investigate the effects of adding semantic annotations including word sense hypernyms to the source text for use as an extra source of information in HPSG parse ranking for the English Resource Grammar. The semantic annotations are coarse semantic categories or entries from a distributional thesaurus, assigned either heuristically or by a pre-trained tagger. We test this using two test corpora in different domains with various sources of training data. The best reduces error rate in dependency F-score by 1% on average, while some methods produce substantial decreases in performance.

1 Introduction

Most start-of-the-art natural language parsers (Charniak, 2000; Clark and Curran, 2004; Collins, 1997) use lexicalised features for parse ranking. These are important to achieve optimal parsing accuracy, and yet these are also the features which by their nature suffer from data-sparseness problems in the training data. In the absence of reliable fine-grained statistics for a given token, various strategies are possible. There will often be statistics available for coarser categories, such as the POS of the particular token. However, it is possible that these coarser representations discard too much, missing out information which could be valuable to the parse ranking. An intermediate level of representation could provide valuable additional information here. For example, assume we wish to correctly attach the prepositional phrases in the following examples:

(1) *I saw a tree with my telescope*

(2) *I saw a tree with no leaves*

The most obvious interpretation in each case has the prepositional phrase headed by *with* attaching in different places: to the verb phrase in the first example, and to the noun *tree* in the second. Such distinctions are difficult for a parser to make when the training data is sparse, but imagine we had seen examples such as the following in the training corpus:

(3) *Kim saw a eucalypt with his binoculars*

(4) *Sandy observed a willow with plentiful foliage*

There are few lexical items in common, but in each case the prepositional phrase attachment follows the same pattern: in (3) it attaches to the verb, and in (4) to the noun. A conventional lexicalised parser would have no knowledge of the semantic similarity between *eucalypt* and *tree*, *willow* and *tree*, *binoculars* and *telescope*, or *foliage* and *leaves*, so would not be able to make any conclusions about the earlier examples on the basis of this training data. However if the parse ranker has also been supplied with information about synonyms or hypernyms of the lexemes in the training data, it could possibly have generalised, to learn that PPs containing nouns related to seeing instruments often modify verbs relating to observation (in preference to nouns denoting inanimate objects), while plant flora can often be modified by PPs relating to appendages of plants such as *leaves*. This is not necessarily applicable only to PP attachment, but may help in a range of other syntactic phenomena, such as distinguishing between complements and modifiers of verbs.

*This research was conducted while the second author was a postdoctoral researcher within NICTA VRL.

†The third author is a visiting scholar on the Erasmus Mundus Masters Program in 'Language and Communication Technologies' (LCT, 2007–0060).

The synonyms or hypernyms could take the form of any grouping which relates word forms with semantic or syntactic commonality – such as a label from the WordNet (Miller, 1995) hierarchy, a subcategorisation frame (for verbs) or closely related terms from a distributional thesaurus (Lin, 1998).

We present work here on using various levels of semantic generalisation as an attempt to improve parse selection accuracy with the English Resource Grammar (ERG: Flickinger (2000)), a precision HPSG-based grammar of English.

2 Related Work

2.1 Parse Selection for Precision Grammars

The focus of this work is on parsing using handcrafted precision HPSG-based grammars, and in particular the ERG. While these grammars are carefully crafted to avoid overgeneration, the ambiguity of natural languages means that there will unavoidably be multiple candidate parses licensed by the grammar for any non-trivial sentence. For the ERG, the number of parses postulated for a given sentence can be anywhere from zero to tens of thousands. It is the job of the parse selection model to select the best parse from all of these candidates as accurately as possible, for some definition of 'best', as we discuss in Section 3.2.

Parse selection is usually performed by training discriminative parse selection models, which 'discriminate' between the set of all candidate parses. A widely-used method to achieve this is outlined in Velldal (2007). We feed both correct and incorrect parses licensed by the grammar to the TADM toolkit (Malouf, 2002), and learn a maximum entropy model. This method is used by Zhang et al. (2007) and MacKinlay et al. (2011) *inter alia*. One important implementation detail is that rather than exhaustively ranking all candidates out of possibly many thousands of trees, Zhang et al. (2007) showed that it was possible to use 'selective unpacking', which means that the exhaustive parse forest can be represented compactly as a 'packed forest', and the top-ranked trees can be successively reconstructed, enabling faster parsing using less memory.

2.2 Semantic Generalisation for parse ranking

Above, we outlined a number of reasons why semantic generalisation of lexemes could enable parsers to make more efficient use of training data, and indeed, there has been some prior work investigating this possibility. Agirre et al. (2008) applied two state-of-the-art treebank parsers to the sense-tagged subset of the Brown corpus version of the Penn Treebank (Marcus et al., 1993), and added sense annotation to the training data to evaluate their impact on parse selection and specifically on PP-attachment. The annotations they used were oracle sense annotations, automatic sense recognition and the first sense heuristic, and it was this last method which was the best performer in general. The sense annotations were either the WordNet synset ID or the coarse *semantic file*, which we explain in more detail below, and replaced the original tokens in the training data. The largest improvement in parsing F-score was a 6.9% reduction in error rate for the Bikel parser (Bikel, 2002), boosting the F-score from 0.841 to 0.852, using the noun supersense only. More recently, Agirre et al. (2011) largely reproduced these results with a dependency parser.

Fujita et al. (2007) add sense information to improve parse ranking with JaCy (Siegel and Bender, 2002), an HPSG-based grammar which uses similar machinery to the ERG. They use baseline syntactic features, and also add semantic features based on dependency triples extracted from the semantic representations of the sentence trees output by the parser. The dataset they use has human-assigned sense tags from a Japanese lexical hierarchy, which they use as a source of annotations. The dependency triples are modified in each feature set by replacing elements of the semantic triples with corresponding senses or hypernyms. In the best-performing configuration, they use both syntactic and semantic features with multiple levels of the the semantic hierarchy from combined feature sets. They achieve a 5.6% improvement in exact match parsing accuracy.

3 Methodology

We performed experiments in HPSG parse ranking using the ERG, evaluating the impact on parse selection of semantic annotations such as coarse sense labels or synonyms from a distributional the-

	WeScience	LOGON
Total Sentences	9632	9410
Parseable Sentences	9249	8799
Validated Sentences	7631	8550
Train/Test Sentences	6149/1482	6823/1727
Tokens/sentence	15.0	13.6
Training Tokens	92.5k	92.8k

Table 1: Corpora used in our experiments, with total sentences, how many of those can be parsed, how many of the parseable sentences have a single gold parse (and are used in these experiments), and average sentence length

saurus. Our work here differs from the aforementioned work of Fujita et al. (2007) in a number of ways. Firstly, we use purely syntactic parse selection features based on the derivation tree of the sentence (see Section 3.4.3), rather than ranking using dependency triples, meaning that our method is in principle able to be integrated into a parser more easily, where the final set of dependencies would not be known in advance. Secondly, we do not use human-created sense annotations, instead relying on heuristics or trained sense-taggers, which is closer to the reality of real-world parsing tasks.

3.1 Corpora

Following MacKinlay et al. (2011), we use two primary training corpora. First, we use the LOGON corpus (Oepen et al., 2004), a collection of English translations of Norwegian hiking texts. The LOGON corpus contains 8550 sentences with exactly one gold parse, which we partitioned randomly by sentence into 10 approximately equal sections, reserving two sections as test data, and using the remainder as our training corpus. These sentences were randomly divided into training and development data. Secondly, we use the WeScience (Ytrestøl et al., 2009) corpus, a collection of Wikipedia articles related to computational linguistics. The corpus contains 11558 sentences, from which we randomly chose 9632, preserving the remainder for future work. This left 7631 sentences with a single gold tree, which we divided into a training set and a development set in the same way. The corpora are summarised in Table 1.

With these corpora, we are able to investigate in-domain and cross-domain effects, by testing on a different corpus to the training corpus, so we can examine whether sense-tagging alleviates the cross-domain performance penalty noted in MacKinlay et al. (2011). We can also use a subset of each training corpus to simulate the common situation of sparse training data, so we can investigate whether sense-tagging enables the learner to make better use of a limited quantity of training data.

3.2 Evaluation

Our primary evaluation metric is Elementary Dependency Match (Dridan and Oepen, 2011). This converts the semantic output of the ERG into a set of dependency-like triples, and scores these triples using precision, recall and F-score as is conventional for other dependency evaluation. Following MacKinlay et al. (2011), we use the EDM_{NA} mode of evaluation, which provides a good level of comparability while still reflecting most the semantically salient information from the grammar.

Other work on the ERG and related grammars has tended to focus on exact tree match, but the granular EDM metric is a better fit for our needs here – among other reasons, it is more sensitive in terms of error rate reduction to changes in parse selection models (MacKinlay et al., 2011). Additionally, it is desirable to be able to choose between two different parses which do not match the gold standard exactly but when one of the parses is a closer match than the other; this is not possible with exact match accuracy.

3.3 Reranking for parse selection

The features we are adding to the parse selection procedure could all in principle be applied by the parser during the selective unpacking stage, since they all depend on information which can be pre-computed. However, we wish to avoid the need for multiple expensive parsing runs, and more importantly the need to modify the relatively complex internals of the parse ranking machinery in the PET parser (Callmeier, 2000). So instead of performing the parse ranking in conjunction with parsing, as is the usual practice, we use a pre-parsed forest of the top-500 trees for each corpus, and rerank the forest afterwards for each configuration shown.

The pre-parsed forests use the same models which were used in treebanking. Using reranking means that the set of candidate trees is held constant, which means that parse selection models never get the chance to introduce a new tree which was not in the original parse forest from which the gold tree was annotated, which may provide a very small performance boost (although when the parse selection models are similar as is the case for most of the models here, this effect is likely to be very small).

3.4 Word Sense Annotations

3.4.1 Using the WordNet Hierarchy

Most experiments we report on here make some use of the WordNet sense inventory. Obviously we need to determine the best sense and corresponding WordNet synset for a given token. We return to this in Section 3.4.2, but for now assume that the sense disambiguation is done.

As we are concerned primarily with making commonalities between lemmas with different base forms apparent to the parse selection model, the fine-grained synset ID will do relatively little to provide a coarser identifier for the token – indeed, if two tokens with identical forms were assigned different synset IDs, we would be obscuring the similarity.[1]

We can of course make use of the WordNet hierarchy, and use hypernyms from the hierarchy to tag each candidate token, but there are a large number of ways this can be achieved, particularly when it is possibly to assign multiple labels per token as is the case here (which we discuss in Section 3.4.3). We apply two relatively simple strategies. We noted in Section 2.2 that Agirre et al. (2008) found that the semantic file was useful. This is the coarse lexicographic category label, elsewhere denoted *supersense* (Ciaramita and Altun, 2006), which is the terminology we use. Nouns are divided into 26 coarse categories such as 'animal', 'quantity' or 'phenomenon', and verbs into 15 categories such as 'perception' or 'consumption'. In some configurations, denoted SS, we tag each open-class token with one of the supersense labels.

Another configuration attempts to avoid making assumptions about which level of the hierarchy will be most useful for parse disambiguation, instead leaving it the MaxEnt parse ranker to pick those labels from the hierarchy which are most useful. Each open class token is labelled with multiple synsets, starting with the assigned leaf synset and travelling as high as possible up the hierarchy, with no distinction made between the different levels in the hierarchy. Configurations using this are designated HP, for 'hypernym path'.

3.4.2 Disambiguating senses

We return now to the question of determination of the synset for a given token. One frequently-used and robust strategy is to lemmatise and POS-tag each token, and assign it the first-listed sense from WordNet (which may or may not be based on actual frequency counts). We POS-tag using TnT (Brants, 2000) and lemmatise using WordNet's native lemmatiser. This yields a leaf-level synset, making it suitable as a source of annotations for both SS and HP. We denote this 'WNF' for 'WordNet First' (shown in parentheses after SS or HP).

Secondly, to evaluate whether a more informed approach to sense-tagging helps beyond the naive WNF method, in the 'SST' method, we use the outputs of SuperSense Tagger (Ciaramita and Altun, 2006), which is optimised for assigning the supersenses described above, and can outperform a WNF-style baseline on at least some datasets. Since this only gives us coarse supersense labels, it can only provide SS annotations, as we do not get the leaf synsets needed for HP. The input we feed in is POS-tagged with TnT as above, for comparability with the WNF method, and to ensure that it is compatible with the configuration in which the corpora were parsed – specifically, the unknown-word handling uses a version of the sentences tagged with TnT. We ignore multi-token named entity outputs from SuperSense Tagger, as these would introduce a confounding factor in our experiments and also reduce comparability of the results with the WNF method.

3.4.3 A distributional thesaurus method

A final configuration attempts to avoid the need for curated resources such as WordNet, instead using an automatically-constructed distributional thesaurus (Lin, 1998). We use the thesaurus from McCarthy et al. (2004), constructed along these lines using the grammatical relations from RASP (Briscoe and Carroll, 2002) applied to 90 millions words of text from the British National Corpus.

[1]This could be useful for verbs since senses interact strongly subcategorisation frames, but that is not our focus here.

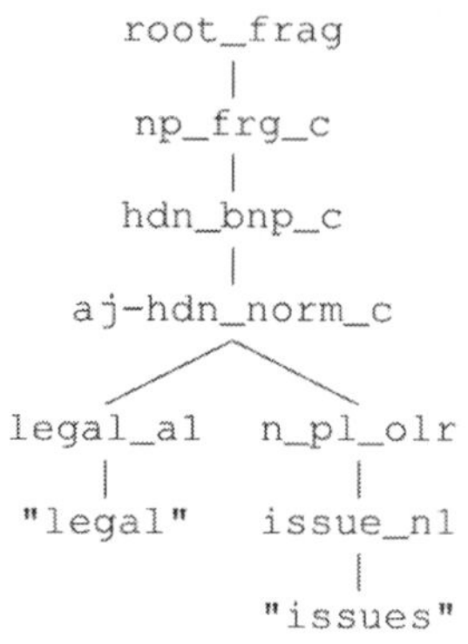

Figure 1: ERG derivation tree for the phrase *Legal issues*

```
[n_-_c_le "issues"]
[n_pl_olr n_-_c_le "issues"]
[aj-hdn_norm_c n_pl_olr n_-_c_le "issues"]
```

(a) Original features

```
[n_-_c_le noun.cognition]
[n_pl_olr n_-_c_le noun.cognition]
[aj-hdn_norm_c n_pl_olr n_-_c_le noun.cognition]
```

(b) Additional features in leaf mode, which augment the original features

```
[noun.cognition "issues"]
[n_pl_olr noun.cognition "issues"]
[aj-hdn_norm_c n_pl_olr noun.cognition "issues"]
```

(c) Additional features in leaf-parent ('P') mode, which augment the original features

Figure 2: Examples of features extracted from for `"issues"` node in Figure 1 with grandparenting level of 2 or less

To apply the mapping, we POS-tag the text with TnT as usual, and for each noun, verb and adjective we lemmatise the token (with WordNet again, falling back to the surface form if this fails), and look up the corresponding entry in the thesaurus. If there is a match, we select the top five most similar entries (or fewer if there are less than five), and use these new entries to create additional features, as well as adding a feature for the lemma itself in all cases. This method is denoted LDT for 'Lin Distributional Thesaurus'. We note that many other methods could be used to select these, such as different numbers of synonyms, or dynamically changing the number of synonyms based on a threshold against the top similarity score, but this is not something we evaluate in this preliminary investigation.

Adding Word Sense to Parse Selection Models

We noted above that parse selection using the methodology established by Velldal (2007) uses human-annotated incorrect and correct derivation trees to train a maximum entropy parse selection model. More specifically, the model is trained using features extracted from the candidate HPSG derivation trees, using the labels of each node (which are the rule names from the grammar) and those of a limited number of ancestor nodes.

As an example, we examine the noun phrase *Legal issues* from the WeScience corpus, for which the correct ERG derivation tree is shown in Figure 1. Features are created by examining each node in the tree and at least its parent, with the feature name set to the concatenation of the node labels. We also generally make used of *grandparenting* features, where we examine earlier ancestors in the derivation tree. A grandparenting level of one means we would also use the label of the grandparent (i.e. the parent's parent) of the node, a level of two means we would add in the great-grandparent label, and so on. Our experiments here use a maximum grandparenting level of three. There is also an additional transformation applied to the tree – the immediate parent of each leaf is, which is usually a lexeme, is replaced with the corresponding *lexical type*, which is a broader parent category from the type hierarchy of the grammar, although the details of this are not relevant here.

For the node labelled `"issues"` in Figure 1 with grandparenting levels from zero to two, we would extract the features as shown in Figure 2(a) (where the parent node `issue_n1` has already been replaced with its lexical type `n_-c_le`).

In this work here, we create variants of these features. A preprocessing script runs over the training or test data, and for each sentence lists variants of each token using standoff markup indexed by character span, which are created from the set of additional semantic tags assigned to each token by the word sense configuration (from those described in Section 3.4) which is currently in use. These sets of semantic tags for a given word could be a single supersense tag, as in SS, a set of synset IDs as in HP or a set of replacement lemmas in LDT. In all cases, the set of semantic tags could also be empty – if either the word has a part of speech which we are not

Test	Train	P/ R/ F	SS (WNF) P/ R/ F	ΔF	SS_p(WNF) P/ R/ F	ΔF
LOG	WESC (23k)	85.02/82.22/83.60	85.09/82.33/83.69	+0.09	84.81/82.20/83.48	−0.11
	WESC (92k)	86.56/83.58/85.05	86.83/84.04/85.41	+0.36	87.03/83.96/85.47	+0.42
	LOG (23k)	88.60/87.23/87.91	88.72/87.20/87.95	+0.04	88.43/87.00/87.71	−0.21
	LOG (92k)	91.74/90.15/90.94	91.82/90.07/90.94	−0.00	91.90/90.13/91.01	+0.07
WESC	WESC (23k)	86.80/84.43/85.60	87.12/84.44/85.76	+0.16	87.18/84.50/85.82	+0.22
	WESC (92k)	89.34/86.81/88.06	89.54/86.76/88.13	+0.07	89.43/87.23/88.32	+0.26
	LOG (23k)	83.74/81.41/82.56	84.02/81.43/82.71	+0.15	84.10/81.67/82.86	+0.31
	LOG (92k)	85.98/82.93/84.43	86.02/82.69/84.32	−0.11	85.89/82.76/84.30	−0.13

Table 2: Results for SS (WNF) (supersense from first WordNet sense), evaluated on 23k tokens (approx 1500 sentences) of either WESCIENCE or LOGON, and trained on various sizes of in-domain and cross-domain training data. Subscript '$_p$' indicates mappings were applied to leaf parents rather than leaves.

Test	Train	P/ R/ F	SS (SST) P/ R/ F	ΔF	SS_p(SST) P/ R/ F	ΔF
LOG	WESC (23k)	85.02/82.22/83.60	84.97/82.38/83.65	+0.06	85.32/82.66/83.97	+0.37
	WESC (92k)	86.56/83.58/85.05	87.05/84.47/85.74	+0.70	86.98/83.87/85.40	+0.35
	LOG (23k)	88.60/87.23/87.91	88.93/87.50/88.21	+0.29	88.84/87.40/88.11	+0.20
	LOG (92k)	91.74/90.15/90.94	91.67/90.02/90.83	−0.10	91.47/89.96/90.71	−0.23
WESC	WESC (23k)	86.80/84.43/85.60	86.88/84.29/85.56	−0.04	87.32/84.48/85.88	+0.27
	WESC (92k)	89.34/86.81/88.06	89.53/86.54/88.01	−0.05	89.50/86.56/88.00	−0.05
	LOG (23k)	83.74/81.41/82.56	84.06/81.30/82.66	+0.10	83.96/81.64/82.78	+0.23
	LOG (92k)	85.98/82.93/84.43	86.13/82.96/84.51	+0.08	85.76/82.84/84.28	−0.16

Table 3: Results for SS (SST) (supersense from SuperSense Tagger)

Test	Train	P/ R/ F	HPWNF P/ R/ F	ΔF	HP_p(WNF) P/ R/ F	ΔF
LOG	WESC (23k)	85.02/82.22/83.60	84.56/82.03/83.28	−0.32	84.74/82.20/83.45	−0.15
	WESC (92k)	86.56/83.58/85.05	86.65/84.22/85.42	+0.37	86.41/83.65/85.01	−0.04
	LOG (23k)	88.60/87.23/87.91	88.58/87.26/87.92	+0.00	88.58/87.35/87.96	+0.05
	LOG (92k)	91.74/90.15/90.94	91.68/90.19/90.93	−0.01	91.66/89.85/90.75	−0.19
WESC	WESC (23k)	86.80/84.43/85.60	86.89/84.19/85.52	−0.08	87.18/84.43/85.78	+0.18
	WESC (92k)	89.34/86.81/88.06	89.74/86.96/88.33	+0.27	89.23/86.88/88.04	−0.01
	LOG (23k)	83.74/81.41/82.56	83.87/81.20/82.51	−0.04	83.47/81.00/82.22	−0.33
	LOG (92k)	85.98/82.93/84.43	85.89/82.38/84.10	−0.33	85.75/83.03/84.37	−0.06

Table 4: Results for HPWNF (hypernym path from first WordNet sense)

Test	Train	P/ R/ F	LDT_p(5) P/ R/ F	ΔF
LOG	WESC (23k)	85.02/82.22/83.60	84.48/82.18/83.31	−0.28
	WESC (92k)	86.56/83.58/85.05	86.36/84.14/85.23	+0.19
	LOG (23k)	88.60/87.23/87.91	88.28/86.99/87.63	−0.28
	LOG (92k)	91.74/90.15/90.94	91.01/89.25/90.12	−0.82
WESC	WESC (23k)	86.80/84.43/85.60	86.17/83.51/84.82	−0.78
	WESC (92k)	89.34/86.81/88.06	88.31/85.61/86.94	−1.12
	LOG (23k)	83.74/81.41/82.56	83.60/81.18/82.37	−0.19
	LOG (92k)	85.98/82.93/84.43	85.74/82.96/84.33	−0.11

Table 5: Results for LDT (5) (Lin-style distributional thesaurus, expanding each term with the top-5 most similar)

attempting to tag semantically, or if our method has no knowledge of the particular word.

The mapping is applied at the point of feature extraction from the set of derivation trees – at model construction time for the training set and at reranking time for the development set. If a given leaf token has some set of corresponding semantic tags, we add a set of variant features for each semantic tag, duplicated and modified from the matching "core" features described above. There are two ways these mappings can be applied, since it is not immediately apparent where the extra lexical generalisation would be most useful. The 'leaf' variant applies to the leaf node itself, so that in each feature involving the leaf node, add a variant where the leaf node surface string has been replaced with the new semantic tag. The 'parent' variant, which has a subscript 'P' (e.g. $SS_P(WNF)$) applies the mapping to the immediate parent of the leaf node, leaving the leaf itself unchanged, but creating variant features with the parent nodes replaced with the tag.

For our example here, we assume that we have an SS mapping for Figure 2(a), and that this has mapped the token for `"issues"` to the WordNet supersense `noun.cognition`. For the leaf variant, the extra features that would be added (either for considering inclusion in the model, or for scoring a sentence when reranking) are shown in Figure 2(b), while those for the parent variant are in Figure 2(c).

3.4.4 Evaluating the contribution of sense annotations

We wish to evaluate whether adding sense annotations improve parser accuracy against the baseline of training a model in the conventional way using only syntactic features. As noted above, we suspect that this semantic generalisation may help in cases where appropriate training data is sparse – that is, where the training data is from a different domain or only a small amount exists. So to evaluate the various methods in these conditions, we train models from small (23k token) training sets and large (96k token) training sets created from subsets of each corpus (WeScience and LOGON). For the baseline, we train these models without modification. For each of the various methods of adding semantic tags, we then re-use each of these training sets to create new models after adding the appropriate additional features as described above, to evaluate whether these additional features improve parsing accuracy

4 Results

We present an extensive summary of the results obtained using the various methods in Tables 2, 3, 4 and 5. In each case we show results for applying to the leaf and to the parent. Aggregating the results for each method, the differences range between substantially negative and modestly positive, with a large number of fluctuations due to statistical noise.

LDT is the least promising performer, with only one very modest improvement, and the largest decreases in performance, of around 1%. The HP-WNF and $HP_P(WNF)$ methods make changes in either direction – on average, over all four training/test combinations, there are very small drops in F-score of 0.02% for HPWNF, and 0.06% for $HP_P(WNF)$, which indicates that neither of the methods is likely to be useful in reliably improving parser performance.

The SS methods are more promising. SS (WNF) and $SS_P(WNF)$ methods yield an average improvement of 0.10% each, while SS (SST) and $SS_P(SST)$ give average improvements of 0.12% and 0.13% respectively (representing an error rate reduction of around 1%). Interestingly, the increase in tagging accuracy we might expect using SuperSense Tagger only translates to a modest (and probably not significant) increase in parser performance, possibly because the tagger is not optimised for the domains in question. Amongst the statistical noise it is hard to discern overall trends; surprisingly, it seems that the size of the training corpus has relatively little to do with the success of adding these supersense annotations, and that the corpus being from an unmatched domain doesn't necessarily mean that sense-tagging will improve accuracy either. There may be a slight trend for sense annotations to be more useful when WeScience is the training corpus (either in the small or the large size).

To gain a better insight into how the effects change as the size of the training corpus changes for the different domains, we created learning curves for the best-performing method, $SS_P(SST)$ (although as noted above, all SS methods give similar levels of improvement), shown in Figure 3. Overall, these

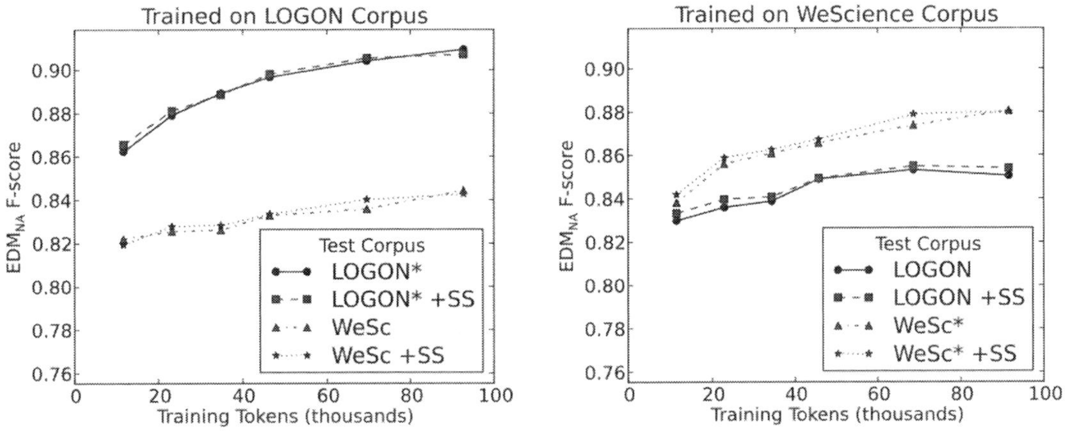

(a) LOGON (b) WESCIENCE

Figure 3: EDM_{NA} learning curves for SS (SST) (supersense from SuperSense Tagger). '*' denotes in-domain training corpus.

graphs support the same conclusions as the tables – the gains we see are very modest and there is a slight tendency for WESCIENCE models to benefit more from the semantic generalisation, but no strong tendencies for this to work better for cross-domain training data or small training sets.

5 Conclusion

We have presented an initial study evaluating whether a fairly simple approach to using automatically-created coarse semantic annotations can improve HPSG parse selection accuracy using the English Resource Grammar. We have provided some weak evidence that adding features based on semantic annotations, and in particular word supersense, can provide modest improvements in parse selection performance in terms of dependency F-score, with the best-performing method SS_p(SST) providing an average reduction in error rate over 4 training/test corpus combinations of 1%. Other approaches were less promising. In all configurations, there were instances of F-score decreases, sometimes substantial.

It is somewhat surprising that we did not achieve reliable performance gains which were seen in the related work described above. One possible explanation is that the model training parameters were suboptimal for this data set since the characteristics of the data are somewhat different than without sense annotations. The failure to improve somewhat mirrors the results of Clark (2001), who was attempting to improve the parse ranking performance of the unification-based based probabilistic parser of Carroll and Briscoe (1996). Clark (2001) used dependencies to rank parses, and WordNet-based techniques to generalise this model and learn selectional preferences, but failed to improve performance over the structural (i.e. non-dependency) ranking in the original parser. Additionally, perhaps the changes we applied in this work to the parse ranking could possibly have been more effective with features based on semantic dependences as used by Fujita et al. (2007), although we outlined reasons why we wished to avoid this approach.

This work is preliminary and there is room for more exploration in this space. There is scope for much more feature engineering on the semantic annotations, such as using different levels of the semantic hierarchy, or replacing the purely lexical features instead of augmenting them. Additionally, more error analysis would reveal whether this approach was more useful for avoiding certain kinds of parser errors (such as PP-attachment).

Acknowledgements

NICTA is funded by the Australian Government as represented by the Department of Broadband, Communications and the Digital Economy and the Australian Research Council through the ICT Centre of Excellence program.

References

E. Agirre, T. Baldwin, and D. Martinez. 2008. Improving parsing and PP attachment performance with sense information. In *Proceedings of ACL-08: HLT*, pages 317–325, Columbus, Ohio, June.

Eneko Agirre, Kepa Bengoetxea, Koldo Gojenola, and Joakim Nivre. 2011. Improving dependency parsing with semantic classes. In *Proceedings of the 49th Annual Meeting of the Association of Computational Linguistics, ACL-HLT 2011 Short Paper, Portland, Oregon"*.

D. M. Bikel. 2002. Design of a multi-lingual, parallel-processing statistical parsing engine. In *Proceedings of the second international conference on Human Language Technology Research*, pages 178–182, San Francisco, CA, USA.

T. Brants. 2000. Tnt – a statistical part-of-speech tagger. In *Proceedings of the Sixth Conference on Applied Natural Language Processing*, pages 224–231, Seattle, Washington, USA, April.

T. Briscoe and J. Carroll. 2002. Robust accurate statistical annotation of general text. In *Proceedings of the 3rd International Conference on Language Resources and Evaluation*, pages 1499–1504.

U. Callmeier. 2000. Pet – a platform for experimentation with efficient HPSG processing techniques. *Nat. Lang. Eng.*, 6(1):99–107.

J. Carroll and E. Briscoe. 1996. Apportioning development effort in a probabilistic lr pars- ing system through evaluation. In *Proceedings of the SIGDAT Conference on Empirical Methods in Natural Language Processing*, pages 92–100, Philadelphia, PA.

E. Charniak. 2000. A maximum-entropy-inspired parser. In *Proceedings of the 1st North American chapter of the Association for Computational Linguistics conference*, pages 132–139.

M. Ciaramita and Y. Altun. 2006. Broad-coverage sense disambiguation and information extraction with a supersense sequence tagger. In *Proceedings of the 2006 Conference on Empirical Methods in Natural Language Processing*, pages 594–602, Sydney, Australia, July.

S. Clark and J.R. Curran. 2004. Parsing the WSJ using CCG and log-linear models. In *Proceedings of the 42nd Meeting of the ACL*, pages 104–111.

S. Clark. 2001. *Class-based Statistical Models for Lexical Knowledge Acquisition*. Ph.D. thesis, University of Sussex.

M. Collins. 1997. Three generative, lexicalised models for statistical parsing. In *Proceedings of the 35th Annual Meeting of the Association for Computational Linguistics*, pages 16–23, Madrid, Spain, July.

R. Dridan and S. Oepen. 2011. Parser evaluation using elementary dependency matching. In *Proceedings of the 12th International Conference on Parsing Technologies*, pages 225–230, Dublin, Ireland, October.

Dan Flickinger. 2000. On building a more efficient grammar by exploiting types. *Nat. Lang. Eng.*, 6 (1):15–28.

S. Fujita, F. Bond, S. Oepen, and T. Tanaka. 2007. Exploiting semantic information for HPSG parse selection. In *ACL 2007 Workshop on Deep Linguistic Processing*, pages 25–32, Prague, Czech Republic, June.

D. Lin. 1998. Automatic retrieval and clustering of similar words. In *Proceedings of the 17th international conference on Computational linguistics-Volume 2*, pages 768–774.

A. MacKinlay, R. Dridan, D. Flickinger, and T. Baldwin. 2011. Cross-domain effects on parse selection for precision grammars. *Research on Language & Computation*, 8(4):299–340.

R. Malouf. 2002. A comparison of algorithms for maximum entropy parameter estimation. In *Proceedings of the Sixth Conference on Natural Language Learning (CoNLL-2002)*, pages 49–55.

M. P. Marcus, M. A. Marcinkiewicz, and B. Santorini. 1993. Building a large annotated corpus of english: the penn treebank. *Comput. Linguist.*, 19(2):313–330.

D. McCarthy, R. Koeling, J. Weeds, and J. Carroll. 2004. Finding predominant word senses in untagged text. In *Proceedings of the 42nd Annual Meeting on Association for Computational Linguistics*, pages 279–es.

G.A. Miller. 1995. WordNet: a lexical database for English. *Communications of the ACM*, 38(11):39–41.

S. Oepen, D. Flickinger, K. Toutanova, and C.D. Manning. 2004. LinGO Redwoods: A rich and dynamic treebank for HPSG. *Research on Language & Computation*, 2(4):575–596.

M. Siegel and E.M. Bender. 2002. Efficient deep processing of japanese. In *Proceedings of the 3rd workshop on Asian language resources and international standardization-Volume 12*, pages 1–8.

E. Velldal. 2007. *Empirical Realization Ranking*. Ph.D. thesis, University of Oslo Department of Informatics.

G. Ytrestøl, D. Flickinger, and S. Oepen. 2009. Extracting and annotating Wikipedia sub-domains – towards a new eScience community resourc. In *Proceedings of the Seventh International Workshop on Treebanks and Linguistic Theories*, Groeningen, The Netherlands, January.

Y. Zhang, S. Oepen, and J. Carroll. 2007. Efficiency in unification-based n-best parsing. In *IWPT '07: Proceedings of the 10th International Conference on Parsing Technologies*, pages 48–59, Morristown, NJ, USA.

A Probabilistic Lexical Model for Ranking Textual Inferences

Eyal Shnarch and **Ido Dagan**
Computer Science Department
Bar-Ilan University
Ramat-Gan 52900, Israel
{shey,dagan}@cs.biu.ac.il

Jacob Goldberger
Faculty of Engineering
Bar-Ilan University
Ramat-Gan 52900, Israel
goldbej@eng.biu.ac.il

Abstract

Identifying textual inferences, where the meaning of one text follows from another, is a general underlying task within many natural language applications. Commonly, it is approached either by generative syntactic-based methods or by "lightweight" heuristic lexical models. We suggest a model which is confined to simple lexical information, but is formulated as a principled generative probabilistic model. We focus our attention on the task of *ranking textual inferences* and show substantially improved results on a recently investigated question answering data set.

1 Introduction

The task of identifying texts which share semantic content arises as a general need in many natural language processing applications. For instance, a paraphrasing application has to recognize texts which convey roughly the same content, and a summarization application needs to single out texts which contain the content stated by other texts. We refer to this general task as *textual inference* similar to prior use of this term (Raina et al., 2005; Schoenmackers et al., 2008; Haghighi et al., 2005).

In many textual inference scenarios the setting requires a classification decision of whether the inference relation holds or not. But in other scenarios ranking according to inference likelihood would be the natural task. In this work we focus on *ranking textual inferences*; given a sentence and a corpus, the task is to rank the corpus passages by their plausibility to imply as much of the sentence meaning as possible. Most naturally, this is the case in question answering (QA), where systems search for passages that cover the semantic components of the question. A recent line of research was dedicated to this task (Wang et al., 2007; Heilman and Smith, 2010; Wang and Manning, 2010).

A related scenario is the task of Recognizing Textual Entailment (RTE) within a corpus (Bentivogli et al., 2010)[1]. In this task, inference systems should identify, for a given *hypothesis*, the sentences which entail it in a given corpus. Even though RTE was presented as a classification task, it has an appealing potential as a ranking task as well. For instance, one may want to find texts that validate a claim such as *cellular radiation is dangerous for children*, or to learn more about it from a newswire corpus. To that end, one should look for additional mentions of this claim such as *extensive usage of cell phones may be harmful for youngsters*. This can be done by ranking the corpus passages by their likelihood to entail the claim, where the top ranked passages are likely to contain additional relevant information.

Two main approaches have been used to address textual inference (for either ranking or classification). One is based on transformations over syntactic parse trees (Echihabi and Marcu, 2003; Heilman and Smith, 2010). Some works in this line describe a probabilistic generative process in which the parse tree of the question is generated from the passage (Wang et al., 2007; Wang and Manning, 2010).

In the second approach, lexical models have been employed for textual inference (MacKinlay and Baldwin, 2009; Clark and Harrison, 2010). Typi-

[1] http://www.nist.gov/tac/2010/RTE/index.html

cally, lexical models consider a text fragment as a bag of terms and split the inference decision into two steps. The first is a *term-level* estimation of the inference likelihood for each term independently, based on direct lexical match and on lexical knowledge resources. Some commonly used resources are WordNet (Fellbaum, 1998), distributional-similarity thesauri (Lin, 1998), and web knowledge resources such as (Suchanek et al., 2007). The second step is making a final *sentence-level* decision based on these estimations for the component terms. Lexical models have the advantage of being fast and easy to utilize (e.g. no dependency on parsing tools) while being highly competitive with top performing systems, e.g. the system of Majumdar and Bhattacharyya (2010).

In this work, we investigate how well such lexical models can perform in textual inference ranking scenarios. However, while lexical models usually apply heuristic methods, we would like to pursue a principled learning-based generative framework, in analogy to the approaches for syntactic-based inference. An attractive work in this spirit is presented in (Shnarch et al., 2011a), that propose a model which is both lexical and probabilistic. Later, Shnarch et al. (2011b) improved this model and reported results that outperformed previous lexical models and were on par with state-of-the-art RTE models.

Whereas their term-level model provides means to integrate lexical knowledge in a probabilistic manner, their sentence-level model depends to a great extent on heuristic normalizations which were introduced to incorporate prominent aspects of the sentence-level decision. This deviates their model from a pure probabilistic methodology.

Our work aims at amending this deficiency and proposes a new probabilistic sentence-level model based on a Markovian process. In that model, all parameters are estimated by an EM algorithm. We evaluate this model on the tasks of ranking passages for QA and ranking textual entailments within a corpus, and show that eliminating the need for heuristic normalizations greatly improves state-of-the-art performance. The full implementation of our model is available for download[2] and can be used as an easy-to-install and highly competitive inference engine that operates only on lexical knowledge, or as a lexical component integrated within a more complex inference system.

2 Background

Wang et al. (2007) provided an annotated data set, based on the Text REtrieval Conference (TREC) QA tracks[3], specifically for the task of ranking candidate answer passages. We adopt their experimental setup and next review the line of syntactic-based works which reported results on this data set.

2.1 Syntactic generative models

Wang et al. (2007) propose a quasi-synchronous grammar formulation which specifies the generation of the question parse tree, loosely conditioned on the parse tree of the candidate answer passage. Their model showed improvement over previous syntactic models for QA: Punyakanok et al. (2004), who computed similarity between question-answer pairs with a generalized tree-edit distance, and Cui et al. (2005), who developed an information measure for sentence similarity based on dependency paths of aligned words. Wang et al. (2007) reproduced these methods and extended them to utilize WordNet.

More recently, Heilman and Smith (2010) improved Wang et al. (2007) results with a classification based approach. Feature for the classifier were extracted from a greedy algorithm which searches for tree-edit sequences which transform the parse tree of the candidate answer into the one of the question. Unlike other works reviewed here, this one does not utilize lexical knowledge resources.

Similarly, Wang and Manning (2010) present an extended tree-edit operations set and search for edit sequences to generate the question from the answer candidate. Their CRF-based classifier models these sequences as latent variables.

An important merit of these methods is that they offer principled, often probabilistic, generative models for the task of ranking candidate answers. Their drawback is the need for syntactic analysis which makes them slower to run, dependent on parsing performance, which is often mediocre in many text genres, and inadequate for languages which lack proper parsing tools.

[2] http://www.cs.biu.ac.il/nlp/downloads/probLexModel.html

[3] http://trec.nist.gov/data/qamain.html

2.2 Lexical models

Lexical models, on the other hand, are faster, easier to implement and are more practical for various genres and languages. Such models derive from knowledge resources *lexical inference rules* which indicate that the meaning of a lexical term can be inferred from the meaning of another term (e.g. *youngsters* → *children* and *harmful* → *dangerous*). They are common in the Recognizing Textual Entailment (RTE) systems and we present some representative methods for that task. We adopt textual entailment terminology and henceforth use *Hypothesis* (denoted H) for the inferred text fragment and *Text* (denoted T) for the text from which it is being inferred[4].

Majumdar and Bhattacharyya (2010) utilized a simple union of lexical rules derived from various lexical resources for the term-level step. They derived their sentence-level decision based on the number of matched hypothesis terms. The results of this simple model were only slightly worse than the best results of the RTE-6 challenge which were achieved by a syntactic-based system (Jia et al., 2010). Clark and Harrison (2010), on the other hand, considered the number of mismatched terms in establishing their sentence-level decision. MacKinlay and Baldwin (2009) represented text and hypothesis as word vectors augmented with lexical knowledge. For sentence-level similarity they used a variant of the cosine similarity score. Common to most of these lexical models is the application of heuristic methods in both the term and the sentence level steps.

Targeted to replace heuristic methods with principled ones, Shnarch et al. (2011a) present a model which aims at combining the advantages of a probabilistic generative model with the simplicity of lexical methods. In some analogy to generative parse-tree based models, they propose a generative process for the creation of the hypothesis from the text.

At the term-level, their model combines knowledge from various input resources and has the advantages of considering the effect of transitive rule application (e.g. *mobile phone* → *cell phone* → *cellular*) as well as the integration of multiple pieces of evidence for the inference of a term (e.g. both the appearance of *harmful* and *risky* in T provide evidence for the inference of *dangerous* in H). We denote this term-level Probabilistic Lexical Model as PLM^{TL}, and have reproduced it in our work as presented in Section 4.1. For the sentence-level decision they describe an AND gate mechanism, i.e. deducing a positive inference decision for H as a whole only if all its terms were inferred from T.

In an extension to that work, Shnarch et al. (2011b) modified PLM^{TL} to improve the sentence-level step. They pointed out some prominent aspects for the sentence-level decision. First, they suggest that a hypothesis as a whole can be inferred from the text even if some of its terms are not inferred. To model this, they introduced a noisy-AND mechanism (Pearl, 1988). Additionally, they emphasized the effect of hypothesis length and the dependency between terms on the sentence-level decision. However, they did not fully achieve their target of presenting a fully coherent probabilistic model, as their model included heuristic normalization formulae.

On the contrary, the model we present is the first along this line to be fully specified in terms of a generative setting and formulated in pure probabilistic terms. We introduce a Markovian-style probabilistic model for the sentence-level decision. This model receives as input term-level probabilistic estimates, which may be provided by any term-level model. In our implementation we embed PLM^{TL} as the term-level model and present a complete coherent Markovian-based Probabilistic Lexical Model, which we term *M-PLM*.

3 Markovian sentence-level model

The goal of a sentence-level model is to integrate term-level inputs into an inference decision for the hypothesis as a whole. For a hypothesis $H = h_1, \ldots, h_n$ and a text T, term-level models first estimate independently for each term h_t its probability to be inferred from T. Let x_t be a binary random variable representing the event that h_t is indeed inferred from T (i.e., $x_t = 1$ if h_t is inferred and 0 otherwise).

Given these term-level probabilities, a sentence-level model is employed to estimate the probability that H as a whole is inferred from T. This step is

[4] In the task of passage ranking for QA, the hypothesis is the question and the text is the candidate passage.

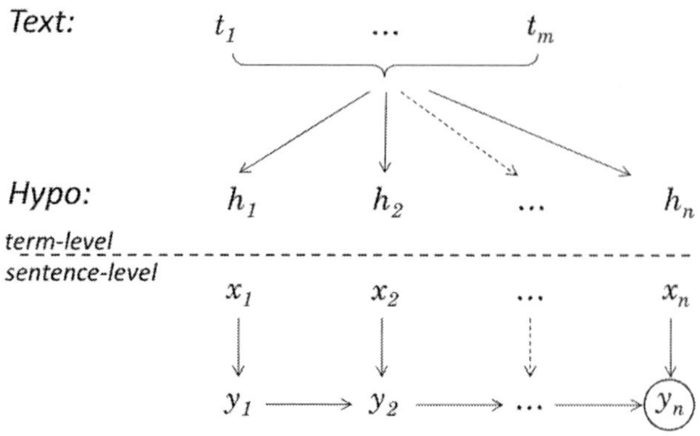

Figure 1: A probabilistic lexical model: the upper part is the term-level input to the sentence-level Markovian process, depicted in the lower part. x_i is a binary variable representing the inference of h_i and y_j is a variable for the accumulative inference decision for the first j terms of *Hypo*. The final sentence-level decision is given by y_n.

the focus of our work. We assume that the term-level probabilities are given as input. Section 4.1 describes PLM^{TL}, as a concrete method for deriving these probabilities.

Our sentence-level model is based on a Markovian process and is described in Section 3.1. In particular, it takes into account, in probabilistic terms, the prominent factors in lexical entailment, mentioned in Section 2. An efficient inference algorithm for our model is given in Section 3.2 and EM-based learning is specified in Section 3.3.

3.1 Markovian sentence-level decision

The motivation for proposing a Markovian process for the sentence-level is to establish an intermediate model, lying between two extremes: assuming full independence between hypothesis terms versus assuming that every term is dependent on all other terms. The former alternative is too weak, while the latter alternative is computationally hard and not very informative, and thus hard to capture in a model. Our model specifies a Markovian dependence structure, which limits the dependence scope to adjacent terms, as follows.

We define a binary variable y_t to be the accumulated sentence-level inference decision up to h_t. In other words, $y_t = 1$ if the subset $\{h_1, \ldots, h_t\}$ of H's terms is inferred as a whole from T.

Note that this means that y_t can be 1 even if some terms amongst $h_1, \ldots, h_t$ are not inferred. As y_n is the decision for the complete hypothesis, our model addresses this way the prominent aspect that the hypothesis as a whole may be inferred even if some of its terms are not inferred. The reason for allowing this is that such un-inferred terms may be inferred from the global context of T, or alternatively, are actually inferred from T but the knowledge resources in use do not contain the proper lexical rule to make such inference.

Figure 1 describes both steps of a full lexical inference model. Its lower part depicts our Markovian process. In the proposed model the inference decision at each position t is a combination of x_t, the variable for the event of h_t being inferred, and y_{t-1}, the accumulated decision at the previous position. Therefore, the *transition* parameters of *M-PLM* can be modeled as:

$$q_{ij}(k) = P(y_t = k | y_{t-1} = i, x_t = j) \quad \forall k, i, j \in \{0, 1\}$$

where $y_1 = x_1$. For instance, $q_{01}(1)$ is the probability that $y_t = 1$, given that $y_{t-1} = 0$ and $x_t = 1$.

Applying the Markovian process on the entire hypothesis we get y_n, which represents the final sentence-level decision, where a soft decision is obtained by computing the probability of $y_n = 1$:

$$P(y_n = 1) = \sum_{\substack{x_1, \ldots, x_n \\ y_2, \ldots, y_{n-1}, y_n = 1}} P(x_1) \prod_{t=2}^{n} P(x_t) P(y_t | y_{t-1}, x_t)$$

The summation is done over all possible binary values of the term-level variables $x_1, \ldots, x_n$ and the accumulated sentence-level variables $y_2, \ldots, y_{n-1}$ where $y_n = 1$. Note that for clarity, in this formula x_t and y_t denote the binary *values* at the corresponding variable positions. A tractable form for computing $P(y_n = 1)$ is presented in Section 3.2.

Overall, the prominent factors in lexical entailment, raised by prior works, are incorporated within the core structure of this probabilistic model, without the need to resort to heuristic normalizations. Reducing the negative affect of hypothesis length on the entailment probability is achieved by having y_t, at each position, being *directly* dependent only on x_t and y_{t-1} as opposed to being affected by all hypothesis terms. The second factor, modeling the dependency between hypothesis terms, is addressed by the *indirect* dependency of y_n on all preceding hypothesis terms. This dependency arises from the recursive nature of the Markovian model, as can be seen in the next section.

Our proposed Markovian process presents a linear dependency between terms which, to some extent, poses an anomaly with respect to the structure of the entailment phenomenon. Yet, as we do want to limit the dependence structure, following the natural order of the sentence words seems the most reasonable choice, as common in many other types of sequential models. We also tried randomizing the word order which, on average, did not improve performance.

3.2 Inference

The accumulated sentence-level inference can be efficiently computed using a typical forward algorithm. We denote the probability of $x_t = j, j \in \{0, 1\}$ by $h_t(j) = P(x_t = j)$. The forward step is given in Eq. (1) and its initialization is defined in Eq. (2).

$$\alpha_t(k) = P(y_t = k) = \sum_{i,j \in \{0,1\}} \alpha_{t-1}(i) h_t(j) q_{ij}(k) \quad (1)$$

$$\alpha_1(k) = P(x_1 = k) \quad (2)$$

where $k \in \{0, 1\}$ and $t = 2, ..., n$.

$\alpha_t(k)$ is the probability that the accumulated decision at position t is k. It is calculated by summing over the probabilities of all four combinations of $\alpha_{t-1}(i)$ and $h_t(j)$, multiplied by the corresponding transition probability, $q_{ij}(k)$.

The soft sentence-level decision can be efficiently calculated by:

$$P(y_n = a) = \alpha_n(a) \qquad a \in \{0, 1\} \quad (3)$$

3.3 Learning

Typically, natural language applications work at the sentence-level. The training data for such applications is, therefore, available as annotations at the sentence-level. Term-level alignments between passage terms and question terms are rarely available. Hence, we learn our term-level parameters from available sentence-level annotations, using the generative process described above to bridge the gap between these two levels.

For learning we use the typical backwards algorithm which is described by Eq. (4) and Eq. (5), where $\beta_t(a|i)$ is the probability that the full hypothesis inference value is a given that $y_t = i$.

$$\beta_n(a|i) = P(y_n = a | y_n = i) = 1_{\{a=i\}} \quad (4)$$

$$\beta_t(a|i) = P(y_n = a | y_t = i) = \sum_{j,k \in \{0,1\}} h_{t+1}(j) q_{ij}(k) \beta_{t+1}(a|k) \quad (5)$$

where $t = n-1, .., 1$, $a \in \{0, 1\}$ and $1_{\{condition\}}$ is the indicator function which returns 1 if *condition* holds and 0 otherwise.

To estimate $q_{ij}(k)$, the parameters of the Markovian process, we employ the EM algorithm:

E-step: For each (T, H) pair in the training data set, annotated with $a \in \{0, 1\}$ as its sentence-level inference value, we evaluate the expected probability of every transition given the annotation value a:

$$w_{tijk}(T, H) = P(y_{t-1} = i, x_t = j, y_t = k | y_n = a) = \frac{\alpha_{t-1}(i) h_t(j) q_{ij}(k) \beta_t(a|k)}{P(y_n = a)} \quad (6)$$

$\forall i, j, k \in \{0, 1\}$ and $t = 2, ..., |H|$.

M-step: Given the values of $w_{tijk}(T, H)$ we can estimate each $q_{ij}(1)$, $i, j \in \{0, 1\}$, by taking the proportion of transitions in which $y_{t-1} = i$, $x_t = j$ and $y_t = 1$, out of the total transitions in which $y_{t-1} = i$ and $x_t = j$:

$$q_{ij}(1) \leftarrow \frac{\sum_{(T,H)} \sum_{t=2}^{|H|} w_{tij1}(T, H)}{\sum_{(T,H)} \sum_{t=2}^{|H|} \sum_{k \in \{0,1\}} w_{tijk}(T, H)} \quad (7)$$

$$q_{ij}(0) = 1 - q_{ij}(1)$$

4 Complete model implementation

We next describe the end-to-end probabilistic lexical inference model we used in our evaluations. We implemented PLM^{TL} as our term-level model to provide us with $h_t(j)$, the term-level probabilities. We chose this model since it is fully lexical, has the advantages of lexical knowledge integration described in Section 2 and achieved top results on RTE data sets. Next, we summarize PLM^{TL}, and in Appendix A we show how to adjust the learning schema to fit into our sentence-level model.

4.1 PLM^{TL}

Shnarch et al. (2011a) provide a term-level model which integrates lexical rules from various knowledge resources. As described below it also considers transitive chains of rule applications as well as the impact of parallel chains which provide multiple evidence that $h \in H$ is inferred from T.

Their model assumes a parameter θ_R for each knowledge resource R in use. θ_R specifies the resource's reliability, i.e. the prior probability that applying a rule from R to an arbitrary text-hypothesis pair would yield a valid inference.

Next, transitive *chains* may connect a text term to a hypothesis term via intermediate term(s). For instance, starting from the text term *T-Mobile*, a chain that utilizes the lexical rules *T-Mobile* $\rightarrow$ *telecom* and *telecom* $\rightarrow$ *cell phone* enables the inference of the term *cell phone* from T. They compute, for each step in a chain, the probability that this step is valid based on the θ_R values. Denoting the resource which provided a rule r by $R(r)$, Eq. (8) specifies that the validity probability of the inference step corresponding to the application of the rule r within the chain c pointing at h_t (as represented by x_{tcr}) is $\theta_{R(r)}$.

Next, for a chain c pointing at h_t (represented by x_{tc}) to be valid, *all* its rule steps should be valid for this pair. Eq. (9) estimates this probability by the joint probability that the applications of all rules $r \in c$ are valid, assuming independence of rules.

Several chains may connect terms in T to h_t, thus providing multiple pieces of evidence that h_t is inferred from T. For instance, both *youngsters* and *kids* in T may indicate the inference of *children* in H. For a term h_t to be inferred from the entire sentence T it is enough that *at least one* of the chains from T to h_t is valid. This is the complement event of h_t not being inferred from T which happens when all chains which suggest the inference of h_t, denoted by $C(h_t)$, are invalid. Eq. (10) specifies this probability (again assuming independence of chains).

$$P(x_{tcr} = 1) = \theta_{R(r)} \tag{8}$$

$$P(x_{tc} = 1) = \prod_{r \in c} P(x_{tcr} = 1) \tag{9}$$

$$\begin{aligned} h_t(1) = P(x_t = 1) &= 1 - P(x_t = 0) \\ &= 1 - \prod_{c \in C(h_t)} P(x_{tc} = 0) \end{aligned} \tag{10}$$

With respect to the contributions of our work, we note that previous works resorted to applying some heuristic amendments on these equations to achieve valuable results. In contrast, our work is the first to present a purely generative model. This achievement shows that it is possible to shift from ad-hoc heuristic methods, which are common practice, to more solid mathematically-based methods.

Finally, for ranking text passages from a corpus for a given hypothesis (question in the QA scenario), our Markovian sentence-level model takes as its input the outcome of Eq. (10) for each $h_t \in H$. For PLM^{TL} we need to estimate the model parameters, that is the various θ_R values. In our Markovian model this is done by the scheme detailed in Appendix A. Given these term-level probabilities, our model computes for each hypothesis its probability to be inferred from each of the corpus passages, namely $P(y_n = 1)$ in Eq (3). Passages are then ranked according to this probability.

5 Evaluations and Results

To evaluate the performance of *M-PLM* for ranking textual inferences we focused on the task of ranking candidate answer passages for question answering (QA) as presented in Section 5.1. Additionally, we demonstrate the added value of our sentence-level model in another ranking experiment based on RTE data sets, described in Section 5.2.

5.1 Answer ranking for question answering

Data set We adopted the experimental setup of Wang et al. (2007) who also provided an annotated data set for answer passage ranking in QA[5].

In their data set an instance is a pair of a factoid question and a candidate answer passage (a single sentence in this data set). It was constructed from the data of the QA tracks at TREC 8–13. The question-candidate pairs were manually judged and a pair was annotated as positive if the candidate passage indicates the correct answer for the question. The training and test sets roughly contain 5700 and 1500 pairs correspondingly.

[5]The data set was kindly provided to us by Mengqiu Wang and is available for download at http://www.cs.stanford.edu/~mengqiu/data/qg-emnlp07-data.tgz.

Method PLM^{TL} utilizes WordNet and the Catvar (Categorial Variation) derivations database (Habash and Dorr, 2003) as generic and publicly available lexical knowledge resources, when question and answer terms are restricted to the first WordNet sense. In order to be consistent with (Shnarch et al., 2011b), the best performing model of prior work, we restricted our model to utilize only these two resources which they used. However, additional lexical resources can be provided as input to our model (e.g. a distributional similarity-base thesaurus).

We report Mean Average Precision (MAP) and Mean Reciprocal Rank (MRR), the standard measures for ranked lists. In the cases of tie we took a conservative approach and ranked positive annotated instances below the negative instances scored with the same probability. Hence, the reported figures are lower-bounds for any tie-breaking method that could have been applied.

Results We compared our model to all 5 models evaluated for this data set, described in Section 2, and to our own implementation of (Shnarch et al., 2011b). We term this model Heuristically-Normalized Probabilistic Lexical Model, *HN-PLM*, since it modifies PLM^{TL} by introducing heuristic normalization formulae. As explained earlier, both *M-PLM* and *HN-PLM* embed PLM^{TL} in their implementation but they differ in their sentence-level model. In our implementation of both models, PLM^{TL} applies chains of transitive rule applications whose maximal length is 3.

As seen in Table 1, *M-PLM* outperforms all prior models by a large margin. A comparison of *M-PLM* and *HN-PLM* reveals the major positive effect of choosing the Markovian process for the sentence-level decision. By avoiding heuristically-normalized formulae and having all our parameters being part of the Markovian model, we managed to increases both MAP and MRR by nearly 2.5%[6].

Ablation Test As an additional examination of the impact of the Markovian process components, we evaluated the contribution of having 4 transition parameters. The AND-logic applied by (Shnarch et al., 2011a) to their sentence-level decision roughly corresponds to 2 of the Markovian parameters. A binary AND outputs 1 if both its inputs are 1. This corresponds to $q_{11}(1)$ which is indeed estimate to be near 1. In any other case an AND gate outputs 0. This corresponds to $q_{00}(1)$ which was estimated to be near zero.

[6]The difference is not significant according to the Wilcoxon test, however we note that given the data set size it is hard to get a significant difference and that both Heilman and Smith (2010) and Wang and Manning (2010) improvements over the results of Wang et al. (2007) were not statistically significant.

System	MAP	MRR
Punyakanok et al.	41.89	49.39
Cui et al.	43.50	55.69
Wang & Manning	59.51	69.51
Wang et al.	60.29	68.52
Heilman & Smith	60.91	69.17
Shnarch et al. *HN-PLM*	61.89	70.24
M-PLM	**64.38**	**72.69**

Table 1: Results (in %) for the task of answer ranking for question answering (sorted by MAP).

The two parameters q_{01} and q_{10} are novel to the Markovian process and do not have counterparts in (Shnarch et al., 2011a). These parameters are the cases in which the sentence-level decision accumulated so far and the term-level decision do not agree. Introducing these 2 parameters enables our model to provide a positive decision for the hypothesis as a whole (or for a part of it) even if some of its terms were not inferred. We performed an ablation test on each of these two parameters by forcing the value of the ablated parameter to be zero. The notable performance drop presented in Table 2 indicates the crucial contribution of these parameters to our model.

Ablated parameter	Δ MAP	Δ MRR
$q_{01}(1) = 0$	-2.61	-4.91
$q_{10}(1) = 0$	-2.12	-2.86

Table 2: Ablation test for the novel parameters of the Markovian process. Results (in %) indicate performance drop when forcing a parameter to be zero.

5.2 RTE evaluations

To assess the added value of our model on an additional ranking evaluation, we utilize the search task data sets of the recent Recognizing Textual Entailment (RTE) benchmarks (Bentivogli et al., 2009; Bentivogli et al., 2010), which were originally constructed for the task of entailment classification. In that task a hypothesis is given with a corpus and the goal is to identify which sentences of the corpus entail the hypothesis. This setting naturally lends itself to a ranking scenario, in which the desired output is a list of the corpus sentences ranked by their probability to entail the given hypothesis.

To that end, we employed the same methodology as described in the previous section. Table 3 presents the improvement of our model over *HN-PLM*, whose classification performance was reported to be on par with best-performing systems on these data sets[7]. As can be seen, the improvement is substantial for both measures on both data sets. These results further assess the contribution of our Markovian sentence-level model.

	RTE-5		RTE-6	
	MAP	MRR	MAP	MRR
HN-PLM	58.0	82.9	54.0	71.9
M-PLM	61.6	84.8	60.0	79.2
Δ	+3.6	+1.9	+6.0	+7.3

Table 3: Improvements of our sentence-level model over *HN-PLM*. Results (in %) are shown for the last RTE and for the search task in RTE-5.

6 Discussion

This paper investigated probabilistic lexical models for ranking textual inferences focusing on passage ranking for QA. We showed that our coherent probabilistic model, whose sentence-level model is based on a Markovian process, considerably improves five prior syntactic-based models as well as a heuristically-normalized lexical model. Therefore, it raises the baseline for future methods.

In future work we would like to further explore a broader range of related probabilistic models. Especially, as our Markovian process is dependent on term order, it would be interesting to investigate models which are not order dependent.

Initial experiments on the classification task show that *M-PLM* performs well above the average system but below *HN-PLM*, since it does not normalize the estimated probability well across hypothesis. We therefore suggest a future work on better classification models.

Finally, we view this work as joining a line of research which develops principled probabilistic models for the task of textual inference and demonstrates their superiority over heuristic methods.

[7]RTE data sets were only used for the classification task so far, therefore there are no state-of-the-art results to compare with, when utilizing them for the ranking task.

A Appendix: Adaptation of *PLM*^{TL} learning

M-PLM embeds *PLM*^{TL} as its term-level model. *PLM*^{TL} introduces θ_R values as additional parameters for the complete model. We show how we modify (Shnarch et al., 2011a) E-step formula to fit our Markovian modeling, described in Section 3.1. The M-step formula remains exactly the same.

Eq. (11) estimates the a-posteriori validity probability of a single application of the rule r in the transitive chain c pointing at h_t, given that the annotation of the pair is a.

$$w_{tcr}(T,H) = P(x_{tcr} = 1|y_n = a) = \tag{11}$$
$$\frac{\sum_{i,j,k\in\{0,1\}} \alpha_{t-1}(i) P(x_t = j|x_{tcr} = 1)\theta_{R(r)} q_{ij}(k)\beta_t(a|k)}{P(y_n = a)}$$

where $t = 2 \dots n$ and $P(x_t = j|x_{tcr} = 1)$ is the probability that the inference value of x_t is j, given that the application of r provides a valid inference step. As appeared in (Shnarch et al., 2011b) this probability can be evaluated as follows:

$$P(x_t = 1|x_{tcr} = 1) = 1 - \frac{P(x_t = 0)}{P(x_{tc} = 0)}\left(1 - \frac{P(x_{tc} = 1)}{\theta_{R(r)}}\right)$$

For $t = 1$ there is no accumulated sentence-level decision at the previous position (i.e. no α_{t-1}) therefore Eq. (11) becomes:

$$w_{1cr}(T,H) = \frac{\sum_{j\in\{0,1\}} P(x_1 = j|x_{1cr} = 1)\theta_{R(r)}\beta_1(a|j)}{P(y_n = a)}$$

Acknowledgments

This work was partially supported by the Israel Science Foundation grant 1112/08, the PASCAL-2 Network of Excellence of the European Community FP7-ICT-2007-1-216886, and the European Community's Seventh Framework Programme (FP7/2007-2013) under grant agreement no. 287923 (EXCITEMENT).

References

Luisa Bentivogli, Ido Dagan, Hoa Trang Dang, Danilo Giampiccolo, and Bernardo Magnini. 2009. The fifth PASCAL recognizing textual entailment challenge. In *Proceedings of the Text Analysis Conference*.

Luisa Bentivogli, Peter Clark, Ido Dagan, Hoa Trang Dang, and Danilo Giampiccolo. 2010. The sixth PASCAL recognizing textual entailment challenge. In *Proceedings of the Text Analysis Conference*.

Peter Clark and Phil Harrison. 2010. BLUE-Lite: a knowledge-based lexical entailment system for RTE6. In *Proceedings of the Text Analysis Conference*.

Hang Cui, Renxu Sun, Keya Li, Min yen Kan, and Tat seng Chua. 2005. Question answering passage retrieval using dependency relations. In *Proceedings of SIGIR*.

Abdessamad Echihabi and Daniel Marcu. 2003. A noisy-channel approach to question answering. In *Proceedings of ACL*.

Christiane Fellbaum, editor. 1998. *WordNet: An Electronic Lexical Database (Language, Speech, and Communication)*. The MIT Press.

Nizar Habash and Bonnie Dorr. 2003. A categorial variation database for english. In *Proceedings of the Conference of the North American Chapter of the Association for Computational Linguistics*.

Aria Haghighi, Andrew Ng, and Christopher Manning. 2005. Robust textual inference via graph matching. In *Proceedings of the Conference on Empirical Methods in Natural Language Processing*.

Michael Heilman and Noah A. Smith. 2010. Tree edit models for recognizing textual entailments, paraphrases, and answers to questions. In *Proceedings of the Conference of the North American Chapter of the Association for Computational Linguistics*.

Houping Jia, Xiaojiang Huang, Tengfei Ma, Xiaojun Wan, and Jianguo Xiao. 2010. PKUTM participation at the Text Analysis Conference 2010 RTE and summarization track. In *Proceedings of the Text Analysis Conference*.

Dekang Lin. 1998. Automatic retrieval and clustering of similar words. In *Proceedings of COLING*.

Andrew MacKinlay and Timothy Baldwin. 2009. A baseline approach to the RTE5 search pilot. In *Proceedings of the Text Analysis Conference*.

Debarghya Majumdar and Pushpak Bhattacharyya. 2010. Lexical based text entailment system for main task of RTE6. In *Proceedings of the Text Analysis Conference*.

Judea Pearl. 1988. *Probabilistic reasoning in intelligent systems: networks of plausible inference*. Morgan Kaufmann.

Vasin Punyakanok, Dan Roth, and Wen tau Yih. 2004. Mapping dependencies trees: An application to question answering. In *Proceedings of the International Symposium on Artificial Intelligence and Mathematics*.

Rajat Raina, Andrew Y. Ng, and Christopher D. Manning. 2005. Robust textual inference via learning and abductive reasoning. In *Proceedings of AAAI*.

Stefan Schoenmackers, Oren Etzioni, and Daniel Weld. 2008. Scaling textual inference to the web. In *Proceedings of the Conference on Empirical Methods in Natural Language Processing*.

Eyal Shnarch, Jacob Goldberger, and Ido Dagan. 2011a. A probabilistic modeling framework for lexical entailment. In *Proceedings of ACL*.

Eyal Shnarch, Jacob Goldberger, and Ido Dagan. 2011b. Towards a probabilistic model for lexical entailment. In *Proceedings of the TextInfer Workshop on Textual Entailment*.

Fabian M. Suchanek, Gjergji Kasneci, and Gerhard Weikum. 2007. Yago: A Core of Semantic Knowledge. In *Proceedings of WWW*.

Mengqiu Wang and Christopher Manning. 2010. Probabilistic tree-edit models with structured latent variables for textual entailment and question answering. In *Proceedings of Coling*.

Mengqiu Wang, Noah A. Smith, and Teruko Mitamura. 2007. What is the Jeopardy model? a quasi-synchronous grammar for QA. In *Proceedings of the Conference on Empirical Methods in Natural Language Processing*.

#Emotional Tweets

Saif M. Mohammad
Emerging Technologies
National Research Council Canada
Ottawa, Ontario, Canada K1A 0R6
saif.mohammad@nrc-cnrc.gc.ca

Abstract

Detecting emotions in microblogs and social media posts has applications for industry, health, and security. However, there exists no microblog corpus with instances labeled for emotions for developing supervised systems. In this paper, we describe how we created such a corpus from Twitter posts using emotion-word hashtags. We conduct experiments to show that the self-labeled hashtag annotations are consistent and match with the annotations of trained judges. We also show how the Twitter emotion corpus can be used to improve emotion classification accuracy in a different domain. Finally, we extract a word–emotion association lexicon from this Twitter corpus, and show that it leads to significantly better results than the manually crafted WordNet Affect lexicon in an emotion classification task.[1]

1 Introduction

We use language not just to convey facts, but also our emotions. Automatically identifying emotions expressed in text has a number of applications, including customer relation management (Bougie et al., 2003), determining popularity of products and governments (Mohammad and Yang, 2011), and improving human-computer interaction (Velásquez, 1997; Ravaja et al., 2006).

Twitter is an online social networking and microblogging service where users post and read messages that are up to 140 characters long. The messages are called *tweets*.

Often a tweet may include one or more words immediately preceded with a hash symbol (#). These words are called *hashtags*. Hashtags serve many purposes, but most notably they are used to indicate the topic. Often these words add to the information in the tweet: for example, hashtags indicating the tone of the message or their internal emotions.

From the perspective of one consuming tweets, hashtags play a role in search: Twitter allows people to search tweets not only through words in the tweets, but also through hashtagged words. Consider the tweet below:

> *We are fighting for the 99% that have been left behind. #OWS #anger*

A number of people tweeting about the Occupy Wall Street movement added the hashtag *#OWS* to their tweets. This allowed people searching for tweets about the movement to access them simply by searching for the *#OWS* hashtag. In this particular instance, the tweeter (one who tweets) has also added an emotion-word hashtag *#anger*, possibly to convey that he or she is angry.

Currently there are more than 200 million Twitter accounts, 180 thousand tweets posted every day, and 18 thousand Twitter search queries every second. Socio-linguistic researchers point out that Twitter is primarily a means for people to converse with other individuals, groups, and the world in general (Boyd et al., 2010). As tweets are freely accessible to all, the conversations can take on non-traditional forms such as discussions developing through many voices rather than just two interlocuters. For example, the use of Twitter and Facebook has been credited with

[1]Email the author to obtain a copy of the hash-tagged tweets or the emotion lexicon: saif.mohammad@nrc-cnrc.gc.ca.

providing momentum to the 2011 Arab Spring and Occupy Wall Street movements (Skinner, 2011; Ray, 2011). Understanding how such conversations develop, how people influence one another through emotional expressions, and how news is shared to elicit certain emotional reactions, are just some of the compelling reasons to develop better models for the emotion analysis of social media.

Supervised methods for emotion detection tend to perform better than unsupervised ones. They use ngram features such as unigrams and bigrams (individual words and two-word sequences) (Aman and Szpakowicz, 2007; Neviarouskaya et al., 2009; Mohammad, 2012b). However, these methods require labeled data where utterances are marked with the emotion they express. Manual annotation is time-intensive and costly. Thus only a small amount of such text exists. Further, supervised algorithms that rely on ngram features tend to classify accurately only if trained on data from the same domain as the target sentences (Mohammad, 2012b). Thus even the limited amount of existing emotion-labeled data is unsuitable for use in microblog analysis.

In this paper, we show how we automatically created a large dataset of more than 20,000 emotion-labeled tweets using hashtags. We compiled labeled data for six emotions—joy, sadness, anger, fear, disgust, and surprise—argued to be the most basic (Ekman, 1992). We will refer to our dataset as the Twitter Emotion Corpus (TEC). We show through experiments that even though the tweets and hashtags cover a diverse array of topics and were generated by thousands of different individuals (possibly with very different educational and socio-economic backgrounds), the emotion annotations are consistent and match the intuitions of trained judges. We also show how we used the TEC to improve emotion detection in a domain very different from social media.

Finally, we describe how we generated a large lexicon of ngrams and associated emotions from TEC. This emotion lexicon can be used in many applications, including highlighting words and phrases in a piece of text to quickly convey regions of affect. We show that the lexicon leads to significantly better results than that obtained using the manually crafted WordNet Affect lexicon in an emotion classification task.

2 Related Work

Emotion analysis can be applied to all kinds of text, but certain domains and modes of communication tend to have more overt expressions of emotions than others. Genereux and Evans (2006), Mihalcea and Liu (2006), and Neviarouskaya et al. (2009) analyzed web-logs. Alm et al. (2005) and Francisco and Gervás (2006) worked on fairy tales. Boucouvalas (2002), John et al. (2006), and Mohammad (2012a) explored emotions in novels. Zhe and Boucouvalas (2002), Holzman and Pottenger (2003), and Ma et al. (2005) annotated chat messages for emotions. Liu et al. (2003) and Mohammad and Yang (2011) worked on email data. Kim et al. (2009) analyzed sadness in posts reacting to news of Michael Jackson's death. Tumasjan et al. (2010) study Twitter as a forum for political deliberation.

Much of this work focuses on six Ekman emotions. There is less work on complex emotions, for example, work by Pearl and Steyvers (2010) that focuses on politeness, rudeness, embarrassment, formality, persuasion, deception, confidence, and disbelief. Bolen et al. (2009) measured tension, depression, anger, vigor, fatigue, and confusion in tweets. One of the advantages of our work is that we can easily collect tweets with hashtags for many emotions, well beyond the basic six.

Go et al. (2009) and González-Ibáñez et al. (2011) noted that sometimes people use the hashtag *#sarcasm* to indicate that their tweet is sarcastic. They collected tweets with hashtags of *#sarcasm* and *#sarcastic* to create a dataset of sarcastic tweets. We follow their ideas and collect tweets with hashtags pertaining to different emotions. Additionally, we present several experiments to validate that the emotion labels in the corpus are consistent and match intuitions of trained judges.

3 Existing Emotion-Labeled Text

The SemEval-2007 Affective Text corpus has newspaper headlines labeled with the six Ekman emotions by six annotators (Strapparava and Mihalcea, 2007). More precisely, for each headline–emotion pair, the annotators gave scores from 0 to 100 indicating how strongly the headline expressed the emotion. The inter-annotator agreement as determined by calculating the Pearson's product moment corre-

emotion	# of instances	% of instances	r
anger	132	13.2	0.50
disgust	43	4.3	0.45
fear	247	24.7	0.64
joy	344	34.4	0.60
sadness	283	28.3	0.68
surprise	253	25.3	0.36
		simple average	0.54
		frequency-based average	0.43

Table 1: Inter-annotator agreement (Pearson's correlation) amongst 6 annotators on the 1000-headlines dataset.

lation (r) between the scores given by each annotator and the average of the other five annotators is shown in Table 1. For our experiments, we considered scores greater than 25 to indicate that the headline expresses the corresponding emotion.

The dataset was created for an unsupervised competition, and consisted of 250 headlines of trial data and 1000 headlines of test data. We will refer to them as the 250-headlines and the 1000-headlines datasets respectively. However, the data has also been used in a supervised setting through (1) tenfold cross-validation on the 1000-headlines dataset and (2) using the 1000 headlines as training data and testing on the 250-headlines dataset (Chaffar and Inkpen, 2011).

Other datasets with sentence-level annotations of emotions include about 4000 sentences from blogs, compiled by Aman and Szpakowicz (2007); 1000 sentences from stories on topics such as education and health, compiled by Neviarouskaya et al. (2009); and about 4000 sentences from fairy tales, annotated by Alm and Sproat (2005).

4 Creating the Twitter Emotion Corpus

Sometimes people use hashtags to notify others of the emotions associated with the message they are tweeting. Table 2 shows a few examples. On reading just the message before the hashtags, most people will agree that the tweeter #1 is sad, tweeter #2 is happy, and tweeter #3 is angry.

However, there also exist tweets such as the fourth example, where reading just the message before the hashtag does not convey the emotions of the tweeter. Here, the hashtag provides information not present (implicitly or explicitly) in the rest of the message.

1. *Feeling left out... #sadness*
2. *My amazing memory saves the day again! #joy*
3. *Some jerk stole my photo on tumblr. #anger*
4. *Mika used my photo on tumblr. #anger*
5. *School is very boring today :/ #joy*
6. *to me.... YOU are ur only #fear*

Table 2: Example tweets with emotion-words hashtags.

There are also tweets, such as those shown in examples 5 and 6, that do not seem to express the emotions stated in the hashtags. This may occur for many reasons including the use of sarcasm or irony. Additional context is required to understand the full emotional import of many tweets. Tweets tend to be very short, and often have spelling mistakes, short forms, and various other properties that make such text difficult to process by natural language systems. Further, it is probable, that only a small portion of emotional tweets are hashtagged with emotion words.

Our goal in this paper is to determine if we can successfully use emotion-word hashtags as emotion labels despite the many challenges outlined above:

- Can we create a large corpus of emotion-labeled hashtags?
- Are the emotion annotations consistent, despite the large number of annotators, despite no control over their socio-economic and cultural background, despite the many ways in which hashtags are used, and despite the many idiosyncracies of tweets?
- Do the hashtag annotations match with the intuitions of trained judges?

We chose to collect tweets with hashtags corresponding to the six Ekman emotions: *#anger, #disgust, #fear, #happy, #sadness,* and *#surprise.*

Eisenstein et al. (2010) collected about 380,000 tweets[2] from Twitter's official API.[3] Similarly, Go et al. (2009) collected 1.6 million tweets.[4] However, these datasets had less than 50 tweets that contained emotion-word hashtags. Therefore, we abandoned the search-in-corpora approach in favor of the one described below.

[2]http://www.ark.cs.cmu.edu/GeoText

[3]https://dev.twitter.com/docs/streaming-api

[4]https://sites.google.com/site/twittersentimenthelp

4.1 Hashtag-based Search on the Twitter Search API

The Archivist[5] is a free online service that helps users extract tweets using Twitter's Search API.[6] For any given query, Archivist first obtains up to 1500 tweets from the previous seven days. Subsequently, it polls the Twitter Search API every few hours to obtain newer tweets that match the query. We supplied Archivist with the six hashtag queries corresponding to the Ekman emotions, and collected about 50,000 tweets from those posted between November 15, 2011 and December 6, 2011.

We discarded tweets that had fewer than three valid English words. We used the *Roget Thesaurus* as the lexicon of English words.[7] This helped filter out most, if not all, of the non-English tweets that had English emotion hashtags. It also eliminated very short phrases, and some expressions with very bad spelling. We discarded tweets with the prefix "Rt", "RT", and "rt", which indicate that the messages that follow are re-tweets (re-postings of tweets sent earlier by somebody else). Like González-Ibáñez et al. (2011), we removed tweets that did not have the hashtag of interest at the end of the message. It has been suggested that middle-of-tweet hashtags may not be good labels of the tweets.[8] Finally, we were left with about 21,000 tweets, which formed the Twitter Emotion Corpus (TEC).

4.2 Distribution of emotion-word hashtags

Table 3 presents some details of the TEC. Observe that the distribution of emotions in the TEC is very different from the distribution of emotions in the 1000-headlines corpus (see Table 1). There are more messages tagged with the hashtag *#joy* than any of the other Ekman emotions.

Synonyms can often be used to express the same concept or emotion. Thus it is possible that the true distribution of hashtags corresponding to emotions is different from what is shown in Table 3. In the future, we intend to collect tweets with synonyms of *joy, sadness, fear,* etc., as well.

[5]http://archivist.visitmix.com

[6]https://dev.twitter.com/docs/using-search

[7]Roget's Thesaurus: www.gutenberg.org/ebooks/10681

[8]End-of-message hashtags are also much more common than hashtags at other positions.

hashtag	# of instances	% of instances
#anger	1,555	7.4
#disgust	761	3.6
#fear	2,816	13.4
#joy	8,240	39.1
#sadness	3,830	18.2
#surprise	3,849	18.3
Total tweets	21,051	100.0
# of tweeters	19,059	

Table 3: Details of the Twitter Emotion Corpus.

5 Consistency and Usefulness of Emotion Hashtagged Tweets

As noted earlier, even with trained judges, emotion annotation obtains only a modest inter-annotator agreement (see Table 1). As shown in Table 3, the TEC has about 21,000 tweets from about 19,000 different people. If TEC were to be treated as manually annotated data (which in one sense, it is), then it is data created by a very large number of judges, and most judges have annotated just one instance. Therefore, an important question is to determine whether the hashtag annotations of the tens of thousands of tweeters are consistent with one another. It will also be worth determining if this large amount of emotion-tagged Twitter data can help improve emotion detection in sentences from other domains.

To answer these questions, we conducted two automatic emotion classification experiments described in the two sub-sections below. For these experiments, we created binary classifiers for each of the six emotions using Weka (Hall et al., 2009).[9] For example, the *Fear–NotFear* classifier determined whether a sentence expressed fear or not. Note that, for these experiments, we treated the emotion hashtags as class labels and removed them from the tweets. Thus a classifier has to determine that a tweet expresses anger, for example, without having access to the hashtag *#anger*.

We chose Support Vector Machines (SVM) with Sequential Minimal Optimization (Platt, 1999) as the machine learning algorithm because of its successful application in various research problems. We used binary features that captured the presence or absence of unigrams and bigrams.

[9]http://www.cs.waikato.ac.nz/ml/weka

Label (X)	#gold	#right	#guesses	P	R	F
I. System using ngrams with freq. > 1						
anger	132	35	71	49.3	26.5	34.5
disgust	43	8	19	42.1	18.6	25.8
fear	247	108	170	63.5	43.7	51.8
joy	344	155	287	54.0	45.1	49.1
sadness	283	104	198	52.5	36.7	43.2
surprise	253	74	167	44.3	29.2	35.2
ALL LABELS	1302	484	912	53.1	37.2	**43.7**
II. System using all ngrams (no filtering)						
ALL LABELS	1302	371	546	67.9	28.5	40.1
III. System that guesses randomly						
ALL LABELS	1302	651	3000	21.7	50.0	30.3

Table 4: Cross-validation results on the 1000-headlines dataset. *#gold* is the number of headlines expressing a particular emotion. *#right* is the number these instances the classifier correctly marked as expressing the emotion. *#guesses* is the number of instances marked as expressing an emotion by the classifier.

In order to set a suitable benchmark for experiments with the TEC corpus, we first applied the classifiers to the SemEval-2007 Affective Text corpus. We executed ten-fold cross-validation on the 1000-headlines dataset. We experimented with using all ngrams, as well as training on only those ngrams that occurred more than once.

The rows under I in Table 4 give a breakdown of results obtained by the *EmotionX–NotEmotionX* classifiers. when they ignored single-occurrence n-grams (where X is one of the six basic emotions). *#gold* is the number of headlines expressing a particular emotion X. *#right* is the number of instances that the classifier correctly marked as expressing X. *#guesses* is the number of instances marked as expressing X by the classifier. Precision (P) and recall (R) are calculated as shown below:

$$P = \frac{\#right}{\#guesses} * 100 \quad (1)$$

$$R = \frac{\#right}{\#gold} * 100 \quad (2)$$

F is the balanced F-score. The ALL LABELS row shows the sums of *#gold*, *#right*, and *#guesses*.

The II and III rows in the table show overall results obtained by a system that uses all ngrams and by a system that guesses randomly.[10] We do not show a breakdown of results by emotions for II and III due to space constraints.

It is not surprising that the emotion classes with the most training instances and the highest inter-annotator agreement (joy, sadness, and fear) are also the classes on which the classifiers perform best (see Table 1).

The F-score of 40.1 obtained using all ngrams is close to 39.6 obtained by Chaffar and Inkpen (2011)—a sanity check for our baseline system. Ignoring words that occur only once in the training data seems beneficial. All classification results shown ahead are for the cases when ngrams that occurred only once were filtered out.

5.1 Experiment I: Can a classifier learn to predict emotion hashtags?

We applied the binary classifiers described above to the TEC. Table 5 shows ten-fold cross-validation results. Observe that even though the TEC was created from tens of thousands of users, the automatic classifiers are able to predict the emotions (hashtags) with F-scores much higher than the random baseline, and also higher than those obtained on the 1000-headlines corpus. Note also that this is despite the fact that the random baseline for the 1000-headlines corpus ($F = 30.3$) is higher than the random baseline for the TEC ($F = 21.7$). The results suggest that emotion hashtags assigned to tweets are consistent to a degree such that they can be used for detecting emotion hashtags in other tweets.

Note that expectedly the *Joy–NotJoy* classifier

[10] A system that randomly guesses whether an instance is expressing an emotion X or not will get half of the *#gold* instances right. Further, the system will mark half of all the instances as expressing emotion X. For ALL LABELS, $\#right = \frac{\#gold}{2}$, and $\#guesses = \frac{\#instances*6}{2}$.

Label	#gold	#right	#guesses	P	R	F
I. System using ngrams with freq. > 1						
anger	1555	347	931	37.3	22.31	27.9
disgust	761	102	332	30.7	13.4	18.7
fear	2816	1236	2073	59.6	43.9	50.6
joy	8240	4980	7715	64.5	60.4	62.4
sadness	3830	1377	3286	41.9	36.0	38.7
surprise	3849	1559	3083	50.6	40.5	45.0
ALL LABELS	21051	9601	17420	55.1	45.6	**49.9**
II. System that guesses randomly						
ALL LABELS	21051	10525	63,153	16.7	50.0	21.7

Table 5: Cross-validation results on the TEC. The highest F-score is shown in bold.

gets the best results as it has the highest number of training instances. The *Sadness–NotSadness* classifier performed relatively poorly considering the amount of training instances available, whereas the *Fear-NotFear* classifier performed relatively well. It is possible that people use less overt cues in tweets when they are explicitly giving it a sadness hashtag.

5.2 Experiment II: Can TEC improve emotion classification in a new domain?

As mentioned earlier, supervised algorithms perform well when training and test data are from the same domain. However, certain domain adaptation algorithms may be used to combine training data in the target domain with large amounts of training data from a different source domain.

The Daumé (2007) approach involves the transformation of the original training instance feature vector into a new space made up of three copies of the original vector. The three copies correspond to the target domain, the source domain, and the general domain. If X represents an original feature vector from the *target domain*, then it is transformed into XOX, where O is a zero vector. If X represents original feature vector from the *source domain*, then it is transformed into OXX. This data is given to the learning algorithm, which learns information specific to the target domain, specific to the source domain, as well as information that applies to both domains. The test instance feature vector (which is from the target domain) is transformed to XOX. Therefore, the classifier applies information specific to the target domain as well as information common to both the target and source domains, but not information specific only to the source domain.

In this section, we describe experiments on using the Twitter Emotion Corpus for emotion classification in the newspaper headlines domain. We applied our binary emotion classifiers on unseen test data from the newspaper headlines domain—the 250-headlines dataset—using each of the following as a training corpus:

- Target-domain data: the 1000-headlines data.
- Source-domain data: the TEC.
- Target and Source data: A joint corpus of the 1000-headlines dataset and the TEC.

Additionally, when using the 'Target and Source' data, we also tested the domain adaptation algorithm proposed in Daumé (2007). Since the *EmotionX* class (the positive class) has markedly fewer instances than the *NotEmotionX* class, we assigned higher weight to instances of the positive class during training.[11] The rows under I in Table 6 give the results. (Row II results are for the experiment described in Section 6, and can be ignored for now.)

We see that the macro-averaged F-score when using target-domain data (row I.a.) is identical to the score obtained by the random baseline (row III). However, observe that the precision of the ngram system is higher than the random system, and its recall is lower. This suggests that the test data has many n-grams not previously seen in the training data. Observe that as expected, using source-domain data produces much lower scores (row I.b.) than when using target-domain training data (row I.a.).

Using both target- and source-domain data produced significantly better results (row I.c.1.) than

[11] For example, for the *anger–NotAnger* classifier, if 10 out of 110 instances have the label anger, then they are each given a weight of 10, whereas the rest are given a weight of 1.

	# of features	P	R	F
I. System using ngrams in training data:				
a. the 1000-headlines text (target domain)	1,181	40.2	32.1	35.7
b. the TEC (source domain)	32,954	29.9	26.1	27.9
c. the 1000-headlines text and the TEC (target and source)				
c.1. no domain adaptation	33,902	41.7	35.5	38.3
c.2. with domain adaptation	101,706	46.0	35.5	**40.1**
II. System using ngrams in 1000-headlines and:				
a. the TEC lexicon	1,181 + 6	44.4	35.3	39.3
b. the WordNet Affect lexicon	1,181 + 6	39.7	30.5	34.5
c. the NRC emotion lexicon	1,181 + 10	46.7	38.6	**42.2**
III. System that guesses randomly	-	27.8	50.0	35.7

Table 6: Results on the 250-headlines dataset. The highest F-scores in I and II are shown in bold.

using target-domain data alone (I.a.). Applying the domain adaptation technique described in Daumé (2007), obtained even better results (row I.c.2.). (We used the Fisher Exact Test and a confidence interval of 95% for all precision and recall significance testing reported in this paper.) The use of TEC improved both precision and recall over just using the target-domain text. This shows that the Twitter Emotion Corpus can be leveraged, preferably with a suitable domain adaptation algorithm, to improve emotion classification results even on datasets from a different domain. It is also a validation of the premise that the self-labeled emotion hashtags are consistent, at least to some degree, with the emotion labels given by trained human judges.

6 Creating the TEC Emotion Lexicon

Word–emotion association lexicons are lists of words and associated emotions. For example, the word *victory* may be associated with the emotions of joy and relief. These emotion lexicons have many applications, including automatically highlighting words and phrases to quickly convey regions of affect in a piece of text. Mohammad (2012b) shows that these lexicon features can significantly improve classifier performance over and above that obtained using ngrams alone.

WordNet Affect (Strapparava and Valitutti, 2004) includes 1536 words with associations to the six Ekman emotions.[12] Mohammad and colleagues compiled emotion annotations for about 14,000 words by crowdsourcing to Mechanical Turk (Mohammad and Turney, 2012; Mohammad and Yang, 2011).[13] This lexicon, referred to as the NRC emotion lexicon, has annotations for eight emotions (six of Ekman, trust, and anticipation) as well as for positive and negative sentiment.[14] Here, we show how we created an ngram–emotion association lexicon from emotion-labeled sentences in the 1000-headlines dataset and the TEC.

6.1 Method

Given a dataset of sentences and associated emotion labels, we compute the *Strength of Association (SoA)* between an n-gram n and an emotion e to be:

$$SoA(n, e) = PMI(n, e) - PMI(n, \neg e) \qquad (3)$$

where PMI is the pointwise mutual information.

$$PMI(n, e) = \log \frac{freq(n, e)}{freq(n) * freq(e)} \qquad (4)$$

where $freq(n, e)$ is the number of times n occurs in a sentence with label e. $freq(n)$ and $freq(e)$ are the frequencies of n and e in the labeled corpus.

$$PMI(n, \neg e) = \log \frac{freq(n, \neg e)}{freq(n) * freq(\neg e)} \qquad (5)$$

where $freq(n, \neg e)$ is the number of times n occurs in a sentence that does not have the label e. $freq(\neg e)$ is the number of sentences that do not have the label e. Thus, equation 4 is simplified to:

$$SoA(n, e) = \log \frac{freq(n, e) * freq(\neg e)}{freq(e) * freq(n, \neg e)} \qquad (6)$$

[12] http://wndomains.fbk.eu/wnaffect.html

[13] http://www.purl.org/net/saif.mohammad/research

[14] Plutchik (1985) proposed a model of 8 basic emotions.

Emotion lexicon	# of word types
1000-headlines lexicon	152
TEC lexicon	11,418
WordNet Affect lexicon	1,536
NRC emotion lexicon	14,000

Table 7: Number of word types in emotion lexicons.

Since PMI is known to be a poor estimator of association for low-frequency events, we ignored ngrams that occurred less than five times.

If an n-gram has a stronger tendency to occur in a sentence with a particular emotion label, than in a sentence that does not have that label, then that ngram–emotion pair will have an SoA score that is greater than zero.

6.2 Emotion lexicons created from the 1000-headlines dataset and the TEC

We calculated SoA scores for the unigrams and bigrams in the TEC with the six basic emotions. All ngram–emotion pairs that obtained scores greater than zero were extracted to form the TEC emotion lexicon. We repeated these steps for the 1000-headlines dataset as well. Table 7 shows the number of word types in the two automatically generated and the two manually created lexicons. Observe that the 1000-headlines dataset produces very few entries, whereas the large size of the TEC enables the creation of a substantial emotion lexicon.

6.3 Evaluating the TEC lexicon

We evaluate the TEC lexicon by using it for classifying emotions in a setting similar to the one discussed in the previous section. The test set is the 250-headlines dataset. The training set is the 1000-headlines dataset. We used binary features that captured the presence or absence of unigrams and bigrams just as before. Additionally, we also used integer-valued affect features that captured the number of word tokens in a sentence associated with different emotions labels in the TEC emotion lexicon and the WordNet Affect lexicon. For example, if a sentence has two joy words and one surprise word, then the joy feature has value 2, surprise has value 1, and all remaining affect features have value 0.[15]

We know from the results in Table 6 (I.a. and I.c) that using the Twitter Emotion Corpus in addition to the 1000-headlines training data significantly improves results. Now we investigate if the TEC lexicon, which is created from TEC, can similarly improve performance. The rows under II in Table 6 give the results.

[15]Normalizing by sentence length did not give better results.

Observe that even though the TEC lexicon is a derivative of the TEC that includes fewer unigrams and bigrams, the classifiers using the TEC lexicon produces an F-score (row II.a.) significantly higher than in the scenarios of I.a. and almost as high as in I.c.2. This shows that the TEC lexicon successfully captures the word–emotion associations that are latent in the Twitter Emotion Corpus. We also find that the the classifiers perform significantly better when using the TEC lexicon (row II.a.) than when using the WordNet Affect lexicon (row II.b.), but not as well as when using the NRC emotion lexicon (row II.c.). The strong results of the NRC emotion lexicon are probably because of its size and because it was created by direct annotation of words for emotions, which required significant time and effort. On the other hand, the TEC lexicon can be easily improved further by compiling an even larger set of tweets using synonyms and morphological variants of the emotion words used thus far.

7 Conclusions and Future Work

We compiled a large corpus of tweets and associated emotions using emotion-word hashtags. Even though the corpus has tweets from several thousand people, we showed that the self-labeled hashtag annotations are consistent. We also showed how the Twitter emotion corpus can be combined with labeled data from a different target domain to improve classification accuracy. This experiment was especially telling since it showed that self-labeled emotion hashtags correspond well with annotations of trained human judges. Finally we extracted a large word–emotion association lexicon from the Twitter emotion corpus. Our future work includes collecting tweets with hashtags for various other emotions and also hashtags that are near-synonyms of the basic emotion terms described in this paper.

Acknowledgments

We thank Tara Small and Peter Turney for helpful discussions. For Archivist, we thank its creators.

References

Cecilia O. Alm and Richard Sproat, 2005. *Emotional sequencing and development in fairy tales*, pages 668–674. Springer.

Cecilia Ovesdotter Alm, Dan Roth, and Richard Sproat. 2005. Emotions from text: Machine learning for text-based emotion prediction. In *Proceedings of the Joint Conference on HLT–EMNLP*, Vancouver, Canada.

Saima Aman and Stan Szpakowicz. 2007. Identifying expressions of emotion in text. In Vclav Matoušek and Pavel Mautner, editors, *Text, Speech and Dialogue*, volume 4629 of *Lecture Notes in Computer Science*, pages 196–205. Springer Berlin / Heidelberg.

Johan Bollen, Alberto Pepe, and Huina Mao. 2009. Modeling public mood and emotion: Twitter sentiment and socio-economic phenomena. *CoRR*.

Anthony C. Boucouvalas. 2002. Real time text-to-emotion engine for expressive internet communication. *Emerging Communication: Studies on New Technologies and Practices in Communication*, 5:305–318.

J. R. G. Bougie, R. Pieters, and M. Zeelenberg. 2003. Angry customers don't come back, they get back: The experience and behavioral implications of anger and dissatisfaction in services. Open access publications from tilburg university, Tilburg University.

Danah Boyd, Scott Golder, and Gilad Lotan. 2010. Tweet, Tweet, Retweet: Conversational Aspects of Retweeting on Twitter. volume 0, pages 1–10, Los Alamitos, CA, USA. IEEE Computer Society.

Soumaya Chaffar and Diana Inkpen. 2011. Using a heterogeneous dataset for emotion analysis in text. In *Canadian Conference on AI*, pages 62–67.

Hal Daumé. 2007. Frustratingly easy domain adaptation. In *Conference of the Association for Computational Linguistics (ACL)*, Prague, Czech Republic.

Jacob Eisenstein, Brendan O'Connor, Noah A. Smith, and Eric P. Xing. 2010. A latent variable model for geographic lexical variation. In *Proceedings of the 2010 Conference on Empirical Methods in Natural Language Processing*, pages 1277–1287, Stroudsburg, PA. Association for Computational Linguistics.

Paul Ekman. 1992. An argument for basic emotions. *Cognition and Emotion*, 6(3):169–200.

Virginia Francisco and Pablo Gervás. 2006. Automated mark up of affective information in english texts. In Petr Sojka, Ivan Kopecek, and Karel Pala, editors, *Text, Speech and Dialogue*, volume 4188 of *Lecture Notes in Computer Science*, pages 375–382. Springer Berlin / Heidelberg.

Michel Genereux and Roger P. Evans. 2006. Distinguishing affective states in weblogs. In *AAAI-2006 Spring Symposium on Computational Approaches to Analysing Weblogs*, pages 27–29, Stanford, California.

Alec Go, Richa Bhayani, and Lei Huang. 2009. Twitter sentiment classification using distant supervision. In *Final Projects from CS224N for Spring 2008–2009 at The Stanford Natural Language Processing Group*.

Roberto González-Ibáñez, Smaranda Muresan, and Nina Wacholder. 2011. Identifying sarcasm in twitter: a closer look. In *Proceedings of the 49th Annual Meeting of the Association for Computational Linguistics: Human Language Technologies: short papers - Volume 2*, pages 581–586, Portland, Oregon.

Mark Hall, Eibe Frank, Geoffrey Holmes, Bernhard Pfahringer, Peter Reutemann, and Ian H. Witten. 2009. The weka data mining software: an update. *SIGKDD*, 11:10–18.

Lars E. Holzman and William M. Pottenger. 2003. Classification of emotions in internet chat: An application of machine learning using speech phonemes. Technical report, Leigh University.

David John, Anthony C. Boucouvalas, and Zhe Xu. 2006. Representing emotional momentum within expressive internet communication. In *Proceedings of the 24th IASTED international conference on Internet and multimedia systems and applications*, pages 183–188, Anaheim, CA. ACTA Press.

Elsa Kim, Sam Gilbert, Michael J. Edwards, and Erhardt Graeff. 2009. Detecting sadness in 140 characters: Sentiment analysis of mourning michael jackson on twitter.

Hugo Liu, Henry Lieberman, and Ted Selker. 2003. A model of textual affect sensing using real-world knowledge. In *Proceedings of the 8th international conference on Intelligent user interfaces*, IUI '03, pages 125–132, New York, NY. ACM.

Chunling Ma, Helmut Prendinger, and Mitsuru Ishizuka. 2005. Emotion estimation and reasoning based on affective textual interaction. In J. Tao and R. W. Picard, editors, *First International Conference on Affective Computing and Intelligent Interaction (ACII-2005)*, pages 622–628, Beijing, China.

Rada Mihalcea and Hugo Liu. 2006. A corpus-based approach to finding happiness. In *AAAI-2006 Spring Symposium on Computational Approaches to Analysing Weblogs*, pages 139–144. AAAI Press.

Saif M. Mohammad and Peter D. Turney. 2012. Crowdsourcing a word–emotion association lexicon. *To Appear in Computational Intelligence*.

Saif M. Mohammad and Tony Yang. 2011. Tracking Sentiment in Mail: How Genders Differ on Emotional Axes. In *Proceedings of the 2nd Workshop on Computational Approaches to Subjectivity and Sentiment Analysis (WASSA 2.011)*, pages 70–79, Portland, Oregon. Association for Computational Linguistics.

Saif M. Mohammad. 2012a. From once upon a time to happily ever after: Tracking emotions in mail and books. *To Appear in Decision Support Systems.*

Saif M. Mohammad. 2012b. Portable features for emotion classification. In *Proceedings of the North American Chapter of the Association for Computational Linguistics: Human Language Technologies (NAACL-HLT 2012)*, Montreal, Canada. Association for Computational Linguistics.

Alena Neviarouskaya, Helmut Prendinger, and Mitsuru Ishizuka. 2009. Compositionality principle in recognition of fine-grained emotions from text. In *Proceedings of the Proceedings of the Third International Conference on Weblogs and Social Media (ICWSM-09)*, pages 278–281, San Jose, California.

Lisa Pearl and Mark Steyvers. 2010. Identifying emotions, intentions, and attitudes in text using a game with a purpose. In *Proceedings of the NAACL-HLT 2010 Workshop on Computational Approaches to Analysis and Generation of Emotion in Text*, Los Angeles, California.

John Platt. 1999. Using analytic qp and sparseness to speed training of support vector machines. In *In Neural Info. Processing Systems 11*, pages 557–563. MIT Press.

Robert Plutchik. 1985. On emotion: The chicken-and-egg problem revisited. *Motivation and Emotion*, 9(2):197–200.

Niklas Ravaja, Timo Saari, Marko Turpeinen, Jari Laarni, Mikko Salminen, and Matias Kivikangas. 2006. Spatial presence and emotions during video game playing: Does it matter with whom you play? *Presence: Teleoperators and Virtual Environments*, 15(4):381–392.

Tapas Ray. 2011. The 'story' of digital excess in revolutions of the arab spring. *Journal of Media Practice*, 12(2):189–196.

Julia Skinner. 2011. Social media and revolution: The arab spring and the occupy movement as seen through three information studies paradigms. *Sprouts: Working Papers on Information Systems*, 11(169).

Carlo Strapparava and Rada Mihalcea. 2007. Semeval-2007 task 14: Affective text. In *Proceedings of SemEval-2007*, pages 70–74, Prague, Czech Republic.

Carlo Strapparava and Alessandro Valitutti. 2004. Wordnet-Affect: An affective extension of WordNet. In *Proceedings of the 4th International Conference on Language Resources and Evaluation (LREC-2004)*, pages 1083–1086, Lisbon, Portugal.

Andranik Tumasjan, Timm O Sprenger, Philipp G Sandner, and Isabell M Welpe. 2010. Predicting elections with twitter : What 140 characters reveal about political sentiment. *Word Journal Of The International Linguistic Association*, pages 178–185.

Juan D. Velásquez. 1997. Modeling emotions and other motivations in synthetic agents. In *Proceedings of the fourteenth national conference on artificial intelligence and ninth conference on Innovative applications of artificial intelligence*, AAAI'97/IAAI'97, pages 10–15. AAAI Press.

Xu Zhe and A Boucouvalas, 2002. *Text-to-Emotion Engine for Real Time Internet CommunicationText-to-Emotion Engine for Real Time Internet Communication*, pages 164–168.

Monolingual Distributional Similarity for Text-to-Text Generation

Juri Ganitkevitch, Benjamin Van Durme, and **Chris Callison-Burch**
Center for Language and Speech Processing
Human Language Technology Center of Excellence
Johns Hopkins University
Baltimore, MD 21218, USA

Abstract

Previous work on paraphrase extraction and application has relied on either parallel datasets, or on distributional similarity metrics over large text corpora. Our approach combines these two orthogonal sources of information and directly integrates them into our paraphrasing system's log-linear model. We compare different distributional similarity feature-sets and show significant improvements in grammaticality and meaning retention on the example text-to-text generation task of sentence compression, achieving state-of-the-art quality.

1 Introduction

A wide variety of applications in natural language processing can be cast in terms of text-to-text generation. Given input in the form of natural language, a text-to-text generation system produces natural language output that is subject to a set of constraints. Compression systems, for instance, produce shorter sentences. Paraphrases, i.e. differing textual realizations of the same meaning, are a crucial components of text-to-text generation systems, and have been successfully applied to tasks such as multi-document summarization (Barzilay et al., 1999; Barzilay, 2003), query expansion (Anick and Tipirneni, 1999; Riezler et al., 2007), question answering (McKeown, 1979; Ravichandran and Hovy, 2002), sentence compression (Cohn and Lapata, 2008; Zhao et al., 2009), and simplification (Wubben et al., 2012).

Paraphrase collections for text-to-text generation have been extracted from a variety of different corpora. Several approaches rely on bilingual parallel data (Bannard and Callison-Burch, 2005; Zhao et al., 2008; Callison-Burch, 2008; Ganitkevitch et al., 2011), while others leverage distributional methods on monolingual text corpora (Lin and Pantel, 2001; Bhagat and Ravichandran, 2008). So far, however, only preliminary studies have been undertaken to combine the information from these two sources (Chan et al., 2011).

In this paper, we describe an extension of Ganitkevitch et al. (2011)'s bilingual data-based approach. We augment the bilingually-sourced paraphrases using features based on monolingual distributional similarity. More specifically:

- We show that using monolingual distributional similarity features improves paraphrase quality beyond what we can achieve with features estimated from bilingual data.

- We define distributional similarity for paraphrase patterns that contain constituent-level gaps, e.g.

  $sim(\text{one } JJ \text{ instance of } NP, \text{a } JJ \text{ case of } NP).$

  This generalizes over distributional similarity for contiguous phrases.

- We compare different types of monolingual distributional information and show that they can be used to achieve significant improvements in grammaticality.

- Finally, we compare our method to several strong baselines on the text-to-text generation task of sentence compression. Our method shows state-of-the-art results, beating a purely bilingually sourced paraphrasing system.

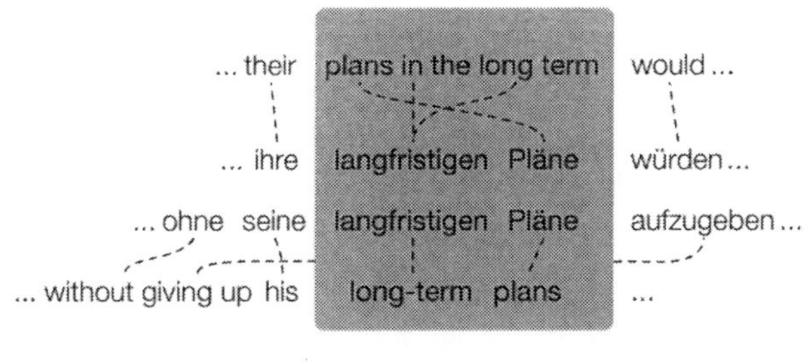

Figure 1: Pivot-based paraphrase extraction for contiguous phrases. Two phrases translating to the same phrase in the foreign language are assumed to be paraphrases of one another.

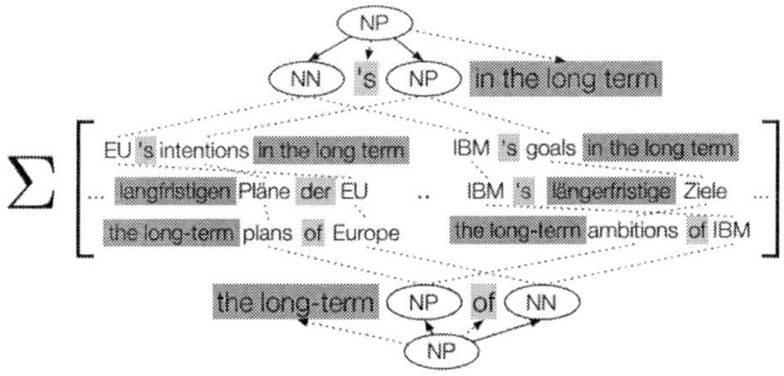

Figure 2: Extraction of syntactic paraphrases via the pivoting approach: We aggregate over different surface realizations, matching the lexicalized portions of the rule and generalizing over the nonterminals.

2 Background

Approaches to paraphrase extraction differ based on their underlying data source. In Section 2.1 we outline pivot-based paraphrase extraction from bilingual data, while the contextual features used to determine closeness in meaning in monolingual approaches is described in Section 2.2.

2.1 Paraphrase Extraction via Pivoting

Following Ganitkevitch et al. (2011), we formulate our paraphrases as a syntactically annotated *synchronous context-free grammar* (SCFG) (Aho and Ullman, 1972; Chiang, 2005). An SCFG rule has the form:

$$\mathbf{r} = C \rightarrow \langle f, e, \sim, \vec{\varphi} \rangle,$$

where the left-hand side of the rule, C, is a nonterminal and the right-hand sides f and e are strings of terminal and nonterminal symbols. There is a one-to-one correspondency between the nonterminals in f and e: each nonterminal symbol in f has to also appear in e. The function $\sim$ captures this bijective mapping between the nonterminals. Drawing on machine translation terminology, we refer to f as the *source* and e as the *target* side of the rule.

Each rule is annotated with a feature vector of feature functions $\vec{\varphi} = \{\varphi_1 ... \varphi_N\}$ that, using a corresponding weight vector $\vec{\lambda}$, are combined in a log-linear model to compute the *cost* of applying $\mathbf{r}$:

$$cost(\mathbf{r}) = -\sum_{i=1}^{N} \lambda_i \log \varphi_i. \quad (1)$$

A wide variety of feature functions can be formulated. We detail the feature-set used in our experiments in Section 4.

To extract paraphrases we follow the intuition that two English strings e_1 and e_2 that translate to the same foreign string f can be assumed to have the same meaning, as illustrated in Figure 1.[1]

First, we use standard machine translation methods to extract a foreign-to-English translation grammar from a bilingual parallel corpus (Koehn, 2010). Then, for each pair of translation rules where the left-hand side C and foreign string f match:

$$\mathbf{r}_1 = C \rightarrow \langle f, e_1, \sim_1, \vec{\varphi}_1 \rangle$$
$$\mathbf{r}_2 = C \rightarrow \langle f, e_2, \sim_2, \vec{\varphi}_2 \rangle,$$

we *pivot* over f to create a paraphrase rule $\mathbf{r}_p$:

$$\mathbf{r}_p = C \rightarrow \langle e_1, e_2, \sim_p, \vec{\varphi}_p \rangle,$$

with a combined nonterminal correspondency function $\sim_p$. Note that the common source side f implies that e_1 and e_2 share the same set of nonterminal symbols.

The paraphrase feature vector $\vec{\varphi}_p$ is computed from the translation feature vectors $\vec{\varphi}_1$ and $\vec{\varphi}_2$ by following the pivoting idea. For instance, we estimate the conditional paraphrase probability $p(e_2|e_1)$ by marginalizing over all shared foreign-language translations f:

$$p(e_2|e_1) = \sum_f p(e_2, f|e_1) \quad (2)$$
$$= \sum_f p(e_2|f, e_1) p(f|e_1) \quad (3)$$
$$\approx \sum_f p(e_2|f) p(f|e_1). \quad (4)$$

[1] See Yao et al. (2012) for an analysis of this assumption.

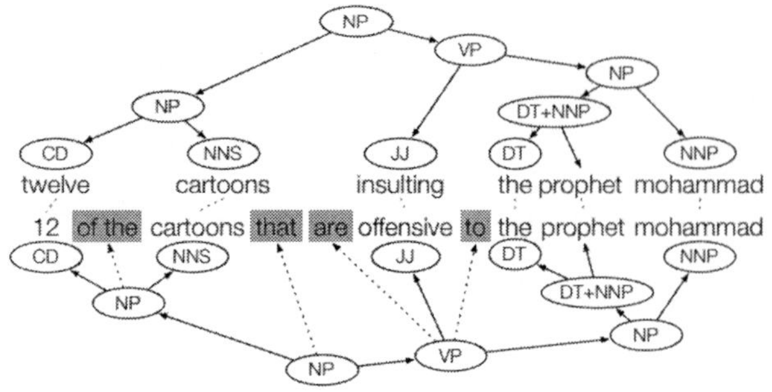

Figure 3: An example of a synchronous paraphrastic derivation, here a sentence compression. Shaded words are deleted in the indicated rule applications.

Figure 2 illustrates syntax-constrained pivoting and feature aggregation over multiple foreign language translations for a paraphrase pattern.

After the SCFG has been extracted, it can be used within standard machine translation machinery, such as the Joshua decoder (Ganitkevitch et al., 2012). Figure 3 shows an example for a synchronous paraphrastic derivation produced as a result of applying our paraphrase grammar in the decoding process.

The approach outlined relies on aligned bilingual texts to identify phrases and patterns that are equivalent in meaning. When extracting paraphrases from monolingual text, we have to rely on an entirely different set of semantic cues and features.

2.2 Monolingual Distributional Similarity

Methods based on monolingual text corpora measure the similarity of phrases based on contextual features. To describe a phrase e, we define a set of features that capture the context of an occurrence of e in our corpus. Writing the context vector for the i-th occurrence of e as $\vec{s}_{e,i}$, we can aggregate over all occurrences of e, resulting in a *distributional* signature for e, $\vec{s}_e = \sum_i \vec{s}_{e,i}$. Following the intuition that phrases with similar meanings occur in similar contexts, we can then quantify the goodness of e' as a paraphrase of e by computing the cosine similarity between their distributional signatures:

$$sim(e, e') = \frac{\vec{s}_e \cdot \vec{s}_{e'}}{|\vec{s}_e||\vec{s}_{e'}|}.$$

A wide variety of features have been used to describe the distributional context of a phrase. Rich, linguistically informed feature-sets that rely on dependency and constituency parses, part-of-speech tags, or lemmatization have been proposed in widely known work such as by Church and Hanks (1991) and Lin and Pantel (2001). For instance, a phrase is described by the various syntactic relations it has with lexical items in its context, such as: "for what verbs do we see with the phrase as the subject?", or "what adjectives modify the phrase?".

However, when moving to vast text collections or collapsed representations of large text corpora, linguistic annotations can become impractically expensive to produce. A straightforward and widely used solution is to fall back onto lexical n-gram features, e.g. "what words or bigrams have we seen to the left of this phrase?" A substantial body of work has focussed on using this type of feature-set for a variety of purposes in NLP (Lapata and Keller, 2005; Bhagat and Ravichandran, 2008; Lin et al., 2010; Van Durme and Lall, 2010).

2.3 Other Related Work

Recently, Chan et al. (2011) presented an initial investigation into combining phrasal paraphrases obtained through bilingual pivoting with monolingual distributional information. Their work investigated a reranking approach and evaluated their method via a substitution task, showing that the two sources of information are complementary and can yield improvements in paraphrase quality when combined.

3 Incorporating Distributional Similarity

In order to incorporate distributional similarity information into the paraphrasing system, we need to calculate similarity scores for the paraphrastic SCFG rules in our grammar. For rules with purely lexical right-hand sides e_1 and e_2 this is a simple task, and the similarity score $sim(e_1, e_2)$ can be directly included in the rule's feature vector $\vec{\varphi}$. However, if e_1 and e_2 are long, their occurrences become sparse and their similarity can no longer be reliably estimated. In our case, the right-hand sides of our rules often contain gaps and computing a similarity score is less straightforward.

Figure 4 shows an example of such a discontinuous rule and illustrates our solution: we decompose the discontinuous patterns that make up the

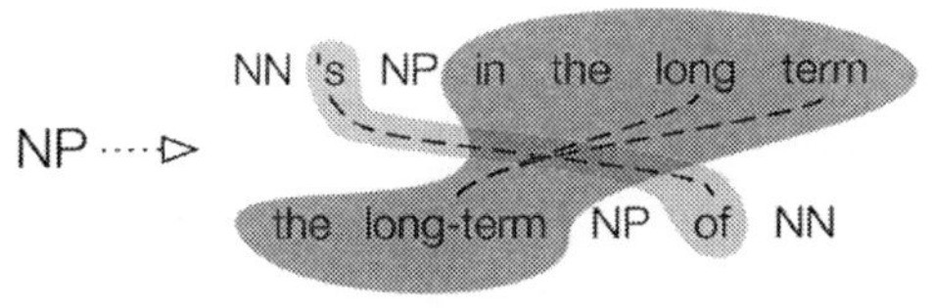

$$sim(\mathbf{r}) = \frac{1}{2}\left(sim\left(\begin{matrix}\text{the long-term}\\ \text{in the long term}\end{matrix}\right) + sim\left(\begin{matrix}\text{'s}\\ \text{of}\end{matrix}\right)\right)$$

Figure 4: Scoring a rule by extracting and scoring contiguous phrases consistent with the alignment. The overall score of the rule is determined by averaging across all pairs of contiguous subphrases.

right-hand sides of a rule $\mathbf{r}$ into pairs of contiguous phrases $\mathcal{P}(\mathbf{r}) = \{\langle e, e' \rangle\}$, for which we can look up distributional signatures and compute similarity scores. This decomposition into phrases is non-trivial, since our sentential paraphrase rules often involve significant reordering or structural changes. To avoid comparing unrelated phrase pairs, we require $\mathcal{P}(\mathbf{r})$ to be consistent with a token alignment $\mathbf{a}$. The alignment is defined analogously to word alignments in machine translation, and computed by treating the source and target sides of our paraphrase rules as a parallel corpus.

We define the overall similarity score of the rule to be the average of the similarity scores of all extracted phrase pairs:

$$sim(\mathbf{r}, \mathbf{a}) = \frac{1}{|\mathcal{P}(\mathbf{a})|} \sum_{(e,e') \in \mathcal{P}(\mathbf{a})} sim(e, e').$$

Since the distributional signatures for long, rare phrases may be computed from only a handful of occurrences, we additionally query for the shorter sub-phrases that are more likely to have been observed often enough to have reliable signatures and thus similarity estimates.

Our definition of the similarity of two discontinuous phrases substantially differs from others in the literature. This difference is due to a difference in motivation. Lin and Pantel (2001), for instance, seek to find new paraphrase pairs by comparing their arguments. In this work, however, we try to add orthogonal information to existing paraphrase pairs. Both our definition of pattern similarity and our feature-set (see Section 4.3) are therefore geared towards comparing the substitutability and context similarity of a pair of paraphrases.

Our two similarity scores are incorporated into the paraphraser as additional rule features in $\vec{\varphi}$, sim_{ngram} and sim_{syn}, respectively. We estimate the corresponding weights along with the other λ_i as detailed in Section 4.

4 Experimental Setup

4.1 Task: Sentence Compression

To evaluate our method on a real text-to-text application, we use the sentence compression task. To tune the parameters of our paraphrase system for sentence compression, we need an appropriate corpus of reference compressions. Since our model is designed to compress by paraphrasing rather than deletion, the commonly used deletion-based compression data sets like the Ziff-Davis corpus are not suitable. We thus use the dataset introduced in our previous work (Ganitkevitch et al., 2011).

Beginning with 9570 tuples of parallel English–English sentences obtained from multiple reference translations for machine translation evaluation, we construct a parallel compression corpus by selecting the longest reference in each tuple as the source sentence and the shortest reference as the target sentence. We further retain only those sentence pairs where the compression ratio cr falls in the range $0.5 < cr \leq 0.8$. From these, we select 936 sentences for the development set, as well as 560 sentences for a test set that we use to gauge the performance of our system.

We contrast our distributional similarity-informed paraphrase system with a pivoting-only baseline, as well as an implementation of Clarke and Lapata (2008)'s state-of-the-art compression model which uses a series of constraints in an integer linear programming (ILP) solver.

4.2 Baseline Paraphrase Grammar

We extract our paraphrase grammar from the French–English portion of the Europarl corpus (version 5) (Koehn, 2005). The Berkeley aligner (Liang et al., 2006) and the Berkeley parser (Petrov and Klein, 2007) are used to align the bitext and parse the English side, respectively. The paraphrase grammar is produced using the Hadoop-based Thrax

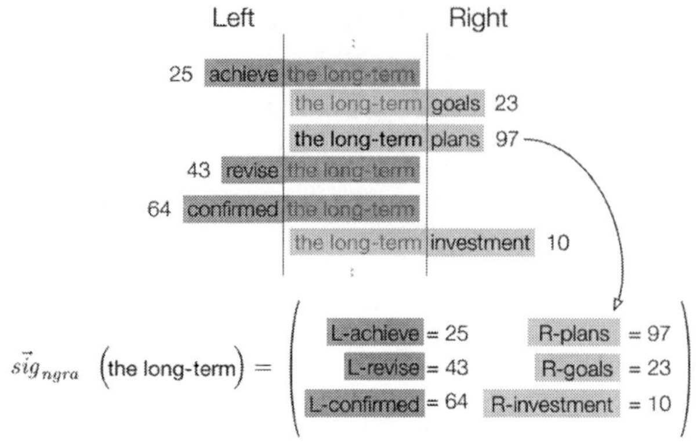

Figure 5: An example of the n-gram feature extraction on an n-gram corpus. Here, "the long-term" is seen preceded by "revise" (43 times) and followed by "plans" (97 times). The corresponding left- and right-side features are added to the phrase signature with the counts of the n-grams that gave rise to them.

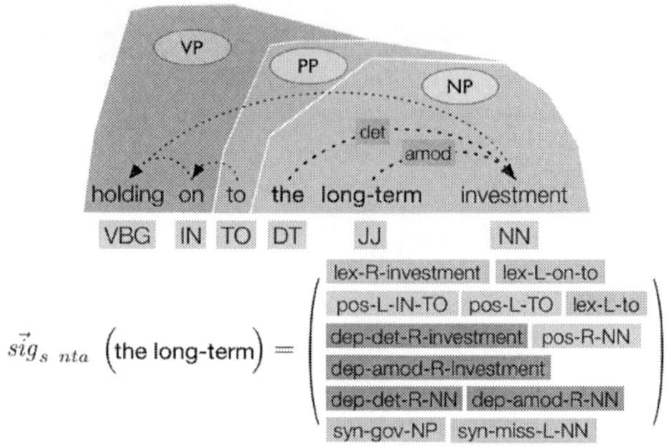

Figure 6: An example of the syntactic feature-set. The phrase "the long-term" is annotated with position-aware lexical and part-of-speech n-gram features (e.g. "on to" on the left, and "investment" and "NN" to its right), labeled dependency links (e.g. $amod - investment$) and features derived from the phrase's CCG label NP/NN.

grammar extractor's paraphrase mode (Ganitkevitch et al., 2012). The syntactic nonterminal labels we allowed in the grammar were limited to constituent labels and CCG-style slashed categories. Paraphrase grammars extracted via pivoting tend to grow very large. To keep the grammar size manageable, we pruned away all paraphrase rules whose phrasal paraphrase probabilities $p(e_1|e_2)$ or $p(e_2|e_1)$ were smaller than 0.001.

We extend the feature-set used in Ganitkevitch et al. (2011) with a number of features that aim to better describe a rule's compressive power: on top of the word count features $wcount_{src}$ and $wcount_{tgt}$ and the word count difference feature $wcount_{diff}$, we add character based count and difference features $ccount_{src}$, $ccount_{tgt}$, and $ccount_{diff}$, as well as log-compression ratio features $word_{cr} = \log \frac{wcount_{tgt}}{wcount_{src}}$ and the analogously defined $char_{cr} = \log \frac{ccount_{tgt}}{ccount_{src}}$.

For model tuning and decoding we used the Joshua machine translation system (Ganitkevitch et al., 2012). The model weights are estimated using an implementation of the PRO tuning algorithm (Hopkins and May, 2011), with PRÉCIS as our objective function (Ganitkevitch et al., 2011). The language model used in our paraphraser and the Clarke and Lapata (2008) baseline system is a Kneser-Ney discounted 5-gram model estimated on the Gigaword corpus using the SRILM toolkit (Stolcke, 2002).

4.3 Distributional Similarity Model

To investigate the impact of the feature-set used to construct distributional signatures, we contrast two approaches: a high-coverage collection of distributional signatures with a relatively simple feature-set, and a much smaller set of signatures with a rich, syntactically informed feature-set.

4.3.1 n-gram Model

The high-coverage model (from here on: n-gram model) is drawn from a web-scale n-gram corpus (Brants and Franz, 2006; Lin et al., 2010). We extract signatures for phrases up to a length of 4. For each phrase p we look at n-grams of the form wp and pv, where w and v are single words. We then extract the corresponding features w_{left} and v_{right}. The feature count is set to the count of the n-gram, reflecting the frequency with which p was preceded or followed, respectively, by w and v in the data the n-gram corpus is based on. Figure 5 illustrates this feature extraction approach. The resulting collection comprises distributional signatures for the 200 million most frequent 1-to-4-grams in the n-gram corpus.

4.3.2 Syntactic Model

For the syntactically informed signature model (from here on: syntax model), we use the constituency and dependency parses provided in the Annotated Gigaword corpus (Napoles et al., 2012). We limit ourselves to the Los Angeles Times/Washington Post portion of the corpus and extract phrases up to a length of 4. The following feature set is used to compute distributional signatures for the extracted phrases:

- Position-aware lexical and part-of-speech unigram and bigram features, drawn from a three-word window to the right and left of the phrase.
- Features based on dependencies for both links into and out of the phrase, labeled with the corresponding lexical item and POS. If the phrase corresponds to a complete subtree in the constituency parse we additionally include lexical and POS features for its head word.
- Syntactic features for any constituents governing the phrase, as well as for CCG-style slashed constituent labels for the phrase. The latter are split in governing constituent and missing constituent (with directionality).

Figure 6 illustrates the syntax model's feature extraction for an example phrase occurrence. Using this method we extract distributional signatures for over 12 million 1-to-4-gram phrases.

4.3.3 Locality Sensitive Hashing

Collecting distributional signatures for a large number of phrases quickly leads to unmanageably large datasets. Storing the syntax model's 12 million signatures in a compressed readable format, for instance, requires over 20GB of disk space. Like Ravichandran et al. (2005) and Bhagat and Ravichandran (2008), we rely on locality sensitive hashing (LSH) to make the use of these large collections practical.

In order to avoid explicitly computing the feature vectors, which can be memory intensive for frequent phrases, we chose the online LSH variant described by Van Durme and Lall (2010), as implemented in the Jerboa toolkit (Van Durme, 2012). This method, based on the earlier work of Indyk and Motwani (1998) and Charikar (2002), approximates the cosine similarity between two feature vectors based on the Hamming distance in a dimensionality-reduced bitwise representation. Two feature vectors u, v each of dimension d are first projected through a $d \times b$ random matrix populated with draws from $\mathcal{N}(0, 1)$. We then convert the resulting b-dimensional vectors into bit-vectors by setting each bit of the signature conditioned on whether the corresponding projected value is less than 0. Now, given the bit signatures $h(\vec{u})$ and $h(\vec{v})$, we can approximate the cosine similarity of u and v as:

$$sim'(u, v) = \cos\left(\frac{D(h(\vec{u}), h(\vec{v}))}{b}\pi\right),$$

where $d(\cdot, \cdot)$ is the Hamming distance. In our experiments we use 256-bit signatures. This reduces the memory requirements for the syntax model to around 600MB.

5 Evaluation Results

To rate the quality of our output, we solicit human judgments of the compressions along two five-point scales: grammaticality and meaning preservation. Judges are instructed to decide how much the meaning from a reference translation is retained in the compressed sentence, with a score of 5 indicating that all of the important information is present, and 1 being that the compression does not retain any of the original meaning. Similarly, a grammar score of 5 indicates perfect grammaticality, while a score of 1 is assigned to sentences that are entirely ungrammatical. We ran our evaluation on Mechanical Turk, where a total of 126 judges provided 3 redundant judgments for each system output. To provide additional quality control, our HITs were augmented with both positive and negative control compressions. For the positive control we used the reference compressions from our test set. Negative control was provided by adding a compression model based on random word deletions to the mix.

In Table 1 we compare our distributional similarity-augmented systems to the plain pivoting-based baseline and the ILP approach. The compression ratios of the paraphrasing systems are tuned to match the average compression ratio seen on the development and test set. The ILP system is configured to loosely match this ratio, as to not overly constrain its search space. Our results indicate that the paraphrase approach significantly outperforms ILP on meaning retention. However, the baseline system shows notable weaknesses in grammaticality. Adding the n-gram distributional similarity model to the paraphraser recovers some of the difference in grammaticality while simultaneously yielding some gain in the compressions' meaning retention. Moving to distributional similarity estimated on the syntactic feature-set yields additional improvement, despite the model's lower coverage.

It is known that human evaluation scores correlate linearly with the compression ratio produced by a sentence compression system (Napoles et al., 2011). Thus, to ensure fairness in our comparisons, we produce a pairwise comparison breakdown that only takes into account compressions of almost identical length.[2] Figure 7 shows the results of this analysis, detailing the number of wins and ties in the human judgements.

We note that the gains in meaning retention over both the baseline and the ILP system are still present in the pairwise breakdown. The gains over the paraphrasing baseline, as well as the improvement in meaning over ILP are statistically significant at $p < 0.05$ (using the sign test).

We can observe that there is substantial overlap between the baseline paraphraser and the n-gram model, while the syntax model appears to yield noticeably different output far more often.

Table 2 shows two example sentences drawn from our test set and the compressions produced by the different systems. It can be seen that both the paraphrase-based and ILP systems produce good quality results, with the paraphrase system retaining the meaning of the source sentence more accurately.

6 Conclusion

We presented a method to incorporate monolingual distributional similarity into linguistically informed paraphrases extracted from bilingual parallel data. Having extended the notion of similarity to discontiguous pattern with multi-word gaps, we investigated the effect of using feature-sets of varying complexity to compute distributional similarity for our paraphrase collection. We conclude that, compared to a simple large-scale model, a rich, syntax-based feature-set, even with significantly lower coverage, noticeably improves output quality in a text-to-text generation task. Our syntactic method significantly improves grammaticality and meaning retention over a strong paraphrastic baseline, and offers substantial gains in meaning retention over a deletion-based state-of-the-art system.

Acknowledgements This research was supported in part by the NSF under grant IIS-0713448 and in part by the EuroMatrixPlus project funded by the European Commission (7th Framework Programme). Opinions, interpretations, and conclusions are the authors' alone.

[2]We require the compressions to be within $\pm 10\%$ length of one another.

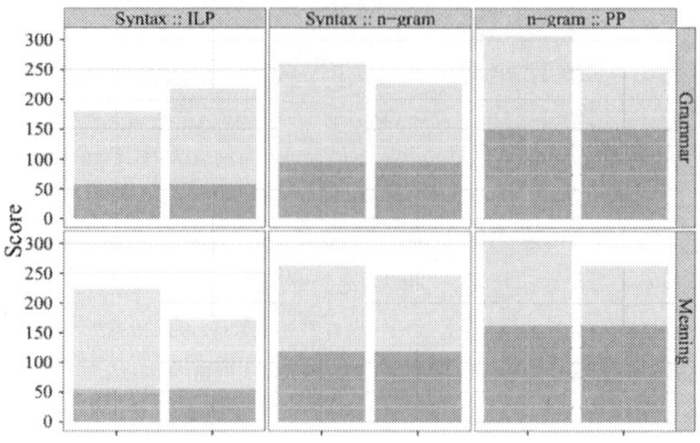

Figure 7: A pairwise breakdown of the human judgments comparing the systems. Dark grey regions show the number of times the two systems were tied, and light grey shows how many times one system was judged to be better than the other.

	CR	Meaning	Grammar
Reference	0.80	4.80	4.54
ILP	0.74	3.44	**3.41**
PP	0.78	3.53	2.98
PP + n-gram	0.80	3.65	3.16
PP + syntax	0.79	**3.70**	3.26
Random Deletions	0.78	2.91	2.53

Table 1: Results of the human evaluation on longer compressions: pairwise compression rates (CR), meaning and grammaticality scores. Bold indicates a statistically significance difference at $p < 0.05$.

Source	should these political developments have an impact on sports ?
Reference	should these political events affect sports ?
Syntax	should these events have an impact on sports ?
n-gram	these political developments impact on sports ?
PP	should these events impact on sports ?
ILP	political developments have an impact
Source	now we have to think and make a decision about our direction and choose only one way . thanks .
Reference	we should ponder it and decide our path and follow it , thanks .
Syntax	now we think and decide on our way and choose one way . thanks .
n-gram	now we have and decide on our way and choose one way . thanks .
PP	now we have and decide on our way and choose one way . thanks .
ILP	we have to think and make a decision and choose way thanks

Table 2: Example compressions produced by our systems and the baselines Table 1 for three input sentences from our test data.

References

Alfred V. Aho and Jeffrey D. Ullman. 1972. *The Theory of Parsing, Translation, and Compiling*. Prentice Hall.

Peter G. Anick and Suresh Tipirneni. 1999. The paraphrase search assistant: terminological feedback for iterative information seeking. In *Proceedings of SI-GIR*.

Colin Bannard and Chris Callison-Burch. 2005. Paraphrasing with bilingual parallel corpora. In *Proceedings of ACL*.

Regina Barzilay, Kathleen R. McKeown, and Michael Elhadad. 1999. Information fusion in the context of multi-document summarization. In *Proceedings of ACL*.

Regina Barzilay. 2003. *Information Fusion for Mutli-document Summarization: Paraphrasing and Generation*. Ph.D. thesis, Columbia University, New York.

Rahul Bhagat and Deepak Ravichandran. 2008. Large scale acquisition of paraphrases for learning surface patterns. In *Proceedings of ACL/HLT*.

Thorsten Brants and Alex Franz. 2006. Web 1T 5-gram version 1.

Chris Callison-Burch. 2008. Syntactic constraints on paraphrases extracted from parallel corpora. In *Proceedings of EMNLP*.

Tsz Ping Chan, Chris Callison-Burch, and Benjamin Van Durme. 2011. Reranking bilingually extracted paraphrases using monolingual distributional similarity. In *EMNLP Workshop on GEMS*.

Moses Charikar. 2002. Similarity estimation techniques from rounding algorithms. In *Proceedings of STOC*.

David Chiang. 2005. A hierarchical phrase-based model for statistical machine translation. In *Proceedings of ACL*.

Kenneth Church and Patrick Hanks. 1991. Word association norms, mutual information and lexicography. *Computational Linguistics*, 6(1):22–29.

James Clarke and Mirella Lapata. 2008. Global inference for sentence compression: An integer linear programming approach. *Journal of Artificial Intelligence Research*, 31:273–381.

Trevor Cohn and Mirella Lapata. 2008. Sentence compression beyond word deletion. In *Proceedings of the COLING*.

Juri Ganitkevitch, Chris Callison-Burch, Courtney Napoles, and Benjamin Van Durme. 2011. Learning sentential paraphrases from bilingual parallel corpora for text-to-text generation. In *Proceedings of EMNLP*.

Juri Ganitkevitch, Yuan Cao, Jonathan Weese, Matt Post,

and Chris Callison-Burch. 2012. Joshua 4.0: Packing, PRO, and paraphrases. In *Proceedings of WMT12*.

Mark Hopkins and Jonathan May. 2011. Tuning as ranking. In *Proceedings of EMNLP*.

Piotr Indyk and Rajeev Motwani. 1998. Approximate nearest neighbors: towards removing the curse of dimensionality. In *Proceedings of STOC*.

Philipp Koehn. 2005. Europarl: A parallel corpus for statistical machine translation. In *MT summit*, volume 5.

Philipp Koehn. 2010. *Statistical Machine Translation*. Cambridge University Press.

Mirella Lapata and Frank Keller. 2005. Web-based models for natural language processing. *ACM Transactions on Speech and Language Processing*, 2(1).

Percy Liang, Ben Taskar, and Dan Klein. 2006. Alignment by agreement. In *Proceedings of HLT/NAACL*.

Dekang Lin and Patrick Pantel. 2001. Discovery of inference rules from text. *Natural Language Engineering*.

Dekang Lin, Kenneth Church, Heng Ji, Satoshi Sekine, David Yarowsky, Shane Bergsma, Kailash Patil, Emily Pitler, Rachel Lathbury, Vikram Rao, Kapil Dalwani, and Sushant Narsale. 2010. New tools for web-scale n-grams. In *Proceedings of LREC*.

Kathleen R. McKeown. 1979. Paraphrasing using given and new information in a question-answer system. In *Proceedings of ACL*.

Courtney Napoles, Chris Callison-Burch, Juri Ganitkevitch, and Benjamin Van Durme. 2011. Paraphrastic sentence compression with a character-based metric: Tightening without deletion. *Workshop on Monolingual Text-To-Text Generation*.

Courtney Napoles, Matt Gormley, and Benjamin Van Durme. 2012. Annotated gigaword. In *Proceedings of AKBC-WEKEX 2012*.

Slav Petrov and Dan Klein. 2007. Improved inference for unlexicalized parsing. In *Proceedings of HLT/NAACL*.

Deepak Ravichandran and Eduard Hovy. 2002. Learning sufrace text patterns for a question answering system. In *Proceedings of ACL*.

Deepak Ravichandran, Patrick Pantel, and Eduard Hovy. 2005. Randomized Algorithms and NLP: Using Locality Sensitive Hash Functions for High Speed Noun Clustering. In *Proceedings of ACL*.

Stefan Riezler, Alexander Vasserman, Ioannis Tsochantaridis, Vibhu Mittal, and Yi Liu. 2007. Statistical machine translation for query expansion in answer retrieval. In *Proceedings of ACL*.

Andreas Stolcke. 2002. SRILM - an extensible language modeling toolkit. In *Proceeding of the International Conference on Spoken Language Processing*.

Benjamin Van Durme and Ashwin Lall. 2010. Online generation of locality sensitive hash signatures. In *Proceedings of ACL, Short Papers*.

Benjamin Van Durme. 2012. Jerboa: A toolkit for randomized and streaming algorithms. Technical Report 7, Human Language Technology Center of Excellence, Johns Hopkins University.

Sander Wubben, Antal van den Bosch, and Emiel Krahmer. 2012. Sentence simplification by monolingual machine translation. In *Proceedings of ACL*.

Xuchen Yao, Benjamin Van Durme, and Chris Callison-Burch. 2012. Expectations of word sense in parallel corpora. In *Proceedings of HLT/NAACL*.

Shiqi Zhao, Haifeng Wang, Ting Liu, and Sheng Li. 2008. Pivot approach for extracting paraphrase patterns from bilingual corpora. In *Proceedings of ACL/HLT*.

Shiqi Zhao, Xiang Lan, Ting Liu, and Sheng Li. 2009. Application-driven statistical paraphrase generation. In *Proceedings of ACL*.

*SEM 2012 Shared Task: Resolving the Scope and Focus of Negation

Roser Morante
CLiPS - University of Antwerp
Prinsstraat 13, B-2000 Antwerp, Belgium
Roser.Morante@ua.ac.be

Eduardo Blanco
Lymba Corporation
Richardson, TX 75080 USA
eduardo@lymba.com

Abstract

The Joint Conference on Lexical and Computational Semantics (*SEM) each year hosts a shared task on semantic related topics. In its first edition held in 2012, the shared task was dedicated to resolving the scope and focus of negation. This paper presents the specifications, datasets and evaluation criteria of the task. An overview of participating systems is provided and their results are summarized.

1 Introduction

Semantic representation of text has received considerable attention these past years. While early shallow approaches have been proven useful for several natural language processing applications (Wu and Fung, 2009; Surdeanu et al., 2003; Shen and Lapata, 2007), the field is moving towards analyzing and processing complex linguistic phenomena, such as metaphor (Shutova, 2010) or modality and negation (Morante and Sporleder, 2012).

The *SEM 2012 Shared Task is devoted to negation, specifically, to resolving its scope and focus. Negation is a grammatical category that comprises devices used to reverse the truth value of propositions. Broadly speaking, *scope* is the part of the meaning that is negated and *focus* the part of the scope that is most prominently or explicitly negated (Huddleston and Pullum, 2002). Although negation is a very relevant and complex semantic aspect of language, current proposals to annotate meaning either dismiss negation or only treat it in a partial manner.

The interest in automatically processing negation originated in the medical domain (Chapman et al., 2001), since clinical reports and discharge summaries must be reliably interpreted and indexed. The annotation of negation and hedge cues and their scope in the BioScope corpus (Vincze et al., 2008) represented a pioneering effort. This corpus boosted research on scope resolution, especially since it was used in the CoNLL 2010 Shared Task (CoNLL ST 2010) on hedge detection (Farkas et al., 2010). Negation has also been studied in sentiment analysis (Wiegand et al., 2010) as a means to determine the polarity of sentiments and opinions.

Whereas several scope detectors have been developed using BioScope (Morante and Daelemans, 2009; Velldal et al., 2012), there is a lack of corpora and tools to process negation in general domain texts. This is why we have prepared new corpora for scope and focus detection. Scope is annotated in Conan Doyle stories (`CD-SCO` corpus). For each negation, the cue, its scope and the negated event, if any, are marked as shown in example (1a). Focus is annotated on top of PropBank, which uses the WSJ section of the Penn TreeBank (`PB-FOC` corpus). Focus annotation is restricted to verbal negations annotated with MNEG in PropBank, and all the words belonging to a semantic role are selected as focus. An annotated example is shown in (1b)[1].

(1) a. [John had] **never** [<u>said</u> as much before]
b. John had never said {as much} before

The rest of this paper is organized as follows. The two proposed tasks are described in Section 2, and the corpora in Section 3. Participating systems and their results are summarized in Section 4. The approaches used by participating systems are described in Section 5, as well as the analysis of results. Finally, Section 6 concludes the paper.

[1]Throughout this paper, negation cues are marked in bold letters, scopes are enclosed in square brackets and negated events are underlined; focus is enclosed in curly brackets.

2 Task description

The *SEM 2012 Shared Task[2] was dedicated to resolving the scope and focus of negation (Task 1 and 2 respectively). Participants were allowed to engage in any combination of tasks and submit at most two runs per task. A pilot task combining scope and focus detection was initially planned, but was cancelled due to lack of participation. We received a total of 14 runs, 12 for scope detection (7 closed, 5 open) and 2 for focus detection (0 closed, 2 open).

Submissions fall into two tracks:

- **Closed track**. Systems are built using exclusively the annotations provided in the training set and are tuned with the development set. Systems that do not use external tools to process the input text or that modify the annotations provided (e.g., simplify parse tree, concatenate lists of POS tags,) fall under this track.
- **Open track**. Systems can make use of any external resource or tool. For example, if a team uses an external semantic parser, named entity recognizer or obtains the lemma for each token by querying external resources, it falls under the open track. The tools used cannot have been developed or tuned using the annotations of the test set.

Regardless of the track, teams were allowed to submit their final results on the test set using a system trained on both the training and development sets. The data format is the same as in several previous CoNLL Shared Tasks (Surdeanu et al., 2008). Sentences are separated by a blank line. Each sentence consists of a sequence of tokens, and a new line is used for each token.

2.1 Task 1: Scope Resolution

Task 1 aimed at resolving the scope of negation cues and detecting negated events. The task is divided into 3 subtasks:

1. Identifying **negation cues**, i.e., words that express negation. Cues can be single words (e.g., *never*), multiwords (e.g., *no longer, by no means*), or affixes (e.g.l *im-*, *-less*). Note that negation cues can be discontinuous, e.g., *neither [. . .] nor*.
2. Resolving the **scope of negation**. This subtask addresses the problem of determining which tokens within a sentence are affected by the negation cue. A scope is a sequence of tokens that can be discontinuous.
3. Identifying the **negated event or property**, if any. The negated event or property is always within the scope of a cue. Only factual events can be negated.

[2]www.clips.ua.ac.be/sem2012-st-neg/

For the sentence in (2), systems have to identify *no* and *nothing* as negation cues, *after his habit he said* and *after mine I asked questions* as scopes, and *said* and *asked* as negated events.

(2) [After his habit he said] **nothing**, and after mine I asked no questions.
After his habit he said nothing, and [after mine I asked] **no** [questions].

2.1.1 Evaluation measures

Previously, scope resolvers have been evaluated at either the token or scope level. The token level evaluation checks whether each token is correctly labeled (inside or outside the scope), while the scope level evaluation checks whether the full scope is correctly labeled. The CoNLL 2010 ST introduced precision and recall at scope level as performance measures and established the following requirements: A true positive (TP) requires an exact match for both the negation cue and the scope. False positives (FP) occur when a system predicts a non-existing scope in gold, or when it incorrectly predicts a scope existing in gold because: (1) the negation cue is correct but the scope is incorrect; (2) the cue is incorrect but the scope is correct; (3) both cue and scope are incorrect. These three scenarios also trigger a false negative (FN). Finally, FN also occur when the gold annotations specify a scope but the system makes no such prediction (Farkas et al., 2010).

As we see it, the CONLL 2010 ST evaluation requirements were somewhat strict because for a scope to be counted as TP, the negation cue had to be correctly identified (strict match) as well as the punctuation tokens within the scope. Additionally, this evaluation penalizes partially correct scopes more than fully missed scopes, since partially correct scopes count as FP and FN, whereas missed scopes count only as FN. This is a standard problem when applying the F measures to the evaluation of sequences. For this shared task we have adopted a slightly different approach based on the following criteria:

- Punctuation tokens are ignored.
- We provide a scope level measure that does not require strict cue match. To count a scope as TP this

measure requires that only one cue token is correctly identified, instead of all cue tokens.

- To count a negated event as TP we do not require correct identification of the cue.
- To evaluate cues, scopes and negated events, partial matches are not counted as FP, only as FN. This is to avoid penalizing partial matches more than missed matches.

The following evaluation measures have been used to evaluate the systems:

- Cue-level F_1-measures (Cue).
- Scope-level F_1-measures that require only partial cue match (Scope NCM).
- Scope-level F_1-measures that require strict cue match (Scope CM). In this case, all tokens of the cue have to be correctly identified.
- F_1-measure over negated events (Negated), computed independently from cues and from scopes.
- Global F_1-measure of negation (Global): the three elements of the negation — cue, scope and negated event — all have to be correctly identified (strict match).
- F_1-measure over scope tokens (Scope tokens). The total of scope tokens in a sentence is the sum of tokens of all scopes. For example, if a sentence has two scopes, one of five tokens and another of seven tokens, then the total of scope tokens is twelve.
- Percentage of correct negation sentences (CNS).

A second version of the measures (Cue/Scope CM/Scope NCM/Negated/Global-B) was calculated and provided to participants, but was not used to rank the systems, because it was introduced in the last period of the development phase following the request of a participant team. In the B version of the measures, precision is not counted as (TP/(TP+FP)), but as (TP / total of system predictions), counting in this way the percentage of perfect matches among all the system predictions. Providing this version of the measures also allowed us to compare the results of the two versions and to check if systems would be ranked in a different position depending on the version.

Even though we believe that relaxing scope evaluation by ignoring punctuation marks and relaxing the strict cue match requirement is a positive feature of our evaluation, we need to explore further in order to define a scope evaluation measure that captures the impact of partial matches in the scores.

2.2 Task 2: Focus Detection

This task tackles focus of negation detection. Both scope and focus are tightly connected. Scope is the part of the meaning that is negated and focus is that part of the scope that is most prominently or explicitly negated (Huddleston and Pullum, 2002). Focus can also be defined as the element of the scope that is intended to be interpreted as false to make the overall negative true.

Detecting focus of negation is useful for retrieving the numerous words that contribute to implicit positive meanings within a negation. Consider the statement *The government didn't release the UFO files* {*until 2008*}. The focus is *until 2008*, yielding the interpretation *The government released the UFO files, but not until 1998*. Once the focus is resolved, the verb *release*, its AGENT *The government* and its THEME *the UFO files* are positive; only the TEMPORAL information *until 2008* remains negated.

We only target verbal negations and focus is always the full text of a semantic role. Some examples of annotation and their interpretation (Int) using focus detection are provided in (3–5).

(3) Even if that deal isn't {revived}, NBC hopes to find another.
Int: Even if that deal is suppressed, NBC hopes to find another.

(4) A decision isn't expected {until some time next year}.
Int: A decision is expected at some time next year.

(5) ...it told the SEC it couldn't provide financial statements by the end of its first extension "{without unreasonable burden or expense}".
Int: It could provide them by that time with a huge overhead.

2.2.1 Evaluation measures

Task 2 is evaluated using precision, recall and F_1. Submissions are ranked by F_1. For each negation, the predicted focus is considered correct if it is a perfect match with the gold annotations.

3 Data Sets

We have released two datasets, which will be available from the web site of the task: CD-SCO for scope detection and PB-FOC for focus detection. The next two sections introduce the datasets.

WL2	108	0	After	After	IN	(S(S(PP*	_	After	_	_	_	_
WL2	108	1	his	his	PRP$	(NP*	_	his	_	_	_	_
WL2	108	2	habit	habit	NN	*))	_	habit	_	_	_	_
WL2	108	3	he	he	PRP	(NP*)	_	he	_	_	_	_
WL2	108	4	said	say	VBD	(VP*	_	said	said	_	_	_
WL2	108	5	nothing	nothing	NN	(NP*)))	nothing	_	_	_	_	_
WL2	108	6	,	,	,	*	_	_	_	_	_	_
WL2	108	7	and	and	CC	*	_	_	_	_	_	_
WL2	108	8	after	after	IN	(S(PP*	_	_	_	_	after	_
WL2	108	9	mine	mine	NN	(NP*))	_	_	_	_	mine	_
WL2	108	10	I	I	PRP	(NP*)	_	_	_	_	I	_
WL2	108	11	asked	ask	VBD	(VP*	_	_	_	_	asked	asked
WL2	108	12	no	no	DT	(NP*	_	_	_	no	_	_
WL2	108	13	questions	question	NNS	*)))	_	_	_	_	questions	_
WL2	108	14	.	.	.	*)	_	_	_	_	_	_

Figure 1: Example sentence from CD-SCO.

3.1 CD-SCO: Scope Annotation

The corpus for Task 1 is CD-SCO, a corpus of Conan Doyle stories. The training corpus contains *The Hound of the Baskervilles*, the development corpus, *The Adventure of Wisteria Lodge*, and the test corpus *The Adventure of the Red Circle* and *The Adventure of the Cardboard Box*. The original texts are freely available from the Gutenberg Project.[3]

CD-SCO is annotated with negation cues and their scope, as well as the event or property that is negated. The cues are the words that express negation and the scope is the part of a sentence that is affected by the negation cues. The negated event or property is the main event or property actually negated by the negation cue. An event can be a process, an action, or a state.

Figure 1 shows an example sentence. Column 1 contains the name of the file, column 2 the sentence #, column 3 the token #, column 4 the word, column 5 the lemma, column 6 the PoS, column 7 the parse tree information and columns 8 to end the negation information. If a sentence does not contain a negation, column 8 contains "***" and there are no more columns. If it does contain negations, the information for each one is encoded in three columns: negation cue, scope, and negated event respectively.

The annotation of cues and scopes is inspired by the BioScope corpus, but there are several differences. First and foremost, BioScope does not annotate the negated event or property. Another important difference concerns the scope model itself: in CD-SCO, the cue is not considered to be part of the scope. Furthermore, scopes can be discontinuous and all arguments of the negated event are considered to be part of the scope, including the subject, which is kept out of the scope in BioScope. A final difference is that affixal negation is annotated in CD-SCO, as in (6).

(6) [He] declares that he heard cries but [is] **un**[{able} to state from what direction they came].

	Training	Dev.	Test
# tokens	65,450	13,566	19,216
# sentences	3644	787	1089
# negation sent.	848	144	235
% negation sent.	23.27	18.29	21.57
# cues	984	173	264
# unique cues	30	20	20
# scopes	887	168	249
# negated	616	122	173

Table 1: CD-SCO Corpus statistics.

Statistics for the corpus is presented in Table 1. More information about the annotation guidelines is provided by Morante et al. (2011) and Morante and Daelemans (2012), including inter-annotator agreement.

The corpus was preprocessed at the University of Oslo. Tokenization was obtained by the PTB-compliant tokenizer that is part of the LinGO English Resource Grammar. [4]

[3] `http://www.gutenberg.org/browse/authors/d\#a37238`

[4] `http://moin.delph-in.net/`

Apart from the gold annotations, the corpus was provided to participants with additional annotations:

- Lemmatization using the GENIA tagger (Tsuruoka and Tsujii, 2005), version 3.0.1, with the '-nt' command line option. GENIA PoS tags are complemented with TnT PoS tags for increased compatibility with the original PTB.
- Parsing with the Charniak and Johnson (2005) reranking parser.[5] For compatibility with PTB conventions, the top-level nodes in parse trees ('S1'), were removed. The conversion of PTB-style syntax trees into CoNLL-style format was performed using the CoNLL 2005 Shared Task software.[6]

3.2 PB-FOC: Focus Annotation

We have adapted the only previous annotation effort targeting focus of negation for PB-FOC (Blanco and Moldovan, 2011). This corpus provides focus annotation on top of PropBank. It targets exclusively verbal negations marked with MNEG in PropBank and selects as focus the semantic role containing the most likely focus. The motivation behind their approach, annotation guidelines and examples can be found in the aforementioned paper.

We gathered all negations from sections 02–21, 23 and 24 and discarded negations for which the focus or PropBank annotations were not sound, leaving 3,544 instances.[7] For each verbal negation, PB-FOC provides the current sentence, and the previous and next sentences as context. For each sentence, along with the gold focus annotations, PB-FOC contains the following additional annotations:

- Token number;
- POS tags using the Brill tagger (Brill, 1992);
- Named Entities using the Stanford named entity recognizer recognizer (Finkel et al., 2005);
- Chunks using the chunker by Phan (2006);
- Syntactic tree using the Charniak parser (Charniak, 2000);
- Dependency tree derived from the syntactic tree (de Marneffe et al., 2006);
- Semantic roles using the labeler described by (Punyakanok et al., 2008); and
- Verbal negation, indicates with 'N' if that token correspond to a verbal negation for which focus must be predicted.

		Train	Devel	Test
	1 role	2,210	515	672
	2 roles	89	15	38
	3 roles	3	0	2
	All	2,302	530	712
Semantic roles focus belongs to	A1	980	222	309
	AM-NEG	592	138	172
	AM-TMP	161	35	46
	AM-MNR	127	27	38
	A2	112	28	36
	A0	94	23	31
	None	88	19	35
	AM-ADV	78	23	26
	C-A1	46	6	16
	AM-PNC	33	8	12
	AM-LOC	25	4	10
	A4	11	2	5
	R-A1	10	2	2
	Other	40	8	16

Table 2: Basic numeric analysis for PB-FOC. The first 4 rows indicate the number of unique roles each negation belongs to, the rest indicate the counts for each role.

Figure 2 provides a sample of PB-FOC. Knowing that the original focus annotations were done on top of PropBank and that focus corresponds to a single role, semantic role information is key to predict the focus. In Table 2, we show some basic numeric analysis regarding focus annotation and the automatically obtained semantic role labels. Most instances of focus belong to a single role in the three splits and the most common role focus belongs to is A1, followed by AM-NEG, M-TMP and M-MNR. Note that some instances have at least one word that does not belong to any role (88 in training, 19 in development and 35 in test).

4 Submissions and results

A total of 14 runs were submitted: 12 for scope detection and 2 for focus detection. The unbalanced number of submissions might be due to the fact that both tasks are relatively new and the tight timeline (six weeks) under which systems were developed.

ErgTokenization, http://moin.delph-in.net/ReppTop

[5]November 2009 release available from Brown University.

[6]http://www.lsi.upc.edu/~srlconll/srlconll-1.1.tgz

[7]The original focus annotation targeted the 3,993 negations marked with MNEG in the whole PropBank.

Marketers	1	NNS	O	B-NP	(S1(S(NP*)	2	nsubj	(A0*)	*	-	*
believe	2	VBP	O	B-VP	(VP*	0	root	(V*)	*	-	*
most	3	RBS	O	B-NP	(SBAR(S(NP*	4	amod	(A1*	(A0*	-	FOCUS
Americans	4	NNPS	O	I-NP	*)	7	nsubj	*	*)	-	FOCUS
wo	5	MD	O	B-VP	(VP*	7	aux	*	(AM-MOD*)	-	*
n't	6	RB	O	I-VP	*	7	neg	*	(AM-NEG*)	-	*
make	7	VB	O	I-VP	(VP*	2	ccomp	*	(V*)	N	*
the	8	DT	O	B-NP	(NP*	10	det	*	(A1*	-	*
convenience	9	NN	O	I-NP	*	10	nn	*	*	-	*
trade-off	10	NN	O	I-NP	*)))))	7	dobj	*)	*)	-	*
...	11	:	O	O	*	2	punct	*	*	-	*
.	12	.	O	O	*))	2	punct	*	*	-	*

Figure 2: Example sentence from PB-FOC.

	Team	Prec.	Rec.	F1
Open	UConcordia, run 1	60.00	56.88	58.40
	UConcordia, run 2	59.85	56.74	58.26

Table 3: Official results for Task 2.

Some participants showed interest in the second task and expressed that they did not participate because of lack of time. In this section, we present the results for each task.

4.1 Task 1

Six teams (UiO1, UiO2, FBK, UWashington, UMichigan, UABCoRAL) submitted results for the closed track with a total of seven runs, and four teams (UiO2, UGroningen, UCM-1, UCM-2) submitted results for the open track with a total of five runs. The evaluation results are provided in Table 4, which contains the official results, and Table 5, which contains the results for evaluation measures B.

The best Global score in the closed track was obtained by UiO1 (57.63 F_1). The best score for Cues was obtained by FBK (92.34 F_1), for Scopes CM by UiO2 (73.39 F_1), for Scopes NCM by UWashington (72.40 F_1), and for Negated by UiO1 (67.02 F_1). The best Global score in the open track was obtained by UiO2 (54.82 F_1), as well as the best scores for Cues (91.31 F_1), Scopes CM (72.39 F_1), Scopes NCM (72.39 F_1), and Negated (61.79 F_1).

4.2 Task 2

Only one team participated in Task 2, UConcordia from CLaC Lab at Concordia University. They submitted two runs and the official results are summarized in Table 3. Their best run scored 58.40 F_1.

5 Approaches and analysis

In this section we summarize the methodologies applied by participants to solve the tasks and we analyze the results.

5.1 Task 1

To solve Task 1 most teams develop a three module pipeline with a module per subtask. Scope resolution and negated event detection are independent of each other and both depend on cue detection. An exception is the UiO1 system, which incorporates a module for factuality detection. Most systems apply machine learning algorithms, either Conditional Random Fields (CRFs) or Support Vector Machines (SVMs), while less systems implement a rule-based approach. Syntax information is widely employed, either in the form of rules or incorporated in the learning model. Multi-word and affixal negation cues receive a special treatment in most cases, and scopes are generally postprocessed.

The systems that participate in the closed track are machine learning based. The UiO1 system is an adaptation of another system (Velldal et al., 2012), which combines SVM cue classification with SVM-based ranking of syntactic constituents for scope resolution. The approach is extended to identify negated events by first classifying negations as factual or non-factual, and then applying an SVM ranker over candidate events. The original treatment of factuality in this system results in the highest score for both the negated event subtask and the global task.

The UiO2 system combines SVM cue classification with CRF-based sequence labeling. An original aspect of the UiO2 approach is the model represen-

Official results for Task 1

		Cues			Scopes CM			Scopes NCM			Scope Tokens			Negated			Global			% CNS
		Prec.	Rec.	F_1	Prec.	Rec.	F_1	Prec.	Rec.	F_1	Prec.	Rec.	F_1	Prec.	Rec.	F_1	Prec.	Rec.	F_1	
Closed track	**UiO1 r2**	89.17	93.56	91.31	83.89	60.64	70.39	83.89	60.64	70.39	75.87	90.08	82.37	60.58	75.00	**67.02**	79.87	45.08	**57.63**	**43.83**
	UiO1 r1	91.42	92.80	92.10	87.43	61.45	72.17	87.43	61.45	72.17	81.99	88.81	**85.26**	60.50	72.89	66.12	83.45	43.94	57.57	42.13
	UiO2	89.17	93.56	91.31	85.71	62.65	**72.39**	85.71	62.65	72.39	86.03	81.55	83.73	68.18	52.63	59.40	78.26	40.91	53.73	40.00
	FBK	93.41	91.29	**92.34**	88.96	58.23	70.39	88.96	58.23	70.39	81.53	82.44	81.98	64.14	56.71	60.20	84.96	36.36	50.93	35.74
	UWashington	88.04	92.05	90.00	82.72	63.45	71.81	82.90	64.26	**72.40**	83.26	83.77	83.51	58.04	50.92	54.25	74.02	35.61	48.09	34.04
	UMichigan	94.31	87.88	90.98	90.00	50.60	64.78	90.00	50.60	64.78	84.85	80.66	82.70	50.00	52.24	51.10	84.27	28.41	42.49	27.23
	UABCoRAL	85.93	85.61	85.77	79.04	53.01	63.46	79.53	54.62	64.76	85.37	68.86	76.23	65.00	38.46	48.33	66.36	27.65	39.04	26.81
Open track	**UiO2**	89.17	93.56	**91.31**	85.71	62.65	**72.39**	85.71	62.65	**72.39**	82.25	82.16	**82.20**	66.90	57.40	**61.79**	78.72	42.05	**54.82**	**41.28**
	UGroningen r2	88.89	84.85	86.82	76.12	40.96	53.26	76.12	40.96	53.26	69.20	82.27	75.17	56.63	65.29	60.65	72.00	27.27	39.56	27.23
	UCM-1	89.26	91.29	90.26	82.86	46.59	59.64	82.86	46.59	59.64	85.37	68.53	76.03	66.67	12.72	21.36	66.28	21.59	32.57	18.72
	UCM-2	81.34	64.39	71.88	67.13	38.55	48.98	66.90	38.96	49.24	58.30	67.70	62.65	46.15	21.18	29.03	42.65	10.98	17.46	11.91
	UGroningen r1	86.90	82.95	84.88	46.38	12.85	20.12	46.38	12.85	20.12	69.69	70.30	69.99	53.94	52.05	52.98	37.74	7.58	12.62	7.66

Table 4: Official results. "r1" stands for run 1 nd "r2" for run 2. CNS stands for Correct Negation Sentences. "CM" stands for Cue Match and "NCM" stands for No Cue Match.

		Cues B			Scopes B CM			Scopes B NCM			Negated B			Global B		
		Prec.	Rec.	F_1	Prec.	Rec.	F_1	Prec.	Rec.	F_1	Prec.	Rec.	F_1	Prec.	Rec.	F_1
Closed track	**UiO1 r2**	86.97	93.56	90.14	56.55	60.64	58.52	56.55	60.64	58.52	58.60	75.00	**65.79**	41.90	45.08	**43.43**
	UiO1 r1	89.09	92.80	90.91	59.30	61.45	60.36	59.30	61.45	60.36	57.62	72.89	64.36	42.18	43.94	43.04
	UiO2	86.97	93.56	90.14	59.32	62.65	60.94	59.32	62.65	60.94	67.16	52.63	59.01	38.03	40.91	39.42
	FBK	91.63	91.29	**91.46**	58.23	58.23	58.23	58.23	58.23	58.23	60.39	56.71	58.49	38.03	40.91	39.42
	UWashington	85.26	92.05	88.52	58.52	63.45	**60.89**	59.26	64.26	**61.66**	53.90	50.92	52.37	32.98	35.61	34.24
	UMichigan	92.80	87.88	90.27	55.51	50.60	52.94	55.51	50.60	52.94	38.25	52.24	44.16	30.00	28.41	29.18
	UABCoRAL	79.58	85.61	82.48	55.23	53.01	54.10	56.90	54.62	55.74	62.50	38.46	47.62	25.70	27.65	26.64
Open track	**UiO2**	86.97	93.56	**90.14**	59.54	62.65	**61.06**	59.54	62.65	**61.06**	63.82	57.40	**60.44**	39.08	42.05	**40.51**
	UGroningen r2	85.82	84.85	85.33	39.84	40.96	40.39	39.84	40.96	40.39	55.22	65.29	59.83	27.59	27.27	27.43
	UCM-1	86.69	91.29	88.93	45.67	46.59	46.13	45.67	46.59	46.13	66.67	12.72	21.36	20.50	21.59	21.03
	UCM-2	72.34	64.39	68.13	41.20	38.55	39.83	41.63	38.96	40.25	44.44	21.18	28.69	12.34	10.98	11.62
	UGroningen r1	83.91	82.95	83.43	12.26	12.85	12.55	12.26	12.85	12.55	52.66	52.05	52.35	7.66	7.58	7.62

Table 5: Results withevaluation measures B. Precision is calculated as: true positives / total of system predictions. "r1" stands for run 1 nd "r2" for run 2. "CM" stands for Cue Match and "NCM" stands for No Cue Match.

Participating institutions:
UiO: University of Oslo; FBK: Fondazione Bruno Kessler & University of Trento; UWashington: University of Washington; UMichigan: University of Michigan; UABCoRAL: CoRAL Lab University of Alabama; UGroningen: University of Groningen; UCM: Complutense University of Madrid.

tation for scopes and negated events, where tokens are assigned a set of labels that attempts to describe their behavior within the mechanics of negation. After unseen sequences are labeled, in-scope and negated tokens are assigned to their respective cues using simple post-processing heuristics.

The FBK system consists of three different CRF classifiers, as well as the UMichigan. A characteristic of the cue model of the UMichigan system is that tokens are assigned five labels in order to represent the different types of negation. Similarly, the UWashington system has a CRF sequence tagger for scope and negated event detection, while the cue detector learns regular expression matching rules from the training set. The UABCoRAL system follows the same strategy, but instead of CRFs it employs SVM Light.

The resources utilized by participants in the open track are diverse. UiO2 reparsed the data with MaltParser in order to obtain dependency graphs. For the rest, the system is the same as in the closed track. The global results obtained by this system in the closed track are higher than the results obtained in the open track, which is mostly due to a higher performance of the scope resolution module. This is the only machine learning system in the open track and the highest performing one.

The UGroningen system is based on tools that produce complex semantic representations. The system employs the C&C tools[8] for parsing and Boxer[9] to produce semantic representations in the form of Discourse Representation Structures (DRSs). For cue detection, the DRSs are converted to flat, non-recursive structures, called Discourse Representation Graphs (DRGs). These DRGs allow for cue detection by means of labelled tuples. Scope detection is done by gathering the tokens that occur within the scope of the negated DRSs. For negated event detection, a basic algorithm takes the detected scope and returns the negated event based on information from the syntax tree within the scope.

UCM-1 and UCM-2 are rule-based systems that rely heavily on information from the syntax tree. The UCM-1 system was initially designed for processing opinionated texts. It applies a dictionary approach to cue detection, with the detection of affixal cues being performed using WordNet. Non-affixal cue detection is performed by consulting a predefined list of cues. It then uses information from the syntax tree in order to get a first approximation to the scope, which is later refined using a set of post-processing rules. In the case of the UCM-2 system an algorithm detects negation cues and their scope by traversing Minipar dependency structures. Finally, the scope is refined with post-processing rules that take into account the information provided by the first algorithm and linguistic clause boundaries.

If we compare tracks, the Global best results obtained in the closed track (57.63 F_1) are higher than the Global best results obtained in the open track (54.82 F_1). If we compare approaches, the best results in the two tracks are obtained with machine learning-based systems. The rule-based systems participating in the open track clearly score lower (39.56 F_1 the best) than the machine learning-based system (54.82 F_1).

Regarding subtasks, systems achieve higher results in the cue detection task (92.34 F_1 the best) and lower results in the scope resolution (72.40 F_1 the best) and negated event detection (67.02 F_1 the best) tasks. This is not surprising, not only because of the error propagation effect, but also because the set of negation cues is closed and comprises mostly single tokens, whereas scope sequences are longer. The best results in cue detection are obtained by the FBK system that uses CRFs and applies a special procedure to detect the negation cues that are subtokens. The best scores for scope resolution (72.40, 72.39 F_1) are obtained by two machine learning components. UWashington uses CRFs with features derived from the syntax tree. UiO2 uses CRFs models with syntactic and lexical features for scopes, together with a set of labels aimed at capturing the behavior of certain tokens within the mechanics of negation. The best scores for negated events (67.02 F_1) are obtained by the UiO1 system that first classifies negations as factual or non-factual, and then applies an SVM ranker over candidate events.

Finally, we would like to draw the attention to the different scores obtained depending on the evaluation measure used. When scope resolution is evaluated with the Scope (NCM, CM) measure, results

[8] `http://svn.ask.it.usyd.edu.au/trac/candc/wiki/Documentation`

[9] `http://svn.ask.it.usyd.edu.au/trac/candc/wiki/boxer`

are much lower than when using the Scope Tokens measure, which does not reflect the ability of systems to deal with sequences. Another observation is related to the difference in precision scores between the two versions of the evaluation measures. Whereas for Cues and Negated the differences are not so big because most cues and negated events span over a single token, for Scopes they are. The best Scope NCM precision score is 90.00 %, whereas the best Scope NCM B precision score is 59.54 %. This shows that the scores can change considerably depending on how partial matches are counted (as FP and FN, or only as FN). As a final remark it is worth noting that the ranking of systems does not change when using the B measures.

5.2 Task 2

UConcordia submitted two runs in the open track. Both of them follow the same three component approach. First, negation cues are detected. Second, the scope of negation is extracted based on dependency relations and heuristics defined by Kilicoglu and Bergler (2011). Third, the focus of negation is determined within the elements belonging to the scope following three heuristics.

6 Conclusions

In this paper we presented the description of the first *SEM Shared Task on Resolving the Scope and Focus of Negation, which consisted of two different tasks related to different aspects of negation: Task 1 on resolving the scope of negation, and Task 2 on detecting the focus of negation. Task 1 was divided into three subtasks: identifying negation cues, resolving their scope, and identifying the negated event. Two new datasets have been produced for this Shared Task: the CD-SCO corpus of Conan Doyle stories annotated with scopes, and the PB-FOC corpus, which provides focus annotation on top of PropBank. New evaluation software was also developed for this task. The datasets and the evaluation software will be available on the web site of the Shared Task. As far as we know, this is the first task that focuses on resolving the focus and scope of negation.

A total of 14 runs were submitted, 12 for scope detection and 2 for focus detection. Of these, four runs are from systems that take a rule-based approach, two runs from hybrid systems, and the rest from systems that take a machine learning approach using SVMs or CRFs. Most participants designed a three component architecture.

For a future edition of the shared task we would like to unify the annotation schemes of the two corpora, namely the annotation of focus in PB-FOC and negated events in CD-SCO. The annotation of more data with both scope and focus would allow us to study the two aspects jointly. We would also like to provide better evaluation measures for scope resolution. Currently, scopes are evaluated in terms of F_1, which demands a division of errors into the categories TP/FP/TN/FN borrowed from the evaluation of information retrieval systems. These categories are not completely appropriate to be assigned to sequence tasks, such as scope resolution.

Acknowledgements

We are very grateful to Vivek Srikumar for preprocessing the PB-FOC corpus with the Illinois semantic role labeler, and to Stephan Oepen for preprocessing the CD-SCO corpus. We also thank the *SEM organisers and the ST participants. Roser Morante's research was funded by the University of Antwerp (GOA project BIOGRAPH).

References

Eduardo Blanco and Dan Moldovan. 2011. Semantic Representation of Negation Using Focus Detection. In *Proceedings of the 49th Annual Meeting of the Association for C omputational Linguistics: Human Language Technologies*, pages 581–589, Portland, Oregon, USA. Association for Computational Linguistics.

Eric Brill. 1992. A simple rule-based part of speech tagger. In *Proceedings of the third conference on Applied natural language processing*, ANLC '92, pages 152–155, Stroudsburg, PA, USA. Association for Computational Linguistics.

Wendy W. Chapman, Will Bridewell, Paul Hanbury, Gregory F. Cooper, and Bruce G. Buchanan. 2001. A simple algorithm for identifying negated findings and diseases in discharge summaries. *J Biomed Inform*, 34:301–310.

Eugene Charniak and Mark Johnson. 2005. Coarse-to-fine n-best parsing and maxent discriminative reranking. In *Proceedings of the 43rd Annual Meeting of the Association for Computational Linguistics*, pages 173–180, Ann Arbor.

Eugene Charniak. 2000. A maximum-entropy-inspired parser. In *Proceedings of the 1st North American chapter of the Association for Computational Linguistics conference*, NAACL 2000, pages 132–139, Stroudsburg, PA, USA. Association for Computational Linguistics.

Marie-Catherine de Marneffe, Bill MacCartney, and Christopher D. Manning. 2006. Generating Typed Dependency Parses from Phrase Structure Parses. In *Proceedings of the IEEE / ACL 2006 Workshop on Spoken Language Technology*. The Stanford Natural Language Processing Group.

Richárd Farkas, Veronika Vincze, György Móra, János Csirik, and György Szarvas. 2010. The CoNLL-2010 Shared Task: Learning to Detect Hedges and their Scope in Natural Language Text. In *Proceedings of the Fourteenth Conference on Computational Natural Language Learning*, pages 1–12, Uppsala, Sweden. Association for Computational Linguistics.

Jenny Rose Finkel, Trond Grenager, and Christopher Manning. 2005. Incorporating non-local information into information extraction systems by gibbs sampling. In *Proceedings of the 43rd Annual Meeting on Association for Computational Linguistics*, ACL '05, pages 363–370, Stroudsburg, PA, USA. Association for Computational Linguistics.

Rodney D. Huddleston and Geoffrey K. Pullum. 2002. *The Cambridge Grammar of the English Language*. Cambridge University Press.

Halil Kilicoglu and Sabine Bergler. 2011. Effective bio-event extraction using trigger words and syntactic dependencies. *Computational Intelligence*, 27(4):583–609.

Roser Morante and Walter Daelemans. 2009. A metalearning approach to processing the scope of negation. In *Proceedings of the 13th Conference on Natural Language Learning*, pages 21–29, Boulder, CO.

Roser Morante and Walter Daelemans. 2012. ConanDoyle-neg: Annotation of negation cues and their scope in Conan Doyle stories. In *Proceedings of LREC 2012*, Istambul.

Roser Morante and Caroline Sporleder. 2012. Special issue on modality and negation: An introduction. *Computational Linguistics*.

Roser Morante, Sarah Schrauwen, and Walter Daelemans. 2011. Annotation of negation cues and their scope. guidelines v1.0. Technical Report Series CTR-003, CLiPS, University of Antwerp, Antwerp, April.

Xuan-Hieu Phan. 2006. Crfchunker: Crf english phrase chunker.

Vasin Punyakanok, Dan Roth, and Wen-tau Yih. 2008. The importance of syntactic parsing and inference in semantic role labeling. *Computational Linguistics*, 34(2):257–287, June.

Dan Shen and Mirella Lapata. 2007. Using Semantic Roles to Improve Question Answering. In *Proceedings of the 2007 Joint Conference on Empirical Methods in Natural Language Processing and Computational Natural Language Learning (EM NLP-CoNLL)*, pages 12–21.

Ekaterina Shutova. 2010. Models of Metaphor in NLP. In *Proceedings of the 48th Annual Meeting of the Association for Computational Linguistics*, pages 688–697, Uppsala, Sweden. ACL.

Mihai Surdeanu, Sanda Harabagiu, John Williams, and Paul Aarseth. 2003. Using Predicate-Argument Structures for Information Extraction. In *Proceedings of the 41st Annual Meeting of the Association for Computational Linguistics*, pages 8–15, Sapporo, Japan. Association for Computational Linguistics.

Mihai Surdeanu, Richard Johansson, Adam Meyers, Lluís Màrquez, and Joakim Nivre. 2008. The conll-2008 shared task on joint parsing of syntactic and semantic dependencies. In *CoNLL 2008: Proceedings of the 12th Conference on Computational Natural Language Learning*, page 159177, Manchester.

Yoshimasa Tsuruoka and Jun'ichi Tsujii. 2005. Bidirectional inference with the easiest-first strategy for tagging sequence data. In *Proceedings of of Human Language Technology Conference and Conference on Empirical Methods in Natural Language Processing*, pages 467–474, Vancouver.

Erik Velldal, Lilja Øvrelid, Jonathon Read, and Stephan Oepen. 2012. Speculation and negation: Rules, rankers, and the role of syntax. *Computational Linguistics*.

Veronika Vincze, Gyorgy Szarvas, Richard Farkas, Gyorgy Mora, and Janos Csirik. 2008. The BioScope corpus: biomedical texts annotated for uncertainty, negation and their scopes. *BMC Bioinformatics*, 9(Suppl 11):S9+.

Michael Wiegand, Alexandra Balahur, Benjamin Roth, Dietrich Klakow, and Andrés Montoyo. 2010. A survey on the role of negation in sentiment analysis. In *Proceedings of the Workshop on Negation and Speculation in Natural Language Processing*, pages 60–68, Uppsala, Sweden. University of Antwerp.

Dekai Wu and Pascale Fung. 2009. Semantic Roles for SMT: A Hybrid Two-Pass Model. In *Proceedings of Human Language Technologies: The 2009 Annual Conference of the North American Chapter of the Association for Computational Linguistics, Companion Volume: Short Papers*, pages 13–16, Boulder, Colorado. Association for Computational Linguistics.

UABCoRAL: A Preliminary study for Resolving the Scope of Negation

Binod Gyawali, Thamar Solorio
CoRAL Lab
Department of Computer and Information Sciences
University of Alabama at Birmingham
Birmingham, Alabama, USA
{bgyawali,solorio}@cis.uab.edu

Abstract

This paper describes our participation in the closed track of the *SEM 2012 Shared Task of finding the scope of negation. To perform the task, we propose a system that has three components: negation cue detection, scope of negation detection, and negated event detection. In the first phase, the system creates a lexicon of negation signals from the training data and uses the lexicon to identify the negation cues. Then, it applies machine learning approaches to detect the scope and negated event for each negation cue identified in the first phase. Using a preliminary approach, our system achieves a reasonably good accuracy in identifying the scope of negation.

1 Introduction

All human language samples, either written or spoken, contain some information in negated form. In tasks such as information retrieval, sometimes, we should consider only the positive information of an event and disregard its negation information, and vice versa. For example, while searching for the patients with diabetes, we should not include a patient who has a clinical report saying *No symptoms of diabetes were observed.* Thus, finding the negation and its scope is important in tasks where the negation and assertion information need to be treated differently. However, most of the systems developed for processing natural language data do not consider negations present in the sentences. Although various works (Morante et al., 2008; Morante and Daelemans, 2009; Li et al., 2010; Councill et al., 2010; Apostolova et al., 2011) have dealt with the identification of negations and their scope in sentences, this is still a challenging task.

The first task in *SEM 2012 Shared Task (Morante and Blanco, 2012) is concerned with finding the scope of negation. The task includes identifying: i) negation cues, ii) scope of negation, and iii) negated event for each negation present in the sentences. Negation cue is a word, part of a word, or a combination of words that carries the negation information. Scope of negation in a sentence is the longest group of words in the sentence that is influenced by the negation cue. Negated event is the shortest group of words that is actually affected by the negation cue. In Example (1) below, word *no* is a negation cue, the discontinuous word sequences 'I gave him' and 'sign of my occupation' are the scopes, and 'gave' is the negated event.

(1) I [gave] him *no* sign of my occupation.

In this paper, we propose a system to detect the scope of negation for the closed track of *SEM 2012 Shared Task. Our system uses a combination of a rule based approach, and a machine learning approach. We use a rule based approach to create a lexicon of all the negation words present in the training data. Then we use this lexicon to detect the negation cues present in the test data. We do a preliminary analysis of finding the scope of negation and the negated events by applying a machine learning approach, and using basic features created from the words, lemmas, and parts-of-speech (POS) tags of words in the sentences. The F-measure scores achieved by our system are about 85% for negation cue detection, 65% in full scope identification, 48% in negated event detection, and 39% in identifying full negation. Our error analysis shows that the use of lexicon is not very appropriate to detect the negation cues. We also describe the challenges in identifying the scope and the negated events.

2 Problem Description

The *SEM 2012 shared task competition provided three data sets: training, development, and test data set. Each sentence in each data set is split into words. The dataset contains the information such as lemma, part of speech, and other syntactic information of each word. Each sentence of training and development data is annotated with negation cues, scopes and negated events. Using the training and the development data, the task is to identify negation cues, scopes and negated events in all unannotated sentences of the test data.

Sentence tokens	Negation cue	Scope	Negated event
I	-	I	-
am	-	am	-
not	not	-	-
sure	-	sure	sure
whether	-	whether	-
I	-	I	-
left	-	left	-
it	-	it	-
here	-	here	-

Table 1: An example of negation cue, scope and the negated event

A sentence can contain more than one negation cue. Negation cues in the data set can be i) a single word token such as $n't$, $nowhere$, ii) a continuous sequence of two or more words, such as *no more*, *by no means* or iii) two or more discontinuous words such as ..$neither$...nor... A negation cue is either a part or same as its corresponding negation word. This corresponding negation word is referred as a negation signal in the remaining sections of the paper. For example, for a negation signal $unnecessary$, the negation cue is un, and similarly, for a negation signal $needless$, the negation cue is $less$.

Scope of a negation in a sentence can be a continuous sequence of words or a discontinuous set of words in the sentence. Scope of negation sometimes includes the negation word. A negation word may not have a negated event. Presence of a negated event in a sentence depends upon the facts described by the sentence. Non-factual sentences such as interrogative, imperative, and conditional do not contain negated events. Morante and Daelemans (2012) describe the details of the negation cue, scope, and negated event, and the annotation guidelines. An example of the task is shown in Table 1.

3 System Description

We decompose the system to identify the scope of negation into three tasks. They are:

1. Finding the negation cue
2. Finding the scope of negation
3. Finding the negated event

The scope detection and the negated event detection tasks are dependent on the task of finding the negation cue. But the scope detection and the negated event detection tasks are independent of each other.

We identify the negation cues present in the test data based on a lexicon of negation signals that are present in the training and the development data. The tasks of identifying scope of negation and negated event are modeled as classification problems. To identify scope and negated event, we train classifiers with the instances created from the training data provided. We create test instances from the test data annotated with negation cues predicted by our cue detection component. Due to the use of test data annotated by our cue detection component, the false negative rate in predicting the negation cues is propagated to the scope detection as well as negated event detection components. The details of all the three components are described in the subsections below.

3.1 Identifying the negation cue

In this task, we identify all the negation cues present in the sentences. We group the negation cues under three types depending upon how they are present in the data. They are: single word cues, continuous multiword cues, and discontinuous multiword cues. All the cues present in the training and development datasets are shown in Table 2.

Cue types	Cues
Single word cues	absence, dis, except, fail, im, in, ir, less, n't, neglected, neither, never, no, nobody, none, nor, not, nothing, nowhere, prevent, refused, save, un, without
Continuous multiword cues	no more, rather than, by no means, nothing at all, on the contrary, not for the world
Discontinuous multiword cues	neither nor, no nor, not not

Table 2: Negation cues present in training and development data

In the training and development data, multiword negation cues account for only 1.40% of the total negation cues. At this stage, we decided to focus on identifying the single word negation cues. The system first creates a lexicon that contains the pairs of negation cues and their corresponding negation signals for all the single word negation cues present in the training and the development datasets. In order to identify a negation cue in the test set, the system searches all the words in the sentences of the test data that match the negation signals of the lexicon. For each word that matches, it assigns the corresponding cue of the signal from the lexicon as its negation cue.

3.2 Identifying the scope of negation

We apply a machine learning technique to identify the scope of negation. For each negation cue present in a sentence, we create the problem instances as the tuple of the negation signal and each word present in the same sentence. To create the instances, we use only those sentences having at least one negation. For training, we create instances from the training data, but we consider only those words that are within a window of size 20 from the negation signal and within the sentence boundary. We restricted the words to be within the window in order to minimize the problem of imbalanced data. This window was chosen following our observation that only 1.26% of the scope tokens go beyond the 20 word window from the negation signal. Including the words beyond this window causes a major increase in the negative instances resulting in a highly imbalanced training set. While creating test instances, we do not restrict the words by window size. This restriction is not done in order to include all the words of the sentences in the test instances. An instance is labeled as positive if the word used to create the instance is the scope of the negation signal; else it is labeled as negative.

We extract 10 features to identify the scope of negation as follows:

1. Negation signal in the tuple
2. Lemma of the negation signal
3. POS tag of the negation signal
4. Word in the tuple
5. Lemma of the word in the tuple
6. POS tag of the word in the tuple
7. Distance between the negation signal and the word in terms of number of words
8. Position of the word from the negation signal (left, right)
9. Whether a punctuation character (',', ':',';') exists between the word and the negation signal
10. Sequence of POS tags in between the negation signal and the word

After the classification, if an instance is predicted as positive, the word used to create the instance is considered as the scope of the negation signal. If a negation signal has prefix such as 'dis', 'un', 'in', 'ir', or 'im', the scope of negation includes only the part of word (signal) excluding the prefix. Thus, for each negation signal having these prefix, we remove the prefix from the signal and consider the remaining part of it as the scope, regardless of whether the classifier classifies the instance pair as positive or negative.

3.3 Identifying the negated event

The task of identifying the negated event is similar to the task of identifying the scope of negation. The process of creating the instances for this task is almost the same to that of finding the scope of negation, except that, we limit the window size to 4 words from the negation signal. 4.24% of the negated events lie away from the 4 word window. Beyond this window, the events are very sparse and a small increment in the window size leads to abrupt increase in negative instances and creates an imbalance in the data. The 4 word window size was selected based on the best result obtained among various experiments performed with different window sizes greater than and equal to 4. The same rule applies while creating instances for training data as well as test data. We use only nine features in this step, excluding the 9th feature used in the scope detection. We also apply the same rule of mapping the negation signals starting with 'dis', 'un', 'in', 'ir', and 'im' to the negated event as in the previous step.

4 Experimental Settings

We evaluated our system only on the test data of the shared task. For the machine learning tasks, we used the SVM light classifier (Joachims, 1999) with 4th degree polynomial kernel and other default parameters. The identification of cues, scopes, negated events, and full negation are evaluated on the basis of the F-measures. We also use 'B' variant for cues, scopes, negated events and the full negation for evaluation. The precision of 'B' variant is calculated as the ratio of true positives to the system count. Identification of cues and negated events are measured independent of any other steps. But the identification of the scopes is measured depending upon the correct identification of cues in three different ways as follows:

i) scopes (cue match): the cue has to be correct for the scope to be correct

ii) scopes (no cue match): the system must identify part of the cue for the scope to be correct

iii) scope tokens (no cue match): a part of the system identified cue must overlap with the gold standard cue for the scope tokens to be correct

The F1 score of the full negation detection was used to rank the systems of the participants. The details about the evaluation measures can be found in Morante and Blanco (2012).

5 Results Analysis

The results obtained by our system over the test data are shown in Table 3. The results obtained by each component, and their analysis are described in the subsections below.

5.1 Identifying the negation cues

The system is able to achieve an 85.77% F1 score in the task of identifying the negation cues using a simple approach based on the lexicon of the negation signals. Because of the system's inability to identify multiword negation cues, it could not detect the multiword cues such as *..neither..nor..*, *..absolutely nothing..*, *..far from..*, *..never more..*, that account for 3.5% of the total negation cues present in the test data.

The accuracy of the system is limited by the coverage of the lexicon. Due to the low coverage of the lexicon, the system fails to identify signals such as $ceaseless$, $discoloured$, $incredulity$, $senseless$, and $unframed$ that are present only in the test data. These signals account for 4.5% of the total negation signals present in the test data. Some words such as $never$, $nothing$, not, $n't$, no, and $without$ are mostly present as the negation signals in the data. But these words are not always the negation signals. The phrase *no doubt* is present nine times in the test data, but the word no is a negation signal in only four of them. This accounts for 1.89% error in the negation cue detection. The word $save$ is present once as a negation signal in the training data, but it is never a negation signal in the test data. Therefore, our lexicon based system invariably predicts two occurrences of $save$ in the test data as negation signals.

5.2 Identifying the scope of negation

The system achieves 63.46% F1 score in identifying scopes with cue match, 64.76% F1 score in identifying scopes with no cue match, and 76.23% F1 score in identifying scope tokens with no cue match. The results show that our system has a higher precision than recall in identifying the scope. As mentioned

	gold	system	tp	fp	fn	precision (%)	recall (%)	F1 (%)
Cues	264	284	226	37	38	85.93	85.61	85.77
Scopes (cue match)	249	239	132	35	117	79.04	53.01	63.46
Scopes (no cue match)	249	239	132	35	113	79.53	54.62	64.76
Scope tokens (no cue match)	1805	1456	1243	213	562	85.37	68.86	76.23
Negated (no cue match)	173	104	65	35	104	65.00	38.46	48.33
Full negation	264	284	73	37	191	66.36	27.65	39.04
Cues B	264	284	226	37	38	79.58	85.61	82.48
Scopes B (cue match)	249	239	132	35	117	55.23	53.01	54.10
Scopes B (no cue match)	249	239	132	35	113	56.90	54.62	55.74
Negated B (no cue match)	173	104	65	35	104	62.50	38.46	47.62
Full negation B	264	284	73	37	191	25.70	27.65	26.64
	Total sentences: 1089							
	Negation sentences: 235							
	Negation sentences with errors: 172							
	% Correct sentences: 81.73							
	% Correct negation sentences: 26.81							

Table 3: Results of the system

earlier, the negation cues identified in the first task are used to identify the scope of negation and the negated events. Using the test data with 15% error in negation cues as the input to this component and some of the wrong predictions of the scope by this component led to a low recall value in the scope detection.

The results show that the system works well when a negation signal has fewer scope tokens and when the scope tokens are closer to the negation signal. There are some cases where the system could not identify the scope tokens properly. It is unable to detect the scope tokens that are farther in distance from the negation signals. The system is not performing well in predicting the discontinuous scopes. When a negation cue has discontinuous scope, mostly the system predicts one sequence of words correctly but could not identify the next sequence. In sentence (2) in the example below, the underlined word sequences are the discontinuous scopes of the negation cue *not*. In the sentence, our system predicts only the second sequence of scope, but not the first sequence. In some cases, our system does not have a good coverage of scope tokens. In sentence (3), the underlined word sequence is the scope of the signal *no*, but our system detects only *at ninety was hardship* as its scope. These inabilities to detect the full scope have led to have a higher accuracy in predicting the partial scope tokens (76.23%) than predicting the full scope (64.76%).

(2) *the box is a half pound box of honeydew tobacco and does **not** help us in any way*

(3) *...a thermometer at ninety was **no** hardship*

(4) *...I can**not** see anything save very vague indications*

Analyzing the results, we see that the error in predicting the scope of the negation is high when the scope is distributed in two different phrases. In the example (2) above, *does not help us in any way* is a single verb phrase and all the scope within the phrase is correctly identified by our system. *The box* being a separate phrase, it is unable to identify it. However, in some cases such as example (4), the system could not identify any scope tokens for negation cue *not*.

Some of the findings of previous works have shown that the features related to syntactic path are helpful in identifying the scope of negation. Li et al. (2010) used the syntactic path from the word to the negation signal and showed that this helped to improve the accuracy of scope detection. Similarly, work by Councill et al. (2010) showed that the accuracy of scope detection could be increased using the features from the dependency parse tree. In our experiment, there was a good improvement in the scope detection rate when we included "sequence of POS tags" between the negation signal and the word as a feature. This improvement after including the sequence of POS tags feature and its consistency with the previous works implies that adding path related features might help to improve the accuracy in scope detection.

5.3 Identifying the negated event

We are able to achieve an F1 score of 48.33% in predicting the negated events, which is the lowest score among all three components. As in the scope detection task, error in negation cue detection led to lower the recall rate of the negated event detection system. The accuracy of full negation is based on the correct identification of the negation cues, scope and the negated events of all the negations present in the sentences. The output shows that there are many cases where negation cues and the scope are correctly identified but there is an error in identifying the negated events. The higher error in predicting the negated events led to reduce the score of full negation and achieve an F1 score of 39.04%.

Our system is unable to detect some negated events even though they are adjacent to the negation signal. This shows that the use of simple features extracted from words, lemmas, and POS tags is not enough to predict the negated events properly. Adding features related to words in left and right of the negation signal and the path feature may help to improve the detection of negated events.

In order to analyze the impact of error in the negation cue detection component upon the scope and negated event detection components, we performed an experiment using the gold standard negation cues to detect the scope and the negated events. F1 scores achieved by this system are 73.1% in full scope detection, 54.87% in negated event detection, 81.46% in scope tokens detection, and 49.57% in full negation detection. The result shows that there is almost 10% increment in the F1 score in all the components. Thus, having an improved cue detection component greatly helps to improve the accuracy of scope and negated event detection components.

6 Discussion and Conclusion

In this paper we outline a combination of a rule based approach and a machine learning approach to identify the negation cue, scope of negation, and the negated event. We show that applying a basic approach of using a lexicon to predict the negation cues achieves a considerable accuracy. However, our system is unable to identify the negation cues such as *never*, *not*, *nothing*, *n't*, and *save* that can appear as a negation signal as well as in other non-negated contexts. It also cannot cover the negation cues of the signals that are not present in the training data. Moreover, in order to improve the overall accuracy of the scope and negated event detection, we need an accurate system to detect the negation cues since the error in the negation cue detection propagates to the next steps of identifying the scope and the negated event. It is difficult to identify the scope of negations that are farther in distance from the negation signal. Detecting the tokens of the scope that are discontinuous is also challenging.

As future work, we would like to extend our task to use a machine learning approach instead of the lexicon of negation signals to better predict the negation cues. The system we presented here uses a preliminary approach without including any syntactic information to detect the scope and negated events. We would also incorporate syntactic information to identify the scope and negated events in our future work. To improve the accuracy of identifying the scope and the negated events, adding other features related to the neighbor words of the negation signal might be helpful. In our tasks, we limit the scope and negated event instances by the window size in order to avoid imbalance data problem. Another interesting work to achieve better accuracy could be to use other approaches of imbalanced dataset classification instead of limiting the training instances by the window size.

References

Emilia Apostolova, Noriko Tomuro, and Dina Demner-Fushman. 2011. Automatic extraction of lexico-syntactic patterns for detection of negation and speculation scopes. In *Proceedings of the 49th Annual Meeting of the Association for Computational Linguistics: Human Language Technologies: short papers - Volume 2*, HLT '11, pages 283–287, Stroudsburg, PA, USA. Association for Computational Linguistics.

Isaac G. Councill, Ryan McDonald, and Leonid Velikovich. 2010. What's great and what's not: learning to classify the scope of negation for improved sentiment analysis. In *Proceedings of the Workshop on Negation and Speculation in Natural Language Pro-*

cessing, NeSp-NLP '10, pages 51–59, Stroudsburg, PA, USA. Association for Computational Linguistics.

Thorsten Joachims. 1999. Making large-scale support vector machine learning practical. In *Advances in kernel methods: support sector searning*, pages 169–184. MIT Press, Cambridge, MA, USA.

Junhui Li, Guodong Zhou, Hongling Wang, and Qiaoming Zhu. 2010. Learning the scope of negation via shallow semantic parsing. In *Proceedings of the 23rd International Conference on Computational Linguistics*, COLING '10, pages 671–679, Stroudsburg, PA, USA. Association for Computational Linguistics.

Roser Morante and Eduardo Blanco. 2012. *SEM 2012 Shared Task: Resolving the Scope and Focus of Negation. In *Proceedings of the First Joint Conference on Lexical and Computational Semantics (*SEM 2012)*, Montreal, Canada.

Roser Morante and Walter Daelemans. 2009. A metalearning approach to processing the scope of negation. In *Proceedings of the Thirteenth Conference on Computational Natural Language Learning*, CoNLL '09, pages 21–29, Stroudsburg, PA, USA.

Roser Morante and Walter Daelemans. 2012. ConanDoyle-neg: Annotation of negation in Conan Doyle stories. In *Proceedings of the Eighth International Conference on Language Resources and Evaluation (LREC)*, Istanbul.

Roser Morante, Anthony Liekens, and Walter Daelemans. 2008. Learning the scope of negation in biomedical texts. In *Proceedings of the Conference on Empirical Methods in Natural Language Processing*, EMNLP '08, pages 715–724. Association for Computational Linguistics.

UCM-I: A Rule-based Syntactic Approach for Resolving the Scope of Negation

Jorge Carrillo de Albornoz, Laura Plaza, Alberto Díaz and Miguel Ballesteros
Universidad Complutense de Madrid
C/ Prof. José García Santesmases, s/n
28040 Madrid (Spain)
{jcalbornoz,lplazam,albertodiaz,miballes}@fdi.ucm.es

Abstract

This paper presents one of the two contributions from the Universidad Complutense de Madrid to the *SEM Shared Task 2012 on Resolving the Scope and Focus of Negation. We describe a rule-based system for detecting the presence of negations and delimitating their scope. It was initially intended for processing negation in opinionated texts, and has been adapted to fit the task requirements. It first detects negation cues using a list of explicit negation markers (such as *not* or *nothing*), and infers other implicit negations (such as affixal negations, e.g, *undeniable* or *improper*) by using semantic information from WordNet concepts and relations. It next uses the information from the syntax tree of the sentence in which the negation arises to get a first approximation to the negation scope, which is later refined using a set of post-processing rules that bound or expand such scope.

1 Introduction

Detecting negation is important for many NLP tasks, as it may reverse the meaning of the text affected by it. In information extraction, for instance, it is obviously important to distinguish negated information from affirmative one (Kim and Park, 2006). It may also improve automatic indexing (Mutalik et al., 2001). In sentiment analysis, detecting and dealing with negation is critical, as it may change the polarity of a text (Wiegand et al., 2010). However, research on negation has mainly focused on the biomedical domain, and addressed the problem of detecting if a medical term is negated or not (Chapman et al., 2001), or the scope of different negation signals (Morante et al., 2008).

During the last years, the importance of processing negation is gaining recognition by the NLP research community, as evidenced by the success of several initiatives such as the Negation and Speculation in Natural Language Processing workshop (NeSp-NLP 2010)[1] or the CoNLL-2010 Shared Task[2], which aimed at identifying hedges and their scope in natural language texts. In spite of this, most of the approaches proposed so far deal with negation in a superficial manner.

This paper describes our contribution to the *SEM Shared Task 2012 on Resolving the Scope and Focus of Negation. As its name suggests, the task aims at detecting the scope and focus of negation, as a means of encouraging research in negation processing. In particular, we participate in Task 1: scope detection. For each negation in the text, the negation cue must be detected, and its scope marked. Moreover, the event or property that is negated must be recognized. A comprehensive description of the task may be found in (Morante and Blanco, 2012).

For the sake of clarity, it is important to define what the organization of the task understands by negation cue, scope of negation and negated event. The words that express negation are called negation cues. *Not* and *no* are common examples of such cues. Scope is defined as the part of the meaning that is negated, and encloses all negated concepts. The negated event is the property that is

[1] http://www.clips.ua.ac.be/NeSpNLP2010/
[2] www.inf.u-szeged.hu/rgai/conll2010st/

negated by the cue. For instance, in the sentence: *[Holmes] did not [**say** anything]*, the scope is enclosed in square brackets, the negation cue is underlined and the negated event is shown in bold. More details about the annotation of negation cues, scopes and negated events may be found in (Morante and Daelemans, 2012).

The system presented to the shared task is an adaptation of the one published in (Carrillo de Albornoz et al., 2010), whose aim was to detect and process negation in opinionated text in order to improve polarity and intensity classification. When classifying sentiments and opinions it is important to deal with the presence of negations and their effect on the emotional meaning of the text affected by them. Consider the sentence (1) and (2). Sentence (1) expresses a positive opinion, whereas that in sentence (2) the negation word *not* reverses the polarity of such opinion.

(1) I liked this hotel.

(2) I didn't like this hotel.

Our system has the main advantage of being simple and highly generic. Even though it was originally conceived for treating negations in opinionated texts, a few simple modifications have been sufficient to successfully address negation in a very different type of texts, such as Conan Doyle stories. It is rule-based and does not need to be trained. It also uses semantic information in order to automatically detect the negation cues.

2 Methodology

As already told, the UCM-I system is a modified version of the one presented in (Carrillo de Albornoz et al., 2010). Next sections detail the modifications performed to undertake the present task.

2.1 Detecting negation cues

Our previous work was focused on explicit negations (i.e., those introduced by negation tokens such as *not*, *never*). In contrast, in the present work we also consider what we call *implicit negations*, which includes affixal negation (i.,e., words with prefixes such as dis-, un- or suffixes such as -less; e.g., *im*patient or care*less*), inffixal negation (i.e., point*less*ness, where the negation cue *less* is in the middle of the noun phrase). Note that we did not

Table 1: Examples of negation cues.

Explicit negation cues			
no	not	non	nor
nobody	never	nowhere	...
Words with implicit negation cues			
unpleasant	unnatural	dislike	impatient
fearless	hopeless	illegal	...

have into account these negation cues when analyzing opinionated texts because these words themselves usually appear in affective lexicons with their corresponding polarity values (i.e., *impatient*, for instance, appears in SentiWordNet with a negative polarity value).

In order to detect negation cues, we use a list of predefined negation signals, along with an automatic method for detecting new ones. The list has been extracted from different previous works (Councill et al., 2010; Morante, 2010). This list also includes the most frequent contracted forms (e.g., *don't*, *didn't*, etc.). The automated method, in turn, is intended for discovering in text new affixal negation cues. To this end, we first find in the text all words with prefixes *dis-*, *a-*, *un-*, *in-*, *im-*, *non-*, *il-*, *ir-* and the suffix *-less* that present the appropriate part of speech. Since not all words with such affixes are negation cues, we use semantic information from WordNet concepts and relations to decide. In this way, we retrieve from WordNet the synset that correspond to each word, using WordNet::SenseRelate (Patwardhan et al., 2005) to correctly disambiguate the meaning of the word according to its context, along with all its antonym synsets. We next check if, after removing the affix, the word exists in WordNet and belongs to any of the antonym synsets. If so, we consider the original word to be a negation cue (i.e., the word without the affix has the opposite meaning than the lexical item with the affix).

Table 1 presents some examples of explicit negation cues and words with implicit negation cues. For space reasons, not all cues are shown. We also consider common spelling errors such as the omission of apostrophes (e.g., *isnt* or *nt*). They are not likely to be found in literary texts, but are quite frequent in user-generated content.

This general processing is, however, improved with two rules:

Table 2: Examples of false negation cues.

no doubt	without a doubt	not merely	not just
not even	not only	no wonder	...

1. **False negation cues**: Some negation words may be also used in other expressions without constituting a negation, as in sentence (3). Therefore, when the negation token belongs to such expressions, this is not processed as a negation. Examples of false negation cues are shown in Table 2.

   (3) ... the evidence may implicate not only your friend Mr. Stapleton but his wife as well.

2. **Tag questions:** Some sentences in the corpora present negative tag questions in old English grammatical form, as it may shown in sentences (4) and (5). We have implemented a specific rule to deal with this type of constructions, so that they are not treated as negations.

   (4) You could easily recognize it, could you not?.
   (5) But your family have been with us for several generations, have they not?

2.2 Delimiting the scope of negation

The scope of a negation is determined by using the syntax tree of the sentence in which the negation arises, as generated by the Stanford Parser.[3] To this end, we find in the syntax tree the first common ancestor that encloses the negation token and the word immediately after it, and assume all descendant leaf nodes to the right of the negation token to be affected by it. This process may be seen in Figure 1, where the syntax tree for the sentence: *[Watson did] not [solve the case]* is shown. In this sentence, the method identifies the negation token *not* and assumes its scope to be all descendant leaf nodes of the common ancestor of the words *not* and *solve* (i.e., *solve the case*).

This modeling has the main advantage of being highly generic, as it serves to delimit the scope of negation regardless of what the negated event is (i.e., the verb, the subject, the object of the verb, an adjective or an adverb). As shown in (Carrillo de Albornoz et al., 2010), it behaves well when determining the scope of negation for the purpose of classifying product reviews in polarity classes. However, we have found that this scope is not enough for the present task, and thus we have implemented a set of post-processing rules to expand and limit the scope according to the task guidelines:

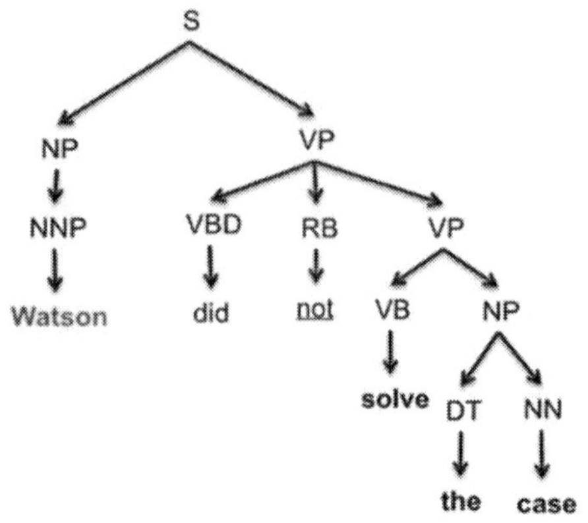

Figure 1: Syntax tree of the sentence: *Watson did not solve the case.*

1. **Expansion to subject.** This rule expands the negation scope in order to include the subject of the sentence within it. In this way, in sentence (6) the appropriate rule is fired to include "This theory" within the negation scope.

   (6) [This theory would] not [work].

   It must be noted that, for polarity classification purposes, we do not consider the subject of the sentence to be part of this scope. Consider, for instance, the sentence: *The beautiful views of the Eiffel Tower are not guaranteed in all rooms.* According to traditional polarity classification approaches, if the subject is considered as part of the negation scope, the polarity of the positive polar expression "beautiful" should be changed, and considered as negative.

2. **Subordinate boundaries.** Our original negation scope detection method works well with coordinate sentences, in which negation cues scope only over their clause, as if a "boundary" exists between the different clauses. This occurs, for instance, in the sentence:

[3]http://nlp.stanford.edu/software/lex-parser.shtml

Table 3: List of negation scope delimiters.

Tokens	POS
so, because, if, while until, since, unless before, than, despite	 IN IN
what, whose	WP
why, where	WRB
however	RB
“,”, - , :, ;, (,), !, ?, .	-

(7) [It may be that you are] not [yourself luminous], but you are a conductor of light.

It also works properly in subordinate sentences, when the negation occurs in the subordinate clause, as in: *You can imagine my surprise when I found that [there was] no [one there].*

However, it may fail in some types of subordinate sentences, where the scope should be limited to the main clause, but our model predict both clauses to be affected by the negation. This is the case for the sentences where the dependent clause is introduced by the subordinate conjunctions in Table 3. An example of such type of sentence is (8), where the conjunction token *because* introduces a subordinate clause which is out of the negation scope. To solve this problem, the negation scope detection method includes a set of rules to delimit the scope in those cases, using as delimiters the conjunctions in Table 3. Note that, since some of these delimiters are ambiguous, their part of speech tags are used to disambiguate them.

(8) [Her father] refused [to have anything to do with her] ***because*** *she had married without his consent.*

3. **Prepositional phrases:** Our original method also fails to correctly determine the negation scope when the negated event is followed by a prepositional phrase, as it may be seen in Figure 2, where the syntax tree for the sentence: *[There was] no [attempt at robbery]* is shown. Note that, according to our original model, the phrase “at robbery” does not belong to the negation scope. This is an error that was not detected before, but has been fixed for the present task.

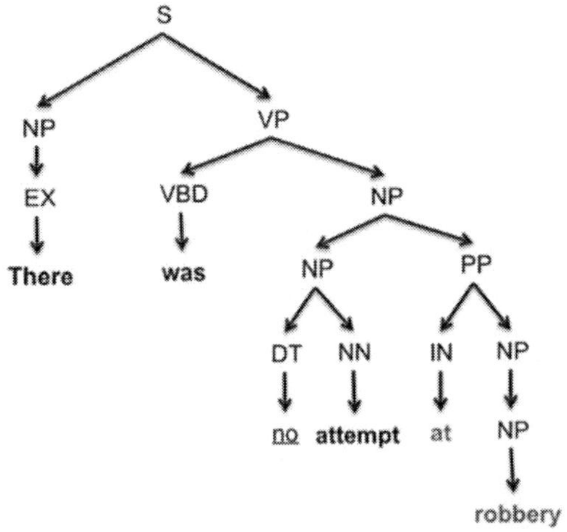

Figure 2: Syntax tree for the sentence: *There was no attempt at robbery.*

2.3 Finding negated events

We only consider a single type of negated events, so that, when a cue word contains a negative affix, the word after removing the affix is annotated as the negated event. In this way, “doubtedly” is correctly annotated as the negated event in sentence (9). However, the remaining types of negated events are relegated to future work.

(9) [The oval seal is] ***undoubtedly*** *[a plain sleeve-link].*

3 Evaluation Setup

The data collection consists of a development set, a training set, and two test sets of 787, 3644, 496 and 593 sentences, respectively from different stories by Conan Doyle (see (Morante and Blanco, 2012) for details). Performance is measured in terms of recall, precision and F-measure for the following subtasks:

- Predicting negation cues.
- Predicting both the scope and cue.
- Predicting the scope, the cue does not need to be correct.
- Predicting the scope tokens, where not a full scope match is required.
- Predicting negated events.
- Full evaluation, which requires all elements to be correct.

Table 4: Results for the development set.

Metric	Pr.	Re.	F-1
Cues	92.55	86.13	89.22
Scope (cue match)	86.05	44.05	58.27
Scope (no cue match)	86.05	44.05	58.27
Scope tokens (no cue match)	88.05	59.05	70.69
Negated (no cue match)	65.00	10.74	18.43
Full negation	74.47	20.23	31.82

4 Evaluation Results

The results of our system when evaluated on the development set and the two test sets (both jointly and separately), are shown in Tables 4, 5, and 6.

It may be seen from these tables that our system behaves quite well in the prediction of negation cues subtask, achieving around 90% F-measure in all data sets, and the second position in the competition. Performance in the scope prediction task, however, is around 60% F-1, and the same results are obtained if the correct prediction of cues is required (*Scope (cue match)*). This seems to indicate that, for all correct scope predictions, our system have also predicted the negation cues correctly. Obviously these results improve for the *Scope tokens* measure, achieving more than 77% F-1 for the Cardboard data set. We also got the second position in the competition for these three subtasks. Concerning detection of negated events, our system gets poor results, 22.85% and 19.81% F-1, respectively, in each test data set. These results affect the performance of the full negation prediction task, where we get 32.18% and 32.96% F-1, respectively. Surprisingly, the result in the test sets are slightly better than those in the development set, and this is due to a better behavior of the WordNet-based cue detection method in the formers than in the later.

5 Discussion

We next discuss and analyze the results above. Firstly, and regarding detection of negation cues, our initial list covers all explicit negations in the development set, while the detection of affixal negation cues using our WordNet-based method presents a precision of 100% but a recall of 53%. In particular, our method fails when discovering negation cues such as *unburned*, *uncommonly* or *irreproachable*, where the word after removing the affix is a derived form of a verb or adjective.

Secondly, and concerning delimitation of the scope, our method behaves considerably well. We have found that it correctly annotates the negation scope when the negation affects the predicate that expresses the event, but sometimes fails to include the subject of the sentence in such scope, as in: *[I know absolutely] nothing [about the fate of this man]*, where our method only recognizes as the negation scope the terms *about the fate of this man*.

The results have also shown that the method frequently fails when the subject of the sentence or the object of an event are negated. This occurs, for instance, in sentences: *I think, Watson, [a brandy and soda would do him] no [harm]* and *No [woman would ever send a reply-paid telegram]*, where we only point to "harm" and "woman" as the scopes.

We have found a further category of errors in the scope detection tasks, which concern some types of complex sentences with subordinate conjunctions where our method limits the negation scope to the main clause, as in sentence: *[Where they came from, or who they are,] nobody [has an idea]* , where our method limits the scope to "has an idea". However, if the negation cue occurs in the subordinate clause, the method behaves correctly.

Thirdly, with respect to negated event detection, as already told our method gets quite poor results. This was expected, since our system was not originally designed to face this task and thus it only covers one type of negated events. Specifically, it correctly identifies the negated events for sentences with affixal negation cues, as in: *It is most improper, most outrageous*, where the negated event is "proper". However, it usually fails to identify these events when the negation affects the subject of the sentence or the object of an event.

6 Conclusions and Future Work

This paper presents one of the two contributions from the Universidad Complutense de Madrid to the *SEM Shared Task 2012. The results have shown that our method successes in identifying negation cues and performs reasonably well when determining the negation scope, which seems to indicate that a simple unsupervised method based on syntactic information and a reduced set of post-processing rules

Table 5: Results for the test sets (jointly).

Metric	Gold	System	Tp	Fp	Fn	Precision	Recall	F-1
Cues	264	278	241	29	23	89.26	91.29	90.26
Scopes (cue match)	249	254	116	24	133	82.86	46.59	59.64
Scopes (no cue match)	249	254	116	24	133	82.86	46.59	59.64
Scope tokens (no cue match)	1805	1449	1237	212	568	85.37	68.53	76.03
Negated (no cue match)	173	33	22	11	151	66.67	12.72	21.36
Full negation	264	278	57	29	207	66.28	21.59	32.57

Table 6: Results for the Cardboard and Circle test sets.

Metric	Cardboard set			Circle set		
	Pr.	Re.	F-1	Pr.	Re.	F-1
Cues	90.23	90.23	90.23	88.32	92.37	90.30
Scope (cue match)	83.33	46.88	60.00	82.35	46.28	59.26
Scope (no cue match)	83.33	46.88	60.00	82.35	46.28	59.26
Scope tokens (no cue match)	84.91	72.08	77.97	85.96	64.50	73.70
Negated (no cue match)	66.67	13.79	22.85	66.67	11.63	19.81
Full negation	68.29	21.05	32.18	64.44	22.14	32.96

is a viable approach for dealing with negation. However, detection of negated events is the main weakness of our approach, and this should be tackled in future work. We also plan to improve our method for detecting affixal negations to increment its recall, by using further WordNet relations such as "derived from adjective", and "pertains to noun", as well as to extend this method to detect infixal negations.

Acknowledgments

This research is funded by the Spanish Ministry of Science and Innovation (TIN2009-14659-C03-01) and the Ministry of Education (FPU program).

References

Jorge Carrillo de Albornoz, Laura Plaza, and Pablo Gervás. 2010. A hybrid approach to emotional sentence polarity and intensity classification. In *Proceedings of the 14th Conference on Computational Natural Language Learning (CoNLL 2010)*, pages 153–161.

W. W. Chapman, W. Bridewell, P. Hanbury, G. F. Cooper, and B.G. Buchanan. 2001. A simple algorithm for identifying negated findings and diseases in discharge summaries. *J Biomed Inform*, 34:301–310.

Isaac Councill, Ryan McDonald, and Leonid Velikovich. 2010. What's great and what's not: learning to classify the scope of negation for improved sentiment analysis. In *Proceedings of the Workshop on Negation and Speculation in Natural Language Processing*, pages 51–59.

Jung-Jae Kim and Jong C. Park. 2006. Extracting contrastive information from negation patterns in biomedical literature. *ACM Trans. on Asian Language Information Processing*, 5(1):44–60.

Roser Morante and Eduardo Blanco. 2012. Sem 2012 shared task: Resolving the scope and focus of negation. In *Proceedings of the 1st Joint Conference on Lexical and Computational Semantics (*SEM 2012)*.

Roser Morante and Walter Daelemans. 2012. Conandoyle-neg: Annotation of negation in conan doyle stories. In *Proceedings of the 8th International Conference on Language Resources and Evaluation.*

Roser Morante, Anthony Liekens, and Walter Daelemans. 2008. Learning the scope of negation in biomedical texts. In *Proceedings of the 2008 Conference on Empirical Methods in Natural Language Processing*, pages 715–724.

Roser Morante. 2010. Descriptive Analysis of Negation Cues in Biomedical Texts. In *Proceedings of the 7th International Conference on Language Resources and Evaluation.*

A.G. Mutalik, A. Deshpande, and P.M. Nadkarni. 2001. Use of general-purpose negation detection to augment concept indexing of medical documents. A quantitative study using the UMLS. *J Am Med Inform Assoc*, 8(6):598–609.

Siddharth Patwardhan, Satanjeev Banerjee, and Ted Pedersen. 2005. SenseRelate::TargetWord: a generalized framework for word sense disambiguation. In *Proceedings of the ACL 2005 on Interactive poster and demonstration sessions*, pages 73–76.

Michael Wiegand, Alexandra Balahur, Benjamin Roth, Dietrich Klakow, and Andrés Montoyo. 2010. A survey on the role of negation in sentiment analysis. In *Proceedings of the Workshop on Negation and Speculation in Natural Language Processing*, pages 60–68.

UCM-2: a Rule-Based Approach to Infer the Scope of Negation via Dependency Parsing

Miguel Ballesteros, Alberto Díaz, Virginia Francisco, Pablo Gervás, Jorge Carrillo de Albornoz and Laura Plaza
Natural Interaction Based on Language Group
Complutense University of Madrid
Spain
{miballes, albertodiaz, virginia}@fdi.ucm.es,
pgervas@sip.ucm.es, {jcalbornoz, lplazam}@fdi.ucm.es

Abstract

UCM-2 infers the words that are affected by negations by browsing dependency syntactic structures. It first makes use of an algorithm that detects negation cues, like *no, not or nothing*, and the words affected by them by traversing Minipar dependency structures. Second, the scope of these negation cues is computed by using a post-processing rule-based approach that takes into account the information provided by the first algorithm and simple linguistic clause boundaries. An initial version of the system was developed to handle the annotations of the Bioscope corpus. For the present version, we have changed, omitted or extended the rules and the lexicon of cues (allowing prefix and suffix negation cues, such as *impossible* or *meaningless*), to make it suitable for the present task.

1 Introduction

One of the challenges of the *SEM Shared Task (Morante and Blanco, 2012) is to infer and classify the scope and event associated to negations, given a training and a development corpus based on Conan Doyle stories (Morante and Daelemans, 2012). Negation, simple in concept, is a complex but essential phenomenon in any language. It turns an affirmative statement into a negative one, changing the meaning completely. We believe therefore that being able to handle and classify negations we would be able to improve several text mining applications.

Previous to this Shared Task, we can find several systems that handle the scope of negation in the state of the art. This is a complex problem, because it requires, first, to find and capture the negation cues, and second, based on either syntactic or semantic representations, to identify the words that are directly (or indirectly) affected by these negation cues. One of the main works that started this trend in natural language processing was published by Morante's team (2008; 2009), in which they presented a machine learning approach for the biomedical domain evaluating it on the Bioscope corpus.

In 2010, a Workshop on Negation and Speculation in Natural Language Processing (Morante and Sporleder, 2010) was held in Uppsala, Sweden. Most of the approaches presented worked in the biomedical domain, which is the most studied in negation detection.

The system presented in this paper is a modification of the one published in Ballesteros et al. (2012). This system was developed in order to replicate (as far as possible) the annotations given in the Bioscope corpus (Vincze et al., 2008). Therefore, for the one presented in the task we needed to modify most of the rules to make it able to handle the more complex negation structures in the Conan Doyle corpus and the new challenges that it represents. The present paper has the intention of exemplifying the problems of such a system when the task is changed.

Our system presented to the Shared Task is based on the following properties: it makes use of an algorithm that traverses dependency structures, it classifies the scope of the negations by using a rule-based approach that studies linguistic clause boundaries and the outcomes of the algorithm for traversing dependency structures, it applies naive and simple solutions to the problem of classifying the negated event and it does not use the syntactic annotation provided in the Conan Doyle corpus (just in an exception for the negated event annotation).

In Section 2 we describe the algorithms that we propose for inferring the scope of negation and the modifications that we needed to make to the previous version. In Section 3 we discuss the evaluation performed with the blind test set and development set and the error analysis over the development set. Finally, in Section 4 we give our conclusions and suggestions for future work.

2 Methodology

Our system consists of two algorithms: the first one is capable of inferring words affected by the negative operators (cues) by traversing dependency trees and the second one is capable of annotating sentences within the scope of negations. This second algorithm is the one in which we change the behaviour in a deeper way. The first one just serves as a consulting point in some of the rules of the second one. By using the training set and development set provided to the authors we modified, omitted or changed the old rules when necessary.

The first algorithm which traverses a dependency tree searching for negation cues to determine the words affected by negations, was firstly applied (at an earlier stage) to a very different domain (Ballesteros et al., 2010) obtaining interesting results. At that time, the Minipar parser (Lin, 1998) was selected to solve the problem in a simple way without needing to carry out several machine learning optimizations which are well known to be daunting tasks. We also selected Minipar because at that moment we only needed unlabelled parsing.

Therefore, our system consists of three different modules: a static negation cue lexicon, an algorithm that from a parse given by Minipar and the negation cue lexicon produces a set of words affected by the negations, and a rule-based system that produces the annotation of the scope of the studied sentence. These components are described in the following sections.

In order to annotate the sentence as it is done in the Conan Doyle corpus, we also developed a postprocessing system that makes use of the outcomes of the initial system and produces the expected output. Besides this, we also generate a very naive rule-based approach to handle the problem of annotating the negated event.

It is worth to mention that we did not make use of the syntactic annotation provided in the Conan Doyle corpus, our input is the plain text sentence. Therefore, the system could work without the columns that are included in the annotation, just with the word forms. We only make use of the annotation when we annotate the negated event, checking the part-of-speech tag to ascertain whether the corresponding word is a verb or not. The system could work without these columns but only the results of the negated event would be affected.

2.1 Negation Cue Lexicon

The lexicon containing the negation cues is static. It can be extended indefinitely but it has the restriction that it does not learn and it does not grow automatically when applying it to a different domain. The lexicon used in the previous system (Ballesteros et al., 2012) was also static but it was very small compared to the one employed by the present system, just containing less than 20 different negation cues.

Therefore, in addition to the previous lexicon, we analysed the training set and development sets and extracted 153 different negation cues (plus the ones already present in the previous system). We stored these cues in a file that feeds the system when it starts. Table 1 shows a small excerpt of the lexicon.

not	no	neither..nor
unnecessary	unoccupied	unpleasant
unpractical	unsafe	unseen
unshaven	windless	without

Table 1: Excerpt of the lexicon

2.2 Affected Wordforms Detection Algorithm

The algorithm that uses the outcomes of Minipar is the same employed in (Ballesteros et al., 2012) without modifications. It basically traverses the dependency structures and returns for each negation cue a set of words affected by the cue.

The algorithm takes into account the way of handling main verbs by Minipar, in which these verbs appear as heads and the auxiliary verbs are dependants of them. Therefore, the system first detects the nodes that contain a word which is a negation cue, and afterwards it does the following:

- If the negation cue is a verb, such as *lack*, it is marked as a negation cue.

- If the negation cue is not a verb, the algorithm marks the main verb (if it exists) that governs the structure as a negation cue.

For the rest of nodes, if a node depends directly on any of the ones previously marked as negation cue, the system marks it as affected. The negation is also propagated until finding leaves, so wordforms that are not directly related to the cues are detected too.

Finally, by using all of the above, the algorithm generates a list of words affected by each negation cue.

2.3 Scope Classification Algorithm

This second algorithm is the one that has suffered the deepest modifications from the first version. The previous version handled the annotation as it is done in the Bioscope corpus. The algorithm works as follows:

- The system opens a scope when it finds a new negation cue detected by the affected wordforms detection algorithm. In Bioscope, only the sentences in passive voice include the subject inside the scope. However, the Conan Doyle corpus does not contain this exception always including the subject in the scope when it exists. Therefore, we modified the decision that fires this rule, and we apply the way of annotating sentences in passive voice for all the negation cues, either passive or active voice sentences.

  Therefore, for most of the negation cues the system goes backward and opens the scope when it finds the subject involved or a marker that indicates another statement, like a comma.

  There are some exceptions to this, such as scopes in which the cue is *without* or *neither...nor*. For them the system just opens the scope at the cue.

- The system closes a scope when there are no more wordforms to be added, i.e.:
  - It finds words that indicate another statement, such as *but* or *because*.
  - No more words in the output of the first algorithm.
  - End of the sentence.

- We also added a new rule that can handle the negation cues that are prefix or suffix of another word, such as *meaning-less*: if the system finds a cue word like this, it then annotates the suffix or prefix as the cue (such as *less*) and the rest of the word as part of the scope. Note that the Affected Wordforms Detection algorithm detects the whole word as a cue word.

2.4 Negated Event Handling

In order to come up with a solution that could provide at least some results in the negated event handling, we decided to do the following:

- When the cue word contains a negative prefix or a negative suffix, we annotate the word as the negated event.

- When the cue word is either *not* or *n't* and the next word is a verb, according to the part-of-speech annotation of the Conan Doyle corpus, we annotate the verb as the negated event.

2.5 Post-Processing Step

The post-processing step basically processes the annotated sentence with Bioscope style, (we show an example for clarification: *<scope>There is <cue>no</cue> problem</scope>*). It tokenizes the sentences, in which each token is a word or a wordform, after that, it does the following:

- If the token contains the string *<scope>*, the system just starts a new scope column reserving three new columns and it puts the word in the first free "scope" column. Because it means that there is a new scope for the present sentence.

- If the token is between a *<cue>* annotation, the system puts it in the corresponding free "cue" column of the scope already opened.

- If the token is annotated as "negated event", the system just puts the word in the last column of the scope already opened.

Note that these three rules are not exclusive and can be fired for the same token, but in this case they are fired in the same order as they are presented.

3 Results and Discussion

In this section we first show the evaluation results and second the error analysis after studying the results on the development set.

3.1 Results

In this section we show the results obtained in two different tables: Table 2 shows the results of the system with the test set, Table 3 shows the results of the system with the development set.

As we can observe, the results for the development set are higher than the ones obtained for the test set. The reason is simple, we used the development set (apart from the training set) to modify the rules and to make the system able to annotate the sentences of the test set.

Note that our system only detects some of the negation cues (around 72% F1 and 76% F1, respectively, for the test and development sets). We therefore believe that one of the main drawbacks of the present system is the static lexicon of cues. In the previous version, due to the simplicity of the task, this was not an issue. However, it is worth noting that once the negation is detected the results are not that bad, we show a high precision in most of the tasks. But the recall suffers due to the coverage of the lexicon.

It is also worth noting that for the measure *Scope tokens*, which takes into account the tokens included in the scope but not a full scope match, our system provides interesting outcomes (around 63% F1 and 73% F1, respectively), showing that it is able to annotate the tokens in a similar way. We believe that this fact evidences that the present system comes from a different kind of annotation and a different domain, and the extension or modification of such a system is a complex task.

We can also observe that the *negated events* results are very low (around 17.46% F1 and 22.53% F1, respectively), but this was expected because by using our two rules we are only covering two cases and moreover, these two cases are not always behaving in the same way in the corpora.

3.2 Error Analysis

In this section we analyse the different errors of our system with respect to the development set. This set contains 787 sentences, of which 144 are negation sentences containing 168 scopes, 173 cues and 122 negation events.

With respect to the negation cue detection we have obtained 58 false negatives (fn) and 16 false positives (fp). These results are not directly derived from the static lexicon of cues. The main problem is related with the management of sentences with more than one scope. The majority of the errors have been produced because in some cases all the cues are assigned to all the scopes detected in the same sentence, generating fp, and in other cases the cues of the second and subsequent scopes are ignored, generating fn. The first case occurs in sentences like (1), *no* and *without* are labelled as cues in the two scopes. The second case occurs in sentences like (2), where neither the second scope nor the second cue are labelled. In sentence (3) *un* is labelled as cue two times (unbrushed, unshaven) but within the same scope, generating a fp in the first scope and a fn in the second one.

- (1) But no [one can glance at your toilet and attire without [seeing that your disturbance dates from the moment of your waking .. ']]
- (2) [You do]n't [mean] - . [you do] n't [mean that I am suspected] ? "
- (3) Our client smoothed down [his] un[brushed hair] and felt [his] un[shaven chin].

We also found false negatives that occur in multi word negation cues as *by no means*, *no more* and *rather than*.

A different kind of false positives is related to modality cues, dialogue elements and special cases (Morante and Blanco, 2012). For example, *no* in (4), *not* in (5) and *save* in (6).

- (4) " You traced him through the telegram , no [doubt]., " said Holmes .

Test set	gold	system	tp	fp	fn	precision (%)	recall (%)	F1 (%)
Cues:	264	235	170	39	94	81.34	64.39	71.88
Scopes(cue match):	249	233	96	47	153	67.13	38.55	48.98
Scopes(no cue match):	249	233	96	48	152	66.90	38.96	49.24
Scope tokens(no cue match):	1805	2096	1222	874	583	58.30	67.70	62.65
Negated(no cue match):	173	81	36	42	134	46.15	21.18	29.03
Full negation:	264	235	29	39	235	42.65	10.98	17.46

Table 2: Test set results.

Development	gold	system	tp	fp	fn	precision (%)	recall (%)	F1 (%)
Cues:	173	161	115	16	58	87.79	66.47	75.66
Scopes(cue match):	168	160	70	17	98	80.46	41.67	54.90
Scopes(no cue match):	168	160	70	17	98	80.46	41.67	54.90
Scope tokens(no cue match):	1348	1423	1012	411	336	71.12	75.07	73.04
Negated(no cue match):	122	71	35	31	82	53.03	29.91	38.25
Full negation:	173	161	24	16	149	60.00	13.87	22.53

Table 3: Development set results.

- (5) " All you desire is a plain statement , [is it] not ? '.
- (6) Telegraphic inquiries ... that [Marx knew] nothing [of his customer save that he was a good payer] .

We can also find problems with affixal negations, that is, bad separation of the affix and root of the word. For example, in (7) *dissatisfied* was erroneously divided in *di-* and *ssatisfied*. Again, it is derived from the use of a static lexicon.

- (7) He said little about the case, but from that little we gathered that [he also was not dis[satisfied] at the course of events].

Finally, we could also find cases that may be due to annotation errors. For example, *incredible* is not annotated as negation cue in (8). The annotation of this cue we think is inconsistent, it appears 5 times in the training corpus, 2 times is labelled as cue, but 3 times is not. According to the context in this sentence, *incredible* means not *credible*.

- (8) "Have just had most incredible and grotesque experience.

With respect to the full scope detection, most of the problems are due again to the management of sentences with more than one scope. We have obtained 98 fn and 17 fp. Most of the problems are related with affixal negations, as in (9), in which all the words are included in the scope, which according to the gold standard is not correct.

- (9) [Our client looked down with a rueful face at his own] un[conventional appearance].

With respect to the scope tokens detection, the results are higher, around 73% F1 in scope tokens compared to 55% in full match scopes. The reason is because our system included tokens for the majority of scopes, increasing the recall until 75% but lowering the precision due to the inclusion of more fp.

4 Conclusions and Future Work

In this paper we presented our participation in the SEM-Shared Task, with a modification of a rule-based system that was designed to be used in a different domain. As the main conclusion we could say that modifying such a system to perform in a different type of texts is complicated. However, taking into account this fact, and the results obtained, we are tempted to say that our system presents competitive results.

We believe that the present system has a lot of room for improvement: (i) improve the management of sentences with more than one scope modifying the scope classification algorithm and the post-processing step, (ii) replacing the dependency parser with a state-of-the-art parser in order to get higher performance, or (iii) proposing a different way of getting a reliable lexicon of cues, by using a semantic approach that informs if the word has a negative meaning in the context of the sentence. Again, this could be achieved by using one of the parsers presented in the ConLL 2008 Shared Task (Surdeanu et al., 2008).

Acknowledgments

This research is funded by the Spanish Ministry of Education and Science (TIN2009-14659-C03-01 Project).

References

Miguel Ballesteros, Raúl Martín, and Belén Díaz-Agudo. 2010. Jadaweb: A cbr system for cooking recipes. In *Proceedings of the Computing Cooking Contest of the International Conference of Case-Based Reasoning*.

Miguel Ballesteros, Virginia Francisco, Alberto Díaz, Jesús Herrera, and Pablo Gervás. 2012. Inferring the scope of negation in biomedical documents. In *Proceedings of the 13th International Conference on Intelligent Text Processing and Computational Linguistics (CICLING 2012)*, New Delhi. Springer.

Dekang Lin. 1998. Dependency-based evaluation of MINIPAR. In *Proceedings of the Workshop on the Evaluation of Parsing Systems*, Granada.

Roser Morante and Eduardo Blanco. 2012. Sem 2012 shared task: Resolving the scope and focus of negation. In *Proceedings of the First Joint Conference on Lexical and Computational Semantics (*SEM 2012), Montreal, Canada.*

Roser Morante and Walter Daelemans. 2009. A metalearning approach to processing the scope of negation. In *Proceedings of the Thirteenth Conference on Computational Natural Language Learning*, CoNLL '09, pages 21–29, Stroudsburg, PA, USA. Association for Computational Linguistics.

Roser Morante and Walter Daelemans. 2012. Conandoyle-neg: Annotation of negation in conan doyle stories. In *Proceedings of the Eighth International Conference on Language Resources and Evaluation (LREC). Istanbul, Turkey.*

Roser Morante and Caroline Sporleder, editors. 2010. *Proceedings of the Workshop on Negation and Speculation in Natural Language Processing*, Uppsala, Sweden.

Roser Morante, Anthony Liekens, and Walter Daelemans. 2008. Learning the scope of negation in biomedical texts. In *Proceedings of the Conference on Empirical Methods in Natural Language Processing*, EMNLP '08, pages 715–724, Stroudsburg, PA, USA. Association for Computational Linguistics.

Mihai Surdeanu, Richard Johansson, Adam Meyers, Lluís Màrquez, and Joakim Nivre. 2008. The CoNLL-2008 shared task on joint parsing of syntactic and semantic dependencies. In *CoNLL 2008: Proceedings of the Twelfth Conference on Natural Language Learning*, pages 159–177, Manchester, United Kingdom.

Veronika Vincze, Gyorgy Szarvas, Richard Farkas, Gyorgy Mora, and Janos Csirik. 2008. The BioScope corpus: biomedical texts annotated for uncertainty, negation and their scopes. *BMC Bioinformatics*, 9(Suppl 11):S9+.

UConcordia: CLaC Negation Focus Detection at *Sem 2012

Sabine Rosenberg and Sabine Bergler
CLaC Lab, Concordia University
1455 de Maisonneuve Blvd West, Montréal, QC, Canada, H3W 2B3
sabin_ro@cse.concordia.ca, bergler@cse.concordia.ca

Abstract

Simply detecting negation cues is not sufficient to determine the semantics of negation, scope and focus must be taken into account. While scope detection has recently seen repeated attention, the linguistic notion of focus is only now being introduced into computational work. The *Sem2012 Shared Task is pioneering this effort by introducing a suitable dataset and annotation guidelines. CLaC's NegFocus system is a solid baseline approach to the task.

1 Introduction

Negation has attracted the attention of the NLP community and we have seen an increased advance in sophistication of processing tools. In order to assess factual information as asserted or not, it is important to distinguish the difference between

(1) (a) *Newt Gingrich Not Conceding Race After Losing Florida Primary*
(b) *Newt Gingrich Conceding Race After Losing Florida Primary*

This distinction is important and cannot be properly inferred from the surrounding context, *not* conceding a race after losing is in fact contrary to expectation in the original headline (1a), and the constructed (1b) is more likely in isolation.

Negation has been addressed as a task in itself, rather than as a component of other tasks in recent shared tasks and workshops. Detection of negation cues and negation scope at CoNLL (Farkas et al., 2010), BioNLP (Kim et al., 2011) and the Negation and Speculation in NLP Workshop (Morante and Sporleder, 2010) laid the foundation for the *Sem 2012 Shared Task. While the scope detection has been extended to fictional text in this task, an important progression from the newspaper and biomedical genres, the newly defined Focus Detection for Negation introduces the important question: what is the intended opposition in (1a)? The negation trigger is *not*, the scope of the negation is the entire verb phrase, but which aspect of the verb phrase is underscored as being at variance with reality, that is, which of the following possible (for the sake of linguistic argument only) continuations is the more likely one:

(2) i ..., *Santorum does.* ($\neg Newt\ Gingrich$)
ii ..., *Doubling Efforts* ($\neg concede$)
iii ..., *Demanding Recount* ($\neg race$)
iv ..., *Texas redistricting at fault* ($\neg Florida$)

This notion of *focus of negation* is thus a pragmatic one, chosen by the author and encoded with various means. Usually, context is necessary to determine focus. Often, different possible interpretations of focus do not change the factual meaning of the overall text, but rather its coherence. In (1 a) the imagined possible contexts (2 ii) and (2 iii) closely correspond to a simple negation of (1 b), (2 i) and (2 iv) do not feel properly represented by simply negating (1 b). This level of interpretation is contentious among people and it is the hallmark of well-written, well-edited text to avoid unnecessary guesswork while at the same time avoiding unnecessary clarifying repetition. The potential for ambiguity is demonstrated by Example (3) from (Partee, 1993), where it is questionable whether the speaker in fact *has possession* of the book in question.

(3) *I didn't get that book from Mary*

Here, if the focus is *from Mary*, it would be likely that the speaker has possion of the book, but received it some other way. If the focus is *that book*, the speaker does not have possession of it.

It is important to note hat this notion of focus is not syntactically determined as shown in (3) (even though we use syntactic heuristics here to approximate it) but pragmatically and it correlates with pronunciation stress, as discussed in linguistics by (Han and Romero, 2001). More recently, focus negation has been identified as a special use (Poletto, 2008). The difference of scope and focus of negation are elaborated by (Partee, 1993), and have been used for computational use by (Blanco and Moldovan, 2011).

The *Sem 2012 Task 2 on Focus Detection builds on recent negation scope detection capabilities and introduces a gold standard to identify the focus item. Focus of negation is annotated over 3,993 sentences in the WSJ section of the Penn TreeBank marked with MNEG in PropBank. It accounts for verbal, analytical and clausal relation to a negation trigger; the role most likely to correspond to the focus was selected as focus. All sentences of the training data contain a negation. A sample annotation from the gold standard is given in (4), where PropBank semantic roles are labelled *A1, M-NEG*, and *M-TMP* and focus is underlined (until June).

(4) $\langle A\ decision_{A_1}\rangle\ is\langle n't_{M-NEG}\rangle\ expected$ $\langle\ \underline{until\ June}\ _{M-TMP}\rangle$

2 Previous Work

A recent study in combining regular pattern extraction with parse information for enhanced indexing of radiology reports showed effective detection of negated noun phrases for that corpus (Huang and Lowe, 2007). NegFinder (Mutalik et al., 2001) detects negated concepts in dictated medical documents with a simple set of corpus specific context-free rules, and they observe that in their corpus "One of the words *no*, *denies/denied*, *not*, or *without* was present in 92.5 percent of all negations." Interestingly, several of their rules concern coordination (*and, or*) or prepositional phrase attachment patterns (*of, for*). NegEx (Chapman et al., 2001) is publicly available and maintained and updated with community-enhanced trigger lists (`http://code.google.com/p/negex/wiki/NegExTerms`). NegEx "locates trigger terms indicating a clinical condition is negated or possible and determines which text falls within the scope of the trigger terms." NegEx uses a simple regular expression algorithm with a small number of negation phrases and focuses on a wide variety of triggers but limits them to domain relevant ones. Consequently, the trigger terms and conditions are heavily stacked with biomedical domain specific terms. Outside the biomedical text community, sentiment and opinion analysis research features negation detection (Wilson, 2008). Current gold standard annotations for explicit negation as well as related phenomena include TIMEBANK (Pustejovsky et al., 2003), MPQA (Wiebe et al., 2005), and Bio-Scope (Vincze et al., 2008).

(Wiegand et al., 2010) presents a flat feature combination approach of features of different granularity and analytic sophistication, since in opinion mining the boundary between negation and negative expressions is fluid.

3 CLaC's NegFocus

CLaC Labs' general, lightweight negation module is intended to be embedded in any processing pipeline. The heuristics-based system is composed of three modules for the GATE (Cunningham et al., 2011) environment: the first component detects and annotates explicit negation cues present in the corpus, the second component detects and annotates the syntactic scope of the detected instances of verbal negation, and the third component implements focus heuristics for negation. The first two steps were developed independently, drawing on data from MPQA (Wiebe et al., 2005) and TIMEBANK (Pustejovsky et al., 2003) with validation on Bio-Scope (Vincze et al., 2008). The third step has been added based on data for the *Sem 2012 challenge and is intended to validate both, the first two "preprocessing" steps and the simple heuristic approximation of focus.

3.1 Data Preprocessing

Parser-based, our focus detection pipeline requires as input entire sentences. Therefore, the first step requires the extraction of each sentence utilizing the supplied token numbers and save them in the correct format. The system then performs standard preprocessing: sentence splitting, tokenization, parsing using the Stanford Parser (Klein and Manning, 2003; de Marneffe and Manning, 2006) and morphological preprocessing. Note that NegFocus does not use any PropBank annotations nor other provided training annotations, resulting in an independent, parser-based stand-alone module.

3.2 Detection of Negation Triggers

The Focus Detection task only considers the explicit negation cues *not, nor, never*. The first step in NegFocus is thus to identify these triggers in the sentences using an explicit negation trigger word list.

3.3 Syntactic Scope Detection

The Focus Detection task only considers negation of verbs. Thus, NegFocus extracts the syntactic complement of the verb to form the negated verb phrase from the dependency graphs (de Marneffe and Manning, 2006). We annotate this as the syntactic scope of the negation. Note that while we use dependency graphs, our syntactic scope is based on the parse tree and differs from the notion of scope encoded in BioScope (Vincze et al., 2008) and the related format used for the *Sem 2012 Negation Scope Annotation task, which represent in our opinion the pragmatic notion of scope for the logical negation operation. Syntactic scope detection is thus considered to be a basic stepping stone towards the pragmatic scope and since the Focus Detection task does not provide scope annotations, we use syntactic scope here to validate this principle.

Our heuristics are inspired by (Kilicoglu and Bergler, 2011). In the majority of cases the dependency relation which identifies the syntactic scope is the *neg* relation. Traditionally, parse trees identify scope as lower or to the right of the trigger term, and our scope module assumes these grammatical constraints, yet includes the verb itself for the purposes of the shared task. Example 5, from the training dataset "The Hound of the Baskervilles" by Conan Doyle for the *Sem 2012 Negation Scope Annotation task, demonstrates our syntactic scope of the negation (underlined), in contrast with the gold standard scope annotation (in brackets). The gold annotation guidelines follow the proposal of Morante et al. (Morante et al., 2011)[1].

(5) *[We did] not [drive up to the door] but got down near the gate of the avenue.*

3.4 Focus Heuristics

The third and final step for NegFocus is to annotate focus in sentences containing verbal negations. Using the verbal negation scope annotations of the previous step, four focus heuristics are invoked:

3.4.1 Baseline

The Baseline heuristic for this component is defined according to notions discussed in (Huddleston and Pullum, 2002), where the last constituent in the verb phrase of a clause is commonly the default location to place the heaviest stress, which we here equate with the focus. Example (6) depicts an instance where both NegFocus results (underlined) and the gold focus annotation (in brackets) match exactly. The baseline heuristic achieves 47.4% recall and 49.4% precision on the training set and 47% recall and 49.7% precision on the test set.

(6) *NBC broadcast throughout the entire night and did not go off the air [until noon yesterday].*

As pointed out in Section 3.3, focus is not always determined by scope (Partee, 1993). The training data gave rise to three additional heuristics.

3.4.2 Adverb

When an adverb is directly preceding and connected through an *advmod* dependency relation to the negated verb, the adverb constituent is determined as the focus of the negation.

(7) *Although it may not be [legally] obligated to sell the company if the buy-out group can't revive its bid, it may have to explore alternatives if the buyers come back with a bid much lower than the group 's original $ 300-a-share proposal.*

[1] http://www.clips.ua.ac.be/sites/default/files/ctrs-n3.pdf

3.4.3 Noun Subject Passive

Passives are frequent in newspaper articles and passive constructions front what would otherwise be the verb complement. Thus the fronted material should be eligible for focus assignment. Passives are flagged through the *nsubjpass* dependency, and for cases where the negated verb participates in an nsubjpass relation and has no other complement, the nsubjpass is determined as the focus.

(8) *[Billings] were n't disclosed.*

3.4.4 Negation Cue

The challenge data has cases where the negation cue itself is its own focus. These cases seem to be pragmatically determined. Error cases were reduced when determining the negation cue to be its own focus in two cases. The first case occurs when the negated verb has an empty complement (and is not a passive construction), as in Example 9.

(9) *Both said the new plan would [n't] work.*

The second case occurs when the negated verb embeds a verb that we identify as an implicit negation. We have a list of implicit negation triggers largely compiled from MPQA (Wiebe et al., 2005). Implicit negations are verbs that lexically encode a predicate and a negation, such as *reject* or *fail*.

(10) *Black activist Walter Sisulu said the African National Congress would [n't] reject violence as a way to pressure the South African government into concessions that might lead to negotiations over apartheid . . .*

4 Results

Ordering the heuristics impacts on recall. We place the most specific heuristics before the more general ones to avoid starvation effects. For example, the *adverb* heuristic followed by the *noun subject passive* heuristic achieved better results at the beginning, since they are more specific then the *negation cue* heuristic.

Table 1 shows the performance of the heuristics of NegFocus on the test set and on the development set. We observe that the heuristics are stable across the two sets with a 60% accuracy on the test set. The worst performer is the baseline, which is very coarse for such a semantically sophisticated task: assuming that the last element of the negated verb phrase is the focus is truly a baseline.

heuristic	corr.	incorr.	acc.
Test Set			
baseline	336	238	.59
adverb	26	4	.87
nsubjpass	10	8	.56
neg. cue	33	20	.62
Development Set			
baseline	257	174	.6
adverb	15	6	.71
nsubjpass	10	6	.63
neg. cue	21	19	.53

Figure 1: Performance of NegFocus heuristics

The overall performance of the system is almost balanced between precision and recall with an f-measure of .58.

	Test Set	
Precision	60.00	[405/675]
Recall	56.88	[405/712]
F-score	58.40	
	Development Set	
Precision	59.65	[303/508]
Recall	57.06	[303/531]
F-score	58.33	

Figure 2: System Results

Our heuristics, albeit simplistic, are based on linguistically sound observations. The heuristic nature allows additional heuristics that are more tailored to a corpus or a task to be added without incurring unmanageable complexity, in fact each heuristic can be tested on the development set and can report on the test set to monitor its performance. The heuristics will also provide excellent features for statistical systems.

5 Error Analysis

We distinguish 11 classes of errors on the test set.

The classes of errors depicted in Table (3) indicates that the classes of errors and their frequencies are consistent across the different data sets. The third error class in Table (3) is of particular inter-

	Error Type	Test Set	Dev Set
1	Precision Errors: Verbal Negation Scope not found by NegFocus	37	23
2	Focus Mismatch: gold focus annotation is the neg. cue	138	112
3	Focus Mismatch: gold focus annotation is a constituent triggered by the *nsubj* dependency to the negated verb	44	16
4	Focus Mismatch: gold focus annotation is the constituent triggered by the *nsubjpass* dependency	7	12
5	Focus Mismatch: gold focus annotation is an adverb triggered by the *advmod* dependency with the verb, but is not adjacent to the verb	14	4
6	Partial Match: the spans of the gold focus annotation and NegFocus annotation overlap	6	8
7	Focus Mismatch: gold focus annotation is not contained within the NegFocus Syntactic Scope	4	5
8	NegFocus Syntactic Scope annotation error	10	9
9	Focus Mismatch: Miscellaneous errors	27	25
10	Focus Mismatch: gold focus annotation matches CLaC baseline heuristic, however another CLaC focus heuristic was chosen	3	3
11	Focus Mismatch: gold focus annotation contains two discontinuous focus annotation spans	17	11
	TOTAL	307	228

Figure 3: System Errors

est to us, as it highlights the different interpretations of verbal negation scope. NegFocus will not include the noun subject in the syntactic negation scope, and therefore the noun subject constituent is never a focus candidate as required in Example (11).

(11) *In New York, [a spokesman for American Brands] would n't comment.*

Similarly, the seventh error class in Table (3) contains focus annotations that are not contained in NegFocus negation scopes. Example (12) shows an error where the sentence begins with a prepositional phrase that is annotated as the gold focus.

(12) *[On some days], the Nucor plant does n't produce anything.*

We disagree with the gold annotations on this and similar cases: the prepositional phrase *on some days* is not negated, it provides a temporal specification for the negated statement *the Nucor plant produces something* and in our opinion, the negation negates *something*, contrasting it with

(13) *[On some days], the Nucor plant does n't produce a lot.*

which allows for some production, which indicates to us that without context information, low focus is warranted here.

NegFocus incorporates a focus heuristic for determining the passive noun subject constituent as the focus of the negation, however only in cases where the negated verb has an empty complement. The fourth error class contains errors in focus determination where this heuristic fails and where the passive subject is the gold focus despite the complement of the negated verb not being empty, requiring further analysis:

(14) *To simplify the calculations , [commissions on the option and underlying stock] are n't included in the table.*

NegFocus determines an adverb directly preceding the verb trigger as the focus of the negation, but, as described in the fifth error class, the gold focus annotations in a few cases determine adverbs to be the focus of the negation even when they don't directly precede the verb, but are linked by the *advmod* relation, as in Example (15). When we experimented with relaxing the adjacency constraint, re-

	Error Type	Test Set	Dev Set
1	NegFocus annotation is adverb	2	3
2	NegFocus annotation is passive noun subject	7	4
3	NegFocus Scope Error	7	14
4	NegFocus baseline heuristic at variance with gold annotation	122	91
	TOTAL	138	112

Figure 4: Negation cue annotation misses

sults suffered. This, too, is an area where we wish to investigate whether any general patterns are possible and what additional resources they require to be reliable.

(15) *" The intervention has been friendly, meaning that they [really] did n't have to do it, " said Maria Fiorini Ramirez, money-market economist at Drexel Burnham Lambert Inc .*

The majority of NegFocus errors occur in the second error class. Table (4) further analyzes the second error class, where the gold annotation puts the negation trigger in the focus but NegFocus finds another focus (usually in the verb complement).

The gold standard annotations place the focus of the negation of verb v on the negation trigger if it cannot be inferred that an action v occurred (Blanco and Moldovan, 2011). NegFocus will only make this assumption when the verb complement constituent is empty, otherwise the baseline focus heuristic will be triggered, as depicted in Example (16).

(16) *AMR declined to comment , and Mr. Trump did [n't] respond to requests for interviews.*

Furthermore, the CLaC system will choose to trigger the subject passive focus heuristic in the case where the verb complement constituent is empty, and the passive noun subject is present. In contrast, the gold standard annotations do not necessarily follow this heuristic as seen in Example (17).

(17) *That is n't 51 %, and the claim is [n't] documented .*

Lastly, the gold focus annotations include focus spans which are discontinuous. NegFocus will only detect one continuous focus span within one instance of a verbal negation. The eleventh error class includes those cases where NegFocus matches one of the gold focus spans but not the other as seen in Example (18).

(18) *[The payments] aren't expected [to have an impact on coming operating results], Linear added .*

These error cases show that more analysis of the data, but also of the very notion of focus, is necessary.

6 Conclusion

We conclude that this experiment confirmed the hypothesis that negation trigger detection, syntactic scope determination, and focus determination are usefully modelled as a pipeline of three simple modules that apply after standard text preprocessing and dependency parsing. Approximating focus from a principled, linguistic point of view proved to be a quick and robust exercise. Performance on development and test sets is nearly identical and in a range around 58% f-measure. While the annotation standards as well as our heuristics warrant revisiting, we believe that the value of the focus annotation will prove its value beyond negation. The challenge data provide a valuable resource in themselves, but we believe that their true value will be shown by using the derived notion of focus in downstream applications. For initial experiments, the simple NegFocus pipeline is a stable prototype.

References

E. Blanco and D. Moldovan. 2011. Semantic representation of negation using focus detection. In *Proceedings of the 49th Annual Meeting of the Association for Computational Linguistics: Human Language Technologies (ACL-HLT 2011)*, Portland, OR.

W. Chapman, W. Bridewell, P. Hanbury, G.F. Cooper, and B. Buchanan. 2001. A simple algorithm for identifying negated findings and diseases in discharge summaries. *Journal of Biomedical Informatics*, 34(5):301-310.

H. Cunningham, D. Maynard, K. Bontcheva, V. Tablan, N. Aswani, I. Roberts, G. Gorrell, A. Funk, A. Roberts, D. Damljanovic, T. Heitz, M.A. Greenwood, H. Saggion, J. Petrak, Y. Li, and Wim P. 2011. *Text Processing with GATE (Version 6)*. GATE (April 15, 2011).

M. de Marneffe and C.D. Manning. 2006. Generating typed dependency parses from phrase structure parses. In *LREC*.

R. Farkas, V. Vincze, G.Móra, J. Csirik, and G.Szarvas. 2010. The conll-2010 shared task: Learning to detect hedges and their scope in natural language text. In *Proceedings of the Fourteenth Conference on Computational Natural Language Learning*.

C-H. Han and M. Romero. 2001. Negation, focus and alternative questions. In K. Megerdoomian and L.A. Bar-el, editors, *Proceedings of the West Coast Conference in Formal Linguistics XX*, Somerville, MA. Cascadilla Press.

Y. Huang and H.J. Lowe. 2007. A novel hybrid approach to automated negation detection in clinical radiology reports. *Journal of the American Medical Informatics Association : JAMIA*, 14(3):304-311.

R.D. Huddleston and G.K. Pullum. 2002. *The Cambridge grammar of the English language*. Cambridge University Press, Cambridge, UK; New York.

H. Kilicoglu and S. Bergler. 2011. Effective bio-event extraction using trigger words and syntactic dependencies. *Computational Intelligence*, 27(4):583–609.

J.-D. Kim, Y. Wang, T. Takagi, and A. Yonezawa. 2011. Overview of genia event task in bionlp shared task 2011. In *Proceedings of BioNLP Shared Task 2011 Workshop at ACL-HLT*.

D. Klein and C.D. Manning. 2003. Accurate unlexicalized parsing. In *Proceedings of the 41st Annual Meeting of the Association for Computational Linguistics*.

R. Morante and C. Sporleder, editors. 2010. *NeSp-NLP '10: Proceedings of the Workshop on Negation and Speculation in Natural Language Processing*, Stroudsburg, PA, USA. Association for Computational Linguistics.

R. Morante, S. Schrauwen, and W. Daelemans. 2011. Annotation of negation cues and their scope. guidelines v1.0. Technical report, CLiPS, University of Antwerp.

P. G. Mutalik, A. Deshpande, and P. M. Nadkarni. 2001. Use of general-purpose negation detection to augment concept indexing of medical documents: a quantitative study using the umls. *Journal of the American Medical Informatics Association : JAMIA*, 8(6):598-609.

B. Partee. 1993. On the "scope of negation" and polarity sensitivity. In E. Hajicova, editor, *Functional Approaches to Language Description*.

C. Poletto. 2008. The syntax of focus negation. *University of Venice Working Papers in Linguistics*, 18.

J. Wiebe, T. Wilson, and C. Cardie. 2005. Annotating expressions of opinions and emotions in language. *Language Resources and Evaluation*, 39(2-3).

M. Wiegand, B. Roth, D. Klakow, A. Balahur, and A. Montoyo. 2010. A survey on the role of negation in sentiment analysis. In *Proceedings of the Workshop on Negation and Speculation in Natural Language Processing (NeSp-NLP 2010)*.

Th. Wilson. 2008. *Fine-Grained Subjectivity Analysis*. Ph.D. thesis, University of Pittsburgh. Intelligent Systems Program.

UGroningen: Negation detection with Discourse Representation Structures

Valerio Basile and **Johan Bos** and **Kilian Evang** and **Noortje Venhuizen**
{v.basile,johan.bos,k.evang,n.j.venhuizen}@rug.nl
Center for Language and Cognition Groningen (CLCG)
University of Groningen, The Netherlands

Abstract

We use the NLP toolchain that is used to construct the Groningen Meaning Bank to address the task of detecting negation cue and scope, as defined in the shared task "Resolving the Scope and Focus of Negation". This toolchain applies the C&C tools for parsing, using the formalism of Combinatory Categorial Grammar, and applies Boxer to produce semantic representations in the form of Discourse Representation Structures (DRSs). For *negation cue detection*, the DRSs are converted to flat, non-recursive structures, called Discourse Representation Graphs (DRGs). DRGs simplify cue detection by means of edge labels representing relations. *Scope detection* is done by gathering the tokens that occur within the scope of a negated DRS. The result is a system that is fairly reliable for cue detection and scope detection. Furthermore, it provides a fairly robust algorithm for detecting the *negated event or property* within the scope.

1 Introduction

Nothing is more home to semantics than the phenomenon of *negation*. In classical theories of meaning all states of affairs are divided in two truth values, and negation plays a central role to determine which truth value is at stake for a given sentence. Negation lies at the heart of deductive inference, of which consistency checking (searching for contradictions in texts) is a prime example in natural language understanding.

It shouldn't therefore come as a surprise that detecting negation and adequately representing its scope is of utmost importance in computational semantics. In this paper we present and evaluate a system that transforms texts into logical formulas – using the C&C tools and Boxer (Bos, 2008) – in the context of the shared task on recognising negation in English texts (Morante and Blanco, 2012).

We will first sketch the background and the basics of the formalism that we employ in our analysis of negation (Section 2). In Section 3 we explain how we detect negation cues and scope. Finally, in Section 4 we present the results obtained in the shared task, and we discuss them in Section 5.

2 Background

The semantic representations that are used in this shared task on detecting negation in texts are constructed by means of a pipeline of natural language processing components, of which the backbone is provided by the C&C tools and Boxer (Curran et al., 2007). This tool chain is currently in use semi-automatically for constructing a large semantically annotated corpus, the Groningen Meaning Bank (Basile et al., 2012).

The C&C tools are applied for tagging the data with part-of-speech and super tags and for syntactic parsing, using the formalism of Combinatory Categorial Grammar, CCG (Steedman, 2001). The output of the parser, CCG derivations, form the input of Boxer, producing formal semantic representations in the form of Discourse Representation Structures (DRSs), the basic meaning-carrying structures in the framework of Discourse Representation Theory (Kamp and Reyle, 1993). DRT is a widely accepted formal theory of natural language meaning that has been used to study a wide range of linguistic

Figure 1: CCG derivation and unresolved semantics for the sentence "I saw nothing suspicious"

phenomena, such as anaphoric pronouns, temporal relations (Kamp and Reyle, 1993), presuppositions (Van der Sandt, 1992), abstract anaphora and rhetorical relations (Asher, 1993; Asher and Lascarides, 2003).

A DRS contains two parts: a set of of discourse referents, and a set of conditions. Negation is represented in a condition by a unary operator in DRT. As an example, Figure 1 shows the derivation for one sentence as produced by the pipeline, illustrating how lexical semantic entries are used to construct a DRS for a whole sentence, guided by the syntactic parse tree. Here, machinery of the λ-calculus is employed to deal with variable renaming when required.

DRSs are recursive structures by nature. They can be produced in several formats (in Prolog or XML) and translated into first-order formulas. The representations can also be generated as a set of tuples, forming together a directed graph equivalent to the original DRS, where discourse referents and symbols are nodes and predicates and relations are viewed as labelled edges. These "flat" Discourse Representation Graphs, DRGs, are often more suitable for certain processing tasks. The tuples also hold additional information, mapping DRS conditions to surface tokens. This mapping is important in tasks where surface realisation plays a role. We also use it in this shared task to get back from complex structures to a flat, token-based annotation of scope.

3 Method

The shared task aims at detecting negation in text — systems are supposed to label tokens that are in the scope of negation, and also identify the token that triggered the negation. The basic idea of our method was to run the existing Boxer system for semantic analysis, then traverse the produced DRSs, and, on encountering an embbeded negated DRS, output the tokens associated with this negation, as well as the token triggering it.

As this isn't what Boxer is usually asked to do, it required some bookkeeping adjustments. Boxer's anaphora resolution feature was turned off because it is not necessary for the task and would lead to unwanted inclusion of antecedents into negation scopes. Also, its features for representing tense information and rhetorical relations were not used.

The rest of this section pays a closer look at how negation cues are detected and how scope is assigned to tokens. We address the issues of translating a formal representation such as DRS into the format required by the shared task — a representation more oriented at the surface form. We submitted two runs of our system, which both used the C&C tools and Boxer. For the second run, we added some postprocessing steps that tune the result towards a higher performance, especially on scope detection. While these postprocessing steps improve performance, many of them may be specific to the genre and style of the texts used in the shared task.

3.1 Cue detection

Since Boxer has been developed as a system to generate full semantic representations, its lexicon implicitly contains a list of negation cues: those words giving rise to semantic representations of the form $\neg B$, where B is the DRS representing the meaning of the scope of the negation. Key examples here are determiners and noun phrases (*no*, *none*, *no-one*), and verb phrase negation (*not*).

However, negation detection is not the primary function of Boxer, as it is part of the larger aim of providing interpretable semantic representation for English texts, and doing so robustly. So for the current task, after investigating the development data made available by the organisers, Boxer's lexicon was revised at a few points to account for particular negation cues that Boxer originally did not detect. This included the detection of *never* as negation cue, as well as words with a negative prefix or suffix (e.g. *inadequate*, *motionless*). These affix negations were detected using an automatically generated list of negatively affixed nouns, adjectives and adverbs from WordNet (Fellbaum, 1998). The list was created by means of an algorithm that returns all nouns, adjectives and adverbs in WordNet that start with one of *a, an, dis, in, il, im, ir, non, non-, un*, or end with one of *less, lessness, lessly*, and have a direct antonym such that the lemma form equals the stem of the affixed negation (i.e., without the affix).

On the other hand, not everything that introduces a negated DRS in Boxer is a typical negation cue. A case in point is the quantifier *all*, which up until the shared task received a semantics similar to $\lambda P \lambda Q. \neg \exists x(P(x) \wedge \neg Q(x))$ in Boxer's lexicon. As a consequence, Boxer predicted *all* to be a negation cue trigger, in contrast to the shared task gold standard data. Such instances were replaced by logically equivalent representations (in the case of *all*: $\lambda P \lambda Q. \forall x(P(x) \rightarrow Q(x))$).

In order to obtain the tokens that triggered the negated DRS, Boxer's DRG output was used. Occurrences of predicates, relations and connectives in the DRG output carry explicit associations with the tokens in the input whose lexical entries they come from. For basic cue detection, the system annotates as a negation cue those tokens (or affixes) associated with the connective $\neg$ (represented in the DRG as the relation subordinates:neg). Example (1) shows a part of the DRG's tuple format that represents the negation cue "no". *Argument structure* tuples (labeled concept and instance) are also shown, corresponding to a noun in the negation scope, as in "no problem". The first and third columns represent nodes of the DRG graph (both discourse units in this example), the second column represents the label of the edge between the nodes, and the fourth column shows the token associated with the relation (if any).

(1)

...	...	...	...
k1	subordinates:neg	k6	no
k6	concept	c1:problem	
c1:problem	instance	k6:x1	problem
...	...	...	...

In this case, the token "no" is detected as negation cue because it is associated with the relation subordinates:neg.

In the case of affix negation, ideally only the affix should be associated with the negation tuple, and the stem with a corresponding instance tuple. However, since the last column contains tokens, this does not easily fit into the format. We therefore associate the whole affix-negated token with the negation tuple and use separate tuples for affix and stem in order to preserve the information which part of the word is the cue and which part is in the scope of the negation. The resulting three tuples from a sentence containing the word "injustice" are shown in the following example:

(2)

...	...	...	...
k3	subordinates:neg	k4	injustice
k4	concept	c2:in:71	
k4	concept	c3:justice:1	
...	...	...	...

The target nodes of the two argument structure tuples (labeled concept because "injustice" is a noun) are labeled with the relevant part of the affix-negated word, and a special ID to indicate the presence of a prefix or suffix. This information is used by the script producing the token-based result format. Although multi-word cues, such as *neither..nor* and *on the contrary*, were not correctly predicted as such by Boxer, no effort was made to include them. Due to the token-based detection approach, the cue detection algorithm would have to be severly complicated to include these cases as one negation cue. Because of the relatively small frequency of multi-word cues, we decided not to include special processing steps to account for them.

The second run includes some postprocessing steps implemented on top of the basic output. Since Boxer is not designed to deal with dialogue, interjections were originally ignored as negation cues. Therefore, the postprocessing script added the word "no" as a negation cue (with empty scope) when it occurred as an interjection (tagged "UH"). It also excluded negations with the cue "no" when occurring as part of the expression "no doubt" and not immediately preceded by a verb with the lemma "have" or "be" as in "I have no doubt that...", which *is* to be annotated as a negation. High precision and recall for cue detection on the training data suggested that no further processing steps were worth the effort.

3.2 Scope detection

The tokens in the scope of a negation are determined on the basis of the detected negation cue. It is associated with the negation connective of some negated DRS $\neg B$, so the system annotates as scope all the tokens (and stems in the case of affix negation) directly or indirectly associated with predicates and relations inside B. This includes tokens directly associated with predicates that appear within the negated DRS, as well as those predicates outside of the negated DRS whose discourse referent occurs within the negation scope as the second argument of a thematic role relation.

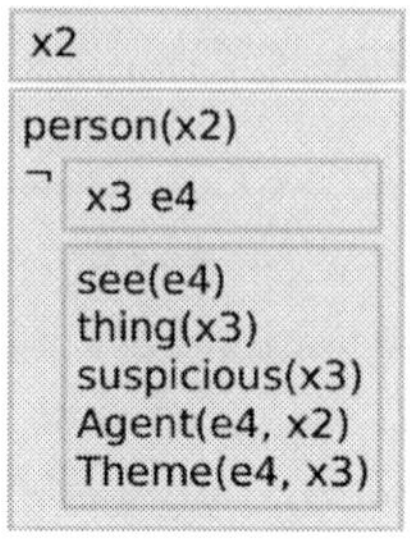

Figure 2: DRS for the sentence "I saw nothing suspicious"

An example is given in Figure 2, where e.g. the tokens *see* and *suspicious* are associated, respectively, with see(e4) and suspicious(x3). Although the predicate person(x2) associated with the pronoun *I* occurs outside of the negated DRS, its referent occurs as an argument within the negated DRS in Agent(e4, x2) and therefore it is taken to be part of the scope of the negation. The desired scope is thus detected, containing the tokens *I*, *saw* and *suspicious*.

Again, in the second run some postprocessing steps were implemented to improve performance. We observed that the scopes in the manually annotated data were usually continuous, except for negation cues within them. However, the scopes produced by the DRS algorithm contained many "gaps" between the tokens of the detected scope, due to an intrinsic feature of the DRS representation. Conventionally, DRSs only explicitly contain content words (i.e. nouns, verbs, adjectives, adverbs), while function words, such as determiners, modals and auxiliary verbs, are represented e.g. as structural properties or temporal features, or not at all, as in the case of the infinitival *to*. Thus, when retrieving the surface representation of the negated scopes from the DRSs, not all structural properties can be directly associated with a surface token and thus not all tokens required for the scope are retrieved. Because in the gold standard annotation these function words were considered part of the negation scope, we designed an ad hoc mechanism to include them, namely filling all the gaps that occur in the negation scope (leaving out the negation cue). For the same reason, determiners immediately preceding the detected scopes were added in postprocessing. Finally, conjunctions were removed from the beginning of negation scopes, because they were sometimes wrongly recognized by our pipeline as adverbs.

3.3 Negated event/property detection

Although not among our main goals, we also addressed the issue of detecting the "negated event or property" in negation scopes within factual statements. This is done using a heuristic algorithm that uses the detected scope, as well as the syntax tree provided as part of the data.

Since the scope is provided as a set of tokens, the first step is to identify what we call the *scope constituent*, i.e. a constituent in the syntax tree that corresponds to the scope. This is done by going through the tokens in the scope from left to right and determining for each token the largest constituent that starts with this token. The first constituent found in this way the category of whose root is one of SBAR, S and VP is taken to be the scope constituent.

In the second step, the *scope VP* is determined as the first VP encountered when doing a pre-order, left-to-right traversal of the scope constituent. The first verb directly dominated by this VP node determines how the process continues: (i) For non-factual modals (e.g. *may, must, should*), no event/property is annotated. (ii) For futurity modals (e.g. *would, will, shall*), the negated event/property is determined recursively by taking the first embedded VP as the new scope VP. (iii) For forms of the verb *be*, the algorithm first looks for the head of an embedded ADJP or NP. If one is found, this is annotated as a negated property. Otherwise, the verb is assumed to be a passive auxiliary and the negated event/property is again determined recursively on the basis of the first embedded VP. (iv) In all other cases, the verb itself is annotated as the negated event.

To limit the undesired detection of negated events/properties outside of factual statements, the algorithm is not applied to any sentence that contains a question mark.

4 Results

Here we discuss our results on the Shared Task as compared to the gold standard annotations provided by (Morante and Daelemans, 2012). The output of our two runs will be discussed with respect to Task 1. The first run includes the results of our system without postprocessing steps and in the second run the system is augmented with the postprocessing steps, as discussed in Section 3.

During the process of evaluating the results of the training data, an issue with the method of evaluation was discovered. In the first version of the evaluation script precision was calculated using the standard formula: $\frac{tp}{tp+fp}$. However, partial matches are excluded from this calculation (they are only counted as false negatives), which means that in the case of *scopes(cue match)*, precision is calculated as the number of exact scope matches (true positives) divided by the number of exact scope matches plus the number of completely wrong instances with no overlap (false positives). As precision is a measure for calculating correctly detected instances among all detected instances, it seems that partial matches should also be taken into account as detected instance. Therefore, we proposed a new evaluation method (B): $\frac{tp}{system}$, where *system* includes all detected negations of the current system (including partial matches). However, this measure may be too strict as it penalizes a system harder for outputting a partially correct scope than for outputting no scope at all.[1] This choice between two evils seems to indicate that precision is too simple a measure for targets where partial matches are possible. Therefore, in our evaluation of scope detection, we will focus on the *scope tokens* measure where there are no partial matches. For cue and negated event/property detection, we use the stricter, but more meaningful B version. The difference here is almost negligible because these targets typically have just one token.

4.1 Run 1 (without postprocessing)

Table 1 shows the results of the basic system without postprocessing, with the most important results for our system highlighted. As we can see, the basic system performs well on cue detection (F1=

[1]This was pointed out by an anonymous reviewer.

Table 1: Results of the first run (without postprocessing)

Task	gold	system	tp	fp	fn	precision (%)	recall (%)	F1 (%)
Cues:	264	261	219	33	45	86.90	82.95	84.88
Scopes(cue match):	249	261	32	37	217	46.38	12.85	20.12
Scopes(no cue match):	249	261	32	37	217	46.38	12.85	20.12
Scope tokens(no cue match):	1805	1821	1269	552	536	**69.69**	**70.30**	**69.99**
Negated(no cue match):	173	169	89	76	82	53.94	52.05	52.98
Full negation:	264	261	20	33	244	37.74	7.58	12.62
Cues B:	264	261	219	33	45	**83.91**	**82.95**	**83.43**
Scopes B (cue match):	249	261	32	37	217	12.26	12.85	12.55
Scopes B (no cue match):	249	261	32	37	217	12.26	12.85	12.55
Negated B (no cue match):	173	169	89	76	82	52.66	52.05	52.35
Full negation B:	264	261	20	33	244	7.66	7.58	7.62

Table 2: Results of the second run (with postprocessing)

Task	gold	system	tp	fp	fn	precision (%)	recall (%)	F1 (%)
Cues:	264	261	224	28	40	88.89	84.85	86.82
Scopes(cue match):	249	256	102	32	147	76.12	40.96	53.26
Scopes(no cue match):	249	256	102	32	147	76.12	40.96	53.26
Scope tokens(no cue match):	1805	2146	1485	661	320	**69.20**	**82.27**	**75.17**
Negated(no cue match):	173	201	111	85	59	56.63	65.29	60.65
Full negation:	264	261	72	28	192	72.00	27.27	39.56
Cues B:	264	261	224	28	40	**85.82**	**84.85**	**85.33**
Scopes B (cue match):	249	256	102	32	147	39.84	40.96	40.39
Scopes B (no cue match):	249	256	102	32	147	39.84	40.96	40.39
Negated B (no cue match):	173	201	111	85	59	55.22	65.29	59.83
Full negation B:	264	261	72	28	192	27.59	27.27	27.43

83.43%), and reasonably well on the detection of scope tokens (F1= 69.99%).

Note that the results for *Scopes(cue match)* and *Scopes(no cue match)* are the same for our system. Since we make use of token-based cue detection, the only cases of partial cue detection are instances of multi-word cues, which, as discussed above, were not accounted for in our system. In these cases, the part of the cue that is not detected has a large chance of becoming part of the scope of the cue that is detected due to collocation. So, we hypothesize that *Scopes(cue match)* and *Scopes(no cue match)* are the same because in all cases of partial cue detection, the scope incorrectly contains part of the gold-standard cue, which affects both measures negatively.

There is a large discrepancy between the detection of scope tokens and the detection of complete scopes, as the latter is low on both precision (12.26%) and recall (12.85%). The relatively high precision and recall for scope tokens (69.69% and 70.30%, respectively) suggests that there are many cases of partial scope detection, i.e. cases where the scope is either under- or overdetected with respect to the gold standard scope. Since the postprocessing steps for scope detection were developed to reduce exactly this under- and overdetection, we expect that the results for the second run are significantly better. The same holds for negated/event property detection (F1= 52.98%) since it uses the results from scope detection.

4.2 Run 2 (with postprocessing)

Table 2 reports the results of the extended system, which extends the basic system with postprocessing steps for cue detection and especially for scope detection. The postprocessing steps indeed result in higher precision and recall for all tasks, except for *Scope tokens*, which shows a negligible decrease in precision (from 69.69% to 69.20%). This suggests that there are more cases of overdetected scopes than underdetected scopes, because the number of wrongly detected tokens (false positives) increased while the number of undetected scope tokens (false negatives) decreased. This is probably due to the gap-filling mechanism that was implemented as a postprocessing step for scope detection, generalizing that all scopes should be continuous. We will elaborate more on this point in the discussion in Section 5.

As expected, the detection of complete scopes shows the highest increase in F1 score (from 12.55% to 40.39%). This indicates that the postprocessing steps effectively targeted the weak points of the basic system.

While there are no postprocessing steps for negated event or property detection, the F1 score for this task also increases (from 52.35% to 59.83%), as expected, due to the improvement in scope detection.

5 Discussion

Overall, we can say that both of our systems perform well on cue detection, with a small increase when including the postprocessing steps. This was expected since the postprocessing for cue detection targeted only two specific types of cues, namely, interjections and occurrences of "no doubt". The scope detection benefits consideraby from adding the postprocessing steps, as was their main goal. In the final results of the shared task, run 2 of our system ended second out of five in the open track, while run 1 was ranked last. We will here discuss some points that deserve special attention.

5.1 Affix Negation

As discussed above, affix negations received a special treatment because they were not originally detected as negation cues in Boxer. In the DRS, the token containing the affixed negation cue is associated with two predicates, representing the negative affix and the negated stem. The algorithm secures that only the affix is annotated as the negation cue and that the negated stem is annotated as part of the scope. An example of a sentence containing affix negation is shown in (3) (cardboard 31).[2]

(3) a. [You <u>do</u> yourself an] **in**[justice]. `gold`
   b. You do yourself an **in**[<u>justice</u>]. `run1`
   c. You do yourself [an] **in**[<u>justice</u>]. `run2`

[2]In the following, boldfaced tokens represent the negation cues, brackets embed the scope and underlining signifies the negated event or property (subscripts added in case of multiple negation cues).

Table 3: Results of negated event/property detection on gold standard cue and scope annotation

Task	prec.(%)	rec.(%)	F1(%)
Negated (no cue match):	64.06	76.88	69.89
Negated B (no cue match):	59.71	76.88	67.22

Note that in neither of the runs the complete scope from the gold standard is detected, although postprocessing increases the recall of scope tokens by adding the determiner "an" to the scope of the negation. However, examples like this are not unambiguous with respect to their negation scope. For example, the sentence in (3) can be interpreted in two ways: "It is *not* the case that you do yourself (something that is) justice" and "It is the case that you do yourself (something that is) *not* justice". While the gold standard annotation assumes the former, wide-scope reading, our system predicts the narrow scope reading for the negation. The narrow scope reading can be motivated by means of Grice's *Maxim of Manner* (Grice, 1975); the choice of an affix negation instead of a verbal negation signals a narrow scope, because in case a wide scope negation is intended, a verbal negation would be more perspicuous. Thus, the difference in the output of our system and the gold standard annotation is in this case caused by a different choice in disambiguating negation scope, rather than by a shortcoming of the detection algorithm.

5.2 Negated event/property detection

Although correct detection of the negated event or property was not our prime concern, the results obtained with our algorithm were quite promising. Among the systems participating in the closed track of task 1, our extended system is ranked third out of seven for negated event/property detection even though the performance on scope detection is lower than all of the other systems in this track. Since negated event/property detection depends on the detected scope, it seems that our heuristic algorithm for detecting the negated event/property is very robust against noisy input. The performance of the detection algorithm on the gold-standard annotation of scopes is shown in Table 3. Although we cannot compare these results to the performance of other systems on the gold standard data, it should be noted that the results shown here are unmatched by the test results of any other system. It would therefore be worthwile for future work to refine the negated event/property detection algorithm outlined here.

5.3 Postprocessing

The results for the two versions of our system showed that the postprocessing steps implemented in the extended system improved the results considerably, especially for scope detection. Example (4) (cardboard 62) shows the effect of postprocessing on the detection of scopes for negative interjections.

(4) a. “**No**$_1$, [I saw]$_2$ **nothing**$_2$.” `gold`
b. “[No], [I saw] **nothing**.” `run1`
c. “[**No**$_1$, I saw]$_2$ **nothing**$_2$.” `run2`

In Run 1, the system correctly detects the cue “nothing” and the event “saw”, although the detected scope is too wide due to an error in the output of the parser we used. In Run 2, postprocessing also correctly recognizes the interjection “no” as a negation cue. Gap filling in this case makes the scope overdetection worse by also adding the comma to the scope. A similar case of the overdetection of scope is shown in (5) (cardboard 85).

(5) a. [The box] is a half-pound box of honeydew tobacco and [does] **not** [help us in any way]. `gold`
b. [The box] is a half-pound box of honeydew tobacco and does **not** [help us in any way]. `run1`
c. [The box is a half-pound box of honeydew tobacco and does] **not** [help us in any way]. `run2`

Note that in Run 1 the first part of the coordinated structure is correctly excluded from the scope of the negation, but the auxiliary “does” is incorrectly not counted as scope. The gap-filling mechanism then adds the intermediary part to the scope of the negation, resulting in an increase in recall for scope tokens detection (since “does” is now part of the scope) but a lower precision because of the overgeneration of the coordinated part.

Nevertheless, the increased precision and recall for scope detection can mainly be ascribed to the gap-filling mechanism implemented in the postprocessing steps for scope detection. As discussed above, the presence of gaps in the original output is due to the non-sequential nature of the DRT representation and the fact that function words are not directly associated with any element in the representations. This suggests that future work on surface realisation from DRSs should focus on translating the structural properties of DRSs into function words.

5.4 Differences between texts

We noted that there was a difference between the performance on text 1 (The Adventure of the Red Circle) and text 2 (The Adventure of the Cardboard Box). The results for text 2 were overall higher than the results for text 1 (except for a 1% decline in recall for *Full negation*). There was a higher scope precision for text 2 and after the postprocessing steps an even larger difference was found for scope detection (15% versus 44% increase in F1 score for *Scopes*). We hypothesize that this difference may be due to a higher number of multiword expressions in text 1 (7 vs. 2) and to the fact that text 1 seems to have more scopes containing gaps. This latter observation is supported by the fact that gap filling results in more overgeneration (more false positives), which is reflected in the ratios of false positives in text 1 (38%) and text 2 (27%). Thus, while the postprocessing steps improve performance, they seem to be genre and style dependent. This motivates further development of the “clean”, theoretically motivated version of our system in order to secure domain-independent broad coverage of texts, which is the goal of the Groningen Meaning Bank project.

6 Conclusion

Participating in this shared task on negation detection gave us a couple of interesting insights into our natural language processing pipeline that we are developing in the context of the Groningen Meaning Bank. It also showed that it is not easy to transfer the information about negation from a formal, logical representation of scope to a theory-neutral surface-oriented approach. The results were in line with what we expected beforehand, with the highest loss appearing in the awkward translation from one formalism to another.

References

Nicholas Asher and Alex Lascarides. 2003. *Logics of conversation*. Studies in natural language processing. Cambridge University Press.

Nicholas Asher. 1993. *Reference to Abstract Objects in Discourse*. Kluwer Academic Publishers.

Valerio Basile, Johan Bos, Kilian Evang, and Noortje Venhuizen. 2012. Developing a large semantically annotated corpus. In *Proceedings of the Eighth International Conference on Language Resources and Evaluation (LREC'12)*. To appear.

Johan Bos. 2008. Wide-Coverage Semantic Analysis with Boxer. In J. Bos and R. Delmonte, editors, *Semantics in Text Processing. STEP 2008 Conference Proceedings*, volume 1 of *Research in Computational Semantics*, pages 277–286. College Publications.

James Curran, Stephen Clark, and Johan Bos. 2007. Linguistically Motivated Large-Scale NLP with C&C and Boxer. In *Proceedings of the 45th Annual Meeting of the Association for Computational Linguistics Companion Volume Proceedings of the Demo and Poster Sessions*, pages 33–36, Prague, Czech Republic.

Christiane Fellbaum, editor. 1998. *WordNet. An Electronic Lexical Database*. The MIT Press.

H. P. Grice. 1975. Logic and conversation. In P. Cole and J. L. Morgan, editors, *Syntax and Semantics: Vol. 3: Speech Acts*, pages 41–58. Academic Press, San Diego, CA.

Hans Kamp and Uwe Reyle. 1993. *From Discourse to Logic; An Introduction to Modeltheoretic Semantics of Natural Language, Formal Logic and DRT*. Kluwer, Dordrecht.

Roser Morante and Eduardo Blanco. 2012. *SEM 2012 Shared Task: Resolving Scope and Focus of Negation. In *Proceedings of the First Joint Conference on Lexical and Computational Semantics (*SEM 2012)*, Montreal, Canada. To appear.

Roser Morante and Walter Daelemans. 2012. ConanDoyle-neg: Annotation of negation in Conan Doyle stories. In *Proceedings of the Eighth International Conference on Language Resources and Evaluation (LREC'12)*. To appear.

Mark Steedman. 2001. *The Syntactic Process*. The MIT Press.

Rob Van der Sandt. 1992. Presupposition Projection as Anaphora Resolution. *Journal of Semantics*, 9:333–377.

UiO_1: Constituent-Based Discriminative Ranking for Negation Resolution

Jonathon Read **Erik Velldal** **Lilja Øvrelid** **Stephan Oepen**
University of Oslo, Department of Informatics
{jread,erikve,liljao,oe}@ifi.uio.no

Abstract

This paper describes the first of two systems submitted from the University of Oslo (UiO) to the 2012 *SEM Shared Task on resolving negation. Our submission is an adaption of the negation system of Velldal et al. (2012), which combines SVM cue classification with SVM-based ranking of syntactic constituents for scope resolution. The approach further extends our prior work in that we also identify factual negated events. While submitted for the closed track, the system was the top performer in the shared task overall.

1 Introduction

The First Joint Conference on Lexical and Computational Semantics (*SEM 2012) hosts a shared task on resolving negation (Morante and Blanco, 2012). This involves the subtasks of (i) identifying *negation cues*, (ii) identifying the in-sentence *scope* of these cues, and (iii) identifying negated (and factual) *events*. This paper describes a system submitted by the Language Technology Group at the University of Oslo (UiO). Our starting point is the negation system developed by Velldal et al. (2012) for the domain of biomedical texts, an SVM-based system for classifying cues and ranking syntactic constituents to resolve cue scopes. However, we extend and adapt this system in several important respects, such as in terms of the underlying linguistic formalisms that are used, the textual domain, handling of morphological cues and discontinuous scopes, and in that the current system also identifies negated events.

The data sets used for the shared task include the following, all based on negation-annotated Conan Doyle (CD) stories (Morante and Daelemans, 2012): a training set of 3644 sentences (hereafter referred to as CDT), a development set of 787 sentences (CDD), and a held-out evaluation set of 1089 sentences (CDE). We will refer to the combination of CDT and CDD as CDTD. An example of an annotated sentence is shown in (1) below, where the cue is marked in bold, the scope is underlined, and the event marked in italics.

(1) There was **no** *answer*.

We describe two different system configurations, both of which were submitted for the closed track (hence we can only make use of the data provided by the task organizers). The systems only differ with respect to how they were optimized. In the first configuration, (hereafter I), all components in the pipeline had their parameters tuned by 10-fold cross-validation across CDTD. The second configuration (II) is tuned against CDD using CDT for training. The rationale for this strategy is to guard against possible overfitting effects that could result from either optimization scheme, given the limited size of the data sets. For the held-out testing all models are estimated on the entire CDTD.

Unless otherwise noted, all reported scores are generated using the evaluation script provided by the organizers, which breaks down performance with respect to cues, events, scope tokens, and two variants of scope-level exact match (one requiring exact match of cues and the other only partial cue match). The latter two scores are identical for our system hence are not duplicated in this paper. Furthermore, as we did not optimize for the scope tokens measure this is only reported for the final evaluation.

Note also that the evaluation actually includes two variants of the metrics mentioned above; a set of primary measures with precision computed as $P = TP/(TP + FP)$ and a set of so-called *B measures* that instead uses $P = TP/S$, where S is the total number of predictions made by the system. The reason why S is not identical with $TP + FP$ is that partial matches are only counted as FNs (and not FPs) in order to avoid double penalties. We do not report the B measures for development testing as they were only introduced for the final evaluation and hence were not considered in our system optimization. We note though, that the relative-ranking of participating systems for the primary and B measures is identical, and that the correlation between the paired lists of scores is nearly perfect ($r = 0.997$).

The paper is structured according to the components of our system. Section 2 details the process of identifying instances of negation through the disambiguation of known cue words and affixes. Section 3 describes our hybrid approach to scope resolution, which utilizes both heuristic and data-driven methods to select syntactic constituents. Section 4 discusses our event detection component, which first applies a classifier to filter out non-factual events and then uses a learned ranking function to select events among in-scope tokens. End-to-end results are presented in Section 5.

2 Cue Detection

Cue identification is based on the light-weight classification scheme presented by Velldal et al. (2012). By treating the set of cue words as a closed class, Velldal et al. (2012) showed that one could greatly reduce the number of examples presented to the learner, and correspondingly the number of features, while at the same time improving performance. This means that the classifier only attempts to 'disambiguate' known cue words, while ignoring any words not observed as cues in the training data.

The classifier applied in the current submission is extended to also handle morphological or affixal negation cues, such as the prefix cue in ***im**patience*, the infix in *care**less**ness*, and the suffix of *colour**less***. The negation affixes observed in CDTD are; the prefixes *un*, *dis*, *ir*, *im*, and *in*; the infix *less* (we internally treat this as the suffixes *lessly* and *lessness*); and the suffix *less*. Of the total set of 1157 cues in the training and development data, 192 are affixal. There are, however, a total of 1127 tokens matching one of the affix patterns above, and while we maintain the closed class assumption also for the affixes, the classifier will need to consider their status as a cue or non-cue when attaching to any such token, as in *image*, *recklessness*, and *bless*.

2.1 Features

In the initial formulation of Velldal (2011), an SVM classifier was applied using simple n-gram features over words, both full forms and lemmas, to the left and right of the candidate cues. In addition to these token-level features, the classifier we apply here includes features specifically targeting affixal cues. The first such feature records character n-grams from both the beginning and end of the base that an affix attaches to (up to five positions). For a context like ***im**possible* we would record n-grams such as {*possi*, *poss*, ...} and {*sible*, *ible*, ...}, and combine this with information about the affix itself (*im*) and the token part-of-speech ("JJ").

For the second type of affix-specific features, we try to emulate the effect of a lexicon look-up of the remaining substring that an affix attaches to, checking its status as an independent base form and its part-of-speech. In order to take advantage of such information while staying within the confines of the closed track, we automatically generate a lexicon from the training data, counting the instances of each PoS tagged lemma in addition to n-grams of word-initial characters (again recording up to five positions). For a given match of an affix pattern, a feature will then record these counts for the substring it attaches to. The rationale for this feature is that the occurrence of a substring such as *un* in a token such as *underlying* should be less likely as a cue given that the first part of the remaining string (e.g., *derly*) would be an unlikely way to begin a word.

It is also possible for a negation cue to span multiple tokens, such as the (discontinuous) pair *neither / nor* or fixed expressions like *on the contrary*. There are, however, only 16 instances of such multiword cues (MWCs) in the entire CDTD. Rather than letting the classifier be sensitive to these corner cases, we cover such MWC patterns using a small set of simple post-processing heuristics. A small stop-list is used for filtering out the relevant words from the examples presented to the classifier (*on*, *the*, etc.). Note that, in terms of training the final classifiers, CDTD provides us with a total of 1162 positive and

Data set	Model	Prec	Rec	F_1
CDTD	Baseline	92.25	88.50	90.34
	$Classifier_I$	94.99	95.07	95.03
CDD	Baseline	90.68	84.39	87.42
	$Classifier_{II}$	93.75	95.38	94.56
CDE	Baseline	87.10	92.05	89.51
	$Classifier_I$	91.42	92.80	92.10
	$Classifier_{II}$	89.17	93.56	91.31

Table 1: Detecting negation cues using the two classifiers and the majority-usage baseline.

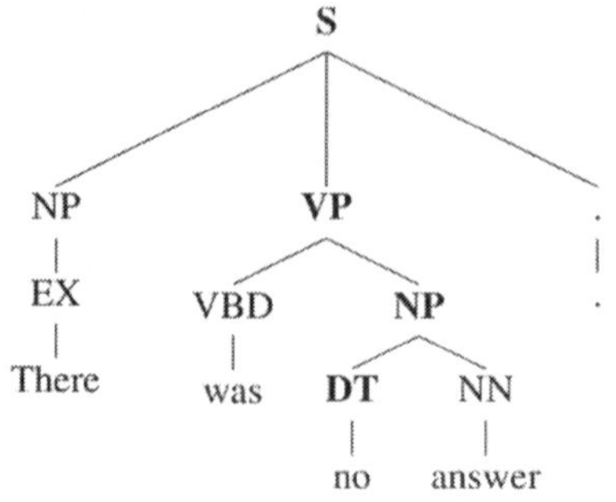

Figure 1: Example parse tree provided in the data, highlighting our candidate scope constituents.

1100 negative training examples, given our closed-class treatment of cues.

Before we turn to the results, note that the difference between the two submitted versions of the classifier (I and II) only concerns the orders of the n-grams used for the token-level features.[1]

2.2 Results

Table 1 presents the results for our cue classifier. As an informed baseline, we also tried classifying each word based on its most frequent use as a cue or non-cue in the training data. (Affixal cue occurrences are counted by looking at both the affix-pattern and the base it attaches to, basically treating the entire token as a cue. Tokens that end up being classified as cues are then matched against the affix patterns observed during training in order to correctly delimit the annotation of the cue.) This simple majority-usage approach actually provides a fairly strong baseline, yielding an F_1 of 90.34 on CDTD. Compare this to the F_1 of 95.03 obtained by the classifier on the same data set. However, when applying the models to the held-out set, with models estimated over the entire CDTD, the classifier suffers a slight drop in performance, leaving the baseline even more competitive: While our best performing final cue classifier (I) achieves F_1=92.10, the baseline achieves F_1=89.51, and even outperforms four of the ten cue detection systems submitted for the shared task (three of the 12 shared task submissions use the same classifier).

[1]Classifier I records the lemma and full form of the target token, and lemmas two positions left/right. Classifier II records the lemma, form, and PoS of the target, full forms three positions to the left and one to the right, PoS one position right/left, and lemmas three positions to the right. The affixal-specific features are the same for both configurations as described above.

Inspecting the predictions of the classifier on CDD, which comprises a total of 173 gold annotated cues, we find that Classifier I mislabels 11 false positives (FPs) and seven false negatives (FNs). Of the FPs, we find five so-called *false negation cues* (Morante et al., 2011), including three instances of the fixed expression *none the less*. The others are affixal cues, of which two are clearly wrong (***un**derworked*, ***un**iversal*) while others might arguably be due to annotation errors (***in**superable*, ***un**happily*, *end**less***, *list**less**ly*). Among the FNs, two are due to MWCs not covered by our heuristics (e.g., *no more*), with the remainder concerning affixes.

3 Constituent-Based Scope Resolution

During the development of our scope resolution system we have pursued both a rule-based and data-driven approach. Both are rooted in the assumption that the scope of negations corresponds to a syntactically meaningful unit. Our starting point here will be the syntactic analyses provided by the task organizers (see Figure 1), generated using the reranking parser of Charniak and Johnson (2005). However, as alignment between scope annotations and syntactic units is not straightforward for all cases, we apply several exception rules that 'slacken' the requirements for alignment, as discussed in Section 3.1. In Sections 3.2 and 3.3 we detail our rule-based and data-driven approaches, respectively. Note that the predictions of the rule-based component will be incorporated as features in the learned model, similarly to the set-up described by Read et al. (2011). Section 3.4 details the post-processing we apply to handle cases of discontinuous scope, before Section 3.5 finally presents development results together with a brief error analysis.

3.1 Constituent Alignment and Slackening

In order to test our initial assumption that syntactic units correspond to scope annotations, we quantify the alignment of scopes with constituents in CDT, excluding 97 negations that do not have a scope. We find that the initial alignment is rather low at 52.42%. We therefore formulate a set of *slackening* heuristics, designed to improve on this alignment by removing certain constituents at the beginning or end of a scope. First of all, removing constituent-initial and -final punctuation improves alignment to 72.83%. We then apply the following slackening rules, with examples indicating the resulting scope following slackening (not showing events):

- Remove coordination (CC) and following conjuncts if the coordination is a rightwards sibling of an ancestor of the cue and it is not directly dominated by an NP.

  (2) Since we have been so **un***fortunate* as to miss him and have no notion [. . .]

- Remove S* to the right of cue, if delimited by punctuation.

  (3) "There is **no** other *claimant*, I presume ?"

- Remove constituent-initial SBAR.

  (4) If it concerned no one but myself I would **not** try to keep it from you."

- Remove punctuation-delimited NPs.

  (5) "But I *ca***n't** forget them, Miss Stapleton," said I.

- Remove constituent-initial RB, CC, UH, ADVP or INTJ.

  (6) And yet it was **not** quite the *last*.

The slackening rules are based on a few observations. First, scope rarely crosses coordination boundaries (with the exception of nominal coordination). Second, scope usually does not cross clause boundaries (indicated by S/SBAR). Furthermore, titles and other nominals of address are not included in the scope. Finally, sentence and discourse adverbials are often excluded from the scope. Since these express semantic distinctions, we approximate this notion syntactically using parts-of-speech and constituent category labels expressing adverbials (RB), coordinations (CC), various types of interjections (UH, INTJ) and adverbial phrases (ADVP). We may note here that syntactic categories are not always sufficient to express semantic distinctions. Prepositional phrases, for instance, are often used to express the same type of discourse adverbials, but can also express a range of other distinctions (e.g., temporal or locative adverbials), which *are* included in the scope. So a slackening rule removing initial PPs was tried but not found to improve overall alignment.

```
RB//VP/SBAR if SBAR\WH*
RB//VP/S
RB//S
DT/NP if NP/PP
DT//SBAR if SBAR\WHADVP
DT//S
JJ//ADJPVP/S if S\VP\VB*[@lemma="be"]
JJ/NP/NP if NP\PP
JJ//NP
UH
IN/PP
NN/NP//S/SBAR if SBAR\WHNP
NN/NP//S
CC/SINV
```

Figure 2: Scope resolution heuristics.

After applying the above slackening rules the alignment rate for CDT improves to 86.13%. This also represents an upper-bound on our performance, as we will not be able to correctly predict a scope that does not align with a (slackened) constituent.

3.2 Heuristics Operating over Constituents

The alignment of constituents and scopes reveal consistent patterns and we therefore formulate a set of heuristic rules over constituents. These are based on frequencies of paths from the cue to the scope-aligned constituent for the annotations in CDT, as well as the annotation guidelines (Morante et al., 2011). The rules are formulated as paths over constituent trees and are presented in Figure 2. The path syntax is based on LPath (Lai and Bird, 2010). The rules are listed in order of execution, showing how more specific rules are consulted before more general ones. We furthermore allow for some additional functionality in the interpretation of rules by enabling simple constraints that are applied to the candidate constituent. For example, the rule `RB//VP/SBAR if SBAR\WH*` will be activated when the cue is an adverb having some ancestor VP which has a parent SBAR, where the SBAR must contain a WH-phrase among its children.

In cases where no rule is activated we use a *default scope* prediction, which expands the scope to both the left and the right of the cue until either the sentence boundary or a punctuation mark is reached. The rules are evaluated individually in Section 3.5 below and the rule predictions are furthermore employed as features for the ranker described below.

3.3 Constituent Ranking

Our data-driven approach to scope resolution involves learning a ranking function over candidate syntactic constituents. The approach has similarities to discriminative parse selection, except that we here rank subtrees rather than full parses.

When defining the training data, we begin by selecting negations for which the parse tree contains a constituent that (after slackening) aligns with the gold scope. We then select an initial candidate by selecting the smallest constituent that spans all the words in the cue, and then generate subsequent candidates by traversing the path to the root of the tree (see Figure 1). This results in a mean ambiguity of 4.9 candidate constituents per negation (in CDTD). Candidates whose projection corresponds to the gold scope are labeled as correct; all others are labeled as incorrect. Experimenting with a variety of feature types (listed in Table 2), we use the implementation of ordinal ranking in the SVM^{light} toolkit (Joachims, 2002) to learn a linear scoring function for preferring correct candidate scopes.

The most informative feature type is the *LPath from cue*, which in addition to recording the full path from the cue to the candidate constituent (e.g., the path to the correct candidate in Figure 1 is `no/DT/NP/VP/S`), also includes delexicalized (`./DT/NP/VP/S`), generalized (`no/DT//S`), and generalized delexicalized versions (`./DT//S`).

Note that the *rule prediction* feature facilitates a hybrid approach by recording whether the candidate matches the boundaries of the scope predicted by the rules of Section 3.2, as well as the degree of overlap.

3.4 Handling Discontinuous Scope

10.3% of the scopes in the training data are what (Morante et al., 2011) refer to as *discontinuous*. This means that the scope contains two or more parts which are bridged by tokens other than the cue.

Feature types	**I**	**II**
LPath from cue	•	•
LPath from cue bigrams and trigrams	•	•
LPath from cue to left/right boundary	•	
LPath to left/right boundary		•
LPath to root	•	
Punctuation to left/right	•	•
Rule prediction		•
Sibling bigrams		•
Size in tokens, relative to sentence (%)	•	•
Surface bigrams	•	•
Tree distance from cue	•	•

Table 2: Features used to describe candidate constituents for scope resolution, with indications of presence in our two system configurations.

(7) I therefore spent the day at my club and did **not** return to Baker Street until evening.

(8) There was certainly **no** physical injury of any kind.

The sentence in (7) exemplifies a common cause of scopal discontinuity in the data, namely ellipsis (Morante et al., 2011). Almost all of these are cases of coordination, as in example (7) where the cue is found in the final conjunct (*did not return [...]*) and the scope excludes the preceding conjunct(s) (*therefore spent the day at my club*). There are also some cases of adverbs that are excluded from the scope, causing discontinuity, as in (8), where the adverb *certainly* is excluded from the scope.

In order to deal with discontinuous scopes we formulate two simple post-processing heuristics, which are applied after rules/ranking: (1) If the cue is in a conjoined phrase, remove the previous conjuncts from the scope, and (2) remove sentential adverbs from the scope (where a list of sentential adverbs was compiled from the training data).

3.5 Results

Our development procedure evaluated all permutations of feature combinations, searching for optimal parameters using gold-standard cues. Table 2 indicates which features are included in our two ranker configurations, i.e., tuning by 10-fold cross-validation on CDTD (I) vs. a train/test-split for CDT/CDD(II).

Table 3 lists the results of our scope resolution approaches applied to gold cues. As a baseline, all

Data set	Model	Prec	Rec	F_1
CDTD	Baseline	98.31	33.18	49.61
	Rules	100.00	71.37	83.29
	$Ranker_I$	100.00	73.55	84.76
CDD	Baseline	100.00	36.31	53.28
	Rules	100.00	69.64	82.10
	$Ranker_{II}$	100.00	70.24	82.52
CDE	Baseline	96.47	32.93	49.10
	Rules	98.73	62.65	76.66
	$Ranker_I$	98.77	64.26	77.86
	$Ranker_{II}$	98.75	63.45	77.26

Table 3: Scope resolution for gold cues using the two versions of the ranker, also listing the performance of the rule-based approach in isolation.

cases are assigned the default scope prediction of the rule-based approach. On CDTD this results in an F_1 of 49.61 (P=98.31, R=33.18); compare to the ranker in Configuration I on the same data set (F_1=84.76, P=100.00, R=73.55). We note that our different optimization procedures do not appear to have made much difference to the learned ranking functions as both perform similarly on the held-out data, though suffering a slight drop in performance compared to the development results. We also evaluate the rules and observe that this approach achieves similar held-out results. This is particularly note-worthy given that there are only fourteen rules plus the default scope baseline. Note that, as the rankers performed better than the rules in isolation on both CDTD and CDD during development, our final system submissions are based on rankers I and II from Table 3.

We performed a manual error analysis of our scope resolution system ($Ranker_{II}$) on the basis of CDD (using gold cues). First, we may note that parse errors are a common sources of scope resolution errors. It is well-known that coordination presents a difficult construction for syntactic parsers, and we often find incorrectly parsed coordinate structures among the system errors. Since coordination is used both in the slackening rules and the analysis of discontinuous scopes, these errors have clear effects on system performance. We may further note that discourse-level adverbials, such as *in the second place* in example (9) below, are often included in the scope assigned by our system, which they should not be according to the gold annotation.

(9) But, in the second place, why did you **not** come at once?

There are also quite a few errors related to the scope of affixal cues, which the ranker often erroneously assigns a scope that is larger than simply the base which the affix attaches to.

4 Event Detection

Our event detection component implements two stages: First we apply a factuality classifier, and then we identify negated events[2] for those contexts that have been labeled as factual. We detail the two stages in order below.

4.1 Factuality Detection

The annotation guidelines of Morante et al. (2011) specify that events should only be annotated for negations that have a scope and that occur in factual statements. This means that we can view the *SEM data sets to implicitly annotate factuality and non-factuality, and take advantage of this to train an SVM factuality classifier. We take positive examples to correspond to negations annotated with both a scope and an event, while negative examples correspond to scope negations with no event. For CDTD, this strategy gives 738 positive and 317 negative examples, spread over a total of 930 sentences. Note that we do not have any explicit annotation of cue words for these examples. All we have are instances of negation that we know to be within a factual or non-factual context, but the indication of factuality may typically be well outside the annotated negation scope. For our experiments here, we therefore use the negation cue itself as a place-holder for the abstract notion of context that we are really classifying. Given the limited amount of data, we only optimize our factuality classifier by 10-fold cross-validation on CDTD (i.e., the same configuration is used for submissions I and II).

The feature types we use are all variations over bag-of-words (BoW) features. We include left- and right-oriented BoW features centered on the negation cue, recording forms, lemmas, and PoS, and using both unigrams and bigrams. The features are ex-

[2]Note that the annotation guidelines use the term *event* rather broadly as referring to a process, action, state, or property (Morante et al., 2011).

Data set	Model	Prec	Rec	F_1	Acc
CDTD	Baseline	69.95	100.00	82.32	69.95
	Classifier	84.51	96.07	89.92	83.98
CDE	Baseline	69.48	100.00	81.99	69.48
	Classifier	77.73	95.91	85.86	78.31

Table 4: Results for factuality detection (using gold negation cues and scopes). Due to the limited training data for factuality, the classifier is only optimized by 10-fold cross-validation on CDTD.

tracted from the sentence as a whole, as well as from a local window of six tokens to each side of the cue.

Table 4 provides results for factuality classification using gold-standard cues and scopes.[3] We also include results for a baseline approach that simply considers all cases to be factual, i.e., the majority class. In this case precision is identical to accuracy and recall is 100%. For precision and accuracy we see that the classifier improves substantially over the baseline on both data sets, although there is a bit of a drop in performance when going from the 10-fold to held-out results. There also seem to be some signs of overfitting, given that roughly 70% of the training examples end up as support vectors.

4.2 Ranking Events

Having filtered out non-factual contexts, events are identified by applying a similar approach to that of the scope-resolving ranker described in Section 3.3. In this case, however, we rank tokens as candidates for events. For simplicity in this first round of development we make the assumption that all events are single words. Thus, the system will be unable to correctly predict the event in the 6.94% of instances in CDTD that are multi-word.

We select candidate words from all those marked as being in the scope (including substrings of tokens with affixal cues). This gives a mean ambiguity of 7.8 candidate events per negation (in CDTD). Then, discarding multi-word training examples, we use SVM^{light} to learn a ranking function for identifying events among the candidates.

Table 5 shows the features employed, with indications as to their presence in our two configurations (after an exhaustive search of feature combinations). The most important feature was *LPath to scope constituent*. For example, in Figure 1 the scope constituent is the `S` root of the tree; the path that describes the correct candidate is `answer/NN/NP/VP/S`. As discussed in Section 3.3, we also record generalized, delexicalized and generalized delexicalized paths.

[3] As this is not singled out as a separate subtask in the shared task itself, these are the only scores in the paper not computed using the script provided by the organizers.

Feature type	I	II
Contains affixal cue	•	
Following lemma		•
Lemma	•	•
LPath to scope constituent	•	•
LPath to scope constituent bigrams	•	•
Part-of-speech	•	•
Position in scope	•	•
Preceding lemma	•	•
Preceding part-of-speech	•	•
Token distance from cue	•	•

Table 5: Features used to describe candidates for event detection, with indications of presence in our two system configurations.

Data set	Model	Prec	Rec	F_1
CDTD	Ranker_{I}	91.49	90.83	91.16
CDD	$\text{Ranker}_{\text{II}}$	92.11	91.30	91.70
CDE	Ranker_{I}	83.73	83.73	83.73
	$\text{Ranker}_{\text{II}}$	84.94	84.95	84.94

Table 6: Event detection for gold scopes and gold factuality information.

Table 6 lists the results of the event ranker applied to gold-standard cues, scopes, and factuality. For a comparative baseline, we implemented a keyword-based approach that simply searches in-scope words for instances of events previously observed in the training set, sorted according to descending frequency. This baseline achieves F_1=29.44 on CDD. For comparison, the ranker (II) achieves F_1=91.70 on the same data set, as seen in Table 6. We also see that Configuration II appears to generalize best, with over 1.2 points improvement over the F_1 of I.

An analysis of the event predictions for CDD indicates that the most frequent errors (41.2%) are instances where the ranker correctly predicts part of the event but our single word assumption is invalid. Another apparent error is that the system fails to

	Submission I			Submission II		
	Prec	**Rec**	**F_1**	**Prec**	**Rec**	**F_1**
Cues	91.42	92.80	92.10	89.17	93.56	91.31
Scopes	87.43	61.45	72.17	83.89	60.64	70.39
Scope Tokens	81.99	88.81	85.26	75.87	90.08	82.37
Events	60.50	72.89	66.12	60.58	75.00	67.02
Full negation	83.45	43.94	57.57	79.87	45.08	57.63
Cues B	89.09	92.80	90.91	86.97	93.56	90.14
Scopes B	59.30	61.45	60.36	56.55	60.64	58.52
Events B	57.62	72.89	64.36	58.60	75.00	65.79
Full negation B	42.18	43.94	43.04	41.90	45.08	43.43

Table 7: End-to-end results on the held-out data.

predict a main verb for the event, and instead predicts nouns (17.7% of all errors), modals (17.7%) or prepositions (11.8%).

5 Held-Out Evaluation

Table 7 presents our final results for both system configurations on the held-out evaluation data (also including the B measures, as discussed in the introduction). Comparing submission I and II, we find that the latter has slightly better scores end-to-end. However, as seen throughout the paper, the picture is less clear-cut when considering the isolated performance of each component. When ranked according to the *Full Negation* measures, our submissions were placed first and second (out of seven submissions in the closed track, and twelve submissions total). It is difficult to compare system performance on subtasks, however, as each component will be affected by the performance of the previous.

6 Conclusions

This paper has presented two closed-track submissions for the *SEM 2012 shared task on negation resolution. The systems were ranked first and second overall in the shared task end-to-end evaluation, and the submissions only differ with respect to the data sets used for parameter tuning. There are four components in the pipeline: (i) An SVM classifier for identifying negation cue words and affixes, (ii) an SVM-based ranker that combines empirical evidence and manually-crafted rules to resolve the in-sentence scope of negation, (iii) a classifier for determining whether a negation is in a factual or non-factual context, and (iv) a ranker that determines (factual) negated events among in-scope tokens.

For future work we would like to try training separate classifiers for affixal and token-level cues, given that largely separate sets of features are effective for the two cases. The system might also benefit from sources of information that would place it in the open track. These include drawing information from other parsers and formalisms, generating cue features from an external lexicon, and using additional training data for factuality detection, e.g., FactBank (Saurí and Pustejovsky, 2009).

From observations on CDTD we note that approximately 14% of scopes will be unresolvable as they are not aligned with constituents (see Section 3.1). This can perhaps be tackled by ranking tokens as candidates for left and right scope boundaries (similar to the event ranker in the current work). This would improve the upper-bound to 100% at the expense of greatly increasing the number of candidates. However, the strong discriminative power of our current approach can still be incorporated using constituent-based features.

Acknowledgments

We thank Roser Morante and Eduardo Blanco for their work in organizing this shared task and commitment to producing quality data. We also thank the anonymous reviewers for their feedback. Large-scale experimentation was carried out with the TITAN HPC facilities at the University of Oslo.

References

Eugene Charniak and Mark Johnson. 2005. Coarse-to-fine n-best parsing and MaxEnt discriminative reranking. In *Proceedings of the Forty-Third Annual Meeting of the Association for Computational Linguistics*, Ann Arbor, MI.

Thorsten Joachims. 2002. Optimizing search engines using clickthrough data. In *Proceedings of the Eighth ACM International Conference on Knowledge Discovery and Data Mining*, Alberta.

Catherine Lai and Steven Bird. 2010. Querying linguistic trees. *Journal of Logic, Language and Information*, 19:53–73.

Roser Morante and Eduardo Blanco. 2012. *SEM 2012 shared task: Resolving the scope and focus of negation. In *Proceedings of the First Joint Conference on Lexical and Computational Semantics*, Montreal.

Roser Morante and Walter Daelemans. 2012. ConanDoyle-neg: Annotation of negation in Conan Doyle stories. In *Proceedings of the Eighth International Conference on Language Resources and Evaluation*, Istanbul.

Roser Morante, Sarah Schrauwen, and Walter Daelemans. 2011. Annotation of negation cues and their scope: Guidelines v1.0. Technical report, University of Antwerp. CLIPS: Computational Linguistics & Psycholinguistics technical report series.

Jonathon Read, Erik Velldal, Stephan Oepen, and Lilja Øvrelid. 2011. Resolving speculation and negation scope in biomedical articles using a syntactic constituent ranker. In *Proceedings of the Fourth International Symposium on Languages in Biology and Medicine*, Singapore.

Roser Saurí and James Pustejovsky. 2009. Factbank: a corpus annotated with event factuality. *Language Resources and Evaluation*, 43(3):227–268.

Erik Velldal, Lilja Øvrelid, Jonathon Read, and Stephan Oepen. 2012. Speculation and negation: Rules, rankers and the role of syntax. *Computational Linguistics*, 38(2).

Erik Velldal. 2011. Predicting speculation: A simple disambiguation approach to hedge detection in biomedical literature. *Journal of Biomedical Semantics*, 2(5).

UiO_2: Sequence-Labeling Negation Using Dependency Features

Emanuele Lapponi **Erik Velldal** **Lilja Øvrelid** **Jonathon Read**
University of Oslo, Department of Informatics
{emanuel,erikve,liljao,jread}@ifi.uio.no

Abstract

This paper describes the second of two systems submitted from the University of Oslo (UiO) to the 2012 *SEM Shared Task on resolving negation. The system combines SVM cue classification with CRF sequence labeling of events and scopes. Models for scopes and events are created using lexical and syntactic features, together with a fine-grained set of labels that capture the scopal behavior of certain tokens. Following labeling, negated tokens are assigned to their respective cues using simple post-processing heuristics. The system was ranked first in the open track and third in the closed track, and was one of the top performers in the scope resolution sub-task overall.

1 Introduction

Negation Resolution (NR) is the task of determining, for a given sentence, which tokens are affected by a negation cue. The data set most prominently used for the development of systems for automatic NR is the BioScope Corpus (Vincze et al., 2008), a collection of clinical reports and papers in the biomedical domain annotated with negation and speculation cues and their scopes. The data sets released in conjunction with the 2012 shared task on NR hosted by The First Joint Conference on Lexical and Computational Semantics (*SEM 2012) are comprised of the following negation annotated stories of Conan Doyle (CD): a training set of 3644 sentences drawn from *The Hound of the Baskervilles* (CDT), a development set of 787 sentences taken from *Wisteria Lodge* (CDD; we will refer to the combination of CDT and CDD as CDTD), and a held-out test set of 1089 sentences from *The Cardboard Box* and *The Red Circle* (CDE). In these sets, the concept of negation scope extends on the one adopted in the BioScope corpus in several aspects: Negation cues are not part of the scope, morphological (affixal) cues are annotated and scopes can be discontinuous. Moreover, in-scope states or events are marked as negated if they are factual and presented as events that did not happen (Morante and Daelemans, 2012). Examples (1) and (2) below are examples of affixal negation and discontinuous scope respectively: The cues are bold, the tokens contained within their scopes are underlined and the negated event is italicized.

(1) Since we have been so **un***fortunate* as to miss him [...]

(2) If he was in the hospital and yet **not** on the staff he could only have been a house-surgeon or a house-physician: little more than a senior student.

Example (2) has no negated events because the sentence is non-factual.

The *SEM shared task thus comprises three subtasks: cue identification, scope resolution and event detection. It is furthermore divided into two separate tracks: one closed track, where only the data supplied by the organizers (word form, lemma, PoS-tag and syntactic constituent for each token) may be employed, and an open track, where participants may employ any additional tools or resources.

Pragmatically speaking, a token can be either *out of scope* or assigned to one or more of the three remaining classes: *negation cue*, *in scope* and *negated event*. Additionally, *in-scope* tokens and *negated events* are paired to the cues they are negated by.

Our system achieves this by remodeling the task as a sequence labeling task. With annotations converted to sequences of labels, we train a Conditional Random Field (CRF) classifier with a range of different feature types, including features defined over dependency graphs. This article presents two submissions for the *SEM shared task, differing only with respect to how these dependency graphs were derived. For our open track submission, the dependency representations are produced by a state-of-the-art dependency parser, whereas the closed track submission employs dependencies derived from the constituent analyses supplied with the shared task data sets through a process of constituent-to-dependency conversion. In both systems, labeling of test data is performed in two stages. First, cues are detected using a token classifier,[1] and secondly, scope and event resolution is achieved by post-processing the output of the sequence labeler.

The two systems described in this paper have been developed using CDT for training and CDD for testing, and differ only with regard to the source of syntactic information. All reported scores are generated using an evaluation script provided by the task organizers. In addition to providing a full end-to-end evaluation, the script breaks down results with respect to identification of cues, events, scope tokens, and two variants of scope-level exact match; one requiring exact match also of cues and another only partial cue match. For our system these two scope-level scores are identical and so are not duplicated in our reporting. Additionally we chose not to optimize for the scope tokens measure, and hence this is also not reported as a development result.

Note also that the official evaluation actually includes two different variants of the metrics mentioned above; a set of *primary measures* with precision computed as P=TP/(TP+FP) and a set of *B measures* where precision is rather computed as P=TP/SYS, where SYS is the total number of predictions made by the system. The reason why SYS is not identical with TP+FP is that partial matches are only counted as FNs (and not FPs) in order to avoid double penalties. We do not report the B measures for development testing as they were introduced for the final evaluation and hence were not considered in our system optimization. We note though, that the relative-ranking of participating systems for the primary and B measures is identical, and that the correlation between the paired lists of scores is nearly perfect (r=0.997).

The rest of the paper is structured as follows. First, the cue classifier, its features and results are described in Section 2. Section 3 presents the system for scope and event resolution and details different features, the model-internal representation used for sequence-labeling, as well as the post-processing component. Error analyses for the cue, scope and event components are provided in the respective sections. Section 4 and 5 provide developmental and held-out results, respectively. Finally, we provide conclusions and some reflections regarding future work in Section 6.

2 Cue detection

Identification of negation cues is based on the light-weight classification scheme presented by Velldal et al. (2012). By treating the set of cue words as a closed class, Velldal et al. (2012) showed that one could greatly reduce the number of examples presented to the learner, and correspondingly the number of features, while at the same time improving performance. This means that the classifier only attempts to "disambiguate" known cue words while ignoring any words not observed as cues in the training data.

The classifier applied in the current submission is extended to also handle affixal negation cues, such as the prefix cue in ***im**patience*, the infix in *care**less**ness*, and the suffix of *colour**less***. The types of negation affixes observed in CDTD are; the prefixes *un*, *dis*, *ir*, *im*, and *in*; the infix *less* (we internally treat this as the suffixes *lessly* and *lessness*); and the suffix *less*. Of the total number of 1157 cues in the training and development set, 192 are affixal. There are, however, a total of 1127 tokens matching one of the affix patterns above, and while we maintain the closed class assumption also for the affixes, the classifier will need to consider its status as a cue

[1]Note that the cue classifier applied in the current paper is the same as that used in the other shared task submission from the University of Oslo (Read et al., 2012), and the two system descriptions will therefore have much overlap on this particular point. For all other components the architectures of the two system are completely different, however.

or non-cue when attaching to any such token, like for instance *image*, *recklessness*, and *bless*.

2.1 Features

In the initial formulation of Velldal (2011), an SVM classifier was trained using simple n-gram features over words, both full forms and lemmas, to the left and right of the candidate cues. In addition to these token-level features, the classifier we apply here includes some features specifically targeting morphological or affixal cues. The first such feature records character n-grams from both the beginning and end of the base that an affix attaches to (up to five positions). For a context like ***impossible*** we would record n-grams such {*possi*, *poss*, *pos*, ...} and {*sible*, *ible*, *ble*, ...}, and combine this with information about the affix itself (*im*) and the token part-of-speech ("JJ").

For the second feature type targeting affix cues we try to emulate the effect of a lexicon look-up of the remaining substring that an affix attaches to, checking its status as an independent base form and its part-of-speech. In order to take advantage of such information while staying within the confines of the closed track, we automatically generate a lexicon from the training data, counting the instances of each PoS tagged lemma in addition to n-grams of word-initial characters (again recording up to five positions). For a given match of an affix pattern, a feature will then record the counts from this lexicon for the substring it attaches to. The rationale for this feature is that the occurrence of a substring such as *un* in a token such as *underlying* should be considered more unlikely to be a cue given that the first part of the remaining string (e.g., *derly*) would be an unlikely way to begin a word.

Note that, it is also possible for a negation cue to span multiple tokens, such as the (discontinuous) pair *neither / nor* or fixed expressions like *on the contrary*. There are, however, only 16 instances of such multiword cues (MWCs) in the entire CDTD. Rather than letting the classifier be sensitive to these corner cases, we cover such MWC patterns using a small set of simple post-processing heuristics. A small stop-list is used for filtering out the relevant words from the examples presented to the classifier (*on*, *the*, etc.).

Data set	Model	Prec	Prec	F_1
CDD	Baseline	90.68	84.39	87.42
	Classifier	93.75	95.38	94.56
CDE	Baseline	87.10	92.05	89.51
	Classifier	89.17	93.56	91.31

Table 1: Cue classification results for the final classifier and the majority-usage baseline, showing test scores for the development set (training on CDT) and the final held-out set (training on CDTD).

2.2 Results

Table 1 presents results for the cue classifier. While the classifier configuration was optimized against CDD, the model used for the final held-out testing is trained on the entire CDTD, which (given our closed-class treatment of cues) provides a total of 1162 positive and 1100 negative training examples. As an informed baseline, we also tried classifying each word based on its most frequent use as cue or non-cue in the training data. (Affixal cue occurrences are counted by looking at both the affix-pattern and the base it attaches to, basically treating the entire token as a cue. Tokens that end up being classified as cues are then matched against the affix patterns observed during training in order to correctly delimit the annotation of the cue.) This simple majority-usage approach actually provides a fairly strong baseline, yielding an F_1 of 87.42 on CDD (P=90.68, R=84.39). Compare this to the F_1 of 94.56 obtained by the classifier on the same data set (P=93.75, R=95.38). However, when applying the models to the held-out set, with models estimated over the entire CDTD, the baseline seems to able to make good use of the additional data and proves to be even more competitive: While our final cue classifier achieves F_1=91.31, the baseline achieves F_1=89.51, almost two percentage points higher than its score on the development data, and even outperforms four of the ten cue detection systems submitted for the shared task (three of the 12 shared task submissions use the same classifier).

When inspecting the predictions of our final cue classifier on CDD, comprising a total of 173 gold annotated cues, we find that our system mislabels 11 false positives (FPs) and 7 false negatives (FNs).

Of the FPs, we find five so-called *false negation cues* (Morante et al., 2011), including three instances of *none* in the fixed expression *none the less*. The others are affixal cues, of which two are clearly wrong (***un**derworked*, ***un**iversal*) while others might arguably be due to annotation errors (***in**superable*, ***un**happily*, *end**less***, *list**less**ly*). Among the FNs, two are due to MWCs not covered by our heuristics (e.g., *no more*), while the remaining errors concern affixes, including one in an interesting context of double negation; ***not dis**satisfied*.

3 Scope and event resolution

In this work, we model negation scope resolution as a special instance of the classical IOB (Inside, Outside, Begin) sequence labeling problem, where negation cues are labeled to be sequence starters and scopes and events as two different kinds of chunks. CRFs allow the computation of $p(\mathbf{X}|\mathbf{Y})$, where $\mathbf{X}$ is a sequence of labels and $\mathbf{Y}$ is a sequence of observations, and have already been shown to be efficient in similar, albeit less involved, tasks of negation scope resolution (Morante and Daelemans, 2009; Councill et al., 2010). We employ the CRF implementation in the Wapiti toolkit, using default settings (Lavergne et al., 2010). A number of features were used to create the models. In addition to the information provided for each token in the CD corpus (lemma, part of speech and constituent), we extracted both left and right token distance to the closest negation cue. Features were expanded to include forward and backward bigrams and trigrams on both token and PoS level, as well as lexicalized PoS unigrams and bigrams[2]. Table 2 presents a complete list of features. The more intricate, dependency-based features are presented in Section 3.1, while the labeling of both scopes and events is detailed in Section 3.2.

General features
Token
Lemma
PoS unigram
Forward token bigram and trigram
Backward token bigram and trigram
Forward PoS trigram
Backward PoS trigram
Lexicalized PoS
Forward Lexicalized PoS bigram
Backward Lexicalized PoS bigram
Constituent
Dependency relation
First order head PoS
Second order head PoS
Lexicalized dependency relation
PoS-disambiguated dependency relation
Cue-dependent features
Token distance
Directed dependency distance
Bidirectional dependency distance
Dependency path
Lexicalized dependency path

Table 2: List of features used to train the CRF models.

3.1 Dependency-based features

For the system submitted to the closed track, the syntactic representations were converted to dependency representations using the Stanford dependency converter, which comes with the Stanford parser (de Marneffe et al., 2006).[3] These dependency representations result from a conversion of Penn Treebank-style phrase structure trees, combining 'classic' head finding rules with rules that target specific linguistic constructions, such as passives or attributive adjectives. The so-called *basic* format provides a dependency graph which is a directed tree, see Figure 1 for an example.

For the open track submission we used Maltparser (Nivre et al., 2006) with its pre-trained parse model for English.[4] The parse model has been trained on a conversion of sections 2-21 of the Wall Street Journal section of the Penn Treebank to Stanford dependencies, augmented with data from Question Bank. The parser was applied to the negation data, using the word tokens and supplied parts-of-speech as input to the parser.

The features extracted via the dependency graphs aim at modeling the syntactic relationship between each token and the closest negation cue. Token distance was therefore complemented with two variants of dependency distance from each token to the lexi-

[2] By *lexicalized PoS* we mean an instance of a PoS-Tag in conjunction with the sentence token.

[3] Note that the converter was applied directly to the phrase-structure trees supplied with the negation data sets, and the Stanford parser was not used to parse the data.

[4] The pre-trained model is available from maltparser.org

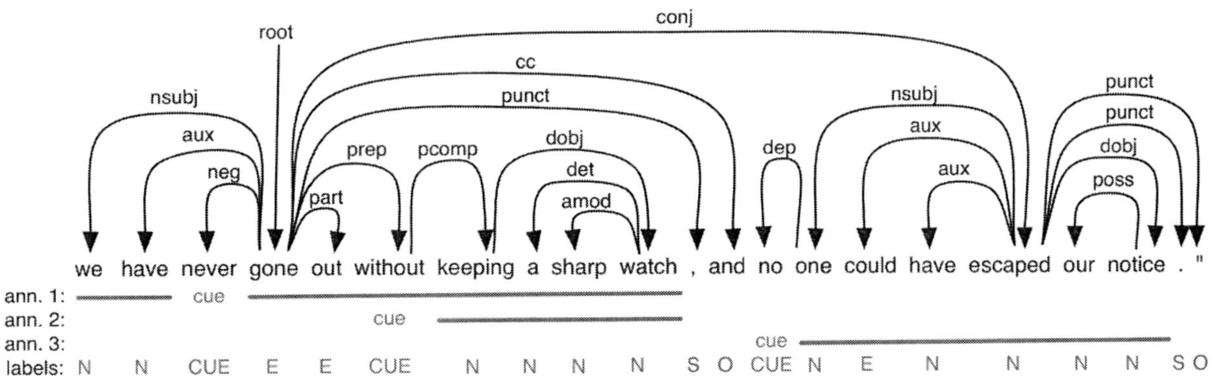

Figure 1: A sentence from the CD corpus showing a dependency graph and the annotation-to-label conversion.

cally closest cue, *Directed Distance* (DD) and *Bidirectional Distance* (BD). DD is extracted by following the reversed, directed edges from token X to the cue. If there is no such path, the value of the feature is -1. BD uses the Dijkstra shortest path algorithm on an undirected representation of the graph. The latter feature proved to be more effective than the former when not used together; using them in conjunction seemed to confuse the model, thus the final model utilizes only BD. We furthermore use the *Dependency Graph Path* (DGP) as a feature. This feature was inspired by the Parse Tree Path feature presented in Gildea and Jurafsky (2002) in the context of Semantic Role Labeling. It represents the path traversed from each token to the cue, encoding both the dependency relations and the direction of the arc that is traversed: for instance, the relation between *our* and *no* in Figure 1 is described as $\uparrow poss \uparrow dobj \downarrow nsubj \downarrow det$. Like Councill et al. (2010), we also encode the PoS of the first and second order syntactic head of each token. For the token *no* in Figure 1, for instance, we record the PoS of *one* and *escaped*, respectively.

3.2 Model-internal representation

The token-wise annotations in the CD corpus contain multiple layers of information. Tokens may or may not be negation cues and they can be either in or out of scope; in-scope tokens may or may not be negated events, and are associated with each of the cues they are negated by. Moreover, scopes may be (partially) overlapping, as in Figure 1, where the scope of *without* is contained within the scope of *never*. We convert this representation internally by assigning one of six labels to each token: O, CUE, MCUE, N, E and S, for out-of-scope, cue, morphological (affixal) cue, in-scope, event and negation stop respectively. The CUE, O, N and E labels parallel the IOB chunking paradigm and are eventually translated in the final annotations by our post-processing component. MCUE and S extend the label set to account for the specific behavior of the tokens they are associated with. The rationale behind the separation of cues in two classes is the pronounced differences between the PoS frequency distributions of standard versus morphological cues. Table 3 presents the frequency distribution of PoS-tags over the different cue types in CDTD and shows that, unsurprisingly, the majority class for morphological cues is adjectives, which typically generate different scope patterns compared to the majority class for standard cues. The S label, a special instance of an out-of-scope token, is defined as the

PoS	# S	PoS	# MCUE	PoS	# CUE
punctuation	1492	JJ	268	RB	1026
CC	52	RB	28	DT	296
IN + TO	46	NN	16	NN	146
RB	38	NN	4	UH	118
PRP	32	IN	2	IN	64
rest	118	rest	-	rest	38

Table 3: Frequency distribution of parts of speech over the S, MCUE and CUE labels in CDTD.

first non-cue, out-of-scope token to the right of one labeled with N, and targets mostly punctuation.

After some experimentation with joint labeling of scopes and events, we opted for separation of the two models, hence training separate models for the two tasks of scope resolution and event detection. In the model for scopes, all E labels are switched to N; conversely, Ns become Os in the event model. Given the nature of the annotations, the predictions provided by the model for events serve a double purpose: finding the negated token in a sentence and deciding whether a sentence is factual or not. The outputs of the two classifiers are merged during post-processing.

3.3 Post-processing

A simple, heuristics-based algorithm was applied to the output of the labelers in order to pair each in-scope token to its negation cue(s) and determine overlaps. Our algorithm works by first determining the overlaps among negation cues. Cue A negates cue B if the following conditions are met:

- B is to the right of A.
- There are no tokens labeled with S between A and B.
- Token distance between A and B does not exceed 10.

In the example in Figure 1, the overlapping condition holds for *never* and *without* but not for *without* and *no*, because of the punctuation between them. The token distance threshold of 10 was determined empirically on CDT. In order to assign in-scope tokens to their respective cue, tokens labeled with N are treated as follows:

- Assign each token T to the closest negation cue A with no S-labeled tokens or punctuation separating it from T.
- If A was found to be negated by cue B, assign T to B as well.
- If T is labeled with E by the event classifier, mark it as an event.

		F_1	
	Configuration	**Closed**	**Open**
(A)	O, N, CUE, MCUE, E, S Dependency Features	**64.85**	**66.41**
(B)	O, N, CUE, MCUE, E, S No Dependency Features	59.35	59.35
(C)	O, N, CUE, E Dependency Features	62.69	63.24
(D)	O, N, CUE, E No Dependency Features	56.44	56.44

Table 4: Full negation results on CDD with gold cues.

This algorithm yields the correct annotations for the example in Figure 1; when applied to label sequences originating from the gold scopes in CDD, the reported F_1 is 95%. We note that this loss of information could have been avoided by presenting the CRF with a version of a sentence for each negation cue. Then, when labeling new sentences, the model could be applied repeatedly (based on the number of cues provided by the cue detection system). However, training with multiple instances of the same sentence could result in a dilution of the evidence needed for scope labeling; this remains to be investigated in future work.

4 Development results

To investigate the effects of the augmented set of labels and that of dependency features comparatively, we present four different configurations of our system in Table 4, using F_1 for the stricter score that counts perfect-match negation resolution for each negation cue. Comparing (B) and (D), we observe that explicitly encoding significant tokens with extra labels does improve the performance of the classifier. Comparing (A) to (B) and (C) to (B) shows the effect of the dependency features with and without the augmented set of labels. With (A) being our top performing system and (D) a kind of internal baseline, we observe that the combined effects of the labels and dependency features is beneficial, with a margin of about 8 and 10 percentage points for our closed and open track systems respectively.

Table 5 presents the results for scope resolution on CDD with gold cues. Interestingly, the constituent

	Closed			Open		
	Prec	**Rec**	**F_1**	**Prec**	**Rec**	**F_1**
Scopes	100.00	70.24	**82.52**	100.00	66.67	80.00
Scope Tokens	94.69	82.16	**87.98**	90.64	81.36	85.75
Negated	82.47	72.07	76.92	83.65	77.68	**80.55**
Full negation	100.00	47.98	64.85	100.00	49.71	**66.41**

Table 5: Results for scope resolution on CDD with gold cues.

trees converted to Stanford dependencies used in the closed track outperform the open system employing Maltparser on scopes, while for negated events the latter is over 5 percentage points better than the former, as shown in Table 5.

4.1 Error analysis

We performed a manual error analysis of the scope resolution on the development data using gold cue information. Since our system does not deal specifically with discontinuous scopes, and seeing that we are employing a sequence classifier with a fairly local window, we are not surprised to find that a substantial portion of the errors are caused by discontinuous scopes. In fact, in our closed track system, these errors amount to 34% of the total number of errors. Discontinuous scopes, as in (3) below, account for 9.3% of all scopes in CDD and the closed task system does not analyze any of these correctly, whereas the open system correctly analyzes one discontinuous scope.

(3) I therefore spent the day at my club and did **not** return to Baker Street until evening.

A similar analysis with respect to event detection on gold scope information indicated that errors are mostly due to either *predicting* an event for a *non-factual* context (false positive) or *not predicting* an event for a *factual* context (false negative), i.e., there are relatively few instances of predicting the wrong token for a factual context (which result in both a false negative and a false positive). This suggests that the CRF has learned what tokens should be labeled as an event for a negation, but has not learned so well how to determine whether the negation is factual or non-factual. In this respect it may be that incorporating information from a separate and dedicated component for factuality detection — as in the system of Read et al. (2012) — could yield improvements for the CRF event model.

5 Held-out evaluation

Final results on held-out data for both closed and open track submissions are reported in Table 6. For the final run, we trained our systems on CDTD. We observe a similar relative performance to our development results, with the open track system outperforming the closed track one, albeit by a smaller margin than what we saw in development. We are also surprised to see that despite not addressing discontinuous scopes directly, our system obtained the best score on scope resolution (according to the metric dubbed "Scopes (cue match)").

6 Conclusions and future work

This paper has provided an overview of our system submissions for the *SEM 2012 shared task on resolving negation. This involves the subtasks of identifying negations cues, identifying the in-sentence scope of these cues, as well as identifying negated (and factual) events. While a simple SVM token classifier is applied for the cue detection task, we apply CRF sequence classifiers for predicting scopes and events. For the CRF models we experimented with a fine-grained set of labels and a wide range of feature types, drawing heavily on information from dependency structures. We have detailed two different system configurations — one submitted for the open track and another for the closed track — and the two configurations only differ with respect to the source used for the dependency parses: For the closed track submission we simply converted the constituent structures provided in the shared task data to Stanford dependencies, while for the open track we apply the Maltparser. For the end-to-end evaluation, our submission was ranked first in the open track and third in the closed track. The system also had the best performance for each individual sub-task in the open track, as well as being among

	Closed			Open		
	Prec	**Rec**	**F₁**	**Prec**	**Rec**	**F₁**
Cues	89.17	93.56	91.31	89.17	93.56	91.31
Scopes	85.71	62.65	72.39	85.71	62.65	72.39
Scope Tokens	86.03	81.55	83.73	82.25	82.16	82.20
Negated	68.18	52.63	59.40	66.90	57.40	61.79
Full negation	78.26	40.91	53.73	78.72	42.05	54.82
Cues B	86.97	93.56	90.14	86.97	93.56	90.14
Scopes B	59.32	62.65	60.94	59.54	62.65	61.06
Negated B	67.16	52.63	59.01	63.82	57.40	60.44
Full negation B	38.03	40.91	39.42	39.08	42.05	40.51

Table 6: End-to-end results on the held-out data.

the top-performers on the scope resolution sub-task across both tracks.

Due to time constraints we were not able to directly address discontinuous scopes in our system. For future work we plan on looking for ways to tackle this problem by taking advantage of syntactic information, both in the classification and in the post-processing steps. We are also interested in developing the CRF-internal label-set to include more informative labels. We also want to test the system design developed for this task on other corpora annotated for negation (or other related phenomena such as speculation), as well as perform extrinsic evaluation of our system as a sub-component to other NLP tasks such as sentiment analysis or opinion mining. Lastly, we would like to try training separate classifiers for affixal and token-level cues, given that largely separate sets of features are effective for the two cases.

Acknowledgements

We thank colleagues at the University of Oslo, and in particular Johan Benum Evensberget and Arne Skjærholt for fruitful discussions and suggestions. We also thank the anonymous reviewers for their helpful feedback.

References

Isaac G. Councill, Ryan McDonald, and Leonid Velikovich. 2010. What's great and what's not: Learning to classify the scope of negation for improved sentiment analysis. In *Proceedings of the Workshop On Negation and Speculation in Natural Language Processing*, pages 51–59.

Marie-Catherine de Marneffe, Bill MacCartney, and Christopher D. Manning. 2006. Generating typed dependency parses from phrase structure parses. In *Proceedings of the 5th International Conference on Language Resources and Evaluation*.

Daniel Gildea and Daniel Jurafsky. 2002. Automatic labeling of semantic roles. *Computational Linguistic*, 28(3):245–288.

Thomas Lavergne, Olivier Cappé, and François Yvon. 2010. Practical very large scale CRFs. In *Proceedings the 48th Annual Meeting of the Association for Computational Linguistics (ACL)*, pages 504–513. Association for Computational Linguistics.

Roser Morante and Walter Daelemans. 2009. A metalearning approach to processing the scope of negation. In *CoNLL '09: Proceedings of the Thirteenth Conference on Computational Natural Language Learning*, pages 21–29. Association for Computational Linguistics.

Roser Morante and Walter Daelemans. 2012. ConanDoyle-neg: Annotation of negation in Conan Doyle stories. In *Proceedings of the Eighth International Conference on Language Resources and Evaluation*, Istanbul.

Roser Morante, Sarah Schrauwen, and Walter Daelemans. 2011. Annotation of negation cues and their scope: Guidelines v1.0. Technical report, University of Antwerp. CLIPS: Computational Linguistics & Psycholinguistics technical report series.

Joakim Nivre, Johan Hall, and Jens Nilsson. 2006. MaltParser: A data-driven parser-generator for dependency parsing. In *Proceedings of the Fifth International Conference on Language Resources and Evaluation*, pages 2216–2219.

Jonathon Read, Erik Velldal, Lilja Øvrelid, and Stephan Oepen. 2012. UiO_1: Constituent-based discriminative ranking for negation resolution. In *Proceedings of the First Joint Conference on Lexical and Computational Semantics*, Montreal. Submission under review.

Erik Velldal, Lilja Øvrelid, Jonathon Read, and Stephan Oepen. 2012. Speculation and negation: Rules, rankers and the role of syntax. *Computational Linguistics*, 38(2).

Erik Velldal. 2011. Predicting speculation: A simple disambiguation approach to hedge detection in biomedical literature. *Journal of Biomedical Semantics*, 2(5).

Veronika Vincze, György Szarvas, Richárd Farkas, György Móra, and János Csirik. 2008. The BioScope corpus: Biomedical texts annotated for uncertainty, negation and their scopes. *BMC Bioinformatics*, 9 (Suppl. 11).

UMichigan: A Conditional Random Field Model for Resolving the Scope of Negation

Amjad Abu-Jbara
EECS Department
University of Michigan
Ann Arbor, MI, USA
amjbara@umich.edu

Dragomir Radev
EECS Department
University of Michigan
Ann Arbor, MI, USA
radev@umich.edu

Abstract

In this paper, we present a system for detecting negation in English text. We address three tasks: negation cue detection, negation scope resolution and negated event identification. We pose these tasks as sequence labeling problems. For each task, we train a Conditional Random Field (CRF) model on lexical, structural, and syntactic features extracted from labeled data. The models are trained and tested using the dataset distributed with the *sem Shared Task 2012 on resolving the scope and focus of negation. The system detects negation cues with 90.98% F1 measure (94.3% and 87.88% recall). It identifies negation scope with 82.70% F1 on token-by-token level and 64.78% F1 on full scope level. Negated events are detected with 51.10% F1 measure.

1 Introduction

Negation is a linguistic phenomenon present in all languages (Tottie, 1993; Horn, 1989). The semantic function of negation is to transform an affirmative statement into its opposite meaning. The automatic detection of negation and its scope is a problem encountered in a wide range of natural language processing applications including, but not limited to, data mining, relation extraction, question answering, and sentiment analysis. For example, failing to account for negation may result in giving wrong answers in question answering systems or in the prediction of opposite sentiment in sentiment analysis systems.

The occurrence of negation in a sentence is determined by the presence of a negation cue. A negation cue is a word, a phrase, a prefix, or a postfix that triggers negation. Scope of negation is the part of the meaning that is negated (Huddleston and Pullum, 2002). The negated event is the event or the entity that the negation indicates its absence or denies its occurrence. For example, in the sentence below ***never*** is the negation cue. The scope is enclosed in square brackets. The negated event is underlined.

> *[Andrew had]* ***never*** *[liked smart phones], but he received one as a gift last week and started to use it.*

Negation cues and scopes may be discontinuous. For example, the negation cue *neither ... nor* is discontinuous.

In this chapter, we present a system for automatically detecting negation cues, negated events, and negation scopes in English text. The system uses conditional random field (CRF) models trained on labeled sentences extracted from two classical English novels. The CRF models are trained using lexical, structural, and syntactic features. The experiments show promising results.

This paper is organized as follows. Section 2 reviews previous work. Section 3 describes the data. Section 4 describes the CRFs models. Section 5 presents evaluation, results, and discussion.

2 Previous Work

Most research on negation has been done in the biomedical domain (Chapman et al., 2001; Mutalik et al., 2001; Kim and Park, 2006; Morante et al.,

Token	Lemma	POS	Syntax	Cue 1	Scope 1	Event 1	Cue 2	Scope 2	Event 2
She	She	PRP	(S(NP*)	-	She	-	-	-	-
would	would	MD	(VP*	-	would	-	-	-	-
not	not	RB	*	not	-	-	-	-	-
have	have	VB	(VP*	-	have	-	-	-	-
said	say	VBD	(VP*	-	said	-	-	-	-
‘	‘	“	(SBAR(S(NP*	-	’	-	-	-	-
Godspeed	Godspeed	NNP	*	-	Godspeed	-	-	-	-
’	’	”	*)	-	’	-	-	-	-
had	have	VBD	(VP*	-	had	-	-	had	-
it	it	PRP	(ADVP*	-	it	-	-	it	-
not	not	RB	*)	-	not	-	not	-	-
been	be	VBN	(VP*	-	been	-	-	been	-
so	so	RB	(ADVP*)))))))	-	so	-	-	so	-
.	.	.	*)	-	-	-	-	-	-

Table 1: Example sentence annotated for negation following sem shared task 2012 format

2008a; Morante and Daelemans, 2009; Agarwal and Yu, 2010; Morante, 2010; Read et al., 2011), mostly on clinical reports. The reason is that most NLP research in the biomedical domain is interested in automatically extracting factual relations and pieces of information from unstructured data. Negation detection is important here because information that falls in the scope of a negation cue cannot be treated as facts.

Chapman et al. (2001) proposed a rule-based algorithm called *NegEx* for determining whether a finding or disease mentioned within narrative medical reports is present or absent. The algorithm uses regular-expression-based rules. Mutalik et al. (2001) developed another rule based system called *Negfinder* that recognizes negation patterns in biomedical text. It consists of two components: a lexical scanner, *lexer* that uses regular expression rules to generate a finite state machine, and a parser. Morante (2008b) proposed a supervised approach for detecting negation cues and their scopes in biomedical text. Their system consists of two memory-based engines, one that decides if the tokens in a sentence are negation signals, and another one that finds the full scope of these negation signals.

Negation has been also studied in the context of sentiment analysis (Wilson et al., 2005; Jia et al., 2009; Councill et al., 2010; Heerschop et al., 2011; Hogenboom et al., 2011). Wiegand et al. (2010) surveyed the recent work on negation scope detection for sentiment analysis. Wilson et al. (2005) studied the contextual features that affect text polarity. They used a machine learning approach in which negation is encoded using several features. One feature checks whether a negation expression occurs in a fixed window of four words preceding the polar expression. Another feature accounts for a polar predicate having a negated subject. They also have disambiguation features to handle negation words that do not function as negation cues in certain contexts, e.g. *not to mention* and *not just*.

Jia et al. (2009) proposed a rule based method to determine the polarity of sentiments when one or more occurrences of a negation term such as not appear in a sentence. The hand-crafted rules are applied to syntactic and dependency parse tree representations of the sentence.

Hogenboom et al. (2011) found that applying a simple rule that considers two words, following a negation keyword, to be negated by that keyword, to be effective in improving the accuracy of sentiment analysis in movie reviews. This simple method yields a significant increase in overall sentiment classification accuracy and macro-level F1 of 5.5% and 6.2%, respectively, compared to not accounting for negation.

This work is characterized by addressing three tasks at once: negation cue detection, negated event identification, and negation scope resolution. Our proposed approach uses a supervised graphical probabilistic model trained using labeled data.

3 Data

We use the dataset distributed by the organizers of the *sem Shared Task 2012 on resolving the scope and focus of negation. This dataset includes two stories by Conan Doyle, The Hound of the Baskervilles, The Adventures of Wisteria Lodge. All occurrences of negation are annotated accounting for negation expressed by nouns, pronouns, verbs, adverbs, determiners, conjunctions and prepositions. For each negation cue, the negation cue and scope are marked, as well as the negated event (if any exists). The annotation guidelines follow the proposal of Morante et al. (2011)[1]. The data is split into three sets: a training set containing 3,644 sentences, a development set containing 787 sentences, and a testing set containing 1,089 sentences. The data is provided in CoNLL format. Each line corresponds to a token and each annotation is provided in a column; empty lines indicate end of sentences. The provided annotations are:

- Column 1: chapter name
- Column 2: sentence number within chapter
- Column 3: token number within sentence
- Column 4: word
- Column 5: lemma
- Column 6: part-of-speech
- Column 7: syntax
- Columns 8 to last:
  - If the sentence has no negations, column 8 has a "***" value and there are no more columns.
  - If the sentence has negations, the annotation for each negation is provided in three columns. The first column contains the word or part of the word (e.g., morpheme "un"), that belongs to the negation cue. The second contains the word or part of the word that belongs to the scope of the negation cue. The third column contains the word or part of the word that is the negated event or property. It can be the case that no negated event or property are marked as negated.

[1]http://www.clips.ua.ac.be/sites/default/files/ctrs-n3.pdf

Token	Lemma	Punc.	Cat.	POS	Label
Since	Since	0	OTH	IN	O
we	we	0	PRO	PRP	O
have	have	0	VB	VBP	O
been	be	0	VB	VBN	O
so	so	0	ADVB	RB	O
unfortunate	unfortunate	0	ADJ	JJ	PRE
as	as	0	ADVB	RB	O
to	to	0	OTH	TO	O
miss	miss	0	VB	VB	O
him	him	0	PRO	PRP	O
and	and	0	OTH	CC	O
have	have	0	VB	VBP	O
no	no	0	OTH	DT	NEG
notion	notion	0	NOUN	NN	O
of	of	0	OTH	IN	O
his	his	0	PRO	PRP$	O
errand	errand	0	NOUN	NN	O
,	,	1	OTH	,	O
this	this	0	OTH	DT	O
accidental	accidental	0	ADJ	JJ	O
souvenir	souvenir	0	NOUN	NN	O
becomes	become	0	VB	VBZ	O
of	of	0	OTH	IN	O
importance	importance	0	NOUN	NN	O
.	.	1	OTH	.	O

Table 2: Example sentence labeled for negation cue detection

Table 1 shows an example of an annotated sentence that contains two negation cues.

4 Approach

The problem that we are trying to solve can be split into three tasks. The first task is to detect negation cues. The second task is to identify the scope of each detected negation cue. The third task is to identify the negated event. We use a machine learning approach to address these tasks. We train a Conditional Random Field (CRF) (Lafferty et al., 2001) model on lexical, structural, and syntactic features extracted from the training dataset. In the following subsections, we describe the CRF model that we use for each task.

4.1 Negation Cue Detection

Negation cues are lexical elements that indicate the existence of negation in a sentence. From lexical point of view, negation cues can be divided into four categories:

1. Prefix (i.e. in-, un-, im-, il-, dis-). For example, **un-** in ***un**suitable*) is a prefix negation cue.

2. Postfix (i.e. -less). for example, **-less** in care**less**.

3. Multi-word negation cues such as *neither...nor*, *rather than*, *by no means*, etc.

4. Single word negation cues such as *not*, *no*, *none*, *nobody*, etc.

The goal of this task is to detect negation cues. We pose this problem as a sequence labeling task. The reason for this choice is that some negation cues may not indicate negation in some contexts. For example, the negation cue *not* in the phrase *not to mention* does not indicate negation. Also, as we saw above, some negation cues may consist of multiple words, some of them are continuous and others are discontinuous. Treating the task as a sequence labeling problem help model the contextual factors that affect the function of negation cues. We train a CRF model using features extracted from the sentences of the training dataset. The token level features that we train the model on are:

- *Token*: The word or the punctuation mark as it appears in the sentence.

- *Lemma*: The lemmatized form of the token.

- *Part-Of-Speech tag*: The part of speech tag of the token.

- *Part-Of-Speech tag category*: Part-of-speech tags reduced into 5 categories: Adjective (ADJ), Verb (VB), Noun (NN), Adverb (ADVB), Pronoun (PRO), and other (OTH).

- *Is punctuation mark*: This feature takes the value 1 if the token is a punctuation mark and 0 otherwise.

- *Starts with negation prefix*: This feature takes the value 1 if the token is a word that starts with un-, in-, im-, il-, or dis- and 0 otherwise.

- *Ends with negation postfix*: This feature takes the value 1 if the token is a word that ends with -less and 0 otherwise.

The CRF model that we use considers at each token the features of the current token, the two preceding tokens, and the two proceeding tokens. The model also uses token bigrams and trigrams, and part-of-speech tag bigrams and trigrams as features.

The labels are 5 types: "O" for tokens that are not part of any negation cue; "NEG" for single word negation cues; "PRE" for prefix negation cue; "POST" for postfix negation cue; and "MULTI-NEG" for multi-word negation cues. Table 2 shows an example labeled sentence.

At testing time, if a token is labeled "NEG" or "MULTI-NEG" the whole token is treated as a negation cue or part of a negation cue respectively. If a token is labeled as "PRE" or "POST", a regular expression is used to determine the prefix/postfix that trigged the negation.

4.2 Negation Scope Detection

Scope of negation is the sequence of tokens (can be discontinuous) that expresses the meaning that is meant to be negated by a negation cue. A sentence may contain zero or more negation cues. Each negation cue has its own scope. It is possible that the scope of two negation cues overlap. We use each negation instance (i.e. each negation cue and its scope) as one training example. Therefore, a sentence that contains two negation cues provides two training examples. We train a CRF model on features extracted from all negation instances in the training dataset. The features that we use are:

- *Token*: The word or the punctuation mark as it appears in the sentence.

- *Lemma*: The lemmatized form of the token.

- *Part-Of-Speech tag*: The part of speech tag of the token.

- *Part-Of-Speech tag category*: Part-of-speech tags reduced into 5 categories: Adjective (ADJ), Verb (VB), Noun (NN), Adverb (ADVB), Pronoun (PRO), and other (OTH).

- *Is punctuation mark*: This feature takes the value 1 if the token is a punctuation mark and 0 otherwise.

- *Type of negation cue*: Possible types are: "NEG" for single word negation cues; "PRE" for prefix negation cue; "POST" for postfix negation cue; and "MULTI" for multi-word negation cues.

- *Relative position*: This feature takes the value 1 if the token position in the sentence is before the position of the negation cue, 2 if the token position is after the position of the negation cue, and 3 if the token is the negation cue itself.

- *Distance*: The number of tokens between the current token and the negation cue.

- *Same segment*: This feature takes the value 1 if this token and the negation cue fall in the segment in the sentence. The sentence is segmented by punctuation marks.

- *Chunk*: This feature takes the value NP-B (VP-B) if this token is the first token of a noun (verb) phrase, NP-I (VP-I) if it is inside a noun (verb) phrase, NP-E (VP-E) if it is the last token of a noun (verb) phrase.

- *Same chunk*: This feature takes the value 1 if this token and the negation cue fall in the same chunk (noun phrase or verb phrase).

- *Is negation*: This feature takes the value 1 if this token is a negation cue, and 0 otherwise.

- *Syntactic distance*: The number of edges in the shortest path that connects the token and the negation in the syntactic parse tree.

- *Common ancestor node*: The type of the node in the syntactic parse tree that is the least common ancestor of this token and the negation cue token.

The CRF model considers the features of 4 tokens to the left and to the right at each position. It also uses bigram and trigram combinations of some of the features.

At testing time a few postprocessing rules are used to fix sure labels if they were labeled incorrectly. For example, if a word starts with a prefix negation cue, the word itself (without the prefix) is always part of the scope and it is also the negated event.

4.3 Negated Event Identification

It is possible that a negation cue comes associated with an event. A negation has an event if it occurs in a factual context. The dataset that we use was labeled for negated events whenever one exists. We used the same features described in the previous subsection to train a CRF model for negated event identification. We have also tried to use one CRF model for both scope resolution and negated event identification, but we noticed that using two separate models results in significantly better results for both tasks.

5 Evaluation

We use the testing set described in Section 3 to evaluate the system. The testing set contains 1089 sentences 235 of which contains at least one negation.

We use the standard precision, recall, and f-measure metrics to evaluate the system. We perform the evaluation on different levels:

1. Cues: the metrics are computed only for cue detection.

2. Scope (tokens): the metrics are calculated at token level. If a sentence has 2 scopes, one with 5 tokens and another with 4, the total number of scope tokens is 9.

3. Scope (full): the metrics are calculated at the full scope level. Both the negation cue and the whole scope should be correctly identified. If a sentence contains 2 negation cues, then 2 scopes are checked. We report two values here one the requires the cue match correctly and one that does not.

4. Negated Events: the metrics are computed only for negated events identification (apart from negation cue and scope).

Variant A								
	gold	system	tp	fp	fn	precision	recall	F1
Cues	264	250	232	14	32	94.31	87.88	90.98
Scope (cue match)	249	227	126	14	123	90.00	50.60	64.78
Scope (no cue match)	249	227	126	14	123	90.00	50.60	64.78
Scope (tokens - no cue match)	1805	1716	1456	260	349	84.85	80.66	82.70
Negated (no cue match)	173	183	70	70	64	50.00	52.24	51.10
Full negation:	264	250	75	14	189	84.27	28.41	42.49
Variant B								
	gold	system	tp	fp	fn	precision	recall	F1
Cues :	264	250	232	14	32	92.80	87.88	90.27
Scope (cue match):	249	227	126	14	123	55.51	50.60	52.94
Scope (no cue match):	249	227	126	14	123	55.51	50.60	52.94
Negated (no cue match):	173	183	70	70	64	38.25	52.24	44.16
Full negation :	264	250	75	14	189	30.00	28.41	29.18
# Sentences	1089							
# Negation sentences	235							
# Negation sentences with errors	171							
% Correct sentences	83.47							
% Correct negation sentences	27.23							

Table 3: Results of negation cue, negated event, and negation scope detection

5. Full negation: the metrics are computed for all the three tasks at once and requiring everything to match correctly.

For cue, scope and negated event to be correct, both the tokens and the words or parts of words have to be correctly identified. The final periods in abbreviations are disregarded. If gold has value "Mr." and system "Mr", system is counted as correct. Also, punctuation tokens are *not* taken into account for evaluation.

Two variants of the metrics are computed. In the first variant (A), precision is calculated as *tp / (tp + fp)* and recall is calculated as *tp / (tp + fn)* where *tp* is the count of true positive labels, *fp* is the count of false positive labels, and *fn* is the count of false negative labels. In variant B, the precision is calculated differently, using the formula *precision = tp / system*.

Table 3 shows the results of our system.

6 Error Analysis

The system used no external resources outside the training data. This means that the system recognizes only negation cues that appeared in the training set. This was the first source of error. For example, the word *unacquainted* that starts with the negation prefix *un* has never been seen in the training data. Intuitively, if no negation cue is detected, the system does not attempt to produce scope levels. This problem can be overcome by using a lexicon of negation words and those words that can be negated by adding a negation prefix to them.

We noticed in several occasions that scope detection accuracy can be improved if some simple rules can be imposed after doing the initial labeling using the CRF model (but we have not actually implemented any such rules in the system). For example, the system can require all the tokens that belong to the same chunk (noun group, verb group, etc.) all have the same label (e.g. the majority vote label). The same thing could be also applied on the segment rather than the chunk level where the boundaries of segments are determined by punctuation marks.

7 Conclusion

We presented a supervised system for identifying negation in English sentences. The system uses three CRF trained models. One model is trained for negation cue detection. Another model is trained for negated event identification. A third one is trained for negation scope identification. The models are trained using features extracted from a labeled dataset. Our experiments show that the system achieves promising results.

References

Shashank Agarwal and Hong Yu. 2010. Biomedical negation scope detection with conditional random fields. *Journal of the American Medical Informatics Association*, 17(6):696–701.

Wendy Webber Chapman, Will Bridewell, Paul Hanbury, Gregory F. Cooper, and Bruce G. Buchanan. 2001. A simple algorithm for identifying negated findings and diseases in discharge summaries. *Journal of Biomedical Informatics*, pages 301–310.

Isaac G. Councill, Ryan McDonald, and Leonid Velikovich. 2010. What's great and what's not: learning to classify the scope of negation for improved sentiment analysis. In *Proceedings of the Workshop on Negation and Speculation in Natural Language Processing*, NeSp-NLP '10, pages 51–59, Stroudsburg, PA, USA. Association for Computational Linguistics.

Bas Heerschop, Paul van Iterson, Alexander Hogenboom, Flavius Frasincar, and Uzay Kaymak. 2011. Analyzing sentiment in a large set of web data while accounting for negation. In *AWIC*, pages 195–205.

Alexander Hogenboom, Paul van Iterson, Bas Heerschop, Flavius Frasincar, and Uzay Kaymak. 2011. Determining negation scope and strength in sentiment analysis. In *SMC*, pages 2589–2594.

Laurence R. Horn. 1989. *A natural history of negation / Laurence R. Horn*. University of Chicago Press, Chicago :.

Rodney D. Huddleston and Geoffrey K. Pullum. 2002. *The Cambridge Grammar of the English Language*. Cambridge University Press, April.

Lifeng Jia, Clement Yu, and Weiyi Meng. 2009. The effect of negation on sentiment analysis and retrieval effectiveness. In *Proceedings of the 18th ACM conference on Information and knowledge management*, CIKM '09, pages 1827–1830, New York, NY, USA. ACM.

Jung-Jae Kim and Jong C. Park. 2006. Extracting contrastive information from negation patterns in biomedical literature. 5(1):44–60, March.

John D. Lafferty, Andrew McCallum, and Fernando C. N. Pereira. 2001. Conditional random fields: Probabilistic models for segmenting and labeling sequence data. In *Proceedings of the Eighteenth International Conference on Machine Learning*, ICML '01, pages 282–289, San Francisco, CA, USA. Morgan Kaufmann Publishers Inc.

Roser Morante and Walter Daelemans. 2009. Learning the scope of hedge cues in biomedical texts. *Proceedings of the Workshop on BioNLP BioNLP 09*, (June):28.

Roser Morante, Anthony Liekens, and Walter Daelemans. 2008a. Learning the scope of negation in biomedical texts. *Proceedings of the Conference on Empirical Methods in Natural Language Processing EMNLP 08*, (October):715–724.

Roser Morante, Anthony Liekens, and Walter Daelemans. 2008b. Learning the scope of negation in biomedical texts. In *Proceedings of the 2008 Conference on Empirical Methods in Natural Language Processing*, pages 715–724, Honolulu, Hawaii, October. Association for Computational Linguistics.

Roser Morante, Sarah Schrauwen, and Walter Daelemans. 2011. Annotation of negation cues and their scope. Technical report.

Roser Morante. 2010. Descriptive analysis of negation cues in biomedical texts. *Language Resources And Evaluation*, pages 1–8.

P. G. Mutalik, A. Deshpande, and P. M. Nadkarni. 2001. Use of general-purpose negation detection to augment concept indexing of medical documents: a quantitative study using the UMLS. *Journal of the American Medical Informatics Association : JAMIA*, 8(6):598–609.

Jonathon Read, Erik Velldal, Stephan Oepen, and Lilja vrelid. 2011. Resolving speculation and negation scope in biomedical articles with a syntactic constituent ranker. In *Proceedings of the Fourth International Symposium on Languages in Biology and Medicine*, Singapore.

Gunnel Tottie. 1993. Negation in English Speech and Writing: A Study in Variation. *Language*, 69(3):590–593.

Michael Wiegand, Alexandra Balahur, Benjamin Roth, Dietrich Klakow, and Andrés Montoyo. 2010. A survey on the role of negation in sentiment analysis. In *Proceedings of the Workshop on Negation and Speculation in Natural Language Processing*, NeSp-NLP '10, pages 60–68, Stroudsburg, PA, USA. Association for Computational Linguistics.

Theresa Wilson, Janyce Wiebe, and Paul Hoffmann. 2005. Recognizing contextual polarity in phrase-level sentiment analysis. In *Proceedings of the conference on Human Language Technology and Empirical Methods in Natural Language Processing*, HLT '05, pages 347–354, Stroudsburg, PA, USA. Association for Computational Linguistics.

UWashington: Negation Resolution using Machine Learning Methods

James Paul White
University of Washington
Department of Linguistics, Box 354340
Seattle, WA 98195, USA
jimwhite@uw.edu

Abstract

This paper reports on a simple system for resolving the scope of negation in the closed track of the *SEM 2012 Shared Task. Cue detection is performed using regular expression rules extracted from the training data. Both scope tokens and negated event tokens are resolved using a Conditional Random Field (CRF) sequence tagger – namely the SimpleTagger library in the MALLET machine learning toolkit. The full negation F_1 score obtained for the task evaluation is 48.09% (P=74.02%, R=35.61%) which ranks this system fourth among the six submitted for the closed track.

1 Introduction

Resolving the scope of negation is an interesting area of research for Natural Language Processing (NLP) systems because many such systems have used methods that are insensitive to polarity. As a result it is fairly common to have a system that treats "X does Y" and "X does not Y" as having the same, or very nearly the same, meaning[1]. A few application areas that have been addressing this issue recently are in sentiment analysis, biomedical NLP, and recognition of textual entailment. Sentiment analysis systems are frequently used in corporate and product marketing, call center quality control, and within "recommender" systems which are all contexts where it is important to recognize that "X does like Y" is contrary to "X does not like Y". Similarly in biomedical text such as research papers and abstracts, diagnostic procedure reports, and medical records it is important to differentiate between statements about what is the case and what is not the case.

The *SEM 2012 Shared Task is actually two related tasks run in parallel. The one this system was developed for is the identification of three features of negation: the cue, the scope, and the factual negated event (if any). The other task is concerned with the focus of negation. Detailed description of both subtasks, including definition of the relevant concepts and terminology (negation, cue, scope, event, and focus) appears in this volume (Morante and Blanco, 2012). Roser Morante and Eduardo Blanco describe the corpora provided to participants with numbers and examples, methods used used to process the data, and briefly describes each participant and analyzes the overall results.

Annotation of the corpus was undertaken at the University of Antwerp and was performed on several Sherlock Holmes works of fiction written by Sir Arthur Conan Doyle. The corpus includes all sentences from the original text, not just those employing negation. Roser Morante and Walter Daelemans provide a thorough explanation of those gold annotations of negation cue, scope, and negated event (if any) (Morante and Daelemans, 2012). Their paper explains the motivations for the particular annotation decisions and describes in detail the guidelines, including many examples.

2 Related Work

Recognition of phrases containing negation, particularly in the medical domain, using regular expressions has been described using several different approaches. Systems such as Negfinder (Mutalik et

[1]A one token difference between the strings surely indicating at least an inexact match.

al, 2001) and NegEx (Chapman et al, 2001) use manually constructed rules to extract phrases from text and classify them as to whether they contain an expression of negation. Rokach et al evaluate several methods and show their highest level of performance (an F_1 of 95.9 ± 1.9%) by using cascaded decision trees of regular expressions learned from labelled narrative medical reports (Rokach et al, 2008).

Those systems perform a different function than that required for this task though. They classify phrases extracted from plain text as to whether they contain negation or not, while the requirement of this shared task for negation cue detection is to identify the particular token(s) or part of a token that signals the presence of negation. Furthermore, those systems only identify the scope of negation at the level of phrasal constituents, which is different than what is required for this task in which the scopes are not necessarily contiguous.

Conditional Random Field (CRF) sequence taggers have been successfully applied to many scope resolution problems, including those of negation. The NegScope system (Agarwal and Yu, 2010) trains a CRF sequence tagger on labelled data to identify both the cue and scope of negation. However, that system only recognizes a whole word as a cue and does not recognize nor generalize negation cues which are affixes. There are also systems that use CRF sequence taggers for detection of hedge scopes (Tang et al, 2010, Zhao et al, 2010). Morante and Daelemans describe a method for improving resolution of the scope of negation by combining IGTREE, CRF, and Support Vector Machines (SVM) (Morante and Daelemans, 2009).

3 System Description

This system is implemented as a three stage cascade with the output from each of the first two stages included as input to the subsequent stage. The stages are ordered as cue detection, scope detection, and finally negated event detection. The format of the inputs and outputs for each stage use the shared task's CoNLL-style file format. That simplifies the use of the supplied gold-standard data for training of each stage separately.

Because this system was designed for the closed track of the shared task, it makes minimal language-specific assumptions and learns (nearly) all language-specific rules from the gold-labelled training data (which includes the development set for the final system).

The CRF sequence tagger used by the system is that implemented in the SimpleTagger class of the MALLET toolkit, which is a Java library distributed under the Common Public License[2].

The system is implemented in the Groovy programming language, an agile and dynamic language for the Java Virtual Machine[3]. The source code is available under the GNU Public License on GitHub[4].

3.1 Cue Detection

Cues are recognized by four different regular expression rule patterns: affixes (partial token), single (whole) token, contiguous multiple token, and gappy (discontiguous) multiple token. The rules are learned by a two pass process. In the first pass, for each positive example of a negation cue in the training data, a rule that matches that example is added to the prospective rule set. Then, in the second pass, the rules are applied to the training data and the counts of correct and incorrect matches are accumulated. Rules that are wrong more often than they are right are removed from the set used by the system.

A further filtering of the prospective rules is done in which gappy multiple token rules that match the same word type more than once are removed. Those prospective rules are created to match cases in the supplied training data where the a repetition has occurred and then encoded by the annotators as a single cue (and thus scope) of negation[5].

The single token and multiple token rules match both the word string feature (ignoring case) and the part-of-speech (POS) feature of each token. And because a single token rule might also match a cue that belongs to a multiple token rule, multiple token rules are checked first.

Affix rules are of two types: prefix cues and non-prefix cues. The distinction is that while prefix cues must match starting at the beginning of the word string, the non-prefix cues may have a suffix following them in the word string that is not part of the cue. Affix rules only match against the word

[2]http://mallet.cs.umass.edu/

[3]http://groovy.codehaus.org/

[4]https://github.com/jimwhite/SEMST2012

[5]Such as baskervilles12 174: "Not a whisper, not a rustle, rose..." which has a cue annotation of "Not" *gap* "not".

string feature of the tokens and are insensitive to the POS feature.

In order to generalize the affix rules, sets are accumulated of both base word strings (the substring following a prefix cue or substring preceding a non-prefix cue) and suffixes (the substring following non-prefix cues, if any). In addition, all other word strings and lemma strings in the training corpus that are at least four characters long are added to the set of possible base word strings[6]. A set of negative word strings is also accumulated in the second pass of the rule training to condition against false positive matches for each affix rule.

A prefix cue rule will match a token with a word string that starts with the cue string and is followed by any of the strings in the base word set. Similarly a suffix cue rule will match a token whose word string contains the cue string preceded by a string in the base word set and is either at the end of the string or is followed by one of the strings in the suffix string set. Affix rules, unlike the other cue-matching rules, also output the string for matched base word as the value of the scope for the matched token. In any case, if the token's word string is in the negative word string set for the rule then it will not be matched.

Following submission of the system outputs for the shared tasked I discovered that a hand written regular expression rule that filters out the (potential) cues detected for "(be|have) no doubt" and "none the (worse|less)" was inadvertently included in the system. Although those rules could be learned automatically from the training data (and such was my intention), the system as reported here does not currently do so.

3.2 Negation Scope Resolution

For each cue detected, scope resolution is performed as a ternary classification of each token in the sentence as to whether it is part of a cue, part of a scope, or neither. The classifier is the CRF sequence tagger implemented in the SimpleTagger class of the MALLET toolkit (McCallum, 2002). Training is performed using the gold-standard data including the gold cues. The output of the tagger is not used to determine the scope value of a token in those cases where an affix rule in the cue detector has matched a token and therefore has supplied the matched base word string as the value of the scope for the token.

For features that are computed in terms of the cue token, the first (lowest numbered) token marked as a cue is used when there is more than one cue token for the scope.

Features used by the scope CRF sequence tagger are:

- Of the per-token data: word string in lowercase, lemma string in lowercase, part-of-speech (POS) tag, binary flag indicating whether the token is a cue, a binary flag indicating whether the token is at the edge of its parent non-terminal node or an internal sibling, a binary flag indicating whether the token is a cue token, and relative position to the cue token in number of tokens.
- Of the cue token data: word string in lowercase, lemma string in lowercase, and POS tag.
- Of the path through the syntax tree from the cue token: an ordered list of the non-terminal labels of each node up the tree to the lowest common parent, an ordered list of the non-terminal labels of each node down the tree from that lowest common parent, a path relation value consisting of the label of the lowest common parent node concatenated with an indication of the relative position of the paths to the cue and token in terms of sibling order.

3.3 Negated Event Resolution

Detection of the negated event or property is performed using the same CRF sequence tagger and features used for scope detection. The only difference is that the token classification is in terms of whether each token in the sentence is part of a factual negated event for each negation cue.

3.4 Feature Set Selection

A comparison of the end-to-end performance of this system using several different sets of per token feature choices for the scope and negated event classifiers is shown in Table 1. In each case the training data is the entire training data and the dev data is the entire dev data supplied by the organizers for this shared task. The scores are computed

[6]This "longer than four character" rule was manually created to correct for over-generalization observed in the training data. If the affix rule learner selected this value using the correct/incorrect counts as it does with the other rule parameters then this bit of language-specific tweaking would be unnecessary.

		Gold	System	TP	FP	FN	Precision (%)	Recall (%)	F1 (%)
Baseline	(train)	984	1034	382	56	602	87.21	38.82	53.73
	(dev)	173	164	34	9	139	79.07	19.65	31.48
Set 1	(train)	984	1034	524	56	460	90.34	53.25	67.00
	(dev)	173	164	60	9	113	86.96	34.68	49.59
Set 2	(train)	984	1034	666	56	318	92.24	67.68	78.07
	(dev)	173	164	61	9	112	87.14	35.26	50.21
System	(train)	984	1034	644	56	340	92.00	65.45	76.49
	(dev)	173	164	68	9	105	88.31	39.31	54.40

Table 1: Comparison of full negation scores for various feature sets.

by the evaluation program also supplied by the organizers. The baseline features are those provided in the data, with the exception of the syntactic tree fragment: word string in lowercase, lemma in lowercase, and POS tag. The "set 1" features are the remainder of the features described in section 3.2, with the exception of those of the path through the syntax tree from the cue token. The "set 2" features are the three baseline features plus the three features of the path through the syntax tree from the cue token: list of non-terminal labels from cue up to the lowest common parent, lowest common parent label concatenated with the relative distance in nodes between the siblings, list of non-terminals from the lowest common parent down to the token. The "system" feature set is the union of set 1 and set 2, and is the one used by the submitted system.

The baseline score is an F_1 of 31.5% (P=79.1%, R=19.7%) on the dev data. Using either feature set 1 or 2 results in substantially better performance. They achieve nearly the same score on the dev set with an F_1 of 50±0.5% (P=87±0.2%, R=35±0.3%) in which the difference is that between one case of true positive vs. false negative out of 173. The combination of those feature sets is better still though with an F_1 of 54.4% (P=88.3%, R=39.3%).

4 Results

Table 2 presents the scores computed for the system output on the held-out evaluation data. The F_1 for full negation is 48.1% (P=74%, R=35.6%), which is noticeably lower than that seen for the dev data (54.4%). That reduction is to be expected because the dev data was used for system tuning. There was also evidence of significant over-fitting to the training data because the F_1 for that was 76.5% (P=92%, R=65.5%). The largest component of the fall off in performance is in the recall.

The worst performing component of the system is the negated event detection which has an F_1 of 54.3% (P=58%, R=51%) on the evaluation data. One contributor to low precision for the negated event detector is that the root word of an affix cue is always output as a negated event, bypassing the negated event CRF sequence classifier. In the combined training and dev data there is a total of 1157 gold cues (and scopes) of which 738 (63.8%) are annotated as having a negated event. Of the 1198 cues the system outputs for that data, 188 (15.7%) are affix cues, each of which will also be output as a negated event. Therefore it would be reasonable to expect that approximately 16 (27.7%) of the false positives for the negated event in the evaluation (60) are due to that behavior.

	Gold	System	TP	FP	FN	Precision (%)	Recall (%)	F1 (%)
Cues	264	285	243	33	21	88.04	92.05	90.00
Scopes (no cue match)	249	270	158	33	89	82.90	64.26	72.40
Scope tokens (no cue match)	1805	1816	1512	304	293	83.26	83.77	83.51
Negated (no cue match)	173	154	83	60	80	58.04	50.92	54.25
Full negation	264	285	94	33	170	74.02	35.61	48.09
Cues B	264	285	243	33	21	85.26	92.05	88.52
Scopes B (no cue match)	249	270	158	33	89	59.26	64.26	61.66
Negated B (no cue match)	173	154	83	60	80	53.9	50.92	52.37
Full negation B	264	285	94	33	170	32.98	35.61	34.24

Table 2: System evaluation on held-out data.

5 Conclusion

This paper describes the system I implemented for the closed track of the *SEM 2012 Shared Task for negation cue, scope, and event resolution. The system's performance on the held-out evaluation data, an F_1 of 48.09% (P=74.02%, R=35.61%) for the full negation, relative to the other entries for the task is fourth among the six teams that participated.

The strongest part of this system is the scope resolver which performs at a level near that of the best-performing systems in this shared task. I think it is likely that the performance on scope resolution would be equivalent to them with a better negation cue detector. That is supported by the "no cue match" version of the scope resolution evaluation for which this system has the highest F_1 (72.4%).

Clearly the weakest link is the negated event detector. Since one obvious source of error is that the root word extracted when an affix cue is detected is always output as a negated event, a promising approach for improvement would be to instead utilize that as a feature for the negated event's CRF sequence tagger so that they have a chance to be filtered out in non-factual contexts.

Acknowledgements

I want to thank Roser Morante and Eduardo Blanco for organizing this task, the reviewers for their thorough and very helpful suggestions, and Emily Bender for her guidance.

References

Shashank Agarwal and Hong Yu. 2010. Biomedical negation scope detection with conditional random fields. *Journal of the American Medical Informatics Association*, *17*(6), 696–701. doi:10.1136/jamia.2010.003228

Chapman, W. W., Bridewell, W., Hanbury, P., Cooper, G. F., & Buchanan, B. G.. 2001. A simple algorithm for identifying negated findings and diseases in discharge summaries. *Journal of Biomedical Informatics*, *34*(5), 301–310. doi:10.1006/jbin.2001.1029

Andrew McCallum. 2002. MALLET: A Machine Learning for Language Toolkit. Retrieved from http://mallet.cs.umass.edu

Roser Morante and Eduardo Blanco. 2012. *SEM 2012 Shared Task: Resolving the Scope and Focus of Negation. *Proceedings of the First Joint Conference on Lexical and Computational Semantics*. Presented at the *SEM 2012, Montreal, Canada.

Roser Morante and Walter Daelemans. 2009. A Metalearning Approach to Processing the Scope of Negation. *Proceedings of the Thirteenth Conference on Computational Natural Language Learning (CoNLL-2009)* (pp. 21–29). Boulder, Colorado: Association for Computational Linguistics.

Roser Morante and Walter Daelemans. 2012. Conan-Doyle-neg: Annotation of negation in Conan Doyle stories. *Proceedings of the Eighth International Conference on Language Resources and Evaluation (LREC)*.

Pradeep G. Mutalik, Aniruddha Deshpande, and Prakash M. Nadkarni. 2001. Use of general-purpose negation detection to augment concept indexing of medical documents: a quantitative study using the UMLS. *Journal of the American Medical Informatics Association: JAMIA*, *8*(6), 598–609.

Lior Rokach, Roni Romano, and Oded Maimon. 2008. Negation recognition in medical narrative reports. *Information Retrieval*, *11*(6), 499–538. doi:10.1007/s10791-008-9061-0

Buzhou Tang, Xiaolong Wang, Xuan Wang, Bo Yuan, and Shixi Fan. 2010. A Cascade Method for Detecting Hedges and their Scope in Natural Language Text. *Proceedings of the Fourteenth Conference on Computational Natural Language Learning* (pp. 13–17). Uppsala, Sweden: Association for Computational Linguistics.

Qi Zhao, Chengjie Sun, Bingquan Liu, and Yong Cheng. 2010. Learning to Detect Hedges and their Scope Using CRF. *Proceedings of the Fourteenth Conference on Computational Natural Language Learning* (pp. 100–105). Uppsala, Sweden: Association for Computational Linguistics.

FBK: Exploiting Phrasal and Contextual Clues for Negation Scope Detection

Md. Faisal Mahbub Chowdhury † ‡
‡ Fondazione Bruno Kessler (FBK-irst), Trento, Italy
† University of Trento, Italy
chowdhury@fbk.eu

Abstract

Automatic detection of negation cues along with their scope and corresponding negated events is an important task that could benefit other natural language processing (NLP) tasks such as extraction of factual information from text, sentiment analysis, etc. This paper presents a system for this task that exploits phrasal and contextual clues apart from various token specific features. The system was developed for the participation in the Task 1 (closed track) of the *SEM 2012 Shared Task (Resolving the Scope and Focus of Negation), where it is ranked 3rd among the participating teams while attaining the highest F_1 score for negation cue detection.

1 Introduction

Negation is a linguistic phenomenon that can alter the meaning of a textual segment. While automatic detection of negation expressions (i.e. cues) in free text has been a subject of research interest for quite some time (e.g. Chapman et al. (2001), Elkin et al. (2005) etc), automatic detection of full scope of negation is a relatively new topic (Morante and Daelemans, 2009; Councill et al., 2010). Detection of negation cues, their scope and corresponding negated events in free text could improve accuracy in other natural language processing (NLP) tasks such as extraction of factual information from text, sentiment analysis, etc (Jia et al., 2009; Councill et al., 2010).

In this paper, we present a system that was developed for the participation in the Scope Detection task of the *SEM 2012 Shared Task[1]. The proposed system exploits phrasal and contextual clues apart from various token specific features. Exploitation of phrasal clues is not new for negation scope detection. But the way we encode this information (i.e. the features for phrasal clues) is novel and differs completely from the previous work (Councill et al., 2010; Morante and Daelemans, 2009). Moreover, the total number of features that we use is also comparatively lower. Furthermore, to the best of our knowledge, automatic negated event/property identification has not been explored prior to the *SEM 2012 Shared Task. So, our proposed approach for this particular sub-task is another contribution of this paper.

The remainder of this paper is organised as follows. First, we describe the scope detection task as well as the accompanying datasets in Section 2. Then in Section 3, we present how we approach the task. Following that, in Section 4, various empirical results and corresponding analyses are discussed. Finally, we summarize our work and discuss how the system can be further improved in Section 5.

2 Task Description: Scope Detection

The Scope Detection task (Task 1) of *SEM 2012 Shared Task deals with intra-sentential (i.e. context is single sentence) negations. According to the guidelines of the task (Morante and Daelemans, 2012; Morante et al., 2011), the scope of a negation cue(s) is composed of all negated concepts and negated event/property, if any. Negation cue(s) is

[1]http://www.clips.ua.ac.be/sem2012-st-neg/

	Training	Development	Test
Total sentence	3644	787	1089
Negation sentences	848	144	235
Negation cues	984	173	264
Cues with scopes	887	168	249
Tokens in scopes	6929	1348	1805
Negated events	616	122	173

Table 1: Various statistics of the training, development and test datasets.

not considered as part of the scope. Cues and scopes may be discontinuous.

The organisers provided three sets of data – training, development and test datasets, all consisting of stories by *Conan Doyle*. The training dataset contains Chapters 1-14 from `The Hound of the Baskervilles`. While development dataset contains `The Adventures of Wisteria Lodge`. For testing, two other stories, `The Adventure of the Red Circle` and `The Adventure of the Cardboard Box`, were released during the evaluation period of the shared task. Table 1 shows various statistics regarding the datasets.

In the training and development data, all occurrences of negation are annotated. For each negation cue, the cue and corresponding scope are marked, as well as the negated event/property, if any. The data is provided in CoNLL-2005 Shared Task format. Table 2 shows an example of annotated data where "un" is the negation cue, "his own conventional appearance" is the scope, and "conventional" is the negated property.

The test data has a format similar to the training data except that only the Columns 1–7 (as shown in Table 2) are provided. Participating systems have to output the remaining column(s).

During a random checking we have found at least 2 missing annotations[2] in the development data. So, there might be few wrong/missing annotations in the other datasets, too.

There were two tracks in the task. For the **closed track**, systems have to be built strictly with information contained in the given training corpus. This includes the automatic annotations that the organizers provide for different levels of analysis (POS tags, lemmas and parse trees). For the **open track**, systems can be developed making use of any kind of external tools and resources.

We participated in the **closed track** of the scope detection task.

3 Our Approach

We approach the subtasks (i.e. cue, scope and negated event detection) of the Task 1 as sequence identification problems and train three different 1st order Conditional Random Field (CRF) classifiers (i.e. one for each of them) using the MALLET machine learning toolkit (McCallum, 2002). All these classifiers use ONLY the information available inside the training corpus (i.e. training and development datasets) as provided by the task organisers, which is the requirement of the closed track.

3.1 Negation Cue Detection

At first, our system automatically collects a vocabulary of all the positive tokens (i.e. those which are not negation cues) of length greater than 3 characters, after excluding negation cue affixes (if any), from the training data and uses them to extract features that could be useful to identify potential negation cues which are subtokens (e.g. *un*able). We also create a list of highly probable negation expressions (henceforth, *NegExpList*) from the training data based on frequencies. The list consists of the following terms – *nor, neither, without, nobody, none, nothing, never, not, no, nowhere,* and *non*.

Negation cue subtokens are identified if the token itself is predicted as a negation cue by the classifier and has one of the following affixes that are collected from the training data – *less, un, dis, im, in, non, ir*.

Lemmas are converted to lower case inside the feature set. Additional post-processing is done to annotate some obvious negation expressions that are seen inside the training data but sometimes missed by the classifier during prediction on the development data. These expressions include *neither, nobody, save for, save upon,* and *by no means*. A spe-

[2]Annotations for the following negation cues (and their corresponding scope/negated events) in the development data are missing – {*cue: "no", token no.: 8, sentence no.: 237, chapter: wisteria01*} and {*cue: "never", token no.: 3, sentence no.: 358, chapter: wisteria02*}.

wisteria01	60	0	Our	Our	PRP$	(S(NP*	_	_	_
wisteria01	60	1	client	client	NN	*)	_	_	_
wisteria01	60	2	looked	look	VBD	(VP*	_	_	_
wisteria01	60	3	down	down	RB	(ADVP*)	_	_	_
wisteria01	60	4	with	with	IN	(PP*	_	_	_
wisteria01	60	5	a	a	DT	(NP(NP*	_	_	_
wisteria01	60	6	rueful	rueful	JJ	*	_	_	_
wisteria01	60	7	face	face	NN	*)	_	_	_
wisteria01	60	8	at	at	IN	(PP*	_	_	_
wisteria01	60	9	his	his	PRP$	(NP*	_	his	_
wisteria01	60	10	own	own	JJ	*	_	own	_
wisteria01	60	11	unconventional	unconventional	JJ	*	un	conventional	conventional
wisteria01	60	12	appearance	appearance	NN	*)))))	_	appearance	_

Table 2: Example of the data provided for *SEM 2012 Shared Task.

Feature name	Description
POS_i	Part-of-speech of $token_i$
$Lemma_i$	Lemma form of $token_i$
$Lemma_{i-1}$	Lemma form of $token_{i-1}$
hasNegPrefix	If $token_i$ has a negation prefix and is found inside the automatically created vocabulary
hasNegSuffix	If $token_i$ has a negation suffix and is found inside the automatically created vocabulary
matchesNegExp	If $token_i$ is found in *NegExpList*

Table 3: Feature set for negation cue classifier

cial check is done for the phrase *"none the less"* which is marked as a non-negation expression inside the training data.

Finally, a CRF model is trained using the collected features (see Table 3) and used to predict negation cue on test instance.

3.2 Scope and Negated Event Detection

Once the negation cues are identified, the next tasks are to detect scopes of the cues and negated events which are approached independently using separate classifiers. If a sentence has multiple negation cues, we create separate training/test instance of the sentence for each of the cues.

Tables 4 and 5 show the feature sets that are used to train classifiers. Both the feature sets exclusively use various phrasal clues, e.g. whether the (closest) NP, VP, S or SBAR containing the token under consideration (i.e. $token_i$) and that of the negation cue are different. Further phrasal clues that are exploited include whether the least common phrase of $token_i$ has no other phrase as child, and also list of the counts of different common phrasal categories (starting from the root of the parse tree) that contain $token_i$ and the cue. These latter two types of phrasal clue features are found effective for the negated event detection but not for scope detection.

We also use various token specific features (e.g. lemma, POS, etc) and contextual features (e.g. lemma of the 1st word of the corresponding sentence, position of the token with respect to the cue, presence of conjunction and special characters between $token_i$ and the cue, etc). Finally, new features are created by combining different features of the neighbouring tokens within a certain range of the $token_i$. The range values are selected empirically.

Once scopes and negated events are identified (separately), the prediction output of all the three classifiers are merged to produce the full negation scope.

Initially, a number of features is chosen by doing manual inspection (randomly) of the scopes/negated events in the training data as well analysing syntactic structures of the corresponding sentences. Some of those features (e.g. POS of previous token for scope detection) which are found (empirically) as not useful for performance improvement have been discarded.

Feature name:	Description
$Lemma_1$	Lemma of the 1st word of the sentence
POS_i	Part-of-speech of $token_i$
$Lemma_i$	Lemma of $token_i$
$Lemma_{i-1}$	Lemma of $token_{i-1}$
isCue	If $token_i$ is negation cue
isCueSubToken	If a subtoken of $token_i$ is negation cue
isCcBetCueAndCurTok	If there is a conjunction between $token_i$ and cue
isSpecCharBetCueAndCurTok	If there is a non-alphanumeric token between $token_i$ and cue
Position	Position of $token_i$: before, after or same w.r.t. the cue
isCueAndCurTokInDiffNP	If $token_i$ and cue belong to different NPs
isCueAndCurTokInDiffVP	If $token_i$ and cue belong to different VPs
isCueAndCurTokInDiffSorSBAR	If $token_i$ and cue belong to different S or SBAR
FeatureConjunctions	New features by combining those of $token_{i-2}$ to $token_{i+2}$

Table 4: Feature set for negation scope classifier. **Bold** features are the phrasal clue features.

Feature name	Description
$Lemma_1$	Lemma of the 1st word of the sentence
POS_i	Part-of-speech of $token_i$
$Lemma_i$	Lemma of $token_i$
POS_{i-1}	POS of $token_{i-1}$
isCue	If $token_i$ is negation cue
isCueSubToken	If a subtoken of $token_i$ is negation cue
isSpecCharBetCueAndCurTok	If there is a non-alphanumeric token between $token_i$ and cue
IsModal	If POS of $token_i$ is MD
IsDT	If POS of $token_i$ is DT
isCueAndCurTokInDiffNP	If $token_i$ and cue belong to different NPs
isCueAndCurTokInDiffVP	If $token_i$ and cue belong to different VPs
isCueAndCurTokInDiffSorSBAR	If $token_i$ and cue belong to different S or SBAR
belongToSamePhrase	If the least common phrase of $token_i$ and cue do not contain other phrase
CPcatBetCueAndCurTok	All common phrase categories (and their counts) that contain $token_i$ and cue
FeatureConjunctions	New features by combining those of $token_{i-3}$ to $token_{i+1}$

Table 5: Feature set for negated event classifier. **Bold** features are the phrasal clue features.

We left behind two verifications unintentionally which should have been included. One of them is to take into account whether a sentence is a factual statement or a question before negated event detection. The other is to check whether a predicted negated event is found inside the predicted scope of the corresponding negation cue.

4 Results and Discussions

In this section, we discuss various empirical results on the development data and test data. Details regarding the evaluation criteria are described in Morante and Blanco (2012).

4.1 Results on the Development Dataset

Our feature sets are selected after doing a number of experiments by combining various potential feature types. In these experiments, the system is trained on the training data and tested on development data. Due to time limitation we could not do parameter tuning for CRF model training which we assume could further improve the results.

Table 8 shows the results[3] on the development data using the feature sets described in Section 3. There are two noticeable things in these results. Firstly, there is a very high F_1 score (93.29%) obtained for negation cue identification. And secondly, the precision obtained for scope detection (97.92%) is very high as well.

Table 6 shows the results (of negated event iden-

[3]All the results reported in this paper, apart from the ones on test data which are directly obtained from the organisers, reported in this paper are computed using the official evaluation script provided by the organisers.

	TP	FP	FN	Prec.	Rec.	F_1
Using only contextual and token specific features	71	16	46	81.61	60.68	69.61
After adding phrasal clue features	81	17	34	82.65	70.43	76.05

Table 6: Negated event detection results on development data with and without the 5 phrasal clue feature types. The results are obtained using gold annotation of negation cues. Note that, TP+FN is not the same. However, since these results are computed using the official evaluation script, we are not sure why there is this mismatch.

Using negation cues annotated by our system						
	TP	FP	FN	Prec.	Rec.	F_1
Scope detection	94	2	74	97.92	55.95	71.21
Event detection	63	19	51	76.83	55.26	64.28
Using gold annotations of negation cues						
	TP	FP	FN	Prec.	Rec.	F_1
Scope detection	103	0	65	100.00	61.31	76.02
Event detection	81	17	34	82.65	70.43	76.05

Table 7: Scope and negated event detection results on development data with and without gold annotations of negation cues. Note that, for negated events, TP+FN is not the same. However, since these results are computed using the official evaluation script, we are not sure why there is this mismatch.

tification) obtained before and after the usage of our proposed 5 phrasal clue feature types (using gold annotation of negation cues). As we can see, there is a significant improvement in recall (almost 10 points) due to the usage of phrasal clues which ultimately leads to a considerable increase (almost 6.5 points) of F_1 score.

4.2 Results on the Official Test Dataset

Table 9 shows official results of our system in the *SEM 2012 Shared Task (closed track) of scope detection, as provided by the organisers. It should be noted that the test dataset is almost 1.5 times bigger than the combined training corpus (i.e. training + development data). Despite this fact, the results of cue and scope detection on the test data are almost similar as those on the development data. However, there is a sharp drop (almost 4 points lower F_1 score) in negated event identification, primarily due to lower precision. This resulted in a lower F_1 score (almost 4.5 points) for full negation identification.

4.3 Further Analyses of the Results and Feature Sets

Our analyses of the empirical results (conducted on the development data) suggest that negation cue identification largely depends on the token itself rather than its surrounding syntactic construction. Although context (i.e. immediate neighbouring tokens) are also important, the significance of a vocabulary of positive tokens (for the identification of negation cue subtokens) and the list of negation cue expressions is quite obvious. In a recently published study, Morante (2010) listed a number of negation cues and argued that their total number are actually not exhaustive. We refrained from using the cues listed in that paper (instead we built a list automatically from the training data) since additional knowledge/resource outside the training data was not allowed for the closed track. But we speculate that usage of such list of expressions as well as an external dictionary of (positive) words can further boost the high performance that we already achieved.

Since scope and negation event detection are dependent on the correct identification of cues, we have done separate evaluation on the development data using the gold cues (instead of predicting the cues first). As the results in Table 7 show, there is a considerable increment in the results for both scope and event detection if the correct annotation of cues are available.

The general trend of errors that we have observed in scope detection is that the more distant a token is from the negation cue in the phrase structure tree (of the corresponding sentence) the harder it becomes for the classifier to predict whether the token should be included in the scope or not. For example, in the sentence "*I am not aware that in my whole life such a thing has ever happened before.*" of the development data, the negation cue "*not*" has scope over the whole sentence. But the scope classifier fails to include the last 4 words in the scope. Perhaps syntactic dependency can provide complementary information in such cases.

As for the negated event identification errors, the majority of the prediction errors (on the development data) occurred for verb and noun tokens which are mostly immediately preceded by the negation cue. Information of syntactic dependency should be

	Gold	System	TP	FP	FN	Prec. (%)	Rec. (%)	F_1 (%)
Cues:	173	156	153	2	20	98.71	88.44	93.29
Scopes (cue match):	168	150	94	2	74	97.92	55.95	71.21
Scopes (no cue match):	168	150	94	2	74	97.92	55.95	71.21
Scope tokens (no cue match):	1348	1132	1024	108	324	90.46	75.96	82.58
Negated (no cue match):	122	90	63	19	51	76.83	55.26	64.28
Full negation:	173	156	67	2	106	97.10	38.73	55.37
Cues B:	173	156	153	2	20	98.08	88.44	93.01
Scopes B (cue match):	168	150	94	2	74	62.67	55.95	59.12
Scopes B (no cue match):	168	150	94	2	74	62.67	55.95	59.12
Negated B (no cue match):	122	90	63	19	51	70.00	55.26	61.76
Full negation B:	173	156	67	2	106	42.95	38.73	40.73
# Sentences: 787			# Negation sentences: 144			# Negation sentences with errors: 97		
% Correct sentences: 87.55						% Correct negation sentences: 32.64		

Table 8: Results on the development data. In the *"B"* variant of the results, *Precision = TP / System*, instead of *Precision = TP / (TP + FP)*.

helpful to reduce such errors, too.

5 Conclusions

In this paper, we presented our approach for negation cue, scope and negated event detection task (*closed track*) of *SEM 2012 Shared Task, where our system ranked 3rd among the participating teams for full negation detection while obtaining the best F_1 score for negation cue detection. Interestingly, according to the results provided by the organisers, our system performs better than all the systems of the *open track* except one (details of these results are described in (Morante and Blanco, 2012)).

The features exploited by our system include phrasal and contextual clues as well as token specific information. Empirical results show that the system achieves very high precision for scope detection. The results also imply that the novel phrasal clue features exploited by our system improve identification of negated events significantly.

We believe the system can be further improved in a number of ways. Firstly, this can be done by incorporating linguistic knowledge as described in Morante (2010). Secondly, we did not take into account whether a sentence is a factual statement or a question before negated event detection. We also did not check whether a predicted negated event is found inside the predicted scope of the corresponding negation cue. These verifications should increase the results more. Finally, previous work reported that usage of syntactic dependency information helps in scope detection (Councill et al., 2010). Hence, this could be another possible direction for improvement.

Acknowledgments

The author would like to thank Alberto Lavelli and the anonymous reviewers for various useful feedback regarding the manuscript.

References

WW Chapman, W Bridewell, P Hanbury, GF Cooper, and BG Buchanan. 2001. A Simple Algorithm for Identifying Negated Findings and Diseases in Discharge Summaries. *Journal of Biomedical Informatics*, 34(5):301–10.

I Councill, R McDonald, and L Velikovich. 2010. Whats Great and Whats Not: Learning to Classify the Scope of Negation for Improved Sentiment Analysis. In *Proceedings of the Workshop on Negation and Speculation in Natural Language Processing*, pages 51–59, Uppsala, Sweden.

P Elkin, S Brown, B Bauer, C Husser, W Carruth, L Bergstrom, and D Wahner-Roedler. 2005. A controlled trial of automated classification of negation from clinical notes. *BMC Medical Informatics and Decision Making*, 5(1):13.

L Jia, C Yu, and W Meng. 2009. The Effect of Negation on Sentiment Analysis and Retrieval Effectiveness. In

	Gold	System	TP	FP	FN	Prec. (%)	Rec. (%)	F_1 (%)
Cues:	264	263	241	17	23	93.41	91.29	92.34
Scopes (cue match):	249	249	145	18	104	88.96	58.23	70.39
Scopes (no cue match):	249	249	145	18	104	88.96	58.23	70.39
Scope tokens (no cue match):	1805	1825	1488	337	317	81.53	82.44	81.98
Negated (no cue match):	173	154	93	52	71	64.14	56.71	60.20
Full negation:	264	263	96	17	168	84.96	36.36	50.93
Cues B:	264	263	241	17	23	91.63	91.29	91.46
Scopes B (cue match):	249	249	145	18	104	58.23	58.23	58.23
Scopes B (no cue match):	249	249	145	18	104	58.23	58.23	58.23
Negated B (no cue match):	173	154	93	52	71	60.39	56.71	58.49
Full negation B:	264	263	96	17	168	36.50	36.36	36.43
# Sentences: 1089		# Negation sentences: 235			# Negation sentences with errors: 151			
% Correct sentences: 84.94					% Correct negation sentences: 35.74			

Table 9: Results on the *SEM 2012 Shared Task (closed track) test data provided by the organisers. In the *"B"* variant of the results, *Precision = TP / System*, instead of *Precision = TP / (TP + FP)*.

Proceedings of the 18th ACM Conference on Information and Knowledge Management (CIKM 2009), pages 1827–1830, Hong Kong, China.

AK McCallum. 2002. MALLET: A machine learning for language toolkit. http://mallet.cs.umass.edu,.

R Morante and E Blanco. 2012. *SEM 2012 Shared Task: Resolving the Scope and Focus of Negation. In *Proceedings of the First Joint Conference on Lexical and Computational Semantics (*SEM 2012)*, Montreal, Canada.

R Morante and W Daelemans. 2009. A Metalearning Approach to Processing the Scope of Negation. In *Proceedings of CoNLL 2009*, pages 28–36, Boulder, Colorado, USA.

R Morante and W Daelemans. 2012. ConanDoyle-neg: Annotation of Negation in Conan Doyle Stories. In *Proceedings of the 8th International Conference on Language Resources and Evaluation (LREC 2012)*, Istanbul, Turkey.

R Morante, S Schrauwen, and W Daelemans. 2011. Annotation of Negation Cues and Their Scope Guidelines v1.0. Technical Report CLiPS Technical Report 3, CLiPS, Antwerp, Belgium.

R Morante. 2010. Descriptive Analysis of Negation Cue in Biomedical Texts. In *Proceedings of the 7th International Conference on Language Resources and Evaluation (LREC 2010)*, Malta.

SemEval-2012 Task 1: English Lexical Simplification

Lucia Specia
Department of Computer Science
University of Sheffield
L.Specia@sheffield.ac.uk

Sujay Kumar Jauhar
Research Group in Computational Linguistics
University of Wolverhampton
Sujay.KumarJauhar@wlv.ac.uk

Rada Mihalcea
Department of Computer Science and Engineering
University of North Texas
rada@cs.unt.edu

Abstract

We describe the English Lexical Simplification task at SemEval-2012. This is the first time such a shared task has been organized and its goal is to provide a framework for the evaluation of systems for lexical simplification and foster research on context-aware lexical simplification approaches. The task requires that annotators and systems rank a number of alternative substitutes – all deemed adequate – for a target word in context, according to how "simple" these substitutes are. The notion of simplicity is biased towards non-native speakers of English. Out of nine participating systems, the best scoring ones combine context-dependent and context-independent information, with the strongest individual contribution given by the frequency of the substitute regardless of its context.

1 Introduction

Lexical Simplification is a subtask of Text Simplification (Siddharthan, 2006) concerned with replacing words or short phrases by simpler variants in a context aware fashion (generally synonyms), which can be understood by a wider range of readers. It generally envisages a certain human target audience that may find it difficult or impossible to understand complex words or phrases, e.g., children, people with poor literacy levels or cognitive disabilities, or second language learners. It is similar in many respects to the task of Lexical Substitution (McCarthy and Navigli, 2007) in that it involves determining adequate substitutes in context, but in this case on the basis of a predefined criterion: simplicity.

A common pipeline for a Lexical Simplification system includes at least three major components: (i) complexity analysis: selection of words or phrases in a text that are considered complex for the reader and/or task at hand; (ii) substitute lookup: search for adequate replacement words or phrases deemed complex in context, e.g., taking synonyms (with the same sense) from a thesaurus or finding similar words/phrases in a corpus using distributional similarity metrics; and (iii) context-based ranking: ranking of substitutes according to how simple they are to the reader/task at hand.

As an example take the sentence: *"Hitler committed terrible atrocities during the second World War."* The system would first identify complex words, e.g. *atrocities*, then search for substitutes that might adequately replace it. A thesaurus lookup would yield the following synonyms: *abomination*, *cruelty*, *enormity* and *violation*, but *enormity* should be dropped as it does not fit the context appropriately. Finally, the system would determine the simplest of these substitutes, e.g., *cruelty*, and use it to replace the complex word, yielding the sentence: *"Hitler committed terrible cruelties during the second World War."*.

Different from other subtasks of Text Simplification like Syntactic Simplification, which have been relatively well studied, Lexical Simplification has received less attention. Although a few recent attempts explicitly address dependency on context (de Belder et al., 2010; Yatskar et al., 2010; Biran et al., 2011; Specia, 2010), most approaches are context-independent (Candido et al., 2009; Devlin and Tait, 1998). In addition, a general deeper understanding of the problem is yet to be gained. As a first attempt to address this problem in the shape of a shared task, the English Simplification task at SemEval-2012 focuses on the third component, which we believe is the core of the Lexical Simplification problem.

The SemEval-2012 shared task on English Lexical Simplification has been conceived with the following main purposes: advancing the state-of-the-art Lexical Simplification approaches, and providing a common framework for evaluation of Lexical Simplification systems for participants and other researchers interested in the field. Another central motive of such a shared task is to bring awareness to the general vagueness associated with the notion of lexical simplicity. Our hypothesis is that in addition to the notion of a target application/reader, the notion of simplicity is highly context-dependent. In other words, given the same list of substitutes for a given target word with the **same sense**, we expect different orderings of these substitutes in different contexts. We hope that participation in this shared task will help discover some underlying traits of lexical simplicity and furthermore shed some light on how this may be leveraged in future work.

2 Task definition

Given a short context, a target word in English, and several substitutes for the target word that are deemed adequate for that context, the goal of the English Simplification task at SemEval-2012 is to rank these substitutes according to how "simple" they are, allowing ties. Simple words/phrases are loosely defined as those which can be understood by a wide range of people, including those with low literacy levels or some cognitive disability, children, and non-native speakers of English. In particular, the data provided as part of the task is annotated by **fluent but non-native speakers of English**.

The task thus essentially involves comparing words or phrases and determining their order of complexity. By ranking the candidates, as opposed to categorizing them into specific labels (simple, moderate, complex, etc.), we avoid the need for a fixed number of categories and for more subjective judgments. Also ranking enables a more natural and intuitive way for humans (and systems) to perform annotations by preventing them from treating each individual case in isolation, as opposed to relative to each other. However, the inherent subjectivity introduced by ranking entails higher disagreement among human annotators, and more complexity for systems to tackle.

3 Corpus compilation

The trial and test corpora were created from the corpus of SemEval-2007 shared task on Lexical Substitution (McCarthy and Navigli, 2007). This decision was motivated by the similarity between the two tasks. Moreover the existing corpus provided an adequate solution given time and cost constraints for our corpus creation. Given existing contexts with the original target word replaced by a placeholder and the lists of substitutes (including the target word), annotators (and systems) are required to rank substitutes in order of simplicity for each context.

3.1 SemEval-2007 - LS corpus

The corpus from the shared task on Lexical Substitution (LS) at SemEval-2007 is a selection of sentences, or *contexts*, extracted from the English Internet Corpus of English (Sharoff, 2006). It contains samples of English texts crawled from the web.

This selection makes up the dataset of a total of $2,010$ contexts which are divided into **Trial** and **Test** sets, consisting of 300 and 1710 contexts respectively. It covers a total of 201 (mostly polysemous) target words, including nouns, verbs, adjectives and adverbs, and each of the target words is shown in 10 different contexts. Annotators had been asked to suggest up to three different substitutes (words or short phrases) for each of the target words within their contexts. The substitutes were lemmatized unless it was deemed that the lemmatization would alter the meaning of the substitute. Annotators were all native English speakers and each annotated the entire dataset. Here is an example of a context for the target word "bright":

> `<lexelt item="bright.a">`
>
> `<instance id="1">`
>
> `<context>`During the siege, George Robertson had appointed Shuja-ul-Mulk, who was a `<head>`bright`</head>` boy only 12 years old and the youngest surviving son of Aman-ul-Mulk, as the ruler of Chitral.`</context>`

```
</instance> ... </lexelt>
```

The gold-standard document contains each target word along with a ranked list of its possible substitutes, e.g., for the context above, three annotators suggested "intelligent" and "clever" as substitutes for "bright", while only one annotator came up with "smart":

bright.a 1:: intelligent 3; clever 3; smart 1;

3.2 SemEval-2012 Lexical Simplification corpus

Given the list of contexts and each respective list of substitutes we asked annotators to rank substitutes for each individual context in ascending order of complexity. Since the notion of textual simplicity varies from individual to individual, we carefully chose a group of annotators in an attempt to capture as much of a common notion of simplicity as possible. For practical reasons, we selected annotators with high proficiency levels in English as second language learners - all with a university first degree in different subjects.

The Trial dataset was annotated by four people while the Test dataset was annotated by five people. In both cases each annotator tagged the complete dataset.

Inter-annotator agreement was computed using an adaptation of the **kappa** index with pairwise rank comparisons (Callison-Burch et al., 2011). This is also the primary evaluation metric for participating systems in the shared task, and it is covered in more detail in Section 4.

The inter-annotator agreement was computed for each pair of annotators and averaged over all possible pairs for a final agreement score. On the Trial dataset, a kappa index of 0.386 was found, while for the Test dataset, a kappa index of 0.398 was found. It may be noted that certain annotators disagreed considerably with all others. For example, on the Test set, if annotations from one judge are removed, the average inter-annotator agreement rises to 0.443. While these scores are apparently low, the highly subjective nature of the annotation task must be taken into account. According to the reference values for other tasks, this level of agreement is considered "moderate" (Callison-Burch et al., 2011).

It is interesting to note that higher inter-annotator agreement scores were achieved between annotators with similar language and/or educational backgrounds. The highest of any pairwise annotator agreement (0.52) was achieved between annotators of identical language and educational background, as well as very similar levels of English proficiency. High agreement scores were also achieved between annotators with first languages belonging to the same language family.

Finally, it is also worth noticing that this agreement metric is highly sensitive to small differences in annotation, thus leading to overly pessimistic scores. A brief analysis reveals that annotators often agree on clusters of simplicity and the source of the disagreement comes from the rankings within these clusters.

Finally, the gold-standard annotations for the Trial and Test datasets – against which systems are to be evaluated – were generated by averaging the annotations from all annotators. This was done context by context where each substitution was attributed a score based upon the average of the rankings it was ascribed. The substitutions were then sorted in ascending order of scores, i.e., lowest score (highest average ranking) first. Tied scores were grouped together to form a single rank. For example, assume that for a certain context, four annotators provided rankings as given below, where multiple candidates between { } indicate ties:

Annotator 1: {clear} {light} {bright} {luminous} {well-lit}

Annotator 2: {well-lit} {clear} {light} {bright} {luminous}

Annotator 3: {clear} {bright} {light} {luminous} {well-lit}

Annotator 4: {bright} {well-lit} {luminous} {clear} {light}

Thus the word "clear", having been ranked 1st, 2nd, 1st and 4th by each of the annotators respectively is given an averaged ranking score of 2. Similarly "light" = 3.25, "bright" = 2.5, "luminous" = 4 and "well-lit" = 3.25. Consequently the gold-standard ranking for this context is:

Gold: {clear} {bright} {light, well-lit} {luminous}

3.3 Context-dependency

As mentioned in Section 1, one of our hypotheses was that the notion of simplicity is context-dependent. In other words, that the ordering of substitutes for different occurrences of a target word with a given sense is highly dependent on the contexts in which such a target word appears. In order to verify this hypothesis quantitatively, we further analyzed the gold-standard annotations of the Trial and Test datasets. We assume that identical lists of substitutes for different occurrences of a given target word ensure that such a target word has the same sense in all these occurrences. For every target word, we then generate all pairs of contexts containing the exact same initial list of substitutes and check the proportion of these contexts for which human annotators ranked the substitutes differently. We also check for cases where only the top-ranked substitute is different. The numbers obtained are shown in Table 1.

	Trial	Test
1) # context pairs	1350	7695
2) # 1) with same list	60	242
3) # 2) with different rankings	24	139
4) # 2) with different top substitute	19	38

Table 1: Analysis on the context-dependency of the notion of simplicity.

Although the proportion of pairs of contexts with the same list of substitutes is very low (less than 5%), it is likely that there are many other occurrences of a target word with the same sense and slightly different lists of substitutes. Further manual inspection is necessary to determine the actual numbers. Nevertheless, from the observed sample it is possible to conclude that humans will, in fact, rank the same set of words (with the same sense) differently depending on the context (on an average in 40-57% of the instances).

4 Evaluation metric

No standard metric has yet been defined for evaluating Lexical Simplification systems. Evaluating such systems is a challenging problem due to the aforementioned subjectivity of the task. Since this is a ranking task, rank correlation metrics are desirable. However, metrics such as Spearman's Rank Correlation are not reliable on the limited number of data points available for comparison on each ranking (note that the nature of the problem enforces a context-by-context ranking, as opposed to a global score), Other metrics for localized, pairwise rank correlation, such as Kendall's Tau, disregard ties, – which are important for our purposes – and are thus not suitable.

The main evaluation metric proposed for this shared task is in fact a measure of inter-annotator agreement, which is used for both contrasting two human annotators (Section 3.2) and contrasting a system output to the average of human annotations that together forms the gold-standard.

Out metric is based on the kappa index (Cohen, 1960) which in spite of many criticisms is widely used for its simplicity and adaptability for different applications. The generalized form of the kappa index is

$$\kappa = \frac{P(A) - P(E)}{1 - P(E)}$$

where $P(A)$ denotes the proportion of times two annotators agree and $P(E)$ gives the probability of agreement by chance between them.

In order to apply the kappa index for a ranking task, we follow the method proposed by (Callison-Burch et al., 2011) for measuring agreement over judgments of translation quality. This method defines $P(A)$ and $P(E)$ in such a way that it now counts agreement whenever annotators concur upon the order of pairwise ranks. Thus, if one annotator ranked two given words 1 and 3, and the second annotator ranked them 3 and 7 respectively, they are still in agreement. Formally, assume that two annotators $A1$ and $A2$ rank two instance a and b. Then $P(A)$ = the proportion of times $A1$ and $A2$ agree on a ranking, where an occurrence of agreement is counted whenever $rank(a < b)$ or $rank(a = b)$ or $rank(a > b)$.

$P(E)$ (the likelihood that annotators $A1$ and $A2$ agree by chance) is based upon the probability that both of them assign the same ranking order to a and b. Given that the probability of getting $rank(a < b)$ by any annotator is $P(a < b)$, the probability that *both* annotators get $rank(a < b)$ is $P(a < b)^2$ (agreement is achieved when $A1$ assigns $a < b$ by chance and $A2$ also assigns $a < b$). Similarly, the probability of chance agreement for $rank(a = b)$ and $rank(a > b)$ are $P(a = b)^2$ and $P(a > b)^2$ respectively. Thus:

$$P(E) = P(a < b)^2 + P(a = b)^2 + P(a > b)^2$$

However, the counts of $rank(a < b)$ and $rank(a > b)$ are inextricably linked, since for any particular case of $a_1 < b_1$, it follows that $b_1 > a_1$, and thus the two counts must be incremented equally. Therefore, over the entire space of ranked pairs, the probabilities remain exactly the same. In essence, after counting for $P(a = b)$, the remaining probability mass is equally split between $P(a < b)$ and $P(a > b)$. Therefore:

$$P(a < b) = P(a > b) = \frac{1 - P(a = b)}{2}$$

Kappa is calculated for every pair of ranked items for a given context, and then averaged to get an overall kappa score:

$$\kappa = \frac{\sum_{n=1}^{|N|} \frac{P_n(A) - P_n(E)}{1 - P_n(E)}}{|N|}$$

where N is the total number of contexts, and $P_n(A)$ and $P_n(E)$ are calculated based on counts extracted from the data on the particular context n.

The functioning of this evaluation metric is illustrated by the following example:

> **Context:** During the siege, George Robertson had appointed Shuja-ul-Mulk, who was a _____ boy only 12 years old and the youngest surviving son of Aman-ul-Mulk, as the ruler of Chitral.
>
> **Gold:** {intelligent} {clever} {smart} {bright}
>
> **System:** {intelligent} {bright} {clever, smart}

Out of the 6 distinct unordered pairs of lexical items, *system* and *gold* agreed 3 times. Consequently, $P_n(A) = \frac{3}{6}$. In addition, $count(a = b) = 1$. Thus, $P_n(a = b) = \frac{1}{12}$. Which gives a $P(E) = \frac{41}{96}$ and the final kappa score for this particular context of 0.13.

The statistical significance of the results from two systems A and B is measured using the method of **Approximate Randomization**, which has been shown to be a robust approach for several NLP tasks (Noreen, 1989). The randomization is run $1,000$ times and if the p-value is ≤ 0.05 the difference between systems A and B is asserted as being statistically significance.

5 Baselines

We defined three baseline lexical simplification systems for this task, as follows.

L-Sub Gold: This baseline uses the gold-standard annotations from the Lexical Substitution corpus of SemEval-2007 as is. In other words, the ranking is based on the *goodness of fit* of substitutes for a context, as judged by human annotators. This method also serves to show that the Lexical Substitution and Lexical Simplification tasks are indeed different.

Random: This baseline provides a randomized order of the substitutes for every context. The process of randomization is such that is allows the occurrence of ties.

Simple Freq.: This simple frequency baseline uses the frequency of the substitutes as extracted from the Google Web 1T Corpus (Brants and Franz, 2006) to rank candidate substitutes within each context.

The results in Table 2 show that the "L-Sub Gold" and "Random" baselines perform very poorly on both Trial and Test sets. In particular, the reason for the poor scores for "L-Sub Gold" can be attributed to the fact that it yields many ties, whereas the gold-standard presents almost no ties. Our kappa metric tends to penalize system outputs with too many ties, since the probability of agreement by chance is primarily computed on the basis of the number of ties present in the two rankings being compared (see Section 4).

The "Simple Freq." baseline, on the other hand, performs very strongly, in spite of its simplistic approach, which is entirely agnostic to context. In fact it surpasses the average inter-annotator agreement on both Trial and Test datasets. Indeed, the scores on the Test set approach the best inter-annotator agreement scores between any two annotators.

	Trial	Test
L-Sub Gold	0.050	0.106
Random	0.016	0.012
Simple Freq.	0.397	0.471

Table 2: Baseline kappa scores on trial and test sets

6 Results and Discussion

6.1 Participants

Five sites submitted one or more systems to the task, totaling nine systems:

ANNLOR-lmbing: This system (Ligozat et al., 2012) relies on language models probabilities, and builds on the principle of the Simple Frequency baseline. While the baseline uses Google n-grams to rank substitutes, this approach uses Microsoft Web n-grams in the same way. Additionally characteristics, such as the contexts of each term to be substituted, were integrated into the system. Microsoft Web N-gram Service was used to obtain log likelihood probabilities for text units, composed of the lexical item and 4 words to the left and right from the surrounding context.

ANNLOR-simple: The system (Ligozat et al., 2012) is based on Simple English Wikipedia frequencies, with the motivation that the language used in this version of Wikipedia is targeted towards people who are not first-language English speakers. Word n-grams (n = 1-3) and their frequencies were extracted from this corpus using the Text-NSP Perl module and a ranking of the possible substitutes of a target word according to these frequencies in descending order was produced.

EMNLPCPH-ORD1: The system performs a series of pairwise comparisons between candidates. A binary classifier is learned purpose using the Trial dataset and artificial unlabeled data extracted based on Wordnet and a corpus in a semi-supervised fashion. A co-training procedure that lets each classifier increase the other classifier's training set with selected instances from the unlabeled dataset is used. The features include word and character n-gram probabilities of candidates and contexts using web corpora, distributional differences of candidate in a corpus of "easy" sentences and a corpus of normal sentences, syntactic complexity of documents that are similar to the given context, candidate length, and letter-wise recognizability of candidate as measured by a trigram LM. The first feature sets for co-training combines the syntactic complexity, character trigram LM and basic word length features, resulting in 29 features against the remaining 21.

EMNLPCPH-ORD2: This is a variant of the EMNLPCPH-ORD1 system where the first feature set pools all syntactic complexity features and Wikipedia-based features (28 features) against all the remaining 22 features in the second group.

SB-mmSystem: The approach (Amoia and Romanelli, 2012) builds on the baseline definition of simplicity using word frequencies but attempt at defining a more linguistically motivated notion of simplicity based on lexical semantics considerations. It adopts different strategies depending on the syntactic complexity of the substitute. For one-word substitutes or common collocations, the system uses its frequency from Wordnet as a metric. In the case of multi-words substitutes the system uses "relevance" rules that apply (de)compositional semantic criteria and attempts to identify a unique content word in the substitute that might better approximate the whole expression. The expression is then assigned the frequency associated to this content word for the ranking. After POS tagging and sense disambiguating all substitutes, hand-written rules are used to decompose the meaning of a complex phrase and identify the most relevant word conveying the semantics of the whole.

UNT-SimpRank: The system (Sinha, 2012) uses external resources, including the Simple English Wikipedia corpus, a set of Spoken English dialogues, transcribed into machine readable form, WordNet, and unigram frequencies (Google Web1T data). SimpRank scores each substitute by a sum of its unigram frequency, its frequency in the Simple English Wikipedia, its frequency in the spoken corpus, the inverse of its length, and the number of senses the substitute has in WordNet. For a given context, the substitutes are then reverse-ranked based on their simplicity scores.

UNT-SimpRankLight: This is a variant of SimpRank which does not use unigram frequencies. The goal of this system is to check whether a memory and time-intensive and non-free resource such as the Web1T corpus makes a difference over other free and lightweight resources.

UNT-SaLSA: The only resource SaLSA depends on is the Web1T data, and in particular only 3-grams from this corpus. It leverages the context provided with the dataset by replacing the target placeholder one by one with each of the substitutes and their inflections thus building sets of 3-grams for each substitute in a given instance. The score of any substitute is then the sum of the 3-gram frequencies of all the generated 3-grams for that substitute.

UOW-SHEF-SimpLex: The system (Jauhar and Specia, 2012) uses a linear weighted ranking function composed of three features to produce a ranking. These include a context sensitive n-gram frequency model, a bag-of-words model and a feature composed of simplicity oriented psycholinguistic features. These three features are combined using an SVM ranker that is trained and tuned on the Trial dataset.

6.2 Pairwise kappa

The official task results and the ranking of the systems are shown in Table 3.

Firstly, it is worthwhile to note that all the top ranking systems include features that use frequency as a surrogate measure for lexical simplicity. This indicates a very high correlation between distributional frequency of a given word and its perceived complexity level. Additionally, the top two systems involve context-dependent and context-independent features, thus supporting our hypothesis of the composite nature of the lexical simplification problem.

Rank	Team - System	Kappa
1	UOW-SHEF-SimpLex	0.496
2	UNT-SimpRank	0.471
	Baseline-Simple Freq.	0.471
	ANNLOR-simple	0.465
3	UNT-SimpRankL	0.449
4	EMNLPCPH-ORD1	0.405
5	EMNLPCPH-ORD2	0.393
6	SB-mmSystem	0.289
7	ANNLOR-lmbing	0.199
8	Baseline-L-Sub Gold	0.106
9	Baseline-Random	0.013
10	UNT-SaLSA	-0.082

Table 3: Official results and ranking according to the pairwise kappa metric. Systems are ranked together when the difference in their kappa score is not statistically significant.

Few of the systems opted to use some form of supervised learning for the task, due to the limited number of training examples given. As pointed out by some participants who checked learning curves for their systems, the performance is likely to improve with larger training sets. Without enough training data, context agnostic approaches such as the "Simple Freq." baseline become very hard to beat.

We speculate that the reason why the effects of context-aware approaches are somewhat mitigated is because of the isolated setup of the shared task. In practice, humans produce language at an even level of complexity, i.e. consistently simple, or consistently complex. In the shared task's setup, systems are expected to simplify a single target word in a context, ignoring the possibility that sometimes simple words may not be contextually associated with complex surrounding words. This not only explains why context-aware approaches are less successful than was originally expected, but also gives a reason for the good performance of context-agnostic systems.

6.3 Recall and top-rank

As previously noted, the primary evaluation metric is very susceptible to penalize slight changes, making it overly pessimistic about systems' performance. Hence, while it may be an efficient way to compare and rank systems within the framework of a shared task, it may be unnecessarily devaluing the practical viability of approaches. We performed two post hoc evaluations that assess system output from a practical point of view. We check how well the top-ranked substitute, i.e., the simplest substitute according to a given system (which is most likely to be used in a real simplification task) compares to the top-ranked candidate from the gold standard. This is reported in the TRnk column of Table 4: the percentage of contexts in which the intersection between the simplest substitute set from a system's output and the gold standard contained *at least* one element. We note that while ties are virtually inexistent in the gold standard data, ties in the system output can affect this metric: a system that naively predicts all substitutes as the simplest (i.e., a single tie including all candidates) will score 100% in this metric.

We also measured the "recall-at-n" values for $1 \leq n \leq 3$, which gives the ratio of candidates from the top n substitute sets to those from the gold-standard. For a given n, we only consider contexts that have at least n+1 candidates in the gold-standard (so that there is some ranking to be done). Table 4 shows the results of this additional analysis.

Team - System	TRnk	n=1	n=2	n=3
UOW-SHEF-SimpLex	0.602	0.575	0.689	0.769
UNT-SimpRank	0.585	0.559	0.681	0.760
Baseline-Simple Freq.	0.585	0.559	0.681	0.760
ANNLOR-simple	0.564	0.538	0.674	0.768
UNT-SimpRankL	0.567	0.541	0.674	0.753
EMNLPCPH-ORD1	0.539	0.513	0.645	0.727
EMNLPCPH-ORD2	0.530	0.503	0.637	0.722
SB-mmSystem	0.477	0.452	0.632	0.748
ANNLOR-lmbing	0.336	0.316	0.494	0.647
Baseline-L-Sub Gold	0.454	0.427	0.667	0.959
Baseline-Random	0.340	0.321	0.612	0.825
UNT-SaLSA	0.146	0.137	0.364	0.532

Table 4: Additional results according to the top-rank (TRnk) and recall-at-n metrics.

These evaluation metrics favour systems that produce many ties. Consequently the baselines "L-Sub Gold" and "Random" yield overly high scores for recall-at-n for n=2 and n= 3. Nevertheless the rest of the results are by and large consistent with the rankings from the kappa metric.

The results for recall-at-2, e.g., show that most systems, on average 70% of the time, are able to find the simplest 2 substitute sets that correspond to the gold standard. This indicates that most approaches are reasonably good at distinguishing very simple substitutes from very complex ones, and that the top few substitutes will most often produce effective simplifications.

These results correspond to our experience from the comparison of human annotators, who are easily able to form clusters of simplicity with high agreement, but who strongly disagree (based on personal biases towards perceptions of lexical simplicity) on the internal rankings of these clusters.

7 Conclusions

We have presented the organization and findings of the first English Lexical Simplification shared task. This was a first attempt at garnering interest in the NLP community for research focused on the lexical aspects of Text Simplification.

Our analysis has shown that there is a very strong relation between distributional frequency of words and their perceived simplicity. The best systems on the shared task were those that relied on this association, and integrated both context-dependent and context-independent features. Further analysis revealed that while context-dependent features are important in principle, their applied efficacy is somewhat lessened due to the setup of the shared task, which treats simplification as an isolated problem.

Future work would involve evaluating the importance of context for lexical simplification in the scope of a simultaneous simplification to all the words in a context. In addition, the annotation of the gold-standard datasets could be re-done taking into consideration some of the features that are now known to have clearly influenced the large variance observed in the rankings of different annotators, such as their background language and the education level. One option would be to select annotators that conform a specific instantiation of these features. This should result in a higher inter-annotator agreement and hence a simpler task for simplification systems.

Acknowledgments

We would like to thank the annotators for their hard work in delivering the corpus on time.

References

Marilisa Amoia and Massimo Romanelli. 2012. SB-mmSystem: Using Decompositional Semantics for Lexical Simplification. In *English Lexical Simplification. Proceedings of the 6th International Workshop on Semantic Evaluation (SemEval 2012)*, Montreal, Canada.

Or Biran, Samuel Brody, and Noemie Elhadad. 2011. Putting it simply: a context-aware approach to lexical simplification. In *Proceedings of the 49th Annual Meeting of the Association for Computational Linguistics: Human Language Technologies*, pages 496–501, Portland, Oregon.

Thorsten Brants and Alex Franz. 2006. The google web 1t 5-gram corpus version 1.1.

Chris Callison-Burch, Philipp Koehn, Christof Monz, and Omar Zaidan. 2011. Findings of the 2011 workshop on statistical machine translation. In *Proceedings of the Sixth Workshop on Statistical Machine Translation*, pages 22–64, Edinburgh, Scotland.

Arnaldo Candido, Jr., Erick Maziero, Caroline Gasperin, Thiago A. S. Pardo, Lucia Specia, and Sandra M. Aluisio. 2009. Supporting the adaptation of texts for poor literacy readers: a text simplification editor for Brazilian Portuguese. In *Proceedings of the Fourth Workshop on Innovative Use of NLP for Building Educational Applications*, pages 34–42, Boulder, Colorado.

J Cohen. 1960. A coefficient of agreement for nominal scales. *Educational and Psychological Measurement*, 20:37–46, April.

Jan de Belder, Koen Deschacht, and Marie-Francine Moens. 2010. Lexical simplification. In *Proceedings of Itec2010: 1st International Conference on Interdisciplinary Research on Technology, Education and Communication*, Kortrijk, Belgium.

Siobhan Devlin and John Tait. 1998. The use of a psycholinguistic database in the simplification of text for aphasic readers. *Linguistic Databases*, pages 161–173.

Sujay Kumar Jauhar and Lucia Specia. 2012. UOW-SHEF: SimpLex - Lexical Simplicity Ranking based on Contextual and Psycholinguistic Features. In *English Lexical Simplification. Proceedings of the 6th International Workshop on Semantic Evaluation (SemEval 2012)*, Montreal, Canada.

Anne-Laure Ligozat, Cyril Grouin, Anne Garcia-Fernandez, and Delphine Bernhard. 2012. ANNLOR: A Naive Notation-system for Lexical Outputs Ranking. In *English Lexical Simplification. Proceedings of the 6th International Workshop on Semantic Evaluation (SemEval 2012)*, Montreal, Canada.

Diana McCarthy and Roberto Navigli. 2007. Semeval-2007 task 10: English lexical substitution task. In *Proceedings of the 4th International Workshop on Semantic Evaluations (SemEval-2007), Prague, Czech Republic*, pages 48–53.

E. Noreen. 1989. Computer-intensive methods for testing hypotheses. New York: Wiley.

Serge Sharoff. 2006. Open-source corpora: Using the net to fish for linguistic data. *International Journal of Corpus Linguistics*, 11(4):435–462.

Advaith Siddharthan. 2006. Syntactic simplification and text cohesion. *Research on Language and Computation*, 4:77–109.

Ravi Sinha. 2012. UNT-SimpRank: Systems for Lexical Simplification Ranking. In *English Lexical Simplification. Proceedings of the 6th International Workshop on Semantic Evaluation (SemEval 2012)*, Montreal, Canada.

Lucia Specia. 2010. Translating from complex to simplified sentences. In *Proceedings of the 9th international conference on Computational Processing of the Portuguese Language*, PROPOR'10, pages 30–39, Berlin, Heidelberg. Springer-Verlag.

Mark Yatskar, Bo Pang, Cristian Danescu-Niculescu-Mizil, and Lillian Lee. 2010. For the sake of simplicity: unsupervised extraction of lexical simplifications from Wikipedia. In *Human Language Technologies: The 2010 Annual Conference of the North American Chapter of the Association for Computational Linguistics*, pages 365–368, Los Angeles, California.

SemEval-2012 Task 2: Measuring Degrees of Relational Similarity

David A. Jurgens
Department of Computer Science
University of California, Los Angeles
jurgens@cs.ucla.edu

Saif M. Mohammad
Emerging Technologies
National Research Council Canada
saif.mohammad@nrc-cnrc.gc.ca

Peter D. Turney
Emerging Technologies
National Research Council Canada
peter.turney@nrc-cnrc.gc.ca

Keith J. Holyoak
Department of Psychology
University of California, Los Angeles
holyoak@lifesci.ucla.edu

Abstract

Up to now, work on semantic relations has focused on relation classification: recognizing whether a given instance (a word pair such as virus:flu) belongs to a specific relation class (such as CAUSE:EFFECT). However, instances of a single relation class may still have significant variability in how characteristic they are of that class. We present a new SemEval task based on identifying the degree of prototypicality for instances within a given class. As a part of the task, we have assembled the first dataset of graded relational similarity ratings across 79 relation categories. Three teams submitted six systems, which were evaluated using two methods.

1 Introduction

Relational similarity measures the degree of correspondence between two relations, where instance pairs that have high relational similarity are said to be analogous, i.e., to express the same relation (Turney, 2006). However, a class of analogous relations may still have significant variability in the degree of relational similarity of its members. Consider the four word pairs dog:bark, cat:meow, floor:squeak, and car:honk. We could say that these four X:Y pairs are all instances of the semantic relation ENTITY:SOUND; that is, X is an entity that characteristically makes the sound Y. Within a class of analogous pairs, certain pairs are more characteristic of the relation. For example, many would agree that dog:bark and cat:meow are better prototypes of the ENTITY:SOUND relation than floor:squeak. Our task requires automatic systems to quantify the degree of prototypicality of a target pair by measuring the relational similarity between it and pairs that are given as defining examples of a particular relation.

So far, most work in semantic relations has focused on differences *between* relation categories for classifying new relation instances. Past SemEval tasks that use relations have focused largely on discrete classification (Girju et al., 2007; Hendrickx et al., 2010) and paraphrasing the relations connecting noun compounds with a verb (Butnariu et al., 2010), which is also a form of discrete classification due to the lack of continuous degrees. However, there is some loss of information in any discrete classification of semantic relations. Furthermore, while some discrete classifiers provide a degree of confidence or probability for a relation classification, there is no *a priori* reason that such values would correspond to human prototypicality judgments. Our proposed task is distinct from these past tasks in that we focus on measuring the *degree* of relational similarity.[1] A graded measure of the degree of relational similarity would tell us that dog:bark is more similar to cat:meow than to floor:squeak. The discrete classification ENTITY:SOUND drops this information.

Systems that are successful at identifying degrees of relation similarity can have a significant impact where an application must choose between multiple instances of the same relation. We illustrate this with two examples. First, consider a relational search task (Cafarella et al., 2006). A user of a relational search engine might give the query,

[1]Task details and data are available at https://sites.google.com/site/semeval2012task2/ .

Subcategory	Relation name	Relation schema	Paradigms	Responses
8(e)	AGENT:GOAL	"Y is the goal of X"	pilgrim:shrine assassin:death climber:peak	patient:health runner:finish astronaut:space
5(e)	OBJECT:TYPICAL ACTION	"an X will typically Y"	glass:break soldier:fight juggernaut:crush	ice:melt lion:roar knife:stab
4(h)	DEFECTIVE	"an X is is a defect in Y"	fallacy:logic astigmatism:sight limp:walk	pimple:skin ignorance:learning tumor:body

Table 1: Examples of the three manually selected paradigms and the corresponding pairs generated by Turkers.

"List all things that are part of a car." SemEval-2007 Task 4 proposed that a relational search engine would use semantic relation classification to answer queries like this one. For this query, a classifier that was trained with the relation PART:WHOLE would be used. However, a system for measuring degrees of relational similarity would be better suited to relational search than a discrete classifier, because the relational search engine could then rank the output list in order of applicability. For the same query, the search engine could rank each item X in descending order of the degree of relational similarity between X:car and a training set of prototypical examples of the relation PART:WHOLE. This would be analogous to how standard search engines rank documents or web pages in descending order of relevance to the user's query.

As a second example, consider the role of relational similarity in analogical transfer. When faced with a new situation, we look for an analogous situation in our past experience, and we use analogical inference to transfer information from the past experience (the source domain) to the new situation (the target domain) (Gentner, 1983; Holyoak, 2012). Analogy is based on relational similarity (Gentner, 1983; Turney, 2008). The degree of relational similarity in an analogy is indicative of the likelihood that transferred knowledge will be applicable in the target domain. For example, past experience tells us that a dog barks to send a signal to other creatures. If we transfer this knowledge to a new experience with a cat meowing, we can predict that the cat is sending a signal, and we can act appropriately with that prediction. If we transfer this knowledge to a new experience with a floor squeaking, we might predict that the floor is sending a signal, which might lead us to act inappropriately. If we have a choice among several source analogies, usually the source pair with the highest degree of relational similarity to the target pair will prove to be the most useful analogy in the target domain, providing practical benefits beyond discrete relational classification.

2 Task Description

Here, we describe our task and the two-level hierarchy of semantic relation classes used for the task.

2.1 Objective

Our task is to rate word pairs by the degree to which they are prototypical members of a given relation class. The relation class is specified by a few paradigmatic (highly prototypical) examples of word pairs that belong to the class and also by a schematic representation of the relation class. The task requires comparing a word pair to the paradigmatic examples and/or the schematic representation. For example, suppose the relation class is REVERSE. We may specify this class by the paradigmatic examples attack:defend, buy:sell, love:hate, and the schematic representation "X is the reverse act of Y" or "X may be undone by Y." Given a pair such as repair:break, we compare this pair to the paradigmatic examples and/or the schematic representation, in order to estimate its degree of prototypicality. The challenges are (1) to infer the relation from the paradigmatic examples and identify what relational or featural attributes best characterize that relation, and (2) to identify the relation of the given pair and rate how similar it is to that shared by the paradigmatic examples.

2.2 Relation Categories

Researchers in psychology and linguistics have considered many different categorizations of semantic relations. The particular relation categorization is often driven by both the type of data and the intended application. Nastase and Szpakowicz (2003) propose a two-level hierarchy for noun-modifier relations, which has been widely used (Nakov and Hearst, 2008; Nastase et al., 2006; Turney and Littman, 2005; Turney, 2005). Others have used classifications based on the requirements for a specific task, such as Information Extraction (Pantel and Pennacchiotti, 2006) or biomedical applications (Stephens et al., 2001).

We adopt the relation classification scheme of Bejar et al. (1991), which includes ten high-level categories (e.g., CAUSE-PURPOSE and SPACE-TIME). Each category has between five and ten more refined subcategories (e.g., CAUSE-PURPOSE includes CAUSE:EFFECT and ACTION:GOAL), for a total of 79 distinct subcategories. Although these categories do not reflect all possible semantic relations, they greatly expand the coverage of relation types from those used in past relation-based SemEval tasks (Girju et al., 2007; Hendrickx et al., 2010), which used only seven and nine relation types, respectively. Furthermore, the classification includes many of the fundamental relations, e.g., TAXONOMIC and PART:WHOLE, while also including relations between a variety of parts of speech and less common relations, such as REFERENCE (e.g., SIGN:SIGNIFICANT) and NONATTRIBUTE (e.g., AGENT:ATYPICAL ACTION). Using such a large relation class inventory enables evaluating the generality of an approach, while still measuring performance on commonly used relations.

3 Task Data

We constructed a new data set for the task, in which word pairs are manually classified into relation categories. Word pairs within a category are manually distinguished according to how well they represent the category; that is, the degree to which they are relationally similar to paradigmatic members of the given semantic relation class. Paradigmatic members of a class were taken from examples provided by Bejar et al. (1991). Due to the large number of annotations needed, we used Amazon Mechanical Turk (MTurk),[2] which is a popular choice in computational linguistics for gathering large numbers of human responses to linguistic questions (Snow et al., 2008; Mohammad and Turney, 2010). We refer to the MTurk workers as Turkers.

Question 1: Consider the following word pairs: pilgrim:shrine, hunter:quarry, assassin:victim, climber:peak. What relation best describes these X:Y word pairs?

(1) "X worships/reveres Y"
(2) "X seeks/desires/aims for Y"
(3) "X harms/destroys Y"
(4) "X uses/exploits/employs Y"

Question 2: Consider the following word pairs: pilgrim:shrine, hunter:quarry, assassin:victim, climber:peak. These X:Y pairs share a relation, "X R Y". Give four additional word pairs that illustrate the same relation, in the same order (X on the left, Y on the right). Please do not use phrases composed of two or more words in your examples (e.g., "racing car"). Please do not use names of people, places, or things in your examples (e.g., "Europe", "Kleenex").

(1) ________ : ________
(2) ________ : ________
(3) ________ : ________
(4) ________ : ________

Figure 1: An example of the two questions for Phase 1.

The data set was built in two phases. In the first phase, Turkers were given three paradigmatic examples of a subcategory and asked to create new pairs that instantiate the same relation as the paradigms. In the second phase, people were asked to distinguish the new pairs from the first phase according to the degree to which they are good representatives of the given subcategory.

Phase 1 In the first phase, we built upon the paradigmatic examples of Bejar et al. (1991), who provided one to ten examples for each subcategory. From these examples, we manually selected three instances to use as seeds for generating new examples, adding examples when a subcategory had less than three. The examples were selected to be balanced across topic domains so as not to bias the Turkers. For each subcategory, we manually created a schematic representation of the relation for the examples. Table 1 gives three examples.

[2]https://www.mturk.com/

To gather new examples of each subcategory, a two-part questionnaire was presented to Turkers (see Figure 1). In the first part, Turkers were shown the three paradigm word pairs for a subcategory along with a list of four relation descriptions (schematic representations of possible relations). One of the four schematic representations accurately described the three paradigm pairs and the other three schematics were distractors (confounding descriptions). Turkers were asked to select which of the four schematic representations best matched the paradigms. The first part of the questionnaire serves as quality control by ensuring that the Turker is capable of recognizing the relation. An incorrect answer to the question is used to recognize and eliminate confused or negligent responses, which were approximately 7% of the responses.

In the second part of the Phase 1 questionnaire, Turkers were shown the three prototypes again and asked to generate four word pairs that expressed the same relation. Turkers were directed to be mindful of the order of the words in each pair, as reversed orderings can have very different degrees of prototypicality in the case of directional relations.

The Turkers provided a total of 3160 additional examples for the 79 subcategories, 2905 of which were unique. We applied minor manual correction to remove spelling errors, which reduced the total number of examples to 2823. A median of 38 examples were found per subcategory with a maximum of 40 and minimum of 23. We note that Phase 1 gathers both high and low quality examples of the relation, which were all included to capture different degrees of prototypicality.

We included an additional 395 pairs by randomly sampling five instances of each subcategory and creating a new pair from the reversed arguments, i.e., adding pair Y:X to the subcategory containing X:Y. Adding reversals was inspired by an observation during Phase 1 that reversed pairs would occasionally be added by the Turkers themselves. We were curious to see what impact reversals would have on Turker responses and on the output of automatic systems. Reversals should reveal order sensitivity with a strongly directional relation, such as PART:WHOLE, but also perhaps there is order sensitivity with more symmetric relations, such as SYNONYMY. Phase 1 produced a total of 3218 pairs.

Question 1: Consider the following word pairs: pilgrim:shrine, hunter:quarry, assassin:victim, climber:peak. What relation best describes these X:Y word pairs?

(1) "X worships/reveres Y"
(2) "X seeks/desires/aims for Y"
(3) "X harms/destroys Y"
(4) "X uses/exploits/employs Y"

Question 2: Consider the following word pairs: pilgrim:shrine, hunter:quarry, assassin:victim, climber:peak. These X:Y pairs share a relation, "X R Y". Now consider the following word pairs:

(1) pig:mud
(2) politician:votes
(3) dog:bone
(4) bird:worm

Which of the above numbered word pairs is the MOST illustrative example of the same relation "X R Y"?

Which of the above numbered word pairs is the LEAST illustrative example of the same relation "X R Y"?

Note: In some cases, a word pair might be in reverse order. For example, tree:forest is in reverse order for the relation "X is made from a collection of Y". The correct order would be forest:tree; a forest is made from a collection of trees. You should treat reversed pairs as BAD examples of the given relation.

Figure 2: An example of the two questions for Phase 2.

Phase 2 In the second phase, the response pairs from Phase 1 were ranked according to their prototypicality. We opted to create a ranking using MaxDiff questions (Louviere, 1991). MaxDiff is a choice procedure consisting of a question about a target concept and four or five alternatives. A participant must choose both the best and worse answers from the given alternatives.

MaxDiff is a strong alternative to creating a ranking from standard rating scales, such as the Likert scale, because it avoids scale biases. Furthermore MaxDiff is more efficient than other choice procedures such as pairwise comparison, because it does not require comparing all pairs.

Like Phase 1, Phase 2 was performed using a two-part questionnaire. The first question was identical to that of Phase 1: four examples of the same relation subcategory generated in Phase 1 were presented and the Turker was asked to select the correct relation from a list of four options. This first question served as a quality control measure for ensuring the Turker could properly identify the relation in question and it also served as a hint, guiding the Turker toward the intended understanding of the shared relation underlying the three paradigms. In the second part, the Turker selects the most and least illustrative example of that relation from among the four examples of pairs generated by Turkers in Phase 1.

We aimed for five Turker responses for each MaxDiff question but averaged 4.73 responses for each MaxDiff question in a subcategory, with a minimum of 3.45 responses per MaxDiff question. Turkers answered a total of 48,846 questions over a period of five months, of which 6,536 (13%) were rejected due to a missing answer or an incorrect response to the first question.

3.1 Measuring Prototypicality

The MaxDiff responses were converted into the prototypicality scores using a counting procedure (Orme, 2009). For each word pair, the prototypicality is scored as the percentage of times it is chosen as most illustrative minus the percentage of times it is chosen as least illustrative (see Figure 2). While methods such as hierarchical Bayes models can be used to compute a numerical rank from the responses, we found the counting method to produce very reasonable results.

3.2 Data Sets

The 79 subcategories were divided into training and testing segments. Ten subcategories were provided as training with both the Turkers' MaxDiff responses and the computed prototypicality ratings. The ten training subcategories were randomly selected. The remaining 69 subcategories were used for testing. All data sets are now released on the task website under the Creative Commons 3.0 license.[3]

Participants were given the list of all pairs gathered in Phase 1 and the Phase 2 responses for the 10 training subcategories. Phase 2 responses for the 69 test categories were not made available. Participants also had access to the set of questionnaire materials provided to the Turkers, the full list of paradigmatic examples provided by Bejar et al. (1991), and the confounding schema relations from the initial questions in Phase 1 and Phase 2, which might serve as negative training examples.

[3] http://creativecommons.org/licenses/by/3.0/

4 Evaluation

Systems are given examples of pairs from a single category and asked to provide numeric ratings of the degree of relational similarity for each pair relative to the relation expressed in that category.

4.1 Scoring

Spearman's rank correlation coefficient, ρ, and a MaxDiff score were used to evaluate the systems. For Spearman's ρ, the prototypicality rating of each pair is used to build a ranking of all pairs in a subcategory. Spearman's ρ is then computed between the pair rankings of a system and the gold standard ranking. This evaluation abstracts away from comparing the numeric values so that only their relative ordering in prototypicality is measured.

In the second scoring procedure, we measure the accuracy of a system at answering the same set of MaxDiff questions as answered by the Turkers in Phase 2 (see Figure 2). Given the four word pairs, the system selects the pair with the lowest numerical rating as *least illustrative* and the pair with the highest numerical rating as *most illustrative*. Ties in prototypicality are broken arbitrarily. Accuracy is measured as the percentage of questions answered correctly. An answer is considered correct when it agrees with the majority of the Turkers. In some cases, two answers may be considered correct. For example, when five Turkers answer a given MaxDiff question, two Turkers might choose one pair as the most illustrative and two other Turkers might choose another pair as the most illustrative. In this case, both pairs would count as correct choices for the most illustrative pair.

4.2 Baselines

We consider two baselines for evaluation: Random and PMI. The Random baseline rates each pair in a subcategory randomly. The expected Spearman correlation for Random ratings is zero. The expected MaxDiff score for Random ratings would be 25% (because there are four word pairs to choose from in Phase 2) if there were always a unique majority, but it is actually about 31%, due to cases where two pairs both get two votes from the Turkers.

Given a MaxDiff question, a Turker might select the pair whose words are most strongly associated

Team	Members	System	Description
Benemérita Universidad Autónoma de Puebla (México) (BUAP)	Mireya T. Vidal, Darnes V. Ayala, Jose A.R. Ortiz, Azucena M. Rendon, David Pinto, and Saul L. Silverio	BUAP	Each pair is represented as a vector over multiple features: lexical, intervening words, WordNet relations between the pair, and syntactic features such as part of speech and morphology. Prototypicality is based on cosine similarity with the class's pairs.
University of Texas at Dallas (UTD)	Bryan Rink and Sanda Harabagiu	NB	Unsupervised learning identifies intervening patterns between all word pairs. Each pattern is then ranked according to its subcategory specificity by learning a generative model from patterns to word pairs. Prototypicality ratings are based on confidence that the highest scoring pattern found for a pair belongs to the subcategory.
		SVM	Intervening patterns are found using the same method as UTD-NB. Word pairs are then represented as feature vectors of matching patterns. An SVM classifier is trained using a subcategory's pairs as positive training data and all other pairs as negative. Prototypicality ratings are based on SVM confidence of class inclusion.
University of Minnesota, Duluth (Duluth)	Ted Pedersen	V0	WordNet is used to build the set of concepts connected by WordNet relations to the pairs' words. Prototypicality is estimated using the vector similarity of the concatenated glosses.
		V1	Same procedure as V0, with one further expansion to related concepts.
		V2	Same procedure as V0, with two further expansions to related concepts.

Table 2: Descriptions of the participating teams and systems.

as the most illustrative and the least associated as the least illustrative. Therefore, we propose a second baseline where pairs are rated according to their Pointwise Mutual Information (PMI) (Church and Hanks, 1990), which measures the statistical association between two words. For this baseline, the prototypicality rating given to a word pair is simply the PMI score for the pair. For two terms x and y, $\text{PMI}(x, y)$ is defined as $\log_2\left(\frac{\text{p}(x,y)}{\text{p}(x)\text{p}(y)}\right)$ where $\text{p}(\cdot)$ denotes the probability of a term or pair of terms. The PMI score was calculated using the method of Turney (2001) on a corpus of approximately 50 billion tokens, indexed by the Wumpus search engine.[4] To calculate $\text{p}(x, y)$, we recorded all co-occurrences of both terms within a ten-word window.

5 Systems

Three teams submitted six systems for evaluation. Table 2 summarizes the teams and systems. Two teams (BUAP and UTD) based their approaches on discovering relation-specific patterns for each category, while the third team (Duluth) used vector space comparisons of the glosses related to the pairs.

[4] http://www.wumpus-search.org/

No single system was able to achieve superior performance on all subcategories. Table 3 reports the averages across all subcategories for Spearman's ρ and MaxDiff accuracy. Five systems were able to perform above the Random baseline, while only one system, UTD-NB, consistently performed above the PMI baseline.

However, the average performance masks superior performance on individual subcategories. Table 3 also reports the number of subcategories in which a system obtained a statistically significant Spearman's ρ with the gold standard ranking. Despite the low average performance, most models were able to obtain significant correlation in multiple subcategories. Furthermore, the significant correlations for different systems were not always obtained in the same subcategories. Across all subcategories, 43 had a significant correlation at $p < 0.05$ and 27 at $p < 0.01$. The broad coverage of significantly correlated subcategories spanned by the combination of all systems and the PMI baseline suggests that high performance on this task may be possible, but that adapting to each of the specific relation types may be very beneficial.

Team	System	Spearman's ρ	# of Subcategories $p < 0.05$	$p < 0.01$	MaxDiff
BUAP	BUAP	0.014	2	0	31.7
UTD	NB	**0.229**	22	16	**39.4**
	SVM	0.116	11	5	34.7
Duluth	V0	0.050	9	3	32.4
	V1	0.039	10	4	31.5
	V2	0.038	7	3	31.1
Baselines	Random	0.018	4	0	31.2
	PMI	0.112	15	7	33.9

Table 3: Average Spearman's ρ and MaxDiff scores for all system across all 69 test subcategories. Columns 4 and 5 denote the number of subcategories with a Spearman's ρ that is statistically significant at the noted level of confidence.

Relation Class	Random	PMI	BUAP	UTD-NB	UTD-SVM	Duluth-V0	Duluth-V1	Duluth-V2
Class-Inclusion	0.057	0.221	0.064	**0.233**	0.093	0.045	0.178	0.168
Part-Whole	0.012	0.144	0.066	**0.252**	0.142	-0.061	-0.084	-0.054
Similar	0.026	0.094	-0.036	**0.214**	0.131	0.183	0.208	0.198
Contrast	-0.049	0.032	0.000	**0.206**	0.162	0.142	0.120	0.051
Attribute	0.037	-0.032	-0.095	**0.158**	0.052	0.044	-0.003	0.008
Non-Attribute	-0.070	**0.191**	0.009	0.098	0.094	0.079	0.066	0.074
Case Relations	0.090	0.168	-0.037	**0.241**	0.187	-0.011	-0.068	-0.115
Cause-Purpose	-0.011	0.130	0.114	**0.183**	0.060	0.021	0.022	0.042
Space-Time	0.013	0.084	0.035	**0.375**	0.139	0.055	-0.004	0.040
Reference	0.142	0.125	-0.001	**0.346**	0.082	0.028	0.074	0.067

Table 4: Average Spearman's ρ correlation with the Turker rankings in each of the high-level relation categories, with the highest average correlation for each subcategory shown in bold.

6 Discussion

Sensitivity to Pair Association The PMI baseline performed much better than anticipated, outperforming all systems but UTD-NB on many of the subcategories, despite treating all relations as directionless. Performance was highest in subcategories where the X:Y pair might reasonably be expected to occur together, e.g., FUNCTIONAL or CONTRADICTORY. However, PMI benefits from the design of our task, which focuses on rating pairs within a given subcategory. In a different task that mixed pairs from a variety of subcategories, PMI would perform poorly, because it would assign high scores to pairs of strongly associated words, regardless of whether they belong to a given subcategory.

Difficulty of Specific Subcategories Performance across the high-level categories was highly varied between approaches. The category-level summary shown in Table 4 reveals high-level trends in difficulty across all submitted systems. The submitted systems performed best for subcategories under the Similar category, while the systems performed worst for Non-Attribute subcategories.

As a further possibility of explaining performance differences between subcategories, we considered the hypothesis that the difficulty of a subcategory is inversely proportional to the range of prototypicality scores, i.e., subcategories with restricted ranges are more difficult. However, we found that the difficulty was uncorrelated with both the size of the interval spanned by prototypicality scores and the standard deviation of the scores.

Sensitivity to Argument Reversal The directionality of a relation can significantly impact the rated prototypicality of a pair whose arguments have been reversed. As an approximate measure of the effect on prototypicality when a pairs' arguments are reversed, we calculated the expected drop in rank

Team	System	Spearman's ρ No Reversals	Spearman's ρ With Reversals
BUAP	BUAP	-0.003	0.014
UTD	NB	0.190	0.229
	SVM	0.104	0.116
Duluth	V0	0.062	0.050
	V1	0.040	0.039
	V2	0.046	0.038
Baselines	Random	0.004	0.018
	PMI	0.143	0.112

Table 5: Average pair ranking correlation for all subcategories when reversed pairs are included and excluded.

between a pair and its reversed form. Based on the Turker rankings, the SEQUENCE (e.g., pregnancy:birth) and FUNCTIONAL (e.g., weapon:knife) subcategories exhibited the strongest sensitivity to argument reversal, while ATTRIBUTE SIMILARITY (e.g., rake:fork) and CONTRARY (e.g., happy:sad) exhibited the least.

The inclusion of reversed pairs potentially adds a small amount of noise to the relation identification process for subcategories with directional relations. Two teams, BUAP and UTD, accounted for relation directionality, while Duluth did not, which resulted in the Duluth systems ranking reversed pairs the same. Therefore, we conducted a post-hoc analysis of the impact of reversals by removing the reversed pairs from the computed prototypicality rankings. Table 5 reports the resulting Spearman's ρ. With Spearman's ρ, we can easily evaluate the impact of the reversals, because we can delete a reversed pair without affecting anything else. For the MaxDiff questions, if there is one reversal in a group of four choices, then we need to delete the whole MaxDiff question. Therefore we do not include the MaxDiff score in Table 5.

Removing reversals decreased performance in the three systems that were sensitive to pair ordering (BUAP, UTD-NB, and UTD-SVM), while only marginally increasing performance in the three systems that ignored the ordering. The performance decrease in systems that use ordering suggests that the reversed pairs are easily identified and ranked appropriately low. As a further estimate of the models' ability to correctly order reversals, we compared the difference in a reversal's rank for both a system's

Team	System	RMSE
BUAP	BUAP	256.07
UT Dallas	NB	257.15
	SVM	209.95
Baseline	Random	227.25

Table 6: RMSE in estimating the difference in rank between a pair and its reversal in the gold standard.

ranking and the ranking computed from Turker Responses. Table 6 reports the Root Mean Squared Error (RMSE) in ranking difference for the three systems that took argument order into account. Although not the best performing system, Table 6 indicates that the UTD-SVM system was most able to appropriately weight reversals' prototypicality. In contrast, the UTD-NB system often had many pairs tied for the lowest rank, which either resulted in pair and its reversal being tied or having a much smaller rank difference, thereby increasing its RMSE.

7 Conclusions

We have introduced a new task focused on rating the degrees of prototypicality for word pairs sharing the same relation. Participants first identify the relation shared between example pairs and then rate the degree to which each pair expresses that relation. As a part of the task, we constructed a dataset of prototypicality ratings for 3218 word pairs in 79 different relation categories.

Participating systems used combinations of corpus-based, syntactic, and WordNet features, with varying degrees of success. The task also included a competitive baseline, PMI, which surpassed all but one system. Several models obtained moderate performance in select relation subcategories, but no one approach succeeded in general, which introduces much opportunity for future improvement. We also hope that both the example pairs and their prototypicality ratings will be a valuable data set for future research in Linguistics as well as Cognitive Psychology. All data sets for this task have been made publicly available on the task website.

Acknowledgements

This research was supported by ONR grant N000140810186.

References

Isaac I. Bejar, Roger Chaffin, and Susan E. Embretson. 1991. *Cognitive and Psychometric Analysis of Analogical Problem Solving*. Springer-Verlag.

Cristina Butnariu, Su Nam Kim, Preslav Nakov, Diarmuid Ó Séaghdha, Stan Szpakowicz, and Tony Veale. 2010. Semeval-2010 task 9: The interpretation of noun compounds using paraphrasing verbs and prepositions. In *Proceedings of the 5th International Workshop on Semantic Evaluation (SemEval-2010)*, pages 39–44. Association for Computational Linguistics.

Michael J. Cafarella, Michele Banko, and Oren Etzioni. 2006. Relational web search. In *WWW Conference*.

Kenneth W. Church and Patrick Hanks. 1990. Word association norms, mutual information, and lexicography. *Computational linguistics*, 16(1):22–29.

Dedre Gentner. 1983. Structure-mapping: A theoretical framework for analogy. *Cognitive science*, 7(2):155–170.

Roxana Girju, Preslav Nakov, Vivi Nastase, Stan Szpakowicz, Peter Turney, and Deniz Yuret. 2007. SemEval-2007 task 04: Classification of semantic relations between nominals. In *Proceedings of the 4th International Workshop on Semantic Evaluation (SemEval-2007)*.

Iris Hendrickx, Su Nam Kim, Zornitsa Kozareva, Preslav Nakov, Diarmuid Ó Séaghdha, Sebastian Padó, Marco Pennacchiotti, Lorenza Romano, and Stan Szpakowicz. 2010. SemEval-2010 task 8: Multi-way classification of semantic relations between pairs of nominals. In *Proceedings of the 5th International Workshop on Semantic Evaluation (SemEval-2010)*, pages 33–38. Association for Computational Linguistics.

Keith J. Holyoak. 2012. Analogy and relational reasoning. In *Oxford handbook of thinking and reasoning*, pages 234–259. Oxford University Press.

Jordan J. Louviere. 1991. Best-worst scaling: A model for the largest difference judgments. Working Paper.

Saif M. Mohammad and Peter D. Turney. 2010. Emotions evoked by common words and phrases: Using mechanical turk to create an emotion lexicon. In *Proceedings of the NAACL-HLT 2010 Workshop on Computational Approaches to Analysis and Generation of Emotion in Text*, pages 26–34. Association for Computational Linguistics.

Preslav Nakov and Marti A. Hearst. 2008. Solving relational similarity problems using the web as a corpus. In *Proceedings of ACL*, volume 8.

Vivi Nastase and Stan Szpakowicz. 2003. Exploring noun-modifier semantic relations. In *Fifth International Workshop on Computational Semantics (IWCS-5)*, pages 285–301. ACL Press Tilburg,, The Netherlands.

Vivi Nastase, Jelber Sayyad-Shirabad, Marina Sokolova, and Stan Szpakowicz. 2006. Learning noun-modifier semantic relations with corpus-based and wordnet-based features. In *Proceedings of AAAI*, volume 21, page 781.

Bryan Orme. 2009. Maxdiff analysis: Simple counting, individual-level logit, and hb.

Patrick Pantel and Marco Pennacchiotti. 2006. Espresso: leveraging generic patterns for automatically harvesting semantic relations. In *Proceedings of the 21st International Conference on Computational Linguistics and the 44th annual meeting of the Association for Computational Linguistics*, pages 113–120. Association for Computational Linguistics.

Rion Snow, Brendan O'Connor, Daniel Jurafsky, and Andrew Y. Ng. 2008. Cheap and fast—but is it good? Evaluating non-expert annotations for natural language tasks. In *Proceedings of the Conference on Empirical Methods in Natural Language Processing*, pages 254–263. Association for Computational Linguistics.

M. Stephens, M. Palakal, S. Mukhopadhyay, R. Raje, J. Mostafa, et al. 2001. Detecting gene relations from medline abstracts. In *Pacific Symposium on Biocomputing*, volume 6, pages 483–495. Citeseer.

Peter D. Turney and Michael L Littman. 2005. Corpus-based learning of analogies and semantic relations. *Machine Learning*, 60(1–3):251–278.

Peter D. Turney. 2001. Mining the Web for synonyms: PMI-IR versus LSA on TOEFL. In *Proceedings of the Twelfth European Conference on Machine Learning (ECML-2001)*, pages 491–502.

Peter D. Turney. 2005. Measuring semantic similarity by latent relational analysis. In *Proceedings of IJCAI*, pages 1136–1141.

Peter D. Turney. 2006. Similarity of semantic relations. *Computational Linguistics*, 32(3):379–416.

Peter D. Turney. 2008. The latent relation mapping engine: Algorithm and experiments. *Journal of Artificial Intelligence Research*, 33(1):615–655.

SemEval-2012 Task 3: Spatial Role Labeling

Parisa Kordjamshidi
Katholieke Universiteit Leuven
parisa.kordjamshidi@cs.kuleuven.be

Steven Bethard
University of Colorado
steven.bethard@colorado.edu

Marie-Francine Moens
Katholieke Universiteit Leuven
sien.moens@cs.kuleuven.be

Abstract

This SemEval2012 shared task is based on a recently introduced spatial annotation scheme called Spatial Role Labeling. The Spatial Role Labeling task concerns the extraction of main components of the spatial semantics from natural language: trajectors, landmarks and spatial indicators. In addition to these major components, the links between them and the general-type of spatial relationships including region, direction and distance are targeted. The annotated dataset contains about 1213 sentences which describe 612 images of the CLEF IAPR TC-12 Image Benchmark. We have one participant system with two runs. The participant's runs are compared to the system in (Kordjamshidi et al., 2011c) which is provided by task organizers.

1 Introduction

One of the essential functions of natural language is to talk about spatial relationships between objects. The sentence *"Give me the book on AI on the big table behind the wall."* expresses information about the *spatial configuration* of the objects (book, table, wall) in some *space*. Particularly, it explains the region occupied by the *book* with respect to the *table* and the direction (orientation) of the *table* with respect to the *wall*. Understanding such spatial utterances is a problem in many areas, including robotics, navigation, traffic management, and query answering systems (Tappan, 2004).

Linguistic constructs can express highly complex, relational structures of objects, spatial relations between them, and patterns of motion through space relative to some reference point. Compared to natural language, formal spatial models focus on one particular spatial aspect such as orientation, topology or distance and specify its underlying spatial logic in detail (Hois and Kutz, 2008). These formal models enable spatial reasoning that is difficult to perform on natural language expressions.

Learning how to map natural language spatial information onto a formal representation is a challenging problem. The complexity of spatial semantics from the cognitive-linguistic point of view on the one hand, the diversity of formal spatial representation models in different applications on the other hand and the gap between the specification level of the two sides has led to the present situation that no well-defined framework for automatic spatial information extraction exists that can handle all of these aspects.

In a previous paper (Kordjamshidi et al., 2010b), we introduced the task of spatial role labeling (SpRL) and proposed an annotation scheme that is language-independent and practically facilitates the application of machine learning techniques. Our framework consists of a set of spatial roles based on the theory of holistic spatial semantics (Zlatevl, 2007) with the intent of covering the main aspects of spatial concepts at a course level, including both static and dynamic spatial semantics. This shared task is defined on the basis of that annotation scheme. Since this is the first shared task on the spatial information and this particular data, we proposed a simplified version of the original scheme. The intention of this simplification was to make this practice feasible in the given timeframe. However, the current task is very challenging particularly for learning the spatial links and relations.

The core problem of SpRL is: i) the *identification* of the words that play a role in describing spatial concepts, and ii) the *classification* of the relational *role* that these words play in the spatial configuration.

For example, consider again the sentence *"Give me the book on AI on the big table behind the wall."*. The phrase headed by the token *book* is referring to a trajector object. The trajector (TR) is an entity whose location is described in the sentence. The phrase headed by the token *table* is referring to the role of a landmark (LM). The landmark is a reference object for describing the location of a trajector. These two spatial entities are related by the spatial expression *on* denoted as spatial indicator (SP). The spatial indicator (often a preposition in English, but sometimes a verb, noun, adjective, or adverb) indicates the existence of spatial information in the sentence and establishes the type of a spatial relation. The spatial relations that can be extracted from the whole sentence are <*on*$_{SP}$ *book*$_{TR}$ *table*$_{LM}$> and <*behind*$_{SP}$ *table*$_{TR}$ *wall*$_{LM}$>. One could also use spatial reasoning to *infer* that the statement <*behind book wall*> holds, however, such inferred relations are not considered in this task. Although the spatial indicators are mostly prepositions, the reverse may not hold- for example, the first preposition *on* only states the topic of the book, so <*on book AI*> is not a spatial relation. For each of the true spatial relations, a general type is assigned. The <*on*$_{SP}$ *book*$_{TR}$ *table*$_{LM}$> relation expresses a kind of topological relationship between the two objects and we assign it a general type named *region*. The <*behind*$_{SP}$ *table*$_{TR}$ *wall*$_{LM}$> relation expresses directional information and we assign it a general type named *direction*.

In general we assume two main abstraction layers for the extraction of spatial information (Bateman, 2010; Kordjamshidi et al., 2010a; Kordjamshidi et al., 2011a): (a) a **linguistic** layer, corresponding to the annotation scheme described above, which starts with unrestricted natural language and predicts the existence of spatial information at the sentence level by identifying the words that play a particular spatial role as well as their spatial relationship; (b) a **formal** layer, in which the spatial roles are mapped onto a spatial calculus model (Galton, 2009). For example, the linguistic layer recognizes that the spatial relation (*on*) holds between *book* and *table*, and the formal layer maps this to a specific, formal spatial representation, e.g., a logical representation like `AboveExternallyConnected(book, table)` or a formal qualitative spatial representation like `EC` (externally connected) in the RCC model (Regional Connection Calculus) (Cohn and Renz, 2008).

In this shared task we focus on the first (linguistic) level which is a necessary step for mapping natural language to any formal spatial calculus. The main roles that are considered here are trajector, landmark, spatial indicator, their links and the general type of their spatial relation. The general type of a relation can be *direction*, *region* or *distance*.

2 Motivation and related work

Spatial role labeling is a key task for applications that are required to answer questions or reason about spatial relationships between entities. Examples include systems that perform text-to-scene conversion, generation of textual descriptions from visual data, robot navigation tasks, giving directional instructions, and geographical information systems (GIS). Recent research trends (Ross et al., 2010; Hois et al., 2011; Tellex et al., 2011) indicate an increasing interest in the area of extracting spatial information from language and mapping it to a formal spatial representation. Although cognitive-linguistic studies have investigated this problem extensively, the computational aspect of making this bridge between language and formal spatial representation (Hois and Kutz, 2008) is still in its elementary stages. The possession of a practical and appropriate annotation scheme along with data is the first requirement. To obtain this one has to investigate and schematize both linguistic and spatial ontologies. This process needs to cover the necessary information and semantics on the one hand, and to maintain the practical feasibility of the automatic annotation of unobserved data on the other hand.

In recent research on spatial information and natural language, several annotation schemes have been proposed such as ACE, GUM, GML, KML, TRML which are briefly described and compared to SpatialML scheme in (MITRE Corporation, 2010). But to our knowledge, the main obstacles for employing machine learning in this context and the very limited usage of this effective approach have been (a) the lack of an agreement on a unique semantic model for spatial information; (b) the diversity of formal spatial relations; and consequently (c) the lack of annotated data on which machine learning can be employed to learn and extract the spatial relations. The most systematic work in this area includes the SpatialML (Mani et al., 2008) scheme which focuses on geographical information, and the work of (Pustejovsky and Moszkowicz, 2009) in which the pivot of the spatial information is the spatial verb. The most recent and active work is the ISO-Space scheme (Pustejovsky et al., 2011) which is based on the above two schemes. The ideas behind ISO-Space are closely related to our annotation scheme in (Kordjamshidi et al., 2010b), however it considers more detailed and fine-grained spatial and linguistic elements which makes the preparation of the data for machine learning more difficult.

Spatial information is directly related to the part of the language that can be visualized. Thus, the extraction of spatial information is useful for multimodal environments. One advantage of our proposed scheme is that it considers this dimension. Because it abstracts the spatial elements that could be aligned with the objects in images/videos and used for annotation of audio-visual descriptions (Butko et al., 2011). This is useful in the multimodal environments where, for example, natural language instructions are given to a robot for finding the way or objects.

Not much work exists on using annotations for learning models to extract spatial information. Our previous work (Kordjamshidi et al., 2011c) is a first step in this direction and provides a domain independent linguistic and spatial analysis to this problem. This shared task invites interested research groups for a similar effort. The idea behind this task is firstly to motivate the application of different machine learning approaches, secondly to investigate effective features for this task, and thirdly to reveal the practical problems in the annotation schemes and the annotated concepts. This will help to enrich the data and the annotation in parallel with the machine learning practice.

3 Annotation scheme

As mentioned in the introduction, the annotation of the data set is according to the general spatial role labeling scheme (Kordjamshidi et al., 2010b). The below example presents the annotated elements in this scheme.

> A woman_{TR} and a child_{TR} are walking_{MOTION} over_{SP} the square_{LM}.
>
> General-type: region
> Specific type: RCC
> Spatial value: PP (proper part)
> Dynamic
> Path: middle
> Frame of reference: –

According to this scheme the main spatial roles are,

Trajectior (TR). The entity, i.e., person, object or event whose location is described, which can be static or dynamic; (also called: *local/figure object*, *locatum*). In the above example *woman* and *child* are two trajectors.

Landmark (LM). The reference entity in relation to which the location or the motion of the trajector is specified. (also called: *reference object* or *relatum*). *square* is the landmark in the above example.

Spatial indicator (SP). The element that defines constraints on spatial properties such as the location of the trajector with respect to the landmark. The spatial indicator determines the type of spatial relation. The preposition *over* is annotated as the spatial indicator in the current example.

Moreover, the links between the three roles are annotated as a spatial **Relation**. Since each spatial relation is defined with three arguments we call it a **spatial triplet**. Each triplet indicates a **relation** between the three above mentioned spatial roles. The sentence contains two spatial relations of $<over_{SP}\ woman_{TR}\ square_{LM}>$ and $<over_{SP}\ child_{TR}\ square_{LM}>$, with the same spatial attributes listed below the example. In spatial information theory the relations and properties are usually grouped into the domains of *topological*, *directional*, and *distance* relations and also shape (Stock,

1997). Accordingly, we propose a mapping between the extracted spatial triplets to the coarse-grained type of spatial relationships including **region**, **direction** or **distance**. We call these types as **general-type** of the spatial relations and briefly describe these below:

Region. refers to a region of space which is always defined in relation to a landmark, e.g. the interior or exterior, e.g. *"the flower is in the vase"*.

Direction. denotes a direction along the axes provided by the different frames of reference, in case the trajector of motion is not characterized in terms of its relation to the region of a landmark, e.g. *"the vase is on the left"*.

Distance. states information about the spatial distance of the objects and could be a qualitative expression such as *close*, *far* or quantitative such as *12 km*, e.g. *"the kids are close to the blackboard"*.

The general-type of the relation in the example is annotated as *region*.

After extraction of these relations a next fine-grained step will be to map each general spatial relationship to an appropriate spatial calculi representation. This step is not intended for this task and the additional tags in the scheme will be considered in the future shared tasks. For example Region Connection Calculus RCC-8 (Cohn and Renz, 2008) representation reflects region-based topological relations. Topological or region-based spatial information has been researched in depth in the area of qualitative spatial representation and reasoning. We assume that the trajectors and landmarks can often be interpreted as spatial regions and, as a consequence, their relation can be annotated with a specific RCC-8 relation. The RCC type in the above example is specifically annotated as the PP (proper part). Similarly, the *direction* and *distance* relations are mapped to more specific formal representations.

Two additional annotations are about motion verbs and dynamism. Dynamic spatial information are associated with spatial movements and spatial changes. In dynamic spatial relations mostly motion verbs are involved. Motion verbs carry spatial information and influence the spatial semantics. In the above example the spatial indicator *over* is related to a motion verb *walking*. Hence the spatial relation is dynamic and *walking* is annotated as the *motion*. In contrast to the dynamic spatial relations, the static ones explain a static spatial configuration such as the example of the previous section $<on_{SP}$ $book_{TR}$ $table_{LM}>$.

In the case of dynamic spatial information a *path* is associated with the location of the trajector. In our scheme the *path* is characterized by the three values of *beginning*, *middle*, *end* and *zero*. The frame of reference can be intrinsic, relative or absolute and is typically relevant for directional relations. For more details about the scheme, see (Kordjamshidi et al., 2010b).

4 Tasks

The SemEval-2012 shared task is defined in three parts.

- The first part considers labeling the spatial indicators and trajector(s) / landmark(s). In other words at this step we consider the extraction of the individual roles that are tagged with TRAJECTOR, LANDMARK and SPATIAL_INDICATOR.

- The second part is a kind of relation prediction task and the goal is to extract triples containing (spatial-indicator, trajector, landmark). The prediction of the tag of RELATION with its three arguments of SP, TR, LM at the same time is considered.

- The third part concerns the classification of the type of the spatial relation. At the most coarse-grained level this includes labeling the spatial relations i.e. the triplets of (spatial indicator, trajector, landmark) with region, direction, and distance labels. This means the **general-type** of the RELATION should be predicted. The **general-type** is an attribute of the RELATION tag, see the example represented in XML format in section 5.1.

5 Preparation of the dataset

The annotated corpus that we used for this shared task is a subset of IAPR TC-12 image Benchmark (Grubinger et al., 2006). It contains 613 text files that include 1213 sentences in total. This is an extension of the dataset used in (Kordjamshidi et al., 2011c). The original corpus was available free of charge and without copyright restrictions. The corpus contains images taken by tourists with descriptions in different languages. The texts describe objects, and their absolute and relative positions in the image. This makes the corpus a rich resource for spatial information. However the descriptions are not always limited to spatial information. Therefore they are less domain-specific and contain free explanations about the images. Table 1 shows the detailed statistics of this data. The average length of the sentences in this data is about 15 words including punctuation marks with a standard deviation of 8.

The spatial roles are assigned both to phrases and their headwords, but only the **headwords** are evaluated for this task. The spatial relations indicate a triplet of these roles. The general-type is assigned to each triplet of spatial indicator, trajector and landmark.

At the starting point two annotators including one task-organizer and another non-expert annotator, annotated 325 sentences for the spatial roles and relations. The purpose was to realize the disagreement points and prepare a set of instructions in a way to achieve highest-possible agreement. From the first effort an inter-annotator agreement (Carletta, 1996) of 0.89 for Cohen's kappa was obtained. We continued with the a third annotator for the remaining 888 sentences. The annotator had an explanatory session and received a set of instructions and annotated examples to decrease the ambiguity in the annotations.

To avoid complexity only the relations that are directly expressed in the sentence are annotated and spatial reasoning was avoided during the annotations. Sometimes the trajectors and landmarks or both are implicit, meaning that there is no word in the sentence to represent them. For example in the sentence *Come over here*, the trajector *you* is only implicitly present. To be consistent with the number of arguments in spatial relations, in these cases we use the term *undefined* for the implicit roles. Therefore, the spatial relation in the above example is $<over_{SP}\ undefined_{TR}\ here_{LM}>$.

5.1 Data format

The data is released in XML format. The original textual files are split into sentences. Each sentence is placed in a <SENTENCE/> tag and assigned an identifier. This tag contains all the other tags which describe the content and spatial relations of one sentence.

The content of the sentence is placed in the <CONTENT/> tag. The words in each sentence are assigned identifiers depending on their specific roles. Trajectors, landmarks and spatial indicators are identified by <TRAJECTOR/>, <LANDMARK/> and <SPATIAL_INDICATOR/> tags, respectively. Each of these XML elements has an "ID" attribute that identifies a related word by its index. The "ID" prefixed by either "TW", "LW" or "SW", respectively for the mentioned roles. For example, a trajector with ID="TW2" corresponds to the word at index 2 in the sentence. Indexes start at 0. Commas, parentheses and apostrophes are also counted as tokens.

Spatial relations are assigned identifiers too, and relate the role-playing words to each other. Spatial relations are identified by the <RELATION/> tag. The spatial indicator, trajector and landmark for the relation are identified by the "SP", "TR" and "LM" attributes, respectively. The values of these attributes correspond to the "ID" attributes in the <TRAJECTOR/>, <LANDMARK/> and <SPATIAL_INDICATOR/> elements. If a trajector or landmark is implicit, then the index of "TR" or "LM" attribute will be set to a dummy index. This dummy index is equal to the index of the last word in the sentence plus one. In this case, the value of TRAJECTOR or LANDMARK is set to "undefined". The coarse-grained spatial type of the relation is indicated by the "GENERAL_TYPE" attribute and gets one value in {REGION, DIRECTION, DISTANCE}. In the original data set there are cases annotated with multiple spatial types. This is due to the ambiguity and/or under-specificity of natural language compared to formal spatial representations (Kordjamshidi et al., 2010a). In this task the general-type with a higher priority by the annotator is provided. Here, by the high priority type, we mean the general type which has been the most informative

	Spatial Roles			Relations	General Types		
Sentences	TR	LM	SP	Spatial triplets	Region	Direction	Distance
1213	1593	1408	1464	1715	1036	644	35

Table 1: Number of annotated components in the data set.

and relevant type for a relation, from the annotator's point of view. This task considers labeling words rather than phrases for all spatial roles. However, in the XML file for spatial indicators often the whole phrase is tagged. In these cases, the index of the indicator refers to one word which is typically the spatial preposition of the phrase. For evaluation only the indexed words are compared and should be predicted correctly.

Below is one example copied from the data. For more examples and details about the general annotation scheme see (Kordjamshidi et al., 2010b).

<SENTENCE ID='S11'>
<CONTENT >
there are red umbrellas in a park on the right .
</CONTENT>
<TRAJECTOR ID='TW3'>
umbrellas
</TRAJECTOR>
<LANDMARK ID='LW6'>
park
</LANDMARK>
<SPATIAL_INDICATOR ID='SW4'>
in
</SPATIAL_INDICATOR>
<RELATION ID='R0' SP='SW4' TR='TW3' LM='LW6' GENERAL_TYPE='REGION'/>
<SPATIAL_INDICATOR ID='SW7'>
on the right
</SPATIAL_INDICATOR>
<RELATION ID='R1' SP='SW7' TR='TW3' LM='LW6' GENERAL_TYPE='DIRECTION'/>
</SENTENCE>

The dataset, both train and test, also the 10-fold splits are made available in the LIIR research group webpage of KU Leuven.[1]

6 Evaluation methodology

According to the usual setting of the shared tasks our evaluation setting was based on splitting the data set into a training and a testing set. Each set contained about 50% of the whole data. The test set released without the ground-truth labels. However, after the systems submission deadline the ground-truth test was released. Hence the participant group performed an additional 10-fold cross validation evaluation too. We report the results of both evaluation settings.

Prediction of each component including TRAJECTORS, LANDMARKS and SPATIAL-INDICATORS is evaluated on the test set using their individual spatial element XML tags. The evaluation metrics of precision, recall and F1-measure are used, which are defined as:

$$recall = \frac{TP}{TP+FN} \quad (1)$$

$$precision = \frac{TP}{TP+FP} \quad (2)$$

$$F1 = \frac{2*recall*precision}{(recall+precision)}, \quad (3)$$

where:

TP = the number of system-produced XML tags that match an annotated XML tag,
FP = the number of system-produced XML tags that do not match an annotated tag,
FN = the number of annotated XML tags that do not match a system-produced tag.

For the roles evaluation two XML tags match when they have exactly same identifier. In fact, when the identifiers are the same then the role and the word index are the same. In addition, systems are evaluated on how well they are able to retrieve triplets of (trajector, spatial-indicator, landmark), in terms of precision, recall and F1-measure. The TP, FP, FN are counted in a similar way but two RELATION tags match if the combination of their TR, LM and SP is exactly the same. In other words a true prediction requires all the three elements are correctly predicted at the same time.

The last evaluation is on how well the systems are able to retrieve the relations and their general type

[1]http://www.cs.kuleuven.be/groups/liir/software/SpRL_Data/

i.e {region, direction, distance} at the same time. To evaluate the GENERAL-TYPE similarly the RELATION tag is checked. For a true prediction, an exact match between the ground-truth and all the elements of the predicted RELATION tag including TR, LM,SP and GENERAL-TYPE is required.

7 Systems and results

One system with two runs was submitted from the University of Texas Dallas. The two runs (Roberts and Harabagiu, 2012), UTDSPRL-SUPERVISED1 and UTDSPRL-SUPERVISED2 are based on the joint classification of the spatial triplets in a binary classification setting. To produce the candidate (indicator, trajector, landmark) triples, in the first stage heuristic rules targeting a high recall are used. Then a binary support vector machine classifier is employed to predict whether a triple is a spatial relation or not. Both runs start with a large number of manually engineered features, and use floating forward feature selection to select the most important ones. The difference between the two runs of UTDSPRL-SUPERVISED1 and UTDSPRL-SUPERVISED2 is their feature set. Particularly, in UTDSPRL-SUPERVISED1 a joint feature based on the conjunctions (e.g. *and*, *but*) is considered before running feature selection but this feature is removed in UTDSPRL-SUPERVISED2.

The submitted runs are compared to a previous system from the task organizers (Kordjamshidi et al., 2011c) which is evaluated on the current data with the same settings. This system, KUL-SKIP-CHAIN-CRF, uses a skip chain conditional random field (CRF) model (Sutton and MacCallum, 2006) to annotate the sentence as a sequence. It considers the long distance dependencies between the prepositions and nouns in the sentence.

The type and structure of the features used in the UTD and KUL systems are different. In the UTD system, the classifier works on triples and the features are of two main types: (a) argument-specific features about the trajector, landmark, or indicator e.g., the landmark's hypernyms, or the indicator's first token; and (b) joint features that consider two or more of the arguments, e.g. the dependency path between indicator and landmark. For more detail, see (Roberts and Harabagiu, 2012). In the KUL system, the classifier works on all tokens in a sentence, and a number of linguistically motivated local and pairwise features over candidate words and prepositions are used. To consider long distance dependencies a template, called a preposition template, is used in the general CRF framework. Loopy belief propagation is used for inference. Mallet[2] and GRMM:[3] implementations are employed there.

Tables 2, 3 and 4 show the results of the three runs in the standard setting of the shared task using the train/test split. In this evaluation setting the UTDSPRL-SUPERVISED2 run achieves the highest performance on the test set, with F1 of 0.573 for the full triplet identification task, and an F1 of 0.566 for additionally classifying the triplet's general-type

Label	Precsion	Recall	F1
TRAJECTOR	0.731	0.621	0.672
LANDMARK	0.871	0.645	0.741
SPATIAL-INDICATOR	0.928	0.712	0.806
RELATION	0.567	0.500	0.531
GENERAL-TYPE	0.561	0.494	0.526

Table 2: UTDSPRL-SUPERVISED1: The University of Texas-Dallas system with a larger number of features,test/train one split.

Label	Precsion	Recall	F1
TRAJECTOR	0.782	0.646	0.707
LANDMARK	0.894	0.680	0.772
SPATIAL-INDICATOR	0.940	0.732	0.823
RELATION	0.610	0.540	0.573
GENERAL-TYPE	0.603	0.534	0.566

Table 3: UTDSPRL-SUPERVISED2: The University of Texas-Dallas system with a smaller number of features, test/train one split.

Label	Precsion	Recall	F1
TRAJECTOR	0.697	0.603	0.646
LANDMARK	0.773	0.740	0.756
SPATIAL-INDICATOR	0.913	0.887	0.900
RELATION	0.487	0.512	0.500

Table 4: KUL-SKIP-CHAIN-CRF: The organizers' system (Kordjamshidi et al., 2011c)- test/train one split.

[2]http://mallet.cs.umass.edu/download.php

[3]http://mallet.cs.umass.edu/grmm/index.php

System	Precsion	Recall	F1
KUL-SKIP-CHAIN-CRF	0.745	0.773	0.758
UTDSPRL-SUPERVISED2	0.773	0.679	0.723

Table 5: The RELATION extraction of KUL-SKIP-CHAIN-CRF (Kordjamshidi et al., 2011c) vs. UTDSPRL-SUPERVISED2 evaluated with 10-fold cross validation

correctly. It also consistently outperforms both the UTDSPRL-SUPERVISED1 run and the KUL-SKIP-CHAIN-CRF system on each of the individual trajector, landmark and spatial-indicator extraction.

The dataset was relatively small, so we released the test data and the two systems were additionally evaluated using 10-fold cross validation. The results of this cross-validation are shown in Table 5. The UTDSPRL-SUPERVISED2 run achieves a higher precision, while the KUL-SKIP-CHAIN-CRF system achieves a higher recall. It should be mentioned the 10-fold splits used by KUL and UTD are not the same. This implies that the results with exactly the same cross-folds may vary slightly from these reported in Table 5.

Using 10-fold cross validation, we also evaluated the classification of the general-type of a relation given the manually annotated positive triplets. The UTDSPRL-SUPERVISED2 system achieved F1= 0.974, and similar experiments using SMO-SVM in (Kordjamshidi et al., 2011b; Kordjamshidi et al., 2011a) achieved F1= 0.973. Thus it appears that identifying the general-type of a relation is a relatively easy task on this data.

Discussion. Since the feature sets of the two systems are different and given the evaluation results in the two evaluation settings, it is difficult to assert which model is better in general. Obviously using joint features potentially inputs richer information to the model. However, it can increase the sparsity in one hand and overfitting on the training data on the other hand. Another problem is that finding heuristics for high recall that are sufficiently general to be used in every domain is not an easy task. By increasing the number of candidates the dataset imbalance will increase dramatically. This can cause a lower performance of a joint model based on a binary classification setting when applied on different data sets. It seems that this task might require a more elaborated structured output prediction model which can consider the joint features and alleviate the problem of huge negatives in that framework while considering the correlations between the output components.

8 Conclusion

The SemEval-2012 spatial role labeling task is a starting point to formally consider the extraction of spatial semantics from the language. The aim is to consider this task as a standalone linguistic task which is important for many applications. Our first practice on this task and the current submitted system to SemEval 2012 clarify the type of the features and the machine learning approaches appropriate for it. The proposed features and models help to perform this task automatically in a reasonable accuracy. Although the spatial scheme is domain independent, the achieved accuracy is dependent on the domain of the used data for training a model. Our future plan is to extend the data for the next workshops and to cover more semantic aspects of spatial information particularly for mapping to formal spatial representation models and spatial calculus.

Acknowledgments

Special thanks to Martijn Van Otterlo for his great cooperation from the initiation phase and in the growth of this task. Many thanks to Sabine Drebusch for her kind and open cooperation in annotating the very first dataset. Thanks to Tigist Kassahun for her help in annotating the current dataset. Thanks the participant team of the University of Texas Dallas and their useful feedback on the annotated data.

References

J. A. Bateman. 2010. Language and space: a two-level semantic approach based on principles of ontological engineering. *International Journal of Speech Technology*, 13(1):29–48.

T. Butko, C. Nadeu, and A. Moreno. 2011. A multilingual corpus for rich audio-visual scenedescription in a meeting-room environment. In *ICMI workshop on multimodal corpora for machine learning: Taking Stock and Roadmapping the Future*.

J. Carletta. 1996. Assessing agreement on classification tasks: the kappa statistic. *Computational Linguistics*, 22(2):249–254.

A. G. Cohn and J. Renz. 2008. Qualitative spatial representation and reasoning. In *Handbook of Knowledge Representation*, volume 3 of *Foundations of Artificial Intelligence*, pages 551 – 596. Elsevier.

A. Galton. 2009. Spatial and temporal knowledge representation. *Journal of Earth Science Informatics*, 2(3):169–187.

M. Grubinger, P. Clough, Henning Müller, and Thomas Deselaers. 2006. The IAPR benchmark: A new evaluation resource for visual information systems. In *International Conference on Language Resources and Evaluation (LREC)*.

J. Hois and O. Kutz. 2008. Natural language meets spatial calculi. In Christian Freksa, Nora S. Newcombe, Peter Gärdenfors, and Stefan Wölfl, editors, *Spatial Cognition*, volume 5248 of *Lecture Notes in Computer Science*, pages 266–282. Springer.

J. Hois, R. J. Ross, J. D. Kelleher, and J. A. Bateman. 2011. Computational models of spatial language interpretation and generation. In *COSLI-2011*.

P. Kordjamshidi, M. van Otterlo, and M. F. Moens. 2010a. From language towards formal spatial calculi. In *Workshop on Computational Models of Spatial Language Interpretation (CoSLI 2010, at Spatial Cognition 2010)*.

P. Kordjamshidi, M. van Otterlo, and M. F. Moens. 2010b. Spatial role labeling: Task definition and annotation scheme. In *Proceedings of the Seventh conference on International Language Resources and Evaluation (LREC'10)*.

P. Kordjamshidi, J. Hois, M. van Otterlo, and M.-F. Moens. 2011a. Machine learning for interpretation of spatial natural language in terms of qsr. Poster Presentation at the 10th International Conference on Spatial Information Theory (COSIT'11).

P. Kordjamshidi, J. Hois, M. van Otterlo, and M.F. Moens. 2011b. Learning to interpret spatial natural language in terms of qualitative spatial relations. *Representing space in cognition: Interrelations of behavior, language, and formal models. Series Explorations in Language and Space, Oxford University Press, submitted*.

P. Kordjamshidi, M. Van Otterlo, and M.F. Moens. 2011c. Spatial role labeling: Towards extraction of spatial relations from natural language. *ACM Trans. Speech Lang. Process.*, 8:1–36, December.

I. Mani, J. Hitzeman, J. Richer, D. Harris, R. Quimby, and B. Wellner. 2008. SpatialML: Annotation scheme, corpora, and tools. In Nicoletta Calzolari, Khalid Choukri, Bente Maegaard, Joseph Mariani, Jan Odjik, Stelios Piperidis, and Daniel Tapias, editors, *Proceedings of the Sixth International Language Resources and Evaluation (LREC'08)*. European Language Resources Association (ELRA).

MITRE Corporation. 2010. SpatialML: Annotation scheme for marking spatial expression in natural language. Technical Report Version 3.0.1, The MITRE Corporation.

J. Pustejovsky and J.L. Moszkowicz. 2009. Integrating motion predicate classes with spatial and temporal annotations. In *CoLing 2008: Companion volume Posters and Demonstrations*, pages 95–98.

J. Pustejovsky, J. Moszkowicz, and M. Verhagen. 2011. Iso-space: The annotation of spatial information in language. In *Proceedings of ISA-6: ACL-ISO International Workshop on Semantic Annotation*.

K. Roberts and S.M. Harabagiu. 2012. Utd-sprl: A joint approach to spatial role labeling. In *Submitted to this workshop of SemEval-2012*.

R. Ross, J. Hois, and J. Kelleher. 2010. Computational models of spatial language interpretation. In *COSLI-2010*.

O. Stock, editor. 1997. *Spatial and Temporal Reasoning*. Kluwer.

C. Sutton and A. MacCallum. 2006. Introduction to conditional random fields for relational learning. In Lise Getoor and Ben Taskar, editors, *Introduction to Statistical Relational Learning*. MIT Press.

D. A. Tappan. 2004. *Knowledge-Based Spatial Reasoning for Automated Scene Generation from Text Descriptions*. Ph.D. thesis.

S. Tellex, T. Kollar, S. Dickerson, M. R. Walter, and N. Roy A. G. Banerjee, S. Teller. 2011. Understanding natural language commands for robotic navigation and mobile manipulation. In *Proceedings of the National Conference on Artificial Intelligence (AAAI), San Francisco, CA*.

J. Zlatevl. 2007. Spatial semantics. *In Hubert Cuyckens and Dirk Geeraerts (eds.) The Oxford Handbook of Cognitive Linguistics, Chapter 13*, pages 318–350.

SemEval-2012 Task 4: Evaluating Chinese Word Similarity

Peng Jin
School of Computer Science
Leshan Normal University
Leshan, 614000, China
jandp@pku.edu.cn

Yunfang Wu
Institute of Computational Linguistics
Peking University
Beijing, 100871, China
wuyf@pku.edu.cn

Abstract

This task focuses on evaluating word similarity computation in Chinese. We follow the way of Finkelstein et al. (2002) to select word pairs. Then we organize twenty undergraduates who are major in Chinese linguistics to annotate the data. Each pair is assigned a similarity score by each annotator. We rank the word pairs by the average value of similar scores among the twenty annotators. This data is used as gold standard. Four systems participating in this task return their results. We evaluate their results on gold standard data in term of Kendall's tau value, and the results show three of them have a positive correlation with the rank manually created while the taus' value is very small.

1 Introduction

The goal of word similarity is to compute the similarity degree between words. It is widely used in natural language processing to alleviate data sparseness which is an open problem in this field. Many research have focus on English language (Lin, 1998; Curran and Moens, 2003; Dinu and Lapata, 2010), some of which rely on the manual created thesaurus such as WordNet (Budanitsky and Hirst, 2006), some of which obtain the similarity of the words via large scale corpus (Lee, 1999), and some research integrate both thesaurus and corpus (Fujii et al., 1997). This task tries to evaluate the approach on word similarity for Chinese language. To the best of our knowledge, this is first release of benchmark data for this study.

In English language, there are two data sets: Rubenstein and Goodenough (1965) and Finkelstein et al. (2002) created a ranking of word pairs as the benchmark data. Both of them are manually annotated. In this task, we follow the way to create the data and annotate the similarity score between word pairs by twenty Chinese native speakers. Finkelstein et al. (2002) carried out a psycholinguistic experiment: they selected out 353 word pairs, then ask the annotators assign a numerical similarity score between 0 and 10 (0 denotes that words are totally unrelated, 10 denotes that words are VERY closely related) to each pair. By definition, the similarity of the word to itself should be 10. A fractional score is allowed.

It should be noted that besides the rank of word pairs, the thesaurus such as Roget's thesaurus are often used for word similarity study (Gorman and Curran, 2006).

The paper is organized as follows. In section 2 we describe in detail the process of the data preparation. Section 3 introduces the four participating systems. Section 4 reports their results and gives a brief discussion.. And finally in section 5 we bring forward some suggestions for the next campaign and conclude the paper.

2 Data Preparation

2.1 Data Set

We use wordsim 353 (Finkelstein et al., 2002) as the original data set. First, each word pair is translated into Chinese by two undergraduates who are fluent in English. 169 word pairs are the same in their translation results. To the rest 184 word pairs, the third undergraduate student check them following the rules:

(i) Single character vs. two characters. If one translator translate one English word into the Chinese word which consists only one Chinese character and the other use two characters to convey the translation, we will prefer to the later provided that these two translations are semantically same. For example, "tiger" is translated into "虎" and "老虎", we will treat them as same and use "老虎" as the final translation. This was the same case in "drug" ("药" and "药物" are same translations).

(ii) Alias. The typical instance is "potato", both "土豆" and "马铃薯" are the correct translations. So we will treat them as same and prefer "土豆" as the final translation because it is more general used than the latter one.

(iii) There are five distinct word pairs in the translations and are removed.

At last, 348 word pairs are used in this task. Among these 348 word pairs, 50 ones are used as the trial data and the rest ones are used as the test data[1].

2.2 Manual Annotation

Each word pair is assigned the similarity score by twenty Chinese native speakers. The score ranges from 0 to 5 and 0 means two words have nothing to do with each other and 5 means they are identically in semantic meaning. The higher score means the more similar between two words. Not only integer but also real is acceptable as the annotated score. We get the average of all the scores given by the annotators for each word pair and then sort them according to the similarity scores. The distribution of word pairs on the similar score is illustrated as table 1.

Score	0.0-1.0	1.0-2.0	2.0-3.0	3.0-4.0	4.0-5.0
# Word pairs	39	90	132	72	13

Table1: The distribution of similarity score

Rank	Word in Chinese/English	Word 2 in Chinese/ English	Similarity score	Std. dev	RSD (%)
1	足球/football	足球/soccer	4.98	0.1	2.0
2	老虎/tiger	老虎/tiger	4.89	0.320	6.55
3	恒星/planet	恒星/star	4.72	0.984	20.8
4	入场券 /admission	门票/ticket	4.60	0.516	11.2
5	钱/money	现金/cash	4.58	0.584	12.7
6	银行/bank	钱/cash	4.29	0.708	16.5
7	手机/cell	电话/phone	4.28	0.751	17.5
8	宝石/gem	珠宝/jewel	4.24	0.767	18.1
9	类型/type	种类/kind	4.24	1.000	23.6
10	运算 / calculation	计算 / computation	4.14	0.780	19.0
Avg	-	-	4.496	0.651	14.80

Table 2: Top ten similar word pairs

Table 2 and table 3 list top ten similar word pairs and top ten un-similar word pairs individually. Standard deviation (Std. dev) and relative standard deviation (RSD) are also computed. Obviously, the relative standard deviation of top ten similar word pairs is far less than the un-similar pairs.

2.3 Annotation Analysis

Figure 1 illustrates the relationship between the similarity score and relative standard deviation. The digits in "x" axes are the average similarity score of every integer interval, for an instance, 1.506 is the average of all word pairs' similarity score between 1.0 and 2.0.

3 Participating Systems

Four systems coming from two teams participated in this task.

[1] In fact there are 297 word pairs are evaluated because one pair is missed during the annotation.

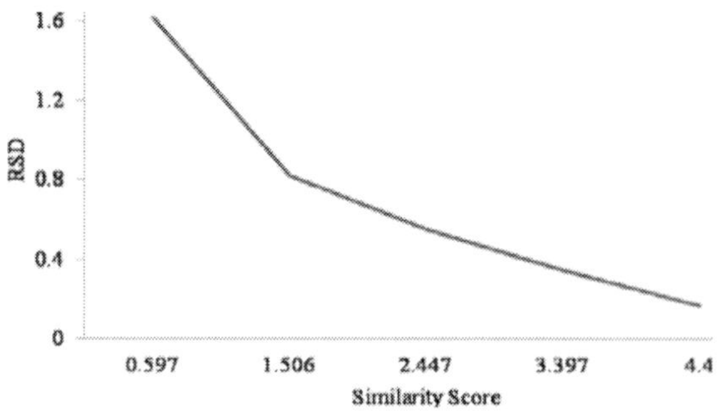

Figure 1. The relationship between RSD and similar score

Rank	Word1 in Chinese/in English	Word2 in Chinese/in English	Similarity score	Std. dev	RSD(%)
1	中午/noon	线绳/string	0.06	.213	338.7
2	国王/king	卷心菜/cabbage	0.16	.382	245.3
3	产品/production	徒步/hike	0.17	.432	247.5
4	延迟/delay	种族主义/racism	0.26	.502	191.1
5	教授/professor	黄瓜/cucumber	0.30	.62	211.1
6	股票/stock	美洲虎/jaguar	0.30	.815	268.2
7	签名/sign	暂停/recess	0.30	.655	215.4
8	股票/stock	CD/CD	0.31	.540	173.6
9	喝/drink	耳朵/ear	0.31	.833	264.8
10	公鸡/rooster	航程/voyage	0.33	.771	236.7
Avg	-	-	0.25	.576	239.2

Table 3: Top ten un-similar word pairs

MIXCC: This system used two machine readable dictionary (MRD), HIT IR-Lab Tongyici Cilin (Extended) (Cilin) and the other is Chinese Concept Dictionary (CCD). The extended CiLin consists of 12 large classes, 97 medium classes, 1,400 small classes (topics), and 17,817 small synonym sets which cover 77,343 head terms. All the items are constructed as a tree with five levels. With the increasing of levels, word senses are more fine-grained. The Chinese Concept Dictionary is a Chinese WordNet produced by Peking University. Word concepts are presented as synsets corresponding to WordNet 1.6. Besides synonym, antonym, hypernym/hyponym, holonym/meronym, there is another semantic relation type named as *attribute* which happens between two words with different part-of-speeches.

They first divide all word pairs into five parts and rank them according to their levels in Cilin in descending order. For each part, they computed word similarity by Jiang and Conrath (1997) method[2].

MIXCD: Different form MIXCC, this system used the trial data to learn a multiple linear regression functions. The CCD was considered as a directed graph. The nodes were synsets and edges were the semantic relations between two synsets. The features for this system were derived from CCD and a corpus and listed as follows:

- the shortest path between two synsets which contain the words
- the rates of 5 semantic relation types
- mutual information of a word pair in the corpus

They used the result of multiple linear regressions to forecast the similarity of other word pairs and get the rank.

GUO-ngram: This system used the method proposed by (Gabrilovich and Markovitch, 2007). They downloaded the Wikipedia on 25th November, 2011 as the knowledge source. In order to bypass the Chinese segmentation, they extract one character (uni-gram) and two sequential characters (bi-gram) as the features.

GUO-words: This system is very similar to GUO-ngram except that the features consist of words rather than n-grams. They implemented a simple index method which searches all continuous character strings appearing in a dictionary. For example, given a text string ABCDEFG in which ABC, BC, and EF appear in the dictionary. The output of the tokenization algorithm is the three words ABC, BC, EF and the two characters E and G.

[2] Because there is no sense-tagged corpus for CCD, the frequency of each concept was set to 1 in this system.

4 Results

Each system is required to rank these 500 word pairs according to their similarity scores. Table 4 gives the overall results obtained by each of the systems.

Rank	Team ID	System ID	Tau's value
1	lib	MIXCC	0.050
2		MIXCD	0.040
3	Gfp1987	Guo-ngram	0.007
4		Guo-words	-0.011

Table 4: The results of four systmes

The ranks returned by these four systems will be compared with the rank from human annotation by the Kendall Rank Correlation Coefficient:

$$\tau = 1 - \frac{2S(\pi,\sigma)}{N(N-1)/2}$$

Where N is the number of objects. π and σ are two distinct orderings of a object in two ranks. $S(\pi,\sigma)$ is the minimum number of adjacent transpositions needing to bring π and σ (Lapata, 2006). In this metric, tau's value ranges from -1 to +1 and -1 means that the two ranks are inverse to each other and +1 means the identical rank.

From table 4, we can see that except the final system, three of them got the positive tau's value. It is regret that the tau's is very small even if the MIXCC system is the best one.

5 Conclusion

We organize an evaluation task focuses on word similarity in Chinese language. Totally 347 word pairs are annotated similarity scores by twenty native speakers. These word pairs are ordered by the similarity scores and this rank is used as benchmark data for evaluation.

Four systems participated in this task. Except the system MIXCD, three ones got their own rank only via the corpus. Kendall's tau is used as the evaluation metric. Three of them got the positive correlation rank compared with the gold standard data

Generally the tau's value is very small, it indicates that obtaining a *good* rank is still difficult. We will provide more word pairs and distinct them relatedness from similar, and attract more teams to participate in the interesting task.

Acknowledgments

This research is supported by National Natural Science Foundation of China (NSFC) under Grant No. 61003206, 60703063.

References

A. Budanitsky and G. Hirst. Evaluating WordNet-based Measures of Lexical Semantic Relatedness. *Computational Linguistics*, 2006, 32(1):13-47.

J. Curran and M. Moens. Scaling Context Space. *Proceedings of ACL*, 2002, pp. 231-238.

G. Dinu and M. Lapata. Measuring Distributional Similarity in Context. *Proceedings of EMNLP*, 2010, pp. 1162-1172.

L. Finkelstein, E. Gabrilovich, Y. Matias, E. Rivlin, Z. Solan, G. Wolfman, and E. Ruppin. 2002. Placing Search in Context: The Concept Revisited. *ACM Transactions on Information Systems*, 20(1):116-131.

A. Fujii, T. Hasegawa, T. Tokunaga and H. Tanaka. Integration of Hand-Crafted and Statistical Resources in Measuring Word Similarity. 1997. *Proceedings of Workshop of Automatic Information Extraction and Building of Lexical Semantic Resources for NLP Applications*. pp. 45-51.

E. Gabrilovich and S. Markovitch, Computing Semantic Relatedness using Wikipedia-based Explicit Semantic Analysis, *Proceedings of IJCAI,* Hyderabad, 2007, pp. 1606—1611.

J. Gorman and J. Curran. Scaling Distributional Similarity to Large Corpora. *Proceedings of ACL*, 2006, pp. 361-368.

J. Jiang and D. Conrath. 1997. Semantic similarity based on corpus statistics and lexical taxonomy. *Proceedings of International Conference on Research in Computational Linguistics*, Taiwan.

M. Lapata. Automatic Evaluation of Information Ordering: Kendall's Tau. *Computational Linguistics*, 2006, 32(4):471-484.

D. Lin. Automatic Retrieval and Clustering of Similar Words. *Proceedings of ACL / COLING*, 1998, pp. 768-774.

L. Lee. Measures of Distributional Similarity. *Proceedings of ACL*, 1999, pp. 25-32.

H. Rubenstein and J.B. Goodenough. 1965. Contextual correlates of synonymy. *Communications of the ACM*, 8(10):627-633.

SemEval-2012 Task 5: Chinese Semantic Dependency Parsing

Wanxiang Che[†], **Meishan Zhang**[†], **Yanqiu Shao**[‡], **Ting Liu**[†]
[†]Research Center for Social Computing and Information Retrieval
Harbin Institute of Technology, China
`{car, mszhang, tliu}@ir.hit.edu.cn`
[‡]Beijing City University, China
`yqshao@bcu.edu.cn`

Abstract

The paper presents the SemEval-2012 Shared Task 5: *Chinese Semantic Dependency Parsing*. The goal of this task is to identify the dependency structure of Chinese sentences from the semantic view. We firstly introduce the motivation of providing Chinese semantic dependency parsing task, and then describe the task in detail including data preparation, data format, task evaluation, and so on. Over ten thousand sentences were labeled for participants to train and evaluate their systems. At last, we briefly describe the submitted systems and analyze these results.

1 Introduction

Semantic analysis is a long-term goal of Natural Language Processing, and as such, has been researched for several decades. A number of tasks for encoding semantic information have been developed over the years, such as entity type recognition and word sense disambiguation. Recently, sentence-level semantics – in particular, semantic role labeling – has received increasing attention. However, some problems concerning the semantic representation method used in semantic role labeling continue to exist (Xue and Palmer, 2005).

1. Semantic role labeling only considers predicate-argument relations and ignores the semantic relations between a noun and its modifier.

2. The meaning of semantic roles is related to special predicates. Therefore, there are infinite semantic roles to be learned, as the number of predicates is not fixed. Although the PropBank (Xue and Palmer, 2003) normalizes these semantic roles into certain symbols, such as Arg0-Arg5, the same symbol can have different semantic meanings when paired with different predicates, and thus cannot be learned well.

Semantic dependency parsing is therefore proposed to solve the two problems above for Chinese. Firstly, the proposed method analyzes all the words' semantic roles in a sentence and specifies the concrete semantic relation of each word pair. Afterward, this work analyzes and summarizes all the possible semantic roles, obtaining over 100 of them, and then uses these semantic roles to specify the semantic relation for each word pair.

Dependency parsing (Kübler et al., 2009) is based on dependency grammar. It has several advantages, such as concise formalization, easy comprehension, high efficiency, and so on. Dependency parsing has been studied intensively in recent decades, with most related work focusing on syntactic structure. Many research papers on Chinese linguistics demonstrate the remarkable difference between semantics and syntax (Jin, 2001; Zhou and Zhang, 2003). Chinese is a meaning-combined language with very flexible syntax, and semantics are more stable than syntax. The word is the basic unit of semantics, and the structure and meaning of a sentence consists mainly of a series of semantic dependencies between individual words (Li et al., 2003). Thus, a reasonable endeavor is to exploit dependency parsing for semantic analysis of Chinese languages. Figure 1 shows an example of Chinese semantic dependency parsing.

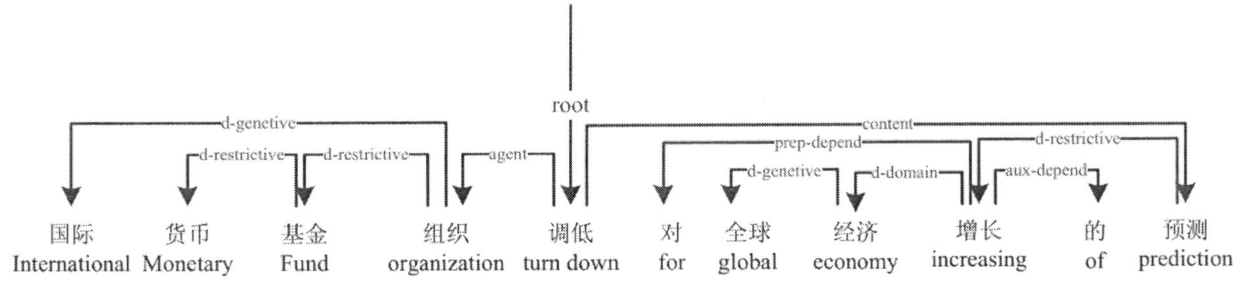

Figure 1: An example of Chinese Semantic Dependency Parsing.

Figure 1 shows that Chinese semantic dependency parsing looks very similar to traditional syntax-dominated dependency parsing. Below is a comparison between the two tasks, dealing with three main points:

1. Semantic relations are more fine-grained than syntactic ones: the syntactic subject can either be the agent or experiencer, and the syntactic object can be the content, patient, possession, and so on. On the whole, the number of semantic relations is at least twice that of syntactic relations.

2. Semantic dependency parsing builds the dependency structure of a sentence in terms of semantics, and the word pairs of a dependency should have a direct semantic relation. This criterion determines many sizeable differences between semantics and syntax, especially in phrases formed by "XP+DEG", "XP+DEV" and prepositional phrases. For example, in "美丽 的 祖国" (beautiful country), the head of "美丽" (beautiful) is "祖国" (country) in semantic dependency parsing, whereas the head is "的" (de) in syntax dependency parsing.

3. Semantic relations are independent of position. For example, in "空气 被 污染" (the air is contaminated) and "污染 了 空气" (contaminate the air), the patient "空气" (the air) can be before or behind a predicate "污染" (contaminate).

The rest of the paper is organized as follows. Section 2 gives a short overview of data annotation. Section 3 focuses on the task description. Section 4 describes the participant systems. Section 5 compares and analyzes the results. Finally, Section 6 concludes the paper.

2 Data Annotation

2.1 Corpus Section

10,068 sentences were selected from the Penn Chinese Treebank 6.0[1] (Xue et al., 2005) (1-121, 1001-1078, 1100-1151) as the raw corpus from which to create the Chinese Semantic Dependency Parsing corpus. These sentences were chosen for the annotation for three reasons. First, gold syntactic dependency structures can be of great help in semantic dependency annotation, as syntactic dependency arcs are often consistent with semantic ones. Second, the semantic role labels in PropBank[2] can be very useful in the present annotation work. Third, the gold word segmentation and Part-Of-Speech can be used as the annotation input in this work.

2.2 Semantic Relations

The semantic relations in the prepared Chinese semantic dependency parsing corpus came mostly from HowNet[3] (Dong and Dong, 2006), a famous Chinese semantic thesaurus. We also referred to other sources. Aside from the relations from HowNet, we defined two kinds of new relations: reverse relations and indirect relations. When a verb modifies a noun, the relation between them is a reverse relation, and r-XXX is used to indicate this kind of relation. For instance, in "打 篮球 的 小 男孩" (the little boy who is playing basketball), the semantic relation between the head word "男孩" (boy)

[1] http://www.ldc.upenn.edu/Catalog/catalogEntry.jsp?catalog\\Id=LDC2007T36

[2] http://verbs.colorado.edu/chinese/cpb/

[3] http://www.keenage.com/

and “打” (playing) is the r-agent. When a verbal noun is the head word, the relation between it and the modifier is the indirect relation j-XXX. For instance, in “企业 管理” (business management), the head word is “管理” (management) and the modifier is “企业” (business), their relation is j-patient.

Finally, we defined 84 single-level semantic relations. The number of multi-level semantic relations that actually appear in the labeled corpus in this work is 39.

Table 1 summarizes all of the semantic relations used for annotation.

2.3 Annotation Flow

Our corpus annotation flow can be divided into the following steps.

1. Conversion of the sentences' constituent structures into dependency structures according to a set of rules similar with those used by the syntactic community to find the head of a phrase (Collins, 1999).

2. Labeling of the semantic relations for each dependency relation according to another set of rules using the functional tags in the Penn Chinese Treebank and the semantic roles in the Chinese PropBank.

3. Six human annotators are asked to check and adjust the structure and semantic relation errors introduced in Step 2.

The first two steps were performed automatically using rules. A high accuracy may be achieved with dependency structures when semantic labels are not considered. However, accuracy declines remarkably when the semantic label is considered. Unlabeled Attachment Score (UAS) and Labeled Attachment Score (LAS) can be used to evaluate the performance of the automatic conversion. Table 2 gives the detailed results.

	UAS	LAS
Conversion Result	90.53	57.38

Table 2: Accuracy after conversion from gold ProbBank.

3 Task Description

3.1 Corpus Statistics

We annotated 10,068 sentences from the Penn Chinese TreeBank for Semantic Dependency Parsing, and these sentences were divided into training, development, and test sections. Table 3 gives the detailed statistical information of the three sections.

Data Set	CTB files	# sent.	# words.
Training	1-10; 36-65;81-121; 1001-1078; 1100-1119; 1126-1140	8301	250311
Devel	66-80; 1120-1125	534	15329
Test	11-35; 1141-1151	1233	34311
Total	1-121; 1001-1078 1100-1151	10068	299951

Table 3: Statistics of training, development and test data.

3.2 Data Format

The data format is identical to that of a syntactic dependency parsing shared task. All the sentences are in one text file, with each sentence separated by a blank line. Each sentence consists of one or more tokens, and each token is represented on one line consisting of 10 fields. Buchholz and Marsi (2006) provide more detailed information on the format. Fields are separated from each other by a tab. Only five of the 10 fields are used: token id, form, pos tagger, head, and deprel. Head denotes the semantic dependency of each word, and deprel denotes the corresponding semantic relations of the dependency. In the data, the lemma column is filled with the form and the cpostag column with the postag. Figure 2 shows an example.

3.3 Evaluation Method

LAS, which is a method widely used in syntactic dependency parsing, is used to evaluate the performance of the semantic dependency parsing system. LAS is the proportion of “scoring” tokens assigned to both the correct head and correct semantic dependency relation. Punctuation is disregarded during the evaluation process. UAS is another important indicator, as it reflects the accuracy of the semantic dependency structure.

Main Semantic Roles	
Subject Roles	agent, experiencer, causer, possessor, existent, whole, relevant
Object Roles	isa, content, possession, patient, OfPart, beneficiary, contrast, partner, basis, cause, cost, scope, concerning
Auxiliary Semantic Roles	
Time Roles	duration, TimeFin, TimeIni, time, TimeAdv
Location and State Roles	LocationFin, LocationIni, LocationThru, StateFin, state, StateIni, direction, distance, location
Others Verb Modifiers	accompaniment, succeeding, frequency, instrument, material, means, angle, times, sequence, sequence-p, negation, degree, modal, emphasis, manner, aspect, comment
Attribute Roles	
Direct modifiers	d-genetive, d-category, d-member, d-domain, d-quantity-p, d-quantity, d-deno-p, d-deno, d-host, d-TimePhrase, d-LocPhrase, d-InstPhrase, d-attribute, d-restrictive, d-material, d-content, d-sequence, d-sequence-p, qp-mod
Verb Phrase	r-{Main Semantic Roles}, eg: r-agent, r-patient, r-possessor
Verb Ellipsis	c-{Main Semantic Roles}, eg: c-agent, c-content, c-patient
Noun as Predication	j-{Main Semantic Roles}, eg: j-agent, j-patient, j-target
Syntactic Roles and Others	
Syntactic Roles	s-cause, s-concession, s-condition, s-coordinate, s-or, s-progression, s-besides, s-succession, s-purpose, s-measure, s-abandonment, s-preference, s-summary, s-recount, s-concerning, s-result
Others	aux-depend, prep-depend, PU, ROOT

Table 1: Semantic Relations defined for Chinese Semantic Dependency Parsing.

ID	FORM	LEMMA	CPOS	PPOS	FEAT	HEAD	REL	PHEAD	PREL
1	钱其琛	钱其琛	NR	NR	_	2	agent	_	_
2	谈	谈	VV	VV	_	0	ROOT	_	_
3	香港	香港	NR	NR	_	4	d-genetive	_	_
4	前景	前景	NN	NN	_	7	s-coordinate	_	_
5	和	和	CC	CC	_	7	aux-depend	_	_
6	台湾	台湾	NR	NR	_	7	d-genetive	_	_
7	问题	问题	NN	NN	_	2	content	_	_

Figure 2: Data format of the Chinese Semantic Dependency Parsing corpus.

4 Participating Systems

Nine organizations were registered to participate in the Chinese Semantic Dependency Parsing task. Finally, nine systems were received from five different participating teams. These systems are as follows:

1. Zhou Qiaoli-1, Zhou Qiaoli-2, Zhou Qiaoli-3
   These three systems propose a divide-and-conquer strategy for semantic dependency parsing. The Semantic Role (SR) phrases are identified (Cai et al., 2011) and then replaced by their head or the SR of the head. The original sentence is thus divided into two types of parts that can be parsed separately. The first type is SR phrase parsing, and the second involves the replacement of SR phrases with either their head or the SR of the head. Finally, the paper takes a graph-based parser (Li et al., 2011) as the semantic dependency parser for all parts. These three systems differ in their phrase identification strategies.

2. NJU-Parser-1, NJU-Parser-2
   The NJU-Parser is based on the state-of-the-art MSTParser (McDonald, 2006). NJU-Parser applies three methods to enhance semantic dependency parsing. First, sentences are split into sub-sentences using commas and semicolons: (a) sentences are split using only commas and semicolons, as in the primary system, and (b) classifiers are used to determine whether a comma or semicolon should be used to split the sentence. Second, the last character in a Chinese word is extracted as the lemma, since it usually contains the main sense or semantic class. Third, the multilevel-label is introduced into the semantic relation, for example, the r-{Main Semantic Roles}, with NJU-Parser exploiting special strategies to handle it. However, this third method does not show positive performance.

3. Zhijun Wu-1
   This system extends the second-order of the MSTParser by adding third-order features, and then applying this model to Chinese semantic dependency parsing. In contrast to Koo and Collins (2010) this system does not implement the third-order model using dynamic programming, as it requires $O(n^4)$ time. It first first obtained the K-best results of second-order models and then added the third-order features into the results.

4. ICT-1
   The ICT semantic dependency parser employs a system-combining strategy to obtain the dependency structure and then uses the classifier from Le Zhang's Maximum Entropy Modeling Toolkit[4] to predict the semantic relation for each dependency. The system-combining strategy involves three steps:

   - Parsing each sentence using Nivre's arc standard, Nivre's arc eager (Nivre and Nilsson, 2005; Nivre, 2008), and Liang's dynamic algorithm (Huang and Sagae, 2010);
   - Combining parses given by the three parsers into a weighted directed graph;
   - Using the Chu-Liu-Edmonds algorithm to search for the final parse for each sentence.

5. Giuseppe Attardi-SVM-1-R, Giuseppe Attardi-SVM-1-rev
   We didn't receive the system description of these two systems.

5 Results & Analysis

LAS is the main evaluation metric in Chinese Semantic Dependency Parsing, whereas UAS is the secondary metric. Table 4 shows the results for these two indicators in all participating systems.

As shown in Table 4, the Zhou Qiaoli-3 system achieved the best results with LAS of 61.84. The LAS values of top systems are very closely. We performed significance tests[5] for top six results. Table 5 shows the results , from which we can see that the performances of top five results are comparative ($p > 0.1$) and the rank sixth system is significantly ($p < 10^{-5}$) worse than top five results.

[4]http://homepages.inf.ed.ac.uk/s0450736/maxenttoolkit.html

[5]http://www.cis.upenn.edu/~dbikel/download/compare.pl

	NJU-Parser-2	NJU-Parser-1	Zhijun Wu-1	Zhou Qiaoli-1	Zhou Qiaoli-2
Zhou Qiaoli-3	$\sim$	$\sim$	$\sim$	$\sim$	$>$
NJU-Parser-2	–	$\sim$	$\sim$	$\sim$	$>$
NJU-Parser-1	–	–	$\sim$	$\sim$	$>$
Zhijun Wu-1	–	–	–	$\sim$	$>$
Zhou Qiaoli-1	–	–	–	–	$>$

Table 5: Significance tests of the top five systems. $\sim$ denotes that the two systems are comparable ($p > 0.1$), and $>$ means the system of this row is significantly ($p < 10^{-5}$) better than the system of this column.

System	LAS	UAS
Zhou Qiaoli-3	61.84	80.60
NJU-Parser-2	61.64	80.29
NJU-Parser-1	61.63	80.35
Zhijun Wu-1	61.58	80.64
Zhou Qiaoli-1	61.15	80.41
Zhou Qiaoli-2	57.55	78.55
ICT-1	56.31	73.20
Giuseppe Attardi-SVM-1-R	44.46	60.83
Giuseppe Attardi-SVM-1-rev	21.86	40.47
Average	54.22	72.82

Table 4: Results of the submitted systems.

The average LAS for all systems was 54.22. Chinese Semantic Dependency Parsing performed much more poorly than Chinese Syntactic Dependency Parsing due to the increased complexity brought about by the greater number of semantic relations compared with syntactic relations, as well as greater difficulty in classifying semantic relations.

In general, all the systems employed the traditional syntax-dominated dependency parsing frameworks. Some new methods were proposed for this task. Zhou Qiaoli's systems first identified the semantic role phrase in a sentence, and then employed graph-based dependency parsing to analyze the semantic structure of the sentence. NJU-Parser first split the sentence into sub-sentences, then trained and parsed the sentence based on these sub-sentences; this was shown to perform well. In addition, ensemble models were also proposed to solve the task using ICT systems.

6 Conclusion

We described the Chinese Semantic Dependency Parsing task for SemEval-2012, which is designed to parse the semantic structures of Chinese sentences.

Nine results were submitted by five organizations, with the best result garnering an LAS score of 61.84, which is far below the performance of Chinese Syntax. This demonstrates that further research on the structure of Chinese Semantics is needed.

In the future, we will check and improve the annotation standards while building a large, high-quality corpus for further Chinese semantic research.

Acknowledgments

We thank the anonymous reviewers for their helpful comments. This work was supported by National Natural Science Foundation of China (NSFC) via grant 61133012 and 61170144, and the National "863" Leading Technology Research Project via grant 2012AA011102.

References

Sabine Buchholz and Erwin Marsi. 2006. Conll-x shared task on multilingual dependency parsing. In *Proceedings of the Tenth Conference on Computational Natural Language Learning (CoNLL-X)*, pages 149–164, New York City, June. Association for Computational Linguistics.

Dongfeng Cai, Ling Zhang, Qiaoli Zhou, and Yue Zhao. 2011. A collocation based approach for prepositional phrase identification. *IEEE NLPKE*.

Michael Collins. 1999. *Head-Driven Statistical Models for Natural Language Parsing*. Ph.D. thesis, Pennsylvania University.

Zhendong Dong and Qiang Dong. 2006. *Hownet And the Computation of Meaning*. World Scientific Publishing Co., Inc., River Edge, NJ, USA.

Liang Huang and Kenji Sagae. 2010. Dynamic programming for linear-time incremental parsing. In *Proceedings of the 48th Annual Meeting of the Association for Computational Linguistics*, pages 1077–1086,

Uppsala, Sweden, July. Association for Computational Linguistics.

Guangjin Jin. 2001. *Theory of modern Chinese verb semantic computation*. Beijing University Press.

Terry Koo and Michael Collins. 2010. Efficient third-order dependency parsers. In *Proceedings of the 48th Annual Meeting of the ACL*, number July, pages 1–11.

Sandra Kübler, Ryan McDonald, and Joakim Nivre. 2009. Dependency Parsing. In *Synthesis Lectures on Human Language Technologies*.

Mingqin Li, Juanzi Li, Zhendong Dong, Zuoying Wang, and Dajin Lu. 2003. Building a large chinese corpus annotated with semantic dependency. In *Proceedings of the second SIGHAN workshop on Chinese language processing - Volume 17*, SIGHAN '03, pages 84–91, Stroudsburg, PA, USA. Association for Computational Linguistics.

Zhenghua Li, Min Zhang, Wanxiang Che, Ting Liu, Wenliang Chen, and Haizhou Li. 2011. Joint models for chinese pos tagging and dependency parsing. In *Proceedings of the 2011 Conference on Empirical Methods in Natural Language Processing*, pages 1180–1191, Edinburgh, Scotland, UK., July. Association for Computational Linguistics.

Ryan McDonald. 2006. *Discriminative learning and spanning tree algorithms for dependency parsing*. Ph.D. thesis, University of Pennsylvania.

Joakim Nivre and Jens Nilsson. 2005. Pseudo-projective dependency parsing. In *Proceedings of the 43rd Annual Meeting of the Association for Computational Linguistics (ACL)*.

Joakim Nivre. 2008. Algorithms for deterministic incremental dependency parsing. *Computational Linguistics*, 34(4):513–553.

Nianwen Xue and Martha Palmer. 2003. Annotating the propositions in the penn chinese treebank. In *Proceedings of the Second SIGHAN Workshop on Chinese Language Processing*.

Nianwen Xue and Martha Palmer. 2005. Automatic semantic role labeling for chinese verbs. In *Proceedings of the 19th International Joint Conference on Artificial Intelligence*.

Nianwen Xue, Fei Xia, Fu-Dong Chiou, and Martha Palmer. 2005. The penn chinese treebank: Phrase structure annotation of a large corpus. *Natural Language Engineering*, 11(2):207–238.

Guoguang Zhou and Linlin Zhang. 2003. *The theory and method of modern Chinese grammar*. Guangdong Higher Education Press.

SemEval-2012 Task 6: A Pilot on Semantic Textual Similarity

Eneko Agirre
University of the Basque Country
Donostia, 20018, Basque Country
e.agirre@ehu.es

Daniel Cer
Stanford University
Stanford, CA 94305, USA
danielcer@stanford.edu

Mona Diab
Center for Computational Learning Systems
Columbia University
mdiab@ccls.columbia.edu

Aitor Gonzalez-Agirre
University of the Basque Country
Donostia, 20018, Basque Country
agonzalez278@ikasle.ehu.es

Abstract

Semantic Textual Similarity (STS) measures the degree of semantic equivalence between two texts. This paper presents the results of the STS pilot task in Semeval. The training data contained 2000 sentence pairs from previously existing paraphrase datasets and machine translation evaluation resources. The test data also comprised 2000 sentences pairs for those datasets, plus two surprise datasets with 400 pairs from a different machine translation evaluation corpus and 750 pairs from a lexical resource mapping exercise. The similarity of pairs of sentences was rated on a 0-5 scale (low to high similarity) by human judges using Amazon Mechanical Turk, with high Pearson correlation scores, around 90%. 35 teams participated in the task, submitting 88 runs. The best results scored a Pearson correlation >80%, well above a simple lexical baseline that only scored a 31% correlation. This pilot task opens an exciting way ahead, although there are still open issues, specially the evaluation metric.

1 Introduction

Semantic Textual Similarity (STS) measures the degree of semantic equivalence between two sentences. STS is related to both Textual Entailment (TE) and Paraphrase (PARA). STS is more directly applicable in a number of NLP tasks than TE and PARA such as Machine Translation and evaluation, Summarization, Machine Reading, Deep Question Answering, etc. STS differs from TE in as much as it assumes symmetric graded equivalence between the pair of textual snippets. In the case of TE the equivalence is directional, e.g. a car is a vehicle, but a vehicle is not necessarily a car. Additionally, STS differs from both TE and PARA in that, rather than being a binary yes/no decision (e.g. a vehicle is not a car), STS incorporates the notion of graded semantic similarity (e.g. a vehicle and a car are more similar than a wave and a car).

STS provides a unified framework that allows for an extrinsic evaluation of multiple semantic components that otherwise have tended to be evaluated independently and without broad characterization of their impact on NLP applications. Such components include word sense disambiguation and induction, lexical substitution, semantic role labeling, multiword expression detection and handling, anaphora and coreference resolution, time and date resolution, named-entity handling, underspecification, hedging, semantic scoping and discourse analysis. Though not in the scope of the current pilot task, we plan to explore building an open source toolkit for integrating and applying diverse linguistic analysis modules to the STS task.

While the characterization of STS is still preliminary, we observed that there was no comparable existing dataset extensively annotated for pairwise semantic sentence similarity. We approached the construction of the first STS dataset with the following goals: (1) To set a definition of STS as a graded notion which can be easily communicated to non-expert annotators beyond the likert-scale; (2) To gather a substantial amount of sentence pairs from diverse datasets, and to annotate them with high quality; (3) To explore evaluation measures for STS; (4) To explore the relation of STS to PARA and Machine Translation Evaluation exercises.

In the next section we present the various sources of the STS data and the annotation procedure used. Section 4 investigates the evaluation of STS systems. Section 5 summarizes the resources and tools used by participant systems. Finally, Section 6 draws the conclusions.

2 Source Datasets

Datasets for STS are scarce. Existing datasets include (Li et al., 2006) and (Lee et al., 2005). The first dataset includes 65 sentence pairs which correspond to the dictionary definitions for the 65 word pairs in Similarity(Rubenstein and Goodenough, 1965). The authors asked human informants to assess the meaning of the sentence pairs on a scale from 0.0 (minimum similarity) to 4.0 (maximum similarity). While the dataset is very relevant to STS, it is too small to train, develop and test typical machine learning based systems. The second dataset comprises 50 documents on news, ranging from 51 to 126 words. Subjects were asked to judge the similarity of document pairs on a five-point scale (with 1.0 indicating "highly unrelated" and 5.0 indicating "highly related"). This second dataset comprises a larger number of document pairs, but it goes beyond sentence similarity into textual similarity.

When constructing our datasets, gathering naturally occurring pairs of sentences with different degrees of semantic equivalence was a challenge in itself. If we took pairs of sentences at random, the vast majority of them would be totally unrelated, and only a very small fragment would show some sort of semantic equivalence. Accordingly, we investigated reusing a collection of existing datasets from tasks that are related to STS.

We first studied the pairs of text from the Recognizing TE challenge. The first editions of the challenge included pairs of sentences as the following:

> T: The Christian Science Monitor named a US journalist kidnapped in Iraq as freelancer Jill Carroll.
> H: Jill Carroll was abducted in Iraq.

The first sentence is the text, and the second is the hypothesis. The organizers of the challenge annotated several pairs with a binary tag, indicating whether the hypothesis could be entailed from the text. Although these pairs of text are interesting we decided to discard them from this pilot because the length of the hypothesis was typically much shorter than the text, and we did not want to bias the STS task in this respect. We may, however, explore using TE pairs for STS in the future.

Microsoft Research (MSR) has pioneered the acquisition of paraphrases with two manually annotated datasets. The first, called MSR Paraphrase (MSRpar for short) has been widely used to evaluate text similarity algorithms. It contains 5801 pairs of sentences gleaned over a period of 18 months from thousands of news sources on the web (Dolan et al., 2004). 67% of the pairs were tagged as paraphrases. The inter annotator agreement is between 82% and 84%. Complete meaning equivalence is not required, and the annotation guidelines allowed for some relaxation. The pairs which were annotated as not being paraphrases ranged from completely unrelated semantically, to partially overlapping, to those that were almost-but-not-quite semantically equivalent. In this sense our graded annotations enrich the dataset with more nuanced tags, as we will see in the following section. We followed the original split of 70% for training and 30% for testing. A sample pair from the dataset follows:

> The Senate Select Committee on Intelligence is preparing a blistering report on prewar intelligence on Iraq.
>
> American intelligence leading up to the war on Iraq will be criticized by a powerful US Congressional committee due to report soon, officials said today.

In order to construct a dataset which would reflect a uniform distribution of similarity ranges, we sampled the MSRpar dataset at certain ranks of string similarity. We used the implementation readily accessible at CPAN[1] of a well-known metric (Ukkonen, 1985). We sampled equal numbers of pairs from five bands of similarity in the [0.4 .. 0.8] range separately from the paraphrase and non-paraphrase pairs. We sampled 1500 pairs overall, which we split 50% for training and 50% for testing.

The second dataset from MSR is the MSR Video Paraphrase Corpus (MSRvid for short). The authors showed brief video segments to Annotators from Amazon Mechanical Turk (AMT) and were asked

[1] http://search.cpan.org/~mlehmann/String-Similarity-1.04/Similarity.pm

- A person is slicing a cucumber into pieces.
- A chef is slicing a vegetable.
- A person is slicing a cucumber.
- A woman is slicing vegetables.
- A woman is slicing a cucumber.
- A person is slicing cucumber with a knife.
- A person cuts up a piece of cucumber.
- A man is slicing cucumber.
- A man cutting zucchini.

Figure 1: Video and corresponding descriptions from MSRvid

Compare Two Similar Sentences

Score how similar two sentences are to each other according to the following scale.

The sentences are:

(5) Completely equivalent, as they *mean the same thing.*
(4) Mostly equivalent, but some *unimportant details differ.*
(3) Roughly equivalent, but some *important information differs/missing.*
(2) Not equivalent, but *share some details.*
(1) Not equivalent, but are *on the same topic.*
(0) On different topics.

Select a similarity rating for each sentence pair below:

Figure 2: Definition and instructions for annotation

to provide a one-sentence description of the main action or event in the video (Chen and Dolan, 2011). Nearly 120 thousand sentences were collected for 2000 videos. The sentences can be taken to be roughly parallel descriptions, and they included sentences for many languages. Figure 1 shows a video and corresponding descriptions.

The sampling procedure from this dataset is similar to that for MSRpar. We construct two bags of data to draw samples. The first includes all possible pairs for the same video, and the second includes pairs taken from different videos. Note that not all sentences from the same video were equivalent, as some descriptions were contradictory or unrelated. Conversely, not all sentences coming from different videos were necessarily unrelated, as many videos were on similar topics. We took an equal number of samples from each of these two sets, in an attempt to provide a balanced dataset between equivalent and non-equivalent pairs. The sampling was also done according to string similarity, but in four bands in the [0.5 .. 0.8] range, as sentences from the same video had a usually higher string similarity than those in the MSRpar dataset. We sampled 1500 pairs overall, which we split 50% for training and 50% for testing.

Given the strong connection between STS systems and Machine Translation evaluation metrics, we also sampled pairs of segments that had been part of human evaluation exercises. Those pairs included a reference translation and a automatic Machine Translation system submission, as follows:

> The only instance in which no tax is levied is when the supplier is in a non-EU country and the recipient is in a Member State of the EU.
>
> The only case for which no tax is still perceived "is an example of supply in the European Community from a third country.

We selected pairs from the translation shared task of the 2007 and 2008 ACL Workshops on Statistical Machine Translation (WMT) (Callison-Burch et al., 2007; Callison-Burch et al., 2008). For consistency, we only used French to English system submissions. The training data includes all of the Europarl human ranked fr-en system submissions from WMT 2007, with each machine translation being paired with the correct reference translation. This resulted in 729 unique training pairs. The test data is comprised of all Europarl human evaluated fr-en pairs from WMT 2008 that contain 16 white space delimited tokens or less.

In addition, we selected two other datasets that were used as out-of-domain testing. One of them comprised of all the human ranked fr-en system submissions from the WMT 2007 news conversation test set, resulting in 351 unique system reference pairs.[2] The second set is radically different as it comprised 750 pairs of glosses from OntoNotes 4.0 (Hovy et al., 2006) and WordNet 3.1 (Fellbaum, 1998) senses. The mapping of the senses of both resources comprised 110K sense pairs. The similarity between the sense pairs was generated using simple word overlap. 50% of the pairs were sampled from senses which were deemed as equivalent senses, the rest from senses which did not map to one another.

3 Annotation

In this first dataset we defined a straightforward likert scale ranging from 5 to 0, but we decided to provide definitions for each value in the scale (cf. Figure 2). We first did pilot annotations of 200 pairs se-

[2]At the time of the shared task, this data set contained duplicates resulting in 399 sentence pairs.

lected at random from the three main datasets in the training set. We did the annotation, and the pairwise Pearson ranged from 84% to 87% among ourselves. The agreement of each annotator with the average scores of the other was between 87% and 89%.

In the future, we would like to explore whether the definitions improve the consistency of the tagging with respect to a likert scale without definitions. Note also that in the assessment of the quality and evaluation of the systems performances, we just took the resulting SS scores and their averages. Using the qualitative descriptions for each score in analysis and evaluation is left for future work.

Given the good results of the pilot we decided to deploy the task in Amazon Mechanical Turk (AMT) in order to crowd source the annotation task. The turkers were required to have achieved a 95% of approval rating in their previous HITs, and had to pass a qualification task which included 6 example pairs. Each HIT included 5 pairs of sentences, and was paid at 0.20$ each. We collected 5 annotations per HIT. In the latest data collection, each HIT required 114.9 second for completion.

In order to ensure the quality, we also performed post-hoc validation. Each HIT contained one pair from our pilot. After the tagging was completed we checked the correlation of each individual turker with our scores, and removed annotations of turkers which had low correlations (below 50%). Given the high quality of the annotations among the turkers, we could alternatively use the correlation between the turkers itself to detect poor quality annotators.

4 Systems Evaluation

Given two sentences, s1 and s2, an STS system would need to return a similarity score. Participants can also provide a confidence score indicating their confidence level for the result returned for each pair, but this confidence is not used for the main results. The output of the systems performance is evaluated using the Pearson product-moment correlation coefficient between the system scores and the human scores, as customary in text similarity (Rubenstein and Goodenough, 1965). We calculated Pearson for each evaluation dataset separately.

In order to have a single Pearson measure for each system we concatenated the gold standard (and system outputs) for all 5 datasets into a single gold standard file (and single system output). The first version of the results were published using this method, but the overall score did not correspond well to the individual scores in the datasets, and participants proposed two additional evaluation metrics, both of them based on Pearson correlation. The organizers of the task decided that it was more informative, and on the benefit of the community, to also adopt those evaluation metrics, and the idea of having a single main evaluation metric was dropped. This decision was not without controversy, but the organizers gave more priority to openness and inclusiveness and to the involvement of participants. The final result table thus included three evaluation metrics. For the future we plan to analyze the evaluation metrics, including non-parametric metrics like Spearman.

4.1 Evaluation metrics

The first evaluation metric is the Pearson correlation for the concatenation of all five datasets, as described above. We will use *overall Pearson* or simply *ALL* to refer to this measure.

The second evaluation metric normalizes the output for each dataset separately, using the linear least squares method. We concatenated the system results for five datasets and then computed a single Pearson correlation. Given $Y = \{y_i\}$ and $X = \{x_i\}$ (the gold standard scores and the system scores, respectively), we transform the system scores into $X' = \{x'_i\}$ in order to minimize the squared error $\sum_i (y_i - x'_i)^2$. The linear transformation is given by $x'_i = x_i * \beta_1 + \beta_2$, where β_1 and β_2 are found analytically. We refer to this measure as *Normalized Pearson* or simply *ALLnorm*. This metric was suggested by one of the participants, Sergio Jimenez.

The third evaluation metric is the weighted mean of the Pearson correlations on individual datasets. The Pearson returned for each dataset is weighted according to the number of sentence pairs in that dataset. Given r_i the five Pearson scores for each dataset, and n_i the number of pairs in each dataset, the weighted mean is given as $\sum_{i=1..5}(r_i * n_i)/\sum_{i=1..5} n_i$ We refer to this measure as *weighted mean of Pearson* or *Mean* for short.

4.2 Using confidence scores

Participants were allowed to include a confidence score between 1 and 100 for each of their scores. We used weighted Pearson to use those confidence scores[3]. Table 2 includes the list of systems which provided a non-uniform confidence. The results show that some systems were able to improve their correlation, showing promise for the usefulness of confidence in applications.

4.3 The Baseline System

We produced scores using a simple word overlap baseline system. We tokenized the input sentences splitting at white spaces, and then represented each sentence as a vector in the multidimensional token space. Each dimension had 1 if the token was present in the sentence, 0 otherwise. Similarity of vectors was computed using cosine similarity.

We also run a random baseline several times, yielding close to 0 correlations in all datasets, as expected. We will refer to the random baseline again in Section 4.5.

4.4 Participation

Participants could send a maximum of three system runs. After downloading the test datasets, they had a maximum of 120 hours to upload the results. 35 teams participated, submitting 88 system runs (cf. first column of Table 1). Due to lack of space we can't detail the full names of authors and institutions that participated. The interested reader can use the name of the runs to find the relevant paper in these proceedings.

There were several issues in the submissions. The submission software did not ensure that the naming conventions were appropriately used, and this caused some submissions to be missed, and in two cases the results were wrongly assigned. Some participants returned Not-a-Number as a score, and the organizers had to request whether those where to be taken as a 0 or as a 5.

Finally, one team submitted past the 120 hour deadline and some teams sent missing files after the deadline. All those are explicitly marked in Table 1. The teams that included one of the organizers are also explicitly marked. We want to stress that in these teams the organizers did not allow the developers of the system to access any data or information which was not available for the rest of participants. One exception is *weiwei*, as they generated the 110K OntoNotes-WordNet dataset from which the other organizers sampled the surprise data set.

After the submission deadline expired, the organizers published the gold standard in the task website, in order to ensure a transparent evaluation process.

4.5 Results

Table 1 shows the results for each run in alphabetic order. Each result is followed by the rank of the system according to the given evaluation measure. To the right, the Pearson score for each dataset is given. In boldface, the three best results in each column.

First of all we want to stress that the large majority of the systems are well above the simple baseline, although the baseline would rank 70 on the Mean measure, improving over 19 runs.

The correlation for the non-MT datasets were really high: the highest correlation was obtained was for MSRvid (0.88 r), followed by MSRpar (0.73 r) and On-WN (0.73 r). The results for the MT evaluation data are lower, (0.57 r) for SMT-eur and (0.61 r) for SMT-News. The simple token overlap baseline, on the contrary, obtained the highest results for On-WN (0.59 r), with (0.43 r) on MSRpar and (0.40 r) on MSRvid. The results for MT evaluation data are also reversed, with (0.40 r) for SMT-eur and (0.45 r) for SMT-News.

The ALLnorm measure yields the highest correlations. This comes at no surprise, as it involves a normalization which transforms the system outputs using the gold standard. In fact, a random baseline which gets Pearson correlations close to 0 in all datasets would attain Pearson of 0.5891[4].

Although not included in the results table for lack of space, we also performed an analysis of confidence intervals. For instance, the best run according to ALL ($r = .8239$) has a 95% confidence interval of [.8123,.8349] and the second a confidence interval of [.8016,.8254], meaning that the differences are not statistically different.

5 Tools and resources used

The organizers asked participants to submit a description file, special emphasis on the tools and resources that they used. Table 3 shows in a simpli-

[3] `http://en.wikipedia.org/wiki/Pearson_product-moment_correlation_coefficient#Calculating_a_weighted_correlation`

[4] We run the random baseline 10 times. The mean is reported here. The standard deviation is 0.0005

Run	ALL	Rank	ALLnrm	Rank	Mean	Rank	MSRpar	MSRvid	SMT-eur	On-WN	SMT-news
00-baseline/task6-baseline	.3110	87	.6732	85	.4356	70	.4334	.2996	.4542	.5864	.3908
aca08ls/task6-University_Of_Sheffield-Hybrid	.6485	34	.8238	15	.6100	18	.5166	.8187	.4859	.6676	.4280
aca08ls/task6-University_Of_Sheffield-Machine_Learning	.7241	17	.8169	18	.5750	38	.5166	.8187	.4859	.6390	.2089
aca08ls/task6-University_Of_Sheffield-Vector_Space	.6054	48	.7946	44	.5943	27	.5460	.7241	.4858	.6676	.4280
acaputo/task6-UNIBA-DEPRI	.6141	46	.8027	38	.5891	31	.4542	.7673	.5126	.6593	.4636
acaputo/task6-UNIBA-LSARI	.6221	44	.8079	30	.5728	40	.3886	.7908	.4679	.6826	.4238
acaputo/task6-UNIBA-RI	.6285	41	.7951	43	.5651	45	.4128	.7612	.4531	.6306	.4887
baer/task6-UKP-run1	.8117	4	.8559	4	.6708	4	.6821	.8708	.5118	.6649	.4672
baer/task6-UKP-run2_plus_postprocessing_smt_twsi	**.8239**	1	**.8579**	2	**.6773**	1	.6830	.8739	.5280	.6641	.4937
baer/task6-UKP-run3_plus_random	.7790	8	.8166	19	.4320	71	.6830	.8739	.5280	-.0620	-.0520
croce/task6-UNITOR-1_REGRESSION_BEST_FEATURES	.7474	13	.8292	12	.6316	10	.5695	.8217	.5168	.6591	.4713
croce/task6-UNITOR-2_REGRESSION_ALL_FEATURES	.7475	12	.8297	11	.6323	9	.5763	.8217	.5102	.6591	.4713
croce/task6-UNITOR-3_REGRESSION_ALL_FEATURES_ALL_DOMAINS	.6289	40	.8150	21	.5939	28	.4686	.8027	.4574	.6591	.4713
csjxu/task6-PolyUCOMP-RUN1	.6528	31	.7642	59	.5492	51	.4728	.6593	.4835	.6196	.4290
danielcer/stanford_fsa†	.6354	38	.7212	70	.4848	66	.3795	.5350	.4377	.6052	.4164
danielcer/stanford_pdaAll†	.4229	77	.7160	72	.5044	62	.4409	.4698	.4558	.6468	.4769
danielcer/stanford_rte†	.5589	55	.7807	55	.4674	67	.4374	.8037	.3533	.3077	.3235
davide_buscaldi/task6-IRIT-pg1	.4280	76	.7379	65	.5009	63	.4295	.6125	.4952	.5387	.3614
davide_buscaldi/task6-IRIT-pg3	.4813	68	.7569	61	.5202	58	.4171	.6728	.5179	.5526	.3693
davide_buscaldi/task6-IRIT-wu	.4064	81	.7287	69	.4898	65	.4326	.5833	.4856	.5317	.3480
demetrios_glinos/task6-ATA-BASE	.3454	83	.6990	81	.2772	87	.1684	.6256	.2244	.1648	.0988
demetrios_glinos/task6-ATA-CHNK	.4976	64	.7160	73	.3215	86	.2312	.6595	.1504	.2735	.1426
demetrios_glinos/task6-ATA-STAT	.4165	79	.7129	75	.3312	85	.1887	.6482	.2769	.2950	.1336
desouza/task6-FBK-run1	.5633	54	.7127	76	.3628	82	.2494	.6117	.1495	.4212	.2439
desouza/task6-FBK-run2	.6438	35	.8080	29	.5888	32	.5128	.7807	.3796	.6228	.5474
desouza/task6-FBK-run3	.6517	32	.8106	25	.6077	20	.5169	.7773	.4419	.6298	.6085
dvilarinoayala/task6-BUAP-RUN-1	.4997	63	.7568	62	.5260	56	.4037	.6532	.4521	.6050	.4537
dvilarinoayala/task6-BUAP-RUN-2	-.0260	89	.5933	89	.1016	89	.1109	.0057	.0348	.1788	.1964
dvilarinoayala/task6-BUAP-RUN-3	.6630	25	.7474	64	.5105	59	.4018	.6378	.4758	.5691	.4057
enrique/task6-UNED-H34measures	.4381	75	.7518	63	.5577	48	.5328	.5788	.4785	.6692	.4465
enrique/task6-UNED-HallMeasures	.2791	88	.6694	87	.4286	72	.3861	.2570	.4086	.6006	.5305
enrique/task6-UNED-SP_INIST	.4680	69	.7625	60	.5615	47	.5166	.6303	.4625	.6442	.4753
georgiana_dinu/task6-SAARLAND-ALIGN_VSSIM	.4952	65	.7871	50	.5065	60	.4043	.7718	.2686	.5721	.3505
georgiana_dinu/task6-SAARLAND-MIXT_VSSIM	.4548	71	.8258	13	.5662	43	.6310	.8312	.1391	.5966	.3806
jan_snajder/task6-takelab-simple	**.8133**	3	**.8635**	1	**.6753**	2	.7343	.8803	.4771	.6797	.3989
jan_snajder/task6-takelab-syntax	**.8138**	2	**.8569**	3	.6601	5	.6985	.8620	.3612	.7049	.4683
janardhan/task6-janardhan-UNL_matching	.3431	84	.6878	84	.3481	83	.1936	.5504	.3755	.2888	.3387
jhasneha/task6-Penn-ELReg	.6622	27	.8048	34	.5654	44	.5480	.7844	.3513	.6040	.3607
jhasneha/task6-Penn-ERReg	.6573	28	.8083	28	.5755	37	.5610	.7857	.3568	.6214	.3732
jhasneha/task6-Penn-LReg	.6497	33	.8043	36	.5699	41	.5460	.7818	.3547	.5969	.4137
jotacastillo/task6-SAGAN-RUN1	.5522	57	.7904	47	.5906	29	.5659	.7113	.4739	.6542	.4253
jotacastillo/task6-SAGAN-RUN2	.6272	42	.8032	37	.5838	34	.5538	.7706	.4480	.6135	.3894
jotacastillo/task6-SAGAN-RUN3	.6311	39	.7943	45	.5649	46	.5394	.7560	.4181	.5904	.3746
Konstantin_Z/task6-ABBYY-General	.5636	53	.8052	33	.5759	36	.4797	.7821	.4576	.6488	.3682
M_Rios/task6-UOW-LEX_PARA	.6397	36	.7187	71	.3825	80	.3628	.6426	.3074	.2806	.2082
M_Rios/task6-UOW-LEX_PARA_SEM	.5981	49	.6955	82	.3473	84	.3529	.5724	.3066	.2643	.1164
M_Rios/task6-UOW-SEM	.5361	59	.6287	88	.2567	88	.2995	.2910	.1611	.2571	.2212
mheilman/task6-ETS-PERP	.7808	7	.8064	32	.6305	11	.6211	.7210	.4722	.7080	.5149
mheilman/task6-ETS-PERPphrases	.7834	6	.8089	27	.6399	7	.6397	.7200	.4850	.7124	.5312
mheilman/task6-ETS-TERp	.4477	73	.7291	68	.5253	57	.5049	.5217	.4748	.6169	.4566
nitish_aggarwal/task6-aggarwal-run1⋆	.5777	52	.8158	20	.5466	52	.3675	.8427	.3534	.6030	.4430
nitish_aggarwal/task6-aggarwal-run2⋆	.5833	51	.8183	17	.5683	42	.3720	.8330	.4238	.6513	.4499
nitish_aggarwal/task6-aggarwal-run3	.4911	67	.7696	57	.5377	53	.5320	.6874	.4514	.5827	.2818
nmalandrakis/task6-DeepPurple-DeepPurple_hierarchical	.6228	43	.8100	26	.5979	23	.5984	.7717	.4292	.6480	.3702
nmalandrakis/task6-DeepPurple-DeepPurple_sigmoid	.5540	56	.7997	41	.5558	50	.5960	.7616	.2628	.6016	.3446
nmalandrakis/task6-DeepPurple-DeepPurple_single	.4918	66	.7646	58	.5061	61	.4989	.7092	.4437	.4879	.2441
parthapakray/task6-JU_CSE_NLP-Semantic_Syntactic_Approach∗	.3880	82	.6706	86	.4111	76	.3427	.3549	.4271	.5298	.4034
rada/task6-UNT-CombinedRegression	.7418	14	.8406	7	.6159	14	.5032	.8695	.4797	.6715	.4033
rada/task6-UNT-IndividualDecTree	.7677	9	.8389	9	.5947	25	.5693	.8688	.4203	.6491	.2256
rada/task6-UNT-IndividualRegression	.7846	5	.8440	6	.6162	13	.5353	.8750	.4203	.6715	.4033
sbdlrhmn/task6-sbdlrhmn-Run1	.6663	23	.7842	53	.5376	54	.5440	.7335	.3830	.5860	.2445
sbdlrhmn/task6-sbdlrhmn-Run2	.4169	78	.7104	77	.4986	64	.4617	.4489	.4719	.6353	.4353
sgjimenezv/task6-SOFT-CARDINALITY	.7331	15	.8526	5	**.6708**	3	.6405	.8562	.5152	.7109	.4833
sgjimenezv/task6-SOFT-CARDINALITY-ONE-FUNCTION	.7107	19	.8397	8	.6486	6	.6316	.8237	.4320	.7109	.4833
siva/task6-DSS-alignheuristic	.5253	60	.7962	42	.6030	21	.5735	.7123	.4781	.6984	.4177
siva/task6-DSS-average	.5490	58	.8047	35	.5943	26	.5020	.7645	.4875	.6677	.4324
siva/task6-DSS-wordsim	.5130	61	.7895	49	.5287	55	.3765	.7761	.4161	.5728	.3964
skamler_/task6-EHU-RUN1v2⋆†	.3129	86	.6935	83	.3889	79	.3605	.5187	.2259	.4098	.3465
sokolov/task6-LIMSI-cosprod	.6392	37	.7344	67	.3940	78	.3948	.6597	.0143	.4157	.2889
sokolov/task6-LIMSI-gradtree	.6789	22	.7377	66	.4118	75	.4848	.6636	.0934	.3706	.2455
sokolov/task6-LIMSI-sumdiff	.6196	45	.7101	78	.4131	74	.4295	.5724	.2842	.3989	.2575
spirin2/task6-UIUC-MLNLP-Blend	.4592	70	.7800	56	.5782	35	.6523	.6691	.3566	.6117	.4603
spirin2/task6-UIUC-MLNLP-CCM	.7269	16	.8217	16	.6104	17	.5769	.8203	.4667	.5835	.4945
spirin2/task6-UIUC-MLNLP-Puzzle	.3216	85	.7857	51	.4376	69	.5635	.8056	.0630	.2774	.2409
sranjans/task6-sranjans-1	.6529	30	.8018	39	.6249	12	.6124	.7240	.5581	.6703	.4533
sranjans/task6-sranjans-2	.6651	24	.8128	22	.6366	8	.6254	.7538	.5328	.6649	.5036
sranjans/task6-sranjans-3	.5045	62	.7846	52	.5905	30	.6167	.7061	.5666	.5664	.3968
tiantianzhu7/task6-tiantianzhu7-1	.4533	72	.7134	74	.4192	73	.4184	.5630	.2083	.4822	.2745
tiantianzhu7/task6-tiantianzhu7-2	.4157	80	.7099	79	.3960	77	.4260	.5628	.1546	.4552	.1923
tiantianzhu7/task6-tiantianzhu7-3	.4446	74	.7097	80	.3740	81	.3411	.5946	.1868	.4029	.1823
weiwei/task6-weiwei-run1⋆†	.6946	20	.8303	10	.6081	19	.4106	.8351	.5128	.7273	.4383
yeh/task6-SRIUBC-SYSTEM1†	.7513	11	.8017	40	.5997	22	.6084	.7458	.4688	.6315	.3994
yeh/task6-SRIUBC-SYSTEM2†	.7562	10	.8111	24	.5858	33	.6050	.7939	.4294	.5871	.3366
yeh/task6-SRIUBC-SYSTEM3†	.6876	21	.7812	54	.4668	68	.4791	.7901	.2159	.3843	.2801
ygutierrez/task6-UMCC_DLSI-MultiLex	.6630	26	.7922	46	.5560	49	.6022	.7709	.4435	.4327	.4264
ygutierrez/task6-UMCC_DLSI-MultiSem	.6529	29	.8115	23	.6116	16	.5269	.7756	.4688	.6539	.5470
ygutierrez/task6-UMCC_DLSI-MultiSemLex	.7213	18	.8239	14	.6158	15	.6205	.8104	.4325	.6256	.4340
yrkakde/task6-yrkakde-DiceWordnet	.5977	50	.7902	48	.5742	39	.5294	.7470	.5531	.5698	.3659
yrkakde/task6-yrkakde-JaccNERPenalty	.6067	47	.8078	31	.5955	24	.5757	.7765	.4989	.6257	.3468

Table 1: The first row corresponds to the baseline. **ALL** for overall Pearson, **ALLnorm** for Pearson after normalization, and **Mean** for mean of Pearsons. We also show the ranks for each measure. Rightmost columns show Pearson for each individual dataset. Note: ∗ system submitted past the 120 hour window, ⋆ post-deadline fixes, † team involving one of the organizers.

Run	ALL	ALL_w	MSRpar	$MSRpar_w$	MSRvid	$MSRvid_w$	SMT-eur	$SMT\text{-}eur_w$	On-WN	$On\text{-}WN_w$	SMT-news	$SMT\text{-}news_w$
davide_buscaldi/task6-IRIT-pg1	.4280	**.4946**	**.4295**	.4082	.6125	**.6593**	.4952	**.5273**	.5387	**.5574**	.3614	**.4674**
davide_buscaldi/task6-IRIT-pg3	.4813	**.5503**	**.4171**	.4033	.6728	**.7048**	.5179	**.5529**	.5526	**.5950**	.3693	**.4648**
davide_buscaldi/task6-IRIT-wu	.4064	**.4682**	**.4326**	.4035	.5833	**.6253**	.4856	**.5138**	**.5317**	.5189	.3480	**.4482**
enrique/task6-UNED-H34measures	**.4381**	.2615	**.5328**	.4494	**.5788**	.4913	**.4785**	.4660	**.6692**	.6440	**.4465**	.3632
enrique/task6-UNED-HallMeasures	**.2791**	.2002	**.3861**	.3802	**.2570**	.2343	.4086	**.4212**	**.6006**	.5947	**.5305**	.4858
enrique/task6-UNED-SP_INIST	**.4680**	.3754	**.5166**	.5082	**.6303**	.5588	.4625	**.4801**	**.6442**	.5761	**.4753**	.4143
parthapakray/task6-JU_CSE_NLP-Semantic_Syntactic_Approach	**.3880**	.3636	.3427	**.3498**	**.3549**	.3353	**.4271**	.3989	**.5298**	.4619	**.4034**	.3228
tiantianzhu7/task6-tiantianzhu7-1	.4533	**.5442**	.4184	**.4241**	**.5630**	**.5630**	.2083	**.4220**	.4822	**.5031**	.2745	**.3536**
tiantianzhu7/task6-tiantianzhu7-2	.4157	**.5249**	.4260	**.4340**	.5628	**.5758**	.1546	**.4776**	.4552	**.4926**	.1923	**.3362**
tiantianzhu7/task6-tiantianzhu7-3	.4446	**.5229**	.3411	**.3611**	**.5946**	.5899	.1868	**.4769**	.4029	**.4365**	.1823	**.4014**

Table 2: Results according to weighted correlation for the systems that provided non-uniform confidence alongside their scores.

fied way the tools and resources used by those participants that did submit a valid description file. In the last row, the totals show that WordNet was the most used resource, followed by monolingual corpora and Wikipedia. Acronyms, dictionaries, multilingual corpora, stopword lists and tables of paraphrases were also used.

Generic NLP tools like lemmatization and PoS tagging were widely used, and to a lesser extent, parsing, word sense disambiguation, semantic role labeling and time and date resolution (in this order). Knowledge-based and distributional methods got used nearly equally, and to a lesser extent, alignment and/or statistical machine translation software, lexical substitution, string similarity, textual entailment and machine translation evaluation software. Machine learning was widely used to combine and tune components. Several less used tools were also listed but were used by three or less systems.

The top scoring systems tended to use most of the resources and tools listed (*UKP*, *Takelab*), with some notable exceptions like *Sgjimenez* which was based on string similarity. For a more detailed analysis, the reader is directed to the papers of the participants in this volume.

6 Conclusions and Future Work

This paper presents the SemEval 2012 pilot evaluation exercise on Semantic Textual Similarity. A simple definition of STS beyond the likert-scale was set up, and a wealth of annotated data was produced. The similarity of pairs of sentences was rated on a 0-5 scale (low to high similarity) by human judges using Amazon Mechanical Turk. The dataset includes 1500 sentence pairs from MSRpar and MSRvid (each), ca. 1500 pairs from WMT, and 750 sentence pairs from a mapping between OntoNotes and WordNet senses. The correlation between non-expert annotators and annotations from the authors is very high, showing the high quality of the dataset. The dataset was split 50% as train and test, with the exception of the surprise test datasets: a subset of WMT from a different domain and the OntoNotes-WordNet mapping. All datasets are publicly available.[5]

The exercise was very successful in participation and results. 35 teams participated, submitting 88 runs. The best results scored a Pearson correlation over 80%, well beyond a simple lexical baseline with 31% of correlation. The metric for evaluation was not completely satisfactory, and three evaluation metrics were finally published. We discuss the shortcomings of those measures.

There are several tasks ahead in order to make STS a mature field. The first is to find a satisfactory evaluation metric. The second is to analyze the definition of the task itself, with a thorough analysis of the definitions in the likert scale.

We would also like to analyze the relation between the STS scores and the paraphrase judgements in MSR, as well as the human evaluations in WMT. Finally, we would also like to set up an open framework where NLP components and similarity algorithms can be combined by the community. All in all, we would like this dataset to be the focus of the community working on algorithmic approaches for semantic processing and inference at large.

Acknowledgements

We would like to thank all participants, specially (in alphabetic order) Yoan Gutierrez, Michael Heilman, Sergio Jimenez, Nitin Madnami, Diana McCarthy and Shrutiranjan Satpathy for their contributions on evaluation metrics. Eneko Agirre was partially funded by the

[5] http://www.cs.york.ac.uk/semeval-2012/task6/

	Acronyms	Dictionaries	Distributional thesaurus	Monolingual corpora	Multilingual corpora	Stop words	Tables of paraphrases	Wikipedia	WordNet	Alignment	Distributional similarity	KB Similarity	Lemmatizer	Lexical Substitution	Machine Learning	MT evaluation	MWE	Named Entity recognition	POS tagger	Semantic Role Labeling	SMT	String similarity	Syntax	Textual entailment	Time and date resolution	Word Sense Disambiguation	Other
aca08ls/task6-University_Of_Sheffield-Hybrid									x			x	x		x							x				x	x
aca08ls/task6-University_Of_Sheffield-Machine_Learning									x			x	x		x							x				x	x
aca08ls/task6-University_Of_Sheffield-Vector_Space									x			x	x													x	x
baer/task6-UKP-run1		x	x	x	x			x	x		x	x	x						x		x	x		x			x
baer/task6-UKP-run2_plus_postprocessing_smt_twsi		x	x	x	x			x	x		x	x	x						x		x	x		x			x
baer/task6-UKP-run3_plus_random		x	x	x	x			x	x		x	x	x						x		x	x		x			x
croce/task6-UNITOR-1_REGRESSION_BEST_FEATURES				x							x		x		x				x				x				
croce/task6-UNITOR-2_REGRESSION_ALL_FEATURES				x							x		x		x				x				x				
croce/task6-UNITOR-3_REGRESSION_ALL_FEATURES_ALL_DOMAINS				x							x		x		x				x				x				
csjxu/task6-PolyUCOMP-RUN								x	x			x							x								
danielcer/stanford_fsa							x		x				x	x			x		x				x				
danielcer/stanford_pdaAll							x		x				x	x			x		x				x				
danielcer/stanford_rte									x	x			x		x		x		x				x				x
davide_buscaldi/task6-IRIT-pg1				x					x			x							x			x					
davide_buscaldi/task6-IRIT-pg3				x					x			x							x			x					
davide_buscaldi/task6-IRIT-wu				x					x			x							x			x					
demetrios_glinos/task6-ATA-BASE									x		x	x							x	x		x					x
demetrios_glinos/task6-ATA-CHNK									x		x	x							x	x		x					x
demetrios_glinos/task6-ATA-STAT									x		x	x							x	x		x					x
desouza/task6-FBK-run1	x			x			x	x	x		x	x	x	x				x	x				x				x
desouza/task6-FBK-run2				x			x	x	x		x	x	x						x								
desouza/task6-FBK-run3				x			x	x	x		x								x								
dvilarinoayala/task6-BUAP-RUN-1		x											x														
dvilarinoayala/task6-BUAP-RUN-2									x																		
dvilarinoayala/task6-BUAP-RUN-3													x														x
jan_snajder/task6-takelab-simple		x	x	x		x		x	x		x	x	x	x	x				x								x
jan_snajder/task6-takelab-syntax				x					x		x	x	x	x				x	x				x				
janardhan/task6-janardhan-UNL_matching									x				x					x	x				x			x	
jotacastillo/task6-SAGAN-RUN1	x			x					x				x	x										x	x	x	
jotacastillo/task6-SAGAN-RUN2	x			x					x				x	x										x	x	x	
jotacastillo/task6-SAGAN-RUN3	x			x					x				x	x										x	x	x	
Konstantin_Z/task6-ABBYY-General																											
M_Rios/task6-UOW-LEX_PARA			x								x		x			x		x	x	x			x				
M_Rios/task6-UOW-LEX_PARA_SEM			x								x		x			x		x	x	x			x				
M_Rios/task6-UOW-SEM			x								x		x					x	x	x			x				
mheilman/task6-ETS-PERP				x					x			x	x	x		x						x					
mheilman/task6-ETS-PERPphrases				x	x				x			x	x	x		x						x					x
mheilman/task6-ETS-TERp				x	x				x			x	x	x													x
parthapakray/task6-JU_CSE_NLP-Semantic_Syntactic_Approach	x					x			x				x				x	x	x				x	x			x
rada/task6-UNT-CombinedRegression								x	x	x	x	x	x		x											x	x
rada/task6-UNT-IndividualDecTree								x	x	x	x	x	x		x											x	x
rada/task6-UNT-IndividualRegression								x	x	x	x	x	x		x											x	x
sgjimenezv/task6-SOFT-CARDINALITY						x						x	x														
sgjimenezv/task6-SOFT-CARDINALITY-ONE-FUNCTION						x						x	x														
skamler_/task6-EHU-RUN1v2							x			x			x						x		x						
sokolov/task6-LIMSI-cosprod				x							x		x		x												
sokolov/task6-LIMSI-gradtree				x							x		x		x												
sokolov/task6-LIMSI-sumdiff				x							x		x		x												
spirin2/task6-UIUC-MLNLP-Blend	x			x			x	x									x	x	x	x			x	x			x
spirin2/task6-UIUC-MLNLP-CCM	x			x			x	x									x	x	x	x			x	x			x
spirin2/task6-UIUC-MLNLP-Puzzle	x			x			x	x									x	x	x	x			x	x			x
sranjans/task6-sranjans-1				x				x	x		x	x	x						x							x	
sranjans/task6-sranjans-2				x				x	x		x	x	x	x				x	x						x	x	
sranjans/task6-sranjans-3				x				x	x		x	x	x	x				x	x				x		x		
tiantianzhu7/task6-tiantianzhu7-1									x			x							x							x	
tiantianzhu7/task6-tiantianzhu7-2									x			x							x								
tiantianzhu7/task6-tiantianzhu7-3						x			x			x							x								
weiwei/task6-weiwei-run1		x		x					x		x		x						x								
yeh/task6-SRIUBC-SYSTEM1			x					x	x		x	x	x						x								
yeh/task6-SRIUBC-SYSTEM2			x					x	x		x	x	x						x								
yeh/task6-SRIUBC-SYSTEM3			x					x	x		x	x	x						x								
ygutierrez/task6-UMCC_DLSI-MultiLex				x					x	x		x	x						x								x
ygutierrez/task6-UMCC_DLSI-MultiSem				x					x			x	x						x							x	x
ygutierrez/task6-UMCC_DLSI-MultiSemLex				x					x	x		x	x						x							x	x
yrkakde/task6-yrkakde-DiceWordnet									x		x		x														
Total	8	6	10	33	5	5	9	20	47	7	31	37	49	13	13	4	7	12	43	9	4	13	17	10	5	15	25

Table 3: Resources and tools used by the systems that submitted a description file. Leftmost columns correspond to the resources, and rightmost to tools, in alphabetic order.

European Communitys Seventh Framework Programme (FP7/2007-2013) under grant agreement no. 270082 (PATHS project) and the Ministry of Economy under grant TIN2009-14715-C04-01 (KNOW2 project). Daniel Cer gratefully acknowledges the support of the Defense Advanced Research Projects Agency (DARPA) Machine Reading Program under Air Force Research Laboratory (AFRL) prime contract no. FA8750-09-C-0181 and the support of the DARPA Broad Operational Language Translation (BOLT) program through IBM. The STS annotations were funded by an extension to DARPA GALE subcontract to IBM # W0853748 4911021461.0 to Mona Diab. Any opinions, findings, and conclusion or recommendations expressed in this material are those of the author(s) and do not necessarily reflect the view of the DARPA, AFRL, or the US government.

References

Chris Callison-Burch, Cameron Fordyce, Philipp Koehn, Christof Monz, and Josh Schroeder. 2007. (meta-) evaluation of machine translation. In *Proceedings of the Second Workshop on Statistical Machine Translation*, StatMT '07, pages 136–158.

Chris Callison-Burch, Cameron Fordyce, Philipp Koehn, Christof Monz, and Josh Schroeder. 2008. Further meta-evaluation of machine translation. In *Proceedings of the Third Workshop on Statistical Machine Translation*, StatMT '08, pages 70–106.

David L. Chen and William B. Dolan. 2011. Collecting highly parallel data for paraphrase evaluation. In *Proceedings of the 49th Annual Meetings of the Association for Computational Linguistics (ACL)*.

B. Dolan, C. Quirk, and C. Brockett. 2004. Unsupervised construction of large paraphrase corpora: Exploiting massively parallel news sources. In *COLING 04: Proceedings of the 20th international conference on Computational Linguistics*, page 350.

Christiane Fellbaum. 1998. *WordNet: An Electronic Lexical Database*. MIT Press.

Eduard Hovy, Mitchell Marcus, Martha Palmer, Lance Ramshaw, and Ralph Weischedel. 2006. Ontonotes: The 90% solution. In *Proceedings of the Human Language Technology Conference of the North American Chapter of the ACL*.

Michael D. Lee, Brandon Pincombe, and Matthew Welsh. 2005. An empirical evaluation of models of text document similarity. In *Proceedings of the 27th Annual Conference of the Cognitive Science Society*, pages 1254–1259, Mahwah, NJ.

Y. Li, D. McLean, Z. A. Bandar, J. D. O'Shea, and K. Crockett. 2006. Sentence similarity based on semantic nets and corpus statistics. *IEEE Transactions on Knowledge and Data Engineering*, 18(8):1138–1150, August.

Herbert Rubenstein and John B. Goodenough. 1965. Contextual correlates of synonymy. *Commun. ACM*, 8(10):627–633, October.

E. Ukkonen. 1985. Algorithms for approximate string matching. *Information and Contro*, 64:110–118.

SemEval-2012 Task 7: Choice of Plausible Alternatives: An Evaluation of Commonsense Causal Reasoning

Andrew S. Gordon
Institute for Creative Technologies
University of Southern California
Los Angeles, CA
gordon@ict.usc.edu

Zornitsa Kozareva
Information Sciences Institute
University of Southern California
Marina del Rey, CA
kozareva@isi.edu

Melissa Roemmele
Department of Linguistics
Indiana University
Bloomington, IN
msroemme@gmail.com

Abstract

SemEval-2012 Task 7 presented a deceptively simple challenge: given an English sentence as a premise, select the sentence amongst two alternatives that more plausibly has a causal relation to the premise. In this paper, we describe the development of this task and its motivation. We describe the two systems that competed in this task as part of SemEval-2012, and compare their results to those achieved in previously published research. We discuss the characteristics that make this task so difficult, and offer our thoughts on how progress can be made in the future.

1 Motivation

Open-domain commonsense reasoning is one of the grand challenges of artificial intelligence, and has been the subject of research since the inception of the field. Until recently, this research history has been dominated by formal approaches (e.g. Lenat, 1995), where logical formalizations of commonsense theories were hand-authored by expert logicians and evaluated using a handful of commonsense challenge problems (Morgenstern, 2012). Progress via this approach has been slow, both because of the inherent difficulties in authoring suitably broad-coverage formal theories of the commonsense world and the lack of evaluation metrics for comparing systems from different labs and research traditions.

Radically different approaches to the commonsense reasoning problem have recently been explored by natural language processing researchers. Speer et al. (2008) describe a novel reasoning approach that applies dimensionality reduction to the space of millions of English-language commonsense facts in a crowd-sourced knowledge base (Liu & Singh, 2004). Gordon et al., (2010) describe a method for extracting millions of commonsense facts from parse trees of English sentences. Jung et al. (2010) describe a novel approach to the extraction of commonsense knowledge about activities by mining online how-to articles. We believe that these new NLP-based approaches hold enormous potential for overcoming the knowledge acquisition bottleneck that has limited progress in commonsense reasoning in previous decades.

Given the growth and enthusiasm for these new approaches, there is increasing need for a common metric for evaluation. A common evaluation suite would allow researchers to gauge the performance of new versions of their own systems, and to compare their approaches with those of other research groups. Evaluations for these new NLP-based approaches should themselves be based in natural language, and must be suitably large to truly evaluate the breadth of different reasoning approaches. Still, each evaluation should be focused on one dimension of the overall commonsense reasoning task, so as not to create a new challenge that no single research group could hope to succeed.

In SemEval-2012 Task 7, we presented a new evaluation for open-domain commonsense reasoning, focusing specifically on commonsense causal reasoning about everyday events.

2 Choice of Plausible Alternatives

Consider the following English sentence, describing a hypothetical state of the world:

The man lost his balance on the ladder.

In addition to parsing this sentence, resolving ambiguities, and constructing a semantic interpretation, human readers also imagine the causal antecedents and consequents that would follow if the statement were true. With such a brief description, readers are left with many questions. How high up on the ladder was this man? What was he doing on the ladder in the first place? How much experience does he have using ladders? Was he intoxicated? The answers to these questions help readers formulate hypotheses for the two central concerns when reasoning about events: *What was the cause of this?* and *What happened as a result?*

As computational linguists, we imagine that our automated natural language processing algorithms will also, eventually, need to engage in similar reasoning processes in order to achieve human-like performance on text understanding tasks. Progress toward the goal of deep semantic interpretation of text has been slow. However, the last decade of natural language processing research has shown that enormous gains can be achieved when there is a clear evaluation metric. A shared task with an automated scoring mechanism allows researchers to compare different approaches, tune system parameters to maximize performance, and assess progress toward broader research objectives. Developing an evaluation metric for causal reasoning poses a number of challenges. It is necessary to formulate a question with answers that can be automatically graded, but can still serve as a proxy for the complex, generative imagination of readers.

Roemmele et al. (2011) offered a solution in the form of a simple binary-choice question. Presented with an English sentence describing a premise, systems must select between two alternatives (also sentences) the one that more plausibly has a causal relation to the premise, as in the following example:

Premise: The man lost his balance on the ladder. *What happened as a result?*
Alternative 1: He fell off the ladder.
Alternative 2: He climbed up the ladder.

Both of these alternatives are conceivable, and neither is entailed by the premise. However, human readers have no difficulty selecting the alternative that is the more plausible of the two. This question asks about a causal consequent, and a complimentary formulation asks for the causal antecedent, as in the following example:

Premise: The man fell unconscious. *What was the cause of this?*
Alternative 1: The assailant struck the man on the head.
Alternative 2: The assailant took the man's wallet.

Roemmele et al. describe their efforts to author a collection of 1000 questions of these two types to create a new causal reasoning evaluation tool: the Choice of Plausible Alternatives (COPA). When presented to humans to select the correct alternative, the inter-rater agreement was extremely high (Cohen's kappa = 0.965). Where disagreements between two raters were found (in 26 of 1000 items), questions were removed and replaced with new ones with perfect agreement.

To develop an automated evaluation tool, the 1000 questions were randomly ordered and sorted into two equally sized sets of 500 questions to serve as development and test sets. The order of the correct alternative was also randomized, such that the expected accuracy of a random baseline would be 50%. Gold-standard answers for each split are used to automatically evaluate a given system's performance.

The distribution of the COPA evaluation includes an automated test of statistical significance of differences seen between two competing systems. This software tool implements a compute-intensive randomized test of statistical significance using stratified shuffling, as described by Noreen (1989). By randomly sorting answers between two systems over thousands of trials, this test computes the likelihood that differences as great as observed differences could be obtained by random chance.

The COPA evaluation is most similar in style to the Recognizing Textual Entailment challenge (Degan et al., 2006), but differs in its focus on causal implication rather than entailment. Instead of asking whether the interpretation of a sentence necessitates the truth of another, COPA concerns the defeasible inferences that can be drawn from the interpretation of a sentence. In this respect, COPA overlaps in its aims with the task of recognizing causal relations in text through automated discourse processing (e.g. Marcu, 1999). Some progress in automated discourse processing has been made using supervised machine learning methods, where system learn the lexical-syntactic patterns that are most correlated with causal relations from a large annotated corpus (Sagae, 2009). Lacking a dedicated training corpus, the COPA evaluation encourages competitors to capture commonsense causal knowledge from any available corpus or existing knowledge repository.

3 SemEval-2012 Systems and Results

The COPA evaluation was accepted as Task 7 of the 6th International Workshop on Semantic Evaluation (SemEval-2012). In several respects, the COPA evaluation was different than the typical shared task offered as part of this series of workshops. First, the task materials were available and distributed long before the evaluation period began, and there were published results of previous systems using this evaluation.[1] Second, the task included no training data, only sets of development and test questions (500 each). Participants were encouraged to use any available text corpus or knowledge repositories in the construction of their systems. Success on the task would not be possible simply through the selection of machine learning algorithms and feature encodings. Instead, some creativity and ingenuity was needed to find a suitable source of commonsense causal information, and determine an automated mechanism for applying this information to COPA questions.

Only one team successfully completed the task and submitted results during the official two-week SemEval-2012 evaluation period. This team was Travis Goodwin, Bryan Rink, Kirk Roberts, and Sanda M. Harabagiu from the University of Texas at Dallas, Human Language Technology Research Institute. This team submitted results from two different systems (Goodwin et al., 2012), which they described to us as follows:

UTDHLT Bigram PMI: The team's first approach selects the alternative with the maximum Pointwise Mutual Information (PMI) statistic (Church & Hanks, 1990) over all pairs of bigrams (at the token level) between the candidate alternative and the premise. PMI statistics were collected using 8.4 million documents from the LDC Gigaword corpus (Graff & Cieri, 2003). A window of 100 terms was used for finding pairs of co-occurring bigrams, and a window/slop size of 2 for the bigram itself.

UTDHLT SVM Combined: The team's second approach augments the first by combining it with several other features and casting the task as a classification problem. To this end, they consider the PMI between events participating in a temporal link on a Time-ML annotated Gigaword corpus. That is, events that occur together frequently will have a higher PMI. They also consider the difference between the number of positive and negative polarity words between an alternative and premise using information from the Harvard Inquisitor. In addition, they used the count of matching cause-effect pairs extracted using patterns on dependency structures from the Gigaword corpus. Combining all of these sources of information, they trained a support vector machine (SVM) learning algorithm to classify the alternative that is most causally related to the premise.

These systems were assessed based on their accuracy on the 500 questions in the test split of the COPA evaluation, presented in Table 1. Both systems significantly outperformed the random baseline (50% accuracy), but the gains seen in the second approach were not significantly different than those of the first.

System	*Accuracy*
UTDHLT Bigram PMI	61.8%
UTDHLT SVM Combined	63.4%

Table 1. SemEval-2012 Task 7 system accuracy on 500 questions in the COPA test split

4 Comparison to Previous Results

In order to better evaluate the success of these two systems, we compared these results with the published results of other systems that have used the COPA evaluation. Three other systems were considered.

PMI Gutenberg (W=5): Described in Roemmele et al. (2011), this approach calculated the PMI between words (unigrams) in the premise and

[1] http://www.ict.usc.edu/~gordon/copa.html

each alternative, and selected the alternative with the stronger correlation. The PMI statistic was calculated using every English-language document in Project Gutenberg (16GB of text), using a window of 5 words.

PMI Story 1M (W=25): Described in Gordon et al. (2011), this approach was identical to that of Roemmele et al. (2011) except that the PMI statistic was calculated using a corpus of nearly one million personal stories extracted from Internet weblogs (Gordon & Swanson, 2009), with 1.9 GB of text. Using this corpus instead of Project Gutenberg, the best results were obtained by using a window of 25 words for the PMI statistic.

PMI Story 10M (W=25): Also described in Gordon et al. (2011), this approach explores the gains that can be achieved by calculating the PMI statistic using a much larger corpus of weblog stories. The story extraction technology used by Gordon and Swanson (2009) was applied to 621 million English-language weblog entries posted to the Internet in 2010 to create a corpus of 10.4 million personal stories (37GB of text). Again, the best results were obtained by using a window of 25 words for the PMI statistic.

Table 2 compares the results of these three previous systems with the two SemEval-2012 systems. Although the last two of these three previous systems achieved higher scores than both of the SemEval-2012 submissions, the differences are not statistically significant.

System	*Accuracy*
PMI Gutenberg (W=5)	58.8%
UTDHLT Bigram PMI	**61.8%**
UTDHLT SVM Combined	**63.4%**
PMI Story 1M (W=25)	65.2%
PMI Story 10M (W=25)	65.4%

Table 2. Comparison of SemEval-2012 Task 7 systems (in bold) with previously published results on the 500 questions in the COPA test split

5 Discussion

The two systems from the University of Texas at Dallas make an important contribution to progress on open-domain commonsense reasoning. Some lessons are evident from the short descriptions of their systems that they provided to us.

As in each of the previously successful systems, this team focused their efforts on calculating correlational statistics between words in COPA questions using very large text corpora. In this case, the Gigaword corpus is used, and the calculation is based on bigrams rather than unigrams. We believe that the content of the news articles that comprise the Gigaword corpus is a step further away from the concerns of COPA questions than both the Project Gutenberg corpus and the weblog story corpora used in previous efforts. Indeed, the gains achieved by Gordon et al. (2011) appear to be entirely due to the relationship between COPA questions and the personal stories that people write about in their public weblogs. However, the use of a large news corpus affords the use of more sophisticated analysis techniques that have been developed for this genre. Here, the Gigaword corpus is annotated using Time-ML relationships, which in turn are used to modify the PMI strength between words.

The use of bigrams is an additional enhancement explored by this team, as is the casting of COPA questions as a classification task using a diverse set of lexical and discourse features. Such an approach can facilitate the combining of diverse systems in the future, where correlational statistics are gathered from a diverse set of text corpora, each suited for specific domains of COPA questions or yielding complimentary feature sets.

Still, the modest COPA performance seen from all existing systems is somewhat discouraging. With the best systems performing in the 60-65% range, we remain much closer to random performance (50%) than human performance (99%). These results cast some doubt that the information necessary to answer COPA questions can be readily obtained from large text corpora. Certainly the use of simple correlational statistics between nearby words is not enough. In the best case, we might wish for perfect identification of causal relationships between events in an extremely large text corpus of narratives similar in content to COPA questions. Semantic similarity between these events and COPA sentences could be computed to gather evidence to select the best alternative. Even if it were possible to achieve this ideal, it is difficult to imagine that such an approach could mirror human performance on this task.

To move closer to human performance, systems may need to stretch beyond corpus statistics into the realm of automated reasoning. Just as human readers do when hearing that "the man lost his balance on the ladder," successful systems may need to treat COPA premises as novel world states, and imagine a broad range of interconnected causal antecedents and consequents. Useful knowledge bases will be those that have adequate *coverage* over commonsense concerns, but also adequate *competency* to support generative inference of the sort more commonly seen in deductive and abductive automated reasoning frameworks. This knowledge may or may not be represented as text, but any successful system must have the capacity to apply this knowledge to the understanding of COPA's textual premises and alternatives. We consider the successful application of commonsense inference to text understanding to be one of the grand challenges of natural language processing, and hope that the COPA evaluation continues to be a useful tool for benchmarking progress toward this goal.

Acknowledgments

The projects or efforts depicted were or are sponsored by the U. S. Army. The content or information presented does not necessarily reflect the position or the policy of the Government, and no official endorsement should be inferred.

References

Church, K. and Hanks, P. (1990) Word Association Norms, Mutual Information, and Lexicography. Computational Linguistics, 16(1):22-29.

Dagan, I., Glickman, O., and Magnini, B. (2006) The PASCAL Recognising Textual Entailment Challenge. In Quiñonero-Candela, J.; Dagan, I.; Magnini, B.; d'Alché-Buc, F. (Eds.), Machine Learning Challenges. Lecture Notes in Computer Science, Vol. 3944, pp. 177-190, Springer, 2006.

Goodwin, T., Rink, B., Roberts, K., and Harabagiu, S. (2012) UTDHLT: COPACETIC System for Choosing Plausible Alternatives. Proceedings of the 6th International Workshop on Semantic Evaluation (SemEval 2012), June 7-8, 2012, Montreal, Canada.

Gordon, A., Bejan, C., and Sagae, K. (2011) Commonsense Causal Reasoning Using Millions of Personal Stories. Twenty-Fifth Conference on Artificial Intelligence (AAAI-11), August 7–11, 2011, San Francisco, CA.

Gordon, A. and Swanson, R. (2009) Identifying Personal Stories in Millions of Weblog Entries. International Conference on Weblogs and Social Media, Data Challenge Workshop, San Jose, CA.

Gordon, J., Van Durme, B., and K. Schubert, L. (2010) Learning from the Web: Extracting General World Knowledge from Noisy Text. Proceedings of the AAAI 2010 Workshop on Collaboratively-built Knowledge Sources and Artificial Intelligence (WikiAI 2010).

Graff, D. and Cieri, C. (2003) English Gigaword. Linguistic Data Consortium, Philadelphia.

Jung, Y., Ryu, J., Kim., K. and Myaeng, S.(2010). Automatic Construction of a Large-Scale Situation Ontology by Mining How-to Instructions from the Web. Journal of Web Semantics 8(2-3):110-124.

Lenat, D. (1995) CYC: A Large-Scale Investment in Knowledge Infrastructure, Communications of the ACM 38:33-38.

Liu, H. and Singh, P. (2004) ConceptNet: A Practical Commonsense Reasoning Toolkit. BT Technology Journal 22(4):211-226.

Marcu, D. (1999). A decision-based approach to rhetorical parsing. The 37th Annual Meeting of the Association for Computational Linguistics (ACL'99), pages 365-372, Maryland, June 1999.

Morgenstern, L. (2012) Common Sense Problem Page. Retrieved April 2012 at http://www-formal.stanford.edu/leora/commonsense/

Noreen, E. (1989) Computer-Intensive Methods for Testing Hypotheses: An Introduction. New York: John Wiley & Sons.

Roemmele, M., Bejan, C., and Gordon, A. (2011) Choice of Plausible Alternatives: An Evaluation of Commonsense Causal Reasoning. AAAI Spring Symposium on Logical Formalizations of Commonsense Reasoning, Stanford University, March 21-23, 2011.

Sagae, K. (2009) Analysis of discourse structure with syntactic dependencies and data-driven shift-reduce parsing. In Proceedings of the 11th International Conference on Parsing Technologies (IWPT), pages 81--84. 2009.

Speer, R., Havasi, C. and Lieberman, H. (2008) AnalogySpace: Reducing the Dimensionality of Common Sense Knowledge. Proceedings of AAAI 2008.

Semeval-2012 Task 8: Cross-lingual Textual Entailment for Content Synchronization

Matteo Negri
FBK-irst
Trento, Italy
negri@fbk.eu

Alessandro Marchetti
CELCT
Trento, Italy
amarchetti@celct.it

Yashar Mehdad
FBK-irst
Trento, Italy
mehdad@fbk.eu

Luisa Bentivogli
FBK-irst
Trento, Italy
bentivo@fbk.eu

Danilo Giampiccolo
CELCT
Trento, Italy
giampiccolo@celct.it

Abstract

This paper presents the first round of the task on *Cross-lingual Textual Entailment for Content Synchronization*, organized within SemEval-2012. The task was designed to promote research on semantic inference over texts written in different languages, targeting at the same time a real application scenario. Participants were presented with datasets for different language pairs, where multi-directional entailment relations ("forward", "backward", "bidirectional", "no_entailment") had to be identified. We report on the training and test data used for evaluation, the process of their creation, the participating systems (10 teams, 92 runs), the approaches adopted and the results achieved.

1 Introduction

The cross-lingual textual entailment task (Mehdad et al., 2010) addresses textual entailment (TE) recognition (Dagan and Glickman, 2004) under the new dimension of cross-linguality, and within the new challenging application scenario of content synchronization.

Cross-linguality represents a dimension of the TE recognition problem that has been so far only partially investigated. The great potential for integrating monolingual TE recognition components into NLP architectures has been reported in several areas, including question answering, information retrieval, information extraction, and document summarization. However, mainly due to the absence of cross-lingual textual entailment (CLTE) recognition components, similar improvements have not been achieved yet in any cross-lingual application. The CLTE task aims at prompting research to fill this gap. Along such direction, research can now benefit from recent advances in other fields, especially machine translation (MT), and the availability of: *i)* large amounts of parallel and comparable corpora in many languages, *ii)* open source software to compute word-alignments from parallel corpora, and *iii)* open source software to set up MT systems. We believe that all these resources can positively contribute to develop inference mechanisms for multilingual data.

Content synchronization represents a challenging application scenario to test the capabilities of advanced NLP systems. Given two documents about the same topic written in different languages (*e.g.* Wiki pages), the task consists of automatically detecting and resolving differences in the information they provide, in order to produce aligned, mutually enriched versions of the two documents. Towards this objective, a crucial requirement is to identify the information in one page that is either equivalent or novel (more informative) with respect to the content of the other. The task can be naturally cast as an entailment recognition problem, where bidirectional and unidirectional entailment judgments for two text fragments are respectively mapped into judgments about semantic equivalence and novelty. Alternatively, the task can be seen as a machine translation evaluation problem, where judgments about semantic equivalence and novelty depend on the possibility to fully or partially translate a text fragment into the other.

```xml
<entailment-corpus languages="spa-eng">
  <pair id="1" entailment="bidirectional">
    <t1>Mozart nació en la ciudad de Salzburgo</t1>
    <t2>Mozart was born in Salzburg</t2>
  </pair>
  <pair id="2" entailment="forward">
    <t1>Mozart nació en la ciudad de Salzburgo</t1>
    <t2>Mozart was born on the 27th January 1756 in Salzburg</t2>
  </pair>
  <pair id="3" entailment="backward">
    <t1>Mozart nació el 27 de enero de 1756 en Salzburgo</t1>
    <t2> Mozart was born in 1756 in the city of Salzburg</t2>
  </pair>
  <pair id="4" entailment="no_entailment">
    <t1>Mozart nació el 27 de enero de 1756 en Salzburgo</t1>
    <t2>Mozart was born to Leopold and Anna Maria Pertl Mozart</t2>
  </pair>
</entailment-corpus>
```

Figure 1: "bidirectional", "forward", "backward" and "no_entailment" judgments for SP/EN CLTE pairs.

The recent advances on monolingual TE on the one hand, and the methodologies used in Statistical Machine Translation (SMT) on the other, offer promising solutions to approach the CLTE task. In line with a number of systems that model the RTE task as a similarity problem (*i.e.* handling similarity scores between T and H as useful evidence to draw entailment decisions), the standard sentence and word alignment programs used in SMT offer a strong baseline for CLTE. However, although representing a solid starting point to approach the problem, similarity-based techniques are just approximations, open to significant improvements coming from semantic inference at the multilingual level (*e.g.* cross-lingual entailment rules such as "perro"→"animal"). Taken in isolation, similarity-based techniques clearly fall short of providing an effective solution to the problem of assigning directions to the entailment relations (especially in the complex CLTE scenario, where entailment relations are multi-directional). Thanks to the contiguity between CLTE, TE and SMT, the proposed task provides an interesting scenario to approach the issues outlined above from different perspectives, and large room for mutual improvement.

2 The task

Given a pair of topically related text fragments (*T1* and *T2*) in different languages, the CLTE task consists of automatically annotating it with one of the following entailment judgments (see Figure 1 for Spanish/English examples of each judgment):

- **bidirectional** ($T1 \rightarrow T2$ & $T1 \leftarrow T2$): the two fragments entail each other (semantic equivalence);
- **forward** ($T1 \rightarrow T2$ & $T1 \not\leftarrow T2$): unidirectional entailment from *T1* to *T2*;
- **backward** ($T1 \not\rightarrow T2$ & $T1 \leftarrow T2$): unidirectional entailment from *T2* to *T1*;
- **no_entailment** ($T1 \not\rightarrow T2$ & $T1 \not\leftarrow T2$): there is no entailment between *T1* and *T2* in both directions;

In this task, both *T1* and *T2* are assumed to be true statements. Although contradiction is relevant from an application-oriented perspective, contradictory pairs are not present in the dataset created for the first round of the task.

3 Dataset description

Four CLTE corpora have been created for the following language combinations: Spanish/English (SP-EN), Italian/English (IT-EN), French/English (FR-EN), German/English (DE-EN). The datasets are released in the XML format shown in Figure 1.

3.1 Data collection and annotation

The dataset was created following the crowdsourcing methodology proposed in (Negri et al., 2011), which consists of the following steps:

1. First, English sentences were manually extracted from copyright-free sources (Wikipedia and Wikinews). The selected sentences represent one of the elements (*T1*) of each entailment pair;
2. Next, each *T1* was modified through crowdsourcing in various ways in order to obtain a corresponding *T2* (*e.g.* introducing meaning-preserving lexical and syntactic changes, adding and removing portions of text);
3. Each *T2* was then paired to the original *T1*, and the resulting pairs were annotated with one of the four entailment judgments. In order to reduce the correlation between the difference in sentences' length and entailment judgments,

only the pairs where the difference between the number of words in *T1* and *T2* (*length_diff*) was below a fixed threshold (10 words) were retained.[1] The final result is a monolingual English dataset annotated with multi-directional entailment judgments, which are well distributed over *length_diff* values ranging from 0 to 9;

4. In order to create the cross-lingual datasets, each English *T1* was manually translated into four different languages (*i.e.* Spanish, German, Italian and French) by expert translators;

5. By pairing the translated *T1* with the corresponding *T2* in English, four cross-lingual datasets were obtained.

To ensure the good quality of the datasets, all the collected pairs were manually checked and corrected when necessary. Only pairs with agreement between two expert annotators were retained. The final result is a multilingual parallel entailment corpus, where *T1*s are in 5 different languages (*i.e.* English, Spanish, German, Italian, and French), and *T2*s are in English. It's worth mentioning that the monolingual English corpus, a by-product of our data collection methodology, will be publicly released as a further contribution to the research community.[2]

3.2 Dataset statistics

Each dataset consists of 1,000 pairs (500 for training and 500 for test), balanced across the four entailment judgments (bidirectional, forward, backward, and no_entailment).

For each language combination, the distribution of the four entailment judgments according to *length_diff* is shown in Figure 2. Vertical bars represent, for each *length_diff* value, the proportion of pairs belonging to the four entailment classes. As can be seen, the *length_diff* constraint applied to the length difference in the monolingual English pairs (step 3 of the creation process) is substantially reflected in the cross-lingual datasets for all language combinations. In fact, as shown in Table 1, the majority of the pairs is always included in the same *length_diff* range (approximately [-5,+5]) and, within this range, the distribution of the four classes is substantially uniform. Our assumption is that such data distribution makes entailment judgments based on mere surface features such as sentence length ineffective, thus encouraging the development of alternative, deeper processing strategies.

	SP-EN	IT-EN	FR-EN	DE-EN
Forward	104	132	121	179
Backward	202	182	191	123
No entailment	163	173	169	174
Bidirectional	175	199	193	209
ALL	644	686	674	685

Table 1: CLTE pairs distribution within the -5/+5 *length_diff* range.

4 Evaluation metrics and baselines

Evaluation results have been automatically computed by comparing the entailment judgments returned by each system with those manually assigned by human annotators. The metric used for systems' ranking is accuracy over the whole test set, *i.e.* the number of correct judgments out of the total number of judgments in the test set. Additionally, we calculated precision, recall, and F1 measures for each of the four entailment judgment categories taken separately. These scores aim at giving participants the possibility to gain clearer insights into their system's behavior on the entailment phenomena relevant to the task.

For each language combination, two baselines considering the length difference between *T1* and *T2* have been calculated (besides the trivial 0.25 accuracy score obtained by assigning each test pair in the balanced dataset to one of the four classes):

- **Composition of binary judgments (Binary).** To calculate this baseline an SVM classifier is trained to take binary entailment decisions ("YES", "NO"). The classifier uses *length(T1)/length(T2)* as a single feature to check for entailment from *T1* to *T2*, and *length(T2)/length(T1)* for the opposite direction. For each test pair, the unidirectional

[1]Such constraint has been applied in order to focus as much as possible on semantic aspects of the problem, by reducing the applicability of simple association rules such as *IF length(T1)>length(T2) THEN T1→T2*.

[2]The cross-lingual datasets are already available for research purposes at http://www.celct.it/resourcesList.php. The monolingual English dataset will be publicly released to non participants in July 2012.

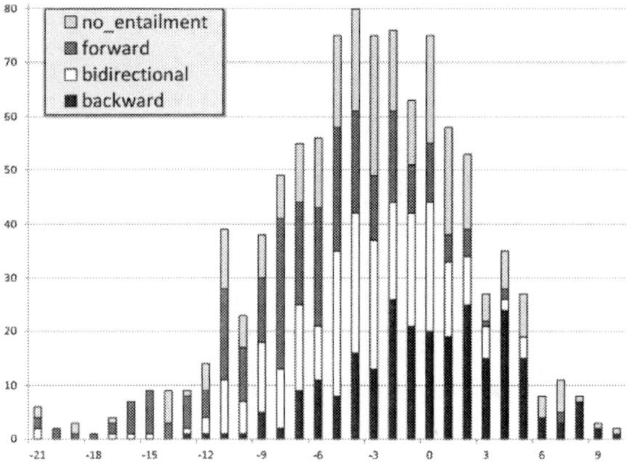

(a) SP-EN

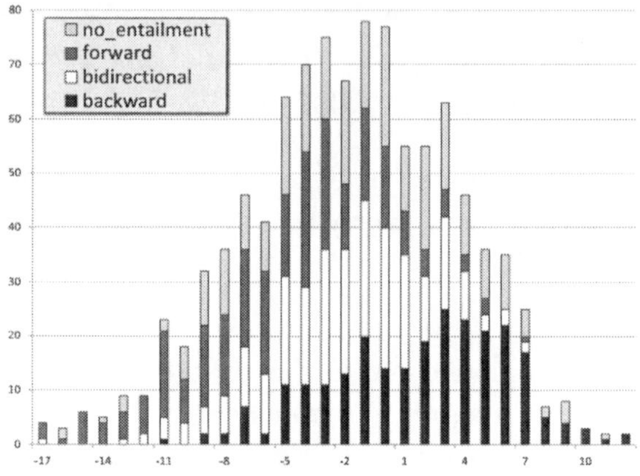

(b) IT-EN

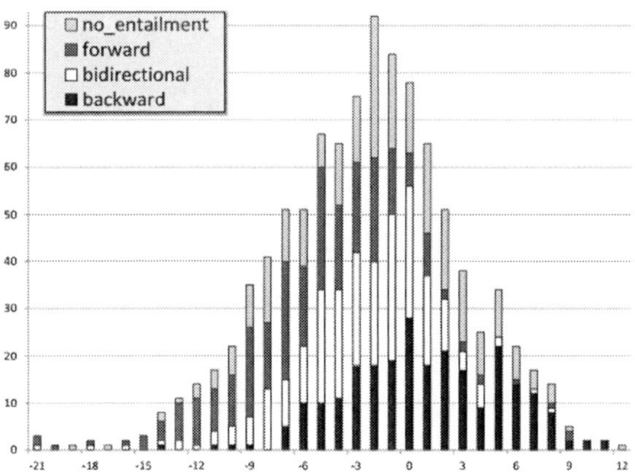

(c) FR-EN

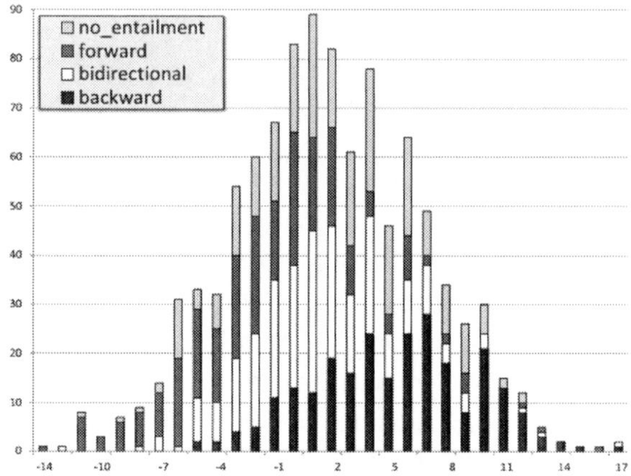

(d) DE-EN

Figure 2: CLTE pairs distribution for different *length_diff* values across all datasets.

judgments returned by the two classifiers are composed into a single multi-directional judgment ("YES-YES"="bidirectional", "YES-NO"="forward", "NO-YES"="backward", "NO-NO"="no_entailment");

- **Multi-class classification (Multi-class).** A single SVM classifier is trained with the same features to directly assign to each pair one of the four entailment judgments.

Both the baselines have been calculated with the LIBSVM package (Chang and Lin, 2011), using a linear kernel with default parameters. Baseline results are reported in Table 2.

Although the four CLTE datasets are derived from the same monolingual EN-EN corpus, baseline results present slight differences due to the effect of translation into different languages.

	SP-EN	IT-EN	FR-EN	DE-EN
1-class	0.25	0.25	0.25	0.25
Binary	0.34	0.39	0.39	0.40
Multi-class	**0.43**	**0.44**	**0.42**	**0.42**

Table 2: Baseline accuracy results.

5 Submitted runs and results

Participants were allowed to submit up to five runs for each language combination. A total of 17 teams registered to participate in the task and downloaded the training set. Out of them, 12 downloaded the test set and 10 (including one of the task organizers) submitted valid runs. Eight teams produced submissions for all the language combinations, while two teams participated only in the SP-EN task. In total, 92 runs have been submitted and evaluated (29 for SP-EN, and 21 for each of the other language pairs).

Despite the novelty and the difficulty of the problem, these numbers demonstrate the interest raised by the task, and the overall success of the initiative.

System_name	SP-EN	IT-EN	FR-EN	DE-EN
BUAP_run1	0.350	0.336	0.334	**0.330**
BUAP_run2	**0.366**	**0.344**	**0.342**	0.268
celi_run1	0.276	0.278	0.278	0.280
celi_run2	**0.336**	**0.338**	**0.300**	**0.352**
celi_run3	0.322	0.334	0.298	0.350
celi_run4	0.268	0.280	0.280	0.274
DirRelCond3_run1	0.300	0.280	0.362	0.336
DirRelCond3_run2	0.300	0.284	0.360	0.336
DirRelCond3_run3	0.300	**0.338**	**0.384**	0.364
DirRelCond3_run4	**0.344**	0.316	**0.384**	**0.374**
FBK_run1*	0.502	-	-	-
FBK_run2*	0.490	-	-	-
FBK_run3*	**0.504**	-	-	-
FBK_run4*	0.500	-	-	-
HDU_run1	0.630	0.554	0.564	**0.558**
HDU_run2	**0.632**	**0.562**	**0.570**	0.552
ICT_run1	**0.448**	**0.454**	**0.456**	**0.460**
JU-CSE-NLP_run1	**0.274**	0.316	0.288	0.262
JU-CSE-NLP_run2	0.266	**0.326**	0.294	**0.296**
JU-CSE-NLP_run3	0.272	0.314	**0.296**	0.264
Sagan_run1	0.342	0.352	**0.346**	**0.342**
Sagan_run2	0.328	0.352	0.336	0.310
Sagan_run3	**0.346**	**0.356**	0.330	0.332
Sagan_run4	0.340	0.330	0.310	0.310
SoftCard_run1	**0.552**	**0.566**	**0.570**	**0.550**
UAlacant_run1_LATE	**0.598**	-	-	-
UAlacant_run2	0.582	-	-	-
UAlacant_run3_LATE	0.510	-	-	-
UAlacant_run4	0.514	-	-	-
Highest	0.632	0.566	0.570	0.558
Average	0.440	0.411	0.408	0.408
Median	0.407	0.350	0.365	0.363
Lowest	0.274	0.326	0.296	0.296

Table 3: Accuracy results (92 runs) over the 4 language combinations. Highest, average, median and lowest scores are calculated considering the best run for each team (*task organizers' system).

Accuracy results are reported in Table 3. As can be seen from the table, overall accuracy scores are quite different across language pairs, with the highest result on SP-EN (0.632), which is considerably higher than the highest score on DE-EN (0.558). This might be due to the fact that most of the participating systems rely on a "pivoting" approach that addresses CLTE by automatically translating *T1* in the same language of *T2* (see Section 6). Regarding the DE-EN dataset, pivoting methods might be penalized by the lower quality of MT output when German *T1*s are translated into English.

The comparison with baselines results leads to interesting observations. First of all, while all systems significantly outperform the lowest 1-class baseline (0.25), both other baselines are surprisingly hard to beat. This shows that, despite the effort in keeping the distribution of the entailment classes uniform across different *length_diff* values, eliminating the correlation between sentences' length and correct entailment decisions is difficult. As a consequence, although disregarding semantic aspects of the problem, features considering such information are quite effective.

In general, systems performed better on the SP-EN dataset, with most results above the binary baseline (8 out of 10), and half of the systems above the multi-class baseline. For the other language pairs the results are lower, with only 3 out of 8 participants above the two baselines in all datasets. Average results reflect this situation: the average scores are always above the binary baseline, whereas only the SP-EN average result is higher than the multi-class baseline(0.44 vs. 0.43).

To better understand the behaviour of each system (also in relation to the different language combinations), Table 4 provides separate precision, recall, and F1 scores for each entailment judgment, calculated over the best runs of each participating team. Overall, the results suggest that the "bidirectional" and "no_entailment" categories are more problematic than "forward" and "backward" judgments. For most datasets, in fact, systems' performance on "bidirectional" and "no_entailment" is significantly lower, typically on recall. Except for the DE-EN dataset (more problematic on "forward"), also average F1 results on these judgments are lower. This might be due to the fact that, for all datasets, the vast majority of "bidirectional" and "no_entailment" judgments falls in a *length_diff* range where the distribution of the four classes is more uniform (see Figure 2).

Similar reasons can justify the fact that "backward" entailment results are consistently higher on all datasets. Compared with "forward" entailment, these judgments are in fact less scattered across the entire *length_diff* range (*i.e.* less intermingled with the other classes).

6 Approaches

A rough classification of the approaches adopted by participants can be made along two orthogonal dimensions, namely:

- **Pivoting vs. Cross-lingual.** Pivoting methods rely on the automatic translation of one of the two texts (either single words or the entire sentence) into the language of the other (typically English) in order perform monolingual TE recognition. Cross-lingual methods assign entailment judgments without preliminary translation.

- **Composition of binary judgments vs. Multi-class classification.** Compositional approaches map unidirectional entailment decisions taken separately into single judgments (similar to the *Binary* baseline in Section 4). Methods based on multi-class classification directly assign one of the four entailment judgments to each test pair (similar to our *Multi-class* baseline).

Concerning the former dimension, most of the systems (6 out of 10) adopted a pivoting approach, relying on Google Translate (4 systems), Microsoft Bing Translator (1), or a combination of Google, Bing, and other MT systems (1) to produce English *T2*s. Regarding the latter dimension, the compositional approach was preferred to multi-class classification (6 out of 10). The best performing system relies on a "hybrid" approach (combining monolingual and cross-lingual alignments) and a compositional strategy. Besides the frequent recourse to MT tools, other resources used by participants include: on-line dictionaries for the translation of single words, word alignment tools, part-of-speech taggers, NP chunkers, named entity recognizers, stemmers, stopwords lists, and Wikipedia as an external multilingual corpus. More in detail:

BUAP [pivoting, compositional] (Vilariño et al., 2012) adopts a pivoting method based on translating *T1* into the language of *T2* and vice versa (Google Translate[3] and the OpenOffice Thesaurus[4]). Similarity measures (*e.g.* Jaccard index) and rules are respectively used to annotate the two resulting sentence pairs with entailment judgments and combine them in a single decision.

CELI [cross_lingual, compositional & multi-class] (Kouylekov, 2012) uses dictionaries for word matching, and a multilingual corpus extracted from Wikipedia for term weighting. Word overlap and similarity measures are then used in different approaches to the task. In one run (Run_1), they are used to train a classifier that assigns separate entailment judgments for each direction. Such judgments are finally composed into a single one for each pair. In the other runs, the same features are used for multi-class classification.

DirRelCond3 [cross_lingual, compositional] (Perini, 2012) uses bilingual dictionaries (Freedict[5] and WordReference[6]) to translate content words into English. Then, entailment decisions are taken combining directional relatedness scores between words in both directions (Perini, 2011).

FBK [cross_lingual, compositional & multi-class] (Mehdad et al., 2012a) uses cross-lingual matching features extracted from lexical phrase tables, semantic phrase tables, and dependency relations (Mehdad et al., 2011; Mehdad et al., 2012b; Mehdad et al., 2012c). The features are used for multi-class and binary classification using SVMs.

HDU [hybrid, compositional] (Wäschle and Fendrich, 2012) uses a combination of binary classifiers for each entailment direction. The classifiers use both monolingual alignment features based on METEOR (Banerjee and Lavie, 2005) alignments (translations obtained from Google Translate), and cross-lingual alignment features based on GIZA++ (Och and Ney, 2000) (word alignments learned on Europarl).

ICT [pivoting, compositional] (Meng et al., 2012) adopts a pivoting method (using Google Translate and an in-house hierarchical MT system), and the open source EDITS system (Kouylekov and Negri, 2010) to calculate similarity scores between monolingual English pairs. Separate unidirectional entailment judgments obtained from binary classifier are combined to return one of the four valid CLTE judgments.

[3]http://translate.google.com/

[4]http://extensions.services.openoffice.org/en/taxonomy/term/233

[5]http://www.freedict.com/

[6]http://www.wordreference.com/

	SP-EN											
	Forward			Backward			No entailment			Bidirectional		
System name	*P*	*R*	*F1*	*P*	*R*	*F1*	*P*	*R*	*F1*	*P*	*R*	F1
BUAP_spa-eng_run2	0,337	0,664	0,447	0,406	0,568	0,473	0,333	0,088	0,139	0,391	0,144	0,211
celi_spa-eng_run2	0,324	0,368	0,345	0,411	0,368	0,388	0,306	0,296	0,301	0,312	0,312	0,312
DirRelCond3_spa-eng_run4	0,358	0,608	0,451	0,444	0,448	0,446	0,286	0,032	0,058	0,243	0,288	0,264
FBK_spa-eng_run3	0,515	**0,704**	0,595	0,546	0,568	0,557	0,447	0,304	0,362	0,482	0,440	0,460
HDU_spa-eng_run2	0,607	0,656	**0,631**	**0,677**	0,704	**0,690**	**0,602**	**0,592**	**0,597**	**0,643**	**0,576**	**0,608**
ICT_spa-eng_run1	**0,750**	0,240	0,364	0,440	0,472	0,456	0,395	0,560	0,464	0,436	0,520	0,474
JU-CSE-NLP_spa-eng_run1	0,211	0,288	0,243	0,272	0,296	0,284	0,354	0,232	0,280	0,315	0,280	0,297
Sagan_spa-eng_run3	0,225	0,200	0,212	0,269	0,224	0,245	0,418	0,448	0,432	0,424	0,512	0,464
SoftCard_spa-eng_run1	0,602	0,616	0,609	0,650	0,624	0,637	0,471	0,448	0,459	0,489	0,520	0,504
UAlacant_spa-eng_run1_LATE	0,689	0,568	0,623	0,645	**0,728**	0,684	0,507	0,544	0,525	0,566	0,552	0,559
AVG.	*0,462*	*0,491*	*0,452*	*0,476*	*0,5*	*0,486*	*0,412*	*0,354*	*0,362*	*0,43*	*0,414*	*0,415*

	IT-EN											
	Forward			Backward			No entailment			Bidirectional		
System name	*P*	*R*	*F1*	*P*	*R*	*F1*	*P*	*R*	*F1*	*P*	*R*	F1
BUAP_ita-eng_run2	0,324	0,456	0,379	0,327	0,672	0,440	0,538	0,056	0,101	0,444	0,192	0,268
celi_ita-eng_run2	0,349	0,360	0,354	0,455	0,36	0,402	0,294	0,320	0,307	0,287	0,312	0,299
DirRelCond3_ita-eng_run3	0,323	0,488	0,389	0,480	0,288	0,360	0,331	0,368	0,348	0,268	0,208	0,234
HDU_ita-eng_run2	0,564	**0,600**	0,581	**0,628**	0,648	0,638	0,551	**0,520**	**0,535**	**0,500**	0,480	0,490
ICT_ita-eng_run1	**0,661**	0,296	0,409	0,554	0,368	0,442	0,427	0,448	0,438	0,383	**0,704**	**0,496**
JU-CSE-NLP_ita-eng_run2	0,240	0,280	0,258	0,339	0,480	0,397	0,412	0,280	0,333	0,359	0,264	0,304
Sagan_ita-eng_run3	0,306	0,296	0,301	0,252	0,216	0,233	0,395	0,512	0,446	0,455	0,400	0,426
SoftCard_ita-eng_run1	0,602	0,616	**0,609**	0,617	**0,696**	**0,654**	**0,560**	0,448	0,498	0,481	0,504	0,492
AVG.	*0,421*	*0,424*	*0,410*	*0,457*	*0,466*	*0,446*	*0,439*	*0,369*	*0,376*	*0,397*	*0,383*	*0,376*

	FR-EN											
	Forward			Backward			No entailment			Bidirectional		
System name	*P*	*R*	*F1*	*P*	*R*	*F1*	*P*	*R*	*F1*	*P*	*R*	F1
BUAP_fra-eng_run2	0,447	0,272	0,338	0,291	**0,760**	0,420	0,250	0,016	0,030	0,449	0,320	0,374
celi_fra-eng_run2	0,316	0,296	0,306	0,378	0,360	0,369	0,270	0,296	0,282	0,244	0,248	0,246
DirRelCond3_fra-eng_run3	0,393	0,576	0,468	0,441	0,512	0,474	0,387	0,232	0,290	0,278	0,216	0,243
HDU_fra-eng_run2	0,564	**0,672**	**0,613**	0,582	0,736	0,650	**0,676**	0,384	0,490	0,500	**0,488**	0,494
ICT_fra-eng_run1	**0,750**	0,192	0,306	0,517	0,496	0,506	0,385	**0,656**	0,485	0,444	0,480	0,462
JU-CSE-NLP_fra-eng_run3	0,215	0,208	0,211	0,289	0,296	0,292	0,341	0,496	0,404	0,333	0,184	0,237
Sagan_fra-eng_run1	0,244	0,168	0,199	0,297	0,344	0,319	0,394	0,568	0,466	0,427	0,304	0,355
SoftCard_fra-eng_run1	0,551	0,608	0,578	**0,649**	0,696	**0,672**	0,560	0,488	**0,521**	**0,513**	**0,488**	**0,500**
AVG.	*0,435*	*0,374*	*0,377*	*0,431*	*0,525*	*0,463*	*0,408*	*0,392*	*0,371*	*0,399*	*0,341*	0,364

	DE-EN											
	Forward			Backward			No entailment			Bidirectional		
System name	*P*	*R*	*F1*	*P*	*R*	*F1*	*P*	*R*	*F1*	*P*	*R*	F1
BUAP_deu-eng_run1	0,395	0,120	0,184	0,248	0,224	0,235	0,344	**0,688**	0,459	0,364	0,288	0,321
celi_deu-eng_run2	0,347	0,416	0,378	0,402	0,392	0,397	0,339	0,312	0,325	0,319	0,288	0,303
DirRelCond3_deu-eng_run4	0,429	0,312	0,361	0,408	0,552	0,469	0,367	0,320	0,342	0,298	0,312	0,305
HDU_deu-eng_run1	0,559	0,528	0,543	0,600	**0,696**	**0,644**	**0,540**	0,488	**0,513**	**0,524**	0,520	**0,522**
ICT_deu-eng_run1	**0,718**	0,224	0,341	0,493	0,552	0,521	0,390	0,512	0,443	0,439	**0,552**	0,489
JU-CSE-NLP_deu-eng_run2	0,182	0,048	0,076	0,307	0,496	0,379	0,315	0,560	0,403	0,233	0,080	0,119
Sagan_deu-eng_run1	0,250	0,168	0,201	0,239	0,256	0,247	0,405	0,600	0,484	0,443	0,344	0,387
SoftCard_deu-eng_run1	0,568	**0,568**	**0,568**	**0,611**	0,640	0,625	0,521	0,488	0,504	0,496	0,504	0,500
AVG.	*0,431*	*0,298*	*0,332*	*0,414*	*0,476*	*0,440*	*0,403*	*0,496*	*0,434*	*0,390*	*0,361*	*0,368*

Table 4: precision, recall and F1 scores, calculated for each team's best run for all the language combinations.

JU-CSE-NLP [pivoting, compositional] (Neogi et al., 2012) uses Microsoft Bing translator[7] to produce monolingual English pairs. Separate lexical mapping scores are calculated (from *T1* to *T2* and vice-versa) considering different types of information and similarity metrics. Binary entailment decisions are then heuristically combined into single decisions.

Sagan [pivoting, multi-class] (Castillo and Cardenas, 2012) adopts a pivoting method using Google Translate, and trains a monolingual system based on a SVM multi-class classifier. A CLTE corpus derived from the RTE-3 dataset is also used as a source of additional training material.

[7] `http://www.microsofttranslator.com/`

SoftCard [pivoting, multi-class] (Jimenez et al., 2012) after automatic translation with Google Translate, uses SVMs to learn entailment decisions based on information about the cardinality of: *T1*, *T2*, their intersection and their union. Cardinalities are computed in different ways, considering tokens in *T1* and *T2*, their IDF, and their similarity (computed with edit-distance)

UAlacant [pivoting, multi-class] (Esplà-Gomis et al., 2012) exploits translations obtained from Google Translate, Microsoft Bing translator, and the Apertium open-source MT platform (Forcada et al., 2011).[8] Then, a multi-class SVM classifier is used to take entailment decisions using information about overlapping sub-segments as features.

7 Conclusion

Despite the novelty of the problem and the difficulty to capture multi-directional entailment relations across languages, the first round of the *Cross-lingual Textual Entailment for Content Synchronization* task organized within SemEval-2012 was a successful experience. This year a new interesting challenge has been proposed, a benchmark for four language combinations has been released, baseline results have been proposed for comparison, and a monolingual English dataset has been produced as a by-product which can be useful for monolingual TE research. The interest shown by participants was encouraging: 10 teams submitted a total of 92 runs for all the language pairs proposed. Overall, the results achieved on all datasets are encouraging, with best systems significantly outperforming the proposed baselines. It is worth observing that the nature of the task, which lies between semantics and machine translation, led to the participation of teams coming from both these communities, showing interesting opportunities for integration and mutual improvement. The proposed approaches reflect this situation, with teams traditionally working on MT now dealing with entailment, and teams traditionally participating in the RTE challenges now dealing with cross-lingual alignment techniques. Our ambition, for the future editions of the CLTE task, is to further consolidate the bridge between the semantics and MT communities.

[8] http://www.apertium.org/

Acknowledgments

This work has been partially supported by the EC-funded project CoSyne (FP7-ICT-4-24853). The authors would also like to acknowledge Giovanni Moretti from CELCT for evaluation scripts and technical assistance, and the volunteer translators that contributed to the creation of the dataset: María Sol Accossato, Laura Barthélémy, Claudia Biacchi, Jane Brendler, Amandine Chantrel, Hanna Cheda Patete, Ellen Clancy, Rodrigo Damian Tejeda, Daniela Dold, Valentina Frattini, Debora Hedy Amato, Geniz Hernandez, Bénédicte Jeannequin, Beate Jones, Anne Kauffman, Marcia Laura Zanoli, Jasmin Lewis, Alicia López, Domenico Losseto, Sabrina Luján Sánchez, Julie Mailfait, Gabriele Mark, Nunzio Pruiti, Lourdes Rey Cascallar, Sylvie Martlew, Aleane Salas Velez, Monica Scalici, Andreas Schwab, Marianna Sicuranza, Chiara Sisler, Stefano Tordazzi, Yvonne.

References

Satanjeev Banerjee and Alon Lavie. 2005. METEOR: An Automatic Metric for MT Evaluation with Improved Correlation with Human Judgments. In *Proceedings of the ACL Workshop on Intrinsic and Extrinsic Evaluation Measures for Machine Translation and/or Summarization*, pages 65–72.

Julio Castillo and Marina Cardenas. 2012. Sagan: A Cross Lingual Textual Entailment system based on Machine Traslation. In *Proceedings of the 6th International Workshop on Semantic Evaluation (SemEval 2012)*.

Chih-Chung Chang and Chih-Jen Lin. 2011. Libsvm: a library for support vector machines. *ACM Transactions on Intelligent Systems and Technology (TIST)*, 2(3):27.

Ido Dagan and Oren Glickman. 2004. Probabilistic Textual Entailment: Generic Applied Modeling of Language Variability. In *Proceedings of the PASCAL Workshop of Learning Methods for Text Understanding and Mining*.

Miquel Esplà-Gomis, Felipe Sánchez-Martínez, and Mikel L. Forcada. 2012. UAlacant: Using Online Machine Translation for Cross-Lingual Textual Entailment. In *Proceedings of the 6th International Workshop on Semantic Evaluation (SemEval 2012)*.

Mikel L. Forcada, Ginestí-Rosell Mireia, Nordfalk Jacob, O'Regan Jim, Ortiz-Rojas Sergio, Pérez-Ortiz Juan A., Sánchez-Martínez Felipe, Ramírez-Sánchez Gema, and Tyers Francis M. 2011. Apertium: a Free/Open-Source Platform for Rule-Based Machine Translation. *Machine Translation*, 25(2):127–144. Special Issue: Free/Open-Source Machine Translation.

Sergio Jimenez, Claudia Becerra, and Alexander Gelbukh. 2012. Soft Cardinality + ML: Learning Adaptive Similarity Functions for Cross-lingual Textual Entailment. In *Proceedings of the 6th International Workshop on Semantic Evaluation (SemEval 2012)*.

Milen Kouylekov and Matteo Negri. 2010. An open-source package for recognizing textual entailment. In *Proceedings of the ACL 2010 System Demonstrations*.

Milen Kouylekov. 2012. CELI: An Experiment with Cross Language Textual Entailment. In *Proceedings of the 6th International Workshop on Semantic Evaluation (SemEval 2012)*.

Yashar Mehdad, Matteo Negri, and Marcello Federico. 2010. Towards Cross-Lingual Textual Entailment. In *Proceedings of the 11th Annual Conference of the North American Chapter of the Association for Computational Linguistics (NAACL HLT 2010)*.

Yashar Mehdad, Matteo Negri, and Marcello Federico. 2011. Using Bilingual Parallel Corpora for Cross-Lingual Textual Entailment. In *Proceedings of the 49th Annual Meeting of the Association for Computational Linguistics: Human Language Technologies (ACL HLT 2011)*.

Yashar Mehdad, Matteo Negri, and José G. C. de Souza. 2012a. FBK: Cross-Lingual Textual Entailment Without Translation. In *Proceedings of the 6th International Workshop on Semantic Evaluation (SemEval 2012)*.

Yashar Mehdad, Matteo Negri, and Marcello Federico. 2012b. Detecting Semantic Equivalence and Information Disparity in Cross-lingual Documents. In *Proceedings of the 50th Annual Meeting of the Association for Computational Linguistics (ACL 2012)*.

Yashar Mehdad, Matteo Negri, and Marcello Federico. 2012c. Match without a Referee: Evaluating MT Adequacy without Reference Translations. In *Proceedings of the 7th Workshop on Statistical Machine Translation (WMT 2012)*.

Fandong Meng, Hao Xiong, and Qun Liu. 2012. ICT: A Translation based Cross-lingual Textual Entailment. In *Proceedings of the 6th International Workshop on Semantic Evaluation (SemEval 2012)*.

Matto Negri, Luisa Bentivogli, Yashar Mehdad, Danilo Giampiccolo, and Alessandro Marchetti. 2011. Divide and Conquer: Crowdsourcing the Creation of Cross-Lingual Textual Entailment Corpora. *Proceedings of the 2011 Conference on Empirical Methods in Natural Language Processing (EMNLP 2011)*.

Snehasis Neogi, Partha Pakray, Sivaji Bandyopadhyay, and Alexander Gelbukh. 2012. JU-CSE-NLP: Language Independent Cross-lingual Textual Entailment System. In *Proceedings of the 6th International Workshop on Semantic Evaluation (SemEval 2012)*.

Franz J. Och and Hermann Ney. 2000. Improved Statistical Alignment Models. In *Proceedings of the 38th Annual Meeting of the Association for Computational Linguistics (ACL 2000)*.

Alpár Perini. 2011. Detecting textual entailment with conditions on directional text relatedness scores. *Studia Universitatis Babes-Bolyai Series Informatica*, LVI(2):13–18.

Alpár Perini. 2012. DirRelCond3: Detecting Textual Entailment Across Languages With Conditions On Directional Text Relatedness Scores. In *Proceedings of the 6th International Workshop on Semantic Evaluation (SemEval 2012)*.

Darnes Vilariño, David Pinto, Mireya Tovar, Saul León, and Esteban Castillo. 2012. BUAP: Lexical and Semantic Similarity for Cross-lingual Textual Entailment. In *Proceedings of the 6th International Workshop on Semantic Evaluation (SemEval 2012)*.

Katharina Wäschle and Sascha Fendrich. 2012. HDU: Cross-lingual Textual Entailment with SMT Features. In *Proceedings of the 6th International Workshop on Semantic Evaluation (SemEval 2012)*.

EMNLP@CPH: Is frequency all there is to simplicity?

Anders Johannsen, Héctor Martínez, Sigrid Klerke†, Anders Søgaard
Centre for Language Technology
University of Copenhagen
{ajohannsen|alonso|soegaard}@hum.ku.dk
sigridklerke@gmail.com†

Abstract

Our system breaks down the problem of ranking a list of lexical substitutions according to how simple they are in a given context into a series of pairwise comparisons between candidates. For this we learn a binary classifier. As only very little training data is provided, we describe a procedure for generating artificial unlabeled data from Wordnet and a corpus and approach the classification task as a semi-supervised machine learning problem. We use a co-training procedure that lets each classifier increase the other classifier's training set with selected instances from an unlabeled data set. Our features include n-gram probabilities of candidate and context in a web corpus, distributional differences of candidate in a corpus of "easy" sentences and a corpus of normal sentences, syntactic complexity of documents that are similar to the given context, candidate length, and letter-wise recognizability of candidate as measured by a trigram character language model.

1 Introduction

This paper describes a system for the SemEval 2012 English Lexical Simplification shared task. The task description uses a loose definition of simplicity, defining "simple words" as "words that can be understood by a wide variety of people, including for example people with low literacy levels or some cognitive disability, children, and non-native speakers of English" (Specia et al., 2012).

Feature	r
NGRAM$_{sf}$	0.33
NGRAM$_{sf+1}$	0.27
NGRAM$_{sf-1}$	0.27
LEN$_{sf}$	-0.26
LEN$_{max}$	-0.26
RI$_{proto(l)}$	-0.18
SYN$_{cn}$	-0.17
SYN$_{w}$	-0.17
SYN$_{cp}$	-0.17

Feature	r
RI$_{proto(f)}$	-0.15
CHAR$_{max}$	-0.14
RI$_{orig(l)}$	-0.11
LEN$_{tokens}$	-0.10
CHAR$_{min}$	0.10
SW$_{freq}$	0.08
SW$_{LLR}$	0.07
CHAR$_{avg}$	-0.04

Table 1: Pearson's r correlations. The table shows the three highest correlated features per group, all of which are significant at the $p < 0.01$ level

2 Features

We model simplicity with a range of features divided into six groups. Five of these groups make use of the distributional hypothesis and rely on external corpora. We measure a candidate's distribution in terms of its lexical associations (RI), participation in syntactic structures (SYN), or corpus presence in order to assess its simplicity (NGRAM, SW, CHAR). A single group, LEN, measures intrinsic aspects of the substitution candidate, such as its length.

The substitution candidate is either an adjective, an adverb, a noun, or a verb, and all candidates within a list share the same part of speech. Because word class might influence simplicity, we allow our model to fit parameters specific to the candidate's part of speech by making a copy of the features for each part of speech which is active only when the candidate is in the given part of speech.

Simple Wikipedia (SW) These two features contain relative frequency counts of the substitution form in Simple English Wikipedia (SW_{freq}), and the log likelihood ratio of finding the word in the simple corpus to finding it in regular Wikipedia (SW_{LLR})[1].

Word length (LEN) This set of three features describes the length of the substitution form in characters (LEN_{sf}), the length of the longest token (LEN_{max}), and the length of the substitution form in tokens (LEN_{tokens}). Word length is an integral part of common measures of text complexity, e.g in the English Flesch–Kincaid (Kincaid et al., 1975) in the form of syllable count, and in the Scandinavian LIX (Bjornsson, 1983).

Character trigram model (CHAR) These three features approximate the reading difficulty of a word in terms of the probabilities of its forming character trigrams, with special characters to mark word beginning and end. A word with an unusual combination of characters takes longer to read and is perceived as less simple (Ehri, 2005).

We calculate the minimum, average, and maximum trigram probability ($CHAR_{min}$, $CHAR_{avg}$, and $CHAR_{max}$).[2]

Web corpus N-gram (NGRAM) These 12 features were obtained from a pre-built web-scale language model[3]. Features of the form $NGRAM_{sf\pm i}$, where $0 < i < 4$, express the probability of seeing the substitution form together with the following (or previous) unigram, bigram, or trigram. $NGRAM_{sf}$ is the probability of substitution form itself, a feature which also is the backbone of our frequency baseline.

Random Indexing (RI) These four features are obtained from measures taken from a word-to-word distributional semantic model. Random Indexing (RI) was chosen for efficiency reasons (Sahlgren, 2005). We include features describing the semantic distances between the candidate and the original form (RI_{orig}), and between the candidate and a prototype vector (RI_{proto}). For the distance between candidate and original, we hypothesize that annotators would prefer a synonym closer to the original form. A prototype distributional vector of a set of words is built by summing the individual word vectors, thus obtaining a representation that approximates the behavior of that class overall (Turney and Pantel, 2010). Longer distances indicate that the currently examined substitution is far from the shared meaning of all the synonyms, making it a less likely candidate. The features are included for both lemma and surface forms of the words.

Syntactic complexity (SYN) These 23 features measure the syntactic complexity of documents where the substitution candidate occurs. We used measures from (Lu, 2010) in which they describe 14 automatic measures of syntactic complexity calculated from frequency counts of 9 types of syntactic structures. This group of syntax-metric scores builds on two ideas.

First, syntactic complexity and word difficulty go together. A sentence with a complicated syntax is more likely to be made up of difficult words, and conversely, the probability that a word in a sentence is simple goes up when we know that the syntax of the sentence is uncomplicated. To model this we search for instances of the substitution candidates in the UKWAC corpus[4] and measure the syntactic complexity of the documents where they occur.

Second, the perceived simplicity of a word may change depending on the context. Consider the adjective "frigid", which may be judged to be simpler than "gelid" if referring to temperature, but perhaps less simple than "ice-cold" when characterizing someone's personality. These differences in word sense are taken into account by measuring the similarity between corpus documents and substitution contexts and use these values to provide a weighted average of the syntactic complexity measures.

3 Unlabeled data

The unlabeled data set was generated by a three-step procedure involving synonyms extracted from Wordnet[5] and sentences from the UKWAC corpus.

[1]Wikipedia dump obtained March 27, 2012. Date on the Simple Wikipedia dump is March 22, 2012.

[2]Trigram probabilities derived from Google T1 unigram counts.

[3]The "jun09/body" trigram model from Microsoft Web N-gram Services.

[4]http://wacky.sslmit.unibo.it/

[5]http://wordnet.princeton.edu/

1) **Collection**: Find synsets for unambigious lemmas in Wordnet. The synsets must have more than three synonyms. Search for the lemmas in the corpus. Generate unlabeled instances by replacing the lemma with each of its synonyms. 2) **Sampling**: In the unlabeled corpus, reduce the number of ranking problems per lemma to a maximum of 10. Sample from this pool while maintaining a distribution of part of speech similar to that of the trial and test set. 3) **Filtering**: Remove instances for which there are missing values in our features.

The unlabeled part of our final data set contains $n = 1783$ problems.

4 Ranking

We are given a number of ranking problems ($n = 300$ in the trial set and $n = 1710$ for the test data). Each of these consists of a text extract with a position marked for substitution, and a set of candidate substitutions.

4.1 Linear order

Let $\mathcal{X}^{(i)}$ be the substitution set for the i-th problem. We can then formalize the ranking problem by assuming that we have access to a set of (weighted) preference judgments, $w(a \prec b)$ for all $a, b \in \mathcal{X}^{(i)}$ such that $w(a \prec b)$ is the value of ranking item a ahead of b. The values are the confidence-weighted pair-wise decisions from our binary classifier. Our goal is then to establish a total order on $\mathcal{X}^{(i)}$ that maximizes the value of the non-violated judgments. This is an instance of the Linear Ordering Problem (Martí and Reinelt, 2011), which is known to be NP-hard. However, with problems of our size (maximum ten items in each ranking), we escape these complexity issues by a very narrow margin—$10! \approx 3.6$ million means that the number of possible orderings is small enough to make it feasible to find the optimal one by exhaustive enumeration of all possibilities.

4.2 Binary classication

In order to turn our ranking problem into binary classification, we generate a new data set by enumerating all point-wise comparisons within a problem and for each apply a transformation function $\Phi(\mathbf{a}, \mathbf{b}) = \mathbf{a} - \mathbf{b}$. Thus each data point in the new set is the difference between the feature values of two candidates. This enables us to learn a binary classifier for the relation "ranks ahead of".

We use the trial set for labeled training data L and, in a transductive manner, treat the test set as unlabeled data U_{test}. Further, we supplement the pool of unlabeled data with artificially generated instances U_{gen}, such that $U = U_{test} \cup U_{gen}$.

Using a co-training setup (Blum and Mitchell, 1998), we divide our features in two independent sets and train a large margin classifier[6] on each split. The classifiers then provide labels for data in the unlabeled set, adding the k most confidently labeled instances to the training data for the other classifier, an iterative process which continues until there is no unlabeled data left. At the end of the training we have two classifiers. The classification result is a mixture-of-experts: the most confident prediction of the two classifiers. Furthermore, as an upper-bound of the co-training procedure, we define an oracle that returns the correct answer whenever it is given by at least one classifier.

4.3 Ties

In many cases we have items a and b that tie—in which case both $a \prec b$ and $b \prec a$ are violated. We deal with these instances by omitting them from the training set and setting $w(a \prec b) = 0$. For the final ranking, our system makes no attempt to produce ties.

5 Experiments

In our experiments we vary feature-split, size of unlabeled data, and number of iterations. The first feature split, SYN–SW, pooled all syntactic complexity features and Wikipedia-based features in one view, with the remaining feature groups in another view. Our second feature split, SYN–CHAR–LEN, combined the syntactic complexity features with the character trigram language model features and the basic word length features. Both splits produced a pair of classifiers with similar performance—each had an F-score of around .73 and an oracle score of .87 on the trial set on the binary decision problem, and both splits performed equally on the ranking task.

[6]Liblinear with L1 penalty and L2 loss. Parameter settings were default. http://www.csie.ntu.edu.tw/~cjlin/liblinear/

System	All	N	V	R	A
MicrosoftFreq	0.449	0.367	0.456	0.487	0.493
Syn–SW$_f$	0.377	0.283	0.269	0.271	0.421
Syn–SW$_l$	0.425	0.355	**0.497**	0.408	0.425
Syn–Char–Len$_f$	0.377	0.284	0.469	0.270	0.421
Syn–Char–Len$_l$	0.435	0.362	0.481	0.465	0.439

Table 2: Performance on part of speech. Unlabeled set was U_{test}. Subscripts tell whether the scores are from the first or last iteration

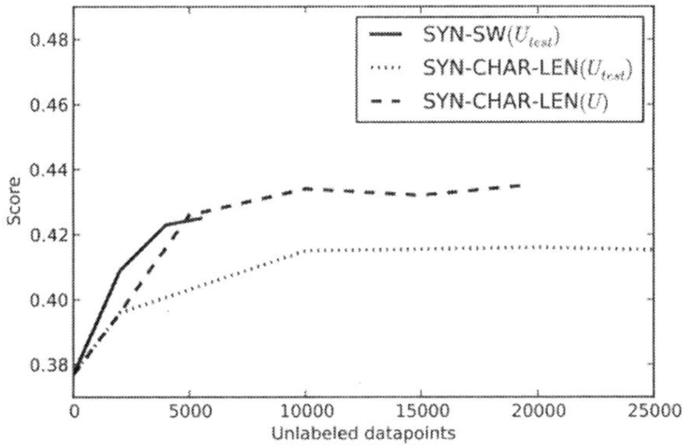

Figure 1: Test set kappa score vs. number of data points labeled during co-training

With a large unlabeled data set available, the classifiers can avoid picking and labeling data points with a low certainty, at least initially. The assumption is that this will give us a higher quality training set. However, as can be seen in Figure 1, none of our systems are benefitting from the additional data. In fact, the systems learn more when the pool of unlabeled data is restricted to the test set.

Our submitted systems, Ord1 and Ord2 scored 0.405 and 0.393 on the test set, and 0.494 and 0.500 on the trial set. Following submission we adjusted a parameter[7] and re-ran each split with both U and U_{test}.

We analyzed the performance by part of speech and compared them to the frequency baseline as shown in Table 2. For the frequency baseline, performance is better on adverbs and adjectives alone, and somewhat worse on nouns. Both our systems benefit from co-training on all word classes. Syn–Char–Len, our best performing system, notably has a score reduction (compared to the baseline) of only 5% on adverbs, eliminates the score reduction on nouns, and effectively beats the baseline score on verbs with a 6% increase.

6 Discussion

The frequency baseline has proven very strong, and, as witnessed by the correlations in Table 1, frequency is by far the most powerful signal for "simplicity". But is that all there is to simplicity? Perhaps it is. For a person with normal reading ability, a simple word may be just a word with which the person is well-acquainted—one that he has seen before enough times to have a good idea about what it means and in which contexts it is typically used. And so an n-gram model might be a fair approximation. However, lexical simplicity in English may still be something very different to readers with low literacy. For instance, the highly complex letter-to-sound mapping rules are likely to prevent such readers from arriving at the correct pronunciation of unseen words and thus frequent words with exceptional spelling patterns may not seem simple at all.

A source of misclassifications discovered in our error analysis is the fact that substituting candidates into the given contexts in a straight-forward manner can introduce syntactic errors. Fixing these can require significant revisions of the sentence, and yet the substitutions resulting in an ungrammatical sentence are sometimes still preferred to grammatical alternatives.[8] Here, scoring the substitution and the immediate context in a language model is of little use. Moreover, while these odd grammatical errors may be preferable to many non-native English speakers with adequate reading skills, such errors can be more obstructing to reading impaired users and beginning language learners.

Acknowledgments

This research is partially funded by the European Commission's 7th Framework Program under grant agreement n° 238405 (CLARA).

[7]In particular, we selected a larger value for the C parameter in the liblinear classifier.

[8]For example sentence 1528: "However, it appears they intend to *pull* out all stops to get what they want." Gold: {try everything} {do everything it takes} {pull} {stop at nothing} {go to any length} {yank}.

References

C. H. Bjornsson. 1983. Readability of Newspapers in 11 Languages. *Reading Research Quarterly*, 18(4):480–497.

A Blum and T Mitchell. 1998. Combining labeled and unlabeled data with co-training. In *Proceedings of the eleventh annual conference on Computational learning theory*, pages 92–100. ACM.

Linnea C. Ehri. 2005. Learning to read words: Theory, findings, and issues. *Scientific Studies of Reading*, 9(2):167–188.

J P Kincaid, R P Fishburne, R L Rogers, and B S Chissom. 1975. Derivation of New Readability Formulas (Automated Readability Index, Fog Count and Flesch Reading Ease Formula) for Navy Enlisted Personnel.

Xiaofei Lu. 2010. Automatic analysis of syntactic complexity in second language writing. *International Journal of Corpus Linguistics*, 15(4):474–496.

Rafael Martí and Gerhard Reinelt. 2011. *The Linear Ordering Problem: Exact and Heuristic Methods in Combinatorial Optimization (Applied Mathematical Sciences)*. Springer.

Magnus Sahlgren. 2005. An introduction to random indexing. In *Methods and Applications of Semantic Indexing Workshop at the 7th International Conference on Terminology and Knowledge Engineering, TKE*, volume 5.

Lucia Specia, Sujay K. Jauhar, and Rada Mihalcea. 2012. SemEval-2012 Task 1: English Lexical Simplification. In *Proceedings of the 6th International Workshop on Semantic Evaluation (SemEval 2012)*, Montreal, Canada.

P. D Turney and P. Pantel. 2010. From frequency to meaning: Vector space models of semantics. *Journal of Artificial Intelligence Research*, 37:141–188.

UTD: Determining Relational Similarity Using Lexical Patterns

Bryan Rink and Sanda Harabagiu
University of Texas at Dallas
P.O. Box 830688; MS EC31
Richardson, TX, 75083-0688, USA
{bryan, sanda}@hlt.utdallas.edu

Abstract

In this paper we present our approach for assigning degrees of relational similarity to pairs of words in the SemEval-2012 Task 2. To measure relational similarity we employed lexical patterns that can match against word pairs within a large corpus of 12 million documents. Patterns are weighted by obtaining statistically estimated lower bounds on their precision for extracting word pairs from a given relation. Finally, word pairs are ranked based on a model predicting the probability that they belong to the relation of interest. This approach achieved the best results on the SemEval 2012 Task 2, obtaining a Spearman correlation of 0.229 and an accuracy on reproducing human answers to MaxDiff questions of 39.4%.

1 Introduction

Considerable prior research has examined and elaborated upon a wide variety of semantic relations between concepts along with techniques for automatically discovering pairs of concepts for which a relation holds (Bejar et al., 1991; Stephens and Chen, 1996; Rosario and Hearst, 2004; Khoo and Na, 2006; Girju et al., 2009). However, most previous work has considered membership assignment for a semantic relation as a binary property. In this paper we discuss an approach which assigns a *degree* of membership to a pair of concepts for a given relation. For example, for the semantic relation CLASS-INCLUSION (Taxonomic), the concept pairs *weapon:spear* and *bird:robin* are stronger members of the relationship than *hair:brown*, because *brown* may describe many things other than hair, and brown is also used much less frequently as a noun than the words in the first two word pairs. Task 2 of SemEval 2012 (Jurgens et al., 2012) was designed to evaluate the effectiveness of automatic approaches for determining the similarity of a pair of concepts to a specific semantic relation. The task focused on 79 semantic relations from Bejar et al. (1991) which broadly fall into the ten categories enumerated in Table 1.

> Consider the following word pairs: *millionaire:money*, *author:copyright*, *robin:nest*. These X:Y pairs share a relation "X R Y". Now consider the following word pairs:
> (1) *teacher:students*
> (2) *farmer:crops*
> (3) *homeowner:door*
> (4) *shrubs:roots*
> Which of the numbered word pairs is the MOST illustrative example of the same relation "X R Y"? ____
> Which of the above numbered word pairs is the LEAST illustrative example of the same relation "X R Y"? ____

Figure 1: Example Phase 2 MaxDiff question for the relation 2h PART-WHOLE: Creature:Possession.

The data for the task was collected in two phases using Amazon Mechanical Turk [1]. During Phase 1, Turkers were asked to provide pairs of words which fit a relation template, such as "*X* possesses/owns/has *Y*". Turkers provided word pairs such as *expert:experience*, *mall:shops*, *letters:words*, and *doctor:degree*. A total of 3,218 word pairs

[1] http://www.mturk.com/mturk/

Category	Example word pairs	Relations
CLASS-INCLUSION	flower:tulip, weapon:knife, clothing:shirt, queen:Elizabeth	5
PART-WHOLE	car:engine, fleet:ship, mile:yard, kickoff:football	10
SIMILAR	car:auto, stream:river, eating:gluttony, colt:horse	8
CONTRAST	alive:dead, old:young, east:west, happy:morbid	8
ATTRIBUTE	beggar:poor, malleable:molded, soldier:fight, exercise:vigorous	8
NON-ATTRIBUTE	sound:inaudible, exemplary:criticized, war:tranquility, dull:cunning	8
CASE RELATIONS	tailor:suit, farmer:tractor, teach:student, king:crown	8
CAUSE-PURPOSE	joke:laughter, fatigue:sleep, gasoline:car, assassin:death	8
SPACE-TIME	bookshelf:books, coast:ocean, infancy:cradle, rivet:girder	9
REFERENCE	smile:friendliness, person:portrait, recipe:cake, astronomy:stars	6

Table 1: The ten categories of semantic relations used in SemEval 2012 Task 2. Each word pair has been taken from a different subcategory of each major category.

across 79 relations were provided by Turkers in Phase 1. Some of these word pairs are naturally more representative of the relationship than others. Therefore, in the second phase, each word pair was presented to a different set of Turkers for ranking in the form of MaxDiff (Louviere and Woodworth, 1991) questions. Figure 1 shows an example MaxDiff question for the relation 2h PART-WHOLE: Creature:Possession ("*X* possesses/owns/has *Y*"). In each MaxDiff question, Turkers were simply asked to select the word pair which was the most illustrative of the relation and the word pair which was the least illustrative of the relation. For the example in Figure 1, most Turkers chose either *shrubs:roots* or *farmer:crops* as the most illustrative of the *Creature:Possession* relation, and *homeowner:door* as the least illustrative. When Turkers select a pair of words they are performing a semantic inference that we wanted to also perform in a computational manner. In this paper we present a method for automatically ranking word pairs according to their relatedness to a given semantic relation.

2 Approach for Determining Relational Similarity

In the vein of previous methods for determining relational similarity (Turney, 2011; Turney, 2008a; Turney, 2008b; Turney, 2005), we propose two approaches using patterns generated from the contexts in which the word pairs occur. Our corpus consists of 8.4 million documents from Gigaword (Parker and Consortium, 2009) and over 4 million articles from Wikipedia. For each word pair, <W1>, <W2> provided by Turkers in Phase 1, as well as the three relation examples, we collected all contexts which matched the schema:

" [0 or more non-content words] <W1> [0 to 7 words] <W2> [0 or more non-content words]"

We also include those contexts where W1 and W2 are swapped. The window size of seven words was determined based on experiments on the training set of ten relations provided by the task organizers. For the non-content words, we considered closed class words such as determiners (*the, who, every*), prepositions (*in, on, instead of*), and conjunctions (*and, but*). Members of these classes were collected from their corresponding Wikipedia pages. Below we provide a sample of the 7,022 contexts found for the word pair *love*:*hate*:

"they <W1> to <W2> it"
"<W1> and <W2> the most . by"
"between <W1> & <W2>"
"<W1> you then i <W2> you and"

We restrict the context before and after the word pair to non-content words in order to match longer contexts without introducing exponential growth in the number of patterns and the consequential sparsity problems. These contexts are directly used as patterns. To generate additional patterns we have one method for shortening contexts and two methods for generating patterns from contexts.

Any contexts which contain words before <W1> or after <W1> are used to create additional shorter contexts by successively removing leading and trailing words. For example, the context "as much <W1> in the <W2> as his" for the word pair *money*:*bank* would generate the following shortened contexts:

"much <W1> in the <W2> as his"
"<W1> in the <W2> as his"

"as much <W1> in the <W2>" as
"as much <W1> in the <W2>"
"much <W1> in the <W2> as"
"<W1> in the <W2> as"
"<W1> in the <W2>"

These shortened contexts are used, along with the original context, to generate patterns.

The first pattern generation method replaces each word between <W1> and <W2> with a wildcard ([^]+ means one or more non-space characters). For example:

"as much <W1> [^]+ the <W2> as"
"as much <W1> in [^]+ <W2> as"

The second pattern generation technique allows for a single word to be matched in the context between the arguments <W1> and <W2>, along with arbitrary matching of other tokens in the context. For example, the context for *red:stop* "the <W1> flag is flagged to indicate a <W2>" will generate new patterns such as:

"the <W1>.* flag .*<W2>"
"the <W1>.* is .*<W2>"
"the <W1>.* flagged .*<W2>"
"the <W1>.* indicate .*<W2>"

After all patterns have been generated, they are used by our two approaches to assign relational similarity scores to word pairs.

2.1 UTD-NB Approach

The first of our two approaches, UTD-NB, assigns weights to patterns which are then used to assign similarity scores to word pairs. The approach begins by obtaining all word pairs associated with a relation. Each relation is associated with a target set (T) of word pairs from two sources: (i) the three or four example word pairs provided for each relation, and (ii) the word pairs provided by Turkers in Phase 1. We collect all of the contexts for those word pairs to generate patterns. The UTD-NB approach assumes that the word pairs provided by Turkers, while noisy, can be used to characterize the relation. As an example, consider these word pairs provided by Turkers for the relation 8a (Cause:Effect) *illness:discomfort*, *fire:burns*, *accident:damage*. A pattern which extracts these word pairs is: "<W1> that caused [^]+ <W2>". This pattern is unlikely to match the contexts of word pairs from other relations. Therefore, we use the statistics about how many target word pairs a pattern extracts versus how many non-target pairs a pattern extracts to assign a weight to the pattern. A pattern which matches many of the word pairs from the target relation and few (or none) of the word pairs from other relations is likely to be a good indicator of that relation. For example, the pattern **P1** for the relation 8a (Cause:Effect): "the <W1>.* caused .*<W2> to his" matches only three word pairs: *explosion:damage*, *accident:damage*, and *injury:pain*, all of them belonging to the target relation. Conversely, the pattern **P2**: "<W1>.* causing .*<W2> but" matches five words pairs. However, only three of them belong to the target relation: *hit:injury*, *explosion:damage*, *germs:sickness*. The remaining two: *city:people*, *action:alarm* belong to other relations: .

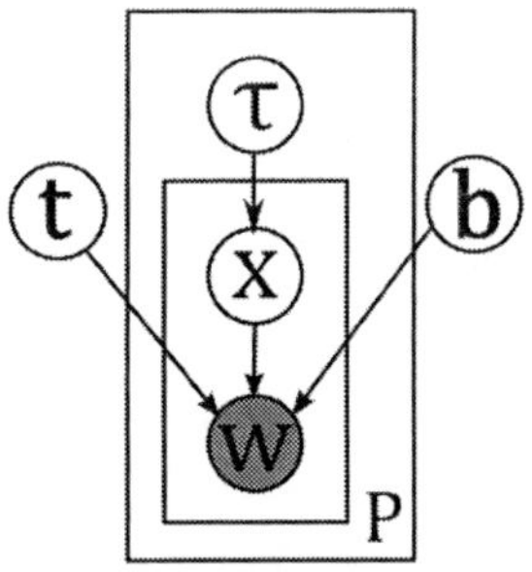

Figure 2: Probabilistic model for the word pairs extracted by patterns, for a single relation.

We use the number of target word pairs extracted, x, and the total number of word pairs extracted, n, to calculate τ: the probability that a word pair extracted by the pattern will belong to the target relation. The maximum likelihood estimate for τ is $\frac{x}{n}$, however for small values of x this estimate has a high variance and can significantly overestimate the true value. Therefore, we used the Wilson interval score for determining a lower bound on τ at a 99.9% confidence level. This gives the pattern **P1** above with $x = 3$ and $n = 3$ a lower bound on τ of 21.7% and **P2** with $x = 3$ and $n = 5$ a lower bound on τ of 16.6%. We use this lower bound as the pattern's weight. These pattern weights are then combined to score each word pair for the target relation.

We model the word pairs extracted by the patterns as a generative process shown in Figure 2. Each pattern, p, is associated with with a precision, τ, which is the probability that a word pair extracted by that pattern is a member of the target relation. The observed word pairs extracted by a pattern are denoted by w. Our model assumes that a word pair extracted by a pattern may be drawn from one of two distinct distributions over word pairs: a distribution for the target relation $\vec{t}$, and a background distribution over word pairs $\vec{b}$. The generation of a word pair begins with a binary variable x drawn from a Bernoulli distribution parametrized by τ (the pattern's precision), which represents whether a word pair is generated according to a relation specific distribution, or a background distribution. More explicitly, if $x = 1$, then a word pair w is generated by the target relation distribution $\vec{t}$, and if $x = 0$, a word pair is generated by the background distribution $\vec{b}$.

We may not yet perform any meaningful inference because no evidence has been observed to correctly infer whether the target distribution or the background distribution generated w. Therefore we use the pattern weights derived above (based on the lower bounds on the pattern precisions) as that pattern's value of τ. For estimating the distributions $\vec{t}$ and $\vec{b}$, we assume that x is 1 (w is generated by $\vec{t}$) if and only if $\tau \geq 0.1$ and the word pair w belongs to the target set of word pairs T. This threshold on τ has a filtering effect on the patterns, and those patterns below the threshold are treated as non-indicative of the relation. These assumptions allow us to estimate the parameters for $\vec{t}$ and $\vec{b}$:

$$P(w|\vec{t}) = \begin{cases} \frac{\#(w,h)}{\#(h)} & \text{if } w \in T \\ 0 & \text{if } w \notin T \end{cases} \quad (1)$$

$$P(w|\vec{b}) = \frac{\#(w, \neg h) + \#(w, h)\mathbf{1}_{w \notin T}}{\sum_u \#(u, \neg h) + \#(u, h)\mathbf{1}_{u \notin T}} \quad (2)$$

where $\#(w, h)$ is the number of times w was extracted by a high precision pattern ($\tau \geq 10\%$), and $\#(h)$ is the number of word pairs extracted by a high precision pattern.

The only remaining hidden variable in the model is x which we can now estimate using the inferred distributions for the other variables. We chose to use the probability of x for a word pair w as the score by which we rank the word pairs. Furthermore, we use only the probability of x for the highest ranking pattern p which extracted w:

$$P(x = 1|p, w) = \frac{P(x = 1, w|p)}{P(w|p)} \quad (3)$$

where $P(x = 1, w|p) = \tau_p \times \vec{t}(w)$ and $P(w|p) = P(x = 1, w|p) + P(x = 0, w|p)$

This method of scoring word pairs accounts for how common a word pair is overall. For example for the relation 4c (CONTRAST: Reverse), the word pair *white:black* occurs very commonly in both high precision patterns and low precision patterns (those more likely associated with other relations). Therefore even though the word pair shares its highest ranking pattern with the pair *eat:fast*, *white:black* receives a score of 0.019 while *eat:fast* receives a score of 0.216 because $\vec{t}(white : black) = 0.006$ and $\vec{b}(white : black) = 0.104$, while $\vec{t}(eat : fast) = 0.0016$ and $\vec{b}(eat : fast) = 0.0018$. However, if a pattern with 100% precision were to extract *white:black*, the pair would appropriately receive a score of 1.0 despite being much more common in the background distribution. This is motivated by our assumption that such a pattern can only extract word pairs which truly belong to the relation. Another motivation for scoring word pairs by their highest ranking pattern is that it does not depend on any assumption of independence between the patterns which extract the pairs. For example, the pattern "<W1> , not <W2> . " extracts largely the same word pairs as "<W1> [^]+ not <W2> ." and thus its matches should not be taken as additional evidence about the word pairs.

2.2 UTD-SVM Approach

Our second approach uses an SVM-rank (Joachims, 2006) model to rank the word pairs. Each word pair from a target relation is represented as a binary feature vector indicating which patterns extracted the word pair. We train the SVM-rank classifier by assigning all word pairs from the target relation rank 2, and all word pairs from other relations with rank 1. The SVM model is then trained and used to classify the word pairs from the target relation. Even though the model is used to classify the same word pairs it was trained on, it still provides higher scores to word pairs more likely to belong to the target relation. We directly rank the word pairs using these scores.

3 Discussion

The organizers of SemEval 2012 Task 2 viewed relational similarity in two different ways. The first

Word pair	% Most illustrative - % Least illustrative
"freezing:warm"	56.0
"earsplitting:quiet"	36.0
"evil:angelic"	18.0
"ancient:modern"	12.0
"disastrous:peaceful"	6.0
"ecstatic:disgruntled"	2.0
"disgusting:tasty"	0.0
"beautiful:plain"	-2.0
"dirty:sterile"	-4.0
"wrinkled:smooth"	-6.0
"sweet:sour"	-20.0
"disgruntled:ecstatic"	-32.0
"white:gray"	-54.0

Table 2: A sample of the 41 word pairs provided by Amazon Mechanical Turk participants for the relation 4f (CONTRAST: Asymmetric Contrary - X and Y are at opposite ends of the same scale). The word pairs are ranked by how illustrative of the relation participants found each pair to be.

view was that of solving a MaxDiff problem, question in which participants are shown a list of four word pairs and asked to select the most and least illustrative pairs. The second view of relation similarity considers the task of assigning scores to a according to their similarity to the relation of interest. The first column of Table 2 provides an example of word pairs that Amazon Turkers said belonged to the 4f: CONTRAST: *Asymmetric Contrary* relation in Phase 1, ranked according to how well other Turkers felt they represented the relation. The score in the second column is calculated as the percentage of how often Turkers rated a word pair as the most illustrative and how often Turkers rated the word pair as the least illustrative.

Both of our approaches for determining relation similarity assign scores directly to the word pairs collected in Phase 1, with the goal of ranking the words in the same order that was induced from the responses by Amazon Mechanical Turkers.

3.1 Evaluation Measures

SemEval-2012 Task 2 had two official evaluation metrics. The first directly measured the accuracy of automatically choosing the most and least illustrative word pairs among a set of four word pairs taken from responses during Phase 1. The accuracy of choosing the most illustrative word pair and the accuracy of choosing the least illustrative word pair were calculated separately and averaged to produce the MaxDiff accuracy.

Team-Algorithm	Spearman	MaxDiff
UTD-NB	0.229	39.4
UTD-SVM	0.116	34.7
Duluth-V0	0.050	32.4
Duluth-V1	0.039	31.5
Duluth-V2	0.038	31.1
BUAP	0.014	31.7
Random	0.018	31.2

Table 3: Results for all systems participating in SemEval 2012 Task 2 on relational similarity, including a random baseline.

The second evaluation metric measured the correlation between an automatic ranking of word pairs for a relation and a ranking induced by the Turkers' responses to the MaxDiff questions. The word pairs were given scores equal to the percentage of times they were chosen by Turkers as the most illustrative example for a relation minus the percentage of times they were chosen as the least illustrative. Systems were then evaluated according to their Spearman rank correlation with the ranking of word pairs induced by that score. Spearman correlations range from -1 for a negative correlation to 1.0 for a perfect correlation.

3.2 Results

Table 3 shows the results for the six systems which participated in SemEval-2012 Task 2, along with the results for a baseline which ranks each word pair randomly. Our two approaches achieved the best results on both evaluation metrics. Our UTD-NB approach achieves much better performance than our UTD-SVM approach, likely due to the unconventional use of the SVM to classify its own training data. That said, the results are still significantly higher than those of other participants. This may be attributed to our incorporation of better patterns or our use of a large corpus. It might also be a consequence of our approaches considering all of the testing word pairs simultaneously.

Table 4 shows the results for each of the ten categories of relations. The best results are achieved on SPACE-TIME relations, while the lowest performance is on the NON-ATTRIBUTE relations. NON-

Category	Rndm	BUAP	UTD NB	UMD V0
1 CLASS-INCLUSION	0.057	0.064	0.233	0.045
2 PART-WHOLE	0.012	0.066	0.252	-0.061
3 SIMILAR	0.026	-0.036	0.214	0.183
4 CONTRAST	-0.049	0.000	0.206	0.142
5 ATTRIBUTE	0.037	-0.095	0.158	0.044
6 NON-ATTRIBUTE	-0.070	0.009	0.098	0.079
7 CASE RELATIONS	0.090	-0.037	0.241	-0.011
8 CAUSE-PURPOSE	-0.011	0.114	0.183	0.021
9 SPACE-TIME	0.013	0.035	0.375	0.055
10 REFERENCE	0.142	-0.001	0.346	0.028

Table 4: Spearman correlation results for the best system from each team, across all ten categories of relations.

ATTRIBUTE relations associate objects and actions with an atypical attribute (*harmony:discordant, immortal:death, recluse:socialize*). Because the pairs of words associated with these relation are not typically associated together, our approach likely performs poorly on these relations because our approach is based on finding the pairs of words together in a large corpus.

An interesting consequence of the 10% precision threshold used in the UTD-NB approach is that 24 relations had no patterns exceeding the threshold and therefore produced zeroes as scores for all word pairs. However, word pairs which never occurred within seven tokens of each other in our corpus received a negative score and were ranked lower. Such rankings tend to produce Spearman scores around 0.0. Our lowest Spearman score was -0.068, while other teams had low scores of -0.344 and -0.266, both occurring on relations for which UTD-NB produced no positive word pair scores. There are two lessons to be learned from this result: (i) the UTD-NB approach does a good job of recognizing when it cannot rank word pairs, and (ii) such relations are likely difficult and worth further investigation.

4 Conclusion

We described the UTD approaches to determining relation similarity using lexical patterns from a large corpus. Combined with a probabilistic model for word pair extraction by those patterns, we were able to achieve the highest performance at the SemEval 2012 Task 2. Our results showed the approach significantly outperformed a model which used an SVM-rank model used to classify its own training set. The approach also performed well across a wide range of relation types and argument classes which included nouns, adjectives, verbs, and adverbs. This implies that the approaches presented in this paper could be successfully applied to other domains which involve semantic relations.

References

Isaac I. Bejar, Roger Chaffin, and Susan E. Embretson. 1991. *Cognitive and psychometric analysis of analogical problem solving. Recent research in psychology.* Springer-Verlag Publishing.

Roxana Girju, Preslav Nakov, Vivi Nastase, Stan Szpakowicz, Peter Turney, and Deniz Yuret. 2009. Classification of semantic relations between nominals. *Language Resources and Evaluation*, 43(2):105–121.

Thorsten Joachims. 2006. Training linear SVMs in linear time. In *Proceedings of the 12th ACM SIGKDD international conference KDD '06*, page 217, New York, New York, USA, August. ACM Press.

David A. Jurgens, Saif M. Mohammad, Peter D. Turney, and Keith J. Holyoak. 2012. SemEval-2012 Task 2: Measuring Degrees of Relational Similarity. In *Proceedings of the 6th International Workshop on Semantic Evaluation (SemEval 2012).*

Christopher S G Khoo and Jin-cheon Na. 2006. Semantic relations in information science. *Annual Review of Information Science and Technology*, 40(1):157–228.

Jordan J Louviere and G G Woodworth. 1991. Best-worst scaling: A model for the largest difference judgments. Technical report, University of Alberta.

Robert Parker and Linguistic Data Consortium. 2009. *English gigaword fourth edition.* Linguistic Data Consortium.

Barbara Rosario and Marti A. Hearst. 2004. Classifying semantic relations in bioscience texts. In *Proceedings of the AACL '04*, pages 430–es, July.

Larry M. Stephens and Yufeng F. Chen. 1996. Principles for organizing semantic relations in large knowledge bases. *IEEE Transactions on Knowledge and Data Engineering*, 8(3):492–496, June.

Peter D. Turney. 2005. Measuring Semantic Similarity by Latent Relational Analysis. In *International Joint Conference On Artificial Intelligence*, volume 19.

Peter D. Turney. 2008a. A Uniform Approach to Analogies, Synonyms, Antonyms, and Associations. In *Proceedings of COLING '08*, August.

Peter D. Turney. 2008b. The Latent Relation Mapping Engine: Algorithm and Experiments. *Journal of Artificial Intelligence Research*, 33:615–655.

Peter D. Turney. 2011. Analogy perception applied to seven tests of word comprehension. *Journal of Experimental & Theoretical Artificial Intelligence*, 23(3):343–362, July.

UTD-SpRL: A Joint Approach to Spatial Role Labeling

Kirk Roberts and Sanda M. Harabagiu
Human Language Technology Research Institute
University of Texas at Dallas
Richardson, TX 75083, USA
{kirk, sanda}@hlt.utdallas.edu

Abstract

We present a joint approach for recognizing spatial roles in SemEval-2012 Task 3. Candidate spatial relations, in the form of triples, are heuristically extracted from sentences with high recall. The joint classification of spatial roles is then cast as a binary classification over the candidates. This joint approach allows for a rich feature set based on the complete relation instead of individual relation arguments. Our best official submission achieves an F_1-measure of 0.573 on relation recognition, best in the task and outperforming the previous best result on the same data set (0.500).

1 Introduction

A significant amount of spatial information in natural language is encoded in spatial relationships between objects. In this paper, we present our approach for detecting the special case of spatial relations evaluated in SemEval-2012 Task 3, Spatial Role Labeling (SpRL) (Kordjamshidi et al., 2012). This task considers the most common type of spatial relationships between objects, namely those described with a spatial preposition (e.g., *in*, *on*, *over*) or a spatial phrase (e.g., *in front of*, *on the left*), referred to as the spatial INDICATOR. A spatial INDICATOR connects an object of interest (the TRAJECTOR) with a grounding location (the LANDMARK). Examples of this type of spatial relationship include:

(1) $[\text{cars}]_T$ parked $[\text{in front of}]_I$ the $[\text{house}]_L$.
(2) $[\text{bushes}]_{T1}$ and small $[\text{trees}]_{T2}$ $[\text{on}]_I$ the $[\text{hill}]_L$.
(3) a huge $[\text{column}]_L$ with a $[\text{football}]_T$ $[\text{on top}]_I$.
(4) $[\text{trees}]_T$ $[\text{on the right}]_I$. $[\emptyset]_L$

SpRL is a type of *semantic role labeling* (SRL) (Palmer et al., 2010), where the spatial INDICATOR is the predicate (or trigger) and the TRAJECTOR and LANDMARK are its two arguments. Previous approaches to SpRL (Kordjamshidi et al., 2011) have largely followed the commonly employed SRL pipeline: (1) find predicates (i.e., the INDICATOR), (2) recognize the predicate's syntactic constituents, and (3) classify the constituent's role (i.e., TRAJECTOR, LANDMARK, or neither). The problem with this approach is that arguments are considered largely in isolation. Consider the following:

(5) there is a picture on the wall above the bed.

This sentence contains three objects (*picture*, *wall*, and *bed*) and two INDICATORS (*on* and *above*). Since the most common spatial relation pattern is simply trajector-indicator-landmark (as in Examples (1) and (2)), the triple *wall-above-bed* is a likely candidate relation. However, the semantics of these objects invalidates the relation (i.e., walls are beside beds, ceilings are above them). Instead the correct relation is *picture-above-bed* because the preposition *above* syntactically attaches to *picture* instead of *wall*. Prepositional attachment, however, is a difficult syntactic problem solved largely through the use of semantics, so an understanding of the consistency of spatial relationships plays an important role in their recognition. Consistency checking is not possible under a pipeline approach that classifies whether *wall* as the TRAJECTOR without any knowledge of its LANDMARK.

We therefore propose an alternative to this pipeline approach that jointly decides whether a given TRAJECTOR-INDICATOR-LANDMARK triple expresses a spatial relation. We utilize a high recall heuristic for recognizing objects capable of participating in a spatial relation as well as a lexicon of INDICATORs. All possible combinations of these arguments (including undefined LANDMARKs) are considered by a binary classifier in order to make a joint decision. This allows us to incorporate features based on all three relation elements such as the relation's semantic consistency.

2 Joint Classification

2.1 Relation Candidate Selection

Previous joint approaches to SpRL have performed poorly relative to the pipeline approach (Kordjamshidi et al., 2011). However, these approaches have issues with data imbalance: if every token could be a TRAJECTOR, LANDMARK, or INDICATOR, then even short sentences may contain thousands of negative relation candidates. Such unbalanced data sets are difficult for classifiers to reason over (Japkowicz and Stephen, 2002). To reduce this imbalance, we propose high recall heuristics to recognize candidate elements (INDICATORs, TRAJECTORs, and LANDMARKs). Since INDICATORs are taken from a closed set of prepositions and a small set of spatial phrases, we simply use a lexicon constructed from the indicators in the training data (e.g., *on*, *in front of*). Thus, our approach is not capable of detecting INDICATORs that were unseen in the training data. The effectiveness of this indicator lexicon is evaluated in Section 3.2. For TRAJECTORs and LANDMARKs, we observe that both may be considered spatial objects, which unlike INDICATORs are not a closed class of words. Instead, we consider noun phrase (NP) heads to be spatial objects. To overcome part-of-speech errors and increase recall, we incorporate three sources: (1) the NP heads from a syntactic parse tree (Klein and Manning, 2003), (2) the NP heads from a chunk parse[1], and (3) words that are marked as nouns in at least 66% of instances in Treebank (Marcus et al., 1993). This approach identifies all nouns, not just spatial nouns. But for the SemEval-2012 Task 3 data, which is composed of image descriptions, most nouns are spatial objects and no further refinements are necessary. Further heuristics (such as using WordNet (Fellbaum, 1998)) could be used to refine the set of spatial objects if other domains (such as newswire) were to be used. Our main emphasis in this step, however, is recall: by utilizing these heuristics we greatly reduce the number of negative instances while removing very few positive spatial relations. The effectiveness of our heuristics are evaluated in Section 3.2.

Once all possible spatial INDICATORs and spatial objects are marked, all possible combinations of these are formed as candidate relations. Additionally, for each spatial object and spatial INDICATOR pair, an additional candidate relation is formed with an undefined LANDMARK (such as in Example (4)).

2.2 Classification Framework

Given candidate spatial relations, we utilize a binary support vector machine (SVM) classifier to indicate which relation candidates are spatial relations. We use the LibLINEAR (Fan et al., 2008) SVM implementation, adjusting the negative outcome weight from 1.0 to 0.8 (tuned via cross-validation on the training data). This adjustment sacrifices precision for recall, but raises the overall F_1 score. For type classification (REGION, DIRECTION, and DISTANCE), we use LibLINEAR as a multi-class SVM with no weight adjustment in order to maximize accuracy. The features used in both classifiers are discussed in Sections 2.3 and 2.4.

2.3 Relation Detection Features

The difference between our two official submissions (supervised1 and supervised2) is that different sets of features were used to detect spatial relations. The features for general type classification, discussed in Section 2.4, were consistent across both submissions. Based on previous approaches to spatial role labeling, our own initial intuitions, and error analysis, we created over 100 different features, choosing the best feature set with a greedy forward/backward automated feature selection technique (Pudil et al., 1994). This greedy method iteratively chooses the best un-used feature to add to the feature set. At the end of each iteration, there is a pruning step to remove any features made redundant by the addition of the latest feature.

Before describing the individual features used in our submission, we first enumerate some basic fea-

[1] http://www.surdeanu.name/mihai/bios/

tures that form the building blocks of many of the features in our submissions (with sample feature values from Example (1)):

(BF.1) The TRAJECTOR's raw string (e.g., *cars*).
(BF.2) The LANDMARK's raw string (*house*).
(BF.3) The INDICATOR's raw string (*in_front_of*).
(BF.4) The TRAJECTOR's lemma (*car*).
(BF.5) The LANDMARK's lemma (*house*).
(BF.6) The dependency path from the TRAJECTOR to the INDICATOR (↑NSUBJ↓PREP). Uses the Stanford Dependency Parser (de Marneffe et al., 2006).
(BF.7) The dependency path from the INDICATOR to the LANDMARK (↓POBJ).

For BF.2, BF.5, and BF.7, if the relation's LANDMARK is undefined, the feature value is simply *undefined*. The features for our first submission (supervised1), in the order they were chosen by the feature selector, are as follows:

(JF1.1) The concatenation of BF.6, BF.3, and BF.7 (i.e., the dependency path from the TRAJECTOR to the LANDMARK including the INDICATOR's raw string), *for all* spatial objects related to the TRAJECTOR under consideration via a conjunction dependency relation (including the TRAJECTOR itself). For instance, TRAJECTOR_1 in Example (2) would have two feature values: ↓CONJ↓PREP↓POBJ and ↓PREP↓POBJ. Since objects connected via a conjunction should participate in the same relation, this allows the classifier to overcome the sparsity related to the low number of training instances containing a conjunction.
(JF1.2) The concatenation of BF.1, BF.3, and BF.2 (*cars::in_front_of::house*).
(JF1.3) Whether or not the LANDMARK is part of a term from the INDICATOR lexicon. Words like *front* and *side* are common LANDMARKs but may also be part of an INDICATOR as well.
(JF1.4) All the words between the left-most argument in the relation and the right-most argument (*parked*, *the*). Does not include any word in the arguments.
(JF1.5) The value of BF.7.
(JF1.6) The first word in the INDICATOR.
(JF1.7) The LANDMARK's WordNet hypernyms.
(JF1.8) The TRAJECTOR's WordNet hypernyms.
(JF1.9) Whether or not the relative order of the relation arguments in the text is INDICATOR, LANDMARK, TRAJECTOR. This order is rare and thus this feature acts as a negative indicator.
(JF1.10) Whether or not the TRAJECTOR is a prepositional object (POBJ from the dependency tree) of a preposition that is *not* the relation's INDICATOR but is in the INDICATOR lexicon. Again, this is a negative indicator.
(JF1.11) The concatenation of BF.4, BF.3, and BF.5 (*car::in_front_of::house*).
(JF1.12) The dependency path from the TRAJECTOR to the LANDMARK. Differs from JF1.1 because it does not consider conjunctions or differentiate between INDICATORs.
(JF1.13) The concatenation of BF.3 and BF.7.
(JF1.14) Whether or not the relation under consideration has an undefined LANDMARK *and* the sentence contains no spatial objects other than the TRAJECTOR under consideration. This helps to indicate relations with undefined LANDMARKs in short sentences.

The first feature selected by the automated feature selector (JF1.1) utilizes conjunctions (e.g., *and*, *or*, *either*). However, conjunctions are difficult to detect with high precision, so we decided to perform another round of feature selection without this particular feature. The chosen features were then submitted separately (supervised2):

(JF2.1) The same as JF1.2.
(JF2.2) The same as JF1.3.
(JF2.3) The same as JF1.4.
(JF2.4) The same as JF1.13.
(JF2.5) The value of BF.1.
(JF2.6) The same as JF1.5.
(JF2.7) Similar to JF1.1, but only using the concatenation of BF.6 and BF.3 (i.e., leaving out the dependency path from the INDICATOR to the LANDMARK).
(JF2.8) The same as JF1.7.
(JF2.9) The same as JF1.8.
(JF2.10) The lexical pattern from the left-most argument to the right-most argument (TRAJECTOR_*parked*_INDICATOR_*the*_LANDMARK).
(JF2.11) The raw string of the preposition in a PREP dependency relation with the TRAJECTOR *if* that preposition is not the relation's INDICATOR.
(JF2.12) The PropBank role types for each argument in the relation (TRAJECTOR=A1;INDICATOR=AM_LOC;LANDMARK=AM_LOC). Uses SENNA (Collobert and Weston, 2009) for the PropBank parse.
(JF2.13) The same as JF1.14.
(JF2.14) The concatenation of BF.4, BF.3, and BF.5.
(JF2.15) The same as JF1.10, but with no requirement to be in the INDICATOR lexicon.

2.4 Type Classification Features

After joint detection of a relation's arguments, a separate classifier determines the relation's general type. The features used to classify a relation's general type (REGION, DIRECTION, and DISTANCE) were also selected using an automated feature selector from the same set of features. Both submissions (supervised1 and supervised2) utilized these

	supervised1			supervised2		
Label	Precision	Recall	F_1	Precision	Recall	F_1
TRAJECTOR	0.731	0.621	0.672	0.782	0.646	0.707
LANDMARK	0.871	0.645	0.741	0.894	0.680	0.772
INDICATOR	0.928	0.712	0.806	0.940	0.732	0.823
Relation	0.567	0.500	0.531	0.610	0.540	0.573
Relation + Type	0.561	0.494	0.526	0.603	0.534	0.566

Table 1: Official results for submissions.

features. The following features were used for classifying a spatial relation's general type:

(TF.1) The last word of the INDICATOR.
(TF.2) The value of BF.3.
(TF.3) The value of BF.5.
(TF.4) The same as JF1.3.
(TF.5) The same as JF2.10.

3 Evaluation

3.1 Official Submission

The official results for both of our submissions is shown in Table 1. The argument-specific results for TRAJECTORs, LANDMARKs, and INDICATORS are difficult to interpret in the joint approach. In a pipeline method, these usually indicate the performance of individual classifiers, but in our approach these results are simply a derivative of our joint classification output. The first submission (supervised1) achieved a triple F_1 of 0.531 for relation detection and 0.526 when the general type is included. Our second submission (supervised2) performed better, with an F_1 of 0.573 for relation detection and 0.566 when the general type is included. This suggests that the feature JF1.1, even though it is the best individual feature, introduces a significant amount of noise.

The only result to compare our official submissions to is that of Kordjamshidi et al. (2011), who utilize a pipeline approach. Their method has a relation detection F_1 of 0.500 (they do not report a score with general type). We further compare our method with theirs in Section 4.

3.2 Relation Candidate Evaluation

The heuristics described in Section 2.1 that enable joint classification were tuned for the training data, but their recall on the test data places a strict upper bound on the recall to our overall approach. It is therefore important to understand the performance loss that occurs at this step.

Table 2 shows the performance of our heuristics on the training and test data. The spatial INDICATOR lexicon has perfect recall on the training data because it was built from this data set. However, it performs at only 0.951 recall on the test data, as almost 5% of the INDICATORs in the test data were not seen in the training data. Most of these are phrasal verbs (e.g., *sailing over*) or include the modifier *very* (e.g., *to the very left*). Our spatial object recognizer performed better, only dropping from 0.998 (2 errors) to 0.989 (16 errors). Some of these errors resulted from mis-spellings (e.g., *housed* instead of *houses*), non-head spatial objects (*mountain* from the NP *mountain landscape*), NPs containing conjunctions (*trees* in *two palm trees, lamps and flags*, which gets marked as one simple NP), as well as parser errors. The significant drop in precision for both spatial indicators and objects is an additional concern. This does not indicate the extracted items were not valid as potential indicators or objects, but rather that no gold relation contained them. As explained in Section 4, this is likely caused by the disparity in sentence length: longer sentences result in more matches, but not necessarily more relations. As evidence of this, despite the training and test data containing almost the same number of sentences, there are 36% more spatial indicators and 20% more spatial objects in the test set.

3.3 Further Experiments

After the evaluation deadline, the task organizers provided the gold test data, allowing us to perform additional experiments. In this process we found several annotation errors which we needed to fix in order to process our gold results. These errors were largely annotations that were given an incorrect token index, resulting in the annotation text not matching the referenced text. These fixes increased our performance, shown on Table 3, improving relation detection for the supervised2 feature set from 0.573

		#	Precision	Recall	F_1
Spatial Indicators	Train	1,488	0.448	1.000	0.619
	Test	2,335	0.328	0.951	0.487
Spatial Objects	Train	2,974	0.448	0.998	0.618
	Test	3,704	0.387	0.989	0.556

Table 2: Results of relation candidate selection heuristics.

Data	Precision	Recall	F_1
Train/Test	0.644	0.556	0.597
Train/Test -NSI	0.644	0.582	0.611
Train CV	0.824	0.743	0.781
Test CV	0.745	0.639	0.688
Train+Test CV	0.774	0.680	0.724

Table 3: Additional experiments on corrected test data using the supervised2 data set. -NSI indicates that the gold spatial INDICATORs that are not in the lexicon are removed. CV indicates 10-fold cross validation.

to 0.597. We use this updated data set for the following experiments. While the results aren't comparable to other methods, the goal of these experiments is to analyze our system under various configurations by their relative performance.

Table 3 also shows a 10-fold cross validation performance on 3 data sets: (1) the training data, (2) the test data, and (3) both the training and test data. While our feature set is tuned to the training data, the test data is clearly more difficult. Section 4 discusses the differences between the training and test data that may lead to such a performance reduction.

Since our lexicon of spatial INDICATORs was built from the training data, our method will not recognize any relations that use unseen INDICATORs. To differentiate between how our method performs on the full test data and just those INDICATORs that are in the lexicon, we removed the 39 gold relations with unseen INDICATORs and re-tested the system. As can be seen in Table 3 (under -NSI), this improves recall by 2.6 points.

3.4 Feature Experiments

To estimate the contribution of our features, we performed an additive experiment to see how each feature contributes to the overall test score. Table 4 shows the feature contributions based on the order they were added by the feature selector. For many of the features the score goes down when added. However, without these features, the final score would drop to 0.578, indicating they still provide valuable information in the context of the other features. Table 5 shows performance on the updated test set when individual features are removed. Here, six features that were useful on the training data did not prove useful on the test data.

Feature	Precision	Recall	F_1
JF2.1	0.333	0.156	**0.212**
+JF2.2	0.347	0.126	0.185
+JF2.3	0.708	0.115	**0.197**
+JF2.4	0.555	0.294	**0.384**
+JF2.5	0.636	0.402	**0.493**
+JF2.6	0.590	0.414	0.486
+JF2.7	0.621	0.553	**0.585**
+JF2.8	0.614	0.568	**0.590**
+JF2.9	0.573	0.568	0.571
+JF2.10	0.612	0.547	**0.578**
+JF2.11	0.625	0.571	**0.597**
+JF2.12	0.660	0.536	0.592
+JF2.13	0.633	0.573	**0.601**
+JF2.14	0.642	0.563	0.600
+JF2.15	0.644	0.556	0.597

Table 4: Additive feature experiment results using the supervised2 features. Bold indicates increases in F_1 over the previous feature set.

Feature	Precision	Recall	F_1
$\emptyset$	0.644	0.556	0.597
JF2.1	0.627	0.571	**0.598**
JF2.2	0.629	0.542	0.582
JF2.3	0.540	0.494	0.516
JF2.4	0.591	0.412	0.485
JF2.5	0.631	0.558	0.592
JF2.6	0.657	0.515	0.577
JF2.7	0.636	0.547	0.589
JF2.8	0.641	0.562	**0.599**
JF2.9	0.678	0.539	**0.601**
JF2.10	0.607	0.569	0.587
JF2.11	0.640	0.565	**0.600**
JF2.12	0.646	0.566	**0.603**
JF2.13	0.646	0.553	0.596
JF2.14	0.618	0.572	0.594
JF2.15	0.642	0.563	**0.600**

Table 5: Results when individual features from the supervised2 submission are removed. Bold indicates improvement when the feature is removed.

4 Discussion

The only available work against which our method may be compared is that of Kordjamshidi et al. (2011). They propose both a pipeline and joint approach to SpRL. In their case, their pipeline approach performs better than their joint approach. Joint approaches increase data sparsity, so their greatest value is in the ability to use a richer set of features that describe the relationships between the arguments. Kordjamshidi et al. (2011) furthermore did not employ heuristics to select relation candidates such as those in Section 2.1. Given this difference it is difficult to assert that a joint approach is better with complete certainty, but we believe the ability to analyze the consistency of the entire relation provides a significant advantage. Many of our features (JF2.1, JF2.3, JF2.10, JF2.12, JF2.13, and JF2.14) were of this joint type.

The drop in performance from the training data to the test data is significant. The possibility that this is entirely due to over-training is dispelled by the cross validation results in Table 3. While different features might work better on the test set, they are unlikely to overcome the cross validation difference of 9.3 points (0.781 vs. 0.688). Much of this comes from the recall limit due to the use of the spatial indicator lexicon. The other significant cause of performance degradation seems to be caused by sentence length and complexity. The test sentences are longer (18 tokens vs. 15 tokens in the training data), and have far more conjunctions (389 *and* tokens vs. 256), indicating greater syntactic complexity. But the largest difference is the number of relation candidates generated by the heuristics: 60,377 relation candidates from the training data vs. 167,925 relation candidates from the test data (the data sets are roughly the same size: 600 training and 613 test sentences). The drop of precision in spatial objects in Table 2 reflects this as well. Since the number of candidate relations is quadratic in the number of spatial objects, it is likely that just a few, long sentences result in this dramatic increase in the number of candidates.

Since more general domains (such as newswire) are likely to have this problem as well, one important area of future work is the reduction of the number of relation candidates (increasing precision) while still maintaining near-perfect recall.

5 Conclusion

We have presented a joint approach for recognizing spatial roles in SemEval-2012 Task 3. Our approach improves over previous attempts at joint classification by extracting a more precise (but still extremely high recall) set of relation candidates, allowing binary classification on a more balanced data set. This joint approach allowed for a rich set of features based on all the relation's arguments. Our best official submission achieved an F_1-measure of 0.573 on relation recognition, best in the task and outperforming all previous work.

Acknowledgments

The authors would like to thank the SemEval-2012 Task 3 organizers for their work preparing the data set and organizing the task.

References

Ronan Collobert and Jason Weston. 2009. Deep Learning in Natural Language Processing. Tutorial at NIPS.

Marie-Catherine de Marneffe, Bill MacCartney, and Christopher D. Manning. 2006. Generating Typed Dependency Parses from Phrase Structure Parses. In *Proceedings of the Fifth International Conference on Language Resources and Evaluation*.

Rong-En Fan, Kai-Wei Chang, Cho-Jui Hsieh, Xiang-Rui Wang, and Chih-Jen Lin. 2008. LIBLINEAR: A Library for Large Linear Classification. *Journal of Machine Learning Research*, 9:1871–1874.

Christiane Fellbaum, editor. 1998. *WordNet: An Electronic Lexical Database*. MIT Press.

Nathalie Japkowicz and Shaju Stephen. 2002. The class imbalance problem: A systematic study. *Intelligent Data Analysis*, 6(5).

Dan Klein and Christopher D. Manning. 2003. Accurate Unlexicalized Parsing. In *Proceedings of the 41st Annual Meeting of the Association for Computational Linguistics*, pages 423–430.

Parisa Kordjamshidi, Martijn Van Otterlo, and Marie-Francine Moens. 2011. Spatial Role Labeling: Towards Extraction of Spatial Relations from Natural Language. *ACM Transactions on Speech and Language Processing*, 8(3).

Parisa Kordjamshidi, Steven Bethard, and Marie-Francine Moens. 2012. SemEval-2012 Task 3: Spatial Role Labeling. In *Proceedings of the 6th International Workshop on Semantic Evaluation (SemEval)*.

Mitchell P. Marcus, Mary Ann Marcinkiewicz, and Beatrice Santorini. 1993. Building a Large Annotated Corpus of English: The Penn Treebank. *Computational Linguistics*, 19(2):313–330.

Martha Palmer, Daniel Gildea, and Nianwen Xue. 2010. *Semantic Role Labeling*. Morgan and Claypool.

Pavel Pudil, Jana Novovičová, and Josef Kittler. 1994. Floating search methods in feature selection. *Pattern Recognition Letters*, 15:1119–1125.

MIXCD: System Description for Evaluating Chinese Word Similarity at SemEval-2012

Yingjie Zhang
Nanjing University
22 Hankou Road
Jiangsu P. R. China
jillzhyj@139.com

Bin Li
Nanjing University
Nanjing Normal University
122 Ninghai Road
Jiangsu P. R. China
gothere@126.com

Xinyu Dai
Nanjing University
22 Hankou Road
Jiangsu P. R. China
dxy@nju.edu.cn

Jiajun Chen
Nanjing University
22 Hankou Road
Jiangsu P. R. China
cjj@nju.eud.cn

Abstract

This document describes three systems calculating semantic similarity between two Chinese words. One is based on Machine Readable Dictionaries and the others utilize both MRDs and Corpus. These systems are performed on SemEval-2012 Task 4: Evaluating Chinese Word Similarity.

1 Introduction

The characteristics of polysemy and synonymy that exist in words of natural language have always been a challenge in the fields of Natural Language Processing (NLP) and Information Retrieval (IR). In many cases, humans have little difficulty in determining the intended meaning of an ambiguous word, while it is extremely difficult to replicate this process computationally. For many tasks in psycholinguistics and NLP, a job is often decomposed to the requirement of resolving the semantic similarity between words or concepts.

There are two ways to get the similarity between two words. One is to utilize the machine readable dictionary (MRD). The other is to use the corpus.

For the 4th task in SemEval-2012 we are required to evaluate the semantic similarity of Chinese word pairs. We consider 3 methods in this study. One uses MRDs only and the other two use both MRD and corpus. A post processing will be done on the results of these methods to treat synonyms.

In chapter 2 we introduce the previous works on the evaluation of Semantic Similarity. Chapter 3 shows three methods used in this task. Chapter 4 reveals the results of these methods. And conclusion is stated in chapter 5.

2 Related Work

For words may have more than one sense, similarity between two words can be determined by the best score among all the concept pairs which their various senses belong to.

Before constructed dictionary is built, Lesk similarity (Lesk, 1986) which is proposed as a solution for word sense disambiguation is often used to evaluating the similarity between two concepts. This method calculates the overlap between the corresponding definitions as provided by a dictionary.

$$sim_{Lesk}(c_1, c_2) = |gloss(c_1) \cap gloss(c_2)|$$

Since the availability of computational lexicons such as WordNet, the taxonomy can be represented as a hierarchical structure. Then we use the structure information to evaluate the semantic similarity. In these methods, the hierarchical structure is often seen as a tree and concepts as the nodes of the tree while relations between two concepts as the edges.

(Resnik, 1995) determines the conceptual similarity of two concepts by calculating the information content (IC) of the least common subsumer (LCS) of them.

$$sim_{res}(c_1, c_2) = IC(LCS(c_1, c_2))$$

where the IC of a concept can be quantified as follow:

$$IC(c) = log^{-1}P(c)$$

This method do not consider the distance of two concepts. Any two concepts have the same LCS will have the same similarity even if the distances between them are different. It is called node-based method.

(Leacock and Chodorow, 1998) develops a similarity measure based on the distance of two senses c_1 and c_2. They focus on hypernymy links and scaled the path length by the overall depth D of the tree.

$$sim_{lch}(c_1, c_2) = -log\frac{length(c_1, c_2)}{2 \times D}$$

(Wu and Palmer, 1994) combines the depth of the LCS of two concepts into a similarity score.

$$sim_{wup}(c_1, c_2) = \frac{2 \times depth(LCS(c_1, c_2))}{depth(c_1) + depth(c_2)}$$

These approaches are regarded as edge-based methods. They are more natural and direct to evaluating semantic similarity in taxonomy. But they treat all nodes as the same and do not consider the different information of different nodes.

(Jiang and Conrath, 1998) uses the information content of concept instead of its depth. So both node and edge information can be considered to evaluate the similarity. It performs well in evaluating semantic similarity between two texts (Zhang et al., 2008; Corley and Mihalcea, 2005; Pedersen, 2010).

$$sim_{jnc}(c_1, c_2) = \frac{1}{IC(c_1)+IC(c_2)-2\times IC(LCS(c_1,c_2))}$$

SemCor is used in Jiang's work to get the frequency of a word with a specific sense treated by the Lagrange Smoothing.

3 Approaches

For SemEval-2012 task 4, we use two MRDs and one corpus as our knowledge resources. One MRD is HIT IR-Lab Tongyici Cilin (Extended) (Cilin) and the other is Chinese Concept Dictionary (CCD). The corpus we used in our system is People's Daily. Three systems are proposed to evaluate the semantic similarity between two Chinese words. The first one utilizes both the MRDs called MIXCC (Mixture of Cilin and CCD) and other two named MIXCD1 (Mixture of Corpus and Dictionary) and MIXCD2 respectively combine the information derived from both corpus and dictionary into the similarity score. A post processing is done to trim the similarity of words with the same meaning.

3.1 Knowledge Resources

HIT IR-Lab Tongyici Cilin (Extended) is built by Harbin Institute of Technology which contained 77343 word items. Cilin is constructed as a tree with five levels. With the increasing of the level, word senses are more fine-grained. All word items in Cilin are located at the fifth level. The larger level the LCS of an item pair has, the closer their concepts are.

Chinese Concept Dictionary (CCD) is a Chinese WordNet produced by Peking University. Word concepts in it are represented as Synsets and one-one corresponding to WordNet 1.6. There are 4 types of hierarchical semantic relations in CCD as follows:

- Synonym: the meanings of two words are equivalence
- Antonym: two synsets contain the words with opposite meaning
- Hypernym and Hyponym: two synsets with the IS-A relation
- Holonym and Meronym: two synsets with the IS-PART-OF relation

Additionally there is another type of semantic relation such as Attribute in CCD This relation type often happens between two words with different part-of-speech. Even though it is not the hierarchical relation, this relation type can make two words with different POS have a path between them. In WordNet it is often shown as a Morphological transform between two words, while it may happen on two different words with closed meaning in CCD.

The corpus we use in our system is People's Daily 2000 from January to June which has been manually segmented.

3.2 MIXCC

MIXCC utilizes both Cilin and CCD to evaluate the semantic similarity of word pair. In this method we get the rank in three steps.

First, we use Cilin to separate the list of word pairs into five parts and sort them in descending order of LCS's level. The word pairs having the same level of LCS will be put in the same part.

Second, for each part we compute the similarity almost by Jiang and Conrath's method mentioned in Section 2 above. Only Synonym and Hypernym-Hyponym relations of CCD concepts are considered in this method. So CCD could be constructed as a forest. We add a root node which combined the forest into a tree to make sure that there is a path between any two concepts.

$$sim_{jnc}(w_1, w_2) = \max_{\substack{c_1 \in concept(w_1) \\ \wedge c_2 \in concept(w_2)}} sim_{jnc}(c_1, c_2)$$

w_1 and w_2 compose a word pair needed to calculate semantic similarity between them. c_1 (c_2) is the Synset in CCD which contains w_1 (w_2).

Because there is no sense-tagged corpus for CCD, the frequency of every word in each concept is always 1.

After $sim_{jnc}(w_1, w_2)$ of all word pairs in the same part are calculated, we sort the scores in a decreasing order again. Then we get five groups of ranked word pairs.

At last the five groups are combined together as the result shown in table 1.

3.3 MIXCD

MIXCD combines the information of corpus and MRDs to evaluate semantic similarity.

In this system we use trial data to learn a multiple linear regression function. There are two classes of features for this study which are derived from CCD and People's Daily respectively. One class of feature is the mutual information of a word pair and the other is the shortest path between two concepts containing the words of which the similarity needed to be evaluated.

We consider CCD as a large directed graph. The nodes of the graph are Synsets and edges are the semantic relations between two Synsets. All five types of semantic relation showed in Section 3.1 will be used to build the graph.

For each word pair, the shortest path between two Synsets which contain the words respectively is found. Then the path is represented in two forms.

In one form we record the vector consisting of the counts of every relation type in the path. The system using this path's form is called MIXCD0.

For example the path between "心理学 (psychology)" and "精神病学 (psychiatry)" is represented as (0, 0, 3, 2, 0). It means that "心理学" and "精神病学" are not synonym and the shortest path between them contained 3 IS-A relations and 2 IS-PART-OF relations.

We suppose that the path's length is a significant feature to measure the semantic similarity of a word pair. So in the other form the length is added into the vector as the first component. And the counts of each relation are recorded in proportion to the length. This form of path representation is used in the submitted system called MIXCD. Then the path between "心理学" and "精神病学" is represented as (5, 0, 0, 0.6, 0.4, 0).

In both forms, the Synonym feature will be 1 if the length of the path is 0.

The mutual information of all word pairs is calculated via the segmented People's Daily.

Last we use the result of multiple linear regression to forecast the similarity of other word pairs and get the rank.

3.4 Post Processing

The word pair with the same meaning may be consisted of two same words or two different words belong to the same concept. It is difficult for both systems to separate one from the other. Therefore we display a post processing on our systems to make sure that the similarity between the same words has a larger rank than two different words of the same meaning.

4 Experiments and Results

We perform our systems on trial data and then use Kendall tau Rank Correlation (Kendall, 1995; Wessa, 2012) to evaluate the results shown in Table 1. The trial data contains 50 word pairs. The similarity of each pair is scored by several experts and the mean value is regarded as the standard answer to get the manual ranking.

Method	Kendall tau	2-sided p value
MIXCC	**0.273469**	0.005208
MIXCD0	0.152653	0.119741
MIXCD	0.260408	0.007813
Manual(upper)	0.441633	6.27E-06

Table 1: Kendall tau Rank Correlation of systems on trial

From Table 1, we can see the tau value of MIXCD0 is 0.1526 and MIXCD is 0.2604. MIXCD performed notably better than MIXCD0. It shows that path's length between two words is on an important position of measuring semantic similarity. This feature does improve the similarity result. The 2-sided p value of MIXCD0 is 0.1197. It is much larger than the value of MIXCD which is 0.0078. So the ranking result of MIXCD0 is much more occasional than result of MIXCD.

The tau value of MIXCC is 0.2735 and it is much smaller than the manual ranking result which is 0.4416 seen as the upper bound. It shows that the similarity between two words in human's minds dose not only depend on their hierarchical relation represented in Dictionary. But the value is larger than that of MIXCD. It seems that the mutual information derived from corpus which is expected to improve the result reduces the correction of rank result contrarily. There may be two reasons on it.

First, because of the use of trial data in MIXCD, the result of similarity ranking strongly depended on this data. The reliability of trial data's ranking may influent the performance of our system. We calculate the tau value between every manual and the correct ranking. The least tau value is 0.4416 and the largest one is 0.8220 with a large disparity. We use the Fleiss' kappa value (Fleiss, 1971) to evaluate the agreement of manual ranking and the result is 0.1526 which showed the significant disagreement. This disagreement may make the regression result cannot show the relation between features and score correctly. To reduce the disagreement's influence we calculate the mean of manual similarity score omitting the maximum and minimum ones and get a new standard rank (trial2). Then we perform MIXCD on trail2 and show the new result as MIXCD-2 in Form 2. MIXCC's result is also compared with trail2 shown as MIXCC-2.

	MIXCC-2	MIXCD-2	MIXCC	MIXCD
Kendall tau	**0.297959**	0.265306	0.273469	0.260408

Table 2: tau value on new standard (omit max/min manual scores)

From Table 2 we can see the tau values of MIXCC rose to 0.2980 and MIXCD to 0.2653. It shows that omitting the maximum and minimum manual scores can reduce some influence of the disagreement of artificial scoring.

Second, the combination method of mutual information and semantic path in MRD may also influent the performance of our system. The ranks between MIXCD and MIXCC are also compared and the tau value is 0.2065. It shows a low agreement of semantic similarity measurements between MRD and Corpus. The mutual information exerts a large influence on the measure of similarity and sometimes may bring the noise to the result making it worse.

We also perform our systems on test data containing 297 words pairs in the same form of trial data and got the follow result:

Method	Kendall tau
MIXCC	0.050
MIXCD0	-0.064
MIXCD	0.040

Table 3 tau values of the result of test data

The ranking on test data of our systems shows an even worse result. Because of the low confidence of trial data ranking, multiple linear regression function learning from the trial data performs bad on other word pairs.

5 Conclusion

In this paper we propose three methods to evaluate the semantic similarity of Chinese word pairs. The first one uses MRDs and the second one adds the information derived from corpus. The third one uses the same knowledge resources as the second one but highlights the path length of the word pair. The results of the systems show a large difference and all have a low score. From the results we can see the similarity showed in corpus is much different from the one expressed in MRD. One reason of the low score is that the manual rank given by the task has a low agreement among them. We get a new manual rank which reduces some influence of disagreement by calculating the mean value of scores omitting the maximum and minimum ones. Comparing the result of our systems with the new ranking, all of them get a higher tau value.

Acknowledgement

This paper is supported in part by National Natural Science Fund of China under contract 61170181, National Social Science Fund of China under contract 10CYY021, State Key Lab. for Novel Software Technology under contract KFKT2011B03, Jiangsu PostDoc Fund under contract 1101065C.

References

Mike E. Lesk, 1986. Automatic sense disambiguation using machine readable dictionaries: How to tell a pine cone from an ice cream cone. In *Proceedings of the SIGDOC Conference* 1986, Toronto, June.

Philip Resnik, 1995. Using information content to evaluate semantic similarity. In *Proceedings of the 14th International Joint Conference on Artificial Intelligence*, Montreal, Canada.

Claudia Leacock and Martin Chodorow, 1998. Combining local context and WordNet sense similiarity for word sense disambiguation. In *WordNet, An Electronic Lexical Database*. The MIT Press.

Zhibiao Wu and Martha Palmer, 1994. Verb semantics and lexical selection. In *Proceedings of the 32nd Annual Meeting of the Association for Computational Linguistics*, Las Cruces, New Mexico.

Jay J. Jiang and David W. Conrath, 1998. Semantic similarity based on corpus statistics and lexical taxonomy. In *Proceedings of the International Conference on Research in Computational Linguistics*.

Ce Zhang , Yu-Jing Wang , Bin Cui , Gao Cong, 2008. Semantic similarity based on compact concept ontology. In *Proceeding of the 17th international conference on World Wide Web*, April 21-25, 2008, Beijing, China

Courtney Corley , Rada Mihalcea, 2005. Measuring the semantic similarity of texts. In *Proceedings of the ACL Workshop on Empirical Modeling of Semantic Equivalence and Entailment*, p.13-18, June 30-30, 2005, Ann Arbor, Michigan.

Ted Pedersen, 2010. Information content measures of semantic similarity perform better without sense-tagged text. In *Human Language Technologies: The 2010 Annual Conference of the North American Chapter of the Association for Computational Linguistics*, p.329-332, June 02-04, 2010, Los Angeles, California.

M. G. Kendall, 1955. *Rank Correlation Methods*. New York: Hafner Publishing Co.

P. Wessa, 2012. *Free Statistics Software, Office for Research Development and Education*, version 1.1.23-r7, URL http://www.wessa.net/

Jordan L. Fleiss, 1971. Measuring nominal scale agreement among many raters. *Psychological Bulletin*, Vol. 76, No. 5 pp. 378–382.

Zhijun Wu: Chinese Semantic Dependency Parsing with Third-Order Features

Zhijun Wu **Xuan Wang** **Xinxin Li**
Computer Application Research Center
School of Computer Science and Technology
Harbin Institute of Technology Shenzhen Graduate School
Shenzhen 518055, P.R.China
mattwu305@gmail.com wangxuan@insun.hit.edu.cn lixin2@gmail.com

Abstract

This paper presents our system participated on SemEval-2012 task: *Chinese Semantic Dependency Parsing*. Our system extends the second-order MST model by adding two third-order features. The two third-order features are grand-sibling and tri-sibling. In the decoding phase, we keep the k best results for each span. After using the selected third-order features, our system presently achieves LAS of 61.58% ignoring punctuation tokens which is 0.15% higher than the result of purely second-order model on the test dataset.

1 Introduction

Recently, semantic role labeling (SRL) has been a hot research topic. CoNLL shared tasks for joint parsing for syntactic and semantic dependencies both in the year 2008 and 2009, cf. (Surdeanu et al., 2008; Hajič et al., 2009; Bohnet, 2009). Same shared tasks in SemEval-2007 (Sameer S., 2007). The SRL is traditionally implemented as two subtasks, argument identification and classification. However, there are some problems for the semantic representation method used by the semantic role labeling. For example, the SRL only considers the predicate-argument relations and ignores the relations between a noun and its modifier, the meaning of semantic roles is related with special predicates. In order to overcome those problems, semantic dependency parsing (SDP) is introduced. Semantic dependencies express semantic links between predicates and arguments and represent relations between entities and events in text. The SDP is a kind of dependency parsing, and its task is to build a dependency structure for an input sentence and to label the semantic relation between a word and its head. However, semantic relations are different from syntactic relations, such as position independent. Table 1 shows the position independent of semantic relations for the sentence *XiaoMing hit XiaoBai with a book today.*

Today, XiaoMing hit XiaoBai with a book.
XiaoBai was hit by XiaoMing today with a book.
With a book, XiaoMing hit XiaoBai today.
XiaoMing hit XiaoBai with a book today.

Table 1: An example position dependency

Although semantic relations are different from syntactic relations, yet they are identical in the dependency tree. That means the methods used in syntactic dependency parsing can also be applied in SDP.

Two main approaches to syntactic dependency paring are *Maximum Spanning Tree* (MST) based dependency parsing and *Transition* based dependency parsing (Eisner, 1996; Nivre et al., 2004; McDonald and Pereira, 2006). The main idea of

MSTParser is to take dependency parsing as a problem of searching a maximum spanning tree (MST) in a directed graph (Dependency Tree). We see MSTParser a better chance to improve the parsing speed and MSTParser provides the state-of-the-art performance for both projective and non-projective tree banks. For the reasons above, we choose MSTParser as our *SemEval-2012* shared task participating system basic framework.

2 System Architecture

Our parser is based on the projective MSTParser using all the features described by (McDonald et al., 2006) as well as some third-order features described in the following sections. Semantic dependency paring is introduced in Section 3. We explain the reasons why we choose projective MSTParser in Section 4 which also contains the experiment result analysis in various conditions. Section 5 gives our conclusion and future work.

3 Semantic Dependency parsers

3.1 First-Order Model

Dependency tree parsing as the search for the maximum spanning tree in a directed graph was proposed by McDonald et al. (2005c). This formulation leads to efficient parsing algorithms for both projective and non-projective dependency trees with the Eisner algorithm (Eisner, 1996) and the Chu-Liu-Edmonds algorithm (Chu and Liu, 1965; Edmonds, 1967) respectively. The formulation works by defining in McDonald et al (2005a). The score of a dependency tree y for sentence x is

$$s(x,y) = \sum_{(i,j)\in y} s(i,j) = \sum w \cdot f(i,j)$$

f(i, j) is a multidimensional feature vector representation of the edge from node i to node j. We set the value of f(i, j) as 1 if there an edge from node i to node j. w is the corresponding weight vector between the two nodes that will be learned during training. Hence, finding a dependency tree with highest score is equivalent to finding a maximum spanning tree. Obviously, the scores are restricted to a single edge in the dependency tree, thus we call this first-order dependency parsing. This is a standard linear classifier. The features used in the first-order dependency parser are based on those listed in (Johansson, 2008). Table 2 shows the features we choose in the first-order parsing. We use some shorthand notations in order to simplify the feature representations: h is the abbreviation for head, d for dependent, s for nearby nodes (may not be siblings), f for form, le for the lemmas, pos for part-of-speech tags, dir for direction, dis for distance, '+1' and '-1' for right and left position respectively. Additional features are built by adding the direction and the distance plus the direction. The direction is left if the dependent is left to its head otherwise right. The distance is the number of words minus one between the head and the dependent in a certain sentence, if ≤ 5, 5 if > 5, 10 if > 10. ◎ means that previous part is built once and the additional part follow ◎ together with the previous part is built again.

Head and Dependent
h-f, h-l, d-pos ◎dir(h, d) ◎dis(h, d)
h-l, h-pos, d-f ◎dir(h, d) ◎dis(h, d)
h-pos, h-f, d-l ◎dir(h, d) ◎dis(h, d)
h-f, d-l, d-pos ◎dir(h, d) ◎dis(h, d)
h-f, d-f, d-l ◎dir(h, d) ◎dis(h, d)
h-f, h-l, d-f, d-l ◎dir(h, d) ◎dis(h, d)
h-f, h-l, d-f, d-pos ◎dir(h, d) ◎dis(h, d)
h-f, h-pos, d-f, d-pos ◎dir(h, d) ◎dis(h, d)
h-l, h-pos, d-l, d-pos ◎dir(h, d) ◎dis(h, d)
Dependent and Nearby
d-pos-1, d-pos, s-pos ◎dir(d, s) ◎dis(d, s)
d-pos-1, s-pos, s-pos+1 ◎dir(d, s) ◎dis(d, s)
d-pos-1, d-pos, s-pos+1 ◎dir(d, s) ◎dis(d, s)
d-pos, s-pos, s-pos+1 ◎dir(d, s) ◎dis(d, s)
d-pos, d-pos+1, s-pos-1 ◎dir(d, s) ◎dis(d, s)
d-pos-1, d-pos, s-pos-1 ◎dir(d, s) ◎dis(d, s)
d-pos, d-pos+1, s-pos ◎dir(d, s) ◎dis(d, s)
d-pos, s-pos-1, s-pos ◎dir(d, s) ◎dis(d, s)
d-pos+1, s-pos-1, s-pos ◎dir(d, s) ◎dis(d, s)
d-pos-1, d-pos, s-pos-1, s-pos ◎ dir(d, s) ◎ dis(d, s)
d-pos, d-pos+1, s-pos-1, s-pos ◎ dir(d, s) ◎ dis(d, s)
d-pos-1, d-pos, s-pos, s-pos+1 ◎ dir(d, s) ◎ dis(d, s)

Table 2: Selected features in first order parsing

3.2 Second-Order Model

A second order model proposed by McDonald (McDonald and Pereira, 2006) alleviates some of the first order factorization limitations. Because the first order parsing restricts scores to a single edge in a dependency tree, the procedure is sufficient. However, in the second order parsing scenario where more than one edge are considered by the parsing algorithm, combinations of two edges might be more accurate which will be described in the Section 4. The second-order parsing can be defined as below:

$$s(x,y)=\sum_{(i,j)\in y} s(i,k,j)$$

where k and j are adjacent, same-side children of i in the tree y. The shortcoming of this definition is that it restricts i on the same side of its sibling. In our system, we extend this restriction by adding the feature that as long as i is another child of k or j. In that case, i may be the child or grandchild of k or j which is shown in Figure 1.

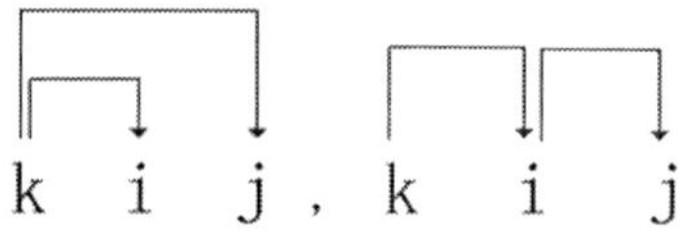

Figure 1: Sibling and grand-child relations.

Siblings
c1-pos, c2-pos◎dir(c1, c2)◎dis(c1, c2)
c1-f, c2-f◎dir(c1, c2)
c1-f, c2-pos◎dir(c1, c2)
c1-pos, c2-f◎dir(c1, c2)
Parent and Two Children
p-pos, c1-pos, c2-pos◎dir(c1, c2)◎dis(c1, c2)
p-f, c1-pos, c2-pos◎dir(c1, c2)◎dis(c1, c2)
p-f, c1-f, c2-pos◎dir(c1, c2) ◎dis(c1, c2)
p-f, c1-f, c2-f ◎dir(c1, c2) ◎dis(c1, c2)
p-pos, c1-f, c2-f◎dir(c1, c2) ◎dis(c1, c2)
p-pos, c1-f, c2-pos◎dir(c1, c2) ◎dis(c1, c2)
p-pos, c1-pos, c2-f◎dir(c1, c2) ◎dis(c1, c2)

Table 3: Selected features in second-order parsing

Shorthand notations are almost the same with the Section 3.1 except for that we use c1 and c2 to represent the two children and p for parent. In second-order parsing, the features selected are shown in Table 3. We divide the dependency distance into six parts which are 1 if> 1, 2 if> 2, … , 5 if > 5, 10 if> 10.

3.3 Third-Order Features

The order of parsing is defined according to the number of dependencies it contains (Koo and Collins, 2010). Collins classifies the third-order as two models, Model 1 is all grand-siblings, and Model 2 is grand-siblings and tri-siblings. A grand-sibling is a 4-tuple of indices (g, h, m, s) where g is grandfather. (h, m, s) is a sibling part and (g, h, m) is a grandchild part as well as (g, h, s). A tri-sibling part is also a 4-tuple of indices (h, m, s, t). Both (h, m, s) and (h, s, t) are siblings. Figure 2 clearly shows these relations.

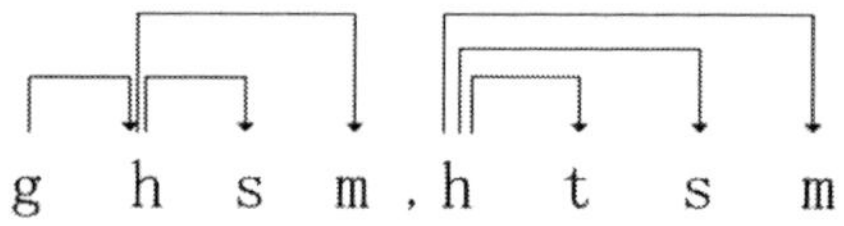

Figure 2: Grand-siblings and tri-siblings dependency.

Collins and Koo implement an efficient third-order dependency parsing algorithm, but still time consuming compared with the second-order (McDonald, 2006). For that reason, we only add third-order relation features into our system instead of implementing the third-order dependency parsing model. These features shown in Table 4 are grand-sibling and tri-sibling described above. Shorthand notations are almost the same with the Section 3.1 and 3.2 except that we use c3 for the third sibling and g represent the grandfather. We attempt to add features of words form and parts-of-speech as well as directions into our system, which is used both in first-order and second-order as features, but result shows that these decrease the system performance.

Tri-Sibling
c1-pos, c2-pos, c3-pos◎dir(c1, c2)
Grandfather and Two Children
g-pos, c1-pos, c2-pos◎dir(c1, c2)
g-pos, p-pos, c1-pos, c2-pos◎dir(c1, c2)

Table 4: Third-order features.

4 Experiment result analysis

As we all know that projective dependency parsing using edge based factorization can be processed by the Einster algorithm (Einster, 1996). The corpus given by SemEval-2012 is consists of 10000 sentences converting into dependency structures from Chinese Penn Treebank randomly. We find that none of non-projective sentence existing by testing the 8301 sentences in training data. For this reason, we set the MSTParser into projective parsing mode.

We perform a number of experiments where we compare the first-order, second-order and second-order by adding third-order features proposed in the previous sections. We train the model on the full training set which contains 8301 sentences totally. We use 10 training iterations and projective decoding in the experiments. Experimental results show that 10 training iterations are better than others. After adjusting the features of third-order, our best result reaches the labeled attachment score of 62.48% on the developing dataset which ignores punctuation. We submitted our currently best result to SemEval-2012 which is 61.58% on the test dataset. The results in Table 5 show that by adding third-order features to second-order model, we improve the dependency parsing accuracies by 1.21% comparing to first-order model and 0.15% comparing to second-order model.

Models	LAS	UAS
First-Order	61.26	80.18
Second-Order	62.33	81.40
Second-Order+	62.48	81.43

Table 5: Experimental results. Second-Order+ means second-order model by adding third-order features. Results are tested under the developping dataset which contains the heads and semantic relations given by organizer.

5 Conclusion and Future Work

In this paper, we have presented the semantic dependency parsing and shown it works on the first-order model, second-order model and second-order model by adding third-order features. Our experimental results show more significant improvements than the conventional approaches of third-order model.

In the future, we firstly plan to implement the third-order model by adding higher-order features, such as forth-order features. We have found that both in the first-order and second-order model of MSTParser, words form and lemmas are recognized as two different features. These features are essential in languages that have different grid, however, which are the same in Chinese in the given dataset. Things are the same in POS (part-of-speech tags) and CPOS (fine-grid POS) which are viewed as different features. For the applications of syntactic and semantic parsing, the parsing time and memory footprint are very important. Therefore, secondly, we decide to remove these repeated features in order to reduce to training time as well as the space if it does not lower the system performance.

Acknowledgments

The authors would like to thank the reviewers for their helpful comments.

References

Mihai Surdeanu, Richard Johansson, Adam Meyers, Lluís Márquez, and JoakimNivre. 2008. The CoNLL-2008 shared task on joint parsing of syntactic andsemantic dependencies. In *Proceedings of the 12th CoNLL-2008.*

Jan Hajič, Massimiliano Ciaramita, Richard Johansson, Daisuke Kawahara, Maria Antonia Martí, Llu'is Márquez, Adam Meyers, Joakim Nivre, SebastianPado, Jan Štepánek, Pavel Straňák, Miahi Surdeanu, Nianwen Xue, and Yi Zhang. 2009. The CoNLL-2009 Shared Task: Syntactic and Semantic Dependencies in Multiple Languages. In *Proceedings of the 13th CoNLL-2009, June 4-5,* Boulder, Colorado, USA.

Bohnet, Bernd. 2009. Efficient parsing of syntactic and semantic dependency structures. In *Proceedings of CoNLL-09.*

Ryan McDonald. 2006. Discriminative Learning and Spanning Tree Algorithms for Dependency Parsing. Ph.D. thesis, University of Pennsylvania.

Ryan McDonald and Fernando Pereira. 2006. Online Learning of Approximate Dependency Parsing Algrithms. In *In Proc. of EACL,* pages 81–88.

Ryan. McDonald, K. Crammer, and F. Pereira. 2005a. Online large-margin training of dependency parsers. In *Proc. of the 43rd Annual Meeting of the ACL.*

Ryan. McDonald, F. Pereira, K. Ribarov, and J. Haji˘c. 2005c. Non-projective dependency parsing using spanning tree algorithms. In *Proc. HLT-EMNLP.*

Richard Johansson. 2008. *Dependency-based Semantic Analysis of Natural-language Text.* Ph.D. thesis, Lund University.

Jason Eisner. 1996. Three new probabilistic models for dependency parsing: An exploration. In *Proceedings of the 16th International Conference on Computational Linguistics (COLING-96)*, pages 340–345, Copenhaen.

Joakim Nivre, Johan Hall, and Jens Nilsson. 2004. Memory-Based Dependency Parsing. In *Proceedings of the 8th CoNLL*, pages 49–56, Boston, Massachusetts.

Terry Koo, Michael Collins. 2010. Efficient Third-order Dependency Parsers. *Proceedings of the 48th Annual Meeting of the Association for Computational Linguistics*, pages 1–11.

UKP: Computing Semantic Textual Similarity by Combining Multiple Content Similarity Measures

Daniel Bär[†], **Chris Biemann**[†], **Iryna Gurevych**[†‡], **and Torsten Zesch**[†‡]

[†]Ubiquitous Knowledge Processing Lab (UKP-TUDA)
Department of Computer Science, Technische Universität Darmstadt

[‡]Ubiquitous Knowledge Processing Lab (UKP-DIPF)
German Institute for Educational Research and Educational Information

www.ukp.tu-darmstadt.de

Abstract

We present the UKP system which performed best in the Semantic Textual Similarity (STS) task at SemEval-2012 in two out of three metrics. It uses a simple log-linear regression model, trained on the training data, to combine multiple text similarity measures of varying complexity. These range from simple character and word n-grams and common subsequences to complex features such as Explicit Semantic Analysis vector comparisons and aggregation of word similarity based on lexical-semantic resources. Further, we employ a lexical substitution system and statistical machine translation to add additional lexemes, which alleviates lexical gaps. Our final models, one per dataset, consist of a log-linear combination of about 20 features, out of the possible 300+ features implemented.

1 Introduction

The goal of the pilot Semantic Textual Similarity (STS) task at SemEval-2012 is to measure the degree of semantic equivalence between pairs of sentences. STS is fundamental to a variety of tasks and applications such as question answering (Lin and Pantel, 2001), text reuse detection (Clough et al., 2002) or automatic essay grading (Attali and Burstein, 2006). STS is also closely related to textual entailment (TE) (Dagan et al., 2006) and paraphrase recognition (Dolan et al., 2004). It differs from both tasks, though, insofar as those operate on binary similarity decisions while STS is defined as a graded notion of similarity. STS further requires a bidirectional similarity relationship to hold between a pair of sentences rather than a unidirectional entailment relation as for the TE task.

A multitude of measures for computing similarity between texts have been proposed in the past based on surface-level and/or semantic content features (Mihalcea et al., 2006; Landauer et al., 1998; Gabrilovich and Markovitch, 2007). The existing measures exhibit two major limitations, though: Firstly, measures are typically used in separation. Thereby, the assumption is made that a single measure inherently captures all text characteristics which are necessary for computing similarity. Secondly, existing measures typically exclude similarity features beyond *content* per se, thereby implying that similarity can be computed by comparing text content exclusively, leaving out any other text characteristics. While we can only briefly tackle the second issue here, we explicitly address the first one by combining several measures using a supervised machine learning approach. With this, we hope to take advantage of the different facets and intuitions that are captured in the single measures.

In the following section, we describe the feature space in detail. Section 3 describes the machine learning setup. After describing our submitted runs, we discuss the results and conclude.

2 Text Similarity Measures

We now describe the various features we have tried, also listing features that did not prove useful.

2.1 Simple String-based Measures

String Similarity Measures These measures operate on string sequences. The *longest common* *substring* measure (Gusfield, 1997) compares the length of the longest contiguous sequence of characters. The *longest common subsequence* measure (Allison and Dix, 1986) drops the contiguity requirement and allows to detect similarity in case of word insertions/deletions. *Greedy String Tiling* (Wise, 1996) allows to deal with reordered text parts as it determines a set of shared contiguous substrings, whereby each substring is a match of maximal length. We further used the following measures, which, however, did not make it into the final models, since they were subsumed by the other measures: *Jaro (1989)*, *Jaro-Winkler* (Winkler, 1990), *Monge and Elkan (1997)*, and *Levenshtein (1966)*.

Character/word n-grams We compare character n-grams following the implementation by Barrón-Cedeño et al. (2010), thereby generalizing the original trigram variant to $n = 2, 3, \ldots, 15$. We also compare word n-grams using the Jaccard coefficient as previously done by Lyon et al. (2001), and the containment measure (Broder, 1997). As high n led to instabilities of the classifier due to their high intercorrelation, only $n = 1, 2, 3, 4$ was used.

2.2 Semantic Similarity Measures

Pairwise Word Similarity The measures for computing word similarity on a semantic level operate on a graph-based representation of words and the semantic relations among them within a lexical-semantic resource. For this system, we used the algorithms by Jiang and Conrath (1997), Lin (1998a), and Resnik (1995) on WordNet (Fellbaum, 1998).

In order to scale the resulting pairwise word similarities to the text level, we applied the aggregation strategy by Mihalcea et al. (2006): The sum of the *idf*-weighted similarity scores of each word with the best-matching counterpart in the other text is computed in both directions, then averaged. In our experiments, the measure by Resnik (1995) proved to be superior to the other measures and was used in all word similarity settings throughout this paper.

Explicit Semantic Analysis We also used the vector space model *Explicit Semantic Analysis* (ESA) (Gabrilovich and Markovitch, 2007). Besides WordNet, we used two additional lexical-semantic resources for the construction of the ESA vector space: Wikipedia and Wiktionary[1].

Textual Entailment We experimented with using the BIUTEE textual entailment system (Stern and Dagan, 2011) for generating entailment scores to serve as features for the classifier. However, these features were not selected by the classifier.

Distributional Thesaurus We used similarities from a Distributional Thesaurus (similar to Lin (1998b)) computed on 10M dependency-parsed sentences of English newswire as a source for pairwise word similarity, one additional feature per POS tag. However, only the feature based on cardinal numbers (CD) was selected in the final models.

2.3 Text Expansion Mechanisms

Lexical Substitution System We used the lexical substitution system based on supervised word sense disambiguation (Biemann, 2012). This system automatically provides substitutions for a set of about 1,000 frequent English nouns with high precision. For each covered noun, we added the substitutions to the text and computed the pairwise word similarity for the texts as described above. This feature alleviates the lexical gap for a subset of words.

Statistical Machine Translation We used the Moses SMT system (Koehn et al., 2007) to translate the original English texts via three bridge languages (Dutch, German, Spanish) back to English. Thereby, the idea was that in the translation process additional lexemes are introduced which alleviate potential lexical gaps. The system was trained on Europarl made available by Koehn (2005), using the following configuration which was not optimized for this task: WMT11[2] baseline without tuning, with MGIZA alignment. The largest improvement was reached for computing pairwise word similarity (as described above) on the concatenation of the original text and the three back-translations.

2.4 Measures Related to Structure and Style

In our system, we also used measures which go beyond content and capture similarity along the structure and style dimensions inherent to texts. However, as we report later on, for this content-

[1] `www.wiktionary.org`

[2] 0-5-grams, grow-diag-final-and alignment, msd-bidirectional-fe reodering, interpolation and kndiscount

oriented task they were not selected by the classifier. Nonetheless, we briefly list them for completeness.

Structural similarity between texts can be detected by computing **stopword n-grams** (Stamatatos, 2011). Thereby, all content-bearing words are removed while stopwords are preserved. Stopword n-grams of both texts are compared using the containment measure (Broder, 1997). In our experiments, we tested n-gram sizes for $n = 2, 3, \ldots, 10$.

We also compute **part-of-speech n-grams** for various POS tags which we then compare using the containment measure and the Jaccard coefficient.

We also used two similarity measures between pairs of words (Hatzivassiloglou et al., 1999): **Word pair order** tells whether two words occur in the same order in both texts (with any number of words in between), **word pair distance** counts the number of words which lie between those of a given pair.

To compare texts along the stylistic dimension, we further use a **function word frequencies** measure (Dinu and Popescu, 2009) which operates on a set of 70 function words identified by Mosteller and Wallace (1964). Function word frequency vectors are computed and compared by Pearson correlation.

We also include a number of measures which capture statistical properties of texts, such as **type-token ratio** (TTR) (Templin, 1957) and **sequential TTR** (McCarthy and Jarvis, 2010).

3 System Description

We first run each of the similarity measures introduced above separately. We then use the resulting scores as features for a machine learning classifier.

Pre-processing Our system is based on DKPro[3], a collection of software components for natural language processing built upon the Apache UIMA framework. During the pre-processing phase, we tokenize the input texts and lemmatize using the TreeTagger implementation (Schmid, 1994). For some measures, we additionally apply a stopword filter.

Feature Generation We now compute similarity scores for the input texts with all measures and for all configurations introduced in Section 2. This resulted in 300+ individual score vectors which served as features for the following step.

[3] http://dkpro-core-asl.googlecode.com

Run	Features
1	Greedy String Tiling Longest common subsequence (2 normalizations) Longest common substring Character 2-, 3-, and 4-grams Word 1- and 2-grams (Containment, w/o stopwords) Word 1-, 3-, and 4-grams (Jaccard) Word 2- and 4-grams (Jaccard, w/o stopwords) Word Similarity (Resnik (1995) on WordNet aggregated according to Mihalcea et al. (2006); 2 variants: complete texts + difference only) Explicit Semantic Analysis (Wikipedia, Wiktionary) Distributional Thesaurus (POS: Cardinal numbers)
2	All Features of Run 1 Lexical Substitution for Word Sim. (complete texts) SMT for Word Sim. (complete texts as above)
3	All Features of Run 2 Random numbers from [4.5, 5] for surprise datasets

Table 1: Feature sets of our three system configurations

Feature Combination The feature combination step uses the pre-computed similarity scores, and combines their log-transformed values using a linear regression classifier from the WEKA toolkit (Hall et al., 2009). We trained the classifier on the training datasets of the STS task. During the development cycle, we evaluated using 10-fold cross-validation.

Post-processing For Runs 2 and 3, we applied a post-processing filter which stripped all characters off the texts which are not in the character range [a-zA-Z0-9]. If the texts match, we set their similarity score to 5.0 regardless of the classifier's output.

4 Submitted Runs

Run 1 During the development cycle, we identified 19 features (see Table 1) which achieved the best performance on the training data. For each of the known datasets, we trained a separate classifier and applied it to the test data. For the surprise datasets, we trained the classifier on a joint dataset of all known training datasets.

Run 2 For the Run 2, we were interested in the effects of two additional features: lexical substitution and statistical machine translation. We added the corresponding measures to the feature set of Run 1 and followed the same evaluation procedure.

Run 3 For the third run, we used the same feature set as for Run 2, but returned random numbers from $[4.5, 5]$ for the sentence pairs in the surprise datasets.

Dim.	Text Similarity Features	PAR	VID	SE
	Best Feature Set, Run 1	.711	.868	.735
	Best Feature Set, Run 2	.724	.868	.742
Content	Pairwise Word Similarity	.564	.835	.527
	Character n-grams	.658	.771	.554
	Explicit Semantic Analysis	.427	.781	.619
	Word n-grams	.474	.782	.619
	String Similarity	.593	.677	.744
	Distributional Thesaurus	.494	.481	.365
	Lexical Substitution	.228	.554	.483
	Statistical Machine Translation	.287	.652	.516
Structure	Part-of-speech n-grams	.193	.265	.557
	Stopword n-grams	.211	.118	.379
	Word Pair Order	.104	.077	.295
Style	Statistical Properties	.168	.225	.325
	Function Word Frequencies	.179	.142	.189

Table 2: Best results for single measures, grouped by dimension, on the training datasets *MSRpar*, *MSRvid*, and *SMTeuroparl*, using 10-fold cross-validation

5 Results on Training Data

Evaluation was carried out using the official scorer which computes Pearson correlation of the human rated similarity scores with the the system's output.

In Table 2, we report the results achieved on each of the training datasets using 10-fold cross-validation. The best results were achieved for the feature set of Run 2, with Pearson's $r = .724$, $r = .868$, and $r = .742$ for the datasets *MSRpar*, *MSRvid*, and *SMTeuroparl*, respectively. While individual classes of content similarity measures achieved good results, a different class performed best for each dataset. However, text similarity measures related to structure and style achieved only poor results on the training data. This was to be expected due to the nature of the data, though.

6 Results on Test Data

Besides the Pearson correlation for the union of all datasets (*ALL*), the organizers introduced two additional evaluation metrics after system submission: *ALLnrm* computes Pearson correlation after the system outputs for each dataset are fitted to the gold standard using least squares, and *Mean* refers to the weighted mean across all datasets, where the weight depends on the number of pairs in each dataset.

In Table 3, we report the offical results achieved on the test data. The best configuration of our system was Run 2 which was ranked #1 for the evaluation metrics *ALL* ($r = .823$)[4] and *Mean* ($r = .677$), and #2 for *ALLnrm* ($r = .857$). An exhaustive overview of all participating systems can be found in the STS task description (Agirre et al., 2012).

$\#_1$	$\#_2$	$\#_3$	Sys.	r_1	r_2	r_3	PAR	VID	SE	WN	SN
1	**2**	**1**	**UKP2**	**.823**	**.857**	**.677**	**.683**	**.873**	**.528**	**.664**	**.493**
2	3	5	TL	.813	.856	.660	.698	.862	.361	.704	.468
3	1	2	TL	.813	.863	.675	.734	.880	.477	.679	.398
4	4	4	UKP1	.811	.855	.670	.682	.870	.511	.664	.467
5	6	13	UNT	.784	.844	.616	.535	.875	.420	.671	.403
⋮	⋮	⋮	⋮	⋮	⋮	⋮	⋮	⋮	⋮	⋮	⋮
87	85	70	B/L	.311	.673	.435	.433	.299	.454	.586	.390

Table 3: Official results on the test data for the top 5 participating runs out of 89 which were achieved on the known datasets *MSRpar*, *MSRvid*, and *SMTeuroparl*, as well as on the surprise datasets *OnWN* and *SMTnews*. We report the ranks ($\#_1$: ALL, $\#_2$: ALLnrm, $\#_3$: Mean) and the corresponding Pearson correlation r according to the three offical evaluation metrics (see Sec. 6). The provided baseline is shown at the bottom of this table.

7 Conclusions and Future Work

In this paper, we presented the UKP system, which performed best across the three official evaluation metrics in the pilot Semantic Textual Similarity (STS) task at SemEval-2012. While we did not reach the highest scores on any of the single datasets, our system was most robust across different data. In future work, it would be interesting to inspect the performance of a system that combines the output of all participating systems in a single linear model.

We also propose that two major issues with the datasets are tackled in future work: (a) It is unclear how to judge similarity between pairs of texts which contain contextual references such as *on Monday* vs. *after the Thanksgiving weekend*. (b) For several pairs, it is unclear what point of view to take, e.g. for the pair *An animal is eating / The animal is hopping*. Is the pair to be considered similar (*an animal is doing something*) or rather not (*eating* vs. *hopping*)?

Acknowledgements This work has been supported by the Volkswagen Foundation as part of the Lichtenberg-Professorship Program under grant No. I/82806, and by the Klaus Tschira Foundation under project No. 00.133.2008.

[4] 99% confidence interval: $.807 \leq r \leq .837$

References

Eneko Agirre, Daniel Cer, Mona Diab, and Aitor Gonzalez-Agirre. 2012. SemEval-2012 Task 6: A Pilot on Semantic Textual Similarity. In *Proceedings of the 6th International Workshop on Semantic Evaluation, in conjunction with the 1st Joint Conference on Lexical and Computational Semantics*.

Lloyd Allison and Trevor I. Dix. 1986. A bit-string longest-common-subsequence algorithm. *Information Processing Letters*, 23:305–310.

Yigal Attali and Jill Burstein. 2006. Automated essay scoring with e-rater v.2.0. *Journal of Technology, Learning, and Assessment*, 4(3).

Alberto Barrón-Cedeño, Paolo Rosso, Eneko Agirre, and Gorka Labaka. 2010. Plagiarism Detection across Distant Language Pairs. In *Proceedings of the 23rd International Conference on Computational Linguistics*, pages 37–45.

Chris Biemann. 2012. Creating a System for Lexical Substitutions from Scratch using Crowdsourcing. *Language Resources and Evaluation: Special Issue on Collaboratively Constructed Language Resources*, 46(2).

Andrei Z. Broder. 1997. On the resemblance and containment of documents. *Proceedings of the Compression and Complexity of Sequences*, pages 21–29.

Paul Clough, Robert Gaizauskas, Scott S.L. Piao, and Yorick Wilks. 2002. METER: MEasuring TExt Reuse. In *Proceedings of 40th Annual Meeting of the Association for Computational Linguistics*, pages 152–159.

Ido Dagan, Oren Glickman, and Bernardo Magnini. 2006. The PASCAL Recognising Textual Entailment Challenge. In *Machine Learning Challenges*, Lecture Notes in Computer Science, pages 177–190. Springer.

Liviu P. Dinu and Marius Popescu. 2009. Ordinal measures in authorship identification. In *Proceedings of the 3rd PAN Workshop. Uncovering Plagiarism, Authorship and Social Software Misuse*, pages 62–66.

William B. Dolan, Chris Quirk, and Chris Brockett. 2004. Unsupervised Construction of Large Paraphrase Corpora: Exploiting Massively Parallel News Sources. In *Proceedings of the 20th International Conference on Computational Linguistics*, pages 350–356.

Christiane Fellbaum. 1998. *WordNet: An Electronic Lexical Database*. MIT Press.

Evgeniy Gabrilovich and Shaul Markovitch. 2007. Computing Semantic Relatedness using Wikipedia-based Explicit Semantic Analysis. In *Proceedings of the 20th International Joint Conference on Artificial Intelligence*, pages 1606–1611.

Dan Gusfield. 1997. *Algorithms on Strings, Trees and Sequences: Computer Science and Computational Biology*. Cambridge University Press.

Mark Hall, Eibe Frank, Geoffrey Holmes, Bernhard Pfahringer, Peter Reutemann, and Ian H. Witten. 2009. The WEKA Data Mining Software: An Update. *SIGKDD Explorations*, 11(1):10–18.

Vasileios Hatzivassiloglou, Judith L. Klavans, and Eleazar Eskin. 1999. Detecting text similarity over short passages: Exploring linguistic feature combinations via machine learning. In *Proceedings of the Joint SIGDAT Conference on Empirical Methods in Natural Language Processing and Very Large Corpora*, pages 203–212.

Matthew A. Jaro. 1989. Advances in record linkage methodology as applied to the 1985 census of Tampa Florida. *Journal of the American Statistical Association*, 84(406):414–420.

Jay J. Jiang and David W. Conrath. 1997. Semantic similarity based on corpus statistics and lexical taxonomy. In *Proceedings of the 10th International Conference on Research in Computational Linguistics*.

Philipp Koehn, Hieu Hoang, Alexandra Birch, Chris Callison-Burch, Marcello Federico, Nicola Bertoldi, Brooke Cowan, Wade Shen, Christine Moran, Richard Zens, Chris Dyer, Ondřej Bojar, Alexandra Constantin, and Evan Herbst. 2007. Moses: Open Source Toolkit for Statistical Machine Translation. In *Proceedings of the ACL 2007 Demo and Poster Sessions*, pages 177–180.

Philipp Koehn. 2005. Europarl: A Parallel Corpus for Statistical Machine Translation. In *Proceedings of the 10th Machine Translation Summit*, pages 79–86.

Thomas K. Landauer, Peter W. Foltz, and Darrell Laham. 1998. An introduction to latent semantic analysis. *Discourse Processes*, 25(2):259–284.

Vladimir I. Levenshtein. 1966. Binary codes capable of correcting deletions, insertions, and reversals. *Soviet Physics Doklady*, 10(8):707–710.

Dekang Lin and Patrick Pantel. 2001. Discovery of Inference Rules for Question Answering. *Natural Language Engineering*, 7(4):343–360.

Dekang Lin. 1998a. An information-theoretic definition of similarity. In *Proceedings of International Conference on Machine Learning*, pages 296–304.

Dekang Lin. 1998b. Automatic Retrieval and Clustering of Similar Words. In *Proceedings of the 36th Annual Meeting of the Association for Computational Linguistics*, pages 768–774.

Caroline Lyon, James Malcolm, and Bob Dickerson. 2001. Detecting short passages of similar text in large document collections. In *Proceedings of Conference on Empirical Methods in Natural Language Processing*, pages 118–125.

Philip M. McCarthy and Scott Jarvis. 2010. MTLD, vocd-D, and HD-D: A validation study of sophisticated approaches to lexical diversity assessment. *Behavior research methods*, 42(2):381–92.

Rada Mihalcea, Courtney Corley, and Carlo Strapparava. 2006. Corpus-based and Knowledge-based Measures of Text Semantic Similarity. In *Proceedings of the 21st National Conference on Artificial Intelligence*, pages 775–780.

Alvaro Monge and Charles Elkan. 1997. An efficient domain-independent algorithm for detecting approximately duplicate database records. In *Proceedings of the SIGMOD Workshop on Data Mining and Knowledge Discovery*, pages 23–29.

Frederick Mosteller and David L. Wallace. 1964. *Inference and disputed authorship: The Federalist*. Addison-Wesley.

Philip Resnik. 1995. Using Information Content to Evaluate Semantic Similarity in a Taxonomy. In *Proceedings of the 14th International Joint Conference on Artificial Intelligence*, pages 448–453.

Helmut Schmid. 1994. Probabilistic part-of-speech tagging using decision trees. In *Proceedings of the International Conference on New Methods in Language Processing*, pages 44–49.

Efstathios Stamatatos. 2011. Plagiarism detection using stopword n-grams. *Journal of the American Society for Information Science and Technology*, 62(12):2512–2527.

Asher Stern and Ido Dagan. 2011. A Confidence Model for Syntactically-Motivated Entailment Proofs. In *Proceedings of the International Conference on Recent Advances in Natural Language Processing*, pages 455–462.

Mildred C. Templin. 1957. *Certain language skills in children*. University of Minnesota Press.

William E. Winkler. 1990. String Comparator Metrics and Enhanced Decision Rules in the Fellegi-Sunter Model of Record Linkage. In *Proceedings of the Section on Survey Research Methods*, pages 354–359.

Michael J. Wise. 1996. YAP3: Improved detection of similarities in computer program and other texts. In *Proceedings of the 27th SIGCSE technical symposium on Computer science education*, pages 130–134.

TakeLab: Systems for Measuring Semantic Text Similarity

**Frane Šarić, Goran Glavaš, Mladen Karan,
Jan Šnajder, and Bojana Dalbelo Bašić**
University of Zagreb
Faculty of Electrical Engineering and Computing
{frane.saric, goran.glavas, mladen.karan, jan.snajder, bojana.dalbelo}@fer.hr

Abstract

This paper describes the two systems for determining the semantic similarity of short texts submitted to the SemEval 2012 Task 6. Most of the research on semantic similarity of textual content focuses on large documents. However, a fair amount of information is condensed into short text snippets such as social media posts, image captions, and scientific abstracts. We predict the human ratings of sentence similarity using a support vector regression model with multiple features measuring word-overlap similarity and syntax similarity. Out of 89 systems submitted, our two systems ranked in the top 5, for the three overall evaluation metrics used (*overall Pearson* – 2nd and 3rd, *normalized Pearson* – 1st and 3rd, *weighted mean* – 2nd and 5th).

1 Introduction

Natural language processing tasks such as text classification (Sebastiani, 2002), text summarization (Lin and Hovy, 2003; Aliguliyev, 2009), information retrieval (Park et al., 2005), and word sense disambiguation (Schütze, 1998) rely on a measure of semantic similarity of textual documents. Research predominantly focused either on the document similarity (Salton et al., 1975; Maguitman et al., 2005) or the word similarity (Budanitsky and Hirst, 2006; Agirre et al., 2009). Evaluating the similarity of short texts such as sentences or paragraphs (Islam and Inkpen, 2008; Mihalcea et al., 2006; Oliva et al., 2011) received less attention from the research community. The task of recognizing paraphrases (Michel et al., 2011; Socher et al., 2011; Wan et al., 2006) is sufficiently similar to reuse some of the techniques.

This paper presents the two systems for automated measuring of semantic similarity of short texts which we submitted to the SemEval-2012 Semantic Text Similarity Task (Agirre et al., 2012). We propose several sentence similarity measures built upon knowledge-based and corpus-based similarity of individual words as well as similarity of dependency parses. Our two systems, *simple* and *syntax*, use supervised machine learning, more specifically the support vector regression (SVR), to combine a large amount of features computed from pairs of sentences. The two systems differ in the set of features they employ.

Our systems placed in the top 5 (out of 89 submitted systems) for all three aggregate correlation measures: 2nd (*syntax*) and 3rd (*simple*) for overall Pearson, 1st (*simple*) and 3rd (*syntax*) for normalized Pearson, and 2nd (*simple*) and 5th (*syntax*) for weighted mean.

The rest of the paper is structured as follows. In Section 2 we describe both knowledge-based and corpus-based word similarity measures. In Section 3 we describe in detail the features used by our systems. In Section 4 we report the experimental results cross-validated on the development set as well as the official results on all test sets. Conclusions and ideas for future work are given in Section 5.

2 Word Similarity Measures

Approaches to determining semantic similarity of sentences commonly use measures of semantic similarity between individual words. Our systems use the knowledge-based and the corpus-based (i.e., distributional lexical semantics) approaches, both of which are commonly used to measure the semantic similarity of words.

2.1 Knowledge-based Word Similarity

Knowledge-based word similarity approaches rely on a semantic network of words, such as WordNet. Given two words, their similarity can be estimated by considering their relative positions within the knowledge base hierarchy.

All of our knowledge-based word similarity measures are based on WordNet. Some measures use the concept of a *lowest common subsumer (LCS)* of concepts c_1 and c_2, which represents the lowest node in the WordNet hierarchy that is a hypernym of both c_1 and c_2. We use the NLTK library (Bird, 2006) to compute the PathLen similarity (Leacock and Chodorow, 1998) and Lin similarity (Lin, 1998) measures. A single word often denotes several concepts, depending on its context. In order to compute the similarity score for a pair of words, we take the maximum similarity score over all possible pairs of concepts (i.e., WordNet synsets).

2.2 Corpus-based Word Similarity

Distributional lexical semantics models determine the meaning of a word through the set of all contexts in which the word appears. Consequently, we can model the meaning of a word using its distribution over all contexts. In the distributional model, deriving the semantic similarity between two words corresponds to comparing these distributions. While many different models of distributional semantics exist, we employ latent semantic analysis (LSA) (Turney and Pantel, 2010) over a large corpus to estimate the distributions.

For each word w_i, we compute a vector x_i using the truncated singular value decomposition (SVD) of a tf-idf weighted term-document matrix. The cosine similarity of vectors x_i and x_j estimates the similarity of the corresponding words w_i and w_j.

Two different word-vector mappings were computed by processing the New York Times Annotated Corpus (NYT) (Sandhaus, 2008) and Wikipedia. Aside from lowercasing the documents and removing punctuation, we perform no further preprocessing (e.g., no stopwords removal or stemming). Upon removing the words not occurring in at least two documents, we compute the tf-idf. The word vectors extracted from NYT corpus and Wikipedia have a dimension of 200 and 500, respectively.

Table 1: Evaluation of word similarity measures

Measure	ws353	ws353-sim	ws353-rel
PathLen	0.29	0.61	-0.05
Lin	0.33	0.64	-0.01
Dist (NYT)	0.50	0.50	0.51
Dist (Wikipedia)	0.62	0.66	0.55

We compared the measures by computing the Spearman correlation coefficient on the WordSim353[1] data set, as well as its similarity and relatedness subsets described in (Agirre et al., 2009). Table 1 provides the results of the comparison.

3 Semantic Similarity of Sentences

Our systems use supervised regression with SVR as a learning model, where each system exploits different feature sets and SVR hyperparameters.

3.1 Preprocessing

We list all of the preprocessing steps our systems perform. If a preprocessing step is executed by only one of our systems, the system's name is indicated in parentheses.

1. All hyphens and slashes are removed;
2. The angular brackets (< and >) that enclose the tokens are stripped (*simple*);
3. The currency values are simplified, e.g., `$US1234` to `$1234` (*simple*);
4. Words are tokenized using the Penn Treebank compatible tokenizer;
5. The tokens *n't* and *'m* are replaced with *not* and *am*, respectively (*simple*);
6. The two consecutive words in one sentence that appear as a compound in the other sentence are replaced by the said compound. E.g., *cater pillar* in one sentence is replaced with *caterpillar* only if *caterpillar* appears in the other sentence;

[1] `http://www.cs.technion.ac.il/~gabr/resources/data/wordsim353/wordsim353.html`

7. Words are POS-tagged using Penn Treebank compatible POS-taggers: NLTK (Bird, 2006) for *simple*, and OpenNLP[2] for *syntax*;
8. Stopwords are removed using a list of 36 stopwords (*simple*).

While we acknowledge that some of the preprocessing steps we take may not be common, we did not have the time to determine the influence of each individual preprocessing step on the results to either warrant their removal or justify their presence.

Since, for example, *sub-par*, *sub par* and *subpar* are treated as equal after preprocessing, we believe it makes our systems more robust to inputs containing small orthographic differences.

3.2 Ngram Overlap Features

We use many features previously seen in paraphrase classification (Michel et al., 2011). Several features are based on the unigram, bigram, and trigram overlap. Before computing the overlap scores, we remove punctuation and lowercase the words. We continue with a detailed description of each individual feature.

Ngram Overlap

Let S_1 and S_2 be the sets of consecutive ngrams (e.g., bigrams) in the first and the second sentence, respectively. The ngram overlap is defined as follows:

$$ngo(S_1, S_2) = 2 \cdot \left(\frac{|S_1|}{|S_1 \cap S_2|} + \frac{|S_2|}{|S_1 \cap S_2|} \right)^{-1} \quad (1)$$

The ngram overlap is the harmonic mean of the degree to which the second sentence covers the first and the degree to which the first sentence covers the second. The overlap, defined by (1), is computed for unigrams, bigrams, and trigrams.

Additionally we observe the *content ngram overlap* – the overlap of unigrams, bigrams, and trigrams exclusively on the content words. The content words are nouns, verbs, adjectives, and adverbs, i.e., the lemmas having one of the following part-of-speech tags: JJ, JJR, JJS, NN, NNP, NNS, NNPS, RB, RBR, RBS, VB, VBD, VBG, VBN, VBP, and VBZ. Intuitively, the function words (prepositions, conjunctions, articles) carry less semantics than content words and thus removing them might eliminate the noise and provide a more accurate estimate of semantic similarity.

In addition to the overlap of consecutive ngrams, we also compute the skip bigram and trigram overlap. Skip-ngrams are ngrams that allow arbitrary gaps, i.e., ngram words need not be consecutive in the original sentence. By redefining S_1 and S_2 to represent the sets of skip ngrams, we employ eq. (1) to compute the skip-n gram overlap.

3.3 WordNet-Augmented Word Overlap

One can expect a high unigram overlap between very similar sentences only if exactly the same words (or lemmas) appear in both sentences. To allow for some lexical variation, we use WordNet to assign partial scores to words that are not common to both sentences. We define the WordNet augmented coverage $P_{WN}(\cdot, \cdot)$:

$$P_{WN}(S_1, S_2) = \frac{1}{|S_2|} \sum_{w_1 \in S_1} score(w_1, S_2)$$

$$score(w, S) = \begin{cases} 1 & \text{if } w \in S \\ \max_{w' \in S} sim(w, w') & \text{otherwise} \end{cases}$$

where $sim(\cdot, \cdot)$ represents the WordNet path length similarity. The *WordNet-augmented word overlap* feature is defined as a harmonic mean of $P_{WN}(S_1, S_2)$ and $P_{WN}(S_2, S_1)$.

Weighted Word Overlap

When measuring sentence similarities we give more importance to words bearing more content, by using the information content

$$ic(w) = \ln \frac{\sum_{w' \in C} freq(w')}{freq(w)}$$

where C is the set of words in the corpus and $freq(w)$ is the frequency of the word w in the corpus. We use the Google Books Ngrams (Michel et al., 2011) to obtain word frequencies because of its excellent word coverage for English. Let S_1 and S_2 be the sets of words occurring in the first and second sentence, respectively. The weighted word coverage of the second sentence by the first sentence is

[2] http://opennlp.apache.org/

given by:

$$wwc(S_1, S_2) = \frac{\sum_{w \in S_1 \cap S_2} ic(w)}{\sum_{w' \in S_2} ic(w')}$$

The *weighted word overlap* between two sentences is calculated as the harmonic mean of the $wwc(S_1, S_2)$ and $wwc(S_2, S_1)$.

This measure proved to be very useful, but it could be improved even further. Misspelled frequent words are more frequent than some correctly spelled but rarely used words. Hence dealing with misspelled words would remove the inappropriate heavy penalty for a mismatch between correctly and incorrectly spelled words.

Greedy Lemma Aligning Overlap

This measure computes the similarity between sentences using the semantic alignment of lemmas. First we compute the word similarity between all pairs of lemmas from the first and the second sentence, using either the knowledge-based or the corpus-based semantic similarity. We then greedily search for a pair of most similar lemmas; once the lemmas are paired, they are not considered for further matching. Previous research by Lavie and Denkowski (2009) proposed a similar alignment strategy for machine translation evaluation. After aligning the sentences, the similarity of each lemma pair is weighted by the larger information content of the two lemmas:

$$sim(l_1, l_2) = \max(ic(l_1), ic(l_2)) \cdot ssim(l_1, l_2) \quad (2)$$

where $ssim(l_1, l_2)$ is the semantic similarity between lemmas l_1 and l_2.

The overall similarity between two sentences is defined as the sum of similarities of paired lemmas normalized by the length of the longer sentence:

$$glao(S_1, S_2) = \frac{\sum_{(l_1,l_2) \in P} sim(l_1, l_2)}{\max(length(S_1), length(S_2))}$$

where P is the set of lemma pairs obtained by greedy alignment. We take advantage of greedy align overlap in two features: one computes $glao(\cdot,\cdot)$ by using the Lin similarity for $ssim(\cdot,\cdot)$ in (2), while the other feature uses the distributional (LSA) similarity to calculate $ssim(\cdot,\cdot)$.

Vector Space Sentence Similarity

This measure is motivated by the idea of compositionality of distributional vectors (Mitchell and Lapata, 2008). We represent each sentence as a single distributional vector $u(\cdot)$ by summing the distributional (i.e., LSA) vector of each word w in the sentence S: $u(S) = \sum_{w \in S} \mathbf{x}_w$, where $\mathbf{x}_w$ is the vector representation of the word w. Another similar representation $u_W(\cdot)$ uses the information content $ic(w)$ to weigh the LSA vector of each word before summation: $u_W(S) = \sum_{w \in S} ic(w)\mathbf{x}_w$. The *simple* system uses $|\cos(u(S_1), u(S_2))|$ and $|\cos(u_W(S_1), u_W(S_2))|$ for the *vector space sentence similarity* features.

3.4 Syntactic Features

We use dependency parsing to identify the lemmas with the corresponding syntactic roles in the two sentences. We also compute the overlap of the dependency relations of the two sentences.

Syntactic Roles Similarity

The similarity of the words or phrases having the same syntactic roles in the two sentences may be indicative of their overall semantic similarity (Oliva et al., 2011). For example, two sentences with very different main predicates (e.g., *play* and *eat*) probably have a significant semantic difference.

Using Lin similarity $ssim(\cdot,\cdot)$, we obtain the similarity between the matching lemmas in a sentence pair for each syntactic role. Additionally, for each role we compute the similarity of the chunks that lemmas belong to:

$$chunksim(C_1, C_2) = \sum_{l_1 \in C_1} \sum_{l_2 \in C_2} ssim(l_1, l_2)$$

where C_1 and C_2 are the sets of chunks of the first and second sentence, respectively. The final similarity score of two chunks is the harmonic mean of $chunksim(C_1, C_2)/|C_1|$ and $chunksim(C_1, C_2)/|C_2|$.

Syntactic roles that we consider are predicates (p), subjects (s), direct (d), and indirect (i) (i.e., prepositional) objects, where we use (o) to mean either (d) or (i). The Stanford dependency parser (De Marneffe et al., 2006) produces the dependency parse of the sentence. We infer (p), (s), and (d) from the syntactic dependencies of type *nsubj* (nominal subject), *nsubjpass* (nominal subject passive), and *dobj* (direct object). By combining the *prep* and *pobj* dependencies (De Marneffe and Manning, 2008), we identify (i). Since the (d) in one sentence often semantically corresponds to (i) in the other sentence, we pair all (o) of one sentence with all (o) of the other sentence and define object similarity between the two sentences as the maximum similarity among all (o) pairs. Because the syntactic role might be absent from both sentences (e.g., the object in sentences "John sings" and "John is thinking"), we introduce additional binary features indicating if the comparison for the syntactic role in question exists.

Many sentences (especially longer ones) have two or more (p). In such cases it is necessary to align the corresponding predicate groups (i.e., the (p) with its corresponding arguments) between the two sentences, while also aggregating the (p), (s), and (o) similarities of all aligned (p) pairs. The similarity of two predicate groups is defined as the sum of (p), (s), and (o) similarities. In each iteration, the greedy algorithm pairs all predicate groups of the first sentence with all predicate groups of the second sentence and searches for a pair with the maximum similarity. Once the predicate groups of two sentences have been aligned, we compute the (p) similarity as a weighted sum of (p) similarities for each predicate pair group. The weight of each predicate group pair equals the larger information content of two predicates. The (s) and (o) similarities are computed in the same manner.

Syntactic Dependencies Overlap

Similar to the ngram overlap features, we measure the overlap between sentences based on matching dependency relations. A similar measure has been proposed in (Wan et al., 2006). Two syntactic dependencies are considered equal if they have the same dependency type, governing lemma, and dependent lemma. Let S_1 and S_2 be the set of all dependency relations in the first and the second sentence, respectively. *Dependency overlap* is the harmonic mean between $|S_1 \cap S_2|/|S_1|$ and $|S_1 \cap S_2|/|S_2|$. *Content dependency overlap* computes the overlap in the same way, but considers only dependency relations between content lemmas.

Similarly to weighted word overlap, we compute the weighted dependency relations overlap. The weighted coverage of the second sentence dependencies with the first sentence dependencies is given by:

$$wdrc(S_1, S_2) = \frac{\sum_{r \in S_1 \cap S_2} \max(ic(g(r)), ic(d(r)))}{\sum_{r \in S_2} \max(ic(g(r)), ic(d(r)))}$$

where $g(r)$ is the governing word of the dependency relation r, $d(r)$ is the dependent word of the dependency relation r, and $ic(l)$ is the information content of the lemma l. Finally, the *weighted dependency relations overlap* is the harmonic mean between $wdrc(S_1, S_2)$ and $wdrc(S_2, S_1)$.

3.5 Other Features

Although we primarily focused on developing the ngram overlap and syntax-based features, some other features significantly improve the performance of our systems.

Normalized Differences

Our systems take advantage of the following features that measure normalized differences in a pair of sentences: (A) sentence length, (B) the noun chunk, verb chunk, and predicate counts, and (C) the aggregate word information content (see *Normalized differences* in Table 2).

Numbers Overlap

The annotators gave low similarity scores to many sentence pairs that contained different sets of numbers, even though their sentence structure was very similar. Socher et al. (2011) improved the performance of their paraphrase classifier by adding the following features that compare the sets of numbers N_1 and N_2 in two sentences: $N_1 = N_2$, $N_1 \cap N_2 \neq \emptyset$, and $N_1 \subseteq N_2 \vee N_2 \subseteq N_1$. We replace the first two features with $\log(1 + |N_1| + |N_2|)$ and $2 \cdot |N_1 \cap N_2|/(|N_1| + |N_2|)$. Additionally, the numbers that differ only in the number of decimal places are treated as equal (e.g., 65, 65.2, and 65.234 are treated as equal, whereas 65.24 and 65.25 are not).

Named Entity Features

Shallow NE similarity treats capitalized words as named entities if they are longer than one character. If a token in all caps begins with a period, it is classified as a stock index symbol. The *simple* system

Table 2: The usage of feature sets

Feature set	*simple*	*syntax*
Ngram overlap	+	+
Content-ngram overlap	-	+
Skip-ngram overlap	-	+
WordNet-aug. overlap	+	-
Weighted word overlap	+	+
Greedy align. overlap	-	+
Vector space similarity	+	-
Syntactic roles similarity	-	+
Syntactic dep. overlap	-	+
Normalized differences*	A,C	A,B
Shallow NERC	+	-
Full NERC	-	+
Numbers overlap	+	+

* See Section 3.5

uses the following four features: the overlap of capitalized words, the overlap of stock index symbols, and the two features indicating whether these named entities were found in either of the two sentences.

In addition to the overlap of capitalized words, the *syntax* system uses the OpenNLP named entity recognizer and classifier to compute the overlap of entities for each entity class separately. We recognize the following entity classes: persons, organizations, locations, dates, and rudimentary temporal expressions. The absence of an entity class from both sentences is indicated by a separate binary feature (one feature for each class).

Feature Usage in TakeLab Systems

Some of the features presented in the previous sections were used by both of our systems (*simple* and *syntax*), while others were used by only one of the systems. Table 2 indicates the feature sets used for the two submitted systems.

4 Results

4.1 Model Training

For each of the provided training sets we trained a separate Support Vector Regression (SVR) model using LIBSVM (Chang and Lin, 2011). To obtain the optimal SVR parameters C, g, and p, our systems employ a grid search with nested cross-validation. Table 3 presents the cross-validated performance (in terms of Pearson correlation) on the training sets. The models tested on the SMTnews test set were trained on the SMTeuroparl train set. For the OnWn test set, the *syntax* model was trained on the MSRpar set, while the *simple* system's model was trained on the union of all train sets. The final predictions were trimmed to a 0–5 range.

Table 3: Cross-validated results on train sets

	MSRvid	MSRpar	SMTeuroparl
simple	0.8794	0.7566	0.7802
syntax	0.8698	0.7144	0.7308

Our development results indicate that the *weighted word overlap*, *WordNet-augmented word overlap*, the *greedy lemma alignment overlap*, and the *vector space sentence similarity* individually obtain high correlations regardless of the development set in use. Other features proved to be useful on individual development sets (e.g., *syntax roles similarity* on MSRvid and *numbers overlap* on MSRpar). More research remains to be done in thorough feature analysis and systematic feature selection.

4.2 Test Set Results

The organizers provided five different test sets to evaluate the performance of the submitted systems. Table 4 illustrates the performance of our systems on individual test sets, accompanied by their rank. Our systems outperformed most other systems on MSRvid, MSRpar, and OnWN sets (Agirre et al., 2012). However, they performed poorly on the SMTeuroparl and SMTnews sets. While the correlation scores on the MSRvid and MSRpar test sets correspond to those obtained using cross-validation on the corresponding train sets, the performance on the SMT test sets is drastically lower than the cross-validated performance on the corresponding train set. The sentences in the SMT training set are significantly longer (30.4 tokens on average) than the sentences in both SMT test sets (12.3 for SMTeuroparl and 13.5 for SMTnews). Also there are several repeated pairs of extremely short and identical sentences (e.g., "Tunisia" – "Tunisia" appears 17 times

Table 4: Results on individual test sets

	simple	*syntax*
MSRvid	0.8803 (1)	0.8620 (8)
MSRpar	0.7343 (1)	0.6985 (2)
SMTeuroparl	0.4771 (26)	0.3612 (63)
SMTnews	0.3989 (46)	0.4683 (18)
OnWN	0.6797 (9)	0.7049 (6)

Table 5: Aggregate performance on the test sets

	All	ALLnrm	Mean
simple	0.8133 (3)	0.8635 (1)	0.6753 (2)
syntax	0.8138 (2)	0.8569 (3)	0.6601 (5)

in the SMTeuroparl test set). The above measurements indicate that the SMTeuroparl training set was not representative of the SMTeuroparl test set for our choice of features.

Table 5 outlines the aggregate performance of our systems according to the three aggregate evaluation measures proposed for the task (Agirre et al., 2012). Both systems performed very favourably compared to the other systems, achieving very high rankings regardless of the aggregate evaluation measure.

The implementation of *simple* system is available at `http://takelab.fer.hr/sts`.

5 Conclusion and Future Work

In this paper we described our submission to the SemEval-2012 Semantic Textual Similarity Task. We have identified some high performing features for measuring semantic text similarity. Although both of the submitted systems performed very well on all but the two SMT test sets, there is still room for improvement. The feature selection was ad-hoc and more systematic feature selection is required (e.g., wrapper feature selection). Introducing additional features for deeper understanding (e.g., semantic role labelling) might also improve performance on this task.

Acknowledgments

This work was supported by the Ministry of Science, Education and Sports, Republic of Croatia under the Grant 036-1300646-1986. We would like to thank the organizers for the tremendous effort they put into formulating this challenging task.

References

Eneko Agirre, Enrique Alfonseca, Keith Hall, Jana Kravalova, Marius Paşca, and Aitor Soroa. 2009. A study on similarity and relatedness using distributional and wordnet-based approaches. In *Proceedings of Human Language Technologies: The 2009 Annual Conference of the North American Chapter of the Association for Computational Linguistics*, pages 19–27. Association for Computational Linguistics.

Eneko Agirre, Daniel Cer, Mona Diab, and Aitor Gonzalez-Agirre. 2012. SemEval-2012 Task 6: A pilot on semantic textual similarity. In *Proceedings of the 6th International Workshop on Semantic Evaluation (SemEval 2012), in conjunction with the First Joint Conference on Lexical and Computational Semantics (*SEM 2012)*. ACL.

Ramiz M. Aliguliyev. 2009. A new sentence similarity measure and sentence based extractive technique for automatic text summarization. *Expert Systems with Applications*, 36(4):7764–7772.

Steven Bird. 2006. NLTK: the natural language toolkit. In *Proceedings of the COLING/ACL on Interactive presentation sessions*, COLING-ACL '06, pages 69–72. Association for Computational Linguistics.

Alexander Budanitsky and Graeme Hirst. 2006. Evaluating wordnet-based measures of lexical semantic relatedness. *Computational Linguistics*, 32(1):13–47.

Chih-Chung Chang and Chih-Jen Lin. 2011. LIBSVM: A library for support vector machines. *ACM Transactions on Intelligent Systems and Technology*, 2:27:1–27:27. Software available at `http://www.csie.ntu.edu.tw/~cjlin/libsvm`.

Marie-Catherine De Marneffe and Christopher D. Manning. 2008. The Stanford typed dependencies representation. In *Coling 2008: Proceedings of the workshop on Cross-Framework and Cross-Domain Parser Evaluation*, pages 1–8. Association for Computational Linguistics.

Marie-Catherine De Marneffe, Bill MacCartney, and Christopher D. Manning. 2006. Generating typed dependency parses from phrase structure parses. In *Proceedings of LREC*, volume 6, pages 449–454.

Aminul Islam and Diana Inkpen. 2008. Semantic text similarity using corpus-based word similarity and string similarity. *ACM Transactions on Knowledge Discovery from Data (TKDD)*, 2(2):10.

Alon Lavie and Michael Denkowski. 2009. The METEOR metric for automatic evaluation of machine translation. *Machine translation*, 23(2):105–115.

Claudia Leacock and Martin Chodorow. 1998. Combining local context and WordNet similarity for word sense identification. *WordNet: An electronic lexical database*, 49(2):265–283.

Chin-Yew Lin and Eduard Hovy. 2003. Automatic evaluation of summaries using n-gram co-occurrence statistics. In *Proceedings of the 2003 Conference of the North American Chapter of the Association for Computational Linguistics on Human Language Technology-Volume 1*, pages 71–78. Association for Computational Linguistics.

Dekang Lin. 1998. An information-theoretic definition of similarity. In *Proceedings of the 15th international conference on Machine Learning*, volume 1, pages 296–304. San Francisco.

Ana G. Maguitman, Filippo Menczer, Heather Roinestad, and Alessandro Vespignani. 2005. Algorithmic detection of semantic similarity. In *Proceedings of the 14th international conference on World Wide Web*, pages 107–116. ACM.

Jean-Baptiste Michel, Yuan Kui Shen, Aviva P. Aiden, Adrian Veres, Matthew K. Gray, et al. 2011. Quantitative analysis of culture using millions of digitized books. *Science*, 331(6014):176.

Rada Mihalcea, Courtney Corley, and Carlo Strapparava. 2006. Corpus-based and knowledge-based measures of text semantic similarity. In *Proceedings of the national conference on artificial intelligence*, volume 21, page 775. Menlo Park, CA; Cambridge, MA; London; AAAI Press; MIT Press; 1999.

Jeff Mitchell and Mirella Lapata. 2008. Vector-based models of semantic composition. *Proceedings of ACL-08: HLT*, pages 236–244.

Jesús Oliva, Jóse Ignacio Serrano, María Dolores Del Castillo, and Ángel Iglesias. 2011. SyMSS: A syntax-based measure for short-text semantic similarity. *Data & Knowledge Engineering*.

Eui-Kyu Park, Dong-Yul Ra, and Myung-Gil Jang. 2005. Techniques for improving web retrieval effectiveness. *Information processing & management*, 41(5):1207–1223.

Gerard Salton, Andrew Wong, and Chung-Shu Yang. 1975. A vector space model for automatic indexing. *Communications of the ACM*, 18(11):613–620.

Evan Sandhaus. 2008. The New York Times annotated corpus. *Linguistic Data Consortium, Philadelphia*, 6(12):e26752.

Hinrich Schütze. 1998. Automatic word sense discrimination. *Computational linguistics*, 24(1):97–123.

Fabrizio Sebastiani. 2002. Machine learning in automated text categorization. *ACM computing surveys (CSUR)*, 34(1):1–47.

Richard Socher, Eric H. Huang, Jeffrey Pennington, Andrew Y. Ng, and Christopher D. Manning. 2011. Dynamic pooling and unfolding recursive autoencoders for paraphrase detection. *Advances in Neural Information Processing Systems*, 24.

Peter D. Turney and Patrick Pantel. 2010. From frequency to meaning: Vector space models of semantics. *Journal of Artificial Intelligence Research*, 37(1):141–188.

Stephen Wan, Mark Dras, Robert Dale, and Cécile Paris. 2006. Using dependency-based features to take the “para-farce” out of paraphrase. In *Proceedings of the Australasian Language Technology Workshop*, volume 2006.

Soft Cardinality: A Parameterized Similarity Function for Text Comparison

Sergio Jimenez
Universidad Nacional
de Colombia, Bogota,
Ciudad Universitaria
edificio 453, oficina 220
sgjimenezv@unal.edu.co

Claudia Becerra
Universidad Nacional
de Colombia, Bogota
cjbecerrac@unal.edu.co

Alexander Gelbukh
CIC-IPN
Av. Juan Dios Bátiz,
Av. Mendizábal, Col.
Nueva Industrial Vallejo,
CP 07738, DF, México
gelbukh@gelbukh.com

Abstract

We present an approach for the construction of text similarity functions using a parameterized resemblance coefficient in combination with a softened cardinality function called soft cardinality. Our approach provides a consistent and recursive model, varying levels of granularity from sentences to characters. Therefore, our model was used to compare sentences divided into words, and in turn, words divided into q-grams of characters. Experimentally, we observed that a performance correlation function in a space defined by all parameters was relatively smooth and had a single maximum achievable by "hill climbing." Our approach used only surface text information, a stop-word remover, and a stemmer to tackle the semantic text similarity task 6 at SEMEVAL 2012. The proposed method ranked 3rd (average), 5th (normalized correlation), and 15th (aggregated correlation) among 89 systems submitted by 31 teams.

1 Introduction

Similarity is the intrinsic ability of humans and some animals to balance commonalities and differences when comparing objects that are not identical. Although there is no direct evidence of how this process works in living organisms, some models have been proposed from the cognitive perspective (Sjöberg, 1972; Tversky, 1977; Navarro and Lee, 2004). On the other hand, several similarity models have been proposed in mathematics, statistics, and computer science among other fields. Particularly in AI, similarity measures play an important role in the construction of intelligent systems that are required to exhibit behavior similar to humans. For instance, in the field of natural language processing, text similarity functions provide estimates of the human similarity judgments related to language. In this paper, we combine elements from the perspective of cognitive psychology and computer science to propose a model for building similarity functions suitable for the task of semantic text similarity.

We identify four main families of text similarity functions: i) resemblance coefficients based on sets (e.g. Jaccard's (1901) and Dice's (1945) coefficients) ii) functions in metric spaces (e.g. cosine *tf-idf* similarity (Salton et al., 1975)); iii) the edit distance family of measures (e.g. Levenstein (1966) distance, LCS (Hirschberg, 1977)); and iv) hybrid approaches ((Monge and Elkan, 1996; Cohen et al., 2003; Corley and Mihalcea, 2005; Jimenez et al., 2010)). All of these measures use a subdivision of the texts in different granularity levels, such as q-grams of words, words, q-grams of characters, syllables, and characters. Among hybrid approaches, Monge-Elkan's measure and soft cardinality methods are recursive and can be used to build similarity functions at any arbitrary range of granularity. For instance, it is possible to construct a similarity function to compare sentences based on a function that compares words, which in turn can be constructed based on a function that compares bigrams of characters. Furthermore, hybrid approaches can integrate similarity functions that are not based on the representation of the surface of text, such as semantic relatedness measures (Pedersen et al., 2004).

Text similarity measures can be static or adaptive whether they are binary functions using only surface information of the two texts, or are functions that suit to a wider set of texts. For instance, measures using *tf-idf* weights adapt their results to the set of texts in which those weights were obtained. Other approaches learn parameters of the similarity function from a set of texts to optimize a particular task. For instance, Ristad and Yianilos (1998) and Bikenko and Mooney (2003) learned the costs of edit operations for all characters for an edit-distance function in a name-matching task. Other machine-learning approaches have also been proposed to build adaptive measures in name-matching (Bilenko and

Mooney, 2003) and textual-entailment tasks.

However, those machine-learning-based methods for adaptive similarity suffer from sparseness and the "curse of dimensionality". For example, the method of Ristad and Yianilos learns $n^2 + 2n$ parameters, where n is the size of the character set. Similarly, dimensionality in the method of Bilenko and Mooney is the size of the data set vocabulary. This issue is addressed primarily through machine-learning algorithms, which reduce the dimensionality of the problem regularizating to achieve enough generalization to get an acceptable performance difference between training and test data. Although machine-learning solutions have proven effective for many applications, the principle of Occam's razor suggests that it should be preferable to have a model that explains the data with a smaller number of significant parameters. In this paper, we seek a simpler adaptive similarity model with few meaningful parameters.

Our proposed similarity model starts with a cardinality-based resemblance coefficient (i.e. Dice's coefficient $2|A\cap B|/|A|+|B|$) and generalizes it to model the effect of asymmetric selection of the referent. This effect is a human factor discovered by Tversky (1977) that affects judgments of similarity, i.e. humans tends to select the more prominent stimulus as the referent and the less salient stimulus as the object. Some of Tversky's examples are "the son resembles the father" rather than "the father resembles the son", "an ellipse is like a circle" not "a circle is like an ellipse", and "North Korea is like Red China" rather than "Red China is like North Korea". Generally speaking, "the variant is more similar to the prototype than vice versa". In the previous example, stimulus salience is associated with the prominence of the country; for text comparison we associate word salience with *tf-idf* weights. At the text level, we associate salience with a combination of word-salience, inter-word similarity, and text length provided by soft cardinality. Experimentally, we observed that this effect also occurs when comparing texts, but not necessarily in the same direction suggested by Tversky. We used this effect to improve the performance of our similarity model. In addition, we proposed a parameter that biases the function to generate greater or lower similarity scores.

Finally, in our model we used a soft cardinality function (Jimenez et al., 2010) instead of the classical set cardinality. Just as classical cardinality counts the number of elements which are not identical in a set, soft cardinality uses an auxiliary inter-element similarity function to make a soft count. For instance, the soft cardinality of a set with two very similar (but not identical) elements should be a real number closer to 1.0 instead of 2.0.

The rest of the paper is organized as follows. In Section 2 we briefly present soft cardinality. In Section 3 the proposed parameterized similarity model is presented. In Section 4 experimental validation is provided using 8 data sets annotated with human similarity judgments from the "Semantic-Text-Similarity" task at SEMEVAL-2012. Finally, a brief discussion is provided in Section 5 and conclusions are presented in Section 6.

2 Soft Cardinality

Let $A = \{a_1, a_2, \ldots, a_{|A|}\}$ and $B = \{b_1, b_2, \ldots, b_{|B|}\}$ be two sets being compared. When each element of a_i or b_j has an associated weight w_{a_i} or w_{b_j} the problem of comparing those sets becomes a weighted similarity problem. This means that such model has to take into account not only the commonalities and diferences, but also their weights. Also, if an $(|A \cup B|) \times (|A \cup B|)$ similarity matrix $\mathbf{S}$ is available, the problem becomes a weighted soft similarity problem because the commonality between A and B has to be computed not only with identical elements, but also with elements with a degree of similarity. The values of $\mathbf{S}$ can be obtained from an auxiliary similarity function $sim(a,b)$ that satisfies at least non-negativity ($\forall a,b,\ sim(a,b) \geq 0$) and reflexivity ($\forall a,\ sim(a,a) = 1$). Other postulates such as symmetry ($\forall a,b,\ sim(a,b) = sim(b,a)$) and triangle inequality[1] ($\forall a,b,c,\ sim(a,c) \geq sim(a,b) + sim(b,c) - 1$) are not strictly necessary.

Jimenez et al. (2010) proposed a set-based weighted soft-similarity model using resemblance coefficients and the soft cardinality function instead of classical set cardinality. The idea of calculating the soft cardinality is to treat elements a_i in set the A as sets themselves and to treat inter-element similarities as the intersections between the elements $sim(a_i, a_j) = |a_i \cap a_j|$. Therefore, the soft cardinality of set A becomes $|A|' = \left|\bigcup_{i=1}^{|A|} a_i\right|$. Since it is not feasible to calculate this union, they proposed the following weighted approximation using $|a_i| = w_{a_i}$:

$$|A|'_{sim} \simeq \sum_{i}^{|A|} w_{a_i} \left(\sum_{j}^{|A|} sim(a_i, a_j)^p \right)^{-1} \quad (1)$$

Parameter $p \geq 0$ in eq.1 controls the "softeness" of the cardinality, taking $p = 1$ its no-effect value and leaving element similarities unchanged for the calculation of soft cardinality. When p is large, all $sim(*,*)$ results lower than 1 are transformed into a number approaching 0. As a result, the soft cardinality behaves like the classical cardinality, returning the addition of all the weights of the elements, i.e $|A|'_{sim} \simeq \sum_i^{|A|} w_{a_i}$. When p is close to 0, all $sim(*.*)$ results are transformed approaching

[1]triangle inequality postulate for similarity is derived from its counterpart for dissimilarity (distance) $distance(a,b) = 1 - sim(a,b)$.

into a number approaching 1, making the soft cardinality returns the average of the weights of the elements, i.e. $|A|'_{sim} \simeq \frac{1}{|A|}\sum_i^{|A|} w_{a_i}$. Jimenez et al. used $p = 2$ and *idf* weights in the same name-matching task proposed by Cohen et al. (Cohen et al., 2003).

3 A Parameterized Similarity Model

As we mentioned above, Tvesky proposed that humans tends to select more salient stimulus as *referent* and less salient stimulus as *object* when comparing two objects A and B. Based on the idea of Tvesrky, the similarity between two objects can be measured as the ratio between *the salience of commonalities* and *the salience of the less salient object*. Drawing an analogy between objects as sets and salience as the cardinality of a set, the salience of commonalities is $|A \cap B|$, and the salience of the less salient object is $\min(|A|, |B|)$. This ratio is known as the overlap coefficient $Overlap(A, B) = \frac{|A \cap B|}{\min(|A|,|B|)}$. However, whether $|A| < |B|$ or whether $|A| \ll |B|$, the similarity obtained by $Overlap(A, B)$ is the same. Hence, we propose to model the selecction of the referent using a parameter α that makes a weighted average between $\min(|A|, |B|)$ and $\max(|A|, |B|)$, controling the degree to which the asymmetric referent-selection effect is considered in the similarity measure.

$$SIM(A, B) = \frac{|A \cap B| + bias}{\alpha \max(|A|, |B|) + (1 - \alpha) \min(|A|, |B|)} \quad (2)$$

The parameter α controls the degree to which the asymmetric referent-selection effect is considered in the similarity measure. Its no-effect value is $\alpha = 0.5$, so the eq.2 becomes the Dice coefficient. Moreover, when $\alpha = 0$ the eq.2 becomes the overlap coefficient, otherwise when $\alpha = 1$ the opposite effect is modeled.

In addition, we introduced a $bias$ parameter in eq. 2 that increases the commonalities of each object pair by the same amount, and so it measures the degree to which all of the objects have commonalities among each other. Clearly, the non-effect value for the $bias$ parameter is 0.

Besides, the $bias$ parameter has the effect of biasing $SIM(A, B)$ by considering any pair $\langle A, B\rangle$ more similar if $bias > 0$ and their cardinalities are small. Conversely, the similarity between pairs with large cardinalities is promoted if $bias < 0$. However, as higher values of $bias$ may result in similarity scores outside the interval $[0, 1]$, additional post-procesing to limit the similarities in this interval may be required.

The proposed parameterized text similarity measure is constructed by combining the proposed resemblance coefficient in eq.2 and the soft cardinality in eq.1. The resulting measure has three parameters: α, $bias$, and p. Weights w_{a_i} can be *idf* weights. This measure takes two texts represented as sets of words and returns their similarity. The auxiliary similarity function $sim(a, b)$ necessary for calculating the soft cardinality is another parameter of the model. This auxiliary function is any function that can compare two words and return a similarity score in $[0, 1]$.

α	Asymetric referent selection at text level
$bias$	Bias parameter at text level
p	Soft cardinality exponent at word level
w_{a_i}	Element weights at word level
q_1, q_2	q_1-grams or $[q_1 : q_2]$spectra word division
α_{sim}	Asymetric referent selection at q-gram level
$bias_{sim}$	Bias parameter q-gram level

Table 1: Parameters of the proposed similarity model

To build this $sim(a, b)$ function, we chose to reuse the eq.2 but representing words as sets of q-grams or ranges of q-grams of different sizes, i.e. $[q_1 : q_2]$ spectra. Q-grams are consecutive overlapped substrings of size q. For instance, the word "*saturday*" divided into trigrams is {◁*sa*, *sat*, *atu*, *tur*, *urd*, *rda*, *day*, *ay*▷}. The character '▷' is a padding character added to differenciate q-grams at the begining or end of the string. A $[2 : 4]$spectra is the combined representation of a word using –in this example– bigrams, trigrams and quadgrams (Jimenez and Gelbukh, 2011). The cardinality function for $sim()$ was the classical set cardinality. Clearly, the soft cardinality could be used again if an auxiliary similarity function for character comparison and a q-gram weighting mechanism are provided to allow another level of recursion. Therefore, the parameters of $sim(a, b)$ are: α_{sim}, $bias_{sim}$. Finally, the entire set of parameters of the proposed similarity model is shown in Table 1.

4 Experimental Setup and Results

The aim of these experiments is to observe the behavior of the parameters of our similarity model and verify if the hypothesis that motivated these parameters can be confirmed experimentally. The experimental data are 8 data sets (3 for training and 5 for test) proposed in the "Semantic Text Similarity" task at SEMEVAL-2012. Each data set consist of a set of pairs of text annotated with human-similarity judgments on a scale of 0 to 5. Each similarity judgment is the average of the judgments provided by 5 human judges. For a comprehensible description of the task see(Agirre et al., 2012).

For the experiments, all data sets were pre-processed by converting to lowercase characters, English stop-words removal and stemming using Porter stemmer (Porter, 1980). The performance measure used for all experiments was the Pearson correlation r.

4.1 Model Parameters

In order to make an initial exploration of the parameters in Table 1, we set $q_1 = 2$ (i.e. bigrams) and used $w_{a_i} = idf(a_i)$. For other parameters, we started with all the non-effect values, i.e. $\alpha = 0.5$, $bias = 0$, $p = 1$, $\alpha_{sim} = 0.5$ and $bias_{sim} = 0$. Plots in Figure 1 show the Pearson correlation measured in each of the data sets. For each graph, the non-effect configuration was used and each parameter varies in the range indicated in each horizontal axis. For best viewing, the non-effect values on each graph are represented by a vertical line.

In this exploration of the parameters it was noted that each parameter defines a function for the performance measure that is smooth and with an unique global maximum. Therefore, we assumed that the join performance function in the space defined by the 5 parameters also had the same properties. The parameters for each data set shown in Table 2 were found using a simple hill-climbing algorithm. Different q-gram and spectra configurations were tested manually.

5 Discussion

It is possible to observe from the results in Figure 1 and Table 2 that the behavior of the parameters is similar in pairs of data sets that have training and test parts. This behavior is evident in both MSRvid and MSRpar data sets, but it is less evident in SMTeuroparl. Furthermore, the optimal parameters for training data sets MSRvid and MSRpar were similar to those of their test data sets. In conclusion, the proposed set of parameters provides a set of features that characterize a data set for the text similarity task.

Regarding the effect of asymmetry in referent selecction proposed by Tvesrky, it was observed that –at text level– the MSRvid data sets were the only ones that supported this hypothesis ($\alpha = 0.32, 0.42$). The remaining data sets showed the opposite effect ($\alpha > 0.5$). That is, annotators chose the most salient document (the longer) as the referent when a pair of texts is being compared.

The Table 2 also shows that the optimal parameters for all data sets were different from the no-effect values combination. This result can also be seen in Figure 1, where curves crossed the vertical line of no-effect value –in most of the cases– in values different to the optimum. Clearly, the proposed set of parameters is useful for adjusting the similarity function for a particular data set and task.

6 Conclusions

We have proposed a new parameterized similarity function for text comparison and a method for finding the optimal values of the parameter set when training data is available. In addition, the parameter α, which was motivated by the similarity model of Tversky, proved effective in obtaining better performance, but we could not confirm the Tvesky's hypothesis that humans tends to select the object (text) with less stimulus salience (text length) as the referent. This result might have occurred because either the stimulus salience is not properly represented by the length of the text, or Tversky's hypothesis cannot be extended to text comparison.

The proposed similarity function proved effective in the task of "Semantic Text Similarity" in SEMEVAL 2012. Our method obtained the third best average correlation on the 5 test data sets. This result is remarkable because our method only used data from the surface of the texts, a stop-word remover, and a stemmer, which can be even be considered as a baseline method.

Acknowledgments

This research was funded by the Systems and Industrial Engineering Department, the Office of Student Welfare of the National University of Colombia, Bogotá, and throught a grant from the Colombian Department for Science, Technology and Innovation Colciencias, proj. 110152128465. The second author recognizes the support from Mexican Government (SNI, COFAA-IPN, SIP 20113295, CONACYT 50206-H) and CONACYT–DST India (proj. "Answer Validation through Textual Entailment").

References

Eneko Agirre, Daniel Cer, Mona Diab, and Gonzalez-Agirre Aitor. 2012. SemEval-2012 task 6: A pilot on semantic textual similarity. In *Proc. of the 6th International Workshop on Semantic Evaluation (SemEval 2012), in conjunction with the First Joint Conference on Lexical and Computational Semantics (*SEM 2012).*, Montreal,Canada.

Mikhail Bilenko and Raymond J. Mooney. 2003. Adaptive duplicate detection using learnable string similarity measures. In *Proc. of the ninth ACM SIGKDD international conference on Knowledge discovery and data mining*, pages 39–48, Washington, D.C. ACM.

William W Cohen, Pradeep Ravikumar, and Stephen E Fienberg. 2003. A comparison of string distance metrics for Name-Matching tasks. In *Proc. of the IJCAI2003 Workshop on Information Integration on the Web II Web03.*

Courtney Corley and Rada Mihalcea. 2005. Measuring the semantic similarity of texts. In *Proc. of the ACL Workshop on Empirical Modeling of Semantic Equivalence and Entailment*, Stroudsburg, PA.

Lee R. Dice. 1945. Measures of the amount of ecologic association between species. *Ecology*, pages 297–302.

Daniel S. Hirschberg. 1977. Algorithms for the longest common subsequence problem. *J. ACM*, 24(4):664–675.

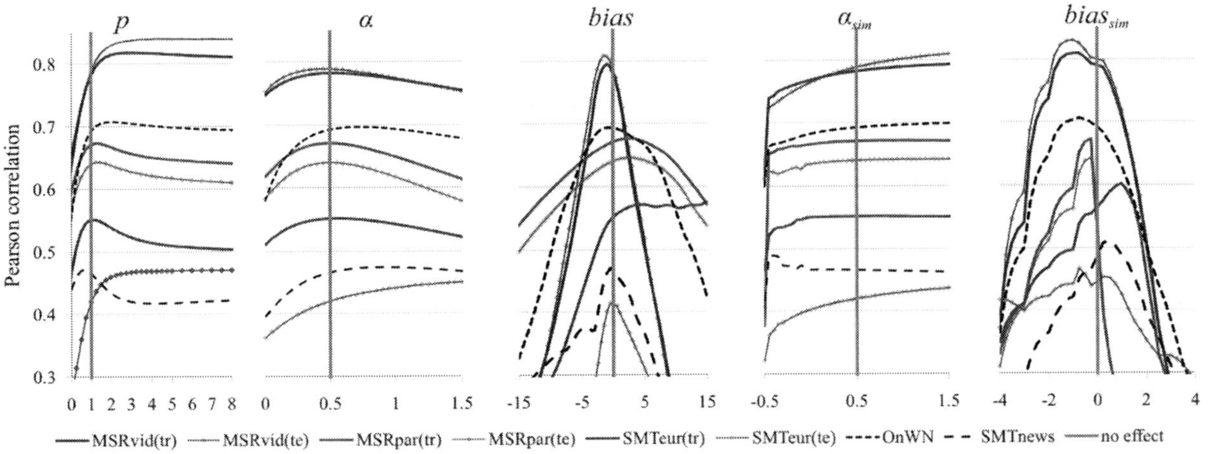

Figure 1: Exploring similarity model parameters around their no-effect values (tr=training, te=test)

	Parameters						correl.	Official Results	
Data set	$[q_1 : q_2]$	α	$bias$	p	α_{sim}	$bias_{sim}$	r	SoftCard	Best
MSRpar.training	[4]	0.62	1.14	0.77	-0.04	-0.38	0.6598	n/a	n/a
MSR.par.test	[4]	0.60	1.02	0.9	-0.02	-0.4	0.6335	0.6405[1]	0.7343
MSRvid.training	[1:4]	0.42	-0.80	2.28	0.18	0.08	0.8323	n/a	n/a
MSRvid.test	[1:4]	0.32	-0.80	1.88	1.08	0.08	0.8579	0.8562	0.8803
SMTeuroparl.training	[2:4]	0.74	-0.06	0.91	1.88	2.90	0.6193	n/a	n/a
SMTeuroparl.test	[2:4]	0.84	-0.16	0.71	1.78	3.00	0.5178	0.5152[2]	0.5666
OnWN.test	[2:5]	0.88	-0.62	1.36	-0.02	-0.70	0.7202	0.7109[1]	0.7273
SMTnews.test	[1:4]	0.88	0.88	1.57	0.80	3.21	0.5344	0.4833[1]	0.6085

[1]Result obtained using Jaro-Winkler (Winkler, 1990) measure as $sim(a, b)$ function between words.
[2]Result obtained using generalized Monge-Elkan measure $p = 4$, no stop-words removal and no term weights (Jimenez et al., 2009).

Table 2: Results with optimized parameters and official SEMEVAL 2012 results

Paul Jaccard. 1901. Etude comparative de la distribution florare dans une portion des alpes et des jura. *Bulletin de la Société Vaudoise des Sciences Naturelles*, pages 547–579.

Sergio Jimenez and Alexander Gelbukh. 2011. SC spectra: a linear-time soft cardinality approximation for text comparison. In *Proc. of the 10th international conference on Artificial Intelligence*, MICAI'11, Puebla, Mexico.

Sergio Jimenez, Claudia Becerra, Alexander Gelbukh, and Fabio Gonzalez. 2009. Generalized Monge-Elkan method for approximate text string comparison. In *Computational Linguistics and Intelligent Text Processing*, volume 5449 of *LNCS*, pages 559–570.

Sergio Jimenez, Fabio Gonzalez, and Alexander Gelbukh. 2010. Text comparison using soft cardinality. In *String Processing and Information Retrieval*, volume 6393 of *LNCS*, pages 297–302.

Vladimir I. Levenshtein. 1966. Binary codes capable of correcting deletions, insertions, and reversals. *Soviet Physics Doklady*, 10(8):707–710.

Alvaro E. Monge and Charles Elkan. 1996. The field matching problem: Algorithms and applications. In *Proc. KDD-96*, pages 267–270, Portland, OR.

Daniel Navarro and Michael D. Lee. 2004. Common and distinctive features in stimulis representation: A modified version of the contrast model. *Psychonomic Bulletin & Review*, 11:961–974.

Ted Pedersen, Siddharth Patwardhan, and Jason Michelizzi. 2004. WordNet::Similarity: measuring the relatedness of concepts. In *Proc. HLT-NAACL–Demonstration Papers*, Stroudsburg, PA.

Martin Porter. 1980. An algorithm for suffix stripping. *Program*, 3(14):130–137.

Eric S. Ristad and Peter N. Yianilos. 1998. Learning string edit distance. *IEEE Transactions on Pattern Analysis and Machine Intelligence*, 20(5):522–532.

Gerard Salton, A. Wong, and C.S. Yang. 1975. A vector space model for automatic indexing. *Com. ACM*, 18(11):613–620.

L. Sjöberg. 1972. A cognitive theory of similarity. *Göteborg Psychological Reports*.

Amos Tversky. 1977. Features of similarity. *Psychological Review*, 84(4):327–352.

William E. Winkler. 1990. String comparator metrics and enhanced decision rules in the Fellegi-Sunter model of record linkage. In *Proc. of the Section on Survey Research Methods*.

UNED: Evaluating Text Similarity Measures without Human Assessments*

Enrique Amigó † Julio Gonzalo † Jesús Giménez ‡ Felisa Verdejo†

† UNED, Madrid
{enrique,julio,felisa}@lsi.uned.es

‡ Google, Dublin
jesgim@gmail.com

Abstract

This paper describes the participation of UNED NLP group in the SEMEVAL 2012 Semantic Textual Similarity task. Our contribution consists of an unsupervised method, Heterogeneity Based Ranking (HBR), to combine similarity measures. Our runs focus on combining standard similarity measures for Machine Translation. The Pearson correlation achieved is outperformed by other systems, due to the limitation of MT evaluation measures in the context of this task. However, the combination of system outputs that participated in the campaign produces three interesting results: (i) Combining all systems without considering any kind of human assessments achieve a similar performance than the best peers in all test corpora, (ii) combining the 40 less reliable peers in the evaluation campaign achieves similar results; and (iii) the correlation between peers and HBR predicts, with a 0.94 correlation, the performance of measures according to human assessments.

1 Introduction

Imagine that we are interested in developing computable measures that estimate the semantic similarity between two sentences. This is the focus of the STS workshop in which this paper is presented. In order to optimize the approaches, the organizers provide a training corpus with human assessments. The participants must improve their approaches and select three runs to participate. Unfortunately, we can not ensure that systems will behave similarly in both the training and test corpora. For instance, some Pearson correlations between system achievements across test corpora in this competition are: 0.61 (MSRpar-MSRvid), 0.34 (MSRvid-SMTeur), or 0.49 (MSRpar-SMTeur). Therefore, we cannot expect a high correlation between the system performance in a specific corpus and the test corpora employed in the competition.

Now, imagine that we have a *magic box* that, given a set of similarity measures, is able to predict which measures will obtain the highest correlation with human assessments without actually requiring those assessments. For instance, suppose that putting all system outputs in the magic box, we obtain a 0.94 Pearson correlation between the prediction and the system achievements according to human assessments, as in Figure 1. The horizontal axis represents the magic box ouput, and the vertical axis represents the achievement in the competition. Each dot represents one system. In this case, we could decide which system or system combination to employ for a certain test set.

Is there something like this magic box? The answer is yes. Indeed, what Figure 1 shows is the results of an unsupervised method to combine measures, the *Heterogeneity Based Ranking* (HBR). This method is grounded on a generalization of the heterogeneity property of text evaluation measures proposed in (Amigó et al., 2011), which states that the more a set of measures is heterogeneous, the

*This work has been partially funded by the Madrid government, grant MA2VICMR (S-2009/TIC- 1542), the Spanish government, grant Holopedia (TIN2010-21128-C02-01) and the European Community's Seventh Framework Programme (FP7/ 2007-2013) under grant agreement nr. 288024 (LiMoSINe project).

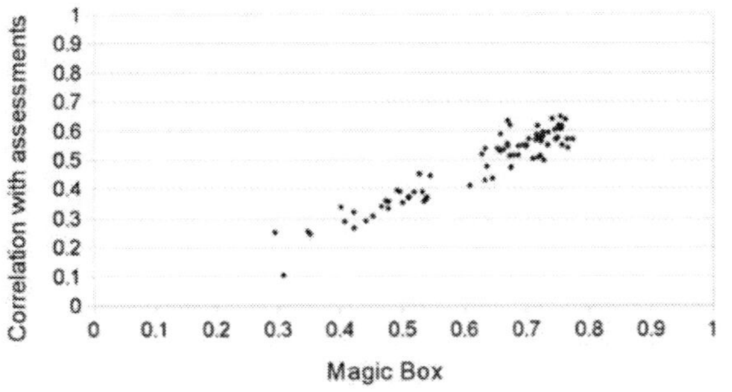

Figure 1: Correspondence between the magic box information and the (unknown) correlation with human assessments, considering all runs in the evaluation campaign.

more a score increase according to all the measures is reliable. In brief, the HBR method consists of computing the heterogeneity of the set of measures (systems) for which a similarity instance (pair of texts) improves each of the rest of similarity instances in comparison. The result is that HBR tends to achieve a similar or higher correlation with human assessments than the single measures. In order to select the most appropriate single measure, we can meta-evaluate measures in terms of correlation with HBR, which is what the previous figure showed.

We participated in the STS evaluation campaign employing HBR over automatic text evaluation measures (e.g. ROUGE (Lin, 2004)), which are not actually designed for this specific problem. For this reason our results were suboptimal. However, according to our experiments this method seem highly useful for combining and evaluating current systems. In this paper, we describe the HBR method and we present experiments employing the rest of participant methods as similarity measures.

2 Definitions

2.1 Similarity measures

In (Amigó et al., 2011) a novel definition of similarity is proposed in the context of automatic text evaluation measures. Here we extend the definition for text similarity problems in general.

Being Ω the universe of texts d, we assume that a similarity measure, is a function $x : \Omega^2 \longrightarrow \Re$ such that there exists a decomposition function $f : \Omega \longrightarrow \{e_1..e_n\}$ (e.g., words or other linguistic units or relationships) satisfying the following constraints; (i) maximum similarity is achieved only when the text decomposition resembles exactly the other text; (ii) adding one element from the second text increases the similarity; and (iii) removing one element that does not appear in the second text also increases the similarity.

$$f(d_1) = f(d_2) \leftrightarrow x(d_1, d_2) = 1$$

$$(f(d_1) = f(d'_1) \cup \{e \in f(d_2) \setminus f(d_1)\}) \\ \rightarrow x(d'_1, d_2) > x(d_1, d_2)$$

$$(f(d_1) = f(d'_1) - \{e \in f(d_1) \setminus f(d_2)\}) \\ \rightarrow x(d'_1, d_2) > x(d_1, d_2)$$

According to this definition, a random function, or the inverse of a similarity function (e.g. $\frac{1}{x(d_1 d_2)}$), do not satisfy the similarity constraints, and therefore cannot be considered as similarity measures. However, this definition covers any kind of overlapping or precision/recall measure over words, syntactic structures or semantic units, which is the case of most systems here.

Our definition assumes that measures are granulated: they decompose text in a certain amount of elements (e.g. words, grammatical tags, etc.) which are the basic representation and comparison units to estimate textual similarity.

2.2 Heterogeneity

Heterogeneity (Amigó et al., 2011) represents to what extent a set of measures differ from each other. Let us refer to a pair of texts $i = (i_1, i_2)$ with a certain degree of similarity to be computed as a *similarity instance*. Then we estimate the Heterogeneity $H(\mathcal{X})$ of a set of similarity measures $\mathcal{X}$ as the probability over similarity instances $i = (i_1, i_2)$ and $j = (j_1, j_2)$ between distinct texts, that there exist two measures in $\mathcal{X}$ that contradict each other. Formally:

$$H(\mathcal{X}) \equiv P_{\substack{i_1 \neq i_2 \\ j_1 \neq j_2}}(\exists x, x' \in \mathcal{X} | x(i) > x(j) \wedge x'(j) < x'(i))$$

where $x(i)$ stands for the similarity, according to measure x, between the texts i_1, i_2.

3 Proposal: Heterogeneity-Based Similarity Ranking

The heterogeneity property of text evaluation measures (in fact, text similarity measures to human references) introduced in (Amigó et al., 2011) states that the quality difference between two texts is lower bounded by the heterogeneity of the set of evaluation measures that corroborate the quality increase. Based on this, we define the *Heterogeneity Principle* which is applied to text similarity in general as: *the probability of a real similarity increase between random text pairs is correlated with the Heterogeneity of the set of measures that corroborate this increase:*

$$P(h(i) \geq h(j)) \sim H(\{x|x(i) \geq x(j)\})$$

where $h(i)$ is the similarity between i_1, i_2 according to human assessments (gold standard). In addition, the probability is maximal if the heterogeneity is maximal:

$$H(\{x|x(i) \geq x(j)\}) = 1 \Rightarrow P(h(i) \geq h(j)) = 1$$

The first part is derived from the fact that increasing Heterogeneity requires additional diverse measures corroborating the similarity increase. The direct relationship is the result of assuming that a similarity increase according to any aspect is always a positive evidence of true similarity. In other words, a positive match between two texts according to any feature can never be a negative evidence of similarity.

As for the second part, if the heterogeneity of a measure set is maximal, then the condition of the heterogeneity definition holds for any pair of distinct documents ($i_1 \neq i_2$ and $j_1 \neq j_2$). Given that all measures corroborate the similarity increase, the heterogeneity condition does not hold. Then, the compared texts in (i_1, i_2) are not different. Therefore, we can ensure that $P(h(i) \geq h(j)) = 1$.

The proposal in this paper consists of ranking similarity instances by estimating, for each instance i, the average probability of its texts (i_1, i_2) being closer to each other than texts in a different instance j:

$$\mathrm{R}(i) = \mathrm{Avg}_j(P(h(i) \geq h(j)))$$

Applying the heterogeneity principle we can estimate this as:

$$\mathrm{HBR}_{\mathcal{X}}(i) = \mathrm{Avg}_j(H(\{x|x(i) \geq x(j)\}))$$

We refer to this ranking function as the *Heterogeneity Based Ranking* (HBR). It satisfies three crucial properties for a measure combining function:

1. HBR is independent from measure scales and it does not require relative weighting schemes between measures. Formally, being f any strict growing function:

   $$\mathrm{HBR}_{x_1..x_n}(i) = \mathrm{HBR}_{x_1..f(x_n)}(i)$$

2. HBR is not sensitive to redundant measures:

   $$\mathrm{HBR}_{x_1..x_n}(i) = \mathrm{HBR}_{x_1..x_n,x_n}(i)$$

3. Given a large enough set of similarity instances, HBR is not sensitive to non-informative measures. Being x_r a random function such that $P(x_r(i) > x_r(j)) = \frac{1}{2}$, then:

   $$\mathrm{HBR}_{x_1..x_n}(i) \sim \mathrm{HBR}_{x_1..x_n,x_r}(i)$$

The first two properties are trivially satisfied: the $\exists$ operator in H and the score comparisons are not affected by redundant measures nor their scales properties. Regarding the third property, the heterogeneity of a set of measures plus a random function x_r is:

$$H(\mathcal{X} \cup \{x_r\}) \equiv$$

$$P_{\substack{i_1 \neq i_2 \\ j_1 \neq j_2}}(\exists x, x' \in \mathcal{X} \cup \{x_r\} | x(i) > x(j) \wedge x'(j) < x'(i)) =$$

$$H(\mathcal{X}) + (1 - H(\mathcal{X})) * \frac{1}{2} = \frac{H(\mathcal{X}) + 1}{2}$$

That is, the heterogeneity grows proportionally when including a random function. Assuming that the random function corroborates the similarity increase in a half of cases, the result is a proportional relationship between HBR and HBR with the additional measure. Note that we need to assume a large enough amount of data to avoid random effects.

4 Official Runs

We have applied the HBR method with excellent results in different tasks such as Machine Translation and Summarization evaluation measures, Information Retrieval and Document Clustering. However, we had not previously applied our method to semantic similarity. Therefore, we decided to apply directly automatic evaluation measures for Machine Translation as single similarity measures to be combined by means of HBR. We have used 64 automatic evaluation measures provided by the ASIYA Toolkit (Giménez and Màrquez, 2010)[1]. This set includes measures operating at different linguistic levels (lexical, syntactic, and semantic) and includes all popular measures (BLEU, NIST, GTM, METEOR, ROUGE, etc.) The similarity formal constraints in this set of measures is preserved by considering lexical overlap when the target linguistic elements (i.e. named entities) do not appear in the texts.

We participated with three runs. The first one consisted of selecting the best measure according to human assessments in the training corpus. It was the INIST measure (Doddington, 2002). The second run consisted of selecting the best 34 measures in the training corpus and combining them with HBR, and the last run consisted of combining all evaluation measures with HBR. The heterogeneity of measures was computed over 1000 samples of similarity instance pairs (pairs of sentences pairs) extracted from the five test sets. Similarity instances were ranked over each test set independently.

In essence, the main contribution of these runs is to corroborate that Machine Translation evaluation measures are not enough to solve this task. Our runs appear at the Mean Rank positions 42, 28 and 77. Apart of this, our results corroborate our main hypothesis: without considering human assessment or any kind of supervised tunning, combining the measures with HBR resembles the best measure (INIST) in the combined measure set. However, when including all measures the evaluation result decreases (rank 77). The reason is that some Machine Translation evaluation measures do not represent a positive evidence of semantic similarity in this corpus. Therefore, the HBR assumptions are not satisfied and the final correlation achieved is lower. In summary, our approach is suitable if we can ensure that all measures (systems) combined are at least a positive (high or low) evidence of semantic similarity.

But let us focus on the HBR behavior when combining participant measures, which are specifically designed to address this problem.

5 Experiment with Participant Systems

5.1 Combining System Outputs

We can confirm empirically in the official results that all participants runs are positive evidence of semantic similarity. That is, they achieve a correlation with human assessments higher than 0. Therefore, the conditions to apply HBR are satisfied. Our goal now is to resemble the best performance without accessing human assessments neither from the training nor the test corpora. Figure 2 illustrates the Pearson correlation (averaged across test sets) achieved by single measures (participants) and all peers combined in an unsupervised manner by HBR (black column). As the figure shows, HBR results are comparable with the best systems appearing in the ninth position. In addition, Figure 4 shows the differences over particular test sets between HBR and the best system. The figure shows that there are not consistent differences between these approaches across test beds.

The next question is why HBR is not able to improve the best system. Our intuition is that, in this test set, average quality systems do not contribute with additional information. That is, the similarity aspects that the average quality systems are able to capture are also captured by the best system.

However, the best system within the combined set is not a theoretical upper bound for HBR. We can prove it with the following experiment. We apply HBR considering only the 40 less predictive systems in the set (the rest of measures are not considered when computing HBR). Then we compare the results of HBR regarding the considered single systems. As Figure 3 shows, HBR improves substantially all single systems achieving the same result than when combining all systems (0.61). The reason is that all these systems are positive evidences but they consider partial similarity aspects. But the most important issue here is that combining the 40 less predictive systems in the evaluation campaign

[1] http://www.lsi.upc.edu/ nlp/Asiya

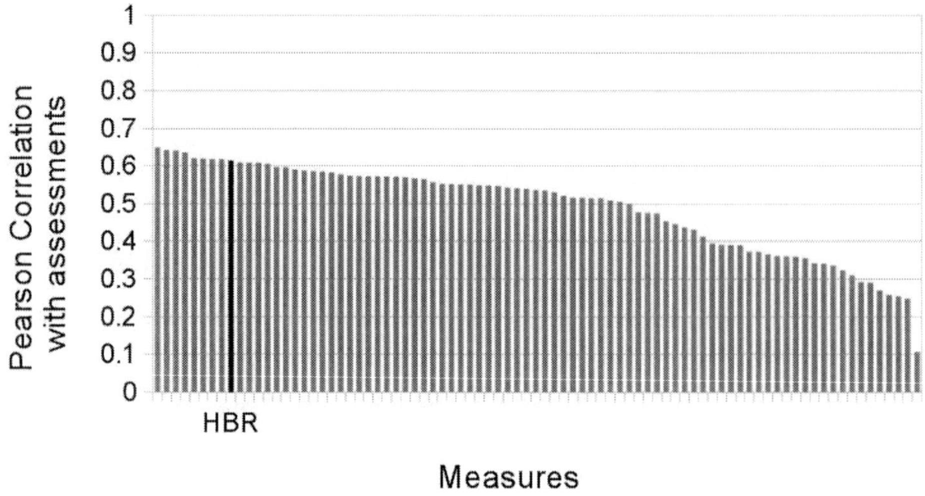

Figure 2: Measures (runs) and HBR sorted by average correlation with human assessments.

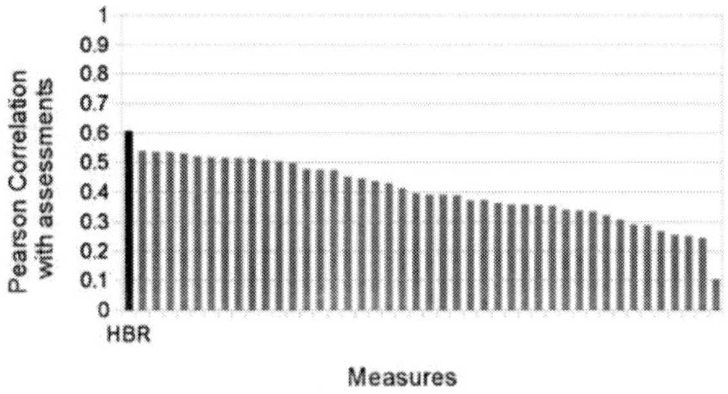

Figure 3: 40 less predictive measures (runs) and HBR sorted by average correlation with human assessments.

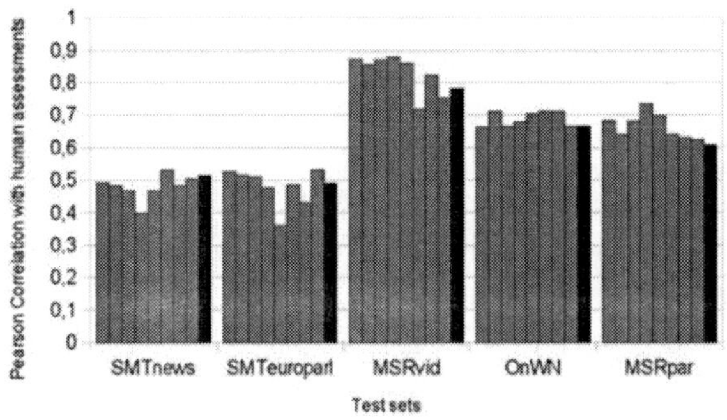

Figure 4: Average correlation with human assessments for the best runs and HBR.

is enough to achieve high final scores. This means that the drawback of these measures as a whole is not what information is employed but how this information is scaled and combined. This drawback is solved by the HBR approach.

In summary, the main conclusion that we can extract from these results is that, in the absence of human assessments, HBR ensures a high performance without the risk derived from employing potentially biased training corpora or measures based on partial similarity aspects.

6 An Unsupervised Meta-evaluation Method

But HBR has an important drawback: its computational cost, which is $\mathcal{O}(n^4 * m)$, being n the number of texts involved in the computation and m the number of measures. The reason is that computing H is quadratic with the number of texts, and the method requires to compute H for every pair of texts. In addition, HBR does not improve the best systems.

However, HBR can be employed as an unsupervised evaluation method. For this, it is enough to compute the Pearson correlation between runs and HBR. This is what Figure 1 showed at the beginning of this article. For each dot (participant run), the horizontal axis represent the correlation with HBR (magic box) and the vertical axis represent the correlation with human assessments. This graph has a Pearson correlation of 0.94 between both variables. In other words, without accessing human assessments, this method is able to predict the quality of

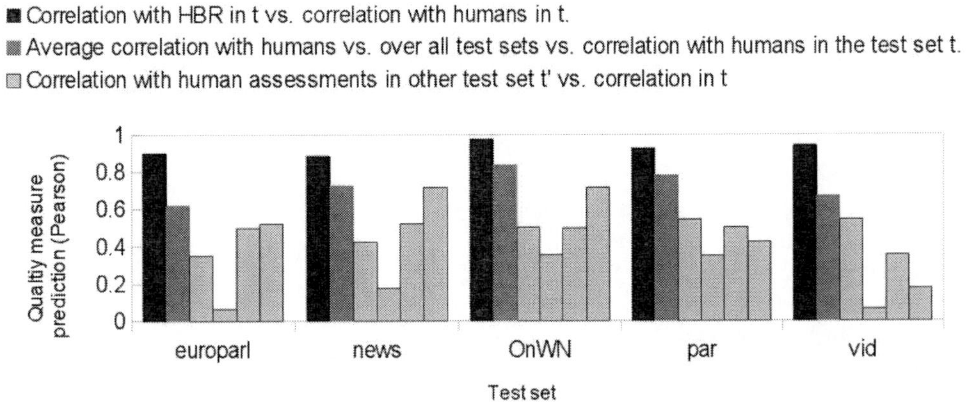

Figure 5: Predicting the quality of measures over a single test set.

textual similarity system with a 0.94 of accuracy in this test bed.

In this point, we have two options for optimizing systems. First, we can optimize measures according to the results achieved in an annotated training corpus. The other option consists of considering the correlation with HBR in the test corpus. In order to compare both approaches we have developed the following experiment. Given a test corpus t, we compute the correlation between system scores in t versus a training corpus t'. This approach emulates the scenario of training systems over a (training) set and evaluating over a different (test) set. We also compute the correlation between system scores in all corpora vs. the scores in t. Finally, we compute the correlation between system scores in t and our predictor in t (which is the correlation system/HBR across similarity instances in t). This approach emulates the use of HBR as unsupervised optimization method.

Figure 5 shows the results. The horizontal axis represents the test set t. The black columns represent the prediction over HBR in the corresponding test set. The grey columns represent the prediction by using the average correlation across test sets. The light grey columns represents the prediction using the correlation with humans in other single test set. Given that there are five test sets, the figure includes four grey columns for each test set. The figure clearly shows the superiority of HBR as measure quality predictor, even when it does not employ human assessments.

7 Conclusions

The Heterogeneity Based Ranking provides a mechanism to combine similarity measures (systems) without considering human assessments. Interestingly, the combined measure always improves or achieves similar results than the best single measure in the set. The main drawback is its computational cost. However, the correlation between single measures and HBR predicts with a high confidence the accuracy of measures regarding human assessments. Therefore, HBR is a very useful tool when optimizing systems, specially when a representative training corpus is not available. In addition, our results shed some light on the contribution of measures to the task. According to our experiments, the less reliable measures as a whole can produce reliable results if they are combined according to HBR.

The HBR software is available at http://nlp.uned.es/~enrique/

References

Enrique Amigó, Julio Gonzalo, Jesus Gimenez, and Felisa Verdejo. 2011. Corroborating text evaluation results with heterogeneous measures. In *Proceedings of the 2011 Conference on Empirical Methods in Natural Language Processing*, pages 455–466, Edinburgh, Scotland, UK., July. Association for Computational Linguistics.

George Doddington. 2002. Automatic Evaluation of Machine Translation Quality Using N-gram Co-Occurrence Statistics. In *Proceedings of the 2nd Inter-*

national Conference on Human Language Technology, pages 138–145.

Jesús Giménez and Lluís Màrquez. 2010. Asiya: An Open Toolkit for Automatic Machine Translation (Meta-)Evaluation. *The Prague Bulletin of Mathematical Linguistics*, (94):77–86.

Chin-Yew Lin. 2004. Rouge: A Package for Automatic Evaluation of Summaries. In Marie-Francine Moens and Stan Szpakowicz, editors, *Text Summarization Branches Out: Proceedings of the ACL-04 Workshop*, pages 74–81, Barcelona, Spain, July. Association for Computational Linguistics.

UTDHLT: COPACETIC System for Choosing Plausible Alternatives

Travis Goodwin, Bryan Rink, Kirk Roberts, Sanda M. Harabagiu
Human Language Technology Research Institute
University of Texas Dallas
Richardson TX, 75080
{travis,bryan,kirk,sanda}@hlt.utdallas.edu

Abstract

The Choice of Plausible Alternatives (COPA) task in SemEval-2012 presents a series of forced-choice questions wherein each question provides a premise and two viable cause or effect scenarios. The correct answer is the cause or effect that is the most plausible. This paper describes the COPACETIC system developed by the University of Texas at Dallas (UTD) for this task. We approach this task by casting it as a classification problem and using features derived from bigram co-occurrences, TimeML temporal links between events, single-word polarities from the Harvard General Inquirer, and causal syntactic dependency structures within the gigaword corpus. Additionally, we show that although each of these components improves our score for this evaluation, the difference in accuracy between using all of these features and using bigram co-occurrence information alone is not statistically significant.

1 The Problem

"The surfer caught the wave." This statement, although almost tautological for human understanding, requires a considerable depth of semantic reasoning. What is a surfer? What does it mean to "catch a wave"? How are these concepts related? What if we want to ascertain, given that the surfer caught the wave, whether the most likely next event is that "the wave carried her to the shore" or that "she paddled her board into the ocean"? This type of causal and temporal reasoning requires a breadth of world-knowledge, often called commonsense understanding.

Question 15 (Find the EFFECT)	
Premise:	I poured water on my sleeping friend.
Alternative 1:	My friend awoke.
Alternative 2:	My friend snored.

Question 379 (Find the CAUSE)	
Premise:	The man closed the umbrella.
Alternative 1:	He got out of the car.
Alternative 2:	He approached the building.

Figure 1: An example of each type of question, one targeting an effect, and another targeting a cause.

The seventh task of SemEval-2012 evaluates precisely this type of cogitation. COPA: Choice of Plausible Alternatives presents 1,000[1] sets of two-choice questions (presented as a premise and two alternatives) provided in simple English sentences. The goal for each question is to choose the most plausible cause or effect entailed by the premise (the dataset provided an equal distribution of cause and effect targetting questions). Additionally, each question is labeled so as to describe whether the answer should be a cause or an effect, as indicated in Figure 1.

The topics of these questions were drawn from two sources:

1. Randomly selected accounts of personal stories taken from a collection of Internet weblogs (Gordon and Swanson, 2009).
2. Randomly selected subject terms from the Library of Congress Thesaurus for Graphic Materials (of Congress. Prints et al., 1980).

Additionally, the incorrect alternatives were authored

[1]This data set was split into a 500 question development (or training) set and a 500 question test set.

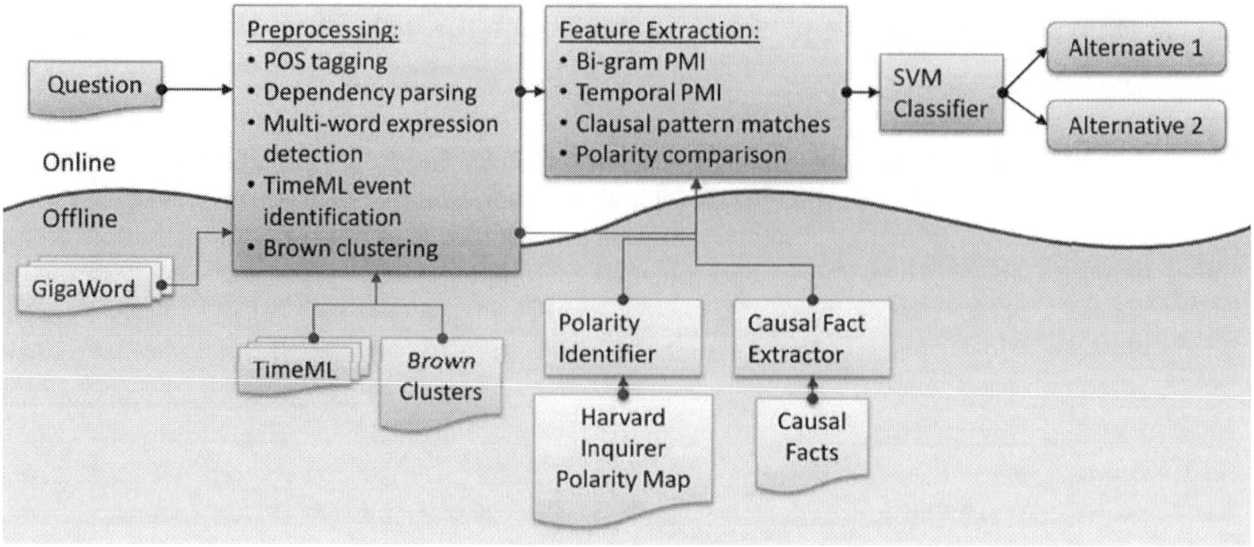

Figure 2: Architecture of the COPACETIC System

with the intent of impeding "purely associative methods" (Roemmele et al., 2011). The task aims to evaluate the state of commonsense causal reasoning (Roemmele et al., 2011).

2 System Architecture

Given a question, such as Question 15 (as shown in Figure 1), our system selects the most plausible alternative by using the output of an SVM classifier, trained on the 500 provided development questions and tested on the 500 provided test questions. The classifier operates with features describing information extracted from the processing of the question's premise and alternatives. As illustrated by Figure 2, the preprocessing involves part of speech (POS) tagging, and syntactic dependency parsing provided by the Stanford parser (Klein and Manning, 2003; Toutanova et al., 2003), multi-word expression detection using Wikipedia, automatic TimeML annotation using TARSQI (Verhagen et al., 2005; Pustejovsky et al., 2003), and Brown clustering as provided in (Turian, 2010).

The architecture of the COPACETIC system is divided into offline (independent of any question) and online (question dependent) processing. The online aspect of our system inspects each question using an SVM and selects the most likely alternative. Our system's offline functions focus on pre-processing resources so that they may be used by components of the online aspect of our system. In the next section, we describe the offline processing upon which our system is built, and in the following section, the online manner in which we evaluate each question.

2.1 Offline Processing

Because the questions presented in this task require a wealth of commonsense knowledge, we first extracted commonsense and temporal facts. This subsection describes the process of mining this information from the fourth edition of the English Gigaword corpus[2] (Parker et al., 2009).

We collected commonsense facts by extracting cause and effect pairs using twenty-four hand-crafted patterns. Rather than lexical patterns, we used patterns over syntactic dependency structures in order to capture the syntactic role each word plays. Figure 3 illuminates two examples of the dependency structures encoded by our causal patterns. Causal Pattern 1 captures all cases of causality indicated by the verb *causes*, while Causal Pattern 2 illustrates a more sophisticated pattern, in which the phrasal verb *brought on* indicates causality.

In order to extract this information, we first parsed the syntactic dependence structure of each sentence using the Stanford parser (Klein and Manning, 2003). Next, we loaded each sentence's dependence tree

[2]The LDC Catalog number of the English Gigaword Fourth Edition corpus is LDC2009T13.

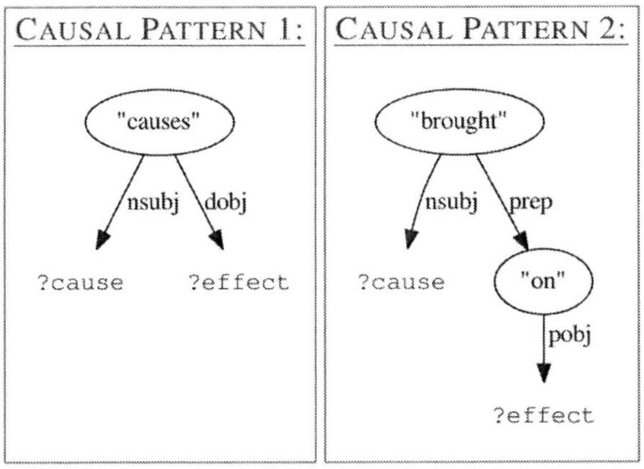

Figure 3: The dependency structures associated with the causal patterns: `?cause` "causes" `?effect`, and `?cause` "brought on" `?effect`.

into the RDF3X (Neumann and Weikum, 2008) implementation of an RDF[3] database. Then, we represented our dependency structures using in the SPARQL[4]query language and extracted cause and effect pairs by issuing SPARQL queries against the RDF3X database. We used SPARQL and RDF representations because they allowed us to easily represent and reason over graphical structures, such as those of our dependency trees.

It has been shown that causality often manifests as a temporal relation (Bethard, 2008; Bethard and Martin, 2008). The questions presented in this task are no exception: many of the alternative-premise pairs necessitate temporal understanding. For example, consider question 63 provided in Figure 4.

Question 63 (Find the EFFECT)
Premise: The man removed his coat.
Alternative 1: He entered the house.
Alternative 2: He loosened his tie.

Figure 4: Example question 63, which illustrates the necessity for temporal reasoning.

[3]The Resource Description Framework (RDF) is is a specification from the W3C. Information on RDF is available at http://www.w3.org/RDF/.

[3]The SPARQL Query Language is defined at `http://www.w3.org/TR/rdf-sparql-query/`. An examples of the `WHERE` clause for a SPARQL query associated with the *brought on* pattern from Figure 3 is provided below:

```
{  ?a   <nsubj>      ?cause ;
        <token>   "brought" ;
        <prep>          ?b .
   ?b   <token>        "on" ;
        <pobj>      ?effect .   }
```

In order to extract this temporal information, we automatically annotated our corpus with TimeML annotations using the TARSQI Toolkit (Verhagen et al., 2005). Unfortunately, the events represented in this corpus were too sparse to use directly. To mitigate this sparsity, we clustered events using the 3,200 Brown clusters[5] described in (Turian, 2010).

After all such offline processing has been completed, we incorporate the knowledge encoded by this processing in the online components of our system (online preprocessing, and feature extraction) as described in the following section.

2.2 Online Processing

We cast the task of selecting the most plausible alternative as a classification problem, using a support vector machine (SVM) supervised classifier (using a linear kernel). To this end, we pre-process each question for lexical information. We extract parts of speech (POS) and syntactic dependencies using the Stanford CoreNLP parser (Klein and Manning, 2003; Toutanova et al., 2003). Stopwords are removed using a manually curated list of one hundred and one common stopwords; non-content words (defined as words whose POS is not a noun, verb, or adjective) are also discarded. Additionally, we extract multi-word expressions (noun collocations[6] and phrasal verbs[7]). Finally, in order to utilize our offline TimeML annotations, we extract events using POS. Examples of the retained content words are underlined in Figures 5, 6, 7 and 8.

After preprocessing each question, we convert it into two premise-alternative pairs (PREMISE-ALTERNATIVE1, and PREMISE-ALTERNATIVE2). For each of these pairs, we attempt to form a bridge from the causal sentence to the effect sentence, without distinction over whether the cause or effect originated from the premise or the alternative. This bridge is provided by four measures, or features, described in the following section.

[5]These clusters are available at `http://metaoptimize.com/projects/wordreprs/`.

[6]These were detected using a list of English Wikipedia article titles available at `http://dumps.wikimedia.org/backup-index.html`.

[7]Phrasal verbs were determined using a list available at `http://www.learn-english-today.com/phrasal-verbs/phrasal-verb-list.htm`.

3 The Features of the COPACETIC System

In determining the causal relatedness between a cause and an effect sentence, we utilize four features. Each feature calculates a value indicating the perceived strength of the causal relationship between a cause and an effect using a different measure of causality. The four features used by our COPACETIC system are described in the following subsections.

3.1 Bigram Relatedness

Our first feature measures the degree of relatedness between all pairs of bigrams (at the token level) in the cause and effect pair. We do this by calculating the point-wise mutual Information (PMI) (Fano, 1961) for all bigram combinations between the candidate alternative and its premise in the English Gigaword corpus (Parker et al., 2009) as shown in Equation 1.

$$PMI(x; y) \equiv \log \frac{p(x, y)}{p(x)p(y)} \qquad (1)$$

Under the assumption that distance words are unlikely to causally influence each other, we only consider co-occurrences within a window of one hundred tokens when calculating the joint probability of the PMI. Additionally, we allow for up to two tokens to occur within a single bigram's occurrence (e.g. the phrase *pierced her ears* would be considered a match for the bigram *pierced ears*). Although these relaxations skew the values of our calculated PMIs by artificially lowering the joint probability, we are only concerned with how the values compare to each other. Note that because we employ no smoothing, the PMI of an unseen bigram is set to zero. The maximum PMI over all pairs of bigrams is retained as the value for this feature. Figure 5 illustrates this feature for Question 495.

Question 495 (Find the EFFECT)
Premise: The girl wanted to wear earrings.
Alternative 1: She got her ears pierced.
Alternative 2: She got a tattoo.

Alternative 1		Alternative 2	
PMI(wear earrings, pierced ears)	= -10.928	PMI(wear earrings, tattoo)	= -12.77
PMI(wanted wear, pierced ears)	= -13.284	PMI(wanted wear, tattoo)	= -14.284
PMI(girl wanted, pierced ears)	= -13.437	PMI(girl wanted, tattoo)	= -14.762
PMI(girl, pierced ears)	= -15.711	PMI(girl, tattoo)	= -14.859
Maximum PMI	= -10.928	Maximum PMI	= -12.77

Figure 5: Example PMI values for bigrams and unigrams (with content words underlined). Alternative 1 is correctly chosen as it has largest maxi mum PMI.

3.2 Temporal Relatedness

Although most of the questions in this task focus on causal relationships, for many questions, the nature of this causal relationship manifests instead as a temporal one (Bethard and Martin, 2008; Bethard, 2008). We use temporal link information from TimeML (Pustejovsky et al., 2005; Pustejovsky et al., 2003) annotations on our corpus to determine how temporally related a given cause and effect sentence are. This is accomplished by using the point-wise mutual information (PMI) between all pairs of events from the cause to the effect (see Equation 1). We define the relevant probabilities as follows:

- The joint probability ($P(x, y)$) of a cause and effect event is defined as the number of times the cause event participates in a temporal link ending with the effect event.
- The probability of a cause event ($P(x)$) is defined as the number of times the cause event precipitates a temporal link to any event.
- The probability of an effect event ($P(y)$) is defined as the number of times the effect event ends a temporal link begun by any event.

We define the PMI to be zero for any unseen pair of events (and for any pairs involving an unseen event). The summation of all pairs of PMIs is used as the value of this feature. Figure 6 shows how this feature behaves.

Question 468 (Find the CAUSE)
Premise: The dog barked.
Alternative 1: The cat lounged on the couch.
Alternative 2: A knock sounded at the door.

Alternative 1	Alternative 2
PMI(lounge, bark) = 5.60436	PMI(knock, bark) = 5.77867
	PMI(sound, bark) = 5.26971

Figure 6: Example temporal PMI values (with content words underlined). Alternative 2 is correctly chosen as it has the highest summation.

3.3 Causal Dependency Structures

We attempted to capture the degree of direct causal relatedness between a cause sentence and an effect sentence. To determine the strength of this relationship, we considered how often phrases from the cause and effect sentences occur within a causal dependency structure. We detect this through the use of twenty-four[8] manually crafted causal patterns (described in Section 2.1). The alternative that has the maximum number of matched dependency structures with the premise is retained as the correct choice. Figure 7 illustrates this feature.

Question 490 (Find the `EFFECT`)
Premise: The man won the lottery.
Alternative 1: He became rich.
Alternative 2: He owed money.

Alternative 1	Alternative 2
won → rich = 15	won → owed = 5

Figure 7: Example casual dependency matches (with content words underlined). Alternative 1 is correctly selected because more patterns extracted "won" causing "rich" than "won" causing "owed".

3.4 Polarity Comparison

We observed that many of the questions involve the dilemma of determining whether a positive premise is more related to a positive or negative alternative (and vice-versa). This differs from sentiment analysis in that rather than determining if a sentence expresses a negative statement or view, we instead desire the overall sentimental connotation of a sentence (and thus of each word). For example, the premise from Question 494 (Figure 8) is "the woman became famous." Although this sentence makes no positive or negative claims about the woman, the word "famous" – when considered on its own – implies positive connotations.

We capture this information using the Harvard General Inquirer (Stone et al., 1966). Originally developed in 1966, the Harvard General Inquirer provides a mapping from English words to their polarity (`POSITIVE`, or `NEGATIVE`). For example, it denotes the word "abandon" as `NEGATIVE`, and the word "abound" as `POSITIVE`. We use this information by summing the score for all words in a sentence (assigning `POSITIVE` words a score of 1.0, `NEGATIVE` words a score of -1.0, and `NEUTRAL` or unseen words a score of 0.0). The difference between these scores between the cause sentence and the effect sentence is used as the value of this feature. This feature is illustrated in Figure 8.

[8]Twenty-four patterns was deemed sufficient due to time constraints.

Question 494 (Find the `CAUSE`)
Premise: The woman became famous.
Alternative 1: Photographers followed her.
Alternative 2: Her family avoided her.

Premise		Alternative 1			Alternative 2		
famous `POSITIVE`	1.0	follow	`NEUTRAL`	0.0	avoid	`NEGATIVE`	−1.0
		photographer	`NEUTRAL`	0.0	family	`NEUTRAL`	0.0
Sum	1.0	Sum		0.0	Sum		−1.0

Figure 8: Example polarity comparison (with content words underlined). Alternative 1 is correctly chosen as it has the least difference from the score of the premise.

4 Results

The COPA task of SemEval-2012 provided participants with 1,000 causal questions, divided into 500 questions for development or training, and 500 questions for testing. We submitted two systems to the COPA Evaluation for SemEval-2012, both of which are trained on the 500 development questions. Our first system uses only the bigram PMI feature and is denoted as `bigram_pmi`. Our second system uses all four features and is denoted as `svm_combined`. The accuracy of our two systems on the 500 provided test questions is provided in Table 1 (Gordon et al., 2012). On this task, accuracy is defined as the quotient of dividing the number of questions for which the correct alternative was chosen by the number of questions. Although multiple groups registered, ours were the only submitted results. Note that the difference in performance between our two systems is not statistically significant ($p = 0.411$) (Gordon et al., 2012).

Team ID	System ID	Score
UTDHLT	`bigram_pmi`	0.618
UTDHLT	`svm_combined`	0.634

Table 1: Accuracy of submitted systems

The primary hindrance to our approach is in combining each feature – that is, determining the confidence of each feature's judgement. Because the questions vary significantly in their subject matter and the nature of the causal relationship between given causes and effects, a single approach is unlikely to satisfy all scenarios. Unfortunately, the problem of determining which feature best applies to a give question requires non-trivial reasoning over implicit semantics between the premise and alternatives.

5 Conclusion

This evaluation has shown that although commonsense causal reasoning is trivial for humans, it belies deep semantic reasoning and necessitates a breadth of world knowledge. Additional progress towards capturing world knowledge by leveraging a large number of cross-domain knowledge resources is necessary. Moreover, distilling information not specific to any domain – that is, a means of inferring basic and fundamental information about the world – is not only necessary but paramount to the success of any future system desiring to build chains of commonsense or causal reasoning. At this point, we are merely approximating such possible distillation.

6 Acknowledgements

We would like to thank the organizers of SemEval-2012 task 7 for their work constructing the dataset and overseeing the task.

References

[Bethard and Martin2008] S. Bethard and J.H. Martin. 2008. Learning semantic links from a corpus of parallel temporal and causal relations. *Proceedings of the 46th Annual Meeting of the ACL-HLT*.

[Bethard2008] S Bethard. 2008. Building a corpus of temporal-causal structure. *Proceedings of the Sixth LREC*.

[Fano1961] RM Fano. 1961. Transmission of Information: A Statistical Theory of Communication.

[Gordon and Swanson2009] A. Gordon and R. Swanson. 2009. Identifying personal stories in millions of weblog entries. In *Third International Conference on Weblogs and Social Media, Data Challenge Workshop, San Jose, CA*.

[Gordon et al.2012] Andrew Gordon, Zornitsa Kozareva, and Melissa Roemmele. 2012. (2012) SemEval-2012 Task 7: Choice of Plausible Alternatives: An Evaluation of Commonsense Causal Reasoning. In *Proceedings of the 6th International Workshop on Semantic Evaluation (SemEval 2012)*, Montreal.

[Klein and Manning2003] D. Klein and C.D. Manning. 2003. Accurate unlexicalized parsing. In *Proceedings of the 41st Annual Meeting on Association for Computational Linguistics-Volume 1*, pages 423–430. Association for Computational Linguistics.

[Neumann and Weikum2008] Thomas Neumann and Gerhard Weikum. 2008. RDF-3X: a RISC-style engine for RDF. *Proceedings of the VLDB Endowment*.

[of Congress. Prints et al.1980] Library of Congress. Prints, Photographs Division, and E.B. Parker. 1980. Subject headings used in the library of congress prints and photographs division. Prints and Photographs Division, Library of Congress.

[Parker et al.2009] Robert Parker, David Graff, Junbo Kong, Ke Chen, and Kazuaki Maeda. 2009. English Gigaword Fourth Edition.

[Pustejovsky et al.2003] J Pustejovsky, J Castano, and R Ingria. 2003. TimeML: Robust specification of event and temporal expressions in text. *AAAI Spring Symposium on New Directions in Question-Answering*.

[Pustejovsky et al.2005] J Pustejovsky, Bob Ingria, Roser Sauri, Jose Castano, Jessica Littman, Rob Gaizauskas, Andrea Setzer, G. Katz, and I. Mani. 2005. The specification language TimeML. *The Language of Time: A Reader*.

[Roemmele et al.2011] Melissa Roemmele, Cosmin Adrian Bejan, and Andrew S. Gordon. 2011. Choice of Plausible Alternatives: An Evaluation of Commonsense Causal Reasoning. *2011 AAAI Spring Symposium Series*.

[Stone et al.1966] P. J. Stone, D.C. Dunphy, and M. S. Smith. 1966. *The General Inquirer: A Computer Approach to Content Analysis*. MIT Press.

[Toutanova et al.2003] K. Toutanova, D. Klein, C.D. Manning, and Y. Singer. 2003. Feature-rich part-of-speech tagging with a cyclic dependency network. In *Proceedings of the 2003 Conference of NAACL-HLT*, pages 173–180. Association for Computational Linguistics.

[Turian2010] J Turian. 2010. Word representations: a simple and general method for semi-supervised learning. *Proceedings of the 48th Annual Meeting of the ACL*, pages 384–394.

[Verhagen et al.2005] M Verhagen, I Mani, and R Sauri. 2005. Automating Temporal Annotation with TARSQI. In *Proceedings of the ACL 2005*, pages 81–84.

HDU: Cross-lingual Textual Entailment with SMT Features

Katharina Wäschle and **Sascha Fendrich**
Department of Computational Linguistics
Heidelberg University
Heidelberg, Germany
{waeschle, fendrich}@cl.uni-heidelberg.de

Abstract

We describe the Heidelberg University system for the Cross-lingual Textual Entailment task at SemEval-2012. The system relies on features extracted with statistical machine translation methods and tools, combining monolingual and cross-lingual word alignments as well as standard textual entailment distance and bag-of-words features in a statistical learning framework. We learn separate binary classifiers for each entailment direction and combine them to obtain four entailment relations. Our system yielded the best overall score for three out of four language pairs.

1 Introduction

Cross-lingual textual entailment (CLTE) (Mehdad et al., 2010) is an extension of textual entailment (TE) (Dagan and Glickman, 2004). The task of recognizing entailment is to determine whether a hypothesis H can be semantically inferred from a text T. The CLTE task adds a cross-lingual dimension to the problem by considering sentence pairs, where T and H are in different languages. The SemEval-2012 CLTE task (Negri et al., 2012) asks participants to judge entailment pairs in four language combinations[1], defining four target entailment relations, *forward*, *backward*, *bidirectional* and *no entailment*.

We investigate this problem in a statistical learning framework, which allows us to combine cross-lingual word alignment features as well as common monolingual entailment metrics, such as bag-of-words overlap, edit distance and monolingual alignments on translations of T and H, using standard statistical machine translation (SMT) tools and resources. Our goal is to address this task without deep processing components to make it easily portable across languages. We argue that the cross-lingual entailment task can benefit from direct alignments between T and H, since a large amount of bilingual parallel data is available, which naturally models synonymy and paraphrasing across languages.

2 Related Work

With the yearly Recognizing Textual Entailment (RTE) challenge (Dagan et al., 2006), there has been a lot of work on monolingual TE. We therefore include established monolingual features in our approach, such as alignment scores (MacCartney et al., 2008), edit distance and bag-of-words lexical overlap measures (Kouylekov and Negri, 2010). So far, the only work on CLTE that we are aware of is Mehdad et al. (2010), where the problem is reduced to monolingual entailment using machine translation, and Mehdad et al. (2011), which exploits parallel corpora for generating features based on phrase alignments as input to an SVM. Our approach combines ideas from both, mostly resembling Mehdad et al. (2011). There are, however, several differences; we use word translation probabilities instead of phrase tables and model monolingual and cross-lingual alignment separately. We also include additional similarity measures derived from the MT evaluation metric Meteor, which was used in Volokh and Neumann (2011) for the monolingual TE task. Con-

[1] Spanish-English (**es-en**), Italian-English (**it-en**), French-English (**fr-en**) and German-English (**de-en**).

versely, Padó et al. (2009) showed that textual entailment features can be used for measuring MT quality, indicating a strong relatedness of the two problems.

The CLTE task is also related to the problem of identifying parallel sentence pairs in a non-parallel corpus, so we adapt alignment-based features from Munteanu and Marcu (2005), where a Maximum Entropy classifier was used to judge if two sentences are sufficiently parallel.

Regarding the view on entailment, MacCartney and Manning (2007) proposed the decomposition of top-level entailment, such as *equivalence* (which corresponds to the CLTE *bidirectional* class), into atomic forward and backward entailment predictions, which is mirrored in our multi-label approach with two binary classifiers.

3 SMT Features for CLTE

The SemEval-2012 CLTE task emerges from the monolingual RTE task; however the perception of entailment differs slightly. In CLTE, the sentences T_1 and T_2 are of roughly the same length and the entailment is predicted in both directions. Negri et al. (2011) states that the CLTE pairs were created by paraphrasing an English sentence E and leaving out or adding information to construct a modified sentence E', which was then translated into a different language[2], yielding sentence F and thus creating a bilingual entailment pair. For this reason, we believe that our system should be less inference-oriented than some previous RTE systems and rather should capture

- paraphrases and synonymy to identify semantic equivalence,
- phrases that have no matching correspondent in the other sentence, indicating missing (respectively, additional) information.

To this end, we define a number of similarity metrics based on different views on the data pairs, which we combine as features in a statistical learning framework. Our features are both cross- and monolingual. We obtain monolingual pairs by translating the English sentence E into the foreign language, yielding $T(E)$ and vice versa $T(F)$ from F, using Google Translate[3].

3.1 Token ratio features

A first indicator for additional or missing information are simple token ratio features, i.e. the fraction of the number of tokens in T_1 and T_2. We define three token ratio measures:

- English-to-Foreign, $\frac{|E|}{|F|}$
- English-to-English-Translation, $\frac{|E|}{|T(F)|}$
- Foreign-to-Foreign-Translation, $\frac{|T(E)|}{|F|}$

3.2 Bag-of-words and distance features

Typical similarity measures used in monolingual TE are lexical overlap metrics, computed on bag-of-words representations of both sentences. We use the following similarities, computing both $\mathrm{sim}(E, T(F))$ and $\mathrm{sim}(F, T(E))$.

- Jaccard coefficient, $\mathrm{sim}(A, B) = \frac{|A \cap B|}{|A \cup B|}$
- Overlap coefficient, $\mathrm{sim}(A, B) = \frac{|A \cap B|}{\min(|A|,|B|)}$

We also compute the lexical overlap on bigrams and trigrams.

In addition, we include a simple distance measure based on string edit distance ed, summing up over all distances between every token a in A and its most similar token b in B, where we assume that the corresponding token is the one with the smallest edit distance:

- $\mathrm{dist}(A, B) = \log \sum_{a \in A} \min_{b \in B} \mathrm{ed}(a, b)$

3.3 Meteor features

The Meteor scoring tool (Denkowski and Lavie, 2011) for evaluating the output of statistical machine translation systems can be used to calculate the similarity of two sentences in the same language. Meteor uses stemming, paraphrase tables and synonym collections to align words between the two sentences and scores the resulting alignment. We include the overall weighted Meteor score both for $(E, T(F))$

[2]We refer to the non-English language sentence as F.

[3]http://translate.google.com/

and $(F, T(E))$[4] as well as separate alignment precision, recall and fragmentation scores for $(E, T(F))$.

3.4 Monolingual alignment features

We use the alignments output by the Meteor-1.3 scorer for $(E, T(F))$[5] to calculate the following metrics:

- number of unaligned words
- percentage of aligned words
- length of the longest unaligned subsequence

3.5 Cross-lingual alignment features

We calculate IBM model 1 word alignments (Brown et al., 1993) with GIZA++ (Och and Ney, 2003) on a data set concatenated from Europarl-v6[6] (Koehn, 2005) and a bilingual dictionary obtained from dict.cc[7] for coverage. We then heuristically align each word e in E with the word f in F for which we find the highest word translation probability $p(e|f)$ and vice versa. Words for which no translation is found are considered unaligned. From this alignment a, we derive the following features both for E and F (resulting in a total of eight cross-lingual alignment features):

- number of unaligned words
- percentage of aligned words
- alignment score $\frac{1}{|E|} \sum_{e \in E} p(e|a(e))$
- length of the longest unaligned subsequence

4 Classification

To account for the different data ranges, we normalized all feature value distributions to the normal distribution $\mathcal{N}(0, \frac{1}{3})$, so that 99% of the feature values are in $[-1, 1]$. We employed SVM^{light} (Joachims, 1999) for learning different classifiers to output the four entailment classes. We submitted a second run to evaluate our recently implemented stochastic learning toolkit Sol (Fendrich, 2012), which implements binary, multi-class, and multi-label classification.

For development, we split the training set in two parts, which were alternatingly used as training and test set. We first experimented with a multi-class classifier that learned all four entailment classes at once. However, although the task defines four target entailment relations, those can be broken down into two atomic relations, namely directional entailment from T_1 to T_2 and from T_2 to T_1 (table 1). We therefore learned a binary classifier for each atomic entailment relation and combined the output to obtain the final entailment class. We found this view to be a much better fit for the problem, improving the accuracy score on the development set by more than 10 percentage points (table 2). This two-classifiers approach can also be seen as a variant of multi-label learning, with the two atomic entailment relations as labels. We therefore also trained a direct implementation of multi-label classification. Although it substantially outperformed the multi-class approach, the system yielded considerably lower scores than the version using two binary classifiers.

$T_1 \rightarrow T_2$	$T_2 \rightarrow T_1$	**entailment**
1	1	*bidirectional*
1	0	*forward*
0	1	*backward*
0	0	*no entailment*

Table 1: Combination of atomic entailment relations.

5 Results

The accuracy scores of our two runs on the SemEval-2012 CLTE test set are presented in table 3. Our system performed best out of ten systems for the language pairs **es-en** and **de-en** and tied in first place for **fr-en**. For **it-en**, our system came in second. Regarding the choice of the learner, our toolkit slightly outperformed SVM^{light} on three of the four language pairs.

To determine the contribution of different feature types for each language combination, we performed ablation tests on the development set, where we switched off groups of features and measured the

[4]Meteor-1.3 supports English, Spanish, French and German. We used the Spanish version for scoring Italian, since those languages are related.

[5]Since the synonymy module is only available for English, we do not use the alignment of $(F, T(E))$.

[6]http://www.statmt.org/europarl/

[7]http://www.dict.cc/

	es-en	it-en	fr-en	de-en
multi-class	0.47	0.456	0.466	0.458
multi-label	0.586	0.526	0.568	0.522
2× binary	0.646	0.614	0.628	0.588

Table 2: Different classifiers on development set.

	es-en	it-en	fr-en	de-en
SVM^{light}	0.630	0.554	0.564	0.558
Sol	0.632	0.562	0.570	0.552

Table 3: Results on test set.

impact on the accuracy score (table 4). We assessed the statistical significance of differences in score with an approximate randomization test[8] (Noreen, 1989), indicating a significant impact in **bold font**. The results show that only in two cases a single feature group significantly impacts the score, namely the Meteor score features for **es-en** and the cross-lingual alignment features for **de-en**. However, no feature group hurts the score either, since negative variations in score are not significant. To ensure that the different feature groups actually express diverse information, we also evaluated our system using only one group of features at a time. The results confirm the most significant feature type for each language pair, but even the best-scoring feature group for each pair always yielded scores 3-6 percentage points lower than the system with all feature groups combined. We therefore conclude that the combination of diverse features is one key aspect of our system.

[8]Using a significance level of 0.05.

6 Conclusions

We have shown that SMT methods can be profitably applied for the problem of CLTE and that combining different feature types improves accuracy. Key to our approach is furthermore the view of the four-class entailment problem as a bidirectional binary or multi-label problem. A possible explanation for the superior performance of the multi-label approach is that the overlap of the bidirectional entailment with forward and backward entailment might confuse the multi-class learner.

Regarding future work, we think that our results can be improved by building on better alignments, i.e. using more data for estimating cross-lingual alignments and larger paraphrase tables. Furthermore, we would like to investigate more thoroughly in what way the representation of the problem in terms of machine learning impacts the system performance on the task – in particular, why the two-classifiers approach substantially outperforms the multi-label implementation.

References

Peter F. Brown, Vincent J. Della Pietra, Stephen A. Della Pietra, and Robert L. Mercer. 1993. The mathematics of statistical machine translation: Parameter estimation. *Computational linguistics*, 19(2):263–311.

Ido Dagan and Oren Glickman. 2004. Probabilistic textual entailment: Generic applied modeling of language variability.

Ido Dagan, Oren Glickman, and Bernado Magnini. 2006. The pascal recognising textual entailment challenge. *Machine Learning Challenges. Evaluating Predictive Uncertainty, Visual Object Classification, and Recognising Tectual Entailment*, pages 177–190.

Michael Denkowski and Alon Lavie. 2011. Meteor 1.3:

	es-en		it-en		fr-en		de-en	
feature group (#/features)	score	impact	score	impact	score	impact	score	impact
Meteor scores (5)	0.616	**0.03**	0.6	0.014	0.618	0.01	0.59	-0.002
distance/bow (10)	0.644	0.002	0.608	0.006	0.62	0.008	0.596	-0.008
token ratio (3)	0.652	-0.006	0.606	0.008	0.62	0.008	0.588	0
cross-lingual alignment (8)	0.638	0.008	0.592	0.022	0.62	0.008	0.526	**0.062**
monolingual alignment (3)	0.648	-0.002	0.624	-0.01	0.59	0.038	0.596	-0.008
all (29)	0.646		0.614		0.628		0.588	

Table 4: Ablation tests on development set.

Automatic Metric for Reliable Optimization and Evaluation of Machine Translation Systems. In *Proceedings of the EMNLP 2011 Workshop on Statistical Machine Translation*.

Sascha Fendrich. 2012. Sol – Stochastic Learning Toolkit. Technical report, Department of Computational Linguistics, Heidelberg University.

Thorsten Joachims. 1999. Making large-scale SVM learning practical. *Advances in Kernel Methods Support Vector Learning*, pages 169–184.

Philipp Koehn. 2005. Europarl: A parallel corpus for statistical machine translation. In *MT summit*, volume 5.

Milen Kouylekov and Matteo Negri. 2010. An open-source package for recognizing textual entailment. In *Proceedings of the ACL 2010 System Demonstrations*, pages 42–47.

Bill MacCartney and Christopher D. Manning. 2007. Natural logic for textual inference. In *Proceedings of the ACL-PASCAL Workshop on Textual Entailment and Paraphrasing*, pages 193–200.

Bill MacCartney, Michel Galley, and Christopher D. Manning. 2008. A phrase-based alignment model for natural language inference. In *Proceedings of the Conference on Empirical Methods in Natural Language Processing*, pages 802–811.

Yashar Mehdad, Matteo Negri, and Marcello Federico. 2010. Towards cross-lingual textual entailment. In *Human Language Technologies: The 2010 Annual Conference of the North American Chapter of the Association for Computational Linguistics*, pages 321–324.

Yashar Mehdad, Matteo Negri, and Marcello Federico. 2011. Using bilingual parallel corpora for cross-lingual textual entailment. *Proceedings of ACL-HLT*.

Dragos Stefan Munteanu and Daniel Marcu. 2005. Improving machine translation performance by exploiting non-parallel corpora. *Computational Linguistics*, 31(4):477–504.

Matteo Negri, Luisa Bentivogli, Yashar Mehdad, Danilo Giampiccolo, and Alessandro Marchetti. 2011. Divide and conquer: crowdsourcing the creation of cross-lingual textual entailment corpora. In *Proceedings of the Conference on Empirical Methods in Natural Language Processing*, pages 670–679.

Matteo Negri, Alessandro Marchetti, Yashar Mehdad, Luisa Bentivogli, and Danilo Giampiccolo. 2012. Semeval-2012 Task 8: Cross-lingual Textual Entailment for Content Synchronization. In *Proceedings of the 6th International Workshop on Semantic Evaluation (SemEval 2012)*.

Eric W. Noreen. 1989. *Computer Intensive Methods for Testing Hypotheses. An Introduction.* Wiley, New York.

Franz Josef Och and Hermann Ney. 2003. A systematic comparison of various statistical alignment models. *Computational linguistics*, 29(1):19–51.

Sebastian Padó, Daniel Cer, Michel Galley, Dan Jurafsky, and Christopher D. Manning. 2009. Measuring machine translation quality as semantic equivalence: A metric based on entailment features. *Machine Translation*, 23(2):181–193.

Alexander Volokh and Günter Neumann. 2011. Using MT-based metrics for RTE. In *The Fourth Text Analysis Conference*. NIST.

UAlacant: Using Online Machine Translation for Cross-Lingual Textual Entailment

Miquel Esplà-Gomis and **Felipe Sánchez-Martínez** and **Mikel L. Forcada**
Departament de Llenguatges i Sistemes Informàtics
Universitat d'Alacant, E-03071 Alacant, Spain
{mespla, fsanchez, mlf}@dlsi.ua.es

Abstract

This paper describes a new method for cross-lingual textual entailment (CLTE) detection based on machine translation (MT). We use sub-segment translations from different MT systems available online as a source of cross-lingual knowledge. In this work we describe and evaluate different features derived from these sub-segment translations, which are used by a support vector machine classifier to detect CLTEs. We presented this system to the SemEval 2012 task 8 obtaining an accuracy up to 59.8% on the English–Spanish test set, the second best performing approach in the contest.

1 Introduction

Cross-lingual textual entailment (CLTE) detection (Mehdad et al., 2010) is an extension of the textual entailment (TE) detection (Dagan et al., 2006) problem. TE detection consists of finding out, for two text fragments T and H in the same language, whether T entails H from a semantic point of view or not. CLTE presents a similar problem, but with T and H written in different languages.

During the last years, many authors have focused on resolving TE detection, as solutions to this problem have proved to be useful in many natural language processing tasks, such as question answering (Harabagiu and Hickl, 2006) or machine translation (MT) (Mirkin et al., 2009; Padó et al., 2009). Therefore, CLTE may also be useful for related tasks in which more than one language is involved, such as cross-lingual question answering or cross-lingual information retrieval. Although CLTE detection is a relatively new problem, it has already been tackled. Mehdad et al. (2010) propose to use machine translation (MT) to translate H from L_H, the language of H, into L_T, the language of T, and then use any of the state-of-the-art TE approaches. In a later work (Mehdad et al., 2011), the authors use MT, but in a more elaborate way. They train a phrase-based statistical MT (PBSMT) system (Koehn et al., 2003) translating from L_H to L_T, and use the translation table obtained as a by-product of the training process to extract a set of features which are processed by a support vector machine classifier (Theodoridis and Koutroumbas, 2009, Sect. 3.7) to decide whether T entails H or not. Castillo (2011) discusses another machine learning approach in which the features are obtained from semantic similarity measures based on WordNet (Miller, 1995).

In this work we present a new approach to tackle the problem of CLTE detection using a machine learning approach, partly inspired by that of Mehdad et al. (2011). Our method uses MT as a source of information to detect semantic relationships between T and H. To do so, we firstly split both T and H into all the possible sub-segments with lengths between 1 and L, the maximum length, measured in words. We then translate the set of sub-segments from T into L_H, and vice versa, and collect all the sub-segment pairs in a single set. We claim that when T-side sub-segments match T and their corresponding H-side sub-segments match H, this reveals a semantic relationship between them, which can be used to determine whether T entails H or not. Note that MT is used as a *black box*, i.e. sub-segment translations may be collected from any MT system, and that our approach could even use any other sources of bilingual sub-sentential information. It is even possible to combine different MT systems as we do in our experiments. This is a key point of our work, since it uses MT in a more elaborate way than Mehdad et al. (2010), and it does not depend on a specific MT approach. Another important difference between this work and that of Mehdad et al. (2011) is the set of features used for classification.

The paper is organized as follows: Section 2 describes the method used to collect the MT information and obtain the features; Section 3 explains the experimental framework; Section 4 shows the results obtained for the different features combination proposed; the paper ends with concluding remarks.

2 Features from machine translation

Our approach uses MT as a *black box* to detect parallelisms between the text fragments T and H by following these steps:

1. T is segmented in all possible sub-segments t_m^{m+p-1} of length p with $1 \leq p \leq L$ and $1 \leq m \leq |T| - p + 1$, where L is the maximum sub-segment length allowed. Analogously, H is segmented to get all the possible sub-segments h_n^{n+q-1} of length q, with $1 \leq q \leq L$ and $1 \leq n \leq |T| - q + 1$.
2. The sub-segments obtained from T are translated using all the available MT systems into L_H. Analogously, the sub-segments from H are translated into L_T, to generate a set of sub-segment pairs (t, h).
3. Those pairs of sub-segments (t, h) such that t is a sub-string of T and h is a sub-string of H are annotated as sub-segment links.

Note that it could be possible to use statistical MT to translate both T and H and then use word alignments to obtain the sub-segment links. However, we use this methodology to ensure that any kind of MT system can be used by our approach. As a result of this process, a sub-segment in T may be linked to more than one sub-segment in H, and vice versa. Based on these sub-segment links we have designed a set of features which may be used by a classifier for CLTE.

2.1 Basic features [Bas]

We used a set of basic features to represent the information from the sub-segment links between T and H, which are computed as the fraction of words in each of them covered by linked sub-segments of length $l \in [1, L]$. We define the feature function $F_l(S)$, applied on a text fragment S (either T or H) as:

$$F_l(S) = \text{Cov}(S, l)/|S|$$

where $\text{Cov}(S, l)$ is a function which obtains the number of words in S covered by at least one sub-segment of length l which is part of a sub-segment link. An additional feature is computed to represent the total proportion of words in each text fragment:

$$F_{\text{total}}(S) = \text{Cov}(S, *)/|S|$$

where $\text{Cov}(S, *)$ is the same as $\text{Cov}(S, l)$ but using sub-segments of any length up to L. $F_{\text{total}}(S)$ provide information about overlapping that $F_l(S)$ cannot grasp. For instance, if we have $F_1(T) = 0.5$ and $F_2(T) = 0.5$, we cannot know if the sub-segments of $l = 1$ and $l = 2$ are covering the same or different words, so $F_{\text{total}}(S)$ represents the actual proportion of words covered in a text fragment S. These feature functions are applied both on T and H, thus obtaining a set of $2 * L + 2$ features, henceforth Bas.

2.2 Extensions to the basic features

Some extensions can be made to the basic features defined above by using additional external resources. In this section we propose two extensions.

Separate analysis of function words and content words [Spl]. In this case, features represent, separately, function words, with poor lexical information, and content words, with richer lexical and semantic information. In this way, $F_l(S)$ is divided into $\text{FF}_l(S)$ and $\text{CF}_l(S)$ defined as:

$$\text{FF}_l(S) = \text{Cov}_\text{F}(S, l)/|\text{FW}(S)|$$

and

$$\text{CF}_l(S) = \text{Cov}_\text{C}(S, l)/|\text{CW}(S)|$$

where $\text{FW}(S)$ is a function that returns the function words in text fragment S and $\text{CW}(S)$ performs the same task for content words. Analogously, $\text{Cov}_\text{F}(S, l)$ and $\text{Cov}_\text{C}(S, l)$ are versions of $\text{Cov}(S, l)$ which only consider function and content words, respectively. This extension can be also be applied to $F_{\text{total}}(T)$ and $F_{\text{total}}(H)$. The set of $4L + 4$ features obtained in this way (henceforth Spl) allows the classifier to use the information from the most relevant words in T and H to detect entailment.

Stemming [Stm and SplStm]. Stemming can also be used when detecting the sub-segment links. Both the table of sub-segment pairs and the text fragment pair (T,H) are stemmed before matching. In this way, conflicts of number or gender disagreement in the translations can be overcome in order to detect more sub-segment links. This new extension can be applied both to Bas, obtaining the set of features Stm, and to Spl, obtaining the set of features SplStm. Although lemmatization could have been used, stemming was preferred because it does not require the part-of-speech ambiguity to be solved, which may be difficult to solve when dealing with very short sub-segments.

2.3 Additional features

Two additional features were defined unrelated with the basic features proposed. The first one, called here R, is the length ratio $|T|/|H|$. Intuitively we can guess that if H is much longer than T it is unlikely that T entails H.

The second additional set of features is the one defined by Mehdad et al. (2011), so we will refer to it as M. The corresponding feature function computes, for the total number of sub-segments of a given length $l \in [1, L]$ obtained from a text fragment S, the fraction of them which appear in a sub-segment link. It is applied both to H and T and is defined as:

$$F'_l(S) = \text{Linked}_l(S)/(|S| - l + 1)$$

where Linked_l is the number of sub-segments from S with length l which appear in a sub-segment link.

3 Experimental settings

The experiments designed for this task are aimed at evaluating the features proposed in Section 2. We evaluate our CLTE approach using the English–Spanish data sets provided in the task 8 of SemEval 2012 (Negri et al., 2012).

Datasets. Two datasets were provided by the organization of SemEval 2012 (Negri et al., 2011): a training set and a test set, both composed by a set of 500 pairs of sentences. CLTE detection is evaluated in both directions, so instances belong to one of these four classes: forward (the sentence in Spanish entails the one in English); backward (the sentence in English entails the one in Spanish); bidirectional (both sentences entail each other); and no entailment (neither of the sentences entails each other).

For the whole data set, both sentences in each instance were tokenized using the scripts[1] included in the Moses MT system (Koehn et al., 2007). Each sentence was segmented to get all possible sub-segments which were then translated into the other language.

External resources. We used three different MT systems to translate the sub-segments from English to Spanish, and vice versa:

- *Apertium*:[2] a free/open-source platform for the development of rule-based MT systems (Forcada et al., 2011). We used the English–Spanish MT system from the project's repository[3] (revision 34706).
- *Google Translate*:[4] an online MT system by Google Inc.
- *Microsoft Translator*:[5] an online MT system by Microsoft.

External resources were also used for the extended features described in Section 2.2. We used the stemmer[6] and the stopwords list provided by the SnowBall project for Spanish[7] and English.[8]

Classifier. We used the implementation of support vector machine included in the WEKA v.3.6.6 data mining software package (Hall et al., 2009) for multiclass classification, and a polynomial kernel.

4 Results and discussion

We tried the different features proposed in Section 2 in isolation, and also different combinations of them. Table 1 reports the accuracy for the different features described in Section 2 on the test set using sub-segments with lengths up to $L = 6$.[9]

[1] http://bit.ly/H4LNux
[2] http://www.apertium.org
[3] http://bit.ly/HCbn8a
[4] http://translate.google.com
[5] http://www.microsofttranslator.com
[6] http://bit.ly/H2HU97
[7] http://bit.ly/JMybmL
[8] http://bit.ly/Iwg9Vm
[9] All the results in this section are computed with $L = 6$, which proved to be the value providing the best accuracy for the dataset available after trying different values of L.

	Bas ∪ Spl ∪ Stm ∪ SplStm ∪ M ∪ R				Bas ∪ Spl ∪ M ∪ R			
	Apertium		**Ap.+Go.+Mi.**		**Apertium**		**Ap.+Go.+Mi.**	
	P	**R**	**P**	**R**	**P**	**R**	**P**	**R**
Backward	64.3%	64.8%	64.5%	72.8%	59.1%	64.8%	57.3%	60.0%
Forward	65.5%	57.6%	68.9 %	56.8%	59.8%	56.0%	58.7%	59.2%
Bidirectional	57.7%	56.8%	56.6%	55.2%	43.7%	41.6%	42.5%	40.8%
No-entailment	47.5%	53.6%	50.7%	54.4%	42.5%	43.2%	44.7%	44.0%
Accuracy	58.2%		59.8%		51.4%		51.0%	

Table 2: Precision (P) and recall (R) obtained by our approach for each of the four entailment classes and total accuracy on the English–Spanish test set using different feature combinations and different MT systems: Apertium, and a combination of Apertium, Google Translate, and Microsoft Translator (Ap.+Go.+Mi.).

Feature set	N_f	**Accuracy**
Bas	14	50.0%
Spl	28	56.0%
Stm	14	49.6%
SplStm	28	56.8%
R	1	45.8%
M	12	47.0%
Bas ∪ Spl	42	56.6%
Bas ∪ Stm	28	51.0%
Bas ∪ Spl ∪ Stm ∪ SplStm	84	57.4%
Bas ∪ Spl ∪ M ∪ R	41	58.2%
Bas ∪ Spl ∪ Stm ∪ ∪ SplStm ∪ M ∪ R	97	**59.8%**

Table 1: Accuracy obtained by the system using the different feature sets proposed in Section 2 for the test set. N_f is the number of features.

As can be seen, the features providing the best results on accuracy are the SplStm features. In addition, results show that all versions of the basic features (Bas, Spl, Stm, and SplStm) provide better results than the M feature alone. Some combinations of features are also reported in Table 1. Although many combinations were tried, we only report the results of the combinations of features performing best because of lack of space.

As can be seen, both feature combinations Bas ∪ Spl and Bas ∪ Stm obtain higher accuracy than the separated features. Combining all these features Bas ∪ Spl ∪ Stm ∪ SplStm provide even better results, thus confirming some degree of orthogonality between them. Combination Bas ∪ Spl ∪ M ∪ R obtains one of the best results, since it produces an improvement of almost 1% over combination Bas ∪ Spl ∪ Stm ∪ SplStm but using less than a half of features. Combining all the features provides the best accuracy as expected, so this seems to be the best combination for the task.

Table 2 reports the results sent for the SemEval 2012 task 8. We chose feature combinations Bas ∪ Spl ∪ M ∪ R and Bas ∪ Spl ∪ Stm ∪ SplStm ∪ M ∪ R since they are the best performing combinations. We sent two runs of our method using all three MT systems described in Section 3 and two more runs using only sub-segment translations from Apertium.

From the ten teams presenting systems for the contest, only one overcomes our best result. Even the results obtained using Apertium as the only MT system overcome seven of the ten approaches presented. This result confirms that state-of-the-art MT is a rich source of information for CLTE detection.

5 Concluding remarks

In this paper we have described a new method for CLTE detection which uses MT as a black-box source of bilingual information. We experimented with different features which were evaluated with the datasets for task 8 of SemEval 2012. We obtained up to 59.8% of accuracy on the Spanish–English test set provided, becoming the second best performing approach of the contest. As future works, we are now preparing experiments for other pairs of languages and we plan to use weights to promote those translations coming from more-reliable MT systems.

Acknowledgements: Work supported by the Spanish government through project TIN2009-14009-C02-01 and by Universitat d'Alacant through project GRE11-20. Google Translate service provided by the *University Research Program for Google Translate*. We thank M. Negri, Y. Mehdad, and M. Federico for encouraging us to participate in SemEval 2012.

References

Julio J. Castillo. 2011. A WordNet-based semantic approach to textual entailment and cross-lingual textual entailment. *International Journal of Machine Learning and Cybernetics*, 2(3):177–189.

Ido Dagan, Oren Glickman, and Bernardo Magnini. 2006. The PASCAL recognising textual entailment challenge. In *Machine Learning Challenges. Evaluating Predictive Uncertainty, Visual Object Classification, and Recognising Tectual Entailment*, volume 3944 of *Lecture Notes in Computer Science*, pages 177–190. Springer Berlin / Heidelberg.

Mikel Forcada, Mireia Ginestí-Rosell, Jacob Nordfalk, Jim O'Regan, Sergio Ortiz-Rojas, Juan Pérez-Ortiz, Felipe Sánchez-Martínez, Gema Ramírez-Sánchez, and Francis Tyers. 2011. Apertium: a free/open-source platform for rule-based machine translation. *Machine Translation*, 25(2):127–144.

Mark Hall, Eibe Frank, Geoffrey Holmes, Bernhard Pfahringer, Peter Reutemann, and Ian H. Witten. 2009. The WEKA data mining software: an update. *SIGKDD Explorations Newsletter*, 11(1):10–18.

Sanda Harabagiu and Andrew Hickl. 2006. Methods for using textual entailment in open-domain question answering. In *Proceedings of the 21st International Conference on Computational Linguistics and the 44th Annual Meeting of the Association for Computational Linguistics*, pages 905–912, Sydney, Australia.

Philipp Koehn, Franz J. Och, and Daniel Marcu. 2003. Statistical phrase-based translation. In *Proceedings of the 2003 Conference of the North American Chapter of the Association for Computational Linguistics on Human Language Technology*, pages 48–54, Edmonton, Canada.

Philipp Koehn, Hieu Hoang, Alexandra Birch, Chris Callison-Burch, Marcello Federico, Nicola Bertoldi, Brooke Cowan, Wade Shen, Christine Moran, Richard Zens, Chris Dyer, Ondřej Bojar, Alexandra Constantin, and Evan Herbst. 2007. Moses: open source toolkit for statistical machine translation. In *Proceedings of the 45th Annual Meeting of the ACL*, pages 177–180, Prague, Czech Republic.

Yashar Mehdad, Matteo Negri, and Marcello Federico. 2010. Towards cross-lingual textual entailment. In *Human Language Technologies: The 11th Annual Conference of the North American Chapter of the Association for Computational Linguistics*, pages 321–324, Los Angeles, USA.

Yashar Mehdad, Matteo Negri, and Marcello Federico. 2011. Using bilingual parallel corpora for cross-lingual textual entailment. In *Proceedings of the 49th Annual Meeting of the Association for Computational Linguistics: Human Language Technologies*, pages 1336–1345, Portland, Oregon.

George A. Miller. 1995. WordNet: a lexical database for english. *Communications of the ACM*, 38(11):39–41.

Shachar Mirkin, Lucia Specia, Nicola Cancedda, Ido Dagan, Marc Dymetman, and Idan Szpektor. 2009. Source-language entailment modeling for translating unknown terms. In *Proceedings of the Joint Conference of the 47th Annual Meeting of the ACL and the 4th International Joint Conference on Natural Language Processing of the Asian Federation of Natural Language Processing*, pages 791–799, Suntec, Singapore.

Matteo Negri, Luisa Bentivogli, Yashar Mehdad, Danilo Giampiccolo, and Alessandro Marchetti. 2011. Divide and conquer: crowdsourcing the creation of cross-lingual textual entailment corpora. In *Proceedings of the Conference on Empirical Methods in Natural Language Processing*, pages 670–679, Edinburgh, United Kingdom.

Matteo Negri, Alessandro Marchetti, Yashar Mehdad, Luisa Bentivogli, and D. Giampiccolo. 2012. Semeval-2012 Task 8: Cross-lingual Textual Entailment for Content Synchronization. In *Proceedings of the 6th International Workshop on Semantic Evaluation (SemEval 2012)*.

Sebastian Padó, Michel Galley, Dan Jurafsky, and Chris Manning. 2009. Robust machine translation evaluation with entailment features. In *Proceedings of the Joint Conference of the 47th Annual Meeting of the ACL and the 4th International Joint Conference on Natural Language Processing of the Asian Federation of Natural Language Processing*, pages 297–305, Suntec, Singapore.

Sergios Theodoridis and Konstantinos Koutroumbas. 2009. *Pattern Recognition*. Elsevier, 4th edition.

UOW-SHEF: SimpLex – Lexical Simplicity Ranking based on Contextual and Psycholinguistic Features

Sujay Kumar Jauhar
Research Group in Computational Linguistics
University of Wolverhampton
Stafford Street, Wolverhampton
WV1 1SB, UK
Sujay.KumarJauhar@wlv.ac.uk

Lucia Specia
Department of Computer Science
University of Sheffield
Regent Court, 211 Portobello
Sheffield, S1 4DP, UK
L.Specia@dcs.shef.ac.uk

Abstract

This paper describes SimpLex,[1] a Lexical Simplification system that participated in the English Lexical Simplification shared task at SemEval-2012. It operates on the basis of a linear weighted ranking function composed of context sensitive and psycholinguistic features. The system outperforms a very strong baseline, and ranked first on the shared task.

1 Introduction

Lexical Simplification revolves around replacing words by their simplest synonym in a context aware fashion. It is similar in many respects to the task of Lexical Substitution (McCarthy and Navigli, 2007) in that it involves elements of selectional preference on the basis of a central predefined criterion (simplicity in the current case), as well as sensitivity to context.

Lexical Simplification envisages principally a human target audience, and can greatly benefit children, second language learners, people with low literacy levels or cognitive disabilities, and in general facilitate the dissemination of knowledge to wider audiences.

We experimented with a number of features that we posited might be inherently linked with textual simplicity and selected the three that seemed the most promising on an evaluation with the trial dataset. These include contextual and psycholinguistic components. When combined using an SVM ranker to build a model, such a model provides results that offer a statistically significant improvement over a very strong context-independent baseline. The system ranked first overall on the Lexical Simplification task.

[1]Developed by co-organizers of the shared task

2 Related Work

Lexical Simplification has received considerably less interest in the NLP community as compared with Syntactic Simplification. However, there are a number of notable works related to the topic.

In particular Yatskar et al. (2010) leverage the relations between Simple Wikipedia and English Wikipedia to extract simplification pairs. Biran et al. (2011) extend this base methodology to apply lexical simplification to input sentences. De Belder and Moens (2010), in contrast, provide a more general architecture for the task, with scope for possible extension to other languages.

These studies and others have envisaged a range of different target user groups including children (De Belder and Moens, 2010), people with low literacy levels (Aluisio et al., 2008) and aphasic readers (Carroll et al., 1998).

The current work differs from previous research in that it envisages a stand-alone lexical simplification system based on linguistically motivated and cognitive principles within the framework of a shared task. Its core methodology remains open to integration into a larger Text Simplification system.

3 Task Setup

The English Lexical Simplification shared task at SemEval-2012 (Specia et al., 2012) required systems to rank a number of candidate substitutes (which were provided beforehand) based on their simplicity of usage in a given context. For example, given the following context with an empty placeholder, and its candidate substitutes:

> **Context:** During the siege , George Robertson had appointed Shuja-ul-Mulk, who was a ____ boy only 12 years old and the youngest surviving son of Aman-ul-Mulk, as the ruler of Chitral.
>
> **Candidates:** {clever} {smart} {intelligent} {bright}

a system is required to produce a ranking, e.g.:

> **System:** {intelligent} {bright} {clever, smart}

Note that ties were permitted and that all candidates needed to be included in the system rankings.

4 The SimpLex Lexical Simplification System

In an approach similar to what Hassan et al. (2007) used for Lexical Substitution, SimpLex ranks candidates based on a weighted linear scoring function, which has the generalized form:

$$s\left(c_{n,i}\right) = \sum_{m \in M} \frac{1}{r^m\left(c_{n,i}\right)}$$

where $c_{n,i}$ is the candidate substitute to be scored, and each r^m is a standalone ranking function that attributes to each candidate its rank based on its uniquely associated features. Based on this scoring, candidates for context are ranked in descending order of scores.

In the development of the system we experimented with a number of these features including ranking based on word length, number of syllables, scoring with a 2-step cluster and rank architecture, latent semantic analysis, and average point-wise mutual information between the candidate and neighboring words in the context.

However, the features which were intuitively the simplest proved, in the end, to give the best results. They were selected based on their superior performance on the trial dataset and their competitiveness with the strong Simple Frequency baseline. These stand-alone features are described in what follows.

4.1 Adapted N-Gram Model

The motivation behind an n-gram model for Lexical Simplification is that the task involves an inherent WSD problem. This is because the same word may be used with different senses (and consequently different levels of complexity) in different contexts.

A blind application of n-gram frequency searching on the shared task's dataset, however, gives suboptimal results because of two main factors:

1. Inconsistently lemmatized candidates.
2. Blind replacement of even correctly lemmatized forms in context producing ungrammatical results.

We infer the correct inflection of all candidates for a given context based on the appearance of the original target word (which is also one of the candidate substitutes) in context. To do this we run a part-of-speech (POS) tagger on the source text and note the POS of the target word. Then handcrafted rules are used to correctly inflect the other candidates based on this POS tag.

To resolve the issue of ungrammatical textual output, we further use a simple approach of *popping* words in close proximity to the placeholder and performing n-gram searches on all possible query combinations. Take for instance the following example:

> **Context:** He was ____ away.
>
> **Candidates:** {going} {leaving}

where "going" is evidently the original word in context, but "leaving" has also been suggested as a substitute (there are many such cases in the datasets). One of the possible outcomes of *popping* context words leads to the correct sequence for the latter substitute, i.e. "He was **leaving**" with the word "away" having been *popped*.

The rationale behind this approach is that if one of the combinations is grammatically correct, the number of n-gram hits it returns will far exceed those returned by ungrammatical ones.

The n-gram ($2 \leq n \leq 5$) searches are performed on the Google Web 1T corpus (Brants and Franz, 2006), and the number of hits is weighted by the length of the n-gram search (such that longer sequences obtain higher weight). This may seem like a simplistic approach, especially when the candidate words appear in long-distance dependency relations to other parts of the sentence. However, it should be noted that since the Web 1T corpus only consists of n-grams with $n \leq 5$, structures that contain longer dependencies than this are in any case not considered, and hence do not interfere with local context.

4.2 Bag-of-Words Model

The limitations of performing queries on the Google Web 1T are that n-grams hits must be in strict linear order of appearance. To overcome this difficulty, we further mimic the functioning of a bag-of-words model by taking all possible ordering of words of a given n-gram sequence. This approach, to some extent, gives the possibility of observing co-occurrences of candidate and context words in various orderings of appearance. This results in a number of inadequate query strings, but possibly a few (as opposed to one in a linear n-gram search) good word orderings with high hits as well.

As with the previous model, only n-grams with $2 \leq n \leq 5$ are taken. For a given substitute the total number of hits for all possible queries involving that substitute are summed (with each hit being weighted by the length of its corresponding query in words). To obtain the final score, this sum is normalized by the actual number of queries.

4.3 Psycholinguistic Feature Model

The MRC Psycholinguistic Database (Wilson, 1988) and the Bristol Norms (Stadthagen-Gonzalez and Davis, 2006) are knowledge repositories that associate scores to words based on a number of psycholinguistic features. The ones that we felt were most pertinent to our study are:

1. Concreteness - the level of abstraction associated with the concept a word describes.

2. Imageability - the ability of a given word to arouse mental images.

3. Familiarity - the frequency of exposure to a word.

4. Age of Acquisition - the age at which a given word is appropriated by a speaker.

We combined both databases and compiled a single resource consisting of all the words from both sources that list at least one of these features. It may be noted that these attributes were compiled in similar fashion in both databases and were normalized to the same scale of scores falling in the range of 100 to 700.

In spite of a combined compilation, the coverage of the resource was poor, with more than half the candidate substitutes on both trial and test sets simply not being listed in the databases. To overcome this difficulty we introduced a fifth *frequency* feature that essentially simulates the "Simple Frequency" baseline, [2] but with scores that were normalized to the same scale of the other psycholinguistic features.

This composite of features was used in a linear weighted function with weights tuned to best performance values on the trial dataset. This function sums the weighted scores for each candidate, and normalizes this sum by the number of non-zero features (in the worst-case scenario, – when no psycholinguistic features are found – the scorer is equivalent to the "Simple Frequency" baseline). It is interesting to note that the frequency feature did not dominate the linear combination; rather there was a nice interplay of features with Concreteness, Imageability, Familiarity, Age of Acquisition and Simple Frequency being weighted (on a scale of -1 to +1) as 0.72, -0.22, 0.87, 0.36 and 0.36, respectively.

4.4 Feature Combination

We combined the three standalone models using the ranking function of the SVM-light package (Joachims, 2006) for building SVM rankers. The parameters of the SVM were tuned on the trial dataset, which consisted of only 300 example contexts. To avoid overfitting, instead of taking the single best parameters, we took parameter values that were the average of the top 10 distinct runs.

It may be noted that the resulting model makes no attempt to tie candidates, although actual ties may be produced by chance. But since ties are rarely used in the gold standard for the trial dataset, we reasoned that this should not affect the system performance in any significant way.

[2]The "Simple Frequency" baseline scores each substitute based on the number of hits it produces in the Google Web 1T

	bline-SFreq	w-ln	n-syll	psycho	a-n-gram	b-o-w	pmi	lsa	SimpLex
Trial	0.398	0.176	0.118	0.388	0.397	0.395	0.340	0.089	–
Test	0.471	0.236	0.163	0.432	0.460	0.460	0.404	0.054	0.496

Table 1: Comparison of Models' Scores

5 Results and Discussion

The results of the SimpLex system trained and tuned on the trial set, in comparison with the Simple Frequency baseline and the other stand-alone features we experimented with are presented in Table 1. The scores are computed through a version of the Kappa index over pairwise rankings, and therefore represent the average agreement between the system and the gold-standard annotation in the ranking of pairs of candidate substitutes.

Table 1 shows that while in isolation the features are unable to beat the Simple Frequency model, together they form a combination which outperforms the baseline. The improvement of SimpLex over the other models is statistically significant (statistical significance was established using a randomization test with 1000 iterations and p-value ≤ 0.05).

We believe that the reason why the context aware features were still unable to score better than the context-independent baseline is the isolated focus on simplifying a single target word. People tend to produce language that contains words of roughly equal levels of complexity. Hence in some cases the surrounding context, instead of helping to disambiguate the target word, introduces further noise to queries, especially when its individual component words have skewed complexity factors. A simultaneous simplification of all the content words in a context could be a possible solution to this problem.

As an additional experiment to assess the importance of the size of the training data in our simplification system, we pooled together the trial and test datasets, and ran several iterations of the combination algorithm with a regular increment of number of training examples and noted the effects it produced on eventual score. Three hundred examples were apportioned consistently to a test set to maintain comparability between experiments. Note that this time, no optimization of the SVM parameters was made. The results were inconclusive, and contrary to expectation, revealed that there is no general improvement with additional training data. This could be because of the difficulty of the learning problem, for which the scope of the combined dataset is still very limited. A more detailed study with a corpus that is orders of magnitude larger than the current one may be necessary to establish conclusive evidence.

6 Conclusion

This paper presented our system SimpLex which participated in the English Lexical Simplification shared-task at SemEval-2012 and ranked first out of 9 participating systems.

Our findings showed that while a context agnostic frequency approach to lexical simplification seems to effectively model the problem of assessing word complexity to a relatively decent level of accuracy, as evidenced by the strong baseline of the shared task, other elements, such as interplay of context awareness with humanly perceived psycholinguistic features can produce better results, in spite of very limited training data.

Finally, a more global approach to lexical simplification that concurrently addresses all the words in a context to normalize simplicity levels, may be a more realistic proposition for target applications, and also help context aware features perform better.

Acknowledgment

This work was supported by the European Commission, Education & Training, Erasmus Mundus: EMMC 2008-0083, Erasmus Mundus Masters in NLP & HLT program.

References

Sandra M. Aluisio, Lucia Specia, Thiago A.S. Pardo, Erick G. Maziero, and Renata P.M. Fortes. 2008. Towards brazilian portuguese automatic text simplification systems. In *Proceeding of the eighth ACM sym-*

posium on Document engineering, DocEng '08, pages 240–248, Sao Paulo, Brazil. ACM.

Or Biran, Samuel Brody, and Noemie Elhadad. 2011. Putting it simply: a context-aware approach to lexical simplification. In *Proceedings of the 49th Annual Meeting of the Association for Computational Linguistics: Human Language Technologies*, pages 496–501, Portland, Oregon, USA, June. Association for Computational Linguistics.

Thorsten Brants and Alex Franz. 2006. The google web 1t 5-gram corpus version 1.1 ldc2006t13.

John Carroll, Guido Minnen, Yvonne Canning, Siobhan Devlin, and John Tait. 1998. Practical simplification of english newspaper text to assist aphasic readers. In *Proceedings of AAAI - 98 Workshop on Integrating Artificial Intelligence and Assistive Technology*, Madison, Wisconsin, July.

Jan De Belder and Marie-Francine Moens. 2010. Text simplification for children. In *Proceedings of the SIGIR workshop on Accessible Search Systems*, pages 19–26. ACM, July.

S. Hassan, A. Csomai, C. Banea, R. Sinha, and R. Mihalcea. 2007. Unt: Subfinder: Combining knowledge sources for automatic lexical substitution. In *Proceedings of the Fourth International Workshop on Semantic Evaluations (SemEval-2007)*, pages 410 – 413. Association for Computational Linguistics, Prague, Czech Republic.

Thorsten Joachims. 2006. Training linear svms in linear time. In *Proceedings of the 12th ACM SIGKDD international conference on Knowledge discovery and data mining*, KDD '06, pages 217–226, New York, NY, USA. ACM.

Diana McCarthy and Roberto Navigli. 2007. Semeval-2007 task 10: English lexical substitution task. In *Proceedings of the 4th International Workshop on Semantic Evaluations (SemEval-2007), Prague, Czech Republic*, pages 48–53.

Lucia Specia, Sujay Kumar Jauhar, and Rada Mihalcea. 2012. Semeval-2012 task 1: English lexical simplification. In *Proceedings of the 6th International Workshop on Semantic Evaluation (SemEval 2012)*, Montreal, Canada.

Hans Stadthagen-Gonzalez and Colin Davis. 2006. The bristol norms for age of acquisition, imageability, and familiarity. *Behavior Research Methods*, 38:598–605.

Michael Wilson. 1988. Mrc psycholinguistic database: Machine-usable dictionary, version 2.00. *Behavior Research Methods*, 20:6–10.

Mark Yatskar, Bo Pang, Cristian Danescu-Niculescu-Mizil, and Lillian Lee. 2010. For the sake of simplicity: unsupervised extraction of lexical simplifications from wikipedia. In *Human Language Technologies: The 2010 Annual Conference of the North American Chapter of the Association for Computational Linguistics*, HLT '10, pages 365–368, Stroudsburg, PA, USA. Association for Computational Linguistics.

SB: mmSystem - Using Decompositional Semantics for Lexical Simplification

Marilisa Amoia
Department of Applied Linguistics
University of Saarland
m.amoia@mx.uni-saarland.de

Massimo Romanelli
DFKI GmBH
Saarbrcken, Germany
romanell@dfki.de

Abstract

In this paper, we describe the system we submitted to the SemEval-2012 Lexical Simplification Task. Our system (mmSystem) combines word frequency with decompositional semantics criteria based on syntactic structure in order to rank candidate substitutes of lexical forms of arbitrary syntactic complexity (one-word, multi-word, etc.) in descending order of (cognitive) simplicity. We believe that the proposed approach might help to shed light on the interplay between linguistic features and lexical complexity in general.

1 Introduction

Lexical simplification is a subtask of the more general text simplification task which attempts at reducing the cognitive complexity of a text so that it can be (better) understood by a larger audience. Text simplification has a wide range of applications which includes applications for the elderly, learners of a second language, children or people with cognitive deficiencies, etc.

Works on text simplification mostly focus on reducing the syntactic complexity of the text (Siddharthan, 2011; Siddharthan, 2006) and only little work has addressed the issue of lexical simplification (Devlin, 1999; Carroll et al., 1999).

The Lexical Simplification Task (Specia et al., 2012) proposed within the SemEval-2012 is the first attempt to explore the nature of the lexical simplification more systematically. This task requires participating systems, given a context and a target word, to automatically generate a ranking of substitutes, i.e. lexical forms conveying similar meanings to the target word, such that cognitively simpler lexical forms are ranked higher than more difficult ones.

In this paper, we describe the system we submitted to the SemEval-2012 Lexical Simplification Task. In order to rank the candidate substitutes of a lexical form in descending order of simplicity, our system (mmSystem) combines word frequency with decompositional semantics criteria based on syntactic structure. The mmSystem achieved an average ranking if compared with the other participating systems and the baselines. We believe that the approach proposed in this paper might help to shed light on the interplay between linguistic features and cognitive complexity in general.

2 The Lexical Simplification Task

The SemEval-2012 Lexical Simplification Task requires participating systems to automatically generate a ranking of lexical forms conveying similar meanings on cognitive simplicity criteria and can be defined as follows. Given a short text C called the context and which generally corresponds to a sentence, a target word T and a list L_S of candidate substitutes for T, i.e. a list of quasi-synonyms of the target word, the task for a system consists in providing a ranking on L_S such that the original list of substitutes is sorted over simplicity, from the cognitively simplest to the cognitively most difficult lexical form.

As the examples from (1) to (3) show, the Lexical Simplification Task includes substitutes of different syntactic complexity which might vary from simple one-word substitutes as in (1) (the lexical forms that can function as substitutes include content words, i.e. nouns (n), verbs (v), adjectives (a) and adverbs (r)) to collocations, negated forms as in (2) or even definition-like paraphrases as for instance *wind* and *knock the breath out of* in example (3).

(1)

C: He suggested building an experimental hypertext 'web' for the *worldwide.a* community of physicists who used CERN and its publications.
T: *worldwide.a*
L$_S$: *worldwide, global, international*

(2)

C: Go to hell! she remembers Paul yelling at her *shortly.r* after their wedding.
T: *shortly.r*
L$_S$: *soon, a little, just, almost immediately, shortly, not long*

(3)

C: Now however she was falling through that skylight, the strong dark figure that had appeared out of nowhere falling through with her, his arms tightly entwined about her, his shoulder having *winded.v* her.
T: *winded.v*
L$_S$: *knock her breathless, knock the wind out of, choke, wind, knock the breath out of, knock the air out of*

The organizers of the Lexical Simplification Task provide a corpus of 300 trial and 1710 test sentences defining the context of the target word and the associated list of candidate substitutes. To produce a gold standard, 5 human annotators manually ranked the list of substitutes associated to each context. Finally, a scoring algorithm is provided for computing agreement between the output of the system and the manually ranked gold standard. The scoring algorithm is based on the Kappa measure for inter-annotator agreement.

3 The mmSystem

Our aim by participating in the SemEval-2012 Lexical Simplification Task (Task 1) was to investigate the nature of lexical simplicity/complexity and to identify the linguistic features that are responsible for it. The system we have developed is a first step in this direction. The idea behind our framework is the following. We build on previous work (Devlin, 1999; Carroll et al., 1999) that approximate simplicity with word frequency, such that the cognitively simpler lexical form is the one that is more frequent in the language. While this definition might easily apply to one-word substitutes or collocations, it poses some problems in the case of multi-word-expressions or of syntactically more complex lexical forms (e.g. definition like paraphrases) like those proposed in the substitute lists in the SemEval-2012 Task 1.

Our approach builds on the baseline definition of simplicity based on word frequency and integrates it with (de)compositional semantics considerations. Therefore, in order to operationalize the notion of simplicity in our system we adopt different strategies depending on the syntactic complexity of the lexical form that forms the substitute.

- In the case of one-word substitutes or common collocations we use the frequency associated by WordNet (Fellbaum, 1998) to the lexical form as a metric to rank the substitutes, i.e. the substitute with the highest frequency is ranked higher. For instance, the lexical item *intelligent* is ranked lower than *clever* as it has a lower frequency in the language (as defined in WordNet).

- In the case of multi-words or syntactic complex substitutes, we apply so-called *relevance rules*. Those are based on (de)compositional semantic criteria and attempt to identify a unique content word in the substitute that better approximates the whole lexical form. Thus, we assign to the whole lexical form the frequency associated to this most relevant content word and use it for ranking the whole substitute. For instance, relevance rules assign to multi-word substitutes such as *most able* or *not able* the same frequency, and namely that associated with the content word *able*.

3.1 Implementation

In this section we describe in more details the implementation of the mmSystem. The system design can be summarized as follows.

Step 1: POS-Tagging In the first step, context and the associated substitutes are parsed[1] so to obtain a flat representation of their syntax. Basically at this level, we collect Part-Of-Speech information for all content words in the context as well as in the substitute list.

Step 2: Relevance Rules In the second step, depending on the syntactic representation of the substitutes, the system selects a relevance rule that identifies the one-word lexical form that will be used for representing the meaning of the whole substitute.

Step 3: Word Sense Tagging The system applies word sense tagging and assigns a WordNet sense to the target words and their candidate substitutes. In this step, we rely on the SenseRelate::TargetWord package (Patwardhan et al., 2005) and use the Lesk algorithm (Lesk, 1986) for word sense disambiguation.

Step 4: Substitute Ranking Following (Carroll et al., 1999) that pointed out that rare words generally have only one sense, in order to associate a frequency index to each candidate substitute (w_i), we use the number of senses associated by WordNet to a lexical item of a given part of speech, as an approximation of its frequency (f_i). Further, we extract from WordNet the frequency of the word sense (f_{wns_i}) associated to the lexical item w_i at step 3. Words not found in WordNet it assigned a null frequency ($f_i = 0$, $f_{wns_i} = 0$). Finally, we rank the substitute in the following way:

- if $f_1 \neq f_2$
  $w_1 < w_2$, if $f_1 > f_2$ and
  $w_2 < w_1$ otherwise,
- else if $f_1 = f_2$
  $w_1 < w_2$, if $f_{wns_1} > f_{wns_2}$ and
  $w_2 < w_1$ otherwise.

Input:
Sentence 993: "It is *light.a* and easy to use." Substitutes: portable;unheavy;not heavy;light
Step 1: POS-Tagging
portable#A; unheavy#A; not#Neg heavy#A; light#A
Step 2: Relevance Rules
portable#A; unheavy#A; heavy#A#; light#A
Step 3: WSD
portable#A#wns:2; unheavy#A#wns:?; heavy#A#wns:2; light#A#wns:25
Step 4: Ranking
portable#f:2; unheavy#f:0; heavy#f:27; light#f:25 not heavy $<$ light $<$ portable $<$ unheavy
Gold Ranking:
light $<$ not heavy $<$ portable $<$ unheavy

Table 1: Example of mmSystem processing steps.

Table 1 shows an example of data processing.

3.2 Relevance Rules

Relying on previous work on compositional semantics of multi-word-expression (Reddy et al., 2011; Venkatapathy and Joshi, 2005; Baldwin et al., 2003) we defined a set of hand-written rules to assign the relevant meaning to a complex substitute. Relevance rules are used to decompose the meaning of a complex structure and identify the most relevant word conveying the semantics of the whole, so that the frequency associated to the whole lexical form is approximated by the frequency of this most relevant form:

- a one-word lexical item is mapped to itself, e.g. $run.v \rightarrow run.v$
- a multi-word lexical form including only one content word is mapped to this content word, e.g. $not.Neg\ nice.a \rightarrow nice.a$ or $be.Cop\ able.a \rightarrow able.a$
- in the case of a multi-word lexical item including more than one content word, we take into account the syntactic structure of the lexical item and apply heuristics to decide which content word is more relevant for the meaning of the whole. The heuristics we used are based on the empirical analysis of the trial data set provided by the Task 1 organizers that contains

[1] We used the Stanford Parser (Klein and Manning, 2003).

about 300 contexts. As an example consider a lexical item including a verb construction with structure $V_1 + to + V_2$ that is mapped by our rules to the second verb form V_2, e.g. $try.V_1$ to $escape.V_2 \rightarrow escape.V_2$.

Table 2 shows some examples of relevance rules defined in the mmSystem.

Syntax	Example	R_Form
V + Prep	engage for	V
Cop + Adj	be able	Adj
Cop + V	be worried	V
Adv + V	anxiously anticipate	Adv
Adj+N	adnormal growth	Adj
N1 + N2	death penalty	N1
N1 + PrepOf + N2	person of authority	N2
V+N	take notice	N
V1+to+V2	try to escape	V2

Table 2: Example of relevance rules.

These relevance rules allow for a preliminary investigation of the nature of lexical complexity. For instance, we found that in many cases, it is the modifying element of a complex expression that is responsible for a shift in lexical complexity:

(4) a. lie<say **falsely**<say **untruthfully**

b. sample< **typical** sample < **representative** sample

4 Results

The Task 1 overall result can be found in (Specia et al., 2012). The mmSystem achieved an average ranking (score=0.289) if compared with the other participating systems and the baselines that corresponds to an absolute inter-annotator agreement between system output and golden-standard around 66%. Interestingly none of the systems achieved an absolute agreement higher than 75% in this task. This confirms that lexical simplification still remains a difficult task and that the nature of the phenomena underlying it should be better explored.

Table 3 shows the performance of our system per syntactic category. The values are a bit higher than in the official results of Task 1 as the system version used for submission was buggy, however the ranking of our system with respect to the other participating systems remains the same. Interestingly, the best score were achieved for adverbs (0.352) and adjectives (0.342). This can be explained with the fact that the decompositional semantics of these category is better accounted for by our rules.

The relative low performance achieved by the mmSystem can be explained by the fact that our rules only select one content word and use its frequency for ranking. This metric alone is clearly not enough to explain all cases of lexical simplification. As an example of the complexity of this issue, consider the interplay of negation and compositional semantics: The negation of a very frequent verb form might not be so simple to understand as its antonym, e.g. *don't, not remember/forget* vs. *omit to, fail to remember/forget*. We believe, that a more systematic analysis of the lexical semantics involved in lexical simplicity might improve the performance of the system.

	Noun	Verb	Adj	Adv	TOT
cAgr:	0.5	0.5	0.5	0.5	0.5
aAgr:	0.658	0.658	0.671	0.676	0.665
Score:	0.316	0.315	0.342	0.352	0.329

Table 3: mmSystem scores per syntactic category. In the table cAgr represents the agreement by chance, aAgr is the absolute inter-annotator agreement between system output and gold ranking and score is the normalized system score. These values corresponds to P(A) and P(E) observed in the data.

5 Conclusion

In this paper we presented the mmSystem for lexical simplification we submitted to the SemEval-2012 Task 1. The system combines simplification strategies based on word frequency with decompositional semantic criteria. The mmSystem achieved an average performance. The aim of our work was in fact a preliminary investigation of the interplay between (de)compositional semantics and lexical or cognitive simplicity in general. Doubtlessly much remain to be done in order to provide a more efficient formalization of such effects. In future work, we want to perform a wider corpus analysis and study the impact of other linguistic features such as lexical semantics on lexical simplicity.

References

Timothy Baldwin, Colin Bannard, Takaaki Tanaka, and Dominic Widdows. 2003. An empirical model of multiword expression decomposability. In *Proceedings of the ACL 2003 workshop on Multiword expressions: analysis, acquisition and treatment - Volume 18*, MWE '03, pages 89–96, Stroudsburg, PA, USA. Association for Computational Linguistics.

John Carroll, Guido Minnen, Darren Pearce, Yvonne Canning, Siobhan Devlin, and John Tait. 1999. Simplifying text for language-impaired readers. In *In Proceedings of the 9th Conference of the European Chapter of the Association for Computational Linguistics (EACL*, pages 269–270.

S. Devlin. 1999. *Simplifying natural language for aphasic readers*. Ph.D. thesis, University of Sunderland, UK.

Christiane Fellbaum. 1998. *WordNet: An Electronic Lexical Database*. Cambridge, MA: MIT Press.

Dan Klein and Christopher D. Manning. 2003. Accurate unlexicalized parsing. In *Proceedings of the 41st Meeting of the Association for Computational Linguistics*, pages 423–430.

M. Lesk. 1986. Automatic sense disambiguation using machine readable dictionaries: How to tell a pine cone from a ice cream cone. In *Proceedings of SIGDOV '86*.

Siddharth Patwardhan, Satanjeev Banerjee, and Ted Pedersen. 2005. Senserelate::targetword - a generalized framework for word sense disambiguation. In *Proceedings of the Demonstration and Interactive Poster Session of the 43rd Annual Meeting of the Association for Computational Linguistics*, pages 73–76, Ann Arbor, MI.

Siva Reddy, Diana McCarthy, and Suresh Manandhar. 2011. An empirical study on compositionality in compound nouns. In *Proceedings of the International Joint Conference on Natural Language Processing 2011 (IJCNLP-2011)*, Thailand.

Advaith Siddharthan. 2006. Syntactic simplification ant text cohesion. *Research on Language and Computation*, 4(1):77–109.

Advaith Siddharthan. 2011. Text simplification using typed dependencies: A comparision of the robustness of different generation strategies. In *Proceedings of the 13th European Workshop on NLG*.

Lucia Specia, Sujay K. Jauhar, and Rada Mihalcea. 2012. Semeval-2012 task 1: English lexical simplification. In *Proceedings of the 6th International Workshop on Semantic Evaluation (SemEval 2012)*, Montreal, Canada.

Sriram Venkatapathy and Aravind K. Joshi. 2005. Measuring the relative compositionality of verb-noun (v-n) collocations by integrating features. In *Proceedings of the conference on Human Language Technology and Empirical Methods in Natural Language Processing*, HLT '05, pages 899–906, Stroudsburg, PA, USA. Association for Computational Linguistics.

ANNLOR: A Naïve Notation-system for Lexical Outputs Ranking

Anne-Laure Ligozat
LIMSI-CNRS/ENSIIE
rue John von Neumann
91400 Orsay, France
annlor@limsi.fr

Cyril Grouin
LIMSI-CNRS
rue John von Neumann
91400 Orsay, France
cyril.grouin@limsi.fr

Anne Garcia-Fernandez
CEA-LIST
NANO INNOV, Bt. 861
91191 Gif-sur-Yvette cedex, France
anne.garcia-fernandez@cea.fr

Delphine Bernhard
LiLPa, Université de Strasbourg
22 rue René Descartes, BP 80010
67084 Strasbourg cedex, France
dbernhard@unistra.fr

Abstract

This paper presents the systems we developed while participating in the first task (English Lexical Simplification) of SemEval 2012. Our first system relies on n-grams frequencies computed from the Simple English Wikipedia version, ranking each substitution term by decreasing frequency of use. We experimented with several other systems, based on term frequencies, or taking into account the context in which each substitution term occurs. On the evaluation corpus, we achieved a 0.465 score with the first system.

1 Introduction

In this paper, we present the methods we used while participating to the Lexical Simplification task at SemEval 2012 (Specia et al., 2012). We experimented with several methods:

- using word frequencies or other statistical figures from the BNC corpus, Google Books NGrams, the Simple English Wikipedia, and results from the Bing search engine (with/without lemmatization);
- using association measures for a word and its context based on language models (with/without inflection);
- making a combination of previous methods with SVMRank.

Depending on the results obtained on the training corpus, we chose the methods that seemed to best fit the data.

2 Task description

2.1 Presentation

The Lexical Simplification task aimed at determining the degree of simplicity of words. The inputs given were a short text, in which a target word was chosen, and several substitutes for the target word that fit the context.

An example of a short text follows; the target word is "outdoor", and other words of this text will be considered as the *context* of this target word.

```
<instance id="270">
  <context>With the growing demand for
      these fine garden furnishings ,
      they found it necessary to dedicate
      a portion of their business to
      <head>outdoor</head> living and
      patio furnishings .</context>
</instance>
```

The substitutes given for this target word were the following: "alfresco;outside;open-air;outdoor;". The objective was to order these words by descending simplicity.

2.2 Corpora

Two corpora were provided: the *trial* corpus with development examples, and the *test* corpus for evaluation.

In the *trial* corpus, a gold standard was also given. For the previous example, it stated that the substitutes had to be in the following order: "outdoor open-air outside, alfresco", "outdoor" being considered as the simplest substitute, and "outside" and "alfresco" being considered as the less simple ones.

Three baselines have been given by the organizers: the first one is a simple randomization of the substitute list, the second one keeps the substitute list as it is, and the third one (called "simple frequency") relies on the use of the Google Web 1T corpus.

3 Preprocessing

3.1 Corpus constitution

In order to use machine-learning based approaches, we produced two sub-corpora respectively for the training and evaluation stages from the *trial* corpus. The training sub-corpus is used to develop and tune the systems we produced while the evaluation sub-corpus is used to evaluate the results of these systems.

For each set from the SemEval trial corpus, if the set is composed of at least eight lexical elements belonging to the same morpho-syntactic category (e.g., a set with at least eight instances of "bright" as an adjective), we extracted three instances from this set for the evaluation sub-corpus, the remaining instances being part of the training sub-corpus. If the set is composed of less than eight instances, all instances are used in the training sub-corpus. We also kept two complete sets of lexical elements for the evaluation sub-corpus in order to test the robustness of our methods on new lexical elements that have not been studied yet. This distribution allows us to benefit from a repartition between training and evaluation sub-corpora where the instances ratio is of 66/33%.

3.2 Corpus cleaning

While studying the trial corpus, we noticed that the texts were not always in plain text, and in particular contained HTML entities. As some of our methods used the context of target words, we decided to create a cleaner version of the corpora. For the dash and quote HTML entities (– “ etc.), we replaced each entity by its refering symbol. When replacing the apostrophe HTML entity ('), we decided to link the abbreviated token with the previous one because all n-grams methods worked better with abbreviated terms of one token-length *(don't)* than two token-length *(do n't)* (see section 5).

3.3 Inflection

In some sentences, the target words are inflected, but the substitutes are given in their lemmatized forms. For example, one of the texts was the following :

```
<context>In fact , during at least six
    distinct periods in Army history
    since World War I , lack of trust and
    confidence in senior leaders caused
    the so-called best and
    <head>brightest</head> to leave the
    Army in droves .</context>
```

For this text and target word, the proposed substitutes were "capable; most able; motivated; intelligent; bright; clever; sharp; promising", and if we want to test the simplicity of the words in context, for example with a 2-words left context, we will obtain unlikely phrases such as "best and capable" (which should be "best and most capable"). We thus used several resources to get inflected forms of words: we used the Lingua::EN::Conjugate and Lingua::EN::Inflect Perl modules, which give inflected forms of verbs and plural forms of nouns, as well as the English dictionary of inflected forms DELA,[1] to validate the Perl modules outputs if necessary, and get comparatives and superlatives of adjectives, and a list of irregular English verbs, also to validate the Perl modules outputs.

4 Simple English Wikipedia based system

Our best system, called ANNLOR-simple, is based on Simple English Wikipedia frequencies. As the challenge focused on substitutions performed by non-native English speakers, we tried to use linguistic resources that best fit this kind of data. In this way, we made the hypothesis that training our system on documents written by or written for non-native English speakers would be useful.

The use of the Simple English version from Wikipedia seems to be a good solution as it is targeted at people who do not have English as their mother tongue. Our hypothesis seems to be correct due to the results we obtained. Morevover, the Simple English Wikipedia has been used previously in work on automatic text simplification, e.g. (Zhu et al., 2010).

[1] `http://infolingu.univ-mlv.fr/DonneesLinguistiques/Dictionnaires/telechargement.html`

First, we produced a plain text version of the Simple English Wikipedia. We downloaded the dump dated February 27, 2012 and extracted the textual contents using the `wikipedia2text` tool.[2] The final plaintext file contains approximately 10 million words.

We extracted word n-grams (n ranging from 1 to 3) and their frequencies from this corpus thanks to the Text-NSP Perl module [3] and its *count.pl* program, which produces the list of n-grams of a document, with their frequencies. Table 1 gives the number of n-grams produced.

Table 1: Number of distinct n-grams extracted from the Simple English Wikipedia

n	#n-grams
1	301,718
2	2,517,394
3	6,680,906
1 to 3	9,500,018

Some of these n-grams are invalid, and result from problems when extracting plain text from Wikipedia, such as "27|ufc 1", which corresponds to wiki syntax. As we would not find these n-grams in our substitution lists, we did not try to clean the n-gram data.

Then, we ranked the possible substitutes of a lexical item according to these frequencies, in descending order. For example, for the substitution list (intelligent, bright, clever, smart), the respective frequencies in the Simple English Wikipedia are (206, 475, 141, 201), and the substitutes will be ranked in descending frequencies: (bright, intelligent, smart, clever).

Several tests were conducted, with varying parameters. We used the plain text version of the Simple English Wikipedia, but also tried to lemmatize it, since substitutes are lemmatized. We used the TreeTagger [4] (Schmid, 1994) and applied it on the whole corpus, before counting n-grams. Moreover, since bigrams and trigrams increase a lot, the size of n-gram data, we evaluated their influence on results. These tests are summed up in table 2.

Table 2: Results obtained with the Simple English Wikipedia based system, on the trial and test corpora

reference n-grams	lemmas	score on trial corpus	score on test corpus
1-grams only	no	0.333	–
1 and 2-grams	no	0.371	–
1 to 3-grams	no	0.381	0.465
1 to 3-grams	yes	0.380	0.462
Simple Frequency baseline		0.398	0.471
WLV-SHEF-SimpLex (best system @SemEval2012)		–	0.496

With unigrams only, 158 substitutes of the trial corpus are absent of the reference dataset, 105 when adding bigrams, and 91 when adding trigrams. Most of the missing n-grams (when using 1 to 3-grams) indeed seem to be very uncommon, such as "undomesticated" or "telling untruths".

The small difference between the lemmatized and inflected versions of Wikipedia is due to two reasons: some substitutes are found in the lemmatized version because substitutes are given in the lemmatized form (for example "abnormal growth" is only present in its plural form "abnormal growths" in the inflected Wikipedia); and some other substitutes are missing in the lemmatized version, mostly because of errors from the TreeTagger (for example "be scared of" becomes "be scare of").

We kept the system that obtained the best scores on the trial corpus, that is with 1 to 3-grams and non-lemmatized n-grams, with a score of 0.381. This system obtained a score of 0.465 on the evaluation corpus, thus ranking second ex-aequo at the SemEval evaluation.

[2]See `http://www.polishmywriting.com/download/wikipedia2text\_rsm\_mods.tgz` and `http://blog.afterthedeadline.com/2009/12/04/generating-a-plain-text-corpus-from-wikipedia`

[3]`http://search.cpan.org/~tpederse/Text-NSP-1.25/lib/Text/NSP.pm`

[4]`http://www.ims.uni-stuttgart.de/projekte/corplex/TreeTagger/`

5 Other frequency-based methods

We tried several other reference corpora, always with the idea that the more frequent a word is, the simpler it is. We used the BNC corpus,[5] as well as the Google Books NGrams.[6] These NGrams were calculated on the books digitized by Google, and contain for each encountered n-gram, its number of occurrences for a given year. As the Google Books NGrams are quite voluminous, we selected a random year (2008), and kept only alphabetical n-grams with potential hyphens, and used n-grams for n ranging from 1 to 4. The dataset used contains 477,543,736 n-grams.

We also used the Microsoft Web N-gram Service (more details on this service are given in the following section) to rank substitutes in descending order. The results of these methods on the trial corpus are given in table 3. The result of the simple frequency baseline is also given: this baseline is also frequency-based, but words are ranked according to the number of hits found when querying the Google Web 1T corpus with each substitute.

Table 3: Results obtained with frequency-based methods, on the trial corpus

reference corpus	score
BNC	0.347
Google Books NGrams	0.367
Microsoft NGrams	0.383
Simple Frequency baseline	0.398

This table shows that all frequency-based methods have lower scores than the Simple Frequency baseline, although the score obtained with the Microsoft NGrams is quite close to the baseline. The results from Microsoft Ngrams and the Simple English are very close. We decided to submit the Simple English Wikipedia-based system because it was more different from the simple frequency baseline.

6 Contextual methods

We also wanted to use contextual information, since, according to the contexts of the target word, different substitutes can be used, or ranked differently. In the following two examples, the same word "film" is targetted, and the same substitutes are proposed "film;picture;movie;"; yet, in the gold standard, "film" is placed before "movie" in instance 19, and after it in instance 15.

```
<instance id="15">
  <context>Film Music Literature
      Cyberplace – Includes
      <head>film</head> reviews , message
      boards , chat room , and images
      from various films .</context>
</instance>
(...)
<instance id="19">
  <context>A fine score by George Fenton
      ( THE CRUCIBLE ) and beautiful
      photograhy by Roger Pratt add
      greatly to the effectiveness of the
      <head>film</head> .</context>
</instance>
```

Ranking substitutes thus depends on the context of the target word. We implemented two systems taking the context of target words into account.

6.1 Language model probabilities

The other system submitted (called ANNLOR-lmbing) relies on language models, which was the method used by the organizers in their Simple Frequency baseline. While the organizers used Google n-grams to rank terms to be substituted by decreasing frequency of use, we used Microsoft Web n-grams in the same way. Nevertheless, we also added the contexts of each term to be substituted.

We used the Microsoft Web N-gram Service[7] to obtain joint probability for text units, and more precisely its Python library.[8] We used the *bing-body/apr10/*) N-Gram model.

We considered a text unit composed of the lexical item and a contextual window of 4 words to the left and 4 words to the right (words being separated by spaces). For example, in the following sentence, we tested "He brings an incredibly rich and diverse background that", and the same unit with the target word replaced by substitutes, for example "He brings an incredibly lush and diverse background that".

[5] http://www.natcorp.ox.ac.uk/

[6] http://books.google.com/ngrams/datasets

[7] http://research.microsoft.com/en-us/collaboration/focus/cs/web-ngram.aspx

[8] http://web-ngram.research.microsoft.com/info/MicrosoftNgram-1.02.zip

```
<instance id="118">
  <context>He brings an incredibly
      <head>rich</head> and diverse
      background that includes everything
      from executive coaching , learning
      &amp; development and management
      consulting , to senior operations
      roles , mixed with a masters in
      organizational
      development.</context>
</instance>
```

We performed several tests, with different N-Gram models, and different context sizes. Some of these results for the trial corpus are given in table 4.

Table 4: Results obtained with Microsoft Web N-gram Service, on the trial corpus

Size of left context	Size of right context	Score
0	3	0.362
3	0	0.358
2	2	0.365
3	3	0.358
4	4	0.370

For the evaluation, this system was our second run, with the parameters that obtained the best scores on the training corpus (contexts of 4 words to the left and to the right). This method obtained a 0.370 score on the trial corpus and a 0.396 score on the test corpus.[9]

7 Combination of methods

As each method seemed to have its own benefits, we tried to combine them using SVMRank [10](Joachims, 2006). The output of each system is converted into a feature file. For example, the output of the Simple English Wikipedia based system begins with:

```
1    bright    475    1
1    intelligent    206    2
1    smart    201    3
1    clever    141    4
2    light    3241    1
2    clear    707    2
2    bright    475    3
2    luminous    14    4
2    well-lit    0    5
```

The first column represent the instance id, the second one the considered substitute, the third one the feature (in this case, the frequency of the substitute in the Simple English Wikipedia), and the last one, the substitute rank according to this method. Then, we combined these files to include all features (after basic query-wise feature scaling). For example, the training file begins with:

```
1 qid:1 2:-0.00461061395325929
    3:0.0345010535723618
    #intelligent
2 qid:1 2:-0.00485010755325339
    3:-0.0213467053270483 #clever
3 qid:1 2:-0.00462903653787422
    3:0.092640777900771 #smart
4 qid:1 2:-0.00361947890097599
    3:0.0489145618699556 #bright
1 qid:4 2:-0.00461061395325929
    3:0.0345010535723618
    #intelligent
```

The first column gives the gold standard rank for the substitute (in training phase), the second one the instance id, and then feature ids and values for each substitute. Default parameters were used.

We used the division of the *trial* corpus into a training corpus and a development corpus. Table 5 gives some examples of scores obtained by combining two methods. The scores are not exactly those presented earlier, since they correspond to a part of the *trial* corpus only. Even though some improvement can be obtained by this combination, it was quite small, and so we did not use it for the evaluation.

Table 5: Results obtained with combination of methods with SVMRank, on the trial corpus

Simple English Wikipedia	Microsoft NGrams	SVM
0.352	0.352	0.354

[9] This result is different from the official one, because an incorrect file was submitted at the time.

[10] http://www.cs.cornell.edu/people/tj/svm_light/svm_rank.html

8 Conclusion

In this paper, we present several systems developed for the English Lexical Simplification task of SemEval 2012. The best results are obtained using frequencies from the Simple English Wikipedia. We found the task quite hard to solve, since none of our experiments significantly outperforms the Simple Frequency baseline. On the trial corpus, our system based upon the Simple English Wikipedia achieved a score of 0.381 (below the 0.399 baseline score); on the test corpus, we achieved a score of 0.465 with the Simple English Wikipedia system while the baseline achieved a score of 0.471 score. All our systems using contextual information did not achieve high scores.

References

Thorsten Joachims. 2006. Training Linear SVMs in Linear Time. In *Proceedings of the ACM Conference on Knowledge Discovery and Data Mining (KDD)*.

Helmut Schmid. 1994. Probabilistic Part-of-Speech Tagging Using Decision Trees. In *Proc. of the International Conference on New Methods in Language Processing*, Manchester, UK.

Lucia Specia, Sujay K. Jauhar, and Rada Mihalcea. 2012. SemEval-2012 Task 1: English Lexical Simplification. In *Proc. of the 6th International Workshop on Semantic Evaluation (SemEval 2012)*, Montréal, Canada.

Zhemin Zhu, Delphine Bernhard, and Iryna Gurevych. 2010. A Monolingual Tree-based Translation Model for Sentence Simplification. In *Proceedings of the 23rd International Conference on Computational Linguistics (COLING 2010)*, pages 1353–1361.

UNT-SimpRank: Systems for Lexical Simplification Ranking

Ravi Sinha
University of North Texas
1155 Union Circle #311277
Denton, Texas
76203-5017
RaviSinha@my.unt.edu

Abstract

This paper presents three systems that took part in the lexical simplification task at SemEval 2012. Speculating on what the concept of simplicity might mean for a word, the systems apply different approaches to rank the given candidate lists. One of the systems performs second-best (statistically significant) and another one performs third-best out of 9 systems and 3 baselines. Notably, the third-best system is very close to the second-best, and at the same time much more resource-light in comparison.

1 Introduction

Lexical simplification (described in (Specia et al., 2012)) is a newer problem that has arisen following a recent surge in interest in the related task of lexical substitution (McCarthy et al., 2007). While lexical substitution aims at making systems generate suitable paraphrases for a target word in an instance, which do not necessarily have to be simpler versions of the original, it has been speculated that one possible use of the task could be lexical simplification, in particular in the realm of making educational text more readable for non-native speakers.

The task of lexical simplification, which thus derives from lexical substitution, uses the same data set, and has been introduced at the 6th International Workshop on Semantic Evaluation (SemEval 2012), in conjunction with the First Joint Conference on Lexical and Computational Semantics (*SEM 2012). Instead of asking systems to provide substitutes, the task provides the systems with all substitutes and asks them to be ranked.

The task provides several instances of triplets of a context C, a target word T, and a set of gold standard substitutes S. The systems are supposed to rank the substitutes $s_i \in S$ from the simplest to the most difficult, and match their predictions against the provided human annotations. The organizers define *simple* loosely as words that can be understood by a wide variety of people, regardless of their literacy and cognitive levels, age, and regional backgrounds.

The task is novel in that so far most work has been done on syntactic simplification and not on lexical simplification. Carroll et. al. (Carroll et al., 1998) seem to have pioneered some methodology and evaluation metrics in this field. Yatskar et. al. (Yatskar et al., 2010) use an unsupervised learning method and metadata from the Simple English Wikipedia.

2 Data

The data (trial and test, no training) have been adopted from the original lexical substitution task (McCarthy et al., 2007). The trial set has 300 examples, each with a context, a target word, and a set of substitutions. The test set has 1710 examples. The organizers provide a scorer for the task, the trial gold standard rankings, and three baselines. The data is provided in XML format, with tags identifying the lemmas, parts of speech, instances, contexts and head words. The substitutions and gold rankings are in plain text format.

3 Resources

Intuitively, a simple word is likely to have a high frequency in a resource that is supposed to contain simple words. Other factors that could intuitively influence simplicity would be the frequency in spoken conversation, and whether the word is polysemous or not. As such, the following resources have been selected to contribute to the metric used in ranking the substitutes.

3.1 Simple English Wikipedia

Simple English Wikipedia has been used before in simplicity analysis, as described in (Yatskar et al., 2010). It is a publicly available, smaller Wikipedia (298MB decompressed), which claims to only consist of words that are somehow *simple*. For all the substitute candidates, I count their frequencies of occurrence in this resource, and these counts serve as a factor in computing the corresponding simplicity scores (refer to Equation 1.)

3.2 Transcribed Spoken English Corpus

A set of spoken dialogues is also utilized in this project to measure simplicity. Spoken language intuitively contains more conversational words, and has the same kind of resolution power as the Simple English Wikipedia when it comes to the relative simplicity of a word. Frequency counts of all the substitute candidates in a set of dialogue corpora is computed, and used as another factor in the Equations 1 and 3.

3.3 WordNet

WordNet, as described in (Fellbaum, 1998), is a lexical knowledge base that combines the properties of a thesaurus with that of a semantic network. The basic entry in WordNet is a *synset*, which is defined as a set of synonyms. I use WordNet 3.0, which has over 150,000 unique words, over 110,000 *synsets*, and over 200,000 word-sense pairs. For each substitute, I extract the raw number of senses (for all parts of speech possible) for that word present in WordNet. This count serves as yet another factor in the proposed simplicity measure, under the hypothesis that a simple word is used very frequently, and is therefore polysemous.

3.4 Web1T Google N-gram Corpus

The Google Web 1T corpus (Brants and Franz, 2006) is a collection of English N-grams, ranging from one to five N-grams, and their respective frequency counts observed on the Web. The corpus was generated from approximately 1 trillion tokens of words from the Web, predominantly English. This corpus is also used in both SIMPRANK and SALSA systems, with the intuition that simpler words will have higher counts on the Web taken as a whole.

3.5 SaLSA

SALSA (Stand-alone Lexical Substitution Analyzer) is an in-house application which accepts as inputs sentences with target words marked distinctly, and then builds all possible 3-grams by substituting the target word with synonyms (and inflections thereof). It then queries the Web1T corpus using an in-house quick lookup application and gathers the counts for all 3-grams. Finally, it sums the counts, and assigns the aggregated scores to each corresponding synonym and outputs a reverse-ranked list of the synonyms. More detail about this methodology can be found in (Sinha and Mihalcea, 2009). SALSA uses the exact same methodology described in the paper, except that it is a stand-alone tool.

4 Experimental Setup

Figure 1 shows the general higher-level picture of how the experiments have been performed. SIMPRANK uses five resources, including the unigram frequency data, while SIMPRANKLIGHT does not use the unigram frequencies.

I hypothesize that the simplicity of a word could be represented as the Equation 1 (here $c_{word}()$ represents the frequency count of the word in a given resource).

$$\begin{aligned} simplicity(word) = \\ \frac{1}{len(word)} + c_{word}(SimpleWiki) \\ + c_{word}(Discourse) + c_{word}(WordNet) \\ + c_{word}(Unigrams) \end{aligned} \quad (1)$$

This formula is very empirical in nature, in that it has been found based on extensive experimentation

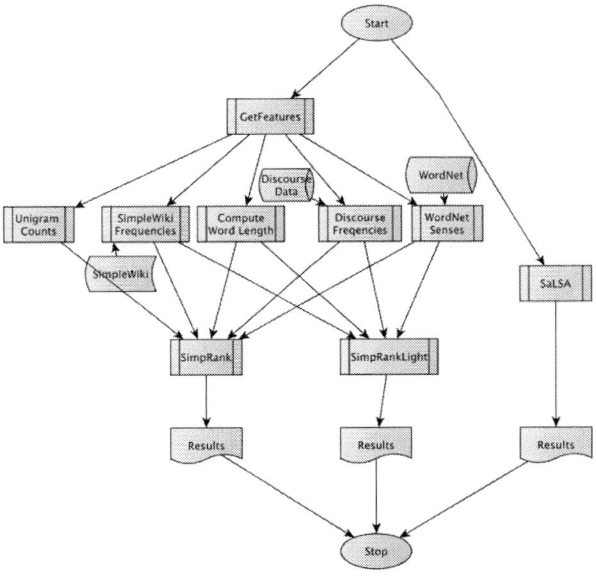

Figure 1: High-level schematic diagram of the experiments

(Table 1). It intuitively makes sense that a simple word is supposed to have high frequency counts in lexical resources that are meant to be simple by design. Formally,

$$\begin{aligned} &simplicity(word) \\ &\quad \propto frequency(SimpleResource) \\ &\quad \propto \frac{1}{length} \end{aligned} \tag{2}$$

Here, SimpleResource could be any resource that contains simple words. Apart from frequency counts, we could possibly also leverage morphology for finding simplicity. Intuitively, a 3-letter word or a 4-letter word would most likely be simpler than a word that has a longer length. This accounts for the length factor in the equations.

As Table 1 depicts, a lot of experiments were performed where the components (counts) were multiplied instead of being added, normalized instead of adding without normalization[1], and also experiments where subsets of the resources were selected. The scores obtained using the gold standard and the trial data are also shown in the table. The best combination found (experiment 8 in the table) is outlined in Equation 1.

Note however, that the Google Web1T corpus is expensive in terms of money, computation time and storage space. Thus, another set of experiments was performed (listed as experiments 1a in Table 1 leaving the unigram counts out, and it was found to work almost just as well. This system has been labeled SIMPRANKLIGHT and uses the formula in Equation 3.

$$\begin{aligned} &simplicity(word) = \\ &\quad \frac{1}{len(word)} + c_{word}(SimpleWiki) \\ &\quad + c_{word}(Discourse) + c_{word}(WordNet) \end{aligned} \tag{3}$$

The substitutes can then be sorted in the decreasing order of simplicity scores. The substitute with the highest simplicity score is hypothesized to be the simplest.

Table 1: Variants of the experiments performed

SN	System components	Method	Remarks	Score
	baseline no-change			0.05
	baseline random			0.01
	baseline unigram count (Web1T)			0.39
1	len, simplewiki, discourse, wordnet	add	normalize	0.20
1a	len, simplewiki, discourse, wordnet	add	don't normalize	**0.37**
2	len, simplewiki, discourse, wordnet	add	normalize, inc sort	-0.20
3	len, simplewiki, discourse, wordnet	multiply	don't normalize	0.25
4	simplewiki, discourse, wordnet	add	don't normalize	0.36
4a	simplewiki, discourse, wordnet	add	normalize	0.22
4b	simplewiki, discourse, wordnet	multiply	don't normalize	0.26
5	len, simplewiki, wordnet	add	don't normalize	0.36
5a	len, simplewiki, wordnet	add	normalize	0.19
5b	len, simplewiki, wordnet	multiply	don't normalize	0.26
6	len, discourse, wordnet	add	don't normalize	0.31
6a	len, discourse, wordnet	add	normalize	0.20
6b	len, discourse, wordnet	multiply	don't normalize	0.25
7	len, simplewiki, discourse	add	don't normalize	0.37
7a	len, simplewiki, discourse	add	normalize	0.22
7b	len, simplewiki, discourse	multiply	don't normalize	0.32
8	len, simplewiki, discourse, wordnet, unigrams	add	don't normalize	**0.39**
8a	len, simplewiki, discourse, wordnet, unigrams	add	normalize	0.22
8b	len, simplewiki, discourse, wordnet, unigrams	multiply	don't normalize	0.26
9	SaLSA			0.36

Experiment 2 in Table 1 shows what happens when an increasing-order ranking of the simplicity scores is used. A negative score here underscores the correctness of both the simplicity score as well as that of the reverse-ranking.

The third system, SALSA (Stand-alone Lexical Substitution Analyzer) is the only system out of the

[1]The normalization is done by dividing by the maximum value obtained for that particular resource

three that takes advantage of the context provided with the data set. It builds all possible 3-grams from the context, replacing the target word one-by-one by a substitute candidate (and inflections of the substitute candidates). It then sums their frequency counts in the Web1T corpus and assigns the sum to the simplicity score of a particular synonym. The synonyms can then be reverse-ranked.

5 System Standings and Discussion

For the test data, Table 2 depicts the system standings, separated by statistical significance.

Table 2: Test data system scores

Rank	Team ID	System ID	Score
1	WLV-SHEF	SimpLex	0.496
2	baseline	Sim Freq	0.471
2	**UNT**	**SimpRank**	**0.471**
2	annlor	simple	0.465
3	**UNT**	**SimpRankL**	**0.449**
4	EMNLPCPH	ORD1	0.405
5	EMNLPCPH	ORD2	0.393
6	SB	mmSystem	0.289
7	annlor	lmbing	0.199
8	baseline	No Change	0.106
9	baseline	Rand	0.013
10	UNT	SaLSA	-0.082

Surprisingly, the systems SIMPRANK and SIMPRANKLIGHT, which do not use the contexts provided, score much better than SALSA, which does use the contexts. Apparently simplicity is rather a statistical concept even for humans (the annotators for the gold standard) and not a contextual one. Also surprisingly, SIMPRANKLIGHT, which does not use Google Web1T data, performs extremely well and within 0.02 of the raw scores.

What is also surprising is the inability of all-but-one systems to beat the baseline of using simple frequency counts from Web1T, which is in turn based entirely on statistical counts and does not take the context into account.

A major contribution of this paper is the discovery that other, lighter, free resources work just as well as the expensive (in money, time and space) Web1T data when it comes to identifying which word is simple and which one is not.

6 Future Work

I plan to extend this experiment by performing ablation studies of all the individual features, playing with new features, and also performing machine learning experiments to see if supervised experiments are a better way of solving the problem of lexical simplicity ranking.

References

Thorsten Brants and Alex Franz. 2006. Web 1T 5-gram Version 1.

John Carroll, Guido Minnen, Yvonne Canning, Siobhan Devlin, and John Tait. 1998. Practical simplification of english newspaper text to assist aphasic readers. In *In Proc. of AAAI-98 Workshop on Integrating Artificial Intelligence and Assistive Technology*, pages 7–10.

Christiane Fellbaum, editor. 1998. *WordNet An Electronic Lexical Database*. The MIT Press, Cambridge, MA ; London, May.

Diana McCarthy, Falmer East Sussex, and Roberto Navigli. 2007. Semeval-2007 task 10: English lexical substitution task. In *In Proceedings of the 4th workshop on Semantic Evaluations (SemEval-2007)*, pages 48–53.

Ravi Sinha and Rada Mihalcea. 2009. Combining lexical resources for contextual synonym expansion. In *Proceedings of the International Conference RANLP-2009*, pages 404–410, Borovets, Bulgaria, September. Association for Computational Linguistics.

Lucia Specia, Sujay K. Jauhar, and Rada Mihalcea. 2012. Semeval-2012 task 1: English lexical simplification. In *Proceedings of the 6th International Workshop on Semantic Evaluation (SemEval 2012)*, Montreal, Canada.

Mark Yatskar, Bo Pang, Cristian Danescu-Niculescu-Mizil, and Lillian Lee. 2010. For the sake of simplicity: Unsupervised extraction of lexical simplifications from Wikipedia. In *Proceedings of the NAACL*, pages 365–368.

Duluth : Measuring Degrees of Relational Similarity with the Gloss Vector Measure of Semantic Relatedness

Ted Pedersen
Department of Computer Science
University of Minnesota
Duluth, MN 55812 USA
tpederse@d.umn.edu

Abstract

This paper describes the Duluth systems that participated in Task 2 of SemEval–2012. These systems were unsupervised and relied on variations of the Gloss Vector measure found in the freely available software package WordNet::Similarity. This method was moderately successful for the Class-Inclusion, Similar, Contrast, and Non-Attribute categories of semantic relations, but mimicked a random baseline for the other six categories.

1 Introduction

This paper describes the Duluth systems that participated in Task 2 of SemEval–2012, Measuring the Degree of Relational Similarity (Jurgens et al., 2012). The goal of the task was to rank sets of word pairs according to the degree to which they represented an underlying category of semantic relation. A highly ranked pair would be considered a good or prototypical example of the relation. For example, given the relation *Y functions as an X* the pair *weapon:knife* (X:Y) would likely be considered more representative of that relation than would be *tool:spoon*.

The task included word pairs from 10 different categories of relational similarity, each with a number of subcategories. In total the evaluation data consisted of 69 files, each containing a set of approximately 40 word pairs. While training examples were also provided, these were not used by the Duluth systems. The system–generated rankings were compared with gold standard data created via Amazon Mechanical Turk.

The Duluth systems relied on the Gloss Vector measure of semantic relatedness (Patwardhan and Pedersen, 2006) as implemented in WordNet::Similarity (Pedersen et al., 2004)[1]. This quantifies the degree of semantic relatedness between two word senses. It does not, however, discover or indicate the nature of the relation between the words. When given two words as input (as was the case in this task), it measures the relatedness of all possible combinations of word senses associated with this pair and reports the highest resulting score. Note that throughout this paper we use *word* and *word sense* somewhat interchangeably. In general it may be assumed that the term *word* or examples of words refers to a word sense.

A key characteristic of this task was that the word pairs in each of the 69 sets were scored assuming a particular specified underlying semantic relation. Given this, the limitation that the Gloss Vector measure does not discover the nature of relations was less of a concern, and led to the hypothesis that a word pair that was highly related would also be a prototypical example of the underlying category of semantic relation. Unfortunately the results from this task do not generally support this hypothesis, although for a few categories at least it appears to have some validity.

This paper continues with a review of the Gloss Vector measure, and explains its connections to the Adapted Lesk measure. The paper then summarizes the results of the three Duluth systems in this task, and concludes with some discussion and analysis of where this method had both successes and failures.

[1] wn-similarity.sourceforge.net

2 Semantic Relatedness

Semantic relatedness is a more general notion than semantic similarity. We follow (Budanitsky and Hirst, 2006) and limit semantic similarity to those measures based on distances and perhaps depths in a hierarchy made up of *is–a* relations. For example, *car* and *motorcycle* are similar in that they are connected via an *is–a* relation with *vehicle*. Semantic similarity is most often applied to nouns, but can also be used with verbs.

Two word senses can be related in many ways, including similarity. *car* and *furnace* might be considered related because they are both made of steel, and *firefighter* and *hose* might be considered related because one uses the other, but neither pair is likely to be considered similar. Measures of relatedness generally do not specify the nature of the relationship between two word senses, but rather indicate that they are related to a certain degree in some unspecified way. As a result, measures of relatedness tend to be symmetric, so A is related to B to the same degree that B is related to A. It should be noted that some of the relations in Task 2 were not symmetric, which was no doubt a complicating factor for the Duluth systems.

3 Adapted Lesk Measure

The Gloss Vector measure was originally developed in an effort to generalize and improve upon the Adapted Lesk measure (Banerjee and Pedersen, 2003).[2] Both the Gloss Vector measure and the Adapted Lesk measure start with the idea of a *supergloss*. A supergloss is the definition (or gloss) of a word sense that is expanded by concatenating it with the glosses of other surrounding senses that are connected to it via some WordNet relation. For example, a supergloss for *car* might consist of the definition of *car*, the definition of *car's* hypernym (e.g., *vehicle*), and the definitions of the meronyms (part-of) of *car* (e.g., *wheel*, *brake*, *bumper*, etc.) Other relations as detailed later in this paper may also be used to expand a supergloss.

In the Adapted Lesk measure, the relatedness between two word senses is a function of the number and length of their matching overlaps in their superglosses. Consecutive words that match are scored more highly than single words, and a higher score for a pair of words indicates a stronger relation. The Adapted Lesk measure was developed to overcome the fact that most dictionary definitions are relatively short, which was a concern noted by (Lesk, 1986) when he introduced the idea of using definition overlaps for word sense disambiguation. While the Adapted Lesk measure expands the size of the definitions, there are still difficulties. In particular, the matches between words in superglosses must be exact, so morphological variants (*run* versus *ran*), synonyms (*gas* versus *petrol*), and closely related words (*tree* versus *shrub*) won't be considered overlaps and will be treated the same as words with no apparent connection (e.g., *goat* and *vase*).

4 Gloss Vector Measure

The Gloss Vector measure[3] is inspired by a 2nd order word sense discrimination approach (Schütze, 1998) which is in turn related to Latent Semantic Indexing or Analysis (Deerwester et al., 1990). The basic idea is to replace each word in a written context with a vector of co-occurring words as observed in some corpus. In this task, the contexts are definitions (and example text) from WordNet. A supergloss is formed exactly as described for Adapted Lesk, and then each word in the supergloss is replaced by a vector of co–occurring words. Then, all the vectors in the supergloss are averaged together to create a new high dimensional representation of that word sense. The semantic relatedness between two word senses is measured by taking the cosine between their two averaged vectors. The end result is that rather than finding overlaps in definitions based on exact matches, a word in a definition is matched to whatever degree its co-occurrences match with the co-occurrences of the words in the other supergloss. This results in a more subtle and fine grained measure of relatedness than Adapted Lesk.

The three Duluth systems only differ in the relations used to create the superglosses, otherwise they are identical. The corpus used to collect co-occurrence information was the complete collection of glosses and examples from WordNet 3.0, which consists of about 1.46 million word tokens and almost 118,000 glosses. Words that appeared in a

[2] WordNet::Similarity::lesk

[3] WordNet::Similarity::vector

stop list of about 200 common words were excluded as co-occurrences, as were words that occurred less than 5 times or more than 50 times in the WordNet corpus. Two words are considered to co-occur if they occur in the same definition (including the example) and are adjacent to each other. These are the default settings as used in WordNet::Similarity.

5 Creating the Duluth Systems

There were three Duluth systems, V0, V1, and V2. These all used the Gloss Vector measure, and differ only in how their superglosses were created. The supergloss is defined using a set of relations that indicate which additional definitions should be included in the definition for a sense. All systems start with a gloss and example for each sense in a pair, which is then augmented with definitions from additional senses as defined for each system.

5.1 Duluth-V0

V0 is identical to the default configuration of the Gloss Vector measure in WordNet::Similarity. This consists of the following relations:

hypernym (hype) : class that includes a member, e.g., a car is a kind of vehicle (hypernym).

hyponym (hypo) : the member of a class, e.g., a car (hyponym) is a kind of vehicle.

holonym (holo) : whole that includes the part, e.g., a ship (holonym) includes a mast.

meronym (mero) : part included in a whole, e.g., a mast (meronym) is a part of a ship.

see also (also) : related adjectives, e.g., egocentric see also selfish.

similar to (sim) : similar adjectives, satanic is similar to evil.

is attribute of (attr) : adjective related to a noun, e.g., measurable is an attribute of magnitude.

synset words (syns) : synonyms of a word, e.g., car and auto are synonyms.[4]

For V0 the definition and example of a noun is augmented with its synonyms and the definitions and examples of any hypernyms, hyponyms, meronyms, and holonyms to which it is directly connected. If the word is a verb it is augmented with its synonyms and any hypernyms/troponyms and hyponyms to which it is directly connected. If the word is an adjective then its definition and example are augmented with those of adjectives directly connected via see also, similar to, and is attribute of relations.

5.2 Duluth-V1

V1 uses the relations in V0, plus the holonyms, hypernyms, hyponyms, and meronyms (X) of the see also, holonym, hypernym, hyponym, and meronym relations (Y). This leads to an additional 20 relations that bring in definitions "2 steps" away from the original word. These take the form of *the holonym of the hypernym of the word sense*, or more generally *the X of the Y* of the word sense, where X and Y are as noted above.

5.3 Duluth-V2

V2 uses the relations in V0 and V1, and then adds the holonym, hypernyms, hyponyms, and meronyms of the 20 relations added for V1. This leads to an additional 80 relations of the form *the hypernyms of the meronym of the hyponym*, or more generally *the X of the X of the Y* of the word.

For example, if the word is *weapon*, then a hypernym of the meronym of the hyponym (of *weapon*) would add the definitions and example of *bow* (hyponym), *bowstring* (meronym of the hyponym), and *cord* (hypernym of the meronym of the hyponym) to the gloss of *weapon* to create the supergloss.

6 Results

There were two evaluation scores reported for the participating systems, Spearman's Rank Correlation Coefficient, and a score based on Maximum Difference Scaling. Since the Gloss Vector measure is based on WordNet, there was a concern that a lack of WordNet coverage might negatively impact the results. However, of the 2,791 pairs used in the evaluation, there were only 3 that contained words unknown to WordNet.

6.1 Spearman's Rank Correlation

The ranking of word pairs in each of the 69 files were evaluated relative to the gold standard using Spearman's Rank Correlation Coefficient. The average of these results over all 10 categories of se-

[4]Since synonyms have the same definition, this relation augments the supergloss with the synonyms themselves.

Table 1: Selected Spearman's Values

Category	rand	v0	v1	v2
SIMILAR	.026	.183	**.206**	.198
CLASS-INCLUSION	.057	.045	**.178**	.168
CONTRAST	-.049	.142	.120	**.198**
average (of all 10)	.018	**.050**	.039	.038

Table 2: Selected MaxDiff Values

Category	rand	v0	v1	v2
SIMILAR	31.5	37.1	**39.2**	37.4
CLASS-INCLUSION	31.0	29.2	**35.6**	33.1
CONTRAST	30.4	**38.3**	36.0	33.8
NON-ATTRIBUTE	28.9	**36.0**	33.0	33.5
average (of all 10)	31.2	**32.4**	31.5	31.1

mantic relations was quite low. Random guessing achieved an averaged Spearman's value 0.018, while Duluth-V0 scored 0.050, Duluth-V1 scored 0.039, and Duluth-V2 scored 0.038.

However, there were specific categories where the Duluth systems fared somewhat better. In particular, results for category 1 (CLASS-INCLUSION), category 3 (SIMILAR) and category 4 (CONTRAST) represent improvements on the random baseline (shown in Table 1) and at least some modest agreement with the gold standard.

The results from the other categories were generally equivalent to what would be obtained with random selection.

6.2 Maximum Difference Scaling

Maximum Difference Scaling is based on identifying the least and most prototypical pair for a given relation from among a set of four pairs. A random baseline scores 31.2%, meaning that it got approximately 1 in 3 of the MaxDiff questions correct. None of the Duluth systems improved upon random to any significant degree : Duluth-V0 scored 32.4, Duluth-V1 scored 31.5, and Duluth-V2 scored 31.1. However, the same categories that did well with Spearman's also did well with MaxDiff (see Table 2). In addition, there is some improvement in category 6 (NON-ATTRIBUTE) at least with MaxDiff scoring.

7 Discussion and Conclusions

The Gloss Vector measure was able to perform reasonably well in measuring the degree of relatedness for the following four categories (where the definitions come from (Bejar et al., 1991)):

CLASS-INCLUSION : one word names a class that includes the entity named by the other word

SIMILAR : one word represents a different degree or form of the ... other

CONTRAST : one word names an opposite or incompatible of the other word

NON-ATTRIBUTE : one word names a quality, property or action that is characteristically not an attribute of the other word

Of these, CLASS-INCLUSION and SIMILAR are well represented by the hypernym/hyponym relations present in WordNet and used by the Gloss Vector measure. WordNet's greatest strength lies in its hypernym tree for nouns, and that was most likely the basis for the success of the CLASS-INCLUSION and SIMILAR categories. While the success with CONTRAST may seem unrelated, in fact it may be that pairs of opposites are often quite similar, for example *happy* and *sad* are both emotions and are similar except for their polarity.

A number of the relations used in Task 2 are not well represented in WordNet. For example, there was a CASE RELATION which could benefit from information about selectional restrictions or case frames that just isn't available in WordNet. The same is true of the CAUSE-PURPOSE relation as there is relatively little information about casual relations in WordNet. While there are part-of relations in WordNet (meronyms/holonyms), these did not prove to be common enough to be a significant benefit for the PART-WHOLE relations in the task.

For many of the relations in the task the Gloss Vector measure was most likely relying primarily on hypernym and hyponym relations, which explains the bias towards categories that featured similarity-based relations. We are however optimistic that a Gloss Vector approach could be more successful given a richer set of relations from which to draw information for superglosses.

References

S. Banerjee and T. Pedersen. 2003. Extended gloss overlaps as a measure of semantic relatedness. In *Proceedings of the Eighteenth International Joint Conference on Artificial Intelligence*, pages 805–810, Acapulco, August.

I. Bejar, R. Chaffin, and S. Embretson. 1991. *Cognitive and Psychometric Analysis of Analogical Problem Solving*. Springer–Verlag, New York, NY.

A. Budanitsky and G. Hirst. 2006. Evaluating WordNet-based measures of semantic distance. *Computational Linguistics*, 32(1):13–47.

S. Deerwester, S.T. Dumais, G.W. Furnas, T.K. Landauer, and R. Harshman. 1990. Indexing by Latent Semantic Analysis. *Journal of the American Society for Information Science*, 41:391–407.

D. Jurgens, S. Mohammad, P. Turney, and K. Holyoak. 2012. Semeval-2012 task 2: Measuring degrees of relational similarity. In *Proceedings of the 6th International Workshop on Semantic Evaluation (SemEval 2012)*, Montreal, June.

M.E. Lesk. 1986. Automatic sense disambiguation using machine readable dictionaries: how to tell a pine cone from an ice cream cone. In *Proceedings of the 5th annual international conference on Systems documentation*, pages 24–26. ACM Press.

S. Patwardhan and T. Pedersen. 2006. Using WordNet-based Context Vectors to Estimate the Semantic Relatedness of Concepts. In *Proceedings of the EACL 2006 Workshop on Making Sense of Sense: Bringing Computational Linguistics and Psycholinguistics Together*, pages 1–8, Trento, Italy, April.

T. Pedersen, S. Patwardhan, and J. Michelizzi. 2004. Wordnet::Similarity - Measuring the relatedness of concepts. In *Proceedings of the Nineteenth National Conference on Artificial Intelligence*, pages 1024–1025, San Jose.

H. Schütze. 1998. Automatic word sense discrimination. *Computational Linguistics*, 24(1):97–123.

BUAP: A First Approximation to Relational Similarity Measuring

Mireya Tovar, J. Alejandro Reyes,
Azucena Montes
CENIDET, Department of
Computer Science
Int. Internado Palmira S/N, Col. Palmira
Cuernavaca, Morelos, México
{mtovar, alexreyes06c, amr}
@cenidet.edu.mx

Darnes Vilariño, David Pinto,
Saul León
B. Universidad Autónoma de Puebla,
Faculty of Computer Science
14 Sur y Av. San Claudio, CU
Puebla, Puebla, México
{darnes, dpinto}@cs.buap.mx
saul.ls@live.com

Abstract

We describe a system proposed for measuring the degree of relational similarity beetwen a pair of words at the Task #2 of Semeval 2012. The approach presented is based on a vectorial representation using the following features: *i)* the context surrounding the words with a windows $size = 3$, *ii)* knowledge extracted from WordNet to discover several semantic relationships, such as meronymy, hyponymy, hypernymy, and part-whole between pair of words, *iii)* the description of the pairs with their POS tag, morphological information (gender, person), and *iv)* the average number of words separating the two words in text.

1 Introduction

The Task # 2 of Semeval 2012 focuses on measuring the degree of relational similarity between the reference words pairs (training) and the test pairs for a given class (Jurgens et al., 2012).

The training data set consists of 10 classes and the testing data set consists of the 69 classes. These datasets as well as the particularities of the task are better described at overview paper (Jurgens et al., 2012). In this paper we report the approach submitted to the competition, which is based on a vector space model representation for each pair (Salton et al., 1975). With respect to the type of features used, we have observed that Fabio Celli (Celli, 2010) considers that contextual information is useful, as well the lexical and semantic information are in the extraction of semantic relationships task. Additionally, in (Chen et al., 2010) and (Negri and Kouylekov, 2010) are proposed WordNet based features with the same purpose.

In the experiments carried out in this paper, we use a set of lexical, semantic, WordNet-based and contextual features which allows to construct the vectors. Actually, we have tested a subset of the 20 contextual features proposed by Celli (Celli, 2010) and some of those proposed by Chen (Chen et al., 2010) and Negri (Negri and Kouylekov, 2010).

The cosine similarity measure is used for determining the degree of relational similarity (Frakes and Baeza-Yates, 1992) among the vectors.

The rest of this paper is structured as follows. Section 2 describes the system employed. Section 3 show the obtained results. Finally, in Section 4 the final conclusions are given.

2 System description

The approach reported in this paper measures the relational similarity of a set of word pairs that belong to the same semantic relationship. Those word pairs are represented by means of the vector space model (Salton et al., 1975). Each value of the vector represents the average value of the corresponding feature. This average is calculated using 100 samples obtained from Internet by employing the Google search engine. The search process is carried out assuming that those words co-occurring in the same context contain some kind of semantic relationship.

Let (w_1, w_2) be a word pair, then the vectorial representation of this pair $(\vec{x})$ using semantic, contextual, lexical, and WordNet-based features may be expressed as it can be seen in Eq. (1).

$$\vec{x} = (avg(f_1), avg(f_2), ..., avg(f_n)) \quad (1)$$

where $avg(f_k)$ is the average value of the feature f_k.

The cardinality of the vector is 42, because we extracted 4 lexical features, 6 semantic features, 7 WordNet-based features and 25 contextual features ($n = 42$). Each word pair is then represented by a unique vector with values associated to each feature. In Figure 1, we show the vectorial representation of the word pair *(transportation, bus)* using a unique text sample (s). In this example, the number and type of features described below is followed, i.e., the first 4 values are lexical, the following 6 are semantic and so on.

$s =$"The Toyama Chih Railway is a **transportation** company that operates railway, tram, and **bus** lines in the eastern part of the prefecture."

$\vec{x} = (6, 1, 0, 0, 27, 4, 4, 4, 4, 5, 2, 4, 5, 25, 0, 0, 0, 0, 0, 0, 0, 0, 0, 0, 0, 0, 0, 0, 0, 0, 0, 0, 0, 0, 0, 4, 4, 0, 4, 4, 4, 4)$

Figure 1: Example of a feature vector for a word pair and its corresponding sentence s.

The previous example is only illustrative, since we have gathered 100 sentence per word pair. In total, we collected a corpus containing 2,054,687 tokens, with a average class terms of 26,684 and with an average class vocabulary of 4,006.

The features extracted are described as follows:

2.1 Lexical features

The lexical features describe morphologically and syntactically the word pair (w_1, w_2). The lexical features extracted are the following:

- Average number of words separating the two words (w_1, w_2) in the text.
- The position of w_1 with respect to w_2 in the text. If w_1 appears before w_2 then the feature value is 1, otherwise, the value is 2.
- The Part of Speech Tag for each word in the pair (two features). We use the FreeLing PoS-tagger (Padró et al., 2010) for obtaining the grammatical category. The possible values are the following: adjective=1; adverb=2; article=3; noun=4; verb=5; pronoun=6; conjunction=7; preposition=8

2.2 Semantic features

The following four semantic features are boolean values (true or false) indicating:

- If w_1 and w_2 are named entities (two features)[1].
- If w_1 and w_2 are entities defined (two features)[2].

The following two semantic features indicate:

- The type of prepositional phrase in case of existing for w_1 and w_2. The feature values are nominal: about=1; after=2; at=3; behind=4; between=5; by=6; except=7; from=8; into=9; near=10; of=11; over=12; through=13; until=14; under=15; upon=16; without=17; above=18; among=19; before=20; below=21; beside=22; but=23; down=24; for=25; in=26; on=27; since=28; to=29; with=30.

2.3 WordNet-based features

The semantic features are boolean values (true or false) indicating whether or not w_2 is contained in:

- the synonym set of w_1
- the antonym set of w_1
- the meronymy set of w_1
- the hyponymy set of w_1
- the hypernymy set of w_1
- the part-whole set of w_1
- the gloss set of w_1

We used WordNet (Fellbaum, 1998) in order to determine the relationship set for word w_1.

[1] A named entity is defined by a Proper Noun Phrase, which was detected using the module NER-Named Entity Recognition of the FreeLing 2.1 tool.

[2] A defined sentence is one that begins with a definite article.

2.4 Contextual features

Contextual features considers values for the words that occur in the context of w_1 and w_2 (in a window size of 3). The description of those features follows.

- Nominal values indicating the Part of Speech Tag (adjective=1; adverb=2; article=3; noun=4; verb=5; pronoun=6; conjunction=7; preposition=8) for the three words at:
  - the left context of w_1 (three features).
  - the right context of w_1 (three features).
  - the left context of w_2 (three features).
  - the right context of w_2 (three features).
- A Nominal value indicating number of the following grammatical categories between w_1 and w_2: verbs, adjectives and nouns (three features).
- Nominal values indicating the frequencies of the verbs: *be, do, have, locate, know, make, use, become, include, take* between w_1 and w_2 (ten features).

2.5 Feature selection

We carried out a feature selection process with the aim of discarding irrelevant features. In this step, we apply the attribute selection filter reported in (Hall, 1999), that evaluates the worth of a subset of attributes by considering the individual predictive ability of each feature along with the degree of redundancy between them and an exhaustive search method.

The following features were obtained as relevant: the average number of words between w_1 and w_2; Named Entity of w_1 and w_2; phrase defined of w_1 and w_2; prepositional phrase type w_1 and w_2; part of speech tag w_1 and w_2; part of speech tag of right context of w_1 with a windows size of 3; occurrences of verbs between w_1 and w_2; frequency of verbs *be, do, make, locate, take*; synonym, antonym, meronymy, hyponymy, hypernymy, part-whole and gloss relationships between w_1 and w_2.

After applying the aforementioned feature selection method, we removed 17 features, and the vectorial representation of each word pair will be done with only 25 values (features).

2.6 Determining the degree of similarity

We have used the features mentioned before for constructing a prototype vector representing a given semantic class. In order to do so, we have employed the training corpus for gathering samples from Internet and, thereafter, we average the feature values in order to construct such prototype vector.

For each word pair in the test dataset, we obtained a vector using the same process explained before. We determined the similarity for each test feature vector with respect to the prototype of the given class by using the cosine similarity coefficient (Frakes and Baeza-Yates, 1992), i.e., measuring the cosine of the angle between the two vectors.

In this way, we obtain a similarity measure of each test word pair with respect to its corresponding class. Finally, we may output a ranking of all the word pairs at the test dataset by sorting these similarity values obtained.

3 Experimental results

The approach submitted to the Task #2 of SemEval 2012 obtained very poor results. The Spearman correlation coefficient, which measured the correlation of the approach with respect to the gold standard, it is quite low (see Table 1).

Team-Algorithm	Spearman	MaxDiff
UTD-NB	0.23	39.4
UTD-SVM	0.12	34.7
DULUTH-V0	0.05	32.4
DULUTH-V1	0.04	31.5
DULUTH-V2	0.04	31.1
BUAP	0.01	31.7
Random	0.02	31.2

Table 1: Spearman and MaxDiff scores obtained at the Task #2 of Semeval 2012

Actually, it shows that the run submitted does not correlate with the gold standard. We consider that this behavior is derived from the nature of the support corpus used for obtaining the features set. The number of sentences (100) used for representing the word pairs was not enough for constructing a real prototype of both, the semantic class and the word pairs. A further analysis will confirm this issue.

Despite this limitation we note that the MaxDiff score was 31.7% slightly above the baseline (31.2%) and not far from the best score of the task (39.4%). That is, we achieved an average of 31.7% of questions answered correctly.

4 Discussion and conclusion

In this paper we report the set of features used in the approach submitted for measuring the degrees of relational similarity between a given reference word pair and a variety of other pairs. The results obtained are not encouraging with a Spearman correlation coefficient close to zero, which mean that there are not correlation between the run submitted and the gold standard. A deeper analysis of the approach is needed in order to determine if the limitation of the system falls in the features used, the similarity measure, or the support corpus used for extracting the features.

Acknowledgments

This project has been partially supported by projects CONACYT #106625, VIEP #PIAD-ING11-II and #VIAD-ING11-II.

References

Fabio Celli. 2010. Unitn: Part-of-speech counting in relation extraction. In *Proceedings of the 5th International Workshop on Semantic Evaluation*, SemEval '10, pages 198–201, Stroudsburg, PA, USA. Association for Computational Linguistics.

Yuan Chen, Man Lan, Jian Su, Zhi Min Zhou, and Yu Xu. 2010. Ecnu: Effective semantic relations classification without complicated features or multiple external corpora. In *Proceedings of the 5th International Workshop on Semantic Evaluation*, SemEval '10, pages 226–229, Stroudsburg, PA, USA. Association for Computational Linguistics.

Christiane Fellbaum. 1998. *WordNet: an electronic lexical database*. MIT Press.

William B. Frakes and Ricardo A. Baeza-Yates, editors. 1992. *Information Retrieval: Data Structures & Algorithms*. Prentice-Hall.

Mark A. Hall. 1999. *Correlation-based Feature Subset Selection for Machine Learning*. Ph.D. thesis, Department of Computer Science, University of Waikato, Hamilton, New Zealand.

David A. Jurgens, Saif M. Mohammad, Peter D. Turney, and Keith J. Holyoak. 2012. Semeval-2012 task 2: Measuring degrees of relational similarity. In *Proceedings of the 6th International Workshop on Semantic Evaluation (SemEval 2012)*, Montreal, Canada.

Matteo Negri and Milen Kouylekov. 2010. Fbk_nk: A wordnet-based system for multi-way classification of semantic relations. In *Proceedings of the 5th International Workshop on Semantic Evaluation*, SemEval '10, pages 202–205, Stroudsburg, PA, USA. Association for Computational Linguistics.

Lluís Padró, Miquel Collado, Samuel Reese, Marina Lloberes, and Irene Castellón. 2010. Freeling 2.1: Five years of open-source language processing tools. In *Proceedings of the Seventh International Conference on Language Resources and Evaluation (LREC'10)*, Valletta, Malta. European Language Resources Association (ELRA).

G. Salton, A. Wong, and C. S. Yang. 1975. A vector space model for automatic indexing. *Commun. ACM*, 18(11):613–620, November.

Zhou qiaoli: A divide-and-conquer strategy for semantic dependency parsing

Qiaoli Zhou **Ling Zhang** **Fei Liu** **Dongfeng Cai** **Guiping Zhang**

Knowledge Engineering
Research Center Shenyang Aerospace University
No.37 Daoyi South Avenue
Shenyang, Liaoning, China

Zhou_qiao_li@hotmail.com 710138892@qq.com fei_12011@163.com caidf@vip.163.com zgp@ge-soft.com

Abstract

We describe our SemEval2012 shared Task 5 system in this paper. The system includes three cascaded components: the tagging semantic role phrase, the identification of semantic role phrase, phrase and frame semantic dependency parsing. In this paper, semantic role phrase is tagged automatically based on rules, and takes Conditional Random Fields (CRFs) as the statistical identification model of semantic role phrase. A projective graph-based parser is used as our semantic dependency parser. Finally, we gain Labeled Attachment Score (LAS) of 61.84%, which ranked the first position. At present, we gain the LAS of 62.08%, which is 0.24% higher than that ranked the first position in the task 5.

1 System Architecture

To solve the problem of low accuracy of long distance dependency parsing, this paper proposes a divide-and-conquer strategy for semantic dependency parsing. Firstly, Semantic Role (SR) phrase in a sentence are identified; next, SR phrase can be replaced by their head or SR of head. Therefore, the original sentence is divided into two kinds of parts, which can be parsed separately. The first kind is SR phrase parsing; the second kind is parsing the sentence in which the SR phrases are replaced by their head or SR of head. Finally, the paper takes graph-based parser as the semantic dependency parser for all parts. They are described in Section 2 and Section 4. Their experimental results are shown in Section5. Section 6 gives our conclusion and future work.

2 SR Phrase Tagging and Frame

To identify SR phrase, SR phrase of train corpus are tagged. SR phrase is tagged automatically based on rules in this paper. A phrase of the sentence is called Semantic Role phrase (SR phrase) when the parent of only one word of this phrase is out of this phrase. The word with the parent out of the phrase is called Head of Phrase (HP). The shortest SR phrase is one word, while the longest SR phrase is a part of the sentence. In this paper, the new sequence in which phrases are replaced by their head or SR of head is defined as the frame. In this paper, firstly, SR phrases of the sentence are identified; secondly, the whole sentence is divided into SR phrases and frame; thirdly, SR phrase and frame semantic dependency are parsed; finally, the dependency parsing results of all components are combined into the dependency parsing result of the whole sentence.

SR of HP is used as the type of this phrase. Only parts of types of SR phrases are tagged. In this paper, the tagged SR phrases are divided into two types: Main Semantic Role (MSR) phrase and Preposition Semantic Role (PSR) phrase.

2.1 MSR Phrase Tagging

In this paper, MSR phrase includes: OfPart, agent, basis, concerning, content, contrast, cost, existent, experiencer, isa, partner, patient, possession, possessor, relevant, scope and whole. MSR phrase tagging rules are shown in figure1&2.

```
Input: wi: word index (ID) in a given sentence.
        N: the number of words.
       Mi: MSR list.
       Vi: POS tags list
Output: the last word ID of MSR phrase
Function: Findmainsemanticword(wi): return word
           ID when wi of semantic belongs to Mi.
           Otherwise return 0.
Function: FindPOSword(wi): return true when wi
           of POS tagging not belongs to Vi. Oth-
           erwise return 0.
Function Findlastword(wi)
    For i←1 to N do begin
      If (Findmainsemanticword(wi)&&
          FindPOSword(wi))
        {
          return wi;
        }
        else {
              i++;
            }
   end
 return 0:
```

Figure1: Tagging Rule of the Last Word of MSR Phrase

Figure 1 shows the rule for identification of the last word of MSR phrase. If the SR of the current word is MSR and its POS is not VV, VE, VC or VA, it is the last word of phrase.

As shown in the figure 2, the first word of phrase is found based on the last word of phrase. The child with the longest distance from the last word of phrase is used as the current word, and if the current word has no child, it is the first word of phrase; otherwise, the child of the current word is found recursively. If the first word of phrase POS is preposition and punctuation, and its parent is the last word, the word following the first word serves as the first word of phrase.

```
Input: Lword: the last word ID of MSR phrase.
Output: Fword: the first word ID of MSR phrase.
Function: Findmaxlenchild (w): return child ID
           with the longest distance from w when w
           has child. Otherwise returns 0.
Fuction: FindPOSword(w): return POS of w.
Fuction:Findparent(w): return parent ID of w.
Function Findfirstword(Lword)
   If(Findmaxlenchild (Lword)= =0)
    {
      return Lword;
    }
    Else {
          Fword=Findmaxlenchildword(Lword);
          If(findPOSword(Fword)==P||
              findPOSword(Fword)= =PU)
            {
              If (findparent(Fword)= =Lword)
                Return Fword +1;
            }
          Findfirstword(Fword);
        }
```

Figure2: Tagging Rule of the First Word of MSR Phrase

29	而	而	CC	CC	_	30	aux-depend	_	_
30	是	是	VC	VC	_	58	s-succession	_	_
31	借鉴	借鉴	VV	VV	_	54	s-succession	_	_
32	发达	发达	JJ	JJ	_	33	d-attribute	_	_
33	国家	国家	NN	NN	_	37	s-coordinate	_	_
34	和	和	CC	CC	_	37	aux-depend	_	_
35	深圳	深圳	NR	NR	_	37	d-member	_	_
36	等	等	ETC	ETC	_	35	aux-depend	_	_
37	特区	特区	NN	NN	_	40	d-genetive	_	_
38	的	的	DEG	DEG	_	37	aux-depend	_	_
39	经验	经验	NN	NN	_	40	s-coordinate	_	_
40	教训	教训	NN	NN	_	31	content	_	_

Figure3: Example of the Tagging MSR Phrase

As shown in the figure 3, the first column is word ID and the seventh column is parent ID of word. SR of ID40 is content, so ID40 is the last word of phrase. Its children include ID39 and ID37, thus ID37 with the longest distance from ID40 is the current word. The child of ID37 is ID33, the child of ID33 is ID32, ID32 has no child, and ID32 is the first word of SR phrase.

The tagged result in the above figure 3 is as follows: 而/CC 是/VC 借鉴/VV content[**发达/JJ 国家/NN 和/CC 深圳/NR 等/ETC 特区/NN 的/DEG** 经验/NN **教训/NN]**

After phrases are tagged, a new sequence generated by replacing the phrase with HP is called MSR frame.

MSR frame: 而/CC 是/VC 借鉴/VV 教训/NN

Example of sentences with nested phrases:

据/P 初步/JJ 统计/NN ，/PU 目前/NT existent[在/P 中国/NR 境内/NN 承包/VV content[工程/NN] 的/DEC 国外/NN 承包商/NN] 已/AD 有/VE 一百三十七/CD 家/M

After phrases are tagged, a new sequence generated by replacing the phrase with HP is called MSR frame.

MSR frame: 据/P 初步/JJ 统计/NN ，/PU 目前/NT 承包商/NN 已/AD 有/VE 一百三十七/CD 家/M

2.2 PSR Phrase Tagging

In this paper, SR phrase containing preposition is defined as PSR phrase. If the POS tags of the current word is Preposition (P), the first word and the last word of PSR phrase are found based on the current word. PSR phrase tagging rule as figure 4 & 5.

```
Input: Pword: the word ID that word POS tags is P.
Output: Fword: the first word ID of PSR phrase.
Function: Findmaxlenchildword(w): return word ID
          with the longest distance from w when w
          has child. Otherwise returns 0.
Function Findfirstword(Pword)
    If(Findmaxlenchildword(Pword)= =0)
     {
       return Pword;
     }
    Else {
          return Fwrod=
           Findmaxlenchildword(Pword);
         }
```

Figure 4: Tagging Rule of the First Word of PSR Phrase

As shown in the figure 4, the child with the longest distance from the current word is the first word of phrase. If the prep has no child, then it is PSR phrase.

As shown in the figure 5, firstly, the parent of the prep is found; next, the parent is taken as the current word, and the child with the longest distance from the current word is found recursively. If no child is found, the current word is the last word of PSR phrase. If preposition of SR is root or parent of preposition is root, and proposition is PSR. If ID of preposition is larger than ID of parent of preposition, and preposition is PSR.

```
Input: Pword: the word ID that word POS tags is P.
Output: Lword: the last word ID of PSR phrase.
Function: Findmaxchild (w): return word ID that
          length is max with w when w has child.
          Otherwise return 0.
Function: Findparent (w): return word ID when w of
          parent is not root. Otherwise return 0.
Function: Findroot(w): return 1 when w of semantic
          role is root. Other wise return 0.
Function Findlastword(Pword)
Var cword: parent ID
   If(Findparentsword(Pword)= =0||
           findroot(Pword)= =1)  {
        return Pword;
   }
   else { cword=Findparent (Pword) )
          If(Pword>cword){
            return Pword;
          }
          else {
               if(Findmaxchild (cword)= =0) {
                    return cword;
               }
               else{
                    Lword=
                       Findmaxchild (cword);
                    Findlastword(Lword);
               }
          }
   }
```

Figure5: Tagging Rule of the Last Word of PSR Phrase

```
1 外商 外商 NN NN _ 2 j-agent _ _
2 投资 投资 NN NN _ 3 r-patient _ _
3 企业 企业 NN NN _ 11 agent _ _
4 在 在 P P _5 prep-depend _ first word
5 改善 改善 VV VV _ 11 duration _ head_
6 中国 中国 NR NR _ 8 d-genetive _ _
7 出口 出口 NN NN _ 8 r-patient _ _
8 商品 商品 NN NN _ 9 d-host _ _
9 结构 结构 NN NN _ 5 patient _ _
10 中 中 LC LC _ 5 aux-depend _ last word_
11 发挥 发挥 VV VV _ 0 ROOT _ _
12 了 了 AS AS _ 11 aspect _ _
13 显著 显著 JJ JJ _ 14 d-attribute _ _
14 作用 作用 NN NN _ 11 content _ _
15 。 。 PU PU _ 11 PU _ _
```

Figure6: Example of the Tagging PSR Phrase

As shown in the figure6, ID4 is prep, and it has no child, so the first word is ID4. The parent of

ID4 is ID5, the child with the longest distance from ID5 is ID10, and ID10 with no child is the last word of phrase.

The tagged result in the above figure 6 is as follows: 外商/NN 投资/NN 企业/NN **duration[在/P 改善/VV 中国/NR 出口/NN 商品/NN 中/LC]** 发挥/VV 了/AS 显著/JJ 作用/NN 。/PU

The position of HP in PSR phrase is not fixed. After phrases are tagged, a new sequence generated by replacing the phrase with SR of HP is called PSR frame.

PSR frame: 外商/NN 投资/NN 企业/NN **duration/duration** 发挥/VV 了/AS 显著/JJ 作用/NN 。/PU

Examples of sentences with nested phrases:

s-cause[由于**/P** 裕隆**/NR s-purpose[** 为**/P** 因应**/VV** Y 2 K**/NT]** 而**/MSP** 决定**/VV** 更新**/VV** 整**/DT** 个**/M** 电脑**/NN** 架构**/NN]**,/PU 因此/AD 资讯/NN 部门/NN 可/VV 谓/VV 人仰马翻/VV 。/PU

PSR frame: **s-cause/s-cause** ,/PU 因此/AD 资讯/NN 部门/NN 可/VV 谓/VV 人仰马翻/VV 。/PU

2.3 SR Phrase Tagging Performance

If the parent of only one word of the tagged phrase is out of this phrase, this phrase is tagged correctly. If each word in the generated frame has one parent (i.e. words out of the phrase are dependent on HP instead of other words of the phrase), the frame is correct.

	Phrase	Frame
MSR	99.99%	100%
PSR	99.98%	99.70%

Table 1. Tagging Performance (P-score)

As shown in the table 1, tagging results were of very high accuracy. The wrong results were not contained in phrase and frame train corpus of dependency parsing.

3 SR Phrase Identification

In this paper, we divide SR phrase into two classes: Max SR phrase and Base SR phrase. Max SR phrase refers to SR phrase is not included in any other SR phrase in a sentence. Base SR phrase refers to SR phrase does not include any other SR phrase in a SR phrase. Therefore, MSR phrase is divided into two classes: Max MSR (MMSR) phrase and Base MSR (BMSR) phrase. PSR phrase was divided into two classes: Max PSR (MPSR) phrase and Base PSR (BPSR) phrase.

3.1 MMSR Phrase Identification based on Cascaded Conditional Random Fields

Reference (Qiaoli Zhou, 2010) is selected as our approach of MMSR phrase identification. The MMSR identifying process is conceptually very simple. The MMSR identification first performs identifying BMSR phrase, and converts the identified phrase to head. It then performs identifying for the updated sequence and converts the newly recognized phrases into head. The identification repeats this process until the whole sequence has no phrase, and the top-level phrase are the MMSR phrases. A common approach to the phrase identification problem is to convert the problem into a sequence tagging task by using the "BIEO" (B for beginning, I for inside, E for ending, and O for outside) representation. If the phrase has one word, the tag is E. This representation enables us to use the linear chain CRF model to perform identifying, since the task is simply assigning appropriate labels to sequence.

There are two differences between our feature set and Qiaoli (2010)'s:

1) We use dependency direction of word as identification feature, while Qiaoli (2010) did not use.
2) We do not use scoring algorithm which is used by Qiaoli (2010).

Direction Unigrams	D_{-3},D_{-2} ,D_{-1} , D_0 , D_{+1} ,D_{+2} ,D_{+3}
Direction Bigrams	D_{-2}D-$_1$, $D_{-1}D_0$, D_0D+1, $D_{+1}D_{+2}$,
Word & Direction	W_0D_0

Table 2. Feature Templates of MMSR Phrase

Table 2 is additional new feature templates based on Qiaoli (2010). W represents a word, and D represents dependency direction of the word. With this approach, nested MSR phrases are identified, and the top-level MMSR phrase is the MMSR that we obtained.

corpus	P	R	F
dev	81.41%	75.40%	78.29%
test	81.23%	73.04%	76.92%

Table 3. MMSR Identification Performance

3.2 BMSR Phrase Identification based on CRFs

We use the tag set "BIEO" the same as that used for MMSR identification.

Word Unigrams	$W_{-3}, W_{-2}, W_{-1}, W_0, W_{+1}, W_{+2}, W_{+3}$
Word Bigrams	$W_{-3}W_{-2}, W_{-2}W_{-1}, W_{-1}W_0, W_0W_{+1}, W_{+1}W_{+2}, W_{+2}W_{+3}$
POS Unigrams	$P_{-3}, P_{-2}, P_{-1}, P_0, P_{+1}, P_{+2}, P_{+3}$
POS Bigrams	$P_{-3}P_{-2}, P_{-2}P_{-1}, P_{-1}P_0, P_0P_{+1}, P_{+1}P_{+2}, P_{+2}P_{+3}$
Word_X	X_0
Word_Y	Y_0
Word_D	D_0
Word_S	$S_{-3}, S_{-2}, S_{-1}, S_0, S_{+1}, S_{+2}, S_{+3}$
Word & POS	$W_{-1}P_{-1}, W_0P_0, W_{+1}P_{+1}$
Word & Word_X	$W_{-3}X_0$
Word & Word_D	$W_0D_0, W_{-3}W_{-2}D_0, W_{-2}W_{-1}D_0, W_{-1}W_0D_0, W_0W_{+1}D_0, W_{+1}W_{+2}D_0, W_{+2}W_{+3}D_0$
Word & Word_S	$W_{-1}S_{-1}, W_0S_0, W_{+1}S_{+1}, W_{+2}S_{+2}$
Word_X & Word_Y	X_0Y_0
POS & Word_D	$P_0D_0, P_{-3}P_{-2}D_0, P_{-2}P_{-1}D_0, P_{-1}P_0D_0, P_0P_{+1}D_0, P_{+1}P_{+2}D_0, P_{+2}P_{+3}D_0$
POS & Word_S	$P_{-1}S_{-1}, P_{-2}S_{-2}, P_{-3}S_{-3}, P_0S_0, P_{+1}S_{+1}, P_{+2}S_{+2}, P_{+3}S_{+3}$
Word_D & Word_S	$D_{-1}S_{-1}, D_{-2}S_{-2}, D_{-3}S_{-3}, D_0S_0, D_{+1}S_{+1}, D_{+2}S_{+2}, D_{+3}S_{+3}$
Word & POS & Word_D	$W_{-1}P_{-1}D_0, W_0P_0D_0, W_{+1}P_{+1}D_0$
Word & POS & Word_D & Word_S	$W_{-3}P_{-3}D_{-3}S_{-3}, W_{-2}P_{-2}D_{-2}S_{-2}, W_{-1}P_{-1}D_{-1}S_{-1}, W_0P_0D_0S_0, W_1P_1D_1S_1, W_2P_2D_2S_2, W_3P_3D_3S_3$

Table 4. Feature Templates of BMSR Phrase

In table 4, "W" represents a word, "P" represents the part-of-speech of the word, "X" represents the fourth word following the current word, "Y" represents the fifth word following the current word, "D" represents the dependency direction of the current word, and "S" represents the paired punctuation feature. "S" consists of "RLIO" (R for the right punctuation, L for the left punctuation, I for the part between the paired punctuation and O for outside).

corpus	P	R	F
dev	79.32%	80.65%	79.98%
test	79.22%	79.96%	79.59%

Table 5. BMSR Identification Performance (F-score)

3.3 MPSR Phrase Identification Based on Collection

Reference (Dongfeng, 2011) is selected as our approach of MPSR phrase identification. The position of HP in PSR phrase is not fixed. Not only PSR phrase is identified, but also PSR phrase type is identified.

There are two major differences between our feature set and Dongfeng (2011)'s:

1) We take the PSR phrase type (the SR of HP) as tag.

2) We use "S-type" represents that the PSR phrase is the single preposition. "Type" represents SR of the preposition.

For example: 工作者/NN location [在/P 甘肃/NR 金川/NR] 发现/VV

O|W	POS	Dongfeng (2011) Tag	Our Tag
*|工作者	NN	O	O
*|在	P	O	O
在|甘肃	NR	I	I
在|金川	NR	E	**Location-E**
在|发现	VV	N	N

Table 6. Example of PSR Phrase Tag Set

In table 6, Dongfeng(2011) takes 'E' as the tag of last word of PSR phrase, but we take **'Location-E'** as the tag of last word of PSR phrase (Location is type of PSR phrase).

With this approach, nested PSR phrases are identified, and the top-level PSR phrase is the MPSR that we obtained.

corpus	MPSR phrase	MPSR phrase & type
dev	84.00%	54.23%
test	83.78%	51.60%

Table 7. MPSR Identification Performance (F-score)

3.4 Combined Identification of MSR Phrase and PSR Phrase

Identification process: MSR phrase and PSR phrase are respectively identified in one sentence, and the results are combined in accordance with this rule: if phrases are nested, only the top-level phrase is tagged; if phrases are same, only the PSR phrase is tagged; if phrases are overlapped, only PSR phrase is tagged.

There are two combinations in this paper:

1) MMSR phrase and MPSR phrase combined result is defined as MMMP phrase. For example as follow ('[ ]'represents MMSR, '{}'represents MPSR):

Example A: [建筑/NN] 是/VC [开发/VV 浦东/NR 的/DEC 一/CD 项/M 主要/JJ 经济/NN 活动/NN] ， /PU 这些/DT 年/M 有/VE [数百/CD 家/M 建筑/NN 公司/NN 、/PU 四千余/CD 个/M 建筑/NN 工地/NN] 遍布/VV location{ 在/P 这/DT 片/M 热土/NN 上/LC } 。/PU

MMMP frame: [**建筑/NN**] 是/VC **活动/NN** ， /PU 这些/DT 年/M 有/VE **工地/NN** 遍布/VV location/location 。/PU

2) BMSR phrase and MPSR phrase combined result is defined as BMMP phrase.

Example B: [建筑/NN] 是/VC 开发/VV [浦东/NR] 的/DEC 一/CD 项/M 主要/JJ 经济/NN 活动/NN ， /PU 这些/DT 年/M 有/VE [数百/CD 家/M 建筑/NN 公司/NN 、/PU 四千余/CD 个/M 建筑/NN 工地/NN] 遍布/VV location{ 在/P 这/DT 片/M 热土/NN 上/LC } 。/PU

BMMP frame: **建筑/NN** 是/VC 开发/VV 浦东**/NR** 的/DEC 一/CD 项/M 主要/JJ 经济/NN 活动/NN ， /PU 这些/DT 年/M 有/VE **工地/NN** 遍布/VV **location/location** 。/PU

corpus	phrase	P	R	F
dev	BMMP	79.48%	81.60%	80.53%
	MMMP	80.00%	76.79%	78.36%
test	BMMP	80.14%	82.48%	81.30%
	MMMP	80.19%	78.53%	79.35%

Table 8. Combination Phrase Identification Performance

3.5 Phrase and Frame Length Distribution

We count phrases, frame and Original Sentence (OS) length distribution in training set and dev set.

	BMMP	MMMP	MMSR	BMSR	OS
[0,5)	80.07%	71.36%	75.36%	85.74%	9.07%
[5,10)	16.15%	21.63%	18.93%	12.33%	8.30%
[10,20)	3.35%	6.13%	5.05%	1.80%	17.23%
20≤	0.43%	0.88%	0.66%	0.13%	65.40%

Table 9. Length Distribution of Phrases and OS

Table 9 shows, about 95% of phrases have less than 10 words, but about 65% of OS has more than 20 words.

	BMMP	MMMP	MMSR	BMSR	OS
[0,5)	16.00%	18.70%	16.43%	14.36%	9.07%
[5,10)	18.87%	24.91%	19.41%	14.11%	8.30%
[10,20)	34.26%	35.42%	33.94%	30.68%	17.23%
20≤	30.87%	20.97%	30.22%	40.85%	65.40%

Table 10. Length Distribution of Frames and OS

Table 10 shows, about 70% of frames have less than 20 words, especially 80% of MMMP frame has less than 20 words, but about 65% of OS has more than 20 words.

	BMMP	MMMP	BMSR	MMSR	OS
phrase	3.07	3.83	2.53	3.44	30.07
frame	16.00	13.21	19.16	15.79	30.07

Table 11. Average Length

We count phrases, frame and Original Sentence (OS) Average Length (AL) in training set and dev set. Table 11 shows phrase of AL accounted for 10% of OS of AL, and frame of AL accounted for 50% of OS of AL. The AL shows that the semantic dependency paring unit length of OS is greatly reduced after dividing an original sentence into SR phrases and frame.

As shown in tables 9, 10 and 11, the length distribution indicates that the divide-and-conquer strategy reduces the complexity of sentences significantly.

4 Semantic Dependency Parsing

Graph-based parser is selected as our basic semantic dependency parser. It views the semantic dependency parsing as problem of finding maximum spanning trees (McDonald, 2006) in directed graphs. In this paper, phrase and frame semantic dependency parsing result was obtained by Graph-based parser. Training set of phrase comes from phrases, and training set of frame comes from frames.

5 Experiments

5.1 Direction of Identification

Dependency direction serves as feature of SR phrase identification, so we need to identify dependency direction of word. We use tag set is {B, F}, B represents backward dependence, F represents forward dependence. The root's dependency direction in sentence is B. Dependency direction identification p-score has reached 94.87%.

Word Unigrams	W_{-4}, W_{-3}, W_{-2}, W_{-1}, W_0, W_{+1}, W_{+2}, W_{+3}, W_{+4}
Word Bigrams	$W_{-3}W_{-2}$, $W_{-2}W_{-1}$, $W_{-1}W_0$, W_0W_{+1}, $W_{+1}W_{+2}$, $W_{+2}W_{+3}$
Word Trigrams	$W_{-1}W_0W_{+1}$
Word Four-grams	$W_{-2}W_{-1}W_0W_{+1}$, $W_0W_{+1}W_{+2}W_{+3}$
Word Five-grams	$W_{-4}W_{-3}W_{-2}W_{-1}W_0$, $W_0W_{+1}W_{+2}W_{+3}W_{+4}$
POS Unigrams	P_{-4}, P_{-3}, P_{-2}, P_{-1}, P_0, P_{+1}, P_{+2}, P_{+3}, P_{+4}
POS Bigrams	$P_{-3}P_{-2}$, $P_{-2}P_{-1}$, $P_{-1}P_0$, P_0P_{+1}, $P_{+1}P_{+2}$, $P_{+2}P_{+3}$
POS Trigrams	$P_{-1}P_0P_{+1}$
POS Four-grams	$P_{-2}P_{-1}P_0P_{+1}$, $P_0P_{+1}P_{+2}P_{+3}$
POS Five-grams	$P_{-4}P_{-3}P_{-2}P_{-1}P_0$, $P_0P_{+1}P_{+2}P_{+3}P_{+4}$
Word & POS	$W_{-2}P_{-2}$, $W_{-1}P_{-1}$, W_0P_0, $W_{+1}P_{+1}$, $W_{+2}P_{+2}$

Table 12. Feature Templates of Dependency Direction

In table12, w represents word, p represents POS.

5.2 System and Model

For a sentence for which phrases has been identified, if phrases can be identified, then the whole sentence semantic dependency parsing result is obtained by phrase parsing model and frame parsing model. Therefore, in this paper, the sentence is divided into the following types based on the phrase identification results: (1) SentMMMP indicates MMSR phrase and MPSR phrase identified in a sentence; (2) SentBMMP indicates BMSR phrase and MPSR phrase identified in a sentence; (3) SentMMSR indicates only MMSR phrase identified in a sentence; (4) SentMPSR indicates only MPSR phrase identified in a sentence; (5) SentBMSR indicates only BMSR phrase identified in a sentence; (6) SentNone indicates no phrase identified in a sentence.

Sentence type	Phrase parsing Model	Frame parsing Model
SentMMMP	MMMP phrase	MMMP frame
SentBMMP	BMMP phrase	BMMP frame
SentMMSR	MMSR phrase	MMSR frame
SentMPSR	MPSR phrase	MPSR frame
SentBMSR	BMSR phrase	BMSR frame
SentNone	Sentence model	

Table 13. Type of Sentence and Parsing Model

Table 13 shows types of sentence, and parsing models for every type of sentence. For example, parsing SentMMMP needs MMMP phrase parsing model and MMMP frame paring model

The corpus contains the sentence type determined by the phrase identification strategy.

Strategy of phrase identification	Sentence type in the corpus
Strategy MMMP	SentMMMP, SentMMSR, SentMPSR, SentNone
Strategy BMMP	SentBMMP, SentMPSR, SentBMSR, SentNone
Strategy BMSR	SentBMSR, SentNone

Table 14. Sentence Types in the Corpus

As shown in table 14, Strategy MMMP indicates that MMMP phrase in the corpus was identified, and sentences in the corpus were divided into SentMMMP, SentMMSR, SentMPSR and SentNone. Strategy BMMP indicates that BMMP phrase in the corpus was identified, and sentences in the corpus were divided into SentBMMP, SentBMSR, SentMPSR and SentNone. Strategy BMSR indicates that BMSR phrase in the corpus was identified, and sentences in the corpus were divided into SentBMSR and SentNone.

5.3 Comparative Experiments

In this paper, we carry out comparative experiments of parsing for the test set by 3 systems.

1) System1 represents strategy MMMP in the table 14.
2) System2 represents strategy BMMP in the table 14.
3) System3 represents strategy BMSR in the table 14.

	Dev	Test
G-parser	62.31%	61.68%
System1(MMMP)	61.98%	61.84%
System2(BMMP)	62.7%	62.08%
System3(BMSR)	62.22%	61.15%

Table 15. Comparative Experiments

As shown in the table 15, system2 result is more accurate than system1, because BMMP phrase identification is more accurate than MMMP as shown in the table 8. Although, BMSR phrase identification is more accurate than MMMP phrase as shown in the table 5 & 8, system 3 result is less accurate than systm1. Compared with BMSR identification, MMMP identification reduces the complexity of sentences significantly, because the table 11 shows that the AL of MMMP frame is about 30% less than that of BMSR frame. G-parser is graph-based parser (Wangxiang Che, 2008).

6 Conclusion and Future Work

To solve the problem of low accuracy of long distance dependency parsing, this paper proposes a divide-and-conquer strategy for semantic dependency parsing. We present our SemEval2012 shared Task 5 system which is composed of three cascaded components: the tagging of SR phrase, the identification of Semantic-role- phrase and semantic dependency parsing.

Divide-and-conquer strategy is influenced by two factors: one is identifying the type of phrase will greatly reduce the sentence complexity; the other is phrase identifying precision results in cascaded errors. The topic of this evaluation is semantic dependency parsing, and word and POS contain less semantic information. If we can make semantic label on words, then it will be more helpful for semantic dependency parsing. In the future, we will study how to solve the long distance dependency parsing problem.

Acknowledgments

The authors would like to thank the reviewers for their helpful comments. This work was supported by National Natural Science Foundation of China (NSFC) via grant 61073123 and Natural Science Foundation of Liaoning province via grant 20102174.

References

Dongfeng Cai, Ling Zhang, Qiaoli Zhou and Yue Zhao. *A Collocation Based Approach for Prepositional Phrase Identification.* IEEE NLPKE, 2011.

McDonald, Ryan. 2006. *Discriminative Learning and Spanning Tree Algorithms for Dependency Parsing.* Ph.D. thesis, University of Pennsylvania.

Guiping Zhang, Wenjing Lang, Qiaoli Zhou and Dongfeng Cai. 2010. *Identification of Maximal-Length Noun Phrases Based on Maximal-Length Preposition Phrases in Chinese,* 2010 International Conference on Asian Language Processing, pages 65-68.

Qiaoli Zhou, Wenjing Lang, Yingying Wang, Yan Wang, Dongfeng Cai. 2010. *The SAU Report for the 1st CIPS-SIGHAN-ParsEval-2010,* Proceedings of the First CIPS-SIGHAN Joint Conference on Chinese Language Processing, pp:304-311.

Wanxiang Che, Zhenghua Li, Yuxuan Hu, Yongqiang Li,Bing Qin, Ting Liu, and Sheng Li. 2008. *A cascaded syntactic and semantic dependency parsing system.* In CoNLL-2008.

ICT:A System Combination for Chinese Semantic Dependency Parsing

Hao Xiong and Qun Liu
Key Lab. of Intelligent Information Processing
Institute of Computing Technology
Chinese Academy of Sciences
P.O. Box 2704, Beijing 100190, China
{xionghao, liuqun}@ict.ac.cn

Abstract

The goal of semantic dependency parsing is to build dependency structure and label semantic relation between a head and its modifier. To attain this goal, we concentrate on obtaining better dependency structure to predict better semantic relations, and propose a method to combine the results of three state-of-the-art dependency parsers. Unfortunately, we made a mistake when we generate the final output that results in a lower score of 56.31% in term of Labeled Attachment Score (LAS), reported by organizers. After giving golden testing set, we fix the bug and rerun the evaluation script, this time we obtain the score of 62.8% which is consistent with the results on developing set. We will report detailed experimental results with correct program as a comparison standard for further research.

1 Introduction

In this year's Semantic Evaluation Task, the organizers hold a task for Chinese Semantic Dependency Parsing. The semantic dependency parsing (SDP) is a kind of dependency parsing. It builds a dependency structure for a sentence and labels the semantic relation between a head and its modifier. The semantic relations are different from syntactic relations. They are position independent, e.g., the patient can be before or behind a predicate. On the other hand, their grains are finer than syntactic relations, e.g., the syntactic subject can be agent or experiencer. Readers can refer to (Wanxiang Che, 2012) for detailed introduction.

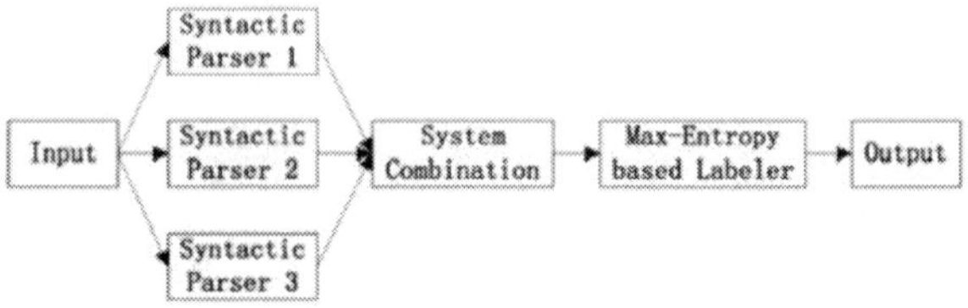

Figure 1: The pipeline of our system, where we combine the results of three dependency parsers and use max-entropy classifier to predict the semantic relations.

Different from most methods proposed in CoNLL-2008 [1] and 2009 [2], in which some researchers build a joint model to simultaneously generate dependency structure and its syntactic relations (Surdeanu et al., 2008; Hajič et al., 2009), here, we first employ several parsers to generate dependency structure and then propose a method to combine their outputs. After that, we label relation between each head and its modifier via the traversal of this refined parse tree. The reason why we use a pipeline model while not a joint model is that the number of semantic relations annotated by organizers is more than 120 types, while in the former task is only 21 types. Compared to the former task, the large number of types will obviously drop the performance of classifier. On the other hand, the performance of syntactic dependency parsing is approaching to perfect, intuitively, that better dependency structure does help to semantic parsing, thus we can concentrate on improving the accuracy of dependency structure construction.

The overall framework of our system is illustrated

[1] http://www.yr-bcn.es/conll2008/
[2] http://ufal.mff.cuni.cz/conll2009-st/

in figure 1, where three dependency parsers are employed to generate the dependency structure, and a maximum entropy classifier is used to predict relation for head and its modifier over combined parse tree. Final experimental results show that our system achieves 80.45% in term of unlabeled attachment score (UAS), and 62.8 % in term of LAS. Both of them are higher than the baseline without using system combinational techniques.

In the following of this paper, we will demonstrate the detailed information of our system, and report several experimental results.

2 System Description

As mentioned, we employ three single dependency parsers to generate respect dependency structure. To further improve the accuracy of dependency structure construction, we blend the syntactic outputs and find a better dependency structure. In the followings, we will first introduce the details of our strategy for dependency structure construction.

2.1 Parsers

We implement three transition-based dependency parsers with three different parsing algorithms: Nivre's arc standard, Nivre's arc eager (see Nivre (2004) for a comparison between the two Nivre algorithms), and Liang's dynamic algorithm(Huang and Sagae, 2010). We use these algorithms for several reasons: first, they are easy to implement and their reported performance are approaching to state-of-the-art. Second, their outputs are projective, which is consistent with given corpus.

2.2 Parser Combination

We use the similar method presented in Hall et al. (2011) to advance the accuracy of parses. The parses of each sentence are combined into a weighted directed graph. The left procedure is similar to traditional graph-based dependency parsing except that the number of edges in our system is smaller since we reserve best edges predicted by three single parsers. We use the popular Chu-Liu-Edmonds algorithm (Chu and Liu, 1965; Edmonds et al., 1968) to find the maximum spanning tree (MST) of the new constructed graph, which is considered as the final parse of the sentence. Specifically, we use the parsing accuracy on developing set to represent the weight of graph edge. Formally, the weight of graph edge is computed as follows,

$$w_e = \sum_{p \in P} Accuracy(p) \cdot I(e,p) \tag{1}$$

where the $Accuracy(p)$ is the parsing score of parse tree p whose value is the score of parsing accuracy on developing set, and $I(e,p)$ is an indicator, if there is such dependency in parse tree p, it returns 1, otherwise returns 0. Since the value of $Accuracy(p)$ ranges from 0 to 1, we doesn't need to normalize its value.

Thus, the detailed procedure for dependency structure construction is,

- Parsing each sentence using Nivre's arc standard, Nivre's arc eager and Liang's dynamic algorithm, respectively.
- Combining parses outputted by three parsers into weighted directed graph, and representing its weight using equation 1.
- Using Chu-Liu-Edmonds algorithm to search final parse for each sentence.

2.3 Features for Labeling

After given dependency structure, for each relation between head and its modifier, we extract 31 types of features, which are typically exploited in syntactic dependency parsing, as our basic features. Based on these basic features, we also add a additional distance metric for each features and obtain 31 types of distance incorporated features. Besides that, we use greedy hill climbing approach to select additional 29 features to obtain better performance. Table 1 shows the basic features used in our system,

And the table 2 gives the additional features. It is worth mentioning, that the distance is calculated as the difference between the head and its modifier, which is different from the calculation reported by most literatures.

2.4 Classifier

We use the classifier from Le Zhang's Maximum Entropy Modeling Toolkit[3] and use the L-BFGS

[3]http://homepages.inf.ed.ac.uk/s0450736/maxent_toolkit .html

	Features
Basic	**mw**:modifier's word **mp**:modifier's POS tag **hw**:head's word **hp**:head's POS tag
Combination	hw|hp,mw|mp,hw|mw hp|mp,hw|mp,hp|mw hw|hp|mw hw|hp|mp hw|mw|mp hp|mw|mp hp|mp|mp-1 hp|mp|mp+1 hp|hp-1|mp hp|hp+1|mp hp|hp-1|mp-1 hp|hp-1|mp+1 hp|hp+1|mp-1 hp|hp+1|mp+1 hp-1|mp|mp-1 hp-1|mp|mp+1 hp+1|mp|mp-1 hp+1|mp|mp+1 hw|hp|mw|mp hp|hp-1|mp|mp-1 hp|hp+1|mp|mp+1 hp|hp+1|mp|mp-1 hp|hp-1|mp|mp+1

Table 1: The basic features used in our system. -1 and +1 indicate the one on the left and right of given word.

parameter estimation algorithm with gaussian prior smoothing(Chen and Rosenfeld, 1999). We set the gaussian prior to 2 and train the model in 1000 iterations according to the previous experience.

3 Experiments

The given corpus consists of 8301 sentences for training(TR), and 569 sentences for developing(DE). For tuning parameters, we just use TR portion, while for testing, we combine two parts and retrain the parser to obtain better results. Surely, we also give results of testing set trained on TR portion for comparison. In the following of this section, we will report the detailed experimental results both on

	Features
Distance	**dist**:basic features with distance
Additional	**lmw**:leftmost word of modifier **rnw**:rightnearest word of modifier **gfw**:grandfather of modifier **lmp,rnp,gfp** lmw|lmp,rnw|rnp,lmw|rnw lmp|rnp,lmw|mw,lmp|mp rnw|mw,rnp|mp,gfw|mw gfp|mp,gfw|hw,gfp|hp gfw|mw|gfp|mp lmw|lmp|mw|mp rnw|rnp|mw|mp lmw|rnw|mw,lmp|rnp|mp gfw|hw|gfp|hp gfw|mw|hw,gfp|mp|hp gfw|mw|hw|gfp|mp|hp lmw|rnw|lmp|rnp|mw|mp lmw|rnw|lmp|rnp

Table 2: The additional features used in our system.

developing and testing set.

3.1 Results on Developing Set

We first report the accuracy of dependency construction on developing set using different parsing algorithms in table 3. Note that, the features used in our system are similar to that used in their published papers(Nivre, 2003; Nivre, 2004; Huang and Sagae, 2010). From table 3 we find that although

	Precision (%)
Nivre's arc standard	78.86
Nivre's arc eager	79.11
Liang's dynamic	79.78
System Combination	**80.85**

Table 3: Syntactic precision of different parsers on developing set.

using simple method for combination over three single parsers, the system combination technique still achieves 1.1 points improvement over the highest single system. Since the Liang's algorithm is a dynamic algorithm, which enlarges the searching space in decoding, while the former two Nivre's arc algorithms actually still are simple beam search algorithm, thus the Liang's algorithm achieves better performance than Nivre's two algorithm, which is consistent with the experiments in Liang's paper.

To acknowledge that the better dependency structure does help to semantic relation labeling, we further predict semantic relations on different dependency structures. For comparison, we also report the performance on golden structure. Since our combinational algorithm requires weight for each edges, we use the developing parsing accuracy 0.7886, 0.7911, and 0.7978 as corresponding weights for each single system. Table 4 shows, that the prediction of semantic relation could benefit from the improvement of dependency structure. We also notice that even given the golden parse tree, the performance of relation labeling is still far from perfect. Two reasons could be explained for that: first is the small size of supplied corpus, second is that the relation between head and its modifier is too fine-grained to distinguish for a classifier. Moreover, here we use golden segmentation for parsing, imagining that an automatic segmenter would further drop the accuracy both on syntactic and semantic parsing.

	Precision (%)
Nivre's arc standard	60.84
Nivre's arc eager	60.76
Liang's dynamic	61.43
System Combination	**62.92**
Golden Tree	**76.63**

Table 4: LAS of semantic relations over different parses on developing set.

3.2 Results on Testing Set

Since there is a bug[4] in our final results submitted to organizers, here, in order to confirm the improvement of our method and supply comparison standard for further research, we reevaluate the correct output and report its performance on different training set. Table 5 and table 6 give the results trained on different corpus. We can see that when increasing the training size, the performance is slightly improved. Also, we find the results on testing set is consistent with that on developing set, where best dependency structure achieves the best performance.

[4]The bug is come from that when we converting the CoNLL-styled outputs generated by our combination system into plain text. While in developing stage, we directly used CoNLL-styled outputs as our input, thus we didn't realize this mistake.

	LAS (%)	**UAS(%)**
Nivre's arc standard	60.38	78.19
Nivre's arc eager	60.78	78.62
Liang's dynamic	60.85	79.09
System Combination	**62.76**	**80.23**
Submitted Error Results	55.26	71.85

Table 5: LAS and UAS on testing set trained on TR.

	LAS (%)	**UAS(%)**
Nivre's arc standard	60.49	78.25
Nivre's arc eager	60.99	78.78
Liang's dynamic	61.29	79.59
System Combination	**62.80**	**80.45**
Submitted Error Results	56.31	73.20

Table 6: LAS and UAS on testing set trained on TR and DE.

4 Conclusion

In this paper, we demonstrate our system framework for Chinese Semantic Dependency Parsing, and report the experiments with different configurations. We propose to use system combination to better the dependency structure construction, and then label semantic relations over refined parse tree. Final experiments show that better syntactic parsing do help to improve the accuracy of semantic relation prediction.

Acknowledgments

The authors were supported by National Science Foundation of China, Contracts 90920004, and High-Technology R&D Program (863) Project No 2011AA01A207 and 2012BAH39B03. We thank Heng Yu for generating parse tree using Liang's algorithm. We thank organizers for their generous supplied resources and arduous preparation. We also thank anonymous reviewers for their thoughtful suggestions.

References

Stanley F. Chen and Ronald Rosenfeld. 1999. A gaussian prior for smoothing maximum entropy models. Technical report, CMU-CS-99-108.

Y.J. Chu and T.H. Liu. 1965. On the shortest arborescence of a directed graph. *Science Sinica*, 14(1396-1400):270.

J. Edmonds, J. Edmonds, and J. Edmonds. 1968. *Optimum branchings*. National Bureau of standards.

J. Hajič, M. Ciaramita, R. Johansson, D. Kawahara, M.A. Martí, L. Màrquez, A. Meyers, J. Nivre, S. Padó, J. Štěpánek, et al. 2009. The conll-2009 shared task: Syntactic and semantic dependencies in multiple languages. In *Proceedings of the Thirteenth Conference on Computational Natural Language Learning: Shared Task*, pages 1–18. Association for Computational Linguistics.

J. Hall, J. Nilsson, and J. Nivre. 2011. Single malt or blended? a study in multilingual parser optimization. *Trends in Parsing Technology*, pages 19–33.

L. Huang and K. Sagae. 2010. Dynamic programming for linear-time incremental parsing. In *Proceedings of the 48th Annual Meeting of the Association for Computational Linguistics*, pages 1077–1086. Association for Computational Linguistics.

J. Nivre. 2003. An efficient algorithm for projective dependency parsing. In *Proceedings of the 8th International Workshop on Parsing Technologies (IWPT*. Citeseer.

J. Nivre. 2004. Incrementality in deterministic dependency parsing. In *Proceedings of the Workshop on Incremental Parsing: Bringing Engineering and Cognition Together*, pages 50–57. Association for Computational Linguistics.

M. Surdeanu, R. Johansson, A. Meyers, L. Màrquez, and J. Nivre. 2008. The conll-2008 shared task on joint parsing of syntactic and semantic dependencies. In *Proceedings of the Twelfth Conference on Computational Natural Language Learning*, pages 159–177. Association for Computational Linguistics.

Ting Liu Wanxiang Che. 2012. Semeval-2012 Task 5: Chinese Semantic Dependency Parsing. In *Proceedings of the 6th International Workshop on Semantic Evaluation (SemEval 2012)*.

NJU-Parser: Achievements on Semantic Dependency Parsing

Guangchao Tang[1] Bin Li[1,2] Shuaishuai Xu[1] Xinyu Dai[1] Jiajun Chen[1]
[1] State Key Lab for Novel Software Technology, Nanjing University
[2] Research Center of Language and Informatics, Nanjing Normal University
Nanjing, Jiangsu, China
{tanggc, lib, xuss, dxy, chenjj}@nlp.nju.edu.cn

Abstract

In this paper, we introduce our work on SemEval-2012 task 5: Chinese Semantic Dependency Parsing. Our system is based on MSTParser and two effective methods are proposed: splitting sentence by punctuations and extracting last character of word as lemma. The experiments show that, with a combination of the two proposed methods, our system can improve LAS about one percent and finally get the second prize out of nine participating systems. We also try to handle the multi-level labels, but with no improvement.

1 Introduction

Task 5 of SemEval-2012 tries to find approaches to improve Chinese sematic dependency parsing (SDP). SDP is a kind of dependency parsing. Currently, there are many dependency parsers available, such as Eisner's probabilistic dependency parser (Eisner, 1996), McDonald's MSTParser (McDonald et al. 2005a; McDonald et al. 2005b) and Nivre's MaltParser (Nivre, 2006).

Despite of elaborate models, lots of problems still exist in dependency parsing. For example, sentence length has been proved to show great impact on the parsing performance. (Li et al., 2010) used a two-stage approach based on sentence fragment for high-order graph-based dependency parsing. Lacking of linguistic knowledge is also blamed.

Three methods are promoted in this paper trying to improve the performance: splitting sentence by commas and semicolons, extracting last character of word as lemma and handling multi-level labels. Improvements could be achieved through the first two methods while not for the third.

2 Overview of Our System

Our system is based on MSTParser which is one of the state-of-the-art parsers. MSTParser tries to obtain the maximum spanning tree of a sentence. For projective parsing task, it takes Eisner's algorithm (Eisner, 1996) to get the dependency tree in $O(n^3)$ time. Meanwhile, Chu-Liu-Edmond's algorithm (Chu and Liu, 1965) is applied for non-projective task, which takes $O(n^2)$ time.

Three methods are adopted to MSTParser in our system:

1) Sentences are split into sub-sentences by commas and semicolons, for which there are two ways. Splitting sentences by all commas and semicolons is used in our primary system. In our contrast system, we use a classifier to determine whether a comma or semicolon can be used to split the sentence. In the primary and contrast system, the proto sentences and the sub-sentences are trained and tested separately and the outputs are merged in the end.
2) In a Chinese word, the last character usually contains main sense or semantic class. We treat the last character of the word as word lemma and find it gets a slightly improvement in the experiment.
3) An experiment trying to solve the problem of multi-level labels was conducted by parsing different levels separately and consequently merging the outputs together.

The experiment results have shown that the first two methods could enhance the system performance while further improvements could be obtained through a combination of them in our sub-submitted systems.

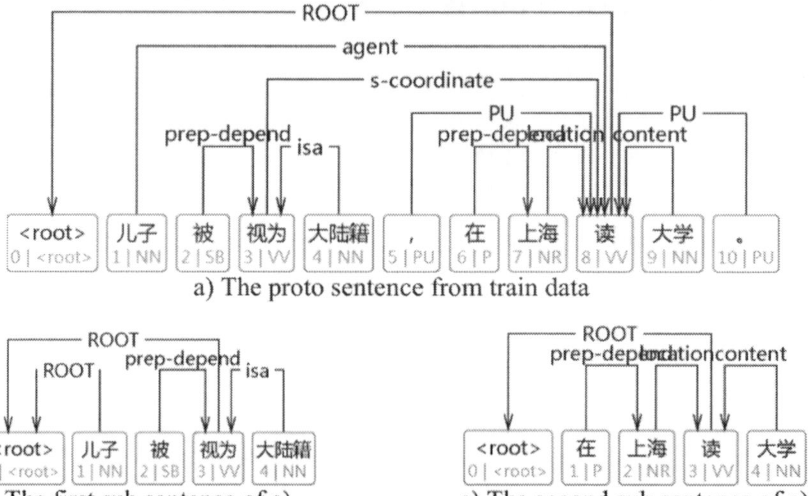

a) The proto sentence from train data

b) The first sub sentence of a)

c) The second sub sentence of a)

Figure 1. An example of the split procedure.

3 Experiments

3.1 Split sentences by commas and semicolons

It is observed that the performance decreases as the length of the sentences increases. Table 1 shows the statistical analysis on the data including SemEval-2012, Conll-07's Chinese corpus and a subset extracted from CTB using Penn2Malt. Long sentence can be split into sub-sentences to get better parsing result.

Items	SemEval -2012	Conll-07 CN	CTB
Postages count	35	13	33
Dependency labels count	122	69	12
Average sentence length	30.15	5.92	25.89
Average dependency length	4.80	1.71	4.36
LAS	61.37	82.89	67.35
UAS	80.18	87.64	79.90

Table 1. Statistical analysis on the data. The CTB data is a subset extracted from CTB using Penn2Malt.

Our work can be described as following steps:

Step 1: Use MSTParser to parse the data. We name the result as ***"normal output"***.

Step 2: Split train and test data by all commas and semicolons. The delimiters are removed in the sub sentences. For train data, a word's dependency relation is kept if the word's head is under the cover of the sub sentence. Otherwise, its head will be set to root and its label will be set to *ROOT* (*ROOT* is the default label of dependency arcs whose head is root). We define the word as ***"sentence head"*** if its head is root. ***"Sub-sentence head"*** indicates the *sentence head* of a sub-sentence. After splitting, there may be more than one *sub-sentence heads* in a sub-sentence. Figure 1 shows an example of the split procedure.

Step 3: Use MSTParser to parse the data generated in step 2. We name the parsing result ***"split output"***. In *split output*, there may be more than one sub-sentences corresponding to a single sentence in *normal output*.

Step 4: Merge the *split output* and the *normal output*. The outputs of sub-sentences are merged with delimiters restored. Dependency relations are recovered for all punctuations and *sub-sentence heads* in *split output* with relations in *normal output*. The sentence head of *normal output* is kept in final output. The result is called ***"merged split output"***. This step need to be consummated because it may result in a dependency tree not well formed with several *sentence heads* or even circles.

The results of experiments on develop data and test data are showed in table 2. For develop data, an improvement of 0.85 could be obtained while 0.93 for test data, both on LAS.

In step 2, there is an alternative to split the sentences, i.e., using a classifier to determine which comma and semicolon can be split. This method is taken in the contrast system. When applying the classifier, all commas and semicolons in train data are labeled with S-IN or S-STOP while other words with NULL. If the sub sentence before the comma or semicolon has only one *sub-sentence head*, it is labeled with S-STOP, otherwise with S-IN. A model is built from train data with CRF++ and test data is evaluated with it. Features used are listed in table 3. Only commas and semicolons with label S-STOP can be used to split the sentence in step 2. Other steps are the same as above. The result is also shown in table 2 as ***"merged split output with CRF++"***.

Data	Methods	LAS	UAS
Develop data	normal output	61.37	80.18
	merged split output	62.22	80.56
	merged split output with CRF++	61.97	80.73
	lemma output	61.64	80.47
	primary system output	**62.41**	80.96
	contrast system output	62.05	80.90
Test data	normal output	60.63	79.37
	merged split output	61.56	80.17
	merged split output with CRF++	61.42	80.20
	lemma output	60.88	79.42
	primary system output	61.63	80.35
	contrast system output	**61.64**	80.29

Table 2. Results of the experiments.

w-4,w-3,w-2,w-1,w,w+1,w+2,w+3,w+4
p-4,p-3,p-2,p-1,p,p+1,p+2,p+3,p+4
wp-4,wp-3,wp-2,wp-1,wp wp+1,wp+2,wp+3,wp+4
w-4|w-3,w-3|w-2,w-2|w-1,w-1|w, w|w+1,w+1|w+2,w+2|w+3,w+3|w+4
p-4|p-3,p-3|p-2,p-2|p-1,p-1|p, p|p+1,p+1|p+2,p+2|p+3,p+3|p+4
first word of sub-sentence before the delimiter

Table 3. Features used in CRF++. w represents for word and p for PosTag. +1 means the index after current while -1 means before.

3.2 Extract last character of word as lemma

In Chinese, the last character of a word usually contains main sense or semantic class, which indicates that it may represent the whole word. For example, "国"(country) can represent "中国"(China) and "恋"(love) can represent "热恋"(crazy love).

The last character is used as lemma in the experiment, with an improvement of 0.27 for LAS on develop data and 0.24 on test data. Details of the scores are listed in table 2 as ***"lemma output"***.

3.3 Multi-level labels experiment

A notable characteristic of SemEval-2012's data is multi-level labels. It introduces four kinds of multi-level labels which are s-X, d-X, j-X and r-X. The first level represents the basic semantic relation of the dependency while the second level shows the second import, except that s-X represents sub-sentence relation.

The r-X label means that a verb modifies a noun and the relation between them is reverse. For example, in phrase "贫户(poor) 出身(born) 的 明星(star)", "出身" is headed to "明星" with label r-agent. It means that "明星" is the agent of "出身".

When a verbal noun is the head word and its child has indirect relation to it, the dependency is labeled with j-X. In phrase "学校(school) 建设(construction)", "建设" is the head of "学校" with label j-content. "学校" is the content of "建设".

The d-X label means that the child modifies the head with an additional relation. For example, in phrase "科技(technology) 企业(enterprise)", "科技" modifies "企业" and the domain of "企业" is "科技".

A heuristic method is tried in the experiment. The multi-level labels of d-X, j-X and r-X are separated into two parts for each level. For example, "d-content" will be separated to "d" and "content". For each part, MSTParser is used to train and test. We call the outputs ***"first-level output"*** and ***"second-level output"***. The outputs of each level and *normal output* are merged then.

In our experiments, only the word satisfies the following conditions need to be merged:

a) The dependency label in *normal output* is started with d-, j- or r-.
b) The dependency label in *first-level output* is d, j or r.
c) The heads in *first-level output* and *second-level output* are of the same.

Otherwise, the dependency relation in *normal output* will be kept. There are also three ways in merging outputs:

a) Label in *first-level output* and label in *second-level output* are merged.
b) First level label in *normal output* and label in *second-level output* are merged.
c) Label in *first-level output* and second level label in *normal output* are merged.

Experiment has been done on develop data. In the experiment, 24% of the labels are merged and 92% of the new merged labels are the same as original. The results of three ways are listed in table 4. All of them get decline compared to *normal output*.

outputs	LAS	UAS
normal output	61.37	80.18
way a)	61.18	80.18
way b)	61.25	80.18
way c)	61.25	80.18

Table 4. Results of multi-level labels experiment on develop data.

3.4 Combined experiment on split and lemma

Improvements are achieved by first two methods in the experiment while a further enhancement is made with a combination of them in the submitted systems. The split method and lemma method are combined as primary system. The split method with CRF++ and lemma method are combined as contrast system. When combining the two methods, last character of the word is firstly extracted as lemma for train data and test data. Then the split or split with CRF++ method is used.

The outputs of the primary system and contrast system are listed in table 2.

4 Analysis and Discussion

The contrast system presented in this paper finally got the second prize among nine systems. The primary system gets the third. There is an improvement of about one percent for both primary and contrast system. The following conclusions can be made from the experiments:

1) Parsing is more effective and accurate on short sentences. A word prefers to depend on another near to it. A sentence can be split to several sub sentences by commas and semicolons to get better parsing output. Result may be improved with a classifier to determine whether a comma or semicolon can be used to split the sentence.
2) Last character of word is a useful feature. In the experiment, the last character is coarsely used as lemma and a minor improvement is achieved. Much more language knowledge can be used in parsing.
3) The label set of the data is worthy to be reviewed. The meanings of the labels are not given in the task. Some of them are confusing especially the multi-level labels. The trying of training and testing multi-level labels separately by levels fails with a slightly decline of the score. Multi-level also causes too many labels: any single-level label can be prefixed to form a new multi-level label. It's a great problem for current parsers. Whether the label set is suitable to Chinese semantic dependency parsing should be discussed.

5 Conclusion and Future Work

Three methods applied in NJU-Parser are described in this paper: splitting sentences by commas and semicolons, taking last character of word as lemma and handling multi-level labels. The first two get improvements in the experiments. Our primary system is a combination of the first two methods. The contrast system is the same as primary system except that it has a classifier implemented in CRF++ to determine whether a comma or a semicolon should be used to split the sentence. Both of the systems get improvements for about one percent on LAS.

In the future, a better classifier should be developed to split the sentence. New method should be applied in merging split outputs to get a well formed dependency tree. And we hope there will be a better label set which are more capable of describing semantic dependency relations for Chinese.

Acknowledgments

This paper is supported in part by National Natural Science Fund of China under contract 61170181, Natural Science Fund of Jiangsu under contract BK2011192, and National Social Science Fund of China under contract 10CYY021.

References

Y.J. Chu and T.H. Liu. 1965. On the shortest arborescence of a directed graph. *Science Sinica*, 14:1396–1400.

MSTParser: http://www.seas.upenn.edu/~strctlrn/MSTParser/MSTParser.html

J. Eisner. 1996. Three new probabilistic models for dependency parsing: An exploration. In *Proc. COLING.*

J. Nivre. 2006. *Inductive Dependency Parsing*. Springer.

R. McDonald, K. Crammer, and F. Pereira. 2005. Online Large-Margin Training of Dependency Parsers. *43rd Annual Meeting of the Association for Computational Linguistics (ACL 2005).*

R. McDonald, F. Pereira, K. Ribarov, and J. Hajič. 2005. Non-projective Dependency Parsing using Spanning Tree Algorithms. *Proceedings of HLT/EMNLP 2005*.

Zhenghua Li, Wanxiang Che, Ting Liu. 2010. Improving Dependency Parsing Using Punctuation. *International Conference on Asian Language Processing(IALP)* 2010.

PolyUCOMP: Combining Semantic Vectors with Skip bigrams for Semantic Textual Similarity

Jian Xu **Qin Lu** **Zhengzhong Liu**
The Hong Kong Polytechnic University
Department of Computing
Hung Hom, Kowloon, Hong Kong
{csjxu, csluqin, hector.liu}@comp.polyu.edu.hk

Abstract

This paper presents the work of the Hong Kong Polytechnic University (PolyUCOMP) team which has participated in the Semantic Textual Similarity task of SemEval-2012. The PolyUCOMP system combines semantic vectors with skip bigrams to determine sentence similarity. The semantic vector is used to compute similarities between sentence pairs using the lexical database WordNet and the Wikipedia corpus. The use of skip bigram is to introduce the order of words in measuring sentence similarity.

1 Introduction

Sentence similarity computation plays an important role in text summarization, classification, question answering and social network applications (Lin and Pantel, 2001; Erkan and Radev, 2004; Ko et al., 2004; Ou et al., 2011). The SemEval 2012 competition includes a task targeted at Semantic Textual Similarity (STS) between sentence pairs (Eneko et al., 2012). Given a set of sentence pairs, participants are required to assign to each sentence pair a similarity score.

Because a sentence has only a limited amount of content words, it is not easy to determine sentence similarities because of the sparseness issue. Hatzivassiloglou et al. (1999) proposed to use linguistic features as indicators of text similarity to address the problem of sparse representation of sentences. Mihalcea et al. (2006) measured sentence similarity using component words in sentences. Li et al. (2006) proposed to incorporate the semantic vector and word order to calculate sentence similarity.

In our approach to the STS task, semantic vector is used and the semantic relatedness between words is derived from two sources: WordNet and Wikipedia. Because WordNet is limited in its coverage, Wikipedia is used as a candidate for determining word similarity.

Word order, however, is not considered in semantic vector. As semantic information are coded in sentences according to its order of writing, and in our systems, content words may not be adjacent to each other, we proposed to use skip bigrams to represent the structure of sentences. Skip bigrams, generally speaking, are pairs of words in a sentence order with arbitrary gap (Lin and Och, 2004a). Different from the previous skip bigram statistics which compare sentence similarities through overlapping skip bigrams (Lin and Och, 2004a), the skip bigrams we used are weighted by a decaying factor of the skipping gap in a sentence, giving higher scores to closer occurrences of skip bigrams. It is reasonable to assume that similar sentences should have more overlapping skip bigrams, and the gaps in their shared skip bigrams should also be similar.

The rest of this paper is organized as followed. Section 2 describes sentence similarity using semantic vectors and the order-sensitive skip bigrams. Section 3 gives the performance evaluation. Section 4 is the conclusion.

2 Similarity between Sentences

Words are used to represent a sentence in the vector space model. Semantic vectors are constructed for sentence representations with each entry corresponding to a word. Since the semantic vector does not consider word order, we further proposed to use skip bigrams to represent sentence structure. Moreover, these skip bigrams are weighted by a decaying factor based on the so called skip distance in the sentence.

2.1 Sentence similarity using Semantic Vector

Given a sentence pair, S_1 and S_2, for example,

S_1: Chairman Michael Powell and FCC colleagues at the Wednesday hearing.

S_2: FCC chief Michael Powell presides over hearing Monday.

The term set of the vector space is first formed by taking only the content words in both sentences,

T={chairman, chief, colleagues, fcc, hearing, michael, monday, powell, presides, wednesday }

Each entry of the semantic vector corresponds to a word in the joint word set (Li et al., 2006). Then, the vector for each sentence is formed in two steps: For a word both in the term set T and in the sentence, the value for this word entry is set to 1. If a word is not in the sentence, the most similar word in the sentence will then be identified, and the corresponding *path* similarity value will be assigned to this entry. Let T be the term set with a sorted list of content words, $T=(t_1, t_2, \ldots, t_n)$. Without loss of generality, let a sentence $S=(w_1\ w_2 \ldots w_m)$ where w_j is a content word and w_j is a word in T. Let the vector space of the sentence S be $VS_s = (v_1, v_2, \ldots, v_n)$. Then the value of v_i is assigned as follows,

$$v_i = \begin{cases} 1 & if\ t_i \in S \\ \arg\max_{w_j \in S}(SIM(t_i, w_j)) & if\ t_i \notin S \end{cases}$$

where the similarity function $SIM(t_i, w_j)$ is calculated according to the *path* measure (Pedersen et al., 2004) using the WordNet, formally defined as,

$$SIM(t_i, w_j) = 1 / dist(t_i, w_j)$$

where $dist(t_i, w_j)$ is the shortest path from t_i, to w_j by counting nodes in the WordNet taxonomy. Based on this, the semantic vectors for the two example sentences will be,

$SV_{S1} = (1, 0.25, 1, 1, 1, 1, 0.33, 1, 0, 1)$ and

$SV_{S2} = (0.25, 1, 0, 1, 1, 1, 1, 1, 1, 0.33)$

Based on the two semantic vectors, the cosine metric is used to measure sentence similarity. In the WordNet, the entry *chairman* in the joint set is most similar to the word *chief* in sentence S_2. In practice, however, this entry might be closer to the word *presides* than to the word *chief*. Therefore, we try to obtain the semantic relatedness using the Wikipedia for sentence T and find that the entry *chairman* is closest to the word *presides*. The Wikipedia-based word relatedness utilizes the hyperlink structure (Milne & Witten, 2008). It first identifies the candidate articles, a and b, that discuss t_i and w_j respectively in this case and then compute relatedness between these articles,

$$rel(a,b) = \frac{\log(\max(|A|, |B|)) - \log(A \cap B)}{\log(|W|) - \log(\min(|A|, |B|))}$$

where A and B are sets of articles that link to a and b. W is the set of all articles in the Wikipedia. Finally, two articles that represent t_i and w_j are selected and their relatedness score is assigned to $SIM(t_i, w_j)$.

2.2 Sentence Similarity by Skip bigrams

Skip bigrams are pairs of words in a sentence order with arbitrary gaps. They contain the order-sensitive information between two words. The skip bigrams of a sentence are extracted as features which will be stacked in a vector space. Each skip bigram is weighted by a decaying factor with its skip distances in the sentence. To illustrate this, consider the following sentences S and T:

$S = w_1 w_2 w_1 w_3 w_4$ and $T = w_2 w_1 w_4 w_5 w_4$

where w denotes a word. It can be used more than once in a sentence. Each sentence above has a $C(5, 2)$[1] $= 10$ skip bigrams.

The sentence S has the following skip bigrams:

"w_1w_2", "w_1w_1", "w_1w_3", "w_1w_4", "w_2w_1", "w_2w_3", "w_2w_4", "w_1w_3", "w_1w_4", "w_3w_4"

The sentence T has the following skip bigrams:

"w_2w_1", "w_2w_4", "w_2w_5", "w_2w_4", "w_1w_4", "w_1w_5", "w_1w_4", "w_4w_5", "w_4w_4", "w_5w_4"

In the sentence S, we have two repeated skip bigrams "w_1w_4" and "w_1w_3". In the sentence T, we have "w_2w_4" and "w_1w_4" repeated twice. In this case, the weight of the recurring skip bigrams will be increased. Hereafter, vectors for S and T will be

[1] Combination: C(5,2)=5!/(2!*3!)=10.

formulated with each entry corresponding to a distinctive skip bigram.

V_S = ("w_1w_2", "w_1w_1", "w_1w_3", "w_1w_4", "w_2w_1", "w_2w_3", "w_2w_4", "w_3w_4")'

V_T = ("w_2w_1", "w_2w_4", "w_2w_5", "w_1w_4", "w_1w_5", "w_4w_5", "w_4w_4", "w_5w_4")'

Now, the question remains how to weight the skip bigrams. Given Σ as a finite word set, let $S=w_1w_2...w_{|S|}$ be a sentence, $w_i \in \Sigma$ and $1 \leq i \leq |S|$. A skip bigram of S, denoted by u, is defined by an index set $I=(i_1, i_2)$ of S ($1 \leq i_1 < i_2 \leq |S|$ and $u=S[I]$). The skip distance of $S[I]$, denoted by $d_u(I)$, is the skip distance of the first word and the second word of u, calculated by i_2-i_1+1. For example, if S is the sentence of $w_1w_2w_1w_3w_4$ and $u = w_1w_4$, then there are two index sets, $I_1=[3,5]$ and $I_2=[1,5]$ such that $u=S[3,5]$ and $u=S[1,5]$, and the skip distances of $S[3,5]$ and $S[1,5]$ are 3 and 5. The weight of a skip bigram u for a sentence S with all its possible occurrences, denoted by $\phi_u(S)$, is defined as:

$$\phi_u(S) = \sum_{I:u=S[I]} \lambda^{d_u(I)}$$

where λ is the decay factor which penalizes the longer skip distance of a skip bigram. By doing so, for the sentence S, the complete word set is $\Sigma=\{w_1, w_2, w_3, w_4\}$. The weights for the skip bigrams are listed in Table 1:

u	$\phi_u(S)$	u	$\phi_u(S)$
w_1w_2	λ^2	w_2w_1	λ^2
w_1w_1	λ^3	w_2w_3	λ^3
w_1w_3	$\lambda^4+\lambda^2$	w_2w_4	λ^4
w_1w_4	$\lambda^5+\lambda^3$	w_3w_4	λ^2

Table 1: Skip bigrams and their Weights in S

In Table 1, if λ is set to 0.25, the weight of the skip bigram w_1w_2 in S is 0.25^2=0.0625, and w_1w_3 is $0.25^4+0.25^2$=0.064. Similarly, the skip bigrams and weights in the sentence T can be obtained. With the skip bigram-based vectors, cosine metric is then used to compute similarity between S and T.

3 Experiments

In the STS task, three training datasets are available: MSR-Paraphrase, MSR-Video and SMTeuroparl (Eneko et al., 2012). The number of sentence pairs for three dataset is 750, 750 and 734.

In the following experiments, Let S_{WN}, S_{WIKI} and S_{SKIP} denote similarity measures of the vector space representation using WordNet, Wikipedia and skip bigrams, respectively. The three similarity measures are linearly combined as S_{COMB}:

$$S_{COMB} = \alpha \times S_{WN} + \beta \times S_{WIKI} + (1-\alpha-\beta) \times S_{SKIP}$$

where α and β are weight factors for S_{WN} and S_{WIKI} in the range [0,1]. If α is set to 1, only the WordNet-based similarity measure is used; if α is 0, the Wikipedia and skip bigram measures are used.

Because each dataset has a different representation for sentences, the parameter configurations for them are different. For the word similarity using the lexical resource WordNet, the *path* measure is used in experiments. To get word relatedness from the English Wikipedia, the Wikipedia Miner tool[2] is used. When computing sentence similarity based on the skip bigrams, the decaying factor (DF) must be specified beforehand. Hence, parameter configurations for the three datasets are listed in Table 2:

Dataset	DF	α	β
MSRpar	0.94	0.01	0.68
SMT-eur	0.9	0.9	0.05
MSRvid	1.4	0.123	0.01

Table 2: Parameter Configurations

In the testing phase, five testing dataset are provided. In addition to three test datasets drawn from the publicly available datasets used in the training phase, two surprise datasets are given. They are SMTnews and OnWN (Eneko et al., 2012). SMTnews has 399 pairs of sentences and OnWN contains 750 sentence pairs. The parameter configurations for these two surprise datasets are the same as those for the dataset MSR-Paraphrase.

The official scoring is based on Pearson correlation. If the system gives the similarity scores close to the reference answers, the system will attain a high correlation value. Besides, three other evaluation metrics (***ALL, ALLnrm, Mean***) based on the Pearson correlation are used (Eneko et al., 2012).

Among the 89 submitted systems, the results of our system are given in Table 3:

Run	ALL	Rank	ALLnrm	RankNrm	Mean	RankMean
PolyUCOMP	0.6528	31	0.7642	59	0.5492	51

Table 3: Performance using Different Metrics

[2] http://wikipedia-miner.cms.waikato.ac.nz/

Using the *ALL* metric, our system ranks 31, but for *ALLnrm* and *Mean* metrics, our system ranking is decreased to 59 and 51. In terms of *ALL* metric, our system achieves a medium performance, implying that our system correlates well with human assessments. In terms of *ALLnrm* and *Mean* metrics, our system performance degrades a lot, implying that our system is not well correlated with the reference answer when each dataset is normalized into the aggregated dataset using the least square error or the weighted mean across the datasets.

To see how well each of the individual vector space models performed on the evaluation sets, we experiment on the five datasets using vectors based on WordNet, Wikipedia (Wiki), SkipBigram and PolyuCOMP (a combination of the three vectors). Table 4 gives detailed results of each dataset.

Run	MSRpar	MSRvid	SMT-eur	On-WN	SMT-news
WordNet	0.4319	0.4586	0.4762	0.6012	0.4155
Wiki	0.4464	0.415	0.4814	0.618	0.4045
SkipBigram	0.4296	0.658	0.4069	0.5317	0.3551
PolyUCOMP	**0.4728**	**0.6593**	**0.4835**	**0.6196**	**0.429**

Table 4: Pearson Correlation for each Dataset

Table 4 shows that after combining three vector representations, each dataset obtains the best performance. The WordNet-based approach gives a better performance than Wikipedia-based approach in MSRvid dataset. The two approaches, however, give similar performance in other four datasets. This is because the sentences in the MSRvid dataset are too short with limited amount of content words. It is difficult to capture the meaning of a sentence without distinguishing words in consecutive positions. This is why the order-sensitive SkipBigram approach gives better performance than the other two approaches. For example,

A woman is playing a game with a man.
A man is playing piano.

Using the semantic vectors, we will get high similarity scores, but the two sentences are dissimilar. If the skip bigram approach is used, the similarity score between sentences will be 0, which correlates with human judgment. In parameter configurations for the MSRvid dataset, higher weight (1-0.123-0.01=0.867) is also given to skip bigrams. It is interesting to note that the decaying factor for this dataset is **1.4** and is not in the range from 0 to 1 inclusive. This is because higher decaying factor helps to capture semantic meaning between words that span afar. For example,

A man is playing a flute.
A man is playing a bamboo flute.

In this sentence pair, the second sentence is entailed by the first one. The similarity can be captured by assigned larger decay factor to weigh the skip bigram "playing flute" in two sentences. Hence, if the value of the decay factor is greater than 1, the two sentences will become much more similar. After careful investigation, these two sentences are similar to a large extent. In this sense, a higher decaying factor would help capture the meaning between sentence pairs. This is quite different from the other four datasets which focus on shared skip bigrams with smaller decaying factor.

4 Conclusions and Future Work

In the Semantic Textual Similarity task of SemEval-2012, we proposed to combine the semantic vector with the order-sensitive skip bigrams to capture the meaning between sentences. First, a semantic vector is derived from either the WordNet or Wikipedia. The WordNet simulates the common human knowledge about word concepts. However, WordNet is limited in its word coverage. To remedy this, Wikipedia is used to obtain the semantic relatedness between words. Second, the proposed approach also considers the impact of word order in sentence similarity by using skip bigrams. Finally, the overall sentence similarity is defined as a linear combination of the three similarity metrics. However, our system is limited in its approaches. In future work, we would like to apply machine learning approach in determining sentence similarity.

References

David Milne , Ian H. Witten. 2008. An Effective, Low-cost Measure of Semantic Relatedness Obtained from Wikipedia Links. In *Proceedings of the first AAAI Workshop on Wikipedia and Artificial Intelligence (WIKIAI'08),* Chicago, I.L

Dekang Lin and Patrick Pantel. 2001. Discovery of Inference Rules for Question Answering. *Natural Language Engineering*, 7(4):343-360.

Eneko Agirre, Daniel Cer, Mona Diab and Aitor Gonzalez-Agirre. 2012. SemEval-2012 Task 6: A Pilot on Semantic Textual Similarity. In *Proceedings of the 6th International Workshop on Semantic Evaluation (SemEval 2012), in conjunction with the First Joint Conference on Lexical and Computational Semantics (*SEM 2012).*

Gunes Erkan and Dragomir R. Radev. 2004. Lexrank: Graph-based Lexical Centrality as Salience in Text Summarization. *Journal of Artificial Intelligence Research*, 22: 457–479.

Lin, Chin-Yew and Franz Josef Och. 2004a. Automatic Evaluation of Machine Translation Quality Using Longest Common Subsequence and Skip bigram Statistics. In *Proceedings of the 42nd Annual Meeting of the Association for Computational Linguistics (ACL 2004)*, Barcelona, Spain.

Ou Jin, Nathan Nan Liu, Yong Yu and Qiang Yang. 2011. Transferring Topical Knowledge from Auxiliary Long Text for Short Text Understanding. In: *Proceedings of the 20th ACM Conference on Information and Knowledge Management (ACM CIKM 2011)*. Glasgow, UK.

Rada Mihalcea and Courtney Corley. 2006. Corpus-based and Knowledge-based Measures of Text Semantic Similarity. In *Proceeding of the Twenty-First National Conference on Artificial Intelligence and the Eighteenth Innovative Applications of Artificial Intelligence Conference*.

Ted Pedersen, Siddharth Patwardhan and Jason Michelizzi. 2004. WordNet::Similarity—Measuring the Relatedness of Concepts. In *Proceedings of the 19th National Conference on Artificial Intelligence (AAAI, San Jose, CA),* pages 144–152.

Vasileios Hatzivassiloglou, Judith L. Klavans , Eleazar Eskin. 1999. Detecting Text Similarity over Short Passages: Exploring Linguistic Feature Combinations via Machine Learning. In *Proceeding of Empirical Methods in natural language processing and Very Large Corpora*.

Youngjoong Ko, Jinwoo Park, and Jungyun Seo. 2004. Improving Text Categorization using the Importance of Sentences. *Information Processingand Management*, 40(1): 65–79.

Yuhua Li, David Mclean, Zuhair B, James D. O'shea and Keeley Crockett. 2006. Sentence Similarity Based on Semantic Nets and Corpus Statistics. *IEEE Transactions on Knowledge and Data Engineering*, 18(8), 1138–1149.

ETS: Discriminative Edit Models for Paraphrase Scoring

Michael Heilman and **Nitin Madnani**
Educational Testing Service
660 Rosedale Road
Princeton, NJ 08541, USA
{mheilman,nmadnani}@ets.org

Abstract

Many problems in natural language processing can be viewed as variations of the task of measuring the semantic textual similarity between short texts. However, many systems that address these tasks focus on a single task and may or may not generalize well. In this work, we extend an existing machine translation metric, TERp (Snover et al., 2009a), by adding support for more detailed feature types and by implementing a discriminative learning algorithm. These additions facilitate applications of our system, called PERP, to similarity tasks other than machine translation evaluation, such as paraphrase recognition. In the SemEval 2012 Semantic Textual Similarity task, PERP performed competitively, particularly at the two surprise subtasks revealed shortly before the submission deadline.

1 Introduction

Techniques for measuring the similarity of two sentences have various potential applications: automated short answer scoring (Nielsen et al., 2008; Leacock and Chodorow, 2003), question answering (Wang et al., 2007), machine translation evaluation (Przybocki et al., 2009; Snover et al., 2009a), etc.

An important aspect of this problem is that similarity is not binary. Sentences can be very semantically similar, such that they might be called paraphrases of each other. They might be completely different. Or, they might be somewhere in between. Indeed, it is arguable that all sentence pairs (except exact duplicates) lie somewhere on a continuum of similarity. Therefore, it is desirable to develop methods that model sentence pair similarity on a continuous, or at least ordinal, scale.

In this paper, we describe a system for measuring the semantic similarity of pairs of short texts. As a starting point, we use the Translation Error Rate Plus (Snover et al., 2009a), or TERp, system, which was specifically developed for machine translation evaluation. TERp takes two sentences as input, finds a set of weighted edits that convert one into the other with low overall weight, and then produces a length-normalized score. TERp also has a greedy, heuristic learning algorithm for inducing weights from labeled sentence pairs in order to increase correlations with human similarity scores.

Some features of the original TERp make adaptation to other semantic similarity tasks difficult, including its largely one-to-one mapping of features to edits and its heuristic, greedy learning algorithm. For example, there is a single feature for lexical substitution, even though it is clear that different types of substitutions have different effects on similarity (e.g., substituting "43.6" with "17" versus substituting "a" for "an"). In addition, the heuristic learning algorithm, which involves perturbing the weight vector by small amounts as in grid search, seems unscalable to larger sets of overlapping features.

Therefore, here, we use TERp's inference algorithms that find low cost edit sequences but use a discriminative learning algorithm based on the Perceptron (Rosenblatt, 1958; Collins, 2002) to estimate edit cost parameters, along with an expanded feature set for broader coverage of the phenomena that are relevant to sentence-to-sentence similarity. We refer to this new approach as Paraphrase Edit Rate with the Perceptron (PERP).

In addition to describing PERP, we discuss how it was applied for the SemEval 2012 Semantic Textual Similarity (STS) task.

2 Problem Definition

In this work, our goal is to create a system that can take as input two sentences (or short texts) x_1 and x_2 and produce as output a prediction $\hat{y}$ for how similar they are. Here, we use the 0 to 5 ordinal scale from the STS task, where increasing values indicate greater semantic similarity.

The STS task data includes five subtasks with text pairs from different sources: the Microsoft Research Paraphrase Corpus (Dolan et al., 2004) (MSRpar), The Microsoft Research Video corpus (Chen and Dolan, 2011) (MSRvid), statistical machine translation output of parliament proceedings (Koehn, 2005) (SMT-eur). For each of these sources, approximately 750 sentence pairs $\mathbf{x_1}$ and $\mathbf{x_2}$ and gold standard similarity values $\mathbf{y}$ were provided for training and development.

In addition, there were two surprise data sources revealed shortly before the submission deadline: pairs of sentences from Ontonotes (Pradhan and Xue, 2009) and Wordnet (Fellbaum, 1998) (OnWN), and machine translations of sentences from news conversations (SMT-news). For all five sources, the held-out test set contained several hundred text pairs. See the task description (Agirre et al., 2012) for additional details.

3 TER, TERp, and PERP

In this section, we briefly describe the TER and TERp machine translation metrics, and how the PERP system extends them in order to better model semantic textual similarity.

TER (Snover et al., 2006) uses a greedy search algorithm to find a set of edits to convert one of the paired input sentences into the other. We can view this set of edits as an alignment a between the two input sentences x_1 and x_2, and when two words in x_1 and x_2, respectively, are part of an edit operation, we say that those words are aligned.[1] Unlike traditional edit distance measures, TER allow for shifts—that is, edits that change the positions of words or phrases in the input sentence x_1. Essentially, TER searches among a set of possible shifts of the phrases in x_1 to find a set of shifts that result in the least cost alignment, using edits of other types, between x_2 and the shifted version of x_1. TER allows one to specify costs for different edit types, but it does not include a method for learning those costs from data.

TERp (Snover et al., 2009b; Snover et al., 2009a) extends TER in two key ways. First, TERp includes new types of edits, including edits for substitution of synonyms, word stems, and phrasal paraphrases extracted from a pivot-based paraphrase table (§3.1). Second, it includes a heuristic learning algorithm for inferring cost parameters from labeled data. TERp includes 8 types of edits: match (M), insertion (I), deletion (D), substitution (S), stemming (T), synonymy (Y), shift (Sh), and phrase substitution (P). The edits are mutually exclusive, such that synonymy edits do not count as substitutions, for example. TERp has 11 total parameters, with a single parameter for each edit except for phrase substition, which has four.

PERP has a general framework similar to that of TERp. It extends TERp, however, by including additional edit parameters, and by using a discriminative learning algorithm (see §5) to learn parameters rather than the heuristic technique used by TERp. Thus, PERP uses the same greedy algorithm as TERp for finding the optimal sets of edits given the cost parameters, but it allows the cost for an individual edit to depend on multiple, overlapping features of that edit. For example, costs for substitution edits depend on whether the aligned words are pronouns, whether the aligned words represent numbers, the lengths of the aligned words, etc. See §4 for the full list of features in PERP.

An alignment from the MSRpar portion of the STS training data is illustrated in Figure 1.

3.1 Phrasal Paraphrases

PERP uses probabilistic phrasal substitutions to align phrases in the hypothesis with phrases in the

[1]For machine translation evaluation with TERp and PERP, x_1 is a system's hypothesis and x_2 is a reference translation. For all STS subtasks, we assigned sentences in the first and second columns of the input files to x_2 and x_1, respectively, so that the hypotheses and references in the SMT-eur subtask would be assigned appropriately.

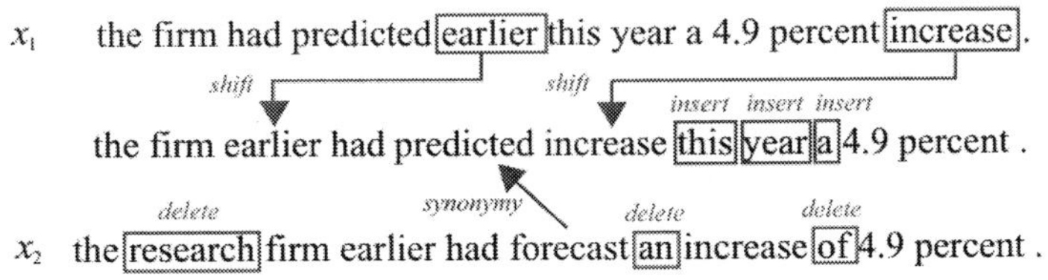

Figure 1: An example of a PERP alignment for a sentence pair from the Microsoft Research Paraphrase Corpus. The search algorithm first performs shifts on x_1 and then performs other edits on x_2. The zero cost edits that match individual words are not shown.

reference. It does so by looking up—in a precomputed phrase table—paraphrases of phrases in the reference and using its associated edit cost as the cost of performing a match against the hypothesis. The paraphrase table used in PERP was identical to the one used by Snover et al. (2009a). It was extracted using the pivot-based method as described by Bannard and Callison-Burch (2005) with several additional filtering mechanisms to increase the precision of the extracted pairs. The pivot-based method utilizes the inherent monolingual semantic knowledge from bilingual corpora: we first identify phrasal correspondences between English and a given foreign language F, then map from English to English by following translation units from English to the other language and back. For example, if the two English phrases $e1$ and $e2$ both correspond to the same foreign phrase f, then they may be considered to be paraphrases of each other with the following probability:

$$p(e1|e2) \approx p(e1|f)p(f|e2)$$

If there are several pivot phrases that link the two English phrases, then they are all used in computing the probability:

$$p(e1|e2) \approx \sum_{f'} p(e1|f')p(f'|e2)$$

We used the same phrasal paraphrase database as in TERp (Snover et al., 2009a), which was extracted from an Arabic-English newswire bitext containing a million sentences. A few examples of the paraphrase pairs used in the MSRpar portion of the STS training data are shown below:

(*commission* → *panel*)
(*the spying* → *espionage*)
(*suffered* → *underwent*)
(*room to* → *space for*)
(*per cent* → *percent*)

4 Features

As discussed in §3, PERP expands on TERp's original features in order to better model semantic textual similarity.

PERP models a pair of sentences x_1 and x_2 using a feature function $\mathbf{f}(a)$ that extracts a vector of real-valued features from an alignment a between x_1 and x_2. This alignment is found with TERp's inference algorithm and consists of a set of edits of various types along with information about the words on which those edits operate. For example, the alignment might contain an edit with the information, "The token 'the' in x_1 was substituted for the token 'an' in x_2." This edit would increment the features in $\mathbf{f}(a)$ for the number of substitutions and the number of substitutions of stopwords, along with other relevant substitution features.

The set of features encoded in $\mathbf{f}(a)$ are described in Table 1.[2] It includes general features that always fire for edits of a particular type (e.g., the "Substitution" feature) as well as specific features that fire only in specific situations (e.g., the "Sub-Pronoun-Both" edit, which fires only when one pronoun is substituted for another).

The function $\mathbf{f}(a)$ is normalized for sentence

[2] All words were converted to lower-case. Word frequencies were calculated from the NYT stories in the fifth edition of the English Gigaword corpus. The stories were tokenized using NLTK and words occurring fewer than 100 times were excluded. Words occurring at least 100 times constituted the vocabulary used for computing the OOV features. The OOV and frequency features only fired for words that consisted only of letters, and the frequency features did not fire for OOV words. The set of negation words including the following: "no", "not", "never", and "n't". The stopword list contained 158 common words and punctuation symbols.

Edits	Feature Name	Description
-	Intercept	Always 1 (and not normalized by text lengths)
T	Stemming	The number of times that two words with the same stem, according to the Porter (1980) stemmer, were aligned.
Y	Synonymy	The number of times that a pair of synonyms, according to WordNet (Fellbaum, 1998), were aligned.
Sh	Shift	The number of shifts.
P	Paraphrase1	The number of phrasal paraphrasing operations.
P	Paraphrase2	The sum of $q \log_{10}(p)$, where p is the probability in the pivot-based paraphrase table for a paraphrase edit and q is the number of edits for that paraphrase edit. See Snover et al. (2009a) for further explanation.
P	Paraphrase3	The sum of pq, where p and q are as above.
P	Paraphrase4	The sum of q, where q is as above.
I	Insertion	The number of insertions.
D	Deletion	The number of deletions.
I, D	Insert-Delete-LogFreq	The sum of $\log_{10} \text{freq}(w)$ over all insertions and deletions, where w is the word being inserted or deleted and freq(w) is the relative frequency of w.
I, D	Insert-Delete-LogWordLen	The sum of $\log_{10} \text{length}(w)$ over all insertions and deletions, where w is the word being inserted or deleted.
I, D	Insert-Delete-X	The number of insertions and deletions of X in alignment, where X is: (a) punctuation, (b) numbers, (c) personal pronouns, (d) negation words, (e) stop words, or (f) out-of-vocabulary (OOV) words (6 features in all).
S	Substitution	The number of substitutions.
S	Sub-X-Both	The number of substitutions where both words are: (a) punctuation, (b) numbers, (c) personal pronouns, (d) negation words, (e) stop words, or (f) OOV words (6 features in all).
S	Sub-X-1only	The number of substitutions where only one word is: (a) punctuation, (b) a number, (c) a personal pronoun, (d) a negation word, (e) a stop word, or (f) an OOV word (6 features in all).
S	Sub-LogFreq-Diff	The sum of $\lvert \log_{10} \text{freq}(w_1) - \log_{10} \text{freq}(w_2)\rvert$ over all substitutions.
S	Sub-Contain	The number of substitutions where both words have more than 5 characters and one is a proper substring of the other.
S	Sub-Diff-By-NonWord	The number of substitutions where the words differ only by non-alphanumeric characters.
S	Sub-Small-LevDist	The number of substitutions where both words have more than 5 characters and the Levenshtein distance between them is 1.
S	Sub-Norm-LevDist	The sum of the following over all substitutions: the Levenshtein distance between the words normalized by the length of the longer word.

Table 1: The set of features in PERP. The first column lists which edits for which each feature is relevant.

lengths by dividing all the values in Table 1 by the sum of the number of words in x_1 and x_2, except for the intercept feature that models the base similarity value in the training data and always has value 1.

There are 36 features and corresponding parameters in all, compared to 11 for TERp.

It is worth pointing out that while the mutual exclusivity between most of the original TERp edits is preserved, PERP does have shared features between insert and delete edits (e.g., "Insert-Delete-Number"), and could in principle share features between substitution, stemming, and synonymy edits.

5 Learning

Given a training set consisting of paired sentences $\mathbf{x_1}$ and $\mathbf{x_2}$ and gold standard semantic similarity ratings $\mathbf{y}$, PERP uses Algorithm 1 to induce a good set

Algorithm 1 `learn`($\mathbf{w}, T, \alpha, \mathbf{x_1}, \mathbf{x_2}, \mathbf{y}$):
An Averaged Perceptron algorithm for learning edit cost parameters. T is the number of iterations through the dataset. α is a learning rate. $\mathbf{x_1}$ and $\mathbf{x_2}$ are paired lists of sentences, and $\mathbf{y}$ is a list of similarities that correspond to those sentence pairs.

$\mathbf{w}_{sum} = \mathbf{0}$
for $t = 1, 2, \ldots, T$ **do**
  $\mathbf{x_1}, \mathbf{x_2}, \mathbf{y} = \text{shuffle}(\mathbf{x_1}, \mathbf{x_2}, \mathbf{y})$
  for $i = 1, 2, \ldots, |\mathbf{y}|$ **do**
    $a = \text{TERpAlign}(\mathbf{w}, x_{1i}, x_{2i})$
    $\hat{y} = \mathbf{w} \cdot \mathbf{f}(a)$
    $\mathbf{w} = \mathbf{w} + \alpha(y_i - \hat{y})\mathbf{f}(a)$
    $\mathbf{w} = \text{applyShiftConstraint}(\mathbf{w})$
    $\mathbf{w}_{sum} = \mathbf{w}_{sum} + \mathbf{w}$
  end for
end for
return $\frac{\mathbf{w}_{sum}}{T|\mathbf{y}|}$

of cost parameters for its various features.[3] The algorithm is a fairly straightforward application of the Perceptron algorithm described by Collins (2002).[4] The only notable difference is that the algorithm constrains PERP's shift parameter to be at least 0.01 in the step labeled "applyShiftConstraint." We found that TERp's inference algorithm would fail if the shift cost reached zero.[5] In our experiments, we initialized all weights to 0, except for the following: the "Substitution," "Insertion," and "Deletion" weights were initialized to 1.0, and the "Shift" weight was initialized to 0.1. Following Collins (2002), the algorithm returns an averaged version of the weights, though this did not appear to substantially impact performance.

[3]The "shuffle" step shuffles the lists of sentence pairs and scores together such that their orderings are randomized but that they stay aligned with each other.

[4]There are a few hyperparameters in the learning algorithms. For our experiments, we set the number of iterations through the training data T to 200. We set the learning rate α to 0.01 to avoid large oscillations in the parameters. We did not systematically tune the hyperparameters. Other values might lead to better performance.

[5]With zero cost shifts, TERp would enter a loop and eventually exceed the amount of available memory. We also set the same minimum cost of 0.01 for shifts in our experiments with the original TERp.

6 Experiments

In this section, we report results for the STS shared task. For a full description of the task, see Agirre et al. (2012).

The task consisted of three known subtasks (MSRpar, MSRvid, and SMT-eur) and two surprise subtasks (On-WN, SMT-news). For the known subtasks, we trained models with task-specific data only. For the On-WN subtask, we used the model trained for MSRpar. For SMT-news, we used the model trained for SMT-eur.

Our submissions to the task included results from two variations, one using the full system (PERPphrases) and one with the paraphrase substitution edits disabled (PERP), in order to isolate the effect of including phrasal paraphrases. In our original submission, the PERPphrases system included a minor bug that affected the calculation of the phrasal paraphrasing features. Here, we report both the original results and a corrected version ("PERPphrases (fix)"), though the correction only minimally affected performance. We also tested two variations of the original TERp system: one with the weights set as reported by Snover et al. (2009a) ("TERp (default)"), and one tuned in the same task-specific manner as PERP ("TERp (tuned)"). We multiplied TERp's predictions by -1 since it produces costs rather than similarities.

The results, in terms of Pearson correlations with test set gold standard scores, are shown in Table 2. In addition to correlations for each subtask, we include the three aggregated measures used for the task. The "ALL" measure is the Pearson correlations on the concatenation of all the data for all five subtasks. It was the original measured used to aggregate the results for the different subtasks. The second aggregated measure is the "Allnrm" measure, which we view as an oracle because it uses the gold standard similarity values from the test set to adjust system predictions. The final aggregate measure is the mean of the correlations for the subtasks, weighted by the number of examples in each subtask's test set ("Mean"). See Agirre et al. (2012) for a full description of the metrics.

For comparison, the table also includes the results from the top-ranked submission according to the "ALL" measure, the results for the word-overlap

	Aggregated Measures			Subtask Measures				
	ALL	ALLnrm	Mean	MSRpar	MSRvid	SMT-eur	On-WN	SMT-news
UKP (top-ranked)	**.8239**	**.8579**	**.6773**	**.6830**	**.8739**	**.5280**	.6641	.4937
PERPphrases (fix) †	.7837	—	.6405	.6410	.7209	.4852	**.7127**	**.5312**
PERPphrases	.7834	.8089	.6399	.6397	.7200	.4850	.7124	**.5312**
PERP	.7808	.8064	.6305	.6211	.7210	.4722	.7080	.5149
TERp (tuned) †	.5558	—	.5582	.5400	.6099	.4967	.5862	.5135
TERp (default)	.4477	.7291	.5253	.5049	.5217	.4748	.6169	.4566
baseline	.3110	.6732	.4356	.4334	.2996	.4542	.5864	.3908
mean of submissions	.5864	.7773	.5286	.4894	.7049	.3958	.5557	.3731

Table 2: Pearson correlations between predictions about the test data and gold standard scores. "†" marks experiments that were not parts of the official SemEval task 6 evaluation. The highest correlation in each column is given in bold. ALLnrm results are not included for all runs because we did not have an implementation of that measure.

baseline from the organizers (Agirre et al., 2012), and the means across all 88 submissions (not including the baseline).

Table 3 shows the rankings in the official results of the PERPphrases submission, for each subtask and overall, along with Pearson correlations from PERP and the best submission for each subtask.

Aggregated Measure	Rank	ρ	ρ_{best}
ALL	6	.7834	.8239
ALLnrm	27	.8089	.8635
Mean	7	.6399	.6773
Subtask Measure	**Rank**	ρ	ρ_{best}
MSRpar	8	.6397	.7343
MSRvid	52	.7200	.8803
SMT-eur	21	.4850	.5666
On-WN	2	.7124	.7273
SMT-news	4	.5312	.6085

Table 3: The ranking and correlation (ρ) obtained by PERPphrases for each of the five datasets as well for all datasets combined. The STS task had a total of 88 submissions. ρ_{best} shows the correlation for the best submission, across all submissions, for each dataset.

7 Conclusion

From the results in §6, PERP appears to be competitive at measuring semantic textual similarity. It performed particularly well on the surprise subtasks, indicating that it generalizes well to new data. Finally, with the exception of the SMT-eur machine translation evaluation subtask, PERP outperformed the TERp system for all of the STS subtasks.

Acknowledgments

We would like to thank the organizers of SemEval and the Semantic Textual Similarity task. We would also like to thank Matt Snover for making the original TERp code available.

References

E. Agirre, D. Cer, M. Diab, and A. Gonzalez-Agirre. 2012. SemEval-2012 task 6: A pilot on semantic textual similarity. In *Proc. of the 6th International Workshop on Semantic Evaluation (SemEval 2012), in conjunction with the First Joint Conference on Lexical and Computational Semantics (*SEM 2012)*.

C. Bannard and C. Callison-Burch. 2005. Paraphrasing with bilingual parallel corpora. In *Proc. of ACL*, pages 597–604.

D. Chen and W. B. Dolan. 2011. Collecting highly parallel data for paraphrase evaluation. In *Proc. of ACL*, pages 190–200.

M. Collins. 2002. Discriminative training methods for hidden Markov models: Theory and experiments with the perceptron algorithm. In *Proc. of EMNLP*.

W. Dolan, C. Quirk, and C. Brockett. 2004. Unsupervised construction of large paraphrase corpora: Exploiting massively parallel news sources. In *Proc. of COLING*, pages 350–356, Geneva, Switzerland.

C. Fellbaum. 1998. *WordNet: An Electronic Lexical Database*. Bradford Books.

P. Koehn. 2005. Europarl: A parallel corpus for statistical machine translation. In *Proc. of Machine Translation Summit*.

C. Leacock and M. Chodorow. 2003. c-rater: Scoring of short-answer questions. *Computers and the Humanities*, 37.

R. D. Nielsen, W. Ward, and J. H. Martin. 2008. Classification errors in a domain-independent assessment system. In *Proc. of the Third Workshop on Innovative Use of Natural Language Processing for Building Educational Applications*.

M. F. Porter. 1980. An algorithm for suffix stripping. *Program*, 3(14):130–137.

S. S. Pradhan and N. Xue. 2009. OntoNotes: The 90% solution. In *Proc. of Human Language Technologies: The 2009 Annual Conference of the North American Chapter of the Association for Computational Linguistics, Companion Volume: Tutorial Abstracts*, pages 11–12.

M. A. Przybocki, K. Peterson, S. Bronsart, and G. A. Sanders. 2009. The NIST 2008 metrics for machine translation challenge - overview, methodology, metrics, and results. *Machine Translation*, 23(2-3):71–103.

F. Rosenblatt. 1958. The perceptron: A probabilistic model for information storage and organization in the brain. *Psychological Review*, 65.

M. Snover, B. Dorr, R. Schwartz, L. Micciulla, and J. Makhoul. 2006. A study of Translation Edit Rate with targeted human annotation. In *Proc. of the Conference of the Association for Machine Translation in the Americas (AMTA)*.

M. Snover, N. Madnani, B. Dorr, and R. Schwartz. 2009a. Fluency, adequacy, or HTER? Exploring different human judgments with a tunable MT metric. In *Proc. of the Fourth Workshop on Statistical Machine Translation at the 12th Meeting of the European Chapter of the Association for Computational Linguistics (EACL-2009)*, March.

M. Snover, N. Madnani, B. Dorr, and R. Schwartz. 2009b. TER-Plus: Paraphrase, semantic, and alignment enhancements to Translation Edit Rate. *Machine Translation*, 23(2–3):117–127.

M. Wang, N. A. Smith, and T. Mitamura. 2007. What is the Jeopardy model? A quasi-synchronous grammar for QA. In *Proc. of of EMNLP*.

Sbdlrhmn: A Rule-based Human Interpretation System for Semantic Textual Similarity Task

Samir AbdelRahman
sbdlrhmn@illinois.edu,
s.abdelrahman@fci-cu.edu.eg

Catherine Blake
clblake@illinois.edu

The Graduate School of Library and Information Science
University Of Illinois at Urbana-Champaign

Abstract

In this paper, we describe the system architecture used in the Semantic Textual Similarity (STS) task 6 pilot challenge. The goal of this challenge is to accurately identify five levels of semantic similarity between two sentences: equivalent, mostly equivalent, roughly equivalent, not equivalent but sharing the same topic and no equivalence. Our participations were two systems. The first system (rule-based) combines both semantic and syntax features to arrive at the overall similarity. The proposed rules enable the system to adequately handle domain knowledge gaps that are inherent when working with knowledge resources. As such one of its main goals, the system suggests a set of domain-free rules to help the human annotator in scoring semantic equivalence of two sentences. The second system is our baseline in which we use the Cosine Similarity between the words in each sentence pair.

1 Introduction

Accurately establishing sentence semantic similarity would provide one of the key ingredients for solutions to many text-related applications, such as automatic grading systems (Mohler and Mihalcea, 2009), paraphrasing (Fernando and Stevenson, 2008), text entailment (Corley et al., 2005) and summarization (Erkan and Radev, 2004). Current approaches for computing semantic similarity between a pair of sentences focus on analyzing their shared words (Salton, 1989), structures (Hu et al. 2011;Mandreoli et al. 2002), semantics (Mihalcea et al. 2006; Le el al. 2006; Hatzivassiloglou, 1999) or any of their combinations (Liu et al. 2008; Foltz et al. 1998). The goal is to arrive at a score which increases proportionally with the relatedness between the two sentences. Yet, they are not concerned with scoring the interpretations of such relatedness (Zhang et al. 2011; Jesus et al. 2011; Wenyin et al. 2010; Liu et al. 2008).

Semantic Textual Similarity (STS), SEMEVAL-12 Task 6 (Agirre et al. 2012), measures the degree of semantic equivalence between a pair of sentences by comparing meaningful contents within a sentence. The assigned scores range from 0 to 5 for each sentence pair with the following interpretations: (5) completely equivalent, (4) mostly equivalent pair with missing unimportant information, (3) roughly equivalent with missing important information, (2) not equivalent, but sharing some details, (1) not equivalent but sharing the same topic and (0) not equivalent and on different topics. The goal of developing our rule-based system was to identify knowledge representations which have possibly all task human interpretations. Meanwhile, the system domain-free rules aim to help the human annotator in scoring semantic equivalence of sentence pair.

The proposed rule-based solution exploits both sentence syntax and semantics. First, it uses Stanford parser (Klein and Manning, 2002) to expose the sentence structure, part-of-speech (POS) word tags, parse tree and Subject-Verb-Object (S-V-O) dependencies. Second, Illinois Coreference Package (Bengtson and Roth, 2008) is used to extract sentence named entities resolving possible mentions. Third, WordNet (Miller, 1995) and Adapted Lesk Algorithm for word sense disambiguation (Banerjee and Pedersen, 2010) are used to compute each sentence word semantic relatedness to the other sentence. ReVerb (Etzioni et al. 2011) augments WordNet in case of uncovered words and helps us to discriminate the topics of sentences. We use (Blake, 2007) thought to compare the sentence pair words with each other. Finally, we evolve a rule-based module to present the human heuristics when he interprets the relatedness of the sentence pair meaningful contents.

Throughout our training and testing experiments, we used Task6 corpora (Agirre et al. 2012) namely MSRpar, MSRvid, SMTeuroparl, OnWN and SMTnews; where:

- MSRpar is 1500 pairs of sentences of MSR-Paraphrase, Microsoft Research Paraphrase Corpus; 750 for training and 750 for testing.
- MSRvid is 1500 pairs of sentences of MSR-Video, Microsoft Research Video Description Corpus; 750 for training and 750 for testing.
- SMTeuroparl is 918 pairs of sentences of WMT2008 development dataset (Europarl section); 459 for training and 459 for testing.
- OnWn is 750 pairs of sentences pairs of sentences where the first sentence comes from Ontonotes and the second sentence from a WordNet definition; it is only a testing corpus.
- SMTnews is 399 pairs of sentences of news conversation sentence pairs from WMT; it is only a testing corpus.

The reminder of this paper is organized as follows: Section 2 describes our two participations; Section 3 discusses their official results; Section 4 draws our conclusion for both systems.

2 The Proposed Systems

In this section, we focus on the rule-based system, Sections 2.1, 2.2, 2.3 and 2.4, as our main task contribution. Further, the section describes our second run, Sections 2.5, to shed light on the role of cosine similarity for solving the task problem. To establish the task semantic textual similarity, we show how the rule-based system exploits the sentence semantic, syntax and heuristics; also, we describe how our base-line system uses the sentence syntax only.

2.1 Definitions

We say the two sentences are on different topics, if all their verbs are mostly (> 50%) unrelated (Table 1). Otherwise, they are on the same topic. For example, the two sentences *"A woman is putting on makeup."*, *"A band is singing."* are on different topics as *"putting"*, *"singing"* are not equivalent. However, the two sentences *"A baby is talking."*, *A boy is trying to say firetruck."* are on the same topics as *"talking"* and *"trying to say"* are semantically equivalent.

We define the sentence important information as its head nouns, named entities or main verbs; where the main verbs are all verbs except auxiliary, model and infinitive ones. Hence, we say that two sentences miss important information if either loses at least one of these mentions from the other. Otherwise, they are candidates to be semantically equivalent. For example, the sentence *"Besides Hampton and Newport News, the grant funds water testing in Yorktown, King George County, Norfolk and Virginia Beach."* misses *"Hampton and Newport News"* compared to the sentence *"The grant also funds beach testing in King George County, Norfolk and Virginia Beach."* However, "on a table" is unimportant information which *"A woman is tapping her fingers."* misses compared to *"A woman is tapping her fingers on a table."*

Finally, we deploy a list of stop words and non-verbs as unimportant information. However, if any exists in both sentences, we match them with each other; otherwise we ignore any occurrences.

2.2 The Syntactic Module

This syntactic module is a preprocessing module in which the system calls Stanford parser, Version 2.0.1, and the Illinois coreference package, Version 1.3.2, to result in the sentence four type representations: 1) part of speech (POS) tags, 2) Subject-Verb-Object (S-V-O), Subject-Verb (S-V) and Verb-Object (V-O) dependencies, 3) parse tree and 4) coreference resolutions. All sentences are lemmatized based on their POSs. Also, verbs and CDs are utilized to determine topics/important information and numbers respectively. All noun and verb phrases are used to boost the sentence word semantic scores (Section 2.3). We consider all occurrences of S-V-O, S-V and V-O to distinguish the topic compatibility between two comparable sentences (Section 2.3 and 2.4).

The coreference package is used to match the equivalent discourse entities between two sentences which improve the matching steps. For example, in the pair of *"Mrs Hillary Clinton explains her plan towards the Middle East countries"* and *"Mrs Clinton meets their ambassadors"*, *"Mrs Hillary Clinton"*, *"her"* and *"Mrs Clinton"* refer to the same entity where *"the Middle East countries"* and *"their"* are equivalent. Moreover, we consider the second sentence doesn't lose *"Hillary"* as missing important information since the related mentions are labeled equivalent.

2.3 The Semantic Matching Module

WordNet, Version 3.0, has approximately 5,947 entries covering around 85% of training corpora words (Agirre et al. 2012). Most of the remaining 15% words are abbreviations, named entities and incorrect POS tags. We use WordNet shortest path measure to compute the semantic similarity between two words. Also, we use Adapted Lesk algorithm to obtain the best WordNet word sense. The disambiguation algorithm compares each pair of words through their contexts (windows) of words coupled with their all overlapping glosses of all WordNet relation types.

The semantic matching module inputs are the sentence pair (S1, S2), their lemmatized words, parse trees, S-V-O/S-V/V-O dependencies and coreference mentions (Section 2.2). It matches syntactically the words with each other. For any uncovered WordNet word, the module calls ReVerb (Section 2.4) and it assigns the returned value to the word score. All numbers, e.g. million, 300,45.6, are mathematically compared with each other. This module compares the noun phrases with single words to handle the compound words, e.g. *"shot gun"* with *"shotgun"* or *"part-of-speech"* with *"part of speech"*. For those words whose scores are not equal to 1, it compares each pair of words from the sentence pair within their Subject-VP (subject with its verb phrase) contexts using Adapted Lesk algorithm to find best sense for each included word. Then, it applies WordNet shortest path measure to score such words. In our disambiguation algorithm implementation, we found that the runtime requirement is directly proportional to the input sentence length. So, we shortened the sentence length to Subject-VP which includes the underlying comparable words.

Relatedness	Score (S1, S2)
unrelated	0 <= Ws <0.3
weakly related	0.3 <= Ws <0.85
strongly related	Ws >= 0.85

Table 1 – Mapping relatedness to wordnet similarity

Table 1 describes the proposed system WordNet thresholds through our relatedness definitions. The thresholds were thoroughly selected depending on our analysis for the WordNet hierarchary and semantic similarity measures (Pedersen et al., 2004). We obsereved that while most of the nearest tree sibilings and parent-child nodes scores have more than 0.85 Wordnet semantic scores, most of the fartherest ones have scores less than 0.3. In between these extremes, there is a group of scattered tree nodes which ranges from 0.3 to 0.85. The number of nodes per each mentioned group is related to the semantic simlarity measure technique.

2.4 Semantics – Using ReVerb

Our working hypothesis is that verbs that use the same arguments are more likely to be similar. To estimate verb usage, the system uses frequencies from the ReVerb (http://openie.cs.washington.edu/) online interface to count the number of times a verb is used with two arguments. For example, consider the sentence pair *"The man fires rifle"* and *"The man cuts lemon"*. The number of sentences in ReVerb that contain the verb *fires* with the argument *rifle* is 538 and the number of sentences for the verb *cuts* with the argument *lemon* is 45, which tell us that you are more likely to find sentences that describe firing a rifle than cutting a lemon on the web. However, there a no ReVerb sentences for the verb *fires* with the argument *lemon* or the verb *cuts* with the argument *rifle*. Which tells us that people generally don't fire lemons or cut rifles.

Reverb provides the system with information about the suitability of using argument in one sentence with verbs from another. Specifically, frequencies from Reverb are retrieved for each subject-verb-object triple in each sentence, e.g. "S1-V1-O1" and "S2-V2-O2". The system then retrieves ReVerb frequencies for the verb-object in each sentence of "V2-O1" and "V1-O2". If at least one of all of these scores equals to 0, they are considered to be weakly similar.

ReVerb is also called for any sentence word that WordNet doesn't cover. The system retrieves the Reverb frequency for is-a relation using the word missing from Wordnet, as Argument1, and each word from the other sentence as Argument2. The largest Reverb retrieved score is taken. Consider the pair of *"A group of girls are exiting a taxi"* and *"A video clip of Rihanna leaving a taxi."*. Since "*Rihanna*" is not a WordNet word, our ReVerb interface hits the web for *"Rihanna is-a girl"*, *"Rihanna is-a group"*, *"Rihanna is-a taxi" and "Rihanna is-a existing"* and it returns *"Rihanna is-a girl"* as the best candidate with strength score equals 0.2.

We explored several relatedness scores which specifically equal to 0, 0.2, 0.4, 0.6, 0.8 or 1 if the frequencies are less than to 10, 50, 100, 500, 1000 or 1000+ respectively.

2.5 The Rule-Based Module

Rule-based module aims at defining human-like rules to interpret how the pair similar or dissimilar from each other. Pair Similarity (P) is based on the strong relatedness values (Table 1) and the Dissimilarity (D) is based on the other types of relatedness values. As we believe that strong and not strong are proportional to the pair similarity and dissimilarity respectively

Rule-based module input is sentence pair S1, S2 word semantic scores, i.e. Ws1s and Ws2s (Table 1). Then, it calculates: 1) their three types of averages for S1 and S2 semantic scores, i.e. all word semantic scores, weakly related only and unrelated values; 2) P as the minimum percentage of strong Wss in (S1 and S1); 3) D as, 100-P, the percentage of not strong Wss in S1 and S1

This module outputs the semantic textual similarity semantic (STS) score which ranges from 0 to 5. Throughout this section, when we use "unrelated", "weak" and strong terminologies, we use Table 1 Relatedness definitions. Also, when we use "important" term, we refer to our definition (Section 2.1)

Human judgments for computing STS score of the sentence pair are based on word similarities and dissimilarities. They consider that two sentences are similar if most (> 50%) of their words are strongly related, otherwise the sentences are candidates to be dissimilar. Since all Wss range from 0 to 1, the average of strong scores is more than the average of weak scores. Likewise, the average of weak scores is more than the average of non-related scores.

Score(Sentence Ws1s, Sentence Ws2s)

```
AllAvg = (Ws1s+ Ws1s)/2
WeakAvg= the averaged weakly related scores of Ws1s and Ws1s
UnRElAvg=the average of unrelated scores of Ws1s and Ws1s
P = minimum (% Ws1s strong scores, % Ws2s strong scores)
D=100-P
Value=0
If 95 <= P <=100 then  Value = 5;
If 80 <= P < 95 then   Value = 4;
If 50 <= P < 80  then  Value = 3;
If 20 <= P < 50  then  Value = 2;
If 0 <= P < 20 then
   If all verbs are strongly related then Value=1
   Else Value= 0.0001;
If (Value in [4, 5]) then
   If all Ds for important words then Value= 3
If (Value ==3) then
   If all Ds for not important words then Value= 2
If (Value <> 5 AND Value <> 0) then
   If all Ds for weakly related words
         Value= Value+ AllAvg
   Else if at least half Ds for weakly related words
         Value= Value+ WeakAvg
   Otherwise
         Value = Value + UnRelAvg
Return Value
```

When we call Score(Ws1s,Ws2s), we take care of the following two special cases where it goes directly to Value 3: 1) if missing some words leads to missing the whole verb/noun phrases and 2) if one sentence has all past tense verbs and the other has present verbs.

When we design P inequalities, we make them have relaxed boundaries conformed with human grading values. For example, we choose P between 95 and 100 in Value (5); where 95 and 100 equal to grades 4.5 and 5 respectively. Value (3) interval are values between more than or equal 2.5 and less than 4. Then, we utilize the important information and verb constraints to direct classifications through different groups.

When we design range conditions between values, we select D to present the distance between the sentence pair. As D weak values increase, the two sentences become closer. As D unrelated values increase, the two sentences become distant.

We carefully analyzed the training corpora to assure that the above thresholds satisfy most of the training sentence pairs. Each threshold output was manually checked and adjusted to satisfy around 55% to 75% of the training corpora.

Applying the above module, the pair of *"A man is playing football"* and *"The man plays football"* STS score equals 5.00. The pair of *"A man is singing and playing"* and *"The man plays"* STS score equals 3.00 since the first one misses *"singing"*. The pair of *"The cat is drinking milk."* and *"A white cat is licking and drinking milk kept on a plate."* STS scores equals to 3.4 since they have P=0.66, *"white"* as unimportant information but *"licking"*, *" kept"*, *"plate"* as important information words.

2.6 Our Baseline System Description

Our goal in the second run is to evaluate the relatedness of the two sentences using only the words in the sentence. Sentences are represented as a vector (i.e. based on the Vector Space Model) and the similarity between the two sentences S1 and S2 is (5* cosine similarity). We take into account all sentence words such that they are lower-case and non-stemmed.

3 Results and Discussion

3.1 Rule-based System Analysis

Our system was implemented in Python and used the Natural Language Toolkit (NLTK, www.nltk.org/), WordNet and lemmatization modules. Table 2 provides in the official results of our system Pearson-Correlation measure.

D	Para	Vid	Europ	OnWn	News
Tr	0.6011	0.7021	0.4528		
Te	0.5440	0.7335	0.3830	0.5860	0.2445

Table 2. Run1 Official Person-Correlation measure

In Table 2, the first row shows the proposed system results namely 0.6011, 0.7021 and 0.4528 for MSRpar, MSRvid and SMTeuropel training corpora respectively. The second row shows the test results, namely 0.5440, 0.7335 and 0.3830, 0.5860 and 0.2445 for MSRpar, MSRvid and SMTeuropel, On-Wn and SMTnews testing corpora respectively.

In the Task-6 results (Agirre et al. 2012), our system was ranked 21th out of 85 participants with 0.6663 Pearson-Correlation ALL competition rank. We tested two WordNet measures, namely the shortest path and WUP, the path length to the root node from the least common subsumer (LCS) of the two concepts, measures on the training corpora. In contrast to the shortest path measure, WUP measure increased the P versus the D scores on the three corpora. This overestimated many training STS scores and negatively affected the correlation with the gold standard corpora. Using WUP measure, the correlations of MSRpar, MSRvid and SMTeuropel corpora were 0.5553, 0.3488 and 0.4819 respectively. We decided to use WordNet shortest path measure due to its better correlation results. When we used WUP measure on testing corpora, the correlations were 0.5103, 0.4617, 0.4810, 0.6422 and 0.4400 for MSRpar, MSRvid and SMTeuropel, On-Wn and SMTnews testing corpora respectively. We observed that when we used WUP measure on MSRvid corpora, the correlations were degraded. This is because most of MSRvid corpus pair sentences talking about human genders which have high WUP scores when comparing with each other. Unfortunately, WordNet shortest path measure underestimated SMTnews pair sentence similarities which affected dramatically the related correlation measure. Hence, the choice of the suitable WordNet metric for the whole corpora is still under our consideration.

Thresholds and Semantic Pattern: Our current efforts are directed towards statistical modeling of the system thresholds. We intend also to use some web semantic patterns or phrases, such as ReVerb patterns, to boost the semantic scores of single words.

3.2 Baseline System Analysis

In Table 3, the first row shows the proposed system results namely 0.4688, 0.4175 and 0.5349 for

MSRpar, MSRvid and SMTeuropel training corpora respectively. The second row shows the proposed system results, namely 0.4617, 0.4489 and 0.4719, 0.6353 and 0.4353 for MSRpar, MSRvid and SMTeuropel, On-Wn and SMTnews testing corpora respectively.

D	Para	Vid	Europ	OnWn	News
Tr	0.4688	0.4175	0.5349		
Te	0.4617	0.4489	0.4719	0.6353	0.4353

Table 3. Run 2 Official Person-Correlation measure

In the Task-6 results (Agirre et al. 2012), Run2 was ranked 72th out of 85 participants with 0.4169 Pearson-Correlation ALL competition rank. As anticipated, Run2 released fair results. Its performance is penalized or awarded proportionally to the number of exact matching pair words. Accordingly, it may record considerable scores for pairs which have highly percentage exact matching words. For example, it provides competitive correlation scores compared to other participants on On-Wn and SMTnews testing corpora. Though, this doesn't imply that it is an ideal solution for STS task. It usually indicates that many corpus pairs may have some substantial exact matching words.

4 Conclusions

In this paper, we presented systems developed for SEMEVAL12- Task6. The first run used both semantics and syntax. The second run, our baseline, uses only the words in the initial two sentences and defines similarity as the cosine similarity between the two sentences. The official task results suggest that semantics and syntax (Run1) supersedes the words alone (Run 2) with 0.2494 which indicates that the words alone are not sufficient to capture semantic similarity.

Acknowledgment

This material is based upon work supported by the National Science Foundation under Grant No. (1115774). Any opinions, findings, and conclusions or recommendations expressed in this material are those of the author(s) and do not necessarily reflect the views of the National Science Foundation.

References

Catherine Blake. 2007. *The Role of Sentence Structure in Recognizing Textual Entailment.* RTE Proceedings of the ACL-PASCAL Workshop on Textual Entailment and Paraphrasing:101-106.

Courtney Corley and Andras Csomai and Rada Mihalcea. 2005. *Text Semantic Similarity, with Applications.* Proceedings of the Conference on Recent Advances in Natural Language Processing (RANLP), Borovetz, Bulgaria.

Dan Klein and Christopher D. Manning. 2002. *Fast Exact Inference with a Factored Model for Natural Language Parsing.* In *Advances in Neural Information Processing Systems 15 (NIPS)*, Cambridge, MA: MIT Press:3-10.

Dong-bin Hu and Jun Ding. 2011. *Study on Similar Engineering Decision Problem Identification Based On Combination of Improved Edit-Distance and Skeletal Dependency Tree with POS.* Systems Engineering Procedia 1: 406–413.

Eneko Agirre, Daniel Cer, Mona Diab and Aitor Gonzalez-Agirre. 2012. SemEval-2012 Task 6: A Pilot on Semantic Textual Similarity. In Proceedings of the 6th International Workshop on Semantic Evaluation (SemEval 2012), in conjunction with the First Joint Conference on Lexical and Computational Semantics (*SEM 2012)

Eric Bengtson and Dan Roth. 2008. *Understanding the Value of Features for Coreference Resolution.* EMNLP:294-303.

Federica Mandreoli and Riccardo Martoglia and Paolo Tiberio. 2002 . *A Syntactic Approach for Searching Similarities within Sentences.* Proceeding of International Conference on Information and Knowledge Management:656–637.

George A. Miller. 1995. *WordNet: A Lexical Database for English.* Communications of the ACM, 38(11): 39-41.

Gerard Salton. 1989. *Automatic Text Processing.* The Transformation, Analysis, and Retrieval of Information by Computer. Wokingham, Mass.Addison-Wesley.

Gunes Erkan and Dragomir R. Radev. 2004. *LexRank: Graph-based Lexical Centrality as Salience in Text Summarization.* Journal of Artificial Intelligence Research 22:457-479.

Junsheng Zhang, Yunchuan Sun, Huilin Wang, Yanqing He. 2011. *Calculating Statistical Similarity between Sentences.* Journal of Convergence Information Technology, Volume 6, Number 2: 22-34.

Liu Wenyin and Xiaojun Quan and Min Feng and Bite Qiu. 2010. *A Short Text Modeling Method Combining Semantic and Statistical Information.* Information Sciences 180: 4031–4041.

Michael Mohler and Rada Mihalcea. 2009. *Text-to-text Semantic Similarity for Automatic Short Answer Grading*. Proceedings of the European Chapter of the Association for Computational Linguistics (EACL).

Oliva Jesus and Serrano I. Jose and María D. del Castillo and Ángel Iglesias .2011. *SyMSS: A Syntax-based Measure for Short-Text Semantic Similarity*. Data and Knowledge Engineering 70: 390–405.

Oren Etzioni, Anthony Fader, Janara Christensen, Stephen Soderland, and Mausam. 2011. *Open Information Extraction: The Second Generation*. Proceedings of the 22nd International Joint Conference on Artificial Intelligence (IJCAI).

Rada Mihalcea and Courtney Corley and Carlo Strapparava. 2006. *Corpus-based and knowledge-based measures of text semantic similarity*. Proceeding of the Twenty-First National Conference on Artificial Intelligence and the Eighteenth Innovative Applications of Artificial Intelligence Conference.

Peter W. Foltz and Walter Kintsch and Thomas K Landauer. 1998. *The measurement of textual coherence with latent semantic analysis*. Discourse Processes Vol. 25, No. 2-3: 285-307.

Samuel Fernando and Mark Stevenson. 2008. *A Semantic Similarity Approach to Paraphrase Detection*. Computational Linguistics (CLUK) 11th Annual Research Colloquium, 2008.

Satanjeev Banerjee and Ted Pedersen. 2010. *An Adapted Lesk Algorithm for Word Sense Disambiguation Using WordNet*. CICLING:136-145.

Ted Pedersen, Siddharth Patwardhan, and Jason Michelizzi. 2004. *WordNet::Similarity-measuring the relatedness of concepts*. In Proceedings of NAACL, 2004.

Vasileios Hatzivassiloglou , Judith L. Klavans , Eleazar Eskin. 1999. *Detecting text similarity over short passages: Exploring linguistic feature combinations via machine learning*. Proceeding of Empirical Methods in natural language processing and Very Large Corpora.

Xiao-Ying Liu and Yi-Ming Zhou and Ruo-Shi Zheng. 2008. *Measuring Semantic Similarity within Sentences*. Proceedings of the Seventh International Conference on Machine Learning and Cybernetics.

Yuhua Li, David McLean, Zuhair A. Bandar, James D. O'Shea, and Keeley Crockett. *Sentence Similarity based on Semantic Nets and Corpus statistics*. 2006. IEEE Transactions on Knowledgeand Data Engineering Vol. 18, No. 8: 1138-1150.

LIMSI: Learning Semantic Similarity by Selecting Random Word Subsets

Artem Sokolov
LIMSI-CNRS
B.P. 133, 91403 Orsay, France
artem.sokolov@limsi.fr

Abstract

We propose a semantic similarity learning method based on Random Indexing (RI) and ranking with boosting. Unlike classical RI, we use only those context vector features that are informative for the semantics modeled. Despite ignoring text preprocessing and dispensing with semantic resources, the approach was ranked as high as 22nd among 89 participants in the SemEval-2012 Task6: Semantic Textual Similarity.

1 Introduction

One of the popular and flexible tools of semantics modeling are vector distributional representations of texts (also known as vector space models, semantic word spaces or distributed representations). The principle idea behind vector space models is to use word usage statistics in different contexts to generate a high-dimensional vector representations for each word. Words are represented by context vectors whose closeness in the vector space is postulated to reflect semantic similarity (Sahlgren, 2005). The approach rests upon the *distributional hypothesis*: words with similar meanings or functions tend to appear in similar contexts. The prominent examples of vector space models are Latent Semantic Analysis (or Indexing) (Landauer and Dutnais, 1997) and Random Indexing (Kanerva et al., 2000).

Because of the heuristic nature of distributional methods, they are often designed with a specific semantic relation in mind (synonymy, paraphrases, contradiction, etc.). This complicates their adaption to other application domains and tasks, requiring manual trial-and-error feature redesigns and tailored preprocessing steps to remove morphology/syntax variations that are not supposed to contribute to the semantics facet in question (e.g., stemming, stopwords). Further, assessing closeness of semantic vectors is usually based on a fixed simple similarity function between distributed representations (often, the cosine function). The cosine function implicitly assigns equal weights to each component of the semantic vectors regardless of its importance for the particular semantic relation and task. Finally, during production of training and evaluation sets, the continuum of possible grades of semantic similarity is usually substituted with several integer values, although often only the relative grade order matters and not their absolute values. Trying to reproduce the same values or the same gaps between grades when designing a semantic representation scheme may introduce an unnecessary bias.

In this paper we address all of the above drawbacks and present a semantic similarity learning method based on Random Indexing. It does not require manual feature design, and is automatically adapted to the specific semantic relations by selecting needed important features and/or learning necessary feature transformations before calculating similarity. In the proof-of-concept experiments on the SemEval-2012 data we deliberately ignored all routine preprocessing steps, that are often considered obligatory in semantic text processing, we did not use any of the semantic resources (like WordNet) nor trained different models for different data domains/types. Despite such over-constrained setting, the method showed very positive performance and was ranked as high as 22nd among 89 participants.

2 Random Indexing

Random Indexing (RI) is an alternative to LSA-like models with large co-occurrence matrices and separate matrix decomposition phase to reduce dimension. RI constructs context vectors on-the-fly based on the occurrence of words in contexts. First, each word is assigned a unique and randomly generated high-dimensional sparse ternary vector. Vectors contain a small number (between 0.1-1%) of randomly distributed +1s and -1s, with the rest of the elements set to 0. Next, the final context vectors for words are produced by scanning through the text with a sliding window of fixed size, and each time the word occurs in the text, the generated vectors of all its neighbors in the sliding context window are added to the context vector of this word[1]. Finally, the obtained context vectors are normalized by the occurrence count of the word.

RI is a practical variant of the well-known dimension reduction technique of the Johnson-Lindenstrauss (JL) lemma (Dasgupta and Gupta, 2003). An Euclidean space can be projected with a random Gaussian matrix R onto smaller dimension Euclidean space, such that with high probability the distance between any pair of points in the new space is within a distortion factor of $1 \pm \varepsilon$ of their original distance. Same or similar guarantees also hold for a uniform $\{-1, +1\}$-valued or ternary (from a certain distribution) random R (Achlioptas, 2003) or for even sparser matrices (Dasgupta et al., 2010)

Restating the JL-lemma in the RI-terminology, one can think of the initial space of characteristic vectors of word sets of all contexts (each component counts corresponding words seen in the context window over the corpus) embedded into a smaller dimension space, and approximately preserving distances between characteristic vectors. Because of the ternary generation scheme, each resulting feature-vector dimension either rewards, penalizes or "switches off" certain words for which the corresponding row of R contained, resp., $+1$, -1 or 0.

So far, RI has been a naïve approach to feature learning – although it produces low-dimensional feature representations, it is unconscious of the learning task behind. There is no guarantee that the Euclidean distance (or cosine similarity) will correctly reflect the necessary semantic relation: for a pair of vectors, not all word subsets are characteristic of a particular semantic relation or specific to it, as presence or absence of certain words may play no role in assessing given similarity type. Implications of RI in the context of learning textual similarity are coming from the feature selection (equivalently, word subset selection) method, based on boosting, that selects only those features that are informative for the semantic relation being learned (Section 4). Thus, the supervision information on sentence similarity guides the choose of word subsets (among all randomly generated by the projection matrix) that happen to be relevant to the semantic annotations.

[1]Although decreasing discounts dampening contribution of far-located context words may by beneficial, we do not use it putting our method in more difficult conditions.

3 Semantic Textual Similarity Task

Let $\{(s_1^i, s_2^i)\}$ be the training set of N pairs of sentences, provided along with similarity labels y_i. The higher the value of y_i the more semantically similar is the pair (s_1^i, s_2^i). Usually absolute values of y_i are chosen arbitrary; only their relative order matters.

We would learn semantic similarity between (s_1^i, s_2^i) as a function $H(\bar{x}^i)$, where $\bar{x}^i$ is a single vector combining sentence context vectors $v(s_1^i)$ and $v(s_2^i)$. Context representation $v(s)$ for a sentence s is defined as an average of the word context vectors $v(w)$ contained in it, found using a large text corpus with the RI approach, described in the previous section: $v(s) = \sum_{w \in s} v(w) / |s|$. Possible transformations into $\bar{x}^i$ include a concatenation of $v(s_1^i)$ and $v(s_2^i)$, concatenation of the sum and difference vectors or a vector composed of component-wise symmetric functions (e.g., a product of corresponding components). In order to learn a symmetric H, one can either use each pair twice during training, or symmetrize the construction of $\bar{x}$.

4 Feature Selection with Boosting

We propose to exploit natural ordering of (s_1^i, s_2^i) according to y^i to learn a parameterized similarity function $H(\bar{x}^i)$. In this way we do not try learning the absolute values of similarity provided in the training. Also, by using boosting approach we allow for gradual inclusion of features into similarity function H, implementing in this way feature selection.

For a given number of training steps T, a boosting ranking algorithm learns a scoring function H, which is a linear combination of T simple, non-linear functions h_t called weak learners: $H(\bar{x}) = \sum_{t=1}^{T} \alpha_t h_t(\bar{x})$, where each α_t is the weight assigned to h_t at step t of the learning process.

Usually the weak learner is defined on only few components of $\bar{x}$. Having build H at step t, the next in turn $(t+1)$'s leaner is selected, optimized and weighted with the corresponding coefficient α_{t+1}. In this way the learning process selects only those features in $\bar{x}$ (or, if viewed from the RI perspective, random word subsets) that contribute most to learning the desired type input similarity.

As the first ranking method we applied the pair-wise ranking algorithm RankBoost (Freund et al., 2003), that learns H by minimizing a convex approximation to a weighted pair-wise loss:

$$\sum_{(s_1^i, s_2^i),(s_1^j, s_2^j): y^i < y^j} P(i,j) [\![H(\bar{x}^i) \geq H(\bar{x}^j)]\!].$$

Operator $[\![A]\!] = 1$ if the $A =$ true and 0 otherwise. Positive values of P weight pairs of $\bar{x}^i$ and $\bar{x}^j$ – the higher is $P(i,j)$, the more important it is to preserve the relative ordering of $\bar{x}^i$ and $\bar{x}^j$. We used the simplest decision stumps that depend on one feature as weak learners: $h(\boldsymbol{x}; \theta, k) = [\![x^k > \theta]\!]$, where k is a feature index and θ is a learned threshold.

The second ranking method we used was a point-wise ranking algorithm, based on gradient boosting regression for ranking (Zheng et al., 2007), called RtRank and implemented by Mohan et al. (2011)[2]. The loss optimized by RtRank is slightly different:

$$\sum_{(s_1^i, s_2^i),(s_1^j, s_2^j): y^i < y^j} (\max\{0, H(\bar{x}^i) - H(\bar{x}^j)\})^2.$$

Another difference is in the method for selecting weak learner at each boosting step, that relies on regression loss and not scalar product as RankBoost. Weak learners for RtRank were regression trees of fixed depth (4 in our experiments).

5 Experiments

We learned context vectors on the GigaWord English corpus. The only preprocessing of the corpus was stripping all tag data, removing punctuation and lowercasing. Stop-words were not removed. Context vectors were built with the JavaSDM package (Hassel, 2004)[3] of dimensionality $N = 100$ and $N = 10^5$, resp., for preliminary and final experiments, with random degree 10 (five +1s and -1s in each initial vector), right and left context window size of 4 words[4] and constant weighting scheme.

	learner	transform	correl.	σ
baseline	pure RI, cos	-	0.264	0.005
	logistic reg.	-	0.508	0.041
	logistic reg.	concat	0.537	0.052
boosting	RankBoost	sumdiff	0.685	0.027
		product	0.663	0.018
		crossprod	0.648	0.028
		crossdiff	0.643	0.023
		concat	0.625	0.025
		absdiff	0.602	0.021
	RtRank	sumdiff	0.730	0.020
		product	0.721	0.023

Table 1: Mean performance of the transformation and boosting methods for $N = 100$ on train data.

Training and test data provided in the SemEval-2012 Task 6 contained 5 training and 5 testing text sets each of different domains or types of sentences (short video descriptions, pairs of outputs of a machine translation system, etc.). Although the 5 sets had very different characteristics, we concatenated all training files and trained a single model. The principal evaluation metrics was Pearson correlation coefficient, that we report here. Two related other measures were also used (Agirre et al., 2012).

Obtained sentence vectors $v(\boldsymbol{s})$ for were transformed into vectors $\bar{x}$ with several methods:

- 'sumdiff': $\bar{x} = (\bar{v}(s_1) + \bar{v}(s_2), sgn(v_1(s_1) - v_1(s_2))(v(s_1) - v(s_2)))$
- 'concat': $\bar{x} = (v(s_1), v(s_2))$, and $\bar{x}' = (v(s_2), v(s_1))$
- 'product': $x_i = v_i(s_1) \cdot v_i(s_2)$
- 'crossprod': $x_{ij} = v_i(s_1) \cdot v_j(s_2)$
- 'crossdiff': $x_{ij} = v_i(s_1) - v_j(s_2)$
- 'absdiff': $x_i = |v_i(s_1) - v_i(s_2)|$.

Methods 'concat' and 'sumdiff' were proposed by Hertz et al. (2004) for distance learning for clus-

[2]http://sites.google.com/site/rtranking

[3]http://www.csc.kth.se/~xmartin/java

[4]Little sensitivity was found to the window sizes from 3 to 6.

learner	transform	train±σ	test	rank	MSRpar	MSRvid	SMTeur	OnWN	SMTnews
RankBoost	product	0.748±0.017	0.6392	32	0.3948	0.6597	0.0143	0.4157	0.2889
	sumdiff	0.735±0.016	0.6196	45	0.4295	0.5724	0.2842	0.3989	0.2575
RtRank	product	0.784±0.017	**0.6789**	**22**	0.4848	0.6636	0.0934	0.3706	0.2455
	sumdiff	0.763±0.014							

Table 2: Mean performance of the best-performing two transformation and two boosting methods for $N = 10^5$.

tering. Comparison of mean performance of different transformation and learning methods on the 5-fold splitting of the training set is given in Table 1 for short context vectors ($N = 100$). The correlation is given for the optimal algorithms' parameters (T for RankBoost and, additionally, tree depth and random ratio for RtRank), found with cross-validation on 5 folds. With these results for small N, two transformation methods were preselected ('sumdiff' and 'product') for testing and submission with $N = 10^5$ (Table 2), as increasing N usually increased performance. Yet, only about 10^3 features were actually selected by RankBoost, meaning that a relatively few random word subsets were informative for approximating semantic textual similarity.

In result, RtRank showed better performance, most likely because of more powerful learners, that depend on several features (word subsets) simultaneously. Performance on machine translation test sets was the lowest that can be explained by very poor quality of the training data[5]: models for these subsets should have been trained separately.

6 Conclusion

We presented a semantic similarity learning approach that learns a similarity function specific to the semantic relation modeled and that selects only those word subsets in RI, presence of which in the compared sentences is indicative of their similarity, by using only relative order of the labels and not their absolute values. In spite of paying no attention to preprocessing, nor using semantic corpora, and with no domain adaptation the method showed promising results.

Acknowledgments

This work has been funded by OSEO under the Quaero program.

[5]A reviewer suggested another reason: more varied or even incorrect lexical choice that is sometimes found in MT output.

References

Dimitris Achlioptas. 2003. Database-friendly random projections: Johnson-Lindenstrauss with binary coins. *Comput. Syst. Sci.*, 66:671–687.

Eneko Agirre, Daniel Cer, Mona Diab, and Aitor Gonzalez. 2012. Semeval-2012 task 6: A pilot on semantic textual similarity. In *Proc. of the Int. Workshop on Semantic Evaluation (SemEval 2012) // Joint Conf. on Lexical & Computational Semantics (*SEM 2012)*.

Sanjoy Dasgupta and Anupam Gupta. 2003. An elementary proof of a theorem of Johnson and Lindenstrauss. *Random Struct. Algorithms*, 22(1):60–65.

Anirban Dasgupta, Ravi Kumar, and Tamás Sarlos. 2010. A sparse Johnson-Lindenstrauss transform. In *Proc. of the ACM Symp. on Theory of Comput.*, pages 341–350.

Yoav Freund, Raj Iyer, Robert E. Schapire, and Yoram Singer. 2003. An efficient boosting algorithm for combining preferences. *Mach.Learn.Res.*, 4:933–969.

Martin Hassel. 2004. JavaSDM - a Java package for working with Random Indexing and Granska.

Tomer Hertz, Aharon Bar-hillel, and Daphna Weinshall. 2004. Boosting margin based distance functions for clustering. In *ICML*, pages 393–400.

Pentti Kanerva, Jan Kristoferson, and Anders Holst. 2000. Random indexing of text samples for latent semantic analysis. In *Proc. of the Conf. of the Cogn. Science Society*.

Thomas K. Landauer and Susan T. Dutnais. 1997. A solution to Plato's problem: The latent semantic analysis theory of acquisition, induction, and representation of knowledge. *Psychol. Rev.*, pages 211–240.

Ananth Mohan, Zheng Chen, and Kilian Q. Weinberger. 2011. Web-search ranking with initialized gradient boosted regression trees. *Mach.Learn.Res.*, 14:77–89.

Magnus Sahlgren. 2005. An introduction to random indexing. In *Workshop on Methods & Applic. of Sem. Indexing // Int. Conf. on Terminol. & Knowl. Eng.*

Zhaohui Zheng, Hongyuan Zha, Tong Zhang, Olivier Chapelle, Keke Chen, and Gordon Sun. 2007. A general boosting method and its application to learning ranking functions for web search. In *NIPS*.

ATA-Sem: Chunk-based Determination of Semantic Text Similarity

Demetrios Glinos
Advanced Text Analytics, LLC
Orlando, Florida, USA
demetrios.glinos@advancedtextanalytics.com

Abstract

This paper describes investigations into using syntactic chunk information as the basis for determining the similarity of candidate texts at the semantic level. Two approaches were considered. The first was a corpus-based method that extracted lexical and semantic features from pairs of chunks from each sentence that were associated through a chunk alignment algorithm. The features were used as input to a classifier trained on the same features extracted from a corpus of gold standard training data. The second approach involved breadth-first chunk association and the application of a rule-based scoring algorithm. Both approaches were evaluated against the test data for the SemEval 2012 Semantic Text Similarity task. The results show that the rule-based chunk approach is superior.

1 Introduction

The task of determining whether two texts are similar in some sense has important applications in the field of natural language processing, including but not limited to document summarization (Evans, et al., 2005), plagiarism detection (Barrón-Cedeño, et al., 2009) and large corpus document retrieval (Charikar, 2002).

While textual similarity can be performed at the purely surface lexical level, as in the "simhash" clustering method described in (Moulton, 2010), similarity also applies at the semantic level, where conceptually similar texts may nevertheless be entirely dissimilar at the surface lexical level. For example, the phrases "restrict or confine" and "place limits on (extent or access)" share no words or morphological roots, yet mean very nearly the same thing at the semantic level.

The Semantic Textual Similarity (STS) task (Task #6) at SemEval-2012 (Agirre, et al., 2012) provided a forum for exploring these issues by furnishing training and evaluation data, and also a common standard for describing degrees of similarity, shown in Table 1.

Score	Description
5	The two sentences are completely equivalent, as they mean the same thing.
4	The two sentences are mostly equivalent, but some unimportant details differ.
3	The two sentences are roughly equivalent, but some important information differs/missing.
2	The two sentences are not equivalent, but share some details.
1	The two sentences are not equivalent, but are on the same topic.
0	The two sentences are on different topics.

Table 1. STS similarity scoring standard.

Our corpus-based chunk similarity method participated in the formal STS evaluation. Our rule-based method was completed after the submittal date, but we report on it here because the method does not involve training on a corpus, nor any parameter tuning, and because it significantly outperformed the corpus-based method.

The remainder of this paper is organized as follows. In the next section, we describe the common processing components for both methods. Section 3 then presents the corpus-based chunk method, followed in Section 4 by a discussion of the rule-based chunk similarity method. Section 5 concludes with a presentation of how the two methods performed against the STS test set, and offers some observations on the viability of chunk-based similarity determination.

2 Common Processing Components

A common processing core supports both of the methods, comprising preprocessing components and also shared components for determining chunk-level similarity. The preprocessing components make use of the U.S. National Library of Medicine's Lexical Tools (NLM 2012) to perform ASCII conversion and tokenization. Candidate sentence pairs are then tagged and chunked using our own tagger and separate chunker, which were both trained on CONLL 2000 data using the CRF++ conditional random field toolkit (Taku-ku 2012). We use chunk labels that augment the standard BIO tags with appropriate Penn-Treebank phrasal tags, for example, "B-NP" and "B-ADVP".

Once the candidate sentences are chunked, the two methods diverge in their approach to classification. However, both approaches use the NLM Lexical Tools and WordNet (Fellbaum, 1998) for term expansion. The NLM's normalization tool is used to reduce terms to lower case, strip them of punctuation, stop words, diacritical marks, etc., and to expand the terms with lexical variants. WordNet's synonyms and hypernyms for the remaining terms are then added to expand the term lists for chunk-level comparisons.

3 Corpus-based Chunk Method

The corpus-based method employs a "chunk alignment" algorithm for selecting pairs of chunks for detailed comparison, one from each candidate sentence. The algorithm operates by initializing pointers to the first chunk in each sentence. Then, noting the chunk type for the indexed chunk in the shorter sentence, the algorithm marches down the longer sentence searching for the first chunk of the same type. Once it is found, the two chunks are marked for comparison and the index into the shorter sentence is incremented to the next chunk. The process repeats until no more chunk pairs can be associated. Figure 1 shows an example of chunk alignment.

The method generates the set of features shown in Table 2 based on the chunk-level comparisons. Features 2 to 4 contain numerical values representing the sums of "matching scores" from the aligned chunks. A four-valued matching score is assigned for each chunk comparison depending on the degree of chunk-level similarity. A value of "3" represents an exact term match or a match on a synonym. The value "2" is given if the head term of one of the chunks is in the hypernym tree for the other chunk. And a value of "1" is given if the two chunk heads have a common hypernym ancestor. The default value "0" is given if none of the above conditions is found. The numbers in brackets in the table identify the unigram features that are associated to compose trigram and 4-gram features, respectively.

Unigrams	0	Total # chunks in Sentence A
	1	Total # chunks in Sentence B
	2	Sum of aligned VP matching scores
	3	Sum of aligned NP matching scores
	4	Sum of aligned PP matching scores
	5	Number of VP chunks in A
	6	Number of NP chunks in A
	7	Number of PP chunks in A
	8	Number of VP chunks in B
	9	Number of NP chunks in B
	10	Number of PP chunks in B
Trigrams		[2, 5, 8], [3, 6, 9], [4, 7, 10]
4-grams		[0, 5, 6, 7], [1, 8, 9, 10]

Table 2. Similarity classifier features.

Once the feature vector is, it is passed to the text similarity classifier, which generates the 0-5 similarity score. The classifier was trained on the gold

Micron's numbers	also	marked	the first quarterly profit	in three years	for the DRAM manufacturer
NP	**ADVP**	**VP**	**NP**	**PP**	**PP**
Micron		has declared	its first quarterly profit	in three years	
NP		**VP**	**NP**	**PP**	

Figure 1. Chunk Alignment Example

standard training data using the CRF++ toolkit using the same feature set described above.

4 Rule-based Chunk Method

The rule-based chunk similarity method employs a breadth-first search method for selecting candidate chunks for further comparison. The algorithm operates by selecting the first chunk of the sentence with the larger number of chunks. It then marches down each chunk of the shorter sentence looking for an exact term match or head term synonym match. If a match is found, a chunk-level score value of 3 is assigned, and the next chunk in the longer sentence is considered. If a match is not found, then a new search is performed, this time searching for a hypernym match. If a match is found in this second pass, a chunk score of 2 is assigned, and the next index chunk is considered. If not, then a third and final pass is performed searching for a related term match. If a match is found after this third pass, a chunk score of 1 is assigned; otherwise, the chunks are deemed dissimilar and receive a chunk score of zero.

We describe this algorithm as "breadth-first" because it has the effect of conducting up to three passes across all of the chunks of the target (shorter) sentence, looking for successively "looser" matches. For these purposes, we consider a hypernym match to be looser than an exact or synynym match, and a common-ancestor (related) term match to be looser than a hypernym match.

The chunk-level matching scores are accumulated in the above manner, just as for the corpus-based method. However, in this case, the results are used directly by the rule-based scoring algorithm. The scoring algorithm treats predicate and argument chunks separately and generates raw scores for each. It then combines them to compute the final similarity score. The predicate raw score is the accumulated score for all VP chunk comparisons, divided by three times the number of such comparisons. This results in a predicate raw score that is in the range [0,1], since the maximum chunk-level matching score is three. The argument raw score is produced in the same manner and multiplied by 5.0, producing a value in the range [0,5].

Where both predicate and argument raw scores exist, the total similarity score for the sentence pair is computed as the product of the two raw scores. This formulation has the benefit of permitting the degree of similarity for each score type to affect the overall score. For example, consider "Sarah bought the book," and "Sarah read the book." Here, the difference in predicate ("bought" versus "read") will temper the otherwise exact match on the arguments. Similarly, for "Sarah bought the book," and "Sarah bought the fish," the inexact match on arguments will soften the perfect predicate score.

Table 3 illustrates how the basic rule-based algorithm works. The table shows the associated chunks from each sentence, their chunk type for scoring purposes, and their chunk-level matching score values. Thus, for example, "The Korean Air deal" and "the final agreement" have a matching score value of 2 because "agreement" is a hypernym of "deal". Moreover, because there is no mention of "Bob Saling" in the first sentence, the corresponding matching value is zero.

Based on the chunk-level scores in the table, the similarity score is calculated as follows. The raw predicate score for the two predicate chunk pairs is 6 (3 for each, from the table), divided by the max-

S1: Boeing said the final agreement is expected to be signed during the next few weeks.
S2: The Korean Air deal is expected to be finalized "in the next several weeks," Boeing spokesman Bob Saling said.

S2 chunk phrase	S1 chunk phrase	Chunk type	Matching score
The Korean Air deal	the final agreement	argument	2
is expected to be finalized	is expected to be signed	predicate	3
in the next several weeks	during the next several weeks	argument	3
Boeing spokesman	Boeing	argument	3
Bob Saling		argument	0
said	said	predicate	3

Table 3. Chunk-level matching scores for rule-based scoring example from training data.

imum possible score, which is also 6, yielding a value of 1.000. The argument raw score is the sum of the scores for the argument pairs, 8 in this case, divided by the maximum possible (12 for the four argument chunks), scaled by 5, yielding a value of 3.333. The final score is their product, 3.333, which compares favorably with the gold standard score value of 3.000 for this sentence pair.

If there are no predicate chunk comparisons for the sentence pair, the rule-based scoring algorithm uses the raw argument score without modification. Similarly, where there are no argument chunk comparisons, the rule uses the raw predicate score multiplied by 5.0 to scale it to cover the range [0,5]. By being robust against zero values in this manner, the algorithm is able to handle comparisons of sentence fragments such as "Tunisia", in the event it is the entirety of the input "sentence".

Additionally, the final score that is reported is the minimum of the combined score described above and an upper limit value that is initialized at 5.0, but which can be reduced as each chunk-level comparison is performed. The upper limit value is reduced to 4.0 if there is a qualifier mismatch (e.g., "uncooked pizza" v. "pizza"). It is reduced to 3.0 if there is a number mismatch, for example, "Two men are playing chess" versus "Three men are playing chess."

5 Results and Discussion

Table 4 shows the results for both algorithms against the STS test suite. The "Corpus-based" and "Rule-based" columns reports results for the two chunk-based similarity algorithm. The five lowest rows represent the five individual data sets in the suite. The values in the table represent Pearson correlation values, which range from -1 to +1, where the closer a value is to 1, the stronger the positive correlation.

The three upper rows represent the three metrics that were used to compute global results across all of the data sets. "All" refers to the computation of a Pearson value where the five gold standards and corresponding results were concatenated. The "Allnrm" row reports correlation values obtained by scaling and translating system outputs in a manner that maintains the individual data set correlation values, yet minimizes the combined data set error. Finally, the "Mean" reports the weighted average of the individual data set correlation values, where the weights used were the numbers of sentence pairs in each data set. There were 750 sentence pairs in each of the MSRpar, MSRvid, and OnWN data sets, but only 459 in the SMT-eur data set and 399 in the SMT-news data set, for a total of 3108 sentence pairs. The characteristics of the different data sets and greater detail on the global scoring metrics are discussed further in the STS task description paper (Agirre, et al., 2012).

Category	Corpus-based	Rule-based	Improvement (%)
All	.4976	.5306	6.63%
Allnrm	.7160	.7646	6.79%
Mean	.3215	.5069	57.67%
MSRpar	.2312	.4536	96.20%
MSRvid	.6595	.7079	7.33%
SMT-eur	.1504	.3996	165.68%
On-WN	.2735	.5149	88.26%
SMT-news	.1426	.3379	136.98%

Table 4. Results against STS test suite.[1]

As Table 4 shows, the rule-based method outperformed the corpus-based method for all individual data sets and for all combined measures. The percentage improvement is noted in the rightmost column in the figure.

We believe the results for the rule-based method are sufficient to show that chunk-based methods may have a role to play in text similarity determinations, particularly in high volume applications where high throughput is essential. Chunking is computationally cheap to perform. It is also robust against sentence fragments and against incomplete or ungrammatical sentence constructions, as may be found in emails, text messages, and blog posts.

However, chunk-based methods may be restricted to such applications since, on an absolute scale, performance was in the bottom one-third of all systems that reported results against the STS data suite. Nevertheless, we recognize that our investigations into chunk-based methods were limited in both time and scope. As a result, we do not believe we have yet encountered the upper limit on performance for chunk-based text similarity systems.

[1] The results for the corpus-based chunk method are reported under the name "demetrios_glinos/task6-ATA-CHNK" on the official STS results page, http://www.cs.york.ac.uk/semeval-2012/task6/index.php?id=results-update.

References

Eneko Agirre, Daniel Cer, Mona Diab and Aitor Gonzalez-Agirre. 2012. SemEval-2012 Task 6: A Pilot on Semantic Textual Similarity. In *Proceedings of the 6th International Workshop on Semantic Evaluation (SemEval 2012), in conjunction with the First Joint Conference on Lexical and Computational Semantics (*SEM 2012).*

Alberto Barrón-Cedeño, Andreas Eiselt, and Paolo Rosso. 2009. Monolingual Text Similarity Measures: A Comparison of Models over Wikipedia Articles Revisions. In *Proceedings of the ICON-2009: 7th International Conference on Natural Language Processing*, pp. 29-38.

Moses S. Charikar. 2002. Similarity Estimation Techniques from Rounding Algorithms. In *STOC '02 Proceedings of the thirty-fourth annual ACM symposium on theory of computing.*

Taku-ku. 2012. CRF++: Yet Another CRF toolkit. http://crfpp.googlecode.com/svn/trunk/doc/index.html.

David K. Evans, Kathleen McKeown, and Judith L. Klavans. 2005. Similarity-based Multilingual Multi-Document Summarization. *IEEE Transactions on Information Theory.*

Christiane Fellbaum. 1998. WordNet: An Electronic Lexical Database. The MIT Press.

Ryan Moulton. 2010. Simple Simhashing: Clustering in linear time. [Internet]. Version 1. Ryan Moulton's Articles. Available from: http://moultano.wordpress.com/article/simple-simhashing-3kbzhsxyg4467-6/.

NLM. 2012. U.S. National Library of Medicine, Lexical Systems Group, Lexical Tools. http://lexsrv3.nlm.nih.gov/LexSysGroup/Projects/lvg/current/web/index.html.

IRIT: Textual Similarity Combining Conceptual Similarity with an N-Gram Comparison Method

Davide Buscaldi, Ronan Tournier, Nathalie Aussenac-Gilles and **Josiane Mothe**
IRIT
118 Route de Narbonne
Toulouse (France)
{davide.buscaldi,ronan.tournier}@irit.fr,
{nathalie.aussenac,josiane.mothe}@irit.fr

Abstract

This paper describes the participation of the IRIT team to SemEval 2012 Task 6 (Semantic Textual Similarity). The method used consists of a n-gram based comparison method combined with a conceptual similarity measure that uses WordNet to calculate the similarity between a pair of concepts.

1 Introduction

The system used for the participation of the IRIT team (composed by members of the research groups SIG and MELODI) to the Semantic Textual Similarity (STS) task (Agirre et al., 2012) is based on two sub-modules:

- a module that calculates the similarity between sentences using n-gram based similarity;
- a module that calculates the similarity between concepts in the two sentences, using a concept similarity measure and WordNet (Miller, 1995) as a resource.

In Figure 1, we show the structure of the system and the connections between the main components. The input phrases are passed on one hand directly to the n-gram similarity module, and on the other they are annoted with the Stanford POS Tagger (Toutanova et al., 2003). All nouns and verbs are extracted from the tagged phrases and WordNet is searched for synsets corresponding to the extracted nouns and nouns associated to the verbs by the *derived terms* relationship. The synsets are the concepts used by the conceptual similarity module to

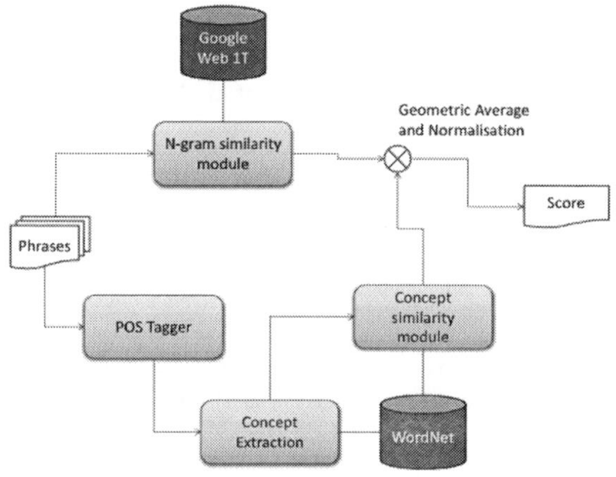

Figure 1: Schema of the system.

calculate the concept similarity. Each module calculates a similarity score using its own method; the final similarity value is calculated as the geometric average between the two scores, multiplied by 5 in order to comply with the task specifications.

The n-gram based similarity relies on the idea that two sentences are semantically related if they contain a long enough sub-sequence of non-empty terms. Google Web 1T (Brants and Franz, 2006) has been used to calculate term idf, which is used as a measure of the importance of the terms. The conceptual similarity is based on the idea that, given an ontology, two concepts are semantically similar if their distance from a common ancestor is small enough. We used three different measures: the Wu-Palmer similarity measure (Wu and Palmer, 1994) and two "Proxigenea" measures (Dudognon et al., 2010). In the following we will explain in detail how each similarity module works.

2 N-Gram based Similarity

N-gram based similarity is based on the Clustered Keywords Positional Distance (CKPD) model proposed in (Buscaldi et al., 2009). This model was originally proposed for passage retrieval in the field of Question Answering (QA), and it has been implemented in the JIRS system[1]. In (Buscaldi et al., 2006), JIRS showed to be able to obtain a better answer coverage in the Question Answering task than other traditional passage retrieval models based on Vector Space Model, such as *Lucene*[2]. The model has been adapted for this task by calculating the idf weights for each term using the frequency value provided by Google Web 1T.

The similarity between a text fragment (or passage) p and another text fragment q is calculated as:

$$Sim(p,q) = \frac{\sum\limits_{\forall x \in Q} h(x,P) \frac{1}{d(x, x_{max})}}{\sum_{i=1}^{n} w_i} \quad (1)$$

Where P is the set of n-grams with the highest weight in p, where all terms are also contained in q; Q is the set of all the possible j-grams in q and n is the total number of terms in the longest passage. The weights for each term and each n-gram are calculated as:

- w_i calculates the weight of the term t_I as:

$$w_i = 1 - \frac{log(n_i)}{1 + log(N)} \quad (2)$$

  Where n_i is the frequency of term t_i in the Google Web 1T collection, and N is the frequency of the most frequent term in the Google Web 1T collection.

- the function $h(x, P)$ measures the weight of each n-gram and is defined as:

$$h(x, P_j) = \begin{cases} \sum_{k=1}^{j} w_k & \text{if } x \in P_j \\ 0 & \text{otherwise} \end{cases} \quad (3)$$

  Where w_k is the weight of the *k-th* term (see Equation 2) and j is the number of terms that compose the n-gram x;

- $\frac{1}{d(x, x_{max})}$ is a distance factor which reduces the weight of the n-grams that are far from the heaviest n-gram. The function $d(x, x_{max})$ determines numerically the value of the separation according to the number of words between a n-gram and the heaviest one. That function is defined as show in Equation 4 :

$$d(x, x_{max}) = 1 + k \cdot ln(1 + L) \quad (4)$$

  Where k is a factor that determines the importance of the distance in the similarity calculation and L is the number of words between a n-gram and the heaviest one (see Equation 3). In our experiments, k was set to 0.1, a default value used in JIRS.

For instance, given the following two sentences: "*Mr. President, enlargement is essential for the construction of a strong and united European continent*" and "*Mr. President, widening is essential for the construction of a strong and plain continent of Europe*", the longest n-grams shared by the two sentences are: "*Mr. President*", "*is essential for the construction of a strong and*", "*continent*".

term	$w(term)$
Mr	0.340
President	0.312
is	0.159
essential	0.353
for	0.153
the	0.104
construction	0.332
of	0.120
a	0.139
strong	0.329
and	0.121
continent	0.427
of	0.120
Europe	0.308
widening	0.464

Table 1: Term weights (idf) calculated using the frequency for each term in Google Web 1T unigrams set.

[1]http://sourceforge.net/projects/jirs/

[2]http://lucene.apache.org/

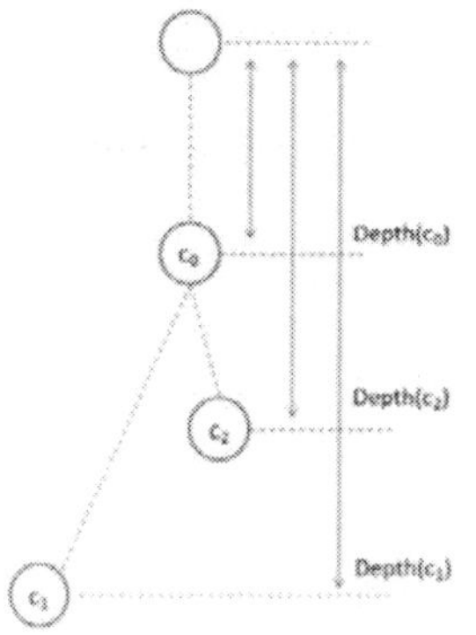

Figure 2: Visualisation of depth calculation.

The weights have been calculated with Formula 2, using the frequencies from Google Web 1T. The weights for each of the longest n-grams are 0.652, 1.809 and 0.427 respectively; their sum is 2.888 which divided by all the term weights contained in the sentence gives 0.764 which is the similarity score between the two sentences as calculated by the n-gram based method.

3 Conceptual Similarity

Given C_p and C_q as the sets of concepts contained in sentence p and q, respectively, with $|C_p| \geq |C_q|$, the conceptual similarity between p and q is calculated as:

$$ss(p,q) = \frac{\sum\limits_{c_1 \in C_p} \max\limits_{c_2 \in C_q} s(c_1, c_2)}{|C_p|} \quad (5)$$

where $s(c_1, c_2)$ is a concept similarity measure. Concept similarity can be calculated by different ways. Wu and Palmer introduced in (Wu and Palmer, 1994) a concept similarity measure defined as:

$$s(c_1, c_2) = \frac{2 \cdot d(c_0)}{d(c_1) + d(c_2)} \quad (6)$$

c_0 is the most specific concept that is present both in the synset path of c_1 and c_2 (see Figure 2 for details). The function returning the depth of a concept is noted with d.

3.1 ProxiGenea

By making an analogy between a family tree and the concept hierarchy in WordNet, (Dudognon et al., 2010; Ralalason, 2010) proposed a concept similarity measure based on the principle of evaluating the proximity between two members of the same family. The measure has been named "ProxiGenea" (from the french Proximité Généalogique, genealogical proximity). We took into account three versions of the ProxiGenea measure:

$$pg_1(c_1, c_2) = \frac{d(c_0)^2}{d(c_1) * d(c_2)} \quad (7)$$

This measure is very similar to the Wu-Palmer similarity measure, but it emphasizes the distances between concepts;

$$pg_2(c_1, c_2) = \frac{d(c_0)}{d(c_1) + d(c_2) - d(c_0)} \quad (8)$$

In this measure, the more are the elements which are not shared between the paths of c_1 and c_2, the more the score decreases. However, if the elements are placed more deeply in the ontology, the decrease is less important.

$$pg_3(c_1, c_2) = \frac{1}{1 + d(c_1) + d(c_2) - 2 \cdot d(c_0)} \quad (9)$$

In Table 2 we show the weights that have been calculated for each concept, using all the above similarity measures, and the concept that provided the maximum weight. No Word Sense Disambiguation process is carried out; therefore, the scores are calculated taking into account all the possible senses for the word. If the same concept is present in both sentences, it obtains always a score of 1. In the other cases, the maximum similarity value obtained with any other concept is retained.

From the example in Table 2 we can see that Wu-Palmer tends to give to the concepts a higher similarity value than Proxigenea3.

The final score for the above example is calculated as the geometric mean between the scores obtained in Table 2 and 0.764 obtained from the n-gram based similarity module, multiplied by 5. Therefore, for each similarity measure, the final scores of the example are, respectively: 4.029, 3.869, 3.921 and 3.703. The correct similarity value, according to the gold standard, was 4.600.

c_1, c_2	wp	pg_1	pg_2	pg_3
Mr Mr	1.000	1.000	1.000	1.000
President President	1.000	1.000	1.000	1.000
construction construction	1.000	1.000	1.000	1.000
continent continent	1.000	1.000	1.000	1.000
Europe continent	0.400	0.160	0.250	0.143
widening enlargement	0.737	0.544	0.583	0.167
score	0.850	0.784	0.805	0.718

Table 2: Maximum conceptual similarity weights using the different formulae for the concepts in the example. c_1: first concept, c_2: concept for which the maximum similarity value was calculated. wp: Wu-Palmer similarity; pg_X: Proxigenea similarity. *score* is the result of (5).

4 Evaluation

Before the official runs we carried out an evaluation to select the best similarity measures over the training set provided by the organisers. The results of this evaluation are shown in Table 3. The measure selected is the normalised Pearson correlation (Agirre et al., 2012). We evaluated also the use of the product instead of the geometric mean for the combination of the two scores.

	Geometric mean			
	MSRpar	MSRvid	SMT-Eur	All
pg1	0.489	0.602	0.587	0.559
pg2	0.490	0.596	0.586	0.558
pg3	0.470	**0.657**	0.552	**0.560**
wp	**0.494**	0.572	**0.592**	0.552
	Scalar product			
	MSRpar	MSRvid	SMT-Eur	All
pg1	0.469	0.601	0.487	**0.519**
pg2	0.471	0.597	0.487	0.518
pg3	0.447	**0.637**	0.459	0.514
wp	**0.476**	0.577	**0.492**	0.515

Table 3: Results on training corpus, comparison of different conceptual similarity measures and combination method. Top: geometric mean, bottom: product.

We used these results to select the final configurations for our participation to the STS task: we selected to exclude Proxigenea 2 and to use the geometric mean to combine the scores of the n-gram based similarity module and the conceptual similarity module. Wu-Palmer similarity allowed to obtain the best results on two train sets but Proxigenea 3 was the similarity measure that obtained the best average score thanks to the good result on MSRvid.

The official results obtained by our system are shown in Table 4, with the ranking obtained for each test set. We could observe that the system was well behind the best system in most test sets, except for SMTeur. This was expected since our system does not use a machine learning approach and is completely unsupervised, while the best systems used supervised learning. We observed also that the behaviour of the concept similarity measures was different from the behaviour on the training sets. In the competition, the best results were always obtained with Proxigenea3 instead of Wu-Palmer, except for the MSRpar test set.

	r	best	pg3	pg1	wp
MSRPar	60	0.734	0.417	0.429	**0.433**
MSRvid	58	0.880	**0.673**	0.612	0.583
SMTeur	**7**	0.567	**0.518**	0.495	0.486
OnWN	64	0.727	**0.553**	0.539	0.532
SMTnews	55	0.608	**0.369**	0.361	0.348
All	58	0.677	**0.520**	0.501	0.490

Table 4: Results obtained on each test set, grouped by conceptual similarity method. r indicates the ranking among all the participants teams.

In Table 4 we extrapolated the results for the composing methods and compared them with the result obtained after their combination. We used the pg3 configuration for the conceptual similarity measure. From these results, we can observe that MSRvid was a test set where the conceptual similarity alone would have resulted better than the combination of scores, while SMT-news was the test set where the CKPD measure obtained the best results in comparison to the result obtained by the conceptual similarity alone. It was quite surprising to observe such a good result for a method that does not take into account any information about the structure of the sentences, actually viewing them as "bags of con-

	Combined	pg3	CKPD
MSRPar	**0.417**	0.412	**0.417**
MSRvid	0.673	**0.777**	0.548
SMTeuroparl	**0.518**	0.486	0.467
OnWN	**0.553**	0.544	0.505
SMTnews	0.369	0.266	**0.408**

Table 5: Results obtained for each test set using only the conceptual similarity measure ($pg3$) and only the structural similarity measure ($CKPD$), compared to the result obtained by the complete system ($Combined$).

cepts". This is probably due to the fact that SMTnews is a corpus composed of automatically translated sentences, where structural similarity is an important clue for determining overall semantic similarity. On the other hand, MSRvid sentences are very short, and CKPD is in most cases unable to capture the semantic similarity.

5 Conclusions

The proposed method combined a measure of structural similarity and a measure of conceptual similarity based on WordNet. With the participation to this task, we were interested in studying the differences between different conceptual similarity measures and in determining whether they can be used to effectively measure the semantic similarity of text fragments. The obtained results showed that Proxigenea 3 allowed us to obtain the best results, indicating that under the test conditions and with WordNet as a resource it overperforms the Wu-Palmer measure. Further studies may be required in order to determine if these results can be generalised to other collections and in using different ontologies. We are also interested in comparing the method to the Lin concept similarity measure (Lin, 1998) which takes into account also the importance of the local root concept.

References

Eneko Agirre, Daniel Cer, Mona Diab, and Aitor Gonzalez. 2012. A pilot on semantic textual similarity. In *Proceedings of the 6th International Workshop on Semantic Evaluation (SemEval 2012), in conjunction with the First Joint Conference on Lexical and Computational Semantcis (*SEM 2012)*, Montreal, Quebec, Canada.

Thorsten Brants and Alex Franz. 2006. Web 1t 5-gram corpus version 1.1.

Davide Buscaldi, José Manuel Gómez, Paolo Rosso, and Emilio Sanchis. 2006. N-gram vs. keyword-based passage retrieval for question answering. In *CLEF*, pages 377–384.

Davide Buscaldi, Paolo Rosso, José Manuel Gómez, and Emilio Sanchis. 2009. Answering questions with an n-gram based passage retrieval engine. *Journal of Intelligent Information Systems (JIIS)*, 34(2):113–134.

Damien Dudognon, Gilles Hubert, and Bachelin Jhonn Victorino Ralalason. 2010. Proxigénéa : Une mesure de similarité conceptuelle. In *Proceedings of the Colloque Veille Stratégique Scientifique et Technologique (VSST 2010)*.

Dekang Lin. 1998. An information-theoretic definition of similarity. In *Proceedings of the Fifteenth International Conference on Machine Learning*, ICML '98, pages 296–304, San Francisco, CA, USA. Morgan Kaufmann Publishers Inc.

George A. Miller. 1995. Wordnet: a lexical database for english. *Commun. ACM*, 38(11):39–41, November.

Bachelin Ralalason. 2010. *Représentation multi-facette des documents pour leur accès sémantique*. Ph.D. thesis, Université Paul Sabatier, Toulouse, September. in French.

Kristina Toutanova, Dan Klein, Christopher D. Manning, and Yoram Singer. 2003. Feature-rich part-of-speech tagging with a cyclic dependency network. In *Proceedings of the 2003 Conference of the North American Chapter of the Association for Computational Linguistics on Human Language Technology - Volume 1*, NAACL '03, pages 173–180.

Zhibiao Wu and Martha Palmer. 1994. Verbs semantics and lexical selection. In *Proceedings of the 32nd annual meeting on Association for Computational Linguistics*, ACL '94, pages 133–138, Stroudsburg, PA, USA. Association for Computational Linguistics.

DSS: Text Similarity Using Lexical Alignments of Form, Distributional Semantics and Grammatical Relations

Diana McCarthy
Saarland University*
diana@dianamccarthy.co.uk

Spandana Gella
University of Malta
spandanagella@gmail.com

Siva Reddy
Lexical Computing Ltd.
siva@sivareddy.in

Abstract

In this paper we present our systems for the STS task. Our systems are all based on a simple process of identifying the components that correspond between two sentences. Currently we use words (that is word forms), lemmas, distributional similar words and grammatical relations identified with a dependency parser. We submitted three systems. All systems only use open class words. Our first system (`alignheuristic`) tries to obtain a mapping between every open class token using all the above sources of information. Our second system (`wordsim`) uses a different algorithm and unlike `alignheuristic`, it does not use the dependency information. The third system (`average`) simply takes the average of the scores for each item from the other two systems to take advantage of the merits of both systems. For this reason we only provide a brief description of that. The results are promising, with Pearson's coefficients on each individual dataset ranging from .3765 to .7761 for our relatively simple heuristics based systems that do not require training on different datasets. We provide some analysis of the results and also provide results for our data using Spearman's, which as a non-parametric measure which we argue is better able to reflect the merits of the different systems (`average` is ranked between the others).

1 Introduction

Our motivation for the systems entered in the STS task (Agirre et al., 2012) was to model the contribution of each linguistic component of both sentences to the similarity of the texts by finding an alignment. Ultimately such a system could be exploited for ranking candidate paraphrases of a chunk of text of any length. We envisage a system as outlined in the future work section. The systems reported are simple baselines to such a system. We have two main systems (`alignheuristic` and `wordsim`) and also a system which simply uses the average score for each item from the two main systems (`average`). In our systems we:

- only deal with open class words as tokens i.e. nouns, verbs, adjectives, adverbs. `alignheuristic` and `average` also use numbers
- assume that tokens have a 1:1 mapping
- match:
  - word forms
  - lemmas
  - distributionally similar lemmas
  - (`alignheuristic` and `average` only) argument or head in a matched grammatical relation with a word that already has a lexical mapping
- score the sentence pair based on the size of the overlap. Different formulations of the score are used by our methods

The paper is structured as follows. In the next section we make a brief mention of related work though of course there will be more pertinent related work presented and published at SemEval 2012. In section 3 we give a detailed account of the systems

*The first author is a visiting scholar on the Erasmus Mundus Masters Program in 'Language and Communication Technologies' (LCT, 2007–0060).

and in section 4 we provide the results obtained on the training data on developing our systems. In section 5 we present the results on the test data, along with a little analysis using the gold standard data. In section 6 we conclude our findings and discuss our ideas for future work.

2 Related Work

Semantic textual similarity relates to textual entailment (Dagan et al., 2005), lexical substitution (McCarthy and Navigli, 2009) and paraphrasing (Hirst, 2003). The key issue for semantic textual similarity is that the task is to determine similarity, where similarity is cast as meaning equivalence. [1] In textual entailment the relation under question is the more specific relation of entailment, where the meaning of one sentence is entailed by another and a system needs to determine the direction of the entailment. Lexical substitution relates to semantic textual similarity though the task involves a lemma in the context of a sentence, candidate substitutes are not provided, and the relation at question in the task is one of substitutability. [2] Paraphrase recognition is a highly related task, for example using comparable corpora (Barzilay and Elhadad, 2003), and it is likely that semantic textual similarity measures might be useful for ranking candidates in paraphrase acquisition.

In addition to various works related to textual entailment, lexical substitution and paraphrasing, there has been some prior work explicitly on semantic text similarity. Semantic textual similarity has been explored in various works. Mihalcea et al. (2006) extend earlier work on word similarity using various WordNet similarity measures (Patwardhan et al., 2003) and a couple of corpus-based distributional measures: PMI-IR (Turney, 2002) and LSA (Berry, 1992). They use a measure which takes a summation over all tokens in both sentences. For each token they find the maximum similarity (WordNet or distributional) weighted by the inverse document frequency of that word. The distributional similarity measures perform at a similar level to the knowledge-based measures that use WordNet. Mohler and Mihalcea (2009) adapt this work for automatic short answer grading, that is matching a candidate answer to one supplied by the tutor. Mohler et al. (2011) take this application forward, combining lexical semantic similarity measures with a graph-alignment which considers dependency graphs using the Stanford dependency parser (de Marneffe et al., 2006) in terms of lexical, semantic and syntactic features. A score is then provided for each node in the graph. The features are combined using machine learning.

The systems we propose likewise use lexical similarity and dependency relations, but in a simple heuristic formulation without a man-made thesaurus such as WordNet and without machine learning.

3 Systems

We lemmatize and part-of-speech tag the data using TreeTagger (Schmid, 1994). We process the tagged data with default settings of the Malt Parser (Nivre et al., 2007) to dependency parse the data. All systems make use of a distributional thesaurus which lists distributionally similar lemmas ('neighbours') for a given lemma. This is a thesaurus constructed using log-dice (Rychlý, 2008) and UkWaC (Ferraresi et al., 2008). [3] Note that we use only the top 20 neighbours for any word in all the methods described below. We have not experimented with varying this threshold.

In the following descriptions, we refer to our sentences as $s1$ and $s2$ and these open classed tokens within those sentences as $t_i \in s1$ and $t_j \in s2$ where each token in either sentence is represented by a word (w), lemma (l), part-of-speech (p) and grammatical relation (gr), identified by the Malt parser, to its dependency head at a given position (hp) in the same sentence.

3.1 `alignheuristic`

This method uses nouns, verbs, adjectives, adverbs and numbers. The algorithm aligns words (w), or lemmas (l) from left to right from $s1$ to $s2$ and vice

[1] See the guidelines given to the annotators at http://www.cs.columbia.edu/~weiwei/workshop/instructions.pdf

[2] This is more or less semantic equivalence since the annotators were instructed to focus on meaning http://www.dianamccarthy.co.uk/files/instructions.pdf.

[3] This is the ukWaC distributional thesaurus available in Sketch Engine (Kilgarriff et al., 2004) at http://the.sketchengine.co.uk/bonito/run.cgi/first_form?corpname=preloaded/ukwac2

versa ( ). If there is no alignment for words or lemmas then it does the same matching process ($s1$ given $s2$ and vice versa) for distributionally similar neighbours using the distributional thesaurus mentioned above ( ) and also another matching process looking for a corresponding grammatical relation identified with the Malt parser in the other sentence where the head (or argument) already has a match in both sentences ( ).

A fuller and more formal description of the algorithm follows:

1. retain nouns, verbs (not *be*), adjectives, adverbs and numbers in both sentences $s1$ and $s2$.

2. :

   (a) look for word matches

   - $w_i \in s1$ to $w_j \in s2$, left to right i.e. the first matching $w_j \in s2$ is selected as a match for w_i.
   - $w_j \in s2$ to $w_i \in s1$, left to right i.e. the first matching $w_i \in s1$ is selected as a match for w_j

   (b) and then lemma matches for any $t_i \in s1$ and $t_j \in s1$ not matched in steps 2a

   - $l_i \in s1$ to $l_j \in s2$, left to right i.e. the first matching $l_j \in s2$ is selected as a match for l_i.
   - $l_j \in s2$ to $l_i \in s1$, left to right i.e. the first matching $l_i \in s1$ is selected as a match for l_j

3. using only $t_i \in s1$ and $t_j \in s2$ not matched in the above steps:

   - : match lemma and PoS ($l + p$) with the distributional thesaurus against the top 20 most similar lemma-pos entries. That is:

     (a) For $l + p_i \in s1$, if not already matched at step 2 above, find the most similar words in the thesaurus, and match if one of these is in $l + p_j \in s2$, left to right i.e. the first matching $l + p_j \in s2$ to any of the most similar words to $l + p_i$ according to the thesaurus is selected as a match for $l + p_i \in s1$.

     (b) For $l + p_j \in s2$, if not already matched at step 2 above, find the most similar words in the thesaurus, and match if one of these is in $l + p_i \in s1$, left to right

   - : match the tokens, if not already matched at step 2 above, by looking for a head or argument relation with a token that has been matched at step 2 to a token with the inverse relation. That is:

     i For $t_i \in s1$, if not already matched at step 2 above, if $hp_i \in s1$ (the pointer to the head, i.e. parent, of t_i) refers to a token $t_x \in s1$ which has at t_k in $s2$, and there exists a $t_q \in s2$ with $gr_q = gr_i$ and $hp_q = t_k$, then match t_i with t_q

     ii For $t_i \in s1$, if not already matched at step 2 or the preceding step (3i) and if there exists another $t_x \in s1$ with a hp_x which refers to t_i (i.e. t_i is the parent, or head, of t_x) with a match between t_x and $t_k \in s2$ from step 2, [4] and where t_k has $gr_k = gr_x$ with hp_k which refers to t_q in $s2$, then match t_i with t_q [5]

     iii we do likewise in reverse for $s2$ to $s1$ and then check all matches are reciprocated with the same 1:1 mapping

Finally, we calculate the score $sim(s1, s2)$:

$$\frac{| \quad | + (wt \times | \quad + \quad |)}{|s1| + |s2|} \times 5 \qquad (1)$$

where wt is a weight of 0.5 or less (see below).

The *sim* score gives a score of 5 where two sentences have the same open class tokens, since matches in both directions are included and the denominator is the number of open class tokens in both sentences. The score is 0 if there are no matches. The thesaurus and grammatical relation matches are counted equally and are considered less important

[4]In the example illustrated in figure 1 and discussed below, t_i could be *rose* in the upper sentence ($s1$) and *Nasdaq* would be t_x and t_k.

[5]So in our example, from figure 1, t_i (*rose*) is matched with t_q (*climb*) as *climb* is the counterpart head to *rose* for the matched arguments (*Nasdaq*).

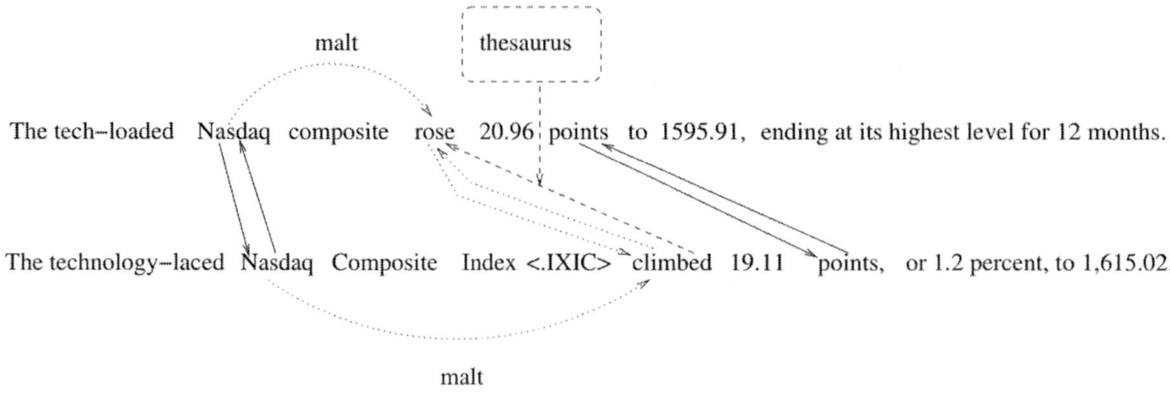

Figure 1: Example of matching with `alignheuristic`

for the score as the exact matches. We set *wt* to 0.4 for the official run, though we could improve performance by perhaps setting a bit lower as shown below in section 4.1.

Figure 1 shows an example pair of sentences from the training data in MSRpar. The solid lines show alignments between words. *Composite* and *composite* are not matched because the lemmatizer assumes that the former is a proper noun and does not decapitalise; we could decapitalise all proper nouns. The dotted arcs show parallel dependency relations in the sentences where the argument (*Nasdaq*) is matched by . The process therefore assumes the corresponding heads (*rise* and *climb*) align. In addition, finds a match from *climb* to *rise* as *rise* is in the top 20 most similar words (neighbours) in the distributional thesaurus. *climb* is not however in the top 20 for *rise* and so a link is not found in the other direction. We have not yet experimented with validating the thesaurus and grammatical relation processes together, though that would be worthwhile in future.

3.2 `wordsim`

In this method, we first choose the shortest sentence based on the number of open words. Let $s1$ and $s2$ be the shortest and longest sentences respectively. For every lemma $l_i \in s1$, we find its best matching lemma $l_j \in s2$ using the following heuristics and assigning an alignment score as follows:

1. if l_i=l_j, then the alignment score of l_i ($algnscr(l_i)$) is one.

2. else $l_i \in s1$ is matched with a lemma $l_j \in s2$ with which it has the highest distributional similarity. [6] The alignment score, $algnscr(l_i)$ is the distributional similarity between l_i and l_j (which is always less than one).

The final sentence similarity score between the pair $s1$ and $s2$ is computed as

$$sim(s1, s2) = \frac{\sum_{l_i \in s1} algnscr(l_i)}{|s1|} \quad (2)$$

3.3 `average`

This system simple uses the average score for each item from `alignheuristic` and `wordsim`. This is simply so we can make a compromise between the merits of the two systems.

4 Experiments on the Training Data

Table 1 displays the results on training data for the system settings as they were for the final test run. We conducted further analysis for the `alignheuristic` system and that is reported in the following subsection. We can see that while the `alignheuristic` is better on the MSRpar and SMT-eur datasets, the `wordsim` outperforms it on the MSRvid dataset, which contains shorter, simpler sentences. One reason might be that the `wordsim` credits alignments in one direction only and this works well when sentences are of a similar length but can loose out on the longer paraphrase and SMT data. This behaviour is

[6] Provided this is within the top 20 most similar words in the thesaurus.

	MSRpar	MSRvid	SMT-eur
alignheuristic	0.6015	0.6994	0.5222
wordsim	0.4134	0.7658	0.4479
average	0.5337	0.7535	0.5061

Table 1: Results on training data

confirmed by the results on the test data reported below in section 5, though we cannot rule out that other factors play a part.

4.1 alignheuristic

We developed the system on the training data for the purpose of finding bugs, and setting the weight in equation 1. During development we found the optimal weight for *wt* to be 0.4. [7] Unfortunately we did not leave ourselves sufficient time to set the weights after resolving the bugs. In table 1 we report the results on the training data for the system that we uploaded, however in table 2 we report more recent results for the final system but with different values of *wt*. From table 2 it seems that results may have been improved if we had determined the final value of *wt* after debugging our system fully, however this depends on the type of data as 0.4 was optimal for the datasets with more complex sentences (MSRpar and SMT-eur).

In table 3, we report results for alignheuristic with and without the distributional similarity thesaurus ( ) and the dependency relations ( ). In table 4 we show the total number of token alignments made by the different matching processes on the training data. We see, from table 4 that the MSRvid data relies on the thesaurus and dependency relations to a far greater extent than the other datasets, presumably because of the shorter sentences where many have a few contrasting words in similar syntactic relations, for example *s*1 *Someone is drawing.* *s*2 *Someone is dancing.* [8] We see from table 3 that the use of these matching processes is less accurate for MSRvid and that while improves performance, seems to degrade performance. From table 2 it would seem that on this type of data we would get the best results by reducing *wt* to a minimum, and perhaps it would make sense to drop . Meanwhile, on the longer more complex MSRpar and SMT-eur data, the less precise and are used less frequently (relative to the) but can be seen from table 3 to improve performance on both training datasets. Moreover, as we mention above, from table 2 the parameter setting of 0.4 used for our final test run was optimal for these datasets.

[7] We have not yet attempted setting the weight on alignment by relation and alignment by distributional similarity separately.

[8] Note that the alignheuristic algorithm is symmetrical with respect to *s*1 and *s*2 so it does not matter which is which.

wt	MSRpar	MSRvid	SMT-eur
0.5	0.5998	0.6518	0.5290
0.4	0.6015	0.6994	0.5222
0.3	0.6020	0.7352	0.5146
0.2	0.6016	0.7577	0.5059
0.1	0.6003	0.7673	0.4964
0	0.5981	0.7661	0.4863

Table 2: Results for the alignheuristic algorithm on the training data: varying *wt*

		MSR par	MSR vid	SMT -eur
-	+	0.6008	0.7245	0.5129
+	-	0.5989	0.7699	0.4959
-	-	0.5981	0.7661	0.4863
+	+	0.6015	0.6994	0.5222

Table 3: Results for the alignheuristic algorithm on the training data: with and without and

	MSRpar	MSRvid	SMT-eur
	10960	2349	12155
	378	1221	964
	1008	965	1755

Table 4: Number of token alignments for the different matching processes

run	ALL	MSRpar	MSRvid	SMT-eur	On-WN	SMT-news
alignheuristic	.5253 (60)	.5735 (24)	.7123 (53)	.4781 (25)	.6984 (7)	.4177 (38)
average	.5490 (58)	.5020 (48)	.7645 (41)	.4875 (16)	.6677(14)	.4324 (31)
wordsim	.5130 (61)	.3765 (75)	.7761 (34)	.4161 (58)	.5728 (59)	.3964 (48)

Table 5: Official results: Rank (out of 89) is shown in brackets

run	ALL	MSRpar	MSRvid	SMT-eur	On-WN	SMT-news	average ρ
alignheuristic	0.5216	0.5539	0.7125	0.5404	0.6928	0.3655	0.5645
average	0.5087	0.4818	0.7653	0.5415	0.6302	0.3835	0.5518
wordsim	0.4279	0.3608	0.7799	0.4487	0.4976	0.3388	0.4756

Table 7: Spearman's ρ for the 5 datasets, 'all' and the average coefficient across the datasets

run	mean	Allnrm
alignheuristic	0.6030 (21)	0.7962 (42)
average	0.5943 (26)	0.8047 (35)
wordsim	0.5287 (55)	0.7895 (49)

Table 6: Official results: Further metrics suggested in discussion. Rank (out of 89) is shown in brackets

5 Results

Table 5 provides the official results for our submitted systems, along with the rank on each dataset. The results in the 'all' column which combine all datasets together are at odds with our intuitions. Our systems were ranked higher in every individual dataset compared to the 'all' ranking, with the exception of `wordsim` and the MSRpar dataset. This 'all' metric is anticipated to impact systems that have different settings for different types of data however we did not train our systems to run differently on different data. We used exactly the same parameter settings for each system on every dataset. We believe Pearson's measure has a significant impact on results because it is a parametric measure and as such the shape of the distribution (the distribution of scores) is assumed to be normal. We present the results in table 6 from new metrics proposed by participants during the post-results discussion: Allnrm (normalised) and mean (this score is weighted by the number of sentence pairs in each dataset). [9] The Allnrm score, proposed by a participant during the discussion phase to try and combat issues with the 'all' score, also does not accord with our intuition given the ranks of our systems on the individual datasets. The mean score, proposed by another participant, however does reflect performance on the individual datasets. Our `average` system is ranked between `alignheuristic` and `wordsim` which is in line with our expectations given results on the training data and individual datasets.

As mentioned above, an issue with the use of Pearson's correlation coefficient is that it is parametric and assumes that the scores are normally distributed. We calculated Spearman's ρ which is the non-parametric equivalent of Pearson's and uses the ranks of the scores, rather than the actual scores. [10] The results are presented in table 7. We cannot calculate the results for other systems, and therefore the ranks for our system, since we do not have the other system's outputs but we do see that the relative performance of our system on 'all' is more in line with our expectations: `average`, which simply uses the average of the other two systems for each item, is usually ranked between the other two systems, depending on the dataset. Spearman's 'all' gives a similar ranking of our three systems as the mean score. We also show average ρ. This is a macro average of the Spearman's value for the 5 datasets without weighting by the number of sentence pairs. [11]

[9]Post-results discussion is archived at `http://groups.google.com/group/sts-semeval/topics`

[10]Note that Spearman's ρ is often a little lower than Pearson's (Mitchell and Lapata, 2008)

[11]We do recognise the difficulty in determining metrics on a new pilot study. The task organisers are making every effort to make it clear that this enterprise is a pilot, not a competition and that they welcome feedback.

6 Conclusions

The systems were developed in less than a week including the time with the test data. There are many trivial fixes that may improve the basic algorithm, such as decapitalising proper nouns. There are many things we would like to try, such as validating the dependency matching process with the thesaurus matching. We would like to match larger units rather than tokens, with preferences towards the longer matching blocks. In parallel to the development of `alignheuristic`, we developed a system which measures the similarity between a node in the dependency tree of $s1$ and a node in the dependency tree of $s2$ as the sum of the lexical similarity of the lemmas at the nodes and the similarity of its children nodes. We did not submit a run for the system as it did not perform as well as `alignheuristic`, probably because the score focused on structure too much. We hope to spend time developing this system in future.

Ultimately, we envisage a system that:

- can have non 1:1 mappings between tokens, i.e. a phrase may be paraphrased as a word for example *blow up* may be paraphrased as *explode*
- can map between sequences of non-contiguous words for example the words in the phrase *blow up* may be separated but mapped to the word *explode* as in *the bomb exploded* ↔ *They blew it up*
- has categories (such as equivalence, entailment, negation, omission ...) associated with each mapping. Speculation, modality and sentiment should be indicated on any relevant chunk so that differences can be detected between candidate and referent
- scores the candidate using a function of the scores of the mapped units (as in the systems described above) but alters the score to reflect the category as well as the source of the mapping, for example entailment without equivalence should reduce the similarity score, in contrast to equivalence, and negation should reduce this still further

Crucially we would welcome a task where annotators would also provide a score on sub chunks of the sentences (or arbitrary blocks of text) that align along with a category for the mapping (equivalence, entailment, negation etc..). This would allow us to look under the hood at the text similarity task and determine the reason behind the similarity judgments.

7 Acknowledgements

We thank the task organisers for their efforts in organising the task and their readiness to take on board discussions on this as a pilot. We also thank the SemEval-2012 co-ordinators.

References

Agirre, E., Cer, D., Diab, M., and Gonzalez-Agirre, A. (2012). Semeval-2012 task 6: A pilot on semantic textual similarity. In *Proceedings of the 6th International Workshop on Semantic Evaluation (SemEval 2012), in conjunction with the First Joint Conference on Lexical and Computational Semantics (*SEM 2012)*.

Barzilay, R. and Elhadad, N. (2003). Sentence alignment for monolingual comparable corpora. In Collins, M. and Steedman, M., editors, *Proceedings of the 2003 Conference on Empirical Methods in Natural Language Processing*, pages 25–32.

Berry, M. (1992). Large scale singular value computations. *International Journal of Supercomputer Applications*, 6(1):13–49.

Dagan, I., Glickman, O., and Magnini, B. (2005). The pascal recognising textual entailment challenge. In *Proceedings of the PASCAL First Challenge Workshop*, pages 1–8, Southampton, UK.

de Marneffe, M.-C., MacCartney, B., and Manning, C. D. (2006). Generating typed dependency parses from phrase structure parses. In *To appear at LREC-06*.

Ferraresi, A., Zanchetta, E., Baroni, M., and Bernardini, S. (2008). Introducing and evaluating ukwac, a very large web-derived corpus of english. In *Proceedings of the Sixth International Conference on Language Resources and Evaluation (LREC 2008)*, Marrakech, Morocco.

Hirst, G. (2003). Paraphrasing paraphrased. Invited talk at the Second International Workshop on Paraphrasing, 41st Annual Meeting of the Association for Computational Linguistics.

Kilgarriff, A., Rychlý, P., Smrz, P., and Tugwell, D. (2004). The sketch engine. In *Proceedings of Euralex*, pages 105–116, Lorient, France. Reprinted in Patrick Hanks (ed.). 2007. Lexicology: Critical concepts in Linguistics. London: Routledge.

McCarthy, D. and Navigli, R. (2009). The English lexical substitution task. *Language Resources and Evaluation Special Issue on Computational Semantic Analysis of Language: SemEval-2007 and Beyond*, 43(2):139–159.

Mihalcea, R., Corley, C., and Strapparava, C. (2006). Corpus-based and knowledge-based measures of text semantic similarity. In *Proceedings of the American Association for Artificial Intelligence (AAAI 2006)*, Boston, MA.

Mitchell, J. and Lapata, M. (2008). Vector-based models of semantic composition. In *Proceedings of ACL-08: HLT*, pages 236–244, Columbus, Ohio. Association for Computational Linguistics.

Mohler, M., Bunescu, R., and Mihalcea, R. (2011). Learning to grade short answer questions using semantic similarity measures and dependency graph alignments. In *Proceedings of the 49th Annual Meeting of the Association for Computational Linguistics: Human Language Technologies*, pages 752–762, Portland, Oregon, USA. Association for Computational Linguistics.

Mohler, M. and Mihalcea, R. (2009). Text-to-text semantic similarity for automatic short answer grading. In *Proceedings of the 12th Conference of the European Chapter of the ACL (EACL 2009)*, pages 567–575, Athens, Greece. Association for Computational Linguistics.

Nivre, J., Hall, J., Nilsson, J., Chanev, A., Eryigit, G., Kübler, S., Marinov, S., and Marsi, E. (2007). Maltparser: A language-independent system for data-driven dependency parsing. *Natural Language Engineering*, 13(2):95–135.

Patwardhan, S., Banerjee, S., and Pedersen, T. (2003). Using measures of semantic relatedness for word sense disambiguation. In *Proceedings of the Fourth International Conference on Intelligent Text Processing and Computational Linguistics (CICLing 2003)*, Mexico City.

Rychlý, P. (2008). A lexicographer-friendly association score. In *Proceedings of 2nd Workshop on Recent Advances in Slavonic Natural Languages Processing, RASLAN 2008*, Brno.

Schmid, H. (1994). Probabilistic Part-of-Speech Tagging Using Decision Trees. In *Proceedings of the International Conference on New Methods in Language Processing*, pages 44–49, Manchester, UK.

Turney, P. D. (2002). Mining the web for synonyms: Pmi-ir versus lsa on toefl. *CoRR*, cs.LG/0212033.

DeepPurple: Estimating Sentence Semantic Similarity using N-gram Regression Models and Web Snippets

Nikos Malandrakis, Elias Iosif, Alexandros Potamianos
Department of ECE, Technical University of Crete, 73100 Chania, Greece
[nmalandrakis,iosife,potam]@telecom.tuc.gr

Abstract

We estimate the semantic similarity between two sentences using regression models with features: 1) n-gram hit rates (lexical matches) between sentences, 2) lexical semantic similarity between non-matching words, and 3) sentence length. Lexical semantic similarity is computed via co-occurrence counts on a corpus harvested from the web using a modified mutual information metric. State-of-the-art results are obtained for semantic similarity computation at the word level, however, the fusion of this information at the sentence level provides only moderate improvement on Task 6 of SemEval'12. Despite the simple features used, regression models provide good performance, especially for shorter sentences, reaching correlation of 0.62 on the SemEval test set.

1 Introduction

Recently, there has been significant research activity on the area of semantic similarity estimation motivated both by abundance of relevant web data and linguistic resources for this task. Algorithms for computing semantic textual similarity (STS) are relevant for a variety of applications, including information extraction (Szpektor and Dagan, 2008), question answering (Harabagiu and Hickl, 2006) and machine translation (Mirkin et al., 2009). Word- or term-level STS (a special case of sentence level STS) has also been successfully applied to the problem of grammar induction (Meng and Siu, 2002) and affective text categorization (Malandrakis et al., 2011). In this work, we built on previous research on word-level semantic similarity estimation to design and implement a system for sentence-level STS for Task6 of the SemEval'12 campaign.

Semantic similarity between words can be regarded as the graded semantic equivalence at the lexeme level and is tightly related with the tasks of word sense discovery and disambiguation (Agirre and Edmonds, 2007). Metrics of word semantic similarity can be divided into: (i) knowledge-based metrics (Miller, 1990; Budanitsky and Hirst, 2006) and (ii) corpus-based metrics (Baroni and Lenci, 2010; Iosif and Potamianos, 2010).

When more complex structures, such as phrases and sentences, are considered, it is much harder to estimate semantic equivalence due to the non-compositional nature of sentence-level semantics and the exponential explosion of possible interpretations. STS is closely related to the problems of paraphrasing, which is bidirectional and based on semantic equivalence (Madnani and Dorr, 2010) and textual entailment, which is directional and based on relations between semantics (Dagan et al., 2006). Related methods incorporate measurements of similarity at various levels: lexical (Malakasiotis and Androutsopoulos, 2007), syntactic (Malakasiotis, 2009; Zanzotto et al., 2009), and semantic (Rinaldi et al., 2003; Bos and Markert, 2005). Measures from machine translation evaluation are often used to evaluate lexical level approaches (Finch et al., 2005; Perez and Alfonseca, 2005), including BLEU (Papineni et al., 2002), a metric based on word n-gram hit rates.

Motivated by BLEU, we use n-gram hit rates and word-level semantic similarity scores as features in a linear regression model to estimate sentence level semantic similarity. We also propose sigmoid scaling of similarity scores and sentence-length dependent modeling. The models are evaluated on the SemEval'12 sentence similarity task.

2 Semantic similarity between words

In this section, two different metrics of word similarity are presented. The first is a language-agnostic, corpus-based metric requiring no knowledge resources, while the second metric relies on WordNet.

Corpus-based metric: Given a corpus, the semantic similarity between two words, w_i and w_j, is estimated as their pointwise mutual information (Church and Hanks, 1990): $I(i,j) = \log \frac{\hat{p}(i,j)}{\hat{p}(i)\hat{p}(j)}$, where $\hat{p}(i)$ and $\hat{p}(j)$ are the occurrence probabilities of w_i and w_j, respectively, while the probability of their co-occurrence is denoted by $\hat{p}(i,j)$. These probabilities are computed according to maximum likelihood estimation. The assumption of this metric is that co-occurrence implies semantic similarity.

During the past decade the web has been used for estimating the required probabilities (Turney, 2001; Bollegala et al., 2007), by querying web search engines and retrieving the number of hits required to estimate the frequency of individual words and their co-occurrence. However, these approaches have failed to obtain state-of-the-art results (Bollegala et al., 2007), unless "expensive" conjunctive AND queries are used for harvesting a corpus and then using this corpus to estimate similarity scores (Iosif and Potamianos, 2010).

Recently, a scalable approach[1] for harvesting a corpus has been proposed where web snippets are downloaded using individual queries for each word (Iosif and Potamianos, 2012b). Semantic similarity can then be estimated using the $I(i,j)$ metric and *within-snippet word co-occurrence frequencies*. Under the maximum sense similarity assumption (Resnik, 1995), it is relatively easy to show that a (more) lexically-balanced corpus[2] (as the one created above) can significantly reduce the semantic similarity estimation error of the mutual information metric $I(i,j)$. This is also experimentally verified in (Iosif and Potamianos, 2012c).

In addition, one can modify the mutual information metric to further reduce estimation error (for the theoretical foundation behind this see (Iosif and Potamianos, 2012a)). Specifically, one may introduce exponential weights α in order to reduce the contribution of $p(i)$ and $p(j)$ in the similarity metric. The modified metric $I_a(i,j)$, is defined as:

$$I_a(i,j) = \frac{1}{2}\left[\log \frac{\hat{p}(i,j)}{\hat{p}^{\alpha}(i)\hat{p}(j)} + \log \frac{\hat{p}(i,j)}{\hat{p}(i)\hat{p}^{\alpha}(j)}\right]. \quad (1)$$

The weight α was estimated on the corpus of (Iosif and Potamianos, 2012b) in order to maximize word sense coverage in the semantic neighborhood of each word. The $I_a(i,j)$ metric using the estimated value of $\alpha = 0.8$ was shown to significantly outperform $I(i,j)$ and to achieve state-of-the-art results on standard semantic similarity datasets (Rubenstein and Goodenough, 1965; Miller and Charles, 1998; Finkelstein et al., 2002). For more details see (Iosif and Potamianos, 2012a).

WordNet-based metrics: For comparison purposes, we evaluated various similarity metrics on the task of word similarity computation on three standard datasets (same as above). The best results were obtained by the Vector metric (Patwardhan and Pedersen, 2006), which exploits the lexical information that is included in the WordNet glosses. This metric was incorporated to our proposed approach. All metrics were computed using the WordNet::Similarity module (Pedersen, 2005).

3 N-gram Regression Models

Inspired by BLEU (Papineni et al., 2002), we propose a simple regression model that combines evidence from two sources: number of n-gram matches and degree of similarity between non-matching words between two sentences. In order to incorporate a word semantic similarity metric into BLEU, we apply the following two-pass process: first lexical hits are identified and counted, and then the semantic similarity between n-grams not matched dur-

[1]The scalability of this approach has been demonstrated in (Iosif and Potamianos, 2012b) for a 10K vocabulary, here we extend it to the full 60K WordNet vocabulary.

[2]According to this assumption the semantic similarity of two words can be estimated as the minimum pairwise similarity of their senses. The gist of the argument is that although words often co-occur with their closest senses, word occurrences correspond to all senses, i.e., the denominator of $I(i,j)$ is overestimated causing large underestimation error for similarities between polysemous words.

ing the first pass is estimated. All word similarity metrics used are peak-to-peak normalized in the [0,1] range, so they serve as a "degree-of-match". The semantic similarity scores from word pairs are summed together (just like n-gram hits) to obtain a BLEU-like semantic similarity score. The main problem here is one of alignment, since we need to compare each non-matched n-gram from the hypothesis with an n-gram from the reference. We use a simple approach: we iterate on the hypothesis n-grams, left-to-right, and compare each with the *most similar* non-matched n-gram in the reference. This modification to BLEU is only applied to 1-grams, since semantic similarity scores for bigrams (or higher) were not available.

Thus, our list of features are the hit rates obtained by BLEU (for 1-, 2-, 3-, 4-grams) and the total semantic similarity (SS) score for 1-grams[3]. These features are then combined using a multiple linear regression model:

$$\hat{D}_L = a_0 + \sum_{n=1}^{4} a_n \, B_n + a_5 \, M_1, \quad (2)$$

where $\hat{D}_L$ is the estimated similarity, B_n is the BLEU hit rate for n-grams, M_1 is the total semantic similarity score (SS) for non-matching 1-grams and a_n are the trainable parameters of the model.

Motivated by evidence of cognitive scaling of semantic similarity scores (Iosif and Potamianos, 2010), we propose the use of a sigmoid function to scale D_L sentence similarities. We have also observed in the SemEval data that the way humans rate sentence similarity is very much dependent on sentence length[4]. To capture the effect of length and cognitive scaling we propose next two modifications to the linear regression model. The sigmoid fusion scheme is described by the following equation:

$$\hat{D}_S = a_6 \hat{D}_L + a_7 \hat{D}_L \left[1 + \exp\left(\frac{a_8 - l}{a_9} \right) \right]^{-1}, \quad (3)$$

where we assume that sentence length l (average length for each sentence pair, in words) acts as a scaling factor for the linearly estimated similarity.

The hierarchical fusion scheme is actually a collection of (overlapping) linear regression models, each matching a range of sentence lengths. For example, the first model D_{L1} is trained with sentences with length up to l_1, i.e., $l \leq l_1$, the second model D_{L2} up to length l_2 etc. During testing, sentences with length $l \in [1, l_1]$ are decoded with D_{L1}, sentences with length $l \in (l_1, l_2]$ with model D_{L2} etc. Each of these partial models is a linear fusion model as shown in (2). In this work, we use four models with $l_1 = 10, l_2 = 20, l_3 = 30, l_4 = \infty$.

4 Experimental Procedure and Results

Initially all sentences are pre-processed by the CoreNLP (Finkel et al., 2005; Toutanova et al., 2003) suite of tools, a process that includes named entity recognition, normalization, part of speech tagging, lemmatization and stemming. The exact type of pre-processing used depends on the metric used. For the plain lexical BLEU, we use lemmatization, stemming (of lemmas) and remove all non-content words, keeping only nouns, adjectives, verbs and adverbs. For computing semantic similarity scores, we don't use stemming and keep only noun words, since we only have similarities between non-noun words. For the computation of semantic similarity we have created a dictionary containing all the single-word nouns included in WordNet (approx. 60K) and then downloaded snippets of the 500 top-ranked documents for each word by formulating single-word queries and submitting them to the Yahoo! search engine.

Next, results are reported in terms of correlation between the automatically computed scores and the ground truth, for each of the corpora in Task 6 of SemEval'12 (paraphrase, video, europarl, WordNet, news). Overall correlation ("Ovrl") computed on the join of the dataset, as well as, average ("Mean") correlation across all task is also reported. Training is performed on a subset of the first three corpora and testing on all five corpora.

Baseline BLEU: The first set of results in Table 1, shows the correlation performance of the plain BLEU hit rates (per training data set and overall/average). The best performing hit rate is the one

[3] Note that the features are computed twice on each sentence in a forward and backward fashion (where the word order is reversed), and then averaged between the two runs.

[4] We speculate that shorter sentences are mostly compared at the lexical level using the short-term memory language buffers, while longer sentences tend to be compared at a higher cognitive level, where the non-compositional nature of sentence semantics dominate.

calculated using unigrams.

Table 1: Correlation performance of BLEU hit rates.

	par	vid	euro	Mean	Ovrl
BLEU 1-grams	**0.62**	**0.67**	**0.49**	**0.59**	**0.57**
BLEU 2-grams	0.40	0.39	0.37	0.39	0.34
BLEU 3-grams	0.32	0.36	0.30	0.33	0.33
BLEU 4-grams	0.26	0.25	0.24	0.25	0.28

Semantic Similarity BLEU (Purple): The performance of the modified version of BLEU that incorporates various word-level similarity metrics is shown in Table 2. Here the BLEU hits (exact matches) are summed together with the normalized similarity scores (approximate matches) to obtain a single B_1+M_1 (Purple) score[5]. As we can see, there are definite benefits to using the modified version, particularly with regards to mean correlation. Overall the best performers, when taking into account both mean and overall correlation, are the WordNet-based and I_a metrics, with the I_a metric winning by a slight margin, earning a place in the final models.

Table 2: Correlation performance of 1-gram BLEU scores with semantic similarity metrics (nouns-only).

	par	vid	euro	Mean	Ovrl
BLEU	0.54	0.60	0.39	0.51	0.58
SS-BLEU WordNet	0.56	**0.64**	**0.41**	**0.54**	0.58
SS-BLEU $I(i,j)$	0.56	0.63	0.39	0.53	**0.59**
SS-BLEU $I_a(i,j)$	**0.57**	**0.64**	0.40	**0.54**	0.58

Regression models (DeepPurple): Next, the performance of the various regression models (fusion schemes) is investigated. Each regression model is evaluated by performing 10-fold cross-validation on the SemEval training set. Correlation performance is shown in Table 3 both with and without semantic similarity. The baseline in this case is the Purple metric (corresponding to no fusion). Clearly the use of regression models significantly improves performance compared to the 1-gram BLEU and Purple baselines for almost all datasets, and especially for the combined dataset (overall). Among the fusion schemes, the hierarchical models perform the best. Following fusion, the performance gain from incorporating semantic similarity (SS) is much smaller. Finally, in Table 4, correlation performance of our submissions on the official SemEval test set is shown. The overall correlation performance of the Hierarchical model ranks somewhere in the middle (43rd out of 89 systems), while the mean correlation (weighted by number of samples per set) is notably better: 23rd out of 89. Comparing the individual dataset results, our systems underperform for the two datasets that originate from the machine translation (MT) literature (and contain longer sentences), while we achieve good results for the rest (19th for paraphrase, 37th for video and 29th for WN).

[5]It should be stressed that the plain BLEU unigram scores shown in this table are not comparable to those in Table 1, since here scores are calculated over only the nouns of each sentence.

Table 3: Correlation performance of regression model with (SS) and without semantic similarities on the training set (using 10-fold cross-validation).

	par	vid	euro	Mean	Ovrl
None (SS-BLEU I_a)	0.57	0.64	0.40	0.54	0.58
Linear ($\hat{D}_L, a_5=0$)	0.62	0.72	0.47	0.60	0.66
Sigmoid ($\hat{D}_S, a_5=0$)	0.64	0.73	0.42	0.60	0.73
Hierarchical	0.64	**0.74**	**0.48**	**0.62**	0.73
SS-Linear ($\hat{D}_L$)	0.64	0.73	0.47	0.61	0.66
SS-Sigmoid ($\hat{D}_S$)	**0.65**	**0.74**	0.42	0.60	**0.74**
SS-Hierarchical	**0.65**	**0.74**	**0.48**	**0.62**	0.73

Table 4: Correlation performance on test set.

	par	vid	euro	WN	news	Mean	Ovrl
None	0.50	0.71	**0.44**	0.49	0.24	0.51	0.49
Sigm.	0.60	0.76	0.26	0.60	0.34	0.56	0.55
Hier.	**0.60**	**0.77**	0.43	**0.65**	**0.37**	**0.60**	**0.62**

5 Conclusions

We have shown that: 1) a regression model that combines counts of exact and approximate n-gram matches provides good performance for sentence similarity computation (especially for short and medium length sentences), 2) the non-linear scaling of hit-rates with respect to sentence length improves performance, 3) incorporating word semantic similarity scores (soft-match) into the model can improve performance, and 4) web snippet corpus creation and the modified mutual information metric is a language agnostic approach that can (at least) match semantic similarity performance of the best resource-based metrics for this task. Future work, should involve the extension of this approach to model larger lexical chunks, the incorporation of compositional models of meaning, and in general the phrase-level modeling of semantic similarity, in order to compete with MT-based systems trained on massive external parallel corpora.

References

E. Agirre and P. Edmonds, editors. 2007. *Word Sense Disambiguation: Algorithms and Applications*. Springer.

M. Baroni and A. Lenci. 2010. Distributional memory: A general framework for corpus-based semantics. *Computational Linguistics*, 36(4):673–721.

D. Bollegala, Y. Matsuo, and M. Ishizuka. 2007. Measuring semantic similarity between words using web search engines. In *Proc. of International Conference on World Wide Web*, pages 757–766.

J. Bos and K. Markert. 2005. Recognising textual entailment with logical inference. In *Proceedings of the Human Language Technology Conference and Conference on Empirical Methods in Natural Language Processing*, page 628635.

A. Budanitsky and G. Hirst. 2006. Evaluating WordNet-based measures of semantic distance. *Computational Linguistics*, 32:13–47.

K. W. Church and P. Hanks. 1990. Word association norms, mutual information, and lexicography. *Computational Linguistics*, 16(1):22–29.

I. Dagan, O. Glickman, and B. Magnini. 2006. The pascal recognising textual entailment challenge. In Joaquin Quionero-Candela, Ido Dagan, Bernardo Magnini, and Florence dAlch Buc, editors, *Machine Learning Challenges. Evaluating Predictive Uncertainty, Visual Object Classification, and Recognising Tectual Entailment*, volume 3944 of *Lecture Notes in Computer Science*, pages 177–190. Springer Berlin / Heidelberg.

A. Finch, S. Y. Hwang, and E. Sumita. 2005. Using machine translation evaluation techniques to determine sentence-level semantic equivalence. In *Proceedings of the 3rd International Workshop on Paraphrasing*, page 1724.

J. R. Finkel, T. Grenager, and C. D. Manning. 2005. Incorporating non-local information into information extraction systems by gibbs sampling. In *Proceedings of the 43rd Annual Meeting on Association for Computational Linguistics*, pages 363–370.

L. Finkelstein, E. Gabrilovich, Y. Matias, E. Rivlin, Z. Solan, G. Wolfman, and E. Ruppin. 2002. Placing search in context: The concept revisited. *ACM Transactions on Information Systems*, 20(1):116–131.

S. Harabagiu and A. Hickl. 2006. Methods for Using Textual Entailment in Open-Domain Question Answering. In *Proceedings of the 21st International Conference on Computational Linguistics and 44th Annual Meeting of the Association for Computational Linguistics*, pages 905–912.

E. Iosif and A. Potamianos. 2010. Unsupervised semantic similarity computation between terms using web documents. *IEEE Transactions on Knowledge and Data Engineering*, 22(11):1637–1647.

E. Iosif and A. Potamianos. 2012a. Minimum error semantic similarity using text corpora constructed from web queries. *IEEE Transactions on Knowledge and Data Engineering* (submitted to).

E. Iosif and A. Potamianos. 2012b. Semsim: Resources for normalized semantic similarity computation using lexical networks. *Proc. of Eighth International Conference on Language Resources and Evaluation* (to appear).

E. Iosif and A. Potamianos. 2012c. Similarity computation using semantic networks created from web-harvested data. *Natural Language Engineering* (submitted to).

N. Madnani and B. J. Dorr. 2010. Generating phrasal and sentential paraphrases: A survey of data-driven methods. *Computational Linguistics*, 36(3):341387.

P. Malakasiotis and I. Androutsopoulos. 2007. Learning textual entailment using svms and string similarity measures. In *Proceedings of of the ACL-PASCAL Workshop on Textual Entailment and Paraphrasing*, pages 42–47.

P. Malakasiotis. 2009. Paraphrase recognition using machine learning to combine similarity measures. In *Proceedings of the 47th Annual Meeting of ACL and the 4th Int. Joint Conference on Natural Language Processing of AFNLP*, pages 42–47.

N. Malandrakis, A. Potamianos, E. Iosif, and S. Narayanan. 2011. Kernel models for affective lexicon creation. In *Proc. Interspeech*, pages 2977–2980.

H. Meng and K.-C. Siu. 2002. Semi-automatic acquisition of semantic structures for understanding domain-specific natural language queries. *IEEE Transactions on Knowledge and Data Engineering*, 14(1):172–181.

G. Miller and W. Charles. 1998. Contextual correlates of semantic similarity. *Language and Cognitive Processes*, 6(1):1–28.

G. Miller. 1990. Wordnet: An on-line lexical database. *International Journal of Lexicography*, 3(4):235–312.

S. Mirkin, L. Specia, N. Cancedda, I. Dagan, M. Dymetman, and S. Idan. 2009. Source-language entailment modeling for translating unknown terms. In *Proceedings of the 47th Annual Meeting of ACL and the 4th Int. Joint Conference on Natural Language Processing of AFNLP*, pages 791–799.

K. Papineni, S. Roukos, T. Ward, and W.-J. Zhu. 2002. Bleu: a method for automatic evaluation of machine translation. In *Proceedings of the 40th Annual Meeting on Association for Computational Linguistics*, pages 311–318.

S. Patwardhan and T. Pedersen. 2006. Using WordNet-based context vectors to estimate the semantic relatedness of concepts. In *Proc. of the EACL Workshop on Making Sense of Sense: Bringing Computational Linguistics and Psycholinguistics Together*, pages 1–8.

T. Pedersen. 2005. WordNet::Similarity. `http://search.cpan.org/dist/WordNet-Similarity/`.

D. Perez and E. Alfonseca. 2005. Application of the bleu algorithm for recognizing textual entailments. In *Proceedings of the PASCAL Challenges Worshop on Recognising Textual Entailment*.

P. Resnik. 1995. Using information content to evaluate semantic similarity in a taxanomy. In *Proc. of International Joint Conference for Artificial Intelligence*, pages 448–453.

F. Rinaldi, J. Dowdall, K. Kaljurand, M. Hess, and D. Molla. 2003. Exploiting paraphrases in a question answering system. In *Proceedings of the 2nd International Workshop on Paraphrasing*, pages 25–32.

H. Rubenstein and J. B. Goodenough. 1965. Contextual correlates of synonymy. *Communications of the ACM*, 8(10):627–633.

I. Szpektor and I. Dagan. 2008. Learning entailment rules for unary templates. In *Proceedings of the 22nd International Conference on Computational Linguistics*, pages 849–856.

K. Toutanova, D. Klein, C. D. Manning, and Y. Singer. 2003. Feature-rich part-of-speech tagging with a cyclic dependency network. In *Proceedings of Conference of the North American Chapter of the Association for Computational Linguistics on Human Language Technology*, pages 173–180.

P. D. Turney. 2001. Mining the web for synonyms: PMI-IR versus LSA on TOEFL. In *Proc. of the European Conference on Machine Learning*, pages 491–502.

F. Zanzotto, M. Pennacchiotti, and A. Moschitti. 2009. A machine-learning approach to textual entailment recognition. *Natural Language Engineering*, 15(4):551582.

JU_CSE_NLP: Multi-grade Classification of Semantic Similarity Between Text Pairs

Snehasis Neogi[1], **Partha Pakray**[2], **Sivaji Bandyopadhyay**[1]
[1]Computer Science & Engineering Department
Jadavpur University, Kolkata, India
[2]Computer Science & Engineering Department
Jadavpur University, Kolkata, India
Intern at Xerox Research Centre Europe
Grenoble, France
{snehasis1981,parthapakray}@gmail.com
sbandyopadhyay@cse.jdvu.ac.in

Alexander Gelbukh
Center for Computing Research
National Polytechnic Institute
Mexico City, Mexico
gelbukh@gelbukh.com

Abstract

This article presents the experiments carried out at Jadavpur University as part of the participation in Semantic Textual Similarity (STS) of Task 6 @ Semantic Evaluation Exercises (SemEval-2012). Task-6 of SemEval- 2012 focused on semantic relations of text pair. Task-6 provides five different text pair files to compare different semantic relations and judge these relations through a similarity and confidence score. Similarity score is one kind of multi way classification in the form of grade between 0 to 5. We have submitted one run for the STS task. Our system has two basic modules - one deals with lexical relations and another deals with dependency based syntactic relations of the text pair. Similarity score given to a pair is the average of the scores of the above-mentioned modules. The scores from each module are identified using rule based techniques. The Pearson Correlation of our system in the task is 0.3880.

1 Introduction

Task-6[1] [1] of SemEval-2012 deals with semantic similarity of text pairs. The task is to find the similarity between the sentences in the text pair (s1 and s2) and return a similarity score and an optional confidence score. There are five datasets in the test data and with tab separated text pairs. The datasets are as follows:

- MSR-Paraphrase, Microsoft Research Paraphrase Corpus (750 pairs of sentences.)
- MSR-Video, Microsoft Research Video Description Corpus (750 pairs of sentences.)
- SMTeuroparl: WMT2008 development dataset (Europarl section) (459 pairs of sentences.)
- SMTnews: news conversation sentence pairs from WMT.(399 pairs of sentences.)
- OnWN: pairs of sentences where the first comes from Ontonotes and the second from a WordNet definition. (750 pairs of sentences.)

Similarity score ranges from 0 to 5 and confidence score from 0 to 100. An s1-s2 pair gets a similarity score of 5 if they are completely equivalent. Similarity score 4 is allocated for mostly equivalent s1-s2 pair. Similarly, score 3 is allocated for roughly equivalent pair. Score 2, 1 and 0 are allocated for non-equivalent details sharing, non-equivalent topic sharing and totally different pairs respectively. Major challenge of this task is to find the similarity score based similarity for the text pair. Generally text entailment tasks refer whether sentence pairs are entailed or not: binary classification (YES, NO) [2] or multi-classification (Forward, Backward, bidirectional or no entailment) [3][4]. But multi grade classification of semantic similarity assigns a score to the sentence pair. Our system considers lexical and dependency based syntactic measures for semantic similarity. Similarity scores are the basic average of these module scores. A subsequent

[1] http://www.cs.york.ac.uk/semeval-2012/task6/

section describes the system architecture. Section 2 describes JU_NLP_CSE system for STS task. Section 3 describes evaluation and experimental results. Conclusions are drawn in Section 4.

2 System Architecture

The system of Semantic textual similarity task has two main modules: one is lexical module and another one is dependency parsing based syntactic module. Both these module have some pre-processing tasks such as stop word removal, co-reference resolution and dependency parsing etc. Figure 1 displays the architecture of the system.

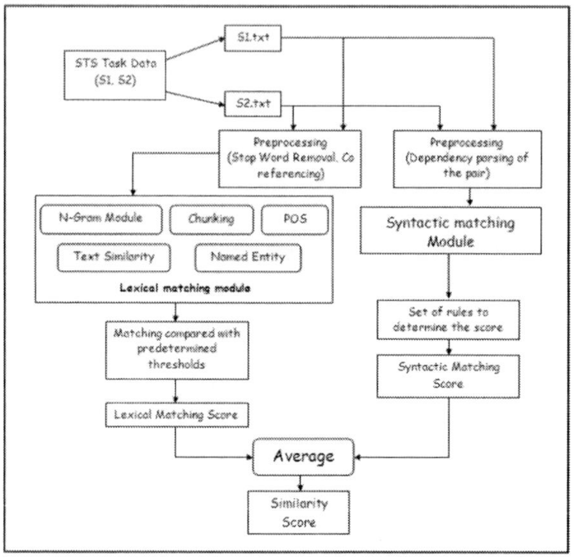

Figure 1: System Architecture

2.1 Pre-processing Module

The system separates the s1-s2 sentence pairs contained in the different STS task datasets. These separated pairs are then passed through the following sub modules:

i. Stop word Removal: Stop words are removed from s1 - s2 sentence pairs.

ii. Co-reference: Co-reference resolutions are carried out on the datasets before passing through the TE module. The objective is to increase the score of the entailment percentage. A word or phrase in the sentence is used to refer to an entity introduced earlier or later in the discourse and both having same things then they have the same referent or co reference. When the reader must look back to the previous context, reference is called "*Anaphoric Reference*". When the reader must look forward, it is termed "*Cataphoric Reference*". To address this problem we used a tool called JavaRAP[2] (A java based implementation of Anaphora Procedure (RAP) - an algorithm by Lappin and Leass (1994)).

iii. Dependency Parsing: Separated s1 – s2 sentences are parsed using Stanford dependency parser[3] to produce the dependency relations in the texts. These dependency relations are used for WordNet based syntactic matching.

2.2 Lexical Matching Module

In this module the TE system calculates different matching scores such as N – Gram match, Text Similarity, Chunk match, Named Entity match and POS match.

i. N-Gram Match module: The N-Gram match basically measures the percentage match of the unigram, bigram and trigram of hypothesis present in the corresponding text. These scores are simply combined to get an overall N – Gram matching score for a particular pair.

ii. Chunk Match module: In this sub module our system evaluates the key NP-chunks of both text (s1) and hypothesis (s2) using NP Chunker v1.1[3] (The University of Sheffield). The hypothesis NP chunks are matched in the text NP chunks. System calculates an overall value for the chunk matching, i.e., number of text NP chunks that match the hypothesis NP chunks. If the chunks are not similar in their surface form then our system goes for wordnet synonyms matching for the words and if they match in wordnet synsets information, it will be encountered as a similar chunk. WordNet [5] is one of most important resource for lexical analysis. The WordNet 2.0 has been used for WordNet based chunk matching. The API for WordNet Searching (JAWS)[4] is an API that provides Java applications with the ability to retrieve data from the WordNet synsets.

iii. Text Similarity Module: System takes into consideration several text similarities calculated

[2] http://aye.comp.nus.edu.sg/~qiu/NLPTools/JavaRAP.html
[3] http://www.dcs.shef.ac.uk/~mark/phd/software/
[4] http://lyle.smu.edu/~tspell/jaws/index.html

over the s1-s2 pair. These text similarity values are summed up to produce a total score for a particular s1-s2 pair. Major Text similarity measures that our system considers are:

- *Cosine Similarity*
- *Lavenstine Distance*
- *Euclidean Distance*
- *MongeElkan Distance*
- *NeedlemanWunch Distance*
- *SmithWaterman Distance*
- *Block Distance*
- *Jaro Similarity*
- *MatchingCoefficient Distance*
- *Dice Similarity*
- *OverlapCoefficient*
- *QGrams Distance*

iv. Named Entity Matching: It is based on the detection and matching of Named Entities in the s1-s2 pair. Stanford Named Entity Recognizer[5] is used to tag the named entities in both s1 and s2. System simply maps the number of hypothesis (s2) NEs present in the text (s1). A score is allocated for the matching.

NE_match = (Number of common NEs in Text and Hypothesis) / (Number of NE in Hypothesis).

v. Part –of – Speech (POS) Matching: This module basically deals with matching the common POS tags between s1 and s2 sentences. Stanford POS tagger[6] is used to tag the part of speech in both s1 and s2. System matches the verb and noun POS words in the hypothesis that match in the text. A score is allocated based on the number of POS matching.

POS_match = (Number of common verb and noun POS in Text and Hypothesis) / (Total number of verb and noun POS in hypothesis).

System calculates the sum of the entire sub module (modules described in section 2.2) scores and forms a single percentage score for the lexical matching. This score is then compared with some predetermined threshold value to assign a final lexical score for each pair. If percentage value is above 0.80 then lexical score 5 is allocated. If the value is between 0.60 to 0.80 then lexical score 4 is allocated. Similarly, lexical score 3 is allocated for percentage score of 0.40 to 0.60 and so on. One lexical score is finally generated for each text pair.

2.3. Syntactic Matching Module:

TE system considers the preprocessed dependency parsed text pairs (s1 – s2) and goes for word net based matching technique. After parsing the sentences, they have some attributes like subject, object, verb, auxiliaries and prepositions tagged by the dependency parser tag set. System uses these attributes for the matching procedure and depending on the nature of matching a score is allocated to the s1-s2 pair. Matching procedure is basically done through comparison of the following features that are present in both the text and the hypothesis.

- *Subject – Subject comparison.*
- *Verb – Verb Comparison.*
- *Subject – Verbs Comparison.*
- *Object – Object Comparison.*
- *Cross Subject – Object Comparison.*
- *Object – Verbs Comparison.*
- *Prepositional phrase comparison.*

Each of these comparisons produces one matching score for the s1-s2 pair that are finally combined with previously generated lexical score to generate the final similarity score by taking simple average of lexical and syntactic matching scores. The basic heuristics are as follows:

(i) If the feature of the text (s1) directly matches the same feature of the hypothesis (s2), matching score 5 is allocated for the text pair.

(ii) If the feature of either text (s1) or hypothesis (s2) matches with the wordnet synsets of the corresponding text (s1) or hypothesis (s2), matching score 4 is allocated.

(iii) If wordnet synsets of the feature of the text (s1) match with one of the synsets of the feature of the hypothesis (s2), matching score 3 is given to the pair.

(iv) If wordnet synsets of the feature of either text (s1) or hypothesis (s2) match with the synsets of the corresponding text (s1) or hypothesis (s2) then matching score 2 is allocated for the pair.

[5] http://nlp.stanford.edu/software/CRF-NER.shtml
[6] http://nlp.stanford.edu/software/tagger.shtml

(v) Similarly if in both the cases match occurs in the second level of wordnet synsets, matching score 1is allocated.
(vi) Matching score 0 is allocated for the pair having no match in their features.
After execution of the module, system generates some scores. Lexical module generates one lexical score and wordnet based syntactic matching module generates seven matching scores. At the final stage of the system all these scores are combined and the mean is evaluated on this combined score. This mean gives the similarity score for a particular s1-s2 pair of different datasets of STS task. Optional confidence score is also allocated which is basically the similarity score multiplied by 10, i.e., if the similarity score is 5.22, the confidence score will be 52.2.

3. Experiments on Dataset and Result

We have submitted one run in SemEval-2012 Task 6. The results for Run on STS Test set are shown in Table 1.

task6-JU_CSE_NLP-Semantic_Syntactic_Approach	**Correlations**
ALL	0.3880
ALLnrm	0.6706
Mean	0.4111
MSRpar	0.3427
MSRvid	0.3549
SMT-eur	0.4271
On-WN	0.5298
SMT-news	0.4034

Table 1: Results of Test Set

ALL: Pearson correlation with the gold standard for the five datasets and the corresponding rank 82.
ALLnrm: Pearson correlation after the system outputs for each dataset are fitted to the gold standard using least squares and the corresponding rank 86.
Mean: Weighted mean across the 5 datasets, where the weight depends on the number of pairs in the dataset and the corresponding rank 76.
The subsequent rows show the pearson correlation scores for each of the individual datasets.

4. Conclusion

Our JU_CSE_NLP system for the STS task mainly focus on lexical and syntactic approaches. There are some limitations in the lexical matching module that shows a correlation that is not higher in the range. In case of simple sentences lexical matching is helpful for entailment but for complex and compound sentences the lexical matching module loses its accuracy. Semantic graph matching or conceptual graph implementation can improve the system. That is not considered in our present work. Machine learning tools can be used to learn the system based on the features. It can also improve the correlation. In future work our system will include semantic graph matching and a machine-learning module.

Acknowledgments

The work was done under support of the DST India-CONACYT Mexico project "*Answer Validation through Textual Entailment*" funded by DST, Government of India.

References

[1] Eneko Agirre, Daniel Cer, Mona Diab and Aitor Gonzalez. SemEval-2012 Task 6: A Pilot on Semantic Textual Similarity. In Proceedings of the 6th International Workshop on Semantic Evaluation (SemEval 2012), in conjunction with the First Joint Conference on Lexical and Computational Semantics (*SEM 2012). (2012)

[2] Dagan, I., Glickman, O., Magnini, B.: *The PASCAL Recognising Textual Entailment Challenge.* Proceedings of the First PASCAL Recognizing Textual Entailment Workshop. (2005).

[3] H. Shima, H. Kanayama, C.-W. Lee, C.-J. Lin,T. Mitamura, S. S. Y. Miyao, and K. Takeda. *Overview of ntcir-9 rite: Recognizing inference in text.* In NTCIR-9 Proceedings,2011.

[4] Pakray, P., Neogi, S., Bandyopadhyay, S., Gelbukh, A.: *A Textual Entailment System using Web based Machine Translation System.* NTCIR-9, National Center of Sciences, Tokyo, Japan. December 6-9, 2011. (2011).

[5] Fellbaum, C.: WordNet: An Electronic Lexical Database. MIT Press (1998).

Tiantianzhu7:System Description of Semantic Textual Similarity (STS) in the SemEval-2012 (Task 6)

Tiantian Zhu
Department of Computer Science and Technology
East China Normal University
51111201046@student.ecnu.edu.cn

Man Lan
Department of Computer Science and Technology
East China Normal University
mlan@cs.ecnu.edu.cn

Abstract

This paper briefly reports our submissions to the Semantic Textual Similarity (STS) task in the SemEval 2012 (Task 6). We first use knowledge-based methods to compute word semantic similarity as well as Word Sense Disambiguation (WSD). We also consider word order similarity from the structure of the sentence. Finally we sum up several aspects of similarity with different coefficients and get the sentence similarity score.

1 Introduction

The task of semantic textual similarity (STS) is to measure the degree of semantic equivalence between two sentences. It plays an increasingly important role in several text-related research and applications, such as text mining, Web page retrieval, automatic question-answering, text summarization, and machine translation. The goal of the Semeval 2012 STS task (task 6) is to build a unified framework for the evaluation of semantic textual similarity modules for different systems and to characterize their impact on NLP applications.

Generally, there are two ways to measure similarity of two sentences, i.e, corpus-based methods and knowledge-based methods. The corpus-based method typically computes sentence similarity based on the frequency of word occurrence or the co-occurrence between collocated words. For example, in (Islam and Inkpen, 2008) they proposed a corpus-based sentence similarity measure as a function of string similarity, word similarity and common word order similarity (CWO). The knowledge-based method computes sentence similarity based on the semantic information collected from knowledge bases. With the aid of a number of successful computational linguistic projects, many semantic knowledge bases are readily available, for example, WordNet, Spatial Date Transfer Standard, Gene Ontology, etc. Among them, the most widely used one is WordNet, which is organized by meanings and developed at Princeton University. Several methods computed word similarity by using WordNet, such as the Lesk method in (Banerjee and Pedersen, 2003), the lch method in (Leacock and Chodorow, 1998)and the wup method in (Wu and Palmer, 1994). Generally, although the knowledge-based methods heavily depend on the knowledge bases, they performed much better than the corpus-based methods in most cases. Therefore, in our STS system, we use a knowledge-based method to compute word similarity.

The rest of this paper is organized as follows. Section 2 describes our system. Section 3 presents the results of our system.

2 System Description

Usually, a sentence is composed of some nouns, verbs, adjectives, adverbs and/or some stop words. We found that these words carry a lot of information, especially the nouns and verbs. Although the adjectives and adverbs also make contribution to the semantic meaning of the sentence, they are much weaker than the nouns and verbs. So we consider to measure the sentence semantic similarities from three aspects. We define the following three types of similarity from two compared sentences to measure the semantic similarity: (1) Noun Similarity to measure the similarity between the nouns from the two compared sentences, (2) Verb Similarity to measure the similarity between Verbs, (3) ADJ-ADV Similarity to measure the similarity between the adjectives and adverbs from each sentence. Besides the semantic information similarity, we also found that the structure of the sentences carry some information which cannot be ignored. Therefore, we define the last aspect of the sentence similarity as Word Order Similarity. In the following we will introduce the different components of our system.

2.1 POS

As a basic natural language processing technique, part of speech tagging is to identify the part of speech of individual words in the sentence. In order to compute the three above semantic similarities, we first identify the nouns, verbs, adjectives, and adverbs in the sentence. Then we can calculate the Noun Similarity, Verb Similarity and ADJ-ADV Similarity from two sentences.

2.2 Semantic similarity between words

The word similarity measurement have important impact on the performance of sentence similarity. Currently, many lexical resources based approaches perform comparatively well to compute semantic word similarities. However, the exact resources they are based are quite different. For example, some are based on dictionary and/or thesaurus, and others are based on WordNet.

WordNet is a machine-readable lexical database. The words in Wordnet are classified into four categories, i.e., nouns, verbs, adjectives and adverbs. WordNet groups these words into sets of synonyms called *synsets*, provides short definitions, and records the various semantic relations between these *synsets*. The *synsets* are interlinked by means of conceptual-semantic and lexical relations. WordNet also provides the most common relationships include *Hyponym/Hypernym* (i.e., is-a relationships) and *Meronym/Holonym* (i.e., part-of relationships). Nouns and verbs are organized into hierarchies based on the hyponymy/hypernym relation between *synsets* while adjectives and adverbs are not.

In this paper, we adopt the wup method in (Wu and Palmer, 1994) to estimate the semantic similarity between two words, which estimates the semantic similarity between two words based on the depth of the two words in WordNet and the depth of their least common subsumer (LCS), where LCS is defined as the common ancestor deepest in the taxonomy.

For example, given two words, w_1 and w_2, the semantic similarity s(w_1,w_2) is the function of their depth in the taxonomy and the depth of their least common subsumer. If d_1 and d_2 are the depth of w_1 and w_2 in WordNet, and h is the depth of their least common subsumer in WordNet, the semantic similarity can be written as:

$$s(w_1, w_2) = \frac{2.0 * h}{d_1 + d_2} \tag{1}$$

2.3 Word Sense Disambiguation

Word Sense Disambiguation (WSD) is to identify the actual meaning of a word according to the context. In our word similarity method, we take the nearest meaning of two words into consideration rather than their actual meaning. More importantly, the nearest meaning does not always represent the actual meaning. In our system, we used a WSD algorithm proposed by (Ted Pedersen et al.,2005), which computes semantic relatedness of word senses using extended gloss overlaps of their dictionary definitions. We utilize this WSD algorithm for each sentence to get the actual meaning of each word before computing the word semantic similarity.

2.4 Semantic Similarity

We adopt a similar way to compute the three types of semantic similarities. Here we take Noun Similarity as an example.

Suppose sentence s_1 and s_2 are the two sentences to be compared, s_1 has a nouns while s_2 has b nouns. Then we get $a * b$ noun pairs and use the word similarity method mentioned in section 2.2 to compute the Noun Similarity of each noun pair. After that, for each noun, we choose its highest score in noun pairs as its similarity score. Then we use the formula below to compute the Noun Similarity.

$$Sim_{Noun} = \frac{(\sum_{i=1}^{c} n_i) * (a + b)}{2ab} \tag{2}$$

where c represents the number of noun words in sequence a and sequence b, $c = min(a, b)$; n_i represents the highest matching similarity score of i-th word in the shorter sequence with respect to one of the words in the longer sequence; and $\sum_{i=1}^{c} n_i$ represents the sum of the highest matching similarity score between the words in sequence a and sequence b. Similarly, we can get Sim_{Verb}. Since there is no *Hyponym/Hypernym* relation for adjectives and adverbs in WordNet, we just compute ADJ-ADV Similarity based on the frequency of overlap of simple words.

2.5 Word Order Similarity

We believe that word order information also make contributions to sentence similarity. In most cases, the longer common sequence (LCS) the two sentences have, the higher similarity score the sentences get. For example the pair of sentences s_1 and s_2, we remove all the punctuation from the sentences:

- s_1: But other sources close to the sale said Vivendi was keeping the door open to further bids and hoped to see bidders interested in individual assets team up
- s_2: But other sources close to the sale said Vivendi was keeping the door open for further bids in the next day or two

Since the length of the longest common sequence is 14, we use the following formula to compute the word order similarity.

$$Sim_{WordOrder} = \frac{lengthofLCS}{shorterlength} \quad (3)$$

where the *shorter length* means the length of the shorter sentence.

2.6 Overall Similarity

After we have the Noun Similarity, Verb Similarity, ADJ-ADV Similarity and Word Order Similarity, we calculate the Overall Similarity of two compared sentences based on these four scores of similarity. We combine them in the following way:

$$\begin{aligned} Sim_{sent} = aSim_{Noun} + bSim_{Verb} + \\ cSim_{ADJ-ADV} + dSim_{WordOrder} \end{aligned} \quad (4)$$

Where a, b, c and d are the coefficients which denote the contribution of each aspect to the overall sentence similarity, For different data collections, we empirically set different coefficients, for example, for the MSR Paraphrase data, the four coefficients are set as $0.5, 0.3, 0.1, 0.1$, because it is hard to get the highest score 5 even when the two sentences are almost the same meaning, We empirically set a threshold, if the score exceeds the threshold we set the score 5.

3 Experiment and Results on STS

Firstly, Stanford parser[1] is used to parse each sentence and to tag each word with a part of speech(POS). Secondly, WordNet SenseRelate AllWords[2], a WSD tool from CPAN is used to disambiguate and to assign a sense for each word based on the assigned POS.

We submitted three runs: run 1 with WSD, run 2 without WSD, run 3 removing stop words and without WSD. The stoplist is available online[3]. Table 1 lists the performance of these three systems as well as the baseline and the rank 1 results on STS task in SemEval 2012.

We can see that run1 gets the best result, which means WSD has improved the accuracy of sentence similarity. Run3 gets better result than run2, which proves that stop words do disturb the computation of sentence similarity, removing them is a better choice in our system.

4 Conclusion

In our work, we adopt a knowledge-based word similarity method with WSD to measure the semantic similarity between two sentences from four aspects: Noun Similarity, Verb Similarity, ADJ-ADV Similarity and Word Order Similarity. The results show that WSD improves the pearson coefficient at some degree. However, our system did not get a good rank. It indicates there still exists many problems such as wrong POS tag and wrong WSD which might lead to wrong meaning of one word in a sentence.

[1] http://nlp.stanford.edu/software/lex-parser.shtml

[2] http://search.cpan.org/Tedpederse/WordNet-SenseRelate-AllWords-0.19

[3] http://jmlr.csail.mit.edu/papers/volume5/lewis04a/a11-smart-stop-list/english.stop

Table 1: STS system configuration and results on STS task.

Run	ALL	ALLnrm	Mean	MSRpar	MSRvid	SMTeur	OnWN	SMTnews
rank 1	.7790	.8579	.6773	.6830	.8739	.5280	.6641	.4937
baseline	.3110	.6732	.4356	.4334	.2996	.4542	.5864	.3908
1	.4533	.7134	.4192	.4184	.5630	.2083	.4822	.2745
2	.4157	.7099	.3960	.4260	.5628	.1546	.4552	.1923
3	.4446	.7097	.3740	.3411	.5946	.1868	.4029	.1823

Acknowledgments

The authors would like to thank the organizers for their invaluable support making STS a first-rank and interesting international event.

References

Chukfong Ho, Masrah Azrifah Azmi Murad, Rabiah Abdul Kadir, Shyamala C. Doraisamy. 2010. *Word Sense Disambiguation-based Sentence Similarity.* In Proc. COLING-ACL, Beijing.

Jin Feng, Yiming Zhou, Trevor Martin. 2008. *Sentence Similarity based on Relevance.* Proceedings of IPMU'08, Torremolinos.

Yuhua Li, David McLean, Zuhair A. Bandar, James D. O'Shea, and Keeley Crockett. 2009. *Sentence Similarity Based on Semantic Nets and Corpus Statistics.*

LIN LI, XIA HU, BI-YUN HU, JUN WANG, YI-MING ZHOU. 2009. *MEASURING SENTENCE SIMILARITY FROM DIFFERENT ASPECTS.*

Islam Aminul and Diana Inkpen. 2008. *Semantic Text Similarity Using Corpus-Based Word Similarity and String Similarity.* ACM Transactions on Knowledge Discovery from Data.

Banerjee and Pedersen. 2003. *Extended gloss overlaps as a measure of semantic relatedness.* In Proceedings of the Eighteenth International Joint Conference on Artificial Intelligence (IJCAI-03), pages805C810, Acapulco, Mexico.

Leacock and Chodorow. 1998. *Combining local context and WordNet similarity for word sense identification.* In Christiane Fellbaum, editor, WordNet: An Electronic Lexical Database. The MIT Press, Cambridge,MA.

Z.Wu and M.Palmer. 1994. *Verbs semantics and lexical selection.* In Proceedings of the 32nd annual meeting on Association for Computional Linguistics,Morristown, NJ, USA.

Ted Pedersen, Satanjeev Banerjee, Siddharth Patwardhan. 2005. *Maximizing Semantic Relatedness to Perform Word Sense Disambiguation.*

sranjans : Semantic Textual Similarity using Maximal Weighted Bipartite Graph Matching

Sumit Bhagwani, Shrutiranjan Satapathy, Harish Karnick
Computer Science and Engineering
IIT Kanpur, Kanpur - 208016, India
{sumitb,sranjans,hk}@cse.iitk.ac.in

Abstract

The paper aims to come up with a system that examines the degree of semantic equivalence between two sentences. At the core of the paper is the attempt to grade the similarity of two sentences by finding the maximal weighted bipartite match between the tokens of the two sentences. The tokens include single words, or multiwords in case of Named Entitites, adjectivally and numerically modified words. Two token similarity measures are used for the task - WordNet based similarity, and a statistical word similarity measure which overcomes the shortcomings of WordNet based similarity. As part of three systems created for the task, we explore a simple *bag of words* tokenization scheme, a more careful tokenization scheme which captures named entities, times, dates, monetary entities etc., and finally try to capture context around tokens using grammatical dependencies.

1 Introduction

Semantic Textual Similarity (STS) measures the degree of semantic equivalence between texts. The goal of this task is to create a unified framework for the evaluation of semantic textual similarity modules and to characterize their impact on NLP applications. The task is part of the Semantic Evaluation 2012 Workshop (Agirre et al., 2012).

STS is related to both Textual Entailment and Paraphrase, but differs in a number of ways and it is more directly applicable to a number of NLP tasks. Also, STS is a graded similarity notion - this graded bidirectional nature of STS is useful for NLP tasks such as MT evaluation, information extraction, question answering, and summarization.

We propose a lexical similarity approach to grade the similarity of two sentences, where a maximal weighted bipartite match is found between the tokens of the two sentences. The approach is robust enough to apply across different datasets. The results on the STS test datasets are encouraging to say the least. The tokens are single word tokens in case of the first system, while in the second system, named and monetary entities, percentages, dates and times are handled too. A token-token similarity measure is integral to the approach and we use both a statistical similarity measure and a WordNet based word similarity measure for the same. In the final run of the task, apart from capturing the aforementioned entities, we heuristically extract adjectivally and numerically modified words. Also, the last run naively attempts to capture the context around the tokens using grammatical dependencies, which in turn is used to measure context similarity.

Section 2 discusses the previous work done in this area. Section 3 describes the datasets, the baseline system and the evaluation measures used by the task organizers. Section 4, 5 and 6 introduce the systems developed and discuss the results of each system. Finally, section 7 concludes the work and section 8 offers suggestions for future work.

2 Related Work

Various systems exist in literature for textual similarity measurement, be it bag of words based models or complex semantic systems. (Achananuparp et al., 2008) enumerates a few word overlap measures, like Jaccard Similarity Coefficient, IDF Overlap measures, Phrasal overlap measures etc, that have been used for sentential similarity.

(Liu et al., 2008) proposed an approach to calculate sentence similarity, which takes into account both semantic information and word order. They define semantic similarity of *sentence 1* relative to *sentence 2* as the ratio of the sum of the word similarity weighted by information content of words in *sentence 1* to the overall information content included in both sentences. The syntactic similarity is calculated as the correlation coefficient between word order vectors.

A similar semantic similarity measure, proposed by (Li et al., 2006), uses a semantic-vector approach to measure sentence similarity. Sentences are transformed into feature vectors having individual words from the sentence pair as a feature set. Term weights are derived from the maximum semantic similarity score between words in the feature vector and words in the corresponding sentence. To utilize word order in the similarity calculation, they define a word order similarity measure as the normalized difference of word order between the two sentences. They have empirically proved that a sentence similarity measure performs the best when semantic measure is weighted more than syntactic measure (ratio $\sim$ 4:1). This follows the conclusion from a psychological experiment conducted by them which emphasizes the role of semantic information over syntactic information in passage understanding.

3 Task Evaluation

3.1 Datasets

The development datasets are drawn from the following sources :

- **MSR Paraphrase :** This dataset consists of pairs of sentences which have been extracted from news sources on the web.
- **MSR Video :** This dataset consists of pairs of sentences where each sentence of a pair tries to summarize the action in a short video snippet.
- **SMT Europarl :** This dataset consists of pairs sentences drawn from the proceedings of the European Parliament, where each sentence of a pair is a translation from a European language to English.

In addition to the above sources, the test datasets also contained the following sources :

- **SMT News :** This dataset consists of machine translated news conversation sentence pairs.
- **On WN :** This dataset consists of pairs of sentences where the first comes from Ontonotes(Hovy et al., 2006) and the second from a WordNet definition. Hence, the sentences are rather phrases.

3.2 Baseline

The task organizers have used the following baseline scoring scheme. Scores are produced using a simple word overlap baseline system. The input sentences are tokenised by splitting at white spaces, and then each sentence is represented as a vector in the multidimensional token space. Each dimension has 1 if the token is present in the sentence, 0 otherwise. Similarity of vectors is computed using the cosine similarity.

3.3 Evaluation Criteria

The scores obtained by the participating systems are evaluated against the gold standard of the datasets using a pearson correlation measure. In order to evaluate the overall performance of the systems on all the five datasets, the organizers use three evaluation measures :

- **ALL :** This measure takes the union of all the test datasets, and finds the Pearson correlation of the system scores with the gold standard of the union.

- **ALL Normalized :** In this measure, a linear fit is found for the system scores on each dataset using a least squared error criterion, and then the union of the linearly fitted scores is used to calculate the Pearson correlation against the gold standard union.

- **Weighted Mean :** The average of the Pearson correlation scores of the systems on the individual datasets is taken, weighted by the number of test instances in each dataset.

4 SYSTEM 1

4.1 Tokenization Scheme

Each sentence is tokenized into words, filtering out punctuations and stop-words. The stop-words are taken from the stop-word list provided by the NLTK Toolkit (Bird et al., 2009). All the word tokens are reduced to their lemmatized form using the Stanford CoreNLP Toolkit (Minnen et al., 2001). The tokenization is basic in nature and doesn't handle named entities, times, dates, monetary entities or multi-word expressions. The challenge with handling multi-word tokens is in calculating multi-word token similarity, which is not supported in a WordNet word-similarity scheme or a statistical word similarity measure.

4.2 Maximal Weighted Bipartite Match

A weighted bipartite graph is constructed where the two sets of vertices are the word-tokens extracted in the earlier subsection. The bipartite graph is made complete by assigning an edge weight to every pair of tokens from the two sentences. The edge weight is based on a suitable word similarity measure. We had two resources at hand - WordNet based word similarity and a statistical word similarity measure.

4.2.1 WordNet Based Word Similarity

The is-a hierarchy of WordNet is used in calculating the word similarity of two words. Nouns and verbs have separate is-a hierarchies. We use the Lin word-sense similarity measure (Lin , 1998a). Adjectives and adverbs do not have an is-a hierarchy and hence do not figure in the Lin similarity measure. To disambiguate the WordNet sense of a word in a sentence, a variant of the Simplified Lesk Algorithm (Kilgarriff and J. Rosenzweig , 2000) is used. WordNet based word similarity has the following drawbacks :

- sparse in named entity content : similarity of named entities with other words becomes infeasible to calculate.

- doesn't support cross-POS similarity.

- applicable only to nouns and verbs.

4.2.2 Statistical Word Similarity

We use DISCO (Kolb , 2008) as our statistical word similarity measure. DISCO is a tool for retrieving the distributional similarity between two given words. Pre-computed word spaces are freely available for a number of languages. We use the English Wikipedia word space. One primary reason for using a statistical word similarity measure is because of the shortcomings of calculating cross-POS word similarity when using a knowledge base like WordNet.

DISCO works as follows : a term-(term, relative position) matrix is constructed with weights being pointwise mutual information scores. From this, a surface level word similarity score is obtained by using Lin's information theoretic measure (Lin , 1998b) for word vector similarity. This score is used as matrix weights to get second order word vectors, which are used to compute a second order word similarity measure . This measure tries to emulate an LSA like similarity giving better performance, and hence is used for the task.

A point to note here is that the precomputed word spaces that DISCO uses are case sensitive, which we think is a drawback. We preserve the case of proper nouns, while all other words are converted to lower case, prior to evaluating word similarity scores.

4.3 Edge Weighting Scheme

Sentences in the MSR video dataset are simpler and shorter than the remaining datasets, with a high degree of POS correspondence between the

Dataset	DISCO	WordNet	DISCO + WordNet
MSR Video	0.61	0.71	0.73
MSR Paraphrase	0.62	0.43	0.57
SMT Europarl	0.58	0.44	0.54

Figure 1: Edge Weight Scheme Evaluation on Development Datasets

Category	NE	Normalized NE
DATE	26th November, November 26	XXXX-11-26
PERCENT	13 percent, 13%	%13.0
MONEY	56 dollars, $56, 56$	$56.0
TIME	3 pm, 15:00	T15:00

Figure 2: Normalization performed by Stanford CoreNLP

tokens of two sentences, as can be observed in the following example :

- *A man is riding a bicycle.* VS *A man is riding a bike.*

This allows for the use of a Knowledge-Base Word Similarity measure like WordNet word similarity. All the other datasets have lengthier sentences, resulting in cross-POS correspondence. Additionally, there is an abundance of named entities in these datasets. The following examples, which are drawn from the MSR Paraphrase dataset, highlight these points :

- *If convicted of the spying charges, he could face the death penalty.* VS *The charges of espionage and aiding the enemy can carry the death penalty.*

- *Microsoft has identified the freely distributed Linux software as one of the biggest threats to its sales.* VS *The company has publicly identified Linux as one of its biggest competitive threats.*

Keeping this in mind, we use DISCO for edge-weighting in all the datasets except MSR Video. For MSR Video, we use the following edge weighting scheme : for same-POS words, WordNet similarity is used, DISCO otherwise. This choice is justified by the results obtained in figure 1 on the development datasets.

4.3.1 Scoring

A maximal weighted bipartite match is found for the bipartite graph constructed, using the Hungarian Algorithm (Kuhn , 1955) - the intuition behind this being that every keyword in a sentence matches injectively to a unique keyword in the other sentence. The maximal bipartite score is normalized by the sentences' length for two reasons - normalization and punishment for extra detailing in either sentence. So the final sentence similarity score between sentences s_1 and s_2 is:

$$sim(s_1, s_2) = \frac{MaximalBipartiteMatchSum(s_1,s_2)}{max(tokens(s_1),tokens(s_2))}$$

4.4 Results

The results are evaluated on the test datasets provided for the STS task. Figure 3 compares the performance of our systems with the top 3 systems for the task. The scores in the figure are Pearson Correlation scores. Figure 4 shows the performance and ranks of all our systems. A total of 89 systems were submitted, including the baseline. The results are taken from the Semeval'12 Task 6 webpage[1]

As can be seen, System 1 suffers slightly on the MSR Paraphrase and Video datasets, while doing comparably well on the other three datasets when compared with the top 3 submissions. Our ALL score suffers because we use

[1]http://www.cs.york.ac.uk/semeval-2012/task6/index.php?id=results-update

System	ALL	MSR Paraphrase	MSR Video	SMT Europarl	OnWN	SMT News
Rank 1	0.8239	0.6830	0.8739	0.5280	0.6641	0.4937
Rank 2	0.8138	0.6985	0.8620	0.3612	0.7049	0.4683
Rank 3	0.8133	0.7343	0.8803	0.4771	0.6797	0.3989
System 1	0.6529	0.6124	0.7240	0.5581	0.6703	0.4533
System 2	0.6651	0.6254	0.7538	0.5328	0.6649	0.5036
System 3	0.5045	0.6167	0.7061	0.5666	0.5664	0.3968
Li et al.	0.4981	0.6141	0.6084	0.5382	0.6055	0.3760
Baseline	0.3110	0.4334	0.2996	0.4542	0.5864	0.3908

Figure 3: Results of top 3 Systems and Our Systems

System	ALL	ALL Rank	All Normalized	All Normalized Rank	Weighted Mean	Weighted Mean Rank
System 1	0.6529	30	0.8018	39	0.6249	12
System 2	0.6651	24	0.8128	22	0.6366	8
System 3	0.5045	62	0.7846	52	0.5905	30

Figure 4: Evaluation of our Systems on different criteria

a combination of WordNet and statistical word similarity measure for the MSR Video dataset, which affects the Pearson Correlation of all the datasets combined. The correlation values for the ALL Normalized criterion are high because of the linear fitting it performs. We get the best performance on the Weighted Mean evaluation criterion.

5 SYSTEM 2

In System 2, in addition to System 1, we capture named entities, dates and times, percentages and monetary entities and normalize them. The tokens resulting from this can be multi-word because of named entities. This tokenization strategy gives us the best results among all our three runs. For capturing and normalizing the above mentioned expressions, we make use of the Stanford NER Toolkit (Finkel et al., 2005). Some normalized samples are mentioned in figure 2.

When grading the similarity of multi-word tokens, we use a second level maximal bipartite match, which is normalized by the smaller of the two multi-word token lengths. Thus, similarity between two multi-word tokens t_1 and t_2 is defined as:
$sim(t_1, t_2) = \frac{MaximalBipartiteMatchSum(t_1,t_2)}{min(words(t_1),words(t_2))}$

This was done to ensure that a complete named entity in the first sentence matches exactly with a partial named entity (indicating the same entity as the first) in the second sentence. For eg. *John Doe vs John* will be given a score of 1. Such occurrences are frequent in the task datasets. For the sentence similarity, the score defined in System 1 is used, where the token length of a sentence is the number of multi-word tokens in it.

5.1 Results

Refer to figures 3 and 4 for results.

This system gives the best results among all our systems. The credit for this improvement can be attributed to recognition and normalization of named entities, dates and times, percentages and monetary entities, as the datasets provided contain these in fairly large numbers.

6 SYSTEM 3

In System 3, in addition to System 2, we heuristically capture compound nouns, adjectivally and numerically modified words like 'passenger plane', 'easy job', '10 years' etc. using the POS based regular expression

$$[JJ|NN|CD]^*NN$$

POS Tagging is done using the Stanford POS Tagger Toolkit (Toutanova et al., 2003).

To make matching more context dependent, rather than just a bag of words approach, we naively attempt to capture the similarity of the contexts of two tokens. We define the context of a word in a sentence as all the words in the sentence which are grammatically related to it. The grammatical relations are all the collapsed dependencies produced by the Stanford Dependency parser (Marneffe et al., 2006). The context of a multi-word token is defined as the union of contexts of all the words in it. We further filter the context by removing stop-words and punctuations in it. The contexts of two tokens are then used to obtain context/syntactic similarity between tokens, which is defined using the Jaccard Similarity Measure:

$$Jaccard(C_1, C_2) = \frac{|C_1 \cap C_2|}{|C_1 \cup C_2|}$$

A linear combination of word similarity and context similarity is taken as an edge weight in the token-token similarity bipartite graph. Motivated by (Li et al., 2006), we chose a ratio of 4:1 for lexical similarity to context similarity.

As in System 2, for multi-word token similarity, we use a second level maximal bipartite match, normalized by smaller of the two token lengths. This helps in matching multi-word tokens expressing the same meaning with score 1, for e.g. *passenger plane* VS *Cuban plane*, *divided Supreme Court* VS *Supreme Court* etc. The sentence similarity score is the same as the one defined in System 2.

6.1 Results

Refer to figures 3 and 4 for results.

This system gives a reduced performance compared to our other systems. This could be due to various factors. Capturing adjectivally and numerically modified words could be done using grammatical dependencies instead of a heuristic POS-tag regular expression. Also, token-token similarity should be handled in a more precise way than a generic second level maximal bipartite match. A better context capturing method can further improve the system.

7 Conclusions

Among the three systems proposed for the task, System 2 performs best on the test datasets, primarily because it identifies named entities as single entities, normalizes dates, times, percentages and monetary figures. The results for System 3 suffer because of naive context capturing. A better job can be done using syntacto-semantic structured representations for the sentences. The performance of our systems are compared with (Li et al., 2006) on the test datasets in figure 3. This highlights the improvement of maximal weighted bipartite matching over greedy matching.

8 Future Work

Our objective is to group words together which share a common meaning. This includes grouping adjectival, adverbial, numeric modifiers with the modified word, group the words of a colloquial phrase together, capture multi-word expressions, etc. These word-clusters will form the vertices of the bipartite graph. The other challenge then is to come up with a suitable cluster-cluster similarity measure. NLP modules such as Lexical Substitution can help when we are using a word-word similarity measure at the core.

Acknowledgments

The authors would like to thank the anonymous reviewers for their valuable comments and suggestions to improve the quality of the paper.

References

Dan Klein and Christopher D. Manning. 2003. *Accurate Unlexicalized Parsing*. Proceedings of the 41st Meeting of the Association for Computational Linguistics, pp. 423-430.

Eduard Hovy, Mitchell Marcus, Martha Palmer, Lance Ramshaw and Ralph Weischedel. 2006. *OntoNotes: The 90% Solution*. Proceedings of HLT/NAACL, New York, 2006.

Eneko Agirre, Daniel Cer, Mona Diab and Aitor Gonzalez-Agirre. 2012. *SemEval-2012 Task 6: A Pilot on Semantic Textual Similarity*. In Proceedings of the 6th International Workshop on Semantic Evaluation (SemEval 2012), in conjunction with the First Joint Conference on Lexical and Computational Semantics (*SEM 2012).

G. Minnen, J. Carroll and D. Pearce. 2001. *Applied morphological processing of English*. Natural Language Engineering, 7(3). 207-223.

Harold W. Kuhn. 1955. *The Hungarian Method for the assignment problem*. Naval Research Logistics Quarterly, 2:8397, 1955.

Jenny Rose Finkel, Trond Grenager, and Christopher Manning. 2005. *Incorporating Non-local Information into Information Extraction Systems by Gibbs Sampling*. Proceedings of the 43nd Annual Meeting of the Association for Computational Linguistics (ACL 2005), pp. 363-370

Kilgarriff and J. Rosenzweig. 2000. *English SENSEVAL : Report and Results*. In Proceedings of the 2nd International Conference on Language Resources and Evaluation, LREC, Athens, Greece.

Kristina Toutanova, Dan Klein, Christopher Manning, and Yoram Singer. 2003. *Feature-Rich Part-of-Speech Tagging with a Cyclic Dependency Network*. In Proceedings of HLT-NAACL 2003, pp. 252-259.

Lin, D. 1998a. *An information-theoretic definition of similarity*. In Proceedings of the International Conference on Machine Learning.

Lin, D. 1998b. *Automatic Retrieval and Clustering of Similar Words.*. In Proceedings of COLING-ACL 1998, Montreal.

Marie-Catherine de Marneffe, Bill MacCartney and Christopher D. Manning. 2006. *Generating Typed Dependency Parses from Phrase Structure Parses*. In LREC 2006.

Palakorn Achananuparp, Xiaohua Hu and Shen Xiajiong. 2008. *The Evaluation of Sentence Similarity Measures*. Science And Technology, 5182, 305-316. Springer.

Peter Kolb. 2008. *DISCO: A Multilingual Database of Distributionally Similar Words*. In Proceedings of KONVENS-2008, Berlin.

Steven Bird, Ewan Klein, and Edward Loper. 2009. *Natural Language Processing with Python - Analyzing Text with the Natural Language Toolkit*. O'Reilly Media, 2009

Xiao-Ying Liu, Yi-Ming Zhou, Ruo-Shi Zheng. 2008. *Measuring Semantic Similarity Within Sentences*. Proceedings of the Seventh International Conference on Machine Learning and Cybernetics, Kunming.

Yuhua Li, David McLean, Zuhair A. Bandar, James D. OShea, and Keeley Crockett. 2006. *Sentence Similarity Based on Semantic Nets and Corpus Statistics*. IEEE Transections on Knowledge and Data Engineering, Vol. 18, No. 8

Weiwei: A Simple Unsupervised Latent Semantics based Approach for Sentence Similarity

Weiwei Guo
Department of Computer Science,
Columbia University,
weiwei@cs.columbia.edu

Mona Diab
Center for Computational Learning Systems,
Columbia University,
mdiab@ccls.columbia.edu

Abstract

The Semantic Textual Similarity (STS) shared task (Agirre et al., 2012) computes the degree of semantic equivalence between two sentences.[1] We show that a simple unsupervised latent semantics based approach, Weighted Textual Matrix Factorization that only exploits bag-of-words features, can outperform most systems for this task. The key to the approach is to carefully handle missing words that are not in the sentence, and thus rendering it superior to Latent Semantic Analysis (LSA) and Latent Dirichlet Allocation (LDA). Our system ranks 20 out of 89 systems according to the official evaluation metric for the task, Pearson correlation, and it ranks 10/89 and 19/89 in the other two evaluation metrics employed by the organizers.

1 Introduction

Identifying the degree of semantic similarity [SS] between two sentences is helpful for many NLP topics. In Machine Translation (Kauchak and Barzilay, 2006) and Text Summarization (Zhou et al., 2006), results are automatically evaluated based on sentence comparison. In Text Coherence Detection (Lapata and Barzilay, 2005), sentences are linked together by similar or related words. For Word Sense Disambiguation, researchers (Banerjee and Pedersen, 2003; Guo and Diab, 2012a) construct a sense similarity measure from the sentence similarity of the sense definitions.

Almost all SS approaches decompose the task into word pairwise similarity problems. For example, Islam and Inkpen (2008) create a matrix for each sentence pair, where columns are the words in the first sentence and rows are the words in the second sentence, and each cell stores the distributional similarity of the two words. Then they create an alignment between words in two sentences, and sentence similarity is calculated based on the sum of the similarity of aligned word pairs. There are two disadvantages with word similarity based approaches: 1. lexical ambiguity as the word pairwise similarity ignores the semantic interaction between the word and sentence/context. 2. word co-occurrence information is not as sufficiently exploited as they are in latent variable models such as Latent Semantic Analysis (LSA) (Landauer et al., 1998) and Latent Dirichilet Allocation (LDA) (Blei et al., 2003). On the other hand, latent variable models can solve the two issues naturally by modeling the semantics of words and sentences simultaneously in the low-dimensional latent space.

However, attempts at addressing SS using LSA perform significantly below word similarity based models (Mihalcea et al., 2006; O'Shea et al., 2008). We believe the reason is that the observed words in a sentence are too few for latent variable models to learn robust semantics. For example, given the two sentences of WordNet sense definitions for $bank\#n\#1$ and $stock\#n\#1$:

bank#n#1: *a financial institution that accepts deposits and channels the money into lending activities*

stock#n#1: *the capital raised by a corporation through the issue of shares entitling holders to an ownership interest (equity)*

LDA can only find the dominant topic (the $financial$ topic) based on the observed words without further discernibility. In this case, many sen-

[1]Mona Diab, co-author of this paper, is one of the task organizers

tences will share the same latent semantics profile, as long as they are in the same topic/domain.

In our work (Guo and Diab, 2012b), we propose to model the missing words (words that are not in the sentence) to address the sparseness issue for the SS task. Our intuition is since observed words in a sentence are too few to tell us what the sentence is about, missing words can be used to tell us what the sentence is **not** about. We assume that the semantic space of both the observed and missing words make up the complete semantic profile of a sentence. We implement our idea using a weighted matrix factorization approach (Srebro and Jaakkola, 2003), which allows us to treat observed words and missing words differently.

It should be noted that our approach is very general (similar to LSA/LDA) in that it can be applied to any genre of short texts, in a manner different from existing work that models short texts by using additional data, e.g., Ramage et al. (2010) model tweets using their metadata (author, hashtag, etc). Also we do not extract additional features such as multiwords expression or syntax from sentences – all we use is bag-of-words feature.

2 Related Work

Almost all current SS methods work in the high-dimensional word space, and rely heavily on word/sense similarity measures. The word/sense similarity measure is either knowledge based (Li et al., 2006; Feng et al., 2008; Ho et al., 2010; Tsatsaronis et al., 2010), corpus-based (Islam and Inkpen, 2008) or hybrid (Mihalcea et al., 2006). Almost all of them are evaluated on a data set introduced in (Li et al., 2006). The LI06 data set consists of 65 pairs of noun definitions selected from the Collin Cobuild Dictionary. A subset of 30 pairs is further selected by LI06 to render the similarity scores evenly distributed. Our approach has outperformed most of the previous methods on LI06 achieving the second best Pearson's correlation and the best Spearman correlation (Guo and Diab, 2012b).

3 Learning Latent Semantics of Sentences

3.1 Intuition

Given only a few observed words in a sentence, there are many hypotheses of latent vectors that are highly related to the observed words. Therefore, missing

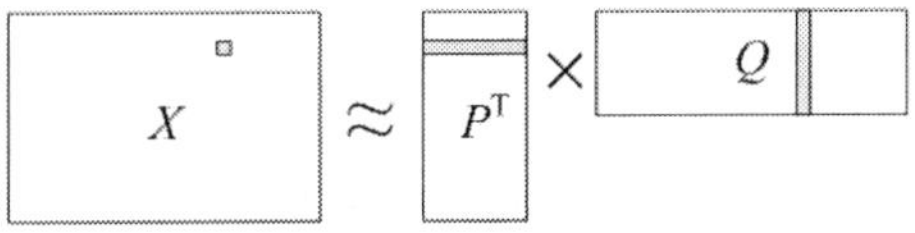

Figure 1: Matrix Factorization

words can be used to prune the hypotheses that are also highly related to the missing words.

Consider the hypotheses of latent vectors in Table 1 for the sentence of the WordNet definition of $bank\#n\#1$. Assume there are 3 dimensions in our latent model: *financial, sport, institution*. We use R_o^v to denote the sum of relatedness between latent vector v and all observed words; similarly, R_m^v is the sum of relatedness between the vector v and all missing words. Hypothesis v_1 is given by topic models, where only the $financial$ sentence is found, and it has the maximum relatedness to observed words in $bank\#n\#1$ sentence $R_o^{v_1}$=20. v_2 is the ideal latent vector, since it also detects that $bank\#n\#1$ is related to $institution$. It has a slightly smaller $R_o^{v_2}$=18, but more importantly, relatedness to missing words $R_m^{v_2}$=300 is substantially smaller than $R_m^{v_1}$=600.

However, we cannot simply choose a hypothesis with the maximum $R_o - R_m$ value, since v_3, which is clearly not related to $bank\#n\#1$ but with a minimum R_m=100, will be our final answer. The solution is straightforward: give a smaller weight to missing words, e.g., so that the algorithm tries to select a hypothesis with maximum value of $R_o - 0.01 \times R_m$. To implement this idea, we model the missing words in the weighted matrix factorization framework [WMF] (Srebro and Jaakkola, 2003).

3.2 Modeling Missing Words by Weighted Matrix Factorization

Given a corpus we represent the corpus as an $M \times N$ matrix X. The row entries of the matrix are the unique N words in the corpus, and the M columns are the sentence ids of all the sentences. The yielded $N \times M$ co-occurrence matrix X comprises the TF-IDF values in each X_{ij} cell, namely that TF-IDF value of word w_i in sentence s_j.

In WMF, the original matrix X is factorized into two matrices such that $X \approx P^{\top}Q$, where P is a $K \times M$ matrix, and Q is a $K \times N$ matrix (Figure 1). In this scenario, the latent semantics of each word w_i or sentence s_j is represented as a K-dimension vector

	financial	sport	institution	R_o	R_m	$R_o - R_m$	$R_o - 0.01R_m$
v_1	1	0	0	***20***	***600***	-580	14
v_2	0.6	0	0.1	18	300	-282	***15***
v_3	0.2	0.3	0.2	5	100	***-95***	4

Table 1: Three possible hypotheses of latent vectors for definition of $bank\#n\#1$

$P_{\cdot,i}$ or $Q_{\cdot,j}$. Note that the inner product of $P_{\cdot,i}$ and $Q_{\cdot,j}$ is used to approximate the semantic relatedness of word w_i and sentence s_j: $X_{ij} \approx P_{\cdot,i} \cdot Q_{\cdot,j}$, as the shaded parts in Figure 1.

In WMF each cell is associated with a weight, so missing words cells (X_{ij}=0) can have a much less contribution than observed words. Assume w_m is the weight for missing words cells. The latent vectors of words P and sentences Q are estimated by minimizing the objective function:

$$\sum_i \sum_j W_{ij} \left(P_{\cdot,i} \cdot Q_{\cdot,j} - X_{ij}\right)^2 + \lambda ||P||_2^2 + \lambda ||Q||_2^2$$
$$\text{where } W_{i,j} = \begin{cases} 1, & \text{if } X_{ij} \neq 0 \\ w_m, & \text{if } X_{ij} = 0 \end{cases} \quad (1)$$

Equation 1 explicitly requires the latent vector of sentence $Q_{\cdot,j}$ to be not related to missing words ($P_{\cdot,i} \cdot Q_{\cdot,j}$ should be close to 0 for missing words $X_{ij} = 0$). Also weight w_m for missing words is very small to make sure latent vectors such as v_3 in Table 1 will not be chosen. In experiments we set $w_m = 0.01$. We refer to our approach as Weighted Textual Matrix Factorization (WTMF).

After we run WTMF on the sentence corpus, the similarity of the two sentences s_j and s_k can be computed by the inner product of $Q_{\cdot,j}$ and $Q_{\cdot,k}$.

3.3 Inference

The latent vectors in P and Q are first randomly initialized, then can be computed iteratively by the following equations (derivation is omitted due to limited space, but can be found in (Srebro and Jaakkola, 2003)):

$$P_{\cdot,i} = \left(Q\tilde{W}^{(i)}Q^\top + \lambda I\right)^{-1} Q\tilde{W}^{(i)}X_{i,\cdot}^\top$$
$$Q_{\cdot,j} = \left(P\tilde{W}^{(j)}P^\top + \lambda I\right)^{-1} P\tilde{W}^{(i)}X_{\cdot,j} \quad (2)$$

where $\tilde{W}^{(i)} = \text{diag}(W_{\cdot,i})$ is an $M \times M$ diagonal matrix containing ith row of weight matrix W. Similarly, $\tilde{W}^{(j)} = \text{diag}(W_{\cdot,j})$ is an $N \times N$ diagonal matrix containing jth column of W.

Since most of the cells have the same value of 0, the inference can be further optimized to save computation, which has been described in (Steck, 2010).

4 Data Preprocessing

The data sets for WTMF comprises two dictionaries WordNet (Fellbaum, 1998), Wiktionary,[2] and the Brown corpus. We did not link the senses between WordNet and Wiktionary, therefore the definition sentences are simply treated as individual documents. We crawl Wiktionary and remove the entries that are not tagged as noun, verb, adjective, or adverb, resulting in 220,000 entries. For both WordNet and Wiktionary, target words are added to the definition (e.g. the word *bank* is added into the definition sentence of $bank\#n\#1$). Also usage examples are appended to definition sentences (hence sentences become short texts). For the Brown corpus, each sentence is treated as a document in order to create more co-occurrence. The importance of words in a sentence is estimated by the TF-IDF schema.

All data is tokenized, pos-tagged[3], and lemmatized[4]. To reduce word sparsity issue, we take an additional preprocessing step: for each lemmatized word, we find all its possible lemmas, and choose the most frequent lemma according to WordNet::QueryData. For example, the word *thinkings* is first lemmatized as *thinking*, then we discover *thinking* has possible lemmas *thinking* and *think*, finally we choose *think* as targeted lemma. The STS data is also preprocessed using the same pipeline.

5 Experiments

5.1 Setting

STS data: The sentence pair data in the STS task is collected from five sources: 1. MSR Paraphrase corpus (Dolan et al., 2004), 2. MSR video data (Chen and Dolan, 2011), 3. SMT europarl data,

[2]http://en.wiktionary.org/wiki/Wiktionary:Main_Page

[3]http://nlp.stanford.edu/software/tagger.shtml

[4]http://wn-similarity.sourceforge.net, WordNet::QueryData

models	MSRpar	MSRvid	SMT-eur	ON-WN	SMT-news
LDA	0.274	0.7682	0.452	0.619	0.366
WTMF	0.411(67/89)	0.835(11/89)	0.513(10/89)	0.727(1/89)	0.438(28/89)

Table 2: Performance of LDA and WTMF on each individual test set of Task 6 STS data

ALL	ALLnrm	Mean
0.695(20/89)	0.830(10/89)	0.608(19/89)

Table 3: Performance of WTMF on all test sets

4. OntoNotes-WordNet data (Hovy et al., 2006), 5. SMT news data.

Evaluation Metrics: Since the systems are required to assigned a similarity score to each sentence pair, Pearson's correlation is used to measure the performance of systems on each of the 5 data sets. However, measuring the overall performance on the concatenation of 5 data sets is rarely discussed in previous work. Accordingly the organizers of STS task provide three evaluation metrics: 1. ALL: Pearson correlation with the gold standard for the combined 5 data sets. 2. ALLnrm: Pearson correlation after the system outputs for each data set are fitted to the gold standard using least squares. 3. Mean: Weighted mean across the 5 data sets, where the weight depends on the number of pairs in the dataset.

WTMF Model: Our model is built on WordNet+Wiktionary+Brown+training data of STS. Each sentence of STS test data is transformed into a latent vector using Equation 2. Then sentence pair similarity is computed by the cosine similarity of the two latent vectors. We employ the parameters used in (Guo and Diab, 2012b) ($\lambda = 20, w_m = 0.01$).

5.2 Results

Table 3 summarizes the overall performance of WTMF on the concatenation of 5 data sets followed by the corresponding rank among all participating systems.[5] There are 88 submitted results in total and 1 baseline which is simply the cosine similarity of surface word vectors.

Table 2 compares the individual performance of LDA (trained on the same corpus) and WTMF on each data set. WTMF outperforms LDA by a large margin. This is because LDA only uses 10 observed words to infer a 100 dimension vector, while WTMF takes advantage of much more missing words to learn more robust latent semantic vectors.

WTMF model achieves great overall performance, with ranks 20, 10, 19 out of 89 reported results in three evaluation metrics respectively. It is worth noting that WTMF is unsupervised in that it does not use the training data similarity values, also the only feature WTMF uses is bag-of-words features without other information such as syntax, sentiment, etc. indicating that these additional features could lead to even more improvement.

Observing the individual performance on each of the 5 data set, we find WTMF ranks relatively high in the four data sets: MSRvid (11/89), SMT-eur (11/89), ON-WN (1/89), SMT-news (28/89). However, WTMF is outperformed by most of the systems on MSRpar data set (67/89). We analyze the data set and find that different from the other four data sets, MSRpar is related to a lot of other NLP topics such as textual entailment or sentiment coherence. Therefore, our feature set (bag of words) is too shallow for this data set indicating that using syntax and more semantically oriented features could be helpful.

6 Conclusions

We introduce a new latent variable model WTMF that is competitive with high dimensional approaches to the STS task. In WTMF model, we explicitly model missing words to alleviate the sparsity problem in modeling short texts. For future work, we would like to combine our methods with existing word similarity based approaches and add more nuanced features incorporating syntax and semantics in the latent model.

Acknowledgments

This research was funded by the Office of the Director of National Intelligence (ODNI), Intelligence Advanced Research Projects Activity (IARPA), through the U.S. Army Research Lab. All statements of fact, opinion or conclusions contained herein are those of the authors and should not be construed as representing the official views or policies of IARPA, the ODNI or the U.S. Government.

[5] http://www.cs.york.ac.uk/semeval-2012/task6/index.php?id=results-update

References

Eneko Agirre, Daniel Cer, Mona Diab, and Aitor Gonzalez-Agirre. 2012. Semeval-2012 task 6: A pilot on semantic textual similarity. In *Proceedings of the 6th International Workshop on Semantic Evaluation (SemEval 2012), in conjunction with the First Joint Conference on Lexical and Computational Semantics (*SEM 2012)*.

Satanjeev Banerjee and Ted Pedersen. 2003. Extended gloss overlaps as a measure of semantic relatedness. In *Proceedings of the 18th International Joint Conference on Artificial Intelligence*, pages 805–810.

David M. Blei, Andrew Y. Ng, and Michael I. Jordan. 2003. Latent dirichlet allocation. *Journal of Machine Learning Research*, 3.

David L. Chen and William B. Dolan. 2011. Collecting highly parallel data for paraphrase evaluation. In *Proceedings of the 49th Annual Meeting of the Association for Computational Linguistics*.

William Dolan, Chris Quirk, and Chris Brockett. 2004. Unsupervised construction of large paraphrase corpora: Exploiting massively parallel news sources. In *Proceedings of the 20th International Conference on Computational Linguistics*.

Christiane Fellbaum. 1998. *WordNet: An Electronic Lexical Database*. MIT Press.

Jin Feng, Yi-Ming Zhou, and Trevor Martin. 2008. Sentence similarity based on relevance. In *Proceedings of IPMU*.

Weiwei Guo and Mona Diab. 2012a. Learning the latent semantics of a concept from its definition. In *Proceedings of the 50th Annual Meeting of the Association for Computational Linguistics*.

Weiwei Guo and Mona Diab. 2012b. Modeling sentences in the latent space. In *Proceedings of the 50th Annual Meeting of the Association for Computational Linguistics*.

Chukfong Ho, Masrah Azrifah Azmi Murad, Rabiah Abdul Kadir, and Shyamala C. Doraisamy. 2010. Word sense disambiguation-based sentence similarity. In *Proceedings of the 23rd International Conference on Computational Linguistics*.

Eduard Hovy, Mitchell Marcus, Martha Palmer, Lance Ramshaw, and Ralph Weischedel. 2006. Ontonotes: The 90% solution. In *Proceedings of the Human Language Technology Conference of the North American Chapter of the ACL*.

Aminul Islam and Diana Inkpen. 2008. Semantic text similarity using corpus-based word similarity and string similarity. *ACM Transactions on Knowledge Discovery from Data*, 2.

David Kauchak and Regina Barzilay. 2006. Paraphrasing for automatic evaluation. In *Proceedings of the Human Language Technology Conference of the North American Chapter of the ACL*.

Thomas K Landauer, Peter W. Foltz, and Darrell Laham. 1998. An introduction to latent semantic analysis. *Discourse Processes*, 25.

Mirella Lapata and Regina Barzilay. 2005. Automatic evaluation of text coherence: Models and representations. In *Proceedings of the 19th International Joint Conference on Artificial Intelligence*.

Yuhua Li, Davi d McLean, Zuhair A. Bandar, James D. O Shea, and Keeley Crockett. 2006. Sentence similarity based on semantic nets and corpus statistics. *IEEE Transaction on Knowledge and Data Engineering*, 18.

Rada Mihalcea, Courtney Corley, and Carlo Strapparava. 2006. Corpus-based and knowledge-based measures of text semantic similarity. In *Proceedings of the 21st National Conference on Articial Intelligence*.

James O'Shea, Zuhair Bandar, Keeley Crockett, and David McLean. 2008. A comparative study of two short text semantic similarity measures. In *Proceedings of the Agent and Multi-Agent Systems: Technologies and Applications, Second KES International Symposium (KES-AMSTA)*.

Daniel Ramage, Susan Dumais, and Dan Liebling. 2010. Characterizing microblogs with topic models. In *Proceedings of the Fourth International AAAI Conference on Weblogs and Social Media*.

Nathan Srebro and Tommi Jaakkola. 2003. Weighted low-rank approximations. In *Proceedings of the Twentieth International Conference on Machine Learning*.

Harald Steck. 2010. Training and testing of recommender systems on data missing not at random. In *Proceedings of the 16th ACM SIGKDD International Conference on Knowledge Discovery and Data Mining*.

George Tsatsaronis, Iraklis Varlamis, and Michalis Vazirgiannis. 2010. Text relatedness based on a word thesaurus. *Journal of Articial Intelligence Research*, 37.

Liang Zhou, Chin-Yew Lin, Dragos Stefan Munteanu, and Eduard Hovy. 2006. Paraeval: Using paraphrases to evaluate summaries automatically. In *Proceedings of Human Language Tech-nology Conference of the North American Chapter of the ACL,*.

UNIBA: Distributional Semantics for Textual Similarity

Annalina Caputo **Pierpaolo Basile** **Giovanni Semeraro**
Department of Computer Science
University of Bari "Aldo Moro"
Via E. Orabona, 4 - 70125 Bari, Italy
{acaputo, basilepp, semeraro}@di.uniba.it

Abstract

We report the results of UNIBA participation in the first SemEval-2012 Semantic Textual Similarity task. Our systems rely on distributional models of words automatically inferred from a large corpus. We exploit three different semantic word spaces: Random Indexing (RI), Latent Semantic Analysis (LSA) over RI, and vector permutations in RI. Runs based on these spaces consistently outperform the baseline on the proposed datasets.

1 Background and Related Research

SemEval-2012 Semantic Textual Similarity (STS) task (Agirre et al., 2012) aims at providing a general framework to "*examine the degree of semantic equivalence between two sentences.*"

We propose an approach to Semantic Textual Similarity based on distributional models of words, where the geometrical metaphor of meaning is exploited. Distributional models are grounded on the *distributional hypothesis* (Harris, 1968), according to which the meaning of a word is determined by the set of textual contexts in which it appears. These models represent words as vectors in a high dimensional vector space. Word vectors are built from a large corpus in such a way that vector dimensions reflect the different uses (or *contexts*) of a word in the corpus. Hence, the meaning of a word is defined by its use, and words used in similar contexts are represented by vectors near in the space. In this way, semantically related words like "basketball" and "volleyball", which occur frequently in similar contexts, say with words "court, play, player", will be represented by near points. Different definitions of contexts give rise to different (semantic) spaces. A context can be a document, a sentence or a fixed window of surrounding words. Contexts and words can be stored through a co-occurrence matrix, whose columns correspond to contexts, and rows to words. Therefore, the strength of the semantic association between words can be computed as the cosine similarity of their vector representations.

Latent Semantic Analysis (Deerwester et al., 1990), BEAGLE (Jones and Mewhort, 2007), Random Indexing (Kanerva, 1988), Hyperspace Analogue to Language (Burgess et al., 1998), WordSpace (Schütze and Pedersen, 1995) are all techniques conceived to build up semantic spaces. However, all of them intend to represent semantics at a word scale. Although vectors addition and multiplication are two well defined operations suitable for composing words in semantic spaces, they miss taking into account the underlying syntax, which regulates the compositionality of words. Some efforts toward this direction are emerging (Clark and Pulman, 2007; Clark et al., 2008; Mitchell and Lapata, 2010; Coecke et al., 2010; Basile et al., 2011; Clarke, 2012), which resulted in theoretical work corroborated by empirical evaluation on how small fragments of text compose (e.g. noun-noun, adjective-noun, and verb-noun pairs).

2 Methodology

Our approach to STS is inspired by the latest developments about semantic compositionality and distributional models. The general methodology is based on the construction of a semantic space endowed with a vector addition operator. The vector addition sums the word vectors of each pair of sentences involved in the evaluation. The result consists of two vectors whose similarity can be computed by cosine similarity. However, this simple methodology translates a text into a mere bag-of-word representation, depriving the text of its syntactic construction, which also influences the overall meaning of the sentence. In order to deal with this limit, we experiment two classical methods for building a semantic space, namely Random Indexing and Latent Semantic Analysis, along with a new method based on vector permutations, which tries to encompass syntactic information directly into the resulting space.

2.1 Random Indexing

Our first method is based on Random Indexing (RI), introduced by Kanerva (Kanerva, 1988). This technique allows us to build a semantic space with no need for (either term-document or term-term) matrix factorization, because vectors are inferred by using an incremental strategy. Moreover, it allows us to solve efficiently the problem of reducing dimensions, which is one of the key features used to uncover the "latent semantic dimensions" of a word distribution.

RI[1] (Widdows and Ferraro, 2008) is based on the concept of Random Projection according to which high dimensional vectors chosen randomly are "nearly orthogonal".

Formally, given an $n \times m$ matrix A and an $m \times k$ matrix R made up of k m-dimensional random vectors, we define a new $n \times k$ matrix B as follows:

$$B^{n,k} = A^{n,m} \cdot R^{m,k} \quad k << m \tag{1}$$

The new matrix B has the property to preserve the distance between points scaled by a multiplicative factor (Johnson and Lindenstrauss, 1984).

Specifically, RI creates the semantic space $B^{n,k}$ in two steps (we consider a fixed window w of terms as context):

1. A *context vector* is assigned to each term. This vector is sparse, high-dimensional and ternary, which means that its elements can take values in {-1, 0, 1}. A context vector contains a small number of randomly distributed non-zero elements, and the structure of this vector follows the hypothesis behind the concept of Random Projection;

2. Context vectors are accumulated by analyzing co-occurring terms in a window w. The *semantic vector* for a term is computed as the sum of the context vectors for terms which co-occur in w.

[1]An implementation of RI can be found at: http://code.google.com/p/semanticvectors/

2.2 Latent Semantic Analysis

Latent Semantic Analysis (Deerwester et al., 1990) relies on the Singular Value Decomposition (SVD) of a term-document co-occurrence matrix. Given a matrix $\mathbf{M}$, it can be decomposed in the product of three matrices $\mathbf{U\Sigma V}^\top$, where $\mathbf{U}$ and $\mathbf{V}$ are the orthonormal matrices and $\mathbf{\Sigma}$ is the diagonal matrix of *singular values* of $\mathbf{M}$ placed in decreasing order. Computing the LSA on the co-occurrence matrix $\mathbf{M}$ can be a computationally expensive task, as a corpus can contain thousands of terms. Hence, we decided to apply LSA to the reduced approximation generated by RI. It is important to point out that no truncation of singular values is performed. Since computing the similarity between any two words is equal to taking the corresponding entry in the $\mathbf{MM}^\top$ matrix, we can exploit the relation

$$\mathbf{MM}^\top = \mathbf{U\Sigma V}^\top\mathbf{V\Sigma}^\top\mathbf{U}^\top = \mathbf{U\Sigma\Sigma}^\top\mathbf{U}^\top = (\mathbf{U\Sigma})(\mathbf{U\Sigma})^\top$$

Hence, the application of LSA to RI makes possible to represent each word in the $\mathbf{U\Sigma}$ space.

A similar approach was investigated by Sellberg and Jönsson (2008) for retrieval of similar FAQs in a Question Answering system. Authors showed that halving the matrix dimension by applying the RI resulted in a drastic reduction of LSA computation time. Certainly there was also a performance price to be paid, however general performance was better than VSM and RI respectively. We also experimented LSA computed on RI versus LSA applied to the original matrix during the tuning of our systems. Surprisingly, we found that LSA applied on the reduced matrix gives better results than LSA. However, these results are not reported as they are not the focus of this evaluation.

2.3 Vector Permutations in RI

The classical distributional models can handle only one definition of context at a time, such as the whole document or the window w. A method to add information about context in RI is proposed in (Sahlgren et al., 2008). The authors describe a strategy to encode word order in RI by the permutation of coordinates in *context vector*. When the coordinates are shuffled using a random permutation, the resulting vector is nearly orthogonal to the original one. That operation corresponds to the generation of a new random vector. Moreover, by applying a predetermined mechanism to obtain random permutations, such as elements rotation, it is always possible to reconstruct the original vector using the reverse permutations. By exploiting this strategy it is possible to obtain different random vectors for each context in which the term occurs.

Our idea is to encode syntactic dependencies using vector permutations. A syntactic dependency between two words is defined as $dep(head, dependent)$, where dep is the syntactic link which connects the $dependent$ word to the $head$ word. Generally speaking, $dependent$ is the modifier, object or complement, while $head$ plays a key role in determining the behavior of the link. For example, $subj(eat, cat)$ means that "cat" is the subject of "eat". In that case the $head$ word is "eat", which plays the role of verb.

The key idea is to encode in the semantic space information about syntactic dependencies which link words together. Rather than representing the kind of dependency, our focus is to encompass information about the existence of such a relation between words in the construction of the space. The method adopted to construct a semantic space that takes into account both syntactic dependencies and Random Indexing can be defined as follows:

1. a context vector is assigned to each term, as described in Section 2.1 (Random Indexing);

2. context vectors are accumulated by analyzing terms which are linked by a dependency. In particular the semantic vector for each term t_i is computed as the sum of the inverse-permuted context vectors for the terms t_j which are dependents of t_i, and the permuted vectors for the terms t_j which are heads of t_i. Moreover, the context vector of t_i, and those of t_j terms which appears in a dependency relation with it, are sum to the final semantic vector in order to provide distributional evidence of co-occurrence. Each permutation is computed as a forward/backward rotation of one element. If Π^1 is a permutation of one element, the inverse-permutation is defined as Π^{-1}: the elements rotation is performed by one left-shifting step.

Formally, denoting with $\mathbf{x}$ the context vector for a term, we compute the semantic vector for the term t_i as follows:

$$\mathrm{s_i} = \mathrm{x_i} + \sum_{\substack{j \\ \forall dep(t_i,t_j)}} (\Pi^{-1}\mathrm{x_j} + \mathrm{x_j}) + \sum_{\substack{k \\ \forall dep(t_k,t_i)}} (\Pi^{1}\mathrm{x_k} + \mathrm{x_k})$$

Adding permuted vectors to the head word and inverse-permuted vectors to the corresponding dependent word allows to encode the information about both heads and dependents into the space. This approach is similar to the one investigated by (Cohen et al., 2010) to encode relations between medical terms.

3 Evaluation

Dataset Description. SemEval-2012 STS is a first attempt to provide a "*unified framework for the evaluation of modular semantic components.*" The task consists in computing the similarity between pair of texts, returning a similarity score. Sentences are extracted from five publicly available datasets: MSR (Paraphrase Microsoft Research Paraphrase Corpus, 750 pairs), MSR (Video Microsoft Research Video Description Corpus, 750 pairs), SMTeuroparl (WMT2008 development dataset, Europarl section, 459 pairs), SMTnews (news conversation sentence pairs from WMT, 399 pairs), and OnWN (pairs of sentences from Ontonotes and WordNet definition, 750 pairs). Humans rated each pair with values from 0 to 5. The evaluation is performed by comparing humans scores against systems performance through Pearson's correlation. The organizers propose three different ways to aggregate values from the datasets:

	ALL	Rank-ALL	ALLnrm	Rank-ALLNrm	Mean	Rank-Mean
baseline	*.3110*	*87*	*.6732*	*85*	*.4356*	*70*
UNIBA-RI	.6285	41	.7951	43	.5651	45
UNIBA-LSARI	.6221	44	.8079	30	.5728	40
UNIBA-DEPRI	.6141	46	.8027	38	.5891	31

Table 1: Evaluation results of Pearson's correlation.

	MSRpar	MSRvid	SMT-eur	On-WN	SMT-news
baseline	*.4334*	*.2996*	*.4542*	*.5864*	*.3908*
UNIBA- RI	.4128	.7612	.4531	.6306	**.4887**
UNIBA- LSARI	.3886	**.7908**	.4679	**.6826**	.4238
UNIBA- DEPRI	**.4542**	.7673	**.5126**	.6593	.4636

Table 2: Evaluation results of Pearson's correlation for individual datasets.

ALL Pearson correlation with the gold standard for the five datasets.

ALLnrm Pearson correlation after the system outputs for each dataset are fitted to the gold standard using least squares.

Mean Weighted mean across the five datasets, where the weight depends on the number of pairs in the dataset.

Experimental Setting. For the evaluation, we built Distributional Spaces using the WaCkypedia_EN corpus[2]. WaCkypedia_EN is based on a 2009 dump of the English Wikipedia (about 800 million tokens) and includes information about: part-of-speech, lemma and a full dependency parsing performed by MaltParser (Nivre et al., 2007). The three spaces described in Section 2 are built exploiting information about term windows and dependency parsing supplied by WaCkypedia. The total number of dependencies amounts to about 200 million.

The RI system is implemented in Java and relies on some portions of code publicly available in the Semantic Vectors package (Widdows and Ferraro, 2008), while for LSA we exploited the publicly available C library SVDLIBC[3].

We restricted the vocabulary to the 50,000 most frequent terms, with stop words removal and forcing the system to include terms which occur in the dataset. Hence, the dimension of the original matrix would have been 50,000×50,000.

[2]http://wacky.sslmit.unibo.it/doku.php?id=corpora

[3]http://tedlab.mit.edu/ dr/SVDLIBC/

Our approach involves some parameters. In particular, each semantic space needs to set up the dimension k of the space. All spaces use a dimension of 500 (resulting in a 50,000×500 matrix). The number of non-zero elements in the random vector is set to 10. When we apply LSA to the output space generated by the Random Indexing we hold all the 500 dimensions since during the tuning we observed a drop in performance when a lower dimension was set. The co-occurrence distance w between terms was set up to 4.

In order to compute the similarity between the vector representations of sentences we used the cosine similarity, and then we multiplied by 5 the obtained value.

Results. Table 1 shows the overall results obtained exploiting the different semantic spaces. We report the three proposed evaluation measures with the corresponding overall ranks with respect to the 89 runs submitted by participants. We submitted three different runs, each exploring a different semantic space: UNIBA-RI (based on Random Indexing), UNIBA-LSARI (based on LSA performed over RI outcome), and UNIBA-DEPRI (based on Random Indexing and vector permutations). Each proposed measure stresses different aspects. ALL is the Pearson's correlation computed over the concatenated dataset. As a consequence this measure ranks higher systems which obtain consistent better results. Conversely, ALLNrm normalizes results by scaling values obtained from each dataset, in this way it tries to give emphasis to systems trained on each dataset.

The result of these different perspective is that our three spaces rank differently according to each measure. It seems that UNIBA-RI is able to work better across all datasets, while UNIBA-LSARI gives the best results on specific datasets, even though all our methods are unsupervised and do not need training steps. A deeper analysis on each dataset is reported on Table 2. Here results seem to be at odds with Table 1.

Considering individual datasets, UNIBA-RI gives only once the best result, while UNIBA-LSARI and UNIBA-DEPRI are able to provide the best results twice. Generally, all results outperform the baseline, based on a simple keyword overlap. Lower results are obtained in MSRpar, we ascribe this result to the notably long sentences here involved. In particular, UNIBA-LSARI gives a result lower than the baseline, and in line with the one obtained by LSA during the tuning. Hence, we ascribe this low performance to the application of LSA method to this specific dataset. Only UNIBA-DEPRI was able to outperform the baseline in this dataset. This shows the usefulness of encoding syntactic features in semantic word space where longer sentences are involved. Generally, it is interesting to be noticed that our spaces perform rather well on short and similarly structured sentences, such as MSRvid and On-WN.

4 Conclusion

We reported evaluation results of our participation in Semantic Textual Similarity task. Our systems exploit distributional models to represent the semantics of words. Two of such spaces are based on a classical definition of context, such as a fixed window of surrounding words. A third spaces tries to encompass more definitions of context at once, as the syntactic structure that relates words in a corpus. Although simple, our methods have achieved generally good results, outperforming the baseline provided by the organizers.

References

Eneko Agirre, Daniel Cer, Mona Diab, and Aitor Gonzalez-Agirre. 2012. Semeval-2012 task 6: A pilot on semantic textual similarity. In *Proceedings of the 6th International Workshop on Semantic Evaluation (SemEval 2012), in conjunction with the First Joint Conference on Lexical and Computational Semantics (*SEM 2012)*.

Pierpaolo Basile, Annalina Caputo, and Giovanni Semeraro. 2011. Encoding syntactic dependencies by vector permutation. In *Proceedings of the EMNLP 2011 Workshop on GEometrical Models of Natural Language Semantics*, GEMS '11, pages 43–51, Stroudsburg, PA, USA. Association for Computational Linguistics.

Curt Burgess, Kay Livesay, and Kevin Lund. 1998. Explorations in context space: Words, sentences, discourse. *Discourse Processes*, 25(2-3):211–257.

Stephen Clark and Stephen Pulman. 2007. Combining symbolic and distributional models of meaning. In *Proceedings of the AAAI Spring Symposium on Quantum Interaction*, pages 52–55.

Stephen Clark, Bob Coecke, and Mehrnoosh Sadrzadeh. 2008. A compositional distributional model of meaning. In *Proceedings of the Second Quantum Interaction Symposium (QI-2008)*, pages 133–140.

Daoud Clarke. 2012. A context–theoretic framework for compositionality in distributional semantics. *Computational Linguistics*, 38(1):41–71.

Bob Coecke, Mehrnoosh Sadrzadeh, and Stephen Clark. 2010. Mathematical foundations for a compositional distributional model of meaning. *CoRR*, abs/1003.4394.

Trevor Cohen, Dominic Widdows, Roger W. Schvaneveldt, and Thomas C. Rindflesch. 2010. Logical leaps and quantum connectives: Forging paths through predication space. In *AAAI-Fall 2010 Symposium on Quantum Informatics for Cognitive, Social, and Semantic Processes*, pages 11–13.

Scott Deerwester, Susan T. Dumais, George W. Furnas, Thomas K. Landauer, and Richard Harshman. 1990. Indexing by latent semantic analysis. *Journal of the American Society for Information Science*, 41(6):391–407.

Zellig Harris. 1968. *Mathematical Structures of Language*. New York: Interscience.

William B. Johnson and Joram Lindenstrauss. 1984. Extensions of Lipschitz mappings into a Hilbert space. *Conference on Modern Analysis and Probability, Contemporary Mathematics*, 26:189–206.

Michael N. Jones and Douglas J. K. Mewhort. 2007. Representing word meaning and order information in a composite holographic lexicon. *Psychological Review*, 114(1):1–37.

Pentti Kanerva. 1988. *Sparse Distributed Memory*. MIT Press.

Jeff Mitchell and Mirella Lapata. 2010. Composition in distributional models of semantics. *Cognitive Science*, 34(8):1388–1429.

Joakim Nivre, Johan Hall, Jens Nilsson, Atanas Chanev, Gülsen Eryigit, Sandra Kübler, Svetoslav Marinov, and Erwin Marsi. 2007. Maltparser: A language-independent system for data-driven dependency parsing. *Natural Language Engineering*, 13(02):95–135.

Magnus Sahlgren, Anders Holst, and Pentti Kanerva. 2008. Permutations as a means to encode order in word space. In V. Sloutsky, B. Love, and K. Mcrae, editors, *Proceedings of the 30th Annual Meeting of the Cognitive Science Society (CogSci'08), July 23-26, Washington D.C., USA*, pages 1300–1305. Cognitive Science Society, Austin, TX.

Hinrich Schütze and Jan O. Pedersen. 1995. Information retrieval based on word senses. In *Proceedings of the 4th Annual Symposium on Document Analysis and Information Retrieval*, pages 161–175.

Linus Sellberg and Arne Jönsson. 2008. Using random indexing to improve singular value decomposition for latent semantic analysis. In Nicoletta Calzolari, Khalid Choukri, Bente Maegaard, Joseph Mariani, Jan Odjik, Stelios Piperidis, and Daniel Tapias, editors, *Proceedings of the Sixth International Conference on Language Resources and Evaluation (LREC2008)*, pages 2335–2338, Marrakech, Morocco. European Language Resources Association (ELRA).

Dominic Widdows and Kathleen Ferraro. 2008. Semantic Vectors: A Scalable Open Source Package and Online Technology Management Application. In Nicoletta Calzolari, Khalid Choukri, Bente Maegaard, Joseph Mariani, Jan Odjik, Stelios Piperidis, and Daniel Tapias, editors, *Proceedings of the 6th International Conference on Language Resources and Evaluation (LREC2008)*, pages 1183–1190, Marrakech, Morocco. European Language Resources Association (ELRA).

UNITOR: Combining Semantic Text Similarity functions through SV Regression

Danilo Croce, Paolo Annesi, Valerio Storch and Roberto Basili
Department of Enterprise Engineering
University of Roma, Tor Vergata
00133 Roma, Italy
{croce,annesi,storch,basili}@info.uniroma2.it

Abstract

This paper presents the UNITOR system that participated to the SemEval 2012 Task 6: Semantic Textual Similarity (STS). The task is here modeled as a Support Vector (SV) regression problem, where a similarity scoring function between text pairs is acquired from examples. The semantic relatedness between sentences is modeled in an unsupervised fashion through different similarity functions, each capturing a specific semantic aspect of the STS, e.g. syntactic vs. lexical or topical vs. paradigmatic similarity. The SV regressor effectively combines the different models, learning a scoring function that weights individual scores in a unique resulting STS. It provides a highly portable method as it does not depend on any manually built resource (e.g. WordNet) nor controlled, e.g. aligned, corpus.

1 Introduction

Semantic Textual Similarity (STS) measures the degree of semantic equivalence between two phrases or texts. An effective method to compute similarity between short texts or sentences has many applications in Natural Language Processing (Mihalcea et al., 2006) and related areas such as Information Retrieval, e.g. to improve the effectiveness of a semantic search engine (Sahami and Heilman, 2006), or databases, where text similarity can be used in schema matching to solve semantic heterogeneity (Islam and Inkpen, 2008).

STS is here modeled as a Support Vector (SV) regression problem, where a SV regressor learns the similarity function over text pairs. Regression learning has been already applied to different NLP tasks. In (Pang and Lee, 2005) it is applied to Opinion Mining, in particular to the rating-inference problem, wherein one must determine an author evaluation with respect to a multi-point scale. In (Albrecht and Hwa, 2007) a method is proposed for developing sentence-level MT evaluation metrics using regression learning without directly relying on human reference translations. In (Biadsy et al., 2008) it has been used to rank candidate sentences for the task of producing biographies from Wikipedia. Finally, in (Becker et al., 2011) SV regressor has been used to rank questions within their context in the multimodal tutorial dialogue problem.

In this paper, the semantic relatedness between two sentences is modeled as a combination of different similarity functions, each describing the analogy between the two texts according to a specific semantic perspective: in this way, we aim at capturing syntactic and lexical equivalences between sentences and exploiting either topical relatedness or paradigmatic similarity between individual words. The variety of semantic evidences that a system can employ here grows quickly, according to the genre and complexity of the targeted sentences. We thus propose to combine such a body of evidence to learn a comprehensive scoring function $y = f(\vec{x})$ over individual measures from labeled data through SV regression: y is the gold similarity score (provided by human annotators), while $\vec{x}$ is the vector of the different individual scores, provided by the chosen similarity functions. The regressor objective is to learn the proper combination of different functions redundantly applied in an unsupervised fashion, without involving any in-depth description of the target domain or prior knowledge. The resulting function selects and filters the most useful information and it is a highly portable method. In fact, it does not depend on manually built resources (e.g. WordNet), but mainly exploits distributional analysis of unlabeled corpora.

In Section 2, the employed similarity functions are described and the application of SV regression is presented. Finally, Section 3 discusses results on the SemEval 2012 - Task 6.

2 Combining different similarity function through SV regression

This section describes the UNITOR systems participating to the SemEval 2012 Task 6: in Section 2.1 the different similarity functions between sentence pairs are discussed, while Section 2.2 describes how the SV regression learning is applied.

2.1 STS functions

Each STS depends on a variety of linguistic aspects in data, e.g. syntactic or lexical information. While their supervised combination can be derived through SV regression, different unsupervised estimators of STS exist.

Lexical Overlap (LO). A basic similarity function is first employed as the *lexical overlap between sentences*, i.e. the cardinality of the set of words occurring in both sentences.

Document-oriented similarity based on Latent Semantic Analysis (LSA). This function captures latent semantic topics through LSA. The adjacency terms-by-documents matrix is first acquired through the distributional analysis of a corpus and reduced through the application of Singular Value Decomposition (SVD), as described in (Landauer and Dumais, 1997). In this work, the individual sentences are assumed as pseudo documents and represented by vectors in the lower dimensional LSA space. The cosine similarity between vectors of a sentence pair is the metric hereafter referred to as *topical similarity*.

Compositional Distributional Semantics (CDS). Lexical similarity can also be extended to account for syntactic compositions between words. This makes sentence similarity to depend on the set of individual compounds, e.g. subject-verb relationship instances. While basic lexical information can still be obtained by distributional analysis, phrase level similarity can be here modeled as a specific function of the co-occurring words, i.e. a complex algebraic composition of their corresponding word vectors. Differently from the document-oriented case used in the LSA function, base lexical vectors are here derived from co-occurrence counts in a word space, built according to the method discussed in (Sahlgren, 2006; Croce and Previtali, 2010). In order to keep dimensionality as low as possible, SVD is also applied here (Annesi et al., 2012). The result is that every noun, verb, adjective and adverb is then projected in the reduced word space and then different composition functions can be applied as discussed in (Mitchell and Lapata, 2010) or (Annesi et al., 2012).

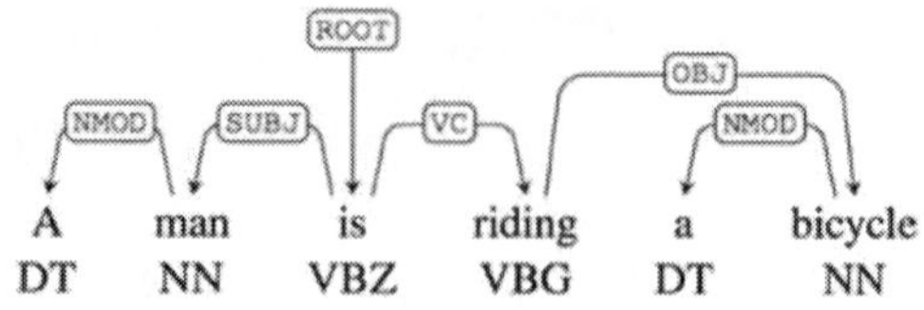

Figure 1: Example of dependency graph

Convolution kernel-based similarity. The similarity function is here the Smoothed Partial Tree Kernel (**SPTK**) proposed in (Croce et al., 2011). This convolution kernel estimates the similarity between sentences, according to the syntactic and lexical information in both sentences. Syntactic representation of a sentence like "*A man is riding a bicycle*" is derived from the dependency parse tree, as shown in Fig. 1. It allows to define different tree structures over which the SPTK operates. First, a tree including only lexemes, where edges encode their dependencies, is generated and called Lexical Only Centered Tree (LOCT), see Fig. 2. Then, we add to each lexical node two leftmost children, encoding the grammatical function and the POS-Tag respectively: it is the so-called Lexical Centered Tree (LCT), see Fig. 3. Finally, we generate the Grammatical Relation Centered Tree (GRCT), see Fig. 4, by setting grammatical relation as non-terminal nodes, while PoS-Tags are pre-terminals and fathers of their associated lexemes. Each tree representation provides a different kernel function so that three different SPTK similarity scores, i.e. LOCT, LCT and GRCT, are here obtained.

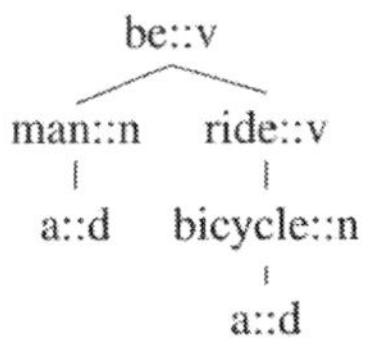

Figure 2: Lexical Only Centered Tree (LOCT)

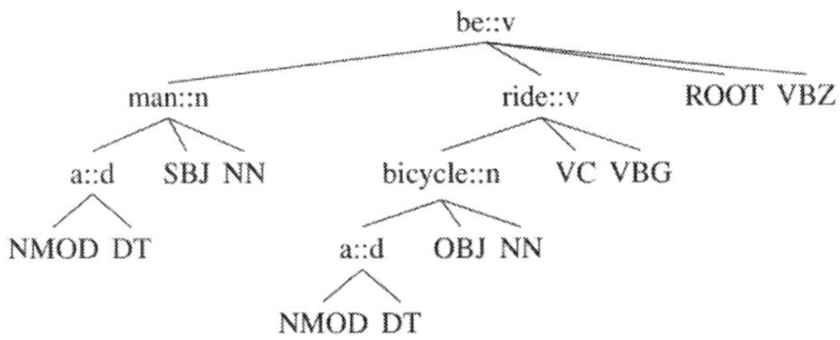

Figure 3: Lexical Centered Tree (LCT)

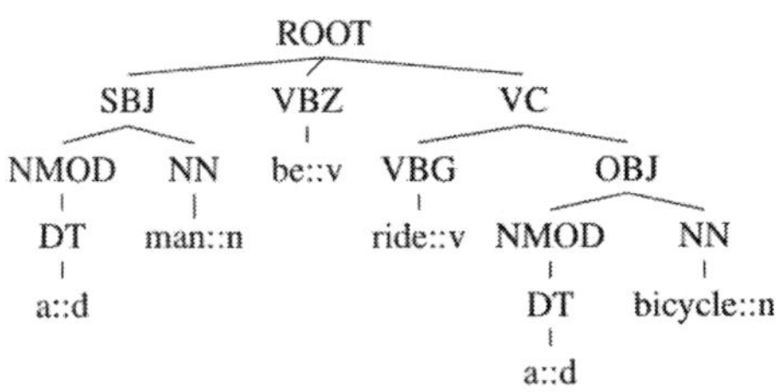

Figure 4: Grammatical Relation Centered Tree (GRCT)

2.2 Combining STSs with SV Regression

The similarity functions described above provide scores capturing different linguistic aspects and an effective way to combine such information is made available by Support Vector (SV) regression, described in (Smola and Schölkopf, 2004). The idea is to learn a higher level model by weighting scores according to specific needs implicit in training data. Given similarity scores $\vec{x}_i$ for the i-th sentence pair, the regressor learns a function $y_i = f(\vec{x}_i)$, where y_i is the score provided by human annotators.

The ε-SV regression (Vapnik, 1995) algorithm allows to define the best f approximating the training data, i.e. the function that has at most ε deviation from the actually obtained targets y_i for all the training data. Given a training dataset $\{(\vec{x}_1, y_1), \ldots, (\vec{x}_l, y_l)\} \in X \times \mathbb{R}$, where X is the space of the input patterns, i.e. the original similarity scores, we can acquire a linear function

$$f(\vec{x}) = \langle \vec{w}, \vec{x} \rangle + b \text{ with } \vec{w} \in X, b \in \mathbb{R}$$

by solving the following optimization problem:

$$\text{minimize } \frac{1}{2}||\vec{w}||^2$$

$$\text{subject to } \begin{cases} y_i - \langle \vec{w}, \vec{x}_i \rangle - b \leq \varepsilon \\ \langle \vec{w}, \vec{x}_i \rangle + b - y_i \leq \varepsilon \end{cases}$$

Since the function f approximating all pairs $(\vec{x}_i, y_i)$ with ε precision, may not exist, i.e. the convex optimization problem is infeasible, slack variables ξ_i, ξ_i^* are introduced:

$$\text{minimize } \frac{1}{2}||\vec{w}||^2 + C \sum_{i=1}^{l} (\xi_i + \xi_i^*)$$

$$\text{subject to } \begin{cases} y_i - \langle \vec{w}, \vec{x}_i \rangle - b \leq \varepsilon + \xi_i \\ \langle \vec{w}, \vec{x}_i \rangle + b - y_i \leq \varepsilon + \xi_i^* \\ \xi_i, \xi_i^* \geq 0 \end{cases}$$

where ξ_i, ξ_i^* measure the error introduced by training data with a deviation higher than ε and the constant $C > 0$ determines the trade-off between the norm $\|\vec{w}\|$ and the amount up to which deviations larger than ε are tolerated.

3 Experimental Evaluation

This section describes results obtained in the SemEval 2012 Task 6: STS. First, the experimental setup of different similarity functions is described. Then, results obtained over training datasets are reported. Finally, results achieved in the competition are discussed.

3.1 Experimental setup

In order to estimate the Latent Semantic Analysis (LSA) based similarity function, the distributional analysis of the English version of the Europarl Corpus (Koehn, 2002) has been carried out. It is the same source corpus of the SMTeuroparl dataset and it allows to acquire a semantic space capturing the same topics characterizing this dataset. A word-by-sentence matrix models the sentence representation space. The entire corpus has been split so that each vector represents a sentence: the number of different sentences is about 1.8 million and the matrix cells contain *tf-idf* scores between words and sentences. The SVD is applied and the space dimensionality is reduced to $k = 250$. Novel sentences are immersed in the reduced space, as described in (Landauer and Dumais, 1997) and the LSA-based similarity between two sentences is estimated according the cosine similarity.

To estimate the Compositional Distributional Semantics (CDS) based function, a co-occurrence Word Space is first acquired through the distributional analysis of the UKWaC corpus (Baroni et al., 2009), i.e. a Web document collection made of about 2 billion tokens. UKWaC is larger than the Europarl corpus and we expect it makes available a more general lexical representation suited for all datasets. An approach similar to the one described in (Croce and Previtali, 2010) has been adopted for the acquisition of the word space. First, all words occurring more than 200 times (i.e. the *targets*) are represented through vectors. The original space dimensions are generated from the set of the 20,000 most frequent words (i.e. *features*) in the UKWaC corpus. One dimension describes the Pointwise Mutual Information score between one feature as it occurs on a left or right window of 3 tokens around a target. Left contexts of targets are treated differently from the right ones, in order to also capture asymmetric syntactic behaviors (e.g., useful for verbs): 40,000 dimensional vectors are thus derived for each target. The particularly small window size allows to better capture paradigmatic relations between targets, e.g. hyponymy or synonymy. Again, the SVD reduction is applied to the original matrix with a $k = 250$. Once lexical vectors are available, a compositional similarity measure can be obtained by combining the word vectors according to a CDS operator, e.g. (Mitchell and Lapata, 2010) or (Annesi et al., 2012). In this work, the adopted compositional representation is the *additive* operator between lexical vectors, as described in (Mitchell and Lapata, 2010) and the similarity function between two sentences is the cosine similarity between their corresponding compositional vectors. Moreover, two additive operators that only sum over nouns and verbs are also adopted, denoted by CDS_V and CDS_N, respectively.

The estimation of the semantically Smoothed Partial Tree Kernel (SPTK) is made available by an extended version of SVM-LightTK software[1] (Moschitti, 2006) implementing the smooth matching between tree nodes. The tree representation described in Sec. 2.1 allows to define 3 different kernels, i.e. SPTK_{LOCT}, SPTK_{LCT} and SPTK_{GRCT}. Similarity between lexical nodes is estimated as the cosine similarity in the co-occurrence Word Space described above, as in (Croce et al., 2011).

In all corpus analysis and experiments, sentences are processed with the LTH dependency parser, described in (Johansson and Nugues, 2007), for Part-of-speech tagging and lemmatization. Dependency parsing of datasets is required for the SPTK application. Finally, SVM-LightTK is employed for the SV regression learning to combine specific similarity functions.

3.2 Evaluating the impact of unsupervised models

Table 1 compares the Pearson Correlation of different similarity functions described in Section 2.1, i.e. mainly the results of the unsupervised approaches, against the challenge training data. Regarding to MSRvid dataset, the topical similarity (LSA function) achieves the best result, i.e. 0.748. Paradigmatic lexical information as in CDS, CDS_N and *LO* provides also good results, confirming the impact of lexical generalization. However, only nouns seem to contribute significantly, as for the poor results of CDS_V suggest. As the dataset is characterized by short sentences with negligible syntactic differences, SPTK-based kernels are not discriminant. On the contrary, the SPTK_{LCT} achieves the best result in the MSRpar dataset, where paraphrasing phenomena are peculiar. Notice that the other SPTK kernels are not equivalently performant, in line with previous results on question classification and semantic role labeling (Croce et al., 2011). Lexical information provides a crucial contribution also for LO, although the contribution of topical or paradigmatic generalization seems negligible over MSRpar. Finally, in the SMTeuroparl, longer sentences are the norm and length seems to compromise the performance of LO. The best results seem to require the lexical and syntactic information provided by CDS and SPTK.

[1] http://disi.unitn.it/moschitti/Tree-Kernel.htm

Models	Dataset		
	MSRvid	MSRpar	SMTeuroparl
CDS	.652	.393	**.681**
CDS_N	.630	.234	.485
CDS_V	.219	.317	.264
LSA	**.748**	.344	.477
$SPTK_{LOCT}$	.300	.251	.611
$SPTK_{LCT}$	.297	**.464**	.622
$SPTK_{GRCT}$	.278	.255	.626
LO	.560	.446	.248

Table 1: Unsupervised results over the training dataset

3.3 Evaluating the role of SV regression

The SV regressors have been trained over a feature space that enumerates the different similarity functions: one feature is provided by the LSA function, three by the CDS, i.e. CDS, CDS_N and CDS_V, three by SPTK, i.e. $SPTK_{LOCT}$, $SPTK_{LCT}$ and $SPTK_{GRCT}$ and one by LO, i.e. the number of words in common. Two more features are obtained by the *sentence lengths* of a pair, i.e. the number of words in the first and second sentence, respectively. Table 2 shows Pearson Correlation results when the regressor is trained according a 10-fold cross validation schema. First, all possible feature combinations are attempted for the SV regression, so that every subset of the 10 features is evaluated. Results of the best feature combination are shown in column $best_{feat}$: for MSRvid, the best performance is achieved when all 10 features are considered; in MSRpar, SPTK combined with LO is sufficient; finally, in the SMTeuroparl the combination is LO, CDS and SPTK. In column all_{feat} results achieved by considering all features are reported. Last column specifies the performance increase with respect to the corresponding best results in the unsupervised settings.

Results of the regressors are always higher with respect to the unsupervised settings, with up to a 35% improvement for the MSRpar, i.e. the most complex domain. Moreover, differences when best and all features are employed are negligible. It means that SV regressor allows to automatically combine and select the most informative similarity aspects, confirming the applicability of the proposed redundant approach to STS.

Dataset	Experiments		Gain
	$best_{feat}$	all_{feat}	
MSRvid	.789	.789	5,0%
MSRpar	.615	.612	32,4%
SMTeuroparl	.692	.691	1,6%

Table 2: SV regressor results over the training dataset

3.4 Results over the SemEval Task 6

According to the above evidence, we participated to the SemEval challenge with three different systems.
Sys_1 - Best Features. Scores between pairs from a specific dataset are obtained by applying a regressor trained over pairs from the same dataset. It means that, for example, the test pairs from the MSRvid dataset are processed with a regressor trained over the MSRvid training data. Moreover, the most representative similarity function estimated for the collection is employed: the feature combination providing the best correlation results over training pairs is adopted for the test. The same is applied to MSRpar and SMTeuroparl. No selection is adopted for the Surprise data and training data for all the domains are used, as described in Sys_3.
Sys_2 - All Features. Relatedness scores between pairs from a specific dataset are obtained using a regressor trained using pairs from the same dataset. Differently from the Sys_1, the similarity function here is employed within the SV regressors trained over all 10 similarity functions (i.e. all features).
Sys_3 - All features and All domains. The SV regressor is trained using training pairs from *all* collections and over *all* 10 features. It means that one single model is trained and employed to score all test data. This approach is also used for the Surprise data, i.e. the OnWN and SMTnews datasets.

Table 3 reports the general outcome for the UNITOR systems. Rank of the individual scores with respect to the other systems participating to the challenge is reported in parenthesis. This allows to draw some conclusions. First, the proposed system ranks around the 12 and 13 system positions (out of 89 systems), and the 6th group. The adoption of all proposed features suggests that more evidence is better, as it can be properly modeled by regression. It seems generally better suited for the variety of semantic phenomena observed in the tests. Regressors seem

Dataset	Results			
	BL	Sys_1	Sys_2	Sys_3
MSRvid	.299	**.821**	**.821**	.802
MSRpar	.433	.569	**.576**	.468
SMTeuroparl	.454	**.516**	.510	.457
surp.OnWN	.586		**.659**	
surp.SMTnews	.390		**.471**	
ALL	.311	.747 (13)	**.747 (12)**	.628 (40)
ALLnrm	.673	.829 (12)	**.830 (11)**	.815 (21)
Mean	.436	.632 (10)	**.632 (9)**	.594 (28)

Table 3: Results over the challenge test dataset

to be robust enough to select the proper features and make the feature selection step (through collection specific cross-validation) useless. Collection specific training seems useful, as Sys_3 achieves lower results, basically due to the significant stylistic differences across the collections. However, the good level of accuracy achieved over the surprise data sets (between 11% and 17% performance gain with respect to the baselines) confirms the large applicability of the overall technique: our system in fact does not depend on *any* manually coded resource (e.g. WordNet) nor on any controlled (e.g. parallel or aligned) corpus. Future work includes the study of the learning rate and its correlation with different and richer similarity functions, e.g. CDS as in (Annesi et al., 2012).

Acknowledgements This research is partially supported by the European Community's Seventh Framework Programme (FP7/2007-2013) under grant numbers 262491 (INSEARCH). Many thanks to the reviewers for their valuable suggestions.

References

Joshua Albrecht and Rebecca Hwa. 2007. Regression for sentence-level mt evaluation with pseudo references. In *Proceedings of ACL*, pages 296–303, Prague, Czech Republic, June.

Paolo Annesi, Valerio Storch, and Roberto Basili. 2012. Space projections as distributional models for semantic composition. In *CICLing (1)*, Lecture Notes in Computer Science, pages 323–335. Springer.

Marco Baroni, Silvia Bernardini, Adriano Ferraresi, and Eros Zanchetta. 2009. The wacky wide web: a collection of very large linguistically processed web-crawled corpora. *Language Resources and Evaluation*, 43(3):209–226.

Lee Becker, Martha Palmer, Sarel van Vuuren, and Wayne Ward. 2011. Evaluating questions in context.

Fadi Biadsy, Julia Hirschberg, and Elena Filatova. 2008. An unsupervised approach to biography production using wikipedia. In *ACL*, pages 807–815.

Danilo Croce and Daniele Previtali. 2010. Manifold learning for the semi-supervised induction of framenet predicates: An empirical investigation. In *Proceedings of the GEMS 2010 Workshop*, pages 7–16, Uppsala, Sweden.

Danilo Croce, Alessandro Moschitti, and Roberto Basili. 2011. Structured lexical similarity via convolution kernels on dependency trees. In *Proceedings of EMNLP*, Edinburgh, Scotland, UK.

Aminul Islam and Diana Inkpen. 2008. Semantic text similarity using corpus-based word similarity and string similarity. *ACM Trans. Knowl. Discov. Data*, 2:10:1–10:25, July.

Richard Johansson and Pierre Nugues. 2007. Semantic structure extraction using nonprojective dependency trees. In *Proceedings of SemEval-2007*, Prague, Czech Republic, June 23-24.

P. Koehn. 2002. Europarl: A multilingual corpus for evaluation of machine translation. *Draft*.

Thomas K Landauer and Susan T. Dumais. 1997. A solution to platos problem: The latent semantic analysis theory of acquisition, induction, and representation of knowledge. *Psychological review*, pages 211–240.

Rada Mihalcea, Courtney Corley, and Carlo Strapparava. 2006. Corpus-based and knowledge-based measures of text semantic similarity. In *In AAAI06*.

Jeff Mitchell and Mirella Lapata. 2010. Composition in distributional models of semantics. *Cognitive Science*, 34(8):1388–1429.

Alessandro Moschitti. 2006. Efficient convolution kernels for dependency and constituent syntactic trees. In *Proceedings of ECML'06*, pages 318–329.

Bo Pang and Lillian Lee. 2005. Seeing stars: Exploiting class relationships for sentiment categorization with respect to rating scales. In *Proceedings of the ACL*.

Mehran Sahami and Timothy D. Heilman. 2006. A web-based kernel function for measuring the similarity of short text snippets. In *Proceedings of the 15th international conference on World Wide Web*, WWW '06, pages 377–386, New York, NY, USA. ACM.

Magnus Sahlgren. 2006. *The Word-Space Model*. Ph.D. thesis, Stockholm University.

Alex J. Smola and Bernhard Schölkopf. 2004. A tutorial on support vector regression. *Statistics and Computing*, 14(3):199–222, August.

Vladimir N. Vapnik. 1995. *The Nature of Statistical Learning Theory*. Springer–Verlag, New York.

Saarland: Vector-based models of semantic textual similarity

Georgiana Dinu
Center of Mind/Brain Sciences
University of Trento
georgiana.dinu@unitn.it

Stefan Thater
Dept. of Computational Linguistics
Universität des Saarlandes
stth@coli.uni-saarland.de

Abstract

This paper describes our system for the Semeval 2012 Sentence Textual Similarity task. The system is based on a combination of few simple vector space-based methods for word meaning similarity. Evaluation results show that a simple combination of these unsupervised data-driven methods can be quite successful. The simple vector space components achieve high performance on short sentences; on longer, more complex sentences, they are outperformed by a surprisingly competitive word overlap baseline, but they still bring improvements over this baseline when incorporated into a mixture model.

1 Introduction

Vector space models are widely-used methods for word meaning similarity which exploit the so-called *distributional hypothesis*, stating that semantically similar words tend to occur in similar contexts. Word meaning is represented by the contexts in which a word occurs, and similarity is computed by comparing these contexts in a high-dimensional vector space (Turney and Pantel, 2010). Distributional models of word meaning are attractive because they are simple, have wide coverage, and can be easily acquired at virtually no cost in an unsupervised way. Furthermore, recent research has shown that, at least to some extent, these models can be generalized to capture similarity beyond the (isolated) word level, either as lexical meaning modulated by context, or as vectorial meaning representations for phrases and sentences. In this paper we evaluate the use of some of these models for the Semantic Textual Similarity (STS) task, which measures the degree of semantic equivalence between two sentences.

In recent work Mitchell and Lapata (2008) has drawn the attention to the question of building vectorial meaning representations for sentences by combining individual word vectors. They propose a family of simple "compositional" models that compute a vector for a phrase or a sentence by combining vectors of the constituent words, using different operations such as vector addition or component-wise multiplication. More refined models have been proposed recently by Baroni and Zamparelli (2010) and Grefenstette and Sadrzadeh (2011).

Thater et al. (2011) and others take a slightly different perspective on the problem: Instead of computing a vector representation for a complete phrase or sentence, they focus on the problem of "disambiguating" the vector representation of a target word based on distributional information about the words in the target's context. While this approach is not "compositional" in the sense described above, it still captures some meaning of the complete phrase in which a target word occurs.

In this paper, we report on the system we used in the Semeval 2012 Sentence Textual Similarity shared task and describe an approach that uses a combination of few simple vector-based components. We extend the model of Thater et al. (2011), which has been shown to perform well on a closely related paraphrase ranking task, with an additive composition operation along the lines of Mitchell and Lapata (2008), and compare it with a simple alignment-based approach which in turn uses vector-based similarity scores. Results show that in particular the alignment-based approach can achieve good performance on the Microsoft Research Video Description dataset. On the other datasets, all vector-based components are outperformed by a surprisingly competitive word overlap baseline, but they still bring improvements over this baseline when incorporated into a mixture model. On the test dataset, the mixture model ranks 10th and 13th on the Microsoft Research Paraphrase and Video Description datasets, respectively, which we take this to be a quite promising result given that we use only few relatively simple vector based components to compute similarity scores for sentences.

The rest of the paper is structured as follows: Section 2 presents the individual vector-based components used by our system. In Section 3 we present detailed evaluation results on the training set, as well as results for our system on the test set, while Section 4 concludes the paper.

2 Systems for Sentence Similarity

Our system is based on four different components: We use two different vector space models to represent word meaning—a basic bag-of-words model and a slightly simplified variant of the contextualization model of Thater et al. (2011)—and two different methods to compute similarity scores for sentences based on these two vector space models—one "compositional" method that computes vectors for sentences by summing over the vectors of the constituent words, and one alignment-based method that uses vector-based similarity scores for word pairs to compute an alignment between the words in the two sentences.

2.1 Vector Space Models

For the basic vector-space model, we assume a set W of words, and represent the meaning of a word $w \in W$ by a vector in the vector space V spanned by the set of basis vectors $\{\vec{e}_{w'} \mid w' \in W\}$ as follows:

$$v_{basic}(w) = \sum_{w' \in W} f(w, w')\, \vec{e}_{w'}$$

where f is a function that assigns a co-occurrence value to the word pair (w, w'). In the experiments reported below, we use pointwise mutual information estimated on co-occurrence frequencies for words within a 5-word window around the target word on either side.[1]

[1] We use a 5-word window here as this setting has been shown to give best results on a closely related task in the literature (Mitchell and Lapata, 2008)

This basic "bag of words" vector space model represents word meaning by summing over all contexts in which the target word occurs. Since words are often ambiguous, this means that context words pertaining to different senses of the target word are mixed within a single vector representation, which can lead to "noisy" similarity scores. The vector for the noun *coach*, for instance, contains context words like *teach* and *tell* (person sense) as well as *derail* and *crash* (vehicle sense).

To address this problem, Thater et al. (2011) propose a "contextualization" model in which the individual components of the target word's vector are reweighted, based on distributional information about the words in the target's context. Let us assume that the context consist of a single word c. The vector for a target w in context c is then defined as:

$$v(w, c) = \sum_{w' \in W} \alpha(c, w')\, f(w, w')\, \vec{e}_{w'}$$

where α is some similarity score that quantifies to what extent the vector dimension that corresponds to w' is compatible with the observed context c. In the experiments reported below, we take α to be the cosine similarity of c and w'; see Section 3 for details.

In the experiments reported below, we use all words in the syntactic context of the target word to contextualize the target:

$$v_{ctx}(w) = \sum_{c \in C(w)} v(w, c)$$

where $C(w)$ is the context in which w occurs, i.e. all words related to w by a dependency relation such as subject or object, including inverse relations.

Remark. The contextualization model presented above is a slightly simplified version of the original model of Thater et al. (2011): it uses standard bag-of-words vectors instead of syntax-based vectors. This simplified version performs better on the training dataset. Furthermore, the simplified model has been shown to be equivalent to the models of Erk and Padó (2008) and Thater et al. (2010) by Dinu and Thater (2012), so the results reported below carry over directly to these other models as well.

2.2 Vector Composition and Alignment

The two vector space models sketched above represent the meaning of *words*, and thus cannot be applied directly to model similarity of phrases or sentences. One obvious and straightforward way to extend these models to the sentence level is to follow Mitchell and Lapata (2008) and represent sentences by vectors obtained by summing over the individual vectors of the constituent words. These "compositional" models can then be used to compute similarity scores between sentence pairs in a straightforward way, simply by computing the cosine of the angle between vectors (or some other similarity score) for the two sentences:

$$sim_{add}(S,S') = cos(\sum_{w \in S} v(w), \sum_{w' \in S'} v(w')) \quad (1)$$

where $v(w)$ can be instantiated either with *basic* or with *ctx* vectors.

In addition to the compositional models, we also experimented with an alignment-based approach: Instead of computing vectors for complete sentences, we compute an alignment between the words in the two sentences. To be more precise, we compute cosine similarity scores between all possible pairs of words (tokens) of the two sentences; based on these similarity scores, we then compute a one-to-one alignment between the words in the two sentences[2], using a greedy search strategy (see Fig. 1). We assign a weight to each link in the alignment which is simply the cosine similarity score of the corresponding word pair and take the sum of the link weights, normalized by the maximal length of the two sentences to be the corresponding similarity score for the two sentences. The final score is then:

$$sim_{align}(S,S') = \frac{\sum_{(w,w') \in \text{ALIGN}(S,S')} cos(v(w),v(w'))}{max(|S|,|S'|)}$$

where $v(w)$ is the vector for w, which again can be either the basic or the contextualized vector.

3 Evaluation

In this section we present our experimental results. In addition to the models described in Section 2, we define a baseline model which simply computes the word overlap between two sentences as:

$$sim_{overlap}(S,S') = \frac{|S \cap S'|}{|S \cup S'|} \quad (2)$$

[2]Note that this can result in some words not being aligned

```
function ALIGN(S1, S2)
    alignment ← ∅
    marked ← ∅
    pairs ← {⟨w,w'⟩ | w ∈ S1, w' ∈ S2}
    while pairs not empty do
        ⟨w,w'⟩ ← highest cosine pair in pairs
        if w ∉ marked and w' ∉ marked then
            alignment ← ⟨w,w'⟩ ∪ alignment
            marked ← {w,w'} ∪ marked
        end if
        pairs ← pairs \ {⟨w,w'⟩}
    end while
    return alignment
end function
```

Figure 1: The alignment algorithm

The score assigned by this method is simply the number of words that the two sentences have in common divided by their total number of words. Finally, we also propose a straightforward mixture model which combines all of the above methods. We use the training data to fit a degree two polynomial over these individual predictors using least squares regression. We report cross-validation scores.

3.1 Evaluation setup

The vector space used in all experiments is a bag-of-words space containing word co-occurrence counts. We use the GigaWord (1.7 billion tokens) as input corpus and extract word co-occurrences within a symmetric 5-word context window. Co-occurrence counts smaller than three are set to 0 and we further apply (positive) pmi weighting.

3.2 Training results

The training data results are shown in Figure 2. The best performance on the video dataset is achieved by the alignment method using a basic vector representation to compute word-level similarity. All vector-space methods perform considerably better than the simple word overlap baseline on this dataset, the alignment method achieving almost 20% gain over this baseline. This indicates that information about the meaning of the words is very beneficial for this type of data, consisting of small, well-structured sentences.

Using the alignment method with contextualized

Component	MSRvid	MSRpar	SMTeur
basic/add	70.9	33.3	31.8
ctx/add	65.7	23.0	30.4
basic/align	**74.6**	40.5	32.1
overlap	56.8	**59.5**	**50.0**
mixture	**78.1**	**61.8**	**54.1**

Figure 2: Results on the training set.

Component	MSRvid	MSRpar	SMTeur
basic/add	−2.1	−0.1	−1.5
ctx/add	−0.6	+1.3	+0.4
basic/align	−4.1	−1.9	−2.6
overlap	−0.1	−17.0	−23.0

Figure 3: Results on the training set when removing individual components from the mixture model.

vector representations (omitted in the table) does not bring any improvement and it performs similarly to the *ctx/add* method. This suggests that aligning similar words in the two sentences does not benefit from further meaning disambiguation through contextualized vectors and that some level of disambiguation may be implicitly performed.

On the paraphrase and europarl datasets, the overlap baseline outperforms, by a large margin, the vector space models. This is not surprising, as it is known that word overlap baselines can be very competitive on Recognizing Textual Entailment datasets, to which these two datasets bare a large resemblance. In particular this indicates that the methods proposed for combining vector representations of words do not provide, in the current state, accurate models for modeling the meaning of larger sentences.

We also report 10-fold cross-validation scores obtained with the mixture model. On all datasets, this outperforms the individual methods, improving by a margin of 2%-4% the best single methods. In particular, on the paraphrase and europarl datasets, this shows that despite the considerably inferior performance of the vector-based methods, these can still help improve the overall performance.

This is also reflected in Table 3, where we evaluate the performance of the mixture method when, in turn, one of the individual components is excluded: with few exceptions, all components contribute to the performance of the mixtures.

3.3 Test results

We have submitted as our official runs the best single vector space model, performing alignment with basic vector similarity, as well as the mixture methods. The mixture method uses weights individually learned for each of the datasets made available during training. For the two surprise datasets we carry over the weights of what we have considered to be the most similar training-available sets: video weights of ontonotes and paraphrase weights for news.

The test data results are given in 4. We report the results for the individual datasets as well as the mean Pearson correlation, weighted by the sizes of the datasets. The table also shows the performance of the official task baseline as well as the top three runs accoring to the overall weighted mean score.

As expected, the mixture method outperforms by a large margin the alignment model, achieving rank 10 and rank 13 on the video and paraphrase datasets. Overall the mixture method ranks 43 according to the weighted mean measure (rank 22 if correcting our official submission which contained the wrong output file for the europarl dataset). The other more controversial measures rank our official, *not* corrected, submission at position 13 (RankNrm) and 71 (Rank), overall. This is an encouraging result, as the individual components we have used are all unsupervised, obtained solely from large amounts of unlabeled data, and with no other additional resources. The training data made available has only been used to learn a set of weights for combining these individual components.

4 Conclusions

This paper describes an approach that combines few simple vector space-based components to model sentence similarity. We have extended the state-of-the-art model for contextualized meaning representations of Thater et al. (2011) with an additive composition operation along the lines of Mitchell and Lapata (2008). We have combined this with a simple alignment-based method and a word overlap baseline into a mixture model.

Our system achieves promising results in particular

Dataset	basic/align	mixture	baseline	Run1	Run2	Run3
MSRvid	77.1	83.1	30.0	87.3	88.0	85.6
MSRpar	40.4	63.1	43.3	68.3	73.4	64.0
SMTeur	26.8	13.9 (37.1*)	45.4	52.8	47.7	51.5
OnWN	57.2	59.6	58.6	66.4	67.9	71.0
SMTnews	35.0	38.0	39.1	49.3	39.8	48.3
ALL	49.5	45.4	31.1	82.3	81.3	73.3
Rank	65	71	87	1	3	15
ALLNrm	78.7	82.5	67.3	85.7	86.3	85.2
RankNrm	50	13	85	2	1	5
Mean	50.6	56.6 (60.0*)	43.5	67.7	67.5	67.0
RankMean	60	43 (22*)	70	1	2	3

Figure 4: Results on the test set. * – corrected score (official results score wrong prediction file we have submitted for the europarl dataset). Official baseline and top three runs according to the weighted mean measure.

on the Microsoft Research Paraphrase and Video Description datasets, on which it ranks 13th and 10th, respectively. We take this to be a promising result, given that our focus has not been the development of a highly-competitive complex system, but rather on investigating what performance can be achieved when using only vector space methods.

An interesting observation is that the methods for combining word vector representations (the vector addition, or the meaning contextualization) can be beneficial for modeling the similarity of the small, well-structured sentences of the video dataset, however they do not perform well on comparing longer, more complex sentences. In future work we plan to further investigate methods for composition in vector space models using the STS datasets, in addition to the small, controlled datasets that have been typically used in this line of research.

Acknowledgments. This work was supported by the Cluster of Excellence "Multimodal Computing and Interaction," funded by the German Excellence Initiative.

References

Marco Baroni and Roberto Zamparelli. 2010. Nouns are vectors, adjectives are matrices: Representing adjective-noun constructions in semantic space. In *Proceedings of the 2010 Conference on Empirical Methods in Natural Language Processing*, Cambridge, MA, October. Association for Computational Linguistics.

Georgiana Dinu and Stefan Thater. 2012. A comparison of models of word meaning in context. In *Proceedings of the 2012 Conference of the North American Chapter of the Association for Computational Linguistics: Human Language Technologies*. Short paper, to appear.

Katrin Erk and Sebastian Padó. 2008. A structured vector space model for word meaning in context. In *Proceedings of the 2008 Conference on Empirical Methods in Natural Language Processing*, Honolulu, HI, USA.

Edward Grefenstette and Mehrnoosh Sadrzadeh. 2011. Experimental support for a categorical compositional distributional model of meaning. In *Proceedings of the 2011 Conference on Empirical Methods in Natural Language Processing*, Edinburgh, Scotland, UK., July. Association for Computational Linguistics.

Jeff Mitchell and Mirella Lapata. 2008. Vector-based models of semantic composition. In *Proceedings of ACL-08: HLT*, Columbus, OH, USA.

Stefan Thater, Hagen Fürstenau, and Manfred Pinkal. 2010. Contextualizing semantic representations using syntactically enriched vector models. In *Proceedings of the 48th Annual Meeting of the Association for Computational Linguistics*, Uppsala, Sweden.

Stefan Thater, Hagen Fürstenau, and Manfred Pinkal. 2011. Word meaning in context: A simple and effective vector model. In *Proceedings of 5th International Joint Conference on Natural Language Processing*, pages 1134–1143, Chiang Mai, Thailand, November. Asian Federation of Natural Language Processing.

Peter D. Turney and Patrick Pantel. 2010. From frequency to meaning: Vector space modes of semantics. *Journal of Artificial Intelligence Research*, 37:141–188.

UMCC_DLSI: Multidimensional Lexical-Semantic Textual Similarity

Antonio Fernández, Yoan Gutiérrez, Alexander Chávez, Héctor Dávila, Andy González, Rainel Estrada , Yenier Castañeda

DI, University of Matanzas
Autopista a Varadero km 3 ½
Matanzas, Cuba

Sonia Vázquez
Andrés Montoyo, Rafael Muñoz,

DLSI, University of Alicante
Carretera de San Vicente S/N
Alicante, Spain

Abstract

This paper describes the specifications and results of UMCC_DLSI system, which participated in the first Semantic Textual Similarity task (STS) of SemEval-2012. Our supervised system uses different kinds of semantic and lexical features to train classifiers and it uses a voting process to select the correct option. Related to the different features we can highlight the resource ISR-WN[1] used to extract semantic relations among words and the use of different algorithms to establish semantic and lexical similarities. In order to establish which features are the most appropriate to improve STS results we participated with three runs using different set of features. Our best approach reached the position 18 of 89 runs, obtaining a general correlation coefficient up to 0.72.

1. Introduction

SemEval 2012 competition for evaluating Natural Language Processing (NLP) systems presents a new task called Semantic Textual Similarity (STS) (Agirre *et al.*, 2012). In STS the participating systems must examine the degree of semantic equivalence between two sentences. The goal of this task is to create a unified framework for the evaluation of semantic textual similarity modules and to characterize their impact on NLP applications.

STS is related to Textual Entailment (TE) and Paraphrase tasks. The main difference is that STS assumes bidirectional graded equivalence between the pair of textual snippets. In the case of TE the equivalence is directional (e.g. a student is a person, but a person is not necessarily a student). In addition, STS differs from TE and Paraphrase in that, rather than being a binary yes/no decision, STS is a similarity-graded notion (e.g. a student and a person are more similar than a dog and a person). This bidirectional gradation is useful for NLP tasks such as Machine Translation, Information Extraction, Question Answering, and Summarization. Several semantic tasks could be added as modules in the STS framework, "such as Word Sense Disambiguation and Induction, Lexical Substitution, Semantic Role Labeling, Multiword Expression detection and handling, Anaphora and Co-reference resolution, Time and Date resolution and Named Entity Recognition, among others"[2]

1.1. Description of 2012 pilot task

In STS, all systems were provided with a set of sentence pairs obtained from a segmented corpus. For each sentence pair, s_1 and s_2, all participants had to quantify how similar s_1 and s_2 were, providing a similarity score. The output of different systems was compared to the manual scores provided by SemEval-2012 gold standard file, which range from 5 to 0 according to the next criterions[3]:

- (5) "The two sentences are equivalent, as they mean the same thing".

[1] Integration of Semantic Resource based on WordNet.

[2] http://www.cs.york.ac.uk/semeval-2012/task6/

[3] http://www.cs.york.ac.uk/semeval-2012/task6/data/uploads/datasets/train-readme.txt

- (4) "The two sentences are mostly equivalent, but some unimportant details differ".
- (3) "The two sentences are roughly equivalent, but some important information differs/missing".
- (2) "The two sentences are not equivalent, but share some details".
- (1) "The two sentences are not equivalent, but are on the same topic".
- (0) "The two sentences are on different topics".

After this introduction, the rest of the paper is organized as follows. Section 2 shows the architecture of our system and a description of the different runs. In section 3 we describe the algorithms and methods used to obtain the features for our system, and Section 4 describe the training phase. The obtained results and a discussion are provided in Section 5, and finally the conclusions and future works in Section 6.

2. System architecture and description of the runs

As we can see in Figure 1 our three runs begin with the pre-processing of SemEval 2012's training set. Every sentence pair is tokenized, lemmatized and POS tagged using Freeling tool (Atserias *et al.*, 2006). Afterwards, several methods and algorithms are applied in order to extract all features for our Machine Learning System (MLS). Each run uses a particular group of features.

The Run 1 (MultiSemLex) is our main run. This takes into account all extracted features and trains a model with a Voting classifier composed by the following techniques: Bagging (using M5P), Bagging (using REPTree), Random SubSpace (using REPTree) and MP5. The training corpus has been provided by SemEval-2012 competition, in concrete by the Semantic Textual Similarity task.

The Runs 2 and 3 use the same classifier, but including different features. Run 2 (MultiLex) uses (see Figure 1) features extracted from Lexical-Semantic Metrics (LS-M) described in section 3.1, Lexical-Semantic Alignment (LS-A) described in section 3.2 and Sentiment Polarity (SP) described in section 3.3.

On the other hand, the Run 3 (MultiSem) uses features extracted only from Semantic Alignment (SA) described in section 3.4 and the textual edit distances named QGram-Distances.

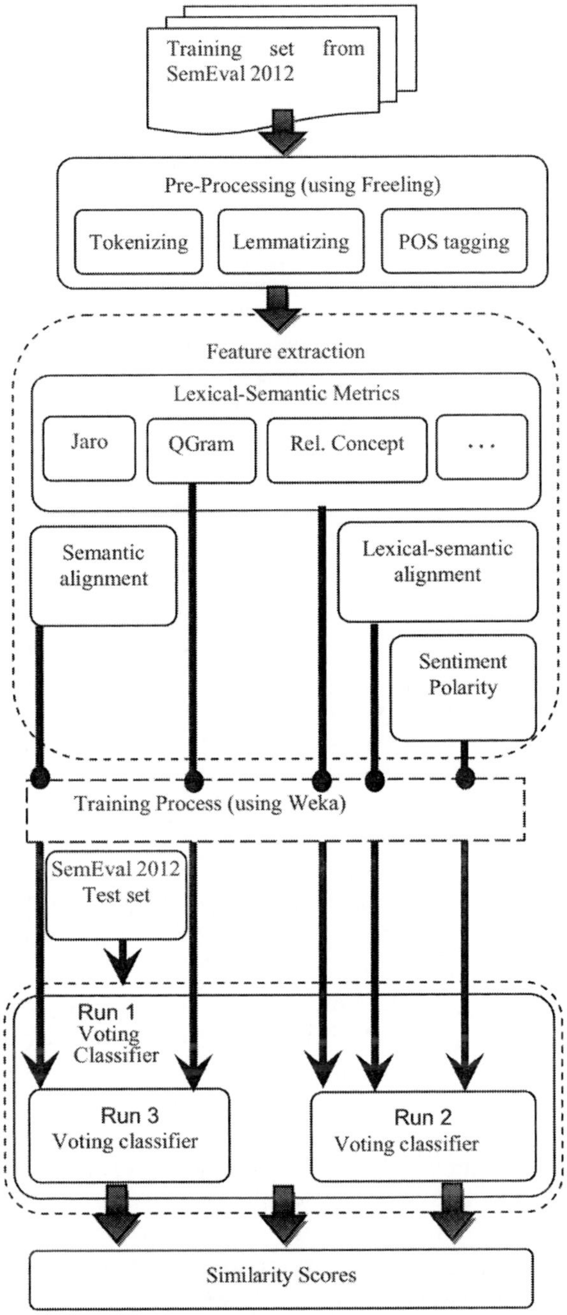

Figure 1. System Architecture.

As a result, we obtain three trained models capable to estimate the similarity value between two sentences.

Finally, we test our system with the SemEval 2012 test set (see Table 7 with the results of our three runs). The following section describes the features extraction process.

3. Description of the features used in the Machine Learning System

Sometimes, when two sentences are very similar, one sentence is in a high degree lexically overlapped by the other. Inspired by this fact we developed various algorithms, which measure the level of overlapping by computing a quantity of matching words (the quantity of lemmas that correspond exactly by its morphology) in a pair of sentences. In our system, we used lexical and semantic similarity measures as features for a MLS. Other features were extracted from a lexical-semantic sentences alignment and a variant using only a semantic alignment.

3.1. Similarity measures

We have used well-known string based similarity measures like: Needleman-Wunch (NW) (sequence alignment), Smith-Waterman (SW) (sequence alignment), Jaro, Jaro-Winkler (JaroW), Chapman-Mean-Length (CMLength), QGram-Distance (QGramD), Block-Distance (BD), Jaccard Similarity (JaccardS), Monge-Elkan (ME) and Overlap-Coefficient (OC). These algorithms have been obtained from an API (*Application Program Interface*) SimMetrics library v1.5[4] for .NET 2.0. Copyright (c) 2006 by Chris Parkinson. We obtained 10 features for our MLS from these similarity measures.

Using Levenshtein's edit distance (LED), we computed also two different algorithms in order to obtain the alignment of the phrases. In the first one, we considered a value of the alignment as the LED between two sentences and the normalized variant named NomLED. Contrary to (Tatu *et al.*, 2006), we do not remove the punctuation or stop words from the sentences, neither consider different cost for transformation operation, and we used all the operations (deletion, insertion and substitution). The second one is a variant that we named Double Levenshtein's Edit Distance (DLED). For this algorithm, we used LED to measure the distance between the sentences, but to compare the similarity between the words, we used LED again. Another feature is the normalized variant of DLED named NomDLED.

The unique difference between classic LED algorithm and DLED is the comparison of similitude between two words. With LED should be: $s[i] = t[i]$, whereas for our DLED we calculate words similarity also with LED (e.g. $DLED(s[i], t[i]) <= 2$). Values above a decision threshold (experimentally 2) mean unequal words. We obtain as result two new different features from these algorithms.

Another distance we used is an extension of LED named Extended Distance (EDx) (see (Fernández Orquín *et al.*, 2009) for details). This algorithm is an extension of the Levenshtein's algorithm, with which penalties are applied by considering what kind of operation or transformation is carried out (insertion, deletion, substitution, or non-operation) in what position, along with the character involved in the operation. In addition to the cost matrixes used by Levenshtein's algorithm, EDx also obtains the Longest Common Subsequence (LCS) (Hirschberg, 1977) and other helpful attributes for determining similarity between strings in a single iteration. It is worth noting that the inclusion of all these penalizations makes the EDx algorithm a good candidate for our approach. In our previous work (Fernández Orquín *et al.*, 2009), EDx demonstrated excellent results when it was compared with other distances as (Levenshtein, 1965), (Needleman and Wunsch, 1970), (Winkler, 1999). How to calculate EDx is briefly described as follows (we refer reader to (Fernández Orquín *et al.*, 2009) for a further description):

$$EDx = \sqrt[8]{\frac{\sum_{i=0}^{l-1} V_{(O_i)} * \left(P_{(c1_j)}, P_{(c2_k)}\right)(2R_{max}+1)^{L-i}}{N}}; \quad (1)$$

Where:
V - Transformations accomplished on the words (O, I, D, S).
O - Not operations at all,
I - Insertion,
D - Deletion,
S - Substitution.
We formalize V as a vector:

$$V = \begin{Bmatrix} (0,0) : o \\ (1,0) : i \\ (0,1) : d \\ (1,1) : s \end{Bmatrix}$$

$c1$ and $c2$ - The examined words
$c1_j$ - The *j-th* character of the word $c1$

[4] http://sourceforge.net/projects/simmetrics/

$c2_k$ - The *k-th* character of the word $c2$
P - The weight of each character

We can vary all this weights in order to make a flexible penalization to the interchangeable characters.

$Pc1_j$ - The weight of characters at $c1_j$
$Pc2_k$ - The weight of characters at $c2_k$

$$j = \begin{Bmatrix} j+1 & si\ O_i \neq I \\ j & si\ O_i = I \end{Bmatrix};\ k = \begin{Bmatrix} k+1 & si\ O_i \neq D \\ k & si\ O_i = D \end{Bmatrix}$$

L - The biggest word length of the language
l - Edit operations length
O_i - Operation at (i) position
$Rmax$ - Greatest value of P ranking

$$N = \sum_{i=0}^{L-1} 2R_{max}(2R_{max}+1)^i \qquad (2)$$

As we can see in the equation (1), the term $V_{(O_i)} * \left(P_{(c1_j)}, P_{(c2_k)}\right)$ *is* the Cartesian product that analyzes the importance of doing *i-th* operation between the characters at *j-th* and *k-th* position

The term $(2R_{max}+1)^{L-i}$ in equation (1) penalizes the position of the operations. The most to the left hand the operation is the highest the penalization is. The term N (see equation (2) normalizes the EDx into [0,1] interval. This measure is also used as a feature for the system.

We also used as a feature the Minimal Semantic Distances (Breadth First Search (BFS)) obtained between the most relevant concepts of both sentences. The relevant concepts pertain to semantic resources ISR-WN (Gutiérrez *et al.*, 2011a; 2010b), as WordNet (Miller *et al.*, 1990), WordNet Affect (Strapparava and Valitutti, 2004), SUMO (Niles and Pease, 2001) and Semantic Classes (Izquierdo *et al.*, 2007). Those concepts were obtained after having applied the Association Ratio (AR) measure between concepts and words over each sentence. The obtained distances for each resource SUMO, WordNet Affect, WordNet and Semantic Classes are named SDist, AffDist, WNDist and SCDist respectively.

ISR-WN, takes into account different kind of labels linked to WN: Level Upper Concepts (SUMO), Domains and Emotion labels. In this work, our purpose is to use a semantic network, which links different semantic resources aligned to WN. After several tests, we decided to apply ISR-WN. Although others resources provide different semantic relations, ISR-WN has the highest quantity of semantic dimensions aligned, so it is a suitable resource to run our algorithm.

Using ISR-WN we are able to extract important information from the interrelations of four ontological resources: WN, WND, WNA and SUMO. ISR-WN resource is based on WN1.6 or WN2.0 versions. In the last updated version, Semantic Classes and SentiWordNet were also included. Furthermore, ISR-WN provides a tool that allows the navigation across internal links. At this point, we can discover the multidimensionality of concepts that exists in each sentence. In order to establish the concepts associated to each sentence we apply Relevant Semantic Trees (Gutiérrez *et al.*, 2010a; Gutiérrez *et al.*, 2011b) approach using the provided links of ISR-WN. We refer reader to (Gutiérrez *et al.*, 2010a) for a further description.

3.2. Lexical-Semantic alignment

Another algorithm that we created is the Lexical-Semantic Alignment. In this algorithm, we tried to align the sentences by its lemmas. If the lemmas coincide we look for coincidences among parts of speech, and then the phrase is realigned using both. If the words do not share the same part of speech, they will not be aligned. Until here, we only have taken into account a lexical alignment. From now on, we are going to apply a semantic variant. After all the process, the non-aligned words will be analyzed taking into account its WorldNet's relations (synonymy, hyponymy, hyperonymy, derivationally – related – form, similar-to, verbal group, entailment and cause-to relation); and a set of equivalencies like abbreviations of months, countries, capitals, days and coins. In the case of the relation of hyperonymy and hyponymy, the words will be aligned if there is a word in the first sentence that is in the same relation (hyperonymy or hyponymy) of another one in the second sentence. For the relations of "cause-to" and "implication" the words will be aligned if there is a word in the first sentence that causes or implicates another one of the second sentence. All the other types of relations will be carried out in bidirectional way, that is, there is an alignment if a word of the first sentence is a synonymous of another one belonging to the second one or vice versa. Finally, we obtain a value we called alignment relation. This value is calculated as $FAV = NAW\ /\ NWSP$. Where FAV is the final alignment value, NAW is the number of aligned word and $NWSP$ is the number of words of the shorter phrase. This value is also another feature for our system.

3.3. Sentiment Polarity Feature

Another feature is obtained calculating SentiWordNet Polarities matches of the analyzed sentences (see (Gutiérrez *et al.*, 2011c) for detail). This analysis has been applied from several dimensions (WordNet, WordNet Domains, WordNet Affect, SUMO, and Semantic Classes) where the words with sentimental polarity offer to the relevant concepts (for each conceptual resource from ISR-WN (e.g. WordNet, WordNet Domains, WordNet Affect, SUMO, and Semantic Classes)) its polarity values. Other analysis were the integration of all results of polarity in a measure and further a voting process where all polarities output are involved (for more details see (Fernández *et al.*, 2012)).

The final measure corresponds to $PV = PolS_1 + PolS_2$, where $PolS_I$ is a polarity value of the sentence S_1 and $PolS_2$ is a polarity value of the sentence S_2. The negative, neutral, and positive values of polarities are represented as -1, 0 and 1 respectively.

3.4. Semantic Alignment

This alignment method depends on calculating the semantic similarity between sentences based on an analysis of the relations, in ISR-WN, of the words that fix them.

First, the two sentences are pre-processed with Freeling and the words are classified according to their parts of speech (noun, verb, adjective, and adverbs.).

We take 30% of the most probable senses of every word and we treat them as a group. The distance between two groups will be the minimal distance between senses of any pair of words belonging to the group. For example:

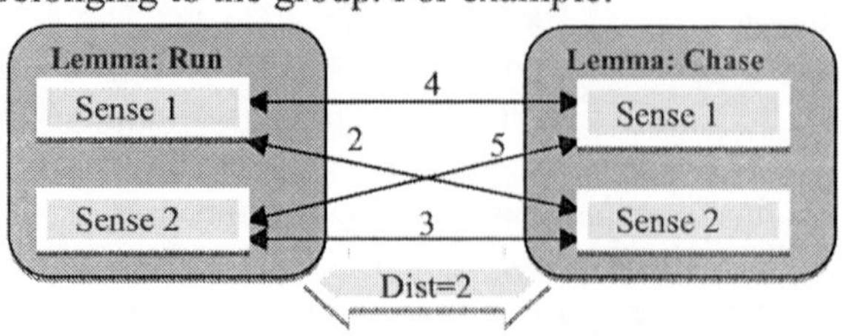

Figure 2. Minimal Distance between "Run" and "Chase".

In the example of Figure 2 the $Dist = 2$ is selected for the pair "Run-Chase", because this pair has the minimal cost=2.

For nouns and the words that are not found in WordNet like common nouns or Christian names, the distance is calculated in a different way. In this case, we used LED.

Let's see the following example:

We could take the pair 99 of corpus MSRvid (from training set) with a litter of transformation in order to a better explanation of our method.

Original pair

A: A polar bear is running towards a group of walruses.

B: A polar bear is chasing a group of walruses.

Transformed pair:

A_1: A polar bear runs towards a group of cats.

B_1: A wale chases a group of dogs.

Later on, using the algorithm showed in the example of Figure 2, a matrix with the distances between all groups of both sentences is created (see Table 1).

GROUPS	polar	bear	runs	towards	group	cats
wale	Dist:=3	Dist:=2	Dist:=3	Dist:=5		Dist:=2
chases	Dist:=4	Dist:=3	Dist:=2	Dist:=4		Dist:=3
group					Dist:=0	
dogs	Dist:=3	Dist:=1	Dist:=4	Dist:=4		Dist:=1

Table 1. Distances between the groups.

Using the Hungarian Algorithm (Kuhn, 1955) for Minimum Cost Assignment, each group of the smaller sentence is checked with an element of the biggest sentence and the rest is marked as words that were not aligned.

In the previous example the words "toward" and "polar" are the words that were not aligned, so the number of non-aligned words is 2. There is only one perfect match: "group-group" (match with $cost = 0$). The length of the shortest sentence is 4. The Table 2 shows the results of this analysis.

Number of exact coincidences (Same)	Total Distances of optimal Matching (Cost)	Number of non-aligned Words (Dif)	Number of lemmas of shorter sentence (Min)
1	5	2	4

Table 2. Features extracted from the analyzed sentences.

This process has to be repeated for the verbs, nouns (see Table 3), adjectives, and adverbs. On the contrary, the tables have to be created only with the similar groups of the sentences. Table 3 shows features extracted from the analysis of nouns.

GROUPS	bear	group	cats
wale	Dist := 2		Dist := 2
group		Dist := 0	
dogs	Dist := 1		Dist := 1

Table 3. Distances between the groups of nouns.

Number of exact coincidences (SameN)	Total Distances of optimal Matching (CostN)	Number of non-aligned Words (DifN)	Number of lemmas of shorter sentence (MinN)
1	3	0	3

Table 4. Feature extracted the analysis of nouns.

Several attributes are extracted from the pair of sentences. Four attributes from the entire sentences, four attributes considering only verbs, only nouns, only adjectives, and only adverbs. These attributes are:

- Number of exact coincidences (Same)
- Total distance of optimal matching (Cost).
- Number of words that do not match (Dif).
- Number of lemmas of the shortest sentence (Min).

As a result, we finally obtain 20 attributes from this alignment method. For each part-of-speech, the attributes are represented adding to its names the characters N, V, A and R to represent features for nouns, verbs, adjectives, and adverbs respectively.

It is important to remark that this alignment process searches to solve, for each word from the rows (see Table 3) its respectively word from the columns.

4. Description of the training phase

For the training process, we used a supervised learning framework, including all the training set (MSRpar, MSRvid and SMTeuroparl) as a training corpus. Using 10 fold cross validation with the classifier mentioned in section 2 (experimentally selected).

As we can see in Table 5, the features: FAV, EDx, CMLength, QGramD, BD, Same, SameN, obtain values over 0.50 of correlation. The more relevant are EDx and QGramD, which were selected as a lexical base for the experiment in Run 3. It is important to remark that feature SameN and Same only using number of exact coincidences obtain an encourage value of correlation.

Feature	Correlation	Feature	Correlation	Feature	Correlation	Correlation using all features (correspond to Run 1)
FAV	0.5064	ME	0.4971	CostV	0.1517	0.8519
LED	0.4572	OC	0.4983	SameN	0.5307	
DLED	0.4782	SDist	0.4037	MinN	0.4149	
NormLED	0.4349	AffDist	0.4043	DifN	0.1132	
NormDLED	0.4457	WNDist	0.2098	CostN	0.1984	
EDx	0.596	SCDist	0.1532	SameA	0.4182	
NW	0.2431	PV	0.0342	MinA	0.4261	
SW	0.2803	Same	0.5753	DifA	0.3818	
Jaro	0.3611	Min	0.5398	CostA	0.3794	
JaroW	0.2366	Dif	0.2588	SameR	0.3586	
CMLength	0.5588	Cost	0.2568	MinR	0.362	
QGramD	0.5749	SameV	0.3004	DifR	0.3678	
BD	0.5259	MinV	0.4227	CostR	0.3461	
JaccardS	0.4849	DifV	0.2634			

Table 5. Correlation of individual features over all training sets.

We decide to include the Sentiment Polarity as a feature, because our previous results on Textual Entailment task in (Fernández *et al.*, 2012). But, contrary to what we obtain in this paper, the influence of the polarity (PV) for this task is very low, its contribution working together with other features is not remarkable, but neither negative (Table 6), So we decide remaining in our system.

In oder to select the lexical base for Run 3 (MultiSem, features marked in bold) we compared the individual influences of the best lexical features (EDx, QGramD, CMLength), obtaining the 0.82, 0.83, 0.81 respectively (Table 6). Finally, we decided to use QGramD.

The conceptual features SDist, AffDist, WNDist, SCDist do not increase the similarity score, this is due to the generality of the obtained concept, losing the essential characteristic between both sentences. Just like with PV we decide to keep them in our system.

As we can see in Table 5, when all features are taking into account the system obtain the best score.

<table>
<tr><th>Feature</th><th colspan="9">Pearson (MSRpar, MSRvid and SMTeuroparl)</th></tr>
<tr><td>SDist</td><td bgcolor="gray"></td><td bgcolor="gray"></td><td bgcolor="gray"></td><td bgcolor="gray"></td><td bgcolor="gray"></td><td bgcolor="gray"></td><td bgcolor="gray"></td><td bgcolor="gray"></td><td rowspan="28">0.8509</td></tr>
<tr><td>AffDist</td><td bgcolor="gray"></td><td bgcolor="gray"></td><td bgcolor="gray"></td><td bgcolor="gray"></td><td bgcolor="gray"></td><td bgcolor="gray"></td><td bgcolor="gray"></td><td bgcolor="gray"></td></tr>
<tr><td>WNDist</td><td bgcolor="gray"></td><td bgcolor="gray"></td><td bgcolor="gray"></td><td bgcolor="gray"></td><td bgcolor="gray"></td><td bgcolor="gray"></td><td bgcolor="gray"></td><td bgcolor="gray"></td></tr>
<tr><td>SCDist</td><td bgcolor="gray"></td><td bgcolor="gray"></td><td bgcolor="gray"></td><td bgcolor="gray"></td><td bgcolor="gray"></td><td bgcolor="gray"></td><td bgcolor="gray"></td><td bgcolor="gray"></td></tr>
<tr><td>EDx</td><td bgcolor="gray"></td><td bgcolor="gray"></td><td bgcolor="gray"></td><td bgcolor="gray"></td><td bgcolor="gray"></td><td></td><td></td><td rowspan="24">0.8507</td></tr>
<tr><td>PV</td><td bgcolor="gray"></td><td bgcolor="gray"></td><td bgcolor="gray"></td><td bgcolor="gray"></td><td rowspan="2"></td><td bgcolor="gray"></td><td bgcolor="gray"></td></tr>
<tr><td>QGramD</td><td bgcolor="gray"></td><td bgcolor="gray"></td><td bgcolor="gray"></td><td></td><td bgcolor="gray"></td><td rowspan="22">0.8491</td></tr>
<tr><td>CMLength</td><td bgcolor="gray"></td><td bgcolor="gray"></td><td rowspan="21">0.8075</td><td bgcolor="gray"></td><td bgcolor="gray"></td><td bgcolor="gray"></td></tr>
<tr><td>Same</td><td rowspan="4">0.7043</td><td rowspan="20">0.795</td><td rowspan="20">0.829</td><td rowspan="20">0.8302</td><td rowspan="20">0.8228</td></tr>
<tr><td>Min</td></tr>
<tr><td>Dif</td></tr>
<tr><td>Cost</td></tr>
<tr><td>SameV</td><td rowspan="4">0.576</td></tr>
<tr><td>MinV</td></tr>
<tr><td>DifV</td></tr>
<tr><td>CostV</td></tr>
<tr><td>SameN</td><td rowspan="4">0.5975</td></tr>
<tr><td>MinN</td></tr>
<tr><td>DifN</td></tr>
<tr><td>CostN</td></tr>
<tr><td>SameA</td><td rowspan="4">0.4285</td></tr>
<tr><td>MinA</td></tr>
<tr><td>DifA</td></tr>
<tr><td>CostA</td></tr>
<tr><td>SameR</td><td rowspan="4">0.3778</td></tr>
<tr><td>MinR</td></tr>
<tr><td>DifR</td></tr>
<tr><td>CostR</td></tr>
</table>

Table 6. Features influence.

Note: Gray cells mean features that are not taking into account.

5. Result and discussion

Semantic Textual Similarity task of SemEval-2012 offered three official measures to rank the systems[5]:

1. ALL: Pearson correlation with the gold standard for the five datasets, and corresponding rank.
2. ALLnrm: Pearson correlation after the system outputs for each dataset are fitted to the gold standard using least squares, and corresponding rank.
3. Mean: Weighted mean across the five datasets, where the weight depends on the number of pairs in the dataset.
4. Pearson for individual datasets.

Using these measures, our main run (Run 1) obtained the best results (see Table 7). This demonstrates the importance of tackling this problem from a multidimensional lexical-semantic point of view.

Run	MSRpar	MSRvid	SMT-eur	On-WN	SMT-news
1	0.6205	0.8104	0.4325	0.6256	0.4340
2	0.6022	0.7709	0.4435	0.4327	0.4264
3	0.5269	0.7756	0.4688	0.6539	0.5470

Table 7. Official SemEval 2012 results.

Run	ALL	Rank	ALLnrm	RankNrm	Mean	RankMean
1	0.7213	18	0.8239	14	0.6158	15
2	0.6630	26	0.7922	46	0.5560	49
3	0.6529	29	0.8115	23	0.6116	16

Table 8. Ranking position of our runs in SemEval 2012.

The Run 2 uses a lot of lexical analysis and not much of semantic analysis. For this reason, the results for Run 2 is poorer (in comparison to the Run 3) (see Table 7) for the test sets: SMT-eur, On-WN and SMT-news. Of course, these tests have more complex semantic structures than the others. However, for test MSRpar it function better and for test MSRvid it functions very similar to Run 3.

Otherwise, the Run 3 uses more semantic analysis that Run 2 (it uses all features mentioned except feature marked in bold on Table 6) and only one lexical similarity measure (QGram-Distance). This makes it to work better for test sets SMT-eur, On-WN and SMT-news (see Table 7). It is important to remark that this run obtains important results for the test SMT-news, positioning this variant in the fifth place of 89 runs. Moreover, it is interesting to notice (Table 7) that when mixing the semantic features with the lexical one (creating Run 1) it makes the system to improve its general results, except for the test: SMT-eur, On-WN and SMT-news in comparison with Run 3. For these test sets seem to be necessary more semantic analysis than lexical in order to improve similarity estimation. We assume that Run 1 is non-balance according to the quantity of lexical and semantic features, because this run has a high quantity of

[5] http://www.cs.york.ac.uk/semeval-2012/task6/index.php?id=results-update

lexical and a few of semantic analysis. For that reason, Run 3 has a better performance than Run 1 for these test sets.

Even when the semantic measures demonstrate significant results, we do not discard the lexical help on Run 3. After doing experimental evaluations on the training phase, when lexical feature from QGram-Distance is not taken into account, the Run 3 scores decrease. This demonstrates that at least a lexical base is necessary for the Semantic Textual Similarity systems.

6. Conclusion and future works

This paper introduced a new framework for recognizing Semantic Textual Similarity, which depends on the extraction of several features that can be inferred from a conventional interpretation of a text.

As mentioned in section 2 we have conducted three different runs, these runs only differ in the type of attributes used. We can see in Table 7 that all runs obtained encouraging results. Our best run was placed between the first 18th positions of the ranking of Semeval 2012 (from 89 Runs) in all cases. Table 8 shows the reached positions for the three different runs and the ranking according to the rest of the teams.

In our participation, we used a MLS that works with features extracted from five different strategies: String Based Similarity Measures, Semantic Similarity Measures, Lexical-Semantic Alignment, Semantic Alignment, and Sentiment Polarity Cross-checking.

We have conducted the semantic features extraction in a multidimensional context using the resource ISR-WN, the one that allowed us to navigate across several semantic resources (WordNet, WordNet Domains, WordNet Affect, SUMO, SentiWorNet and Semantic Classes).

Finally, we can conclude that our system performs quite well. In our current work, we show that this approach can be used to correctly classify several examples from the STS task of SemEval-2012. Comparing with the best run (UKP_Run2 (see Table 9)) of the ranking our main run has very closed results. In two times we increased the best UKP's run (UKP_Run 2), for MSRvid test set in 0.2824 points and for On-WN test set in 0.1319 points (see Table 10).

Run	ALL	Rank	ALLnrm	RankNrm	Mean	RankMean
(UKP) Run 2	0.8239	1	0.8579	2	0.6773	1

Table 9. The best run of SemEval 2012.

It is important to remark that we do not expand any corpus to train the classifier of our system. This fact locates us at disadvantage according to other teams that do it.

Run	ALL	MSRpar	MSRvid	SMT-eur	On-WN	SMT-news
(UKP) Run 2	0.8239	0.8739	0.528	0.6641	0.4937	0.4937
(Our) Run 1	0.721	0.6205	0.8104	0.4325	0.6256	0.434

Table 10. Comparison of our distance with the best.

As future work we are planning to enrich our semantic alignment method with Extended WordNet (Moldovan and Rus, 2001), we think that with this improvement we can increase the results obtained with texts like those in On-WN test set.

Acknowledgments

This paper has been supported partially by Ministerio de Ciencia e Innovación - Spanish Government (grant no. TIN2009-13391-C04-01), and Conselleria d'Educación - Generalitat Valenciana (grant no. PROMETEO/2009/119 and ACOMP/2010/288).

Reference

Antonio Fernández, Yoan Gutiérrez, Rafael Muñoz and Andrés Montoyo. 2012. *Approaching Textual Entailment with Sentiment Polarity*. In ICAI'12 - The 2012 International Conference on Artificial Intelligence, Las Vegas, Nevada, USA.

Antonio Celso Fernández Orquín, Díaz Blanco Josval, Alfredo Fundora Rolo and Rafael Muñoz Guillena. 2009. *Un algoritmo para la extracción de características lexicográficas en la comparación de palabras*. In IV Convención Científica Internacional CIUM, Matanzas, Cuba.

Carlo Strapparava and Alessandro Valitutti. 2004. *WordNet-Affect: an affective extension of WordNet*. In Proceedings of the 4th International Conference on Language Resources and Evaluation (LREC 2004), Lisbon, 1083-1086.

Daniel S. Hirschberg. 1977. Algorithms for the longest common subsequence problem *Journal of the ACM*, 24: 664–675.

Dan I. Moldovan and Vasile Rus. 2001. Explaining Answers with Extended WordNet *ACL*.

Eneko Agirre, Daniel Cer, Mona Diab and Aitor Gonzalez-Agirre. 2012. *SemEval-2012 Task 6: A Pilot on Semantic Textual Similarity*. In Proceedings of the 6th International Workshop on Semantic Evaluation (SemEval 2012), in conjunction with the First Joint Conference on Lexical and Computational Semantics (*SEM 2012), Montreal, Canada, ACL.

George A. Miller, Richard Beckwith, Christiane Fellbaum, Derek Gross and Katherine Miller. 1990. Introduction to WordNet: An On-line Lexical Database *International Journal of Lexicography, 3(4):235-244.*

Harold W. Kuhn. 1955. The Hungarian Method for the assignment problem *Naval Research Logistics Quarterly*, 2: 83–97.

Ian Niles and Adam Pease. 2001. *Origins of the IEEE Standard Upper Ontology*. In Working Notes of the IJCAI-2001 Workshop on the IEEE Standard Upper Ontology, Seattle, Washington, USA.

Jordi Atserias, Bernardino Casas, Elisabet Comelles, Meritxell González, Lluís Padró and Muntsa Padró. 2006. *FreeLing 1.3: Syntactic and semantic services in an open source NLP library*. In Proceedings of the fifth international conference on Language Resources and Evaluation (LREC 2006), Genoa, Italy.

Marta Tatu, Brandon Iles, John Slavick, Novischi Adrian and Dan Moldovan. 2006. *COGEX at the Second Recognizing Textual Entailment Challenge*. In Proceedings of the Second PASCAL Recognising Textual Entailment Challenge Workshop, Venice, Italy, 104-109.

Rubén Izquierdo, Armando Suárez and German Rigau. 2007. A Proposal of Automatic Selection of Coarse-grained Semantic Classes for WSD *Procesamiento del Lenguaje Natural*, 39: 189-196.

Saul B. Needleman and Christian D. Wunsch. 1970. A general method applicable to the search for similarities in the amino acid sequence of two proteins *Journal of Molecular Biology*, 48(3): 443-453.

Vladimir Losifovich Levenshtein. 1965. *Binary codes capable of correcting spurious insertions and deletions of ones. Problems of information Transmission*. pp. 8-17.

William E. Winkler. 1999. *The state of record linkage and current research problems. Technical Report*. U.S. Census Bureau, Statistical Research Division.

Yoan Gutiérrez, Antonio Fernández, Andés Montoyo and Sonia Vázquez. 2010a. *UMCC-DLSI: Integrative resource for disambiguation task*. In Proceedings of the 5th International Workshop on Semantic Evaluation, Uppsala, Sweden, Association for Computational Linguistics, 427-432.

Yoan Gutiérrez, Antonio Fernández, Andrés Montoyo and Sonia Vázquez. 2010b. Integration of semantic resources based on WordNet *XXVI Congreso de la Sociedad Española para el Procesamiento del Lenguaje Natural*, 45: 161-168.

Yoan Gutiérrez, Antonio Fernández, Andrés Montoyo and Sonia Vázquez. 2011a. Enriching the Integration of Semantic Resources based on WordNet *Procesamiento del Lenguaje Natural*, 47: 249-257.

Yoan Gutiérrez, Sonia Vázquez and Andrés Montoyo. 2011b. *Improving WSD using ISR-WN with Relevant Semantic Trees and SemCor Senses Frequency*. In Proceedings of the International Conference Recent Advances in Natural Language Processing 2011, Hissar, Bulgaria, RANLP 2011 Organising Committee, 233--239.

Yoan Gutiérrez, Sonia Vázquez and Andrés Montoyo. 2011c. *Sentiment Classification Using Semantic Features Extracted from WordNet-based Resources*. In Proceedings of the 2nd Workshop on Computational Approaches to Subjectivity and Sentiment Analysis (WASSA 2.011), Portland, Oregon., Association for Computational Linguistics, 139--145.

SRIUBC: Simple Similarity Features for Semantic Textual Similarity

Eric Yeh
SRI International
Menlo Park, CA USA
yeh@ai.sri.com

Eneko Agirre
University of the Basque Country
Donostia, Basque Country
e.agirre@ehu.es

Abstract

We describe the systems submitted by SRI International and the University of the Basque Country for the Semantic Textual Similarity (STS) SemEval-2012 task. Our systems focused on using a simple set of features, featuring a mix of semantic similarity resources, lexical match heuristics, and part of speech (POS) information. We also incorporate precision focused scores over lexical and POS information derived from the BLEU measure, and lexical and POS features computed over split-bigrams from the ROUGE-S measure. These were used to train support vector regressors over the pairs in the training data. From the three systems we submitted, two performed well in the overall ranking, with split-bigrams improving performance over pairs drawn from the MSR Research Video Description Corpus. Our third system maintained three separate regressors, each trained specifically for the STS dataset they were drawn from. It used a multinomial classifier to predict which dataset regressor would be most appropriate to score a given pair, and used it to score that pair. This system underperformed, primarily due to errors in the dataset predictor.

1 Introduction

Previous semantic similarity tasks, such as paraphrase identification or recognizing textual entailment, have focused on performing binary decisions. These problems are usually framed in terms of identifying whether a pair of texts exhibit the needed similarity or entailment relationship or not. In many cases, such as producing a ranking over similarity scores, a soft measure of similarity between a pair of texts would be more desirable.

We contributed three systems for the 2012 Semantic Textual Similarity (STS) task (Agirre et al., 2012). These are:

1. **System 1**, which used a combination of semantic similarity, lexical similarity, and precision focused part-of-speech (POS) features.

2. **System 2**, which used features from System 1, with the addition of skip-bigram features derived from the ROUGE-S (Lin, 2004) measure. POS variants of skip-bigrams were incorporated as well.

3. **System 3**, used the features from above to first classify the dataset the pair was drawn from, and then applied regressors trained for that dataset.

Our systems characterize sentence pairs as feature vectors, populated by a variety of scorers that will be described below. During training, we used support vector regression (SVR) to train regressors against these vectors and their associated similarity scores.

The STS training data is divided into three datasets, reflecting their origin: Microsoft Research Paraphrase Corpus (MSRpar), MSR Research Video Description Corpus (MSRvid), and WMT2008 Development dataset (SMTeuroparl). We trained individual regressors for each of these datasets, and applied them to their counterparts in the testing set.

Both Systems 1 and 2 used the following types of features:

1. Resource based word to word semantic similarities.
2. Cosine-based lexical similarity measure.
3. Bilingual Evaluation Understudy (BLEU) (Papineni et al., 2002) lexical overlap.
4. Precision focused Part of Speech (POS) features.

System 2 added the following features:

1. Lexically motivated skip-bigram overlap.
2. Precision focused skip-bigram POS features.

One of the primary motivations for our the choice of features was to use relatively simple and fast features, which can be scaled up to large datasets, given appropriate caching and pre-generated lookups. As the test phase included surprise datasets, whose origin was not disclosed, we also trained a fourth model using all of the training data from all three datasets. Systems 1 and 2 employed this strategy for the surprise data.

Since the statistics for each of the training datasets varied, directly pooling them together may not be the best strategy when scoring the surprise data, whose origins were unknown. To account for this, System 3 treated this as a gated regression problem, where pairs are considered to originate strictly from one dataset, and to score using a model specifically tailored for that dataset. We first trained regressors on each of the datasets separately. Then we trained a classifier to predict which dataset a given pair is likeliest to have been drawn from, and then applied the matching trained regressor to obtain its score.

This team included one of the organizers. We want to stress that we took all measures to make our participation on the same conditions as the rest of participants. In particular, the organizer did not allow the other member of the team to access any data or information which was not already available for the rest of participants.

For the rest of this system description, we first outline the scorers used to populate the feature vectors used for Systems 1 and 2. We then describe the setup for performing the regression. We follow with an explanation of our strategies for dealing with the surprise data, including a description of System 3. We then summarize performance over the the datasets, and discuss future avenues of investigation.

2 Resource Based Similarity

Our system uses several resources for assessing the word to word similarity between a pair of sentences. In order to pool together the similarity scores for a given pair, we employed the Semantic Matrix (Fernando and Stevenson, 2008) framework. To generate the scores, we used several resources, principally those derived from the relation graph of WordNet (Fellbaum, 1998), and those derived from distributional resources, namely Explicit Semantic Analysis (Gabrilovich and Markovitch, 2009), and the Dekang Lin Proximity-based Thesaurus [1]. We now describe the Semantic Matrix method, and follow with descriptions of each of the resources used.

2.1 Semantic Matrix

The Semantic Matrix is a method for pooling all of the pairwise similarity scores between the tokens found in two input strings. In order to score the similarity between a pair of strings s_1 and s_2 we first identify all of the unique vocabulary words from these strings to derive their corresponding occurrence vectors $\mathbf{v_1}$ and $\mathbf{v_2}$. Each dimension of these vectors corresponds to a unique vocabulary word, and binary values were used, corresponding to whether that word was observed. The similarity score for pair, $\mathrm{sim}(s_1, s_2)$, is given by Formula 1.

$$\mathrm{sim}(s_1, s_2) = \frac{\mathbf{v_1}^T \mathbf{W} \mathbf{v_2}}{\|\mathbf{v_1}\| \, \|\mathbf{v_2}\|} \qquad (1)$$

with $\mathbf{W}$ being the symmetric matrix marking the similarity between pairs of words in the vocabulary. We note that this is similar to the Mahalanobis distance, except adjusted to produce a similarity. For this experiment, we normalized matrix entries so all values lay in the 0-1 range.

As named entities and other words encountered may not appear in one or more of the resources used, we applied the identity to $\mathbf{W}$. This is equivalent to adding a strict lexical match fallback on top of the similarity measure.

[1] http://webdocs.cs.ualberta.ca/ lindek/downloads.htm

Per (Fernando and Stevenson, 2008), a filter was applied over the values of $\mathbf{W}$. Any entries that fell below a given threshold value were flattened to zero, in order to prevent low scoring similarities from overwhelming the score. From previous studies over MSRpar, we applied a threshold of 0.9.

For our experiments, each of the word to word similarity scorers described below were used to generate a corresponding word similarity matrix $\mathbf{W}$, with scores generated using the Semantic Matrix.

2.2 WordNet Similarity

We used several methods to obtain word to word similarities from WordNet. WordNet is a lexical-semantic resource that describes typed relationships between *synsets*, semantic categories a word may belong to. Similarity scoring methods identify the synsets associated with a pair of words, and then use this relationship graph to generate a score.

The first set of scorers were generated from the Leacock-Chodorow, Lin, and Wu-Palmer measures from the WordNet Similarity package (Pedersen et al., 2004). For each of these measures, we averaged across all of the possible synsets between a given pair of words.

Another scorer we used was Personalized PageRank (PPR) (Agirre et al., 2010), a topic sensitive variant of the PageRank algorithm (Page et al., 1999) that uses a random walk process to identify the significant nodes of a graph given its link structure. We first derived a graph $\mathbf{G}$ from WordNet, treating synsets as the vertices and the relationships between synsets as the edges. To obtain a signature for a given word, we apply topic sensitive PageRank (Haveliwala, 2002) over $\mathbf{G}$, using the synsets associated with the word as the initial distribution. At convergence, we convert the stationary distribution into a vector. The similarity between two words is the cosine similarity between their vectors.

2.3 Distributional Resources

In contrast with the structure based WordNet based methods, distributional methods use statistical properties of corpora to derive similarity scores. We generated two scorers, one based on Explicit Semantic Analysis (ESA), and the other on the Dekang Lin Proximity-based Thesaurus. For a given word, ESA generates a *concept vector*, where the concepts are Wikipedia articles, and the score measures how closely associated that word is with the textual content of the article. To score the similarity between two words, we computed the cosine similarity of their concept vectors. This method proved to give state-of-the-art performance on the WordSim-353 word pair relatedness dataset (Finkelstein et al., 2002).

The Lin Proximity-based Thesaurus identifies the neighborhood around words encountered in the Reuters and Text Retrieval Conference (TREC). For a given word, the Thesaurus identifies the top 200 words with the most similar neighborhoods, listing the score based on these matches. For our experiments, we treated these as feature vectors, with the intuition being similar words should share similar neighbors. Again, the similarity score between two words was scored using the cosine similarity of their vectors.

3 Cosine Similarity

Another scorer we used was the cosine similarity over the lemmas found in the sentences in a pair. For generating the vectors used in the cosine similarity computation, we used the term frequency of the lemmas.

4 BLEU Features

BLEU is a measure developed to automatically assess how closely sentences generated by machine translation systems match reference human generated texts. BLEU is a directional measurement, and works on the assumption that the more lexically similar a *system* generated sentence is to a *reference* sentence, a human generated translation, the better the system sentence is. This can also be seen as a stand-in for the semantic similarity of the pairs, as was shown when BLEU was applied to the paraphrase identification identification problem in (Finch et al., 2005).

The BLEU score for a given system sentence and reference sentence of order N is computed using Formula 2.

$$\text{BLEU}(sys, ref) = B \cdot \exp \sum_{n=1}^{N} \frac{1}{N} \log(p_n) \quad (2)$$

B is a brevity penalty used to prevent degenerate translations. Given this has little bearing on our experiments, we set its value to 1 for our experiments. Following (Papineni et al., 2002), we give each order n equal weight in the geometric mean. The probability of an order n-gram from the system sentence being found in the reference, p_n, is given in Formula 3.

$$p_n = \frac{\sum_{ngram \in sys} \text{count}_{sys \wedge ref}(ngram)}{\sum_{ngram \in sys} \text{count}_{sys}(ngram)} \quad (3)$$

$\text{count}_{sys}(ngram)$ is frequency of occurrence for the given n-gram in the system sentence. The numerator term is computed as $\text{count}_{sys \wedge ref}(ngram) = \min(\text{count}_{sys}(ngram), \text{count}_{ref}(ngram))$ where $\text{count}_{ref}(ngram)$ is the frequency of occurrence of that n-gram in the reference sentence. This is equivalent to having each n-gram have a 1-1 mapping with a matching n-gram in the reference (if any), and counting the number of mappings.

As there is a risk of higher order system n-grams having no matches in the reference, we apply Laplacian smoothing to the n-gram counts.

BLEU is considered to be a precision focused measure, as it only measures how much of the system sentence matches a reference sentence. Following (Finch et al., 2005), we obtain a modified BLEU score for strings s_1 and s_2 of a pair by averaging the BLEU scores where each takes a turn as the system sentence, as given in Formula 4.

$$\text{Score}(s_1, s_2) = \frac{1}{2}\text{BLEU}(s_1, s_2) \cdot \text{BLEU}(s_2, s_1) \quad (4)$$

For our experiments, we used BLEU scores of order $N = 1..4$, over n-grams formed over the sentence lemmas, and used these as features for characterizing a given pair.

4.1 Precision Focused POS Features

From past experiments with paraphrase identification over the MSR Paraphrase Corpus, we have found including POS information to be beneficial. To this capture this kind of information, we generated precision focused POS features, which measures the following between the sentences in a problem pair:

1. The overlap in POS tags.
2. The mismatch in POS tags.

We follow the formulation for POS vectors given in (Finch et al., 2005). For a given sentence pair, we identify the set of words whose lemmas were matched in both the system and reference sentences, W_{match} and those with no matches, W_{miss}. Using the directional notion of system and reference sentences from BLEU, for each word $w \in W_{match}$,

$$\text{POSMatch}(t, sys, ref) = \frac{\sum_{w \in W_{match}} \text{count}_t(w)}{|sys|} \quad (5)$$

where count_t is 1 if word w has the matching POS tag, and 0 otherwise. $|sys|$ is the token count of the system sentence. This is deemed to be precision-focused, as this computation is done over candidates found in the system sentence.

To generate the score for missing POS tags, we perform a similar computation,

$$\text{POSMiss}(t, sys, ref) = \frac{\sum_{w \in W_{miss}} \text{count}_t(w)}{|sys|} \quad (6)$$

To score the POS match and misses between a pair, we follow Formula 4 and average the scores for each POS tag, where the sentences in a given pair swap positions as the system and reference sentences.

5 Split-Bigram Features

System 2 added split-bigram features, which were derived from the ROUGE-S measure. Like bigrams, split-bigrams consist of an ordered pair of distinct tokens drawn from a source sentence. Unlike bigrams, split-bigrams allow for a number of intervening tokens to appear between the split-bigram tokens. For example, *"The cat ate fish."* would generate the following split-bigrams *the→cat*, *the→ate*, *the→fish*, *cat→ate*, *cat→fish*, and *ate→fish*. The intent of split-bigrams is to quickly capture long range dependencies, without requiring a parse of the sentence.

Similar to ROUGE-S, we used lexical overlap of the split-bigrams as an approximation of semantic similarity. As our pairs are bidirectional, we used the same framework (Formula 2) for obtaining BLEU scores to generate split-bigram overlap scores for our pairs. Here, counts are obtained over split-bigrams found in the system and reference sentences, and the order was set to 1.

For generating the skip-bigram overlap score for a pair, we used a maximum distance of three.

5.1 Skip-Bigram POS Features

In the same vein as the precision focused POS features, we used the POS tags of matched split-bigrams as features, where the frequency of the POS tags in split-bigrams, $t \rightarrow t'$, were used. Here, B_{match} represents the split-bigrams which were found in both the system and reference sentences, matched on lexical content.

$$\text{SBMatch}(t \rightarrow t', sys, ref) = \frac{\sum\limits_{b \in B_{match}} \text{count}_{t \rightarrow t'}(b)}{|sys|} \quad (7)$$

Due to sparsity, we only considered scores from split-bigram matches between the system and reference sentences, and do not model split-bigram misses. As before, we generate scores for each split-bigram tag sequence by averaging the scores where both sentences in a pair have swapped positions. For our experiments, we only considered split-bigram POS features of up to distance 3. In our initial experiments we found split-bigram POS features helped only in the case of shorter sentence pairs, so we only generated features if both the sentences in a given pair contained ten tokens or less.

6 Experimental Setup

For all three systems, we used the Stanford CoreNLP (Toutanova et al., 2003) package to perform lemmatization and POS tagging of the input sentences. For regressors, we used LibSVM's (Chang and Lin, 2011) support vector regression capability, using radial basis kernels. Based off of tuning on the training set, we set $\gamma = 1$ and the default slack value.

From previous experience with paraphrase identification over the MSR Paraphrase Corpus, we retained stop words in all of our experiments.

Dataset	Mean	Std.Dev
MSRpar	3.322	0.9294
MSRvid	2.135	1.595
SMTeur	4.307	0.7114

Table 1: Means and standard deviations of similarity scores for each of the training datasets.

7 Dealing with Surprise Data

As the STS training data was broken into three separate datasets, each with their own distinct statistics, we developed three regressors trained individually on each of these datasets. This presented a problem when dealing with surprise datasets, whose statistics were not known.

The approach taken by Systems 1 and 2 was simply to pool together all three training datasets into a single dataset and train a single regressor on that unified model. We then applied that regressor against the two surprise datasets, OnWN and SMTnews.

Analysis of the similarity score statistics showed that they varied greatly between each of the training sets, as given in Table 1. Thus combining the datasets blindly, as with Systems 1 and 2, may prove to be a suboptimal strategy. The approach taken by System 3 was to consider the feature vectors themselves as capturing information about which dataset they were drawn from, and to use a classifier to predict that dataset. We then emit the score from the regressor trained on just that matching dataset. We used the Stanford Classifier's (Manning and Klein, 2003) multinomial logistic regression as our dataset predictor, using the feature vectors from System 2.

Five-fold cross validation over the training data showed the dataset predictor to have an overall accuracy of 91.75%.

In order to assess performance over the known datasets at test time, System 3 also applied the same strategy for the MSRpar, MSRvid, and SMTeuroparl test sets.

Sys	All	Allnorm	Mean	MSRpar	MSRvid	SMTeur	OnWN	SMTnews
1	0.7513 / 11	0.8017 / 40	0.5997 / 22	**0.6084**	0.7458	**0.4688**	**0.6315**	**0.3994**
2	0.7562 / 10	0.8111 / 24	0.5858 / 33	0.6050	**0.7939**	0.4294	0.5871	0.3366
3	0.6876 / 21	0.7812 / 54	0.4668 / 68	0.4791	0.7901	0.2159	0.3843	0.2801

Table 2: Pearson correlation of described systems against test data, by dataset. Overall measures are *All* indicates the combined Pearson, *Allnorm* the normalized variant, and *Mean* the macro average of Pearson correlations. Rank for the system in the overall measure is given after the slash.

Guess/Gold	MSRpar	MSRvid	SMTeur
MSRpar	664	7	75
MSRvid	7	737	10
SMTeur	79	6	649

Table 3: Confusion for the dataset predictor, used to predict which dataset a pair was drawn from. This was ddrawn using five-fold cross validation over the training set, with columns representing golds and guesses as rows.

Dataset	Prec	Rec	F1
MSRpar	0.8901	0.8853	0.8877
MSRvid	0.9775	0.9827	0.9801
SMTeur	0.8842	0.8842	0.8842

Table 4: Results on classifying pairs by source dataset, using five-fold cross validation over training data.

8 Results and Discussion

Results on the test data for each of the systems against the individual datasets, are given in Table 2, given in Pearson linear correlation with the gold standard scores. Overall measures for the systems are given, along with their overall ranking.

The split-bigram features in System 2 contributed primarily to performance over the MSRvid dataset, while degrading performance on the other datasets slightly. This is likely a result of increasing sparsity in the feature space, but overall this system performed well. System 3 underperformed on most datasets, asides from its performance on MSRvid. The confusion generated over five-fold cross validation over the training set is given in Table 3, and precision, recall, and F1 scores by dataset label from five-fold cross validation over the training set are given in Table 4. As these show, predictor errors lay primarily in confusing MSRpar for SMTeuroparl, and vice versa. This error was significant enough to reduce performance on both the MSRpar and SMTeuroparl test sets. This proved to be enough to reduce the scores between these two datasets.

9 Conclusion and Future Work

Our STS systems have shown that relatively simple syntax free methods can be employed to the STS task. Future avenues of investigation would be to include the use of syntactic information, in order to obtain better predicate-argument information. Syntactic information has proven useful for the paraphrase identification task over MSRpar, as demonstrated in studies such as (Das and Smith, 2009) and (Socher et al., 2011). Furthermore, a qualitative assessment of the pairs across different datasets showed relatively significant differences, which would strengthen the argument for developing features and methods specific to each dataset. Another improvement would be to develop a better dataset predictor for System 3. Also recognizing there may be ways to normalize and rescale scores across datasets so the regression models used do not have to account for differing means and standard deviations.

Finally, there are other bodies of source data that may be adapted for use with the STS task, such as the paraphrasing pairs of the Recognizing Textual Entailment challenges, human generated reference translations for machine translation evaluation, and human generated summaries used for summarization evaluations. Although these are gold decisions, at the very least they could provide a source of high similarity pairs, from which one could manufacture lower scoring variants.

Acknowledgments

The authors would like to thank the Semantic Textual Similarity organizers for all of their hard work and effort.

One of the authors was supported by the Intelligence Advanced Research Projects Activity (IARPA) via Air Force Research Laboratory (AFRL) contract number FA8650-10-C-7058. The U.S. Government is authorized to reproduce and distribute reprints for Governmental purposes notwithstanding any copyright annotation thereon. The views and conclusions contained herein are those of the authors and should not be interpreted as necessarily representing the official policies or endorsements, either expressed or implied, of IARPA, AFRL, or the U.S. Government.

Eneko Agirre was partially funded by the European Communitys Seventh Framework Programme (FP7/2007-2013) under grant agreement no. 270082 (PATHS project) and the Ministry of Economy under grant TIN2009-14715-C04-01 (KNOW2 project)

References

Eneko Agirre, Montse Cuadros, German Rigau, and Aitor Soroa. 2010. Exploring knowledge bases for similarity. In *Proceedings of the International Conference on Language Resources and Evaluation 2010*.

Eneko Agirre, Daniel Cer, Mona Diab, and Aitor Gonzalez-Agirre. 2012. Semeval-2012 task 6: A pilot on semantic textual similarity. In *Proceedings of the 6th International Workshop on Semantic Evaluation (SemEval 2012), in conjunction with the First Joint Conference on Lexical and Computational Semantics (*SEM 2012)*.

Chih-Chung Chang and Chih-Jen Lin. 2011. LIBSVM: A library for support vector machines. *ACM Transactions on Intelligent Systems and Technology*, 2:27:1–27:27.

Dipanjan Das and Noah A. Smith. 2009. Paraphrase identification as probabilistic quasi-synchronous recognition. In *In Proceedings of the Joint Conference of the Annual Meeting of the Association for Computational Linguistics and the International Joint Conference on Natural Language Processing(ACL 2009)*, pages 468–476, Singapore.

Christine Fellbaum. 1998. *WordNet - An Electronic Lexical Database*. MIT Press.

Samuel Fernando and Mark Stevenson. 2008. A semantic similarity approach to paraphrase detection. In *Computational Linguistics UK (CLUK 2008) 11th Annual Research Colloqium*.

Andrew Finch, Young-Sook Hwang, and Eiichio Sumita. 2005. Using machine translation evaluation techniques to determine sentence-level semantic equivalence. In *Proceedings of the Third International Workshop on Paraphrasing (IWP 2005)*, pages 17–24, Jeju Island, South Korea.

Lev Finkelstein, Evgeniy Gabrilovich, Yossi Matias, Ehud Rivlin, Zach Solan, Gadi Wolfman, and Eytan Ruppin. 2002. Placing search in context: The concept revisited. *ACM Transactions on Information Systems*, 20(1):116–131.

Evgeniy Gabrilovich and Shaul Markovitch. 2009. Wikipedia-based semantic interpretation. *Journal of Artificial Intelligence Research*, 34:443–498.

Taher H. Haveliwala. 2002. Topic-sensitive pagerank. In *WWW '02*, pages 517–526, New York, NY, USA. ACM.

Chin-Yew Lin. 2004. Rouge: A package for automatic evaluation of summaries. pages 74–81, Barcelona, Spain, jul. Association for Computational Linguistics.

Christopher Manning and Dan Klein. 2003. Optimization, maxent models, and conditional estimation without magic. In *Proceedings of the 2003 Conference of the North American Chapter of the Association for Computational Linguistics on Human Language Technology: Tutorials - Volume 5*, NAACL-Tutorials '03, pages 8–8, Stroudsburg, PA, USA. Association for Computational Linguistics.

Lawrence Page, Sergey Brin, Rajeev Motwani, and Terry Winograd. 1999. The pagerank citation ranking: Bringing order to the web. Technical Report 1999-66, Stanford InfoLab, November. Previous number = SIDL-WP-1999-0120.

Kishore Papineni, Salim Roukos, Todd Ward, and Wei-Jing Zhu. 2002. Bleu: a method for automatic evaluation of machine translation. In *Proceedings of the 40th Annual Meeting on Association for Computational Linguistics*, ACL '02, pages 311–318, Stroudsburg, PA, USA. Association for Computational Linguistics.

Ted Pedersen, Siddharth Patwardhan, and Jason Michelizzi. 2004. WordNet::Similarity - Measuring the Relatedness of Concepts. In *Proceedings of the Nineteenth National Conference on Artificial Intelligence (Intelligent Systems Demonstrations)*, pages 1024–1025, San Jose, CA, July.

Richard Socher, Eric H. Huang, Jeffrey Pennington, Andrew Y. Ng, and Christopher D. Manning. 2011. Dynamic pooling and unfolding recursive autoencoders for paraphrase detection. In *Advances in Neural Information Processing Systems 24*.

Kristina Toutanova, Dan Klein, Christopher D. Manning, and Yoram Singer. 2003. Feature-rich part-of-speech tagging with a cyclic dependency network. In *Proceedings of HLT-NAACL 2003*, pages 252–259.

FBK: Machine Translation Evaluation and Word Similarity metrics for Semantic Textual Similarity

José Guilherme C. de Souza
Fondazione Bruno Kessler
University of Trento
Povo, Trento, Italy
desouza@fbk.eu

Matteo Negri
Fondazione Bruno Kessler
Povo, Trento
Italy
negri@fbk.eu

Yashar Mehdad
Fondazione Bruno Kessler
Povo, Trento
Italy
mehdad@fbk.eu

Abstract

This paper describes the participation of FBK in the Semantic Textual Similarity (STS) task organized within Semeval 2012. Our approach explores lexical, syntactic and semantic machine translation evaluation metrics combined with distributional and knowledge-based word similarity metrics. Our best model achieves 60.77% correlation with human judgements (*Mean* score) and ranked 20 out of 88 submitted runs in the *Mean* ranking, where the average correlation across all the sub-portions of the test set is considered.

1 Introduction

The Semantic Textual Similarity (STS) task proposed at SemEval 2012 consists of examining the degree of semantic equivalence between two sentences and assigning a score to quantify such similarity ranging from 0 (the two texts are about different topics) to 5 (the two texts are semantically equivalent). The complete description of the task, the datasets and the evaluation methodology adopted can be found in (Agirre et al., 2012).

Typical approaches to measure semantic textual similarity exploit information at the lexical level. The proposed solutions range from calculating the overlap of common words between the two text segments (Salton et al., 1997) to the application of knowledge-based and corpus-based word similarity metrics to cope with the low recall achieved by on simple lexical matching (Mihalcea et al., 2006).

Our participation in the STS task is inspired by previous work on paraphrase recognition, in which machine translation (MT) evaluation metrics are used to identify whether a pair of sentences are semantically equivalent or not (Finch and Hwang, 2005; Wan et al., 2006). Our approach to semantic textual similarity makes use of not only lexical information but also syntactic and semantic information. To this aim, our metrics are based on different natural language processing tools that provide syntactic and semantic annotation. These include shallow parsing, constituency parsing, dependency parsing, semantic roles labeling, discourse representation analyzer, and named entities recognition. In addition, we employed distributional and knowledge-based word similarity metrics in an attempt to improve the results given by the MT metrics. The computed scores are used as features to train a regression model in a supervised learning framework.

Our best run model achieves 60.77% correlation with human judgements when evaluating the semantic similarity of texts from the entire test set and was ranked in the 20th position (out of 88 submitted runs) in the *Mean* ranking.

2 System Description

The system has been designed following a machine learning based approach in which a regression model is induced using different shallow and deep linguistic features extracted from the datasets. The STS training corpora are first preprocessed using different tools that annotate the texts at different levels. Using the preprocessed data, the features are extracted for each pair and used to train a model that will be applied to unseen test pairs. The training set is composed by three datasets (*MSRpar*, *MSRvid* and *SMTeuroparl*) which combined contain a total of 2234 instances. The test data is composed by a different sample of the same three datasets plus instances derived from two additional corpora (*OnWN* and *SMTnews*). The datasets construction and annotation are described in (Agirre et al., 2012).

Our system exploits two sets of features which respectively build on MT evaluation metrics (2.1) and word similarity metrics (2.2). The whole feature set is summarized in figure 1.

2.1 Machine Translation Evaluation Metrics

MT evaluation metrics are designed to assess whether the output of a MT system is semantically equivalent to a set of reference translations. The MT evaluation metrics described in this section, implemented in the Asiya Open Toolkit for Automatic Machine Translation (Meta-) Evaluation[1] (Giménez and Màrquez, 2010) are used to extract features at different linguistic levels: lexical, syntactic and semantic. For the syntactic and semantic levels, Asiya calculates similarity measures based on the linguistic elements provided by each kind of annotation. Linguistic elements are defined as "the linguistic units, structures, or relationships" (Giménez, 2008) (e.g. dependency relations, discourse relations, named entities, part-of-speech tags, among others). (Giménez, 2008) defines two simple measures using the linguistic elements of a given linguistic level: overlapping and matching. `Overlapping` is a measure of the proportion of items inside the linguistic elements of a certain type shared by both texts. `Matching` is defined in the same way with the difference that the order between the items inside a linguistic element is taken into consideration. That is, the items of a linguistic element are concatenated in a single unit from left to right.

2.1.1 Lexical Level

At the lexical level we explored different n-gram and edit distance based metrics. The difference among them is in the way each algorithm calculates the lexical similarity, which yields to different results. We used the following n-gram-based metrics: BLEU (Papineni et al., 2002), NIST (Doddington, 2002), ROUGE (Lin and Och, 2004), GTM (Melamed et al., 2003), METEOR (Banerjee and Lavie, 2005). Besides those, we also used metrics based on edit distance. Such metrics calculate the number of edit operations (e.g. insertions, deletions, and substitutions) necessary to transform one text into the other (the lower the number of edit operations, the higher the similarity score). The edit-distance-based metrics used were: WER (Nieß en et al., 2000), PER (Tillmann et al., 1997), TER (Snover et al., 2006) and TER-Plus (Snover et al., 2009). The lexical metrics form a group of metrics that we hereafter call `lex`.

2.1.2 Syntactic Level

The syntactic level was explored by running constituency parsing (`cp`), dependency parsing (`dp`), and shallow parsing (`sp`). Constituency trees were produced by the Max-Ent reranking parser (Charniak, 2005). The **constituency parse** trees were exploited by using three different classes of metrics that were designed to calculate the similarities between the trees of two texts: `overlapping` in function of a given part-of-speech; `matching` in function of a given constituency type; and syntactic tree matching (STM) metric proposed by (Liu and Gildea, 2005).

Dependency trees were obtained using MINIPAR (Lin, 2003). Two types of metrics were used to calculate the similarity between two texts using dependency trees. In the first, different similarity measures were calculated taking into consideration three different perspectives: overlap of words that hang in the same level or in a deeper level of the dependency tree; overlap between words that hang directly from terminal nodes given a specified part-of-speech; and overlap between words that are ruled by non-terminal nodes given a specified grammatical relation (subject, object, relative clause, among others). The second type is an implementation of the head-word chain matching introduced in (Liu and Gildea, 2005).

The **shallow syntax** approach proposed by (Giménez, 2008) uses three different tools to explore the parts-of-speech, word lemmas and base phrases chunks, respectively: SVMTool (Giménez and Màrquez, 2004), Freeling (Carreras et al., 2004) and Phreco (Carreras et al., 2005). In this type of metrics the idea is to measure the similarity between the two texts using parts-of-speech and chunk types. The following metrics were used: `overlapping` according to the part-of-speech; `overlapping` according to the chunk type; the accumulated NIST metric (Doddington, 2002) scores over different

[1] `http://nlp.lsi.upc.edu/asiya/`

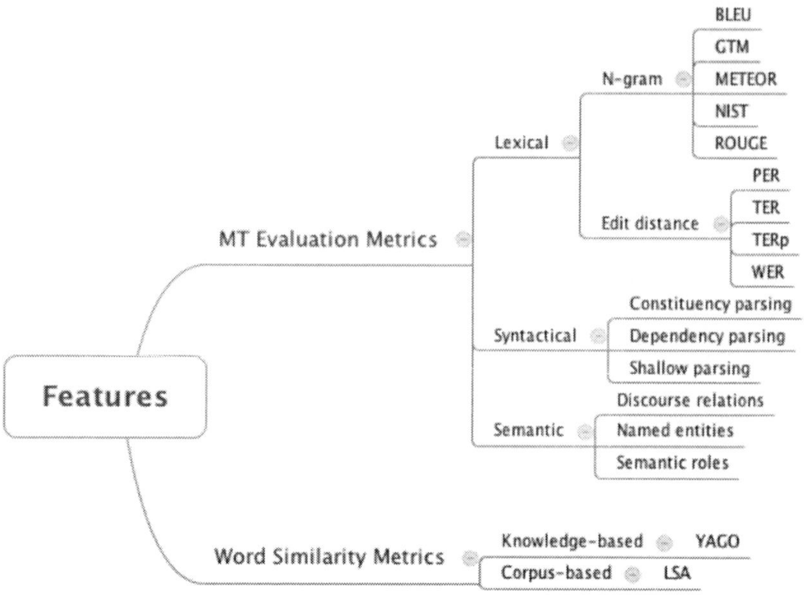

Figure 1: A summary of the class of features explored.

sequences (lemmas, parts-of-speech, base phrase chunks and chunk IOB labels).

2.1.3 Semantic Level

At the semantic level we aplored three different types of information, namely: discourse representations, named entities and semantic roles. Hereafter they are respectively referred to as `dr`, `ne`, and `sr` features. The discourse relations are automatically annotated using the C&C Tools (Clark and Curran, 2004). The following metrics using semantic tree representations were proposed by (Giménez, 2008). A metric similar to the STM in which semantic trees are used instead of constituency trees; the `overlapping` between **discourse representation** structures according to their type; and the morphosyntactic `overlapping` of discourse representation structures that share the same type.

Named entities metrics are calculated by comparing the entities that appear in each text. The named entities were annotated using the BIOS package (Surdeanu et al., 2005). Two types of metrics were used: the `overlapping` between the named entities in each sentence according to their type and the `matching` between the named entities in function of their type.

Semantic roles were automatically annotated using the SwiRL package (Surdeanu and Turmo, 2005). The arguments and adjuncts annotated in each sentence are compared according to three different metrics: `overlapping` between the semantic roles according to their type; the `matching` between the semantic roles according to their type; and the `overlapping` of the roles without taking into consideration their lexical realization.

2.2 Word Similarity Metrics

Besides the MT evaluation metrics, we experimented with lexical semantics by calculating word similarity metrics. For that, we followed a distributional and a knowledge-based word similarity approach.

2.2.1 Distributional Word Similarity

As some previous work on semantic textual textual similarity (Mihalcea et al., 2006) and textual entailment (Kouylekov et al., 2010; Mehdad et al., 2010) have shown, distributional word similarity measures can improve the performance of both tasks by allowing matches between terms that are lexically different. We measure the word similarity computing a set of Latent Semantic Analysis (LSA) metrics over Wikipedia. The 200,000 most visited articles of Wikipedia were extracted and cleaned to build the term-by-document matrix using the jLSI tool[2].

Using this model we designed three different similarity metrics that compute the similarity between all elements in one text with all elements in the other text. For two metrics we calculate the similarities between different parts-of-speech: (i) similarity over nouns and adjectives, and (ii) similarity over verbs. The third metric computes the similarity between all words in the two sentences. The similarity is computed by averaging the pairwise similarity using the LSA model between the elements of each text. These metrics are hereafter called `lsa`.

2.2.2 Knowledge-based Word Similarity

In order to incorporate world knowledge information about entities (persons, organizations, locations, among others) into our model we experimented with knowledge-based (thesaurus-based) word similarity metrics. Usually such approaches have a very limited coverage of concepts due to the reduced size of the available thesauri. In order to increase the coverage we extracted concepts from the YAGO2 semantic knowledge base (Hoffart et al., 2011) derived from Wikipedia, Wordnet (Miller, 1995) and Geonames[3]. YAGO2 contains knowledge about 10 million entities and more than 120 million facts about these entities.

In order to link the entities in the text to the entities in YAGO2 we have used "The Wiki Machine" (TWM) tool[4]. The tool solves the linking problem by disambiguating each entity mention in the text (excluding pronouns) using Wikipedia to provide the sense inventory and the training data (Giuliano et al., 2009). After preprocessing the datasets with TWM the entities are annotated with their respective Wikipedia entries represented by their URLs. Using the entity's URL it is possible to retrieve the Wordnet synsets related to the entity's entry in YAGO2 and explore different knowledge-based metrics to compute word similarity between entities.

In our experiments we selected three different algorithms to calculate word similarity using YAGO2: Wu-Palmer (Zhibiao and Palmer, 1994), the Leacock-Chodorow (Leacock et al., 1998) and the path distance (score based on the shortest path that connects the senses in the Wordnet hypernym/hyponym taxonomy). Two classes of metrics were designed: (i) the average of the similarity between all the entities in each sentence and (ii) the similarity of the pair of elements which have the shortest path in the Wordnet taxonomy among all possible pairs. There are six different metrics using the three algorithms in total. An extra metric was designed using only TWM. The metric is calculated by taking the number of common entities in the two sentences divided by the total number of entities annotated in the two sentences. The metrics described in this section are part of the `yago` group.

[2]`http://hlt.fbk.eu/en/technology/jlsi`

[3]`http://www.geonames.org/`

[4]`http://thewikimachine.fbk.eu/html/index.html`

3 Experiments and Discussion

In this section we present our experiments settings, the configuration of the runs submitted and discuss the results obtained. All our experiments were made using half of the training set for training and half for testing (development). Ten different randomizations were run over the training data in order to obtain ten different pairs of train/development sets and reduce overfitting. We tried several different regression algorithms and the best performance was achieved with the implementation of Support Vector Machines (SVM) of the SVMLight package (Joachims, 1998). We used the radial basis function kernel with default parameters without any special tuning for the different datasets.

3.1 Submitted Runs and Results

Based on the results achieved with different feature sets over training data we have selected the best combinations for our submission. The feature sets for each run are:

> **Run 1:** `lex`, `lsa`, `yago`, and a selection of features in the `cp`, `dp`, `sp`, `dr`, `ne` and `sr` groups, forming a total of 286 features.
>
> **Run 2:** `lex`, `lsa`, and `yago`, in a total of 50 features.
>
> **Run 3:** `lex` and `lsa`, forming a total of 43 features.

The results obtained by our three submitted runs are summarized in table 1. The table reports the

		Runs submitted				
		Run 1	Run 2	Run 3	Base	PE
Development		0.885	0.863	0.859	-	-
Test	MSp	0.249	0.512	**0.516**	0.433	0.577
	MSv	0.611	**0.780**	0.777	0.299	0.818
	SMTe	0.149	0.379	**0.441**	0.454	0.450
	Wn	0.421	0.622	**0.629**	0.586	0.629
	SMTn	0.243	0.547	**0.608**	0.390	0.608
	All	0.563	0.643	**0.651**	0.310	0.789
	Allnrm	0.712	0.808	**0.810**	0.673	0.633
	Mean	0.362	0.588	**0.607**	0.435	0.829

Table 1: Results of each run for each dataset (MSRpar, MSRvid, SMTeuroparl, OnWn, SMTnews) calculated with the Pearson correlation between the system's outputs and the gold standard annotation. Official scores obtained using the three evaluation scores *All*, *Allnrm* and *Mean*. Development row presents the average results for each run in the whole training dataset. Base is the official baseline system. Post Evaluation is the experiment ran after the evaluation period with models trained for the specific datasets.

Pearson correlation between the system output and the gold standard annotation provided by the task organizers. The table also presents the official scores used to rank the systems and described in (Agirre et al., 2012). Our best model, Run 3, was ranked 20th according to the *Mean* score, 25th according to the *RankNrm* score and 32th according to the *All* score among 88 submitted runs.

The "Development" row reports the results of our three best models in the development phase. The results obtained for the three training datasets are higher than the results obtained for the testing. One hypothesis that might explain this behavior is overfitting during the training phase due to the way we divided the training set and carried out the experiments. A different experiment setting to carry out the development should be tried to evaluate this hypothesis.

To our surprise, in the test datasets the results of Run 1 and Run 3 swapped positions: in the training setting Run 1 was the best model and Run 3 the third best. The performance of Run 3 was relatively stable across the five datasets ranging from about the 30th to the 48th position the exception being the *SMTnews* dataset. In this dataset Run 3 was the best performing run of the evaluation exercise (and Run 2 the second). One possible explanation for this behavior is the fact that Run 3 is based on lexical features that do not take into consideration the syntactic structure of the two texts and therefore is not penalized by the noise introduced by the texts generated by MT systems. This hypothesis, however, does not explain why Run 3 score for the *SMTeuroparl* dataset was below the baseline score. Error analysis of the effects of different group of features in the test datasets is required to better understand such behaviors.

3.2 Post-evaluation Experiments

After the evaluation period, as a first step towards the required error analysis and a better comprehension of the potential of our approach, we performed an experiment to assess the impact of having models trained for specific datasets. In this experiment, each training dataset (*MSRpar*, *MSRvid* and *SMTeuroparl*) was used to train a model. Each dataset's model was tested on its respective test dataset. The model for the surprise datasets (*OnWn* and *SMTnews*) were trained using the whole training dataset. We used the Run 3 feature set (the best run in the official evaluation). The results of the experiment are reported in the column "Exp" of table 1. The impact of having specific models for each dataset is high. The *Mean* score goes from .607 to .829 and improvements are also observed in the *All* score (0.789). These scores would rank our system at the 7th position in the *Mean* rank. However, it is important to notice that in a real-world setting, knowledge about the source of data is not always available. We consider that having a general model that does not rely on this kind of information represents a more realistic way to confront with real-world applications.

4 Final Remarks

In this paper we described FBK's participation in the STS Semeval 2012 task. Our approach is based on a combination of MT evaluation metrics, distributional, and knowledge-based word similarity metrics. Our best run achieved the 20th position among 88 runs in the *Mean* overall ranking. An error analysis of the problematic test pairs is required to understand the potential of our feature sets and improve the overall performance of our approach. Along this direction, a first experiment with our best features and a different strategy already led to significant improvements in the *Mean* and *All* scores (from .651 to

.789 and from .607 to .829, respectively).

Acknowledgments

This work has been partially supported by the EC-funded project CoSyne (FP7-ICT-4-24853).

The authors would like to thank Claudio Giuliano for kindly helping us to preprocess the datasets with the Wiki Machine.

References

Eneko Agirre, Daniel Cer, Mona Diab, and Aitor Gonzalez. 2012. SemEval-2012 Task 6: A Pilot on Semantic Textual Similarity. In *6th International Workshop on Semantic Evaluation (SemEval 2012), in conjunction with the First Joint Conference on Lexical and Computational Semantics (*SEM 2012)*.

Satanjeev Banerjee and Alon Lavie. 2005. METEOR: An automatic metric for MT evaluation with improved correlation with human judgments. In *ACL 2005 Workshop on Intrinsic and Extrinsic Evaluation Measures for MT and/or Summarization*.

Xavier Carreras, Isaac Chao, Lluís Padro, and Muntsa Padró. 2004. Freeling: An open-source suite of language analyzers. In *4th International Conference on Language Resources and Evaluation (LREC)*, pages 239–242.

Xavier Carreras, Lluís Màrquez, and Jorge Catro. 2005. Filtering-Ranking Perceptron Learning. *Machine Learning*, 60:41–75.

Eugene Charniak. 2005. Coarse-to-fine n-best parsing and MaxEnt discriminative reranking. In *Proceedings of the 43rd Annual Meeting on*, volume 1, pages 173–180.

Stephen Clark and James R. Curran. 2004. Parsing the WSJ using CCG and log-linear models. In *ACL '04 Proceedings of the 42nd Annual Meeting on Association for Computational Linguistics*.

George Doddington. 2002. Automatic evaluation of machine translation quality using n-gram co-occurrence statistics. In *Proceedings of the Second International Conference on Human Language Technology Research*, pages 138–145. Morgan Kaufmann Publishers Inc.

Andrew Finch and YS Hwang. 2005. Using machine translation evaluation techniques to determine sentence-level semantic equivalence. In *Third International Workshop on Paraphrasing*, pages 17–24.

Jesús Giménez and Lluís Màrquez. 2004. SVMTool: A general POS tagger generator based on Support Vector Machines. In *4th International Conference on Language Resources and Evaluation (LREC)*, pages 43–46.

Jesús Giménez and Lluís Màrquez. 2010. Asiya: An Open Toolkit for Automatic Machine Translation (Meta-) Evaluation. *The Prague Bulletin of Mathematical Linguistics*, (94):77–86.

J. Giménez. 2008. *Empirical Machine Translation and its Evaluation*. Ph.D. thesis.

Claudio Giuliano, Alfio Massimiliano Gliozzo, and Carlo Strapparava. 2009. Kernel methods for minimally supervised wsd. *Computational Linguistics*, 35(4):513–528.

Johannes Hoffart, Fabian M. FM Suchanek, Klaus Berberich, Edwin Lewis Kelham, Gerard de Melo, and Gerhard Weikum. 2011. YAGO2: Exploring and Querying World Knowledge in Time, Space, Context, and Many Languages. In *20th International World Wide Web Conference (WWW 2011)*, pages 229–232.

Thorsten Joachims. 1998. Making Large-Scale SVM Learning Practical. In Bernhard Scholkopf, Christopher J. C. Burges, and Alexander J. Smola, editors, *Advances in Kernel Methods - Support Vector Learning*, pages 41–56. MIT Press, Cambridge, USA.

Milen Kouylekov, Yashar Mehdad, and Matteo Negri. 2010. Mining Wikipedia for Large-Scale Repositories of Context-Sensitive Entailment Rules. In *Seventh international conference on Language Resources and Evaluation (LREC 2010)*, pages 3550–3553, La Valletta, Malta.

Claudia Leacock, George A. Miller, and Martin Chodorow. 1998. Using corpus statistics and WordNet relations for sense identification. *Computational Linguistics*, 24(1):147–166.

C.Y. Lin and F.J. Och. 2004. Automatic evaluation of machine translation quality using longest common subsequence and skip-bigram statistics. In *Proceedings of the 42nd Annual Meeting on Association for Computational Linguistics*, page 605. Association for Computational Linguistics.

Dekang Lin. 2003. Dependency-Based Evaluation of Minipar. *Text, Speech and Language Technology*, 20:317–329.

Ding Liu and Daniel Gildea. 2005. Syntactic features for evaluation of machine translation. In *ACL Workshop on Intrinsic and Extrinsic Evaluation Measures for Machine Translation and/or Summarization*, number June, pages 25–32.

Yashar Mehdad, Alessandro Moschitti, and Fabio Massimo Zanzotto. 2010. Syntactic/semantic structures for textual entailment recognition. In *Human Language Technologies: The 2010 Annual Conference of the North American Chapter of the ACL*, number June, pages 1020–1028.

I. Dan Melamed, Ryan Green, and Joseph P. Turian. 2003. Precision and Recall of Machine Translation. In

Proceedings of the Joint Conference on Human Language Technology and the North American Chapter of the Association for Computational Linguistics (HLT-NAACL).

Rada Mihalcea, Courtney Corley, and Carlo Strapparava. 2006. Corpus-based and knowledge-based measures of text semantic similarity. In *Proceedings of the American Association for Artificial Intelligence*, pages 775–780.

George A. Miller. 1995. WordNet: A Lexical Database for English. *Communications of the ACM*, 38(11):39–41.

Sonja Nieß en, Franz Josef Och, Gregor Leusch, and Hermann Ney. 2000. An evaluation tool for machine translation: Fast evaluation for MT research. In *Language Resources and Evaluation*, pages 0–6.

Kishore Papineni, Salim Roukos, Todd Ward, and Wei-jing Zhu. 2002. BLEU: a Method for Automatic Evaluation of Machine Translation. In *Proceedings of the 40th Annual Meeting of the Association for Computational Linguistics (ACL)*, number July, pages 311–318.

Gerard Salton, Amit Singhal, and Mandar Mitra. 1997. Automatic text structuring and summarization. *Information Processing &*, 33(2):193–207.

Matthew Snover, Bonnie Dorr, Richard Schwartz, Linnea Micciulla, and John Makhoul. 2006. A Study of Translation Edit Rate with Targeted Human Annotation. In *Association for Machine Translation in the Americas*.

Matthew G. Snover, Nitin Madnani, Bonnie Dorr, and Richard Schwartz. 2009. TER-Plus: paraphrase, semantic, and alignment enhancements to Translation Edit Rate. *Machine Translation*, 23(2-3):117–127, December.

Mihai Surdeanu and Jordi Turmo. 2005. Semantic role labeling using complete syntactic analysis. In *9th Conference on Computational Natural Language Learning (CoNLL)*, number June, pages 221–224.

Mihai Surdeanu, Jordi Turmo, and Eli Comelles. 2005. Named Entity Recognition from Spontaneous Open-domain Speech. In *9th International Conference on Speech Communication and Technology (Interspeech)*, pages 3433–3436.

C Tillmann, S Vogel, H Ney, A. Zubiaga, and H. Sawaf. 1997. Accelerated DP Based Search for Statistical Translation. In *Fifth European Conference on Speech Communication and Technology*, pages 2667–2670.

Stephen Wan, Mark Dras, Robert Dale, and Cécile Paris. 2006. Using Dependency-Based Features to Take the "Para-farce" out of Paraphrase. In *2006 Australasian Language Technology Workshop (ALTW2006)*, number 2005, pages 131–138.

Wu Zhibiao and Martha Palmer. 1994. Verb Semantics and Lexical Selection. In *ACL '94 Proceedings of the 32nd annual meeting on Association for Computational Linguistics*, pages 133–138.

BUAP: Three Approaches for Semantic Textual Similarity

Maya Carrillo, Darnes Vilariño, David Pinto, Mireya Tovar, Saul León, Esteban Castillo
Benemérita Universidad Autónoma de Puebla,
Faculty of Computer Science
14 Sur & Av. San Claudio, CU
Puebla, Puebla, México
{cmaya, darnes, dpinto, mtovar}@cs.buap.mx
saul.ls@live.com, ecjbuap@gmail.com

Abstract

In this paper we describe the three approaches we submitted to the Semantic Textual Similarity task of SemEval 2012. The first approach considers to calculate the semantic similarity by using the Jaccard coefficient with term expansion using synonyms. The second approach uses the semantic similarity reported by Mihalcea in (Mihalcea et al., 2006). The third approach employs Random Indexing and Bag of Concepts based on context vectors. We consider that the first and third approaches obtained a comparable performance, meanwhile the second approach got a very poor behavior. The best ALL result was obtained with the third approach, with a Pearson correlation equal to 0.663.

1 Introduction

Finding the semantic similarity between two sentences is very important in applications of natural language processing such as information retrieval and related areas. The problem is complex due to the small number of terms involved in sentences which are tipically less than 10 or 15. Additionally, it is required to "understand" the meaning of the sentences in order to determine the "semantic" similarity of texts, which is quite different of finding the lexical similarity.

There exist different works at literature dealing with semantic similarity, but the problem is far to be solved because of the aforementioned issues. In (Mihalcea et al., 2006), for instance, it is presented a method for measuring the semantic similarity of texts, using corpus-based and knowledge-based measures of similarity. The approaches presented in (Shrestha, 2011) are based on the Vector Space Model, with the aim to capture the contextual behavior, senses and correlation, of terms. The performance of the method is better than the baseline method that uses vector based cosine similarity measure.

In this paper, we present three different approaches for the Textual Semantic Similarity task of Semeval 2012 (Agirre et al., 2012). The task is described as follows: Given two sentences s_1 and s_2, the aim is to compute how similar s_1 and s_2 are, returning a similarity score, and an optional confidence score. The approaches should provide values between 0 and 5 for each pair of sentences. These values roughly correspond to the following considerations, even when the system should output real values:

5: The two sentences are completely equivalent, as they mean the same thing.

4: The two sentences are mostly equivalent, but some unimportant details differ.

3: The two sentences are roughly equivalent, but some important information differs/missing.

2: The two sentences are not equivalent, but share some details.

1: The two sentences are not equivalent, but are on the same topic.

0: The two sentences are on different topics.

The description of the runs submitted to the competition follows.

2 Experimentation setup

The three runs submitted to the competition use completely different mechanisms to find the degree of semantic similarity between two sentences. The approaches are described as follows:

2.1 Approach BUAP-RUN-1: Term expansion with synonyms

Let $s_1 = w_{1,1}w_{1,2}...w_{1,|s_1|}$ and $s_2 = w_{2,1}w_{2,2}...w_{2,|s_2|}$ be two sentences. The synonyms of a given word $w_{i,k}$, expressed as $synonyms(w_{i,k})$, are obtained from online dictionaries by extracting the synonyms of $w_{i,k}$. A better matching between the terms contained in the text fragments and the terms at the dictionary are obtained by stemming all the terms (using the Porter stemmer).

In order to determine the semantic similarity between any pair of terms of the two sentences ($w_{1,i}$ and $w_{2,j}$) we use Eq. (1).

$$sim(w_{1,i}, w_{2,j}) = \begin{cases} 1 & \text{if } (w_{1,i} == w_{2,j}) \;||\; w_{1,i} \in synonyms(w_{2,j}) \;||\; w_{2,j} \in synonyms(w_{1,i}) \\ 0 & \text{otherwise} \end{cases} \quad (1)$$

The similarity between sentences s_1 and s_2 is calculated as shown in Eq. (2).

$$similarity(s_1, s_2) = \frac{5 * \sum_{i=1}^{n} \sum_{j=1}^{n} sim(w_{1i}, w_{2j})}{|s_1 \cup s_2|} \quad (2)$$

2.2 Approach BUAP-RUN-2

In this approach, the similarity of s_1 and s_2 is calculated as shown in Eq. (3) (Mihalcea et al., 2006).

$$similarity(s_1, s_2) = \frac{1}{2}\left(\frac{\sum_{w\in\{s_1\}}(maxSim(w,s_2)*idf(w))}{\sum_{w\in\{s_1\}} idf(w)} + \frac{\sum_{w\in\{s_2\}}(maxSim(w,s_1)*idf(w))}{\sum_{w\in\{s_2\}} idf(w)}\right) \quad (3)$$

where $idf(w)$ is the inverse document frequency of the word w, and $maxSim(w, s_2)$ is the maximum lexical similarity between the word w in sentence s_2 and all the words in sentence s_2 calculated by means of the Eq. (4) reported by (Wu and Palmer, 1994). The sentence terms are assumed to be concepts, LCS is the depth of the least common subsumer, and the equation is calculated using the NLTK libraries[1].

$$Sim_{wup} = \frac{2 * depth(LCS)}{depth(concept_1) + depth(concept_2)} \quad (4)$$

2.3 Approach BUAP-RUN-3: Random Indexing and Bag of Concepts

The vector space model (VSM) for document representation supporting search is probably the most well-known IR model. The VSM assumes that term vectors are pair-wise orthogonal. This assumption is very restrictive because words are not independent. There have been various attempts to build representations for documents that are semantically richer than only vectors based on the frequency of terms occurrence. One example is Latent Semantic Indexing (LSI), a method of word co-occurrence analysis to compute semantic vectors (context vectors) for words. LSI applies singular-value decomposition (SVD) to the term-document matrix in order to construct context vectors. As a result the dimension of the produced vector space will be significantly smaller; consequently the vectors that represent terms cannot be orthogonal. However, dimension reduction techniques such as SVD are expensive in terms of memory and processing time. Performing the SVD takes time *O (nmz)*, where *n* is the vocabulary size, *m* is the number of documents, and *z* is the number of nonzero elements per column in the words-by-documents matrix. As an alternative, there is a vector space methodology called Random Indexing (RI) (Sahlgren, 2005), which presents an efficient, scalable, and incremental method for building context vectors. Its computational complexity is *O (nr)* where *n* is as previously described and *r* is the vector dimension. Particularly, we apply RI to capture the inherent semantic structure using Bag of Concepts representation (BoC) as proposed by Sahlgren and Cöster (Sahlgren and Cöster, 2004), where the meaning of a term is considered as the sum of contexts in which it occurs.

[1] http://www.nltk.org/

2.3.1 Random Indexing

Random Indexing (RI) is a vector space methodology that accumulates context vectors for words based on co-occurrence data. The technique can be described as:

- First a unique random representation known as index vector is assigned to each context (document). Index vectors are binary vectors with a small number of non-zero elements, which are either +1 or -1, with equal amounts of both. For example, if the index vectors have twenty non-zero elements in a 1024-dimensional vector space, they have ten +1s and ten -1s. Index vectors serve as indices or labels for documents

- Index vectors are used to produce context vectors by scanning through the text and every time a target word occurs in a context, the index vector of the context is added to the context vector of the target word. Thus, at each encounters of the target word t with a context c the context vector of t is updated as follows: ct $+=ic$ where ct is the context vector of t and ic is the index vector of c. In this way, the context vector of a word keeps track of the contexts in which it occurred.

RI methodology is similar to latent semantic indexing (LSI) (Deerwester et al., 1990). However, to reduce the co-occurrence matrix no dimension reduction technique such as SVD is needed, since the dimensionality d of the random index vectors is pre-established as a parameter (implicit dimension reduction). Consequently d does not change once it has been set; as a result, the dimensionality of context vectors will never change with the addition of new data.

2.3.2 Bag of Concepts

Bag of Concepts (BoC) is a recent representation scheme proposed by Sahlgren and Cöster in (Sahlgren and Cöster, 2004), which is based on the perception that the meaning of a document can be considered as the union of the meanings of its terms. This is accomplished by generating term context vectors from each term within the document, and generating a document vector as the weighted sum of the term context vectors contained within that document. Therefore, we use RI to represent the meaning of a word as the sum of contexts (entire documents) in which it occurs. Illustrating this technique, suppose you have two documents: *D1: A man with a hard hat is dancing*, and *D2: A man wearing a hard hat is dancing*. Let us suppose that they have index vectors *ID1* and *ID2*, respectively: the context vector for *hat* will be the $ID1 + ID2$, because this word appears in both documents. Once the context vectors have been built by RI, they are used to represent the document as BoC. For instance, supposing *CV1, CV2, CV3, ...* and *CV8*, are the context vectors of each word in *D1*, then document *D1* will be represented as the weighted sum of these eight context vectors.

2.3.3 Implementation

The sentences of each file were processed to generate the BoC representations of them. BoC representations were generated by first stemming all words in the sentences. We then used random indexing to produce context vectors for each word in the files (i.e. STS.input.MSRpar, STS.input.MSRvid, etc.), each file was considered a different corpus and documents were the sentences in them. The dimension of the context vectors was fixed at 2048, determined by experimentation using the training set. These context vectors were then $tf \times idf$-weighted, according to the corpus, and added up for each sentence, to produce BoC representations. Therefore the similarity values were calculated by the cosine function. Finally cosine values were multiplied by 5 to produce values between 0 and 5.

3 Experimental results

In Table 1 we show the results obtained by the three approaches submitted to the competition. The columns of Table 1 stand for:

- **ALL**: Pearson correlation with the gold standard for the five datasets, and corresponding rank.

- **ALLnrm**: Pearson correlation after the system outputs for each dataset are fitted to the gold standard using least squares, and corresponding rank.

Run	ALL	Rank	ALL nrm	Rank Nrm	Mean	Rank Mean	MSR par	MSR vid	SMT eur	On - WN	SMT-news
BUAP-RUN-1	0.4997	63	0.7568	62	0.4892	57	0.4037	0.6532	0.4521	0.605	0.4537
BUAP-RUN-2	-0.026	89	0.5933	89	0.0669	89	0.1109	0.0057	0.0348	0.1788	0.1964
BUAP-RUN-3	0.663	25	0.7474	64	0.488	59	0.4018	0.6378	0.4758	0.5691	0.4057

Table 1: Results of approaches of BUAP in Task 6.

- **Mean**: Weighted mean across the 5 datasets, where the weight depends on the number of pairs in the dataset.

Followed by Pearson for individual datasets.

At this moment, we are not aware of the reasons because the second approach obtained a very poor performance. The way in which the $idf(w)$ is calculated could be one of the reasons, because the corpus used is relatively small and also from a different domain. With respect to the other two approaches, we consider that they (first and third) obtained a comparable performance, even when the third approach obtained the best ALL result with a Pearson correlation equal to 0.663.

4 Discussion and conclusion

We have presented three different approaches for tackling the problem of Semantic Textual Similarity. The use of term expansion by synonyms performed well in general and obtained a comparable behavior than the third approach which used random indexing and bag of concepts. It is interesting to observe that these two approaches performed similar when the two term expansion mechanism are totally different. As further, it is important to analyze the poor behavior of the second approach. We would like also to introduce semantic relationships other than synonyms in the process of term expansion.

Acknowledgments

This project has been partially supported by projects CONACYT #106625, #VIAD-ING11-II, PROMEP/103.5/11/4481 and VIEP #PIAD-ING11-II.

References

E. Agirre, D. Cer, M. Diab, and B. Dolan. 2012. SemEval-2012 Task 6: Semantic Textual Similarity. In *Proceedings of the 6th International Workshop on Semantic Evaluation (SemEval 2012)*.

Scott C. Deerwester, Susan T. Dumais, Thomas K. Landauer, George W. Furnas, and Richard A. Harshman. 1990. Indexing by Latent Semantic Analysis. *Journal of the American Society of Information Science*, 41(6):391–407.

Rada Mihalcea, Courtney Corley, and Carlo Strapparava. 2006. Corpus-based and knowledge-based measures of text semantic similarity. In *proceedings of AAAI'06*, pages 775–780.

Magnus Sahlgren and Rickard Cöster. 2004. Using bag-of-concepts to improve the performance of support vector machines in text categorization. In *Proceedings of the 20th international conference on Computational Linguistics*, COLING '04, Stroudsburg, PA, USA. Association for Computational Linguistics.

M. Sahlgren. 2005. An Introduction to Random Indexing. *Methods and Applications of Semantic Indexing Workshop at the 7th International Conference on Terminology and Knowledge Engineering, TKE 2005*.

Prajol Shrestha. 2011. Corpus-based methods for short text similarity. In *TALN 2011*, Montpellier, France.

Zhibiao Wu and Martha Palmer. 1994. Verb semantics and lexical selection. In *32nd. Annual Meeting of the Association for Computational Linguistics*, pages 133 –138, New Mexico State University, Las Cruces, New Mexico.

UNT: A Supervised Synergistic Approach to Semantic Text Similarity

Carmen Banea, Samer Hassan, Michael Mohler, Rada Mihalcea
University of North Texas
Denton, TX, USA
{CarmenBanea,SamerHassan,MichaelMohler}@my.unt.edu, rada@cs.unt.edu

Abstract

This paper presents the systems that we participated with in the Semantic Text Similarity task at SEMEVAL 2012. Based on prior research in semantic similarity and relatedness, we combine various methods in a machine learning framework. The three variations submitted during the task evaluation period ranked number 5, 9 and 14 among the 89 participating systems. Our evaluations show that corpus-based methods display a more robust behavior on the training data, yet combining a variety of methods allows a learning algorithm to achieve a superior decision than that achievable by any of the individual parts.

1 Introduction

Measures of text similarity have been used for a long time in applications in natural language processing and related areas. One of the earliest applications of text similarity is perhaps the vector-space model used in information retrieval, where the document most relevant to an input query is determined by ranking documents in a collection in reversed order of their similarity to the given query (Salton and Lesk, 1971). Text similarity has also been used for relevance feedback and text classification (Rocchio, 1971), word sense disambiguation (Lesk, 1986; Schutze, 1998), and more recently for extractive summarization (Salton et al., 1997), and methods for automatic evaluation of machine translation (Papineni et al., 2002) or text summarization (Lin and Hovy, 2003). Measures of text similarity were also found useful for the evaluation of text coherence (Lapata and Barzilay, 2005).

Earlier work on this task has primarily focused on simple lexical matching methods, which produce a similarity score based on the number of lexical units that occur in both input segments. Improvements to this simple method have considered stemming, stop-word removal, part-of-speech tagging, longest subsequence matching, as well as various weighting and normalization factors (Salton and Buckley, 1997). While successful to a certain degree, these lexical similarity methods cannot always identify the *semantic* similarity of texts. For instance, there is an obvious similarity between the text segments *I own a dog* and *I have an animal*, but most of the current text similarity metrics will fail in identifying any kind of connection between these texts.

More recently, researchers have started to consider the possibility of combining the large number of word-to-word semantic similarity measures (e.g., (Jiang and Conrath, 1997; Leacock and Chodorow, 1998; Lin, 1998; Resnik, 1995)) within a semantic similarity method that works for entire texts. The methods proposed to date in this direction mainly consist of either bipartite-graph matching strategies that aggregate word-to-word similarity into a text similarity score (Mihalcea et al., 2006; Islam and Inkpen, 2009; Hassan and Mihalcea, 2011; Mohler et al., 2011), or data-driven methods that perform component-wise additions of semantic vector representations as obtained with corpus measures such as Latent Semantic Analysis (Landauer et al., 1997), Explicit Semantic Analysis (Gabrilovich and Markovitch, 2007), or Salient Semantic Analysis (Hassan and Mihalcea, 2011).

In this paper, we describe the system with which

we participated in the SEMEVAL 2012 task on semantic text similarity (Agirre et al., 2012). The system builds upon our earlier work on corpus-based and knowledge-based methods of text semantic similarity (Mihalcea et al., 2006; Hassan and Mihalcea, 2011; Mohler et al., 2011), and combines all these previous methods into a meta-system by using machine learning. The framework provided by the task organizers also enabled us to perform an in-depth analysis of the various components used in our system, and draw conclusions concerning the role played by the different resources, features, and algorithms in building a state-of-the-art semantic text similarity system.

2 Related Work

Over the past years, the research community has focused on computing semantic relatedness using methods that are either knowledge-based or corpus-based. Knowledge-based methods derive a measure of relatedness by utilizing lexical resources and ontologies such as WordNet (Miller, 1995) to measure definitional overlap, term distance within a graphical taxonomy, or term depth in the taxonomy as a measure of specificity. We explore several of these measures in depth in Section 3.3.1. On the other side, corpus-based measures such as Latent Semantic Analysis (LSA) (Landauer et al., 1997), Explicit Semantic Analysis (ESA) (Gabrilovich and Markovitch, 2007), Salient Semantic Analysis (SSA) (Hassan and Mihalcea, 2011), Pointwise Mutual Information (PMI) (Church and Hanks, 1990), PMI-IR (Turney, 2001), Second Order PMI (Islam and Inkpen, 2006), Hyperspace Analogues to Language (Burgess et al., 1998) and distributional similarity (Lin, 1998) employ probabilistic approaches to decode the semantics of words. They consist of unsupervised methods that utilize the contextual information and patterns observed in raw text to build semantic profiles of words. Unlike knowledge-based methods, which suffer from limited coverage, corpus-based measures are able to induce a similarity between any given two words, as long as they appear in the very large corpus used as training.

3 Semantic Textual Similarity System

The system we proposed for the SEMEVAL 2012 Semantic Textual Similarity task builds upon both knowledge- and corpus-based methods previously described in (Mihalcea et al., 2006; Hassan and Mihalcea, 2011; Mohler et al., 2011). The predictions of these independent systems, paired with additional salient features, are leveraged by a meta-system that employs machine learning. In this section, we will elaborate further on the resources we use, our features, and the components of our machine learning system. We will start by describing the task setup.

3.1 Task Setup

The training data released by the task organizers consists of three datasets showcasing two sentences per line and a manually assigned similarity score ranging from 0 (no relation) to 5 (semantically equivalent). The datasets[1] provided are taken from the Microsoft Research Paraphrase Corpus ($MSRpar$), the Microsoft Research Video Description Corpus ($MSRvid$), and the WMT2008 development dataset (Europarl section)($SMTeuroparl$); they each consist of about 750 sentence pairs with the class distribution varying with each dataset. The testing data contains additional sentences from the same collections as the training data as well as from two additional unknown sets ($OnWN$ and $SMTnews$); they range from 399 to 750 sentence pairs. The reader may refer to (Agirre et al., 2012) for additional information regarding this task.

3.2 Resources

Wikipedia[2] is a free on-line encyclopedia, representing the outcome of a continuous collaborative effort of a large number of volunteer contributors. Virtually any Internet user can create or edit a Wikipedia web page, and this "freedom of contribution" has a positive impact on both the quantity (fast-growing number of articles) and the quality (potential mistakes are quickly corrected within the collaborative environment) of this on-line resource. The basic entry in Wikipedia is an *article* which describes an entity or an event, and which, in addition to untagged

[1] `http://www.cs.york.ac.uk/semeval-2012/task6/data/uploads/datasets/train-readme.txt`

[2] `www.wikipedia.org`

content, also consists of hyperlinked text to other pages within or outside of Wikipedia. These hyperlinks are meant to guide the reader to pages that provide additional information / clarifications, so that a better understanding of the primary concept can be achieved. The structure of Wikipedia in terms of pages and hyperlinks is exploited directly by semantic similarity methods such as ESA (Gabrilovich and Markovitch, 2007), or SSA (Hassan and Mihalcea, 2011).

WordNet (Miller, 1995) is a manually crafted lexical resource that maintains semantic relationships between basic units of meaning, or *synsets*. A synset groups together senses of different words that share a very similar meaning, which act in a particular context as synonyms. Each synset is accompanied by a *gloss* or definition, and one or two examples illustrating usage in the given context. Unlike a traditional thesaurus, the structure of WordNet is able to encode additional relationships beside synonymy, such as antonymy, hypernymy, hyponymy, meronymy, entailment, etc., which various knowledge-based methods use to derive semantic similarity.

3.3 Features

Our meta-system uses several features, which can be grouped into knowledge-based, corpus-based, and bipartite graph matching, as described below. The abbreviations appearing between parentheses by each method allow for easy cross-referencing with the evaluations provided in Table 1.

3.3.1 Knowledge-based Semantic Similarity Features

Following prior work from our group (Mihalcea et al., 2006; Mohler and Mihalcea, 2009), we employ several WordNet-based similarity metrics for the task of sentence-level similarity. Briefly, for each open-class word in one of the input texts, we compute the maximum semantic similarity (using the WordNet::Similarity package (Pedersen et al., 2004)) that can be obtained by pairing it with any open-class word in the other input text. All the word-to-word similarity scores obtained in this way are summed and normalized to the length of the two input texts. We provide below a short description for each of the similarity metrics employed by this system[3].

The **shortest path** ($Path$) similarity is determined as:

$$Sim_{path} = \frac{1}{length} \qquad (1)$$

where $length$ is the length of the shortest path between two concepts using node-counting (including the end nodes).

The **Leacock & Chodorow** (Leacock and Chodorow, 1998) (LCH) similarity is determined as:

$$Sim_{lch} = -\log \frac{length}{2 * D} \qquad (2)$$

where $length$ is the length of the shortest path between two concepts using node-counting, and D is the maximum depth of the taxonomy.

The **Lesk** ($Lesk$) similarity of two concepts is defined as a function of the overlap between the corresponding definitions, as provided by a dictionary. It is based on an algorithm proposed by Lesk (1986) as a solution for word sense disambiguation.

The **Wu & Palmer** (Wu and Palmer, 1994) (WUP) similarity metric measures the depth of two given concepts in the WordNet taxonomy, and the depth of the least common subsumer (LCS), and combines these figures into a similarity score:

$$Sim_{wup} = \frac{2 * depth(LCS)}{depth(concept_1) + depth(concept_2)} \qquad (3)$$

The measure introduced by **Resnik** (Resnik, 1995) (RES) returns the information content (IC) of the LCS of two concepts:

$$Sim_{res} = IC(LCS) \qquad (4)$$

where IC is defined as:

$$IC(c) = -\log P(c) \qquad (5)$$

and $P(c)$ is the probability of encountering an instance of concept c in a large corpus.

The measure introduced by **Lin** (Lin, 1998) (Lin) builds on Resnik's measure of similarity, and adds a normalization factor consisting of the information content of the two input concepts:

$$Sim_{lin} = \frac{2 * IC(LCS)}{IC(concept_1) + IC(concept_2)} \qquad (6)$$

[3]We point out that the similarity metric proposed by Hirst & St. Onge was not considered due to the time constraints associated with the STS task.

We also consider the **Jiang & Conrath** (Jiang and Conrath, 1997) (JCN) measure of similarity:

$$Sim_{jnc} = \frac{1}{IC(concept_1) + IC(concept_2) - 2 * IC(LCS)} \quad (7)$$

Each of the measures listed above is used as a feature by our meta-system.

3.3.2 Corpus-based Semantic Similarity Features

While most of the corpus-based methods induce semantic profiles in a word-space, where the semantic profile of a word is expressed in terms of its co-occurrence with other words, LSA, ESA and SSA stand out as different, since they rely on a concept-space representation. In these methods, the semantic profile of a word is expressed in terms of the implicit (LSA), explicit (ESA), or salient (SSA) concepts. This departure from the sparse word-space to a denser, richer, and unambiguous concept-space resolves one of the fundamental problems in semantic relatedness, namely the vocabulary mismatch. In the experiments reported in this paper, all the corpus-based methods are trained on the English Wikipedia download from October 2008, with approximately 6 million articles, and more than 9.5 million hyperlinks.

Latent Semantic Analysis (LSA) (Landauer et al., 1997). In LSA, term-context associations are captured by means of a dimensionality reduction operated by a singular value decomposition (SVD) on the term-by-context matrix $\mathbf{T}$, where the matrix is induced from a large corpus. This reduction entails the abstraction of meaning by collapsing similar contexts and discounting noisy and irrelevant ones, hence transforming the real world term-context space into a word-latent-concept space which achieves a much deeper and concrete semantic representation of words.

Explicit Semantic Analysis (ESA) (Gabrilovich and Markovitch, 2007). ESA uses encyclopedic knowledge in an information retrieval framework to generate a semantic interpretation of words. Since encyclopedic knowledge is typically organized into concepts (or topics), each concept is further described using definitions and examples. ESA relies on the distribution of words inside the encyclopedic descriptions. It builds semantic representations for a given word using a word-document association, where the document represents a Wikipedia article (concept). ESA is in effect a Vector Space Model (VSM) built using Wikipedia corpus, where vectors represents word-articles association.

Salient Semantic Analysis (SSA) (Hassan and Mihalcea, 2011). SSA incorporates a similar semantic abstraction and interpretation of words as ESA, yet it uses salient concepts gathered from encyclopedic knowledge, where a "concept" represents an unambiguous word or phrase with a concrete meaning, and which affords an encyclopedic definition. Saliency in this case is determined based on the word being hyperlinked (either trough manual or automatic annotations) in context, implying that they are highly relevant to the given text. SSA is an example of Generalized Vector Space Model (GVSM), where vectors represent word-concepts associations.

In order to determine the similarity of two text fragments , we employ two variations: the typical cosine similarity (cos) and a best alignment strategy ($align$), which we explain in more detail below. Both variations were paired with the LSA, ESA, and SSA systems resulting in six similarity scores that were used as features by our meta-system, namely LSA_{cos}, LSA_{align}, ESA_{cos}, ESA_{align}, SSA_{cos}, and SSA_{align}.

Best Alignment Strategy ($align$). Let T_a and T_b be two text fragments of size a and b respectively. After removing all stopwords, we first determine the number of shared terms (ω) between T_a and T_b. Second, we calculate the semantic relatedness of all possible pairings between non-shared terms in T_a and T_b. We further filter these possible combinations by creating a list φ which holds the strongest semantic pairings between the fragments' terms, such that each term can only belong to one and only one pair.

$$Sim(T_a, T_b) = \frac{(\omega + \sum_{i=1}^{|\varphi|} \varphi_i) \times (2ab)}{a + b} \quad (8)$$

where ω is the number of shared terms between the text fragments and φ_i is the similarity score for the ith pairing.

3.3.3 Bipartite Graph Matching

In an attempt to move beyond the bag-of-words paradigm described thus far, we attempt to compute a set of dependency graph alignment scores based on previous work in automatic short-answer grading (Mohler et al., 2011). This score, computed in two stages, is used as a feature by our meta-system.

In the first stage, the system is provided with the dependency graphs for each pair of sentences[4]. For each node in one dependency graph, we compute a similarity score for each node in the other dependency graph based upon a set of lexical, semantic, and syntactic features applied to both the pair of nodes and their corresponding subgraphs (i.e. the set of nodes reachable from a given node by following directional governor-to-dependant links). The scoring function is trained on a small set of manually aligned graphs using the averaged perceptron algorithm.

We define a total of 64 features[5] to be used to train a machine learning system to compute subgraph-subgraph similarity. Of these, 32 are based upon the bag-of-words semantic similarity of the subgraphs using the metrics described in Section 3.3.1 as well as a Wikipedia-trained LSA model. The remaining 32 features are lexico-syntactic features associated with the parent nodes of the subgraphs and are described in more detail in our earlier paper.

We then calculate weights associated with these features using an averaged version of the perceptron algorithm (Freund and Schapire, 1999; Collins, 2002) trained on a set of 32 manually annotated instructor/student answer pairs selected from the short-answer grading corpus (MM2011). These pairs contain 7303 node pairs (656 matches, 6647 non-matches). Once the weights are calculated, a similarity score for each pair of nodes can be computed by taking the dot product of the feature vector with the weights.

In the second stage, the node similarity scores calculated in the previous step are used to find an optimal alignment for the pair of dependency graphs. We begin with a bipartite graph where each node in one graph is represented by a node on the left side of the bipartite graph and each node in the other graph is represented by a node on the right side. The weight associated with each edge is the score computed for each node-node pair in the previous stage. The bipartite graph is then augmented by adding dummy nodes to both sides which are allowed to match any node with a score of zero. An optimal alignment between the two graphs is then computed efficiently using the Hungarian algorithm. Note that this results in an optimal matching, not a mapping, so that an individual node is associated with at most one node in the other answer. After finding the optimal match, we produce four alignment-based scores by optionally normalizing by the number of nodes and/or weighting the node-alignments according to the idf scores of the words.[6] This results in four alignment scores listed as $graph_{none}$, $graph_{norm}$, $graph_{idf}$, $graph_{idfnorm}$.

3.3.4 Baselines

As a baseline, we also utilize several lexical bag-of-words approaches where each sentence is represented by a vector of tokens and the similarity of the two sentences can be computed by finding the cosine of the angle between their representative vectors using term frequency (tf) or term frequency multiplied by inverse document frequency ($tf.idf$)[6], or by using simple overlap between the vectors' dimensions ($overlap$).

3.4 Machine Learning

3.4.1 Algorithms

All the systems described above are used to generate a score for each training and test sample (see Section 3.1). These scores are then aggregated per sample, and used in a supervised learning framework. We decided to use a regression model, instead of classification, since the requirements for the task specify that we should provide a score in the range of 0 to 5. We could have used classification paired with bucketed ranges, yet classification does not take into consideration the underlying ordinality of the scores (i.e. a score of 4.5 is closer to either 4 or 5, but farther away from 0), which is a noticeable handicap in this scenario. We tried both linear and sup-

[4] We here use the output of the Stanford Dependency Parser in collapse/propagate mode with some modifications as described in our earlier work.

[5] With the exception of the four features based upon the Hirst & St.Onge similarity metric, these are equivalent to the features used in previous work.

[6] The document frequency scores were taken from the British National Corpus (BNC).

port vector regression[7] by performing 10 fold cross-validation on the train data, yet the latter algorithm consistently performs better, no matter what kernel was chosen. Thus we decided to use support vector regression (Smola and Schoelkopf, 1998) with a Pearson VII function-based kernel.

Due to its different learning methodology, and since it is suited for predicting continuous classes, our second system uses the M5P decision tree algorithm (Quinlan, 1992; Wang and Witten, 1997), which outperforms support vector regression on the 10 fold cross-validation performed on the SMTeuroparl train set, while providing competitive results on the other train sets (within .01 Pearson correlation).

3.4.2 Setup

We submitted three system variations, namely $IndividualRegression$, $IndividualDecTree$, and $CombinedRegression$. The first word describes the training data; for **individual**, for the *known test sets* we trained on the corresponding train sets, while for the *unknown test sets* we trained on all the train sets combined; for **combined**, for each test set we trained on all the train sets combined. The second word refers to the learning methodology, where **Regression** stands for support vector regression, and **DecTree** stands for M5P decision tree.

4 Results and Discussion

We include in Table 1 the Pearson correlations obtained by comparing the predictions of each feature to the gold standard for the three train datasets. We notice that the corpus based metrics display a consistent performance across the three train sets, when compared to the other methods, including knowledge-based. Furthermore, the best alignment strategy ($align$) for corpus based models outperforms similarity scores based on traditional cosine similarity. It is interesting to note that simple baselines such as tf, $tf.idf$ and $overlap$ offer significant correlations with all the train sets without access to additional knowledge inferred by knowledge or corpus-based methods. In the case of the bipartite graph matching, the $graph_{norm}$ variation provides the strongest correlation results across all the datasets.

System	MSRpar	MSRvid	SMTeuroparl
$Path$	0.49	0.62	0.50
LCH	0.48	0.49	0.45
$Lesk$	0.48	0.59	0.50
WUP	0.46	0.38	0.42
RES	0.47	0.55	0.48
Lin	0.49	0.54	0.48
JCN	0.49	0.63	0.51
LSA_{align}	0.44	0.57	0.61
LSA_{cos}	0.37	**0.74**	0.56
ESA_{align}	**0.52**	0.70	0.62
ESA_{cos}	0.30	0.71	0.53
SSA_{align}	0.46	0.61	**0.65**
SSA_{cos}	0.22	0.63	0.39
$graph_{none}$	0.42	0.50	0.21
$graph_{norm}$	0.48	0.43	0.59
$graph_{idf}$	0.16	0.67	0.16
$graph_{idfnorm}$	0.08	0.60	0.19
$tf.idf$	0.45	0.63	0.41
tf	0.45	0.69	0.51
$overlap$	0.44	0.69	0.27

Table 1: Correlation of individual features for the training sets with the gold standards

We include the evaluation results provided by the task organizers in Table 2. They indicate that our intuition in using a support vector regression strategy was correct. While the $IndividualRegression$ was our strongest system on the training data, the same ranking applies to the test data (including the additional two surprise datasets) as well, earning it the fifth place among the 89 participating systems, with a Pearson correlation of 0.7846.

Regarding the decision tree based learning ($IndividualDecTree$), despite its more robust behavior on the train sets, it achieved slightly lower outcome on the test data, at 0.7677 correlation. We believe this happened because decision trees have a tendency to overfit training data, as they generate a rigid structure which is unforgiving to minor deviations in the test data. Nonetheless, this second variation still ranks in the top 10% of the submitted systems.

As an alternative approach to handle unknown test data (e.g. different distributions, genres), we opted

[7] Implementations provided through the Weka framework (Hall et al., 2009).

Run	ALL	Rank	Mean	RankMean	MSRpar	MSRvid	SMTeuroparl	OnWN	SMTnews
IndividualRegression	**0.7846**	5	0.6162	13	0.5353	0.8750	0.4203	0.6715	0.4033
IndividualDecTree	**0.7677**	9	0.5947	25	0.5693	0.8688	0.4203	0.6491	0.2256
CombinedRegression	**0.7418**	14	0.6159	14	0.5032	0.8695	0.4797	0.6715	0.4033

Table 2: Evaluation results and ranking published by the task organizers

to also include the *CombinedRegression* strategy as our third variation. This seems to have been fruitful for *MSRvid*, *SMTeuroparl*, and the two surprise datasets (*ONWn* and *SMTnews*). In the case of *SMTeuroparl*, this expanded training set achieves a better performance than learning from the corresponding training set alone, gaining an improvement of 0.0776 correlation points. Unfortunately, the variation has some losses, particularly for the *MSRpar* dataset (0.0321), yet it is able to consistently model and handle a wider variety of text types.

5 Conclusion

This paper describes the three system variations our team participated with in the Semantic Text Similarity task in SEMEVAL 2012. Our focus has been to produce a synergistic approach, striving to achieve a superior result than attainable by each system individually. We have considered a variety of methods for inferring semantic similarity, including knowledge and corpus-based methods. These were leveraged in a machine-learning framework, where our preferred learning algorithm is support vector regression, due to its ability to deal with continuous classes and to dampen the effect of noisy features, while augmenting more robust ones. While it is always preferable to use similar test and train sets, when information regarding the test dataset is unavailable, we show that a robust performance can be achieved by combining all train data from different sources into a single set and allowing a machine learner to make predictions. Overall, it was interesting to note that corpus-based methods maintain strong results on all train datasets in comparison to knowledge-based methods. Our three systems ranked number 5, 9 and 14 among the 89 systems participating in the task.

Acknowledgments

This material is based in part upon work supported by the National Science Foundation CAREER award #0747340 and IIS award #1018613. Any opinions, findings, and conclusions or recommendations expressed in this material are those of the authors and do not necessarily reflect the views of the National Science Foundation.

References

E. Agirre, D. Cer, M. Diab, and A. Gonzalez. 2012. Semeval-2012 task 6: A pilot on semantic textual similarity. In *Proceedings of the 6th International Workshop on Semantic Evaluation (SemEval 2012), in conjunction with the First Joint Conference on Lexical and Computational Semantics (*SEM 2012)*.

C. Burgess, K. Livesay, and K. Lund. 1998. Explorations in context space: words, sentences, discourse. *Discourse Processes*, 25(2):211–257.

K. Church and P. Hanks. 1990. Word association norms, mutual information, and lexicography. *Computational Linguistics*, 16(1):22–29.

M. Collins. 2002. Discriminative training methods for hidden Markov models: Theory and experiments with perceptron algorithms. In *Proceedings of the 2002 Conference on Empirical Methods in Natural Language Processing (EMNLP-02)*, Philadelphia, PA, July.

Y. Freund and R. Schapire. 1999. Large margin classification using the perceptron algorithm. *Machine Learning*, 37:277–296.

E. Gabrilovich and S. Markovitch. 2007. Computing semantic relatedness using Wikipedia-based explicit semantic analysis. In *Proceedings of the 20th International Joint Conference on Artificial Intelligence*, pages 1606–1611, Hyderabad, India.

M. Hall, E. Frank, G. Holmes, B. Pfahringer, P. Reutemann, and I. H. Witten. 2009. The WEKA Data Mining Software: An Update. *SIGKDD Explorations*, 11(1).

S. Hassan and R. Mihalcea. 2011. Measuring semantic relatedness using salient encyclopedic concepts. *Artificial Intelligence, Special Issue*, xx(xx).

A. Islam and D. Inkpen. 2006. Second order co-occurrence PMI for determining the semantic similarity of words. In *Proceedings of the Fifth Conference on Language Resources and Evaluation*, volume 2, Genoa, Italy, July.

A. Islam and D. Inkpen. 2009. Semantic Similarity of Short Texts. In Nicolas Nicolov, Galia Angelova, and Ruslan Mitkov, editors, *Recent Advances in Natural Language Processing V*, volume 309 of *Current Issues in Linguistic Theory*, pages 227–236. John Benjamins, Amsterdam & Philadelphia.

J. J. Jiang and D. W. Conrath. 1997. Semantic similarity based on corpus statistics and lexical taxonomy. In *International Conference Research on Computational Linguistics (ROCLING X)*, pages 9008+, September.

T. K. Landauer, D. Laham, B. Rehder, and M. E. Schreiner. 1997. How well can passage meaning be derived without using word order? a comparison of latent semantic analysis and humans.

M. Lapata and R. Barzilay. 2005. Automatic evaluation of text coherence: Models and representations. In *Proceedings of the 19th International Joint Conference on Artificial Intelligence*, Edinburgh.

C. Leacock and M. Chodorow, 1998. *Combining local context and WordNet similarity for word sense identification*, pages 305–332.

M. Lesk. 1986. Automatic sense disambiguation using machine readable dictionaries: how to tell a pine cone from an ice cream cone. In *SIGDOC '86: Proceedings of the 5th annual international conference on Systems documentation*, pages 24–26, New York, NY, USA. ACM.

C. Y. Lin and E. H. Hovy. 2003. Automatic evaluation of summaries using n-gram co-occurrence statistics. In *Proceedings of Human Language Technology Conference (HLT-NAACL 2003)*, Edmonton, Canada, May.

D. Lin. 1998. An information-theoretic definition of similarity. In *Proceedings of the Fifteenth International Conference on Machine Learning*, pages 296–304, Madison, Wisconsin.

R. Mihalcea, C. Corley, and C. Strapparava. 2006. Corpus-based and knowledge-based measures of text semantic similarity. In *Proceedings of the American Association for Artificial Intelligence (AAAI 2006)*, pages 775–780, Boston, MA, US.

G. A. Miller. 1995. WordNet: a Lexical database for english. *Communications of the Association for Computing Machinery*, 38(11):39–41.

M. Mohler and R. Mihalcea. 2009. Text-to-text semantic similarity for automatic short answer grading. In *Proceedings of the European Association for Computational Linguistics (EACL 2009)*, Athens, Greece.

M. Mohler, R. Bunescu, and R. Mihalcea. 2011. Learning to grade short answer questions using semantic similarity measures and dependency graph alignments. In *Proceedings of the Association for Computational Linguistics – Human Language Technologies (ACL-HLT 2011)*, Portland, Oregon, USA.

K. Papineni, S. Roukos, T. Ward, and W. Zhu. 2002. Bleu: a method for automatic evaluation of machine translation. In *Proceedings of the 40th Annual Meeting of the Association for Computational Linguistics*, pages 311–318, Philadelphia, PA.

T. Pedersen, S. Patwardhan, and J. Michelizzi. 2004. WordNet:: Similarity-Measuring the Relatedness of Concepts. *Proceedings of the National Conference on Artificial Intelligence*, pages 1024–1025.

R. J. Quinlan. 1992. Learning with continuous classes. In *5th Australian Joint Conference on Artificial Intelligence*, pages 343–348, Singapore. World Scientific.

P. Resnik. 1995. Using information content to evaluate semantic similarity in a taxonomy. In *In Proceedings of the 14th International Joint Conference on Artificial Intelligence*, pages 448–453.

J. Rocchio, 1971. *Relevance feedback in information retrieval*. Prentice Hall, Ing. Englewood Cliffs, New Jersey.

G. Salton and C. Buckley. 1997. Term weighting approaches in automatic text retrieval. In *Readings in Information Retrieval*. Morgan Kaufmann Publishers, San Francisco, CA.

G. Salton and M.E. Lesk, 1971. *The SMART Retrieval System: Experiments in Automatic Document Processing*, chapter Computer evaluation of indexing and text processing. Prentice Hall, Ing. Englewood Cliffs, New Jersey.

G. Salton, A. Singhal, M. Mitra, and C. Buckley. 1997. Automatic text structuring and summarization. *Information Processing and Management*, 2(32).

H. Schutze. 1998. Automatic word sense discrimination. *Computational Linguistics*, 24(1):97–124.

A. J. Smola and B. Schoelkopf. 1998. A tutorial on support vector regression. NeuroCOLT2 Technical Report NC2-TR-1998-030.

P. D. Turney. 2001. Mining the Web for Synonyms: PMI-IR versus LSA on TOEFL. In *Proceedings of the 12th European Conference on Machine Learning*, pages 491–502, Freiburg, Germany.

Y. Wang and I. H. Witten. 1997. Induction of model trees for predicting continuous classes. In *Poster papers of the 9th European Conference on Machine Learning*. Springer.

Z. Wu and M. Palmer. 1994. Verbs semantics and lexical selection. In *Proceedings of the 32nd annual meeting on Association for Computational Linguistics*, pages 133—-138, Las Cruces, New Mexico.

DERI&UPM: Pushing Corpus Based Relatedness to Similarity: Shared Task System Description

Nitish Aggarwal* **Kartik Asooja°** **Paul Buitelaar***

*Unit for Natural Language Processing
Digital Enterprise Research Institute
National University of Ireland, Galway, Ireland
firstname.lastname@deri.org

°Ontology Engineering Group
Universidad Politecnica de Madrid
Madrid, Spain
asooja@gmail.com

Abstract

In this paper, we describe our system submitted for the semantic textual similarity (STS) task at SemEval 2012. We implemented two approaches to calculate the degree of similarity between two sentences. First approach combines corpus-based semantic relatedness measure over the whole sentence with the knowledge-based semantic similarity scores obtained for the words falling under the same syntactic roles in both the sentences. We fed all these scores as features to machine learning models to obtain a single score giving the degree of similarity of the sentences. Linear Regression and Bagging models were used for this purpose. We used Explicit Semantic Analysis (ESA) as the corpus-based semantic relatedness measure. For the knowledge-based semantic similarity between words, a modified WordNet based Lin measure was used. Second approach uses a bipartite based method over the WordNet based Lin measure, without any modification. This paper shows a significant improvement in calculating the semantic similarity between sentences by the fusion of the knowledge-based similarity measure and the corpus-based relatedness measure against corpus based measure taken alone.

1 Introduction

Similarity between sentences is a central concept of text analysis, however previous studies about semantic similarities have mainly focused either on single word similarity or complete document similarity. Sentence similarity can be defined by the degree of semantic equivalence of two given sentences, where sentences are typically 10-20 words long. The role of sentence semantic similarity measures in text-related research is increasing due to potential number of applications such as document summarization, question answering, information extraction & retrieval and machine translation.

One plausible limitation of existing methods for sentence similarity is their adaptation from long text (e.g. documents) similarity methods, where word co-occurrence plays a significant role. However, sentences are too short, thats why taking syntactic role of each word with its narrow semantic meaning into account, can be highly relevant to reflect the semantic equivalence of two sentences. These narrow semantics can be reflected from any existing large lexicons [(Wu and Palmer, 1994) and (Lin, 1998)]; nevertheless, these lexicons can not provide the semantics of words which are out of lexicon (e.g. guy) or multiword expressions. These semantics can be represented by a large distributed semantic space such as Wikipedia and similarity can be reflected by relatedness of these extracted semantics. However, relatedness covers broader space than similarity, which forced us to tune the Wikipedia based relatedness with lexical structure (e.g. WordNet) based similarities driven by linguistic syntactic structure, in reflecting more sophisticated similarity of two given sentences.

In this work, we present a sentence similarity using ESA and syntactic similarities. The rest of this paper is organized as follows. Section 2 explores the related work. Section 3 describes our approaches in detail. Section 4 explains our three different submitted runs for STS task. Section 5 shows the results and finally we conclude in section 6.

2 Related Work

In recent years, there have been a variety of efforts in improving semantic similarity measures, however most of these approaches address this problem from the viewpoint of large document similarity based on word co-occurrence using string pattern or corpus statistics. Corpus based approaches such as Latent Semantic Analysis (LSA) [(Landauer et. al, 1998) and (Foltz et. al, 1998)] and ESA (Gabrilovich and Markovitch, 2007) use corpus statistics information about all words and reflect their semantics in distributional high semantic space. However, these approaches perform quite well for long texts as they use word co-occurrence and relying on the principle that words which are used in the same contexts tend to have related meanings. In case of short text similarities, syntactic role of each word with its meaning plays an important role.

There are several linguistic measures [(Achananuparp et. al, 2008) and (Islam and Inkpen, 2008)], which can account for pseudo-syntactic information by analyzing their word order using n-gram. To do this, Islam and Inkpen defined a syntactic measure, which considers the word order between two strings by computing the maximal ordered word overlapping. (Oliva et. al, 2011) present a similarity measure for sentences and short text that takes syntactic information, such as morphology and parsing tree, into account and calculate similarities between words with same syntactic role, by using WordNet.

Our work takes inspiration from existing approaches that exploit a combination of Wikipedia based relatedness with lexical structure based similarities driven by linguistic syntactic structure.

3 Methodology

We implemented two approaches for the STS task [(Agirre et. al, 2012)]. First approach is a fusion of corpus-based semantic relatedness and knowledge-based semantic similarity measures. The core of this combination is the corpus-based measure because the combination includes the corpus-based semantic relatedness score over the whole sentences and the knowledge-based semantic similarity scores for the words falling under the same syntactic roles in both the sentences. Machine learning models are trained by taking all these scores as different features. For the submission, we used Linear regression and Bagging models. Also, the equation obtained after training the linear regression model shows more weightage to the score obtained by the corpus-based relatedness measure as this is the only score (feature), which reflects the semantic relatedness/similarity score over the full sentences, out of all the considered features for the model. We used ESA as the corpus based semantic relatedness measure and modified WordNet-based Lin measure as the knowledge-based similarity. The WordNet-based Lin relatedness measure was modified to reflect better the similarity between the words. For the knowledge-based similarity, currently we considered only the words lying in the three major syntactic role categories i.e. subjects, actions and the objects. We see the first approach as the corpus-based measure ESA tuned with the knowledge-based measure. Thus, it is referred as TunedESA later in the paper.

Our second approach is based on the bipartite method over the WordNet based semantic relatedness measures. WordNet-based Lin measure (without any modification) was used for calculating the relatedness scores for all the possible corresponding pair of words appearing in both the sentences. Then, the similarity/relatedness score for the sentences is calculated by perceiving the problem as the computation of a maximum total matching weight of a bipartite graph having the words as nodes and the relatedness scores as the weight of the edges between the nodes. To solve this, we used Hungarian method. Later, we refer this method as WordNet-Bipartite.

3.1 TunedESA

In this approach, the ESA based relatedness score for the full sentences is combined with the modified WordNet-based Lin similarity scores calculated for the words falling under the corresponding syntactic role category in both the sentences.

	ALL	Rank-ALL	ALLnrm	RankNrm	Mean	RankMean
Baseline	0.3110	87	0.6732	85	0.4356	70
Run1	0.5777	52	0.8158	20	0.5466	52
Run2	0.5833	51	0.8183	17	0.5683	42
Run3	0.4911	67	0.7696	57	0.5377	53

Table 1: Overall Rank and Pearson Correlation of all runs

	MSRpar	MSRvid	SMTeuro	OnWN	SMTnews
Baseline	0.4334	0.2996	0.4542	0.5864	0.3908
ESA*	0.2778	0.8178	0.3914	0.6541	0.4366
Run1	0.3675	**0.8427**	0.3534	0.6030	0.4430
Run2	0.3720	0.8330	0.4238	**0.6513**	**0.4489**
Run3	**0.5320**	0.6874	**0.4514**	0.5827	0.2818

Table 2: Pearson Correlation of all runs with all five STS test datasets

TunedESA could be summarized as these four basic steps:

- Calculate the ESA relatedness score between the sentences.
- Find the words corresponding to the linguistic syntactical categories like subject, action and object of both the sentences.
- Calculate the semantic similarity between the words falling in the corresponding subjects, actions and objects in both the sentences using modified WordNet-based measure Lin.
- Combine these four scores for ESA, Subject, Action and Object to get the final similarity score on the basis of an already learned machine learning model with the training data.

ESA is a promising technique to find the relatedness between documents. The texts which need to be compared are represented as high dimensional vectors containing the TF-IDF weight between the term and the Wikipedia article. The semantic relatedness measure is calculated by taking the cosine measure between these vectors. In this implementation of ESA [1], the score was calculated by considering the full sentence at a time for making the Wikipedia article vector while in the standard ESA, vectors are made for each word of the text followed by the addition of all these vectors to represent the final vector for the text/sentence. It was done just to reduce the time complexity.

To calculate the lexical similarity between the words, we implemented WordNet-based semantic relatedness measure Lin. This score was modified to reflect a better similarity between the words. In the current system, basic linguistic syntactic categories i.e. subjects, actions and objects were used. For instance, below is a sentences pair from the training MSRvid dataset with the gold standard score and the syntactic roles.

Sentence 1: A man is playing a guitar.
Subject: Man, Action: play, Object: guitar

Sentence 2: A man is playing a flute.
Subject: Man, Action: play, Object: flute

Gold Standard Score (0-5): 2.2

As the modification, the scores given by Lin measure were used only for the cases where subsumption relation or hypernymy/hyponymy exists

[1]ESA* considering full sentence at a time to make the vector i.e. different from standard ESA

between the words. This modification was done only for the words falling under the category of subjects and objects.

3.2 WordNet Bipartite

WordNet-based semantic relatedness measure was used for the second approach.

Following steps are performed :

- Each sentence is tokenized to obtain the words.
- Semantic relatedness between every possible pair of words in both the sentences is calculated using WordNet-based measure e.g. Lin.
- Using the scores obtained in the second step, the semantic similarity/relatedness between the sentences is calculated by transforming the problem as that of computing the maximum total matching weight of a bipartite graph, which can be done by using Hungarian method.

4 System Description

We submitted three runs in the semantic textual similarity task. The first two runs are based on the first approach i.e. TunedESA and they differ only in the machine learning algorithm used for obtaining the final similarity score based on all the considered scores/features.

ESA was implemented on the current Wikipedia dump. WordNet based relatedness measure Lin was modified to give a better semantic similarity degree. Stanford Core-NLP library was used for obtaining the words with their syntactic roles. All the required scores/feature i.e. ESA based relatedness for the complete sentences and modified WordNet-based Lin similarity scores were calculated for the corresponding words lying in the same syntactic categories. Bagging and Linear Regression models were built using the training data for the first and second runs respectively. Based on the category of the test dataset, model was trained on the corresponding training dataset.

For the surprise test datasets, we trained our model with the training dataset of the MSRvid data based on the fact that we obtained good results with this category. Then the built models were used for calculating the similarity scores for the test data.

For the third run, WordNet Bipartite method was used to calculate the similarity scores. It didn't require any training.

5 Results and Discussion

All above described runs are evaluated on STS test dataset. Table 1 shows the overall results[2] of our three runs against the baseline system which follows the bag of words approach. Table 2 shows the Pearson correlation on different test datasets for all the three runs. It provides a comparison between corpus based relatedness measure ESA and our system TunedESA (Run 1 & Run 2).

The results show significant improvement against ESA. Although, it can be seen that the baseline results are even better than of the ESA in the cases of MSRpar and SMTeuro. It may be because this implementation of ESA is not the standard one.

6 Conclusion

We presented a method to calculate the degree of sentence similarity based on tuning the corpus based relatedness measure with the knowledge-based similarity measure over the syntactic roles. The results show a definite improvement by the fusion. As future work, we plan to improve the syntactic role handling and considering more syntactical categories. Also, experimentation[3] with standard ESA and other semantic similarity/relatedness measures needs to be performed.

Acknowledgments

This work is supported in part by the European Union under Grant No. 248458 for the Monnet project as well as by the Science Foundation Ireland under Grant No. SFI/08/CE/I1380 (Lion-2).

[2]results can also be found at `http://www.cs.york.ac.uk/semeval-2012/task6/index.php?id=results-update` with the name **nitish_aggarwal**

[3]We plan to provide the further results and information at `http://www.itssimilar.com/`

References

Achananuparp Palakorn and Xiaohua Hu and Xiajiong Shen 2008 The Evaluation of Sentence Similarity Measures, In: DaWaK. pp. 305-316

Agirre Eneko , Cer Daniel, Diab Mona and Gonzalez-Agirre Aitor 2012 SemEval-2012 Task 6: A Pilot on Semantic Textual Similarity. In: Proceedings of the 6th International Workshop on Semantic Evaluation (SemEval 2012), in conjunction with the First Joint Conference on Lexical and Computational Semantics (*SEM 2012).

Foltz P. W., Kintsch W. and Landauer T. K. 1998. *In: journal of the Discourse Processes. pp. 285-307,* The measurement of textual Coherence with Latent Semantic Analysis,

Gabrilovich Evgeniy and Markovitch Shaul 2007 Computing Semantic Relatedness using Wikipedia-based Explicit Semantic Analysis, In: Proceedings of The Twentieth International Joint Conference for Artificial Intelligence. pp. 1606–1611,

Islam, Aminul and Inkpen, Diana 2008 Semantic text similarity using corpus-based word similarity and string similarity, In: journal of ACM Trans. Knowl. Discov. Data. pp. 10:1–10:25

Landauer Thomas K. ,Foltz Peter W. and Laham Darrell 1998. An Introduction to Latent Semantic Analysis, *In: Journal of the Discourse Processes. pp. 259-284,*

Lin Dekang 1998 Proceeding of the 15th International Conference on Machine Learning. pp. 296–304 An information-theoretic definition of similarity

Oliva, Jesús and Serrano, José Ignacio and del Castillo, María Dolores and Iglesias, Ángel April, 2011 SyMSS: A syntax-based measure for short-text semantic similarity In: journal of Data Knowledge Engineering. pp. 390–405

Wu, Zhibiao and Palmer, Martha 1994 Verbs semantics and lexical selection, In: Proceedings of the 32nd annual meeting on Association for Computational Linguistics,

Stanford: Probabilistic Edit Distance Metrics for STS

Mengqiu Wang and **Daniel Cer***
Computer Science Department
Stanford University
Stanford, CA 94305 USA
{mengqiu,danielcer}@cs.stanford.edu

Abstract

This paper describes Stanford University's submission to SemEval 2012 Semantic Textual Similarity (STS) shared evaluation task. Our proposed metric computes probabilistic edit distance as predictions of semantic similarity. We learn weighted edit distance in a probabilistic finite state machine (pFSM) model, where state transitions correspond to edit operations. While standard edit distance models cannot capture long-distance word swapping or cross alignments, we rectify these shortcomings using a novel pushdown automaton extension of the pFSM model. Our models are trained in a regression framework, and can easily incorporate a rich set of linguistic features. The performance of our edit distance based models is contrasted with an adaptation of the Stanford textual entailment system to the STS task. Our results show that the most advanced edit distance model, pPDA, outperforms our entailment system on all but one of the genres included in the STS task.

1 Introduction

We describe a probabilistic edit distance based metric, which was originally designed for evaluating machine translation quality, for computing semantic textual similarity (STS). This metric models weighted edit distance in a probabilistic finite state machine (pFSM), where state transitions correspond to edit operations. The weights of the edit operations are automatically learned in a regression framework. One of the major contributions of this paper is a novel extension of the pFSM model into a probabilistic Pushdown Automaton (pPDA), which enhances traditional edit-distance models with the ability to model phrase shift and word swapping. Furthermore, we give a new log-linear parameterization to the pFSM model, which allows it to easily incorporate rich linguistic features. We contrast the performance of our probabilistic edit distance metric with an adaptation of the Stanford textual entailment system to the STS task.

* Daniel Cer is one of the organizers for the STS task. The STS test set data was not used in any way for the development or training of the systems described in this paper.

2 pFSMs for Semantic Textual Similarity

We start off by framing the problem of semantic textual similarity in terms of weighted edit distance calculated using probabilistic finite state machines (pFSMs). A FSM defines a language by accepting a string of input tokens in the language, and rejecting those that are not. A probabilistic FSM defines the probability that a string is in a language, extending on the concept of a FSM. Commonly used models such as HMMs, *n*-gram models, Markov Chains and probabilistic finite state transducers all fall in the broad family of pFSMs (Knight and Al-Onaizan, 1998; Eisner, 2002; Kumar and Byrne, 2003; Vidal et al., 2005). Unlike all the other applications of FSMs where tokens in the language are words, in our language tokens are edit operations. A string of tokens that our FSM accepts is an edit sequence that transforms one side of the sentence pair (denoted as $\mathbf{s^1}$) into the other side ($\mathbf{s^2}$).

Our pFSM has a unique start and stop state, and one state per edit operation (i.e., *Insert*, *Delete*, *Substitution*). The probability of an edit sequence **e** is generated by the model is the product of the state transition probabilities in the pFSM, formally de-

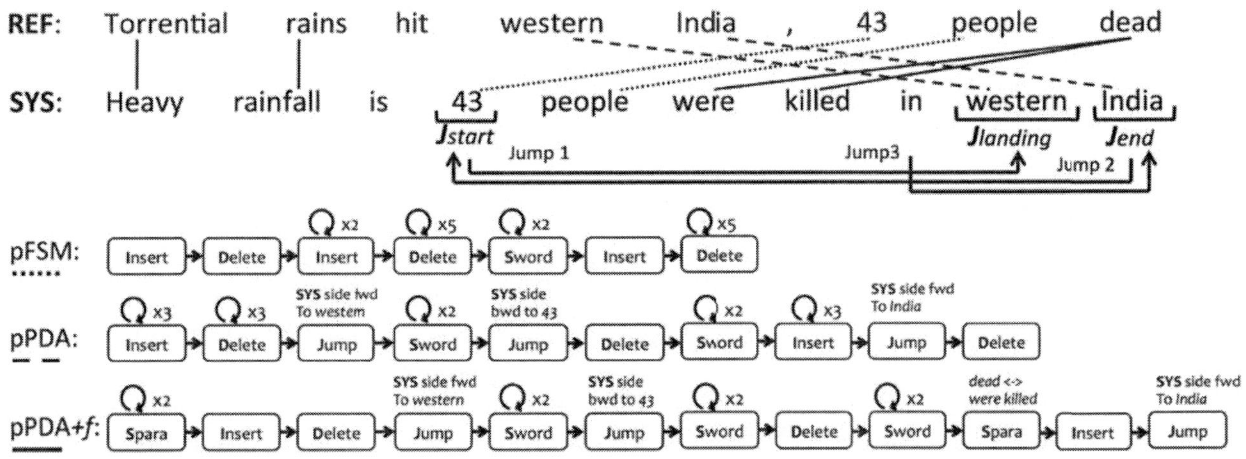

Figure 1: This diagram illustrates an example sentence pair from the statistical machine translation subtask of STS. The three rows below are the best state transition (edit) sequences that transforms REF to SYS, according to the basic pFSM model, the extended pPDA model, and pPDA model with synonym and paraphrase linguistic features. The corresponding alignments generated by the models (pFSM, pPDA, pPDA+*f*) are shown with different styled lines, with later models in the order generating strictly more alignments than earlier ones. The gold human evaluation score is 6.5, and model predictions are: pPDA+f 5.5, pPDA 4.3, pFSM 3.1.

scribed as:

$$w(\mathbf{e} \mid \mathbf{s^1}, \mathbf{s^2}) = \frac{\prod_{i=1}^{|\mathbf{e}|} \exp \theta \cdot \mathbf{f}(e_{i-1}, e_i, \mathbf{s^1}, \mathbf{s^2})}{Z} \quad (1)$$

We featurize each of the state changes with a log-linear parameterization; **f** is a set of binary feature functions defined over pairs of neighboring states (by the Markov assumption) and the input sentences, and θ are the associated feature weights; Z is a partition function. In this basic pFSM model, the feature functions are simply identity functions that emit the current state, and the state transition sequence of the previous state and the current state.

The feature weights are then automatically learned by training a global regression model where the human judgment score for each sentence pair is the regression target ($\hat{y}$). Since the "gold" edit sequence are not given at training or prediction time, we treat the edit sequences as hidden variables and sum over them in our model. We introduce a new regression variable $y \in \mathbb{R}$ which is the log-sum of the unnormalized weights (Eqn. (1)) of all edit sequences, formally expressed as:

$$y = \log \sum_{\mathbf{e'} \subseteq \mathbf{e^*}} \prod_{i=1}^{|\mathbf{e'}|} \exp \theta \cdot \mathbf{f}(e_{i-1}, e_i, \mathbf{s^1}, \mathbf{s^2}) \quad (2)$$

$\mathbf{e^*}$ is the set of all possible alignments. The sum over an exponential number of edit sequences in $\mathbf{e^*}$ is solved efficiently using a forward-backward style dynamic program. Any edit sequence that does not lead to a complete transformation of the sentence pair has a probability of zero in our model. Our regression target then seeks to minimize the least squares error with respect to $\hat{y}$, plus a L_2-norm regularizer term parameterized by λ:

$$\theta^* = \min_{\theta} \{ \sum_{\mathbf{s_i^1}, \mathbf{s_i^2}} [\hat{y}_i - (\frac{y}{|\mathbf{s_i^1}| + |\mathbf{s_i^2}|} + \alpha)]^2 + \lambda \|\theta\|^2 \} \quad (3)$$

The $|\mathbf{s_i^1}| + |\mathbf{s_i^2}|$ is a length normalization term for the ith training instance, and α is a scaling constant whose value is to be learned. At test time, $y/(|\mathbf{s^1}| + |\mathbf{s^2}|) + \alpha$ is computed as the predicted score.

We replaced the standard substitution edit operation with three new operations: S_{word} for same word substitution, S_{lemma} for same lemma substitution, and S_{punc} for same punctuation substitution. In other words, all but the three matching-based substitutions are disallowed. The start state can transition into any of the edit states with a constant unit cost, and each edit state can transition into any other edit state if and only if the edit operation involved is valid at the current edit position (e.g., the model cannot transition into *Delete* state if it is already at the end of $\mathbf{s^1}$; similarly it cannot transition into S_{lemma} unless the lemma of the two words under edit in $\mathbf{s^1}$ and $\mathbf{s^2}$ match). When the end of both sentences are reached, the model transitions into the stop state and ends the edit sequence. The first row in Figure 1 starting with pFSM shows a state transition sequence for an example sentence pair. [1] There exists a one-to-one correspondence between substitution edits and word alignments. Therefore this example state transition sequence correctly generates an alignment for the word *43* and *people*.

2.1 pPDA Extension

A shortcoming of edit distance models is that they cannot handle long-distance word swapping — a pervasive phenomenon found in most natural languages. [2] Edit operations in standard edit distance models need to obey strict incremental order in their edit position, in order to admit efficient dynamic programming solutions. The same limitation is shared by our pFSM model, where the Markov assumption is made based on the incremental order of edit positions. Although there is no known solution to the general problem of computing edit distance where long-distance swapping is permitted (Dombb et al., 2010), approximate algorithms do exist. We present a simple but novel extension of the pFSM model to a probabilistic pushdown automaton (pPDA), to capture non-nested word swapping within limited distance, which covers a majority of word swapping in observed in real data (Wu, 2010).

A pPDA, in its simplest form, is a pFSM where each control state is equipped with a stack (Esparza and Kucera, 2005). The addition of stacks for each transition state endows the machine with memory, extending its expressiveness beyond that of context-free formalisms. By construction, at any stage in a normal edit sequence, the pPDA model can "jump" forward within a fixed distance (controlled by a max distance parameter) to a new edit position on either side of the sentence pair, and start a new edit subsequence from there. Assuming the jump was made on the $\mathbf{s^2}$ side, [3] the machine remembers its current edit position in $\mathbf{s^2}$ as J_{start}, and the destination position on $\mathbf{s^2}$ after the jump as $J_{landing}$.

We constrain our model so that the only edit operations that are allowed immediately following a "jump" are from the set of substitution operations (e.g., S_{word}). And after at least one substitution has been made, the device can now "jump" back to J_{start}, remembering the current edit position as J_{end}. Another constraint here is that after the backward "jump", all edit operations are permitted except for *Delete*, which cannot take place until at least one substitution has been made. When the edit sequence advances to position $J_{landing}$, the only operation allowed at that point is another "jump" forward operation to position J_{end}, at which point we also clear all memory about jump positions and reset.

An intuitive explanation is that when pPDA makes the first forward jump, a gap is left in $\mathbf{s^2}$ that has not been edited yet. It remembers where it left off, and comes back to it after some substitutions have been made to complete the edit sequence. The second row in Figure 1 (starting with pPDA) illustrates an edit sequence in a pPDA model that involves three "jump" operations, which are annotated and indexed by number 1-3 in the example. "Jump 1" creates an un-edited gap between word *43* and *western*, after two substitutions, the model makes "jump 2" to go back and edit the gap. The only edit permitted immediately after "jump 2" is deleting the comma in $\mathbf{s^1}$, since inserting the word *43* in $\mathbf{s^2}$ before any substitution is disallowed. Once the gap is completed, the model resumes at position J_{end} by making "jump 3", and completes the jump sequence.

The "jumps" allowed the model to align words such as *western India*, in addition to the alignments of *43 people* found by the pFSM. In practice, we found that our extension gives a big boost to model performance (*cf.* Section 4), with only a modest increase in computation time. [4]

[1] It is safe to ignore the second and third row in Figure 1 for now, their explanations are forthcoming in Section 2.1.

[2] The edit distance algorithm described in Cormen et al. (2001) can only handle adjacent word swapping (transposition), but not long-distance swapping.

[3] Recall that we transform $\mathbf{s^1}$ into $\mathbf{s^2}$, and thus on the $\mathbf{s^2}$ side, we can only insert but not delete. The argument applies equally to the case where the jump was made on the other side.

[4] The length of the longest edit sequence with jumps only increased by $0.5 * max(|\mathbf{s^1}|, |\mathbf{s^2}|)$ in the worst case, and by and large swapping is rare in comparison to basic edits.

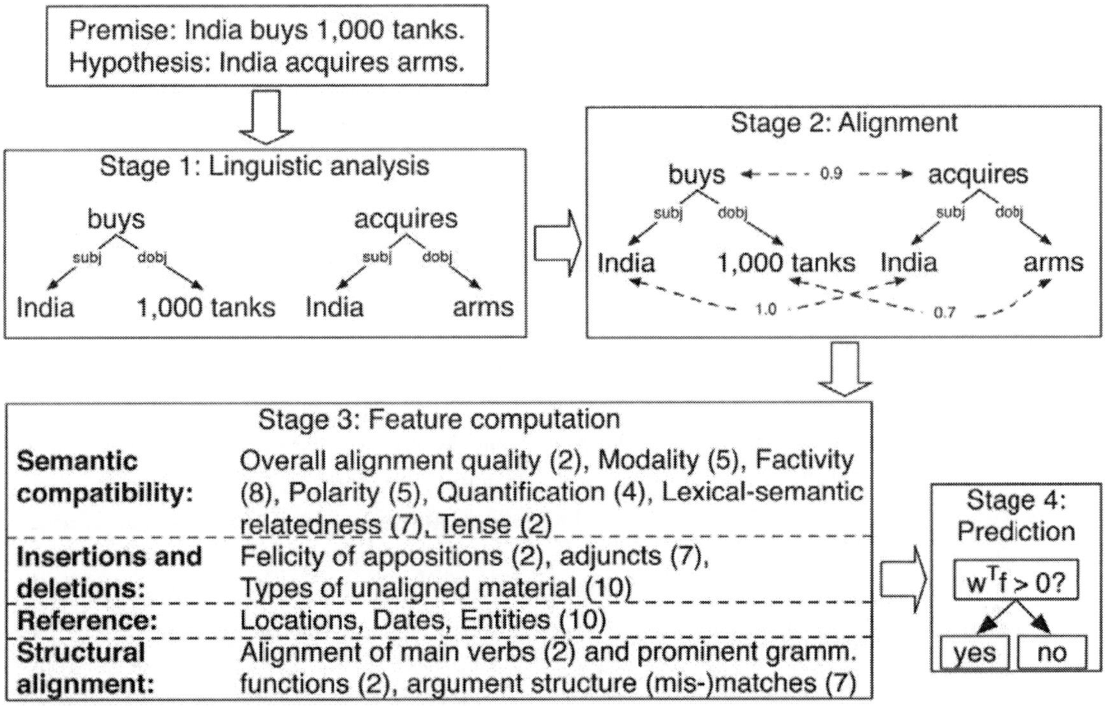

Figure 2: **Stanford Entailment Recognizer:** The pipelined approach used by the Stanford entailment recognizer to analyze sentence pairs and determine whether or not an entailment relationship is present. The entailment recognizer first obtains dependency parses for both the passage and the hypothesis. These parses are then aligned based upon lexical and structural similarity between the two dependency graphs. From the aligned graphs, features are extracted that suggest the presence or absence of an entailment relationship. Figure courtesy of (Pado et al., 2009).

2.2 Parameter Estimation

Since the least squares operator preserves convexity, and the inner log-sum-exponential function is convex, the resulting objective function is also convex. For parameter learning, we used the limited memory quasi-newton method (Liu and Nocedal, 1989) to find the optimal feature weights and scaling constant for the objective. We initialized $\theta = \vec{0}$, $\alpha = 0$, and $\lambda = 5$. We also threw away features occurring fewer than five times in training corpus. Gradient calculation was similar to other pFSM models, such as HMMs, we omitted the details here, for brevity.

2.3 Rich Linguistic Features

We add new substitution operations beyond those introduced in Section 2, to capture synonyms and paraphrase in the sentence pair. Synonym relations are defined according to WordNet (Miller et al., 1990), and paraphrase matches are given by a lookup table. To better take advantage of paraphrase information at the multi-word phrase level, we extended our substitution operations to match longer phrases by adding one-to-many and many-to-many bigram block substitutions. In our experiments on machine translation evaluation task, which our metric was originally developed for, we found that most of the gain came from unigrams and bigrams, with little to no additional gains from trigrams. Therefore, we limited our experiments to bigram pFSM and pPDA models, and pruned the paraphrase table adopted from TERplus [5] to unigrams and bigrams, resulting in 2.5 million paraphrase pairs. Trained on all available training data, the resulting pPDA model has a total of 218 features.

2.4 Model Configuration

We evaluate both the pFSM and pPDA models with the addition of rich linguistic features, as described in the previous section. For pPDA model, the jump distance is set to five. For each model, we experimented with two different training schemes. In the

[5] Available from www.umiacs.umd.edu/~snover/terp.

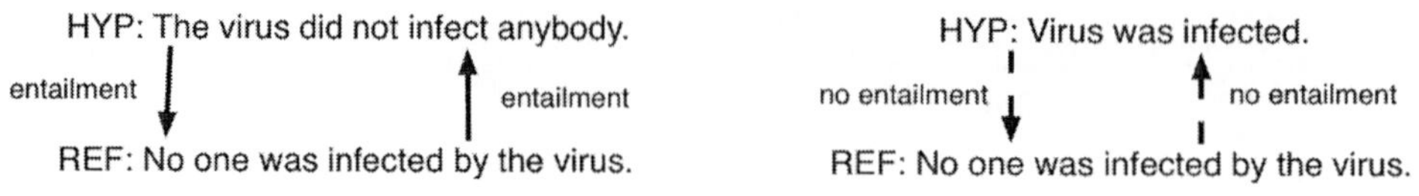

Figure 3: Semantic similarity as determined by mutual textual entailment. Figure courtesy of (Pado et al., 2009).

first scheme, we train a separate model for each section of the training dataset (i.e., MSRpar, MSRvid, and SMTeuroparl), and use that model to test on their respective test set. For the two unseen test sets (SMTnews and OnWN), we used a joint model trained on all of the available training data. We refer to this scheme as *Indi* henceforth. In the second scheme, we used the joint model trained on all training data to make preditions for all test sets (we refer to this scheme as *All*). Our official submission contains two runs – pFSM with scheme *Indi*, and pPDA with scheme *All*.

3 Textual Entailment for STS

We contrast the performance of the probabilistic edit distance metrics with an adaptation of the Stanford Entailment Recognizer to the STS task. In this section, we review the textual entailment task, the operation of the Stanford Entailment Recognizer, and describe how we adapted our entailment system to the STS task.

3.1 Recognizing Textual Entailment

The Recognizing Textual Entailment (RTE) task (Dagan et al., 2005) involves determining whether the meaning of one text can be inferred from another. The text providing the ground truth for the evaluation is known as the passage while the text being tested for entailment is known as the the hypothesis. A passage entails a hypothesis if a casual speaker would consider the inference to be correct. This intentionally side-steps strict logical entailment and implicitly brings in all of the world knowledge speakers use to interpret language.

The STS task and RTE differ in two significant ways. First, the RTE task is one directional. If a hypothesis sentence is implied by a passage, the inverse does not necessarily hold (e.g., "John is outside in the snow without a coat." casually implies "John is cold", but not vice versa). Second, the RTE task forces systems to make a boolean choice about entailment, rather than the graded scale of semantic relatedness implied by STS.

3.2 Textual Entailment System Description

Shown in Figure 2, the Stanford entailment system uses a linguistically rich multi-stage annotation pipeline. Incoming sentence pairs are first dependency parsed. The dependency parse trees are then transformed into semantic graphs containing additional annotations such as named entities and coreference. The two semantic graphs are then aligned based upon structural overlap and lexical semantic similarity using a variety of word similarity metrics based on WordNet, vector space distributional similarity as calculated by InfoMap, and a specialized module for matching ordinal values. The system then supplies the aligned semantic graphs as input to a number of feature producing modules. Some modules produce gross aggregate scores, such as returning the alignment quality between the two sentences. Others look for specific phenomena that suggest the presence or absence of an entailment relationship, such as a match or mismatch in polarity (e.g., "died" vs. "didn't die"), tense, quantification, and argument structure. The resulting features are then passed on to a down stream classifier to predict whether or not an entailment relationship exists.

3.3 Adapting RTE to STS

In order to adapt our entailment recognition system to STS, we follow the same approach Pado et al. (2009) used to successfully adapt the entailment system to machine translation evaluation. As shown in Figure 3, for each pair of sentences presented to the system, we run the entailment system in both directions and extract features that describe whether the first sentence entails the second and vice versa for the opposite direction. This setup effectively treats the STS task as a bidirectional variant of the RTE task. The extracted bidirectional entailment features are then passed on to a support vec-

Models	All	MSRpar	MSRvid	SMTeuro	OnWn	SMTnews
pFSMIndi	$0.6354^{(38)}$	0.3795	0.5350	0.4377	-	-
pFSMAll	0.3727	0.3769	0.4569	0.4256	0.6052	0.4164
pPDAIndi	**0.6808**	0.4244	0.5051	0.4554	-	-
pPDAAll	$0.4229^{(77)}$	**0.4409**	0.4698	**0.4558**	**0.6468**	**0.4769**
Entailment	$0.5589^{(55)}$	0.4374	**0.8037**	0.3533	0.3077	0.3235

Table 1: Absolute score prediction results on STS12 test set. Numbers in this table are Pearson correlation scores. Best result on each test set is highlighted in bold. Numbers in *All* column that has superscript are the official submissions. Their relative rank among 89 systems in shown in parentheses.

tor machine regression (SVR) model, which predicts the STS score for the sentence pair. As in Pado et al. (2009), we augment the bidirectional entailment features with sentence level BLEU scores, in order to improve robustness over noisy non-grammatical data. We trained the SVR model using libSVM over all of the sentence pairs in the STS training set. The model uses a Gaussian kernel with $\gamma = 0.125$, an SVR ε-loss of 0.25, and margin violation cost, C, of 2.0. These hyperparameters were selected by cross validation over the training set.

4 Results

From Table 1, we can see that the pPDA model performed better than the pFSM model on all test sets except the MSRvid section. This result clearly demonstrates the power of the pPDA extension in modeling long-distance word swapping. The MSRvid test set has the shortest overall sentence length (13, versus 35 for MSRpar), and therefore it is not too surprising that long distance word swapping did not help much here. Furthermore, the pPDA model shows a much more pronounced performance gain than pFSM when tested on unseen datasets (OnWn and SMTnews), suggesting that the pPDA model is more robust across domain. A second observation is that the *Indi* training scheme seems to work better than the *All* approach, which shows having more training data does not compensate the different characteristics of each training portion. Our best metric on all test set is the pPDAIndi model, with a Pearson's correlation score of 0.6808. If interpolated into the official submitted runs ranking, it would be placed at the 22nd place among 89 runs. Among the three official runs submitted to the shared task (pPDAAll, pFSMIndi and Entailment), pFSMIndi performs the best, placed at 38th place among 89 runs. Since our metrics were originally designed for statistical machine translation (MT) evaluation, we found that on the unseen SMTNews test set, which consists of news conversation sentence pairs from the MT domain, our pPDA model placed at a much higher position (13 among 89 runs).

In comparison to results on MT evaluation task (Wang and Manning, 2012), we found that the pPDA and pFSM models work less well on STS. Whereas in MT evaluation it is common to have access to thousands of training examples, there is an order of magnitude less available training data in STS. Therefore, learning hundreds of feature parameters in our models from such few examples are likely to be ill-posed.

Overall, the RTE system did not perform as well as the regression based models except for MSRvid domain , which has the shortest overall sentence length. Our qualitative evaluation suggests that MSRvid domain seems to exhibit the least degree of lexical divergence between the sentence pairs, thus making this task *easier* than other domains (the median score of all 89 official systems for MSRvid is 0.7538, while the median for MSRpar and SMTeuroparl is 0.5128 and 0.4437, respectively). The relative rank of RTE for MSRvid is 21 among 89, whereas the pFSM and pPDA systems ranked 80 and 83, respectively. The low performance of pFSM and pPDA on this task significantly affected the ranking of these two systems on the *ALL* evaluation measure. We do not have a clear explanation why RTE system thrives on this *easier* task while pPDA and pFSM suffers. In the future, we aim to gain a better understanding of the characteristics of the two different systems, and explore combination techniques.

5 Conclusion

We describe a metric for computing sentence level semantic textual similarity, which is based on a probabilistic finite state machine model that computes weighted edit distance. Our model admits a rich set of linguistic features, and can be trained to learn feature weights automatically by optimizing a regression objective. A novel pushdown automaton extension was also presented for capturing long-distance word swapping. Our models outperformed Stanford textual entailment system on all but one of the genres on the STS task.

Acknowledgements

We gratefully acknowledge the support of the Defense Advanced Research Projects Agency (DARPA) Machine Reading Program under Air Force Research Laboratory (AFRL) prime contract no. FA8750-09-C-0181 and the support of the DARPA Broad Operational Language Translation (BOLT) program through IBM. Any opinions, findings, and conclusion or recommendations expressed in this material are those of the author(s) and do not necessarily reflect the view of the DARPA, AFRL, or the US government.

References

T. H. Cormen, C. E. Leiserson, R. L. Rivest, and C. Stein. 2001. *Introduction to Algorithms, Second Edition*. MIT Press.

I. Dagan, O. Glickman, and B. Magnini. 2005. The PASCAL recognising textual entailment challenge. In *Proceedings of the PASCAL Challenges Workshop on Recognising Textual Entailment*.

Y. Dombb, O. Lipsky, B. Porat, E. Porat, and A. Tsur. 2010. The approximate swap and mismatch edit distance. *Theoretical Computer Science*, 411(43).

J. Eisner. 2002. Parameter estimation for probabilistic finite-state transducers. In *Proceedings of ACL*.

J. Esparza and A. Kucera. 2005. Quantitative analysis of probabilistic pushdown automata: Expectations and variances. In *Proceedings of the 20th Annual IEEE Symposium on Logic in Computer Science*.

K. Knight and Y. Al-Onaizan. 1998. Translation with finite-state devices. In *Proceedings of AMTA*.

S. Kumar and W. Byrne. 2003. A weighted finite state transducer implementation of the alignment template model for statistical machine translation. In *Proceedings of HLT/NAACL*.

D. C. Liu and J. Nocedal. 1989. On the limited memory BFGS method for large scale optimization. *Math. Programming*, 45:503–528.

G. A. Miller, R. Beckwith, C. Fellbaum, D. Gross, and K. J. Miller. 1990. WordNet: an on-line lexical database. *International Journal of Lexicography*, 3(4).

S. Pado, D. Cer, M. Galley, D. Jurafsky, and C. Manning. 2009. Measuring machine translation quality as semantic equivalence: A metric based on entailment features. *Machine Translation*, 23:181–193.

E. Vidal, F. Thollard, C. de la Higuera, F. Casacuberta, and R. C. Carrasco. 2005. Probabilistic finite-state machines part I. *IEEE Transactions on Pattern Analysis and Machine Intelligence*, 27(7):1013–1025.

M. Wang and C. Manning. 2012. SPEDE: Probabilistic edit distance metrics for sentence level MT evaluation. In *Proceedings of WMT*.

D. Wu, 2010. *CRC Handbook of Natural Language Processing*, chapter How to Select an Answer String?, pages 367–408. CRC Press.

University_Of_Sheffield: Two Approaches to Semantic Text Similarity

Sam Biggins, Shaabi Mohammed, Sam Oakley,
Luke Stringer, Mark Stevenson and **Judita Priess**
Department of Computer Science
University of Sheffield
Sheffield
S1 4DP, UK
{aca08sb, aca08sm, coa07so, aca08ls,
r.m.stevenson, j.preiss}@shef.ac.uk

Abstract

This paper describes the University of Sheffield's submission to SemEval-2012 Task 6: Semantic Text Similarity. Two approaches were developed. The first is an unsupervised technique based on the widely used vector space model and information from WordNet. The second method relies on supervised machine learning and represents each sentence as a set of n-grams. This approach also makes use of information from WordNet. Results from the formal evaluation show that both approaches are useful for determining the similarity in meaning between pairs of sentences with the best performance being obtained by the supervised approach. Incorporating information from WordNet also improves performance for both approaches.

1 Introduction

This paper describes the University of Sheffield's submission to SemEval-2012 Task 6: Semantic Text Similarity (Agirre et al., 2012). The task is concerned with determining the degree of semantic equivalence between a pair of sentences.

Measuring the similarity between sentences is an important problem that is relevant to many areas of language processing, including the identification of text reuse (Seo and Croft, 2008; Bendersky and Croft, 2009), textual entailment (Szpektor et al., 2004; Zanzotto et al., 2009), paraphrase detection (Barzilay and Lee, 2003; Dolan et al., 2004), Information Extraction/Question Answering (Lin and Pantel, 2001; Stevenson and Greenwood, 2005), Information Retrieval (Baeza-Yates and Ribeiro-Neto, 1999), short answer grading (Pulman and Sukkarieh, 2005; Mohler and Mihalcea, 2009), recommendation (Tintarev and Masthoff, 2006) and evaluation (Papineni et al., 2002; Lin, 2004).

Many of the previous approaches to measuring the similarity between texts have relied purely on lexical matching techniques, for example (Baeza-Yates and Ribeiro-Neto, 1999; Papineni et al., 2002; Lin, 2004). In these approaches the similarity of texts is computed as a function of the number of matching tokens, or sequences of tokens, they contain. However, this approach fails to identify similarities when the same meaning is conveyed using synonymous terms or phrases (for example, "The dog sat on the mat" and "The hound sat on the mat") or when the meanings of the texts are similar but not identical (for example, "The cat sat on the mat" and "A dog sat on the chair").

Significant amounts of previous work on text similarity have focussed on comparing the meanings of texts longer than a single sentence, such as paragraphs or documents (Baeza-Yates and Ribeiro-Neto, 1999; Seo and Croft, 2008; Bendersky and Croft, 2009). The size of these texts means that there is a reasonable amount of lexical items in each document that can be used to determine similarity and failing to identify connections between related terms may not be problematic. The situation is different for the problem of semantic text similarity where the texts are short (single sentences). There are fewer lexical items to match in this case, making it more important that connections between related terms are identified. One way in which this information has been incorporated in NLP systems has been to make use of WordNet to provide information about similarity between word meanings, and this approach has been shown to be useful for computing text similarity (Mihalcea and Corley, 2006; Mohler and Mihalcea, 2009).

This paper describes two approaches to the semantic text similarity problem that use WordNet (Miller et al., 1990) to provide information about relations between word meanings. The two approaches are based on commonly used techniques for computing semantic similarity based on lexical matching. The first is unsupervised while the other requires annotated data to train a learning algorithm. Results of the SemEval evaluation show that the supervised approach produces the best overall results and that using the information provided by WordNet leads to an improvement in performance.

The remainder of this paper is organised as follows. The next section describes the two approaches for computing semantic similarity between pairs of sentences that were developed. The system submitted for the task is described in Section 3 and its performance in the official evaluation in Section 4. Section 5 contains the conclusions and suggestions for future work.

2 Computing Semantic Text Similarity

Two approaches for computing semantic similarity between sentences were developed. The first method, described in Section 2.1, is unsupervised. It uses an enhanced version of the vector space model by calculating the similarity between word senses, and then finding the distances between vectors constructed using these distances. The second method, described in Section 2.2, is based on supervised machine learning and compares sentences based on the overlap of the *n*-grams they contain.

2.1 Vector Space Model

The first approach is inspired by the vector space model (Salton et al., 1975) commonly used to compare texts in Information Retrieval and Natural Language Processing (Baeza-Yates and Ribeiro-Neto, 1999; Manning and Schütze, 1999; Jurafsky and Martin, 2009).

2.1.1 Creating vectors

Each sentence is tokenised, stop words removed and the remaining words lemmatised using NLTK (Bird et al., 2009). (The `WordPunctTokenizer` and `WordNetLemmatizer` are applied.) Binary vectors are then created for each sentence.

The similarity between sentences can be computed by comparing these vectors using the cosine metric. However, this does not take account of words with similar meanings, such as "dog" and "hound" in the sentences "The dog sat on the mat" and "The hound sat on the mat". To take account of these similarities WordNet-based similarity measures are used (Patwardhan and Pedersen, 2006).

Any terms that occur in only one of the sentences do not contribute to the similarity score since they will have a 0 value in the binary vector. Any words with a 0 value in one of the binary vectors are compared with all of the words in the other sentence and the similarity values computed. The highest similarity value is selected and use to replace the 0 value in that vector, see Figure 1. (If the similarity score is below the set threshold of 0.5 then the similarity value is not used and in these cases the 0 value remains unaltered.) This substitution of 0 values in the vectors ensures that similarity between words can be taken account of when computing sentence similarity.

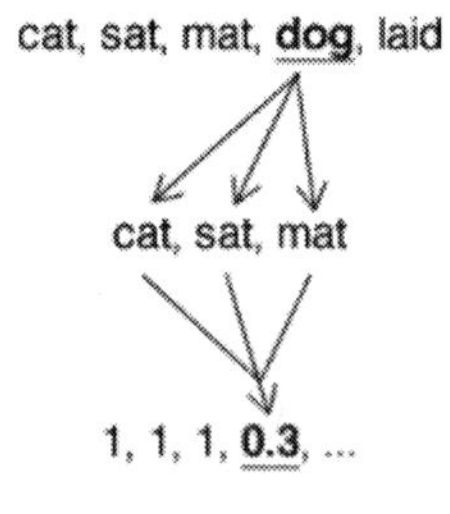

Figure 1: Determining word similarity values for vectors

Various techniques were explored for determining the similarity values between words. These are described and evaluated in Section 2.1.3.

2.1.2 Computing Sentence Similarity

The similarity between two sentences is computed using the cosine metric. Since the cosine metric is a distance measure, which returns a score of 0 for identical vectors, its complement is used to produce the similarity score. This score is multiplied by 5 in order to generate a score in the range required for the task.

2.1.3 Computing Word Similarity

The similarity values for the vectors are computed by first disambiguating each sentence and then applying a similarity measure. Various approaches for carrying out these tasks were explored.

Word Sense Disambiguation Two simple and commonly used techniques for Word Sense Disambiguation were applied.

Most Frequent Sense (MFS) simply selects the first sense in WordNet, i.e., the most common occurring sense for the word. This approach is commonly used as a baseline for word sense disambiguation (McCarthy et al., 2004).

Lesk (1986) chooses a synset by comparing its definition against the sentence and selecting the one with the highest number of words in common.

Similarity measures WordNet-based similarity measures have been found to perform well when used in combination with text similarity measures (Mihalcea and Corley, 2006) and several of these were compared. Implementations of these measures from the NLTK (Bird et al., 2009) were used.

Path Distance uses the length of the shortest path between two senses to determine the similarity between them.

Leacock and Chodorow (1998) expand upon the path distance similarity measure by scaling the path length by the maximum depth of the WordNet taxonomy.

Resnik (1995) makes use of techniques from Information Theory. The measure of relatedness between two concepts is based on the Information Content of the Least Common Subsumer.

Jiang and Conrath (1997) also uses the Information Content of the two input synsets.

Lin (1998) uses the same values as Jiang and Conrath (1997) but takes the ratio of the shared information content to that of the individual concepts.

Results produced by the various combinations of word sense disambiguation strategy and similarity measures are shown in Table 1. This table shows the Pearson correlation of the system output with the gold standard over all of the SemEval training data. The row labelled 'Binary' shows the results using binary vectors which are not augmented with any similarity values. The remainder of the table shows the performance of each of the similarity measures when the senses are selected using the two word sense disambiguation algorithms.

Metric	MFS	Lesk
Binary	0.657	
Path Distance	0.675	0.669
Leacock and Chodorow (1998)	0.087	0.138
Resnik (1995)	0.158	0.153
Jiang and Conrath (1997)	0.435	0.474
Lin (1998)	0.521	0.631

Table 1: Performance of Vector Space Model using various disambiguation strategies and similarity measures

The results in this table show that the only similarity measure that leads to improvement above the baseline is the path measure. When this is applied there is a modest improvement over the baseline for each of the word sense disambiguation algorithms. However, all other similarity measures lead to a drop in performance. Overall there seems to be little difference between the performance of the two word sense disambiguation algorithms. The best performance is obtained using the paths distance and MFS disambiguation.

Table 2 shows the results of the highest scoring method broken down by the individual corpora used for the evaluation. There is a wide range between the highest (0.726) and lowest (0.485) correlation scores with the best performance being obtained for the MSRvid corpus which contains short, simple sentences.

Metric	Correlation
MSRpar	0.591
MSRvid	0.726
SMTeuroparl	0.485

Table 2: Correlation scores across individual corpora using Path Distance and Most Frequent Sense.

2.2 Supervised Machine Learning

For the second approach the sentences are represented as sets of n-grams of varying length, a common approach in text comparison applications which preserves some information about the structure of the document. However, like the standard vector space model (Section 2.1) this technique also fails to identify similarity between texts when an alternative choice of lexical item is used to express the same, or similar, meaning. To avoid this problem WordNet is used to generate sets of alternative n-grams. After the n-grams have been generated for each sentence they are augmented with semantic alternatives created using WordNet (Section 2.2.1). The overlap scores between the n-grams from the two sentences are used as features for a supervised learning algorithm (Section 2.2.2).

2.2.1 Generating n-grams

Preprocessing is carried out using NLTK. Each sentence is tokenised, lemmatised and stop words removed. A set of n-grams are then extracted from each sentence. The set of n-grams for the sentence S is referred to as S_o.

For every n-gram in S_o a list of alternative n-grams is generated using WordNet. Each item in the n-gram is considered in turn and checked to determine whether it occurs in WordNet. If it does then a set of alternative lexical items is constructed by combining all terms that are found in all synsets containing that item as well as their immediate hypernyms and hyponyms of the terms. An additional n-gram is created for each item in this set of alternative lexical items by substituting each for the original term. This set of expanded n-grams is referred to as S_a.

2.2.2 Sentence Comparison

Overlap metrics to determine the similarity between the sets of n-grams are used to create features for the learning algorithm. For two sentences, $S1$ and $S2$, four sets of n-grams are compared: $S1_o$, $S2_o$, $S1_a$ and $S2_a$ (i.e., the n-grams extracted directly from sentences $S1$ and $S2$ as well as the modified versions created using WordNet).

The n-grams that are generated using WordNet (S_a) are not as important as the original n-grams (S_o) for determining the similarity between sentences and this is accounted for by generating three different scores reflecting the overlap between the two sets of n-grams for each sentence. These scores can be expressed using the following equations:

$$\frac{|S1_o \cap S2_o|}{\sqrt{|S1_o| \times |S2_o|}} \quad (1)$$

$$\frac{|(S1_o \cap S2_a) \cap (S2_o \cap S1_a)|}{\sqrt{|(S1_o \cap S2_a)| \times |(S2_o \cap S1_a)|}} \quad (2)$$

$$\frac{|S1_a \cap S2_a|}{\sqrt{|S1_a| \times |S2_a|}} \quad (3)$$

Equation 1 is the cosine measure applied to the two sets of original n-grams, equation 2 compares the original n-grams in each sentence with the alternative n-grams in the other while equation 3 compares the alternative n-grams with each other.

Other features are used in addition to these similarity scores: the mean length of $S1$ and $S2$, the difference between the lengths of $S1$ and $S2$ and the corpus label (indicating which part of the SemEval training data the sentence pair was drawn from). We found that these additional features substantially increase the performance of our system, particularly the corpus label.

3 University of Sheffield's entry for Task 6

Our entry for this task consisted of three runs using the two approaches described in Section 2.

Run 1: Vector Space Model (VS) The first run used the unsupervised vector space approach (Section 2.1). Comparison of word sense disambiguation strategies and semantic similarity measures on the training data showed that the best results were obtained using the Path Distance Measure combined with the Most Frequent Sense approach (see Tables 1 and 2) and these were used for the official run. Post evaluation analysis also showed that this strategy produced the best performance on the test data.

Run 2: Machine Learning (NG) The second run used the supervised machine learning approach (Section 2.2.2). The various parameters used by this approach were explored using 10-fold cross-validation applied to the SemEval training data. We varied the lengths of the n-grams generated, experimented with various pre-processing strategies and machine learning algorithms. The best performance was obtained using short n-grams, unigrams and bigrams, and these were used for the official run. Including longer n-grams did not lead to any improvement in performance but created significant computational cost due to the number of alternative n-grams that were created using WordNet. When the pre-processing strategies were compared it was found that the best performance was obtained by applying both stemming and stop word removal before creating n-grams and this approach was used in the official run. The Weka[1] `LinearRegression` algorithm was used for the official run and a single model was created by training on all of the data provided for the task.

Run 3: Hybrid (VS + NG) The third run is a hybrid combination of the two methods. The supervised approach (NG) was used for the three data sets that had been made available in the training data (MSRpar, MSRvid and SMT-eur) while the vector space model (VS) was used for the other two data sets. This strategy was based on analysis of performance of the two approaches on the training data. The NG approach was found to provide the best performance. However it was sensitive to the data set from which the training data was obtained from while VS, which does not require training data, is more robust.

A diagram depicting the various components of the submitted entry is shown in Figure 2.

4 Evaluation

The overall performance (ALLnrm) of NG, VG and the hybrid systems is significantly higher than the official baseline (see Table 3). The table also includes separate results for each of the evaluation corpora (rows three to seven): the unsupervised VS model performance is significantly higher than the baseline (p-value of 0.06) over all corpus types, as is that of the hybrid model.

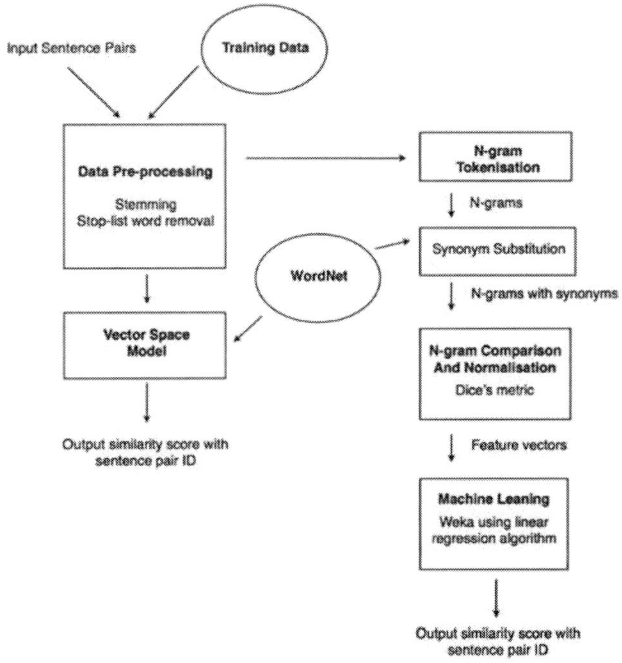

Figure 2: System Digram for entry

However, the performance of the supervised NG model is below the baseline for the (unseen in training data) SMT-news corpus. Given a pair of sentences from an unknown source, the algorithm employs a model trained on all data combined (i.e., omits the corpus information), which may resemble the input (On-WN) or it may not (SMT-news).

After stoplist removal, the average sentence length within MSRvid is 4.5, whereas it is 6.0 and 6.9 in MSRpar and SMT-eur respectively, and thus the last two corpora are expected to form better training data for each other. The overall performance on the MSRvid data is higher than for the other corpora, which may be due to the small number of adjectives and the simpler structure of the shorter sentences within the corpus.

The hybrid system, which selects the supervised system (NG)'s output when the test sentence pair is drawn from a corpus within the training data

[1] `http://www.cs.waikato.ac.nz/ml/weka/`

Corpus	Baseline	Vector Space (VS)	Machine Learning (NG)	Hybrid (NG+VS)
ALL	.3110	.6054	.7241	.6485
ALLnrm	.6732	.7946	.8169	.8238
MSRpar	.4334	.5460	.5166	.5166
MSRvid	.2996	.7241	.8187	.8187
SMT-eur	.4542	.4858	.4859	.4859
On-WN	.5864	.6676	.6390	.6676
SMT-news	.3908	.4280	.2089	.4280

Table 3: Correlation scores from official SemEval results

Rank (/89)	Rank	Ranknrm	RankMean
Baseline	87	85	70
Vector Space (VS)	48	44	29
Machine Learning (NG)	17	18	37
Hybrid	34	15	20

Table 4: Ranks from official SemEval results

and selects the unsupervised system (VS)'s answer otherwise, outperforms both systems in combination. Contrary to expectations, the supervised system did not always outperform VS on phrases based on training data – the performance of VS on MSRpar, with its long and complex sentences, proved to be slightly higher than that of NG. However, the unsupervised system was clearly the correct choice when the source was unknown.

5 Conclusion and Future Work

Two approaches for computing semantic similarity between sentences were explored. The first, unsupervised approach, uses a vector space model and computes similarity between sentences by comparing vectors while the second is supervised and represents the sentences as sets of n-grams. Both approaches used WordNet to provide information about similarity between lexical items. Results from evaluation show that the supervised approach provides the best results on average but also that performance of the unsupervised approach is better for some data sets. The best overall results for the SemEval evaluation were obtained using a hybrid system that attempts to choose the most suitable approach for each data set.

The results reported here show that the semantic text similarity task can be successfully approached using lexical overlap techniques augmented with limited semantic information derived from WordNet. In future, we would like to explore whether performance can be improved by applying deeper analysis to provide information about the structure and semantics of the sentences being compared. For example, parsing the input sentences would provide more information about their structure than can be obtained by representing them as a bag of words or set of n-grams. We would also like to explore methods for improving performance of the n-gram overlap approach and making it more robust to different data sets.

Acknowledgements

This research has been supported by a Google Research Award.

References

E. Agirre, D. Cer, M Diab, and A. Gonzalez-Agirre. 2012. Semeval-2012 task 6: A pilot on semantic textual similarity. In *Proceedings of the 6th International Workshop on Semantic Evaluation (SemEval 2012), in conjunction with the First Joint Conference on Lexical and Computational Semantics (*SEM 2012).*

R. Baeza-Yates and B. Ribeiro-Neto. 1999. *Modern Information Retrieval.* Addison Wesley Longman Limited, Essex.

R. Barzilay and L. Lee. 2003. Learning to paraphrase: An unsupervised approach using multiple-sequence alignment. In *Proceedings of the 2003 Human Language Technology Conference of the North American Chapter of the Association for Computational Linguistics*.

M. Bendersky and W.B. Croft. 2009. Finding text reuse on the web. In *Proceedings of the Second ACM International Conference on Web Search and Data Mining*, pages 262–271. ACM.

S. Bird, E. Klein, and E. Loper. 2009. *Natural Language Processing with Python*. O'Reilly.

B. Dolan, C. Quirk, and C. Brockett. 2004. Unsupervised construction of large paraphrase corpora: Exploiting massively parallel news sources. In *Proceedings of Coling 2004*, pages 350–356, Geneva, Switzerland.

J.J. Jiang and D.W. Conrath. 1997. Semantic Similarity Based on Corpus Statistics and Lexical Taxonomy. In *International Conference Research on Computational Linguistics (ROCLING X)*.

D. Jurafsky and J. Martin. 2009. *Speech and Language Processing*. Pearson, second edition.

C. Leacock and M. Chodorow, 1998. *Combining local context and WordNet similarity for word sense identification*, pages 305–332. In C. Fellbaum (Ed.), MIT Press.

M. Lesk. 1986. Automatic sense disambiguation using machine readable dictionaries: how to tell a pine cone from an ice cream cone. In *Proceedings of ACM SIGDOC Conference*, pages 24–26, Toronto, Canada.

D. Lin and P. Pantel. 2001. Discovery of interence rules for question answering. *Natural Language Engineering*, 7(4):343–360.

D. Lin. 1998. An information-theoretic definition of similarity. In *In Proceedings of the 15th International Conference on Machine Learning*, pages 296–304.

C. Lin. 2004. Rouge: A package for automatic evaluation of summaries. In *Text Summarization Branches Out: Proceedings of the ACL-04 Workshop*, pages 74–81, Barcelona, Spain, July.

C. Manning and H. Schütze. 1999. *Foundations of Statistical Natural Language Processing*. MIT Press, Cambridge, MA.

D. McCarthy, R. Koeling, J. Weeds, and J. Carroll. 2004. Finding predominant senses in untagged text. In *Proceedings of the 42nd Annual Meeting of the Association for Lingusitics (ACL-2004)*, pages 280–287, Barcelona, Spain.

R. Mihalcea and C. Corley. 2006. Corpus-based and knowledge-based measures of text semantic similarity. In *In AAAI06*, pages 775–780.

G.A. Miller, R. Beckwith, C. Fellbaum, D. Gross, and K.J. Miller. 1990. WordNet: An On-line Lexical Database. *International Journal of Lexicography*, 3(4):235–312.

M. Mohler and R. Mihalcea. 2009. Text-to-text semantic similarity for automatic short answer grading. In *Proceedings of the 12th Conference of the European Chapter of the ACL (EACL 2009)*, pages 567–575, Athens, Greece.

K. Papineni, S. Roukos, T. Ward, and W. Zhu. 2002. Bleu: a method for automatic evaluation of machine translation. In *Proceedings of 40th Annual Meeting of the Association for Computational Linguistics*, pages 311–318, Philadelphia, Pennsylvania, USA.

S. Patwardhan and T. Pedersen. 2006. Using WordNet-based context vectors to estimate the semantic relatedness of concept. In *Proceedings of the workshop on "Making Sense of Sense: Bringing Psycholinguistics and Computational Linguistics Together" held in conjunction with the EACL 2006*, pages 1–8.

S.G. Pulman and J.Z. Sukkarieh. 2005. Automatic short answer marking. In *Proceedings of the Second Workshop on Building Educational Applications Using NLP*, pages 9–16, Ann Arbor, Michigan.

P. Resnik. 1995. Using information content to evaluate semantic similarity in a taxonomy. In *In Proceedings of the 14th International Joint Conference on Artificial Intelligence*, pages 448–453.

G. Salton, A. Wong, and C. S. Yang. 1975. A vector space model for automatic indexing. *Commun. ACM*, 18(11):613–620.

J. Seo and W.B. Croft. 2008. Local text reuse detection. In *Proceedings of the 31st Annual International ACM SIGIR Conference on Research and Development in Information Retrieval*, pages 571–578.

M. Stevenson and M. Greenwood. 2005. A Semantic Approach to IE Pattern Induction. In *Proceedings of the 43rd Annual Meeting of the Association for Computational Linguistics (ACL-05)*, pages 379–386, Ann Arbour, MI.

I. Szpektor, H. Tanev, I. Dagan, and B. Coppola. 2004. Scaling web-based acquisition of entailment relations. In *Proceedings of the 2004 Conference on Empirical Methods in Natural Language Processing*, pages 41–48, Barcelona, Spain.

N. Tintarev and J. Masthoff. 2006. Similarity for news recommender systems. In *In Proceedings of the AH'06 Workshop on Recommender Systems and Intelligent User Interfaces*.

F.M. Zanzotto, M. Pennacchiotti, and A. Moschitti. 2009. A machine learning approach to textual entailment recognition. *Natural Language Engineering*, 15-04:551–582.

janardhan: Semantic Textual Similarity using Universal Networking Language graph matching

Janardhan Singh
IIT Bombay,
Mumbai, India
janardhan
@cse.iitb.ac.in

Arindam Bhattacharya
IIT Bombay,
Mumbai, India
arindamb
@cse.iitb.ac.in

Pushpak Bhattacharyya
IIT Bombay,
Mumbai, India
pb
@cse.iitb.ac.in

Abstract

Sentences that are syntactically quite different can often have similar or same meaning. The SemEval 2012 task of Semantic Textual Similarity aims at finding the semantic similarity between two sentences. The semantic representation of Universal Networking Language (UNL), represents only the inherent meaning in a sentence without any syntactic details. Thus, comparing the UNL graphs of two sentences can give an insight into how semantically similar the two sentences are. This paper presents the UNL graph matching method for the Semantic Textual Similarity(STS) task.

1 Introduction

Universal Networking language (UNL) gives the semantic representation of sentences in a graphical form. By comparing the similarity of these graphs, we inherently compare only the semantic content of the two sentences, rather than comparing the similarities in the syntax. Thus, the UNL graph matching strategy is a natural choice for the Semantic Textual Similarity(STS) task of SemEval 2012. UNL graphs are also used in textual entailment and interlingua based machine translation tasks. We use the UNL enconverter system at: `http://www.cfilt.iitb.ac.in /UNL_enco` to generate the UNL graphs of the sentences. For the two graphs, generated from the two sentences, we give a similarity score by matching the two graphs.

In the following sections we describe UNL matching strategy. section 2 describes the UNL system and why this approach is useful, section 3 describes the matching algorithm, section 4 describes the challenges faced in this approach, section 5 gives the results and finally section 6 gives the conclusion and the future scope.

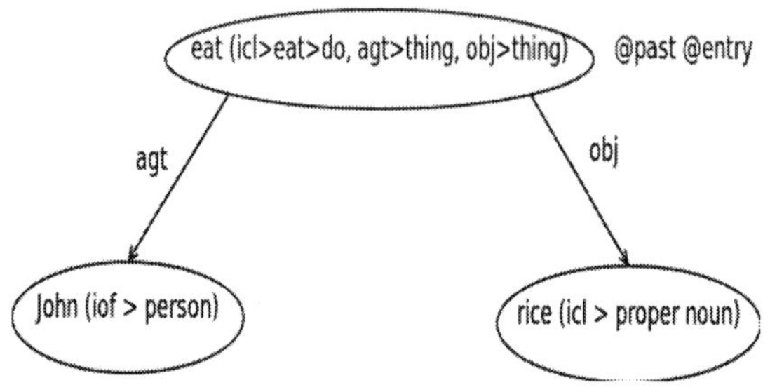

Figure 1: UNL graph for "John eats rice"

2 Universal Networking Language

The Universal Networking Language gives a graphical representation of the semantics of a text in the form of hypergraphs. The representation is at the semantic level which allows mapping of the similar meaning sentences having different syntax to the same representation. To exemplify this point, consider the UNL graphs generated for the following sentences:

Sentence 1: John ate rice.

Sentence 2: Rice was eaten by John.

The UNL graph generated from the system are given in figures 1 and 2 respectively.

The UNL graph consists of three components:

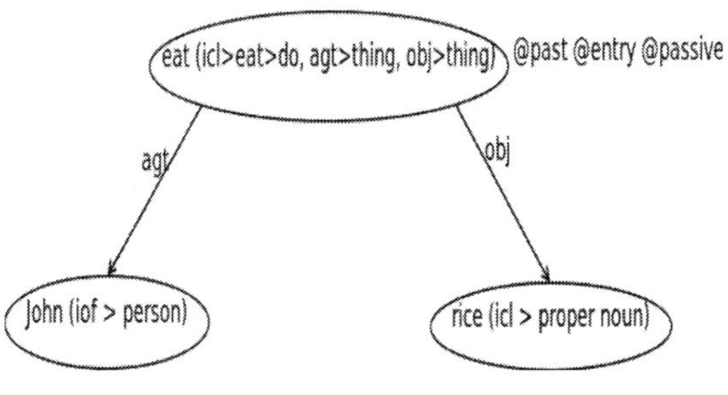

Figure 2: UNL graph for "Rice was eaten by John"

- Universal Words
- Relations
- Attributes

2.1 Universal Words

The Universal Words (UWs) form the vocabulary of the Universal Networking Language. They form the nodes of the UNL graph. The words are normalized to their basic lemma, for example, *eats* becomes *eat*. The Universal Word is, usually, followed by a disambiguating constraint list which is mainly used for disambiguating the sense of the Universal Word. For example, *John (iof> person)*, here the word *John* is disambiguated as an instance of (iof) a *person* and *rice* is disambiguated to be in the class of (icl) proper noun. The UNL generation system, uses a Universal word dictionary created using the wordnet.

2.2 Relations

The UNL manual describes 46 binary semantic relations among the Universal Words as given in UNL manual. These form the labelled arcs of the UNL graph. In the example of figures 1 and 2, the relations agent (agt) and object (obj) are shown. *John* is the *agent* of the action *eat* and *rice* is the object of the action *eat*. The UNL generation system generated these relations using complex rules based on the dependency and constituency parser outputs, Wordnet features and Named Entity recognizer output.

2.3 Attributes

Attributes are attached to the Universal Words to show the speakers perspective for some subjective information in the text. For the given example, with respect to the speaker of the text, the action of *eat* happened in the *past* with respect to the speaker. This is represented by the attribute *@past*.
The detailed description of the UNL standard can be found in the UNL manual available online at `http://www.undl.org/unlsys/unl/unl2005/`.

The two sentences listed above, have the same semantic content, although their syntax is different. One sentence is in the active voice, while the other sentence is in the passive. But if we compare the UNL graphs of the two sentences, they are almost identical, with an extra attribute *@passive* on the main verb *eat* in the second graph. The graph matching of the two sentences results in a high score near to 5. Like voice, most of the syntactic variations are dropped when we move from syntactic to semantic representation. Thus, comparing the semantic representation of the sentences, is useful, to identify their semantic similarity. The UNL generation system generates the attributes using similar features to those for relation generation.

3 UNL matching

The UNL system available online at: `http://www.cfilt.iitb.ac.in/UNL_enco` produces graphs for the sentences by listing the binary relations present in the graph. An example of such a listing is :

Sentence 3: A man is eating a banana by a tree.

```
[unl:1]
agt ( eat(icl>eat>do, agt>thing,
obj>thing):4.@present.@progress
.@entry,
 man(icl>male>thing,
equ>adult_male):2.@indef )
ins ( eat(icl>eat>do, agt>thing,
obj>thing):4.@present.@progress
.@entry,
 tree(icl>woody_plant>thing)
:9.@indef )
obj ( eat(icl>eat>do, agt>thing,
obj>thing):4.@present.@progress
.@entry,
 banana(icl>herb>thing,
equ>banana_tree):6.@indef )
[\unl]
```

Sentence 4 : A man is eating a banana.

```
[unl:1]
agt ( eat(icl>eat>do, agt>thing,
obj>thing):4.@present.@progress
.@entry,
 man(icl>male>thing,
equ>adult_male):2.@indef )
obj ( eat(icl>eat>do, agt>thing,
obj>thing):4.@present.@progress
.@entry,
 banana(icl>herb>thing,
equ>banana_tree):6.@indef )
[\unl]
```

We treat the UNL graph of one sentence as *goldunl* and the other as *testunl*. The matching score between the two is found using the following formulation (Mohanty, 2008):

$$score(testunl, goldunl) = \frac{(2*precision*recall)}{(precision+recall)} \quad (1)$$

$$precision = \frac{\sum_{relation \in testunl} relation\_score(relation)}{(count(relations \in testunl))} \quad (2)$$

$$recall = \frac{\sum_{relation \in testunl} relation\_score(relation)}{(count(relations \in goldunl))} \quad (3)$$

$$relation\_score(relation) = avg(rel\_match, uw1score, uw2score) \quad (4)$$

$$rel\_match = \begin{cases} 1 & \text{if relation name matches} \\ 0 & \text{otherwise} \end{cases} \quad (5)$$

$$uwscore = avg(word\_score, attribute\_score) \quad (6)$$

$$word\_score = \begin{cases} 1 & \text{if universal word matches} \\ 0 & \text{otherwise} \end{cases} \quad (7)$$

$$attribute\_score = F1score(testunl\_attr, goldunl\_attr) \quad (8)$$

The matching scheme is based on the idea of the F1 score. The two UNL graphs are a list of UNL relations each. Considering, one as the gold UNL graph and the other as the test UNL graph, we can find the precision and recall of the total relations that have matched. For the example given in section 2.4, the sentence 3 has three relations while sentence 4 has two relations. A correspondence between the relations *agt* of the two graphs and also the relation *obj* of the two graphs can be established based on the *universal words* that they connect. Each such relation match is given a score, explained later, which is used in the calculation of the precision and recall. From the precision and recall the F1 score can be easily calculated which becomes the total matching score of the two graphs.

The relation score is obtained by averaging the scores of relation match, and the score of the two universal word matches. The universal word match score has a component of the attributes that match between the corresponding universal words. This attribute matching is again the F1 score calculation similar to relation matching. Matching the attributes of the universal words, contributes to the score of the matched universal word, which in turn contributes to the score of the matched relation. Thus, matching of the semantic relations has more weight than the matching of the attributes.

The score obtained by this formulation is between 0 and 1. Another score between 0 and 1 is obtained by flipping the *goldunl* graph to *testunl* and *testunl* to *goldunl*. Average of these two scores is then multiplied by 5 to give the final score.

By this formulation, the score obtained by matching graphs for sentences 3 and 4 is 4.0

4 Challenges in the approach

In the UNL graph matching startegy we faced the following challenges:

4.1 Sentences with grammatical errors

Many of the sentences, especially, from the MSRpar dataset, had minor grammatical errors. The UNL generation requires grammatical correctness. Some of the examples of such sentences are:

- *The no-shows were Sens. John Kerry of Massachusetts and Bob Graham of Florida.*

- *She countersued for $125 million, saying G+J broke its contract with her by cutting her out of key editorial decisions and manipulated the magazine's financial figures.*

- *"She was crying and scared,' said Isa Yasin, the owner of the store.*

Here, terms like *G+J* and punctuation errors as in the third example lead to the generation of improper UNL graphs. To handle such cases, the UNL generation needs to get robust.

4.2 Scoping errors

UNL graphs are hypergraphs, in which, a node can in itself be a UNL graph. Scopes are given identity numbers like *:01,:02* and so on. While matching two different UNL graphs, this matching of scope identity numbers cannot be directly achieved. Also, one graph may have different number of scopes as compared to the other. Hence, eventhough the UNL graphs are generated correctly, due to scoping mismatches the matching score goes down. To tackle this problem, the UNL graphs generated are converted into scopeless form before the matching is performed. Every UNL graph has an entry node, which is the starting node of the graph. This is denoed by an *@entry* attribute on the node. Every scope, too, has an entry node. The idea for converting the UNL graphs into scopeless form is to replace the scope nodes by the graphs that these nodes represent, with the connection to the original scope node going to the entry node of the replacing graph.

4.3 Incomplete or no graph generation

It was observed that for some of the sentences, the UNL generation system did not produce UNL graphs or the generation was incomplete. Some of these sentences are:

- *The Metropolitan Transportation Authority was given two weeks to restore the $1.50 fare and the old commuter railroad rates, York declared.*

- *Long lines formed outside gas stations and people rushed to get money from cash machines Sunday as Israelis prepared to weather a strike that threatened to paralyze the country.*

These, are due to some internal system errors of the UNL generation system. To improve on this, the UNL generation system itself has to improve.

5 Results

By adopting the methodology described in section 3, the following results were obtained on the different datasets.

MSRpar	0.1936
MSRvid	0.5504
SMT-eur	0.3755
On-WN	0.2888
SMT-news	0.3387

As observed, the performance is good for the MSRvid dataset. This dataset consists of small and simple sentences which are grammatically correct. The performance on this dataset should further improve by capturing the synonyms of the Universal words while matching the UNL relations. The performance for MSRpar dataset is low. The sentences in this dataset are long and sometimes with minor grammatical errors resulting in incomplete or no UNL graphs. As the UNL generation system becomes more robust, the performance is expected to improve quickly. The overall result over all the datasets is given in the following table.

ALL	ALLnrm	Mean
0.3431	0.6878	0.3481

6 Conclusion and Future Scope

The UNL graph matching approach works well with grammatically correct sentences. The approach depends on the accuracy of the UNL generation system itself. With the increase in the robustness of the UNL generation system, this approach seems natural. Since, the approach is unsupervised, it does not require any training data. The matching algorithm can be extended to include the synonyms of the Universal Words while matching relations.

References

Mohanty, R. and Limaye, S. and Prasad, M.K. and Bhattacharyya, P. 2008. *Semantic Graph from English Sentences*, Proceedings of ICON-2008: 6th International Conference on Natural Language Processing Macmillan Publishers, India

UNL Center of UNDL Foundation 2005 Universal Networking Language (UNL) Specifications Version 2005 *Online URL:* `http://www.undl.org/unlsys/unl/unl2005/`

UNL enconversion system. 2012. Online URL: `http://www.cfilt.iitb.ac.in/UNL_enco`

SAGAN: An approach to Semantic Textual Similarity based on Textual Entailment

Julio Castillo[†‡] **Paula Estrella**[‡]
[‡]FaMAF, UNC, Argentina
[†]UTN-FRC, Argentina
jotacastillo@gmail.com
pestrella@famaf.unc.edu.ar

Abstract

In this paper we report the results obtained in the Semantic Textual Similarity (STS) task, with a system primarily developed for textual entailment. Our results are quite promising, getting a run ranked 39 in the official results with overall Pearson, and ranking 29 with the Mean metric.

1 Introduction

For the last couple of years the research community has focused on a deeper analysis of natural languages, seeking to capture the meaning of the text in different contexts: in machine translation preserving the meaning of the translations is crucial to determine whether a translation is useful or not, in question-answering understanding the question leads to the desired answers (while the opposite case makes a system rather frustrating to the user) and the examples could continue. In this newly defined task, Semantic Textual Similarity, there is hope that efforts in different areas will be shared and united towards the goal of identifying meaning and recognizing equivalent, similar or unrelated texts. Our contribution to the task, is from a textual entailment point of view, as will be described below.

The paper is organized as follows: Section 2 describes the relevant tasks, Section 3 describes the architecture of the system, then Section 4 shows the experiments carried out and the results obtained, and Section 5 presents some conclusions and future work.

2 Related work

In this section we briefly describe two different tasks that are closely related and in which our system has participated with very promising results.

2.1 Textual Entailment

Textual Entailment (TE) is defined as a generic framework for applied semantic inference, where the core task is to determine whether the meaning of a target textual assertion (hypothesis, H) can be inferred from a given text (T). For example, given the pair (T,H):
T: Fire bombs were thrown at the Tunisian embassy in Bern
H: The Tunisian embassy in Switzerland was attacked
we can conclude that T entails H.

The recently created challenge "Recognising Textual Entailment" (RTE) started in 2005 with the goal of providing a binary answer for each pair (H,T), namely whether there is entailment or not (Dagan et al., 2006). The RTE challenge has mutated over the years, aiming at accomplishing more accurate and specific solutions; for example, in 2008 a three-way decision was proposed (instead of the original binary decision) consisting of "entailment", "contradiction" and "unknown"; in 2009 the organizers proposed a pilot task, the Textual Entailment Search (Bentivogli et al, 2009), consisting in finding all the sentences in a set of documents that entail a given Hypothesis and since 2010 there is a Novelty Detection Task, which means that RTE systems are required to judge whether the information contained in each H is novel with respect to (i.e., not entailed by) the information contained in the corpus.

2.2 Semantic Textual Similarity

The pilot task STS was recently defined in Semeval 2012 (Aguirre et al., 2012) and has as main objective measuring the degree of semantic equivalence between two text fragments. STS is related to both Recognizing Textual Entailment (RTE) and Paraphrase Recognition, but has the advantage of being a more suitable model for multiple NLP applications.

As mentioned before, the goal of the RTE task (Bentivogli et al, 2009) is determining whether the meaning of a hypothesis H can be inferred from a text T. Thus, TE is a directional task and we say that T entails H, if a person reading T would infer that H is most likely true. The difference with STS is that STS consists in determining how similar two text fragments are, in a range from 5 (total semantic equivalence) to 0 (no relation). Thus, STS mainly differs from TE in that the classification is graded instead of binary. In this manner, STS is filling the gap between several tasks.

3 System architecture

Sagan is a RTE system (Castillo and Cardenas, 2010) which has taken part of several challenges, including the Textual Analysis Conference 2009 and TAC 2010, and the Semantic Textual Similarity and Cross Lingual Textual Entailment for content synchronization as part of the Semeval 2012.

The system is based on a machine learning approach and it utilizes eight WordNet-based (Fellbaum, 1998) similarity measures, as explained in (Castillo, 2011), with the purpose of obtaining the maximum similarity between two WordNet concepts. A concept is a cluster of synonymous terms that is called a synset in WordNet. These text-to-text similarity measures are based on the following word-to-word similarity metrics: (Resnik, 1995), (Lin, 1997), (Jiang and Conrath, 1997), (Pirrò and Seco, 2008), (Wu & Palmer, 1994), Path Metric, (Leacock & Chodorow, 1998), and a semantic similarity to sentence level named SemSim (Castillo and Cardenas,2010).

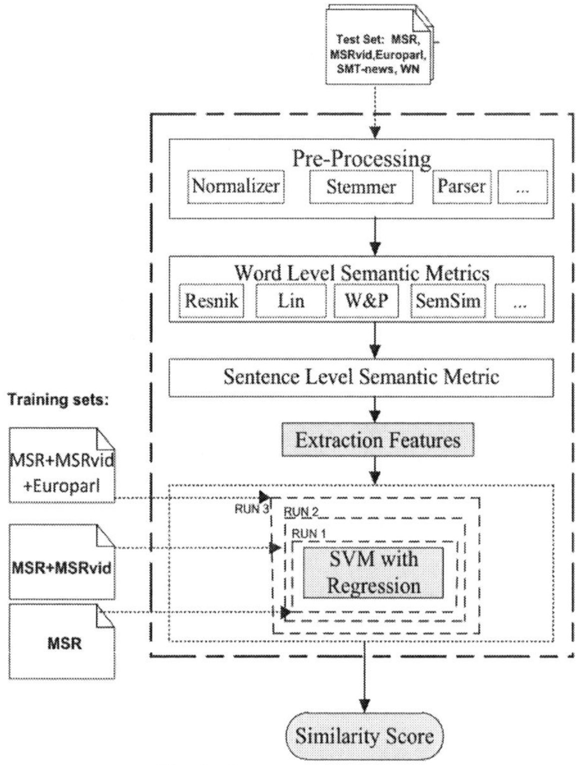

Fig.1. System architecture

The system construct a model of the semantic similarity of two texts (T,H) as a function of the semantic similarity of the constituent words of both phrases. In order to reach this objective, we used a text to text similarity measure which is based on word to word similarity. Thus, we expect that combining word to word similarity metrics to text level would be a good indicator of text to text similarity.

Additional information about how to produce feature vectors as well as each word- and sentence-level metric can be found in (Castillo, 2011). The architecture of the system is shown in Figure 1.

The training set used for the submitted runs are those provided by the organizers of the STS. However we also experimented with RTE datasets as described in the next Section.

4 Experiments and Results

For preliminary experiments before the STS Challenge, we used the training set provided by the organizers, denoted with "_train", and consisting of 750 pairs of sentences from the MSR Paraphrase Corpus (MSRpar), 750 pairs of sentences from the MSRvid Corpus (MSRvid), 459 pairs of sentences of the Europarl WMT2008 development set (SMT-eur). We also used the RTE datasets from Pascal RTE Challenge (Dagan et al., 2006) as part of our training sets. Additionally, at the testing stage, we used the 399 pairs of news conversation (SMT-news) and 750 pairs of sentences where the first one comes from Ontonotes and the second one from a WordNet definition (On-WN).

In STS Challenge it was required that participating systems do not use the test set of MSR-Paraphrase, the text of the videos in MSR-Video, and the data from the evaluation tasks at any WMT to develop or train their systems. Additionally, we also assumed that the dataset to be processed was unknown in the testing phase, in order to avoid any kind of tuning of the system.

4.1 Preliminary Experiments

In a preliminary study performed before the final submission, we experimented with three machine learning algorithms Support Vector Machine (SVM) with regression and polynomial kernel, Multilayer perceptron (MLP), and Linear Regression (LR). Table 1 shows the results obtained with 10-fold cross validation technique and Table 2 shows the results of testing them with two datasets and 3 classifiers over MSR_train.

Classifier	Pearson c.c
SVM with regression	0.54
MLP	0.51
LinearRegression	0.54

Table 1. Results obtained using MSR training set (MSRpar + MSRvid) with 10 fold-cross validation.

Training set & ML algorithm	Pearson c.c
Europarl + SVM w/ regression	0.61
Europarl + MLP	0.44
Europarl + linear regression	0.61
MSRvid + SVM w/ regression	0.70
MSRvid + MLP	0.52
MSRvid + linear regression	0.69

Table 2. Results obtained using MSR training set

Results reported in Table 1 show that we achieved the best performance with SVM with regression and Linear Regression classifiers and using MLP we obtained the worst results to predict each dataset. To our surprise, a linear regression classifier reports better accuracy that MLP, it may be mainly due to the correlation coefficient used, namely Pearson, which is a measure of a linear dependence between two variables and linear regression builds a model assuming linear influence of independent features. We believe that using Spearman correlation should be better than using the Pearson coefficient given that Spearman assumes non-linear correlation among variables. However, it is not clear how it behaves when several dataset are combined to obtain a global score. Indeed, further discussion is needed in order to find the best metric to the STS pilot task. Given these results, in our submission for the STS pilot task we used a combination of STS datasets as training set and the SVM with regression classifier.

Because our approach is mainly based on machine learning the quality and quantity of dataset is a key factor to determine the performance of the system, thus we decided to experiment with RTE datasets too (Bentivogli et el., 2009) with the aim of increasing the size of the training set.

To achieve this goal, first we chose the RTE3 dataset because it is simpler than subsequent datasets and it was proved to provide a high accuracy predicting other datasets (Castillo, 2011). Second, taking into account that RTE datasets are binary classified as YES or NO entailment, we assumed that a non entailment can be treated as a value of 2.0 in the STS pilot task and an entailment can be thought of as a value of 3.0 in STS. Of course, many pairs classified as 3.0 could be mostly equivalent (4.0) or completely equivalent (5.0) but we ignored this fact in the following experiment.

Training set	Test set	Pearson c.c.
RTE3	MSR_train	0.4817
RTE3	MSRvid_train	0.5738
RTE3	Europarl_train	0.4746
MSR_train+RTE3	MSRvid_train	0.5652
MSR_train+RTE3	Europarl_train	0.5498
MSRvid_train+RTE3	MSR_train	0.4559
MSRvid_train+RTE3	Europarl_train	0.4964

Table 3. Results obtained using RTE in the training sets and SVM w/regression as classifier

From these experiments we conclude that RTE3 alone is not enough to adequately predict neither of the STS datasets, and it is understandable if we note that only one pair with 2.0 and 3.0 scores are present in this dataset.

On the other hand, by combining RTE3 with a STS corpus we always obtain a slight decrease in performance in comparison to using STS alone. It is likely due to an unbalanced set and possible contradictory pairs (e.g: a par in RTE3 classified as 3.0 when it should be classified 4.3). Thus, we conclude that in order to use the RTE datasets our system needs a manual annotation of the degree of semantic similarity of every pair <T,H> of RTE dataset.

Having into account that in our training phase we obtained a decrease in performance using RTE datasets we decided not to submit any run using the RTE datasets.

4.2 Submission to the STS shared task

Our participation in the shared task consisted of three different runs using a SVM classifier with regression; the runs were set up as follows:
- Run 1: system trained on a subset of the Microsoft Research Paraphrase Corpus (Dolan and Brockett, 2005), named MSR and consisting of 750 pairs of sentences marked with a degree of similarity from 5 to 0.
- Run 2: in addition to the MSR corpus we incorporated another 750 sentences extracted from the Microsoft Research Video Description Corpus (MSRvid), annotated in the same way as MSR.
- Run 3: to the 1500 sentences from the MSR and MSRvid corpus we incorporated 734 pairs of sentences from the Europarl corpus used as development set in the WMT 2008; all sentences are annotated with the degree of similarity from 5 to 0.

It is very interesting to note that we used the same system configurations for every dataset of each RUN. In this manner, we did not perform any kind of tuning to a particular dataset before our submission. We decided to ignore the "name" of each dataset and apply our system regardless of the particular dataset. Surely, if we take into account where each dataset came from we can develop a particular strategy for every one of them, but we assumed that this kind of information is unknown to our system.

The official scores of the STS pilot task is the Pearson correlation coefficient, and other variations of Pearson which were proposed by the organizers with the aim of better understanding the behavior of the competing systems among the different scenarios.

These metric are named ALL (overall Pearson), ALLnrm (normalized Pearson) and Mean (weighted mean), briefly described below:
- ALL: To compute this metric, first a new dataset with the union of the five gold datasets is created and then the Pearson correlation is calculated over this new dataset.
- ALLnrm: In this metric, the Pearson correlation is computed after the system outputs for each dataset are fitted to the gold standard using least squares.
- Mean: This metric is a weighted mean across the five datasets, where the weight is given by the quantity of pairs in each dataset.

Table 5 report the results achieved with these metrics followed by an individual Pearson correlation for each dataset.

Interestingly, if we analyze the size of data sets, we see that the larger the training set used, the greater the efficiency gains with ALL metric. In effect, RUN3 used 2234 pairs, RUN2 used 1500 pairs and RUN1 was composed by 750 pairs. This highlights the need for larger datasets for the purpose of building more accurate models.

With ALLnrm our system achieved better results but since this metric is based on normalized Pearson correlation which assumes a linear correlation, we believe that this metric is not representative of the underlying phenomenon. For example, conducting manual observation we can see that pairs from SMT-news are much harder to classify than MSRvid pairs. This results can also be evidenced from others participating teams who almost always achieved better results with MSRvid than SMT-news dataset.

The last metric proposed is the Mean and we are ranked 29 among participating teams. It is probably due to the weight of SMT-news (399 pairs) is smaller than MSR or MSRvid.

Mean metrics seems to be more suitable for this task but lack an important issue, do not have into account the different "complexity" of the datasets. It is also a issue for all metrics proposed. We believe that incorporating to Mean metric a complexity factor weighting for each dataset based on a human judge assignment could be more suitable for the STS evaluation. We think in complexity as an underlying concept referring to the difficulty of determine how semantically related two sentences are to one another. Thus, two sentences with high lexical overlap should have a low complexity and instead two sentences that requires deep inference to determine similarity should have a high complexity. This should be heighted by human annotators and could be a method for a more precise evaluation of STS systems.

Finally, we suggested measuring this new challenging task using a weighted Mean of the Spearman's rho correlation coefficient by incorporating a factor to weigh the difficulty of each dataset.

Run	ALL	Rank	ALLnrm	Rank Nrm	Mean	Rank Mean	MSR par	MSR vid	SMT-eur	On-WN	SMT-news
Best Run	,8239	1	,8579	2	,6773	1	,6830	,8739	,5280	,6641	,4937
Worst Run	-,0260	89	,5933	89	,1016	89	,1109	,0057	,0348	,1788	,1964
Sagan-RUN1	,5522	57	,7904	47	,5906	29	,5659	,7113	,4739	,6542	,4253
Sagan-RUN2	,6272	42	,8032	37	,5838	34	,5538	,7706	,4480	,6135	,3894
Sagan-RUN3	,6311	39	,7943	45	,5649	46	,5394	,7560	,4181	,5904	,3746

Table 5. Official results of the STS challenge

5 Conclusions and future work

In this paper we present Sagan, an RTE system applied to the task of Semantic Textual Similarity. After a preliminary study of the classifiers performance for the task, we decided to use a combination of STS datasets for training and the classifier SVM with regression. With this setup the system was ranked 39 in the best run with overall Pearson, and ranked 29 with Mean metric. However, both rankings are based on the Pearson correlation coefficient and we believe that this coefficient is not the best suited for this task, thus we proposed a Mean Spearman's rho correlation coefficient weighted by complexity, instead. Therefore, further application of other metrics should be one in order to find the most representative and fair evaluation metric for this task. Finally, while promising results were obtained with our system, it still needs to be tested on a diversity of settings. This is work in progress, as the system is being tested as a metric for the evaluation of machine translation, as reported in (Castillo and Estrella, 2012).

References

Christoph Tillmann, Stephan Vogel, Hermann Ney, Arkaitz Zubiaga, and Hassan Sawaf. 1997. *Accelerated DP Based Search For Statistical Translation.* In Proceedings of the 5th European Conference on Speech Communication and Technology (EUROSPEECH-97).

Kishore Papineni, Salim Roukos, Todd Ward, and Wei-Jing Zhu. 2002. *BLEU: A Method for Automatic Evaluation of Machine Translation.* In Proceedings of the 40th AnnualMeeting of the Association for Computational Linguistics(ACL-02), pages 311–318.

Sonja Nießen, Franz Josef Och, Gregor Leusch, and Hermann Ney. 2000. *A Evaluation Tool for Machine Translation:Fast Evaluation for MT Research.* In Proceedings of the 2nd International Conference on Language Resources and Evaluation (LREC-2000).

G. Doddington. 2002. *Automatic Evaluation of Machine Translation Quality using N-gram Co-occurrence Statistics.* In Proceedings of the 2nd International Conference on Human Language Technology Research (HLT-02), pages 138–145, San Francisco, CA, USA.

Satanjeev Banerjee and Alon Lavie. 2005. *METEOR: An Automatic Metric for MT Evaluation with Improved Correlation with Human Judgments.* In Proceedings of the 43th Annual Meeting of the Association of Computational Linguistics (ACL-05), pages 65–72.

Michael Denkowski and Alon Lavie. 2011. METEOR-NEXT and the METEOR Paraphrase Tables: Improved Evaluation Support For Five Target Languages. Proceedings of the ACL 2010 Joint Workshop on Statistical Machine Translation and Metrics MATR.

He Yifan, Du Jinhua, Way Andy, and Van Josef . 2010. *The DCU dependency-based metric in WMT-MetricsMATR 2010.* In: WMT 2010 - Joint Fifth Workshop on Statistical Machine Translation and Metrics MATR, ACL, Uppsala, Sweden.

Chi-kiu Lo and Dekai Wu. 2011. *MEANT: inexpensive, high-accuracy, semi-automatic metric for evaluating translation utility based on semantic roles.* 49th Annual Meeting of the Association for Computational Linguistic (ACL-2011). Portland, Oregon, US.

Matthew Snover, Bonnie J. Dorr, Richard Schwartz, Linnea Micciulla, and John Makhoul. 2006. *A Study of Translation Edit Rate with Targeted Human Annotation.* In Proceedings of the 7th Conference of the Association for Machine Translation in the Americas (AMTA-06), pages 223–231.

Ido Dagan, Oren Glickman and Bernardo Magnini. 2006. *The PASCAL Recognising Textual Entailment Challenge.* In Quiñonero-Candela, J.; Dagan, I.; Magnini, B.; d'Alché-Buc, F. (Eds.) Machine Learning Challenges. Lecture Notes in Computer Science , Vol. 3944, pp. 177-190, Springer.

Shachar Mirkin, Lucia Specia, Nicola Cancedda, Ido Dagan, Marc Dymetman, and Idan Szpektor. 2009. *Source-language entailment modeling for translating unknown terms.* In Proceedings of the Joint Conference of the 47th Annual Meeting of the ACL. Stroudsburg, PA, USA, 791-799.

Wilker Aziz and Marc Dymetmany and Shachar Mirkin and Lucia Specia and Nicola Cancedda and Ido Dagan. 2010. *Learning an Expert from Human Annotations in Statistical Machine Translation: the Case of Out-of-VocabularyWords.* In: Proceedings of the 14th annual meeting of the European Association for Machine Translation (EAMT), Saint-Rapha, France.

Dahlmeier, Daniel and Liu, Chang and Ng, Hwee Tou. 2011.TESLA at WMT 2011: Translation Evaluation and Tunable Metric.In: Proceedings of the Sixth Workshop on Statistical Machine Translation. ACL, pages 78-84, Edinburgh, Scotland.

S. Pado, D. Cer, M. Galley, D. Jurafsky and C. Manning. 2009. *Measuring Machine Translation Quality as Semantic Equivalence: A Metric Based on Entailment Features.* Journal of MT 23(2-3), 181-193.

S. Pado, M. Galley, D. Jurafsky and C. Manning. 2009a. *Robust Machine Translation Evaluation with Entailment Features.* Proceedings of ACL 2009.

Eneko Agirre, Daniel Cer, Mona Diab and Aitor Gonzalez-Agirre. 2012. *SemEval-2012 Task 6: A Pilot on Semantic Textual Similarity.* In Proceedings of the 6th International Workshop on Semantic Evaluation (SemEval 2012), in conjunction with the First Joint Conference on Lexical and Computational Semantics (*SEM 2012).

Bentivogli, Luisa, Dagan Ido, Dang Hoa, Giampiccolo, Danilo, Magnini Bernardo.2009.*The Fifth PASCAL RTE Challenge.* In: Proceedings of the Text Analysis Conference.

Fellbaum C. 1998. *WordNet: An Electronic Lexical Database*, volume 1. MIT Press.

Castillo Julio. 2011. *A WordNet-based semantic approach to textual entailment and cross-lingual textual entailment.* International Journal of Machine Learning and Cybernetics - Springer, Volume 2, Number 3.

Castillo Julio and Cardenas Marina. 2010. *Using sentence semantic similarity based onWordNet in recognizing textual entailment.* Iberamia 2010. In LNCS, vol 6433. Springer, Heidelberg, pp 366–375.

Castillo Julio. 2010. *A semantic oriented approach to textual entailment using WordNet-based measures.* MICAI 2010. LNCS, vol 6437. Springer, Heidelberg, pp 44–55.

Castillo Julio. 2010. *Using machine translation systems to expand a corpus in textual entailment.* In: Proceedings of the Icetal 2010. LNCS, vol 6233, pp 97–102.

Resnik P. 1995. *Information content to evaluate semantic similarity in a taxonomy.* In: Proceedings of IJCAI 1995, pp 448–453 907.

Castillo Julio, Cardenas Marina. 2011. *An Approach to Cross-Lingual Textual Entailment using Online Machine Translation Systems.* Polibits Journal. Vol 44.

Castillo Julio and Estrella Paula. 2012. Semantic *Textual Similarity for MT evaluation.* NAACL 2012 Seventh Workshop on Statistical Machine Translation. WMT 2012, Montreal, Canada.

Lin D. 1997. *An information-theoretic definition of similarity.* In: Proceedings of Conference on Machine Learning, pp 296–304 909.

Jiang J, Conrath D.1997. *Semantic similarity based on corpus statistics and lexical taxonomy.* In: Proceedings of theROCLINGX 911

Pirro G., Seco N. 2008. *Design, implementation and evaluation of a new similarity metric combining feature and intrinsic information content.* In: ODBASE 2008, Springer LNCS.

Wu Z, Palmer M. 1994. *Verb semantics and lexical selection.* In: Proceedings of the 32nd ACL 916.

Leacock C, Chodorow M. 1998. *Combining local context and WordNet similarity for word sense identification.* MIT Press, pp 265–283 919

Hirst G, St-Onge D . 1998. *Lexical chains as representations of context for the detection and correction of malapropisms.* MIT Press, pp 305–332 922

Banerjee S, Pedersen T. 2002. *An adapted lesk algorithm for word sense disambiguation using WordNet.* In: Proceeding of CICLING-02

William B. Dolan and Chris Brockett.2005. *Automatically Constructing a Corpus of Sentential Paraphrases.* Third International Workshop on Paraphrasing (IWP2005). Asia Federation of Natural Language Processing.

UOW: Semantically Informed Text Similarity

Miguel Rios and Wilker Aziz
Research Group in Computational Linguistics
University of Wolverhampton
Stafford Street, Wolverhampton,
WV1 1SB, UK
{M.Rios, W.Aziz}@wlv.ac.uk

Lucia Specia
Department of Computer Science
University of Sheffield
Regent Court, 211 Portobello,
Sheffield, S1 4DP, UK
L.Specia@sheffield.ac.uk

Abstract

The UOW submissions to the Semantic Textual Similarity task at SemEval-2012 use a supervised machine learning algorithm along with features based on lexical, syntactic and semantic similarity metrics to predict the semantic equivalence between a pair of sentences. The lexical metrics are based on word-overlap. A shallow syntactic metric is based on the overlap of base-phrase labels. The semantically informed metrics are based on the preservation of named entities and on the alignment of verb predicates and the overlap of argument roles using inexact matching. Our submissions outperformed the official baseline, with our best system ranked above average, but the contribution of the semantic metrics was not conclusive.

1 Introduction

We describe the UOW submissions to the Semantic Textual Similarity (STS) task at SemEval-2012. Our systems are based on combining similarity scores as features using a regression algorithm to predict the degree of semantic equivalence between a pair of sentences. We train the regression algorithm with different classes of similarity metrics: i) lexical, ii) syntactic and iii) semantic. The lexical similarity metrics are: i) cosine similarity using a bag-of-words representation, and ii) precision, recall and F-measure of content words. The syntactic metric computes BLEU (Papineni et al., 2002), a machine translation evaluation metric, over a labels of base-phrases (chunks). Two semantic metrics are used: a metric based on the preservation of Named Entities and TINE (Rios et al., 2011). Named entities are matched by type and content: while the type has to match exactly, the content is compared with the assistance of a distributional thesaurus. TINE is a metric proposed to measure adequacy in machine translation and favors similar semantic frames. TINE attempts to align verb predicates, assuming a one-to-one correspondence between semantic roles, and considering ontologies for inexact alignment. The surface realization of the arguments is compared using a distributional thesaurus and the cosine similarity metric. Finally, we use METEOR (Denkowski and Lavie, 2010), also a common metric for machine translation evaluation, that also computes inexact word overlap as at way of measuring the impact of our semantic metrics.

The lexical and syntactic metrics complement the semantic metrics in dealing with the phenomena observed in the task's dataset. For instance, from the MSRvid dataset:

S1 *Two men are playing football.*

S2 *Two men are practicing football.*

In this case, as typical of paraphrasing, the situation and participants are the same while the surface realization differs, but *playing* can be considered similar to *practicing*. From the SMT-eur dataset:

S3 *The Council of Europe, along with the Court of Human Rights, has a wealth of experience of such forms of supervision, and we can build on these.*

S4 *Just as the European Court of Human Rights, the Council of Europe has also considerable experience with regard to these forms of control; we can take as a basis.*

Similarly, here although with different realizations, the *Court of Human Rights* and the *European Court of Human Rights* represent the same entity.

Semantic metrics based on predicate-argument structure can play a role in cases when different realization have similar semantic roles:

S5 *The right of a government arbitrarily to set aside its own constitution is the defining characteristic of a tyranny.*

S6 *The right for a government to draw aside its constitution arbitrarily is the definition characteristic of a tyranny.*

In this work we attempt to exploit the fact that superficial variations such the ones in these examples should still render very similarity scores.

In Section 2 we describe the similarity metrics in more detail. In Section 3 we show the results of our three systems. In Section 4 we discuss these results and in Section 5 we present some conclusions.

2 Similarity Metrics

The metrics used in this work are as follows:

2.1 Lexical metrics

All our lexical metrics use the same surface representation: words. However, the cosine metric uses bag-of-words, while all the other metrics use only content words. We thus first represent the sentences as bag-of-words. For example, given the pair of sentences S7 and S8:

S7 *A man is riding a bicycle.*

S8 *A man is riding a bike.*

the bag-of-words are S7 = {*A, man, is, riding, a, bicycle,.*} and S8 = {*A, man, is, riding, a, bike, .*}, and the bag-of-content-words are S7 = {*man, riding, bicycle*} and S8 = {*man, riding, bike*}.

We compute similarity scores using the following metrics between a pair of sentences A and B: cosine distance (Equation 1), precision (Equation 2), recall (Equation 3) and F-measure (Equation 4).

$$cosine(A, B) = \frac{|A \bigcap B|}{\sqrt{|A| \times |B|}} \tag{1}$$

$$precision(A, B) = \frac{|A \bigcap B|}{|B|} \tag{2}$$

$$recall(A, B) = \frac{|A \bigcap B|}{|A|} \tag{3}$$

$$F(A, B) = 2 \cdot \frac{precision(A, B) \cdot recall(A, B)}{precision(A, B) + recall(A, B)} \tag{4}$$

2.2 BLEU over base-phrases

The BLEU metric is used for the automatic evaluation of Machine Translation. The metric computes the precision of exact matching of n-grams between a hypothesis and reference translations. This simple procedure has limitations such as: the matching of non-content words mixed with the counts of content words affects in a perfect matching that can happen even if the order of sequences of n-grams in the hypothesis and reference translation are very different, changing completely the meaning of the translation. To account for similarity in word order we use BLEU over base-phrase labels instead of words, leaving the lexical matching for other lexical and semantic metrics. We compute the matchings of 1-4-grams of base-phrase labels. This metric favors similar syntactic order.

2.3 Named Entities metric

The goal of the metric is to deal with synonym entities. First, named entities are grouped by class (e.g. Organization), and then the content of the named entities within the same classes is compared through cosine similarity. If the surface realization is different, we retrieve words that share the same context with the named entity using Dekang Lin's distributional thesaurus (Lin, 1998). Therefore, the cosine similarity will have more information than just the named entities themselves. For example, from the sentence pair S9 and S10:

S9 *Companies include IBM Corp. ...*

S10 *Companies include International Business Machines ...*

The entity from S9: *IBM Corp.* and the entity from S10: *International Business Machines* have the same tag *Organization*. The metric groups them and adds words from the thesaurus resulting in the following bag-of-words. S9: {*IBM Corp.,... Microsoft, Intel, Sun Microsystems, Motorola/Motorola, Hewlett-Packard/Hewlett-Packard, Novell, Apple Computer...*} and S10: {*International Business Machines,... Apple Computer, Yahoo, Microsoft, Alcoa...*}. The metric then computes the cosine similarity between this expanded pair of bag-of-words.

2.4 METEOR

This metric is also a lexical metric based on unigram matching between two sentences. However, matches can be exact, using stems, synonyms, or paraphrases of unigrams. The synonym matching is computed using WordNet (Fellbaum, 1998) and the paraphrase matching is computed using paraphrase tables (Callison-Burch et al., 2010). The structure of the sentences is not not directly considered, but similar word orders are rewarded through higher scores for the matching of longer fragments.

2.5 Semantic Role Label metric

Rios et al. (2011) propose TINE, an automatic metric based on the use semantic roles to align predicates and their respective arguments in a pair of sentences. The metric complements lexical matching with a shallow semantic component to better address adequacy in machine translation evaluation. The main contribution of such a metric is to provide a more flexible way of measuring the overlap between shallow semantic representations (semantic role labels) that considers both the semantic structure of the sentence and the content of the semantic components.

This metric allows to match synonym predicates by using verb ontologies such as VerbNet (Schuler, 2006) and VerbOcean (Chklovski and Pantel, 2004) and distributional semantics similarity metrics, such as Dekang Lin's thesaurus (Lin, 1998), where previous semantic metrics only perform exact match of predicate structures and arguments. For example, in VerbNet the verbs *spook* and *terrify* share the same class *amuse-31.1*, and in VerbOcean the verb *dress* is related to the verb *wear*, so these are considered matches in TINE.

The main sources of errors in this metric are the matching of unrelated verbs and the lack of coverage of the ontologies. For example, for S11 and S12, *remain* and *say* are (incorrectly) related as given by VerbOcean.

S11 *If snow falls on the slopes this week, Christmas will sell out too, says Schiefert.*

S12 *If the roads remain snowfall during the week, the dates of Christmas will dry up, said Schiefert.*

For this work the matching of unrelated verbs is a particularly crucial issue, since the sentences to be compared are not necessarily similar, as it is the general case in machine translation. We have thus modified the metric with a preliminary optimization step which aligns the verb predicates by measuring two degrees of similarity: i) how similar their arguments are, and ii) how related the predicates' realizations are. Both scores are combined as shown in Equation 5 to score the similarity between the two predicates (A_v, B_v) from a pair of sentences (A, B).

$$\begin{aligned}\mathrm{sim}(\mathrm{A_v}, \mathrm{B_v}) &= (w_{lex} \times lexScore(A_v, B_v)) \\ &+(w_{arg} \times argScore(A_{arg}, B_{arg}))\end{aligned} \quad (5)$$

where w_{lex} and w_{arg} are the weights for each component, $argScore(A_{arg}, B_{arg})$ is the similarity, which is computed as in Equation 7, of the arguments between the predicates being compared and $lexScore(A_v, B_v)$ is the similarity score extracted from the Dekang Lin's thesaurus between the predicates being compared. The Dekang Lin's thesaurus is an automatically built thesaurus, and for each word it has an entry with the most similar words and their similarity scores. If the verbs are related in the thesaurus we use their similarity score as $lexScore$ otherwise $lexScore = 0$. The pair of predicates with the maximum sim score is aligned. The alignment is an optimization problem where predicates are aligned 1-1: we search for all 1-1 alignments that lead to the maximum average sim for the pair of sentences. For example, S13 and S14 have the following list of predicates: S13 = {loaded, rose, ending} and S14 = {laced, climbed}. The metric compares each pair of predicates and it aligns the predicates *rose* and *climbed* because they are related in the thesaurus with a similarity score $lexScore = 0.796$ and a $argScore = 0.185$ given that the weights are set to 0.5 and sum up to 1 the predicates reach the maximum $\text{sim} = 0.429$ score. The output of this step results in a set of aligned verbs between a pair of sentences.

S13 *The tech - loaded Nasdaq composite rose 0 points to 0 , ending at its highest level for 0 months.*

S14 *The technology - laced Nasdaq Composite Index IXIC climbed 0 points , or 0 percent , to 0.*

The SRL similarity metric $semanticRole$ between two sentences A and B is then defined as:

$$semanticRole(A, B) = \frac{\sum_{v \in V} verbScore(A_v, B_v)}{|V_B|} \quad (6)$$

The $verbScore$ in Equation 6 is computed over the set of aligned predicates from the previous optimization step and for each aligned predicate the argument similarity is computed by Equation 7.

$$verbScore(A_v, B_v) = \frac{\sum_{arg \in Arg_A \cap Arg_B} argScore(A_{arg}, B_{arg})}{|Arg_B|} \quad (7)$$

In Equation 6, V is the set of verbs aligned between the two sentences A and B, and $|V_B|$ is the number of verbs in one of the sentences.[1] The similarity between the arguments of a verb pair (A_v, B_v) in V is measured as defined in Equation 7, where Arg_A and Arg_B are the sets of labeled arguments of the first and the second sentences and $|Arg_B|$ is the number of arguments of the verb in B.[2] The $argScore(A_{arg}, B_{arg})$ computation is based on the cosine similarity as in Equation 1. We treat the tokens in the argument as a bag-of-words.

[1]This is inherited from the use of the metric focusing on recall in machine translation, where the B is the reference translation. In this work a better approach could be to compute this metric twice, in both directions.

[2]Again, from the analogy of a recall metric for machine translation.

3 Experiments and Results

We use the following state-of-the-art tools to preprocess the data for feature extraction: i) TreeTagger[3] for lemmas and ii) SENNA (Collobert et al., 2011)[4] for Part-of-Speech tagging, Chunking, Named Entity Recognition and Semantic Role Labeling. SENNA has been reported to achieve an F-measure of 75.79% for tagging semantic roles on the CoNLL-2005 [2] benchmark. The final feature set includes:

- Lexical metrics
  - Cosine metric over bag-of-words
  - Precision over content words
  - Recall over content words
  - F-measure over content words
- BLEU metric over chunks
- METEOR metric over words (with stems, synonyms and paraphrases)
- Named Entity metric
- Semantic Role Labeling metric

The Machine Learning algorithm used for regression is the LIBSVM[5] Support Vector Machine (SVM) implementation using the radial basis kernel function. We used a simple genetic algorithm (Back et al., 1999) to tune the parameters of the SVM. The configuration of the genetic algorithm is as follows:

- Fitness function: minimize the mean squared error found by cross-validation
- Chromosome: real numbers for SVM parameters γ, *cost* and ϵ
- Number of individuals: 80
- Number of generations: 100
- Selection method: roulette
- Crossover probability: 0.9

[3]http://www.ims.uni-stuttgart.de/projekte/corplex/TreeTagger/

[4]http://ml.nec-labs.com/senna/

[2]http://www.lsi.upc.edu/ srlconll/

[5]http://www.csie.ntu.edu.tw/ cjlin/libsvm/

- Mutation probability: 0.01

We submitted three system runs, each is a variation of the above feature set. For the official submission we used the systems with optimized SVM parameters. We trained SVM models with each of the following task datasets: MSRpar, MSRvid, SMT-eur and the combination of MSRpar+MSRvid. For each test dataset we applied their respective training models, except for the new test sets, not covered by any training set: for On-WN we used the combination MSRpar+MSRvid, and for SMT-news we used SMT-eur.

Tables 1 to 3 focus on the Pearson correlation of our three systems/runs for individual datasets of the predicted scores against human annotation, compared against the official baseline, which uses a simple word overlap metric. Table 4 shows the average results over all five datasets, where ALL stands for the Pearson correlation with the gold standard for the five dataset, Rank is the absolute rank among all submissions, ALLnrm is the Pearson correlation when each dataset is fitted to the gold standard using least squares, RankNrm is the corresponding rank and Mean is the weighted mean across the five datasets, where the weight depends on the number of sentence pairs in the dataset.

3.1 Run 1: All except SRL features

Our first run uses the lexical, BLEU, METEOR and Named Entities features, without the SRL feature. Table 1 shows the results over the test set, where Run 1-A is the version without SVM parameter optimization and Run 1-B are the official results with optimized parameters for SVM.

Task	Run 1-A	Run 1-B	Baseline
MSRpar	0.455	0.455	0.433
MSRvid	0.706	0.362	0.300
SMT-eur	0.461	0.307	0.454
On-WN	0.514	0.281	0.586
SMT-news	0.386	0.208	0.390

Table 1: Results for Run 1 using lexical, chunking, named entities and METEOR as features. A is the non-optimized version, B are the official results

3.2 Run 2: SRL feature

In this run we use only the SRL feature in order to analyze whether this feature on its own could be sufficient or lexical and other simpler features are important. Table 2 shows the results over the test set without parameter optimization (Run 2-A) and the official results with optimized parameters for SVM (Run 2-B).

Task	Run 2-A	Run 2-B	Baseline
MSRpar	0.335	0.300	0.433
MSRvid	0.264	0.291	0.300
SMT-eur	0.264	0.161	0.454
On-WN	0.281	0.257	0.586
SMT-news	0.189	0.221	0.390

Table 2: Results for Run 2 using the SRL feature only. A is the non-optimized version, B are the official results

3.3 Run 3: All features

In the last run we use all features. Table 3 shows the results over the test set without parameter optimization (Run 3-A) and the official results with optimized parameters for SVM (Run 3-B).

Task	Run 3-A	Run 3-B	Baseline
MSRpar	0.472	0.353	0.433
MSRvid	0.705	0.572	0.300
SMT-eur	0.471	0.307	0.454
On-WN	0.511	0.264	0.586
SMT-news	0.410	0.116	0.390

Table 3: Results for Run 3 using all features. A is the non-optimized version, B are the official results

4 Discussion

Table 4 shows the ranking and normalized official scores of our submissions compared against the baseline. Our submissions outperform the official baseline but significantly underperform the top systems in the shared task. The best system (Run 1) achieved an above average ranking, but disappointingly the performance of our most complete system (Run 3) using the semantic metric is poorer. Surprisingly, the results of the non-optimized versions outperform the optimized versions used in our official submission. One possible reason for that is the overfitting of the optimized models to the training sets.

Run 1 and Run 3 have very similar results: the overall correlation between all datasets of these two systems is 0.98. One of the reasons for these results is that the SRL metric is compromised by the length

System	ALL	Rank	ALLnrm	RankNrm	Mean	RankMean
Run 1	0.640	36	0.719	71	0.382	80
Run 2	0.536	59	0.629	88	0.257	88
Run 3	0.598	49	0.696	82	0.347	84
Baseline	0.311	87	0.673	85	0.436	70

Table 4: Official results and ranking over the test set for Runs 1-3 with SVM parameters optimized

of the sentences. In the MSRvid dataset, where the sentences are simple such as "*Someone is drawing*", resulting in a good semantic parsing, a high performance for this metric is achieved. However, in the SMT datasets, sentences are much longer (and often ungrammatical, since they are produced by a machine translation system) and the performance of the metric drops. In addition, the SRL metric makes mistakes such as judging as highly similar sentences such as "*A man is peeling a potato*" and "*A man is slicing a potato*", where the arguments are the same but the situations are different.

5 Conclusions

We have presented our systems based on similarity scores as features to train a regression algorithm to predict the semantic similarity between a pair of sentences. Our official submissions outperform the baseline method, but have lower performance than most participants, and a simpler version of the systems without any parameter optimization proved more robust. Disappointingly, our main contribution, the addition of a metric based on Semantic Role Labels shows no improvement as compared to simpler metrics.

Acknowledgments

This work was supported by the Mexican National Council for Science and Technology (CONACYT), scholarship reference 309261.

References

Thomas Back, David B. Fogel, and Zbigniew Michalewicz, editors. 1999. *Evolutionary Computation 1, Basic Algorithms and Operators*. IOP Publishing Ltd., Bristol, UK, 1st edition.

Chris Callison-Burch, Philipp Koehn, Christof Monz, Kay Peterson, Mark Przybocki, and Omar Zaidan. 2010. Findings of the 2010 joint workshop on statistical machine translation and metrics for machine translation. In *Proceedings of the Joint Fifth Workshop on Statistical Machine Translation and MetricsMATR*, pages 17–53, Uppsala, Sweden, July.

Timothy Chklovski and Patrick Pantel. 2004. VerbOcean: Mining the Web for Fine-Grained Semantic Verb Relations. In Dekang Lin and Dekai Wu, editors, *Proceedings of EMNLP 2004*, pages 33–40, Barcelona, Spain, July.

Ronan Collobert, Jason Weston, Leon Bottou, Michael Karlen, Koray Kavukcuoglu, and Pavel Kuksa. 2011. Natural Language Processing (almost) from Scratch.

Michael Denkowski and Alon Lavie. 2010. Meteor-next and the meteor paraphrase tables: Improved evaluation support for five target languages. In *Proceedings of the Joint Fifth Workshop on Statistical Machine Translation and MetricsMATR*, pages 339–342, July.

Christiane Fellbaum, editor. 1998. *WordNet An Electronic Lexical Database*. Cambridge, MA ; London, May.

Dekang Lin. 1998. Automatic retrieval and clustering of similar words. In *Proceedings of the 36th Annual Meeting of the Association for Computational Linguistics and 17th International Conference on Computational Linguistics - Volume 2*, ACL '98, pages 768–774, Stroudsburg, PA, USA.

Kishore Papineni, Salim Roukos, Todd Ward, and Wei-Jing Zhu. 2002. Bleu: a method for automatic evaluation of machine translation. In *Proceedings of the 40th Annual Meeting on Association for Computational Linguistics*, ACL '02, pages 311–318, Stroudsburg, PA, USA.

Miguel Rios, Wilker Aziz, and Lucia Specia. 2011. Tine: A metric to assess mt adequacy. Proceedings of the Sixth Workshop on Statistical Machine Translation.

Karin Kipper Schuler. 2006. *VerbNet: A Broad-Coverage, Comprehensive Verb Lexicon*. Ph.D. thesis, University of Pennsylvania.

Penn: Using Word Similarities to better Estimate Sentence Similarity

Sneha Jha and **H. Andrew Schwartz** and **Lyle H. Ungar**
University of Pennsylvania
Philadelphia, PA, USA
{jhasneha, hansens, ungar}@seas.upenn.edu

Abstract

We present the Penn system for SemEval-2012 Task 6, computing the degree of semantic equivalence between two sentences. We explore the contributions of different vector models for computing sentence and word similarity: Collobert and Weston embeddings as well as two novel approaches, namely *eigenwords* and *selectors*. These embeddings provide different measures of distributional similarity between words, and their contexts. We used regression to combine the different similarity measures, and found that each provides partially independent predictive signal above baseline models.

1 Introduction

We compute the semantic similarity between pairs of sentences by combining a set of similarity metrics at various levels of depth, from surface word similarity to similarities derived from vector models of word or sentence meaning. Regression is then used to determine optimal weightings of the different similarity measures. We use this setting to assess the contributions from several different word embeddings.

Our system is based on similarities computed using multiple sets of features: (a) naive lexical features, (b) similarity between vector representations of sentences, and (c) similarity between constituent words computed using WordNet, using the *eigenword* vector representations of words , and using *selectors*, which generalize words to a set of words that appear in the same context.

2 System Description

This section briefly describes the feature sets used to arrive at a similarity measure between sentences. We compare the use of word similarities based on three different embeddings for words neural embeddings using recursive autoencoders, *eigenwords* and *selectors*.

2.1 Neural Models of Word Representation

An increasingly popular approach is to learn representational embeddings for words from a large collection of unlabeled data (typically using a generative model), and to use these embeddings to augment the feature set of a supervised learner. These models are based on the distributional hypothesis in linguistics that words that occur in similar contexts tend to have similar meanings. The similarities between these vectors indicate similarity in the meanings of corresponding words.

The state of the art model in paraphrase detection uses an unsupervised recursive autoencoder (RAE) model based on an unfolding objective that learn feature vectors for phrases in syntactic parse trees (Socher et al., 2011). The idea of neural language models is to jointly learn an embedding of words into an n-dimensional vector space that capture distributional syntactic and semantic information via the words co-occurrence statistics. Further details and evaluations of these embeddings are discussed in Turian et al. (2010).

Once the distributional syntactic and semantic matrix is learned on an unlabeled corpus, one can use it for subsequent tasks by using each words vector to represent that word. For initial word embeddings, we used the 100-dimensional vectors computed via the unsupervised method of Collobert and Weston (2008). These word embeddings are matrices of size $|V| \times n$ where $|V|$ is the size of the vocabulary and n is the dimensionality of the semantic space. This matrix usually captures co-occurrence statistics and its values are learned. We used the embeddings provided by Socher et al. (2011). Although the original paper employed a dynamic pooling layer in addition to the RAE that captures the global structure of the similarity matrix, we found the resulting sentence-level RAE itself was useful. In turn, we use these vector representations at the sentence level where the cosine similarity between the sentence vectors serves as a measure of sentence similarity. All parameters for the RAE layer are kept same as described by Socher et al. (2011).

2.2 Eigenword Similarity

Recent spectral methods use large amounts of unlabeled data to learn word representations, which can then be used as features in supervised learners for linguistic tasks. *Eigenwords*, a spectral method for computing word embeddings based on context words that characterize the meanings of words, can be efficiently computed by a set of methods based on singular value decomposition (Dhillon et al., 2011).

Such representations are dense, low dimensional and real-valued like the vector representations in the previous section except that they are induced using eigen-decomposition of the word co-occurrence matrix instead of neural networks. This method uses Canonical Correlation Analysis (CCA) between words and their immediate contexts to estimate word representations from unlabeled data. CCA is the analog to Principal Component Analysis (PCA) for pairs of matrices. It computes the directions of maximal correlation between a pair of matrices. CCAs invariance to linear data transformations enables proofs showing that keeping the dominant singular vectors faithfully captures any state information. (For this work, we used the Google n-gram collection of web three-grams as the unlabeled data.) Each dimension of these representations captures latent information about a combination of syntactic and semantic word properties. In the original paper, the word embeddings are context-specific. For this task, we only use context-oblivious embeddings i.e. one embedding per word type for this task, based on their model. Word similarity can then be calculated as cosine similarity between the eigenword representation vectors for any two words.

To move from word-level similarity to sentence-level a few more steps are necessary. We adapted the method of matrix similarity given by Stevenson and Greenwood (2005). One calculates similarity between all pairs of words, and each sentence is represented as a binary vector (with elements equal to 1 if a word is present and 0 otherwise). The similarity between these sentences vectors $\vec{a}$ and $\vec{b}$ is given by:

$$s(\vec{a}, \vec{b}) = \frac{\vec{a}W\vec{b}}{|\vec{a}||\vec{b}|} \qquad (1)$$

where W is a semantic similarity matrix containing information about the similarity of word pairs. Each element in matrix W represents the similarity of words according to some lexical or spectral similarity measure.

2.3 Selector Similarity

Another novel method to account for the similarity between words is via comparison of Web selectors (Schwartz and Gomez, 2008). *Selectors* are words that take the place of an instance of a target word within its local context. For example, in "he addressed the strikers at the rally", selectors for 'strikers' might be 'crowd', 'audience', 'workers', or 'students' words which can realize the same constituent position as the target word. Since selectors are determined based on the context, a set of selectors is an abstraction for the context of a word instance. Thus, comparing selector sets produces a measure of word instance similarity. A key difference between selectors and the eigenwords used in this paper are that selectors are instance specific. This has the benefit that selectors can distinguish word senses, but the drawback that each word instance requires its own set of selectors to be acquired.

Although selectors have previously only been used for worse sense disambiguation, one can also use them to compute similarity between two word instances by taking the cosine similarity of vectors containing selectors for each instance. In our case, we compute the cosine similarity for each pair of noun instances and populate the semantic similarity matrix in formula (1) to generate a sentence-level similarity estimate. Combining web selector- based word similarity features with the word embeddings from the neural model gave us the best overall performance on the aggregated view of the data sets.

2.4 Other Similarity Metrics

Knowledge-Based. We use WordNet to calculate semantic distances between all open-class words in the sentence pairs. There are three classifications of similarity metrics over WordNet: path-based, information- content based, and gloss-based (Pederson et al., 2004). We chose to incorporate those measures performing best in the Schwartz & Gomez (2011) application-oriented evaluation: (a) the path-based measure of Schwartz & Gomez (2008); (b) the information-content measure of Jiang & Conrath (1997) utilizing the difference in information content between concepts and their point of intersection; (c) the gloss-based measure of Patwardhan & Pedersen (2006). By including metrics utilizing different sources of information, we suspect they will each have something novel to contribute.

Because WordNet provides similarity between concepts (word senses), we take the maximum similarity between all senses of each word to be the similarity between the two words. Such similarity can then be computed between multiple pairs of words to populate the semantic similarity matrix W in formula (1) and generate sentence-level similarity estimates as described above. The information-content and path-based measures are restricted to comparing nouns and verbs and only across the same part of speech. On the other hand, the gloss-based measure, which relies on connections through concept definitions, is more general and can compare words across parts of speech.

Surface Metrics. We added the following set of lexical features to incorporate some surface information lost in the vector-based representations.

- difference in the lengths of the two sentences
- average length of the sentences
- number of common words based on exact string match
- number of content words in common
- number of common words in base form
- number of similar numerals in the sentences

3 Evaluation and Results

We combine the similarity metrics discussed previously via regression (Pedregosa et al., 2011). We included the following sets of features:

- **System-baseline:** surface metrics, knowledge-based metrics. (discussed in section 2.4).
- **Neu:** Neural Model similarity (section 2.1)
- **Ew:** Eigenword similarity (section 2.2)
- **Sel:** Selector similarity (section 2.3)

To capture possible non-linear relations, we added a squared and square-rooted column corresponding to each feature in the feature matrix. We also tried to combine all the features to form composite measures by defining multiple interaction terms. Both these sets of additional features improved the performance of our regression model. We used all features to train both a linear regression model and a regularized model based on ridge regression. The regularization parameter for ridge regression was set via cross-validation over the training set. All predictions of similarity values were capped within the range [0,1]. Our systems were trained on the following data sets:

- MSR-Paraphrase, Microsoft Research Paraphrase Corpus-750 pairs of sentences.
- MSR-Video, Microsoft Research Video Description Corpus-750 pairs of sentences.
- SMT-Europarl, WMT2008 development data set (Europarl section)-734 pairs of sentences.

Our performance in the official submission for the SemEval task can be seen in Table 1. **LReg** indicates the run with linear regression, **ELReg** adds the eigenwords feature and **ERReg** also uses eigenwords but with ridge regression. At the time of submission, we were not ready to test with the selector features yet. Ridge regression consistently outperformed linear regression for every run of our system, but overall Pearson score for our system using linear regression scored the highest. Table 2 presents a more thorough examination of results.

	MSRpar	MSRvid	SMT-eur	On-WN	SMT-news	**ALLnrm**	**Mean**	**ALL**
task-baseline	.4334	.2996	**.4542**	.5864	.3908	.6732 (85)	.4356 (70)	.3110 (87)
LReg	.5460	.7818	.3547	.5969	**.4137**	.8043 (36)	.5699 (41)	.6497 (33)
ELReg	.5480	.7844	.3513	.6040	.3607	.8048 (34)	.5654 (44)	**.6622** (27)
ERReg	**.5610**	**.7857**	.3568	**.6214**	.3732	**.8083** (28)	**.5755** (37)	.6573 (28)

Table 1: Pearson's r scores for the official submission. ALLnrm: Pearson correlation after the system outputs for each dataset are fitted to the gold standard using least squares, and corresponding rank. Mean: Weighted mean across the 5 datasets, where the weight depends on the number of pairs in the dataset. ALL: Pearson correlation with the gold standard for the five datasets, and corresponding rank. Parentheses indicate official rank out of 87 systems.

	MSRpar	MSRvid	SMT-eur	On-WN	SMT-news	**Mean**	**ALL**
system-baseline	.5143	.7736	.3574	.5017	.3867	.5343	.6542
+Neu	.5243	.7811	.3772	.4860	.3410	.5318	.6643
+Ew	.5267	.7787	**.3853**	.5237	**.4495**	.5560	.6724
+Sel	.4973	.7684	.3129	.4812	.4016	.5306	.6492
+Neu, +Ew	**.5481**	.7831	.2751	.5576	.3424	.5404	.6647
+Neu, +Sel	.5230	.7775	.3724	.5327	.3787	**.5684**	**.6818**
+Ew, +Sel	.5239	.7728	.2842	.5191	.4038	.5320	.6554
+Neu, +Ew, +Sel	.5441	**.7835**	.2644	**.5877**	.3578	.5472	.6645

Table 2: Pearson's r scores for runs based on various combinations of features. Mean: Weighted mean across the 5 datasets, where the weight depends on the number of pairs in the dataset. ALL: Pearson correlation with the gold standard for the five datasets, and corresponding rank.

Discussion. In the aggregate, we see that each of the similarity metrics has the ability to improve results when used with the right combination of other features. For example, while selector similarity by itself does not seem to help overall, using this metric in conjunction with the neural model of similarity gives us our best results. Interestingly, the opposite is true of eigenword similarity, where the best results are seen when they are independent of selectors or the neural models. The decreased correlations can be accounted for by the new features introducing over fitting, and one should note that no such reductions in performance are significant compared to the baseline, where as our best performance is a significant ($p < 0.05$) improvement.

There are a few potential directions for future improvements. We did not tune our system differently for different data sets although there is evidence of specific features favoring certain data sets. In the case of the neural model of similarity we expect that deriving phrase level representations from the sentences and utilizing the dynamic pooling layer should give us a more thorough measure of similarity beyond the sentence-level vectors we used in this work. For eigenwords, we would like to experiment with context-aware vectors as was described in (Dhillon et. al, 2011). Lastly, we were only able to acquire selectors for nouns, but we believe introducing selectors for other parts of speech will increase the power of the selector similarity metric.

4 Conclusion

In this paper, we described two novel word-level similarity metrics, namely *eigenword similarity* and *selector similarity*, that leverage Web-scale corpora in order to build word-level vector representations. Additionally, we explored the use of a vector-model at the sentence-level by unfolding a neural model of semantics. We utilized these metrics in addition to knowledge-based similarity, and surface-level similarity metrics in a regression system to estimate similarity at the sentence level. The performance of the features varies significantly across corpora but at the aggregate, eigenword similarity, selector similarity, and the neural model of similarity all are shown to be capable of improving performance beyond standard surface-level and WordNet similarity metrics alone.

References

Eneko Agirre, Daniel Cer, Mona Diab and Aitor Gonzalez. 2012. The SemEval-2012 Task-6 : A Pilot on Semantic Textual Similarity. *In Proceedings of the 6th International Workshop on Semantic Evaluation (SemEval 2012).*

Ronan Collobert and Jason Weston. 2008. A unified architecture for natural language processing : deep neural networks with multitask learning. *In International Conference on Machine Learning.* Pages 160-167.

Paramveer Dhillon, Dean Foster and Lyle Ungar. 2011. Multiview learning of word embeddings via CCA. *In Proceedings of Neural Information Processing Systems.*

Jay Jiang and David Conrath. 1997. Semantic similarity based on corpus statistics and lexical taxonomy. *In Proceedings on International Conference on Research in Computational Linguistics*, pages 1933.

Dekang Lin. 1997. Using syntactic dependency as local context to resolve word sense ambiguity. *In Proceedings of the 35th annual meeting of Association for Computational Linguistics*, pages 64-71.

Ted Pedersen, Siddharth Patwardhan and Jason Michelizzi. 2004. WordNet::Similarity-measuring the relatedness of concepts. *In Proceedings of the North American Chapter of the Association for Computational Linguistics.*

F. Pedregosa, G. Varoquaux, A. Gramfort, V. Michel, B. Thirion, G. Grisel, M. Blondel, P. Prettenhofer, R. Weiss, V. Dubourg, J. Vanderplas, A. Passos, D. Cournapeau, M. Brucher, M. Perrot, E. Duchesnay. 2011. Scikit-learn: Machine Learning in Python. *Journal of Machine Learning Research.* Vol 12.2825-2830

Hansen A. Schwartz and Fernando Gomez. 2008. Acquiring knowledge from the web to be used as selectors for noun sense disambiguation. *In Proceedings of the Twelfth Conference on Computational Natural Language Learning.*

Hansen A. Schwartz and Fernando Gomez. 2011. Evaluating semantic metrics on tasks of concept similarity. *In Proceedings of the twenty-fourth Florida Artificial Intelligence Research Society.* Palm Beach, Florida: AAAI Press.

Richard Socher, Eric H. Huang, Jeffrey Pennington, Andrew Y. Ng and Christopher Manning. 2011. Dynamic Pooling and Unfolding Recursive Autoencoders for Paraphrase Detection. *In Advances in Neural Information Processing Systems.*

Mark Stevenson and Mark A. Greenwood. 2005. A Semantic Approach to IE Pattern Induction. *In Proceedings of the 43rd Annual Meeting on Association for Computational Linguistics*, pages 379386.

Joseph Turian, Lev Ratinov, and Yoshua Bengio. 2010. Word representations: a simple and general method for semi-supervised learning. *In Proceedings of the annual meeting of Association for Computational Linguistics.*

Soft Cardinality + ML: Learning Adaptive Similarity Functions for Cross-lingual Textual Entailment

Sergio Jimenez
Universidad Nacional
de Colombia, Bogota,
Ciudad Universitaria
edificio 453, oficina 220
sgjimenezv@unal.edu.co

Claudia Becerra
Universidad Nacional
de Colombia, Bogota
cjbecerrac@unal.edu.co

Alexander Gelbukh
CIC-IPN
Av. Juan Dios Bátiz,
Av. Mendizábal, Col.
Nueva Industrial Vallejo,
CP 07738, DF, México
gelbukh@gelbukh.com

Abstract

This paper presents a novel approach for building adaptive similarity functions based on cardinality using machine learning. Unlike current approaches that build feature sets using similarity scores, we have developed these feature sets with the cardinalities of the commonalities and differences between pairs of objects being compared. This approach allows the machine-learning algorithm to obtain an asymmetric similarity function suitable for directional judgments. Besides using the classic set cardinality, we used soft cardinality to allow flexibility in the comparison between words. Our approach used only the information from the surface of the text, a stop-word remover and a stemmer to address the cross-lingual textual entailment task 8 at SEMEVAL 2012. We have the third best result among the 29 systems submitted by 10 teams. Additionally, this paper presents better results compared with the best official score.

1 Introduction

Adaptive similarity functions are those functions that, beyond using the information of two objects being compared, use information from a broader set of objects (Bilenko and Mooney, 2003). Therefore, the same similarity function may return different results for the same pair of objects, depending on the context of where the objects are. Adaptability is intended to improve the performance of the similarity function in relation to the task in question associated with the entire set of objects. For example, adaptiveness improves relevance of documents retrieved for a query in an information retrieval task for a particular document collection.

In text applications there are mainly three methods to provide adaptiveness to similarity functions: term weighting, adjustment or learning the parameters of the similarity function, and machine learning. Term weighting is a common practice that assigns a degree of importance to each occurrence of a term in a text collection (Salton and Buckley, 1988; Lan et al., 2005). Secondly, if a similarity function has parameters, these can be adjusted or learned to adapt to a particular data set. Depending on the size of the search space defined by these parameters, they can be adjusted either manually or using a technique of AI. For instance, Jimenez et al. manually adjusted a single parameter in the generalized measure of Monge-Elkan (1996) (Jimenez et al., 2009) and Ristrad and Yanilios (1998) learned the costs of editing operations between particular characters for the Levenshtein distance (1966) using HMMs. Thirdly, the machine-learning approach aims to learn a similarity function based on a vector representation of texts using a subset of texts for training and a learning function (Bilenko and Mooney, 2003). The three methods of adaptability can also be used in a variety of combinations, e.g. term weighting in combination with machine learning (Debole and Sebastiani, 2003; Lan et al., 2005). Finally, to achieve adaptability, other approaches use data sets considerably larger, such as large corpora or the Web, e.g. distributional similarity (Lee, 1999).

In the machine-learning approach, a vector representation of texts is used in conjunction with an algorithm of classification or regression (Alpaydin, 2004). Each vector of features $\langle f_1, f_2, \ldots, f_m \rangle$ is associated to each pair $\langle T_i, T_j \rangle$ of texts. Thus, Bilenko et al. (2003) proposed a set of features indexed by the data set vocabulary, similar to Zanzotto et al., (2009) who used fragments of parse trees. However, a more common approach is to select as features the scores of different similarity functions. Using these features, the machine-learning algorithm discovers the relative importance of each feature and a combination mechanism that maximizes the alignment of the final result with a gold standard for the particular task.

In this paper, we propose a novel approach to extract feature sets for a machine-learning algorithm using cardinalities rather than scores of similarity functions. For instance, instead of using as a feature the score obtained by the Dice's coefficient (i.e. $2\times|T_i \cap T_j|/|T_i|+|T_j|$), we use $|T_i|$, $|T_j|$ and $|T_i \cap T_j|$ as features. The rationale behind this idea is that despite the similarity scores being suitable for learning a combined function of similarity, they hide the information imbalance between the original pair of texts. Our hypothesis is that the information coded in this imbalance could provide the machine-learning algorithm with better information to generate a combined similarity score. For instance, consider these pairs of texts: ⟨ *"The beach house is white."*, *"The house was completely empty."*⟩ and ⟨ *"The house"*, *"The beach house was completely empty and isolated"*⟩. Both pairs have the same similarity score using the Dice coefficient, but it is evident that the latter has an imbalance of information lost in that single score. This imbalance of information is even more important if the task requires to identify directional similarities, such as "T_1 is more similar to T_2, than T_2 is to T_1".

However, unlike the similarity functions, which are numerous, there is only one set cardinality. This issue can be addressed using the soft cardinality proposed by Jimenez et al. (2010), which uses an auxiliary function of similarity between elements to make a soft count of the elements in a set. For instance, the classic cardinality of the set $A = \{$ *"Sunday"*, *"Saturday"* $\}$ is $|A| = 2$; and the soft cardinality of the same set, using a normalized edit-distance as auxiliary similarity function, is $|A|'_{sim} = 1.23$ because of the commonalities between both words. Furthermore, soft cardinality allows weighting of elements giving it additional capacity to adapt.

We used the proposed approach to participate in the cross-lingual textual-entailment task 8 at SEMEVAL 2012. The task was to recognize bidirectional, forward, backward or lack of entailment in pairs of texts written in five languages. We built a system based on the proposed method and the use of surface information of the text, a stop-word remover and a stemmer. Our system achieved the third best result in official classification and, after some debugging, we are reporting better results than the best official scores.

This paper is structured as follows. Section 2 briefly describes soft cardinality and other cardinalities for text applications. Section 3 presents the proposed method. Experimental validation is presented in Section 4. A brief discussion is presented in Section 5. Finally, conclusions are drawn in Section 6.

2 Cardinalities for text

Cardinality is a measure of counting the number of elements in a set. The cardinality of classical set theory represents the number of non-repeated elements in a set. However, this cardinality is rigid because it counts in the same manner very similar or highly differentiated elements. In text applications, text can be modeled as a set of words and a desirable cardinality function should take into account the similarities between words. In this section, we present some methods to soften the classical concept of cardinality.

2.1 Lemmatizer Cardinality

The simplest approach is to use a stemmer that collapses words with common roots in a single lemma. Consider the sentence: *"I loved, I am loving and I will love you"*. The plain word counting of this sentence is 10 words. The classical cardinality collapses the three occurrences of the pronoun *"I"* giving a count of 8. However, a lemmatizer such as Porter's stemmer (1980) also collapses the words *"loved"*, *"loving"* and *"love"* in a single lemma *"love"* for a count of 6. Thus, when a text is lemmatized, it induces a relaxation of the classical cardinality of a text. In addition, to provide corpus adaptability, a weighted version of this cardinality can add weights associated with each word occurrence instead of adding 1 for each word (e.g. tf-idf).

2.2 LCS cardinality

Longest common subsequence (LCS) length is a measure of the commonalities between two texts, unlike set intersection, taking into account the order. Therefore, a cardinality function of a pair of texts A and B could be $|A \cap B| = len(LCS(A, B))$, $|A| = len(A)$ and $|B| = len(B)$. Functions $len(*)$ and $LCS(*, *)$ calculate length and LCS respectively, either in character or word granularity.

2.3 Soft Cardinality

Soft cardinality is a function that uses an auxiliary similarity function to make a soft count of the elements (i.e. words) in a set (i.e. text) (Jimenez et al., 2010). The auxiliary similarity function can be any measure or metric that returns scores in the interval $[0, 1]$, with 0 being the lowest degree of similarity and 1 the highest (i.e. identical words). Clearly, if the auxiliary similarity function is a rigid comparator that returns 1 for identical words and 0 otherwise, the soft cardinality becomes the classic set cardinality.

The soft cardinality of a set $A = \{a_1, a_2, \ldots, a_{|A|}\}$ can be calculated by the following expression: $|A|'_{sim} \simeq \sum_i^{|A|} w_{a_i} \left(\sum_j^{|A|} sim(a_i, a_j)^p\right)^{-1}$. Where $sim(*, *)$ is the auxiliary similarity function for approximate word comparison, w_{a_i} are weights associated with each word a_i, and p is a tuning parameter that controls the degree of smoothness of the cardinality, i.e. if $0 \leftarrow p$ all elements in a set are considered identical and if $p \rightarrow \infty$ soft cardinality becomes classic cardinality.

2.4 Dot-product VSM "Cardinality"

Resemblance coefficients are cardinality-based similarity functions. For instance, the Dice coefficient is the ratio between the cardinality of the intersection divided by the arithmetic mean of individual cardinalities: $2\times|A\cap B|/|A|+|B|$. The cosine coefficient is similar but instead of using the arithmetic mean it uses the geometric mean: $|A\cap B|/\sqrt{|A|}\times\sqrt{|B|}$. Furthermore, the cosine similarity is a well known metric used in the vector space model (VSM) proposed by Salton et al. (1975) $cosine(A,B) = \frac{\sum w_{a_i}\times w_{b_i}}{\sqrt{\sum w_{a_i}^2}\times\sqrt{\sum w_{b_i}^2}}$. Clearly, this expression can be compared with the cosine coefficient interpreting the dot-product operation in the cosine similarity as a cardinality. Thus, the obtained cardinalities are: $|A\cap B|_{vsm} = \sum w_{a_i}^p \times w_{b_i}^p$, $|A|_{vsm} = \sum w_{a_i}^{2p}$ and $|B|_{vsm} = \sum w_{b_i}^{2p}$. The exponent p controls the effect of weighting providing no effect if $0 \leftarrow p$ or emphasising the weights if $p > 0$. In a similar application, Gonzalez and Caicedo (2011) used $p = 0.5$ and normalization justified by the quantum information retrieval theory.

3 Learning Similarity Functions from Cardinalities

Different similarity measures use different knowledge, identify different types of commonalities, and compare objects with different granularity. In many of the automatic text-processing applications, the qualities of several similarity functions may be required to achieve the final task. The combination of similarity scores with a machine-learning algorithm to obtain a unified effect for a particular task is a common practice (Bilenko et al., 2003; Malakasiotis and Androutsopoulos, 2007; Malakasiotis, 2009). For each pair of texts for comparison, there is provided a vector representation based on multiple similarity scores as a set of features. In addition, a class attribute is associated with each vector which contains the objective of the task or the gold standard to be learned by the machine-learning algorithm.

However, the similarity scores conceal important information when the task requires dealing with directional problems, i.e. whenever the order of comparing each pair of texts is related with the class attribute. For instance, textual entailment is a directional task since it is necessary to recognize whether the first text entails the second text or vice versa. This problem can be addressed using asymmetric similarity functions and including scores for $sim(A,B)$ and $sim(B,A)$ in the resulting vector for each pair $\langle A,B\rangle$. Nevertheless, the similarity measures that are more commonly used are symmetric, e.g. edit-distance (Levenshtein, 1966), LCS (Hirschberg, 1977), cosine similarity, and many of the current semantic relatedness measures (Pedersen et al., 2004). Although, there are asymmetric measures such as the Monge-Elkan measure (1996) and the measure proposed by Corley and Mihalcea (Corley and Mihalcea, 2005), they are outnumbered by the symmetric measures. Clearly, this situation restricts the use of the machine learning as a method of combination for directional problems.

Alternatively, we propose the construction of a vector for each pair of texts using cardinalities instead of similarity scores. Moreover, using cardinalities rather than similarity scores allows the machine-learning algorithm to discover patterns to cope with directional tasks.

Basically, we propose to use a set with six features for each cardinality function: $|A|$, $|B|$, $|A\cap B|$, $|A\cup B|$, $|A-B|$ and $|B-A|$.

4 Experimental Setup

4.1 Cross-lingual Textual Entailment (CLTE) Task

This task consist of recognizing in a pair of topically related text fragments T_1 and T_2 in different languages, one of the following possible entailment relations: i) *bidirectional* $T_1 \Rightarrow T_2 \wedge T_1 \Leftarrow T_2$, i.e. semantic equivalence; ii) *forward* $T_1 \Rightarrow T_2 \wedge T_1 \not\Leftarrow T_2$; iii) *backward* $T_1 \not\Rightarrow T_2 \wedge T_1 \Leftarrow T_2$; and iv) *no entailment* $T_1 \not\Rightarrow T_2 \wedge T_1 \not\Leftarrow T_2$. Besides, both T_1 and T_2 are assumed to be true statements; hence contradictory pairs are not allowed.

Data sets consist of a collection of 1,000 text pairs (500 for training and 500 for testing) each one labeled with one of the possible entailment types. Four balanced data sets were provided using the following language pairs: German-English (deu-eng), French-English (fra-eng), Italian-English (ita-eng) and Spanish-English (spa-eng). The evaluation measure for experiments was accuracy, i.e. the ratio of correctly predicted pairs by the total number of predictions. For a comprehensive description of the task see (Negri et al., 2012).

4.2 Experiments

Given that each pair of texts $\langle T_1,T_2\rangle$ are in different languages, a pair of translations $\langle T_1^t,T_2^t\rangle$ were provided using Google Translate service. Thus, each one of the text pairs $\langle T_1,T_2^t\rangle$ and $\langle T_1^t,T_2\rangle$ were in the same language. Then, all produced pairs were pre-processed by removing stop-words in their respective languages. Finally, all texts were lemmatized using Porter's stemmer (1980) for English and Snowball stemmers for other languages using an implementation provided by the NLTK (Loper and Bird, 2002).

Then, different set of features were generated using similarity scores or cardinalities. While each symmetric similarity function generates 2 features i)$sim(T_1,T_2^t)$ and ii)$sim(T_1^t,T_2)$, asymmetric functions generate two additional features iii)$sim(T_2^t,T_1)$ and iv)$sim(T_2,T_1^t)$.

On the other hand, each cardinality function generates 12 features: i) $|T_1|$, ii) $|T_2^t|$, iii) $|T_1 \cap T_2^t|$, iv) $|T_1 \cup T_2^t|$, v) $|T_1 - T_2^t|$, vi) $|T_2^t - T_1|$, vii) $|T_1^t|$, viii) $|T_2|$, ix) $|T_1^t \cap T_2|$, x) $|T_1^t \cup T_2|$, xi) $|T_1^t - T_2|$, and xii) $|T_2 - T_1^t|$. Various combinations of cardinalities, symmetric and asymmetric functions were used to generate the following feature sets:

Sym.simScores: scores of the following symmetric similarity functions: Jaccard, Dice, and cosine coefficients using classical cardinality and soft cardinality (edit-distance as auxiliar sim. function). In addition, cosine similarity, softTFIDF (Cohen et al., 2003) and edit-distance (total 18 features).

Asym.LCS.sim: scores of the following asymmetric similarity functions: $sim(T_1, T_2) = {}^{lcs(T_1,T_2)}/_{len(T_1)}$ and $sim(T_1, T_2) = {}^{lcs(T_1,T_2)}/_{len(T_2)}$ at character level (4 features).

Classic.card: cardinalities using classical set cardinality (12 features).

Dot.card.w: dot-product cardinality using idf weights as described in Section 2.4, using $p = 1$ (12 features).

LCS.card: LCS cardinality at word-level using idf weights as described in Section 2.1 (12 features).

SimScores: combined features sets from Sym.SimScores, Asym.LCS.sim and the generalized Monge-Elkan measure (Jimenez et al., 2009) using $p = 1, 2, 3$ (30 features).

Dot.card.w.0.5: same as Dot.card.w using $p = 0.5$.

Classic.card.w: classical cardinality using idf weights (12 features).

Soft.card.w: soft cardinality using idf weights as described in Section 2.3 using $p = 1, 2, 3, 4, 5$ (60 features).

The machine-learning classification algorithm for all feature sets was SVM (Cortes and Vapnik, 1995) with the complexity parameter $C = 1.5$ and a linear polynomial kernel. All experiments were conducted using WEKA (Hall et al., 2009).

4.3 Results

In Semeval 2012 exercise, participants were given a particular subdivision into training and test subsets for each data set. For official results, participants received only the gold-standard labels for the subset of training, and accuracies of each system in the test subset was measured by the organizers. In Table 1, the results for that particular division are shown. At the bottom of that table, the official results for the first three systems are shown. Our system, "3rd.Softcard" was configured using soft cardinality with edit-distance as auxiliary similarity function and $p = 2$. Erroneously, at the time of the submission, all texts in the 5 languages were lemmatized using an English stemmer and stop-words in all languages were aggregated into a single set before the withdrawal. In spite of these bugs, our system was the third best score.

FEATURES	SPA	ITA	FRA	DEU	avg.
Sym.simScores	0.404	0.410	0.410	0.410	0.409
Asym.LCS.sim	0.490	0.492	0.482	0.474	0.485
Classic.card	0.560	0.534	0.570	0.542	0.552
Dot.card.w	0.562	0.568	0.550	0.548	0.557
LCS.card	0.606	0.566	0.568	0.558	0.575
SimScores	0.600	0.562	0.568	0.572	0.576
Dot.card.w.0.5	0.584	0.574	0.586	0.572	0.579
Classic.card.w	0.584	0.576	0.588	0.590	0.585
Soft.card.w	0.598	**0.602**	**0.624**	**0.604**	**0.607**
SEMEVAL 2012 OFFICIAL RESULTS					
1st.HDU.run2	**0.632**	0.562	0.570	0.552	0.579
2nd.HDU.run1	0.630	0.554	0.564	0.558	0.577
3rd.Softcard	0.552	0.566	0.570	0.550	0.560

Table 1: Accuracy results for Semeval2012 task 8

Soft.card.w	**60.174(1.917)%**	imprv.	Sign.
Sym.simScore	39.802(1.783)%	51.2%	<0.001
Asym.LCS.sim	48.669(1.820)%	23.6%	<0.001
Classic.card	55.278(2.422)%	8.9%	0.010
Dot.card.w	54.906(2.024)%	9.6%	0.004
LCS.card	55.131(2.471) %	9.1%	0.015
SimScores	56.889(2.412) %	5.8%	0.124
Dot.card.w.0.5	57.114(2.141)%	5.4%	0.059
Classic.card.w	56.708(2.008)%	6.1%	0.017

Table 2: Average accuracy comparison vs. Soft.card.w in 100 runs

To compare our approach of using feature sets based on soft cardinality versus other approaches, we generated 100 random training-test subdivisions (50%-50%) of each data set. The average results were compared and tested statistically with the paired T-tested corrected test. Results, deviations, the percentage of improvement, and its significance in comparison with the Soft.card.w system are shown in Table2.

5 Discusion

Results in Table 2 show that our hypothesis that feature sets obtained from cardinalities should outperform features sets obtained from similarity scores was demostrated when compared versus similarity functions alternatively symmetrical or asymetrical. However, when our approach is compared with a feature set obtained by combining symmetric and asymmetric functions, we obtained an improvement of 5.8% but only with a significance of 0.124. Regarding soft cardinality compared to alternative cardinalities, soft cardinality outperformed others in all cases with significance <0.059.

6 Conclusions

We have proposed a new method to compose feature sets using cardinalities rather than similarity scores. Our approach proved to be effective for directional text comparison tasks such as textual entailment. Furthermore, the soft cardinality function proved to be the best for obtaining such sets of features.

Acknowledgments

This research was funded by the Systems and Industrial Engineering Department, the Office of Student Welfare of the National University of Colombia, Bogotá, and throught a grant from the Colombian Department for Science, Technology and Innovation Colciencias, proj. 110152128465. The second author recognizes the support from Mexican Government (SNI, COFAA-IPN, SIP 20113295, CONACYT 50206-H) and CONACYT–DST India (proj. "Answer Validation through Textual Entailment").

References

Ethem Alpaydin. 2004. *Introduction to Machine Learning*. MIT press.

Mikhail Bilenko and Raymond J. Mooney. 2003. Adaptive duplicate detection using learnable string similarity measures. In *Proc. of the ninth ACM SIGKDD international conference on Knowledge discovery and data mining*, Washington, D.C.

Mikhail Bilenko, Raymond Mooney, William Cohen, Pradeep Ravikumar, and Stephen Fienberg. 2003. Adaptive name matching in information integration. *IEEE Intelligent Systems*, 18(5):16–23.

William W Cohen, Pradeep Ravikumar, and Stephen E Fienberg. 2003. A comparison of string distance metrics for Name-Matching tasks. In *Proc. of the IJCAI2003 Workshop on Information Integration on the Web II Web03*.

Courtney Corley and Rada Mihalcea. 2005. Measuring the semantic similarity of texts. In *Proceedings of the ACL Workshop on Empirical Modeling of Semantic Equivalence and Entailment*, Stroudsburg, PA.

Corinna Cortes and Vladimir N. Vapnik. 1995. Support-Vector networks. *Machine Learning*, 20(3):273–297.

Franca Debole and Fabrizio Sebastiani. 2003. Supervised term weighting for automated text categorization. In *Proc. of the 2003 ACM symposium on applied computing*, New York, NY.

Fabio A. Gonzalez and Juan C. Caicedo. 2011. Quantum latent semantic analysis. In *Proc. of the Third international conference on Advances in information retrieval theory*.

Mark Hall, Frank Eibe, Geoffrey Holmes, and Bernhard Pfahringer. 2009. The WEKA data mining software: An update. *SIGKDD Explorations*, 11(1):10–18.

Daniel S. Hirschberg. 1977. Algorithms for the longest common subsequence problem. *J. ACM*, 24(4):664–675.

Sergio Jimenez, Claudia Becerra, Alexander Gelbukh, and Fabio Gonzalez. 2009. Generalized Monge-Elkan method for approximate text string comparison. In *Computational Linguistics and Intelligent Text Processing*, volume 5449 of *LNCS*, pages 559–570.

Sergio Jimenez, Fabio Gonzalez, and Alexander Gelbukh. 2010. Text comparison using soft cardinality. In *String Processing and Information Retrieval*, volume 6393 of *LNCS*, pages 297–302.

Man Lan, Chew-Lim Tan, Hwee-Boon Low, and Sam-Yuan Sung. 2005. A comprehensive comparative study on term weighting schemes for text categorization with support vector machines. In *Special interest tracks and posters of the 14th international conference on World Wide Web*, New York, NY.

Lillian Lee. 1999. Measures of distributional similarity. In *Proc. of the 37th annual meeting of the Association for Computational Linguistics on Computational Linguistics*, College Park, Maryland.

Vladimir I. Levenshtein. 1966. Binary codes capable of correcting deletions, insertions, and reversals. *Soviet Physics Doklady*, 10(8):707–710.

Edward Loper and Steven Bird. 2002. NLTK: the natural language toolkit. In *In Proceedings of the ACL Workshop on Effective Tools and Methodologies for Teaching Natural Language Processing and Computational Linguistics*, Philadelphia, PA.

Prodromos Malakasiotis and Ion Androutsopoulos. 2007. Learning textual entailment using SVMs and string similarity measures. In *Proc. of the ACL-PASCAL Workshop on Textual Entailment and Paraphrasing*, Stroudsburg, PA.

Prodromos Malakasiotis. 2009. Paraphrase recognition using machine learning to combine similarity measures. In *Proc. of the ACL-IJCNLP 2009 Student Research Workshop*, Stroudsburg, PA.

Alvaro E. Monge and Charles Elkan. 1996. The field matching problem: Algorithms and applications. In *Proc. KDD-96*, Portland, OR.

Matteo Negri, Alessandro Marchetti, Yashar Mehdad, Luisa Bentivogli, and Danilo Giampiccolo. 2012. 2012. semeval-2012 task 8: Cross-lingual textual entailment for content synchronization. In *In Proc. of the 6th International Workshop on Semantic Evaluation (SemEval 2012)*, Montreal, Canada.

Ted Pedersen, Siddharth Patwardhan, and Jason Michelizzi. 2004. WordNet::Similarity: measuring the relatedness of concepts. In *Proc. HLT-NAACL–Demonstration Papers*, Stroudsburg, PA.

Martin Porter. 1980. An algorithm for suffix stripping. *Program*, 3(14):130–137.

Eric S. Ristad and Peter N. Yianilos. 1998. Learning string edit distance. *IEEE Transactions on Pattern Analysis and Machine Intelligence*, 20(5):522–532.

Gerard Salton and Christopher Buckley. 1988. Term-weighting approaches in automatic text retrieval. *Information Processing & Management*, 24(5):513–523.

Gerard Salton, Andrew K. C. Wong, and Chung-Shu Yang. 1975. A vector space model for automatic indexing. *Commun. ACM*, 18(11):613–620.

Fabio Massimo Zanzotto, Marco Pennacchiotti, and Alessandro Moschitti. 2009. A machine learning approach to textual entailment recognition. *Natural Language Engineering*, 15(Special Issue 04):551–582.

JU_CSE_NLP: Language Independent Cross-lingual Textual Entailment System

Snehasis Neogi[1], Partha Pakray[2], Sivaji Bandyopadhyay[1], Alexander Gelbukh[3]
[1]Computer Science & Engineering Department
Jadavpur University, Kolkata, India
[2]Computer Science & Engineering Department
Jadavpur University, Kolkata, India
Intern at Xerox Research Centre Europe
Grenoble, France
[3]Center for Computing Research
National Polytechnic Institute
Mexico City, Mexico
{snehasis1981,parthapakray}@gmail.com
sbandyopadhyay@cse.jdvu.ac.in
gelbukh@gelbukh.com

Abstract

This article presents the experiments carried out at Jadavpur University as part of the participation in Cross-lingual Textual Entailment for Content Synchronization (CLTE) of task 8 @ Semantic Evaluation Exercises (SemEval-2012). The work explores cross-lingual textual entailment as a relation between two texts in different languages and proposes different measures for entailment decision in a four way classification tasks (forward, backward, bidirectional and no-entailment). We set up different heuristics and measures for evaluating the entailment between two texts based on lexical relations. Experiments have been carried out with both the text and hypothesis converted to the same language using the Microsoft Bing translation system. The entailment system considers Named Entity, Noun Chunks, Part of speech, N-Gram and some text similarity measures of the text pair to decide the entailment judgments. Rules have been developed to encounter the multi way entailment issue. Our system decides on the entailment judgment after comparing the entailment scores for the text pairs. Four different rules have been developed for the four different classes of entailment. The best run is submitted for Italian – English language with accuracy 0.326.

1 Introduction

Textual Entailment (TE) (Dagan and Glickman, 2004) is one of the recent challenges of Natural Language Processing (NLP). The Task 8 of SemEval-2012[1] [1] defines a textual entailment system that specifies two major aspects: the task is based on cross-lingual corpora and the entailment decision must be four ways. Given a pair of topically related text fragments (T1 and T2) in different languages, the CLTE task consists of automatically annotating it with one of the following entailment judgments:

i. *Bidirectional (T1 ->T2 & T1 <- T2)*: the two fragments entail each other (semantic equivalence)
ii. *Forward (T1 -> T2 & T1!<- T2)*: unidirectional entailment from T1 to T2 .
iii. *Backward (T1! -> T2 & T1 <- T2)*: unidirectional entailment from T2 to T1.
iv. *No Entailment (T1! -> T2 & T1! <- T2)*: there is no entailment between T1 and T2.

CLTE (Cross Lingual Textual Entailment) task consists of 1,000 CLTE dataset pairs (500 for

[1]http://www.cs.york.ac.uk/semeval2012/index.php?id=tasks

training and 500 for test) available for the following language combinations:

- Spanish/English (spa-eng)
- German/English (deu-eng).
- Italian/English (ita-eng)
- French/English (fra-eng)

Seven Recognizing Textual Entailment (RTE) evaluation tracks have already been held: RTE-1 in 2005 [2], RTE-2 [3] in 2006, RTE-3 [4] in 2007, RTE-4 [5] in 2008, RTE-5 [6] in 2009, RTE-6 [7] in 2010 and RTE-7 [8] in 2011. RTE task produces a generic framework for entailment task across NLP applications. The RTE challenges have moved from 2 – way entailment task (YES, NO) to 3 – way task (YES, NO, UNKNOWN). EVALITA/IRTE [9] task is similar to the RTE challenge for the Italian language. So far, TE has been applied only in a monolingual setting. Cross-lingual Textual Entailment (CLTE) has been proposed ([10], [11], [12]) as an extension of Textual Entailment. In 2010, Parser Training and Evaluation using Textual Entailment [13] was organized by SemEval-2. Recognizing Inference in Text (RITE)[2] organized by NTCIR-9 in 2011 is the first to expand TE as a 5-way entailment task (forward, backward, bi-directional, contradiction and independent) in a monolingual scenario [14].
We have participated in RTE-5 [15], RTE-6 [16], RTE-7 [17], SemEval-2 Parser Training and Evaluation using Textual Entailment Task and RITE [18].
Section 2 describes our Cross-lingual Textual Entailment system. The various experiments carried out on the development and test data sets are described in Section 3 along with the results. The conclusions are drawn in Section 4.

2 System Architecture

Our system for CLTE task is based on a set of heuristics that assigns entailment scores to a text pair based on lexical relations. The text and the hypothesis in a text pair are translated to the same language using the Microsoft Bing machine translation system. The system separates the text pairs (T1 and T2) available in different languages and preprocesses them. After preprocessing we have used several techniques such as Word Overlaps, Named Entity matching, Chunk matching, POS matching to evaluate the separated text pairs. These modules return a set of score statistics, which helps the system to go for multi-class entailment decision based on the predefined rules. We have submitted 3 runs for each language pair for the CLTE task and there are some minor differences in the architectures that constitute the 3 runs. The three system architectures are described in section 2.1, section 2.2 and section 2.3.

2.1 System Architecture 1: CLTE Task with Translated English Text

The system architecture of Cross-lingual textual entailment consists of various components such as Preprocessing Module, Lexical Similarity Module, Text Similarity Module. Lexical Similarity module again is divided into subsequent modules like POS matching, Chunk matching and Named Entity matching. Our system calculates these measures twice once considering T1 as text and T2 as hypothesis and once T2 as text and T1 as hypothesis. The mapping is done in both directions T1-to-T2 and T2-to-T1 to arrive at the appropriate four way entailment decision using a set of rules. Each of these modules is now being described in subsequent subsections. Figure 1 shows our system architecture where the text sentence is translated to English.

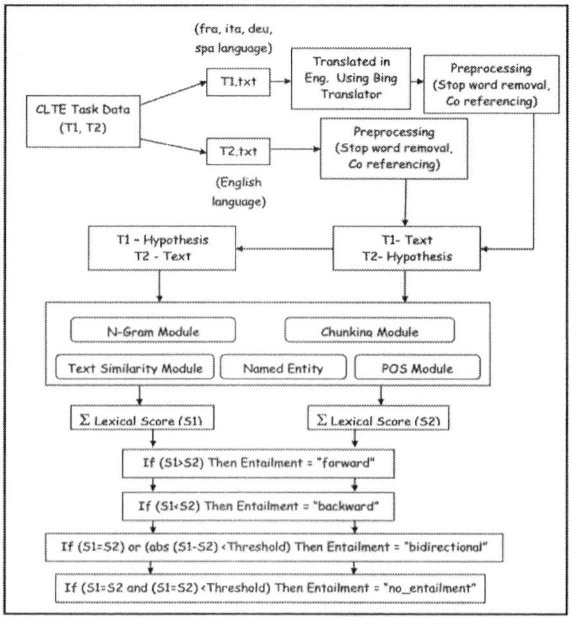

Figure 1: System Architecture

[2] http://artigas.lti.cs.cmu.edu/rite/Main_Page

2.1.1 Preprocessing Module

The system separates the T1 and T2 pair from the CLTE task data. T1 sentences are in different languages (In French, Italian, German and Spanish) where as T2 sentences are in English. Microsoft Bing translator[3] API for Bing translator (microsoft-translator-java-api-0.4-jar-with-dependencies.jar) is being used to translate the T1 text sentences into English. The translated T1 and T2 sentences are passed through the two sub modules.

i. Stop word Removal: Stop words are removed from the T1 and T2 sentences.

ii. Co-reference: Co–reference chains are evaluated for the datasets before passing them to the TE module. The objective is to increase the entailment score after substituting the anaphors with their antecedents. A word or phrase in the sentence is used to refer to an entity introduced earlier or later in the discourse and both having same things then they have the same referent or co-reference. When the reader must look back to the previous context, co-reference is called "*Anaphoric Reference*". When the reader must look forward, it is termed "*Cataphoric Reference*". To address this problem we used a tool called JavaRAP[4] (A java based implementation of Anaphora Procedure (RAP) - an algorithm by Lappin and Leass (1994)). It has been observed that the presence of co – referential expressions are very small in sentence based paradigm.

2.1.2 Lexical Based Textual Entailment (TE) Module

T1 - T2 pairs are the inputs to the system. The TE module is executed once by considering T1 as text and T2 as hypothesis and again by considering T2 as text and T1 as hypothesis. The overall TE module is a collection of several lexical based sub modules.

i. N-Gram Match module: The N-Gram match basically measures the percentage match of the unigram, bigram and trigram of hypothesis present in the corresponding text. These scores are simply combined to get an overall N – Gram matching score for a particular pair. By running the module we get two scores, one for T1-T2 pair and another for T2-T1 pair.

ii. Chunk Similarity module: In this sub module our system evaluates the key NP-chunks of both text and hypothesis identified using NP Chunker v1.1[5]. Then our system checks the presence of NP-Chunks of hypothesis in the corresponding text. System calculates the overall value for the chunk matching, i.e., number of text NP-chunks that match with hypothesis NP-chunks. If the chunks are not similar in their surface form then our system goes for WordNet matching for the words and if they match in WordNet synsets information, the chunks are considered as similar.

WordNet [19] is one of most important resource for lexical analysis. The WordNet 2.0 has been used for WordNet based chunk matching. The API for WordNet Searching (JAWS)[6] is an API that provides Java applications with the ability to retrieve data from the WordNet database. Let us consider the following example taken from training data:

T1: *Due/JJ to/TO [an/DT error/NN of/IN communication/NN] between/IN [the/DT police/NN]* ...

T2: *On/IN [Tuesday/NNP] [a/DT failed/VBN communication/NN] between/IN...*

The chunk in T1 [error communication] matches with T2 [failed communication] via WordNet based synsets information. A weight is assigned to the score depending upon the nature of chunk matching.

$$\text{score (S)} = \sum_{i=1}^{N} M[i] / N$$

$$M[i] = W_m[i] * \rho / Wc[i]$$

Where N= Total number of chunk containing hypothesis.

M[i] = Match Score of the ith Chunk.

$W_m[i]$ = Number of words matched in the ith chunk.

$W_c[i]$ = Total words in the ith chunk.

$$\text{and } \rho = \begin{cases} 1 & \text{if surface word matches.} \\ \tfrac{1}{2} & \text{if matche via WordNet} \end{cases}$$

[3] http://code.google.com/p/microsoft-translator-java-api/

[4] http://aye.comp.nus.edu.sg/~qiu/NLPTools/JavaRAP.html

[5] http://www.dcs.shef.ac.uk/~mark/phd/software/

[6] http://lyle.smu.edu/~tspell/jaws/index.html

System takes into consideration several text similarity measures calculated over the T1-T2 pair. These text similarity measures are summed up to produce a total score for a particular text pair. Similar to the Lexical module, text similarity module is also executed for both T1-T2 and T2-T1 pairs.

iii. Text Distance Module: The following major text similarity measures have been considered by our system. The text similarity measure scores are added to generate the final text distance score.

- *Cosine Similarity*
- *Levenshtein Distance*
- *Euclidean Distance*
- *MongeElkan Distance*
- *NeedlemanWunch Distance*
- *SmithWaterman Distance*
- *Block Distance*
- *Jaro Similarity*
- *MatchingCoefficient Similarity*
- *Dice Similarity*
- *OverlapCoefficient*
- *QGrams Distance*

iv. Named Entity Matching: It is based on the detection and matching of Named Entities in the T1-T2 pair. Stanford Named Entity Recognizer[7] (NER) is used to tag the Named Entities in both T1 and T2. System simply matches the number of hypothesis NEs present in the text. A score is allocated for the matching.

NE_match = (Number of common NEs in Text and Hypothesis)/(Number of NEs in Hypothesis).

v. Part-of-Speech (POS) Matching: This module basically deals with matching the common POS tags between T1 and T2 pair. Stanford POS tagger[8] is used to tag the part of speech in both T1 and T2. System matches the verb and noun POS words in the hypothesis that match in the text. A score is allocated based on the number of POS matching.

POS_match = (Number of verb and noun POS in Text and Hypothesis)/(Total number of verb and noun POS in hypothesis).

[7] http://nlp.stanford.edu/software/CRF-NER.shtml

[8] http://nlp.stanford.edu/software/tagger.shtml

System adds all the lexical matching scores to evaluate the total score for a particular T1- T2 pair, i.e.,

Pair1: (T1 – Text and T2 – Hypothesis)

Pair2: (T1 – Hypothesis and T2 - Text).

Total lexical score for each pair can be mathematically represented by:

$$Score(S2) = \sum (Lexical\ Scores\ of pair2)$$

$$Score(S1) = \sum (Lexical\ Scores\ of pair1)$$

where S1 represents the score for the pair with T1 as text and T2 as hypothesis while S2 represents the score from T1 to T2. The figure 2 shows the sample output values of the TE module.

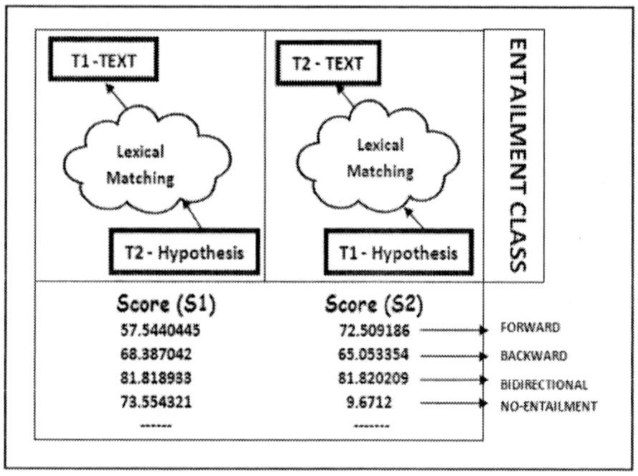

Figure 2: output values of this module

The system finally compares the above two values S1 and S2 as obtained from the lexical module to go for four-class entailment decision. If score S1, i.e., the mapping score with T1 as text and T2 as hypothesis is greater than the score S2, i.e., mapping score with T2 as text and T1 as hypothesis, then the entailment class will be "forward". Similarly if S1 is less than S2, i.e., T2 now acts as the text and T1 acts as the hypothesis then the entailment class will be "backward". Similarly if both the scores S1 and S2 are equal the entailment class will be "bidirectional" (entails in both directions). Measuring "bidirectional" entailment is much more difficult than any other entailment decision due to combinations of different lexical scores. As our system produces a final score (S1 and S2) that is basically the sum over different similarity measures, the tendency of identical S1 – S2 will be quite small. As a result we establish another heuristic for "bidirectional" class. If the absolute value difference between S1 and S2 is below the threshold value, our system recognizes the pair as "bidirectional" *(abs (S1 – S2) < threshold)*. This threshold has been set as 5 based on observation from the training file. If the individual scores S1 and S2 are below a certain threshold, again set based on the observation in the training file, then system concludes the entailment class as "no_entailment". This threshold has been set as 20 based on observation from the training file.

2.2 System Architecture 2: CLTE Task with translated hypothesis

System Architecture 2 is based on lexical matching between the text pairs (T1, T2) and basically measures the same attributes as in the architecture 1. In this architecture, the English hypothesis sentences are translated to the language of the text sentence (French, Italian, Spanish and German) using the Microsoft Bing Translator. The CLTE dataset is preprocessed after separating the (T1, T2) pairs. Preprocessing module includes stop word removal and co-referencing. After preprocessing, the system executes the TE module for lexical matching between the text pairs. This module comprises N-Gram matching, Text Similarity, Named Entity Matching, POS matching and Chunking. The TE module is executed once with T1 as text and T2 as hypothesis and again with T1 as hypothesis and T2 as text. But in this architecture N-Gram matching and text similarity modules differ from the previous architecture. In system architecture 1, the N-Gram matching and text similarity values are calculated on the English text translated from T1 (i.e., Text in Spanish, German, French and Italian languages). In system architecture 2, the Microsoft Bing translator is used to translate T2 texts (in English) to different languages (i.e. in Spanish, German, French and Italian) and calculate N – Gram matching and Text Similarity values on these (T1 – newly translated T2) pairs. Other lexical sub modules are executed as before. These lexical matching scores are stored and compared according to the heuristic defined in section 2.1.

2.3 System Architecture 3: CLTE task using Voting

The system considers the output of the previous two systems (Run 1 from System architecture 1 and Run 2 from System architecture 2) as input. If the entailment decision of both the runs agrees then this is output as the final entailment label. Otherwise, if they do not agree, the final entailment label will be "no_entailment". The voting rule can be defined as the ANDing rule where logical AND operation of the two inputs are considered to arrive at the final evaluation class.

3 Experiments on Datasets and Results

Three runs (Run 1, Run 2 and Run 3) for each language were submitted for the SemEval-3 Task 8. The descriptions of submissions for the CLTE task are as follows:

- *Run1:* Lexical matching between text pairs (Based on system Architecture – 1).
- Run2: Lexical matching between text pairs (Based on System Architecture – 2).
- *Run3:* ANDing Module between *Run1* and *Run2*. (Based on System Architecture –3).

The CLTE dataset consists of 500 training CLTE pairs and 500 test CLTE pairs. The results for Run 1, Run 2 and Run 3 for each language on CLTE Development set are shown in Table 1.

Run Name	Accuracy
JU-CSE-NLP_deu-eng_run1	0.284
JU-CSE-NLP_deu-eng_run2	0.268
JU-CSE-NLP_deu-eng_run3	0.270
JU-CSE-NLP_fra-eng_run1	0.290
JU-CSE-NLP_fra-eng_run2	0.320
JU-CSE-NLP_fra-eng_run3	0.278
JU-CSE-NLP_ita-eng_run1	0.302
JU-CSE-NLP_ita-eng_run2	0.298
JU-CSE-NLP_ita-eng_run3	0.298
JU-CSE-NLP_spa-eng_run1	0.270
JU-CSE-NLP_spa-eng_run2	0.262
JU-CSE-NLP_spa-eng_run3	0.262

Table 1: Results on Development set

The comparison of the runs for different languages shows that in case of deu-eng language pair system architecture – 1 is useful for development data whereas system architecture – 2 is more accurate for test data. For fra-eng language pair, system architecture - 2 is more accurate for development data whereas voting helps to get more accurate results for test data. Similar to the deu-eng language pair, ita-eng language pair shows same trends, i.e., system architecture – 1 is more helpful for development data and system architecture – 2 is more accurate for test data. In case of spa-eng language pair system architecture – 1 is helpful for both development and test data.

The results for Run 1, Run 2 and Run 3 for each language on CLTE Test set are shown in Table 2.

Run Name	Accuracy
JU-CSE-NLP_deu-eng_run1	0.262
JU-CSE-NLP_deu-eng_run2	0.296
JU-CSE-NLP_deu-eng_run3	0.264
JU-CSE-NLP_fra-eng_run1	0.288
JU-CSE-NLP_fra-eng_run2	0.294
JU-CSE-NLP_fra-eng_run3	0.296
JU-CSE-NLP_ita-eng_run1	0.316
JU-CSE-NLP_ita-eng_run2	0.326
JU-CSE-NLP_ita-eng_run3	0.314
JU-CSE-NLP_spa-eng_run1	0.274
JU-CSE-NLP_spa-eng_run2	0.266
JU-CSE-NLP_spa-eng_run3	0.272

Table 2: Results on Test Set

4 Conclusions and Future Works

We have participated in Task 8 of Semeval-2012 named Cross Lingual Textual Entailment mainly based on lexical matching and translation of text and hypothesis sentences in the cross lingual corpora. Both lexical matching and translation have their limitations. Lexical matching is useful for simple sentences but fails to retain high accuracy for complex sentences with number of clauses. Semantic graph matching or conceptual graph is a good substitution to overcome these limitations. Machine learning technique is another important tool for multi-class entailment task. Features can be trained by some machine learning tools (such as SVM, Naïve Bayes or Decision tree etc.) with multi-way entailment (forward, backward, bi-directional, no-entailment) as its class. Works have been started in these directions.

Acknowledgments

The work was carried out under partial support of the DST India-CONACYT Mexico project "*Answer Validation through Textual Entailment*" funded by DST, Government of India and partial support of the project *CLIA Phase II (Cross Lingual Information Access)* funded by DIT, Government of India.

References

[1] Negri, M., Marchetti, A., Mehdad, Y., Bentivogli, L., and Giampiccolo, D.: *Semeval-2012 Task 8: Cross-lingual Textual Entailment for Content Synchronization.* In Proceedings of the 6th International Workshop on Semantic Evaluation (SemEval 2012).

[2] Dagan, I., Glickman, O., Magnini, B.: *The PASCAL Recognising Textual Entailment Challenge.* Proceedings of the First PASCAL Recognizing Textual Entailment Workshop. (2005).

[3] Bar-Haim, R., Dagan, I., Dolan, B., Ferro, L., Giampiccolo, D., Magnini, B., Szpektor, I.: *The-Seond PASCAL Recognising Textual Entailment Challenge.* Proceedings of the Second PASCAL Challenges Workshop on Recognising Textual Entailment, Venice, Italy (2006).

[4] Giampiccolo, D., Magnini, B., Dagan, I., Dolan, B.: *The Third PASCAL Recognizing Textual Entailment Challenge.* In Proceedings of the ACL-PASCAL Workshop on Textual Entailment and Paraphrasing, Prague, Czech Republic. (2007).

[5] Giampiccolo, D., Dang, H. T., Magnini, B., Dagan, I., Cabrio, E.: *The Fourth PASCAL Recognizing Textual Entailment Challenge.* In TAC 2008 Proceedings. (2008)

[6] Bentivogli, L., Dagan, I., Dang. H.T., Giampiccolo, D., Magnini, B.: *The Fifth PASCAL Recognizing Textual Entailment Challenge.* In TAC 2009 Workshop, National Institute of Standards and Technology Gaithersburg, Maryland USA. (2009).

[7] Luisa Bentivogli, Peter Clark, Ido Dagan, Hoa Trang Dang,Danilo Giampiccolo: *The Sixth PASCAL Recognizing Textual Entailment Chal-*

lenge. In TAC 2010 Notebook Proceedings. (2010)

[8] Bentivogli, L., Clark, P., Dagan, I., Dang, H., Giampiccolo, D.: *The Seventh PASCAL Recognizing Textual Entailment Challenge*. In TAC 2011 Notebook Proceedings. (2011)

[9] Bos, Johan, Fabio Massimo Zanzotto, and Marco Pennacchiotti. 2009. *Textual Entailment at EVALITA 2009*: In Proceedings of EVALITA 2009.

[10] Mehdad, Yashar, Matteo Negri, and Marcello Federico.2010. *Towards Cross-Lingual Textual entailment*. In Proceedings of the 11th Annual Conference of the North American Chapter of the Association for Computational Linguistics, NAACL-HLT 2010. LA, USA.

[11] Negri, Matteo, and Yashar Mehdad. 2010. *Creating a Bilingual Entailment Corpus through Translations with Mechanical Turk: $100 for a 10-day Rush*. In Proceedings of the NAACL-HLT 2010, Creating Speech and Text Language Data With Amazon's Mechanical Turk Workshop. LA, USA.

[12] Mehdad, Yashar, Matteo Negri, Marcello Federico. 2011. *Using Bilingual Parallel Corpora for Cross-Lingual Textual Entailment*. In Proceedings of ACL 2011.

[13] Yuret, D., Han, A., Turgut, Z.: *SemEval-2010 Task 12: Parser Evaluation using Textual Entailments*. Proceedings of the SemEval-2010 Evaluation Exercises on Semantic Evaluation. (2010).

[14] H. Shima, H. Kanayama, C.-W. Lee, C.-J. Lin,T. Mitamura, S. S. Y. Miyao, and K. Takeda. *Overview of ntcir-9 rite: Recognizing inference in text*. In NTCIR-9 Proceedings,2011.

[15] Pakray, P., Bandyopadhyay, S., Gelbukh, A.: *Lexical based two-way RTE System at RTE-5*. System Report, TAC RTE Notebook. (2009)

[16] Pakray, P., Pal, S., Poria, S., Bandyopadhyay, S., , Gelbukh, A.: *JU_CSE_TAC: Textual Entailment Recognition System at TAC RTE-6*. System Report, Text Analysis Conference Recognizing Textual Entailment Track (TAC RTE) Notebook. (2010)

[17] Pakray, P., Neogi, S., Bhaskar, P., Poria, S., Bandyopadhyay, S., Gelbukh, A.: *A Textual Entailment System using Anaphora Resolution*. System Report. Text Analysis Conference Recognizing Textual Entailment Track Notebook, November 14-15. (2011)

[18] Pakray, P., Neogi, S., Bandyopadhyay, S., Gelbukh, A.: *A Textual Entailment System using Web based Machine Translation System*. NTCIR-9, National Center of Sciences, Tokyo, Japan. December 6-9, 2011. (2011)

[19] Fellbaum, C.: WordNet: An Electronic Lexical Database. MIT Press (1998).

CELI: An Experiment with Cross Language Textual Entailment

Milen Kouylekov
Celi S.R.L.
via San Quintino 31
Torino, Italy
kouylekov@celi.it

Luca Dini
Celi S.R.L.
via San Quintino 31
Torino, Italy
dini@celi.it

Alessio Bosca
Celi S.R.L.
via San Quintino 31
Torino, Italy
bosca@celi.it

Marco Trevisan
Celi S.R.L.
via San Quintino 31
Torino, Italy
trevisan@celi.it

Abstract

This paper presents CELI's participation in the SemEval Cross-lingual Textual Entailment for Content Synchronization task.

1 Introduction

The Cross-Lingual Textual Entailment task (CLTE) is a new task that addresses textual entailment (TE) (Bentivogli et. al., 2011), targeting the cross-lingual content synchronization scenario proposed in (Mehdad et. al., 2011) and (Negri et. al., 2011). The task has interesting application scenarios that can be investigated. Some of them are content synchronization and cross language query alignment. The task is defined by the organizers as follows: Given a pair of topically related text fragments (T1 and T2) in different languages, the CLTE task consists of automatically annotating it with one of the following entailment judgments:

- Bidirectional: the two fragments entail each other (semantic equivalence)
- Forward: unidirectional entailment from T1 to T2
- Backward: unidirectional entailment from T2 to T1
- No Entailment: there is no entailment between T1 and T2

In this task, both *T1* and *T2* are assumed to be TRUE statements; hence in the dataset there are no contradictory pairs.

Example for Spanish English pairs:

- **bidirectional**
  Mozart naci en la ciudad de Salzburgo
  Mozart was born in Salzburg.
- **forward**
  Mozart naci en la ciudad de Salzburgo
  Mozart was born on the 27th January 1756 in Salzburg.
- **backward**
  Mozart naci el 27 de enero de 1756 en Salzburgo
  Mozart was born in 1756 in the city of Salzburg
- **no_entailment**
  Mozart naci el 27 de enero de 1756 en Salzburgo
  Mozart was born to Leopold and Anna Maria Pertl Mozart.

2 Our Approach to CLTE

In our participation in the 2012 SemEval Cross-lingual Textual Entailment for Content Synchronization task (Negri et. al., 2012) we have developed an approach based on cross-language text similarity. We have modified our cross-language query similarity system TLike to handle longer texts.

Our approach is based on four main resources:

- A system for Natural Language Processing able to perform for each relevant language basic tasks such as part of speech disambiguation, lemmatization and named entity recognition.
- A set of word based bilingual translation modules.

- A semantic component able to associate a semantic vectorial representation to words.

- We use Wikipedia as multilingual corpus.

NLP modules are described in (Bosca and Dini, 2008), and will be no further detailed here.

Word-based translation modules are composed by a bilingual lexicon look-up component coupled with a vector based translation filter, such as the one described in (Curtoni and Dini, 2008). In the context of the present experiments, such a filters has been deactivated, which means that for any input word the component will return the set of all possible translations. For unavailable pairs, we make use of triangular translation (Kraaij, 2003).

As for the semantic component we experimented with a corpus-based distributional approach capable of detecting the interrelation between different terms in a corpus; the strategy we adopted is similar to Latent Semantic Analysis (Deerwester et. al., 1990) although it uses a less expensive computational solution based on the Random Projection algorithm (Lin et. al., 2003) and (Bingham et. al., 2001). Different works debate on similar issues: (Turney, 2001) uses LSA in order to solve synonymy detection questions from the well-known TOEFL test while the method presented by (Inkpen, 2001) or by (Baroni and Bisi, 2001) proposes the use of the Web as a corpus to compute mutual information scores between candidate terms.

More technically, Random Indexing exploits an algebraic model in order to represent the semantics of terms in a Nth dimensional space (a vector of length N); approaches falling into this category, actually create a Terms By Contexts matrix where each cell represents the degree of memberships of a given term to the different contexts. The algorithm assigns a random signature to each context (a highly sparse vector of length N, with few, randomly chosen, non-zero elements) and then generates the vector space model by performing a statistical analysis of the documents in the domain corpus and by accumulating on terms rows all the signatures of the contexts where terms appear.

According to this approach if two different terms have a similar meaning they should appear in similar contexts (within the same documents or surrounded by the same words), resulting into close coordinates in the so generated semantic space.

In our case study semantic vectors have been generated taking as corpus the set of metadata available via the CACAO project (Cacao Project, 2007) federation (about 6 millions records). After processing for each word in the corpus we have:

- A vector of float from 0 to 1 representing its contextual meaning;

- A set of neighbors terms selected among the terms with a higher semantic similarity, calculated as cosine distance among vectors.

We use Wikipedia as a corpus for calculating word statistics in different languages. We have indexed using Lucene[1] the English, Italian, French, German, Spanish distributions of the resource.

The basic idea behind our algorithm is to detect the probability for two texts to be one a translation of the other. In the simple case we expect that if all the words in text TS have a translation in text TT and if TS and TT have the same number of terms, then T_S and T_T are entailed. Things are of course more complex than this, due to the following facts:

- The presence of compound words make the constraints on cardinality of search terms not feasible (e.g. the Italian Carta di Credito vs. the German KreditCarte).

- One or more words in T_S could be absent from translation dictionaries.

- One or more words in T_S could be present in the translation dictionaries, but contextually correct translation might be missing.

- There might be items which do not need to be translated, notably Named Entities.

The first point, compounding, is only partially an obstacle. NLP technology developed during CACAO Project, which adopted translation dictionaries, deals with compound words both in terms of identification and translation. Thus the Italian *"Carta di Credito"* would be recognized and correctly translated into *"KreditCarte"*. So, in an ideal

[1] *http://lucene.apache.org*

word, the cardinality principle could be considered strict. In reality, however, there are many compounding phenomena which are not covered by our dictionaries, and this forces us to consider that a mismatch in text term cardinality decrease the probability that the two translations are translation of each other, without necessarily setting it to zero.

Concerning the second aspect, the absence of source (T1) words in translation dictionaries, it is dealt with by accessing the semantic repository described in the previous section. We first obtain the list of neighbor terms for the *untranslatable* source word. This list is likely to contain many words that have one or more translations. For each translation, again, we consult our semantic repository and we obtain its semantic vector.

Finally, we compose all vectors of all available translations and we search in the target text (T2) for the word whose semantic vector best matches the composed one (cosine distance). Of course we cannot assume that the best matching vector is a translation of the original word, but we can use the distance between the two vectors as a further weight for deciding whether the two texts are translations one of the other.

There are of course cases when the source word is correctly missing in the source dictionary. This is typically the case of most named entities, such as geographical and person names. These entities should be appropriately recognized and searched as exact matches in the target text, thus by-passing any dictionary look-up and any semantic based matching. Notice that the recognition of named entities it is not just a matter of generalizing the statement according to which *"if something is not in the dictionaries, it is a named entity"*. Indeed there are well known cases where the named entity is homograph with common words (e.g. the French author *"La Fontaine"*), and in these cases we must detect them in order to avoid the rejection of likely translation pairs. In other words we must avoid that the two texts *"La fontaine fables"* and *"La Fontaine favole"* are rejected as translation pairs, just by virtue of the fact that *"La fontaine"* is treated as a common word, thus generating the Italian translation *"La fontana"*. Fortunately CACAO disposes of a quite accurate subsystem for recognizing named entities in texts, mixing standard NLP technologies with statistical processing and other corpus-oriented heuristics.

We concentrated our work on handling cases where two texts are candidates to be mutual translations, but one or more words receive a translation which is not contained in the target text. Typically these cases are a symptom of a non-optimal quality in translation dictionaries: the lexicographer probably did not consider some translation candidate. To address this problem we have created a solution based on a weighting scheme. For each word of the source language we assign a weight that reflects its importance to the semantic interpretation of the text. We define a $match_{weight}$ of a word using the formula represented in Figure 2.In this formula wi_s is a word from the source text, wk_t is a word from the target text, w is a word in the source language and trans is a boolean function that searches in the dictionary for translations between two words.

The $match_{weight}$ is relevant to the matching of a translation of a word from the source with one of the words of the target. If the system finds a direct correspondence the weight is 0. If the match was made using random indexing the weight is inverse to the cosine similarity between the vectors.

In order to make an approximation of the significance of the word to the meaning of the phrase we have used as its cost the inverse document frequency (IDF) of the word calculated using Wikipedia as a corpus. IDF is a most popular measure (a measure commonly used in Information Retrieval) for calculating the importance of a word to a text. If N is the number of documents in a text collection and N_w is the number of documents of the collection that contain w then the IDF of w is given by the formula:

$$weight(wi_s) = idf(w) = log(\frac{N}{N_w}) \quad (2)$$

Using the $match_{weight}$ and $weight$ we define the $match_{score}$ of a source target pair as:

$$match_{score}(T_s, T_t) = \frac{\sum match_{weigth}(wi_s)}{\sum weight(wi_s)} \quad (3)$$

If all the words of the source text have a translation in the target text the score is 0. If none is found the score is 1. We have calculated the scores for each

$$match_{weight}(wi_s) = \begin{cases} 0 & \exists wk_t\ trans(wi_s) = wk_t \\ w * (wi_s) * (1 - d) & \exists w\ \&wk_t\ distance(wi_s, w) = d\&trans(w) = wk_t \\ w * (wi_s) & otherwise \end{cases} \quad (1)$$

Figure 1: Match Weight of a Word

pair taking t1 as a source and t2 as a target and vice versa.

3 Systems

We have submitted **four** runs in the SemEval CLTE challenge. We used the NaiveBayse algorithm implemented in Mallet[2] to create a classifier that will produce the output for each of the four categories Forward , Backward , Bidirectional and No Entailment.

System 1 As our first system we have created a binary classifier in the classical RTE (Bentivogli et. al., 2011) classification (YES & NO) for each direction Forward and Backward. We assigned the Bidirectional category if both classifiers returned YES. As features the classifiers used only the match scores obtained for the corresponding direction as one and only numeric feature.

System 2 For the second system we trained a classifier using all *four* categories as output. Apart of the scores obtained matching the texts in both directions we have included also a set of eight simple surface measures. Some of these are:

- The length of the two texts.
- The number of common words without translations.
- The cosine similarity between the tokens of the two texts without translation.
- Levenshtein distance between the texts.

System 3 For the third system we trained a classifier using all *four* categories as output. We used as features scores obtained matching the texts in both directions without the surface features used in the System 2.

[2] *http://mallet.cs.umass.edu/*

System 4 In the last system we trained a classifier using all *four* categories as output. We used as features the simple surface measures used in System 2.

The results obtained are shown in Table 1.

4 Analysis

Analyzing the results of our participation we have reached several important conclusions.

The dataset provided by the organizers presented a significant challenge for our system which was adapted from a query similarity approach. The results obtained demonstrate that only a similarity based approach will not provide good results for this task. This fact is also confirmed by the poor performance of the simple similarity measures by themselves (System 4) and by their contribution to the combined run (System 2).

The poor performance of our system can be partially explained also by the small dimensions of the cross-language dictionaries we used. Expanding them with more words and phrases can potentially increase our results.

The classifier with *four* categories clearly outperforms the two directional one (System 1 vs. System 3).

Overall we are not satisfied with our experiment. A radically new approach is needed to address the problem of Cross-Language Textual Entailment, which our similarity based system could not model correctly.

In the future we intend to integrate our approach in our RTE open source system EDITS (Kouylekov et. al., 2011) (Kouylekov and Negri, 2010) available at *http://edits.sf.net*.

Acknowledgments

This work has been partially supported by the ECfunded project Galateas (CIP-ICT PSP-2009-3-250430).

	SPA-ENG	ITA-ENG	FRA-ENG	DEU-ENG
System 1	0.276	0.278	0.278	0.280
System 2	**0.336**	**0.336**	**0.300**	**0.352**
System 3	0.322	0.334	0.298	0.350
System 4	0.268	0.280	0.280	0.274

Table 1: Results obtained.

References

Baroni M., Bisi S. 2004. Using cooccurrence statistics and the web to discover synonyms in technical language In Proceedings of LREC 2004

Bentivogli L., Clark P., Dagan I., Dang H, Giampiccolo D. 2011. The Seventh PASCAL Recognizing Textual Entailment Challenge In Proceedings of TAC 2011

Bingham E., Mannila H. 2001. Random projection in dimensionality reduction: Applications to image and text data. In Knowledge Discovery and Data Mining, ACM Press pages 245250

Bosca A., Dini L. 2008. Query expansion via library classification system. In CLEF 2008. Springer Verlag, LNCS

Cacao Project CACAO - project supported by the eContentplus Programme of the European Commission. *http://www.cacaoproject.eu/*

Curtoni P., Dini L. 2006. Celi participation at clef 2006 Cross language delegated search. In CLEF2006 Working notes.

Deerwester S., Dumais S.T., Furnas G.W., Landauer T.K., Harshman R. 1990. Indexing by latent semantic analysis. Journal of the American Society for Information Science 41 391407

Inkpen D. 2007. A statistical model for near-synonym choice. ACM Trans. Speech Language Processing 4(1)

Kraaij W. 2003. Exploring transitive translation methods. In Vries, A.P.D., ed.: Proceedings of DIR 2003.

Kouylekov M., Negri M. An Open-Source Package for Recognizing Textual Entailment. 48th Annual Meeting of the Association for Computational Linguistics (ACL 2010) ,Uppsala, Sweden. July 11-16, 2010

Kouylekov M., Bosca A., Dini L. 2011. EDITS 3.0 at RTE-7. Proceedings of the Seventh Recognizing Textual Entailment Challenge (2011).

Lin J., Gunopulos D. 2003. Dimensionality reduction by random projection and latent semantic indexing. In proceedings of the Text Mining Workshop, at the 3rd SIAM International Conference on Data Mining.

Mehdad Y.,Negri M., Federico M.. 2011. Using Parallel Corpora for Cross-lingual Textual Entailment. In Proceedings of ACL-HLT 2011.

Negri M., Bentivogli L., Mehdad Y., Giampiccolo D., Marchetti A. 2011. Divide and Conquer: Crowdsourcing the Creation of Cross-Lingual Textual Entailment Corpora. In Proceedings of EMNLP 2011.

Negri M., Marchetti A., Mehdad Y., Bentivogli L., Giampiccolo D. Semeval-2012 Task 8: Cross-lingual Textual Entailment for Content Synchronization. In Proceedings of the 6th International Workshop on Semantic Evaluation (SemEval 2012). 2012.

Turney P.D. 2001. Mining the web for synonyms: Pmi-ir versus lsa on toefl. In EMCL 01: Proceedings of the 12th European Conference on Machine Learning, London, UK, Springer-Verlag pages 491502

FBK: Cross-Lingual Textual Entailment Without Translation

Yashar Mehdad
FBK-irst
Trento , Italy
mehdad@fbk.eu

Matteo Negri
FBK-irst
Trento , Italy
negri@fbk.eu

José Guilherme C. de Souza
FBK-irst & University of Trento
Trento, Italy
desouza@fbk.eu

Abstract

This paper overviews FBK's participation in the Cross-Lingual Textual Entailment for Content Synchronization task organized within SemEval-2012. Our participation is characterized by using cross-lingual matching features extracted from lexical and semantic phrase tables and dependency relations. The features are used for multi-class and binary classification using SVMs. Using a combination of lexical, syntactic, and semantic features to create a cross-lingual textual entailment system, we report on experiments over the provided dataset. Our best run achieved an accuracy of 50.4% on the Spanish-English dataset (with the average score and the median system respectively achieving 40.7% and 34.6%), demonstrating the effectiveness of a "pure" cross-lingual approach that avoids intermediate translations.

1 Introduction

So far, cross-lingual textual entailment (CLTE) (Mehdad et al., 2010) has been applied to: *i)* available TE datasets (*"YES"/"NO"* uni-directional relations between monolingual pairs) transformed into their cross-lingual counterpart by translating the hypotheses into other languages (Negri and Mehdad, 2010), and *ii)* machine translation evaluation datasets (Mehdad et al., 2012b). The content synchronization task represents a challenging application scenario to test the capabilities of CLTE systems, by proposing a richer inventory of phenomena (i.e. *"Bidirectional"/"Forward"/"Backward"/"No entailment"* multi-directional entailment relations).

Multi-directional CLTE recognition can be seen as the identification of semantic equivalence and information disparity between two topically related sentences, at the cross-lingual level. This is a core aspect of the multilingual content synchronization task, which represents a challenging application scenario for a variety of NLP technologies, and a shared research framework for the integration of semantics and MT technology.

The CLTE methods proposed so far adopt either a "pivoting approach" (translation of the two input texts into the same language, as in (Mehdad et al., 2010)), or an "integrated solution" that exploits bilingual phrase tables to capture lexical relations and contextual information (Mehdad et al., 2011). The promising results achieved with the integrated approach still rely on phrasal matching techniques that disregard relevant semantic aspects of the problem. By filling this gap integrating linguistically motivated features, in our participation, we propose an approach that combines lexical, syntactic and semantic features within a machine learning framework (Mehdad et al., 2012a).

Our submitted runs have been produced by training and optimizing multiclass and binary SVM classifiers, over the Spanish-English (Spa-Eng) development set. In both cases, our results were positive, showing significant improvements over the median systems and average scores obtained by participants. The overall results confirm the difficulty of the task, and the potential of our approach in combining linguistically motivated features in a "pure" cross-lingual approach that avoids the recourse to external MT components.

2 Experiments

In our experiment we used the Spa-Eng portion of the dataset described in (Negri et al., 2012; Negri et al., 2011), consisting of 500 multi-directional entailment pairs which was provided to train the systems and 500 pairs for the submission. Each pair in the dataset is annotated with "Bidirectional", "Forward", "Backward" or "No entailment" judgements.

2.1 Approach

Our system builds on the integration of lexical, syntactic and semantic features in a supervised learning framework. Our model builds on three main feature sets, respectively derived from: *i)* phrase tables, *ii)* dependency relations, and *iii)* semantic phrase tables.

1. Phrase Table (PT) matching: through these features, a semantic judgement about entailment is made exclusively on the basis of lexical evidence. The matching features are calculated with a phrase-to-phrase matching process. A phrase in our approach is an *n-gram* composed of one or more (up to 5) consecutive words, excluding punctuation. Entailment decisions are assigned combining phrasal matching scores calculated for each level of *n-grams* (*i.e.* considering the number of *1-grams*, *2-grams*,..., *5-grams* extracted from H that match with *n-grams* in T). Phrasal matches, performed either at the level of tokens, lemmas, or stems, can be of two types:

1. **Exact**: in the case that two phrases are identical at one of the three levels (token, lemma, stem).
2. **Lexical**: in the case that two different phrases can be mapped through entries of the resources used to bridge T and H (*i.e.* phrase tables).

For each phrase in H, we first search for exact matches at the level of token with phrases in T. If no match is found at a token level, the other levels (lemma and stem) are attempted. Then, in case of failure with exact matching, lexical matching is performed at the same three levels. To reduce redundant matches, the lexical matches between pairs of phrases which have already been identified as exact matches are not considered.

Once the matching phase for each *n-gram* level has been concluded, the number of matches $Match_n$ and the number of phrases in the hypothesis $H(n)$ is used to estimate the portion of phrases in H that are matched at each level n (Equation 1).[1] Since languages can express the same meaning with different amounts of words, a phrase with length n in H can match a phrase with any length in T.

$$Match_n = \frac{Match_n}{|H(n)|} \tag{1}$$

In order to build English-Spanish phrase tables for our experiments, we used the freely available Europarl V.4, News Commentary and United Nations Spanish-English parallel corpora released for the WMT10 Shared Translation Task.[2] We run the TreeTagger (Schmid, 1995) and Snowball stemmer (Porter, 2001) for preprocessing, and used the Giza++ (Och and Ney, 2000) toolkit to align the tokenized corpora at the word level. Subsequently, we extracted the bi-lingual phrase table from the aligned corpora using the Moses toolkit (Koehn et al., 2007).

2. Dependency Relation (DR) matching targets the increase of CLTE precision. By adding syntactic constraints to the matching process, DR features aim to reduce wrong matches often occurring at the lexical level. For instance, the contradiction between "*Yahoo acquired Overture*" and "*Overture compró Yahoo*" is evident when syntax (in this case subject-object inversion) is taken into account, but can not be caught by bag-of-words methods.

We define a dependency relation as a triple that connects pairs of words through a grammatical relation. For example, *"nsubj (loves, John)"* is a dependency relation with head *loves* and dependent *John* connected by the relation *nsubj*, which means that *"John"* is the *subject* of *"loves"*. DR matching captures similarities between dependency relations, by combining the syntactic and lexical level. In a valid match, while the relation has to be the same ("exact"

[1] When checking for entailment from H to T, the normalization is carried out dividing the number of n-grams in H by the number of n-grams in T. The same holds for dependency relation and semantic phrase table matching.

[2] http://www.statmt.org/wmt10/

match), the connected words must be either the same or semantically equivalent in the two languages. For example, *"nsubj (loves, John)"* can match *"nsubj (ama, John)"* and *"nsubj (quiere, John)"* but not *"dobj (quiere, John)"*.

Given the dependency tree representations of T and H, for each grammatical relation (*r*) we calculate a DR matching score ($Match_r$, see Equation 2) as the number of matching occurrences of *r* in T and H (respectively $DR_r(T)$ and $DR_r(H)$), divided by the number of occurrences of *r* in H.

$$match_r = \frac{|match(DR_r(T), DR_r(H))|}{|DR_r(H)|} \quad (2)$$

In our experiments, in order to extract dependency relation (DR) matching features, the dependency tree representations of English and Spanish texts have been produced with DepPattern (Otero and Lopez, 2011). We then mapped the sets of dependency relation labels for the English-Spanish parser output into: Adjunct, Determiner, Object, Subject and Preposition. The dictionary, containing about 9M bilingual word pairs, created during the alignment of the English-Spanish parallel corpora provided the lexical knowledge to perform matches when the connected words are different.

3. Semantic Phrase Table (SPT) matching: represents a novel way to leverage the integration of semantics and MT-derived techniques. To this aim, SPT improves CLTE methods relying on pure lexical match, by means of "generalized" phrase tables annotated with shallow semantic labels. Semantically enhanced phrase tables, with entries in the form "*[LABEL]* $word_1 ... word_n$ *[LABEL]*" (*e.g.* "*[ORG] acquired [ORG]*"), are used as a recall-oriented complement to the lexical phrase tables used in machine translation (token-based entries like "*Yahoo acquired Overture*"). The main motivation for this augmentation is that word replacement with semantic tags allows to match T-H tokens that do not occur in the original bilingual parallel corpora used for phrase table extraction. Our hypothesis is that the increase in recall obtained from relaxed matches through semantic tags in place of "out of vocabulary" terms (*e.g.* unseen person, location, or organization names) is an effective way to improve CLTE performance, even at the cost of some loss in precision. Semantic phrase tables, however, have two additional advantages. The first is related to their smaller size and, in turn, its positive impact on system's efficiency, due to the considerable search space reduction. Semantic tags allow to merge different sequences of tokens into a single tag and, consequently, different phrase entries can be unified to one semantic phrase entry. As a result, for instance, the SPT used in our experiments is more than 30% smaller than the original token-based one. The second advantage relates to their potential impact on the confidence of CLTE judgements. Since a semantic tag might cover more than one token in the original entry phrase, SPT entries are often short generalizations of longer original phrases. Consequently, the matching process can benefit from the increased probability of mapping higher order n-grams (*i.e.* those providing more contextual information) from H into T and vice-versa.

Like lexical phrase tables, SPTs are extracted from parallel corpora. As a first step, we annotate the corpora with named-entity taggers (FreeLing in our case (Carreras et al., 2004)) for the source and target languages, replacing named entities with general semantic labels chosen from a coarse-grained taxonomy including the categories: person, location, organization, date and numeric expression. Then, we combine the sequences of unique labels into one single token of the same label, and we run Giza++ (Och and Ney, 2000) to align the resulting semantically augmented corpora. Finally, we extract the semantic phrase table from the augmented aligned corpora using the Moses toolkit (Koehn et al., 2007).

For the matching phase, we first annotate T and H in the same way we labeled our parallel corpora. Then, for each n-gram order (n=1 to 5, excluding punctuation), we use the SPT to calculate a matching score (SPT_match_n, see Equation 3), as the number of n-grams in H that match with phrases in T divided by the number of n-grams in H. The matching algorithm is same as the phrase table matching one.

$$SPT\_match_n = \frac{|SPT_n(H) \cap SPT(T)|}{|SPT_n(H)|} \quad (3)$$

Run	Features	Classification	Parameter selection	Result
1	PT+SPT+DR	Multiclass	Entire training set	0.502
2	PT+SPT+DR	Multiclass	2-fold cross validation	0.490
3	PT+SPT+DR	Binary	Entire training set	**0.504**
4	PT+SPT+DR	Binary	2-fold cross validation	0.500

Table 1: Summary of the submitted runs and results for Spa-Eng dataset.

Forward			**Backward**			**No entailment**			**Bidirectional**		
P	*R*	*F1*	*P*	*R*	*F1*	*P*	*R*	*F1*	*P*	*R*	F1
0.515	**0.704**	0.595	0.546	0.568	0.557	0.447	0.304	0.362	0.482	0.440	0.460

Table 2: Best run's Precision/Recall/F1 scores.

In our supervised learning framework, the computed PT, SPT and DR scores are used as separate features, giving to an SVM classifier, LIBSVM (Chang and Lin, 2011), the possibility to learn optimal feature weights from training data.

2.2 Submitted runs

In order to test our models under different conditions, we set the CLTE problem both as two-way and multiclass classification tasks.

Two-way classification casts multidirectional entailment as a unidirectional problem, where each pair is analyzed checking for entailment both from left to right and from right to left. In this condition, each original test example is correctly classified if both pairs originated from it are correctly judged ("YES-YES" for bidirectional, "YES-NO" for forward, "NO-YES" for backward entailment, and "NO-NO" for no entailment). Two-way classification represents an intuitive solution to capture multidirectional entailment relations but, at the same time, a suboptimal approach in terms of efficiency since two checks are performed for each pair.

Multiclass classification is more efficient, but at the same time more challenging due to the higher difficulty of multiclass learning, especially with small datasets. We also tried to use the parameter selection tool for C-SVM classification using the RBF (radial basis function) kernel, available in LIBSVM package. Our submitted runs and results have been obtained with the settings summarized in table 1.

As can be seen from the table, our best result has been achieved by Run 3 (50.4% accuracy), which is significantly higher than the average and median score over the best runs obtained by participants (44.0% and 40.7% respectively). The detailed results achieved by the best run are reported in Table 2. We can observe that our system is performing well for recognizing the unidirectional entailment (i.e. forward and backward), while the performance drops over no_entailment pairs. The low results for bidirectional cases also reflect the difficulty of discriminating the no_entailment pairs from the bidirectional ones. Looking at the detailed results, we can observe a high recall in the forward and backward entailment cases, which could be explained by the effectiveness of the semantic phrase table matching features aiming at coverage increase over lexical methods. Adding more linguistically motivated features and weighting the non-matched phrases can be a starting point to improve the overall results for other cases (bidirectional and no entailment).

3 Conclusion

In this paper we described our participation to the cross-lingual textual entailment for content synchronization task at SemEval-2012. We approached this task by combining lexical, syntactic and semantic features, at the cross-lingual level without recourse to intermediate translation steps. In spite of the difficulty and novelty of the task, our results on the Spanish-English dataset (0.504) prove the effectiveness of the approach with significant improvements over the reported average and median accuracy scores for the 29 submitted runs (respectively 40.7% and 34.6%).

Acknowledgments

This work has been partially supported by the EU-funded project CoSyne (FP7-ICT-4-248531).

References

X. Carreras, I. Chao, L. Padró, and M. Padró. 2004. FreeLing: An Open-Source Suite of Language Analyzers. In *Proceedings of the 4th International Conference on Language Resources and Evaluation (LREC'04)*.

C.C. Chang and C.J. Lin. 2011. LIBSVM: A Library for Support Vector Machines. *ACM Transactions on Intelligent Systems and Technology (TIST)*, 2(3).

P. Koehn, H. Hoang, A. Birch, C. Callison-Burch, M. Federico, N. Bertoldi, B. Cowan, W. Shen, C. Moran, R. Zens, C. Dyer, O. Bojar, A. Constantin, and E. Herbst. 2007. Moses: Open Source Toolkit for Statistical Machine Translation. In *Proceedings of the 45th Annual Meeting of the ACL on Interactive Poster and Demonstration Sessions (ACL 2007)*.

Y. Mehdad, M. Negri, and M. Federico. 2010. Towards Cross-Lingual Textual Entailment. In *Proceedings of the 11th Annual Conference of the North American Chapter of the Association for Computational Linguistics (NAACL HLT 2010)*.

Y. Mehdad, M. Negri, and M. Federico. 2011. Using Bilingual Parallel Corpora for Cross-Lingual Textual Entailment. In *Proceedings of the 49th Annual Meeting of the Association for Computational Linguistics: Human Language Technologies (ACL HLT 2011)*.

Y. Mehdad, M. Negri, and M. Federico. 2012a. Detecting Semantic Equivalence and Information Disparity in Cross-lingual Documents. In *Proceedings of the ACL'12*.

Y. Mehdad, M. Negri, and M. Federico. 2012b. Match without a Referee: Evaluating MT Adequacy without Reference Translations. In *Proceedings of the Machine Translation Workshop (WMT2012)*.

M. Negri and Y. Mehdad. 2010. Creating a Bi-lingual Entailment Corpus through Translations with Mechanical Turk: $100 for a 10-day rush. In *Proceedings of the NAACL HLT 2010 Workshop on Creating Speech and Language Data with Amazon's Mechanical Turk*, pages 212–216. Association for Computational Linguistics.

M. Negri, L. Bentivogli, Y. Mehdad, D. Giampiccolo, and A. Marchetti. 2011. Divide and conquer: Crowdsourcing the creation of cross-lingual textual entailment corpora. In *Proceedings of EMNLP 2011*.

M. Negri, A. Marchetti, Y. Mehdad, L. Bentivogli, and D. Giampiccolo. 2012. Semeval-2012 Task 8: Cross-lingual Textual Entailment for Content Synchronization. In *Proceedings of the 6th International Workshop on Semantic Evaluation (SemEval 2012)*.

F.J. Och and H. Ney. 2000. Improved Statistical Alignment Models. In *Proceedings of the 38th Annual Meeting of the Association for Computational Linguistics (ACL 2000)*.

P.G. Otero and I.G. Lopez. 2011. A Grammatical Formalism Based on Patterns of Part-of-Speech Tags. *International journal of corpus linguistics*, 16(1).

M. Porter. 2001. Snowball: A language for stemming algorithms.

H. Schmid. 1995. Treetaggera language independent part-of-speech tagger. *Institut für Maschinelle Sprachverarbeitung, Universität Stuttgart*.

BUAP: Lexical and Semantic Similarity for Cross-lingual Textual Entailment

Darnes Vilariño, David Pinto, Mireya Tovar, Saul León, Esteban Castillo
Benemérita Universidad Autónoma de Puebla,
Faculty of Computer Science
14 Sur & Av. San Claudio, CU
Puebla, Puebla, México
{darnes, dpinto, mtovar}@cs.buap.mx
saul.ls@live.com, ecjbuap@gmail.com

Abstract

In this paper we present a report of the two different runs submitted to the task 8 of Semeval 2012 for the evaluation of Cross-lingual Textual Entailment in the framework of Content Synchronization. Both approaches are based on textual similarity, and the entailment judgment (bidirectional, forward, backward or no entailment) is given based on a set of decision rules. The first approach uses textual similarity on the translated and original versions of the texts, whereas the second approach expands the terms by means of synonyms. The evaluation of both approaches show a similar behavior which is still close to the average and median.

1 Introduction

Cross-lingual Textual Entailment (CLTE) has been recently proposed by (Mehdad et al., 2010; Mehdad et al., 2011) as an extension of the Textual Entailment task (Dagan and Glickman, 2004). Given a text (T) and an hypothesis (H) in different languages, the CLTE task consists of determining if the meaning of H can be inferred from the meaning of T. In this paper we present a report of the obtained results after submitting two different runs for the Task 8 of Semeval 2012, named "Cross-lingual Textual Entailment for Content Synchronization" (Negri et al., 2012). In this task, the Cross-Lingual Textual Entailment addresses textual entailment recognition under a new dimension (cross-linguality), and within a new challenging application scenario (content synchronization). The task 8 of Semeval 2012 may be formally defined as follows:

Given a pair of topically related text fragments (T_1 and T_2) in different languages, the task consists of automatically annotating it with one of the following entailment judgments:

- Bidirectional ($T_1 \rightarrow T_2$ & $T_1 \leftarrow T_2$): the two fragments entail each other (semantic equivalence)
- Forward ($T_1 \rightarrow T_2$ & $T1 \, ! \leftarrow T_2$): unidirectional entailment from T_1 to T_2
- Backward ($T_1 \, ! \rightarrow T_2$ & $T_1 \leftarrow T_2$): unidirectional entailment from T_2 to T_1
- No Entailment ($T_1 \, ! \rightarrow T_2$ & $T_1 \, ! \leftarrow T_2$): there is no entailment between T_1 and T_2

In this task, both T_1 and T_2 are assumed to be *TRUE* statements; hence in the dataset there are no contradictory pairs. Cross-lingual datasets are available for the following language combinations:

- Spanish/English (SPA-ENG)
- German/English (DEU-ENG)
- Italian/English (ITA-ENG)
- French/English (FRA-ENG)

The remaining of this paper is structured as follows: Section 2 describes the two different approaches presented in the competition. The obtained results are shown and dicussed in Section 3. Finally, the findings of this work are given in Section 4.

2 Experimental setup

For this experiment we have considered to tackle the CLTE task by means of textual similarity and textual length. In particular, the textual similarity is used to determine whether some kind of entailment exists or not. We have established the threshold of 0.5 for the similarity function as evidence of textual entailment. Since the two sentences to be evaluated are written in two different languages, we have translated each sentence to the other language, so that, we have two sentences in English, and two sentences in the original language (Spanish, German, Italian and French). We have used the Google translate for this purpose [1].

The corpora used in the experiments comes from a cross-lingual Textual Entailment dataset presented in (Negri et al., 2011), and provided by the task organizers. We have employed the training dataset only for adjust some parameters of the system, but the approach is knowledge-based and, therefore, it does not need a training corpus. Both, the training and test corpus contain 500 sentences for each language.

The textual length is used to determine the entailment judgment (bidirectional, forward, backward, no entailment). We have basically, assumed that the length of a text may give some evidence of the type of entailment. The decision rules used for determining the entailment judgment are described in Section 2.3.

In this competition we have submitted two different runs which differ with respect to the type of textual similarity used (lexical vs semantic). The first one, calculates the similarity using only the translated version of the original sentences, whereas the second approach uses text expansion by means of synonyms and, thereafter, it calculates the similarity between the pair of sentences.

Let T_1 be the sentence in the original language, T_2 the T_1 topically related text fragment (written in English). Let T_3 be the English translation of T_1, and T_4 the translation of T_2 to the original language (Spanish, German, Italian and French). The formal description of these two approaches are given as follows.

[1] http://translate.google.com.mx/

2.1 Approach 1: Lexical similarity

The evidence of textual entailment between $T1$ and $T2$ is calculated using two formulae of lexical similarity. Firstly, we determine the similarity between the two texts written in the source language ($SimS$). Additionally, we calculate the lexical similarity between the two sentences written in the target language ($SimT$), in this case English.

Given the limited text length of the text fragments, we have used the Jaccard coefficient as similarity measure. Eq. (1) shows the lexical similarity for the two texts written in the original language, whereas, Eq. (2) presents the Jaccard coefficient for the texts written in English.

$$simS = simJaccard(T_1, T_4) = \frac{|T_1 \cup T_4|}{|T_1 \cap T_4|} \quad (1)$$

$$simT = simJaccard(T_2, T_3) = \frac{|T_2 \cup T_3|}{|T_2 \cap T_3|} \quad (2)$$

2.2 Approach 2: Semantic similarity

In this case we calculate the semantic similarity between the two texts written in the original language ($simS$), and the semantic similarity between the two text fragments written in English ($simT$). The semantic level of similarity is given by considering the synonyms of each term for each sentence (in the original and target language). For this purpose, we have employed five dictionaries containing synonyms for the five different languages considered in the competition (English, Spanish, German, Italian, and French)[2]. In Table 1 we show the number of terms, so as the number of synonyms in average by term considered for each language.

Let $T_1 = w_{1,1}w_{1,2}...w_{1,|T_1|}$, $T_2 = w_{2,1}w_{2,2}...w_{2,|T_2|}$ be the source and target sentences, and let $T_3 = w_{3,1}w_{3,2}...w_{3,|T_3|}$, $T_4 = w_{4,1}w_{4,2}...w_{4,|T_4|}$ be translated version of the original source and target sentences, respectively. The synonyms of a given word $w_{i,k}$, expressed as $synset(w_{i,k})$, are obtained from the aforementioned dictionaries by extracting the synonyms of $w_{i,k}$. In order to obtain a better matching between the terms contained in the text fragments and the terms in the

[2] http://extensions.services.openoffice.org/en/dictionaries

Table 1: Dictionaries of synonyms used for term expansion

Language	*Terms*	*synonyms per term (average)*
English	2,764	60
Spanish	9,887	45
German	21,958	115
Italian	25,724	56
French	36,207	93

dictionary, we have stemmed all the terms using the Porter stemmer.

In order to determine the semantic similarity between two terms of sentences written in the source language ($w_{1,i}$ and $w_{4,j}$) we use Eq. (3). The semantic similariy between two terms of the English sentences are calculated as shown in Eq. (4).

$$sim(w_{1,i}, w_{4,j}) = \begin{cases} 1 & \text{if}\,(w_{1,i} == w_{4,j})\ || \\ & w_{1,i} \in synset(w_{4,j})\ || \\ & w_{4,j} \in synset(w_{1,i}) \\ 0 & \text{otherwise} \end{cases} \tag{3}$$

$$sim(w_{2,i}, w_{3,j}) = \begin{cases} 1 & \text{if}\,(w_{2,i} == w_{3,j})\ || \\ & w_{2,i} \in synset(w_{3,j})\ || \\ & w_{3,j} \in synset(w_{2,i}) \\ 0 & \text{otherwise} \end{cases} \tag{4}$$

Both equations consider the existence of semantic similarity when the two words are identical, or when the some of the two words appear in the synonym set of the other word.

The semantic similarity of the complete text fragments T_1 and T_4 ($simS$) is calculated as shown in Eq. (5). Whereas, the semantic similarity of the complete text fragments T_2 and T_3 ($simT$) is calculated as shown in Eq. (6).

$$simS(T_1, T_4) = \frac{\sum_{i=1}^{|T_1|}\sum_{j=1}^{|T_4|} sim(w_{1,i}, w_{4,j})}{|T_1 \cup T_4|} \tag{5}$$

$$simT(T_2, T_3) = \frac{\sum_{i=1}^{|T_2|}\sum_{j=1}^{|T_3|} sim(w_{2,i}, w_{3,j})}{|T_2 \cup T_3|} \tag{6}$$

2.3 Decision rules

Both approches used the same decision rules in order to determine the entailment judgment for a given pair of text fragments (T_1 and T_2). The following algorithm shows the decision rules used.

Algorithm 1.

If $|T_2| < |T_3|$ then
If ($simT > 0.5$ and $simS > 0.5$)
then **forward**
ElseIf $|T_2| > |T_3|$ then
If ($simT > 0.5$ and $simS > 0.5$)
then **backward**
ElseIf ($|T_1| == |T_4|$ and $|T_2| == |T_3|$) then
If ($simT > 0.5$ and $simS > 0.5$)
then **bidirectional**
Else **no entailment**

As mentioned above, the rules employed the lexical or semantic textual similarity, and the textual length for determining the textual entailment.

3 Results

In Table 2 we show the overall results obtained by the two approaches submitted to the competition. We also show the highest, lowest, average and median overall results obtained in the competition.

	SPA-ENG	*ITA-ENG*	*FRA-ENG*	*DEU-ENG*
Highest	0.632	0.566	0.57	0.558
Average	0.407	0.362	0.366	0.357
Median	0.346	0.336	0.336	0.336
Lowest	0.266	0.278	0.278	0.262
BUAP_run1	0.35	0.336	0.334	0.33
BUAP_run2	0.366	0.344	0.342	0.268

Table 2: Overall statistics obtained in the Task 8 of Semeval 2012

The runs submitted perform similar, but the semantic approach obtained a slightly better performance. The two results are above the median but below the average. We consider that better results may be obtained if the two features used (textual similarity and textual length) were introduced into a supervised classifier, so that, the decision rules were approximated on the basis of a training dataset, instead of the empirical setting done in this work. Future experiments will be carried out in this direction.

4 Discussion and conclusion

Two different approaches for the Cross-lingual Textual Entailment for Content Synchronization task of Semeval 2012 are reported in this paper. We used two features for determining the textual entailment judgment between two texts T_1 and T_2 (written in two different languages). The first approach proposed used lexical similarity, meanwhile the second used semantic similarity by means of term expansion with synonyms.

Even if the performance of both approaches is above the median and slighly below the average, we consider that we may easily improve this performance by using syntactic features of the text fragments. Additionally, we are planning to integrate some supervised techniques based on decision rules which may be trained in a supervised dataset. Future experiments will be executed in this direction.

Acknowledgments

This project has been partially supported by projects CONACYT #106625, #VIAD-ING11-II and VIEP #PIAD-ING11-II.

References

Ido Dagan and Oren Glickman. 2004. Probabilistic Textual Entailment: Generic Applied Modeling of Language Variability. In *Learning Methods for Text Understanding and Mining*, January.

Yashar Mehdad, Matteo Negri, and Marcello Federico. 2010. Towards Cross-Lingual Textual Entailment. In *Human Language Technologies: The 2010 Annual Conference of the North American Chapter of the Association for Computational Linguistics*, pages 321–324, Los Angeles, California, June. Association for Computational Linguistics.

Yashar Mehdad, Matteo Negri, and Marcello Federico. 2011. Using bilingual parallel corpora for cross-lingual textual entailment. In *Proceedings of the 49th Annual Meeting of the Association for Computational Linguistics: Human Language Technologies - Volume 1*, HLT '11, pages 1336–1345, Stroudsburg, PA, USA. Association for Computational Linguistics.

Matteo Negri, Luisa Bentivogli, Yashar Mehdad, Danilo Giampiccolo, and Alessandro Marchetti. 2011. Divide and conquer: crowdsourcing the creation of cross-lingual textual entailment corpora. In *Proceedings of the Conference on Empirical Methods in Natural Language Processing*, EMNLP '11, pages 670–679, Stroudsburg, PA, USA. Association for Computational Linguistics.

M. Negri, A. Marchetti, Y. Mehdad, L. Bentivogli, and D. Giampiccolo. 2012. Semeval-2012 Task 8: Cross-lingual Textual Entailment for Content Synchronization. In *Proceedings of the 6th International Workshop on Semantic Evaluation (SemEval 2012)*.

DirRelCond3: Detecting Textual Entailment Across Languages With Conditions On Directional Text Relatedness Scores

Alpár Perini
'Babeş-Bólyai' University
Cluj-Napoca, Romania
palpar at gmail.com

Abstract

There are relatively few entailment heuristics that exploit the directional nature of the entailment relation. Cross-Lingual Text Entailment (CLTE), besides introducing the extra dimension of cross-linguality, also requires to determine the exact direction of the entailment relation, to provide content synchronization (Negri et al., 2012). Our system uses simple dictionary lookup combined with heuristic conditions to determine the possible directions of entailment between the two texts written in different languages. The key members of the conditions were derived from (Corley and Mihalcea, 2005) formula initially for text similarity, while the entailment condition used as a starting point was that from (Tatar et al., 2009). We show the results obtained by our implementation of this simple and fast approach at the CLTE task from the SemEval-2012 challenge.

1 Introduction

Recognizing textual entailment (TE) is a key task for many natural language processing (NLP) problems. It consists in determining if an entailment relation exists between two texts: the text (T) and the hypothesis (H). The notation $T \rightarrow H$ says that the meaning of H can be inferred from T, in order words, H does not introduce any novel information with respect to T.

Even though RTE challenges lead to many approaches for finding textual entailment, fewer authors exploited the directional character of the entailment relation. Due to the fact that the entailment relation, unlike the equivalence relation, is not symmetric, if $T \rightarrow H$, it is less likely that the reverse $H \rightarrow T$ can also hold (Tatar et al., 2009).

The novel Cross-Lingual Text Entailment (CLTE) approach increases the complexity of the traditional TE task in two way, both of which have been only partially researched and have promise for great potential (Negri et al., 2012):

- the two texts are no longer written in the same language (cross-linguality);
- the entailment needs to be queried in both directions (content synchronization).

Mehdad et al. (2010) presented initial research directions and experiments for the cross-lingual context and explored possible application scenarios.

2 Theoretical Background

The semantic similarity formula from (Corley and Mihalcea, 2005) defines the similarity of a pair of documents differently depending on with respect to which text it is computed. The formula involves only the set of open-class words (nouns, verbs, adjectives and adverbs) from each text.

Based on this text-to-text similarity metric, Tatar et al. (2009) have derived a textual entailment recognition system. The paper demonstrated that in the case when $T \rightarrow H$ holds, the following relation will take place:

$$sim(T, H)_H > sim(T, H)_T \qquad (1)$$

however, the opposite of this statement is not always true, nevertheless it is likely. In (Tatar et al., 2007) a simpler version for the calculus of $sim(T, H)_T$ is used: namely the only case of similarity is the identity (a symmetric relation) and/or the occurrence of a word from a text in the synset of a word in the other text (not symmetric relation).

Perini and Tatar (2009) used the earlier semantic similarity formula (Corley and Mihalcea, 2005) to derive a formula for directional text relatedness score as follows:

$$rel(T, H)_T = \frac{\sum_{pos} \sum_{T_i \in WS^T_{pos}} (maxRel(T_i) \times idf(T_i))}{\sum_{pos} \sum_{T_i \in WS^T_{pos}} idf(T_i)} \quad (2)$$

A mathematically similar formula could be given for $rel(T, H)_H$ (by swapping T for H in the RHS of (2)) which would normally produce a different score. In (2), $maxRel(T_i)$ was defined as the highest *relatedness* between (in this order) word T_i and words from H having the same part of speech as T_i. The relatedness between a pair of words was computed by taking the weight of the highest-ranked WordNet relation that takes place between them. It should be noted that the word order in the pair was strict and that most of the WordNet relations involved in the calculus were not symmetric.

After defining the relatedness of two texts, which depends on the *direction*, Perini and Tatar (2009) introduced a new directional entailment condition, derived from the one in (Tatar et al., 2009):

$$rel(T, H)_T + \sigma > rel(T, H)_H > rel(T, H)_T > \theta \, . \quad (3)$$

3 The DirRelCond3 System

After having presented the necessary theoretical background, in this section we give an overview of our system for CLTE.

The application was implemented in the Java programming language. XML input and output was performed using the DocumentBuilder and the DOM parser from Java.

The first step was to tag both the English and the foreign language sentence using the TreeTagger (Schmid, 1995), which had the advantage that it was fast and it supported all the languages required by this task by providing it with the necessary parameter file, and also had a nice Java wrapper for it (annolab, 2011). The output of the tagger was used to obtain the necessary POS information needed to distinguish the set of open-class words for each sentence. Because the tagset used for each language was different, it was necessary to adapt all the different variants to the four generic classes: noun, verb, adjective and adverb.

The translation step followed for the foreign language sentence, which took words only from these classes and translated them using two dictionaries in some cases. The base dictionary used for word lookup was the FreeDict (FreeDictProject, 2012), for which it was possible to download the language files and use them locally with the help of a server (ktulu, 2006) and a Java client (SourceForge, 2001). The disadvantage of this dictionary was that it had rather few headwords mainly for the Italian and Spanish languages. A later improvement was to use an additional online dictionary as a fall-back, WordReference.com (WordReference.com, 2012), which had a very good headword count for the Italian and French languages, it also provided a very nice JSON API to access it and there was a ready-to-use Java API (SourceForge, 2011) for it that supported caching the results. Although the number of queries per hour was limited, it was very helpful that they approved the caching of the results for the duration of the development. The dictionary lookup process attached to each foreign word that was found the set of English meanings, corresponding to each sense that was found.

The penultimate step was to compute the text relatedness scores with respect to each sentence, $rel(T, H)_T$ and $rel(T, H)_H$, by applying (2). The only modification compared to the original formula was that in the case of the translated word, all the obtained meanings were used and the one producing the maximum relatedness was kept. We have used the following weights (assigned intuitively) for the different WordNet relations in the final *word relatedness score*:

- equals: 1.0;
- same synset: 0.9;
- similar to: 0.85

- hypernyms: 0.8;
- hyponyms: 0.7;
- entailment: 0.7;
- meronyms: 0.5;
- holonyms: 0.5;
- not in WordNet or dictionaries: 0.01.

The final step was to devise a condition based on these two text relatedness scores, similar to (3), but one that would be able to report the entailment vote for both directions:

$$\begin{cases} \text{noentail}, & \text{if } rel(T,H)_T \text{ or } rel(T,H)_H < \theta \\ \text{bidir}, & \text{if } abs(rel(T,H)_T, rel(T,H)_H) < \delta \\ \text{forward}, & \text{if } rel(T,H)_H > rel(T,H)_T + \sigma \\ \text{backwd}, & \text{otherwise} \end{cases} \tag{4}$$

4 Experimental Results

The CLTE task provided researchers with training sets of 500 sentence pairs (one English, one foreign) already annotated with the type of entailment that exists between them ('Forward', 'Backward', 'Bidirectional', 'No entailment'). There was one training set for each French-English, German-English, Italian-English, Spanish-English language combination (Negri et al., 2011). The test set consisted in a similarly structured 500 pairs for each language pair but without annotations. The mentioned entailment judgment types were uniformly distributed, both in the case of the development and the test dataset.

The DirRelCond3 system participated at the CLTE task with four runs for each of the above language combinations. Regarding the results, the accuracies obtained are summarized in table 1 as percentages.

Figures 1, 2, 3, 4 show the precision, recall and F-measure for the 'Forward', 'Backward', 'No entailment' and 'Bidirectional' judgments for each of the language pair combinations in the case of the best run that the DirRelCond3 system has obtained:

The earlier figures pointed out that generally the unidirectional 'Forward' and 'Backward' judgements produced better results than the remaining ones that involved bi-directionality. This is somewhat expected because in this case it is more difficult to correctly judge since there could more possibility for error.

Regarding the individual runs, run 2 added slightly improved dictionary search in addition to run 1, by attempting to look for the lemma form of the word as well, that was available thanks to the

System	*Spa-En*	*Ita-En*	*Fra-En*	*Deu-En*
Run 1	30.0	28.0	36.2	33.6
Run 2	30.0	28.4	36.0	33.6
Run 3	30.0	*33.8*	*38.4*	36.4
Run 4	*34.4*	31.6	*38.4*	*37.4*

Table 1: DirRelCond3 accuracies obtained for CLTE task. Best results are with italic.

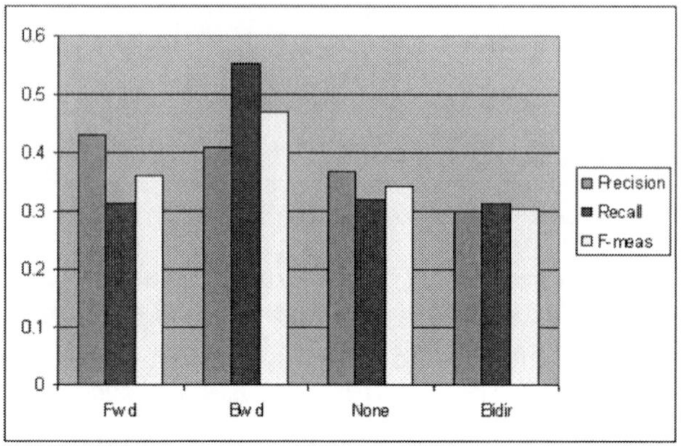

Figure 1: DirRelCond3 German-English pair precision, recall and F-measure values for the different judgments.

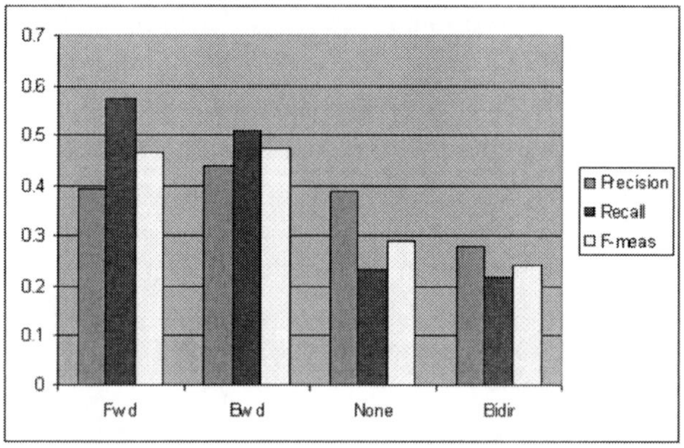

Figure 2: DirRelCond3 French-English pair precision, recall and F-measure values for the different judgments.

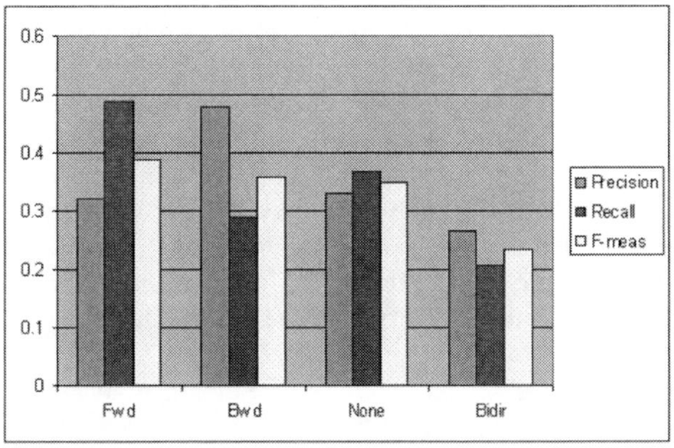

Figure 3: DirRelCond3 Italian-English pair precision, recall and F-measure values for the different judgments.

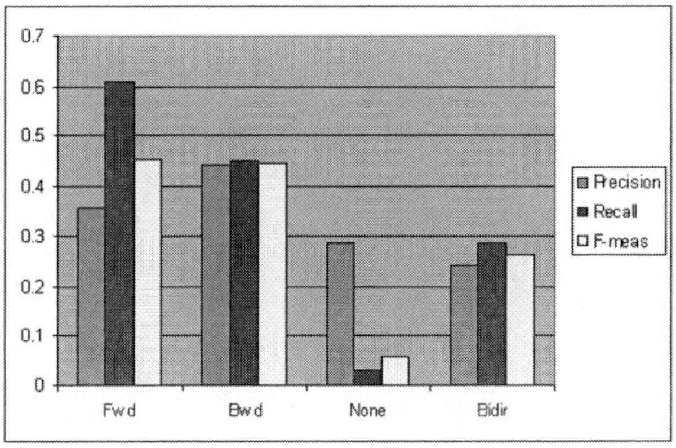

Figure 4: DirRelCond3 Spanish-English pair precision, recall and F-measure values of the different judgments.

TreeTagger tool (Schmid, 1995). In case the word was still not found, but the language was French or Italian and the word contained apostrophe, a lookup was attempted for the part following it.

Run 3 added another slight improvement for German, in case there was still no match for the word, tried to see if the word was a composite containing two parts found in the dictionary, and if so, used the first one.

The first two runs were only using the FreeDict (FreeDictProject, 2012) dictionary, while starting with run 3, Italian and French language words, in case not found, could also be searched in the WordReference (WordReference.com, 2012) online dictionary.

The first three runs were using entailment conditions common to all language combinations. The values of the parameters were chosen based on the CLTE development dataset (Negri et al., 2011) and were as follows:
$\theta = 0.5, \delta = 0.03, \sigma = 0.0$.
The final run used empirically-tuned conditions for each language pair in the dataset. The θ threshold needed to be lowered for Spanish since many words were not found in FreeDict, which was the only one we had available for use, so the relatedness scores were rather smaller. The values are summarized in table 2 below:

Param	*Spa-En*	*Ita-En*	*Fra-En*	*Deu-En*
θ	0.25	0.55	0.5	0.45
δ	0.03	0.025	0.03	0.04
σ	0.0	0.2	0.0	0.0

Table 2: DirRelCond3 – Run 4 condition parameters.

5 Conclusions and Future Work

In this paper we have presented the DirRelCond3 systems that participated at the CLTE task (Negri et al., 2012) from SemEval-2012. The system was a good example of how an approach for mono-lingual text entailment can be adapted to the new dimension of cross-linguality. It would have been possible to use a MT tool and then do the entailment detection steps all in English as was the original approach, however we expected that that would introduce more possibility for error than translating and comparing words with the same POS.

The overall best result for each language that we have obtained was around the median of all the system runs that were submitted to the CLTE task. The best accuracy obtained by our system was for the French-English pair with 38.4%, but well below the accuracy of the best systems. Generally the results involving German and French were somewhat better than the other two languages. In the case of Spanish this could easily be caused by the significantly smaller dictionary that was available, while for Italian, after relying also on WordReference.com this was no longer the case. A possiblity is that some language particularities were affecting the results (e.g. high usage of apostrophe) but perhaps the entailment heuristic thresholds were not the best either.

Finally, there are several possible improvements.

Firstly, in case the dictionary provides POS information for the translation, that could be used to retain only those senses that have the same POS as the original word. For some languages, particularly for Spanish, it would be helpful to rely on dictionaries with more headwords. Secondly, we can use the inverse document frequency counts for words, obtained either from the CLTE development corpus or from web searches, because currently that was simply one. Thirdly, both the empirically obtained conditions can be further tuned, manually or by means of learning, separately for each language pair. Fourthly, when computing the word relatedness scores, the weights of the WordNet relations could be further adjusted for each language, empirically, or again by learning.

References

annolab. 2011. tt4j – TreeTagger for Java. http://code.google.com/p/tt4j/.

Courtney Corley and Rada Mihalcea. 2005. Measuring the semantic similarity of texts. In Ann Arbor, editor, *Proceedings of the ACL Workshop on Empirical Modeling of Semantic Equivalence and Entailment*, pages 13–18.

FreeDictProject. 2012. FreeDict – free bilingual dictionaries. http://www.freedict.org/en/.

ktulu. 2006. JavaDICT – Java DICT Client. http://ktulu.com.ar/blog/projects/javadictd/.

Yashar Mehdad, Matteo Negri, and Marcello Federico. 2010. Towards cross-lingual textual entailment. In *Human Language Technologies: The 2010 Annual Conference of the North American Chapter of the Association for Computational Linguistics*, pages 321–324, Los Angeles, California, June. Association for Computational Linguistics.

Matteo Negri, Luisa Bentivogli, Yashar Mehdad, Danilo Giampiccolo, and Alessandro Marchetti. 2011. Divide and conquer: Crowdsourcing the creation of cross-lingual textual entailment corpora. In *Proceedings of the 2011 Conference on Empirical Methods in Natural Language Processing*, pages 670–679, Edinburgh, Scotland, UK., July. Association for Computational Linguistics.

M. Negri, A. Marchetti, Y. Mehdad, L. Bentivogli, and D. Giampiccolo. 2012. Semeval-2012 Task 8: Cross-lingual Textual Entailment for Content Synchronization. In *Proceedings of the 6th International Workshop on Semantic Evaluation (SemEval 2012)*.

Alpar Perini and Doina Tatar. 2009. Textual entailment as a directional relation revisited. *Knowledge Engineering: Principles and Techniques*, pages 69–72.

Helmut Schmid. 1995. TreeTagger – a language independent part-of-speech tagger. http://www.ims.uni-stuttgart.de/projekte/corplex/TreeTagger/.

SourceForge. 2001. JDictClient – JAVA dict server client. http://sourceforge.net/projects/jdictclient/.

SourceForge. 2011. WordReference Java API. http://sourceforge.net/projects/wordrefapi/.

Doina Tatar, Gabriela Serban, and M. Lupea. 2007. Text entailment verification with text similarities. In Babes-Bolyai University, editor, *Knowledge Engineering: Principles and Techniques*, pages 33–40. Cluj University Press.

Doina Tatar, Gabriela Serban, A. Mihis, and Rada Mihalcea. 2009. Textual entailment as a directional relation. *Journal of Research and Practice in Information Technology*, 41(1):17–28.

WordReference.com. 2012. WordReference.com – Online Language Dictionaries. http://www.wordreference.com/.

ICT: A Translation based Method for Cross-lingual Textual Entailment

Fandong Meng, Hao Xiong and Qun Liu
Key Lab. of Intelligent Information Processing
Institute of Computing Technology
Chinese Academy of Sciences
P.O. Box 2704, Beijing 100190, China
{mengfandong,xionghao,liuqun}@ict.ac.cn

Abstract

In this paper, we present our system description in task of Cross-lingual Textual Entailment. The goal of this task is to detect entailment relations between two sentences written in different languages. To accomplish this goal, we first translate sentences written in foreign languages into English. Then, we use EDITS[1], an open source package, to recognize entailment relations. Since EDITS only draws monodirectional relations while the task requires bidirectional prediction, thus we exchange the hypothesis and test to detect entailment in another direction. Experimental results show that our method achieves promising results but not perfect results compared to other participants.

1 Introduction

In Cross-Lingual Textual Entailment task (CLTE) of 2012, the organizers hold a task for Cross-Lingual Textual Entailment. The Cross-Lingual Textual Entailment task addresses textual entailment (TE) recognition under a new dimension (cross-linguality), and within a new challenging application scenario (content synchronization) Readers can refer to M. Negri et al. 2012.s., for more detailed introduction. [1]

Textual entailment, on the other hand, recognize, generate, or extract pairs of natural language expressions, and infer that if one element is true, whether the other element is also true. Several methods are proposed by previous researchers. There have been some workshops on textual entailment in recent years. The recognizing textual entailment challenges (Bar-Haim et al. 2006; Giampiccolo, Magnini, Dagan, & Dolan, 2007; Giampiccolo, Dang, Magnini, Dagan, & Dolan, 2008), currently in the 7th year, provide additional significant thrust. Consequently, there are a large number of published articles, proposed methods, and resources related to textual entailment. A special issue on textual entailment was also recently published, and its editorial provides a brief overview of textual entailment methods (Dagan, Dolan, Magnini, & Roth, 2009).

Textual entailment recognizers judge whether or not two given language expressions constitute a correct textual entailment pair. Different methods may operate at different levels of representation of the input expressions. For example, they may treat the input expressions simply as surface strings, they may operate on syntactic or semantic representations of the input expressions, or on representations combining information from different

[1]http://edits.fbk.eu/

levels. Logic-based approach is to map the language expressions to logical meaning representations, and then rely on logical entailment checks, possibly by invoking theorem provers (Rinaldi et al., 2003; Bos & Markert, 2005; Tatu & Moldovan, 2005, 2007). An alternative to use logical meaning representations is to start by mapping each word of the input language expressions to a vector that shows how strongly the word co-occurs with particular other words in corpora (Lin, 1998b), possibly also taking into account syntactic information, for example requiring that the co-occurring words participate in particular syntactic dependencies (Pad´o & Lapata, 2007). Several textual entailment recognizing methods operate directly on the input surface strings. For example, they compute the string edit distance (Levenshtein, 1966) of the two input strings, the number of their common words, or combinations of several string similarity measures (Malakasiotis & Androutsopoulos, 2007). Dependency grammar parsers (Melcuk, 1987; Kubler, McDonald, & Nivre, 2009) are popular in textual entailment research. However, cross-lingual textual entailment brings some problems on past algorithms. On the other hand, many methods can't be applied to it directly.

In this paper, we propose a translation based method for cross-lingual textual entailment, which has been described in Mehdad et al. 2010. First, we translate one part of the text, which termed as "t1" and written in one language, into English, which termed as "t2". Then, we use EDITS, an open source package, to recognize entailment relations between two parts. Large-scale experiments are conducted on four language pairs, French-English, Spanish-English, Italian-English and German-English. Although our method achieves promising results reported by organizers, it is still far from perfect compared to other participants.

The remainder of this paper is organized as follows. We describe our system framework in section 2. We report experimental results in section 3 and draw our conclusions in the last section.

2 System Description

Figure 1 illustrates the overall framework of our system, where a machine translation model is employed to translate foreign language into English, since original EDITS could only deal with the text in the same language pairs.

In the following of this section, we will describe the translation module and configuration of EDITS in details.

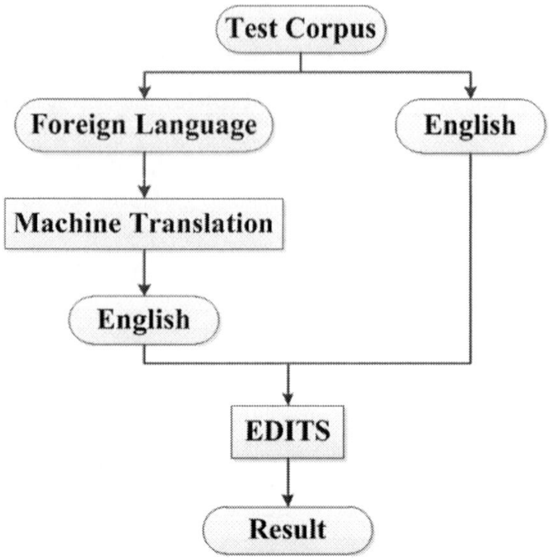

Figure 1: The framework of our system.

2.1 Machine Translation

Recently, machine translation has attracted intensive attention and has been well studied in natural language community. Effective models, such as Phrase-Based model (Koehn et al., 2003), Hierarchical Phrase-Based model (HPB) (Chiang, 2005), and Syntax-Based (Liu et al., 2006) model have been proposed to improve the translation quality. However, since current translation models require parallel corpus to extract translation rules, while parallel corpus on some language pairs such as Italian-English and Spanish-English are hard to obtain, therefore, we could use Google Translation Toolkit (GTT) to generate translation.

Specifically, WMT[2] released some bilingual corpus for training, thus we use some portion to train a French-English translation engine using hierarchical phrase-based model. We also exploit system combination technique (A Rosti et al., 2007) to improve translation quality via blending the translation of our models and GTT's. It is worth noting that GTT only gives 1-best translation, thus we duplicate 50 times to generate 50-best for system combination.

[2] http://www.statmt.org/wmt12/

2.2 Textual Entailment

Many methods have been proposed to recognize textual entailment relations between two expressions written in the same language. Since edit distance algorithms are effective on this task, we choose this method. And we use popular toolkit, EDITS, to accomplish the textual entailment task.

EDITS is an open source software, which is used for recognizing entailment relations between two parts of text, termed as "T" and "H". The system is based on the edit distance algorithms, and computes the "T"-"H" distance as the cost of the edit operations (i.e. insertion, deletion and substitution) that are necessary to transform "T" into "H". EDITS requires that three modules are defined: an edit distance algorithm, a cost scheme for the three edit operations, and a set of rules expressing either entailment or contradiction. Each module can be easily configured by the user as well as the system parameters. EDITS can work at different levels of complexity, depending on the linguistic analysis carried on over "T" and "H". Both linguistic processors and semantic resources that are available to the user can be integrated within EDITS, resulting in a flexible, modular and extensible approach to textual entailment.

T: "Yahoo acquired Overture"
H: "Yahoo owns Overture"

Figure 2: An Example of two expressions EDITS can recognize.

Figure 2 shows an example of two expressions that EDITS can recognize. EDITS will give an answer that whether expression "H" is true given that expression "T" is true. The result is a Boolean value. If "H" is true given "T" is true, then the result is "YES", otherwise "NO".

EDITS implements a distance-based framework which assumes that the probability of an entailment relation between a given "T"-"H" pair is inversely proportional to the distance between "T" and "H" (i.e. the higher the distance, the lower is the probability of entailment). Within this framework the system implements and harmonizes different approaches to distance computation, providing both edit distance algorithms, and similarity algorithms. Each algorithm returns a normalized distance score (a number between 0 and 1). At a training stage, distance scores calculated over annotated "T"-"H" pairs are used to estimate a threshold that best separates positive from negative examples. The threshold, which is stored in a Model, is used at a test stage to assign an entailment judgment and a confidence score to each test pair.

```
<module name="distance">
  <module name="overlap">
    <module name="default_matcher">
      <option name="ignore_case" value="true"/>
      <option name="optimize" value="METRIC"/>
    </module>
    <module name="default_weight">
      <option name="idf_index" value="en"/>
      <option name="stopwords" value="en"/>
    </module>
  </module>
</module>
```

Figure 3: Our configured file for training

Figure 3 shows our configuration file for training models, we choose "distance" algorithm in EDITS, and "default_matcher", and "ignore_case" , and some other default but effective configured parameters.

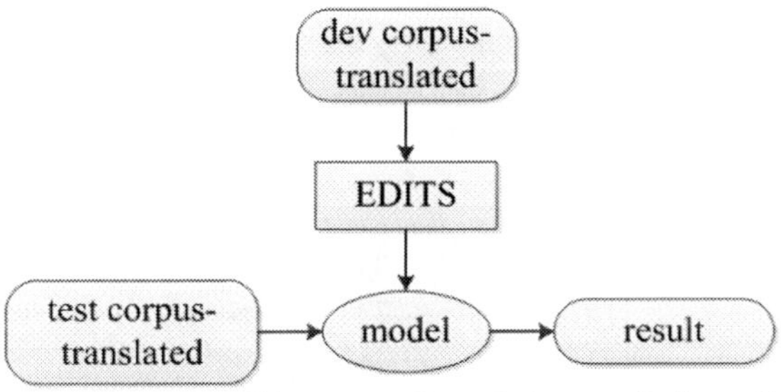

Figure 4: The overall training and decoding procedure in our system.

Figure 4 shows our training and decoding procedure. As EDITS can only recognize textual entailment from one part to the other, we manually change the tag "H" with "T", and generate the results again, and then compute two parts' entailment relations. For example, if "T"-"H" is "YES", and "H"-"T" is "NO", then the entailment result between them is "forward"; if "T"-"H" is "NO", and "H"-"T" is "YES", then the entailment result between them is "backward"; if both "T"-"H" and "H"-"T" are "YES", the result is "bidirectional";

otherwise "no_entailment".

3 Experiments and Results

Since organizers of SemEval 2012 task 8 supply a piece of data for training, we thus exploit it to optimize parameters for EDITS. Table 1 shows the F-measure score of training set analyzed by EDITS, where "FE" represents French-English, "SE" represents Spanish-English, "IE" represents Italian-English and "GE" represents Italian-English.

Judgment	FE	SE	IE	GE
forward	0.339	0.373	0.440	0.327
backward	0.611	0.574	0.493	0.552
no_entailment	0.533	0.535	0.494	0.494
bidirectional	0.515	0.502	0.506	0.495
Overall	**0.516**	**0.506**	**0.488**	**0.482**

Table 1: Results on training set.

From Table 1, we can see that the performance of "forward" prediction is lower than others. One explanation is that the "T" is translated from foreign language, which is error unavoidable. Thus some rules used for checking "T", such as stopword list will be disabled. Then it is possible to induce a "NO" relation between "T" and "H" that results in lower recall of "forward".

Since for French-English, we build a system combination for improving the quality of translation. Table 2 shows the results of BLEU score of translation quality, and F-score of entailment judgment.

System	BLEU4	F-score
HPB	28.74	0.496
GTT	30.08	0.508
COMB	**30.57**	**0.516**

Table 2: Performance of different translation model, where COMB represents system combination.

From table 2, we find that the translation quality slightly affect the correctness of entailment judgment. However, the difference of performance in entailment judgment is smaller than that in translation quality. We explain that the translation models exploit phrase-based rules to direct the translation, and the translation errors mainly come from the disorder between each phrases. While a distance based entailment model generally considers the similarity of phrases between test and hypothesis, thus the disorder of phrases influences the judgment slightly.

Using the given training data for tuning parameters, table 3 to table 6 shows the detailed experimental results on testing data, where P represents precision and R indicates recall, and both of them are calculated by given evaluation script.

French -- English			
Judgment	**P**	**R**	**F-measure**
forward	0.750	0.192	0.306
backward	0.517	0.496	0.506
no_entailment	0.385	0.656	0.485
bidirectional	0.444	0.480	0.462
Overall	0.456		
Best System	0.570		

Table 3: Test results on French-English

Spanish -- English			
Judgment	**P**	**R**	**F-measure**
forward	0.750	0.240	0.364
backward	0.440	0.472	0.456
no_entailment	0.395	0.560	0.464
bidirectional	0.436	0.520	0.474
Overall	0.448		
Best System	0.632		

Table 4: Test results on Spanish-English

Italian – English			
Judgment	**P**	**R**	**F-measure**
forward	0.661	0.296	0.409
backward	0.554	0.368	0.442
no_entailment	0.427	0.448	0.438
bidirectional	0.383	0.704	0.496
Overall	0.454		
Best System	0.566		

Table 5: Test results on Italian-English

German – English			
Judgment	**P**	**R**	**F-measure**
forward	0.718	0.224	0.341
backward	0.493	0.552	0.521
no_entailment	0.390	0.512	0.443
bidirectional	0.439	0.552	0.489
Overall	0.460		
Best System	0.558		

Table 6: Test results on German-English

After given golden testing reference, we also investigate the effect of training set to testing set. We choose testing set from RTE1 and RTE2, both are English text, as our training set for optimization of EDITS, and the overall results are shown in table 7 to table 10, where CLTE is training set given by this year's organizers.

French -- English			
Judgment	**CLTE**	**RTE1**	**RTE2**
forward	0.306	0.248	0.289
backward	0.506	0.425	0.440
no_entailment	0.485	0.481	0.485
bidirectional	0.462	**0.472**	**0.485**
Overall	0.456	0.430	0.444

Table 7: Test results on French-English given different training set.

Spanish – English			
Judgment	**CLTE**	**RTE1**	**RTE2**
forward	0.364	0.293	0.297
backward	0.456	0.332	0.372
no_entailment	0.464	0.386	0.427
bidirectional	0.474	**0.484**	**0.503**
Overall	0.448	0.400	0.424

Table 8: Test results on Spanish-English given different training set.

Italian -- English			
Judgment	**CLTE**	**RTE1**	**RTE2**
forward	0.409	0.333	0.335
backward	0.442	0.394	0.436
no_entailment	0.438	0.410	0.421
bidirectional	0.496	0.474	0.480
Overall	0.454	0.420	0.432

Table 9: Test results on Italian-English given different training set.

German – English			
Judgment	**CLTE**	**RTE1**	**RTE2**
forward	0.341	**0.377**	**0.425**
backward	0.521	0.372	0.460
no_entailment	0.443	0.437	**0.457**
bidirectional	0.489	0.487	**0.508**
Overall	0.460	0.434	**0.470**

Table 10: Test results on German-English given different training set.

Results in table 7 and table 8 shows that models trained on "CLTE" have better performance than those trained on RTE1 and RTE2, except "bidirectional" judgment type. In Table 9, all results decoding by models trained on "CLTE" are the best. And in Table 10, only a few results decoding by models trained on "RTE1" and "RTE2" have higher score. The reason may be that, the test corpora are bilingual, there are some errors in the machine translation procedure when translate one part of the test from its language into the other. When training on these bilingual text and decoding these bilingual text, these two procedure have error consistency. Some errors may be counteracted. If we train on RTE, a standard monolingual text, and decode a bilingual text, more errors may exist between the two procedures. So we believe that, if we use translation based strategy (machine translation and monolingual textual entailment) to generate cross-lingual textual entailment, we should use translation based strategy to train models, rather than use standard monolingual texts.

4 Conclusion

In this paper, we demonstrate our system framework for this year's cross-lingual textual entailment task. We propose a translation based model to address cross-lingual entailment. We first translate all foreign languages into English, and then employ EDITS to induce entailment relations. Experiments show that our method achieves promising results but not perfect results compared to other participants.

Acknowledgments

The authors were supported by National Science Foundation of China, Contracts 90920004, and High-Technology R&D Program (863) Project No 2011AA01A207 and 2012BAH39B03. We thank organizers for their generous supplied resources and arduous preparation. We also thank anonymous reviewers for their thoughtful suggestions.

References

Bar-Haim, R., Dagan, I., Dolan, B., Ferro, L., Giampiccolo, D., Magnini, B., & Szpektor, I. 2006.*The 2nd PASCAL recognising textual entailment challenge.* In Proc. of the 2nd PASCAL ChallengesWorkshop on Recognising Textual Entailment, Venice, Italy.

Bos, J., & Markert, K. 2005. *Recognising textual entailment with logical inference.* In Proc. Of the Conf. on HLT and EMNLP, pp. 628–635, Vancouver, BC, Canada.

Dagan, I., Dolan, B., Magnini, B., & Roth, D. 2009. Recognizing textual entailment: Rational,evaluation and approaches. Nat. Lang. Engineering, 15(4), i–xvii. Editorial of the special issue on Textual Entailment.

David Chiang. 2005. A hierarchical phrase-based model for statistical machine translation. In Proceedings of ACL 2005, pages 263–270.

Giampiccolo, D., Dang, H., Magnini, B., Dagan, I., & Dolan, B. 2008. *The fourth PASCAL recognizing textual entailment challenge.* In Proc. of the Text Analysis Conference, pp. 1–9, Gaithersburg, MD.

Giampiccolo, D., Magnini, B., Dagan, I., & Dolan, B. 2007. *The third PASCAL recognizing textual entailment challenge.* In Proc. of the ACL-Pascal Workshop on Textual Entailment and Paraphrasing, pp. 1–9, Prague, Czech Republic.

I. Dagan and O. Glickman.2004. *Probabilistic Textual Entailment: Generic Applied Modeling of Language Variability.* Proceedings of the PASCAL Workshop of Learning Methods for Text Understanding and Mining.

Ion Androutsopoulos and Prodromos Malakasiotis. 2010.*A Survey of Paraphrasing and Textual Entailment Methids.* Journal of Artificial Intelligence Research, 32, 135-187.

Kouylekov, M. and Negri, M. 2010. *An open-source package for recognizing textual entailment.* Proceedings of the ACL 2010 System Demonstrations, 42-47.

Kubler, S., McDonald, R., & Nivre, J. 2009. *Dependency Parsing. Synthesis Lectures on HLT.* Morgan and Claypool Publishers.

Levenshtein, V. 1966. *Binary codes capable of correcting deletions, insertions, and reversals.* Soviet Physice-Doklady, 10, 707–710.

Lin, D. 1998b. *An information-theoretic definition of similarity.* In Proc. of the 15th Int. Conf. on Machine Learning, pp. 296–304, Madison, WI. Morgan Kaufmann, San Francisco, CA.

Malakasiotis, P., & Androutsopoulos, I. 2007. *Learning textual entailment using SVMs and string similarity measures.* In Proc. of the ACL-PASCAL Workshop on Textual Entailment and Paraphrasing, pp. 42–47, Prague. ACL.

Mehdad, Y. and Negri, M. and Federico, M.2010. *Towards Cross-Lingual Textual Entailment. Human Language Technologies.*The 2010 Annual Conference of the NAACL. 321-324.

Mehdad, Y. and Negri, M. and Federico, M.2011. *Using bilingual parallel corpora for cross-lingual textual entailment.* Proceedings of ACL-HLT

Melcuk, I. 1987. *Dependency Syntax: Theory and Practice.* State University of New York Press.

M. Negri, A. Marchetti, Y. Mehdad, L. Bentivogli, and D. Giampiccolo.2012. *Semeval-2012 Task 8: Crossligual Textual Entailment for Content Synchronizatio n.* In Proceedings of the 6th International Workshop on Semantic Evaluation (SemEval 2012).

Negri, M. and Bentivogli, L. and Mehdad, Y. and Giampiccolo, D. and Marchetti, A.2011. *Divide and conquer: crowdsourcing the creation of cross-lingual textual entailment corpora.* Proceedings of the Conference on Empirical Methods in Natural Language Processing.

Pad′o, S., & Lapata, M. 2007. *Dependency-based construction of semantic space models.* Comp. Ling., 33(2), 161–199.

Philipp Koehn, Franz J. Och, and Daniel Marcu. 2003. *Statistical phrase-based translation.* In Proceedings of the 2003 Human Language Technology Conference of the North American Chapter of the Association for Computational Linguistics, Edmonton, Canada, July.

Rinaldi, F., Dowdall, J., Kaljurand, K., Hess, M., & Molla, D. 2003. *Exploiting paraphrases in a question answering system.* In Proc. of the 2nd Int. Workshop in Paraphrasing, pp. 25–32, Saporo, Japan.

Rosti, A. and Matsoukas, S. and Schwartz, R. *Improved word-level system combination for machine translation,* ANNUAL MEETING-ASSOCIATION FOR COMPUTATIONAL LINGUISTICS,2007

Tatu, M., & Moldovan, D. 2005. *A semantic approach to recognizing textual entailment.* In Proc. of the Conf. on HLT and EMNLP, pp. 371–378, Vancouver, Canada.

Tatu, M., & Moldovan, D. 2007. *COGEX at RTE 3.* In Proc. of the ACL-PASCAL Workshop on Textual Entailment and Paraphrasing, pp. 22–27, Prague, Czech Republic.

Yang Liu, Qun Liu, and Shouxun Lin. 2006. Tree–to string alignment template for statistical machine translation. In Proceedings of ACL 2006, pages 609–616, Sydney, Australia, July.

SAGAN: A Machine Translation Approach for Cross-Lingual Textual Entailment

Julio Castillo[1,2] **and Marina Cardenas**[2]
[1]UNC-FaMAF, Argentina
[2]UTN-FRC, Argentina
{jotacastillo, ing.marinacardenas}@gmail.com

Abstract

This paper describes our participation in the task denominated Cross-Lingual Textual Entailment (CLTE) for content synchronization. We represent an approach to CLTE using machine translation to tackle the problem of multilinguality. Our system resides on machine learning and in the use of WordNet as semantic source knowledge. Results are very promising always achieving results above mean score.

1 Introduction

This paper describes the participation of Sagan, a TE and CLTE system, in the new task of Cross Lingual Textual Entailment for Content Synchronization.

The objective of the Recognizing Textual Entailment (RTE) task (Dagan et al., 2006) is determining whether the meaning of a text fragment that we call hypothesis H can be inferred from another text fragment T. In this manner, we say that T entails H, if a person reading T would infer that H is most likely true. Thus, this definition assumes common human understanding of language and common background knowledge.

In that context, Cross-Lingual Textual Entailment addresses textual entailment recognition in the challenging application scenario of content synchronization. Thus, CLTE constitutes a generalization of Textual Entailment task (also Monolingual Textual Entailment) , but envisioning a larger number of application areas in NLP, including question answering, information retrieval, information extraction, and document summarization, across different languages.

Content synchronization could be used to keep consistence among documents written in different languages. For example, a CLTE system can be used in Wikipedia articles to inform lectors which information is absent or inconsistent in comparison to other page in a different language.

This new task has to face more additional issues than monolingual TE. Among them, we emphasize the ambiguity, polysemy, and coverage of the resources. Another additional problem is the necessity for semantic inference across languages, and the limited availability of multilingual knowledge resources.

The CLTE for content synchronization specifically consist on determining the entailment relationship between two text fragment T1 and T2 which are assumed belong a related topic.

Four alternatives are possible in this relationship:

- Bidirectional : It is a semantic equivalence between T1 and T2.
- Forward : It is an unidirectional entailment from T1 to T2.
- Backward: It is an unidirectional entailment from T2 to T1.
- No Entailment: It means that there is no entailment between T1 and T2.

The paper is organized as follows: Section 2 describes the relevant work done on cross-lingual textual entailment and related tasks, Section 3 describes the architecture of the system, then Section 4 shows experiments and results; and finally Section 5 summarize some conclusions and future work.

2 Related work

In this section we briefly describe two tasks that are closely related to CLTE.

2.1 Textual Entailment

The objective of the recognizing textual entailment (RTE) task (Dagan et al., 2006) is determining whether or not the meaning of a ''hypothesis'' (H) can be inferred from a ''text'' (T).

The two-way RTE task consists of deciding whether: T entails H, in which case the pair will be marked as ''Entailment'', otherwise the pair will be marked as ''No Entailment''. This definition of entailment is based on (and assumes) average human understanding of language as well as average background knowledge.

Recently the RTE4 Challenge has changed to a three-way task (Bentivogli et al, 2009) that consists in distinguishing among ''Entailment'', ''Contradiction'' and ''Unknown'' when there is no information to accept or reject the hypothesis.

The RTE challenge has mutated over the years, aiming at accomplishing more accurate and specific solutions; in 2009 the organizers proposed a pilot task, the Textual Entailment Search (Bentivogli et al, 2009), consisting in finding all the sentences in a set of documents that entail a given Hypothesis and since 2010 there is a Novelty Detection Task, which means that RTE systems are required to judge whether the information contained in each H is novel with respect to (i.e., not entailed by) the information contained in the corpus.

Thus, the new CLTE task can be thought as a generalized problem of RTE, which has to face new challenges as scarcity of resources to multilingual scenario, among others issues.

2.2 Semantic Textual Similarity

The pilot task STS was recently defined in Semeval 2012 (Aguirre et al., 2012) and has as main objective measuring the degree of semantic equivalence between two text fragments. STS is related to both Recognizing Textual Entailment (RTE) and Paraphrase Recognition, but has the advantage of being a more suitable model for multiple NLP applications.

As mentioned before, the goal of the RTE task (Bentivogli et al, 2009) is determining whether the meaning of a hypothesis H can be inferred from a text T. The main difference with STS is that STS consists in determining how similar two text fragments are, in a range from 5 (total semantic equivalence) to 0 (no relation). Thus, STS mainly differs from TE and Paraphrasing in that the classification is graded instead of binary and also STS assumes bidirectional equivalence but in TE the equivalence is only directional. In this manner, STS is filling the gap between TE and Paraphrase.

2.3 Cross-Lingual Textual Entailment

There are a few previous works on CLTE, the first one was the definition of this new task (Mehdad et al., 2010). Afterwards, the creation of CLTE corpus by using Mechanical Turk is described on (Negri et al., 2011) and a corpus freely available for CLTE is published (Castillo, 2011).

To our knowledge, two approach are proposed to address this new challenging task, one consist of using machine translation to move on towards monolingual textual entailment scenario and then apply classic techniques for RTE (Mehdad et al., 2010; Castillo and Cardenas, 2011), and the other is based on exploit databases of paraphrases (Mehdad et al., 2011). Both techniques obtained similar results and the accuracy achieved by them is not a statically significant difference.

In previous work (Castillo, 2010; Castillo and Cardenas, 2011) we addressed the CLTE focusing on English-Spanish language pair and released a bilingual textual entailment corpus. This paper is based on that work in order to tackling the problem across different language pairs Spanish-English (SPA-ENG), Italian-English (ITA-ENG), French-English (FRA-ENG) and German-English (GER-ENG) and we also used an approach based on machine translation.

3 System architecture

Sagan is a CLTE system (Castillo and Cardenas, 2010) which has taken part of several challenges, including the Textual Analysis Conference 2009 and TAC 2010, and the Semantic Textual Similarity Semeval 2012 (Aguirre et al., 2012; Castillo and Estrella, 2012) and Cross Lingual Textual Entailment for content synchronization as part of the Semeval 2012 (Negri et al., 2012).

The system is based on a machine learning approach and it utilizes eight WordNet-based (Fellbaum, 1998) similarity measures with the purpose of obtaining the maximum similarity between two concepts. We used SVM as classifier with polynomial kernel. The system determines the entailment based on the semantic similarity of two texts (T,H) viewed as a function of the semantic similarity of the constituent words of both phrases. Thereby, we expect that combining word to word similarity metrics to text level would be a good indicator of text to text similarity.

These text-to-text similarity measures are based on the following word-to-word similarity metrics: (Resnik, 1995), (Lin, 1997), (Jiang and Conrath, 1997), (Pirrò and Seco, 2008), (Wu and Palmer, 1994), Path Metric, (Leacock and Chodorow, 1998), and a semantic similarity to sentence level named SemSim (Castillo and Cardenas, 2010).

Additional information about how to produce feature vectors as well as each word- and sentence-level metric can be found in (Castillo, 2011). The architecture of the system is shown in Figure 1.

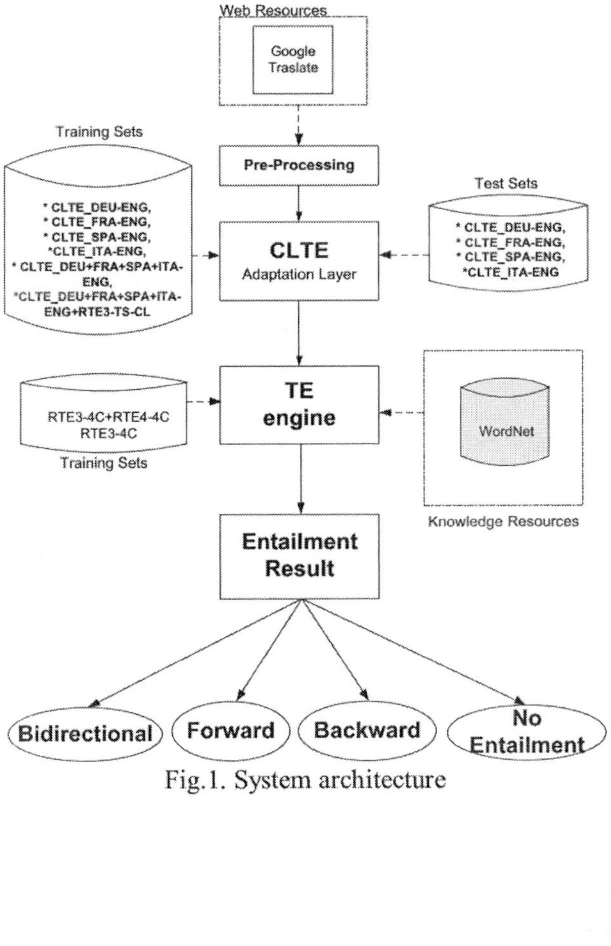

Fig.1. System architecture

In the preprocessing module we performed string normalization across different languages by using a lookup table for lexical entries, and then date and time normalization is carried out.

CLTE adaption layer is composed by four machine translation sub-modules that bring back each <T_i ,H> pair into the monolingual case ENG-ENG. Where T_i can be given in Spanish, German, Italian or French.

The training set used to the submitted runs are whose provided by the organizers of the CLTE for Content Synchronization Task and a combination of RTE datasets, such as it is described in the Section Experiments and Results.

4 Experiments and Results

The dataset provided by the organizers consists of 500 CLTE pairs translated to four languages following the crowdsourcing-based methodology proposed in (Negri et al., 2011). Also, for test purpose additional 500 pairs are provided. Both datasets are balanced with respect to the four entailment judgments (bidirectional, forward, backward, and no entailment).

We also performed experiments using traditional RTE datasets. Because of the RTE datasets are binary classified as NO (no-entailment) and YES (entailment), then we assumed that NO class is "no-entailment" and YES class is "forward" in the CLTE task. Certainly, the corpus tagged in this way will have contradictory information, since several pairs classified as forward should be classified as bidirectional, and also several pairs classified as no-entailment could be backwards, but the objective is experimenting whether we can gain accuracy in our RTE system despite of these (few) contradictory cases.

Additionally, in our experiments we used an algorithm (Castillo,2010) to generate additional training data, in other words to expand a data set. It is based on a Double Translation Process (dtp) or round-trip translation. Double translation process can be defined as the process of starting with an S (String in English), translating it to a foreign language F(S), for example Spanish, and finally back into the English source language F-1(S).

We applied the algorithm starting with RTE3 and RTE4 datasets. Thus, the augmented corpus is denoted RTE3-4C which is tagged according to the three-way task composed of: 340 pairs Contradiction, 1520 pairs Yes, and 1114 pairs Unknown. In the case of the two-way task, it is composed by 1454 pairs No, and 1520 pairs Yes.

The other dataset augmented is denoted RTE4-4C, and has the following composition: 546 pairs Contradiction, 1812 pairs Entailment, and 1272 pairs Unknown. Therefore, in the two-way task, there are 1818 pairs No (No Entailment), and 1812 pairs Yes (Entailment) in this data set.

The idea behind using RTE3-4C and RTE3-4C is providing to our system an increased dataset aiming to acquire more semantic variability.

In our system submission we report the experiments performed with the test sets provided by CLTE organizers which is composed by four datasets of 500 pairs each one.

4.1 Submission to the CLTE shared task

With the aims of applying the monolingual textual entailment techniques, in the CLTE domain, we utilized the Google translate as MT system to bring back the <T,H> pairs into the monolingual case.

Then we generated a feature vector for every <T,H> pair with both training and test sets, and used monolingual textual entailment engine to classify the pairs. First we described the dataset used and then explain each submitted run.

The datasets used are listed below:

- CLTE_Esp+Fra+Ita+Ger: dataset composed by all language pairs.
- RTE3-TS-CL: a ENG-SPA cross lingual textual entailment corpus (Castillo,2011) composed by 200 pairs (108 Entailment, 32 Contradiction, 60 Unknown).
- RTE3-4C: an augmented dataset based on RTE3.
- RTE4-4C: an augmented dataset based on RTE4.

Our participation in the shared task consisted of four different runs produced with the same feature set, and the main differences rely on the amount and type of training data. Each run is described below:

- RUN1: system trained on CLTE_Esp+ Fra+Ger+Ita corpus in addition to the RTE3-TS-CL dataset.
- RUN2: system trained on CLTE_Esp, CLTE_Fra, CLTE_Ger and CLTE_Ita corpus. At testing phase, the system chooses the right dataset according to the language that it is processing.
- RUN3: system trained using all training data that came from different language pairs.

We remark that we can combine the training data because of we used a machine translation submodule that bring back each <T,H> pair into the monolingual case ENG-ENG.

- RUN4: In RUN4 the training set is composed by all pairs of CLTE_Esp+Fra+Ita+Ger and RTE3-4C+ RTE4-4C datasets.

Ten teams participated in this CLTE task, eight submitting runs to all language pairs. For Spanish 28 runs were submitted and 20 runs were submitted for the other languages. The results achieved by our system is showed in Table 1.

Team id	Team system id	Score (Accuracy)				Run Rank			
		SPA-ENG	*ITA-ENG*	*FRA-ENG*	*DEU-ENG*	*SPA*	*ITA*	*FRA*	*DEU*
Sagan	*run1*	0.342	0.352	**0.346**	**0.342**	16	6	**9**	**9**
Sagan	*run2*	0.328	0.352	0.336	0.310	19	7	11	13
Sagan	*run3*	**0.346**	**0.356**	0.330	0.332	**14**	**5**	12	12
Sagan	*run4*	0.340	0.330	0.310	0.310	17	12	13	14
System Rank		7	4	5	6				

The results reported show that our best run is ranking above the average for all languages. The same situation occurs when ranking the systems, except for Spanish where the system is placed on 7th among 10 teams.

We achieved the highest result of 0.356 with RUN3 in the pair ITA-ENG which is placed fourth among participating systems.

We also note that, in general, training the system with the pairs of all datasets achieved better results than training separately for each dataset. Furthermore, if we analyze RUN4 vs. RUN3 we can conclude that incorporating additional RTE dataset produces a very unbalanced dataset resulting in a decrease in performance. In (Castillo, 2011) we experimented with these expanded datasets over monolingual RTE and CLTE tasks and we showed gain in performance, thus we suspect that the decrease is more due to unbalanced dataset than to noise introduced by the double translation process.

Interesting, the Corpus RTE3-TS-CL dataset utilized in the RUN1 helps to improve the results in FRA-ENG and DEU-ENG language pairs.

The Table 2 shows that our system predict with high F-measure to *bidirectional* and *no-entailment* entailment judgments in all language pairs, but has problems to distinguish the *forward* and *backward* entailment judgments.

It is probably due to our systems is based on semantic overlap between T and H, resulting the backwards particularly difficult to predict to our system.

Run id	Language pair	Precision				Recall				F-measure				Score (Accuracy)	Mean Score-all runs
		F	*B*	*NE*	*BI*	*F*	*B*	*NE*	*BI*	*F*	*B*	*NE*	*BI*		
Run3	SPA-ENG	0.23	0.27	**0.42**	0.42	0.20	0.22	0.45	0.51	0.21	0.25	0.43	0.46	**0.346**	**0.346**
Run3	ITA-ENG	**0.31**	0.25	0.40	**0.46**	0.30	0.22	0.51	0.40	0.30	0.23	0.45	0.43	**0.356**	**0.336**
Run1	FRA-ENG	0.24	**0.30**	0.39	0.43	0.17	0.34	0.57	0.30	0.20	0.32	0.47	0.36	**0.346**	**0.336**
Run1	DEU-ENG	0.25	0.23	0.41	0.44	0.17	0.26	0.60	0.34	0.20	0.25	0.49	0.39	**0.342**	**0.336**

Table 2. Official results for Precision, Recall and F-measure

5 Conclusions and future work

In this paper we explained our participation in the new challenging task of Cross-Lingual Textual Entailment (CLTE) for Content Synchronization. This task also could presents benefit as a metric for machine translation evaluation, as reported in (Castillo and Estrella, 2012).

This work focuses on CLTE based on Machine translation to bring back the problem into the monolingual Textual Entailment (TE) scenario. This decoupled approach between Textual Entailment and Machine Translation has several advantages, such as taking benefits of the most recent advances in machine translation, the ability to test the efficiency of different MT systems, as well as the ability to scale the system easily to any language pair.

Results achieved are promising and additional work is needed in order to address the problem of distinguish among *forward*, *backward* and *bidirectional* entailment judgments.

Future work will be oriented to tackle the problem with backwards. Finally, we remark the necessity of bigger corpus tagged in four-way classification, for all language pairs.

References

Ido Dagan, Oren Glickman and Bernardo Magnini. 2006. *The PASCAL Recognising Textual Entailment Challenge*. In Quiñonero-Candela, J.; Dagan, I.; Magnini, B.; d'Alché-Buc, F. (Eds.) Machine Learning Challenges. Lecture Notes in Computer Science , Vol. 3944, pp. 177-190, Springer.

M. Negri, A. Marchetti, Y. Mehdad, L. Bentivogli, and D. Giampiccolo. 2012. *Semeval-2012 Task 8: Cross-lingual Textual Entailment for Content Synchronization*. In Proceedings of the 6th International Workshop on Semantic Evaluation (SemEval 2012).

L. Bentivogli, P. Clark, I. Dagan, H. T. Dang, and D. Giampiccolo. 2010. *The Sixth PASCAL Recognizing Textual Entailment Challenge*. In TAC 2010 Workshop Proceedings, NIST, Gaithersburg, MD, USA.

Y. Mehdad, M. Negri, and M. Federico. 2010. *Towards Cross-Lingual Textual Entailment*. In Proceedings of NAACL-HLT 2010.

Eneko Agirre, Daniel Cer, Mona Diab and Aitor Gonzalez-Agirre. 2012. *SemEval-2012 Task 6: A Pilot on Semantic Textual Similarity*. In Proceedings of the 6th International Workshop on Semantic Evalua-tion (SemEval 2012), in conjunction with the First Joint Conference on Lexical and Computational Semantics (*SEM 2012).

Bentivogli, Luisa, Dagan Ido, Dang Hoa, Giampiccolo, Danilo, Magnini Bernardo.2009.*The Fifth PASCAL RTE Challenge*. In: Proceedings of the Text Analysis Conference.

Fellbaum C. 1998. *WordNet: An Electronic Lexical Database*, volume 1. MIT Press.

Castillo Julio. 2011. *A WordNet-based semantic approach to textual entailment and cross-lingual textual entailment*. International Journal of Machine Learning and Cybernetics - Springer, Volume 2, Number 3.

Castillo Julio and Cardenas Marina. 2010. *Using sentence semantic similarity based onWordNet in recognizing textual entailment*. Iberamia 2010. In LNCS, vol 6433. Springer, Heidelberg, pp 366–375.

Castillo Julio. 2010. *A semantic oriented approach to textual entailment using WordNet-based measures*. MICAI 2010. LNCS, vol 6437. Springer, Heidelberg, pp 44–55.

Castillo Julio. 2010. *Using machine translation systems to expand a corpus in textual entailment*. In: Proceedings of the Icetal 2010. LNCS, vol 6233, pp 97–102.

M. Negri, L. Bentivogli, Y. Mehdad, D. Giampiccolo, and A. Marchetti. 2011. *Divide and Conquer: Crowdsourcing the Creation of Cross-Lingual Textu-*

al Entailment Corpora. In Proceedings of the Conference on Empirical Methods in Natural. EMNLP 2011.

Resnik P. 1995. *Information content to evaluate semantic similarity in a taxonomy*. In: Proceedings of IJCAI 1995, pp 448–453.

Castillo Julio, Cardenas Marina. 2011. *An Approach to Cross-Lingual Textual Entailment using Online Machine Translation Systems*. Polibits Journal. Vol 44.

Castillo Julio and Estrella Paula. 2012. *Semantic Textual Similarity for MT evaluation*. NAACL 2012 Seventh Workshop on Statistical Machine Translation. WMT 2012, Montreal, Canada.

Lin D. 1997.*An information-theoretic definition of similarity*. In: Proceedings of Conference on Machine Learning, pp 296–304.

Jiang J, Conrath D.1997. *Semantic similarity based on corpus statistics and lexical taxonomy*. In: Proceedings of the ROCLINGX.

Pirro G., Seco N. 2008. *Design, implementation and evaluation of a new similarity metric combining feature and intrinsic information content*. In: ODBASE 2008, Springer LNCS.

Wu Z, Palmer M. 1994. *Verb semantics and lexical selection*. In: Proceedings of the 32nd ACL 916.

Leacock C, Chodorow M. 1998. *Combining local context and WordNet similarity for word sense identification*. MIT Press, pp 265–283.

Hirst G, St-Onge D . 1998. *Lexical chains as representations of context for the detection and correction of malapropisms*. MIT Press, pp 305–332.

Banerjee S, Pedersen T. 2002. *An adapted lesk algorithm for word sense disambiguation using WordNet*. In: Proceeding of CICLING-02.

William B. Dolan and Chris Brockett.2005. *Automatically Constructing a Corpus of Sentential Paraphrases*. Third International Workshop on Paraphrasing (IWP2005). Asia Federation of Natural Language Processing.

Castillo Julio and Estrella Paula. 2012. *SAGAN: An approach to Semantic Textual Similarity based on Textual Entailment*. In Proceedings of the 6th International Workshop on Semantic Evaluation (SemEval 2012), in conjunction with the First Joint Conference on Lexical and Computational Semantics (*SEM 2012).

Mehdad Y., M. Negri, and M. Federico. 2011. *Using Parallel Corpora for Cross-lingual Textual Entailment*. In Proceedings of ACL-HLT 2011.

Author Index

Association for Computational Linguistics
209 N. Eighth Street
Stroudsburg, Pennsylvania 18360

18th International Conference on Cognition and Exploratory Learning in Digital Age (CELDA 2021)

Online
13-15 October 2021

iadis